Textbook of Community Psychiatry

Wesley E. Sowers
Hunter L. McQuistion
Jules M. Ranz
Jacqueline Maus Feldman
Patrick S. Runnels
Editors

Textbook of Community Psychiatry

American Association for Community Psychiatry

Second Edition

Editors
Wesley E. Sowers
Clinical Professor of Psychiatry
University of Pittsburgh Medical Center
Pittsburgh, PA, USA

Jules M. Ranz
Clinical Professor of Psychiatry
Columbia University, Vagelos College of Physicians and Surgeons
New York, NY, USA

Patrick S. Runnels
Vice Chair/Professor, Department of Psychiatry
Case Western Reserve School of Medicine
Ohio, OH, USA

Hunter L. McQuistion
Clinical Professor of Psychiatry
New York University Grossman School of Medicine | NYU Langone Health
New York, NY, USA

Jacqueline Maus Feldman
Professor Emerita of Psychiatry, Department of Psychiatry and Behavioral Neurobiology
University of Alabama at Birmingham
Birmingham, AL, USA

ISBN 978-3-031-10238-7 ISBN 978-3-031-10239-4 (eBook)
https://doi.org/10.1007/978-3-031-10239-4

This Springer imprint is published by the registered company Springer Nature Switzerland AG
The registered company address is: Gewerbestrasse 11, 6330 Cham, Switzerland

Much has changed since the publication of the Handbook of Community Psychiatry in 2012. We are indebted to the many contributors to this edition which has morphed into a textbook. There are many new chapters and new authors who have joined in this attempt to produce a comprehensive accounting of the work and ideas of the multitude of psychiatrists working in the field and dedicated to serve the community at large. There has been growing recognition of the primacy of the community service perspective in meeting the needs of our population and increasing interest among young psychiatrists entering the profession.

This work stands on the shoulders of many of the giants of community psychiatry who have passed before us. There are too many for us to mention them all here. We are especially saddened by the loss of three of these paragons of our profession who contributed to the first edition of this book. Carl Bell, Joel Feiner, and Richard Warner were tireless in their efforts to promote social justice and to serve distressed communities. They were advocates, mentors, and superb clinicians, and they will long serve as examples for all of us who continue to have the pleasure of doing this work. We hope that the pages of this book will serve as a memorial to their lives and work.

Contents

Part III Core Competencies for Community Psychiatrists

Part IV Effective and Established Interventions

About the Authors

Wesley E. Sowers MD, is Clinical Professor of Psychiatry at the University of Pittsburgh Medical Center and is the director of the Center for Public Service Psychiatry and its associated fellowship program at Western Psychiatric Hospital. He is board certified in adult psychiatry with subspecialty certifications in addiction, and administrative and community psychiatry. He is a past president of the American Association for Community Psychiatry and has served on the Board of Directors of that organization since 1988. He has also been on the Board of the American Association of Psychiatric Administrators since 1999. He has served as co-chair of the Mental Health Services Committee of the Group for Advancement of Psychiatry since 2009. From 2008 to 2016, he was co-director of the SAMHSA-sponsored Recovery to Practice curriculum development project for psychiatry.Dr. Sowers is a graduate of Brown University and Northwestern University Medical School. He completed residencies at the Cook County Hospital in Chicago and the Albert Einstein College of Medicine, Department of Psychiatry, in New York City. Clinically, he has extensive experience in the provision of treatment and services to special populations such as homeless men and women, people with criminal records, LGBTQ individuals, and people with substance use disorders. He has published several articles, editorials, and book chapters on topics related to his clinical activities and healthcare systems management. He was the chief architect of the Level of Care Utilization System (LOCUS) and its counterpart for children and adolescents (CALOCUS), instruments widely used to guide service intensity decisions.

Hunter L. McQuistion MD, is Clinical Professor of Psychiatry at New York University (NYU) Grossman School of Medicine and senior attending psychiatrist at NYU Langone Health. He is medical director of the SAMHSA-funded Engagement, Treatment, and Recovery (EnTRy) Program at Family Health Centers at NYU Langone, which provides FQHC-based multidisciplinary and recovery-oriented services to underserved Brooklyn residents experiencing serious mental health challenges. He recently completed a successful and satisfying stewardship as chief of psychiatry and behavioral health at NYC Health+Hospitals|Gouverneur. Among other roles in systems management and clinical policy, Dr. McQuistion has also served at a high level in the City of New York Department of Health & Mental Hygiene.As an academic community psychiatrist, he has focused much of his career on program development and scholarship concerning people who experience homelessness and mental illnesses, but has also turned energies to other underserved populations, including interest in efforts on racial and ethnic issues as related to clinical competencies. Spanning roles in advocacy, administration, epidemiological and services research, and education, Dr. McQuistion has published and presented widely. He offers program and educational consultation as well as providing direct clinical services. Among other accomplishments, Dr. McQuistion is a past president of the American Association for Community Psychiatry, is recognized as an Exemplary Psychiatrist by the National Alliance on Mental Illness, is a Distinguished Life Fellow of the American Psychiatric Association, a Fellow of the New York Academy of Medicine, and a member of the Group for Advancement of Psychiatry.

Jules M. Ranz MD, is Clinical Professor of Psychiatry at Columbia. He was director of the Public Psychiatry Fellowship at NYS Psychiatric Institute/Columbia University Medical Center from 1992 to 2017 and continues as a member of its faculty and mentor to many of the over 300 psychiatrists who completed the fellowship. The Public Psychiatry Fellowship is generally acknowledged to be the premier program of its kind in the country. In the past decade, 20 other public/community psychiatry fellowships have been created, most modeled on the Columbia program. During this time, Dr. Ranz has created a network of directors of these programs and has encouraged six of the fellowships to publish articles describing their individual programs.Dr. Ranz was principal author of a 2006-published article written by the Mental Health Services Committee of the Group for the Advancement of Psychiatry, utilizing data to demonstrate that early and mid-career psychiatrists spend more time in publicly funded organizational settings than in solo office practice. A follow-up paper described a 12 site study conducted by Dr. Ranz and that same committee: “A Four Factor Model of Systems-Based Practices in Psychiatry” published in 2012. In recognition of his long career as a public psychiatry educator, Dr. Ranz received the 2013 APA/NIMH Vestermark Psychiatry Educator Award. Following his semiretirement from the Columbia Fellowship, Dr. Ranz helped to create a Community Psychiatry Nurse Practitioner fellowship at a Federally Qualified Health Center, which was described in a 2021 publication in *Psychiatric Services*. He is continuing to serve as an advocate for bringing psychiatric nurse practitioners and psychiatrists together to collaborate on both academic and advocacy levels.

Jacqueline Maus Feldman MD, is professor emerita in the School of Medicine, Department of Psychiatry and Behavioral Neurobiology, University of Alabama at Birmingham (UAB). She retired in July 2014, as the Patrick H. Linton Professor, the medical director of the UAB Community Psychiatry Program, the executive director of the UAB Comprehensive Community Mental Health Center, the director of the division of public psychiatry, and the vice chair for clinical affairs. She continues to provide clinical and administrative services for the department, has consulted with Alabama Medicaid, and serves as the National Alliance on Mental Illness (NAMI) national associate medical director. She has also served as the federal court monitor for women's mental health in the Alabama Department of Corrections and participated with the Department of Justice in its investigation of Georgia State Hospitals. She has also served on numerous national and regional planning and review committees, is a past president of the Alabama Psychiatric Physicians Association and past president of the American Association for Community Psychiatry, and has served on the board of the American Psychiatric Foundation, as well as the Alabama NAMI Board. She has served on the American Psychiatric Association Annual Meeting Scientific Program Committee as member and chair. Her areas of research included effectiveness of ACT, dual diagnosis, jail diversion, and treatment of perinatal depression. She has published and spoken extensively on affective disorders, schizophrenia, dual diagnosis, public policy development, advocacy, mental health and criminal justice, and recovery, and is the immediate past editor-in-chief of the *Community Mental Health Journal*.Dr. Feldman has been listed numerous times in "Best Doctors in America" and named by NAMI three times as an Exemplary Psychiatrist.

Patrick S. Runnels MD, MBA, serves as both chief medical officer of population health and vice chair of psychiatry for University Hospitals in Cleveland. Additionally, he holds an academic appointment as professor at the Case Western Reserve University School of Medicine, where he founded the Public and Community Psychiatry Fellowship. Additionally, he was the founding chair and remains an active member the National Council on Mental Wellness Medical Director Institute. He has served in the past on the board of trustees of the American Psychiatric Association, the National Alliance on Mental Illness (Ohio Chapter), and the American Association for Community Psychiatry. He has also served as chair of the Council on Advocacy and Government Relations for the American Psychiatric Association. Dr. Runnels received his medical degree from the University of Missouri, Columbia, had his psychiatric residency at the Mount Sinai Hospital in New York City, and then completed the Columbia University's Fellowship in Public Psychiatry. He received his executive MBA from Case Western Reserve University Weatherhead School of Management. He has published several articles, editorials, and book chapters, as well as given numerous national talks and presentations in the areas of healthcare leadership and clinical transformation.

Part I

Introduction and Background

Introduction: Community Psychiatry on the Move

Hunter L. McQuistion, Wesley E. Sowers, Jules M. Ranz, Jacqueline Maus Feldman, and Patrick S. Runnels

This Textbook is a key expansion of 2012's *American Association of Community Psychiatrists Handbook of Community Psychiatry* (McQuistion et al. 2012). With this edition, we aim to deliver a comprehensive examination of the many phases of public and community psychiatry, offering a foundational resource for anyone working for community well-being in behavioral health. While the volume primarily focuses on psychiatry's role in community behavioral health, the bulk of chapters are relevant to training and ongoing education for a range of allied professionals and policymakers. At the core of this textbook is a commitment to document and expand the range of professional knowledge, skills, and awareness of those who themselves dedicate their work to communities of people.

Concerning the role of psychiatry, community psychiatry itself as a field or subspecialty is so broad that it handily encompasses domains of public policy, teaching and research, program management and administration, and, of course, clinical work. Self-identified community psychiatrists flexibly work in multiple roles over their careers and not infrequently covering multiple domains simultaneously. This bestows the benefit of breadth of view in their work and enables them to address patient care from all 360 degrees of biopsychosocial and to some, arguably, spiritual conceptualization.

An important, and unique, dimension affecting the need to diligently update the field is how community psychiatry is affected by social, cultural, and political changes. For example, the past 10 years have brought deep turmoil to America, with a widened political division that challenges consensus on how to solve both old and new social problems. As of this writing, in mid-2022, cardinal issues include an overdue re-examination of the cultural status quo, most particularly defined by the crucible of human rights: the struggles of Black and other people of color. This is compounded by an international humanitarian crisis of refugee migration owing to war and social violence, including American immigration

H. L. McQuistion (✉)
New York University Grossman School of Medicine | NYU Langone Health, New York, NY, USA
e-mail: hunter.mcquistion@nyulangone.org

W. E. Sowers
University of Pittsburgh Medical Center, Pittsburgh, PA, USA
e-mail: sowerswe@upmc.edu

J. M. Ranz
Columbia University, Vagelos College of Physicians and Surgeons, New York, NY, USA
e-mail: Jmr1@cumc.columbia.edu

J. M. Feldman
University of Alabama at Birmingham, Gravois Mills, MO, USA
e-mail: jfeldman@uabmc.edu

P. S. Runnels
Department of Psychiatry, Case Western Reserve School of Medicine, Shaker Heights, OH, USA
e-mail: patrick.runnels1@UHhospitals.org

W. E. Sowers et al. (eds.), *Textbook of Community Psychiatry*,
https://doi.org/10.1007/978-3-031-10239-4_1

and asylum-seeking. Continuing are wholly inadequate efforts to improve the lives of people with mental illnesses who are homeless or incarcerated. A demoralizing viral pandemic has raged across all social strata, too, compounding traumatic loss, both personally and economically, with effects on well-being that are yet evolving. In our view, the COVID-19 pandemic has exacerbated a political crisis that separates communities, sometimes even with hateful speech and action. Additionally, the specter of war has threatened international stability as not other conflict since World War II. And finally, there is accelerating urgency to address climate change, itself an ultimate social determinant of mental health, and indeed the most serious existential threat facing humanity.

The picture may feel dystopian, but we would be mistaken to discount efforts to adapt and even thrive by using both time-honored and developing ways to promote community wellness. The above-noted issues, and others, affect how today's community psychiatry focuses its energy. These efforts are duly addressed throughout the chapters of this book's Edition. Resonant with this is this *Textbook's* thread of focusing attention on the domain of primordial prevention (Association of the Faculties of Medicine of Canada 2022), otherwise described as addressing social determinants of health. Over the past 10 years, the concept of social determinants of health has, at last, advanced to the level of accepted terminology, giving community psychiatry's expertise even greater recognition through its role in exploring them in research together with the social sciences.

Similarly, community psychiatrists are often sought in their daily work to ameliorate or eliminate the human cost of these problems, through roles in direct service, clinical administration, governmental policy, and organized psychiatry and even in overseeing quality in managed care. Because these psychiatrists understand that the parts of behavioral healthcare *are* always moving, they hold systems-savviness and are therefore sought out as experts for practice adaptation and change.

This overlaps a crucial aspect of community psychiatry also weaved into this book: advocacy. This book is a vehicle for the American Association of Community Psychiatry (AACP) and in this way reflects advocacy as a foundational value. As testament and illustration of this, AACP recently modified its name from "…of Community Psychiatrists" to "*…for Community Psychiatry*," accentuating the value of advocating for population health and the integrity of communities. This name change also reflects the need for a broader vision of community psychiatry in which a multidisciplinary collaboration prevails.

While the *Textbook's* attention to societal events strongly reflects the spirit and substance of community-oriented service delivery and its research, technical and phenomenological developments have also affected practice, some in direct relation to these events. The rapid growth of virtual and other electronic technologies is a prime example, expanding exponentially during the pandemic. Similarly, over the past decade, the electronic health record (EHR) has become commonplace, enabling enhanced clinical communication, including directly with patients. Paradoxically, the burdens of EHR documentation can also be tagged as contributors to physician burnout, yet another development causing many psychiatrists to experience a sense of less time spent with their patients, compounding the continuing pressure for service volume driven by reimbursement in organized practice settings. Indeed, the last decade has evolved a growing concern about a diminishing and aging psychiatric workforce in the public sector, even as demand increases. It is hoped that this will be offset by the prospect that recruitment of medical students to psychiatry is on the rise (Psychiatric News, April 21 2021), that psychiatric residency programs are increasingly sensitive to the effect of social determinants of mental health, and that community/public psychiatry fellowships have increased in number, from 2 in 2007 to 26 in 2022.

So, despite serious challenges to practice, community psychiatry has firmly established itself within today's profession, and there is reason for optimism in its role on the future panorama of behavioral healthcare. This highlights another of this *Textbook's* functions: it is a guide for trainees and early career professionals as they begin to shape the contours of community psychiatry's influence on both macro- and micro-level changes in healthcare.

In this manner, this *Textbook* also helps fulfill this aspect of AACP's mission:

> …to promote health, recovery and resilience in people, families and communities by inspiring and supporting community psychiatric care providers, and in transforming behavioral health care;

while it pursues this element of its Vision Statement:

> [to] develop and disseminate knowledge and skills for effective and sustainable practices and systems to advance population health.

With the *Textbook* as a tool not only for the present practice environment, the rising generation of practitioners and leaders in community psychiatry will have a solid and uniform basis of knowledge and reference for their efforts to advance their clinical work and advocacy, continuing to build the subspecialty as times change.

Therefore, this edition offers an exposition and elaboration of the AACP's goals by examining the historical, philosophical, and scientific basis and development of community and public service psychiatry. The *Textbook* helps the AACP's efforts to effect technology transfer and professional development, and it does so by supporting the AACP Certification in Community and Public Psychiatry. It is an updated study guide for the Certification examination, with many examination questions arising from its chapters.

In terms of content, we have keenly focused on a consistency of approach to patient care, in systems management, public policy, training and education, and research priorities among the chapters. We have drawn on expert chapter authors, especially AACP members, who share the organization's goals. We are deeply indebted to them for their energy, vision, and hard work in preparing their ideas for our readers. We are particularly honored by those authors who are not psychiatrists – colleagues in psychology, social work, nursing, and the peer community – who have been crucial in assuring comprehensiveness and perspective within the volume while also reflecting the inherently multidisciplinary and collaborative nature of community psychiatry. Finally, we are indebted and pay homage to those contributors to the 2012 Handbook who are now deceased and missed, leaders and mentors in our field who are noted throughout the book.

How the Book Is Organized

The *Textbook* is organized into nine sections, or parts, that cover topics that are relevant to the conceptualization and practice of clinical work, but also give a theoretical basis, as well as historical context, to the various topics within community psychiatry.:

Part I: Introduction and Background

After this Introduction, chapter "History of Community Psychiatry" sets the stage by describing the historical evolution of community psychiatry, offering chronological development of where behavioral health services are today. The emphasis is on the US behavioral healthcare system, but that system could not have itself evolved without traditions and initiatives going back centuries, primarily in the Western world.

Part II: The Basics: Central Pillars of Community Psychiatry

Part II covers essential features of practicing in community-oriented systems, and it represents our view of what are cardinal values in today's behavioral healthcare: recovery and person-centeredness, population health and prevention, leadership and collaboration, advocacy and social justice, and care integration and comprehensive services.

Part III: Core Competencies for Community Psychiatrists

Once basic principles have been understood, essentials of successful clinical practice can be gathered. These include creating a service culture that is welcoming to people seeking help, developing enlightened service planning that is an also trauma-informed, and how to employ techniques and clinical skills to address challenges commonly experienced by those we serve.

Part IV: Effective and Established Interventions

Expanding on technique, Part IV examines clinical and rehabilitative practices that have been shown to be particularly effective in helping people pursue personal recovery goals. These span a discussion of evidence-based practices (EBPs) and their tension with the "practice-based evidence" that grows out of clinical experience, wisdom, and quasi-experimental data. How EBPs inform interventions for co-occurring mental illnesses and substance misuse is examined in this light. Included in practical approaches, the section also covers the ascendance of cognitive behavioral therapy, both for general psychiatric populations and its important emergence for psychosis (discussed in Part VII). Also covered here is the critical tool of psychiatric rehabilitation, not infrequently glossed over in psychiatric training, with specific references to other chapters in this book that, together, thoroughly discuss all its aspects. The section also includes the role of emergency services as well as reviewing the current state of assertive community treatment. Often not emphasized, but so important to community well-being, is a chapter on families and the interventions tailored to them.

Part V: Creating Healthy Communities

In the end, supporting community health is a central mission of public service. Its application to community psychiatry is given detail in Part V. The stage is set by the basic science of community psychiatry, epidemiology. It then moves from the quantitative to the equally significant qualitative effects of community, political, and social effects on community well-being. Operationalizing community psychiatric principles is explored in the chapter on community collaboration, as well as with one presenting services research precepts and methodology. Part V also examines the specific community disruptions caused by incarceration, disasters, and the impending global effect of an 800-pound gorilla: climate change.

Part VI: Supportive Services for Community Living

In coping with societal realities, Part VI addresses responses by advocates, policymakers, and behavioral health program planners to address social determinants of mental health challenges, with the goal of blunting their effect. This section therefore delves into issues that affect housing and employment and the challenges of service coordination. Because the recovery experience cannot progress in isolation, particularly with the vicissitudes of societal impediments, this section discusses social supports through the clubhouse movement, with peers, as well as how a person can mobilize personal wellness.

Part VII: Special Populations

So much of community psychiatry is defined by conceptualizing and working with clinical populations. From a clinical service vantage point, local communities manifest population needs, and any treatment of them in a volume like this one can never cover them all. However, Part VII focuses on how clinicians and organized systems of care can address the needs of ten prominent clinical populations based on demographics, rural residence, veteran status, sexual orientation, homelessness, and migration status. Also included in this section is detail regarding populations with a first episode or early psychotic challenge, along with practical description of cognitive behavioral therapy of psychosis.

Part VIII: The Development and Administration of Services

Extending the systems expertise inherent in public and community psychiatry into management is the business of Part VIII. Many public and community psychiatrists enter this arena in the interest of advocating for necessary change and the need to affect population health. The section covers an overall vision for a public mental health system, the role of medical director, the challenges of workforce development, the financing of behavioral health, how to successfully wrestle with clinical value, and, then, how to evaluate programming. It also explores the burgeoning universe of technology in behavioral health, an area that, as noted above, has expanded dramatically over the past decade.

Part IX: Shaping the Future

As we shape the future, three chapters are necessarily dedicated to the process of education and training, including how mentorship might even begin before medical school and how public and community psychiatry fellowships have a key role in mounting sophistication for work in publicly funded clinical environments. Consequently, we pull together all the elements embraced by the textbook and deeply discuss future prospects in community psychiatry, including on an international level.

Finally, though this book does not attempt to minimize contributions of other recent treatments of community psychiatry (Rowe et al. 2011; Jacobs and Steiner 2016), it aims to reinforce and, in many respects, deepen the conversations emerging from them, offering an enlightening and comprehensive view. We hope the chapters in this book are rewarding for you, enabling the *Textbook* to meet its goals.

References

Association of the Faculties of Medicine of Canada. *AFMC Primer on Population Health*, Chapter 4. Available at: https://phprimer.afmc.ca/en/part-i/chapter-4/. Accessed February 6, 2022

McQuistion HL, Sowers WE, Ranz J, Feldman JM (2012). *Handbook of Community Psychiatry* (eds.). Springer, New York City,

Jacobs S & Steiner JL (2016). *Yale Textbook of Community Psychiatry* (Eds.). Oxford University Press, New York City

Psychiatric News, April 21, 2021. Psychiatry Residency Match Numbers Climb Again After Unprecedented Year in Medical Education. Available at: https://psychnews.psychiatryonline.org/doi/full/10.1176/appi.pn.2021.5.27. Accessed February 2, 2022.

Rowe M, Lawless M, Thompson K, Davidson L (2011). *Classics of Community Psychiatry: Fifty Years of Public Mental Health Outside the Hospital* (Eds.). Oxford University Press, New York City.

History of Community Psychiatry

Jacqueline Maus Feldman

Introduction

Since antiquity, mental illnesses have proven challenging for individuals suffering with them, for families who wish to support them, and for communities in which they live. Evolution in the development of community services and supports has been predicated on the understanding or interpretation of mental illness, aided by acceptance and innovation, but often anchored in ignorance, stigma, and short-sightedness. Regardless of how one defines community psychiatry (by provider, by setting, by duration of care, by diagnosis, by set of principles, by finances/payer of services), multiple facets are important in the evolutions of the field. A historical review of community psychiatry is imperative to comprehend the variables that impact the lives of those touched by mental illness and may suggest how systems of care should be organized to enhance recovery.

As early as the Neolithic era, evidence exists that many attempts were made to treat and cure mental illness. Skeletal remains with large burr holes in their skulls from that era have been speculated to reflect interventions in brain disorders (Brothwell 1981). Records from ancient Egypt reported clinical presentations of depression and somatization, with trials of magical spells, applications of body fluids, use of hallucinogens, and religious retreats to ameliorate these conditions (Nassar 1987). Hindu religious texts denoted interpretations of mental illness as reflections of supernatural beings imbued with magical powers, or as a result of the body being out of balance; the religious community responded with application of prayers, herbs, or persuasion (an early attempt at therapy?) (Bhuga 1992). Bodily imbalance was also embraced as an explanation for mental disorders by the ancient Chinese; treatment like herbs and acupuncture sought to being these back in alignment (Yizhuang 2005). Ancient Jewish cultures viewed mental illness as a reflection of a discordant relationship with G-d. Eschewing theories that the etiologies of mental illness were supernatural or divine in nature, Hippocrates recommended close observation; accurately described numerous mental maladies; noted contributory roles of environment, diet, and lifestyle; and suggested treatment be focused on balancing bodily fluids. Ultimately Plato embraced the theory that all mental illness was predicated on physical problems, and a Greek physician became the first to suggest humane treatment, including releasing agitated patients from restraints (von Staden 1996).

During the Middle Ages, the Quran reflected the need to treat those who were mentally challenged with humane protectiveness; some Muslim physicians encouraged the development

J. M. Feldman (✉)
University of Alabama at Birmingham,
Birmingham, AL, USA
e-mail: jfeldman@uabmc.edu

W. E. Sowers et al. (eds.), *Textbook of Community Psychiatry*,
https://doi.org/10.1007/978-3-031-10239-4_2

of trusting counseling relationships and developed patient-centered, supportive asylums from 700 to 1200 AD (Million 2004). Unfortunately, such forbearance was not as readily apparent in Europe during the Middle Ages, where interpretation of mental illness again became tied to a "mixture of the divine, diabolical, magical and transcendental" (Millon, p. 38). Humors, spirits, and demons were all thought responsible for mental disorders, and the suffering individual was thought to be morally unfit and suffering from sin and punishment for a lapse in his relationship with G-d or possessed by the devil. During this time, the challenge of providing care for these individuals fell to families, although in England the courts often provided additional supports. Others were not so lucky and were the target of witch hunts; the "more" fortunate were removed (or pushed) from family care and shipped off to and restrained in almshouses, jails, or mad houses (Wright 1997).

The Age of Enlightenment marked a resurgence in the belief that mental illness was predicated on physical not moral problems, though patients were often seen as wild animals, needing restraint and physical punishment to ameliorate their animalistic furies. In America in the 1700s, the general medical Pennsylvania Hospital began to offer services for those with mental illness (though in its basement), and colonial Virginia opened the first mental health asylum in Williamsburg designated specifically for citizens with mental illness. Towards the end of the 1700s, the moral treatment movement occurred, with leadership provided by Phillipe Pinel in France and Tuke and the Quakers in England. Rees (1987) describes Pinel's philosophy:

> the insane came to be regarded as normal people who had lost their reason as a result of having been exposed to severe psychological and social stress. These stressors were called the moral causes of insanity and moral treatment relieves the patient by friendly association, discussion of his difficulties and the daily pursuit of purposeful activity; in other words, social therapy, individual therapy, and occupational therapy." (pp. 306–307)

Before further exploring moral treatment in the United States and the evolution of psychiatric care that eventually culminated in expansion of community psychiatry, a brief sojourn into the history of Geel is imperative, as it illustrates the potential and capacity for a community to embrace and support people with mental illness in a recovery-oriented fashion. Over 700 years ago, a city in Belgium, Geel, established a system of community care for those with mental illness that has been sustained, in some fashion, through this very day. By legend, it is told that in the sixteenth-century Dymphna, the daughter of an Irish king, fled to the forests of Geel to escape her recently widowed father, who in a grief-stricken delusion, demanded she marry him. Instead of acquiescing, she chose to be beheaded; named the patron saint of those with mental illness, the site of her martyrdom became a chapel that witnessed cures of mental illness. Pilgrims seeking miracle cures overwhelmed the region and the church onsite became their housing; at the bequest of the overwhelmed church, villagers from the surrounded area open their homes and thus began the tradition of "integrated, community residential care" (Goldstein and Godemont 2003). These often trans-generational foster families provided mental health care and support with virtually no formal training, and by the late 1930s over 3800 boarders were living with Geel families; for the most part "the role of the family as caretaker, teacher, natural supportive parent, and behavioral model allows the boarder to function in the normal social world" (p. 449).

By the 1950s, however, boarder populations began to decline. A study was initiated in Belgium in the mid-1960s to study Geel and its mental health-care system, as its original leader was expressing fears that the Colony would dwindle away. Instead, legislation has elevated the Colony to autonomous status, and new physician administrators have inspired evolution in the services rendered. More recent research reflects the majority of boarders are male, ages ranging from 15 to 75, half have intellectual disabilities, and over 20% are diagnosed with schizophrenia. Non-adherence rates are low, and a relatively low incidence of violence is reported. Each family has a psychiatric nurse assigned to them, and hospitalization is available if necessary. Of interest, boarders are not kept out of pubs (taverns), which are "an important part of community social life" (p. 455). Historically largely agrarian (which offered boarders opportunity for farming jobs), Geel is now industrialized; boarders still are "given the opportunity to do meaningful work" (p. 456). Geel

> acknowledges and accepts the human needs of the boarders and responds to those needs rather than acting on unfounded or exaggerated fears...because of their exposure to and experience with mental illness, the entire population protects rather than fears members of their community who are mentally ill. The living legend of Geel offers an opportunity to learn lessons that can encourage effective mental health care—community caring in caring communities." (p. 456)

A more recent study of Geel (von Bilsen 2016) reflects the importance of "radical compassion and kindness" and "social integration, care in the community, and normalization" as instrumental for successful functioning in the community, as well as offering opportunities for destigmatization and acceptance of those living with mental illness.

Unfortunately, communities like Geel are difficult to replicate, but dedicated individuals continued to strive to enhance mental health care in America in the mid-1800s. Inspired by Phillippe Pinel, Dorthea Dix promulgated moral treatment reform in America. After failing to convince the federal government to embrace responsibility for those with mental illness (in 1854 President Franklin Pierce vetoed a bill that would have set up federally funded construction of mental hospitals), Dorthea Dix continued her campaign, begun in the 1840s, to convince state governments "to provide that which many of the ill patients lacked: stable housing, nutritious meals, supportive care in kind and calming environment….to provide asylum for those needing support and nurturing to cope with their mental illness" (Feldman 2010, p. 193). Asylums were constructed and patients admitted and "treated" (with kindness, housing, food, and work). While initially capable of providing succor and support, the institutions were quickly overwhelmed by an influx of society's less fortunate (those with chronic medical illnesses like syphilis and dementia, orphans, and those who were impoverish); battling excessive caseloads and inadequate funding, humane treatment floundered in asylums, and patients were warehoused with little to no treatment or care offered (Crossley 2006). Although the introduction of ECT and insulin shock therapy ensued, many patients spent the remainder of their lives incarcerated in state hospitals. By the mid-1950s, the numbers of patients housed in American mental institutions peaked at over 550,000.

In the late 1800s and early 1900s, other reforms and treatments in mental health blossomed that set the stage for the evolution of institutional care ultimately transitioning to community-based care. The Mental Hygiene movement was led by Clifford Beers, a brilliant young financier who developed bipolar disorder, attempted suicide, and spent 3 terrible years in a state hospital in Connecticut. Against the recommendation of most of his friends and supporters, he felt compelled to document his course of care (even going so far as to get himself locked down on the freezing violent ward), hoping to improve care, to demonstrate to the general public that people with mental illness could recover, and to prevent mental illness and institutionalization. He was instrumental in the formation of the National Committee on Mental Hygiene, which ultimately evolved into the NMHA, now known as Mental Health America. This group performed and published surveys of state hospitals and patient treatment and treatment conditions and proved instrumental in changing conditions in state hospitals across the nation (Beers 1981).

In the late 1940s, a clubhouse model of psychosocial rehabilitation burst on the scene in New York City. Based on the belief that those with mental illness were capable of helping each other, the Fountain House (detailed in chapter "Fountain House and the Clubhouse Movement"), a membership organization run for and by persons with mental illness, was established. It aimed to achieve many things for its members that became the backbone of the principle of psychosocial rehabilitation: establishing relationships, increasing productivity and self-confidence, re-entrance into society, learning self-advocacy, and fighting stigma. It has spawned numerous organizations locally and has served as a role model for many as they develop their own club house models (Fountain House).

The use of psychoanalysis to treat patients with neuroses blossomed in the 1930s and 1940s, and the creation of a veteran population afflicted by PTSD in World War II underscored not only personal vulnerability to horrendous stress but also the protective power of the unit (community) and incentivized the government to step up efforts at treatment (Marlowe 1996). See also chapter "Veterans' Services" on veterans' issues. Until the middle of the twentieth century, however, the systems of care for those with serious mental illness evolved slowly, and little significant progress was made towards actual treatment of mental illness; instead, the major focus continued to be segregation of those with mental illness from the general public. However, the mid-1950s and early 1960s were the beginning of a massive transition of those with serious mental illness back into the community. Although the introduction of the discovery and use of major tranquilizers (chlorpromazine) have often been touted as the major influence in de-institutionalization (movement of state hospitalized patients into the community), it is entirely possible that finances and politics were major players as well. Grazier et al. (2005) noted:

> efforts to transfer responsibility/costs between and among agencies, states and the federal government, with persistent funding sources that were inadequate to meet the kind of resource and service needs of adults with serious mental illness... resulted in confusion, complexity in access to payment for services, created a burden on consumers and their families and disincentive from grass root providers to meet services needs…what developed was a lack of consistent national mental health policies…that led to a piecemeal financial system that diffused accountability, encouraged cost-shifting, and obscured service responsibility resulting in vulnerable populations being poorly served or abandoned. (p. 549)

State and federal legislation was passed that moved the development of *community*-based systems of care forward. In 1948 the National Mental Health Act created the National Institutes of Mental Health with the goal of supporting and sustaining innovative mental health-care programs and "scientific" treatment. In 1958, Congress passed the Mental Health Study Act, which was to "provide for an objective, thorough, and nationwide analysis and re-evaluation of the human and economic problems of mental illness" (Public Law 84-192). A resultant report (Action for Mental Health) delineated necessary funding, staffing, and treatment that President Kennedy used as a springboard to recommend a National Mental Health Program, calling for the building of two thousand mental health centers to provide comprehensive community-based programs to serve those with severe mental illness *and* adults, children and families suffering from stress (Ewalt 1961). In 1963, the Mental Retardation Facilities and Community Mental Health Center Construction (CMHC) Act was signed into law; unfortunately, proposed funding for staff was revised downward in 1965, and only substantial funding for the building of community mental health centers remained. Still, these centers were to provide both inpatient and outpatient services, consultation and education, and day treatment and crisis services. Centers serving rural areas and poor urban areas received additional funding. Worried that federal support would eventually disappear, there was some reluctance on the part of states to embrace these funds; by the time the program was terminated in 1981, only 754 catchment areas had applied for funding. It is worth noting that CMHC funding bypassed state authorities and was provided directly to local community authorities and agencies, since it was felt that states mostly provided inpatient services and that local community agency would be more responsive to the needs of local communities. Indeed, local communities were more interested in serving the larger number of people with common mental disorders rather than the smaller number of people with serious mental disorders served by state hospitals. As a result, many of these mental health centers focused care on those who were not seriously mentally ill. "These times reflected the beginning of a philosophical shift in treatment; psychiatric predicated care fell to psychologists, and effective interventions were thought not be medical or biologic in nature, but to be social or educational, and where it was proffered, that early intervention could prevent mental illness" (Feldman 2010, p. 194).

The passage of Medicaid and Medicare in the mid-1960s offered some provision of care and service, although these programs were not designed for patients with serious mental illness. Without continuous employment, SSDI was not available to these patients, and lower payment and higher co-pays existed for mental health until recently. IMD (Institution for Mental Disease) restrictions kept (and still keep) patients with Medicaid from accessing free-standing psychiatric hospital services, though there is considerable advocacy for such services to be paid for by Medicaid. Further elaborations on funding for mental health care are offered in chapter "Financing of Community Behavioral Health Services" concerning behavioral health financing.

Eventually hospital closures and/or downsizing meant the state hospital populations went from a high of over 558,00 to 62,000 in 1996. In spite of promised assistance with treatment, medication, housing, and vocational training, during the 1970s and 1980s, local mental health centers proved at best inconsistent in providing said treatment, and patients often found themselves facing "trans-institutionalization (placement in nursing homes, boarding homes, foster care, jails or prisons).

While President Nixon was successful in withdrawing some public support of mental health care, in 1977, President Carter empowered a Commission on Mental Health to review services and funding across the nation. It discovered that community services had increased over the last 15 years, but that substantial numbers of populations (ethnic minorities, the urban poor, women, children, veterans, those with physical handicaps, adults with chronic mental illness) were underserved, living without basic necessities, limited aftercare or medical care, and increased rates of hospital recidivism. The report encouraged the development of services for those with chronic mental illness, proposing federal grants for said development; the National Mental Health Service Systems Act of 1980 called for – and funded – a massive overhaul of the nation's mental health-care system to focus priorities on services for these underserved populations. Unfortunately, it was underfunded by President Reagan and by 1981 deleted entirely by the Omnibus Budget Reconciliation Act, decimating years of federal leadership, serving to further dismantle the regional impact of NIMH, and reducing staff and services at local mental health centers. Criteria for SSDI also changed then; while patients with serious mental illness made up 11% of SSDI recipients, they were 30% of those who lost program eligibility (Feldman 2010).

The 1980s and 1990s were also decades of imposition of managed care on the service provision for mental health patients in the community. Capitation systems were put in place, ostensibly to maintain quality services while controlling costs. Standardization of assessments and treatment, limited enrollment rates, risk-sharing, and external regulation (all often predicated on minimization of hospitalization) placed enormous burdens on local MHCs. But "managed care, which fostered a system in which choice was limited, care was managed to decrease costs, and continuity was threatened, was particularly troublesome for individuals with socially stigmatized, poorly understood illnesses that had traditionally been treated separately from standard medical care" (Feldman 2010, p. 196). Many state systems of care funded by Medicaid were decimated, and equivocal results from this experiment continue to be reported.

Declared the decade of the brain by President George H W Bush, the 1990s *did* reflect a revival in interest in biological treatment of serious mental illness and ushered in a plethora of new medications, including the atypical antipsychotic medications, which were touted as being superior to older antipsychotic medication; they did seem to have a reduced (though still present) probability of causing tardive dyskinesia, a dramatic movement disorder side effect. However, as a class they also carried with them a propensity for placing patients at risk for weight gain and development of diabetes, hyperlipidemia, and/or metabolic syndrome. While promising to enhance treatment, these new medications also imposed huge financial burdens on formulary costs and "opened the door for massive influence by pharmaceutical companies" (Feldman 2010, p. 196). The Medicaid Rehabilitation option did encourage a focus on those with serious mental illness and encouraged development of a broader array of services by offering payment for supports such as case managers, day treatment, and ACT (assertive community treatment teams). Many mental health centers utilized Medicare funding to provide partial hospitalization services in an attempt to minimize hospitalization and re-hospitalization. It should be underscored that the focus of treatment during this time was on symptom control.

By the early 1990s, there were limited tool kits to guide clinical interventions, primitive evidence-based practices, few nuanced outcome measures, and an increasing demand for service in the face of an under-developed psychiatric workforce. In response, the federal government in 1992 directed NIMH to be reorganized under NIH (the National Institutes of Health) to strengthen mental health-care research. At the same time, CMHS (Center for Mental Health Services) was moved under SAMHSA (Substance Abuse Mental Health Services Administration), to encourage and support workforce development. The philosophy of a community supports system was embraced. Forays into vocational rehabilitation blossomed. Psychosocial and psychiatric rehabilitation models were developed which emphasized the development of vocational rehabilitation plans; they focused on characteristics of work that were desired, the skills and knowledge necessary to perform the work successfully, the current level of readiness, and the methods to be used to help close the identified gaps (Wallace 1993; Lamb 1994; Liberman 1992). A wide variety of skills training (see chapter "Psychiatric Rehabilitation"), family psycho-education (chapter "Family Systems Care in Public Sector Settings"), and supported employment modules (chapter "Supported Employment") have been developed since then. Barton (1999) reported that multiple programs focusing on empowerment, competency, and recovery had proven helpful: "the range of social, educational, occupational, behavioral and cognitive training has improved the role performance of persons with serious mental illness, and noted an average of 50% decrease in cost of care due to reduced hospitalizations" (p. 526).

The report of the US Surgeon General in 1999 (US Department of HHS) denoted the gap between research and practice and made recommendations "emphasizing a scientific base, overcoming stigma, public awareness, adequate services, cultural competence, and real parity" (p. 467–8, Cohen et al. 2003). President Clinton's attempt at health-care reform, which included parity between medical and mental health, proved unsuccessful. It was not until 2008 that Congress ultimately passed legislation requiring parity. More recently, tool kits and clinical guidelines have suggested evidence-based treatment interventions (APA practice guidelines), and since 2000 there has been an increasing push for the development of means to assess efficacy of treatment and the push for evidence-based practice (SAMHSA).

During the latter part of the 1990s and into the present, the major focus of treatment has shifted from symptom control to rehabilitation to recovery addressing needs of the whole person, "with the goal to help people pursue independence, self-management, personally meaningful activities and better quality of life" (p. 427, Drake et al. 2003). Core guidelines for recovery-oriented services included development of trusting consumer/professional partnerships less focused on hierarchy than on strength-based assessments, shared decision-making (Torrey and Drake 2010), psycho-education, relapse prevention, and consumer-centered treatment planning. Involvement and engagement with families as collaborators have occurred. NAMI's use of family-to-family educational techniques has supported its efficacy (Mercado et al. 2016). Addressing co-occurring disorders (substance use/abuse/dependence and medical illnesses concomitantly with mental illness) is proving challenging, and yet without addressing these co-existing illnesses, patients will continue to be at higher risk for relapse and rehospitalization

(SAMHSA 2009). Cognitive behavioral therapy, dialectical behavioral therapy, and peer support (utilization of consumers as peer specialists, bridge programs) have offered consumers innovative therapies (see chapter "Peer Service Providers as Colleagues") that can enhance recovery (Kart et al. 2021). As community providers seek to endorse and support rehabilitation and recovery, the use of assertive community treatment teams (see chapter "Case Management and Assertive Community Treatment") reinforces and supports the skills sets necessary for recovery (Bond and Drake 2015). Attention to the imperative issue of stable housing (see chapter "Housing First and the Role of Psychiatry in Supported Housing") has moved to the forefront, with multiple models of housing (dry vs damp vs wet; housing first, transitional housing, permanent housing) being attempted (Sylvestre et al. 2017). Utilization of telehealth (particularly during this era of COVID-19) has expanded capacity (see chapter "Telehealth and Technology") to respond to the mental health needs of the community in a more timely fashion (Kopec et al. 2020). In addition, addressing the impact of social determinants and mental health equity on the development and maintenance of mental illness (see chapter "Social and Political Determinants of Health and Mental Health") has come to the forefront of developing services for those living with mental illness (Compton and Shim 2017; Feldman 2020). Workforce development (or the lack there-in) continues to plague opportunities to plan expansions in access and treatment options (Hoge 2017).

Several salient court decisions have had a tremendous impact on the development of improved services for mental health patients. These are well summarized on a timeline in chapter "Advocacy in Evolution: The Push and Pull of Psychiatrists". Suffice it to say, each federal ruling underscores the movement along the spectrum of the right to receive the least restrictive treatment by those committed to the states for mental health care. Recent court decisions (e.g., Wit v United Behavioral Health, 2019) reflect there continue to be people living with mental illness who experience discriminatory policies and practices by insurance companies that restrict timely access to appropriate care.

Legislation continues to affect community psychiatry. The Medicare Modernization Act of 2005 proffered means by which those who had Medicare were able to purchase their medication, including psychiatric medication. In 2008 the Mental Health Parity and Addiction Equity Act Parity was passed that legislated that payment (and limits) for mental health and provision of mental health services (including substance abuse services) had to be essentially equivalent for medical and mental health care. Despite concerns that costs would rise precipitously, research reflects little impact on utilization, cost, or quality of care (Azzone et al. 2011). Of note, final rules for the Parity Act were not released until November 2013, and industry research still reflects considerable discrepancies in behavioral health access, provision, and reimbursement (Davenport et al. 2019).

In terms of mental health care, the passage of the landmark Patient Protection and Affordable Care Act (aka Obama Care, ACA) in 2010 expanded capacity of Americans to purchase health insurance; by law, behavioral health-care services were required to provide certain benefits. The ACA originally included Medicaid expansion for all states, but the US Supreme Court made Medicaid expansion voluntary. If states chose to expand Medicaid, this in turn expanded access to mental health services. Millions have been able to do so (Beronio et al. 2014) though there are still millions without access, particularly in states that did not expand Medicaid eligibility.

Almost 20 years ago, in 2003, President George W. Bush assembled the New Freedom Commission on Mental Health. This group of health-care practitioners were empowered to survey services across the United States, identifying programs that were particularly successful: "It reviewed the science of mental health, and mental health services, and offered an indictment of the mental health service system, which included fragmentation/gaps in care for children and adolescents, increased unemployment and disability (in those with SPMI) and noted that neither mental health nor suicide prevention were a national priority." Many, many examples of successful programs were highlighted. The commission recommended six general goals: (1) mental health is essential to overall health; (2) mental health care should be consumer/family driven; (3) disparities (like funding and access) had to be eliminated; (4) early mental health screening assessments/ referrals needed to be common; (5) quality care should be delivered and research increased; and (6) community mental health should enhance the use of technology (Grob and Goldman 2007). No monies were attached to the report or its recommendations, so the report's capacity to provide tangible influence to support evidence-based practice was limited. To its credit, the federal Center for Medicaid and Medicare Services embraced and promulgated a mantra of moving science into service and has focused funding on that research which could do so.

There have been other changes over the last 10 years that have significantly impacted those living with mental illness:

1. Engagement with the criminal justice system (GAP Committee, Psychiatry and the Community 2016). Educational training for law enforcement and the judiciary, innovative diversion policies, and treatment instead of incarceration are some of the strategies that are being utilized to enhance safe, recovery-oriented engagement and treatment (see chapter "Collaborative Reduction of Criminal Justice Involvement for Persons with Mental Illness").
2. Programs that enhance the identification and recovery-oriented treatment for those with first-episode psychosis have been established nationwide (see chapter "Early Psychosis and the Prevention and Mitigation of Serious Mental Illness").
3. In the face of climate change devastations such as drought and famine, storms, and wildfires that are already striking in all regions of an unprepared world, climate change is rapidly becoming acknowledged as the existential threat to humankind. In turn, mental health consequences of climate change are finally being recognized and assessment and treatment options considered (see chapter "Climate Change: Impact on Community Mental Health").

As the third decade of the twenty-first century progresses, multiple determinants are converging on the provision of mental health care. It is no longer acceptable to believe only prescribed medications are the sole considerations in the treatment of serious mental illness. Instead the hierarchical relationship of physician to patient must evolve into one of partnership, predicated on consumer strengths and self-defined desires for recovery goals. Easy-to-access evidence-based recovery-orientated services that address social determinants and mental health equity must be organized, funded, and coordinated and the consumer supported in the community. Stigma continues to hold powerful sway over lawmakers and common citizens, and society, health administrators, and financial systems have withheld adequate funding and service for centuries. By understanding the history of neglect and abuse of those living with mental illness, community psychiatrists can embrace the role of advocate and push to surmount the extant disparities in our systems of care to enable an evolution towards an embrace of and support for recovery: "to achieve the promise of community living for everyone (with) new service delivery patterns and initiatives that ensure every American has easy and consistent access to the most current treatment and best support services" (New Freedom Commission 2003).

References

Azzone, V., Frank, R.G., Normand, S-L. T., & Burham, M.A. (2011) Effect of insurance parity on substance abuse treatment. *Psychiatric Services*, 62, 129-134.

Barton, R. (1999) Psychosocial rehabilitation services in community support systems: A review of outcomes and policy recommendations. *Psychiatric Services*, 50, 524-534.

Beers, C. W. (1981; first published in 1921) A *Mind That Found Itself.* Pittsburgh: University of Pittsburgh Press.

Beronio, K, Glied, S, Frank, R. (2014) How the affordable care act and mental health parity and addiction equity act greatly expand coverage of behavioral health care. *Journal of Behavioural Health Services Research.* 41,410-428.

Brothwell, D. R. (1981). *Digging Up Bones: The Excavation, Treatment and Study of Human Skeletal Remains.* Ithaca, NY: Cornell University Press.

Bhuga, D. (1992). Psychiatry in ancient Indian texts: A review. *History of Psychiatry*, 3, 167-186.

Bond, GR. Drake, RE. (2015). The critical ingredients of assertive community treatment. *World Psychiatry.* 14, 240-242.

Cohen, C. I., Feiner, J. S., Huffine, C., Moffic, H. S., & Thompson, K. S. (2003). The future of community psychiatry. *Community Mental Health Journal*, 39, 459-471.

Compton, MT, Shim, RS (Eds). (2017). *The social determinants of mental health.* Washington, DC: American Psychiatric Publishing.

Crossley, N. (2006). Contextualizing contention. *Contesting Psychiatry: Social Movements in Mental Health.* New York, NY: Routledge.

Davenport, S., Gray, TJ, Melek, SP. (2019). Addiction and mental health vs. physical health: Widening disparities in network use and provider reimbursement. *Milliman Research Report.*

Drake, R.E, Green, A. I. Mueser, K.T., & Goldman, H. The history of community mental health treatment and rehabilitation for persons with severe mental illness. (2003). *Community Mental Health Journal*, 39, 427-440.

Ewalt, J. (1961) Action *for Mental Health: Final Report of the Joint Commission on Mental Illness and Health.* New York: Basic Books.

Feldman, JM. (2020). Achieving mental health equity: Community psychiatry. In Stewart, AJ, Shim, RS (Eds) *Achieving mental health equity; Psychiatric Clinics of North America.* 43, 511-524.

Feldman, J.M. (2010) Chronic mentally ill populations. In Ruiz, P. & Primm, A. (Eds) *Disparities in Psychiatric Care: Clinical and Cross-Cultural Perspectives.* 2010: Baltimore: Lippincott, Williams & Williams, 189-197.

Fountain House. https://www.fountainhouse.org. Accessed 5/6/11.

GAP Committee, Psychiatry and the Community. (2016) *People with Mental Illness in The Criminal Justice System.* Arlington, VA: APPI.

Goldstein, J. L. & Godemont, M. M. L. (2003). The legend and lessons of Geel, Belgium: A 1500-year-old legend, a 21st-century model. *Community Mental Health Journal*, 39, 441-458.

Grazier, K.L., Mowbray, C.T., & Holter, M. C. (2005). Rationing psychosocial treatments in the United States. *International Journal of Law and Psychiatry*, 28, 545-560.

Grob, G. N., & Goldman, H. (2007). *The dilemma of federal mental health policy: Radical Reform or incremental change?* New Brunswick, NJ: Rutgers University Press.

Hoge, MA. (2017). Workforce development in behavioural health. Available at https://www.hrsa.gov/Sites/default/virtual-behavioral-health-conference/files/keynote_workforce_development_in_behavioral_health.pdf. Accessed December 21, 2021.

Kart, A, et al. (2021). Cognitive behavioural therapy in treatment of schizophrenia. *Archives Of Neuropsychiatry.* 58, 61-65.

Kopec, K, et al. (2020) . Rapid transition to telehealth in a community mental health service provider during the COVID-19 pandemic. *Primary Care Companion CNS Disorders.* 22, 20bro2787.

Lamb, H. R. (1994) A century and a half of psychiatric rehabilitation in the United States. *Hospital and Community Psychiatry*, 45, 1015-1020,

Liberman, R. P. (1992) *Handbook of Psychiatric Rehabilitation.* Boston: Allyn and Bacon.

Mercado, M. et al. 2016 Generalizability of the NAMI family-to-family education program: Evidence From an efficacy study. *Psychiatric Services.* 67, 591-593.

Marlowe, D. H. (1996) Psychological and psychosocial consequences of combat and deployment with, 1special emphasis on the Gulf War. http://www.gulflink.osd.mil/library/randrep/marlowe_paper/index.html [accessed 5/6/11].

Million, T. (2004). *Masters of the Mind: Exploring the Story of Mental Illness from Ancient Times to the New Millennium.* Hoboken, N.J.: John Wiley & Sons.

Nassar, M. (1987). Psychiatry in ancient Egypt. *Psychiatric Bulletin*, 11, 420.

New Freedom Commission on Mental Health (2003). *Achieving the promise: Transforming mental health care in America: Final report.* (DHHS Publication SMA-20-3832). Rockville, MD.

Rees, T. P. (1987). Back to moral treatment and community care. *Journal of Mental Science,* 103, 303-313.

Sylvestre, J, Nelson, G, Aubry, T. (eds) (2017*). Housing, citizenship, and communities for people with serious mental Illness: Theory, research, practice and policy perspectives.* New York City, New York: Oxford University Press, Inc.

SAMHSA (2009) Integrated treatment for co-occurring disorders: Building your program, DHHS Publication number SMA-08-4366, Rockville, MD:CMSSAMHSA, US Department of Health and Human Services.

SAMHSA National Mental Health Information. About evidence-based practices: Shaping Mental health services toward recovery. https://www.samhsa.gov/resource-search/ebp/mentalhealth.samhsa.gov/cmhs/communitysupport/toolkits/about.asp [accessed March 7, 2022].

Torrey, WC, Drake, RE. (2010). Psychiatric shared-decision making in the outpatient psychiatric care of adults with severe mental illnesses: Redesigning care for the future. *Community Mental Health Journal.* 46, 433-445.

U.S. Department of Health and Human Services. (1999). *Mental health: A report of the surgeon general.* Rockville, MD: U.S. Department of Health and

Human Services, Substance Abuse, and Mental Health Services Administration, Center for Mental Health Services, National Institutes of Health, National Institute of Mental Health.

von Bilsen, HPJG. (2016). Lessons to be learned from the oldest community psychiatric service in the world: Geel in Belgium. *British Journal of Psychiatry Bulletin*. 40, 207-211.

von Staden, H. (1996). Liminal perils: Early Roman receptions of Greek medicine. In (Eds) Ragep, F. J., Ragep, S. P., & Livesey, S. J. *Tradition, Transmission, Transformation*. Leiden, the Netherlands: E. J. Brill. 369-418.

Wallace CJ. (1993). Psychiatric Rehabilitation. *Psychopharmacology Bulletin*, 29, 537-548.

Wright, D. (1997). Discussion point. Getting out of the asylum: Understanding the confinement of the insane in the nineteenth century. *Social History of Medicine*. 10, 137-155.

Yizhuang, M. D. (2005). History of Chinese psychiatry. *Chinese Society of Psychiatry*. http://www.cma-mh.org/english/index.asp [accessed 5/2/2011].

Part II

The Basics: The Pillars of Community Psychiatry

Recovery and Person-Centered Care: Empowerment, Collaboration, and Integration

Wesley E. Sowers

Introduction

The concept of recovery is not a new one in behavioral health, but it has experienced resurgence since the release of the President's New Freedom Commission Report (PNFCR) in 2003 (Hogan 2003). The belief that persons with mental illness or substance use disorders can lead productive and satisfying lives has been part of the philosophic core of community psychiatry for many years and was practiced most notably in psychiatric rehabilitation paradigms through the latter part of the twentieth century. While variations on the theme of recovery have been noted since the nineteenth century and perhaps even earlier, they were established more formally in the 1930s with the establishment of the Alcoholics Anonymous and Recovery, Inc. (Sowers 2003).

Brief Historical Perspective

The idea of recovery has been a mainstay of the addiction community for many years. It has its roots in the 12-step movement that began in the 1930s (White 1998). It became clear to the founders of Alcoholics Anonymous that overcoming the disease of addiction was much more than establishing abstinence. They recognized that addictive disorders create thought processes and conditioned responses that are far more powerful than the physiological manifestations of dependence. They offered an alternative to professional offerings that appeared to be more effective (Laudet et al. 2000). The 12 steps and the various slogans related to thought processes common in persons with addictions are all related to current concepts about recovery.

Although recovery has had a less prominent role in the mental health community in the past, it has been part of the scene for nearly as long as it has been part of the addiction field. Abraham Low, MD, a psychiatrist, began developing recovery-enhancing techniques in 1937, and by 1952, Recovery, Inc was established (Lowe 1950; Sachs 1997). Recovery, Inc. is an organization run by mental health consumers that employs many of the ideas developed by Dr. Low. It offers a peer-assisted healing program that focuses on changing thought processes, developing autonomy, and regaining productive and satisfying lives. Like the 12-step approach, it attempts to empower people to take responsibility for managing their illness or disability. In contrast to 12-step program, Recovery, Inc. has recognized the value of developing a partnership with helping professionals and has attempted to support this relationship (Sowers 2003).

An anti-psychiatry movement originated within the profession in the later part of the twen-

W. E. Sowers (✉)
University of Pittsburgh Medical Center, Bradford Woods, PA, USA

W. E. Sowers et al. (eds.), *Textbook of Community Psychiatry*,
https://doi.org/10.1007/978-3-031-10239-4_3

tieth century, questioning the controlling and judgmental nature of common practices. The legitimacy of diagnosis was also questioned, in light of the lack of biologic or etiologic explanation for them as in other branches of medicine. Who should define "normal" experience? These threads were picked up by survivors of treatment and embellished to the extent that psychiatrists have been vilified in general in some circles, such as Scientology. Laing and Szasz did not see a problem with treatment so long as people were interested in receiving it. The movement as it evolved began to ostracize those who sought and participated in treatment, depicting them as brainwashed. These controversies continue today as diagnostic systems evolve (Rissmiller and Rissmiller 2006).

There are many people with mental illness or substance use disorders who have felt that they have been mistreated by the system, and they have become more organized and more vocal in recent years regarding their rights as individuals and their conviction that they must control their own destiny. They assert that they should not be oppressed by authorities whose primarily interests are control and public safety. The "Recovery Movement" has emerged from these convictions, and while it is not necessarily a unified movement, it has become a significant political force impacting policy and practice in the administration of behavioral health services. Persons in "recovery" have asserted that systems of care and professional attitudes must change if they are hoping to engage with them. Only then will they find meaningful assistance in their struggle to attain autonomy and meaning in their lives (Borkin 2000).

System transformation has emerged as a major priority in federal and state behavioral health services administrations since the issue of the PNFCR and the Surgeon General's report on mental health issues (SAMHSA 2003; US Department of Health and Human Services 1999). Penetration to policy makers and administrators has been fairly broad, but much work remains to be done with regard to training and actual practice (Jacobson and Curtis 2000). The movements mentioned above have been progenitors of the current emphasis on "social inclusion" and securing the civil rights of persons with behavioral health disorders and have significant impact on the evolution of services today. This "transformation" aims to replace a system that has been described as prescriptive and paternalistic with one that is collaborative and empowering and recognizes the potential for growth and change in the individuals that it serves. While there are few that oppose this transformation in principle, there are many who feel the obstacles to achieving the ideal are too formidable to overcome and that is not applicable to everyone who suffers these maladies.

This chapter will consider the nature of recovery and resiliency and their usefulness as organizing concepts in the evolution of our systems of care. It will examine the principles and practices which may be most helpful in moving people toward recovery and the value of incorporating them into the way that services are delivered.

The Elements of Recovery

The concept of recovery has a long history as noted earlier, but it is not a monolithic one, and there have been many variations in how persons or groups have defined it. If recovery is an individual experience as most contend, then each person who has experienced it may define it somewhat differently. Even though recovery has individual meanings and is a dynamic concept, there are certain elements that can be identified that are commonly included in the definitions and that remain fairly stable through changing circumstances (Whitley and Drake 2010). This section will attempt to identify some of those common elements and consider their significance (SAMHSA 2005).

The term "recovery" implies that a person who has been disabled for some period of time returns to their previous level of function, but it has come to take on a much broader significance with regard to persons with behavioral health disorders. There are many who feel that the term is inadequate because in many cases people have not ever developed good capability and are working toward establishing it for the first time. This is especially true for children with emotional disturbances. Another objection is the implication that there is an end point, or cure. This point remains controversial, and there are many who claim that recovery, even from severe mental illness, may be complete, while others contend that it is an ongoing process, which, for most people, is lifelong.

Whichever position is adopted, being "in" recovery, as opposed to being "recovered," describes a process. As various aspects of this process are considered, it may be of interest to consider how they mirror other theories of development, mature coping strategies, and self-actualization. Even though the idea of recovery has been applied most commonly to situations in which a person is struggling to overcome an identifiable (or diagnosable) condition, in its most basic sense, recovery is about a growth and maturation process, not distinct from what all people must negotiate at some time in their lives (Erikson 1950; Vogel-Scibilia et al. 2009). As such, it can be considered a developmental process leading to a "mature" state of being (Mead and Copeland 2000).

By contrast, people who do not engage in a recovery process often appear to be "stuck" in a cycle of making the same decisions over and over, despite the fact that they are not happy with the results. Most of us experience this state at some time in our lives or in some aspect of our living and find that we are afraid of uncertainty and the possibility that we could be even unhappier if we choose to do something unfamiliar. This state will be referred to as "Stagnation" for the purposes of our discussion.

The Aims of a Recovery Process

Change

A person enters a recovery process as an attempt to break patterns of behavior that have been detrimental to their well-being. There are almost always choices that can be made about how to think and act regardless of what type of limitations or disabilities with which one is confronted. Change must often be radical in order to escape the rigidity of past patterns of behavioral, and "reinventing oneself" is a challenging and daunting prospect.

Growth

Change leads to growth, to an expanding sense of self and of the world. A growth or maturation process begins when one is able to embrace change and continues in an incremental fashion as new experiences and behaviors are added to an individual's palette. A state of stagnation implies a closed world of repetition circumscribed around sets of stereotyped behaviors. Recovery, in contrast, implies expanding world, new possibilities, and customized responses to the significant challenges presented by a changing environment (Deegan 1988).

Autonomy and Resilience

Growth and the development of a broader array of behaviors allow people to adapt to a wide variety of circumstances. Adaptability and the capacity to influence the environment lead to a greater sense of personal effectiveness. The way that one understands their reality changes from one in which they believe that they have no control over or responsibility for what happens to them to one in which they believe that the choices that they make and things they do are the most important determinants of their experience and circumstance. As the process of recovery progresses, there is a growing capacity to act independently and to make responsible decisions (Mead et al. 2001).

Purpose and Meaning

Ultimately, satisfaction in life must be derived from the ideas and activities that give it meaning. We derive meaning from a number of sources: spiritual connections, work, relationships, social structures, education, recreation, and artistic endeavors (King 2004; Green et al. 1997). As growth progresses and we see ourselves as the agents that shape our world, we begin to create a set of beliefs to replace a nihilistic void that characterizes a stagnant life.

Development of Enabling Qualities

In order to initiate and sustain a recovery process, a person must develop several qualities to enable it. These may be described in various ways, but however they are conceived; there is an evolution in the thinking process as people progress toward the changes they wish to make. Many of these qualities are included in various formulations of stages of change. The most common of these elements will be presented here as a progression, but in reality, they do not always appear in a linear or predictable chronologic order.

Acceptance and Responsibility

Before a desire to change can take hold, a person must recognize their limitations and/or disabilities. While there is often tremendous tenacity in resistance to admitting vulnerability and to giving up the belief that factors outside one's self is responsible for your trouble, once it is surmounted, there is a possibility for change. With acceptance comes responsibility, the recognition that we must depend on ourselves to do what is required to make changes.

Desire and Determination

In order for change to occur, people must move beyond ambivalence and even willingness and develop a genuine desire to live differently and a determination to do whatever is needed to do so.

Hope and Faith

When people are stuck and stagnant, they are often unable to see that things can be any different and feel helpless to change their circumstances. When a person decides to enter a recovery process, they are embracing the possibility of change, and they must develop the belief that they are capable of it.

Courage, Diligence, and Tolerance

Change requires intense and consistent effort and causes a great deal of discomfort and pain. A person must find the courage to face/experience this challenge and the tenacity to persevere under physical and emotional stress.

Integrity, Honesty, and Trust

A person engaging in a recovery process is most successful when able to consistently pursue and represent the truth and judicious values and avoiding misrepresentation and deception. Achieving this, it is possible to gain respect and trust in oneself and from others. These qualities make it possible to join a community and find meaning beyond immediate self-interests (Kaufmann et al. 1989).

Tolerance, Humility, and Forgiveness

To be human is to make mistakes; sometimes they may be egregious mistakes that cause a great deal of suffering. In order to progress in a recovery process, a person must develop some capacity to accept the weaknesses of others and to recognize their own. Freedom and equanimity come with the capacity to forgive both oneself and others.

Characteristics of a Mature Recovery

The development of the foregoing virtues is obviously an extended process which is likely to proceed in fits and starts, and it may take many years to achieve great consistency. For most people, it is a lifelong struggle to stay on track. This process, when successfully negotiated, leads ultimately to a certain balance and satisfaction in life in which a person is also a reliable and trusted member of a community. As these qualities become more and more consistent, confidence grows, as does the ability to adapt to and make changes. People find new ways to manage their lives and relationships, drawing on growing resources and a willingness to accept some of the risk that comes with self-disclosure and emotional investment. Openness to new ideas, self-observation and assessment, a capacity for kindness and empathy, thoughtfulness and flexibility, and the realization that one need not denigrate others to value one's self would all be aspects of a maturity in recovery, whether in mental health or with substance use disorders.

Resiliency and Recovery

As someone progresses with recovery, they become more resilient or better able to cope with adversity (Unger 2011). These two concepts share many common elements, and they both imply an ability to thrive. They are generally used in different contexts. "Resiliency" is most often used by clinicians and other stakeholders when referring to the characteristics of children and adolescents. The negative implications of recovery, described earlier, are more significant for this age group. "Recovery," on the other hand, is more often used when referring to adult development, but it is not easily separated from the resiliency concept. Many have commented on the inadequacy of the terminology, but it has not been easy to find broadly acceptable alternatives. While the two terms are similar, there are some qualities that distinguish them:

- Resiliency describes a *characteristic* or *state* that allows positive adaptation within the context of significant adversity. Each person has his or her own unique level of resilience.
- Recovery describes a *process* that allows restoration or renewal following personal setbacks related to disabling circumstances. Individuals may or may not engage in a recovery process.
- Resiliency is partly determined by one's genetic makeup and partly developed through experience and environmental influences (i.e., nurturing vs. neglectful).
- Recovery is independent of biological determinants and is largely characterized by attitudes and values rather than abilities.
- Developing resiliency is an essential aspect of a successful recovery process.
- Resiliency may occur in the absence of a recovery process.

Universal Aspects of Recovery

Over the years, the definitions of recovery and what it represents have been variable, and different groups may conceive of it in different ways. This raises the question of whether recovery is the same for everyone, regardless of their affliction, or is it distinct for people recovering from a particular type of disability? Recovery may be defined narrowly or broadly. For example, recovery from an addiction might be conceived of as attaining abstinence or it may be defined more broadly as life satisfaction and growth. Likewise in mental health, recovery may be seen as the absence of symptoms and a reduction in the use of services or alternatively as the ability to live autonomously and make healthy choices.

While there has been some controversy around who "owns" recovery and how it should be formulated, there is a growing consensus on the main elements that constitute a recovery process. This is fortunate, because it makes obvious sense to have a unified understanding of recovery, especially as we struggle to better integrate services for persons with behavioral health issues.

These elements of recovery provide a blueprint for change, regardless of individual circumstances. Whether someone has a mental illness, has a substance use disorder, has a physical disability, had a traumatic experience, or is simply struggling against patterns of behavior that make managing their daily lives difficult, the recipe for change is more or less the same. Although the degree of disability and the difficulty of engaging in a recovery process may vary considerably, recognizing that everyone must follow a common pathway to accomplish change has significant implications for clinical processes, service delivery, and social stigma.

The Value of the Recovery Paradigm

Recovery creates a framework for change that can be applied in a variety of circumstances and settings, so it provides a common language which all clinicians and service users can understand and use to promote health and wellness. As such, it can be the basis for integration of an often diverse array of providers that may be involved in a person's care (Mueser et al. 2002). In clinical settings, it can be the foundation for empathy and collaboration through its formulation of shared human emotions, experience, and ambition. In the broader community, its universal aspects form a strong weapon to wield against stigma. As the community comes to recognize the common experiences of all its constituents, it becomes the basis for acceptance and inclusion and the protection of every individual's human rights. Many observers have noted that the recovery movement is ultimately a civil rights struggle.

Developing Person-Centered, Recovery-Oriented Services

Having considered what constitutes a recovery process, we can now turn our attention to how psychiatrists and other clinicians can promote and facilitate recovery and how we can create services that support it. The development of recovery-oriented services (ROS) begins with the recognition that services must be constructed to meet the needs of individuals and that individuals should not be expected to benefit from programs or treatments designed for stereotypic patients with preconceived needs (Anthony 2000). Person-centered care is sometimes used interchangeably with recovery-oriented services, but may also be seen as an aspect of these services that particularly emphasize the key concept described above. The following principles provide further description of ROS:

- *Hopeful-Optimistic:* The clinician's role is to inspire hope and create an atmosphere that assertively recognizes the possibility for change in every individual (8).
- *Respectful-Strength Based:* The attitude of service providers must be respectful and focused on the positive attributes that define an individual. They must be sensitive to and avoid the subtle condescension that has generally characterized paternalistic approaches of the past (Borkin 2000).
- *Empowering:* ROS encourage service users to take control of their lives, accept responsibility for change, and use shared information to make informed choices (Fisher 1994).
- *Collaborative:* Treatment is conceived of as a partnership between the person seeking assistance and those offering care. Discarding the traditional roles of a controlling provider and a passive consumer, in this paradigm the two work as a team to accomplish the consumer's goals (Noordsy et al. 2000).
- *Supportive-Nurturing:* Disabilities are destructive to self-esteem and confidence. Recovery is a progressive process and requires gradual fortification of these qualities through support, encouragement, recognition of achievements, and trust (Mead et al. 2001).
- *Capacitating:* Growth implies an expanding ability to live, learn, work, create, and interact. ROS should help every individual to define and reach their potential with regard to these activities (Carlson et al. 2001).
- *Inclusive*: ROS should offer and encourage inclusion of disabled individuals in all administrative processes that govern the operation of services. They will also encourage involvement in the larger community (Townsend et al. 2000).
- *Comprehensive*: People should have access to a complete array of clinical and supportive services to meet their basic needs as well as their emotional and spiritual needs. In the

planning process, these services should be tailored to fit individual issues.

- *Outcome Informed*: To make informed health choices, people must have access to information related to the likely results associated with available treatments. There should be opportunities for them to learn about outcomes and evidence and how to evaluate them (Roberts 2002).
- *Culturally Sensitive:* Individuals may have multiple cultural influences in their lives, including spiritual concerns (Huguelet et al. 2011). ROS should celebrate diversity, explore cultural experience, and value the unique contributions that it makes to how one operates in the world and how people understand and experience a disability.
- *Integrated:* It may require several different providers to meet the needs of a particular person. ROS recognize the need to coordinate and, if possible, consolidate the services provided into a coherent and interactive plan with the consumer at its center.
- *Voluntary:* The use of seclusion, restraint, and coercion is not consistent with ROS and is only used if there are clearly no other alternatives. ROS recognize that individuals may have periods of incapacity and encourage the formulation of appropriate plans for these circumstances (Davis 2002).

A significant aspect of person-centered care is its focus on *information sharing* and offering choices that are informed by that knowledge. It encourages individuals to formulate a personal vision for their lives and to create plans that will give them an opportunity to fulfill those ideals. The central role of the relationship in healing processes is also a critical aspect of person-centered care and ROS. The *relationship building* process is ultimately the source of trust that is essential for a clinical partnership. This partnership is what allows engagement in a collaborative planning process, which is the best guarantor of investment in the product of that process (Manfred-Gilham et al. 2002).

A focus on *health and wellness* as opposed to illness and disability is another hallmark of ROS. The prevention or the mitigation of relapse to active illness is accomplished by developing skills that facilitate making healthy choices and exercising effective health management. In this regard, it mirrors the *chronic care and disease management models* promulgated in physical health care. Recognition of the interaction of mental and physical processes as an important determinant of overall well-being leads to an *integrated or holistic approach to service delivery* which fits with recent concepts of medical/mental health homes, or centralized, coordinated care models (Beardslee et al. 2011). The great disparity in health status and life expectancy between those with behavioral health issues and the general population makes this aspect of recovery-oriented care ever more critical. Health cannot be subdivided into its components, as all aspects are interdependent. ROS recognize that people can be healthy, even with an active illness, just as they maybe unhealthy without identifiable disease.

Concerns are often raised about the applicability of ROS to persons with very severe mental illnesses who have periods of cognitive deficits rendering them unable to make prudent choices. They may consistently make choices that place them at risk of harm (Davidson and O'Connell 2006). It is important to recall in these instances that recovery is a developmental process, and it is not always a linear one. We might think of "stages" of recovery as analogous to the stages of change often referred to in the addiction literature. Just as we would not offer a young child complete freedom to do as they please, we would not offer this to someone who has uncontrolled and severe symptoms of mental illness. The operating principle in cases where a person has diminished capacity is to gradually extend their capacity to make wise and responsible choices. Gradually increasing degrees of freedom and choice are required to accomplish this. In the most severe cases of mental illness and intellectual disability, this may be a very slow process. The intention of ROS is to consistently attempt to extend an individual's capacity for self-management and self-agency. When this is not possible, the use of *advanced directives* can be a very valuable tool to allow individuals to exercise some control even when they are most debilitated (Srebnik et al. 2005; Henderson et al. 2008).

Finally, ROS must find ways to challenge individuals to recognize their own possibilities and to pursue their vision without creating overwhelming stress. Much of this work will be accomplished through motivational techniques, allowing individuals to gradually define their own needs, desires, and solutions. Rather than striving for compliance or adherence, ROS hope to create *investment* in a shared plan for change. Change is disruptive and frightening, calling many beliefs and practices into question. ROS must be comfortable in helping people to confront and find answers to spiritual/existential questions; and it must help them to find ways to become part of a community and develop satisfying relationships with others.

Implementation and System Transformation

The characteristics described above provide a basic idea of the nature of services provided by organizations that wish to promote recovery. The American Association of Community Psychiatrists developed the "Guidelines for Recovery Oriented Services." This document provides a further elaborated description of ROS by delineating 17 separate characteristics and dividing them into three categories: administrative, treatment, and support (AACP 2001a). For each characteristic, a set of measurable indicators follows a descriptive paragraph. This document provides a "blueprint" for organizations that would like to develop this model. Its companion "Recovery Oriented Services Evaluation (ROSE)" is a self-assessment tool, which translates the indicators of the guidelines into anchors in its rating process (AACP 2001b). While not validated, the use of this tool creates capacity to enable organizations to measure their progress in developing ROS over time. There have been several other tools that have become available recently, which provide similar guidance (Winarski et al. 2018; Yale 2020).

Several other issues will be encountered by organizations wishing to implement ROS in place of traditional practices. The existing behavioral health workforce has, for the most part, not been well trained to work in a collaborative, egalitarian manner with the people that they serve. As noted above, change is very difficult to embrace, and it is commonly experienced as a threat. Clinicians can often be resistant to change that is not self-initiated, or they may minimize differences between these proposed practices and those currently in place. Full implementation of ROS usually constitutes a cultural change, and it is very difficult to uproot established practices and attitudes.

In this context, it requires visionary or transformational leadership to move organizations toward person-centered, recovery-focused care (Corrigan and Garman 1999). Leaders and teachers will be most successful by taking a motivational approach, helping their staff to find incentives for and value in making changes to their practice. To do so, there must be a significant investment of time and energy to allow not only adequate information transfer but opportunities to process the information and its implications. Significant change occurs most readily when people see that it will further their own interests, so it will be important to help staff define what those interests are.

Leadership, in moving the organization toward ROS, has an opportunity to model facilitative and collaborative practices rather than directive, authoritarian methods. Transparency, informality, flexibility, and suggestibility all contribute to the empowerment of staff and eventually contribute to their ability to treat their clients reciprocally. Solicitation of input and participation in administrative activities and program design and development also allow staff to feel invested in the organization and to take pride in its success. As one might expect, this idea of participation is one that facilitates clients' investment in a treatment planning process and adherence to the collaborative plan developed from it. Having this experience in the workplace begins to create a different culture and will make a translation to clinical processes much easier.

Non-traditional approaches to training may also help to overcome some of the resistance to change. One method that has been well received and successful is the promotion of dialogues between consumers and providers outside their usual roles in the clinical context. Fears about the consequences of honesty can be minimized if participants feel that they have no real-life relationship with their counterparts. This arrangement allows a genuine sharing of experience both from the person in recovery (PIR) and the behavioral health professional and is inevitably appreciated by the participants. It promotes empathy and trust and helps participants to understand that they are less different from one another than they imagined (ACCR 2020).

Another aid to the transformation process is the Recovery to Practice Curricula, developed through the support of Substance Abuse and Mental Health Services Administration. This group of discipline-specific curricula (nursing, social work, psychology, peer professionals, and psychiatry) were developed to advance the principles set forth in the PNFC report. The curriculum for psychiatry was developed by the AACP and the APA and consists of nine modules that have transdisciplinary relevance. Each module consists of an audio-visual introduction to its topic and is designed to be used in a group setting with prepared discussion questions to guide an interactive exchange facilitated by a professional PIR team. This format models the collaborative relationship that characterize ROS and allows participants to express both concerns and positive reactions they have had related to potential changes in their practice (AACP/APA 2011). These modules are well suited to introduce trainees to ROS by residency training programs.

Creating a competent workforce for ROS is a long-term process, but can be expedited with organizational commitment and consistency in applying the principles of ROS at all levels of the organization. Even with these conditions in place, there may be some individuals in the organization who do not feel comfortable with this new paradigm and will want to leave. In most cases it is wise to facilitate these wishes and accept the idea that not everyone is ready for change or well suited to work in this way.

Changing the content of professional training to incorporate the principles of ROS in both didactic and practical aspects of training will ensure that a new generation of clinicians becomes available to replace those leaving the workforce (Peebles et al. 2009). Although it may seem daunting to insert this new content into the already overcrowded curricula commonly encountered in psychiatric training programs, this is an overarching attitudinal shift that will not necessarily replace other topics, but instead should enhance them all. It will require commitment from academic institutions to implement these necessary changes in curricula, and incentives are needed to facilitate movement in this direction.

The concept of ROS received a great deal of attention during the early 2000s and into the 2010s. Unfortunately, this attention has faded significantly during the latter part of the 2010s. This may be due to a number of factors. The recovery movement was overshadowed during this period to some degree by the rise in attention to integrated care and anti-racist interventions, even though recovery principles are relevant to both. In addition, there may have been a general sense of complacency, combined with a lack of appreciation for the complexity and nuances of recovery principles or the breadth of their application. For many providers and professional educators, there was a sense of "mission accomplished" when only shared decision-making was incorporated more broadly into clinical practice. As we have seen, recovery-oriented service principles are much more diverse than that and can be applied in a wide variety of situations and circumstances. In the vernacular, "walking the walk" is much more difficult than "talking the talk." The need to reignite interest in ROS principles will be an important strategy in the struggle to deliver equitable and comprehensive services to distressed communities.

Evidence, Quality, and Recovery-Oriented Services

As discussed above, one of the important elements of ROS is to provide information to consumers and allow them to choose among available options based on what they have learned (Farkas et al. 2005). A full discussion of evidence-based practices is discussed elsewhere in this book (Chapter "Evidence-Based Practice and Practice-Based Evidence"), but it is important to state that the strength of evidence for the effectiveness of each available clinical option is an essential part of ROS.

But what is the evidence for the effectiveness of ROS? There is not yet a clear answer to that question. Many people believe that, intuitively, if people have more control over their care, they will be more invested and more likely to adhere to the plans that they have made to progress in their recovery. A variation of that theme is that ROS is not a "treatment," but provides a *context* and an *attitude* for the delivery of services. If ROS promote equality and justice for persons with behavioral health disorders, then the issue of "evidence" needs not be relevant.

Others note that ROS are complex and multifaceted, and as a result, it would be extremely difficult to generate evidence for its effectiveness using standard approaches. Furthermore, if "recovery" is the desired outcome, then traditional measures of successful treatment may no longer be appropriate. This would apply equally to quality improvement processes. Indicators of success would be more closely aligned with consumer satisfaction and quality of life, rather than service needs and utilization (Drake et al. 2003). While evidence-informed interventions are an important element of ROS, the nature of "valid" evidence must be scrutinized, and perhaps broadened, to accurately reflect the benefits of these approaches (Torrey et al. 2005).

Recovery-oriented services consist of an array of interventions and techniques. Another way to think about the evidence for ROS is through the investigation of the elements that promote it to assess their effectiveness. These elements include interventions such as motivational interviewing, supported employment, shared decision-making, and peer support, all of which have a strong evidentiary base (SAMHSA 2009; SAMHSA 2011; Davidson et al. 2012; Frost et al. 2011).

Recovery and ROS are recurrent themes throughout this text, and the concepts presented here provide a foundation for thinking about the many implications these perspectives will have on the typical activities of the community psychiatrist. They inform our relationships with clients, our approach to service design and delivery, and the scope of our involvement in the community. As noted earlier, a recovery perspective has long been an aspect of good community psychiatry, and indeed, it is hard to imagine how it could be otherwise.

References

AACP: Guidelines for Recovery Oriented Services. 2001a Available at: https://sites.google.com/view/aacp123/publications/archived-documents?authuser=1. Accessed October 25, 2020

AACP: ROSE (Recovery Oriented Services Evaluation) 2001b Available at: https://drive.google.com/file/d/0B89glzXJnn4cZDRxVDBoMExtb2s/view. Accessed October 25, 2020

AACP/APA: Recovery to Practice Curriculum for Psychiatry. 2011 Available at: https://sites.google.com/view/aacp123/resources/recovery-to-practice_1?authuser=1. Accessed October 22, 2020

ACCR (2020) Collaborative for Recovery Dialogues, available at http://coalitionforrecovery.org/committees/consumer-provider-collaborative/. Accessed July 18, 2022

Anthony W A., (2000), A Recovery-Oriented Service System: Setting Some System Level Standards. Psychiatric Rehabilitation Journal, Vol. 24:159-168

Beardslee WR, Chien PI, Bell CC (2011) Prevention of mental disorders, substance abuse, and problem behaviors: a developmental perspective. Psychiatric Services 62:247-254

Borkin, J.R. (2000) Recovery Attitudes Questionnaire: Development and Evaluation. Psychosocial Rehabilitation Journal, Vol.24:95-1003

Carlson LS, Rapp CA, McDiarmid D; (2001) Hiring consumer-providers: barriers and alternative solutions. Community Mental Health Journal 37:199-213

Corrigan, P.W., and Garman, A.N (1999)., "Transformational and Transactional Leadership Skills for Mental Health Teams", Community Mental Health Journal, 35:301-312

Davidson L, O'Connell, Tandora J, et. al (2006)., "Top Ten Concerns About Recovery," Psychiatric Services, 57:640-645

Davidson L, Belamy C, Guy K, & Miller R (2012) Peer support among persons with severe mental illness: a review of evidence and experience; World Psychiatry 11(2) 123-128

Davis S. (2002), Autonomy Versus Coercion: Reconciling Competing Perspectives in Community Mental Health. Community Mental Health Journal, 38:239-250

Deegan P E. (1988) Recovery: The Lived Experience of Rehabilitation. Psychosocial Rehabilitation Journal, Vol. 11:11-19

Drake RE, Green AI, Muesser KT, Goldman HH (2003): The history of community mental health and rehabilitation for persons with severe mental illness. Comm Ment. Health J. 39: 427-440

Erikson, E.H. (1950). Childhood and Society. New York: Norton.

Farkas M, Gagne C, Anthony A, Chamberlain J, (2005) Implementing recovery oriented evidence based programs: identifying the critical dimensions. Community Ment. Health J. 41:141-157

Fisher D B., (1994) Health Care Reform Based on an Empowerment Model of Recovery by People With Psychiatric Disabilities. Hospital and Community Psychiatry, 45:913-915

Frost L, Heinz T, Bach DH (2011): Promoting Recovery-oriented Mental Health Services Through a Peer Specialist Employer Learning Community Journal of Participatory Medicine 2011;3

Green LL, Fullilove MT, Fullilove RE: (1997) Stories of Spiritual Awakening: the nature of spirituality in recovery. J. of Subst Abuse Treatment 15:325-331

Henderson C, Swanson JW, Szmukler G, et al, (2008) A typology of advance statements in mental health care, Psychiatric Serv 69:63-71

Hogan FH, (2003) The President's New Freedom Commission: Recommendations to Transform Mental Health Care in America, Psychiatr Serv 54:1467-1474

Huguelet P, Mohr S, Betrisey C, et al (2011) A randomized trial of spiritual assessment of outpatients with schizophrenia: patients' and clinicians' experience Psychiatric Services 62:79-86

Jacobson N, Curtis L., (2000), Recovery as Policy in Mental Health Services: Strategies Emerging from the States. Psychiatric Rehabilitation Journal, Vol. 23:333-341

King GA: The meaning of life experiences: application of a meta-model to rehabilitation sciences and services. Amer. J of Orthopsychiatry 74:72-88 (2004)

Kaufmann C L, Freund P D, Wilson J., (1989), Self Help in the Mental Health System: A Model for service user-Provider Collaboration. Psychosocial Rehabilitation Journal, 13:5-21

Laudet A B, Magura S, Vogel H S, Knight E., (2000), Addictions Services: Support, Mutual Aid and Recovery from Dual Diagnosis. Community Mental Health Journal, Vol. 36:457-476

Lowe AA, (1950) Mental health through will training, North Quincy, MA, Christopher, 136

Manfred-Gilham JJ, Sales E, Koeske G: (2002) Therapist and case manager perceptions of client barriers to treatment participation and use of engagement strategies. Community Mental Health J. 38: 213-221

Mead S, Copeland, M E., (2000), What Recovery Means to Us: Service user's Perspectives. Community Mental Health Journal, Vol 36:315-331

Mead S, Hilton D, Curtis L., (2001), Peer Support: A Theoretical Perspective. Psychiatric Rehabilitation Journal, Vol. 25:134-141

Mueser K T, Corrigan P W, Hilton D W, Tanzman B, Schaub A, Gingerich S, Essock S M, Tarrier N, Morey B, Vogel-Scibilia S, Herz M I., (2002), Illness Management and Recovery: A Review of the Research. Psychiatric Services, 53:1272-83

Noordsy DL, Torrey WC, Mead S, Brunette M, Potenza D, Copeland MS: (2000) Recovery Oriented psychopharmacology: redefining the goals of antipsychotic treatment J. Clin Psychiatry 61 (supp 3): 22-29

Peebles S, Mabe PA, Fenley G, Buckley PF et al (2009)., "Immersing Practitioners in the Recovery Model: An Educational Program Evaluation," Community Ment Health J, vol. 45: 23-45,

Rissmiller, D.J. and Rissmiller, J.H (2006.), "Evolution of the Antipsychiatry Movement into Mental Health Consumerism." Psychiatric Services, vol. 57:863-866

Roberts L W., (2002) Informed Consent and the Capacity for Voluntarism. Am J Psychiatry 159:705-851

Sachs S (1997) Recovery, Inc.: a wellness model for self-help mental health, Developments in Ambulatory Mental Health Care Continuum, 4

SAMHSA (2003), Transforming MH Care in America, www.samhsa.gov/Federalactionagenda/NFC_EXECSUM.aspx

SAMHSA (2005) National Consensus Statement on Mental Health Recovery. http://store.samhsa.gov/shin/content//SMA05-4129/SMA05-4129.pdf, Washington DC

SAMHSA. *Supported Employment: The Evidence.* DHHS Pub. No. SMA-08-4364, Rockville, MD: Center for Mental Health Services, Substance Abuse and Mental Health Services Administration, U.S. Department of Health and Human Services, 2009.

SAMHSA *Consumer-Operated Services: The Evidence.* HHS Pub. No. SMA-11-4633, Rockville, MD: Center for Mental Health Services, Substance Abuse and Mental Health Services Administration, U.S. Department of Health and Human Services, 2011.

Sowers W (2003) Transforming Systems of Care: AACP Guidelines for Recovery Oriented Services, Community Mental Health Journal 41:757-774

Srebnik DS, Rutherford LT, Peto T, et al (2005) The content and clinical utility of psychiatric advance directives. Psychiatric Services 56:592-598

Torrey WC, Rapp CA, Van Tosh L et al,(2005) "Recovery Principles and Evidence-Based Practice: Essential Ingredients of Service Improvement." Community Mental Health Journal, vol. 41:91-100

Townsend W, Boyd S, Griffin G., (2000) Emerging Best Practices in Mental Health Recovery. The Ohio Department of Mental Health, Columbus, Ohio

Unger M (2011) The social ecology of resilience: addressing contextual and cultural ambiguity of a nascent construct Amer. J. of Orthopsychiatry 81:1-17

Vogel-Scibilia SE, McNulty KC, Baxter B (2009) The Recovery Process Utilizing Erikson's Stages of Human Development, Comm Mental Health Journ; 45:405-414

White WL, (1998) Slaying the Dragon: The history of addiction treatment and recovery in America. Chestnut Health Systems/Lighthouse Institute. Bloomington, IL, US:

Whitley R, Drake RE (2010): Recovery: a dimensional approach. Psychiatric Services 61:1248-1249

Winarski, J., Dow, M, Hendry, P., & Robinson, P. (2018). Self Assessment/Planning Tool for Implementing Recovery-Oriented Services (SAPT) Adapted for Florida's Recovery Oriented System of Care Initiative (ROSC). Tampa, FL: Louis de la Parte Florida Mental Health Institute, University of South Florida.

U.S. Department of Health and Human Services. (1999) *Mental Health: A Report of the Surgeon General—Executive Summary*. Rockville, MD: U.S. Department of Health and Human Services, Substance Abuse and Mental Health Services Administration, Center for Mental Health Services, National Institutes of Health, NIMH, http://www.surgeongeneral.gov/library/mentalhealth/home.html#preface

Yale School of Medicine: Recovery self-assessment, Yale Program for Recovery and Community Health; available at https://medicine.yale.edu/psychiatry/prch/tools/rec_selfassessment/. Accessed October 20, 2020

Population Health, Prevention, and Community Psychiatry

Peter Chien, Michael T. Compton, and Patrick S. Runnels

Introduction

> If someone comes to the emergency room with a rat bite, you treat them. If another comes, you treat that bite, and then you do something about the rats. – Carl C. Bell, MD, community psychiatrist, 1947–2019

Community psychiatry strongly values treating and caring for all people. This includes working with those who might otherwise have difficulty accessing healthcare, such as those experiencing a serious mental illness, homelessness, or poverty. Care delivery often takes place outside of formal healthcare settings – the homes, streets, neighborhoods, and communities where people live – and can involve working with individuals, groups, and family members. In addition to treating individuals, community psychiatry directly confronts the upstream social factors that negatively impact mental health (like poverty and inadequate housing) by developing solutions to address them, such as supported employment and housing first. Finally, the field advocates for policies to prevent mental distress and mental illnesses. This chapter gives an overview of these approaches with some examples.

P. Chien (✉)
Loyola University Medical Center, Acute Recovery Center, Edward Hines Jr. VA Hospital, Hines, IL, USA

M. T. Compton
New York State Psychiatric Institute, Columbia University Vagelos College of Physicians & Surgeons, New York, NY, USA
e-mail: mtc2176@cumc.columbia.edu

P. S. Runnels
Case Western Reserve University School of Medicine, Population Health, University Hospitals, Shaker Heights, OH, USA
e-mail: patrick.runnels1@uhhospitals.org

Population Mental Health

The current system of mental healthcare serves many in need, but not everyone. Epidemiological surveys show that one in five US adults report experiencing a mental health disorder in a given year, though only about half receive any mental health treatment (SAMHSA 2020). Only 10% of those reporting a substance use disorder receive any treatment (SAMHSA 2020). One contributing factor is a behavioral health workforce shortage, which would only intensify if more people were to seek care (HRSA 2015). Treating everyone who would benefit is currently not feasible; thus, population mental health approaches are needed.

A common definition of population health is, "the health outcomes of a group of people, including the distribution of such outcomes within the group" (Kindig and Stoddart 2003). Several elements of population health management distinguish it from traditional clinical care, but the focus of efforts is on the health of a

W. E. Sowers et al. (eds.), *Textbook of Community Psychiatry*,
https://doi.org/10.1007/978-3-031-10239-4_4

group, which might be those served in a particular health system, a racial or demographic group, or people living in a particular geographic area (Purtle et al. 2020). Accountability extends beyond the services or activities performed, with a focus on outcomes, including achieving an equitable distribution of outcomes.

Interventions that are more efficient in reaching more of the service population and those that are more effective in achieving results contribute to population mental health. Conceptually, population mental health can be improved in four domains – at the level of an individual clinician; at the level of a healthcare system; at the level of a public mental health system; and at the level of public policy approaches aimed at common causes of mental health problems, including preventive approaches.

Graphically, a pyramid diagram can help us envision opportunities to move toward population-level treatment and prevention at four levels of care – clinical work, healthcare systems, public mental health systems, and social determinants of health. Interventions at each deeper level increase the number of people reached, with a greater population-level benefit. Each level can be best understood by exploring examples. These examples of population mental health focus on groups of people, defined in these cases as those in a certain healthcare system or geography. The interventions to improve mental health differ; yet they share common underlying principles. They define target outcomes and indicators and collect this data on an accessible dashboard to measure progress, and interventions are adjusted over time based on their effectiveness for achieving better population mental health outcomes.

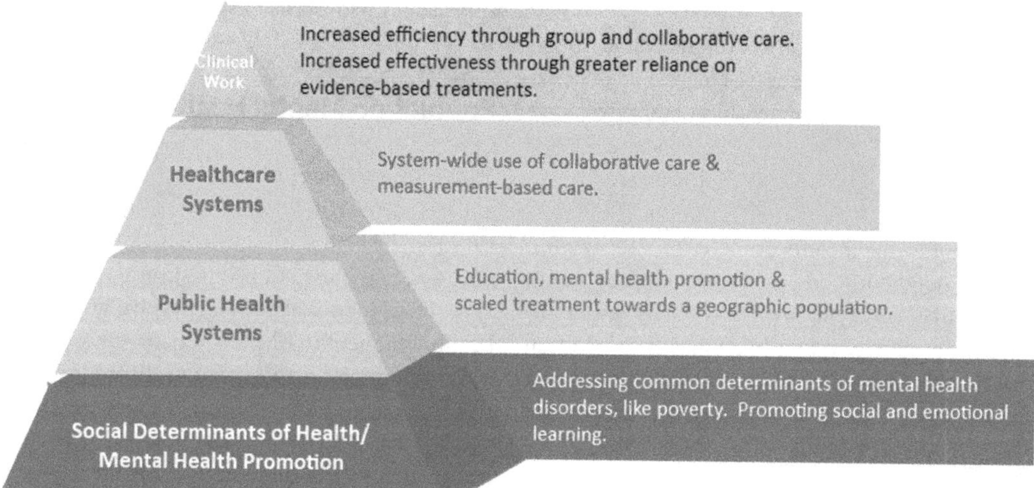

At the individual level, a clinician might employ several ways to improve efficiency or effectiveness, like treating multiple people at a time in group settings, adhering carefully to evidence-based interventions, or engaging in active collaboration with other clinicians.

Even greater proportional gains in population health can be realized through re-design of system workflows. One powerful intervention is measurement-based care, in which numerical data is gathered through standardized workflows. Treatment algorithms are then applied based on that data to help guide clinical decisions. Scores on symptom measures provide regular, objective feedback and can detect small changes in symptoms. This prompts frequent clinical reassessment and can highlight subtherapeutic treatment responses in need of modification.

Measurement-based care produces better outcomes than relying solely on clinical judgment – which is more subjective and leads to greater variability in clinical decisions – particularly in the treatment response and remission of depression (Hong et al. 2021). Additionally, it allows clinicians to more efficiently prioritize their time. For individuals still experiencing a high burden of symptoms, clinicians can quickly focus on key symptom domains in greater depth. At the same time, clinicians can quickly identify people doing consistently well as candidates to have less frequent appointments, tapering treatment, or transition care to their primary care provider in order to spend time with others in need.

At the healthcare system level, the collaborative care approach embeds social workers or other mental health professionals to work alongside primary care physicians within primary care practices to address mental health needs. This approach efficiently engages more people and focuses more attention to mental health needs in a primary care setting (Thota et al. 2012). Collaborative care has traditionally focused on conditions that are highly prevalent in primary care setting, such as depression, which is charted on 9% of visits (Rui and Okeyode 2016). The embedded mental health professional keeps a registry of patients, monitors symptoms and medication response, provides care coordination and brief counselling, consults with a psychiatrist to discuss difficult cases, and partners with the primary care provider, who prescribes the medication. Collaborative care has more than doubled the effectiveness of depression treatment over usual care (Unützer et al. 2002) and has been shown to lead to greater long-term improvements in both depression and anxiety outcomes (Archer et al. 2012), as well as physical health outcomes such as diabetes and cardiovascular measures (Katon et al. 2010).

In the realm of public health systems, New York City has been engaging in a multi-year, multi-faceted, $850 million effort called ThriveNYC. Starting with population-level mapping of mental health needs and assets, ThriveNYC engaged in 54 different initiatives targeting mental health, which are described as "data-driven mitigation of risk factors and threats; scaled implementation of prevention and treatment pathways; strategies to close gaps in access, risk reduction, and health promotion; and action through other sectors than healthcare on structural drivers of inequity and disparities in outcome" (Belkin and McCray 2019). One way that ThriveNYC promotes action is through task-sharing partnerships. In this strategy, mental health professionals teach skills and support people who are not mental health professionals – including police, juvenile justice staff, homeless shelter staff, public school teachers, childcare workers, parents, and other medical clinicians – to promote mental health, implement rating scales, and refer for further treatment when needed (Belkin 2020). These partnerships have generally been well-received, promoting a positive culture of mental health at the community organizations (Dunbar et al. 2017). Thrive NYC also includes a distinct focus on young children through the Early Child Mental Health Network, which promotes pro-social and emotional skills for childcare providers, parents, and their children. Initial results show reduced behavioral needs in the high-risk children targeted by this network (Belkin 2020).

Social Determinants of Mental Health

Social determinants can be thought of as root causes that increase or exacerbate the risk factors for mental illnesses. For example, poverty, discrimination, and adverse childhood experiences such as childhood trauma can precede and increase risk factors for depression such as stress, dysfunctional family interactions, and interpersonal difficulties. They are ideally addressed upstream through public policies (e.g., state and federal laws) and social programs. Other examples of social determinants include poor education, unemployment and financial strain, adverse features of the built environment, food insecurity, and housing instability, among others (Compton and Shim 2015). At an individual level, clinicians already address many malleable social and environmental factors through biopsychosocial plans. For instance, when unemployment affects a person's mental health, evidence-based vocational rehabilitation or supported employment could be an important part of their plan.

Poverty is a good example of how addressing a societal problem can affect the health and mental health of many individuals. Poverty leads to a number of stressors for children and their parents, causes less supportive parenting behaviors and less secure attachment, and creates more relationship conflict across multiple important developmental periods for children. This can be compounded by neighborhood and institutional factors like lower-quality schools, more family and job instability, fewer neighborhood resources, and less access to healthcare (Yoshikawa et al. 2012). The result is that poverty leads to worse cognitive, behavioral, and attentional outcomes, higher rates of depression and anxiety, and less mental, emotional, and behavioral health among youth (Yoshikawa et al. 2012). As is the case with many social determinants, poverty is also associated with numerous poorer physical health outcomes (Kondo et al. 2009) and lower life expectancy (Chetty et al. 2016).

Efforts to reduce poverty have resulted in improved mental health for children. In the midst of the Great Smoky Mountains longitudinal cohort study, a casino opened, giving direct income to each Native American in the region. The children of families who subsequently moved out of poverty had significantly reduced behavioral and psychiatric symptoms compared to those of families who remained in poverty (Costello et al. 2003). This is consistent with analyses of dozens of anti-poverty efforts, which have led to the conclusion that reducing poverty has a positive effect on the mental, emotional, and behavioral health of children (Yoshikawa et al. 2012).

Mental Illness Prevention

Mental health prevention commonly addresses both risk factors, which increase the risk for mental illnesses, and protective factors, which decrease risk. For example, risk factors for depressive disorders include stress, negative cognitive styles, family history of depression (particularly being the offspring of a depressed parent), dysfunctional family interactions, interpersonal difficulties, and lack of social support (Hammen 2018). Population-based efforts at improving any of these addressable risk factors have the potential to lower population rates of depressive disorders.

At a more granular level, prevention can be divided into three traditional categories: primary, secondary, and tertiary. Primary prevention aims to prevent a disease or adverse outcome from occurring, thereby reducing the incidence of a disorder. Secondary prevention refers to screening, early detection, and treatment with the goal to reduce the prevalence of a condition or disease. And through rehabilitative treatments, tertiary prevention aims to reduce disability from an ongoing disease process. Whereas secondary and tertiary prevention can be classified as important forms of treatment, primary prevention is the term referring to actual prevention (NRC 2009).

When working with populations, prevention can be further subdivided based on how the group receiving the preventive intervention is defined (Gordon 1987).

- Universal interventions target an entire population, regardless of level of risk.
- Selective interventions target groups at increased risk for a disease.
- Indicated interventions target individuals identified as at particularly increased risk for a disorder, through known vulnerabilities, combinations of risk factors, or early signs of developing a problem.

The methods of preventive interventions depend on the scope of the population. Universal interventions, which are delivered to an entire population, can emphasize mental health principles or common mental health risk or protective factors. Indicated interventions, on the other hand, tailor interventions to people with early symptoms or clear risk factors. Selective interventions are in between, targeted to specific groups at elevated risk for mental illnesses.

Diverse programs across all three types of preventive interventions are needed. An illustration of universal prevention is social and emotional learning for school-age children, which can improve self-regulation, prosocial relationship, academic outcomes, and general social and emotional competence at later ages (Blewitt et al. 2018). One example of a selective preventive intervention is done for perinatal women throughout the state of New York. After universal screening for depressive symptoms in pregnant and postpartum women, those who screen positive can receive early psychosocial treatment or other interventions, which help prevent the later onset of a depressive disorder (Dennis and Dowswell 2013), which antidepressant treatment has not been shown to do (Molyneaux et al. 2018). An example of an indicated preventive intervention approach is the extensive research, and treatment trials, pertaining to youth and young adults with symptoms consistent with the prodrome of schizophrenia (called clinical high risk, or ultra-high risk). By improving the specificity of early detection, researchers hope to deploy early treatments that will reduce the onset of a psychotic disorder.

Mental Health Promotion

In addition to prevention, mental health promotion is a resilience-building approach that increases protective factors like better social-emotional skills and better social support. Mental health promotion can be developed and nurtured as a positive attribute through actions that improve psychological well-being (WHO 2002). This might include "efforts to [enhance] individuals' ability to achieve developmentally appropriate tasks and a positive sense of self-esteem, mastery, well-being, and social inclusion and to strengthen their ability to cope with adversity" (NRC 2009) and can best be integrated into broader wellness and health promotion efforts (Druss et al. 2010).

For instance, improved psychological well-being can occur through strengthening people's support systems. Various forms of parenting training have been shown to benefit for the development of children. In several studies, this has correlated with comparatively lower rates of physical and mental disorders many years after the original parenting interventions (Siegenthaler et al. 2012). Additionally, good nutrition may promote mental health by avoiding micronutrient deficiencies and providing sufficient nutritional building blocks to promote both physical well-being and improved mood (Sarris et al. 2015). New York State is addressing continued child development by integrating family and development professionals into pediatric and family medicine practices to help identify, monitor, and address emerging behavioral or developmental health concerns in young children (Kaye et al. 2017). Promoting mental health and youth development has the potential for later preventive effects on mental health disorders (Min et al. 2013).

Supporting a Shift Toward Population Health

Integrating population health interventions into practice will require significant change in training, culture and identity, workflows, team composition, and reimbursement. While changes in workflows and team composition have been described in previous sections, here we explore changes in training, culture and identity, and reimbursement through the lens of population health practice.

Training

Clinical training in psychiatry traditionally centers around identifying and treating disease at the individual level, where individual patients must adapt to the circumstances and workflows of the healthcare setting in order to receive care. Population health training has been underemphasized and inconsistent (Koo and Thacker 2008). While understanding and treating disease is important, training must also emphasize system-based practice, described as "an awareness of and responsiveness to the larger context and system of health care, including the social determinants of health, as well as the ability to call effectively on other resources to provide optimal health care" (ACGME 2020). Teaching structural competence could shift training "from a focus on technological intervention toward provision of more comprehensive healthcare—care in which students, interns, residents, fellows, and faculty engage with neighborhood organizations, non-health sector institutions (e.g., schools, corrections, housing), and policymakers to promote patient and community health" (Hansen and Metzl 2017). This training could also focus more on social responsibility (attitudes) and the skills and structural actions needed to make a difference in our communities (Castillo et al. 2020).

Culture and Identity

Community psychiatrists identify direct clinical engagement as among the most important aspects of their work. Indeed, they often engage their patients over the span of many years, developing strong bonds through the shared journey of addressing symptoms, achieving goals, and removing barriers to care in partnership with those they serve. These bonds are central to what brings them joy in their practice. In the collaborative care model, on the other hand, as a consultant to primary care physicians, you may never meet the people whose health you are affecting. Professional satisfaction is related, instead, to being part of a high-functioning team achieving good patient outcomes (Saba et al. 2012), multiplied by the increased number of patients affected. Measurement-based care as a part of population-based mental health services delivery allows for the satisfaction of seeing large numbers of people improve through improving aggregate ratings (Hong et al. 2021). Likewise, community-based task-sharing partnerships that address social determinants and prevent illness never reveal the people who would otherwise have become ill; yet, they provide compelling stories of community impact. In fact, mental health professionals could certainly derive satisfaction from the ability to expand their reach to geographies and entire communities of people.

Even so, shifting toward a population-based approach to mental health service delivery might feel more impersonal and, initially, might feel less fulfilling. Certainly, psychiatrists will always be involved in direct clinical care, but as systems shift to population health paradigms in order to more efficiently and effectively manage demand, psychiatrists can expect that the jobs of the future may involve less direct clinical care overall, that their clinical care may be more time-limited, and that much of their job may involve making an impact indirectly by influencing others in team-based settings. To ensure that psychiatrists are able to maintain job satisfaction, care must be taken to help providers process the loss or diminishment of old roles while elevating and highlighting the value of new roles.

Reimbursement

Reimbursement for healthcare remains grounded primarily in the fee-for-service model, which pays individual clinicians for delivering specific services or interventions targeting specific illnesses. This clinician- and disease-centric model of payment inhibits the expansion of population-based workflows and interventions. Experiments in payment reform to solve this problem have been ongoing for the past decade and steadily expanding over the past 5 years. Conceptually, efforts to promote population health interventions through alternative payment methods focus on paying for value, which is defined simply as getting better population outcomes at lower cost (Porter 2010). All value-based payment models require providers to document the overall illness burden of an attributed population and then take responsibility for achieving predetermined outcomes.

On the front end, payers can give providers per-person payments – referred to as capitated payments – in return for agreeing to provide either specific services that aren't reimbursed through fee-for-service mechanisms (targeted capitation, more common) or that even replace fee-for-service payments in part or in whole (global capitation, less common). In targeted capitation models, providers are constrained in the growth of additional services by the amount they receive per member/per month across their attributed population. For example, if a provider receives $8 per member/per month to deliver care management services to an attributed population of 1000 individuals, they would be able to hire one care manager at a cost of around $96,000. That constraint would push them to either target care management services to those patients with the highest need rather than providing care management to all patients, or to try and negotiate for a higher capitated payment to hire more care managers. In a global capitated model, providers are responsible for excess costs beyond the "per-member per-month" when such care is warranted (i.e., if the cost of delivering services to their population that conform to agreed-upon quality metrics exceeds the amount of capitated payments they receive in aggregate for their attributed population, they would be responsible for absorbing those extra costs) (James and Poulsen 2016).

On the back end, payers can provide bonus incentives to providers that achieve set outcomes under predetermined annual spending caps or penalize providers that fail to achieve set quality metrics or bill fee-for-service too much. This payment model is exemplified by Accountable Care Organizations (CMS 2022). Other variations exist (most notably the prospective payment model used by Federally Qualified Health Centers and Certified Community Behavioral Health Centers), and further details are explored elsewhere in this book (chapter "Financing of Community Behavioral Health Services"). Importantly, no one value-based payment model has emerged as providing a clear pathway toward sustainable, high-value care. Yet, shifting to value-based payment models in community behavioral health settings offers the clearest pathway for scaling the population health interventions outlined in this chapter and securing the outcomes that the populations we serve deserve.

Conclusion: Relevance to Community Psychiatry

Community psychiatry has always used the best clinical skills to help those with some of the most serious mental illnesses. It has long recognized the importance of psychosocial needs for an individual's health. And along the way, it has developed innovative, effective, efficient models to address complex needs. The field has directly addressed social issues through programs like housing first for individuals experiencing homelessness, supported employment to improve people's work and financial situation, and assertive community treatment teams for holistic care for serious mental illnesses.

This clinical work provides a firm base from which to advocate for more efficient and effective healthcare systems and for policies that address the fundamental social determinants of mental health. Reducing poverty, childhood trauma, and discrimination can have a preventive effect to reduce mental distress for many. Coupled with efforts to promote social and emotional development, psychological health, as well as good nutrition and physical health, community psychiatry can have an even greater effect on population mental health.

Population mental healthcare has the potential to affect us all, continuing community psychiatry's value of caring for everyone, leaving no one out. Look for these themes of population health, social determinants, and mental health promotion throughout your individual practice, your practice system, and the many chapters in this handbook. As you look for ways to support more effective or efficient care, include advocacy for policies that address the social determinants of health and common risk and protective factors. Doing so will move us all toward improved mental health.

References

Accreditation Council for Graduate Medical Education, 2020. *ACGME Common Program Requirements Residency).* https://www.acgme.org/globalassets/PFAssets/ProgramRequirements/400_Psychiatry_2020.pdf?ver=2020-06-19-123110-817&ver=2020-06-19-123110-817 Published 2020. Accessed December 5, 2021.

Archer, J., Bower, P., Gilbody, S., Lovell, K., Richards, D., Gask, L., Dickens, C., Coventry, P., 2012. Collaborative care for depression and anxiety problems. Cochrane Database of Systematic Reviews. https://doi.org/10.1002/14651858.cd006525.pub2

Belkin, G., 2020. A path for psychiatry to thrive. Psychiatric Services 71, 852–854. https://doi.org/10.1176/appi.ps.201900105

Belkin, G., McCray, C., 2019. ThriveNYC: Delivering on Mental Health. American Journal of Public Health 109. https://doi.org/10.2105/ajph.2019.305040

Blewitt, C., Fuller-Tyszkiewicz, M., Nolan, A., Bergmeier, H., Vicary, D., Huang, T., McCabe, P., McKay, T., Skouteris, H., 2018. Social and emotional learning associated with Universal Curriculum-based interventions in early childhood education and care centers. JAMA Network Open 1. https://doi.org/10.1001/jamanetworkopen.2018.5727

Castillo, E.G., Isom, J., DeBonis, K.L., Jordan, A., Braslow, J.T., Rohrbaugh, R., 2020. Reconsidering systems-based practice: Advancing structural competency, Health Equity, and Social Responsibility in graduate medical education. Academic Medicine 95, 1817–1822. https://doi.org/10.1097/acm.0000000000003559

Chetty, R., Stepner, M., Abraham, S., Lin, S., Scuderi, B., Turner, N., Bergeron, A., Cutler, D., 2016. The Association Between Income and Life Expectancy in the United States, 2001-2014. JAMA 315, 1750. https://doi.org/10.1001/jama.2016.4226

CMS 2022 - Center for Medicare and Medicaid Services (2022). Accountable Care Organizations: General Information. Last accessed on April 12th, 2022 at: https://innovation.cms.gov/innovation-models/aco

Compton, M.T., Shim, R.S., 2015. The social determinants of mental health. American Psychiatric Publishing, a division of American Psychiatric Association, Washington, DC.

Costello, E.J., Compton, S.N., Keeler, G., Angold, A., 2003. Relationships Between Poverty and Psychopathology. JAMA 290, 2023. https://doi.org/10.1001/jama.290.15.2023

Dennis, C.-L., Dowswell, T., 2013. Psychosocial and psychological interventions for preventing postpartum depression. Cochrane Database of Systematic Reviews. https://doi.org/10.1002/14651858.cd001134.pub3

Druss, B.G., Perry, G.S., Presley-Cantrell, L.R., Dhingra, S., 2010. Mental Health Promotion in a Reformed Health Care System. American Journal of Public Health 100, 2336–2336. https://doi.org/10.2105/ajph.2010.205401

Dunbar, M., Towe, V., Ayer, L., Martineau, M., 2017. Connections to care (C2C): The Perspectives of leaders at community-based organizations that are integrating mental health supports. https://doi.org/10.7249/rr2119

Gordon, R., 1987. An Operational Classification of Disease Prevention in J. A. Steinberg & M. M. Silverman (Eds.), *Preventing mental disorders: A research perspective* (pp. 20–26). National Institute of Mental Health. https://doi.org/10.1037/e659532007-006

Hammen, C., 2018. Risk Factors for Depression: An Autobiographical Review. Annual Review of Clinical Psychology 14, 1–28. https://doi.org/10.1146/annurev-clinpsy-050817-084811

Hansen, H., Metzl, J.M., 2017. New Medicine for the U.S. health care system. Academic Medicine 92, 279–281. https://doi.org/10.1097/acm.0000000000001542

Health Resources Service Administration (HRSA), National Center for Health Workforce Analysis, Substance Abuse and Mental Health Services Administration, 2015. National projections of supply and demand for behavioral health practitioners: 2013–2025. Health Resources Service Administration, Rockville, MD.

Hong, R.H., Murphy, J.K., Michalak, E.E., Chakrabarty, T., Wang, Z., Parikh, S., Culpepper, L., Yatham, L.N., Lam, R.W., Chen, J., 2021. Implementing measurement-based care for depression: Practical solutions for psychiatrists and Primary Care Physicians. Neuropsychiatric Disease and Treatment Volume 17, 79–90. https://doi.org/10.2147/ndt.s283731

James, B.C., Poulsen, G.P. 2016. The Case for Capitation. Harvard Business Review, last accessed on April 12th, 2022 at: https://hbr.org/2016/07/the-case-for-capitation

Katon, W.J., Lin, E.H.B., Von Korff, M., Ciechanowski, P., Ludman, E.J., Young, B., Peterson, D., Rutter, C.M., McGregor, M., McCulloch, D., 2010. Collaborative Care for Patients with Depression and Chronic Illnesses. New England Journal of Medicine 363, 2611–2620. https://doi.org/10.1056/nejmoa1003955

Kaye, D.L., Fornari, V., Scharf, M., Fremont, W., Zuckerbrot, R., Foley, C., Hargrave, T., Smith, B.A., Wallace, J., Blakeslee, G., Petras, J., Sengupta, S., Singarayer, J., Cogswell, A., Bhatia, I., Jensen, P., 2017. Description of a multi-university education and collaborative care child psychiatry access program: New York State's CAP PC. General Hospital Psychiatry 48, 32–36. https://doi.org/10.1016/j.genhosppsych.2017.06.003

Kindig, D., Stoddart, G., 2003. What Is Population Health? American Journal of Public Health 93, 380–383. https://doi.org/10.2105/ajph.93.3.380

Kondo, N., Sembajwe, G., Kawachi, I., van Dam, R.M., Subramanian, S.V., Yamagata, Z., 2009. Income inequality, mortality, and self rated health: meta-analysis of multilevel studies. BMJ 339. https://doi.org/10.1136/bmj.b4471

Koo, D., Thacker, S.B., 2008. The Education of Physicians: A CDC perspective. Academic Medicine 83, 399–407. https://doi.org/10.1097/acm.0b013e3181667e9a

Min, J.-A., Lee, C.-U., Lee, C., 2013. Mental Health Promotion and Illness Prevention: A Challenge for Psychiatrists. Psychiatry Investigation 10, 307. https://doi.org/10.4306/pi.2013.10.4.307

Molyneaux, E., Telesia, L.A., Henshaw, C., Boath, E., Bradley, E., Howard, L.M., 2018. Antidepressants for preventing postnatal depression. Cochrane Database of Systematic Reviews. https://doi.org/10.1002/14651858.cd004363.pub3

National Research Council, Institute of Medicine Committee on the Prevention of Mental Disorders and Substance Abuse Among Children, Youth, and Young Adults, 2009. Preventing mental, emotional, and behavioral disorders among young people: progress and possibilities. National Academies Press, Washington, D.C.

Porter, M.E. 2010. What Is Value in Health Care?. New England Journal of Medicine 363(26), 2477–2481. https://doi.org/10.1056/NEJMp1011024

Purtle, J., Nelson, K.L., Counts, N.Z., Yudell, M., 2020. Population-Based Approaches to Mental Health: History, Strategies, and Evidence. Annual Review of Public Health 41, 201–221. https://doi.org/10.1146/annurev-publhealth-040119-094247

Rui, P., Okeyode, T., 2016 National Ambulatory Medical Care Survey: 2016 National Summary Tables. Accessed March 15, 2021.

Saba, G.W., Villela, T.J., Chen, E., Hammer, H., Bodenheimer, T., 2012. The myth of the lone physician: Toward a collaborative alternative. The Annals of Family Medicine 10, 169–173. https://doi.org/10.1370/afm.1353

Sarris, J., Logan, A.C., Akbaraly, T.N., Amminger, G.P., Balanzá-Martínez, V., Freeman, M.P., Hibbeln, J., Matsuoka, Y., Mischoulon, D., Mizoue, T., Nanri, A., Nishi, D., Ramsey, D., Rucklidge, J.J., Sanchez-Villegas, A., Scholey, A., Su, K.-P., Jacka, F.N., 2015. Nutritional medicine as mainstream in psychiatry. The Lancet Psychiatry 2, 271–274. https://doi.org/10.1016/s2215-0366(14)00051-0

Siegenthaler, E., Munder, T., Egger, M., 2012. Effect of Preventive Interventions in Mentally Ill Parents on the Mental Health of the Offspring: Systematic Review and Meta-Analysis. Journal of the American Academy of Child & Adolescent Psychiatry 51. https://doi.org/10.1016/j.jaac.2011.10.018

Substance Abuse and Mental Health Services Administration, 2020 (publication), Key substance use and mental health indicators in the United States: Results from the 2019 National Survey on Drug Use and Health. Center for Behavioral Health Statistics and Quality, Substance Abuse and Mental Health Services Administration, Rockville, MD.

Thota, A.B., Sipe, T.A., Byard, G.J., Zometa, C.S., Hahn, R.A., McKnight-Eily, L.R., Chapman, D.P., Abraido-Lanza, A.F., Pearson, J.L., Anderson, C.W., Gelenberg, A.J., Hennessy, K.D., Duffy, F.F., Vernon-Smiley, M.E., Nease, D.E., Williams, S.P., 2012. Collaborative Care to Improve the Management of Depressive Disorders. American Journal of Preventive Medicine 42, 525–538. https://doi.org/10.1016/j.amepre.2012.01.019

Unützer, J., Katon, W., Callahan, C.M., Williams, Jr, J.W., Hunkeler, E., Harpole, L., Hoffing, M., Della Penna, R.D., Noël, P.H., Lin, E.H., Areán, P.A., Hegel, M.T., Tang, L., Belin, T.R., Oishi, S., Langston, C., for the IMPACT Investigators, 2002. Collaborative Care Management of Late-Life Depression in the Primary Care Setting. JAMA 288, 2836. https://doi.org/10.1001/jama.288.22.2836

World Health Organization (WHO), 2002. (rep.), Prevention and Promotion in Mental Health. http://www.who.int/mental_health/media/en/545.pdf, Accessed March 15, 2021.

Yoshikawa, H., Aber, J.L., Beardslee, W.R., 2012. The effects of poverty on the mental, emotional, and behavioral health of children and youth: Implications for prevention. American Psychologist 67, 272–284. https://doi.org/10.1037/a0028015

Exercising Effective Leadership

Patrick S. Runnels, Jacqueline Maus Feldman, and Hunter L. McQuistion

Introduction

In order to exercise effective leadership in community psychiatry, one must be and do a variety of things: enjoy interacting with people, be motivated and passionate about working in systems of care; be creative and innovative; be ready and willing to be an advocate for one's self, one's staff, and one's patients in terms of providing quality care; practice a specific skill set; be willing to undergo training in a wide variety of topics; and be open to receiving and changing from feedback. This chapter will review the extant literature which describes the desired attributes of an effective leader, suggest venues of training necessary to support skills acquisition, and identify system-of-care requirements to facilitate growth in leaders who understand and embrace community-based, recovery-oriented systems of care.

P. S. Runnels (✉)
Psychiatry, Case Western Reserve University School of Medicine, Population Health, University Hospitals, Shaker Heights, OH, USA
e-mail: patrick.runnels1@uhhospitals.org

J. M. Feldman
Department of Psychiatry and Behavioral Neurobiology, University of Alabama at Birmingham, Gravois Mills, MO, USA
e-mail: jfeldman@uabmc.edu

H. L. McQuistion
New York University Grossman School of Medicine | NYU Langone Health, New York, NY, USA
e-mail: hunter.mcquistion@nyulangone.org

The Case for Psychiatric Leadership in Community Behavioral Health

With the move towards de-institutionalization in the mid-1960s, massive numbers of patients were discharged to the community where they continued to need mental health follow-up. Fostered by federal legislation, a system of care consisting of networks of community mental health centers (CMHCs) rapidly grew, requiring new leaders to direct clinical care, plan community supports, and advocate for a vulnerable population. Training mental health leaders became a high priority to the US federal government from 1977 to 1984. The National Institute of Mental Health Staff College was funded to promulgate the goals of the Community Mental Health Center Act of 1963 through the development of "The Advanced Training Program in Mental Health Administration" to train CMHC directors. The program included ten, 4-day retreats with pre- and post-activities and provided training for hundreds of people (Mazade 2006). Unfortunately, since that time, coordinated, recovery-based organized training has not occurred on a consistent national level, while federal funding for mental health leadership

W. E. Sowers et al. (eds.), *Textbook of Community Psychiatry*,
https://doi.org/10.1007/978-3-031-10239-4_5

training fell from $117 million in 1972 to less than $1 million by 2005 (Mazade 2005).

Then, in 2007, the Annapolis Coalition released *An Action Plan for Behavioral Health Workforce Development* that put forth recommendations for change. The Coalition targeted training the next generation of mental health leaders as imperative, particularly underscoring the need for leadership in order to respond to the national embrace of rehabilitation and recovery-oriented philosophies. Interestingly, the Coalition recommended training the entire behavioral health workforce, *including:*

> persons in recovery and families, educators, prevention specialists, treatment providers, policy makers, and the individuals who manage accreditation, certification, and licensure systems. In fact, developing and expanding a cadre of leaders among persons in recovery, youth, and family members is particularly critical in achieving transformation of current service systems and models of care. Leadership must be broadly defined to encompass not only organizational and change management, but also coalition and community building, team and program management, and the provision of supervision. (Annapolis Coalition 2007, 19)

Meanwhile, multiple studies project that the number of psychiatrists will be inadequate for mental health demands in America. The average age of the current workforce of around 45,000 psychiatrists is over 55, with 1/3 of psychiatrists within 5 years of retirement age. Impending retirement is likely to cause a reduction in the absolute number of psychiatrists just as demand is increasing (National Council Medical Director's Institute 2018). The most recent estimates project a shortage of 10,000 to 25,000 psychiatrists when factoring in growth in psychiatric advanced practice nurses, an incredibly grim number. And problems with access are compounded by misdistribution of psychiatrists, who are highly concentrated in urban centers and often opt out of taking insurance at all, with nearly 40% operating cash-only practices that cater primarily to individuals who are most financially stable.

Finally, the global burden of disease attributable to mental, neurological, and substance use disorders is expected to rise from 12.3% in 2000 to 14.7% in 2020 (Murray and Lopez 1997). Barriers to psychiatric access will be compounded in the United States by several factors:

- Continued migration of patients moving from institutions (state hospitals, jails, and prisons) to the community
- Persistently high numbers of patients with serious mental illness (schizophrenia, bipolar disorder, major depression) whose lives can be very challenging and whose care is complex and demanding
- Increased demand for access to psychiatry as payment models tied to cost and outcomes force health systems to address the impact of mental illness on physical health outcomes
- Increased demand for access to psychiatry caused by the expansion of Medicaid under the Patient Accountability and Affordable Care Act, which total around 19 million additional lives as of 2021 (Health and Human Services 2021)
- The persistence of individual financial burden and poor regional access that force people to both put off or avoid seeking planned mental healthcare and result in increased utilization of unplanned care in higher cost settings
- As of this writing in early 2022, the as yet not fully understood impact of mental health issues associated with the COVID-19 pandemic

Solving for these problems will require significant changes to psychiatric practice and significant overall system redesign. Those changes must include leadership voices from a variety of professions working together. Yet, the voice of psychiatrist leaders will be critical to ensuring successful practice transformation. The educational background in both medicine and behavioral health, along with the extensive duration of training in mental illness diagnosis and treatment, provides perspective and capability other professions do not have. These will be of paramount importance as health system siloes continue to break down, with inpatient care yielding less financial benefit in behavioral health and outpatient community providers being asked to assume more responsibility for the total health outcomes of the populations they serve. Moreover, the motivation and commitment to the concepts of inclusion, evidence-based practice, harm reduction, and recovery orientation central to the identity of community psychiatrists will be necessary to counteract forces that might seek to marginalize these values in service of more narrow financial considerations or outdated models of care. In an era of transformation, system redesign provides an opportunity to avoid duplicating the poorly designed systems of the past; to that end, community psychiatrists must be prepared to step up to leadership roles and carry them out effectively.

What Is Leadership?

> Leadership is one of the most observed and least understood phenomena on earth. – Burns 1978

Leadership has been defined in many ways, some by attributes of the leader, some by the goals or products that leadership should produce, some by the followers, and some by the environment in which they exist. The noted Harvard psychologist Howard Gardner defined leadership as "the process of persuasion or example by which an individual (or leadership team) induces a group to pursue objectives held by the leader or shared by the leader and his or her followers" while adding that "effective leadership is a combination of a particular context and the attributes needed to lead in that context" (Gardner 1995). Leaders in these situations need to inspire commitment and action, lead as peer problem-solvers, build broad-based involvement, and sustain hope and participation – focusing relentlessly on goals and doing so while communicating selflessness, not self-aggrandizement (Collins 2001). More specifically, Jim Collins (2006) has written about effective leadership in the non-profit sector, noting that this sector often struggles with a diffuse power structure and that successful non-profit leaders recognize the need for legislative skills (persuasion/motivation) to influence not only their direct subordinates but a wide variety of constituencies. Non-profit organizations move from "good to great" by (1) measuring success not necessarily in the money that is made, but the resources they can expand, (2) employing passionate workers who "are down to earth, pragmatic, and committed to excellence," and (3) recruiting leaders who have "humility, defined as burning ambition, transferred into the cause, with brutal, stoic will." And finally, specific to mental health, William Anthony prefaced the superb book *Principled Leadership in Mental Health Systems and Programs* with this statement: "Leadership remains an art as well as a science—some of the tools of leadership are not simply the tools of science—some are tools of the self," while also noting that "...leadership creates a shared vision and mobilizes others toward specific organizational goals consistent with that vision" (Anthony and Huckshorn 2008).

Personal Attributes and Skills of Effective Leaders

Over the past 50 years, a robust literature exploring and understanding effective leadership has emerged. To summarize all relevant paradigms is beyond the scope of one chapter. Yet, most leadership models converge around specific core concepts. To start, nearly all models recognize the overwhelming research linking emotional intelligence with highly effective leadership (importantly the converse is also true: low emotional intelligence has been linked with ineffective leadership). Emotional intelligence is not one concept but can actually be usefully divided into multiple domains; the domains that most impact leadership are (1) self-awareness, (2) self-regulation, (3) motivation, (4) empathy, and (5) social skills. Emotional intelligence in each domain is not fixed. Research has demonstrated that individuals can build emotional intelligence capacity in each of these domains and thereby improve their leadership skills (Goleman 2001).

Yet, leadership styles are not simply a random aggregation of individual emotional and management capabilities. Much work has been done to identify archetypes for how these skills come together to produce different approaches to leadership. Perhaps the most well-known and referenced were elucidated by Goleman (2001). Their team identified six predominant leadership styles:

1. The Coercive Style – this top-down style places an emphasis on giving directives and expecting compliance, which can be very useful in crisis situations.
2. The Authoritative Style – in contrast to the coercive style, this style seeks to inspire people to act around a larger vision or goal, which is very well suited for situations that require system-level transformation.
3. The Affiliative Style – this style seeks to develop harmony both with and between individuals and teams as a route to better results, often leveraged when morale is low or conflict is high.
4. The Democratic Style – as suggested, this style seeks to build consensus and ensure that all voices are heard, which can be particularly important when answers are not clear or change will be complex.
5. The Pacesetting Style – this style involves setting high standards and then embodying those standards through personal practice, best used for teams of highly skilled, highly motivated people who are looking to push to the "next level."
6. The Coaching Style – a style that approaches work by developing individuals rather than accomplishing tasks, which is hugely important unless you happen to have a pre-assembled team of highly developed and experienced individuals and managers.

These styles are not rigid categories into which leaders are sorted. Rather, they represent different approaches that leaders can take based on the specific circumstances in which they are operating. In fact, the most effective leaders leverage three or more styles regularly.

Notably, two styles were identified as being successful less than half the time: coercion and pacesetting. Not surprisingly trying to command people or creating expectations that might feel unattainable has the effect of demotivating individuals more than driving results. Despite that knowledge, leaders in some organizations, including community behavioral health settings, commonly lean into coercion and pacesetting as default styles, which are the simplest to implement and often do achieve short-term results. Such organizations, however, are often beset by high turnover and low morale, with transient gains that evaporate quickly over time, replaced by missed targets and spiraling results, including financial insolvency.

Healthcare environments, and specifically community behavioral health settings, have a unique staffing composition in that, albeit with a special role, clinical leaders are professional *peers* with the people they lead. This equality places leaders in the position that frequently requires them to use a leadership style that accentuates integration of democratic, coaching, and authoritative elements. The integration of authoritative aspects enables the communication of a vision that not only embraces the values of those who are led but introduces the ways (and means) those values can be creatively actualized by the organization's members.

The psychologist Richard Boyatzis and his colleagues have addressed these principles on a more elemental level. They developed a model called resonant leadership. Leveraging the same underlying concepts related to emotional intelligence, they defined resonant leadership as being a combination of true understanding and empathy for the circumstances of the team, paired with communicating and driving a positive vision of what an organization is trying to accomplish that resonates with the hopes and ideals of the team.

Their research showed that resonant leaders not only had high scores on each of the subcategories of emotional intelligence listed above, but, importantly, got much better results by utilizing what they called positive emotional attractors (PEA) across all settings to get those results. When leaders use language and actions that emphasize PEA, they elicit a positive response from those they are leading, which cascades into improved performance as the workforce establishes security in their position, belief in their power to effect positive change in their job, and confidence in their capabilities. In a community mental health setting, PEA might be generated by asking people to recall their motivation for helping marginalized populations, uncovering their career aspirations and then facilitating opportunities to achieve them (e.g., by carving out an opportunity to teach other professionals or start a specialized clinic for a sub-population about which they are passionate), or sharing stories of success and togetherness to build a sense of team. Thoughtful commiseration with people over adversity and tragedy can create positive resonance and improve performance in even the toughest circumstances (Boyatzis et al. 2010).

On the other hand, when leaders use negative emotional attractors (NEA), the opposite happens. Pointing out failures, demanding unreasonable schedules or patient volume goals that create stress and compromise patient care, and focusing on results that staff don't personally connect with or feel are out of their control are all examples of NEA that ultimately demotivate people and interfere with achieving the mission. Some community mental health organizations may even lean into demagoguery, which involves pitting internal groups against each other, leveraging empathy for one group to motivate them antagonistically against another group rather than toward a shared common vision. Readers may have experienced working in community mental health settings where the psychiatric team was regularly the punching bag for a frustrated case management staff, who were nonetheless pushed relentlessly to achieve tight patient volume goals. While this might have bolstered case manager solidarity and rallied individuals to achieve tough targets under tough circumstances in the short term, the toxicity of these environments most often leads to disillusionment and high turnover and can rarely be sustained effectively over time.

Leaning into positivity doesn't work or isn't possible all the time. In fact, a little stress here and there can be important in motivating us to get things done. But research shows that utilizing PEA at least 75% of the time is correlated with higher performing teams (Boyatzis and McKee 2005).

These concepts are echoed by those who have looked more specifically at mental health leadership. Anthony and Huckshorn (2008), referenced earlier, suggest that the focus for mental health leaders should be on actions and principles and that "mental health leaders universally seem to be characterized by commitment, credibility, and capacity to make change." They interviewed 50 leaders in mental health, distilled their responses, and derived 8 principles of leadership in mental health settings:

- *Principle 1:* Leaders communicate a shared vision.
- *Principle 2:* Leaders centralize by mission and decentralize by operations.
- *Principle 3:* Leaders create an organizational culture that identifies and tries to live by key values.
- *Principle 4:* Leaders create an organizational structure and culture that empowers their employees and them.
- *Principle 5:* Leaders ensure that staff is trained in a human technology that can translate vision into reality.
- *Principle 6:* Leaders relate constructively to employees.
- *Principle 7:* Leaders access and use information to make change a constant ingredient of their organization.
- *Principle 8:* Leaders build their organization around exemplary performers.

These principles can be directly mapped to the core tasks of leadership: the need to establish meaningful *visions* (what future the organization is trying to create), *missions* (the role the organization has in creating that future), *operations* (daily activities to accomplish the mission), and *values* (templates that guide the organizational decisions made that direct the daily operations) (Anthony and Huckshorn 2008).

Based on combined years of leaderships in community psychiatry, the American Association for Community Psychiatry (AACP) has promulgated principles and standards for systems of care to enhance and sustain quality of services while ensuring that psychiatric leadership has sufficient supports to maintain these standards (AACP 1995). A further exploration of the roles and duties of a medical director for a community behavioral health organization can be reviewed in this book's chapter "The Medical Director in Community-Based Mental Health Care".

Transactional Versus Transformational Leadership

In parallel with leadership across other settings, leadership in mental health has been in transition for many years, evolving from *transactional* to more *transformative* models (Van Slyke and Alexander 2006). Transactional leaders work with followers to exchange one thing for another. A transactional leader stresses efficiency, planning and goal setting, focusing on competency, structure, and maintaining the organization. They may be more reactive than proactive and often supportive of the status quo (Burns 1978). The transforming leader, by contrast, looks for what motivates followers, seeks to gratify higher needs, and works to engage the *whole* person (intellect, energy, passion, values). Transformational leaders move followers into being leaders and may convert leaders into moral agents. They are responsive to others' needs and interests and are responsible and accountable to stakeholders (Alimo-Metcalfe and Alimo-Metcalfe 2006). These leaders focus less on hierarchy and more on relationships, teamwork, and innovation; they display humility, a generous spirit, honesty, and integrity. Transformational leaders develop a clear, resonant vision and focus relentlessly on communicating that vision to those they lead. Organizations that are highly transactional are shaped by rules and regulations, rigid structure, contracts, and controls, while those that are more transformative are characterized by strong vision and purpose, support for change, and trusting, cooperative interactions between staff and leaders (Alimo-Metcalfe et al. 2007; Bass and Avolo 1993; Bass 1998; Burns 1978).

While some believe that transformational leadership is superior to transactional leadership, others claim that effective leadership requires a balance between transactional and transformative leadership, with effective leaders using both forms of leadership depending on the needs of the situation. Luke (1998) has coined the term of this combined pragmatic approach "catalytic leadership." In his description, catalytic leaders set the stage, pull people together, decide what to do, make plans, make them happen, and create an effective work culture by balancing a hierarchical approach with an approach that engages and incentivizes.

Leadership Development and Training

For those lucky enough to experience working for a great leader, beyond intentional observation, we recommend that individuals not be shy about seeking out direct interaction and even asking for mentorship – even if a leader is busy, most will be flattered and make time. Yet, even without direct exposure, our connected digital world offers abundant videos and recordings of leaders from which to learn. Furthermore, a host of books – from *Principle-Centered Leadership* (1990) by Steven Covey to *Start with Why* (2009) and *The Infinite Game* (2019) by Simon Sinek – offer outstanding meditations on leadership that can both inspire action and help to develop leadership voice.

As importantly, interactions on a day-to-day basis with patients, family members, staff, and systems of care can open one's eyes to the effectiveness of leadership that underscores the importance of embracing a recovery-oriented philosophy, as opposed to the unfortunate consequences of uninspired or feckless leadership that ignores the importance of service user-driven services. The AACP Keystones for Collaboration and Leadership (2007) delineates both a process for transformation of community psychiatry in one of the United States and the issues that must be considered, including transformation to recovery-focused systems of care.

The basis of much current health leadership training in the United States is the model developed by the National Center for Healthcare Leadership (NCHL 2005). A benchmarked, researched, and validated model, NCHL takes 26 leadership competencies critical to the field of health and assigns them to one of 3 domains – Transformation, Execution, and People – that serve to capture the complexity and dynamic quality of the health leader's role.

More formally, one can pursue training through a variety of routes. Most prominently for community psychiatrists are public/community psychiatry fellowships. While just 2 operated as late as 2007, the last 15 years has resulted in a relative explosion to 26 in 2022, and some have expanded to include opportunities for virtual training for those who don't have one located near them. The fellowship model is covered in detail in chapter "Public/Community Psychiatry Fellowships". For those looking for more exposure to business principles, pursuit of an MBA, MPH, or another similar program has become popular, particularly for those who aspire to higher-level leadership positions, though the cost and investment of time might be prohibitive for some. Meanwhile, there are local, regional, and national programs that offer special training in leadership and especially for work in the public sector. One recent example is sponsored by NYC Health+Hospitals (https://www.nychealthandhospitals.org/nyc-health-hospitals-nyu-public-psychiatry-program/).

Conclusion: Transforming Leadership in Community Psychiatry

By almost any measure, the system of healthcare in the United States has not produced adequate results. This is also clearly true for the behavioral health system, including at the more specific level of community mental health settings. That reality cannot be seen as an indictment of providers, who have largely been delivering amazing, even heroic, care to individuals despite working under multiple systemic impairments and inadequacies. At the most elemental level, the impetus for transforming our healthcare system stems from a recognition that we have been measuring the wrong things. By shifting away from measuring units of services delivered and toward measuring cost and outcomes, we are shining a light on our models of care that enable practitioners of all types to fully employ their creativity and skill. Part of this, as well, is operationalizing cultural and racial diversity among community behavioral health staff, enabling a broadening of professional skillsets. This requires leaders to have special understanding of how institutional racism has historically affected administrative power structures and to be proactive in changing that status quo.

Because we have not been good at delivering care designed to achieve results valued by so many patients, the needed changes are enormous in magnitude. It will also challenge the current workforce to get outside its comfort zone. Therefore, transformational leadership is likely to dominate in organizations that succeed in navigating an evolving landscape of care.

The future leaves little doubt that community psychiatrists will be called to step forward and assume leadership positions. With increasing demand for access, together with a threat of dwindling numbers of psychiatrists, processes for planning to respond to new challenges must be put in place by leaders skilled in transformational flexibility and the qualities it demands to "get the job done" while embracing philosophies of rehabilitation, recovery, and inclusion.

References

Alimo-Metcalfe B, Alimo-Metcalfe J, Samele C, Bradley M, et al (2007). The impact of leadership factors in implementing change in complex health and social care environments. NHS Plan: Clinical priority for mental health crisis resolutions (CRTs). Department of Health, NHS SDO, Project 22/2002.

Alimo-Metcalfe RJ, Alimo-Metcalfe, B (2006). The transformational leadership Questionnaire: A convergent and discriminant validity study. *Leadership and Organisation Development Journal*, 21, 280-296.

American Association for Community Psychiatry 1995: Guidelines for Psychiatric Leadership in Organized Delivery Systems for Treatment of Psychiatric and Substance Disorders. Available at: https://www.communitypsychiatry.org/publications/archived-documents . Accessed April 24, 2022.

American Association for Community Psychiatry (2007) *AACP Keystones for Collaboration and Leadership: Issues and Recommendations for the Transformation of Community Psychiatry*. Available at https://www.ispraisrael.org.il/sites/ispra/UserContent/files/%D7%9E%D7%93%D7%99%D7%A0%D7%99%D7%95%D7%AA%20%D7%91%D7%91%D7%A8%D7%99%D7%90%D7%95%D7%AA%20%D7%94%D7%A0%D7%A4%D7%A9/TransformationofPsychiatryReport%5B1%5D.pdf. Accessed April 24, 2022.

Annapolis Coalition (2007). An Action Plan for Behavioral Health Workforce Development: A Framework for Discussion: Executive Summary. Available at: *https://www.drugsandalcohol.ie/19450/1/2007_SAMHSA_Annanpolis_Coalition_WorkforceActionPlan.pdf.* Accessed April 24, 2022.

Anthony W, Huckshorn, KA (2008). *Principled Leadership in Mental Health Systems and Programs.* Boston: Boston University Center for Psychiatric Rehabilitation.

Bass BM, Avolo, BJ (1993). Transformational leadership and organizational culture. *Public Administration Quarterly*, 17, 112-122.

Bass BM (1998). *Transformational Leadership: Industrial, Military, and Educational Impact.* Mahwah, N. J.: Erlbaum.

Boyatzis R, McKee A (2005). *Resonant Leadership.* Harvard Business School Press, Boston MA

Boyatzis REE, Lingham T, Passarelli A (2010). Inspiring the development of emotional, social, and cognitive intelligence competencies in managers. In Rothstein MG & Burke, RJ (eds.), *Self-Management and Leadership Development.* Cheltenham, UK, Edward Elgar. Publishing Ltd.

Burns JM (1978). *Leadership.* New York: Harper & Row.

Collins J (2001) *Good to Great.* New York, NY: HarperCollins

Collins J (2006). *Good to Great and the Social Sectors.* New York, NY: Random House Business Books

Covey S (1990) *Principle-Centered Leadership.* New York, NY: Rosetta Books LLC

Gardner H (1995). *Leading Minds: An Anatomy of Leadership.* New York, NY: Basic Books, Inc.

Goleman D (2001). Leadership That Gets Results. Harvard Business Review, March/April, p.1-15

Health and Human Services (2021) https://www.hhs.gov/about/news/2021/06/05/new-hhs-data-show-more-americans-than-ever-have-health-coverage-through-affordable-care-act.html

Luke JS (1998). *Catalytic Leadership: Strategies for an Interconnected World.* San Francisco: Jossey-Bass, Inc.

Mazade NA (2005). Concepts of "Transformation". Alexandria, VA: *National Association of State Mental Health Program Directors Research Institute, Inc.* Available at: https://citeseerx.ist.psu.edu/viewdoc/download?doi=10.1.1.392.3579&rep=rep1&type=pdf. Accessed April 24, 2022.

Mazade N (2006). *The NIMH Staff College.* Presentation to the IIMHL meeting, Rockville, MD.

Murray CJL, Lopez AD (1997). Alternative projections of mortality and disability by cause 1990-2020: Global burden of disease study. *Lancet*, 349, 1498-1504.

National Center for Healthcare Leadership (NCHL) (2005). Healthcare Leadership. Available at https://www.nchl.org/#. Accessed April 24, 2022.

National Council for Mental Wellbeing (2018). The Medical Director Institute. Available at: https://www.thenationalcouncil.org/about-us/leadership-experts/medical-director-institute/. Accessed April 24, 2022.

Sinek S (2009). *Start with Why.* New York, NY: Penguin Group.

Sinek S (2019). *The Infinite Game.* New York, NY: Penguin Random House LLC.

Van Slyke DM, Alexander RW (2006). Public service leadership: opportunities for clarity and coherence. *American Review of Public Administration* 36(4). 362-37

Advocacy in Evolution: The Push and Pull of Psychiatrists

Jeffrey Geller and Isabel Norian

In the areas of mental health and mental illness, advocacy has been neither a unitary concept nor a simple activity at any point in history. The *methods* by which individuals and groups advocate for causes are many, yet—after taking into account revolutionary changes in technology—have been largely consistent among these parties throughout American history. On the other hand, the *focus* of advocacy efforts regarding mental health matters and mental illness shows a distinct evolution over time, as illustrated by these excerpts from history:

> If the insane are sick people, and the asylum a judicial hospital, make it more and more possible for the insane patient to have early treatment and early discharge. (Stephen Smith, M.D., NY State, Commissioner in Lunacy 1883)
>
> The feeble-minded are a parasitic, predatory class, never capable of self-support or of managing their own affairs. The great majority ultimately become public charges in some form....It is certain that the feeble-minded and the progeny of the feeble-minded constitute one of the great social and economic burdens of modern times. (Walter Fenald, superintendent of the Massachusetts School for the Feeble-Minded 1912)
>
> A national mental health program should recognize that major mental illness is the core problem and unfinished business of the mental health movement. (Joint Commission on Mental Illness and Health 1961)
>
> There is not one institutional psychiatrist alive who...could not be arraigned and convicted of extortion, mayhem and murder. (L. Ron Hubbard 1969)
>
> After 200 years of working to improve conditions for the mentally ill, American psychiatrists must not abandon their advocate role either to the legal profession or to consumer groups, nor renounce their obligation as physicians to treat the whole patient within the context of his clinical and legal rights. (Louis E. Kopolow, MD, NIMH 1977)
>
> Legal advocates for the mentally ill have not been willing to consider seriously the needs of the mentally ill and to formulate those needs as legal rights. Instead, they have done the reverse. They have treated rights as if they constituted the needs of the mentally ill. (Alan A. Stone, MD, President of APA 1979)
>
> [In the 1970s, ex-patients] began to recognize a pattern they referred to as "mentalism" and "sane chauvinism" a set of assumptions which most people seemed to hold about mental patients: that they were incompetent, unable to do things for themselves, constantly in need of supervision and assistance, unpredictable, likely to be violent or irrational and so forth. (Judy Chamberlain, National Empowerment Center 1990)
>
> Propelled by consumerism, the once marginalized ex-patient self-help alternatives, developed as *political opposition to* the mental health system, became institutionalized as consumer options within that system. (Althena Helen McLean 2000)
>
> Advocacy is not just calling on others to do what we want; it is shining a light for others to follow. (Steven S. Sharfstein, MD, President of APA 2006)

J. Geller (✉)
University of Massachusetts Medical School, Worcester, MA, USA
e-mail: Jeffrey.geller@umassmed.edu

I. Norian
Iris Telehealth, Austin, TX, USA

W. E. Sowers et al. (eds.), *Textbook of Community Psychiatry*,
https://doi.org/10.1007/978-3-031-10239-4_6

> The economic costs of mental illness will be more than cancer, diabetes, and respiratory ailments put together. (Thomas Insel, Director of NIMH 2015)
> The effect of racism and racial trauma on mental health is real and cannot be ignored. The disparity in access to mental health care in communities of color cannot be ignored. The inequality and lack of cultural competency in mental health treatment cannot be ignored. (Dan Gillison, CEO of NAMI 2020)

This chapter will offer an overview and historical perspective of who advocates in the area of mental health and mental illness, what they advocate for, methods commonly used, and what the outcome of influential advocacy efforts has been across the history of psychiatry in the USA. Where interrelated, key aspects of Canadian psychiatry history will be considered.

Who Advocates?

Since the first asylum in America was opened about 250 years ago, there have been three main cohorts of advocates in this arena: professionals, persons with mental illnesses (or having been identified as having mental illness), and families of persons with mental illness (Table 1). The strengths of these different voices have varied from one decade to the next. Similarly, local, state, and national reception of and responses to these voices have varied over time. In 1881, Orpheu Everts wrote:

> Men and women of intellectual and social distinction who may have themselves (unhappily) suffered the humiliation, and possibly some errors, of hospital treatment, after apparently recovering the use of their faculties, have given tone and color of veracity to stories of ill-usage, and vigorous expression to mental concepts of hospital administration, tinged by memories and imaginations, the morbid parentage of which may be unsuspected by others or even by themselves. (Everts 1881)

In 1883, John Chapin opined:

> It is a common occurrence that managers of sensational newspapers, pandering to a morbid appetite for wretched personalities, admit to their columns without hesitation the most improbable statements of persons who have been inmates of asylums for insane…Discharged patients and employees,

Table 1 Who advocates, and what might they advocate for?

Psychiatrists
Advocacy for patients
Rights
Entitlements (income, healthcare coverage (including parity), disability benefits)
Employment
Housing
Adequate treatment (available, accessible, evidence-based, best practice)
Health equity
Stigma, discrimination
Advocacy for profession
Scope of practice
Licensing and professional description
Work conditions: Environment (safety including infection control, support services), caseload, productivity, supervision
Renumeration
Workforce: expansion, equity, training, lifelong learning
Board certification and maintenance of certification (MOC)
Advocacy for public health and prevention
Community level
State level
National level
Advocacy for health equity and social justice
Persons with mental illness
Self-advocacy on individual basis for individual rights, self-determination
Advocacy as a group/movement for class rights
Advocacy regarding treatment
Accepting treatment
Declining treatment
Advocacy for nondiscrimination
Services
Housing
Employment
Healthcare coverage, benefits (including parity)
Citizen rights
Social justice
Family members
Advocacy regarding treatment
Treatment with consent
Treatment "over objection"
Advocacy regarding access to information
Advocacy regarding access to services, adequate numbers of psychiatric beds, crisis services in lieu of police response
Advocacy for better entitlements

(continued)

Table 1 (continued)

Advocacy regarding social justice
Advocacy against stigma and discrimination
Government representatives
Municipal/county
Mayor/other executives
Sheriff and police
State
State mental health authority
Department of corrections
Department of children and families
Legislative
Judiciary: judges, attorneys
Law enforcement: probation officers, state troopers, corrections officers
Federal
Executive branch: President, SAMHSA, NIMH, NIDA, NIAAA
Judicial branch
Legislative branch: Congress

> persons with real or supposed grievances, or disaffected from various causes have been ready to join together or act singly to bring about legislative investigations of asylums. (Chapin 1883a)

Today, the voices of the current and former patients could not be received more differently.

A fourth, albeit more dispersed, cohort would be representatives of government, ranging from local to federal levels. In addition to these cohorts of advocates, we might consider a fifth: legal counsel. Attorneys as an advocacy force had become organized and funded by the US Department of Health and Human Services on a state-by-state basis as of 1986 (Sundram 1995). This organization was a culmination of efforts born in the 1960s (Freddolino and Appelbaum 1984). Attorneys represent powerful forces of advocacy in mental health and mental illness matters. Here, we will not consider them separately, as they typically work in concert with other cohorts on any given cause.

Arguably, there are two major impediments to effective advocacy for improved care, treatment, community opportunities (work, housing, social integration), and interpretation of rights. First, lack of cooperation among cohorts can slow progress on any given cause. At its best, such lack of cooperation yields fragmented and disjointed, even redundant efforts around a similar objective. At its worst, this dynamic can deteriorate into antagonism and hostility between cohorts. Second, internal dissent among members of a given cohort can present formidable barriers to progress on a common cause. Examples include fractures between psychiatrists and psychologists, family members for and against assisted outpatient treatment, and individuals who have experienced mental illness who stand for or against the use of psychotropic medications. Historically, guild issues often interfere with coordinated efforts, or disagreement over one issue interferes with joint advocacy on issues where there is agreement.

Unless, and until, various cohorts can advocate with a unitary voice, and different cohorts can join forces to rally together around specific issues, advocacy for mental health matters will be significantly hampered. When different groups speak at cross-purposes, they unwittingly offer cover to those in positions of influence who are reluctant to take meaningful action (e.g., a legislator takes no position, indicating, "I couldn't figure out what 'they' wanted," or "Nothing I could do would please them").

Methods of Advocacy

Cohorts of advocates utilize a variety of advocacy methods. All groups use all methods, but the mainstay of each group's armamentarium is different. Professions emphasize lobbying through professional organizations, which often involves funded lobbying efforts and legal counsel. Consumer groups have come together in the form of non-profits and grassroots organizations, the largest of which is the National Alliance on Mental Illness (NAMI) (https://www.nami.org/). Of note, consumer groups have found strengthening voice and organizing power in online presences including social media platforms in particular. Families, in addition to participating in such organizations, tend to come together to educate and lobby policymakers themselves.

Table 2 Methods of advocacy

Psychiatry
Professional organizations
Lobbying, e.g., political action committees, paid lobbyists, advocacy days
Testimonies
Constituent contact, e.g., letters to senators
Education, e.g., publications
Listservs
Social media platforms, groups
Phone banks
Professional meetings
Surveys
Persons with mental illness
Consumer movements
Social media platforms, groups
Protests, rallies, fundraisers
Legislative action, e.g., letter writing/e-mail campaigns
Publications, e.g., newsletters, online resources/websites
Paid positions, e.g., consumer advocates, peer specialists
Surveys
Peer support groups
Testimonies
Family
Non-profit/grassroots organizations
Social media platforms, groups
Rallies, marches, fundraisers
Constituent pressure
Testimonies
Joint action: Psychiatry, persons with mental illness, family
Joining committee in another group's organization
Educating each other, attending each other's annual meeting, other conferences
Joint education of public
Joint lobbying
Colocation for shared work
Voices of individuals with membership in more than one group, e.g., prosumer
Joint testimonies

Common methods of advocacy are outlined in Table 2. Once again it is worth noting that joint advocacy is the most effective advocacy (e.g., inclusion of persons with mental illness in higher-level positions within state mental health authorities) (Geller et al. 1998).

Points of Impact: Advocacy in History

It is not possible to truly understand contemporary advocacy by, for, and about persons with mental illness without developing a familiarity with the history of these endeavors. The Appendix to this chapter (*Advocacy Timeline*) provides key points in the evolution of advocacy in this area. In reviewing the timeline, note how often the agendas of cohorts of advocates have overlapped, yet how frequently outcomes appeared to appease all or none of the cohorts.

Advocacy at the Beginning of the Twenty-First Century

This first decade of the twenty-first century saw the emergence of strong advocacy around a number of key themes pertinent to mental health and mental illness. Here we review dominant themes, including:

- Recovery
- Empowerment
- Treatment and treatment resources
- Involuntary or "coercive" treatment
- Employment
- Housing

Of note, the concept of "stigma" is not explored separately, as it is our assertion that effective and meaningful advocacy in mental health and mental illness matters results in fundamental, sustainable change in each of the topics explored and in the process effectively reduces stigma. Paolo del Vecchio describes "hegemonic stigma and discrimination," proclaiming "stigma and discrimination and recovery are inexorably linked: no justice, no recovery" (del Vecchio 2006a).

Recovery

The US Department of Health and Human Services defines "recovery" as a process of change through which individuals improve their health and wellness, live a self-directed life, and strive to achieve their full potential (DHHS 2022). It further defines recovery as involving four domains: health, home, purpose, and community. Recovery, probably the fundamental concept in contemporary mental health advocacy, is not a new principle in American psychiatry. The so-called lunatic asylums were founded on a principle of "recovery." Psychiatrists (then called "alienists") working in these asylums were not expected to provide lifelong care, and Dorothea Dix did not advocate to state legislative bodies and the US Congress for domiciliary care for "the insane," Rather, the idea was "removing" a suffering individual from the sources of stress (family, work, almshouse, jail) placing them in a "healing" environment (i.e., asylum) where the presumably knowledgeable, "beneficent" superintendent could cure the individual and return her/him back to their community (Dix 1843; Gollaher 1995). The belief was that the earlier the treatment occurred, the greater the likelihood of recovery. It was Pliny Earle, Superintendent of the asylum in Northampton, Massachusetts, who debunked the reported cure rates by documenting the fallacies in the superintendent's statistics (Earle 1887). As late as the 1880s, superintendents and commissioners were still talking about "recovery" (Smith 1883; Chapin 1883a).

The principle of recovery was lost to American psychiatry from the end of the 1880s to the end of World War II as the size of state hospital populations—largely comprising, at that time, individuals with mental illnesses, those with neurosyphilis, those who were elderly, and those who simply had nowhere else to go—exploded. Recovery efforts made a brief appearance in the 1950s as evidenced by scores of articles in the pages of the journal *Hospital and Community Psychiatry* of that era. The focus on hospital-based recovery was quickly lost, however, as just getting patients out of the hospital became the clarion call of an era retrospectively labeled "deinstitutionalization."

The rebirth of recovery is largely due to a few consumers, a few prominent "prosumers" (advocates who are mental health professionals and have serious mental illness), and an additional professional or two. These individuals advocated for recovery to become the guiding principle of mental health reform, predominantly through education, publications, speeches, mentoring, and modeling. Those in the vanguard included Judy Chamberlin of the National Empowerment Center (Chamberlin 1995); Dan Fisher, MD, PhD, of the National Empowerment Center (Fisher 1994); Pat Deegan, PhD, of the Institute for the Study of Human Resilience (Deegan 1988); Fred Frese, PhD, of the Northeastern Ohio Universities College of Medicines (Frese et al. 2001); and William Anthony, PhD, of the Center for Psychiatric Rehabilitation (Anthony 2000). Anthony's was arguably the most stentorian voice coming from someone not self-identified as being or having been a person with serious mental illness.

Professionals who had not been past or present utilizers of psychiatric services for serious mental illness have followed. Larry Davidson, PhD, and his colleagues at Yale have written prolifically about recovery (Davidson et al. 2006). The American Psychiatric Association adopted a position statement on recovery in July 2005 (American Psychiatric Association 2005), and the American Association of Community Psychiatrists published one in 2001 (AACP Guidelines for Recovery Oriented Services 2001). Recovery started to become integrated into psychiatric training, initially in public sector fellowships (Ranz and Mancini 2008). Recovery became the focus of research, with investigators starting to study specific methods of recovery (Cook et al. 2009).

Recovery, then, is an example where advocacy, initiated largely by those with personal psychiatric histories along with a handful of maverick professionals and directed at professionals and policymakers, has both transformed the contemporary practice of psychiatry and returned the practice of psychiatry to its roots.

Empowerment

There have been numerous definitions of empowerment, and these may vary depending on context. The National Empowerment Center offers a multifaceted definition, which includes such elements as having decision-making power, having access to information and resources, and having a range of options from which to make choices (Chamberlin1997b). There is no recovery without empowerment, but the goal of empowerment is more complicated and fractious than simply a component of recovery. Advocacy for empowerment has meant different things to different people and has been the keystone in the consumer movement.

For some, empowerment means freeing oneself from all the "shackles" of psychiatry. Leonard Frank wrote,

> We of the psychiatric inmate's liberation movement affirm the statement that the policies and practices of American psychiatry are oppressive… [we are] human beings whose lives psychiatry has damaged, whose lives psychiatry has ruined, whose lives psychiatry has shortened, and whose lives psychiatry has taken… The roots of psychiatric authority are fraud, fear and force, psychiatry's unholy trinity. (Frank 1986)

For others, the effort is not so much directed *against* psychiatry, as it is *toward* freedom. As Chamberlin said, "Wanting to be free is not a delusion"—nor is not wanting to be *defined* by a psychiatric diagnosis (Chamberlin 1997a).

Chamberlin (1997b) and Fisher (1994) have each defined empowerment in highly useful terms. In Fisher's definition, empowerment embodies hope, personhood, achievement of self-defined goals, choices, the opportunity to speak for oneself, peer support, an end to discrimination, self-control of symptoms, well-being, liberty and freedom, and healing from within (Fisher 1994). Fisher advocates for:

1. Facilitating recovery through education and inspiration of hope
2. Developing alternatives to hospitalization
3. Providing state funding of involuntary admission under the public safety budget rather than the healthcare budget
4. Maximizing survivor and consumer involvement in all aspects of treatment
5. Establishing self-help and consumer-run services
6. Ensuring that survivors and consumers are genuinely and effectively involved in the protection of human rights and the improvement of quality of services
7. Favoring the role of personal care attendants rather than case managers
8. Viewing the life experiences of recovery from a serious psychiatric disability as an asset—not a liability—in hiring
9. Promoting consumer control and choice of access to housing and financial, educational, vocational, and social services
10. Providing staff training based on the needs of survivors and consumers
11. Basing total quality improvement of mental health services on outcome measures designed by survivors and consumers (Fisher 1994)

Del Vecchio makes the point that "today's consumer movement is not 'radical'" (del Vecchio 2006b). He points out that "rather than fighting against pharmacological treatment the movement supports the consumer's choice of treatments—including medications—and is often active in promoting increased funding for mental health funding…" (del Vecchio 2006b). Organized psychiatry has consistently advocated for patients' empowerment, although not as unambivalently nor as articulately as persons with lived experience. For example, in 1896, John Chapin, MD, of the Pennsylvania Hospital stressed that "patients lose none of their civil rights when they enter the door of his institution" (Chapin 1896). In 1981, Richard Lamb strenuously advocated for "securing patients' rights responsibly" (Lamb 1981). It was George Brooks, superintendent of Vermont State Hospital, who started the work (subsequently picked up by Courtenay Harding (Brooks and Deane 1965; Harding et al. 1987) to demonstrate that schizophrenia was not, of its absolute nature, a progressively disabling condition rendering an individual powerless.

For the psychiatrist practicing in the community, advocacy for empowerment can occur on an everyday basis wherever one provides services to a patient. Psychiatrists have the capacity to empower patients, for example, through shared decision-making. The American Medical Association acknowledged the concepts of empowerment in what it termed "participatory medicine" (Moyer 2010).

Treatment and Treatment Resources

Advocacy concerning treatment has two main facets: advocacy for the right to treatment and advocacy for the right to refuse treatment. Ironically, there has been greater success with the right to refuse than the right to receive treatment.

Repeatedly, the US Supreme Court has failed to find a constitutional right to treatment. However, for inpatients, various entities such as the federal Center for Medicare and Medicaid Services, the Joint Commission, and the US Department of Justice have set minimal standards for treatment. On the outpatient side, there appears to be more attention to increasing productivity: pressure to see more patients per hour, rather than on the quality of the treatment experience. Law enforcement officers are becoming providers of mental health services as resources dwindle at community mental health centers (Zezima 2010). No matter where one is on the advocacy spectrum, all should advocate for high-quality services that are accessible and affordable, accountable and respectful, and delivered in a partnership between patient and practitioner. The health reforms that have addressed parity (Paul Wellstone and Pete Domenici Mental Health Parity and Addiction Equity Act of 2008) and insurability (The Patient Protection and Affordable Care Act 2010) set a platform, but do not guarantee any aspect of quality mental health services. It is here that advocacy needs to be strong and continuous. It can be disheartening to realize that one is hard-pressed to find any mental health reform that was clearly acknowledged, at its outset, to improve treatment *and* cost more money. At a time when mental health services were quite poorly funded, the President's New Freedom Commission's mandate was to be cost-neutral (Hogan 2003).

The right to refuse treatment has really been a movement for the right to refuse treatment when one has the capacity to refuse and the right to have some procedure to override refusal after a procedure to determine the individual is not competent to consent or refuse. At this point in time, both psychiatrist and patient cohorts have generally endorsed this principle. These practices vary state to state, with a trend toward court involvement—rather than physician determination—to override refusal.

A formidable challenge in the face of advocacy by patients, former patients, families, and practitioners has been a severe workforce shortage. The need to train a workforce to meet the needs of persons with serious mental illness has been long-standing. In 1947, Harris and Otto observed: "It has been our conviction for a great many years that there existed a critical need for more undergraduate training in psychiatry designed primarily to equip the general practitioner to deal more adequately with the very types of psychiatric disorders that ordinarily do not require care in a psychopathic hospital (Harris and Otto 1947).

Little has changed. Coordinated advocacy among all cohorts is urgently needed. It has been found that greater involvement of patients in their own treatment produces better outcomes (Freddolino et al. 1989). Opportunities for collaborative advocacy have also arisen through the increased integration of psychiatry and medicine. The demonstrated higher rates of general medical morbidity and mortality in persons with serious mental illness, compounded by psychotropic medication effects (Felker et al. 1996), highlight the need for advocacy in this area.

Involuntary/Coercive Treatment

Perhaps the most divisive issue among the three main cohorts of advocates is that of involuntary/coercive treatment. Advocacy and "counter-advocacy" have played out most dramatically in the areas of hospitalization, medication, seclusion and restraint, and assisted outpatient treatment (AOT).

On the matter of involuntary hospitalization, Kraepelin wrote at the turn of the twentieth century, "Does the general attempt to bring about better care of our insane by placing them in institutions represent a practical philanthropy and is it a healthy sign of our social life? In other words, should one aid or oppose this movement?" (Kraepelin 1900). The matter of seclusion and restraint was considered at the first meeting of the Association of Medical Superintendents of American Institutions for the Insane (AMSAII) (predecessor to APA): "At its first meeting, the Association, by resolutions expressing its unanimous sense, declared its position manfully regarding a question which has perhaps provoked more animated and sometimes acrimonious controversy, than any other connected with the management of the insane, holding as it did, that the true interests of the insane forbade the abandonment of all means of personal restraint in the treatment" (Callender 1883). The members of the AMSAII were quite aware that this position was not going to be popular with restraint abolitionists. They noted, "The clamor for the institution of so-called reform in the total abolition of restraint, incited in mingled ignorance and malevolence, has vented much objurgation against this position of the Association" (Callender 1883). One view from 1845 was described as follows:

> In most cases where the chemical restraints are now used in American hospitals, I have no hesitation in saying that they are far preferable to the vigilance or force of attendants. The object is gained more surely, more effectually, and with far less annoyance to the patient. A mechanical contrivance performs its office steadily, uniformly, and thoroughly and is submitted to as something inevitable. The will and strength of an attendant are capricious and variable in their operation. It is objected to mechanical restraints that they leave disagreeable impressions on the mind of the patient who regards them, even after recovery, as marks of degradation and kindness. That such feelings may have been observed in patients whose recovery was quite imperfect, and who consequently regarded restraints, as they might a thousand other things, in a very false light, is very probable, but not a single instance of such feeling has come to my knowledge, in patients who had attained healthy views on every other subject. It is also objected to them that they are liable to be abused; that they are often applied to save trouble, and even to gratify the light of attendants…It is our rule to use no more, and continue it no longer, than is necessary to affect the object in view, and in all cases, it is the com- fort of the patient, not the attendant, which is consulted. (Anonymous 1845)

The modern resurrection of the seclusion and restraint debate owes a great deal to the efforts of the federal Substance Abuse and Mental Health Services Administration (SAMHSA). SAMHSA has called for the elimination of seclusion and restraint (Curie 2005). SAMHSA advocates for a "transformation of the system of care" and for recovery and posits that the elimination of seclusion and restraint is fundamental to a culture shift. SAMHSA adds: "seclusion and restraint must be used only when the potential exists for imminent physical danger to the patient or others" (Curie 2005). SAMHSA has offered guidelines for the use of seclusion and restraint that many view as unworkable, e.g., "physical restraint may not exceed 10 min."

Advocacy against involuntary medication has been conducted under the banners of "the right to refuse treatment" and "nothing about us without us" (see section "Treatment and Treatment Resources"). Advocacy for involuntary treatment has long argued against the risk of depriving patients of indicated treatment, such that—as it has been phrased—they are "rotting with their rights on" (Applebaum and Gutheil 1979).

Perhaps the hottest subject for advocacy on both sides of the treatment issue over the beginning of this century has been the use of involuntary treatment in the community, otherwise known as "outpatient commitment" or assisted outpatient treatment (AOT). While there is a history of involuntary or coercive community-based treatment throughout the twentieth century when hundreds of individuals were placed on "visit status" from state hospitals (still legally patients of the hospital, but allowed to live in the community), the modern era of advocacy, for and against involuntary outpatient treatment, really began in the 1980s (Geller 1986). The most potent advocacy organization in favor of involuntary community treatment has been the Treatment Advocacy Center (http://www.treatmentadvocacycenter.org) started by E. Fuller Torrey (http://www.treatmentadvocacycenter.org/index.php?option=com_content&task=view&id=16&Itemid=45). Opponents of involuntary community treatment have been led by attorney-advocates, e.g., Bazelon Center (http://www.bazelon.org) and Center for Public Representation (http://www.centerforpublicrep.org). Both sides have used studies to bolster their arguments (Honig and Stefan 2005; Geller and Stanley 2005).

Issues under the heading of voluntary only, versus involuntary only when necessary, have not only divided the three cohorts of advocates, but also have created divisions within each group. Psychiatrists against any involuntary treatment are exemplified by Thomas Szasz (http://www.szasz.com). The Board of the Treatment Advocacy Center counts consumers among its members (http://www.treatmentadvocacycenter.org). Does one believe anosognosia is a valid and significant phenomenon? (Gilleen et al. 2010). Does the AOT law in New York State (Kendra's Law) work due to coercive components, or simply because patients under AOT receive more community resources? (Phelan et al. 2010). Will outpatient commitment widen the net of involuntariness (Geller et al. 2006)? To effectively take a position on the issues of involuntary versus voluntary interventions, one must thoroughly review the data and form one's own conclusions.

As of 2018, there were 47 US states with statutes authorizing AOT (Cripps and Swartz 2018). Cripps and Swartz noted, "the future of AOT in the United States is still somewhat uncertain and will largely depend on the effectiveness and sustainability of the SAMHSA AOT grant programs" (Cripps and Swartz 2018).

Housing

In the 1980s, advocating to end homelessness was generally straightforward and was the predominant housing issue of the decade (Lamb 1992). Providing better housing for persons who already had room and board in psychiatric facilities proved to be more complex. In order to advocate for appropriate housing, one needs to understand the array of housing options available, including "supportive housing," "supported housing," "housing first," and "permanent" versus "transitional" housing." One needs to be familiar with requirements of the Americans with Disabilities Act (ADA) (1990), the *Olmstead* case (1999), Medicaid, etc. Then one needs to apply this knowledge to questions such as:

- Are the assumptions made by the US Supreme Court in the *Olmstead* case clinically valid?
- Does Housing First, designed for individuals experiencing homelessness and substance use disorders, work equally well for persons with serious mental illness?
- What models of housing in a state would be a "fundamental alteration" of services as defined by ADA?
- Is it true that all (or most) individuals with serious mental illness in institutions, if provided information they could understand about housing options, would choose supported housing and move forward with relocating?
- When are the costs of relocating and supporting one specific individual in the community so high that they interfere with providing comparable resources to multiple other individuals?

Employment

Employment is another area where there is general agreement among the three cohorts of advocacy: employment is an important part of recovery. Employment of persons with mental illness has a long and evolutionary history. In the nineteenth century, asylum patients worked for two basic reasons: work was considered to be beneficial to patients' recovery, and the asylums could not function without patient labor. Through the first half of the twentieth century, patients worked simply to keep a state hospital, with its 1000 to 15,000 patients, operational. In the 1950s, state hospitals established programs aimed at equipping patients for work in the community (see *Hospital and Community Psychiatry* throughout the 1950s). This focus was lost with "deinstitutionalization" (see above).

Since the late 1980s, advocates have pushed to support getting individuals affected by mental illness into the mainstream work force. (There were isolated efforts to this end before that time; see Fountain House and the clubhouse movement). This agenda has been augmented by advocacy efforts by patients and ex-patients to obtain employment in the mental health field itself (i.e., peer support, peer survivor positions).

In 2002, Mechanic et al. found that, according to collected survey data, about half of individuals diagnosed with mental illness were employed, and only about a third of individuals diagnosed with mental illness worked full-time (versus 60% of those without a diagnosed mental illness) (Mechanic et al. 2002)). According to a national survey in 2014, increased severity of mental illness correlated with decreased employment rates, ranging from 68.8% for those with "mild" mental illness to 54.5% in those with "serious" mental illness (Luciano and Meara, 2014). In the same survey, it was found that over a third of people with serious mental illness had incomes below $10,000 (versus 23% among those without mental illness) (Luciano and Meara, 2014).

Advocacy for increasing access to competitive work placements for individuals diagnosed with mental illness has been bolstered by studies (including those about supported employment programs) demonstrating the effectiveness of efforts to achieve this objective (Drake et al. 1999).

Peer Support

Peer support has been defined by SAMHSA as follows:

> Peer support encompasses a range of activities and interactions between people who share similar experiences of being diagnosed with mental health conditions, substance use disorders, or both. This mutuality—often called "peerness"—between a peer support worker and person in or seeking recovery promotes connection and inspires hope. Peer support offers a level of acceptance, understanding, and validation not found in many other professional relationships (Mead and McNeil 2006)). By sharing their own lived experience and practical guidance, peer support workers help people to develop their own goals, create strategies for self-empowerment, and take concrete steps towards building fulfilling, self-determined lives for themselves. (SAMHSA 2017)

Peer support can be described as consisting of six categories: peer-delivered services, peer employees, peer-run and peer-operated services, peer partnerships, self-help groups, and Internet support groups (Solomon 2004). Those that are directed at work have been shown to be beneficial in many ways. For example, peer-provided services have been found to be as effective as non-peer-provided services (Solomon 2004). Peer services have benefited the mental health system in many ways: direct labor cost-savings, decreased hospitalization, shorter hospital stays, getting outpatient services to those who would not avail themselves of traditional services, and wellness benefits to both the giver and the receiver of the services (Geller et al. 1998).

Peer services are an example of where different groups may advocate for the same end, but for very different reasons. Patients/ex-patients may advocate for peer services as a keystone to recovery. Mental health administrators may advocate for peer services as a significant labor force cost reduction (while essentially paying lip service to the concept of recovery). One way to keep the two groups on the same track is to have patients/ex-patients working in state mental health authorities (Solomon 2004). The ultimate purpose of any advocacy effort needs to be clear to all parties involved in that effort (Geller et al. 1998).

In recent years, recognition of the value and role of peer support in mental health and recovery has been extended to the value of family involvement and peer support, as well:

> Peer support services are services designed and delivered by individuals who have experienced a mental or substance use disorder and are in recovery. They also include services designed and delivered by family members of those in recovery...The widespread adoption of peer services has led to greater deployment across services for both physical and behavioral health. Peer-support services are provided in a variety of settings and across different models of care. They may be provided in consumer and peer-run settings, and in agency or facility-based programs. Services can be divided into three categories: crisis and respite services; level-of-care transition services; and community-based services, including outreach, engagement, and ongoing recovery supports. (SAMHSA 2020)

Advocacy Trends of the Last Decade

While much has continued to evolve in areas of advocacy in the past 10 years, two particularly powerful trends deserve mention here and will no doubt be the subject of focus of future iterations of this chapter.

First, a tremendous shift of advocacy efforts into social media and other online forums has redefined how advocates of all kinds communicate about causes important to them. Social media groups and platforms, such as Twitter, Facebook, and Instagram, have allowed professionals, patients, and family members to come together in new ways and share their stories directly with others like never before. The ease with which information can be posted, updated, and shared is unparalleled in the history of advocacy:

> We live in a digital age where information can be found instantaneously via the Internet. Studies have shown that consumers search for much of their medical information on the Internet, particularly utilizing blogs and social media platforms. As the mental health field is riddled with misinformation and stigma, this offers a unique opportunity for psychiatrists and mental health professionals to reach a broad audience for mental health education and advocacy (Peek et al. 2015)

Second, a powerful movement to advance health equity, including mental health equity, across populations has gained significant (and long overdue) momentum, particularly starting in 2020. This work is part of a greater movement to address structural racism and other manifestations of racism in our communities and community systems, and—on an even broader scale—social justice. In its Catalyst Brief of 2019, the Urban Institute noted:

> Racist policies and practices have been part of the nation since its inception, practiced by "founding fathers" and presidents who wrote and spoke about equality while engaging in the purchase, bondage, and sale of people of African descent. These policies were intended to subjugate people of color and afford dominance to white people. Ibram Kendi (2016) asserts that these policies led to racist ideas to justify the systemic barriers that created racial inequity and that each period of progress has been followed by a backlash of racist policies and practices…Looking ahead, major disruptive forces—technological innovation, increasingly frequent and severe climate events, and global economic change—could further widen today's equity gaps. Moreover, demographic changes are making the nation more racially and ethnically diverse (Colby and Ortman 2015) …In the face of these profound challenges, civic leaders, advocates, elected officials, and philanthropists are confronting our country's history of unjust and oppressive policies and taking action to promote equity and expand access to opportunity. Many approaches, like those that equip people of color with information and tools to successfully navigate existing systems, modify policies and practices to expand access and options, or enforce antidiscrimination protections, are making some progress. Other emerging strategies focus intentionally on the detrimental effects of past policies and offer bolder remedies that more directly address the roots of persistent inequities. (Kilolo Kijakazi et al. 2019)

The effects of structural racism and mental health inequity extend well into the territory of community psychiatry work. Psychiatrists working in community settings, with their rich and inextricable immersion into psychosocial aspects and realities (including barriers) of those served, have a unique opportunity to participate in the front lines of this work and truly act, alongside patients and families, as agents of change.

As part of mental health advocacy work, psychiatrists are also joining efforts to advance social justice causes across other minoritized and underserved communities, including those who identify as LBGTQ. Much work is to be done in coming years to bring psychiatry to the forefront of this critical advocacy work.

Also important to acknowledge is significant activity and engagement by advocates in the area of mental health in topics related to firearms and gun-related violence. Incidents of mass shootings seen in the media have heightened attention and urgency to advocacy efforts in these areas. Increasingly, generally trained psychiatrists are being asked to weigh in on these debates, on local, state, and national scales. Further, legislators and other potential advocates are expecting psychiatrists to engage in implementation and scrutiny of so-called "red flag" laws (regarding Extreme Risk Protective Orders), laws which allow police or family members to petition a court to order temporary confiscation of firearms from a person who may be considered to present a risk of danger to self or others (Segers 2019). These vital topics intersect inevitably with social justice-related causes including increased attention paid to matters of police brutality, in particular as they relate to impact on Black individuals and communities, as well as other persons and communities of color. Again, psychiatrists have an opportunity to play a potentially pivotal role in advocacy around these issues if they seize the (historic) opportunities afforded by their positions of influence and leadership.

Conclusion

The state of advocacy for causes related to mental illness at the beginning of the twenty-first century was well articulated by David Mechanic:

> Too often I've seen excellent scientists and well-informed clinicians undermine the value of their knowledge and their positive influence with patients through inattention to the power of empathic communication. Second, I've learned that popular ideas that seem intuitively correct and seductive are often wrong and sometimes are harmful…I am impressed that mental health advocates too often talk primarily to one another and to those already committed to their positions…Too often, enthusiastic hype far exceeds real advances or the likelihood of tangible help in the foreseeable future, a problem that characterizes advocacy for biomedical science—and indeed all science—in the American political context. We would be well served by being more humble in our claims and accepting that we still know relatively little about causes, processes, cures, or even good management of the major mental illnesses. (Mechanic et al. 2002)

Interestingly, in advocacy on behalf of persons with serious mental illness, we perpetually revisit issues as though they had never been considered before. Note these nineteenth-century comments:

> The asylums, instead of being regarded as hospitals and asylums for the medical treatment of a disordered condition, have come to be regarded as objects of suspicion; as convenient places for the "incarceration" of persons by designing relatives, and lunatic prisons, proper only for the detention of the criminal and dangerous insane. (Chapin 1883b)
> We need have no fears of public sentiment if we take the pains of educating the public. The public will trust us if we trust it, show it what we are doing—and why we do so. There are a great many things that take place in our hospitals that have no parallel in institutions, the population of which are sane. Yet the public holds us responsible for conduct, and results, based upon estimates, leaving insanity, as an element, entirely out. If the whole truth were known about our institutions, we would have no trouble at all. (Anonymous 1885)
> We desire to say here, and in behalf of the insane themselves to impress upon all *doctrinaires* and public agitators upon this subject, that the most obvious right of the insane in any state of society where private life is respected, and the peace of the domestic fireside is held sacred, is the right not to be meddled with and annoyed one jot more than is necessary (italics in original). (Rights of the Insane 1883)

If advocacy is going to be both different from and more effective than it has proven to be in the past, disparate interest groups are going to have to work together. There are obvious challenges in doing so, as different groups of advocates work primarily from different ethical perspectives: patient autonomy, medical paternalism, and role integrity (Eth et al. 1984). Even among groups often considered aligned, sprouts of difference can uproot fields of agreement.

Disagreements among mental health advocacy groups facilitate nonaction by those who advocate need to act on their interests. Thus, when different advocacy groups visit a Congressman's office and advocate at cross-purposes, it becomes easy for a Congressman to say he has "no position" on the issue (author's personal experience as Robert Wood Johnson Health Policy Fellow 1994).

As we join together in the partnerships of collaborative advocacy, we need to remember our task is of yeomen proportion:

> Adopting an advocacy role means vigorously challenging the status quo. It means not accepting the unrealistic limitations that government agencies place on resources for the poor and other vulnerable segments of society. It means rejecting political expediency that might lead to short-term financial gain. It means convincing the power establishment that preventive services are cost-effective. And it means challenging quiescent peers to join in advocacy efforts. (DeFries 1993)

May we continue to challenge ourselves, and our peers, to join in these critical conversations and causes, for the sake of the individuals, families, and communities we serve.

Historical Appendix

Advocacy timeline	
1842	Elizabeth T. Stone publishes, *A Sketch of the Life of Elizabeth T. Stone* describing the deprivation of her liberty when hospitalized at McLean Asylum
1844	Thirteen superintendents (from the then existing 24 public and private mental hospitals) meet in Philadelphia and form the Association of Medical Superintendents of American Institutions for the Insane. In 1921, the association changed its name to the American Psychiatric Association (APA)
1849	Dorothea Dix visits the East Cambridge, Massachusetts, jail and finds insane prisoners confined under inhumane conditions
1851–1860	Patients of Utica State Lunatic Asylum publish a periodical, *OPAL*
1866	Elizabeth Packard publishes her first book *Martial Power Exemplified*; 3 years earlier, she founded the Anti-Insane Asylum Society (Illinois)
1880	Formation of the National Association for the Protection of the Insane. The reasons for this association included increase in the types of diseases of the nervous system; increase in the incidence of insanity; "the peculiar helplessness of the insane"; help bring about central government supervision in all states; raising the standard of treatment in and out of asylums; and obtain and diffuse knowledge about insanity
1887	Nelly Bly/Elizabeth Cochrane Seaman wrote *Ten Days in a Mad House*, documenting her stay in a "lunatic asylum" on Blackwell Island
1892	Charlotte Perkins Gilman publishes *The Yellow Wallpaper*, a fictionalized account of her treatment by S. Weir Mitchell's rest cure
1908	Clifford Beers publishes his autobiography, *A Mind That Found Itself*. In 1919, with funding from the Commonwealth Fund and the Rockefeller Foundation, Beers forms the International Committee for Mental Hygiene (ICMH), the forerunner of the World Federation for Mental Health (WFMH) (1948)
1909	Beers founds the National Committee for Mental Hygiene, renamed Mental Health Association in 1976, National Mental Health Association in 1980, and Mental Health America in 2006
1930	May 5–10. First International Congress on Mental Hygiene (Washington, DC) 1935.
	June 10 is considered the founding date of Alcoholics Anonymous (AA)
1937	Recovery, Inc. is founded by Neuropsychiatrist Abraham Low (Chicago)
Mid 1940s	Patients at Rockland State Hospital (NY) form We Are Not Alone which morphs into Fountain House 1946.
	Mary Jane Ward publishes *The Snake Pit*
1948	Albert Deutsch publishes *The Shame of the States (Mental illness and social policy: the American experience)* describing conditions in state mental hospitals
1949	Passage of the National Mental Health Act (PL 79-87) leads to the establishment of the National Institute of Mental Health (NIMH) as one component of the National Institute of Health
1951	NIMH publishes *The Draft Act Governing Hospitalization of the Mentally Ill*
1952	The APA publishes its first *Diagnostic and Statistical Manual of Mental Diseases (DSM I)*
1955	Formation of the Joint Commission on Mental Illness and Health 1956
	Inception of the Social Security Disability Insurance (SSDI) program
	Passage of the Health Amendments Act of 1956 (PL 84-911) paves the way for the passage of
	comprehensive community mental health center legislation
1960	Thomas Szasz publishes "The Myth of Mental Illness" in the *American Psychologist*. A year later he publishes a book with the same title
1961	Erving Goffman publishes *Asylums: Essays on the Social Situation of Mental Patients and Other Inmates*
	A US Senate investigates and publishes its findings on Constitutional Rights of the Mentally Ill
1962	Ken Kesey publishes *One Flew Over the Cuckoo's Nest*
1963	Mental Retardation Facilities and Community Mental Health Centers Construction Act of 1963 (PL 88-164). Bill contains funding for constructing community mental health center (CMHCs), but no funds for staffing them
1964	*Dixon v. Weinberger* (District Court of the District of Columbia) finds patients at St. Elizabeth's Hospital have a statutory right to treatment and that those involuntarily committed must be placed in the least restrictive setting consistent with suitable treatment

1965	Medicare legislation is passed. It includes limited coverage for patients receiving active treatment in state hospitals in addition to those in general hospitals
1966	The Social Security Amendments of 1965 (PL 89-97) adds Title XIX, Medicaid, to the Social Security Act *Lake v. Cameron*. An individual cannot be committed until hospital officials determined there is no less restrictive facility available to care for that individual
	Rouse v. Cameron. Criminal defendant who is acquitted by reason of insanity and involuntarily committed to a psychiatric hospital has a legally enforceable right to adequate and suitable treatment
1970	Insane Liberation Front is formed by Dorothy Weiner, Tom Wittick, and others (OR) April. The first issue of *The Radical Therapist* is published
	Wyatt v. Stickney. Three fundamental conditions are necessary for adequate and effective treatment in public psychiatric hospitals: a humane psychological and physical environment, enough qualified staff to administer adequate treatment, and individualized treatment plans
1971	Mental Patient Liberation Project (New York) is founded with one of its creators being well-known advocate, Howie the Harp (Howard Geld). The Mental Patients Liberation Front is founded in Boston
	Mental Patients' Association is founded in Vancouver, Canada. Almost immediately MPA begins operating a drop-in center and community residence. The USA lagged beyond the Canadian consumer-run services model by 5–10 years
	Soteria Research Project, founded by psychiatrist Loren Mosher, opens its first house. Soteria is an early model of client-centered, recovery-based treatment with minimal use of antipsychotic medications
1972	A group of former mental patients circulate a newsletter, *Madness Network News*
	Bruce Ennis, a staff attorney with the ACLU (NY), publishes *Prisoners of Psychiatry* exposing extralegal uses of psychiatry
	Founding of the Mental Health Law Project, subsequently known as of 1993 as the Judge David L. Bazelon Center for Mental Health Law, aka Bazelon Center
	Lessard v. Schmidt. Persons facing involuntary civil commitment are guaranteed the full array of procedural safeguards formerly guaranteed only to individuals charged with a crime
	A US district court judge in the District of Columbia orders an outpatient commitment
1973	An APA Committee passes a resolution that homosexuality per se should not be considered a psychiatric disorder
	First conference on Human Rights and Psychiatric Oppression
	The North American Conference for Human Rights and Against Psychiatric Oppression holds its first Annual Meeting
	Souder v. Brennan. Patient-workers are entitled to minimum wages and overtime compensation, thus ending most state hospital work programs
1974	The book *The Madness Network News Reader* is published by former mental patients and anti-psychiatry activists
1975	*Donaldson v. O'Connor*. A person who is involuntarily civilly committed to a psychiatric hospital has a constitutional right "to such treatment as will help him be cured or to improve his mental condition" *Roger v. Okin*. The first class-action suit on the right to refuse treatment
1977	Mental Patients' Rights Association founded by Sally Zinman (Florida)
	NIMH initiates the Community Support Programs (CSP) to address problems created by poorly executed removal of long-term state hospital patients from their institutions. NIMH awards contracts to 16 states under CSP
	President Carter signs an executive order creating the President's Commission on Mental Health
	The General Accounting Office publishes the first governmental study of the problems of deinstitutionalization, called *Returning the Mentally Disabled to the Community: Government Needs to Do More*
1978	Judy Chamberlin publishes *On Our Own: Patient Controlled Alternatives to the Mental Health System*
	President Carter's Commission on Mental Health publishes *Report to the President*
	Leonard Roy Frank edits and publishes *The History of Shock Treatment*
	First CSP Learning Conference
1979	September. Almost 300 people attended a conference on advocacy for persons with chronic mental illness sponsored by the Dane County Alliance for the Mentally Ill and the University of Wisconsin-Extension in Madison, WI. This conference spurns the birth of the National Alliance on Mental Illness (NAMI)

	Community Support System (CSS) is formed growing out of a series of meetings at NIMH. Components of a CSS were identified as treatment, rehabilitation, case management, basic support, enrichment, crisis intervention, self-help, and rights protection
	Addington v. Texas. The minimum standard of proof to be met in civil commitment hearings is "clear and convincing evidence"
1980	"Phoenix Rising: The Voice of the Psychiatrized" began publication by former psychiatric inpatients (Canada)
	Suzuki v. Yuen. Involuntary civil commitment solely on the grounds of danger to property is unconstitutional
	The Civil Rights of Institutionalized Persons Act allows the federal government to initiate actions against states whose public institutions – such as hospitals, prisons, nursing homes, and jails – -deny residents their constitutional rights
	The Social Security Amendments of 1980 (PL 96-265) mandate review of all Social Security Disability Insurance (SSDI) beneficiaries, except those determined to be permanently disabled, once every 3 years. The Mental Health Systems Act, the major accomplishment in mental health of the Carter administration, creates a comprehensive federal-state effort to care for persons with mental illness Surgeon General Julius B. Richmond, M.D., releases *Toward a National Plan for the Chronically Mentally Ill*
1981	*Pennhurst State School and Hospital v. Halderman*. Court denies that a federal statute had established a right to treatment for persons with developmental disabilities
	US Supreme Court rules inpatients of public psychiatric institutions are not eligible for Supplemental Security Income (SSI) payments granted to persons with mental illness
	The Omnibus Budget Reconciliation Act (OBRA) of 1981 eviscerates the Mental Health Systems Act. The Act lumps together all remaining categorical mental health programs into a huge block grant
1982	Founding of the Carter Center
	Mills v. Rogers. US Supreme Court does not decide on a constitutional right to treatment
	Youngberg v. Romeo. A person in an institution has a constitutionally guaranteed "right to personal security," "a right to freedom from bodily restraint," and the right to receive "such training as an appropriate professional would consider reasonable to ensure his safety and to facilitate his ability to function free from bodily restraints." The effect is to narrowly define any constitutional "right to treatment"
	May 14–18. At the tenth annual International Conference on Human Rights and Psychiatric Oppression (Toronto, Canada), participants promulgated a set of 30 principles
	November 2. Berkeley, CA, voters pass a referendum banning electroconvulsive therapy within the city 1983 May. The California Department of Mental Health, through its Community Support System Project, funds the development of the Consumer Steering Committee
	Academic Consortium is founded to advocate for expanded federal research dollars for mental illness. 1984 The Disability Benefit Reform Act of 1984 requires the Social Security Administration to develop new health criteria for disability determination
1985	NAMI forms a subgroup called NAMI Client Council, renamed NAMI Consumer Council
	April. A consent decree is signed in a Maryland case, *Coe v. Hughes* that establishes that indigent patients in the 12 public inpatient psychiatric facilities have a right to access to the judicial system. June. The First National Mental Health Consumers' Conference is held in Baltimore, MD
	Formation of the National Depressive and Manic-Depressive Association (NDMDA), subsequently the Depressive and Bipolar Support Alliance (DBSA), a patient-directed national organization focused on advocacy, outreach, and education
	American Association of Community Psychiatrists (AACP) is founded. The mission of AACP is to encourage, equip, and empower community and public psychiatrists to develop and implement policies and high-quality practices that promote individuals, family, and community resilience and recovery
	US Senate Subcommittee on the Handicapped issues a report of its investigation of conditions in psychiatric institutions, documenting lack of treatment, abuse, neglect, exploitation, and deplorable living conditions throughout the USA. The Subcommittee chair proclaims, "Protection for these frailest of our society exists largely on paper"
1986	National Mental Health Consumers' Self-Help Clearing House is founded by Joseph Rogers Public Law 99-319 creates a protection and advocacy system for persons with mental illness

	The State Comprehensive Mental Health Services Plan Act (PL99-660) calls on each state to prepare a detailed plan for the care of persons with severe mental illnesses. The plan's development was to include participation by consumers, families, and advocates
1987	*Board of Nassau County v. Arline.* "Society's accumulated myths and fears about disease are as handicapping as the physical limitations"
1988	Formation of Support Coalition International, which subsequently became Mind Freedom
	Shrink-Resistant: The Struggle Against Psychiatry in Canada, edited by Don Weitz and Bonnie Burstow, is published
1989	November 23–26. Canada's first national conference for survivors of psychiatric "services" is attended by about 200 psychiatric survivors
1990	Spring/Summer. *The Journal of Mind and Behavior* publishes an issue, "Challenging the therapeutic state; critical perspectives on psychiatry and the mental health system" with contributor including Phyllis Chesler, Andrew Scull, Peter Breggin, Leonard Frank, Judi Chamberlin, and Thomas Szasz
	Medicaid expands to include a case management option and redefines rehabilitation to include psychiatric rehabilitation services
	The Americans with Disabilities Act (ADA) is enacted to eliminate discrimination against disabled persons. Title II says, "No qualified individual with a disability, shall, by reason of such disability, be excluded from participation in or be denied the benefits of the services, programs, or activities of a public entity, or be subjected to discrimination by any such entity"
1991	Formation of the World Federation of Psychiatric Users (WFPU), later to become the World Network of Users and Survivors of Psychiatry (WNUSP) (International), now a consultant organization to the United Nations
	United Nations adopts Principles for the Protection of Persons with Mental Illness and the Improvement of Mental Health Care
	The Inspector General of the General Accounting Office concludes that NIMH needs to address the findings of "blatant" noncompliance among a fourth of the CMHCs reviewed in the scope and volume of services provided to those unable to pay for them
	The Patient Self-Determination Act, part of the Omnibus Budget and Reconciliation Act of 1990, requires healthcare facilities that receive Medicare and Medicaid funding to provide information to adult patients about their right to make their own healthcare decisions, including the right to accept or refuse treatment and to execute advance directives about medical care
1992	Center for Mental Health Services (CMHS) is formed within the Substance Abuse and Mental Health Services Administration (SAMHSA)
	National Empowerment Center is formed by cofounders Daniel B. Fisher, M.D., Ph.D. and Patricia E. Deegan, Ph.D., both of whom were diagnosed with schizophrenia
	A group of consumers, who are also researchers, initiate the Consumer/Survivor Research and Policy Workgroup. This group works to redefine the national mental health agenda through collaboration with mental health professionals and policymakers
1996	The Domenici-Wellstone Illness Parity Amendment means that businesses with more than 50 employees will have to offer health insurance plans with equal annual and lifetime limits for mental and physical illnesses
	Public Law 104-21 prohibits payment of SSDI and SSI benefits to persons whose disability is based on drug addiction or alcoholism
1997	*Kansas v. Hendricks.* Sex offenders can be civilly committed
	Charles Q. v. Houston (Pennsylvania). State psychiatric hospital patients with the dual diagnoses of mental illness and mental retardation can be served in the community
1988	*Kathleen S. v. Department of Public Welfare* (Pennsylvania). Under the ADA, former patients of the former Haverford State Hospital have a right to placement in the most integrated setting appropriate for their needs
1999	December. Release of the first Surgeon General's report on mental health
	Olmstead v. L.C. and E.W. The ADA requires states to provide community placement for persons with mental disabilities if the state's treatment professionals have determined it is appropriate, if it is not opposed by the individuals affected, and if it can reasonably be provided considering state resources and the needs of other disabled persons
	First White House Conference on Mental Health

2000	Ticket to Work and Work Improvement Act increases level of income disabled persons can earn before losing Medicaid and extends period of time an individual can work and continue to receive Medicare. President Clinton signs a bill authorizing $10 million for mental health courts over 4years
2001	February 1. President George W. Bush announces the New Freedom Initiative, a broad plan to provide
	$5 billion over 5five years to help Americans with disabilities become better integrated into communities and workplaces
	Released as a supplement to the 1999 report, the Surgeon General's report, *Mental Health: Culture, Race and Ethnicity*, documents a disproportionately high burden of disability from mental illness among African Americans, American Indians, Asian Americans, and Hispanic Americans
2002	*Toyota Motor Manufacturing, Kentucky, Inc. v. Williams.* ADA must be strictly interpreted to limit the number of people who can qualify as disabled
	November. Release of *the Interim Report of the President's New Freedom Commission on Mental Health.* Report highlights five areas 1. Fragmentation and gaps in care for children 2. Same for adults 3. High unemployment and disability for people with mental illness 4. Older adults with mental illness are not receiving treatment 5. Mental health and suicide prevention are not national priorities
2003	Formation of the Coalition Against Psychiatric Assault (CAPA), a Toronto (Canada)-based organization whose members are "committed to dismantling the psychiatric system," "see the very concept of mental illness as flawed," and "oppose the violation of human rights which is endemic to psychiatry"
	May: President's New Freedom Commission submits *Achieving the Promise: Transforming Mental Health Care*. Released by the White House in July, the report suggests six goals and recommendations for a transformed mental health system 1. Americans understand that mental health is essential to overall health 2. Mental healthcare is consumer- and family-driven 3. Disparities in mental health services are eliminated 4. Early mental health screening, assessment, and referral are common practice 5. Excellent mental healthcare is delivered and research is accelerated 6. Technology is used to access mental healthcare and information
	Passage of Medicare Prescription Drug, Improvement and Modernization Act of 2003 introduces Medicare Part D with an implementation date of 2006
2005	APA honors Dorothea Dix with its first Posthumous Fellowship
	APA launches HealthyMinds.org, a consumer-oriented website to educate the public about mental health resources and treatment
	Institute of Medicine (IOM) publishes *Improving the Quality of Health Care for Mental and Substance-Use Conditions: Quality Chasm Series*
2006	NAMI publishes *Grading the States: A Report Card on America's Health Care System for Seniors Mental Illness*. Nationally, the grade was D. No state received an A and only five states obtained a B
	From Study to Action: A Strategic Plan for Transformation of Mental Health Care sets out *models* for understanding and organizing transformative systems change
	Roadmap to Seclusion and Restraint Free Mental Health Services emphasizes culture change within organizations as the fundamental change to reducing restrictive interventions
	DBSA publishes a workbook to help individuals set goals for their recovery: *Next Steps: Getting the Treatment You Need to Reach Real Recovery*
	Mental health consumer-survivors form a national coalition of organizations run by consumers, representing 28 states and the District of Columbia, to ensure they have a major role in the development and implementation of national and state policies
2008	March 5. US House of Representatives passes H.R. 1424, the Paul Wellstone Mental Health and Addiction Equity Act. This legislation expands the 1996 Mental Health Parity Act. The Senate had previously passed S.558, Mental Health Parity Act of 2007
	May 3. Enactment by the United Nations of "The Convention of the Rights of Persons with Disabilities"
	July 9. US Senate joins US House of Representatives in voting to end discriminatory copay for psychiatric outpatient visits by passing the Medicare Improvements for Patients and Providers Act. Coinsurance differential to be phased out by 2014

	October 3. President Obama signs the Paul Wellstone and Pete Domenici Mental Health and Addiction Equity Act of 2008. The effective date of the law is January 1, 2010
	US Congress overturns Supreme Court decisions that narrowed the applicability of the ADA by the ADA Amendments Act
	President Bush signs the Genetic Information Nondiscrimination Act of 2008 which prohibits discrimination by insurers and employers due to genetic makeup or family history
	SAMHSA publishes, *Self-Disclosure and Its Impact on People Who Receive Mental Health Services*
2010	March 1. The decision in *DAI v. Patterson* means that the 4,000 residents of New York State adult homes of 120 or more beds are qualified to live in supported housing. NYS is ordered to create 1500 supported housing units per year for 3 years. The state must employ peer bridgers to assist in the process
	March 23. President Obama signs the Patient Protection and Affordable Care Act
2010–2014	Implementation of the Patient Protection and Affordable Care Act
2015	Mental Health and Safe Communities Act of 2015, supporting assisted outpatient treatment, mental health courts, training police about mental illness, court supervised treatment for released prisoners with mental illness, forensic assertive community treatment
	Mental Health Reform Act of 2015, requiring programs to be evidence-based and focused on reducing homelessness, arrest, incarceration, and suicide. (https://mentalillnesspolicy.org/federalmentalhealthlegislation.html)
2016	April 18. SAMHSA announces Assisted Outpatient Treatment Grant Program for Individuals with Serious Mental Illness
2016–2017	21st Century Cures Act (Helping Families in Mental Health Crisis Act), including provisions for Assisted Outpatient Treatment, criminal justice reforms (mental health courts, Crisis Intervention Training (CIT), Mentally Ill Offender and Crime Treatment Reduction Act), creation of a SAMHSA Assistant Secretary of Mental Health
2017	February: House passes bill to roll back gun regulations, voting to overturn a rule that would bar gun ownership for some who have been deemed mentally impaired by the Social Security Administration
	September-December: Interdepartmental Serious Mental Illness Coordinating Committee (ISMICC) established as part of the Cures Act, with representation from numerous agencies and the public
2018	Congress passes HR6, the SUPPORT for Patients and Communities Act, which includes removal of geographic and site of service restrictions for mental health and substance use disorders for telehealth, creation of an interagency task force on childhood trauma, barring states from terminating Medicaid eligibility for minors post-incarceration. (APA 2020)
2019	March 5. The decision in *Wit vs. United Behavioral Health* (UBH) concluded that UBH used flawed medical review criteria to wrongly reject the claims of more than 50,000 people who were attempting to obtain coverage for mental health and addiction treatment. (Webb 2019)
	Congress passes the 2019 Federal Funding Bill, including funding increases for NIMH, SAMHSA, CDC, and other agencies, extended funding for CCBHCs, and allocating funds for states to address the opioid crisis. (APA 2020)
2020	Congress passes HR6074/2020 CARES Act which facilitates temporary expansion of telehealth including for mental health/substance use disorders. (APA 2020)
	Congress passes HR748/2020 CARES Act which increases funding to SAMHSA by $425 million due to the COVID-19 pandemic. (APA 2020)
	Congress passes HR 748 and 6074, providing for emergency funding due to the COVID-19 pandemic, including for the Provider Relief Fund, National Health Service Corp, and Community Health Centers. (APA 2020)
	Congress passes S 785 which seeks to reduce Veteran suicide through investment in suicide prevention programs, mental health resources, establishment of practice guidelines for Veterans with serious mental illness. (APA 2020)
	Congress passes S2661/2020, establishing a three-digit national number for mental health emergencies. (APA 2020)

References

AACP Guidelines for Recovery Oriented Services, 2001. www.communitypsychiatry.org.

American Psychiatric Association. (2005). Use of the concept of recovery, APA Position Statement, Retrieved July 2005 from www.psych.org.

Anonymous. (1845). Lunatic asylums of the United States. *American Journal of Insanity,* 2:46–68.

Anonymous. (1885). Proceedings of the Association of Medical Superintendents. *American Journal of Insanity*, 40:247–325

Anthony, W. A. (2000). A recovery-oriented service system: Setting some system level standards. *Psychiatric Rehabilitation Journal, 24*, 159–168.

APA Successes 2010-2020. Furnished courtesy APA administration to Dr. Geller upon request. Excerpts used in timeline with permission.

Applebaum, P, Gutheil, G. (1979). "Rotting With Their Rights On": Constitutional Theory and Clinical Reality in Drug Refusal by Psychiatric Patients". *Bulletin of the AAPL*, 306-315.

Bazelon Center. http://www.bazelon.org. Retrieved January 4, 2011.

Brooks, G. W., & Deane, W. N. (1965). The chronic patients in the community. *Diseases of the Nervous System, 26*, 85–90.

Callender, J. H. (1883). History and work of the Association of Medical Superintendents of American Institutions for the Insane-Press's address. *American Journal of Insanity, 40*, 1–32.

Center for Public Representation. http://www.centerforpublicrep.org. Retrieved January 4, 2011.

Chamberlin, J. (1990). The ex-patients' movement: Where we've been and where we're going. *The Journal of Mind and Behavior, 11*, 323–336.

Chamberlin, J. (1997a). Citizenship rights and psychiatric disability. *Psychiatric Rehabilitation Journal, 21*, 405–408.

Chamberlin, J. (1997b). A working definition of empowerment. *Psychiatric Rehabilitation Journal, 20*(4), 43–46.

Chamberlin J. Judi Chamberlin is the 1995 Pike Prize recipient. http://www.power2u.org/articles/empower/pike_prize.html. Retrieved November 15, 2010.

Chapin, J. B. (1883a). Public complaints against asylums for the insane, and the commitment of the insane. *American Journal of Insanity, 40*, 33–49.

Chapin, J. B. (1883b). Public complaints against asylums. *American Journal of Insanity, 40*, 33–49.

Chapin, J. B. (1896). On the detention of the insane and the writ of habeas corpus. *American Journal of Insanity, 53*, 242–255.

Cook JA, Copland ME., Hamilton MM, Jonikas J.A, Razzano LA. Initial outcomes of a mental illness self-management program based on wellness recovery action planning. Psychiatric Services 60:246-249, 2009

Colby, Sandra L. and Jennifer M. Ortman, Projections of the Size and Composition of the U.S. Population: 2014 to 2060, Current Population Reports, P25-1143, U.S. Census Bureau, Washington, DC, 2014.

Curie, C. G. (2005). SAMHSA's commitment to eliminating the use of seclusion and restraint. *Psychiatric Services, 56*, 1139–1140.

Cripps, S., Swartz, M. Update on Assisted Outpatient Treatment. October 13, 2018. Springer. *Current Psychiatry Reports* (2018). 20:112. Retrieved November 29, 2020.

Davidson, L., O'Connell, M., Tondora, J., Styron, T., & Kangas, K. (2006). The top ten concerns about recovery encountered in mental health system transformation. *Psychiatric Services, 57*, 640–645.

Deegan, P. E. (1988). Recovery: The lived experience of rehabilitation. *Psychosocial Rehabilitation Journal II, 4*, 11–19.

DeFries, Z. (1993). A call to advocacy. *Hospital and Community Psychiatry, 44*, 101.

del Vecchio, P. (2006a). All we are saying is give people with mental illness a chance. *Psychiatric Services, 57*, 646.

del Vecchio, P. (2006b). The evolution of the consumer movement (Ltr to Edit). *Psychiatric Services, 57*, 1212–1213.

Dix, D. Lynde. (1843). *Memorial: To the Legislature of Massachusetts [protesting against the confinement of insane persons and idiots in almshouses and prisons].* Boston: Printed by Munroe & Francis. https://archive.org/stream/memorialtolegis00dixd/memorialtolegis00dixd_djvu.txt. Retrieved 11/10/2020

Drake, R. E., McHugo, G. J., Bebout, R. R., Becker, D. R., Harris, M., Bond, G. R., & Quimby, E. (1999). A randomized clinical trial of supported employment for inner-city patients with severe mental illness. *Archives of General Psychiatry, 56*, 627–633.

Earle, P. (1887). *The curability of insanity: A series of studies*. Philadelphia: J.B. Lippincott.

Eth, S., Levine, M. L., & Lyon-Levine, M. (1984). Ethical conflicts at the interface of advocacy and psychiatry. *Hospital and Community Psychiatry, 35*, 665–666.

Everts, O. (1881). The American system of public provision for the insane, and despotism in lunatic asylums. *American Journal of Insanity, 38*, 113–139.

Federal Mental Illness Legislation. *Mental Illness Policy Org.* https://mentalillnesspolicy.org/federalmentalhealthlegislation.html. Retrieved December 4, 2020.

Fernald, Walter E. "The Burden of Feeble-Mindedness." The Boston Medical and Surgical Journal 166, no. 25 (1912): 911–15. https://www.massmed.org/About/MMS-Leadership/History/The-Burden-of-Feeble-Mindedness/.

Felker, B., Yazel, J. J., & Short, D. (1996). Mortality and medical comorbidity among psychiatric patients: A review. *Psychiatric Services, 47*, 1356–1363.

Fisher, D. B. (1994). Health care reform based on an empowerment model of recovery by people with psychiatric disabilities. *Hospital and Community Psychiatry, 45*, 193–915.

Frank, L. R. (1986). The policies and practices of American psychiatry are oppressive. *Hospital and Community Psychiatry, 37*, 497–501.

Freddolino, P. P., & Appelbaum, P. S. (1984). Rights protection and advocacy: The need to do more with less. *Hospital and Community Psychiatry, 35*, 319–320.

Freddolino, P. P., Moxley, D. P., & Fleishman, J. A. (1989). An advocacy model for people with long-term psychiatric disabilities. *Psychiatric Services, 40*, 1169–1174.

Frese, F. J., Stanley, J., Kress, K., & Vogel-Scibilia, S. (2001). Integrating evidence-based practices and recovery model. *Psychiatric Services, 52*, 1462–1468.

Geller, J. L. (1986). Rights, wrongs, and the dilemma of coerced community treatment. *American Journal of Psychiatry, 143*, 1259–1264.

Gaudiano, N. House votes to strike rule banning guns for some deemed mentally impaired. *USA Today*, February 2, 2017. https://www.usatoday.com/story/news/2017/02/02/house-votes-strike-rule-banning-guns-some-deemed-mentally-impaired/97299756/. Retrieved December 4, 2020.

Geller, J. L., Brown, J. M., Fisher, W. H., Grudzinskas, A. J., & Manning, T. D. (1998). A national survey of "consumer empowerment" at the state level. *Psychiatric Services, 49*, 498–503.

Geller, J. L., Fisher, W. H., Grudzinskas, A. J., Clayfield, J. C., & Lawlor, T. (2006). Involuntary outpatient treatment as 'Deinstitutionalized Coercion': The net-widening concern. *International Journal of Law and Psychiatry, 29*, 551–562.

Geller, J. L., & Stanley, J. A. (2005). Response to: New research continues to challenge the need for outpatient commitment. *New England Journal of Criminal and Civil Confinement, 31*, 123–126.

Gilleen, J., Greenwood, K., & David, A. S. (2010). Anosognosia in schizophrenia and other neuropsychiatric disorders: Similarities and differences. In G. P. Prigatano (Ed.), *The Study of Anosognosia* (pp. 255–290). Oxford: Oxford University Press.

Gillison Jr, D. (2020). NAMI's statement on recent racist incidents and mental health resources for African Americans. https://www.nami.org/About-NAMI/NAMI-News/2020/NAMI-s-Statement-On-Recent-Racist-Incidents-and-Mental-Health-Resources-for-African-Americans. Retrieved November 30, 2020

Gollaher, D. (1995). Voices for the Mad. New York, Free Press.

Harding, C. M., Brooks, G. W., Ashikaga, T., Strauss, J. S., & Breier, A. (1987). The Vermont longitudinal study of persons with severe mental illness. *II: Long- term outcome of subjects who retrospectively met DSM-III criteria for schizophrenia. American Journal of Psychiatry, 144*, 728–735.

Harris, T. H., & Otto, J. L. (1947). The use of private patients for psychiatric teaching in a medical school. *American Journal of Psychiatry, 103*, 649–652.

Hogan, M. F. (2003). The President's New Freedom Commission: Recommendations to transform mental health care in America. *Psychiatric Services, 54*, 1467–1474.

Honig, J., & Stefan, S. (2005). New research continues to challenge the need for outpatient commitment. *New England Journal of Criminal and Civil Confinement, 31*, 109–110.

Hubbard, L. R. Crime and psychiatry, June 23, 1969. Available at http://freedom.lronhubbard.org/page080.htm. Retrieved May 10, 2012.

Insel T. (2015). 4 things leaders need to know about mental health. World Economic Forum, Davos, Switzerland. https://www.weforum.org/agenda/2015/01/four-things-leaders-need-to-know-about-mental-health. Retrieved November 30, 2020.

Joint Commission on Mental Illness and Health. (1961). *Action for mental health*. New York: Basic Books.

Kendi, Ibram. Stamped from the Beginning: The Definitive History of Racist Ideas in America. New York: Nation Books, 2016.

Kopolow, L. E. (1977). Meeting the patients' rights challenge through mental health advocacy. *Hospital and Community Psychiatry, 28*, 383.

Kilolo Kijakazi, K., Brown, S., Charleston, D., Runes, C. (2019). What would it take to overcome the damaging effects of structural racism and ensure a more equitable future? *Catalyst Brief*, May 2019. *Urban Institute. https://next50.urban.org/sites/default/files/2019-05/2019.05.12_Next50%20structural%20racism_finalized%20%281%29.pdf.* Retrieved November 29, 2020.

Kraepelin, E. (1900). The duty of the state in the care of the insane. *American Journal of Insanity, 57*, 235–280.

Lamb, H. R. (1981). Securing patients' rights-responsibly. *Hospital and Community Psychiatry, 32*, 393–397.

Lamb, H. R. (1992). Perspectives on effective advocacy for homeless mentally ill persons. *Hospital and Community Psychiatry, 43*, 1209–1212.

Luciano, Alison and Ellen Meara (2014). Employment status of people with mental illness: National survey data from 2009 and 2010. Psychiatric Services. 2014 Oct;65(10):1201–9.

McLean, A. H. (2000). From ex-patient alternatives to consumer options: Consequences of consumerism for psychiatric consumers and the ex-patient movement. *International Journal of Health Services, 30*, 821–847.

Mechanic, D., Bilder, S., & McAlpin, D. D. (2002). Employing persons with mental illness. *Health Affairs, 21*, 242–253.

Mead, S., & McNeil, C.. Peer support: What makes it unique. International Journal of Psychosocial Rehabilitation. 2006. 10(2), 29–37.

Moyer, C. (2010). Has participatory medicine's time arrived? *American Medical News, 43*(21), 19–20.

National Alliance on Mental Illness. https://nami.org/. Accessed November 29, 2020.

Patient Protection and Affordable Care Act, The. (2010) PL 111-148.

Paul Wellstone and Pete Domenici Mental Health Parity and Addiction Equity Act of 2008. (P.L. 110-343).

Peer Support. SAMHSA. Peer Support infographic (samhsa.gov). https://www.samhsa.gov/sites/default/files/

programs_campaigns/brss_tacs/peer-support-2017.pdf. Accessed November 7, 2021.

Peek, H.S., Richards, MD., Muir, O., et al (2015). Blogging and social media for Mental Health Education and Advocacy: A Review for Psychiatrists. *Current Psychiatry.* 2015 Nov;17(11):88.

Person- and family-centered care and peer support. SAMHSA. Updated April 22, 2020. https://www.samhsa.gov/section-223/care-coordination/person-family-centered. Retrieved November 29, 2020.

Phelan, J. C., Sinkewicz, M., Castille, D. M., Huz, S., & Link, B. G. (2010). Effectiveness and outcomes of assisted outpatient treatment in New York State. *Psychiatric Services, 61*, 137–143.

Ranz, J. M., & Mancini, A. D. (2008). Public psychiatrists' report of their own recovery-oriented practices. *Psychiatric Services, 59*, 100–104.

Recovery Is Possible. U.S. Department of Health and Human Services. Updated March 14, 2019. https://www.mentalhealth.gov/basics/recovery-possible. Retrieved November 28, 2020.

Rights of the Insane. *American Journal of Insanity*, 39:411–432, 1883

Segers, G (2019). What are the "red flag" laws, and which states have implemented them? CBS News. Updated August 9, 2010. https://www.cbsnews.com/news/what-are-red-flag-laws-and-which-states-have-implemented-them/ Retrieved November 29, 2020.

Sharfstein, S. S. (2006). Presidential address: Advocacy as leadership. *American Journal of Psychiatry, 163*, 1712–1715.

Smith, S. (1883). Remarks on the lunacy laws of the State of New York, as regards the provisions for commitment and discharge of the insane. *American Journal of Insanity, 40*, 50–70.

Solomon, P. (2004). Peer support/peer provided services underlying processes, benefits and critical ingredients. *Psychiatric Rehabilitation Journal, 27*, 392–401.

Stone, A. A. (1979). The myth of advocacy. *Hospital and Community Psychiatry, 30*, 819–822.

Sundram, C. J. (1995). Implementation and activities of protection and advocacy programs for persons with mental illness. *Psychiatric Services, 46*, 702–706.

U.S. Department of Health & Human Services. (2022). https://www.mentalhealth.gov/basics/recovery-possible. Last updated: 3/1/22.

Thomas Szasz, M.D. Cybercenter for Liberty and Responsibility. http://www.szasz.com. Retrieved January 4, 2011.

Treatment Advocacy Center. http://www.treatmentadvocacycenter.org. Retrieved January 4, 2011.

Treatment Advocacy Center: Dr. E. Fuller Torrey. http://www.treatmentadvocacycenter.org/index.php?option=com_content&task=view&id=16&Itemid=45. Retrieved January 4, 2011.

Webb, C (2019). Important Ruling in Wit v. United Behavioral Health Enforces the Right of Individuals to Obtain Treatment for Mental Health and Addiction. *Legal Reader* April 30. 2019. https://www.legalreader.com/wit-v-united-behavioral-health-treatment-mental-health-addiction/ Retrieved November 29, 2020.

What Is Peer Support? SAMHSA. Value of Peers Infographics: General Peer Support (samhsa.gov) https://www.bing.com/search?q=peer+support&cvid=ccba217f999342e982e708387ca00dab&pglt=43&FORM=ANSPA1&PC=LCTS

Zezima K. (2010). State cuts put officers on front lines of mental care. http://www.nytimes.com/2010/12/5us/05mental.html?_r=1&hpw=&pagewanted=point. Retrieved December 6, 2010.

Comprehensive Integrated Systems of Care

Designing Systems and Services for People with Co-occurring Conditions and Complex Needs

Kenneth Minkoff and Nancy H. Covell

Introduction

The vision of community psychiatry is to organize services and systems to prioritize access and engagement for those "most in need and least able to pay" (Stern and Minkoff 1979). When this vision was first articulated, during the era of deinstitutionalization, the target population being prioritized as "most in need" were those adults with the most serious and persistent mental illnesses, who were being transitioned from institutions (state hospitals) into community settings, as well as children/youth with serious emotional disturbance, who also might otherwise be placed in long-term residential settings.

During the past four decades, however, our understanding of who is "most in need" has evolved considerably. We have come to recognize that the population of people with poor outcomes, high costs, and difficulty with access and engagement is much broader and is characterized as much by comorbidity and complexity as by severity in a single domain. Adults may have combinations of mental health, substance use, and cognitive conditions, along with chronic medical issues and disabilities, as well as human service needs (social determinants of health) related to domestic violence, multi-generational trauma, housing, criminal justice, employment, finances, and cultural and racial health disparities. Children and youth may be even more complex, as they are embedded in "complex" families, in which different members have different combinations of traumas, disorders, challenges, and conditions, as well as family system involvement with child protective services, juvenile justice, and school systems in addition to involvement with behavioral health services.

In accordance with our vision, our job in community psychiatry in the current decade should be to organize services and systems for those "most in need" by virtue of their complexity. This "job" is often described as creating "integrated" systems for those with complex needs. However, this job has rarely, if ever, been realized successfully. In fact, although there are notable examples of success in various components of integrated service delivery, we have not had a consistent framework for either design or implementation of comprehensive integrated systems to meet the complex needs of individuals, communities, or populations. The framework can be conceptualized as noted in Fig. 1.

The goal of this chapter is to articulate such a framework and to provide some guidance to practitioners, administrators, and policy makers on how to make progress in the direction of universal implementation of comprehensive integrated systems for "those most in need due to

K. Minkoff (✉)
Zia Partners, Inc., Tucson, AZ, USA

N. H. Covell
New York State Psychiatric Institute; Department of Psychiatry, Vagelos College of Physicians and Surgeons, Columbia University, New York, NY, USA
e-mail: Nancy.covell@nyspi.columbia.edu

W. E. Sowers et al. (eds.), *Textbook of Community Psychiatry*,
https://doi.org/10.1007/978-3-031-10239-4_7

Co-occurring disorders	Trauma	Human service needs	Relationships
Substance use	Physical (including domestic violence) Emotional Sexual	Housing Finances Transportation Food insecurity	Parenting
Medical problems	Criminal justice Welfare interface	Education/employment	Family Other relationships
Cognitive challenges	Immigration	Cultural/racial disparities	LGBTQ

Fig. 1 Complexities framework

complexity." We will recommend who should be prioritized for access to, and engagement in, ongoing services, within available resources, to best meet their needs for help and hope.

Person-Centered Design of Integrated Systems

In this chapter, we are going to describe the design of an integrated system using a person-centered (or family-centered) approach. We do not mean that just as a value statement; we mean that literally. Most discussions of integrated systems begin with consideration of how the administrative entities coordinate, the funding streams are blended, and the agencies collaborate, but this chapter will not do that. To best explain how to design comprehensive integrated systems, it is better to begin with understanding how to help individuals and families with complex needs and then build understanding from the "bottom" up, or from the person at the center out.

Begin with the Basics

There are basic definitions and concepts that are helpful in designing integrated services within any community behavioral health program or organization (or any type of program or organization). Shared and clearly communicated definitions, commitment to system design fundamentals, and embrace of basic service elements will ensure effective and efficient system design processes and products,

Definitions Preliminary agreed-upon nomenclature will provide clarity in communication and planning and development.

Co-occurring Conditions: Any person of any age experiencing any combination of one or more of the following: any mental health (MH) condition, including trauma; any substance use (SUD) addictive condition, including gambling, or nicotine addiction; any cognitive condition, including intellectual/developmental disorders I/DD, acquired brain injury, and/or dementia; any chronic physical health (PH) condition or disability, including vision, hearing, and mobility challenges, infectious diseases, as well as more usual medical illnesses (CSAT 2006).

Complexity: Any person of any age experiencing any combination of one or more of the above conditions with social challenges, including (but not limited to) cultural/racial minority status, immigration concerns, LGBTQ issues, education/employment issues, housing issues, legal issues, domestic violence concerns, parenting/relationship issues, food insecurity, and financial challenges (Zia Partners 2016).

Co-occurring or Complex Families: A family where one person might experience one kind of issue, like a child with an emotional disturbance or intellectual disability, and another member might experience another kind of problem, like a family member or caregiver with a substance use issue, so the family system needs an integrated approach (Zia Partners 2016).

Integrated Services Definition: (adapted from the Center for Integrated Health Solutions, National Council Center of Excellence 2021): Integrated services provide a full spectrum of appropriately matched interventions for multiple conditions in the context of a relationship with the treatment or service team in the setting in which the person is most naturally engaged.

Service Design Fundamentals

In any service setting in our system, individuals and families with co-occurring conditions and other complex needs need to be identified as priorities for engagement and intervention. As previously noted, individuals and families with any combination of conditions are more likely to have poorer outcomes and higher costs in multiple domains than those with a single condition (Dickey and Azeni 1996; Drake and Brunette 1998; Minkoff and Drake 1991; Rosenberg et al. 2001; Swartz et al. 1998). Individuals and families with any co-occurring conditions are more likely to have others, and the more complex you are, the worse you are likely to be doing. Further, complexity predicts trajectory more than condition per se (Glynn et al. 2011). Unfortunately, in the way our systems and services are currently designed, those with complexity tend to be experienced more as misfits at multiple levels than as priorities for care. To design systems within limited resources that are more effectively matched to people in need, this needs to change.

In any service setting in our system, complexity is an expectation not an exception. Consequently, services in any setting must be designed with the expectation of providing appropriately matched integrated services to the people with complexity that are the expectation in that setting. The prevalence data on these overlaps are well recognized. Here are just a few examples: prevalence of substance use issues in people with serious mental illness (RachBeisel et al. 1999), prevalence of trauma and mental health conditions in people with SUD (Sells et al. 2003), prevalence of serious medical issues in people with serious mental illness or SUD (Walker and Druss 2017), prevalence of substance use among people with I/DD (Carroll Chapman and Wu 2012), prevalence of BH needs in the justice system (Steadman et al. 2009), prevalence of behavioral health (BH) needs in people who are homeless (Hossain et al. 2020), and prevalence of SUD (NCASAC 1999) and COD (Stromwall et al. 2008) in the families of children in the child protective services system. The list is endless. The most compelling evidence is reflected when one looks at the service population in any setting. We already know that complexity is an expectation; the tragedy is that in the face of that knowledge, in a system with limited resources, we continue to design services based on one problem at a time, as if complexity were rare. Then, we try to find extra resources for the "special" people to work around our base system or try to have people with multiple needs served in multiple settings with multiple staff, guaranteeing that we use our resources even less efficiently than we already do. To design systems within limited resources that are more effectively matched to people in need, this too needs to change.

Therefore, all programs in a "comprehensive integrated system" must be designed to be "co-occurring capable" or "complexity capable" (Zia Partners 2016). This concept of co-occurring capability (originally termed dual diagnosis capability) originated in the literature on treatment of co-occurring MH and SUD (ASAM 2001; McGovern et al. 2007; Minkoff and Cline 2004, 2005), but has more recently begun to expand to accommodate the recognition that person- or family-centered services routinely involve helping people with all types of complex needs (Zia Partners 2016). Further, recent efforts addressing system change in a variety of "subsystems" are moving from a focus on "special programs" to developing more universal capacity or capabilities. Examples include developing efforts such as evolving frameworks for all types of BH and PH programs to make progress in integrated PH/BH services (Goldman et al. 2020); state of Iowa project in universal implementation of multi-occurring (MH, SUD, I/DD, BI, trauma) capability across services (K. Minkoff and C. Cline, personal communication March 2021); and development of criminal justice/BH redesign moving from a focus on "specialty court dockets" to design of all court pathways on the assumption that BH conditions are an expectation (Peters et al. 2012; Sarteschi et al. 2011).

**Co-occurring Capability/Complexity Capability*: For any program, within its existing mission and resources, organizing that program on every level must assume that the next person/family coming in the door will have multiple needs and design every aspect of that program (policy, procedure, practice, paperwork) and every person providing help, with every penny available, to have clear instructions for how to provide properly matched integrated services to the people with complexity that routinely present (Zia Partners 2016).

**Integrated System*: An integrated system is one in which all programs are designed to be co-occurring or complexity capable and in which all people with complex needs can receive appropriately matched integrated services within any door (Minkoff and Cline 2004, 2005; Engelhardt et al. 2009). Services within an integrated system may focus on specific age groups or types of co-occurring conditions or complex issues, such as co-occurring MH and SUD, co-occurring BH and PH, co-occurring BH and CJ, and co-occurring BH, educational, juvenile justice, and child protective needs (Children's System of Care).

**Comprehensive:* An integrated system is intentional about ALL ages and ALL forms of complexity within any service setting and brings all types of service settings into the partnership. While such comprehensive integrated systems are largely aspirational at present, increasingly community coalitions (e.g., Humowiecki et al. 2018) are recognizing the importance of addressing complexity comprehensively in order to achieve overall progress toward a healthy community within limited resources and significant social challenges.

Basic Service Elements

Although it seems at first glance that designing programs and services to be complexity capable is an impossible challenge, it is not. The secret to success is to NOT get stuck in thinking about how to restructure organization charts, to blend multiple funding streams, or to hire staff with every single type of expertise. Rather, it starts with looking at the research to discover "what works" for individuals and families who come in any door and then beginning to consider how to "implement what works" in a person/family-centered manner inside each of the program's existing services and workflows. This requires building infrastructure for practice support about "what works" into every program, rather than, as we commonly do, build our infrastructure around one problem at a time, and then need to work around ourselves (or spend extra resources to work around our own system) in order to respond to the people with complex challenges who regularly present. The following elements are foundational interventions in designing integrated person/family-centered services for people with complexity:

**Welcoming and Engagement*: In an integrated program or service, individuals and families with complexity are welcomed for help, as a priority, exactly as they are, wherever and whenever they present. "Every door is the right door" and everyone has specific "customer service" instructions, through policy and procedure and practice, to know exactly what to say to make it more likely that the person with multiple needs will experience the type of welcoming connection that counters their past trauma and makes it more likely they will continue to be engaged. (See chapter "Inspiring a Welcoming, Hopeful Culture" for a deeper discussion of Welcoming.)

**Screening and Identification of Multiple Issues*: In an integrated program or service, individuals and families are routinely screened for all co-occurring conditions and complex human service needs, and there is an opportunity to document each issue that requires attention, with level of urgency.

Person/Family-Centered Hopeful Strength-Based Framework: In integrated services, the starting place after welcoming is to build hope. Every person, especially those who have the greatest numbers of challenges, should be inspired when they meet us that we will partner with them over time to help them achieve their most important and meaningful goals for wellness and success. It is critical, in a recovery/resiliency-oriented framework (Recovery-Oriented Systems, Children's System of Care, Trauma-Informed Systems), that we document the person's vision of hope and continue to reinforce that vision. Further, application of evidence-based strength-based framework is most relevant for those who have many challenges. In a strength-based framework, we recognize that the more challenges you face, the more strength it takes for you to be just getting through the day, let alone coming for help, and the things that you are currently doing right for each issue are the building blocks of further progress toward your goals.

Relationship with an Integrated Team: In integrated services in any setting, the service provider(s) work as a team to help you with all your issues. Everyone is given instructions to understand how to be an "integrated partner" with each client. This doesn't mean that everyone is an expert in everything; in fact, people on the team may not be experts in anything or most things. Just the same, everyone joins with each client in a relationship in which each of us works with the clients to help them identify each of their issues and to figure out how to help them find the best next steps to address each of those issues over time in order to reach their goals.

Care Coordination at Appropriate Intensity Over Time: In providing integrated services in any setting, we recognize that the team (or a designated person on the team) is responsible for so-called "high touch" or "low touch" care coordination and tracking of the person's progress over time. The level of intensity of care coordination varies according to the person's level of complexity and ability to do this for themselves. Data systems may help in large organizations to track large cohorts of individuals with specific needs and metrics, but even without a specialized data system, a team can develop mechanisms for keeping track of the clients for which it is responsible.

Access to, Coordination with, and Integration of Specialty Consultation and Resources as Indicated: In an integrated service, the treatment team has organized and routine access to specialty resources within the community. These resources may range from specialty consultation for medical issues or certain types of BH issues (e.g., SUD in a MH setting, or vice versa), to resources for housing, education, and employment, and relationships with criminal justice and child/adult protective services. Routine procedures for information sharing are necessary and may benefit from "health information exchange" protocols and the like, but it is important to remember that information sharing may be facilitated by, but does not REQUIRE, a fancy data system. These specialty resources are not just referral resources, so much as collaborative partnerships in which the expertise is brought into the team, and shared with the client by the team, in a way that helps clients be successful in addressing all of their issues in an integrated fashion.

Small Steps of Progress Over Time for Each Issue: In integrated service provision, it is recognized that individuals with multiple long-standing conditions make progress in small steps over time. The classic illustration of this concept is in the Integrated Dual Diagnosis Treatment (IDDT) research literature, which documented that using evidence-based IDDT for individuals with serious mental illness and co-occurring SUD who were not initially engaged in help, applying the best known interventions resulted in taking about 3–4 years for about half the clients to achieve stable abstinence, with most of the rest making progress in other life domains, even though they were still using (Drake et al. 1998). Unfortunately, our services are often designed so that clients who don't get "better" quickly are regarded as failing, so we put pressure on ourselves and on them to improve quicker, leading to frustration and burnout.

Individualized Issue-Specific Best Practice Interventions for Each Issue: In integrated services, it is understood that there is not a one-size-fits-all approach or model for "integrated care." Rather, integrated service delivery is helping an individual or family find the right next SMALL step forward for EACH of their issues, building on their strengths, in the direction of their goals. In integrated services, each disorder or condition is considered primary, and the "best practice" for anyone is the right next step for that person for EACH condition, with continued small steps of progress over time.

Tracking Progress of Each Issue with Data Over Time: Integrated service delivery is grounded in being able to routinely measure progress for EACH issue over time. In some instances, like using PHQ-9 depression scores in primary health settings, there are specific symptom tools that can measure progress. In other instances, like monitoring diabetes in BH, there are lab tests (HbA1c) that are effective for measurement-based care. In most instances, however, the steps of progress need to be individualized, but still can be tracked concretely and measured around each issue. The key element is to incorporate routine monitoring of small steps of progress into all interventions, so it's easy for the service team to keep track and to attend to places where something is not working well.

Stage-Matching for Each Issue: Integrated care requires a partnership with the individual or family in which priorities for action are determined by the individual, and people have to make choices about how to move through the multiple issues they have in order to achieve their goals. The language for describing progress has been termed "moving through stages of change." However, when individuals have multiple issues, they are commonly NOT in the same stage of change for each issue. That is, stage of change is "issue-specific," not person specific, and integrated interventions in any setting need to be integrated and stage matched for EACH issue. A person with a complex set of issues and needs is likely to be best engaged in integrated services in the setting that is most aligned with the issue for which they are in the most active stage of change in relation to their goals. The structure for establishing stage of change for each primary issue and ensuring that next step interventions and outcomes are routinely stage matched can be built into a service planning framework in an integrated program.

Self-Efficacy and Skill-Building for Each Issue: Integrated services in any setting rely on building self-efficacy for individuals managing their own conditions and disorders. For medical issues, this is termed "chronic disease management," and enabling self-efficacy is a key element of Person-Centered Medical Homes. Tools such as PROMIS (Gruber-Baldini et al. 2017) have been designed to measure progress in this domain. In integrated service delivery, however, self-efficacy must translate to all of the issues with which the person is dealing. Nonetheless, the same approach must be applied. Self-efficacy is directly connected to skill building. Individuals and families do not simply need sets of recommendations and referrals; they need help to learn the skills they need to succeed in making progress for any issue and the confidence to carry out those skills. Skills may include self-management skills and skills in asking for help, whether from family, professionals, or peers. Skills may include skills in using medication or medical equipment, psychosocial skills for weight loss, exercise, maintaining housing, parenting, and so on. The key to skill acquisition is having the team be able to assist the client to learn necessary skills in small practical steps by following the principles of adult learning: practice, rehearsal, and repetition, with big rounds of applause (positive contingencies) for each small step of progress. There are numerous examples of skill manuals for helping people learn crossover skills that support integrated programming in any setting (Bellack et al. 2007; Cook et al. 2020; Copeland 2012; Golden et al. 2006; Najavits 2002; Roberts et al. 1999; Shaner et al. 2003).

Connection to Peer Supports and Natural Supports for Each Issue. Progress in any issue is facilitated when the individual does not need to rely on limited access to professional interventions alone. For almost any issue, there may be some form of peer support or natural support in the community, which might be helpful to the individual with complex needs. These may range from 12-step recovery programs, to church groups, to family support programs, to disease-specific support groups for various types of medical issues, etc. Integrated service programs not only routinely have lists of such resources; they also focus on helping individuals who are interested to make those connections to build effective supports.

How Do We Start the Planning Process and Move Forward

Self-Assessment Questions for Readers

Given the predicates for planning that we have offered, you might be at a loss of where and how to begin. Indeed, this may look like an overwhelming "To-Do" list, but it becomes easier to imagine designing services this way when we step out of our usual "box" and think a bit differently. Ask yourself the following questions about your own services or programs or agency:

1. Is complexity an expectation in the population you serve?
2. If yes, what is your primary mission (e.g., MH) and what types of complexity do you routinely encounter?
3. Given the above, how much of your ROUTINE service delivery is designed with the expectation of complexity, incorporating ANY of the above elements? How much of your ROUTINE service delivery is designed as if the people you serve were NOT complex?

What you are likely to realize is that many of your current services are mis-designed, as if you were mostly serving people with one problem only, or only one problem at a time; when people show up with complex needs, it seems like lots of extra effort to help them. Not only that, you may have discovered that much of your current service design is built backwards, so that you are taking hope away, focusing on deficits, moving too quickly, and ignoring both stage matching and skill building in efforts to send the person to multiple resources and referrals that may or may not exist.

Conversely, if all of your services were designed on the assumption that the next person coming in the door had many issues and your practice protocols were designed to welcome them as they are, screen and identify their issues, build hope, recognize strengths, engage partners, and help with stage-matched, skill-based small steps of progress for each issue, including linkage to peer and natural supports, your work would be much simpler, and your staff and clients would be having an easier time.

Moving Toward Complexity Capability as a Community BH Organization

Becoming "complexity capable" is a transformational process that can be best conceptualized using "customer-oriented continuous quality improvement" (CO-CQI, or CQI for short) as a framework for organizational change. CQI can be considered an evidence-based "recovery process" for organizations, as it involves the organization following a structured data-driven "one day at a time" process to becoming better organized at every level to be about what customers need and want. There are many different methodologies for CQI, but they share common elements (McLaughlin and Kaluzny 2004).

The elements of this transformation process (independent of content) involve the following:

- Establishing the vision for the agency
- Developing a horizontal and vertical partnership to achieve the vision
  - Horizontal means all divisions and programs are welcomed to participate.
  - Vertical means that all levels of staff, as well as service recipients, are welcomed as

partners in change, and staff/peers from each program are empowered as a team of champions or change agents.

- Connecting each program and staff member to the vision
- Organizing a CQI Team – agency wide, and within each division or program unit
- Measuring the current baseline "capability" of each program
- Developing an achievable, measurable improvement plan for each program
- Creating an agency-wide learning community and team of champions or change agents
- Identifying initial agency-wide priorities for progress – welcoming and hope, integrated screening, strength-based assessment, integrated teamwork, stage matching, skill building
- Measuring and celebrating progress
- Developing new policies, procedures, and practice supports to anchor progress
- Continuing the change cycle over time

The good news about this process is that many CBHOs are already engaging in various value-driven transformational activities. These activities have many names reflecting *specific areas of focus, as follows*:

- Recovery-Oriented (focusing on hope, empowerment, strength-based interventions, and peers)
- Trauma-Informed (focusing on responding to the expectation of trauma with safety and healing)
- Children's System of Care (using wraparound principles)
- Co-occurring MH/SUD Capability (integrating MH/SUD)
- Multi-occurring Capability (integrating MH/SUD/IDD/ABI)
- Physical Health/Behavioral Health Integration
- Cultural Competency/Fluency/Humility; Anti-Racism
- Complexity Care: Addressing Health Disparities and Social Determinants
- Accountable Health Communities

For each of these types of transformation, there are measurement tools and emerging literature. Each of these tools helps to organize a quality improvement process for a program or organization by measuring baseline policy, procedure, and practice to support the delivery of the specific type of service throughout the organization and then providing guidance for next steps of progress. For example:

Recovery-oriented tools (ROSI) (Dumont et al. 2005)

Trauma-informed care (Harris and Fallot 2001)

Capability to treat co-occurring mental health and substance use disorders (Gotham et al. 2009; McGovern et al. 2007; Minkoff and Cline 2004, 2005; ZiaPartners 2016)

Continuum-based framework for behavioral health integration into primary care (Chapman et al. 2017; Goldman et al. 2020)

Center for Integrated Health Solutions Organizational Toolkit for Primary and Behavioral Health Integration (CIHS 2014)

Quality Measures for Complex Care (Walton et al. 2020)

The Self-Assessment for Modification of Anti-Racism Tool (SMART) (Shoyinka et al. 2021)

Developing "Comprehensive Integrated Systems of Care," using the concept of complexity capability, builds on all these current approaches, but takes it one step further. The vision of service design that is being described in this chapter is about ALL the above efforts. That is, complexity capability is a shorthand for all the elements that should be built into the design of every program and process, within each program, agency, or community: The most efficient and effective way to do that is to have ONE overarching quality improvement initiative in the organization address all the issues that need attention and to find the one tool or if needed two tools that seem to offer the best way forward for the organization to get started. Once the quality improvement infrastructure has been developed, other tools can be added as indicated within one "integrated" improvement initiative. The reason that addressing all the issues together can make sense in an organization is that ultimately all the issues are commonly present in all the people served – complexity (including trauma and cultural/racial/linguistic challenges) is an expectation, and all people served can benefit from welcoming, hopeful, strength-based, integrated services to help them with all their issues to achieve their goals.

An example: A BH organization may want to use the COMPASS-EZ 2.0 tool from the CCISC toolkit (available from the lead author) to guide this process. This tool was originally developed with a focus on co-occurring MH/SUD, but the authors have updated it to include the option to focus on "complexity capability" more broadly. It assists an enterprise or organization to "engage in a process of organizing everything we do at every level, with every scarce resource we have, to be about ALL the complex needs of the people and families seeking help. By doing a self-assessment of its own capability to routinely address complexity in an integrated manger, each program can begin an organized process to become a welcoming recovery-oriented, complexity capable program" (Refer to ZiaPartners website for a description of the tool).

Within the CCISC toolkit, there are other tools more specifically designed for primary health providers, IDDT providers, and nonclinical system of care partners. Other types of tools and toolkits can be used as well, provided the application of the QI process overall is consistently on improving ability to address complexity (rather than just one or two issues) in the clients being served. One example is that in the Comprehensive Healthcare Integration (CHI) Framework (National Council for Mental Wellbeing, 2022), a PHBH tool, there is a specific focus on attending to "social determinants of health" within the integrated care team. Another example is that in using a tool to develop trauma-informed services in a MH center, it is important to be purposeful about recognizing how easy it is to retraumatize people with co-occurring SUD conditions who do not "follow our recommendations" about discontinuing substance use and may present to our MH center in crisis, smelling of alcohol and unsteady on their feet. How do we make it our most important business in that moment to have that person feel really happy that when they were in crisis they had the good sense to show up in the place where people are paid to help them, rather than thinking our job is to send them away as quickly as possible?

In summary, break the big vision down into small steps for the organization.

In addition to engaging the enterprise in recognizing and embracing the expectation of complexity and the vision of complexity capability as a goal, organizations must help build a horizontal and vertical partnership for change, identify a team that is willing to slowly plan how to make progress, identify opportunities for change and some change agents or champions at all levels of the organization, including people with lived experience, and find one or two programs that are willing to pilot using a self-assessment tool to see if there is value in the conversation and in starting to make change.

Comprehensive Integrated Systems of Care for Communities and Populations

How Do We Get There?

The next section of this chapter will move from a focus on individual programs and organizations to the development of comprehensive integrated systems of care for a community or population, but remember: you don't need to have the whole system committed to making progress in order to get started.

Moving toward organizational and community partnerships for complexity capability.

Start with a design of integrated services for individuals and families, and then move up to programs, organizations, and systems. Using the concept of "complexity capability" for programs, we can begin to apply this to "system design" and "population management" by using the following precept: in an organization, or in a system of care for a population, each program should become "complexity capable," but each program is likely to have a different job. The job of each program starts with what it is already designed to be doing (e.g., adult MH case management program, residential SUD program, school-based services, primary care clinic, homeless outreach, adult probation for offenders with MH/SUD, etc.) and organizing itself to provide integrated services to the people with complex needs who are already showing up. In addition to serving its own clientele, part of its job is being a great partner to help other programs with *their* people, through consultation, in-reach, and effective inter-program teamwork. The goal is NOT to increase referrals, so much as to help more people get what they need in a single door (or as few doors as possible) and have fewer people need duplicate or parallel services, or to fall between the cracks. *Remember: it is easier for staff to move around in a system so that clients don't have to.*

Example: Comprehensive Integrated BH Organization

We can start by illustrating this concept first in a single large community BH organization that has many different types of programs for people with MH and SUD issues and is helping all programs become co-occurring/complexity capable.

In this large BH organization, the adult MH program provides integrated services to individuals who present with MH concerns and may have co-occurring substance use issues with varying degrees of severity and various stages of change. By and large, these clients do NOT want referral to an SUD program. The adult SUD program provides integrated services to individuals who present with a request (or mandate) for SUD services and have a variety of co-occurring MH issues and trauma that will require integrated attention during SUD treatment. The child MH program provides integrated services to adolescents with MH issues, many of whom may be initiating substance use, as well as to the parents and caregivers of children with SED, many of whom may have substance use challenges, but are not requesting SUD treatment for themselves.

In this simple scenario, each program has a job to serve the individuals and families that it usually sees, plus to provide consultation and in-reach to its partners. The adult MH program can provide consultation to the SUD program, by embedding its own clinicians or prescribers on the SUD team, as well as consulting to the child MH program, by providing in-reach for parents who have more severe MH needs. The adult SUD program can provide consultation to the adult MH program and to the child MH program in the same way. The child MH program can provide consultation to either program concerning parenting issues for adult clients and in-reach to help with identification and engagement of any children that may be in need or at risk.

Consequently, when an organization wants to become "complexity capable," it means that it creates an organization-wide quality improvement initiative in which each program makes progress (using the tools and processes described earlier) on its own but also in which part of its progress is being a great team member or partner to other programs. That is, the organization creates an "inter-program learning community" or an "integrated" team across all its programs, so that (just like an integrated team of clinicians) all the programs make progress in working collaboratively to help all the clients of that organization receive the best possible integrated services within the "door" in which they feel most comfortably or naturally engaged.

Comprehensive Integrated System of Care for a Community

Setting goals: All programs and agencies within the community make progress to be complexity capable. Each program improves its ability to provide integrated assistance to the complex people it routinely serves, as well as being a great partner in helping other agencies and programs with their complex people. The goal is that more people can get what they need in a single door (or in as few doors as possible) and fewer people need duplicate or parallel services in the community (which makes poor use of limited resources) or fall through the cracks.

Organizing community partnerships for comprehensive integrated system development:

A framework: Community partnerships for creation of integrated systems begin by bringing programs and agencies together to build successful and continuing collaborations for success. Community BH organizations can often be the initiators and leaders of such collaborative efforts and may benefit from investing resources in helping to staff and sustain the partnership.

Within the framework described in this chapter, here are some simple do's and don'ts of this collaboration:

1. Identify the shared population of interest and invite all the key players to the table. The shared population may be everyone, or just adults or children, or just people involved in the CJ system who have BH needs. Clearly, the larger the population, the more comprehensive will be the system approach, but do not let the goal of perfection be the enemy of making progress in a way that is feasible for your community.
2. Communicate a shared vision that is about the heart and soul of what everyone does: We are coming together to work as partners to improve our ability to welcome, inspire, and provide integrated services to the individuals and families with complex needs who are the expectation in all of our settings.
3. Start with the goal of improving within base resources, before focusing on new resources: Our first step is to work collectively to improve each of our programs' ability to provide integrated helpfulness to the people we are already serving, within the resources that we already have, and then use that framework to make the best use of any additional resources that we may acquire along the way.

   Be aware: Many collaboratives begin by focusing on obtaining a grant to set up a new program, and then that effort absorbs all their energy, so that the fundamental steps of leveraging existing resources to create sustainable change never take place.
4. Our goal is to learn to help people get what they need within as few doors as possible, rather than to have every person with multiple needs attach to multiple agencies, multiple staff, and multiple funding streams, so we get more broke than we already are and make all of our collaborative work unbearably complicated. Many collaboratives focus on making and coordinating multiple referrals for each client, which is complicated for the client and the staff. Alternatively, many collaboratives focus on creating unique interagency teams for each client, which is very inefficient, rather than building each team to be complexity capable for ALL its clients. This is a bit more challenging in the beginning but works much better in the long run.
5. This is a quality improvement partnership. Each agency and program can make progress on its own, whether any of the others make progress or not. The good news is that we can help each other, but we don't have to be stuck waiting for everyone to show up.
6. We can get started with whoever is at the table. If some partners do not come at the beginning, let's get started building something of value and then attracting them to join us. This is a "recovery process" for the system in our community, and just like 12-step programs of recovery, it is a "program of attraction."
7. It is helpful to have a high level "CEO group" that creates an empowered collaboration and authorizes the process while also having a team of "champions" that work collaboratively across the community who are more in the details of making change. These champions and change agents may represent program leaders, front line staff, and service recipients and are empowered within their own agencies or programs to make change, as well as work in partnership with each other across the community to transform the way the whole community works together.
8. In addition to how each program improves within its own resources, let's figure out creative ways for each program to treat the others as "priority partners." For example, if the homeless outreach team has an "expectation" of finding clients with MH and/or SUD, let's embed BH in-reach from the CBHO into the homeless outreach program, rather than trying to refer those clients for intake (where they probably won't show up). Similarly, if we have a high volume of BH need in our proba-

tion programs, let's embed BH staff in those programs, as well as provide probation officer linkages to our BH teams.

Within this framework, it may be helpful for the partners to create a charter agreement for the system improvement collaboration, in which each partner agency agrees to make progress toward complexity capability (or whatever language appeals to the community) and identifies specific steps that agency will take to bring all its programs and staff along. Usually, there are one or two programs that volunteer to be the "pilots" in using one of the self-assessment tools mentioned above and then come back to the collaborative table to illustrate what they learned and how they are beginning to make progress. These "front runners" make it easier for those programs or agencies who are somewhat nervous to get started more safely. The collaboration needs to be very strength-based at the beginning, to applaud the efforts of each organization to get involved and make progress. Early steps of progress usually involve welcoming people with complexity, inspiring hope in every door, and improving the ability to identify and quantify the complex needs of the people who are presenting for help.

An example: Within the CCISC toolkit, an approach that organizes this process for nonclinical and clinical partners within either adult or child system of care collaborations (including CSOC, as described below) is a tool called System of Care Assessment Tool (SOCAT), which provides for self-assessment and improvement by each community partner agency in terms of both its participation in the community collaboration AND its ability to improve the delivery of value-driven complexity-capable services within its own services. The evidence-based SAMHSA model that was first described 40 years ago has been subsequently updated to include more collaboration with SUD service partners and with a more focused lens on addressing cultural, racial, and linguistic diversity and disparities (SAMHSA 2019). In this approach in an integrated Children's System of Care, a community brings together child-serving partners in a formal collaboration around shared values and principles, labelled "wraparound" principles, emphasizing the importance of services being hopeful, strength-based, family-driven, trauma-informed, and resiliency-oriented as well as addressing multiple domains of need in an integrated manner. These partners may include school systems, child protection, juvenile justice, MH services, I/DD services, SUD services (for parents and caregivers of children in need), as well as natural support settings in the community (e.g., faith-based entities). The partners come together in a sustained collaborative structure to adopt the shared principles and to make a commitment to using the principles to serve the children and families with complexity within each agency, as well as to work together to address the most complicated and challenging families using a "wraparound" approach. Successful systems achieve sustainability through embedding this approach into "business as usual" within each partner's base resources across the community.

Conclusion

Individual clients and families with complexity can be served in organizations that go down the path of becoming complexity capable, as well as illustrating the framework for how multiple community partners can come together, over time, to make collective progress toward having a "comprehensive integrated system of care" for that community, within whatever resources that are available. Building organizations and community systems this way is slow and painstaking, but ultimately rewarding work, as existing services, within limited resources, become progressively better able to provide appropriately matched integrated services to individuals and families with complex needs. As a result, these individuals and families are better able to make progress on all their issues to achieve the hopeful, meaningful, and successful lives they are capable of achieving and deserve to have.

References

American Society of Addiction Medicine. (2001). Patient Placement Criteria 2nd Edition Revised. Washington, DC: ASAM.

Bellack AS, Bennett ME, & Gearon JS. (2007) *Behavioral treatment for substance abuse in people with SPMI.* Routledge: New York.

Carroll Chapman SL, Wu L. (2012). Substance Abuse of Individuals with Intellectual Disabilities. *Res Dev Disabil.* 33(4): 1147–1156.

Center for Integrated Health Solutions. (2014). Organizational Assessment for Treatment Integration (OATI), National Council for Behavioral Healthcare, Washington DC.

Chapman E, Chung H, Pincus HA. (2017) Using a continuum-based framework for behavioral health integration into primary care in New York State. *Psychiatric Services.* 68(8):756-8.

Cook JA, Jonikas JA, Burke-Miller JK, Hamilton M, Powell IG, Tucker SJ, Wolfgang JB, Fricks, L, Weidenaar J, Morris E, Powers DL. (2020). Whole Health Action Management: A Randomized Controlled Trial of a Peer-Led Health Promotion Intervention. *Psychiatric Services.* 71(10):1039-46.

Copeland ME. (2012). *WRAP (Wellness Recovery Action Plan) for Addictions.* Dummerston VT: Peach Press.

CSAT. (2006). Definitions and Terms Relating to Co-Occurring Disorders. *COCE Overview Paper 1. DHHS Publication* No. (SMA) 06-4163. Rockville, MD: SAMHSA, CMHS/CMHS.

Dickey B, Azeni H. (1996) Persons with dual diagnoses of substance abuse and major mental illness: their excess costs of psychiatric care. *American Journal of Public Health.* 86(7):973-7.

Drake RE, Brunette MF. (1998). Complications of severe mental illness related to alcohol and drug use disorders. *Recent Developments in Alcoholism.* 285-99.

Drake RE, McHugo GJ, Clark RE, Teague GB, Xie H, Miles K, Ackerson TH. (1998). Assertive community treatment for patients with co-occurring severe mental illness and substance use disorder: A clinical trial. *American journal of Orthopsychiatry.* 68(2):201.

Dumont JM, Ridgway P, Onken SJ, Dornan DH, Ralph RO. (2005). Recovery oriented systems indicators measure (ROSI). *Measuring the promise: A compendium of recovery measures.* 2:229-43.

Engelhardt MA, Hills H, Monroe M. (2009). Comprehensive Continuous Integrated System of Care development: Tampa-Hillsborough County, Florida. *J. Dual Diagnosis* 5:110-116.

Glynn LG, Valderas JM, Healy P, Burke E, Newell J, Gillespie P, et al. (2011). The prevalence of multimorbidity in primary care and its effect on health care utilization and cost. *Family Practice.* 28(5).

Golden LS, Gatchel RJ, Cahill MA. (2006). Evaluating the effectiveness of the National Institute of Corrections "Thinking for a Change" program among probationers. *Journal of Offender Rehabilitation.* 43(2):55-73.

Goldman ML, Smali E, Richkin T, Pincus HA, Chung H. (2020). A novel continuum-based framework for translating behavioral health integration to primary care settings. *Translational Behavioral Medicine.* 10(3):580-9.

Gotham HJ, Brown JL, Comaty JE, McGovern MP, Claus RE. (2009) The dual diagnosis capability in mental health treatment (DDCMHT) index. In *Addiction Health Services Research Annual Meeting*, San Francisco, CA.

Gruber-Baldini AL, Velozo C, Romero S, Shulman LM. (2017). Validation of the PROMIS® measures of self-efficacy for managing chronic conditions. *Quality of Life Research.* 26(7):1915-24.

Harris M, Fallot R. (2001). Creating cultures of trauma-informed care (CCTIC): A self-assessment and planning protocol.

Hossain MM, Sultana A, Tasnim S, Fan Q, Ma P, McKyer EL, (2020). Purohit N. Prevalence of mental disorders among people who are homeless: An umbrella review. *International Journal of Social Psychiatry.* 66(6):528-41.

Humowiecki M, Kuruna T, Sax R, Hawthorne M, Hamblin A, Turner S, Mate K, Sevin C, Cullen K. (2018). Blueprint for complex care: advancing the field of care for individuals with complex health and social needs. *www.nationalcomplex.care/blueprint.*

McGovern MP, Matzkin AL, Giard J. (2007). Assessing the dual diagnosis capability of addiction treatment services: The Dual Diagnosis Capability in Addiction Treatment (DDCAT) Index. *Journal of Dual Diagnosis.* 22;3(2):111-23.

McLaughlin CP, Kaluzny AD. (2004). *Continuous quality improvement in health care: theory, implementation, and applications.* Burlington, MA: Jones & Bartlett Learning.

Minkoff K, Cline CA. (2004). Changing the world: The design and implementation of comprehensive continuous integrated systems of care for individuals with co-occurring disorders. *Psychiatric Clinics.* 1;27(4):727-43.

Minkoff K, Cline CA. (2005). Developing welcoming systems for individuals with co-occurring disorders: The role of the comprehensive continuous integrated system of care model. *Journal of Dual Diagnosis.* 17;1(1):65-89.

Minkoff K, Drake RE, eds. (1991). Dual *Diagnosis of Major Mental Illness and Substance Disorder.* New Directions for Mental Health Services, No 50. San Francisco, CA: Jossey-Bass.

Najavits L, (2002) *Seeking Safety, A Treatment Manual for PTSD and Substance Abuse.* New York, NY: Guilford Press,

National Center on Addiction and Substance Abuse at Columbia University (CASA), & United States of America. (1999). *No Safe Haven: Children of Substance-Abusing Parents.*

National Council Center of Excellence. (2021). *Organizational Assessment Toolkit for Primary and Behavioral Health Care Integration.*

National Council for Mental Wellbeing. (2022). Designing, Implementing and Sustaining Physical Health-Behavioral Health Integration: Comprehensive Healthcare Integration Framework. Washington, DC.

Peters RH, Kremling J, Bekman NM, Caudy MS. (2012) Co-occurring disorders in treatment-based courts: Results of a national survey. *Behavioral Sciences & the Law*. 30(6):800-20.

RachBeisel J, Scott J, Dixon L. (1999). Co-occurring severe mental illness and substance use disorders: a review of recent research. *Psychiatric Services*. 50(11):1427-34.

Roberts LJ, Shaner A, Eckman TA. (1999). *Overcoming addictions: Skills training for people with schizophrenia*. New York City, NY:WW Norton & Company.

Rosenberg SD, Goodman LA, Osher FC, Swartz MS, Essock SM, Butterfield MI,Constantine NT, Wolford GL, Salyers MP. (2001). Prevalence of HIV, hepatitis B, and hepatitis C in people with severe mental illness. *American Journal of Public Health*. 91(1):31.

Sarteschi CM, Vaughn MG, Kim K. (2011). Assessing the effectiveness of mental health courts: A quantitative review. *Journal of Criminal Justice*. 1;39(1):12-20.

Sells DJ, Rowe M, Fisk D, Davidson L. (2003). Violent victimization of persons with co-occurring psychiatric and substance use disorders. *Psychiatric Services*. 54(9):1253-7.

Shaner A, Eckman T, Roberts LJ, Fuller T. (2003). Feasibility of a skills training approach to reduce substance dependence among individuals with schizophrenia. *Psychiatric Services*. 54(9):1287-9.

Shoyinka S, Talley RM, Minkoff K. (2021). Self-assessment for modification of anti-racism tool (SMART). *The American Association for Community Psychiatry* (AACP), 2021.

Steadman HJ, Osher FC, Robbins PC, Case B, Samuels S. (2009). Prevalence of serious mental illness among jail inmates. *Psychiatric Services*. 60(6):761-5.

Stern R, Minkoff K. (1979) Paradoxes in programming for chronic patients in a community clinic. *Psychiatric Services*. 30(9):613-7.

Stromwall LK, Larson NC, Nieri T, Holley LC, Topping D, Castillo J, Ashford JB. (2008). Parents with co-occurring mental health and substance abuse conditions involved in Child Protection Services: clinical profile and treatment needs. *Child Welfare*. 87(3).

Substance Abuse and Mental Health Services Administration, (2019) Intensive Care Coordination for Children and Youth with Complex Mental and Substance Use Disorders: State and Community Profiles. *SAMHSA Publication* No. PEP19-04-01-001. Rockville, MD: Substance Abuse and Mental Health Services Administration.

Swartz MS, Swanson JW, Hiday VA, Borum R, Wagner R, Burns BJ. (1998). Taking the wrong drugs: the role of substance abuse and medication noncompliance in violence among severely mentally ill individuals. *Social Psychiatry and Psychiatric Epidemiology*. 33(1):S75-80.

Walker ER, Druss BG. (2017). Cumulative burden of comorbid mental disorders, substance use disorders, chronic medical conditions, and poverty on health among adults in the USA. *Psychology, Health & Medicine*. 22(6):727-35.

Walton H, Spector A, Williamson M, Tombor I, Michie S. (2020). Developing quality fidelity and engagement measures for complex health interventions. *British Journal of Health Psychology*. 25(1):39-60.

ZiaPartners. (Cline & Minkoff). (2016). CCISC Toolkit: COMPASS-EZ - Creating Welcoming Recovery-Oriented Co-occurring Capable Services for Adults, Children, Youth and Families with Complex Needs: A Self-Assessment Tool for Behavioral Health Programs. *COMPASS-EZ 2.0 (second edition)*: ZiaPartners.

Part III

Core Competencies for Community Psychiatrists

Inspiring a Welcoming, Hopeful Culture

Christie A. Cline and Kenneth Minkoff

Introduction: Welcoming, Hope, and the Vision of Community Psychiatry

Community psychiatry has unique values and a unique vision, which radically sets it apart from other behavioral health "disciplines." Community psychiatry provides a safety net service for a "community"—for a defined population that may need help with behavioral health issues of all kinds. This is critically important: as a safety net provider, anyone who is not "caught" (engaged) in your net will not receive services anywhere. The consequences of not being engaged may be dire and, in fact, may be a matter of life and death. Consequently, the pride of community psychiatry is its capacity to be responsive to the needs of people and families—"customers"—who have serious needs and would not be able to receive services anywhere else. This responsibility extends not just to the "easy" customers, the ones who neatly fit into our existing service packages, but particularly to "complicated" customers, the ones who may not fit *at all* and yet are desperate for help and hope.

In the 10 years since this chapter was written for the First Edition of this Handbook, recognition of the importance of engagement as a foundation for services and systems has become ever more powerful. In 2016, the National Alliance on Mental Illness (NAMI) issued a clarion call for emphasis on this issue: Engagement: A New Standard for Mental Health Care (NAMI 2016). Here is the opening statement of that powerful monograph:

> As an organization of individuals with MH conditions and their families, NAMI knows that the US system of mental health care is failing to engage people who seek help. The facts say it all: **many people who seek mental health care drop out. 70% that drop out do so after their first or second visit.** (Olfson et al. 2009)
>
> The first moments of interaction between a service provider and a person seeking care for a mental health condition can set the tone and course of treatment. This first interaction can start a journey to recovery and a satisfying life – or it can leave a person unsure or hopeless about their future and unwilling to go back a second time. (NAMI 2016, p. 2)

NAMI emphasizes further the importance of "Welcoming" (p.8), not just at the beginning of care, but throughout, and describes that the risk of disengagement can be present throughout the challenges of ongoing service in a service system that is frequently mis-designed.

Further, the focus on "engagement" has expanded to an understanding of the core vision of all health care. The Triple Aim (Institute for Health Improvement) emphasizes customer experience as well as cost and outcomes as one of

C. A. Cline · K. Minkoff (✉)
ZiaPartners, Inc., Catalina, AZ, USA
e-mail: ccline@ziapartners.com;
http://www.ziapartners.com/

W. E. Sowers et al. (eds.), *Textbook of Community Psychiatry*,
https://doi.org/10.1007/978-3-031-10239-4_8

the three major objectives of any health delivery system. Dr. Donald Berwick, the founder of the Institute for Health Improvement, has taken this even further, in recognizing the connection between the ultimate aims of the health system and the need to address social determinants of health and the systemic racism and other discriminatory factors that contribute to dramatic health inequities and disparities. He describes the "moral determinants of health" (Berwick 2020), reminding all of us that those on the front lines have a moral responsibility to design systems that are responsive on all levels to people with the greatest needs.

These values—a vision of hope and help for those most in need, especially those with the greatest combinations of challenges, often those that *no one else is designed to serve*—are what gives community psychiatry its true heart. Yet, the implementation of this set of values, the articulation of this vision, in community psychiatric practice, programs, and settings is not a trivial matter. It requires deliberate attention, at every level of organization structure, process, program, and practice, to ensure that those most in need, that those most likely to be "misfits" in other settings, are not only tolerated and "accepted," but specifically and proactively *welcomed* for care—and inspired with the hope and promise of recovery—wherever, whenever, and however they present. Consider the following situation:

Carlos is a 49-year-old Mexican man who has been referred to your community behavioral health program following his parole from state prison after serving 5 years of a 10-year sentence for an armed robbery to obtain drugs during a time when he was actively addicted to cocaine. Carlos has a 15-year history of schizoaffective disorder and has been receiving antipsychotic and mood-stabilizing medication in prison. Under parole supervision, he lives in a residential program for individuals with mental illness in your community and is sent to your program for case management, medication, and rehabilitative services. Carlos used to work as a welder until his addiction to alcohol and cocaine, as well as persistent psychosis, caused him to lose his job. He has two children in their late teens that live with his ex-wife; she wants nothing to do with him. He has a large extended family that has maintained contact with him in prison. The family members care about Carlos, but do not want to provide him with any financial help or with a place to live. Carlos' primary language is Spanish; he speaks English with limited proficiency. He also is suffering from hepatitis C and is overweight.

Carlos came to his first appointment at your program 2 weeks ago, within a few days of his release from prison and moving into his residence. He had been given a 30-day supply of medication and did not need a refill. He had an initial appointment with a case manager, but was not very talkative about his symptoms, or his life. He seemed a little suspicious and said that his main goal was to not go back to prison. He wanted to try to get a job and somehow be re-connected to his family. He said he wanted to make sure to do what his parole officer wanted him to do. He also said that he did not like living in the group home, but "I guess I'm going to have to put up with it." He stated that he was committed to not using drugs, but did not like going to "those NA meetings." "I am strong; I have a lot of will power." "I don't really want a case manager; I am a man who can take care of himself." He said he would come back for medications and was willing to get help with reinstating his disability.

This morning, Carlos appears, unscheduled, in your waiting room. He is disheveled, agitated, and reeking of alcohol. He states that he got kicked out of the residence last night and spent the night on the street. "They said I was drunk when I only had a few." "Those assholes were stealing my stuff, and I said I would get someone, but good, if they didn't cut it out." He is demanding to see his case manager immediately, saying he needs a place to stay so he won't go back to prison.

Question: What should your clinic staff do first?

The Challenge of Welcoming

Given that this is a chapter on "welcoming and hope," it is easy to see that "the right answer" to the question posed above would be "Welcome him!" It is also easy to see that welcoming him would be a significant challenge, clinically and organizationally.

On one hand, the consequences for Carlos of not being welcomed, engaged, and inspired with hope in the middle of this major crisis could be catastrophic. The wrong approach could result in violence, involuntary commitment, homelessness, and/or reincarceration.

On the other hand, Carlos is exactly the kind of person that most staff at the program might experience as "impossible" to welcome. He is big, drunk, scary, potentially violent, and a parolee with a history of violence. He is also homeless, paranoid, and "behaving inappropriately." He does not even speak English very well.

Yet, if our values in the world of community behavioral health care involve holding ourselves to the *highest possible standard* for welcoming customers like Carlos, then we not only recognize "welcoming" him as a priority, but we deliberately organize welcoming, hopeful engagement, empowerment, and partnership for people like Carlos as a core customer-oriented, value-driven "business practice" for our entire agency.

What Would "Welcoming" Look Like in This Situation?

As soon as Carlos comes in the door, and it is clear that he is in crisis, the program (starting with the receptionist) needs to initiate an immediate response plan that makes it most likely that Carlos will have a successful experience and come away thinking that he made a very good decision to come to the clinic this morning.

The receptionist, seeing him come into the waiting room clearly agitated, would contact a person "on duty" available for immediate response. She might say: "Welcome Carlos. It looks like you need help immediately. I am calling someone to come and see you who should be out here in a few minutes. Would you like something to eat or drink?"

The on-duty clinical staff person would come out and explain that Carlos' regular case manager is not available at the moment, but that he or she is pleased to talk to Carlos. Then the staff person might thank Carlos for coming in when he was in a crisis and ask Carlos if he would mind going to an office to sit down and talk, as well as repeating the offer of something to eat or drink.

Once in the office, the clinician would recognize that Carlos is having a very hard time and is probably very scared and feeling out of control. Carlos needs to feel not only welcomed but empowered and respected. He needs to feel that we will treat him as a partner, not a victim. He needs to feel hope, rather than feel that what is left of his hope is being taken away. In order to reinforce that Carlos made a good decision coming in, the clinician might say, looking Carlos right in the eyes:

> I want you to know that I am very impressed that you came into see us, since you hardly know us. Thank you for your trust. It's amazing that you had the courage to come in here. I don't know what happened, but it looks like a serious crisis. Let's sit down and talk so you can tell me your story, and we can figure out together how to help you. The fact that you came for help is a wonderful thing. I know we want to do everything we can to help you to stay out of prison and help you to achieve your goals.

This "welcoming, hopeful" approach would be the best chance to help Carlos to calm down and feel safe, rather than challenged, to take time to figure out a solution to his crisis, to get him through the next few hours, and to help him plan for some positive next steps to find housing and stay out of prison.

On the other hand, if Carlos is not "proactively welcomed," it is highly likely that the situation could get much worse. It wouldn't be hard to think of a number of things that the staff could say to Carlos that would increase his chance of becoming *more* agitated and even violent. Here are some common examples:

- "You need to go to the emergency room right away. We can't help you here if you're like this."
- "You can't just walk in and be seen on demand. You need to have an appointment."
- "We have a rule that says that you can't be seen if you are intoxicated."
- "You are behaving inappropriately (or threateningly, or in a way that's scary). You need to calm down right away or we won't be able to help you."
- "You are using bad language. That's not allowed here."
- "Your case manager isn't free now. Can you come back in a few hours when s/he might have an opening?"
- "You should know that we can't find you housing at the drop of a hat. I don't think we

can find you a place to stay now that you've lost the group home."

- "Since you've been drinking, you need to go to the ER to be medically cleared before we can see you."
- "Before we talk to you, we need to let you know that we have to call your parole officer to let him know that you have probably violated your parole."

It is important to keep in mind that Carlos' life might very well be at stake here. If Carlos is upset enough, he can just storm out of the clinic without being seen. He is desperate and losing hope. He could easily do something that would hurt someone seriously or get himself hurt or killed.

But ensuring that Carlos is highly likely to have a welcoming experience in our community program requires a deliberate and organized approach. The rest of this chapter will describe basic steps to build a welcoming environment and welcoming hopeful practice, as core features of any community behavioral health program.

Welcoming Systems and Welcoming Practice

During the past decade, increasing attention has been given to the use of organized strategies for building welcoming, hopeful, recovery-oriented programs and practices, such as the Comprehensive Continuous Integrated System of Care (CCISC) (Minkoff and Cline 2004, 2005). We have recognized that our systems and practices have been mis-designed, particularly for people with challenging co-occurring mental health, substance use, and health conditions who are often experienced as "misfits." The goal of "transformation" is to design systems with limited resources to be organized at *every level* (system policy, program design, clinical practice, and staff competency) to welcome our customers as they are, with all their complexity and desperation, to respond to their needs, and to inspire their hopes and dreams. A recent comprehensive review for NASMHPD of implementation of integrated systems and services for individuals with co-occurring MH and SUD (Minkoff and Covell 2019) emphasized the role of systematic approaches such as CCISC for prioritizing welcoming, engagement, and integrated service delivery as core elements of system design.

Welcoming and hope as practice and philosophy are embedded in opportunities for improvement in systems, programs, and practices, many of which are discussed in more detail in other chapters.

- *Recovery-Oriented Systems* are built on a foundation that everyone is welcomed into empowered partnerships and inspired with the hope of recovery (Gagne et al. 2007).
- *Trauma-Informed Systems and Services* recognize the importance of building welcoming partnerships for vulnerable individuals and families (Finkelstein and Markoff 2004; Elliott et al. 2005; National Center for Trauma-Informed Care (http://mentalhealth.samhsa.gov/ncitc/)).
- *Restraint Reduction and Non-violent De-escalation* succeed most effectively in the context of creating a welcoming culture of partnership in an institution (Council of State Governments 2002).
- *The Network for Improvement of Addiction Treatment (NIATx)* has been successful in working with both addiction and mental health programs to use Continuous Quality Improvement to increase welcoming, access, and retention (NIATx outcomes).
- *Homeless Outreach and Family Wraparound Programs* are built on a foundation of welcoming individuals and families who are difficult to engage (Gillig and McQuistion 2006; Friedman and Drews 2005).
- *Motivational Interviewing* (Miller and Rollnick 2002) as a clinical practice begins with welcoming and engaging individuals who do not share our goals.
- *Shared Decision-Making* as a component of psychiatric practice (Torrey and Drake 2010)

formalizes welcoming partnerships to promote adherence.

Comprehensive Continuous Integrated Systems of Care (CCISC)

For the past decade, the authors of this chapter have been working with state and county systems in over 40 states and 7 Canadian provinces, with all types of programs and clinical and nonclinical staff, to build welcoming, recovery-oriented, and integrated systems, programs, and services, designed to be about the needs, hopes, and goals of people and families with complex lives and co-occurring conditions of all kinds (Minkoff and Cline 2004, 2005). CCISC is an organized quality improvement process for system re-design in which every program and every person delivering care becomes welcoming, recovery- or resiliency-oriented (i.e., hopeful and strength-based), and capable of working with co-occurring behavioral health disorders (Minkoff and Covell 2019).

In this chapter, we outline some of the strategies that have been used by systems and programs to not only make progress in welcoming the people served but also to inspire hope in and support the values of the people delivering service.

Strategies to Implement Welcoming, Hopeful Environments and Practices

As the preceding section suggests, "welcoming" is not just a matter of everyone being nicer. Welcoming involves a deliberate approach to both organizing welcoming as a "clinical practice" and to building a welcoming environment and organizational culture. If you are thinking that complex financially challenged behavioral health organizations cannot help everyone to be welcoming, you probably have never been to a hotel, a restaurant, or even a discount department store, because the starting place for welcoming involves basic customer service. There are well-designed organizational technologies for implementing "customer service" as a routine practice and for developing value-driven customer-oriented organizations. These strategies have been studied for years in the fields of management science and organizational development. What is striking is that in behavioral health we have not paid much attention to these strategies at all, even though we are in a "business" where whether or not people are welcomed, inspired, and engaged may be—as we said earlier—a matter of life and death.

Customer service strategies begin with looking at the whole organization from the perspective of the customer, beginning with the "easy" or "routine" customer and then progressing to evaluating the experience and improving the service for customers who may have a harder time. A strategy used by NIATx, for example, is to experience the program or organization by performing what is called a "walk-through," in which management and staff, often accompanied by consumers or customers (as partners in the improvement process), "walk through" the experience of entering the program and being "admitted" to service. For most behavioral health organizations, the "walk-through" is not only "eye-opening"; it is "mind-opening." An administrator of a community mental health center in Oklahoma "walked through" admission to his own facility as part of a CCISC project and said to us afterwards: "I felt fine when I started, but within an hour and a half I wanted to hit somebody." He immediately began a project to redesign the whole admitting area, and the admitting process, to be more welcoming.

Creating a Welcoming Environment

Many organizations begin the process of improving "welcoming" by conducting a "walk-through" of their physical space. The goal of the walk-through is to experience the space through the eyes of a "customer" who may be scared, mistrustful, or angry, who may have multiple issues (e.g., substance abuse and health as well as mental health), who may have experienced past trauma at the hands of caregivers, and who may have cultural or linguistic barriers to care. Common improvement opportunities range from addressing interior decoration (plants, posters, and paint), to removing obviously unwelcoming signs ("Clients are prohibited from…"), to adding hopeful, culturally relevant signs and decorations that address recovery from multiple issues.

It is often surprising what clients perceive to be unwelcoming. In one of our CCISC projects, a drug and alcohol program in South Dakota was working on welcoming clients with co-occurring mental health conditions. The program change team decided to remove a huge rug in the admitting area that was embossed with "Say No to Drugs." Their idea was that this might be perceived as unwelcoming to clients who were on psychotropic medication. After they removed the rug, they were surprised how many clients came up to them and said "thank you." A typical comment was: "I'm so glad you got rid of that rug. Every time I walked in the door I was thinking that I'm someone who uses drugs and you were saying "no" to me."

One of the most challenging issues in developing a welcoming environment has to do with the question of removing "security items" such as metal detectors, glass barriers in the waiting area or in front of the receptionist, and uniformed security guards. While there are clearly settings in which metal detectors and security personnel are expected (e.g., criminal justice settings), the value of such environmental barriers in improving safety in a usual community behavioral health setting is highly questionable. Research on violence reduction indicates that although staff may "feel" safer as a result of these devices, it is likely that any deterrent effect on the unlikely event of violent or unsafe behavior is counterbalanced by a general increase in "adversarial" or "unwelcoming" tone, which in fact increases the overall risk of violence from all clients (Council of State Governments 2002). However, as we shall discuss below, under no circumstances should the first step in improving "welcoming" be to remove those barriers over staff objections. The process of developing the partnership to create a major culture shift requires a well-considered organizational strategy, which will be discussed in more detail later in this chapter.

Defining and Implementing Welcoming Practice

In any "business," ensuring welcoming practice or good customer service requires great attention to detail. It requires that good customer service is defined and organizationally supported as a practice, with purposeful "practice support" strategies and tools. Further, as will be addressed below, it involves a deliberate organizational implementation strategy that "welcomes and empowers" staff to produce the "product" of welcoming and empowering practice with customers (clients, families, etc.).

One way to think of welcoming practice is to divide "welcoming" into a number of different levels—basic, intermediate, and advanced or radical welcoming—and then consider how specific strategies and practices at each level are likely to challenge current behavior and create an improvement opportunity. This approach is designed to partner with staff, not to criticize them. Almost everyone working in behavioral health, including support staff, comes with a sincere desire to be helpful and is usually distressed to not only see "unwelcoming" behavior all around but also to receive little guidance on how to be welcoming in challenging situations.

Basic Welcoming One way of modeling basic welcoming is to develop a script and then use the script to help develop a "guideline" for welcoming practice. The script should specifically push the envelope of common practice and push the envelope of which customers are proactively welcomed. The following script illustrates basic welcoming in a typical community behavioral health organization for individuals who might normally be experienced as "misfits" due to their co-occurring conditions.

> Hi, there! Welcome to our clinic. You seem to be someone who has many issues at the same time: mental health, substance use, medical, housing, etc. You know, you're a person we most enjoy serving here, because you're the kind of person who is often having the hardest time. We know it's not easy for you to come in asking us for help. Thank you for coming. You're in the right place. We're really glad you're here. We know our job is not to know how to fix you the moment we meet you. Our job is to get to know you, inspire you with hope, and help you to figure out how to help you address all of your issues, over time, so you can have the happiest, most hopeful, and successful life you possibly can.

There is no "rocket science" in this speech. It takes less than a minute to say. The question to ask ourselves is: as a community program, how well-organized are we, by policy, procedure, and practice, so that everyone knows that when a person comes in the door, particularly someone who is challenging and feels like a misfit, that this is exactly what we are supposed to say, and from the heart. "Basic welcoming" scripts can be developed, adapted, modified, and written down as guidance for everyone meeting clients at the front door, just like other "customer service" organizations do.

Intermediate Welcoming Intermediate welcoming addresses common practices that support an unwelcoming culture. For example, what if the organization develops a rule that says that no one can "trash talk" about clients or families in any way, even when they are not listening, including in chart documentation, just like no one may use racial slurs behind people's backs?

Negative and unwelcoming language is often routine practice in many community behavioral health organizations. We use terms like "antisocial," "non-compliant," "manipulative," and "inappropriate" to express displeasure and frustration with clients who are seen as hard to engage and/or not doing what we want. We may use "borderline" or "Axis 2" as an epithet rather than as a diagnosis. We may refer to people with substance use disorders as "drunks," or write: "All he wants is to get high."

Language *is* important. How we talk and write about people affects the way we relate to them and can have a profound effect on our ability to engage and inspire. For example, if we say that someone is "noncompliant," it implies that our job is to use whatever power we have to make that person do what we think is good for them. On the other hand, if we say: "He or she is not finding what we are "selling" to be of great value in their efforts to have a happy life," it tells us that our job is to better understand the person's vision and how to best attach anything we have to offer to his or her own goals.

Advanced (or Radical) Welcoming Advanced welcoming, or radical welcoming, refers to those situations, as exemplified by the situation with Carlos described above, in which welcoming practices and strategies are needed for those individuals and families who appear initially to be hardest to welcome. What happens, for example, when someone comes to the door of one part of the service system displaying symptoms in the "other" domain? For example, a client comes to the door of the substance abuse service system displaying mental health symptoms that make it hard to "participate appropriately in care." Or, a client comes to the mental health door—or either door for that matter—smelling of alcohol and unsteady on his feet. Or a mother drops her child off for a mental health appointment, and she smells of alcohol, or marijuana. How do we make it our most important business, in that moment, to have that person feel really happy, that when they were in crisis, or challenged, or scared, that they were in the presence of people being paid to help them, rather than thinking our job is to tell them they have behaved badly and inappropriately and to either kick them out as quickly as we can or to threaten them with consequences? Strategies to support advanced welcoming practice in a community behavioral health organization require at least the same level of attention and organization as do strategies to support "customer service" for challenging customers in a hotel or in a retail store. This requires both attention to modeling or role-playing "radical welcoming" practice (as illustrated with Carlos, earlier in this chapter) and attention to policies or rules that may inadvertently make "welcoming" more difficult, if not impossible (e.g., "No client will be seen who is under the influence of substances").

Radical welcoming has long been a routine characteristic of services such as homeless outreach, or a best practice intervention such as "Pathways to Housing" (Tsemberis and Eisenberg 2000). In these situations, welcoming strategies involve entering the world of—and partnering with—someone who may be experiencing psychosis and/or using drugs, does not share our view of "the problem," and is unwilling to accept conventional services. A "radical welcoming" relationship begins with simple conversation, or an offer of a sandwich, and progresses to address other issues as trust builds. The "radical welcoming" of the person *exactly as they are* is a critical feature of engagement.

Welcoming and Safety

In many community settings, being welcoming is viewed as in conflict with "ensuring safety." Thus, "welcoming" becomes somewhat self-limited: "We will be welcoming *unless* you do something unsafe." This approach must be viewed through an entirely different lens.

As the research on restraint reduction and non-violent de-escalation has taught, welcoming *enhances* safety (Council of State Governments 2002). In fact, the most important time to engage in welcoming practice is when a person is at highest risk. This does not mean that clinicians should put themselves in harm's way when a client is violent or ignore the need for reporting abuse and neglect. What it means instead is the application of the following adage:

> The more risky the situation, and the more the client may need an involuntary intervention, the more attention should be paid to welcoming practice.

Each community behavioral health organization should not only have a procedure for identifying when involuntary interventions are required but ensure that proactive effort is made to have the client experience a welcoming, positive human contact in the context of that intervention. If a client becomes violent to the point that the police or ambulance is called, it is important for the lead clinicians to look the client in the eye and say something like:

> I know this is a terrible situation for you. We want you to know that you are a valuable person, and we care about you very much. We want you to be safe, so you don't hurt anyone or do something you might regret later. Most important, we want you to know that as soon as you are able to be more in control, we will be welcoming you back and working with you on how to make progress toward your goals.

Similarly, a clinic may have a "welcoming" statement for families that creates a context for the process of mandated reporting of abuse or neglect situations.

In every instance, methodical attention to welcoming policy, procedure, and practice becomes a priority for reducing risk and increasing safety in potentially volatile situations. Furthermore, as we now describe, welcoming is more than clinical practice development. It goes much deeper and involves all aspects of organizational culture and the culture of the community itself.

Creating a Welcoming Organizational Culture

When community behavioral health organizations begin to improve welcoming, they often fall into a common "organizational trap." The trap is assuming that the problem of "unwelcoming" belongs to someone else in the organization. For example, clinical staff may say: "We need to train the receptionists to be welcoming" (as if the clinicians are already as welcoming as they could be). Similarly, program supervisors may assume that the case managers or clinicians "need to be trained" in welcoming.

A fundamental rule of organizational theory relates to customer service: If you want to produce a certain type of relational model with your customer, then you need to build a similar relational model internally in your organization. In other words, if we want to welcome our clients as partners, we have to welcome ourselves as partners in the entire process. This may be a radical culture shift for many behavioral health organizations. Building a "welcoming" organization is intertwined with organizational "best practice" strategies for developing vision-driven customer-oriented businesses strategies, like continuous quality improvement or total quality management that many businesses have been using for decades, but have not been very well implemented in behavioral health.

Continuous quality improvement (discussed in detail in chapter "Program Evaluation and CQI"; chapter "Creating Value: Resource and Quality Management") is not just a project that is done to satisfy behavioral health systems regulators and is certainly not the same as "quality assurance" (which is another term for "compliance monitoring"). It is a mechanism for engaging and empowering all levels of the organization in an empowered partnership to create more successful engagement, interventions, and outcomes for customers at every level. The organization of this partnership is deliberate and structured and involves purposefully identifying and empowering representatives from all different levels of the organization to be engaged in the culture shift.

For example, in the NIATx process referenced above, the NIATx consultants help the organization develop an initial CQI project team to look at welcoming and access. This would be considered a small beginning step to help the organization learn how to use CQI techniques, with the hope that these CQI skills continue to expand and thrive within the organization in order to better serve the customers. The initial project team usually includes managers, supervisors, front-line staff, support staff (such as receptionists), and often consumers or families. Everyone has an important (and equal or democratic) perspective on the team. Receptionists in particular may be viewed as "welcoming experts" because they are constantly observing what works and doesn't work at the "front door." For many organizations, just the process of "welcoming" front-line staff and consumers to be equal members of the change team represents a culture shift.

The team begins by engaging in a structured CQI process. The parameters of welcoming and access are identified. Markers of progress may be identified, such as "improvement in the rate of return" (i.e., the percentage of people who come back after an initial appointment). The members of the team may conduct a "walk-through" where they role-play the experience of customers coming in the door. They may use techniques like "secret shopper" to collect information about "baseline" welcoming over the phone. The team discusses the data it has gathered and identifies multiple contributors (positive and negative) to welcoming and access. The team then learns how to use a basic CQI technique (e.g., *Plan-Do-Check-Act* or PDCA) to identify "improvement opportunities" and attempt to make progress. In the course of this process, members of the CQI team experience increased empowerment and excitement by virtue of having been welcomed to be part of the change process.

In our CCISC projects, we work with large systems and agencies to develop not just a single CQI project, but a comprehensive organizational culture shift. This process is described as engaging the organization in an ongoing CQI process where *every* program and *every* person providing care becomes welcoming, recovery- or resiliency-oriented (hopeful and strength-based), and co-occurring-competent (organized to work successfully with challenging people who have multiple needs). This framework takes longer to build, but has deeper results in creating a sustainable culture shift.

In this process, all the internal partners in the organization (all programs, all levels of staff, consumers/families) are welcomed to come to the table and start to develop a representative CQI structure for the whole agency. Each program does its own "self-assessment" or "walk-through" to determine its baseline and then develops its own improvement plan, beginning with improvement in welcoming for people who are challenging or who may be otherwise experienced as "misfits." Each program identifies front-line people who are formally empowered as change agents. The change agents become a team, who work in partnership with leadership, over time, to dramatically change the culture of the organization, both in relation to its customers and to itself (Minkoff and Cline 2005).

The motto for many organizations becomes: "If we want to welcome the people we serve, we need to welcome ourselves as well." In this culture, every staff member is a valued partner in the learning community, who may have something to learn but also something to teach. Welcoming can become a common language through which all aspects of clinical and organizational behavior are vetted, and welcoming becomes "owned" as a positive value by all levels of staff. The best part of this, organizationally, is that "quality" and "welcoming" are not just the responsibility of the "quality department," but become a vision to which everyone contributes. Here is an example from one of our projects:

> The members of a case management team wished to create an initiative to improve its welcoming posture. A designated "change agent" on the team worked out a mechanism to help her teammates improve "welcoming" discussions in team meetings. She carried with her a small red feather. Whenever someone made an "unwelcoming" remark about client or staff, she would quietly and politely hand them the feather. The team experienced this as a welcoming intervention to help them start in process of being more aware of how they thought and talked about people who were having a hard time.

Creating Welcoming Communities

Community psychiatry is, after all, about "communities." And "welcoming" as a framework extends well beyond the boundaries of the individual organization. All community behavioral health organizations operate in partnerships with other service providers in their communities (behavioral health providers, housing, criminal justice, health, child welfare, and so on).

Within these communities, welcoming occurs at two different levels. The first level is the application of welcoming practice to community partners. In this framework, community partners are identified as "organizational customers," just like clients and families. In crisis services, for example, success would be defined as helping a customer (a referring agency) solve a problem, rather than "diverting the client from the hospital" or "preventing an agency from dumping on us."

The second level is that the whole community system may make a collective commitment to improving welcoming, recovery-oriented, co-occurring-capable, trauma-informed care. This can be organized by a public behavioral health authority or it can be organized as a collaborative network of providers (Engelhardt et al. 2009; Konyndyk et al. 2010; Chichester et al. 2006). For examples of current county-level initiatives working on a welcoming integrated system of care, with the engagement of more than a thousand "change agents" over a decade, readers can go to www.mc3milwaukee.org (MC3 stands for Milwaukee Comprehensive Care Collaborative) or www.cadresandiego.org (which describes the nearly 20-year history of the San Diego County Co-occurring Cadre). In either case, the effect of building a welcoming culture is dramatically enhanced when there is a partnership among providers to adopt a common language and approach, in which each provider works on improving its own capacity to be welcoming while all the providers join in a learning community to support each other and hold each other accountable for continuing progress. These types of collaborations are described in more detail in the chapter on Comprehensive Integrated Systems.

Conclusion: Carlos, Revisited

The story of Carlos is fictional, but it is based on many real stories of people like Carlos who come to our doors in community behavioral health settings, essentially putting their lives in our hands. When resources are limited, and we are all under stress, welcoming can easily take a back seat if we do not organize our priorities. Carlos could become another statistic—hospitalization, homelessness, re-incarceration, or death. But another outcome can occur, as a result of providing welcoming, hopeful intervention, from the heart, to people in great distress. We have experienced outcomes like this in our work with both individuals and systems.

After his "welcoming" encounter with the clinician, Carlos calmed down considerably, got something to eat, and was able to think through his options more calmly. He eventually took some extra medication, agreed to go to a crisis bed which "welcomed" him with alcohol still on board, and began to think about where he wanted to live in lieu of the group home. He role-played how to talk with his parole officer to ask for more help and for another chance to find a place to live. He agreed to check in with the clinic every day as part of getting help. He was still having a very hard time and was guarded and paranoid at times, but he also started to trust the clinic staff to help him. About a month later, during one of his routine visits, he ran into the clinician he had seen during the initial crisis. Carlos looked so much better that the clinician barely recognized him. Carlos asked if he could talk to him for a minute. The clinician said, "Sure, what do you need?" Carlos said, "I don't really need anything; I just want to tell you something. I want to thank you. That day, when I came in here, I thought that no one really cared about me, and that you people would just treat me like a screwed up ex-con and send me back to prison. When you sat down, looked me in the eye and told me you were proud of me, I was blown away. My life changed at that moment. I started to believe that there was some hope that someday I could actually feel human again."

References

Berwick D, (2020) The Moral Determinants of Health. *JAMA*, 324(3), 225–26

Chichester C, Hornsby H, et al. (2006) *Final report and evaluation: A project to establish a More welcoming system for people with co-occurring disorders in Maine*. Hornsby-Zeller: Portland, ME.

Council of State Governments. (2002) *Criminal justice / mental health consensus project*. Lexington, KY: Council of State Governments, 62–63.

Elliott DE, et al. (2005) Trauma-informed or trauma-denied: Principles and implementation of Trauma informed services for women (with co-occurring disorders). *J. Comm Psychol*, 3, 461–77.

Engelhardt MA, Hills H., Monroe M. (2009) Comprehensive continuous integrated system of care development: Tampa-Hillsborough County, Florida. *J. Dual Diagnosis*, 5, 110–116.

Finkelstein, N, Markoff LS. (2004) The Women Embracing Life and Living (WELL) Project. Using the relational model to develop integrated systems of care for women with alcohol/drug use and mental health disorders with histories of violence. *Alcoholism Treatment Quarterly*, 22, 63–80.

Friedman, RM, Drews, DA (2005) Research and Training Center for Children's Mental Health, *Evidence-based practices, systems of care, & individualized care*. Tampa, FL: Louis de la Parte Florida Mental Health Institute University of South Florida.

Gagne C, White W, Anthony W. (2007) Recovery: A common vision for the fields of mental health and addictions. *Psych Rehab J*, 31, 32–37.

Gillig, P, McQuistion, HL (eds.). (2006). *Clinical guide to the treatment of the mentally ill homeless person*. American Psychiatric Publishing, Inc: Washington, DC.

Konyndyk J, Murphy N, Witte M. (2010) Journeys of change: Successes and challenges in implementation of an integrated county system of care in Michigan. *J. Dual Diagnosis*, 5, 425–435.

Miller, WR, Rollnick S. (2002) *Motivational Interviewing*, 2nd Edition. Guilford Press: New York.

Minkoff K, Cline C, (2004) Changing the world: the design and implementation of comprehensive continuous integrated systems of care for individuals with co-occurring disorders. *Psychiat Clin N Am*, 27, 727–743.

Minkoff, K, Cline C, (2005) Developing welcoming systems for individuals with co-occurring disorders: the role of the Comprehensive Continuous Integrated System of Care model. *J Dual Diagnosis*, 1, 63–89.

Minkoff, K, Covell N. (2019) *Integrated systems and services for people with co-occurring MH and SUD, What's known, what's new. What now:* (Technical Assistance Paper #8). National Association of State Mental Health Program Directors,

National Alliance on Mental Illness, (2016) *Engagement: A New Standard for Mental Health Care*. NAMI: Washington, DC.

National Center for Trauma-Informed Care. http://mentalhealth.samhsa.gov/ncitc/.

Olfson, M, et al. (2009) Dropout from outpatient MH care in the US. *Psychiatric Services*, 60(7), 898–907.

Torrey, WC, Drake, RE (2010). Practicing shared decision making in the outpatient psychiatric care of adults with severe mental illnesses: Redesigning care for the future. *Community Mental Health Journal*, 46(5), 433–440.

Tsemberis, S, Eisenberg, RF. (2000) Pathways to housing: Supported housing for street dwelling homeless individuals with psychiatric disabilities. *Psychiatric Services*, 51(4), 487–95.

Motivational Interviewing as a Core Communication Style

Michael Flaum

Introduction

So much of what we do in community psychiatry involves facilitating change. Whether that involves working with patients[1] to help them to live full and meaningful lives in the context of a serious mental illness or trying to improve the systems and communities in which we work, we are, in many ways, agents of change. As such, it is critical that we optimize our skills and effectiveness in that role. Motivational interviewing (MI) is an evidence-based, person-centered communication style and set of technical skills and processes, all directed at facilitating change.

It is useful to think about MI in terms of two broad components, commonly referred to as the "spirit" and the "technique" of MI. The spirit is the mind-set, stance, or overall "way of being" in which we may approach our role as helping professionals who collaborate with, rather than direct, those with whom we work. That "spirit" draws heavily from the work of Carl Rogers and colleagues and shares fundamental features with many person-centered counseling styles (Rogers 1951, 1980; Miller and Moyers 2017). It is the technical aspect of MI, involving an intentional and strategic use of language, that differentiates it from other person- or client-centered counseling approaches (Miller and Rose 2009; Wagner 2013).

The combination of the spirit and technique of MI is useful for many of the most common clinical issues that present in community psychiatry settings, ranging from unhealthy lifestyle choices to unhealthy relationships, problems with medication use, work or school related difficulties, etc. And while it is important to understand which kinds of clinical issues may or may not be appropriate for an MI approach from the technical perspective, the MI spirit or "way of being" is particularly well-suited as a default communication style for community psychiatry. It is not only helpful in working with our patients in a strengths-based, recovery-oriented manner but also with their families or other supporters, as well as with our teams and co-workers, community partners, and others within systems that affect our patients' lives.

A Brief Review of the Development and Evidence Base of MI

The term motivational interviewing was first coined in the early 1980s as an approach to help

[1] A note on language: Throughout this chapter, the words "patient," "person," and "client" are used interchangeably to refer to the person receiving services and "psychiatrist," "clinician," and "helper" as the one in the provider role, in a manner that is somewhat context-dependent, but admittedly arbitrary.

M. Flaum (✉)
University of Iowa Carver College of Medicine, Iowa City, IA, USA
e-mail: michael-flaum@uiowa.edu

W. E. Sowers et al. (eds.), *Textbook of Community Psychiatry*,
https://doi.org/10.1007/978-3-031-10239-4_9

"problem drinkers" (Miller 1983). Over the following decade, the focus of research and practice targeted those with addiction problems (Miller and Rollnick 1991; Noonan and Moyers 1997). By the mid-1990s, interest in MI began to spread to other behavioral problems including HIV risk/safe sex, gambling, cigarette smoking, and diet and exercise (Dunn et al. 2001; Burke et al. 2003; Lundahl and Kunz 2010). By the early 2000s, MI was being widely used and studied in the carceral system (e.g., parole and probation officers with a focus on reducing recidivism) (Stinson and Clark 2017), in primary care management of chronic physical illnesses (Knight et al. 2006; VanBuskirk and Wetherell 2014), and in dental care (Kay et al. 2016; Faustino-Silva et al. 2019; Tervalon and Murray-Garcia 1998). Its use over the past decade has expanded markedly, within and outside of healthcare, most notably in education (Rollnick et al. 2016), leadership (Marshall and Sogaard Nielsen 2020) and most recently as an approach to vaccine hesitancy (Gagneur 2020; Gabarda and Butterworth 2021). As of 2020, a cumulative bibliography of controlled clinical outcome studies involving MI lists over 1600 such trials, more than two-thirds of which show a significant benefit relative to a control or alternative approaches (Miller 2020). The trend in clinical studies involving MI is moving away from those comparing MI as a stand-alone treatment to another treatment, but rather using an MI approach as an adjunct to other interventions or therapies.

Research on MI in psychiatric settings and populations has been surprisingly limited (Chanut et al. 2005), with only a handful of small studies involving patients with serious mental illnesses (Chien et al. 2015; Fiszdon et al. 2016) most of which focus on co-occurring mental health and substance use disorders (e.g., Bechdolf et al. 2005; Smeerdijk et al. 2015). A survey of psychiatric educators indicated broad support for its inclusion in psychiatric training curricula (Abele et al. 2016), although many curricula include MI as just one more tool in the toolkit, to be pulled out for specific clinical issues, i.e., for patients with co-occurring substance use issues, rather than as a core communication style, as is suggested herein.

Key Concepts of MI: Ambivalence, the "Paradoxical Effect of Coercion" and "Resisting the Righting Reflex"

Fundamental to MI is the presumption that people do not persistently engage in problematic, unhealthy, or risky behaviors (or indeed any behaviors that are counter to their values and goals) without compelling reasons to do so. They may not take otherwise helpful medications because of problematic side effects or because they struggle with the idea that something is "wrong" with them. They may use illicit substances to help numb them to physical or emotional discomfort or eat mostly unhealthy foods because they are more affordable, accessible, and familiar than what they recognize would be better for them. They may not exercise because they are exhausted from working long hours and then taking care of their children. The list goes on and on, and conversations about these kinds of issues make up more and more of what healthcare professionals find themselves discussing with patients. If the problematic behavior was driven simply by a lack of awareness or knowledge, then providing clear information and direction should help, but how often does that prove to be the case? It is unlikely the behavior would be sustained in the absence of compelling reasons, especially when that behavior has clear negative consequences. People get stuck in these behaviors because there are indeed two legitimate and opposing sides, both of which they are usually keenly aware of. This is the common problem of ambivalence: Helping people get unstuck from ambivalence so as to move toward the healthier choice is the overriding goal of MI.

The pivotal basis of MI that turns a traditional directive counseling approach on its head begins with two interrelated ideas: The first is that if there are two legitimate and opposing sides to an issue (i.e., ambivalence) and two people are discussing that issue, *when one person takes up one side, it is an invitation for the other person to take up the other.* Just like two children approaching a seesaw, if one sits down on one seat, it is an invitation for the other child to sit down on the opposite side. Second, behavioral research consistently demonstrates that *what people tend to remember and act upon most from a conversation about something they are ambivalent about are those things they heard themselves say or argue for* (Magill et al. 2014).

With those two ideas in mind, consider the implications in healthcare or, for that matter, in any helping relationship. If we assume that by virtue of being healthcare providers, it is always our job to take up the pro-health or "good" side of any problematic issue or behavior, are we not inviting our patients to take up the other side? Most experienced clinicians recognize that while a small minority of patients may make needed changes from long-standing problematic behaviors as a result of the advice of a perceived authority figure, for the most part, lecturing, directing, pleading with, or trying to frighten our patients into making changes they are ambivalent about doesn't work most of the time. But what else are we to do, and the assumption is that there is no harm in doing so. Indeed, these two ideas suggest that doing so may actually get in the way of the needed change. The more the helper tries to convince a person to make a change they are ambivalent about, the more that person tends to "dig in" and focus on all the reasons not to do so. This so-called "paradoxical effect of coercion" is central to the rationale for what differentiates MI from other counseling approaches, i.e., the strategy of *structuring conversations in such a way that it is not the helper but rather the person being helped who is more likely to voice the argument for change.*

How do we do so? Surely, we as helping professionals are not about to play some sort of "reverse psychology" game and take the opposing anti-health side of the issue. Instead, rather than sitting on the pro-health side of the metaphorical seesaw, we position ourselves in the middle, recognizing the legitimacy of both sides, and by doing so, normalizing the ambivalence.

How does positioning ourselves in this way help the person move in the direction of the healthier side of that ambivalence? First, we invite them to have the conversation that they have likely been having repeatedly within their own minds, but now have it *out-loud and interpersonally*. With a nonjudgmental, empathic, and curious attitude, we engage in a specific strategy: We listen carefully as they express each side of the argument, but we respond very differently to the pro-change side than we do to the anti-change (or "sustain") side of the argument. When we hear anything on the pro-change side, what in MI parlance is called "change talk," we shine a bright light on it; we reflect it, explore it, ask open-ended questions about it, affirm it, etc. Basically, we do whatever we can to have them elaborate upon it further.

What do we do when we hear the other side, i.e., all the reasons not to change, or in MI parlance, the "sustain talk"? Perhaps it is what we don't do that is more important than what we do in response to sustain talk: We don't argue with it, because if we did, we'd be inviting the person to dig in and defend that side of the ambivalence even more. The temptation to do so is often so strong that we have to actively suppress the impulse to take up the change side of the issue in response to hearing sustain talk. In the lexicon of MI, this is known as "resisting the righting reflex," i.e., actively resisting the impulse that most people, and especially most helping professionals, have in their desire to help a person who seems to be going in the wrong direction. Rather, we listen with what we hope is accurate empathy, we might nod our head or otherwise quietly indicate that we understand there are two sides, but we avoid responding in a manner that would likely elicit further elaboration about it. In MI parlance, we simply "roll with it."

In doing so, we are striving to structure the conversation such that the patient spends more time voicing their desire, ability, reasons, and need to change the behavior and less time voicing all the corresponding desire, ability, reasons, and need to maintain the status quo. This encapsulates the basic theoretical framework of MI, which at its simplest level postulates that the more "change talk" a person hears themselves say, the more likely they are to act on that change, and conversely, the more "sustain talk" they express, the less likely they are to act on the change (Miller and Rose 2009; Magill et al. 2014).

This admittedly oversimplified model is presented here in an effort to highlight the basic paradigm that differentiates MI from other person-centered counseling approaches in terms of its technique. But MI is not simply a set of techniques. It is also an overall mind-set, approach, or way of being, and if the techniques are not utilized within the intended spirit, they run the risk of becoming a hollow or manipulative tactic that is unlikely to be helpful. The core elements of the spirit of MI overlap largely with most person-centered counseling styles. In the following section, the way those components are currently organized, discussed, researched, and disseminated within the world of MI are summarized.

The Spirit of MI

The spirit of MI is currently described in terms of four major components: collaboration, acceptance, evocation, and compassion.

Collaboration MI is a partnership between experts: The helper brings to the table the expertise from their field gathered through their training and experience, and the person being helped is the expert on themselves. Indeed, the term "interview" was chosen as a part of the name for this approach in order to reflect the idea of viewing issues from two vantage points – the "inter-view." The patient is empowered to recognize the value of their own expertise in knowing what matters to them, what has and has not been helpful in the past, what is realistic for them, and what their role is in creating a path going forward. This is a very different power differential than in a traditional or directive medical model, and it requires different expectations and behaviors on the part of both parties. From the patient's perspective, especially for those who have not typically been empowered, this may be initially confusing and/or be met with doubts about the genuineness of the invitation to meaningfully collaborate on their own care. As such, that genuineness is critical and must be consistently demonstrated. This is not about political correctness or following recommended trends toward a person-centered approach in healthcare. The MI clinician recognizes that a genuinely equal partnership is indeed an essential element to the potential for the clinician to be optimally helpful. This calls for humility and curiosity about the vast body of knowledge and experience that the patient has about themselves, their environment, their culture, etc. and the conviction that this information is critical in order for the helper to be effective.

Evocation In the collaborative atmosphere described above, the path forward will be evoked from, rather than imposed upon, the person we are working with. The MI clinician aims to understand what really matters to the person they are working with, what are their core values, what is their self-image or their desired self-image, what do they look forward to, what do they fear? What do they want to be remembered for? Once these kinds of factors are voiced and understood, an opportunity emerges for the clinician to emphasize any discrepancies between the person's current behaviors and those core aspects of their identity and aspirations. The cognitive dissonance of the patient's recognition of those discrepancies is a powerful motivator of change, far more powerful than being told that change is needed for some external reason (Bem 1967).

Acceptance Although acceptance is referred to as one component of the spirit of MI, it includes several subcomponents: accurate empathy, absolute worth, affirmation, and autonomy support.

Accurate Empathy[2] involves the helper's desire to see the world *as if* they are seeing it

[2]The importance of accurate empathy was underscored for William Miller by an observation he made in a study

through the other person's eyes and communicating that to the person. It is distinct from sympathy (i.e., feeling badly for the person's situation) or identification (e.g., thinking or saying something like "yes, I can relate to that, or I understand what that feels like because I have felt that way…"). It requires deep and sustained listening and ongoing reflection to test the accuracy of what you think you are hearing and the capacity to communicate your understanding of both the content and the feelings that the patient is giving voice to and experiencing. Accurate empathy has been shown to have greater effect sizes on clinical outcomes across a wide variety of psychotherapeutic approaches than any other identified therapeutic factors (Miller and Moyers 2021).

Absolute worth is rooted in the belief that every person, despite whatever behaviors they may have engaged in, or perhaps continue to engage in, is inherently worthy of respect. Even in cases in which the person may appear to lack remorse over prior or continuous problematic behaviors, the notion of absolute worth suggests that all people have inherent value, and at their core, most know what the "right thing to do" is and want to do the right thing. Communicating this expectation is often extremely helpful in and of itself, and it can be especially so in situations in which there are perceived and/or real structural power differentials in play.

Affirmation is a related aspect of acceptance in that the clinician expects, looks for, and communicates strengths and capacities that they see in the person. This may take many forms, for example, reframing a person's repeated setbacks as exhibiting qualities of resilience and determination. Communicating the appreciation of those strengths to individuals, especially when they may have a hard time seeing those qualities in themselves, can be transformative. As such, in the teaching of MI, affirmation is included as both one of the core technical skills and a crucial part of its spirit. It is a part of the strength-based view of all people that underlies MI.

The final aspect of "acceptance" is *autonomy support*, which is rooted in the recognition that people are indeed autonomous: they are ultimately responsible for their own choices. We may be able to delay or in some way influence the specifics of how those choices will play out, but at some point, people are going to do what they are going to do. This is even the case in settings in which there are real structural power differentials and behavioral constraints such as in working with involuntary patients or in carceral settings. Within the spirit of MI, we transparently and fully acknowledge our own limits in the face of the individuals' inherent autonomy, trusting that we can be most helpful by supporting and reinforcing the client's autonomy to make choices that will be in greater alignment with their core values.

Compassion Effective sales people have long recognized that "hard sells," i.e., telling people why they need a product and which product they must buy, tend to be less successful than approaching customers collaboratively with respect, evoking what they are looking for in a product, and gently guiding them toward making the decision to buy in a manner that feels like it was their choice. But "using" any aspect of MI to manipulate or otherwise influence people toward a direction that is not driven primarily by their interests is anathema to its fundamental spirit. In an effort to reinforce and make explicit the centrality of this idea, compassion, defined as the "deliberate commitment to pursue the welfare and best interests of the other," was added as a fourth pillar to the spirit of MI in the most recent edition of the Miller and Rollnick text (Miller and Rollnick 2013).

he had been conducting just prior to the publication of his first paper on MI in the early 1980s. Among nine substance use counselors involved in this study of different forms of outpatient treatment for people with problematic drinking, the rating of therapists' accurate empathy in a single MI session prior to entering the study predicted a greater amount of the variance in both short- and long-term outcome, than did which arm of the study the patient was randomized into. There is something about both the desire and capacity to see the world through our clients' eyes and to communicate that back to the client that helps people change or perhaps helps people to be more open to and make more effective use of other therapeutic resources.

Core Skills of MI

The spirit of MI is enacted through the practice and implementation of specific communication skills. In MI training, much of the work involves honing these skills. What follows is an introductory sketch of the four most commonly used means of communication in an MI-consistent manner, which are typically referred to by the acronym "OARS."

Open-ended Questions Perhaps the simplest measure of fidelity to motivational interviewing is the amount of time the helper is talking versus the client. An overall goal of MI is to activate and empower the person being helped toward change, so it is desirable for that person to do most of the talking. Open-ended vs. closed questions are consistent with this, as well as the overall spirit of collaboration and curiosity. Closed questions tend to reinforce the more traditional power dynamics of a directive approach, i.e., the patient's job is to provide unelaborated data in the order that the clinician chooses, so as to provide the information that the clinician feels is necessary for them to assess and recommend a plan of action.

As an example, it would be more MI-consistent to obtain a smoking history with an open-ended question like: "What, if any, has been your experience with cigarettes or nicotine-related products throughout your life?", rather than the usual half dozen or so closed-ended questions (e.g., *do you smoke, have you ever smoked, how many packs per day, when did you start, stop,* etc.). There is nothing inherently wrong with closed questions, which can be useful to fill in gaps, but generally, open-ended questions are more consistent with an MI style.

Affirmations are both part of the spirit of MI and a core skill within the technique. The mindset that all people have strengths is the spirit element; the technique involves the active effort to recognize and communicate particular strengths and capacities at strategic moments within a conversation. Affirmations are statements that express and bring attention to a strength or an admirable or useful quality that a person has. It is important that affirmations be genuine – if not, they can do more harm to the relationship than good. Affirmations can often be especially powerful in situations in which they might not be expected. For example, imagine a psychiatrist called to see a patient in the emergency room who makes it clear in his first sentence that he is not interested in being seen by psychiatry:

> Patient: Doc, I'm sure you are just trying to do your job, but I don't buy into this head shrinker business. No offense, it's just not for me and it never has been.
> Psychiatrist: You are someone who tells it like it is, and you are not interested in wasting either your time or mine.

In MI conversations, we actively seek what may be affirmed, even when the quality we are affirming may be buried within or adjacent to what otherwise may seem problematic. Well-timed, genuine affirmations can help to open many doors that might otherwise remained tightly shut.

Reflections From a technical perspective, perhaps the biggest difference between an MI conversation and those using other approaches involves the use of reflections as modal form of verbalization by the helper. By definition, a reflection is a statement, not a question. It is an implied hypothesis indicating "…this is what I am hearing you say…," or "…this is what I am perceiving you are feeling…Is that right?" A reflection invites the person to elaborate upon, confirm, clarify, or correct the hypothesis. It tends to keep the conversation moving, encouraging the patient to remain actively rather than passively engaged. Reflections can be as simple as repeating or paraphrasing what the person has said or reflecting a guess at an underlying meaning or feeling (simple vs. complex reflections). There are many types of reflective statements that have different goals and usages. Some examples are shown in Table 1.

Becoming fluent with the use of reflections is one of the most important skills of MI and often makes up a good deal of training in MI, espe-

Table 1 Types and examples of reflective listening statements commonly used in MI:

Paraphrasing
Client: These meds don't seem to be working
Clinician: You are not feeling any benefit
Simple reflections often repeat or paraphrase what a person has said, inviting them to elaborate further
Amplified reflection
Client: I've never found medicines to be helpful in any way
Clinician: You are convinced that no medications could ever be helpful for you
Here the goal is to reflect sustain talk in an overstated manner, so that the patient is likely to pick up on the other side of any ambivalence expressed. This can be useful when someone seems to be taking a near absolute position
Affective reflection
Client: I've never found medicines to be helpful in any way
Clinician: You are feeling discouraged about whether anything is ever going to help
Reflecting the affect is often helpful in communicating empathy and clarifying both the feelings a person may be having
Double-sided reflections
Client: The only medicines that have worked for me made me gain so much weight that I ended up feeling even worse
Clinician: On the one hand, you don't like the side effects that you've encountered so far, and on the other you feel you really need the help that these medicines may offer
Double-sided reflections are used very commonly in MI conversations, as they help to recognize and normalize the person's ambivalence. Note that an MI-consistent manner of delivering a double-sided reflection is to reflect the sustain side first and the change side second to make it more likely that the client would pick up on the latter rather than the former in continuing the conversation

Table 2 Simple examples of MI-consistent vs. MI-inconsistent questions

Examples of MI consistent questions:	Examples of MI-inconsistent questions
Why would you want to make this change? What are the three best reasons to do so? How might you go about making the change if you decided to do it?	Why haven't you changed? What keeps you from doing this? Why can't you… Why don't you…

cially early on. Indeed, moving from a primarily question-based interviewing style to one in which reflections become the modal type of communication from the helper is a core part of MI technical proficiency. A commonly used measure of MI fidelity suggests that a 1:1 ratio of reflections to questions indicates "beginning proficiency" in MI, whereas a ratio of 2:1 would indicate MI "competency" (Moyers et al. 2005).

Summaries A summary is a selection of individual reflections grouped together to present a bigger picture of what the clinician has heard. In addition to demonstrating that he or she has been listening carefully and attentively, an effective summary can be used to collect, link together, and reinforce material that has been discussed in a manner that is accessible to the patient. Consistent with the notion of elaborating change talk and "rolling with" sustain talk, MI summaries typically include more of the former than the latter. Summaries can also be very useful in transitioning to another topic or in bringing a session to a close.

Eliciting Change Talk and Responding to Sustain Talk Another set of skills one would learn and practice in MI training involves eliciting change talk and responding to sustain talk. In teaching these skills of MI to psychiatry residents, I sometimes pose the following question as a thought experiment: If we imagined a financial reimbursement model in which you were paid a set amount of money for every change talk statement a patient expressed about a problematic behavior, and you had to pay back some amount for every sustain talk statement, how would you spend your time with patients? It is unlikely that you'd spend much time lecturing, advising, or going through checklists. Rather, you would do what you could to get the patient to do most of the talking and structure your questions and reflections in such a way that made change talk more likely than sustain talk. You'd naturally ask more MI-consistent than inconsistent questions. Simple examples of MI consistent and inconsistent questions are shown in Table 2.

There are a variety of other strategies to elicit change talk such as querying worst- and best-case scenarios or looking back and forward (i.e., asking the person to imagine what life would be like in the future if they did vs. did not make the change). Often, simply asking evocative questions about a person's desire, ability, reason or need to make the change yields change talk. One particularly useful and practical strategy, especially early on in conversations or if change talk is not being expressed spontaneously, is to employ the "importance and confidence rulers," as shown in Table 3.

Understanding and Responding to Sustain Talk and Discord What if a person responds to the importance ruler with a "0"? While this is not common, it certainly does happen and is an example of what appears to be an extreme example of sustain talk. How do we respond in an MI-consistent manner? There are several considerations and options. First, the clinician would want to be aware of and careful to avoid acting upon their "righting reflex," i.e., the impulse to take up the pro-change side of the issue which such a response may naturally trigger within the clinician, for reasons previously explained. With that awareness in mind, the clinician might respond in a variety of ways, including reflecting the person's expression of clarity and lack of ambivalence, perhaps with an amplified reflection, such as: *There is no reason at all for you to consider making this change either now or at any time in your life.*

Table 3 Importance and confidence rulers

Importance ruler: *On a scale of 0–10, how important would you say it is it for you to make this change now? (0 is not at all important, 5 is somewhat important and 10 is extremely important)*
The person's response is then followed by the clinician asking why the person gave the number they gave, but doing so in a strategic manner, specifically asking why a lower number was not chosen. For example, if the person chose a "5," then the MI consistent follow-up question would be: "Why did you choose a 5 rather than perhaps a 2 or 3?" This question elicits change talk, naturally inviting the person to describe some of their reasons for wanting to make the change. On the other hand, an example of an MI-inconsistent follow-up question would be, "why did you choose a 5 rather than a 7 or an 8," as that would elicit discussion of the opposing side of ambivalence, i.e., sustain talk
Confidence ruler: *On a scale of 0–10, how confident would you would feel in being able to make the change, if you decided to make it now? (0 is not at all confident, 5 is somewhat confident, and 10 is extremely confident)*
This question allows exploration of a person' sense of their capacity to make the change, which may be more what is getting in their way than their perceived importance in doing so. Similar to the "importance ruler," i.e., asking about why the confidence number they chose wasn't lower invites them to discuss their strengths and abilities, which can be an opportunity for affirmations and support

Another option might be to do what in MI parlance is termed coming alongside, i.e., simply acknowledging that at this time the issue is not at all important to the patient and that you respect their autonomy and inquire as to whether there are other ways you might be helpful at this time. If the person is in a position in which they do not have the freedom to make those choices, e.g., a patient who is involuntarily committed or incarcerated, then it would be important to attempt to express accurate empathy about what it might feel like to be potentially forced to do something that is diametrically opposed to one's choice.

An important consideration is whether such a response is a genuine, normal, and expected expression of one side of the ambivalence or perhaps represents something having to do with the relationship between the patient and clinician. Up until the past decade, those separate phenomena had been lumped together under the term "resistance" within the lexicon of MI. However, research and clinical experience have shown that what had formerly been thought of as resistance is better understood a manifestation of two very different processes: One, it may be a normal and expected part of the change process when someone is ambivalent, or, two, it may reflect discord between the patient and clinician. It may also reflect a combination of both.

In either case, in response to any sustain talk statement, the clinician would avoid argumentation. If in the clinician's judgement, the statement appeared to be a normal expression of the ambivalence, then they would simply avoid drawing unnecessary attention to it and perhaps recognize and reflect the affect or ask other evocative questions that may elicit change talk. If on the other hand, the clinician suspects that the sustain talk may at least partially be a manifestation of discord (such as if the sustain talk persists perhaps more strongly than ever before or in the absence of any change talk), then it would be appropriate to step back and consider what aspects of the relationship may be underlying that discord. In the next section, we will look at a set of meta-processes that are a helpful way of thinking about that relationship in a dynamic manner.

The "Meta-Processes" of MI: Engagement, Focusing, Evoking, and Planning

In addition to the spirit and technique of MI, over the past decade, a series of 4 "meta-processes" have been recognized as a general guide to where one is at within an MI conversation – both in the moment and over time. A useful metaphor in thinking about these overarching processes is two people taking a walk as shown in Fig. 1. The stairstep imagery in the figure indicates the fact that each one of the processes provides a necessary foundation for the next; however, it is also the case that the processes tend to be interactive rather than discreet.

Engagement MI is inherently relational – whether that relationship lasts a few minutes or many years. As it something that is done with people and not to people, any MI conversation requires at least a tacit agreement between the parties. As such, engagement is foundational. Can you look a person in the eye and either ask verbally or nonverbally whether or not he or she will engage with you? Will the two of you do something together, even if that something is agreeing to have a brief conversation? If yes, then you can begin to discuss where you might go and why you might go there (i.e., focusing and evoking). However, if it is not clear that any kind of engagement can be established, then the work of MI at that point involves understanding the barriers to engagement and seeking ways to overcome or mitigate them. For example, patients being seen for the first time in emergency or crisis setting may be too exhausted, agitated, disorganized, or paranoid for any kind of meaningful engagement to be achieved. Simply recognizing those barriers and stepping back can often be an entrée to at least some engagement (e.g., saying quietly to someone who appears exhausted and who hasn't responded to initial introductory remarks, something like: "I can see how tired you are… I wonder if you'd prefer it if I let you rest for a while and I stopped back a bit later; would that help?"). We may not always have the luxury of time necessary to do something like this, and there are certainly barriers that prevent engagement on an ongoing basis, but without engagement, there can be no MI.

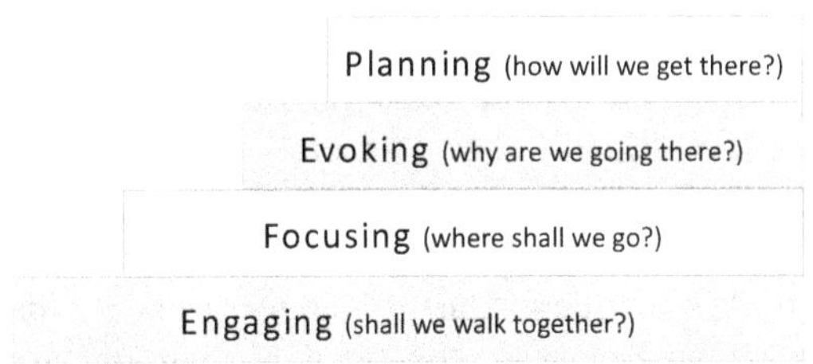

Fig. 1 The "meta-processes" of an MI conversation (Miller and Rollnick 2013)

Focusing As with all aspects of MI, the process of focusing is collaborative. One or more areas of potential focus may be readily apparent or implied (e.g., an intake at a substance use treatment center), or there may be no clear focus, requiring a more explorative process, possibly including a menu of potential options provided by the clinician. Once areas of focus begin to come into clearer view, it is important to see which of these goals are shared by both the patient and clinician. For the sake of ongoing engagement, it is helpful to try to identify at least one area of shared focus.

Returning to the example above of the sedated person in an emergency setting, assume that we learned that he had been brought to the emergency room by his parents because he had stopped taking his antipsychotic medication weeks ago and had been increasingly isolating in his apartment, not eating regularly, and disturbing his neighbors by talking loudly to himself through the night. He had been agitated on admission and had been given an injection of a sedating medication by ER staff and is now awake enough and willing to engage in a conversation. We learn that the person did not feel that he needed any psychiatric help at this time and just wanted to go home as soon as possible. That alone might be an opportunity for an initial shared focus, i.e., both the patient and clinician are looking for a resolution for the short-term problem of what comes next. Developing a plan that includes getting the patient home sooner rather than later may be that shared short-term focus and provide an opportunity for further engagement.

It may also be apparent that there are going to be areas of focus that are not shared. In this case, if the patient's history involved a repeated pattern of rapid decompensation leading to severe negative consequences following discontinuation of medications, the clinician might envision a focus of moving toward a treatment plan that included long-acting injectable medication. Having identified at least two potential areas of focus, one shared, and one not, the opportunity to combine these in a manner that is likely to be successful would involve further understanding of what is most important to the patient through evoking.

Evoking As noted earlier, evocation is one of the core elements of the spirit of MI. It is included within the meta-processes as well because it is part of the dynamic, interactive work of understanding a person's specific reasons for the choices that they make. From a process perspective, once we have established at least some degree of engagement and identified one or more initial areas of focus, we now seek to elucidate why the person might want to go there. What's in it for them? What specifically might motivate them to want to make whatever change we are discussing? In the example above, through the process of evocation, we might learn that one reason this patient wants to get home as soon as possible and avoid hospitalization is that he knows he won't be able to smoke cigarettes in the hospital. We might also learn that the most important relationship in his life is with his dog, and he is afraid that if he doesn't care for him, the dog will be taken away. In other cases, it may take the form of "…I want to be the best role model I can be for my kids"; or "…I want to be around to interact with my grandchildren, and maybe even my great-grandchildren." It is rarely as simple as "I want to be healthier, or I want to do better." Only after we have a sense of what actually matters most to the person are we in a position to help the person recognize the discrepancies between what matters most to them and the choices they may be making that are in opposition to them.

Planning The final meta-process is something that clinicians often tend to be most comfortable with, planning. From an MI perspective, good planning is critical. The problem is that we often jump to it prematurely without the foundation established in the earlier steps, thereby limiting its utility when it comes to issues involving ambivalence. But when there is real engagement, a clear focus, and an understanding of what is most important to the patient, then our role as content experts can be most effectively and efficiently utilized. Like all other aspects of MI, the process of planning is something that is done with a collaborative, accepting, and evocative spirit.

The planning stage is a time when it is often appropriate for the clinician to provide information, offer suggestions, strategize about next steps, etc. An MI-consistent approach to doing so involves three basic steps, referred to as "Elicit-Provide-Elicit" or more simply as "Ask-Tell-Ask."

1. Ask or Elicit: Start by inquiring about what the person may already know about the content; then ask permission to fill in relevant gaps.

2. Tell or Provide: Choose "bite-sized" or easily digestible amounts of content in a manner that will likely be most accessible for the person to process.
3. Ask or elicit: Follow up with questions to see what the person makes of the information or what questions they might have about it.

Thinking about the meta-processes can be particularly useful when the flow of an MI conversation begins to wane or become derailed or when discord may be appearing. If this is noted during planning, for example, it may be necessary to go back and do something to support one of the earlier processes, perhaps with a need to re-engage or refocus or further evoking the person's reasons for change. The stairstep imagery in Fig. 1 reminds us that like most, if not all, psychotherapeutic modalities, MI tends to be an iterative rather than linear process. Each of the metaprocess builds on the preceding ones, and each may have to be reinforced many times.

Issues of Particular Relevance to Community Psychiatry

With the basics laid out above, we now touch briefly on a few areas of particular relevance to community psychiatry.

Does MI "Work" with Those with Serious Mental Illness?

We lack an evidence-based answer to this question, as there has been very little in the way of research directed at if and how traditional MI strategies may have to be adapted or changed for individuals with psychotic disorders. Given that terms like "serious mental illness" and diagnoses such as schizophrenia encompass very heterogenous groups of people with different capacities, strengths, and limitations, a more useful way to think about this question is to ask: What specific aspects or ramifications of having a serious mental illness may present potential barriers to an MI approach and how might those barriers be mitigated or overcome? The MI metaprocesses are useful in thinking through these questions. Am I able to engage the person in any way? If not, what are the barriers to engagement? Might the person be either too paranoid or withdrawn to have any kind of meaningful engagement? If so, might there be other approaches to enhance engagement? Can I change my stance, either physically or verbally in some manner that might facilitate engagement? Similarly, am I able to establish a focus and/or evoke? Is the person perhaps too disorganized in their speech and thinking to allow for a conversation about what we might do together or to evoke and understand their unique desires, abilities, reasons, and needs to make any kind of changes? Without a focus toward one or more goals and/or the capacity to evoke one's motivation, there is no MI.

In most cases, with repeated effort tailored to the identified barriers, adequate engagement, focus, and evocation can usually be achieved with most individuals despite the presence of a serious mental illness (Flaum et al. 2017). It may require a change in the usual MI technical approaches. For example, in working with patients who are very disorganized in their speech and thought processes, we may rely on mostly closed questions. This may be the case for those with prominent negative symptoms as well, in which open-ended questions or reflections may fall flat. We may want to avoid reflections altogether with people who are acutely paranoid, as they may experience them as overly intrusive. We may do more affirming with dysphoric patients and less for those who are manic, more summarizing for those with pressured speech, etc. Just like in any other modality, we do what we can to optimize the therapeutic alliance with whoever we are working with.

Whether or not we can successfully engage, focus, or evoke an individual patient, we can maintain an MI spirit with every patient we see, every time we see them. A respectful, autonomy-supporting, and accepting attitude is often most welcomed and appreciated by those whose experience has taught them to expect otherwise.

Other Applications and Advantages of MI

Cultural humility and structural racism: The spirit of MI described above may also have relevance to the long-standing health disparities experienced by underrepresented minority groups and the effects of structural racism on health outcomes. Approaches such as MI that are grounded in curiosity and prioritize empowering and evoking rather than directing and imposing may provide greater benefit for those who have been traditionally victimized by structural power differentials. This may account for some evidence suggesting that MI may be more successful (i.e., greater effect sizes compared to other approaches) in underrepresented minority than for non-minority white samples (Hettema et al. 2005; Lundahl and Kunz 2010; Montgomery et al. 2011; Clair et al. 2013).

Burnout: It is now widely recognized that burnout is a major problem among healthcare providers. Estimates of burnout among physicians vary widely according to the methodology used, with most studies reporting rates >40% (Shanafelt et al. 2019) and those rates may be higher among psychiatrists (Summers et al. 2020). Burnout is perhaps more of a concern in mental health, as the transmission of hopefulness has a prominent impact on patient outcomes. One of the unexpected benefits of practicing in an MI-consistent manner may be a decrease in burnout. While this has not yet been adequately explored in the academic literature, the anecdotal evidence is remarkably consistent among clinicians who have transitioned to an MI approach as their default way of being with their patients or clients. The struggle to convince people to do something they are ambivalent about can be exhausting. If we are able to partner with people with curiosity, and those partnerships result in new conversations about how they might go about changing, that can be energizing and restorative and perhaps remind us of the reasons we chose to do this work initially.

Leadership: Community psychiatrists often find themselves in leadership positions, ranging from leading small teams to large organizations and systems. Many are thrust into those positions early in their careers without training, formal or otherwise, in what makes good leadership. Recently the consonance between MI and those approaches to organizational change that have long been researched and taught in business has begun to be recognized and explored (Marshall and Sogaard Nielsen 2020). Just like individuals, organizations get stuck and change is hard. While it is clearly an oversimplification to suggest that MI can be directly applied to organizational change, there are clearly some commonalities and there is growing interest and research in this area.

When Is MI Not Appropriate?

MI is not a panacea, and the technique of MI is certainly not applicable in all clinical situations and is indeed *contraindicated* in some. Specifically, the technique of MI is not appropriate for situations in which there are multiple reasonable options and the helper is neutral with respect to the outcome. An example is working with someone who is struggling over the decision about whether or not to go through with a pregnancy or pursue an abortion. The clinician may want to stay neutral and not steer the person in one direction or another. They would want to ensure that they were NOT differentially responding to one side of the patient's ambivalence or the other. In such situations, a Shared Decision Making (SDM) approach (Barry and Edgman-Levitan 2012) may be more appropriate. While there is a lot of overlap between the spirit of MI and SDM (i.e., both are highly collaborative, autonomy-supporting, and evocative), the techniques and goals are different (Elwyn et al. 2014). An understanding of MI allows the clinicians to apply these techniques discriminately, depending on the circumstances.

Learning and Teaching MI

It is one thing to understand the general principles of MI and how it might differ from other approaches, but how do we incorporate it into our daily practice? Like learning a musical instrument or a sport, it takes practice and tends to get better, more fluid, and natural with time. It also helps to have a teacher or coach who can provide feedback while watching you play. Just as one would not take piano lessons by describing to the teacher how they played, the use of audio and video tapes markedly facilitates learning and progress in MI. Supervision through such observation is especially effective when combined with ratings on specific measures of fidelity (Moyers et al. 2005, 2016; Jelsma et al. 2015).

MI is now taught and practiced all in over 50 languages worldwide. This is partly due to active dissemination through the Motivational Interviewing Network of Trainers (MINT), which is an excellent resource for training in MI. The dominant model of training up until recently was through in-person workshops of varied length and sophistication. There are more and more high-quality online materials and opportunities in various formats, ranging from demonstration videos, virtual workshops, and individual coaching to podcasts. The availability of such opportunities expanded markedly during the COVID-19 and is likely to become the dominant form of ongoing training in MI. Finally, there are several very useful books to learn, hone, and practice MI skills (e.g., Rosengren 2017; Miller and Rollnick 2013).

A model of learning and deepening MI skills that is a good complement to, or continuation of, other approaches is the formation of MI learning communities.[3] These are typically ongoing opportunities for small groups, either within or across systems to present and discuss cases, bring in new resources, and support each other's learning within the style and spirit of MI.

Like learning a new instrument or language, it may feel awkward at first, but with ongoing practice and feedback, both the technical aspect and the spirit of MI usually start to feel like second nature. How long does that fluency take and how do you know when you get there? One answer to this was given by Bill Miller in response to the question: "What is the difference between 'doing MI' and 'being MI,'" to which he famously responded, "...about ten years."

[3]A useful guide for starting a learning community can be found on the MINT website here: https://motivationalinterviewing.org/sites/default/files/learning_communities_guidelines_june_2019.pdf

References

Abele, M., Brown, J., Ibrahim H, & Jha MK. (2016) Teaching Motivational Interviewing Skills to Psychiatry Trainees: Findings of a National Survey. *Acad Psychiatry* 40(1):149-52. https://doi.org/10.1007/s40596-014-0149-0

Bechdolf A, Pohlmann B, Geyer C, Ferber C, Klosterkötter J, & Gouzoulis-Mayfrank E. (2005) Motivational interviewing for patients with comorbid schizophrenia and substance abuse disorders: A review. *Fortschr Neurol Psychiatr.* 73(12):728-35. German. https://doi.org/10.1055/s-2004-830258

Barry MJ and S Edgman-Levitan. (2012) Shared Decision Making: The Pinnacle of Patient-Centered Care. *N Engl JMed.* 366:780-81.

Bem D.J. (1967) Self-perception: An alternative interpretation of cognitive dissonance phenomena. *Psychological Review.* 74(3):183–200

Burke, BL, Arkowitz, H, and Menchola M. (2003). The efficacy of motivational interviewing: A meta-analysis of controlled clinical trials. *Journal of Consulting and Clinical Psychology, [s. l.]*, v. 71, n. 5, p. 843–861, 2003. https://doi.org/10.1037/0022-006X.71.5.843

Chanut F, Brown TG, Donguier M. (2005) Motivational interviewing and clinical psychiatry. *Can J Psychiatry.* 50(11):715-21. https://doi.org/10.1177/070674370505001111. PMID: 16366007.

Chien WT, Mui JH, Cheung EF, Gray R. (2015) Effects of motivational interviewing-based adherence therapy for schizophrenia spectrum disorders: a randomized controlled trial. *Trials* 16:270. https://doi.org/10.1186/s13063-015-0785-z

Clair M, Stein LA, Soenksen S, Martin RA, Lebeau R, Golembeske C. (2013) Ethnicity as a moderator of motivational interviewing for incarcerated adolescents after release. *J Subst Abuse Treat.* 2013;45(4):370-375.

Dunn, C., DeRoo, L., & Rivara, F. P. (2001). The use of brief interventions adapted from motivational interviewing across behavioral domains: A systematic review. *Addiction, 96*, 1725–1742.

Elwyn G, Dehlendorf C, Epstein RM, Marrin K, White J & Frosch DL. (2014) Shared decision making and motivational interviewing: Achieving patient-centered care across the spectrum of problems. *Ann Fam Med.* 12(3):270-5

Faustino-Silva D, Colvara D, Carriconde B, Meyer E, et al: (2019) Motivational interviewing effects on caries prevention in children differ by income: A randomized cluster trial. Community dentistry and oral epidemiology. Vol.47(6), p.477-484ISSN: 0301-5661, 1600-0528; https://doi.org/10.1111/cdoe.12488

Fiszdon JM, Kurtz MM, Choi J, Bell MD, Martino S. (2016) Motivational Interviewing to Increase Cognitive Rehabilitation Adherence in Schizophrenia. Schizophr Bull.42(2):327-34. https://doi.org/10.1093/schbul/sbv143

Flaum M, Chanut F, Hurley B, Undrill, G and Vasilev (2017) The role of MI in serious mental illness: Practical challenges and strategies in clinical work and training. Presented as a full day Pre-forum workshop at the 20th annual meeting of the Motivational Interviewing Network of Trainers Forum, Oct 4, 2017, Malahide, Ireland.

Gabarda A, Butterworth SW. (2021) Using Best Practices to Address COVID-19 Vaccine Hesitancy: The Case for the Motivational Interviewing Approach. Health Promotion Practice.;22(5):611-615. https://doi.org/10.1177/15248399211016463

Gagneur A. (2020) Motivational interviewing: A powerful tool to address vaccine hesitancy. Can Commun Dis Rep. 2020;46(4):93-97.

Hettema J, Steele J, Miller WR. (2005) Motivational interviewing. Annu Rev Clin Psychol. 2005;1:91-111. https://doi.org/10.1146/annurev.clinpsy.1.102803.143833. PMID: 17716083.

Jelsma GM, Mertens V, Forsberg L Lars Forsberg L. (2015) How to Measure Motivational Interviewing Fidelity in Randomized Controlled Trials: Practical Recommendations. Contemporary Clinical Trials, Volume 43,Pages 93-99, ISSN 1551-7144, https://doi.org/10.1016/j.cct.2015.05.001

Kay, E., Vascott, D., Hocking, A. et al (2016) Motivational interviewing in general dental practice: A review of the evidence. *Br Dent J* 221, 785–791 (2016). https://doi.org/10.1038/sj.bdj.2016.952

Knight KM, McGowan L, Dickens C, & Bundy C. (2006) A systematic review of motivational interviewing in physical health care settings. *Br J Health Psychol.* 11(Pt 2):319-32. https://doi.org/10.1348/135910705X52516. PMID: 16643702.

Lundahl BH, C Kunz C, Brownell C, Tollefson D, and BL Burke: (2010) A Meta-Analysis of Motivational Interviewing: Twenty-Five Years of Empirical Studies. *Research on Social Work Practice* 20(2) 137-160. https://doi.org/10.1177/1049731509347850

Magill M, Gaume J, Apodaca TR, Walthers J, Mastroleo NR, Borsari B & Longabaugh R. (2014) The technical hypothesis of motivational interviewing: a meta-analysis of MI's key causal model. *J Consult Clin Psychol.*;82(6):973-83. https://doi.org/10.1037/a0036833

Marshall, C. and A Sogaard Nielsen (2020): *Motivational Interviewing for Leaders in the Helping Professions: Facilitating Change in Organizations.* Guilford Press, New York, NY

Miller WR, Moyers TB. (2017) Motivational interviewing and the clinical science of Carl Rogers. *J Consult Clin Psychol.* 85(8):757-766.

Miller WR and Moyers TB. (2021). Accurate Empathy, in *Effective Psychotherapists*. New York, NY: Guilford Press, p 19-32.

Miller WR. (2020) Controlled Clinical Trials Involving Motivational Interviewing Updated 11/16/2020: downloaded from MINT website at: https://motivationalinterviewing.org/sites/default/files/mi_controlled_trials_2020_nov.pdf

Miller WR. (1983) Motivational interviewing with problem drinkers. *Behavioral Psychotherapy.* 11:147–172.

Miller, W. R., & Rollnick, S. (1991) *Motivational interviewing: Preparing people to change* Addictive Behavior. New York, NY: Guilford Press.

Miller, W. R., & Rollnick, S. (2013). *Motivational interviewing: Helping people change* (3rd ed.). New York, NY: Guilford Press.

Miller, W. R., & Rose, G. S. (2009). Toward a theory of motivational interviewing. American Psychologist, 64, 527–537.

Montgomery L, Burlew AK, Wilson J, and Hall, R. (2011) Promising Evidence-Based Treatments for African Americans: Motivational Interviewing/Motivational Enhancement Therapy. In: *Advances in Psychology Research*. Volume 85 Editor: Alexandra M. Columbus.

Moyers TB, Martin T, Manuel JK, Hendrickson SM, Miller WR. (2005) Assessing competence in the use of motivational interviewing. *J Subst Abuse Treat*; 28:19-26.

Moyers T.B. Rowell L.N. Manuel J.K. Ernst D. Houck J.M. (2016). The motivational interviewing treatment integrity code (MITI 4): Rationale, preliminary reliability and validity. *Journal of Substance Abuse Treatment.*; 65: 36-42 https://doi.org/10.1016/j.jsat.2016.01.001

Noonan, W. C., & Moyers, T. B. (1997). Motivational interviewing: A review. *Journal of Substance Misuse*, *2*, 8–16.

Rogers, C. (1951) *Client-centered therapy*. Boston: Houghton-Mifflin.

Rogers, Carl R. (1980). *A Way of Being*. Boston: Houghton-Mifflin, Also published in 1995 with a new introduction by Irvin Yalom, M.D.

Rollnick, S, Kaplan, S.G. & R. Rutschman *(2016) Motivational Interviewing in Schools: Conversations to Improve Behavior and Learning. New York, NY: The Guilford Press,* https://doi.org/10.1080/07317107.2017.1307682

Rosengren D. (2017) *Building Motivational Interviewing Skills: A Practitioner Workbook.* (2nd ed.) New York, NY: Guilford Press.

Shanafelt TD, West C, Sinsky C, Trockel M, Michael Tutty M, Satele DV, Carlasare LE, Dyrbye L. (2019) Changes in Burnout and Satisfaction with Work-Life Integration in Physicians and the General US Working Population Between 2011 and 2017. *Mayo Clin Proc.* 94(9):1681-1694. https://doi.org/10.1016/j.mayocp.2018.10.023.

Smeerdijk M, Keet R, van Raaij B, Koeter M, Linszen D, de Haan L, Schippers G. (2015) Motivational interviewing and interaction skills training for parents of young adults with recent-onset schizophrenia and co-occurring cannabis use: 15-month follow-up. *Psychol Med.* 45(13):2839-48. https://doi.org/10.1017/S0033291715000793. Epub 2015 May 11. PMID: 25959502.

Stinson, Jill D., and Michael D. Clark. (2017). *Motivational Interviewing with Offenders: Engagement, Rehabilitation, and Reentry / Jill D. Stinson, Michael D. Clark.* New York, NY: Guilford Press.

Summers RF, Gorrindo T, Hwang S, Aggarwal R & Guille C. (2020) Well-Being, Burnout, and Depression Among North American Psychiatrists: The State of Our Profession. *Am J Psychiatry*, 177: 955-964.

Tervalon, M., Murray-Garcia, J. (1998). Cultural humility versus cultural competence: A critical distinction in defining physician training outcomes in multicultural education. *Journal of Health Care for the Poor and Underserved*, 9, 117-125.

VanBuskirk KA, Wetherell JL. (2014) Motivational interviewing with primary care populations: a systematic review and meta-analysis. *J Behav Med.* 37(4):768-80. https://doi.org/10.1007/s10865-013-9527-4. Epub 2013 Aug 11. PMID: 23934180; PMCID: PMC4118674.

Wagner C.C. (2013) Motivational Interviewing and Client-Centered Therapy. In: Cornelius-White J., Motschnig-Pitrik R., Lux M. (eds) *Interdisciplinary Applications of the Person-Centered Approach*. Springer, New York, NY.

Person-Centered Recovery Planning as a Roadmap to Recovery

Janis Tondora, Neal Adams, Diane Grieder, and Larry Davidson

Introduction and Framing the Problem

Beginning in 2002 with the release of the Institute of Medicine's Quality Chasm series (2001 & 2006), followed by the President's New Freedom Commission Report in 2003, the urgent need to transform the US mental health service delivery system became abundantly clear to all involved. The system was described as being "in shambles" (U.S. Department of Health and Human Services 2003) and failing to meet the needs of adults, children, and families seeking services.

The growing consensus was that the system needed to be far more recovery-oriented and person-centered – focusing not only on the pursuit of clinical stability but rather the more aspirational pursuit of a good life as defined by each individual based on their unique values and priorities. While there are multiple definitions of recovery and recovery-oriented practice (Anthony 1993), the Federal Substance Abuse and Mental Health Services Administration's (SAMHSA) consensus definition captures the essence of what is meant by "recovery" from mental health and substance use problems (SAMHSA 2010):

> Recovery is a process of change through which individuals improve their health and wellness, live a self-directed life, and strive to reach their full potential.

This definition, and its associated *10 Guiding Principles of Recovery*, specifically highlights the need for systems to be "person-driven," in which individuals optimize their autonomy and independence to the greatest extent possible by leading, controlling, and exercising choice over the services and supports with which they engage. Person-centered recovery planning (PCRP) represents one critical opportunity to translate this person-driven philosophy into person-driven practice.

The values-based demand for PCRP coupled with an emerging evidence base (Tondora et al. 2010; Stanhope et al. 2013) has established the practice as a cornerstone of quality in any recovery-oriented system of care. It is increasingly demanded by consumer advocacy organizations (Bazelon and UPENN 2008); endorsed by professional and provider associations (including the American Psychiatric Association) (American Psychiatric Association and American Association of Community Psychiatrists n.d.); and required by national accrediting bodies (The Joint Commission 2010) and state behavioral

J. Tondora (✉) · L. Davidson
Program for Recovery and Community Health, Yale Department of Psychiatry, New Haven, CT, USA
e-mail: janis.tondora@yale.edu; larry.davidson@yale.edu

N. Adams
Nappa, CA, USA

D. Grieder
Charlottesville, VA, USA

W. E. Sowers et al. (eds.), *Textbook of Community Psychiatry*,
https://doi.org/10.1007/978-3-031-10239-4_10

health authorities (Connecticut Department of Mental Health and Addiction Services 2008). Perhaps most significantly, PCRP was explicitly identified as a requirement by the nation's largest funder of long-term services and supports, i.e., the Centers for Medicare and Medicaid Services (CMS 2014), and it has more recently been identified as a core component of the Certified Community Behavioral Health Clinics (SAMHSA 2016) established by the Excellence in Mental Health Act.

The promise of person-centered care and planning is, however, a far cry from the current realities of our nation's mental healthcare system. Mental health services—including the pivotal process of treatment planning—continue to be oriented primarily to the requirements of bureaucracies rather than to the goal of providing individuals with real and meaningful opportunities for choice and self-determination. A range of implementation barriers contribute to this dilemma (Lodge et al. 2017), including complex administrative requirements and organizational business practices. For example, providers often view strengths-based, person-centered approaches as inconsistent with the clinical documentation requirements and "medical necessity" criteria of various fiscal and regulatory oversight bodies. In addition, the perpetuation of poorly designed templates in electronic health records (EHRs) that remain rooted in traditional, problem-focused approaches to care planning remains significant obstacles to the advancement of PCRP (Tondora et al. 2021).

Practitioners express feelings of tension between their deep personal investment in their work—which is often aligned with the principles of person-centered care—and feeling constrained by bureaucratic demands. While a complete discussion of these systemic implementation barriers is beyond the scope of this chapter, it is important to acknowledge that even the most competent and committed practitioners may be unable to fully actualize their clinical ideals in the absence of systems characteristics that align workflows with person-centered recovery planning. The reader is referred to the work of the National Center for the Advancement of Person-Centered Systems and Practices (https://ncapps.acl.gov/home.html) for a more thorough discussion of person-centered systems transformation along with a wealth of resources to support it. For the remainder of the chapter, we turn our attention back to the essential functions of PCRP and how the principles of person-driven care have been translated into practice guidelines which shape both the process and documentation of recovery planning.

Functions of the Recovery Plan

The person-centered recovery plan (PCRP) serves multiple purposes for providers as well as individuals in recovery and their family members. Written plans function as:

- The social "contract" between the person served and the provider
- A means to support utilization management
- A tool to decrease fragmentation and assure coordination between multiple providers
- Support for medical necessity through identification of areas of need and associated interventions
- A means of promoting accountability by identifying everyone's role in the recovery process, including the person receiving services and/or their natural supports
- An opportunity to enhance the cultural responsiveness of care based on the individual's unique values and worldview
- A means for measuring recovery progress and articulating intended outcomes/transition criteria

A pretty tall order for one document! Yet, done well, this written document can be a valuable clinical tool as well as an essential part of the record that satisfies multiple administrative and regulatory requirements. The creation, implementation, and ongoing modification of the PCRP is *the essence of recovery work* – not, as regarded by many providers, merely a paperwork requirement keeping them from their "real" clinical responsibilities. If one thinks of recovery as a

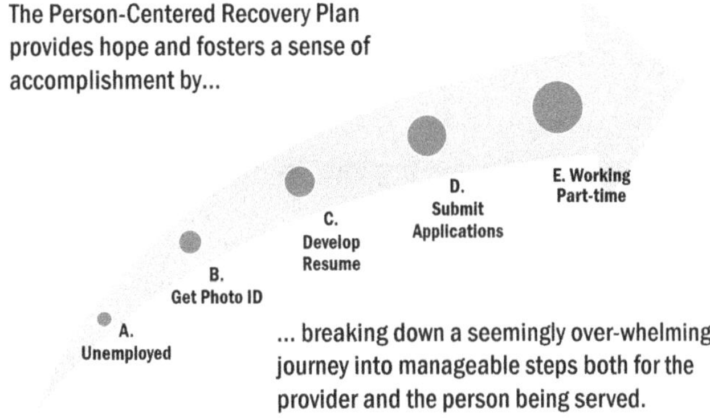
The Person-Centered Recovery Plan
provides hope and fosters a sense of
accomplishment by...
A.
Unemployed
B.
Get Photo ID
C.
Develop
Resume
D.
Submit
Applications
E. Working
Part-time
... breaking down a seemingly over-whelming
journey into manageable steps both for the
provider and the person being served.

Fig. 1 The PCRP as a roadmap to recovery

journey, the PCRP becomes each individual's roadmap so that everyone involved can know the direction and purpose of the journey and what is required to get under way.

The metaphor of recovery as a journey, and PCRP as the roadmap to help guide that expedition, is quite apt. In Fig. 1, *A* is the "starting point" and *E* the "end-point": the transition to another level of care or attainment of the goal – in this case the person's desire to return to work. The question to ask is: "why can't the person simply travel from *A* to E" on their own? How does their experience of mental health challenges interfere with their journey? In order to make sure the person is overcoming these roadblocks, we identity mid-point "destinations," *B, C*, and *D*, which are reflected in the PCRP as short-term objectives or the person's accomplishments along the way. The solid arrow running throughout represents the range of professional services, natural support contributions, and self-directed actions that come together to the help the individual move toward their final destination – in this case getting back to part-time work.

What Is PCRP and How Is It Different?

Person-centered recovery planning (PCRP) is an ongoing process of collaboration between an individual and his or her professional providers and natural supporters that reflects consumer preferences and results in the co-creation of a recovery-oriented care plan (Adams and Grieder 2005). A person-centered approach to care planning differs from more traditional methods of treatment planning in the following ways: the plan…

1. Is oriented toward promoting recovery rather than only minimizing symptoms and dysfunction
2. Is based on the person's own goals and aspirations
3. Articulates the person's own role and the role of both paid and natural supports in assisting the person to achieve valued goals
4. Focuses and builds on the person's capacities, strengths, and interests
5. Maximizes the use of natural community settings and relationships wherever possible
6. Allows for uncertainty, setbacks, and disagreements as inevitable steps on the path to recovery (Tondora et al. 2005; Tondora et al. 2014; O'Brien and Lovett 1992)

Quality Process in PCRP

Best practice PCRP is about much more than the treatment plan document itself. Person-centered planning must be fundamentally rooted in a mutually respectful and healing relationship between a practitioner and a person served. Accreditation standards (CARF International 2011) clearly state that a signature alone is not "sufficient evidence" of meaningful participation in the plan's development and PCRP must involve significant shifts in how we partner with service users and their natural supporters.

Defining and Gathering the Team

- *Professional Supporters:* The recovery team responsible for the creation and implementation of the plan should include representatives from several professions and clinical traditions, including but not limited to psychiatry, nursing, psychology, social work, and occupational therapy working collaboratively in a range of roles (CARF International 2011; Liberman et al. 2001). While these professionals continue to play a valuable role in the PCRP process, there is increased emphasis on the role of family and other natural supporters as well as the person themselves as key members of the team.
- *Natural Supporters:* Natural supporters are those individuals that the person counts on outside the formal treatment system, e.g., friends, family members, neighbors, or even fellow parishioners who collectively make up the person's natural recovery network. If it is the person's preference, natural supporters should be encouraged to attend the PCRP meeting and educated in advance about their rights and responsibilities as a team member. Their contributions can include providing the team with a strengths-based view of the individual, corroborating data that the individual may not be able to express themselves, supporting the individual, and committing to assist with some tasks (natural support actions) on the plan to help further the person's attainment of their goals.
- *Person in Recovery:* The person served is the most essential – but all too often overlooked if not excluded – member of the team. Ideally, the person directing the planning meeting should be the person receiving services, and some individuals may already be comfortable in the "driver's seat." In other words, they are their own best advocates and can effectively articulate their preferences and priorities with confidence. However, others may benefit from some "driver's education." This is often the case when working with someone who has used services for many years. During this time, they may have become accustomed to the role of a "passenger" given the high value placed on compliance in traditional treatment environments. In addition, the degree of participation and self-direction for each person inevitably varies based on a number of factors including individual and cultural preference, clinical status, communication abilities, confidence level, stage of change, skills and experiences, etc. Recognizing that the concept of being in the "driver's seat" might not come naturally to many individuals, providing advance support and education can greatly enhance participant engagement. In various places around the country, peer specialists have proven to be particularly effective in this role offering coaching to help prepare individuals for upcoming PCRP meetings. Strategies such as this provide a practical and meaningful contribution to the team as a whole. "Pre-planning" with the individual gets the conversation started in advance of the team meeting itself – thereby promoting both quality and efficiency.

Person-Centered Assessment and Plan Documentation

Prior to discussing what many would refer to as the "core" of the treatment plan (i.e., goals/objectives, and interventions), a brief discussion about the quality of clinical assessments is necessary. A recovery plan is only as good as the assessment on which it is based! Two commonly neglected areas in the ongoing assessment process are the exploration of the person's strengths and assets as well as identification of the person's stage of change.

Strengths and Resources

The emphasis on individual and/or family "strengths" rather than their deficits or problems is sometimes a difficult process for professional service providers as well as the focus person themselves! It is not uncommon, for example, for individuals to have difficulty identifying their "strengths" as this has not historically been the focus of professional services and assessments. As a result, individuals may have also lost sight of their gifts and talents through years of struggles with their illness and recovery.

Simply asking the question "What are your strengths?" is often not enough to solicit information regarding resources and capabilities that can be built upon in the planning process. Sample questions to be used in strengths-based interviewing often involve probing in an indirect way, e.g., "What are you most proud of in your life?" or "What is the best compliment you ever received?" An additional strategy can be to prompt the person to think back to a time before their life became so difficult: what were they doing, what did they enjoy, what did they dream of doing when they grew up? etc. These are the types of questions which can unlock buried interests and generate sparks that can perhaps reignite hope in the person-centered planning process.

Strengths-based assessments are developed through an in-depth discussion with the individual as well as attempts to solicit collateral information from others in the person's life (or referral sources). Thoughtful consideration should be given to not only the individual's current strengths and resources but also to those that are part of the person's past. This may include consideration of talents, interests, accomplishments, previously effective coping strategies, as well as those that are available in the family, support network, service system, and the community at large.

Stage of Change

A second commonly neglected area in the comprehensive assessment includes consideration of the person's "stage of change" as it relates to various aspects of their life and recovery. Increasingly there is recognition of the importance of understanding the individual's readiness for change in order to be most effective in promoting and supporting a person's recovery journey. In the early 1990s, Prochaska and DiClemente (Prochaska 1992) promoted their trans-theoretical model with stages that help to provide a nonlinear view of the process of change. Another approach to thinking about stages of change was developed at Boston University's Center for Psychiatric Rehabilitation (Anthony and Liberman 1986). In this framework, a person may initially feel overwhelmed by their diagnosis of mental illness and unable to see the possibility of change, but then gradually find hope and take action as they advance in their recovery.

The purpose of assessing the various stages of change is not to "label" people but to reach a richer understanding of the person which then informs the development of the recovery plan. For example, it is not unusual in the mental health field to find plans written as if everyone is in the action stage of change: ready, willing, and able to meet dynamic objectives and be an active participant in their own treatment. However, in some instances, people have a limited sense of their own recovery potential, and they may be overwhelmed or "externally motivated" for services (legal mandates). A well-intended plan that includes a multitude of intensive treatment activity groups 5 days a week is of little value and relevance for an individual who already feels besieged by their illness. Not considering the person's stage of change can lead to frustration and failure for the individual as well as for the provider. In these situations, it's not unusual to hear someone who does not engage in recommended services described as "non-compliant" or "in denial." A more person-centered understanding would be to appreciate that the person was not yet ready for those interventions and that the plan did not align with their stage of change.

The Importance of Understanding

Data collection alone is not sufficient to build a quality PCRP. At the conclusion of the assessment process, the data must be woven together in an integrated understanding of who the person is and what's important to them. This transitional step in plan development can be thought of as moving from the *what* (i.e., simple data and facts) to the *so what* (i.e., how do you make sense of all that data and what are the key themes). This type of deeper understanding is documented in a section of the chart titled narrative diagnostic, interpretative, or integrative summary.

Conceptually, it is important to understand the role of the summary as it reflects both the practitioner's professional interpretation of the data and the person's unique perspective based on his or her lived experience. A well-written summary helps to clarify the individual's primary motivation for change (i.e., most valued recovery goals) and should include what is known about the person's strengths, cultural world view, stage of change, challenges and symptoms, and any interrelationships or themes within the data – especially for individuals who have co-occurring disorders (Prochaska 1992). The summary is an essential transitional step between assessment and planning. It helps to establish common ground and should guide the creation of a highly individualized and responsive set of services and supports.

Developing the depth of understanding reflected in an integrated summary typically requires some degree of clinical skill and experience. Ideally, it is shared with the person as a way of building a healing partnership based on transparency, respect, and compassion. Despite the importance of this planning component, the integrated summary is all too often overlooked in community mental health practice as practitioners struggle with the burden of its documentation. Models for documenting the integrated summary have been offered that outline a useful framework for capturing the relevant information for a person-centered summary in a manner that incorporates the individual's own understanding and perspective (Adams and Grieder 2005).

The Role of Culture in PCRP and Person-Centered Understanding

The experience of individuals from a marginalized identity group, such as people of color, may be more fully captured through the Cultural Formulation Interview (CFI) of the Diagnostic and Statistical Manual of Mental Disorders (DSM) (Lewis-Fernández et al. 2016). The use of more culturally responsive tools such as the CFI is critical in PCRP as an individual's level of participation in the process, preferences around decision-making, and personally valued vision of recovery is inevitably influenced by their cultural worldview. In addition, cultural factors related to the individual's psychosocial environment must be considered, including their potential experience of trauma and discrimination.

At its core, person-centered care and planning aim to increase one's degree of freedom: freedom to build a good life in a community of your choice, freedom to realize your full potential, freedom from oppression, freedom to control choices that impact your life and your experience in care. Now more than ever before, both the COVID-19 pandemic and recent violence against people of color have made painfully clear the fact that not all people are equally free.

Even treatment systems that strive to be recovery-oriented and person-centered are challenged by staggering disparities in access to care, health, and recovery outcomes, as well as the use of involuntary and restrictive treatment interventions. In this sense, people of color and other individuals who are frequently marginalized based upon their sexual orientation, gender, religion, national origin, etc. often experience – both individually and collectively – an additional layer of trauma, both inside and outside mental health treatment systems.

Truly committing to person-centered care and planning means accepting our vulnerability to the types of oppression and discrimination that plague our broader communities. This fact can further complicate the ability to form the trusting and healing partnerships that are the foundation of PCRP. The full impact of person-centered recovery planning will never be realized unless the mental health system is explicitly talking – and doing something – about discrimination, social injustice, and trauma. While a complete discussion of this urgent topic is beyond the scope of this chapter, the American Psychiatric Association's Presidential Task Force to Address Structural Racism Throughout Psychiatry is a valuable source of materials and resources (https://www.psychiatry.org/psychiatrists/structural-racism-task-force).

Core Elements of the PCRP

The person-centered plan can be thought of as a written contract between a person and his/her network of supporters – a contract that outlines a more hopeful vision for the future and how all will work together to achieve it. The development of the plan should be a stepwise process in which each step builds on the one that proceeds it. Sometimes referred to as a logic model, the stacked pyramid (Adams and Grieder 2005) in Fig. 2 is a useful image to reinforce this notion: if one step is skipped or neglected, the foundation to support what follows is compromised and the quality of the process as a whole is at risk.

We have touched on a number of these elements throughout the chapter and will now offer more detailed information around the "core" documentation tasks of the PCRP itself.

Prioritization

Treatment plans are often created with an unrealistic multitude of goals. These plans are cumbersome for the practitioner to write. More importantly, they are overwhelming to the person served and do not serve as a reasonable roadmap to recovery. There can be tension between the viewpoint of the professional service provider and the perspective of the person served on the priorities to be pursued in the plan. From the provider point of view, assuring the ultimate health and safety of the individual typically takes precedence over the preferences of the person served. However, even in those situations in which there is disagreement, recovery-oriented practitioners remain engaged and support the person's right to take reasonable risks to further their growth and recovery.

Goals

The creation of the PCRP should begin with, and flow from, a meaningful and motivating goal statement which reflects something the individual would like to achieve. Before determining the types of services that might be helpful for a person, we must first consider what kind of life they

Fig. 2 Logic model for PCRP

want for themselves. Put simply, in the person-centered world, you can't know what a person *needs* until you first understand what they *want* (ViaHope n.d.). Goals reflect a person's longer-term vision of recovery along with a person's hopes and dreams for the future.

When crafting the goal statements, it is perfectly acceptable, and in fact encouraged, to support the person in "thinking BIG." Providers should NOT become overly concerned about whether or not the goal statement is "realistic." Determining what is realistic (or not) is a slippery slope and often allows unspoken biases or assumptions to come into play. Ideally, the goal is expressed in the person's own words, and it is based on the person's unique interests, preferences, strengths, culturally informed values, and their vision of a good life – not simply the amelioration of symptoms.

Strengths and Resources

Strengths play a vital role in a person-centered plan. Strengths serve as major source of hope throughout the recovery process, and the plan writer must be creative in actively using them within the PCRP itself. Strengths should not be solicited only to sit on a shelf! Rather, a woman with a love of animals who is struggling with her weight and social isolation might be motivated around regular walks to the dog park. An individual who is deeply spiritual might prefer to be connected to the agency's chaplain or a local faith-based healer. The essential point is to think creatively about how best to use the individual's strengths and interests as a way to help them move forward in their recovery.

Barriers

While person-centered planning strives to capitalize on the strengths of the person served, it is also true that the "roadblocks" which interfere with goal attainment often take the shape of mental health-related limitations, experiences, or symptoms. These, too, have a place in the comprehensive person-centered plan. Barriers should be acknowledged alongside assets and strengths as this is essential for justifying care and the "medical necessity" of the professional supports we provide. A recognition of barriers can inform the development of various professional interventions and natural supports, which might be advantageous to the individual in the service of his or her recovery. The difference in a person-centered plan is that the barrier does not become the *exclusive and dominant* focus of the plan. It only takes on meaning to the extent that it is interfering with the attainment of larger life goals.

Objectives

Objectives, sometimes referred to as "short-term goals," are best thought of as milestones that break down longer-term aspirations into meaningful and positive short-term changes. They should reflect a concrete change in functioning, change in behavior, or change in quality of life, that, when achieved, are "proof" that the person is overcoming barriers and making progress. Since objectives serve as a source of measurement, they must be specific, measurable, attainable, relevant, and time-framed – qualities often referred to using the SMART acronym.

Short-term objectives are often the most challenging component in the plan to develop, as plan writers need to honor these technical criteria while at the same time crafting person-centered objectives that feel meaningful and authentic to the person. As with all aspects of the plan, objectives on person-centered plans are co-created with the person served as a way to demonstrate that meaningful progress is being made. In other words, they need to reflect a "step in the right direction" that is valued by the person as this helps build momentum going forward.

Perhaps the most frequent problem seen in creating a quality PCRP is the confusion between objectives and services or interventions. Service participation should not be the default objective! Attending a group session or individual therapy appointment does not in and of itself automatically lead to meaningful changes in the person's life or behavior. Incorporating the phrase "as evidenced by" can be a useful tool in describing objectives. Consider, for example, a woman with cutting behaviors associated with a trauma history who wishes to reconcile with her estranged husband. In this case, the objective is NOT that she will attend dialectical behavior therapy. DBT is the *intervention*. Instead, the objective should focus on the positive behavior that may develop as a result of DBT participation. A meaningful objective might be that she will learn how to use mindfulness techniques to reduce instances of self-injury *as evidenced by* reducing instances of self-harming behavior to no more than one episode of cutting per week for 2 consecutive weeks. Crafting the objectives in this way is necessary both to demonstrate the medical necessity of the plan and to truly promote positive change.

Services/Interventions

Last but not least, we consider the final element of the person-centered recovery plan, i.e., the interventions section which may also be referred to as the "methods," "actions," or "services" section. These elements of a person-centered recovery plan specify the activities of multidisciplinary staff, family, peers, and other natural supports in the person's life community. Specific examples might be medications, psychotherapy, self-help and peer support, exercise and nutrition guidance, wellness activities, spiritual practices and affiliations, homeopathic and naturopathic remedies, cultural healing practices/involvement of indigenous healers, and a range of rehabilitation opportunities such as supported housing, supported education, and supported employment.

While these types of services vary widely in terms of their design and intended purpose, certain quality criteria are applicable across all services. These criteria include assuring that services:

- Respect the individual's choices and preferences
- Are congruent with the person's assessed stage of change, e.g., individuals who are in the early phases of their recovery journey might prefer interventions such as outreach, relationship building, practical help, and crisis intervention. An individual in a more action-oriented stage may be ready to engage in counseling, skills training, self-help groups, etc.
- Clearly describe how the service is intended to overcome barriers identified in the assessment process
- Directly address the objective that they are associated with
- Promote accountability by detailing WHO is delivering the service, WHAT the professional service is (e.g., a title), WHEN it is delivered (i.e., frequency and duration), and WHY (i.e., individualized intent/purpose of the intervention as it relates to a specific objective).

One primary distinction between a more traditional treatment plan and a comprehensive person-centered plan is the inclusion of documented action steps in the PCRP by the person and any involved natural supporters. Traditional treatment plans often limit the interventions section of the planning document to reflect only those treatments that clinical, rehabilitation, medical, and other professionals are paid to deliver to the person served. They miss a key opportunity to capitalize on the resources and talents of the person themselves and other members of their recovery network. While professional services *are* an essential part of the plan, a high-quality, comprehensive PCRP *also* highlights the role of natural supporters and/or the person served.

Evaluating Progress and Updating the Plan

Progress notes serve multiple functions. They provide a written record of treatment activities and are part of the documentation required in billing for the service being provided. In order to meet payer and regulatory requirements, documentation for all billable services should link back to the assessment, narrative summary, and plan. Specifically, progress notes should reference which objective is being addressed by the service and what was the immediate impact of that intervention. Each progress note is in essence a mini-assessment that evaluates the effectiveness of services and informs the next steps for continued support of the individual's recovery.

The recovery plan as a whole should also be considered a living document – if it stays in a file drawer until the next time it's due for revision, it becomes simply a paperwork exercise and loses its impact and value in guiding the daily work. It should be utilized and reviewed for relevance regularly based on the emergence of new information, enhanced understanding, and unexpected developments or stressors. Reviews of the recovery plan should not be triggered only by "crisis" events but also by the successful attainment of goals and objectives and the need to plan for next steps.

The Role of a Psychiatrist in PCRP

While every member of the treatment team has an important contribution to make in the creation and implementation of a PCRP, the psychiatrist role carries with it unique skills and opportunities as well as, at times, frustrations. Issues that impact how psychiatrists participate in PCRP include organizational culture and leadership. Workloads, productivity demands, and time constraints are also influential, as well as the physician's interest and skill.

Psychiatrists often express frustration that their role is limited to that of being merely a prescriber. Unfortunately, in many settings this is a reality. Physicians are often the highest paid individual in a provider organization, and there is a lot of pressure to assure that the psychiatrist's work is cost-effective. At the same time, psychiatric services are billed at a higher rate than other psychosocial interventions, and their work represents an important source of revenue for the organization, which helps to offset expenses. Moreover, the demand for physician time often exceeds availability, and any tasks or responsibilities, which take a doctor away from one-to-one patient contacts that usually focus on psychopharmacology and related medical concerns, are viewed as problematic and costly.

While the psychiatrist may be considered to be a member of the treatment team, the ability of the psychiatrist to actually participate in team meetings and treatment planning with the person served and other members of the team is often limited. Sometimes the psychiatrist is asked to sign off on a treatment plan although they have had very limited involvement in the process. One result of this separation of roles and participation is that psychopharmacologic interventions are not well integrated into an overall multidisciplinary approach to support each individual's unique recovery journey. Medications work best when they are part of an overall plan and the relationship between symptom reduction and other interventions in achieving objectives is clear. As with any other intervention or service, the expected contribution and purpose of psychiatric services as part of an overall plan need to be explicit.

Beyond a doctor's ability to prescribe, psychiatrists often have important training and skills to contribute to PCRP. Sometimes, the psychiatrist can be an effective team leader and facilitate team meetings. Many psychiatrists are especially good at developing formulations which then serve as the foundation of a plan. Often there are medical issues that impact a person served, and the psychiatrist can help the team to understand how these impact recovery. Coordinating services with an individual's primary care provider is another role for the team psychiatrist. This role is especially critical for persons with co-occurring substance use disorders, particularly in light of the increasing prevalence of MAT (medically assisted treatment).

In order to assure that the unique and valuable contributions of psychiatrists in promoting person-centered planning is maximized, their real-time participation in team meetings is essential. Making this a priority and allowing for the time and resources to support this level of involvement are largely a function of organizational leadership and establishing the right operational and clinical priorities. Simply stated, participation in PCRP and treatment team meetings needs to be an explicit part of the psychiatrists' job description, duties, and responsibilities, as well as an element of their performance evaluation.

In many provider organizations, this is already happening. Both persons served and team colleagues are reaping the benefits of this level of physician participation in PCRP. In settings where this is not the usual practice, psychiatrists need to become advocates for change in policies and practice within the treatment systems where they work. Time needs to be allocated, and expectations need to be clear to all members of the staff. Ideally, training in PCRP and how to work effectively in a multidisciplinary team should be part of the curriculum during psychiatry residency programs. Psychiatrists who feel that they lack the skills necessary to promote and practice PCRP can avail themselves of many available training opportunities, including the *Recovery-Oriented Care in Psychiatry Curriculum* offered online by the American Psychiatric Association and the American Association of Community Psychiatrists (https://www.psychiatry.org/psychiatrists/practice/professional-interests/recovery-oriented-care/recovery-oriented-care-in-psychiatry-curriculum).

In summary, if psychiatrists want to play a greater role in the care of persons served and be more than just prescribers, active participation in PCRP provides a potentially powerful strategy for enhancing organizational performance, improving clinical outcomes, and increasing personal job satisfaction.

Summary

The potential power of person-centered recovery planning has led to a call for its widespread adoption by many stakeholders around the world. Despite this sense of urgency, there remains much confusion regarding what PCRP looks like in practice and how exactly it differs from traditional models of treatment planning and clinical practice. This chapter has attempted to address this confusion and move past the legacy of low expectations that has dominated mental health treatment systems for far too long.

PCRP holds high expectations for meaningful outcomes across a broad range of quality-of-life areas that go far beyond the reduction of hospitalization or the maintenance of clinical stability. People receiving mental health services essentially want, and deserve, the same things out of life as anyone else – a home, family, faith, health, etc. People want to *thrive* in their recovery, not just to *survive* their illnesses. Person-centered recovery planning is one tool the system can use to help people in this process.

PCRP Illustration: Roma Example

The following pages demonstrate how the practice of PCRP might be applied using the experience of "Roma" as an example. Roma's traditional, problem-focused treatment plan is followed by a sample person-centered recovery plan as a means of illustrating the stark contrast between these two approaches.

Assessment

History, Demographics, and Presenting Issue

- 29-year-old, Puerto Rican female treated on and off in the XYZ system of care for 15 years.
- Diagnosis of major depression, post-traumatic stress disorder, and poly-substance abuse.
- History of incarceration for drug-related offenses (possession of cocaine, theft, prostitution) and risk of injury to a minor (repeated DUI with children in her car; leaving children unattended during drug use).

- Mother to a 14-year-old daughter and a 9-year-old son who are in the custody of her cousin who is a supportive family member.
- Resided with her cousin and children upon release from prison 6 months ago when she was also referred to a variety of community-based health services.
- While living with her cousin, Roma started drinking, stole money to buy alcohol, and left the children unattended while she was supposed to be supervising them. There are frequent verbal "blow-outs" with her teenage daughter. On one occasion, Roma slapped her across the face when she was drunk. Roma's cousin is willing to let Roma visit with her children, but she asked Roma to leave the apartment until she "cleaned up her act."
- Department of Children and Families (DCF) is involved. When Roma had to leave her cousin's apartment, her DCF worker suggested she seek temporary housing and services at a local transitional shelter. She has been at the shelter now for a month, and she makes it clear that she wants to work toward regaining custody of her children.

Family Background/Early Childhood

- Born in Puerto Rico, the 4th of 5 children.
- Mother reportedly suffered from serious mental illness and abandoned the children when Roma was 6 years old. She was then raised by her maternal grandmother until the age of 8 when the grandmother passed away suddenly. Roma moved in with her biological father, who began sexually abusing her until she became pregnant by him at the age of 14. Roma ran away from home, contacted extended family in the USA, and relocated to Massachusetts to live with a maternal aunt and uncle. The aunt and uncle are now deceased, but Roma continues to be close with her cousin.

Education/Employment

- Average student but avid reader who also excelled in creative writing and arts classes.
- Roma dropped out of high school midway in her junior year when she became involved in a number of abusive relationships and turned to drugs and alcohol as she became increasingly depressed.
- Has worked off and on as a housecleaner for the past decade; however, difficulties with mental health issues and substance abuse have made it difficult for her to finish school or maintain a job for any period of time. While at the Shelter, Roma has been volunteering to help with some clerical and reception tasks.

Health Status

- Hepatitis C due to history of IV drug use. Reports chronic fatigue, joint pain, and GI issues. Primary care doctor is concerned about liver damage and has referred Roma to a male specialist for evaluation and treatment, but Roma has been unwilling to attend appointments with him.

Mental Health Symptoms and Treatment

- Long history of suicidal ideation. On two occasions (over 5 years ago), she overdosed on her meds requiring both medical and psychiatric hospitalization. Currently, Roma denies suicidal ideation, and she has been using her meds effectively to alleviate her symptoms.
- Reports severe sleep disturbance (unable to sleep through the night due to nightmares) and severe fatigue (unable to get out of bed in the morning).
- Struggling to look for work or find an apartment as she is feeling very overwhelmed. In

the past, Roma has had difficulty staying organized around her bills and focusing on her budget. Her inability to pay rent on time has led to instability in housing for her and children. In addition, she admits to being irritable and having volatile interpersonal relationships, especially with her eldest daughter, with whom she is having frequent verbal (and on one occasion, physical) arguments.

Alcohol/Drug Use

- History of polysubstance use, but her drug of choice for the past 10 years has been alcohol. When drinking, judgment can be significantly impaired, and behavior can be aggressive. Roma has been unable to sustain her sobriety for an extended period of time. Reports she drinks to "numb out" when she can't handle the stress of her life. Roma does admit to recent "slips," and her cousin reports that her attendance at AA/NA has dropped off in the past 2 months. Roma says she has been clean since staying at the shelter, and she seems motivated to stay sober and to find alternative, healthy ways to manage her health and stress levels.

Strengths, Interests, and Goals

- Motivated to put her "life back together."
- Deeply loving mother – strong desire to improve her relationships with her children and "be a good role model."
- Supportive cousin who has helped her provide for her children through the years.
- Well-liked by other clients at the Shelter. Doing well as a volunteer in the reception area.
- "Escapes" through painting as well as reading and writing poetry. Enjoys all forms of artistic expression. Would like to finish high school and someday find work in an environment where she can be around books or artists.

Integrated Summary

Roma is a 29-year-old Puerto Rican woman and a deeply loving mother. Through the years, she has relied on the support of a cousin to provide for her minor age children as she struggled to manage a serious trauma history and subsequent medical and behavioral health issues (hepatitis C, major depression, PTSD, poly-substance abuse). She was recently referred to a comprehensive care coordination program by a representative from DCF after she was asked to leave her cousin's apartment, with whom she had been living, due to frequent volatile arguments with her 14-year-old daughter and a suspected relapse on alcohol. Roma's daughter is currently at the same age that Roma was when she became pregnant with her as a result of sexual abuse and incest at the hands of her own father. Unresolved trauma issues appear to be triggering an increase in symptoms and making it particularly difficult for Roma to parent her daughter and manage her recovery. In addition, Roma has been reluctant to follow up on treatment for her hepatitis C which may be due to her trauma history and discomfort with male providers.

Roma is living in a Transitional Shelter, and while she is feeling very overwhelmed and distressed by her situation, she is hopeful regarding the program and has made it clear that her priority goal is to work toward regaining custody of her children. She is in the action stage of change and is motivated to work with her providers in order to develop the stability and skills needed to be the best mother she can be. High-priority assessed needs include connection to specialty medical services as well as the development of parenting and communication skills, symptom management/coping skills, and independent living skills associated with household management (e.g., budgeting).

Roma has a number of strengths and interests to draw upon in her recovery. She is a devoted mother who has demonstrated significant resilience having survived multiple traumas and losses in her life. Consistent with her culture of origin, she places a high value on family support, has benefitted from a close relationship with her cousin, and may prefer natural supports to formal treatment services. Roma is highly creative and artistic and has found refuge in painting, which she uses as a coping skill.

Roma Traditional Treatment Plan

Problem #1: Chronic psychiatric issues (depression and PTSD; noncompliance with treatment and medications; impulse control issues and poor judgment in parenting role); unable to live independently or manage activities of daily living on her own due to co-occurring disorder.

Goal: Achieve and maintain psychiatric stability

Objectives:

1. Roma will be med-compliant for the next 90 days.
2. Roma will have increased insight into her symptoms and behavior

Interventions:

1. Case Manager will communicate with shelter staff to verify Roma's compliance with medication.
2. Therapist provide twice monthly depression treatment to address Roma's irritability and aggression.
3. Psychiatrist will provide medication evaluation and management and monitor response.

Problem #2: Long history of poly-substance use (can become aggressive when under the influence; abuse and neglect of children led to their removal of children by DCF; not attending 12-step as directed; minimizes role of substances in her life despite hepatitis C illness)

Goal: Abstinence from all drugs including alcohol

Objectives:

1. Roma will attend AA/NA meetings 3× per week
2. Roma will stay home at night and try to sleep throughout the night without use of substances
3. Roma will submit weekly urine screens to her probation officer.

Interventions:

1. Case manager will monitor Roma's attendance at 12-step meetings and secure urine screens for her P.O.
2. Substance abuse counselor will provide weekly relapse prevention meetings and report absences to PO.
3. Psychiatrist will prescribe Antabuse to deter Roma's drinking and remind her of dangers of continued drinking due to her liver damage.

Roma's Person-Centered Recovery Plan

There are *many* possible ways that a quality PCRP might come together. This sample is organized around Roma's overarching life goal of being a better mother and getting her kids back. Although she says she wants to go back to school to complete her degree, that is clearly a longer-term goal. Her first priority is reuniting with her children. It is also possible for the plan to be split up into more than one focus area. Note that while there are only two interventions in this sample plan for the psychiatrist, there is clearly the potential for additional medical interventions, e.g., psychiatric evaluation, medication management, perhaps a prescription for Naltrexone, etc. It is also important to remember that "our" Roma is in the active stage of change and is eager to participate in a range of services that may help her to achieve her objectives. If she was precontemplative about her illnesses, a much simpler plan may have been developed, typically with fewer objectives and interventions. Any of these structures can be appropriate provided they are mutually negotiated in partnership with the person in recovery.

Recovery Goal

> I want to be a better mother for my kids and work toward getting them back.

Objective 1 (Targeting Conflicts with Daughter)

Roma will have a minimum of three successful supervised (by cousin) visits with her daughter within 30 days as evidenced by cousin's report that Roma visited without verbal or physical altercations

Interventions and Action Steps

1. Sally Rodriquez, Primary Clinician, will meet with Roma one-time weekly for the next 3 months in order to assist her in identifying and managing mental health and trauma symptoms which impact her parenting and trigger her angry reactions with her daughter.
2. Bob Smith, Rehabilitation Specialist, will provide twice monthly anger management group for 3 months in order to teach Roma conflict resolution and positive coping strategies.
3. Audrey Jenkins, Peer Community Connector, will meet with Roma two times over 2 weeks in order to help Roma to identify and access parenting-support groups/organizations in the community so she can develop a healthy peer network. In addition, Ms. Jenkins will assist Roma in learning about arts-related events/activities in the local community that Roma and her daughter might attend together on their visits.

   Client Self-Directed Wellness and/or Natural Support Actions:
4. Within 2 weeks, Roma will develop a list of preferred arts-related activities she'd like to engage in with her daughter in order to help structure visits and draw upon their shared passion for the arts and creative expression
5. Roma's cousin will work with Roma and shelter staff in order to schedule visits and will report back to Team re: Roma's progress toward the above objective. Roma's cousin will also participate in NAMI-sponsored family-to-family program to receive education and support re: Roma's issues with depression and post-traumatic stress.

Objective 2: (Targeting Alcohol Use Which Complicates Serious Medical Issues)

Roma will maintain abstinence for the next 3 months as evidenced by self-report and feedback from her cousin.

Interventions

1. John Casey, Substance Abuse Coordinator, will provide one-time weekly Relapse Prevention group in order to teach Roma positive coping skills to deal with cravings and manage stressors/symptoms without substance use
2. Anthony Sells, M.D., will make a referral to a female hepatologist within the next 2 weeks, so that Roma can get connected to medical care for her hepatitis C.
3. Audrey Jenkins, Peer Community Connector, will meet with Roma to determine if she would like to see a female hepatologist and help her connect as needed. If Roma would like to stay with her current specialist, Ms. Jenkins will attend scheduled appointments with her to increase her sense of safety. Hepatologist will provide evaluation/ treatment and educate Roma about the dangers of continued drinking on her liver functioning to increase motivation for recovery.

   Client Self-Directed Wellness and/or Natural Support Actions
4. Roma to attend a minimum of 3 local AA/NA groups within 2 weeks to explore if 12-step program can be helpful source of support in learning positive ways to manage stressors without substance use

5. Roma's cousin will buy her a writing journal and book of poetry readings within 2 weeks in order to help Roma in practicing her preferred relaxation strategies daily before bed (as an alternative to drinking).

Objective 3 (Targeting Budgeting)

Roma will manage her monthly budget successfully as evidenced by her paying her Transitional Housing rental fee in full by the 5th of every month each month for the next 6 months. ("I need to learn how to stretch my money and pay my bills, so I can show DCF I can keep a roof over my kids' heads.")

Interventions and Action Steps

1. Anthony Sells, M.D., to provide medication evaluation and monitoring two times per month for the next 3 months for purpose of identifying possible medications to address Roma's complaints of inability to focus during periods of depression.
2. Mary Tomason, Rehab Specialist, to provide skill-building once a week for the next 6 months in order to build Roma's independence in managing her personal budget, e.g., providing instruction re: the process of writing checks and tracking balances in her check register.

   Client Self-Directed Wellness and/or Natural Support Actions
3. Within 1 week, Roma will identify any preferred priorities she has for limited "spending" money (e.g., art and painting supplies) so that she and her cousin can accurately report income to Rehab Specialist assisting with budgeting skills.
4. Within 2 weeks, Roma's cousin has agreed to help her outline and bring in records of her bills in order to assist Roma and Rehab Specialist in creating a budget.

References

Adams, N and Grieder, D. (2005). *Treatment Planning for Person-Centered Care: The Road to Mental Health and Addiction Recovery.* Elsevier/Academic Press.

American Psychiatric Association & American Association of Community Psychiatrists. (n.d.) *Person-Centered Planning and Shared Decision-Making: Recovery-Oriented Care in Psychiatry Curriculum, Module 3.* https://www.psychiatry.org/psychiatrists/practice/professional-interests/recovery-oriented-care/recovery-oriented-care-in-psychiatry-curriculum

Anthony, W. A., Liberman, R. P. (1986). The practice of psychiatric rehabilitation: historical, conceptual, and research base. *Schizophrenia Bulletin,* (12), 542–559.

Anthony, W. A. (1993). Recovery from mental illness: The guiding vision of the mental health service system in the 1990's. *Psychosocial Rehabilitation Journal,* (16) 11–23.

Bazelon Center for Mental Health Law & UPENN Collaborative on Community Integration, (2008). *In the Driver's Seat A Guide to Self-Directed Mental Health Care.* http://www.bazelon.org/wp-content/uploads/2017/01/Drivers-seat.pdf

CARF International (2011). Behavioral Health Standards Manual. Tucson, Arizona.

Center for Medicare and Medicaid Services, (2014). *Guidance to HHS Agencies for Implementing Principles of Section 2403(a) of the Affordable Care Act: Standards for Person-Centered Planning and Self-Direction in Home and Community-Based Services Programs. U.S. Department of Health & Human Services.* https://acl.gov/sites/default/files/programs/2017-03/2402-a-Guidance.pdf http://www.acl.gov/Programs/CDAP/OIP/docs/2402-a-Guidance.pdf (old link)

Connecticut Department of Mental Health and Addiction Services, (2008). *Commissioner's Policy Statement #33 on Individualized Recovery Planning.* http://www.ct.gov/dmhas/cwp/view.asp?a=2907&q=334664

Institute of Medicine. (2001). *Crossing the quality chasm: A new health system for the 21st century.* The National Academies Press. https://doi.org/10.17226/10027.

Institute of Medicine. (2006). *Improving the quality of health care for mental and substance-use conditions: Quality chasm series.* The National Academies Press. https://doi.org/10.17226/11470.

Lewis-Fernández, R., Krishan Aggarwal, N., Hinton, L., Hinton, D. E., & Kirmayer, L. J. (Eds.). (2016). *DSM-5® Handbook on the Cultural Formulation Interview.* American Psychiatric Association.

Liberman, R.P. et al. (2001). Requirements for Multidisciplinary Teamwork in Psychiatric Rehabilitation. *Psychiatric Services*, (52), 1333–42.

Lodge, A. C., Kaufman, L., & Manser, S. S. (2017). Barriers to implementing person-centered recovery planning in public mental health organizations in Texas: Results from nine focus groups. *Administration and Policy in Mental Health and Mental Health Services Research*, 44(3), 413–429. https://doi.org/10.1007/s10488-016-0732-7. PMID: 27037701.

O'Brien J, Lovett H. (1992). Finding a way toward everyday lives: The contribution of person-centered planning. *Pennsylvania Office of Mental Retardation.*

Prochaska, J.O. (1992). In search of how people change: Applications to addictive behaviors. *American Psychologist*, (47), 1102–1114.

Stanhope V, Ingoglia C, Schmelter B, et al., (2013). Impact of person-centered planning and collaborative documentation on treatment adherence. *Psychiatric Services*, 64(1),76–79.

Substance Abuse and Mental Health Services Administration, (2010). *SAMHSA's Working definition of recovery.* U.S. Department of Health and Human Services. https://store.samhsa.gov/sites/default/files/d7/priv/pep12-recdef.pdf

Substance Abuse and Mental Health Addiction Services Administration. (2016). *Criteria for the Demonstration Program to Improve Community Mental Health Centers and to Establish Certified Community Behavioral Health Clinics.* U.S. Department of Health and Human Services. https://www.samhsa.gov/sites/default/files/programs_campaigns/ccbhc-criteria.pdf

The Joint Commission, (2010). *Advancing Effective Communication, Cultural Competence, and Patient- and Family-Centered Care: A Roadmap for Hospitals.* https://www.jointcommission.org/-/media/tjc/documents/resources/patient-safety-topics/health-equity/aroadmapforhospitalsfinalversion727pdf.pdf?db=web&hash=AC3AC4BED1D973713C2CA6B2E5ACD01B

Tondora J, Pocklington S, Gorges A, et al. (2005). Implementation of person-centered care and planning. From policy and practice to evaluation. *Substance Abuse and Mental Health Services Administration.*

Tondora, J., O'Connell, M., Miller, R., Dinzeo, T., Bellamy, C., Andres-Hyman, R., & Davidson, L. (2010). A clinical trial of peer-based culturally responsive person-centered care for psychosis for African Americans and Latinos. *Clinical Trials*, 7(4), 368–379.

Tondora J, Miller R, Slade M, et al. (2014). *Partnering for recovery in mental health: A practical guide to person-centered planning.* John Wiley & Sons.

Tondora, J., Stanhope, V., Grieder, D. et al. (2021). The Promise and Pitfalls of Electronic Health Records and Person-Centered Care Planning. *Journal of Behavioral Health Services and Research.* https://doi.org/10.1007/s11414-020-09743-z

U.S. Department of Health and Human Services. (2003). Achieving the promise: Transforming mental health care in America. President's New Freedom Commission on Mental Health, Final Report (Pub. No. SMA-03–3832).

Via Hope. (n.d.). *Person Centered Recovery Planning Curriculum and Resources.* https://www.viahope.org/programs/recovery-institute-2/person-centered-recovery-planning-implementation/

Cultural and Linguistic Competence

Russell F. Lim and Francis G. Lu

Introduction

The diversity of the United States has increased dramatically over the last 30 years and will continue to change in the next 40 years. According to the US Census population estimates in 2019, only 60.1% of the population is White alone, not Hispanic or Latino; 18.5% Hispanic or Latino; 13.4% Black or African-American alone; 1.3% American Indian or Alaskan Native alone; 5.9% Asian alone; 0.2% Native Hawaiian or other Pacific Islander alone; and 2.8% two or more (US Census Bureau 2019). The fastest-growing racial or ethnic group in the United States is people who are two or more races, who are projected to grow over 200% by 2060 to 6.2%. The next fastest is the Asian alone population, which is projected to almost double to 9.1%, followed by Hispanics whose population will increase to 27.5%. In 2060, 44.3% of the population will be White alone, not Hispanic or Latinx; 15.0% Black or African-American; 1.4% American Indian or Alaskan Native alone; and 0.3% Native Hawaiian or other Pacific Islander alone (Vespa et al. 2020). Immigrants and their US-born children number approximately 85.7 million people, or 26% of the US population, according to the 2020 Current Population Survey (CPS), a slight decline from 2019. The Pew Research Center has projected that the immigrant-origin share of the population will rise to about 36% by 2065 (Batalova et al. 2021).

These population demographic projections have significant implications for community mental health, as many immigrant and ethno-racial populations have their mental health needs taken care of by the public sector, bringing up issues of limited English proficiency (LEP), the use of interpreters, understanding the patient's explanatory models, and the use of complementary and alternative medicine. Further, the Institute of Medicine's report, *Unequal Treatment* (Smedley et al. 2002), indicated that ethno-racial patients have reduced access to services and receive a lower quality of medical and psychiatric treatment than mainstream patients even when socioeconomic status is matched with mainstream patients. Providers in community and other public sector settings will need to develop a set of culturally and linguistically competent attitudes and assessment/treatment skills to properly assess and treat the increasingly culturally diverse patient population. The use of the Outline for Cultural Formulation (OCF) that originally appeared in the *Diagnostic and Statistical Manual, Fourth Edition* (DSM-IV) (American Psychiatric Association 1994) and revised in the DSM-5 (American Psychiatric Association 2013) is helpful in this

R. F. Lim
Comprehensive Psychiatric Services, Chula Vista, CA, USA

F. G. Lu (✉)
University of California, Davis, Cupertino, CA, USA

W. E. Sowers et al. (eds.), *Textbook of Community Psychiatry*,
https://doi.org/10.1007/978-3-031-10239-4_11

regard. This chapter concludes with a look at examples of state legislation affecting the practice of culturally competent community psychiatry.

Stigma, Recovery, and Cultural Competence

Before addressing how to provide culturally appropriate care, we must address the barriers that create the mental health disparities minorities experience. These have been documented in *Unequal Treatment*, the *Surgeon General's Supplement to the Report on Mental Health: Culture, Race, and Ethnicity* (US Dept. of Health and Human Services, Office of the Surgeon General 2001), and *Achieving the Promise: Transforming Mental Health Care in America* (New Freedom Commission on Mental Health 2003). One major barrier is the stigma of mental illness, which can be defined as a cluster of negative attitudes and beliefs that motivate the public to fear, reject, avoid, and discriminate against people with mental illnesses. Stigma leads others to avoid living, socializing, working with, renting to, or employing people with mental disorders. This especially affects people with severe disorders. These negative attitudes are often internalized, leading to low self-esteem, isolation, and hopelessness, which may lead to concealed symptoms and failure to seek treatment. At a systems level, it deters the public from seeking and wanting to pay for care. People of color, women, LGBT persons, and/or those of religious faiths including Christianity can experience a "double stigma." That is to say that they are discriminated against for belonging to non-mainstream groups, and they still experience the stigma of having a mental illness.

Recovery-based practices (see chapter "Recovery and Person Centered Care: Empowerment, Collaboration and Integration") can be thought of as the antidote to stigma and can be defined as practices supporting a personal process of overcoming the negative impact of a psychiatric disability despite its continued presence. The elements of recovery include the instilling of hope; the use of appropriate medication and treatments; client empowerment; the use of community support; mental health education; self-help and spirituality/religion; and obtaining employment and meaningful activity. Service providers can apply the principles of cultural competence to recovery-based treatment, which involves assessment of the cultural background or identity of the patient and their experiences of *racism, sexism, colonialism, or homophobia*. Discrimination may be based on gender, sexual orientation, religious beliefs, ethnicity, language, age, or country of origin among other factors.

Clinicians can begin to build a patient's self-esteem and help them to develop coping skills that shield them from stigma and discrimination and help them make their community a safer place to be themselves. These include reducing the isolation caused by cultural differences and limited English proficiency (LEP) by providing community and peer support, as well as linguistically appropriate services and mental health education, and even encouraging clients to learn more English. Cultural competence in recovery would mean patient-centered service plans accounting for each person's individual cultural experience and avoiding stereotypical ideas that all people belonging to an ethnic group or speaking the same language have the same cultural beliefs. Trauma associated with discrimination, violence, or displacement must be acknowledged and addressed for healing to take place, along with medical needs and substance abuse. Treatment plans may include the use of traditional healers such as curanderos, shamans, medicine men, midwives, and alternative medicine such as acupuncture, ayurvedic or herbal medicine, meditation, tai chi, and yoga. Spirituality plays an important role and may or may not involve an organized religion and could be a belief in God, or a higher power, worshiping and respecting one's ancestors, or a belief in the spirit world. Recovery may also require the acquisition of new skills, job training, language proficiency, or obtaining decent housing, eligible entitlements, and US citizenship. Finally, culturally competent recovery-based practices mean to help the patient to reclaim their cultural identity, which they may have tried to deny due to internalized racism. By providing support to culturally diverse individuals and valuing their differences, providers in the community can promote healing through self-acceptance and stop the internalization of stigma (Ida 2007).

Definitions

Definitions of cultural and linguistic competence have evolved over the past 30 years. The practice of culturally appropriate assessment and treatment can be described as culturally competent, as first described by Terry Cross and others (Cross et al. 1989). The Federal Department of Health and Human Services' (DHHS) Agency for Healthcare Quality and Research noted these definitions based on 1998 and 2000 reports (Agency for Healthcare Research and Quality, Content last reviewed 2019):

Cultural Competence A set of congruent behaviors, attitudes, and policies that come together in a system or agency or among professionals that enables effective interactions in a cross-cultural framework.

Linguistic Competence Providing readily available, culturally appropriate oral and written language services to LEP (limited English proficiency) members through such means as bilingual/bicultural staff, trained medical interpreters, and qualified translators.

Cultural and Linguistic Competence The ability of healthcare providers and healthcare organizations to understand and respond effectively to the cultural and linguistic needs brought by the patient to the healthcare encounter.

Cultural competence requires organizations and their personnel to:

- Value diversity.
- Assess themselves.
- Manage the dynamics of difference.
- Acquire and institutionalize cultural knowledge.
- Adapt to diversity and the cultural contexts of individuals and communities served.

In 2013, the *National Standards for CLAS in Health and Health Care: A Blueprint for Advancing and Sustaining CLAS Policy and Practice* provided these more detailed, nuanced, and actionable definitions (US Department of Health and Human Services, Office of Minority Health 2013):

Culture The integrated pattern of thoughts, communications, actions, customs, beliefs, values, and institutions associated, wholly or partially, with racial, ethnic, or linguistic groups as well as religious, spiritual, biological, geographical, or sociological characteristics. Culture is dynamic in nature, and individuals may identify with multiple cultures over the course of their lifetimes.

Cultural and Linguistic Competency The capacity for individuals and organizations to work and communicate effectively in cross-cultural situations through the adoption and implementation of strategies to ensure appropriate awareness, attitudes, and actions and using policies, structures, practices, procedures, and dedicated resources that support this capacity.

- Cultural Competency: A developmental process in which individuals or institutions achieve increasing levels of awareness, knowledge, and skills along a cultural competence continuum. Cultural competence involves valuing diversity, conducting self-assessments, avoiding stereotypes, managing the dynamics of difference, acquiring and institutionalizing cultural knowledge, and adapting to diversity and cultural contexts in communities.

- Linguistic Competency: The capacity of individuals or institutions to communicate effectively at every point of contact. Effective communication includes the ability to convey information—both written and oral—in a manner that is easily understood by diverse groups, including persons of limited English proficiency, those who have low literacy skills or who are not literate, those having low health literacy, those with disabilities, and those who are deaf or hard of hearing.

Culturally and Linguistically Appropriate Services (CLAS) Services that are respectful of and responsive to individual cultural health beliefs and practices, preferred languages, health literacy levels, and communication needs and employed by all members of an organization (regardless of size) at every point of contact.

Another important concept is cultural humility, defined by Tervalon and Murray-García (1998) as a lifelong process of self-reflection and self-critique. The provider of culturally competent care is encouraged to develop a respectful partnership with each patient through person-centered interviewing that explores similarities and differences between his or her own and each patient's priorities, goals, and capacities. Ideally, the conclusion of this cross-cultural exploration would be to develop an approach to managing clinical problems based on negotiation between the two culturally distinct perspectives. A culturally competent provider is open and flexible enough to identify the importance of differences between his or her orientation and that of each patient and to explore compromises that would be acceptable to both. Thus, a clinician applying the principles of cultural humility would not expect himself or herself to be an expert in cultural details or to take on other healer's roles such as a minister or an herbalist.

Federal Policies and National Standards

The federal government, as represented by Congress, and the agencies they fund, determines funding priorities and the delivery of services. In 1998, the DHHS Office of Minority Health conducted a national level review of existing cultural and linguistic competence standards and measures in order to propose a draft of national standards, known as the CLAS (culturally and linguistically appropriate services) Standards; in 2013, this document was revised and enhanced (US Department of Health and Human Services, Office of Minority Health 2013). The standards for health and healthcare organizations were informed by a careful review of key legislation, regulations, contracts, and standards currently in use by federal and state agencies and other national organizations. Proposed standards were then developed with input from a national advisory committee of policy administrators, healthcare providers, and health services researchers. Increasing from 14 to 15 standards, an overarching Principal Standard was added: "1. Provide effective, equitable, understandable, and respectful quality care and services that are responsive to diverse cultural health beliefs and practices, preferred languages, health literacy, and other communication needs" (see Table 1). It is important to note that standards 5–8 are about Communication and Language Assistance which were created for those individuals with LEP, defining care that is compatible with cultural health beliefs and in the patient's preferred language. These standards include providing signage, literature, and interpretation in the patient's preferred language so that family members do not have to be used as interpreters. In addition,

Table 1 National Standards for Culturally and Linguistically Appropriate Services (CLAS) in Health and Health Care

The CLAS Standards are intended to advance health equity, improve quality, and help eliminate healthcare disparities by establishing a blueprint for health and healthcare organizations to:
Principal Standard:
1. Provide effective, equitable, understandable, and respectful quality care and services that are responsive to diverse cultural health beliefs and practices, preferred languages, health literacy, and other communication needs.
Governance, Leadership, and Workforce:
2. Advance and sustain organizational governance and leadership that promotes CLAS and health equity through policy, practices, and allocated resources.
3. Recruit, promote, and support a culturally and linguistically diverse governance, leadership, and workforce that are responsive to the population in the service area
4. Educate and train governance, leadership, and workforce in culturally and linguistically appropriate policies and practices on an ongoing basis.
Communication and Language Assistance:
5. Offer language assistance to individuals who have limited English proficiency and/or other communication needs, at no cost to them, to facilitate timely access to all healthcare and services.
6. Inform all individuals of the availability of language assistance services clearly and in their preferred language, verbally and in writing.
7. Ensure the competence of individuals providing language assistance, recognizing that the use of untrained individuals and/or minors as interpreters should be avoided.
8. Provide easy-to-understand print and multimedia materials and signage in the languages commonly used by the populations in the service area.
Engagement, Continuous Improvement, and Accountability:
9. Establish culturally and linguistically appropriate goals, policies, and management accountability, and infuse them throughout the organization's planning and operations.
10. Conduct ongoing assessments of the organization's CLAS-related activities, and integrate CLAS-related measures into measurement and continuous quality improvement activities.
11. Collect and maintain accurate and reliable demographic data to monitor and evaluate the impact of CLAS on health equity and outcomes and to inform service delivery.
12. Conduct regular assessments of community health assets and needs and use the results to plan and implement services that respond to the cultural and linguistic diversity of populations in the service area.
13. Partner with the community to design, implement, and evaluate policies, practices, and services to ensure cultural and linguistic appropriateness.
14. Create conflict and grievance resolution processes that are culturally and linguistically appropriate to identify, prevent, and resolve conflicts or complaints.
15. Communicate the organization's progress in implementing and sustaining CLAS to all stakeholders, constituents, and the general public.

Note. Source: USDHHS, OMH, CLAS Standards, 2013, https://www.thinkculturalhealth.hhs.gov

they include supporting organizational cultural competence, such as strategic planning that specifies hiring and retention practices that encourage diversity with that matches the patient population. Training in cultural competence principles includes how to work effectively with the community and performing ongoing assessment of patient population demographics. A review process should be in place that is available to the public (see Table 1).

The first report on culturally competent mental healthcare created by a government agency was *Cultural Competence Standards in Managed Care Mental Health Services: Four Underserved/Underrepresented Racial/Ethnic Groups*, first published in 1998, and later distributed by the Substance Abuse and Mental Health Services Administration in 2001 (Western Intercollegiate Commission for Higher Education 1998). It detailed overall system standards and implementation guidelines, such as cultural competence planning, community outreach and education, and quality monitoring and improvement, as well as human resource development. These also included clinical standards, like access, triage, assessment, treatment, and discharge planning, and case management. Finally, it delineated guidelines for communication and patient self-help and carefully outlined the provider competencies of culturally specific knowledge and culturally generic attitudes and skills.

In 2000, the Office of Civil Rights empowered by White House Executive Order 13166 "Improving Access to Services for Persons with Limited English Proficiency (LEP)" required that all federal agencies formally address how they would provide access to their services to people with LEP; the 2004 revision is still in effect. DHHS issued guidance that included an "Effective Plan on Language Assistance for LEP Persons," stating that programs receiving federal funds must (1) identify individuals who need language services; (2) have language assistance services; (3) train staff to appropriately work with clients who need language assistance; (4) provide notice for people that services are available, such as signs in their language; and (5) be monitored and updated (US Department of Health and Human Services, Office of Civil Rights, Content last reviewed 2013).

The next report to be released was the Supplement to the Surgeon General's Report on Mental Health, *Mental Health: Culture, Race, and Ethnicity* (US Dept. of Health and Human Services, Office of the Surgeon General 2001), which established that ethnic minorities do not utilize mental health services as much as the majority population and that "culture counts." The supplement documented striking disparities in mental healthcare for racial and ethnic minorities involving access to care, appropriateness of treatment, overall quality of care, and treatment outcomes, as well as the fact that minorities are poorly represented in research studies. Together, these mental health disparities impose a greater burden of disability on racial and ethnic minorities. Some examples from each of the four chapters on the major racial and ethnic groups follow:

- Disproportionate numbers of African-Americans are overrepresented in the most vulnerable segments of the population—people who are homeless, incarcerated, in the child welfare system, victims of trauma—all populations with increased risks for mental disorders.
- As many as 40% of Hispanic Americans report LEP. Because few mental health professionals identify themselves as Spanish-speaking, most Hispanic Americans have limited access to ethnically or linguistically similar providers.
- The suicide rate among American Indians/Alaska Natives is 50% higher than the national rate; rates of co-occurring mental illness and substance abuse (especially alcohol) are also higher among Native youth and adults. Because few data have been collected, the full nature, extent, and sources of these disparities remain a matter of conjecture.
- Asian Americans/Pacific Islanders who seek care for a mental illness often present with more severe illnesses than other racial or ethnic groups. This, in part, suggests that stigma

and shame are critical deterrents to service utilization. It is also possible that mental illnesses may be undiagnosed or treated later in their course because they are expressed in symptoms of a physical nature.

The report concluded with "A Vision for the Future," in which recommendations were grouped in six areas: (1) continue to expand the science base, (2) improve access to treatment, (3) reduce barriers to treatment, (4) improve quality of care, (5) support capacity development, and (6) promote mental health.

Ruiz and Primm (2010) essentially updated this landmark 2001 report and extended its perspective to additional underserved populations beyond the four main US ethno-racial groups. Discussed in their book were issues related to underserved populations such as migrants, refugees, incarcerated individuals, and people experiencing homelessness. The book also addressed issues related to gender, sexual orientation, and age. Brief sections on training, education, and policy laid the foundation for assessing evidence-based approaches and outcomes in these diverse populations.

In 2003, the President's New Freedom Commission on Mental Health issued its report noted above. Through this document, the Bush Administration created policy to guide how mental health and health professionals ought to be recruited and trained to deliver services to diverse populations. Of the six goals discussed as strategies to transform the mental health system, two are most relevant to minority mental health disparities. The first is that mental healthcare is consumer and family driven, and the second is that disparities in mental health services are to be eliminated. Some of the specific recommendations included improved access to quality care that is culturally competent by recruiting and retaining racial and ethnic minority and bilingual professionals, developing and including curricula in all federally funded health and mental health training programs that address the impact of culture, race, and ethnicity on mental health, developing training and research programs targeting services to multicultural populations, and engaging minority consumers and families in workforce development, training, and advocacy.

Clinical Approaches

Staff Training: Diversity Training Versus Cultural Competence Training

Providing mental health services to a diverse population requires training that encompasses culturally relevant knowledge, attitudes, and skills. Cultural knowledge can be obtained from books, such as *Ethnicity and Family Therapy third edition,* edited by McGoldrick et al. (2005), but these references can also be used to create stereotypical lists of qualities and generalities that trainees memorize and may give trainees a false sense of security that they "know" everything about a particular group after reading a single chapter. The references may also give a good starting place for trainees to understand what is normative for an ethnic group and how to begin asking more culturally pertinent questions to understand the client that they have in the office.

In order to use resources like *Ethnicity and Family Therapy*, trainees should have diversity training, which helps them to develop attitudes that are accepting of cultural differences, then cultural competence training that teaches culturally generic skills, and then culturally specific knowledge. The reader is referred to the excellent books suggested as resources at the end of this chapter.

Concerning training in attitudes, our view is that cultural competence training for staff begins with creating an atmosphere where differences are acknowledged and celebrated. This begins with hiring staff from representative groups to allow the cultural perspective to be shared with other staff members, as well as providing culturally appropriate assessment and treatment planning, a process which begins with the use of the DSM-5 Outline for Cultural Formulation (OCF) and Cultural Formulation Interview (CFI) (American Psychiatric Association 2013), as discussed in the next section). Briefly, this means taking a person-centered approach, with a focus on the individual's cultural identity, cultural concepts of distress, and expected treatment. This requires more than just using the DSM-5 diagnosis by simply checking off diagnostic criteria. Clinicians must also review both the Culture-Related and Gender-Related Diagnostic Issues sections of the narrative descriptions of the disorders. The clinic can have case conferences that highlight the cultural aspects of cases through use of the OCF to provide much needed examples of its value to the differential diagnosis and treatment plan. The clinical environment should have signage in the appropriate languages and artwork representative of the patient population.

Diversity training exercises help staff to recognize similarities and differences in their cultural identities and become aware of subtle, unintentional, or implicit prejudices and biases that staff may have. A common 1-hour training exercise is to have staff introduce themselves in groups of six to eight in a way that does not just chronicle their training and jobs, but reveals where they are from, what languages they speak, and what are the important parts of their identity. They may even talk about the origin of their names and its meaning(s). On another occasion, a potluck can be scheduled when staff may also bring in a comfort food from their cultural group, explain to others what is in it, and how their family explained to them how it would help to make them feel better. Another approach is to celebrate ethnic holidays, like Cinco de Mayo, Chinese New Year, Chanukah, Kwanza, and Ramadan, and have a brief presentation on the holiday's meaning and customs. Finally, an hour can be taken with a small group to explore discussion questions from *Understanding Race, Ethnicity, and Power: The Key to Efficacy in Clinical Practice* by Elaine Pinderhughes (1989).

DSM- IV and DSM-5 Outline for Cultural Formulation (OCF)

DSM-IV initiated the OCF (located in Appendix I), and DSM-5 (located in Sect. III) revised it. While DSM-IV had a Glossary of Culture-Bound Syndromes in Appendix I, DSM-5 substituted a Glossary of Cultural Concepts of Distress that included nine well-studied examples in the Appendix. This latter term is much broader to encompass idioms of distress and explanatory models or perceived causes of illness as well as cultural syndromes. The DSM-5 OCF is a useful framework for organizing a culturally competent assessment of a culturally diverse patient, and it contains five sections or parts (Table 3). Clinicians are asked to obtain information on the first four fields of interrelated information and finally to summarize and apply it to the differential diagnosis and treatment plan. *The Clinical Manual of Cultural Psychiatry, second edition* (Lim 2015), provides several case examples and video vignettes of its use with persons from diverse backgrounds involving ethnicity/race, gender, sexual orientation and gender identity, and religion/spirituality in its overview of the OCF.

Part A: Cultural Identity of the Individual

Asking a patient about their cultural identity can be accomplished by performing a social and developmental history with attention being paid to the patient's country of birth, ethnicity of his or her parents, grandparents, and language(s) spoken. Ethnicity may also be assessed by asking the

Table 2 Discussion questions from "Understanding Race, Ethnicity, and Power"

1. What was your first experience with feeling different?
2. What is your ethnic background? What has it meant to belong to your ethnic group? How has it felt to belong to your ethnic group? What do you like about your ethnic identity? What do you dislike?
3. What are your feelings about being White or a person-of-color? How do you think others feel?

Note. Adapted from Pinderhughes (1989)

Table 3 The DSM-5 Outline for Cultural Formulation

A. Cultural identity of the individual
B. Cultural conceptualizations of distress
C. Psychosocial stressors and cultural features of vulnerability and resilience
D. Cultural features of the relationship between the individual and the clinician
E. Overall cultural assessment

Note. Source: American Psychiatric Association (2013)

Table 4 ADDRESSING framework

*A*ge and generational influences
*D*evelopmental or other
*D*isability
*R*eligion and spirituality
*E*thnic and racial identity
*S*ocioeconomic status/social class
*S*exual orientation
*I*ndigenous heritage
*N*ational origin
*G*ender

Note. Source: Hays (2022)

patient directly: what his or her name means or what is his or her ethnic background. The ADDRESSING framework from Hays (2022) can be a useful start as an acronym of cultural identity variables to explore, using the letters of the word "Addressing" as seen in Table 4.

This list is not meant to be exclusive of other cultural identity variables such as language, migration, political orientation, and vocational identity, among other factors. Clinicians need to understand that cultural identity can change over time or when an individual moves to living in different parts of the world. Clinicians also need to appreciate the intersectionality of these cultural identity variables for the individual rather viewing them as discreet silos. Lastly, clinicians should strive to understand the meanings of these cultural variables for the individual and ask them what is most important to them rather than assume what is most important.

Table 5 Kleinman's eight questions

1. What do you call your illness? What name does it have?
2. What do you think has caused the illness?
3. Why and when did it start?
4. What do you think the illness does? How does it work?
5. How severe is it? Will it have a short or long course?
6. What kind of treatment do you think the patient should receive? What are the most important results you hope she receives from this treatment?
7. What are the chief problems the illness has caused?
8. What do you fear most about the illness?

Note. Source: Kleinman et al. (1978)

Table 6 DSM-5 Cultural Conceptualizations of Distress

1. *Cultural syndrome* is a cluster or group of co-occurring, relatively invariant symptoms found in a specific cultural group, community, or context.... The syndrome may or may not be recognized as an illness within the culture...but such cultural patterns of distress and features of illness may nevertheless be recognizable by an outside observer
2. *Cultural idiom of distress* is a linguistic term, phrase, or way of talking about suffering among individuals of a cultural group... referring to shared concepts of pathology and ways of expressing, communicating, or naming essential features of distress
3. *Cultural explanation or perceived cause* is a label, attribution, or feature of an explanatory model that provides a culturally conceived etiology or cause symptoms, illness, or distress.... Causal explanations may be salient features of folk classifications of disease used by laypersons or healers.

Note. Adapted from American Psychiatric Association (2013)

Part B: Cultural Conceptualizations of Distress

The clinician's task is to identify how a person experiences, understands, and communicates their distress or problems to others in addition to understanding how this distress may be symptoms of mental disorders that may align with the diagnostic criteria of DSM-5 mental disorders. Arthur Kleinman et al. (1978) wrote about the distinction between the disease, which is an observable physical phenomenon, and the illness, which is how the patient experiences the disease through his or her cultural viewpoint. They went on to describe a set of eight questions that involve asking the patient what they think is the explanation for their illness: its name, how it works, how severe it is, and what problems it has caused. The clinician continues by asking about what kind of treatment is expected, both by the person and by the person's family (see Table 5). By inquiring about the person's understanding of the illness in their terms, clinicians can gain important insights into how people understand their disease and gain information that will be useful in the negotiation of their treatment with the person. At this time, the clinician may inquire about other healers that the person may have consulted prior to coming to the clinician's office, as many cultural groups have indigenous healers or alternative explanations for the causes of illness. The clinician can then inquire about herbal or organic treatments that may not be compatible with prescribed medications, as well as show interest in the person's journey into health.

DSM-5 broadened this part of the OCF to include idioms of distress, cultural syndromes, and cultural explanation or perceived cause; these three terms are defined on page 14 in the Introduction of DSM-5.

Part C: Psychosocial Stressors and Cultural Features of Vulnerability and Resilience

Part C of the DSM-5's OCF (p.750) includes the "key stressors and supports in the individual social environment (which may include local and distant events) and the role of religion, family, and other social networks (e.g., friends, neighbors and coworkers)." This section focuses on understanding how an individual fits within their community, including nuclear and extended family and other primary social supports. Important things to ask about are the person's primary relationships, educational level, occupational, functional levels, and goals. Also important is relationship to parents, aunts and uncles, cousins, and religious community. People may have ambivalent relationships between their parents and/or religious/ethnic communities, such that the very group that they derive their support from is also a stressor.

Religious and spiritual beliefs are a part of an individual's cultural identity and must be explored because they may guide his or her decision-making about mental health treatment. Social determinants of mental health such as adverse childhood events, discrimination, food insecurity, housing insecurity, and poverty, among others, are important to assess as part of this section. While in their landmark book, Compton and Shim (2015) noted 10 social determinants of mental health, and in 2020, they cited 16, including climate change (Shim and Compton 2020).

Part D: Cultural Features of the Relationship Between the Individual and the Clinician

The fourth part of the DSM-5 OCF refers to how the interaction of the clinician's cultural identity and that of the patient affect communication, diagnosis, and treatment—including the therapeutic relationship. One operationalizes this section by firstly understanding the clinician's own cultural identity, biases, and prejudices through self-reflection. Secondly, the clinician can compare and contrast cultural identity variables of the patient with that of the clinician looking for similarities and differences. Thirdly, the clinician would assess how the similarities and differences affect communication and the therapeutic alliance: rapport, verbal and nonverbal communication, ability to gather history, managing stigma and shame, and transference and countertransference, among other factors (Comas-Diaz and Jacobsen 1991; Comas-Diaz 2012). Added in DSM-5 was this important sentence relevant to some of our patients: "Experiences of racism and discrimination in the larger society may impede establishing trust and safety in the clinical diagnostic encounter."

Part E: Overall Cultural Assessment

The final part of the DSM-5 OCF is the overall cultural assessment for the differential diagnosis and the treatment plan. First, clinicians summarize the information gathered in the first four parts of the OCF to inform the differential diagnosis. For example, they review both culture and gender-related diagnostic issues concerning illness prevalence, differential diagnosis at both phenomenological and disorder levels, associated features, clinical course, and outcomes. Clinicians may consider diagnosing V codes relevant to the social determinants of mental health in addition to mental disorders. The DSM-5 V codes are "other conditions and problems that may be a focus of clinical attention or that may otherwise affect the diagnosis, course, prognosis, or treatment of a patient's mental disorder…." "The conditions or problems listed in this chapter are not mental disorders" (American Psychiatric Association 2013, p. 715). DSM-5 lists these categories of V codes among others: Relational Problems, Abuse and Neglect, Educational and Occupational Problems, Housing and Economic Problems, Problems Related to the Social Environment, Problems Related to Crime or Interaction with the Legal System. For example, one may consider the diagnosis of V62.4 Target of (Perceived) Adverse Discrimination or Persecution that corresponds to the social determinant of mental health of discrimination and exclusion that the clinician may have discovered by applying section C.

With the aim of maximizing adherence, clinicians need to understand the patient's cultural concepts of distress including coping and help-seeking to skillfully negotiate a treatment plan using both Western and indigenous explanations of illness, using the clinician as the bridge between them. Having the services of a cultural consultant (Kirmayer et al. 2013) or cultural broker, or a clinician familiar with the cultural group of the person, can be helpful in determining cultural norms. This role provides important context for the interpretation of symptoms of illness and healing beliefs and practices and understanding of the person's role in family, community, and dominant culture. Review of published literature online and books can also be useful.

Lastly, the clinician needs to ask what would help or hinder treatment when looking at the cultural features of the relationship between the clinician and the patient. For example, cultural identity matches between the clinician and the patient such as language when the patient has limited English proficiency would be extremely important for optimal communication that affects the therapeutic relationship. If this cultural identity match cannot be provided, then a trained interpreter is essential (Chang et al. 2021).

DSM-5 Cultural Formulation Interview (CFI)

In Section III of DSM-5 entitled "Emerging Measures and Models," there is a chapter on "Cultural Formulation" where both the OCF and the CFI are defined and described (American Psychiatric Association 2013, p. 749–759 and Lewis-Fernandez et al. 2016). The CFI is a brief semi-structured interview of 16 questions for systematically gathering information for the OCF: cultural definition of the problem (questions 1–3); cultural perceptions of cause, context, and support (questions 4–10); cultural factors affecting self-coping and past help seeking (questions 11–13); and cultural factors affecting current help seeking (questions 14–16). There is a CFI for use with patients, a CFI for use with informants, and 11 supplementary modules available online (American Psychiatric Association 2013b). These supplementary modules are lists of additional questions that clinicians can utilize to explore in more detail various aspects of the OCF such as cultural identity and the cultural features of the clinician-patient relationship. In addition, there are modules to be used with school-aged children and adolescents, older adults, immigrants and refugees, and caregivers.

While the CFI is an outstanding person-centered approach to obtain information for the OCF beginning in the first interview, clinicians will need to use the supplementary modules for more detailed understanding of the OCF as well as collateral sources of information, such as medical records. Furthermore, there are no CFI questions for Part E of the OCF, since the overall cultural assessment is a synthetic process by the clinician of the cultural information obtained.

Applications of Culturally Effective Treatment

In this section, through examples, we further illustrate the clinical principles described above and how the key to engaging people in ethnic minorities into mental health services is to combine the principles of adapting services and systems to population needs and by understanding and accepting their cultural beliefs about illness.

Southeast Asian Communities

J. David Kinzie (2001) and Kinzie and Keepers (2020) wrote about "The Therapist Variable" in which he described the trauma experienced by Southeast Asian patients and that they have four primary needs: *safety*, both physical and emotional and predictable, *stable personal relationships*, *reduction of symptoms*, and the re-establishment of *social relationships*. According to Kinzie, the therapist must be able to listen to a person's trauma without interruption and be present as a dependable and stable relationship. The therapist is required to believe the evil that humankind has done to their fellow humans, yet still believe that healing is possible, and to receive gifts of modest value from traumatized Southeast Asians, such as prayers, seasonal dishes, or social invitations. Despite clinician training to the contrary, it is therapeutic for them and represents a culturally appropriate way for a person to honor the therapist-patient relationship.

Hinton and Otto (2006) described a way of modifying cognitive behavioral therapy (CBT) for the treatment of post-traumatic stress disorder in Cambodians who conceived of their illness as being caused by *wind*. An example offered by these authors is if there is muscle tension in a limb (caused by forced labor, chronic starvation, and sleep deprivation experienced in the killing fields), there is blockage of vascular "tubes" at or near a related joint. Along with a possible death of the limb distal to the blockage, caused by a lack of blood flow, there can also be a dangerous ascent of wind into the body's core. The catastrophic cognition would be that wind could cause a heart attack or the person's breathing to stop or rupture of the blood vessels in the neck or into the head, leading to fainting, blindness, or death. Treatment for the wind is "cupping" or causing redness on the skin by applying negative pressure through a heated glass bulb applied to the skin, or coining, using coins to rub the skin, causing a red or purple streak on the skin. In the adapted CBT protocol (Otto and Hinton 2006), the therapist introduces the "Limbic Kid" to explain the automatic responses and thoughts associated with the catastrophic cognitions. The therapist then induces dizziness by having the person play a childhood game called "hung," where she or he holds his or her breath while running to retrieve a stick, experiencing dizziness, but no other ill effects, allowing a disconnection of the physical sensation from catastrophic cognitions. Finally, the clinician incorporates a Buddhist ritual, the three bows, with three statements. Thus, the first bow acknowledges the pain. The second is the acceptance that it has lingering effects, and the third is returning a focus to the present, planning to have a good life now.

Hispanic Communities

Other examples of groups for ethnic minorities include CBT of depression adapted for use in Spanish-speaking patients. Miranda et al. (2006) reported that in an ethnically diverse clinical sample diagnosed with major depressive disorder, those randomized to CBT or medication management did better than those simply referred to a community mental health center. In reporting this study, the authors noted, too, that community outreach was needed to educate people about their illness and the types of treatment. Nevertheless, despite providing transportation and childcare, only slightly over one-third were able to attend more than six Spanish language sessions for those who were monolingual, illustrating the difficulties encountered by the study's participants in making appointments. The subsample taking medications did slightly better, implying that psychopharmacology was still effective, but less so without outreach and support.

Ruiz and Langrod (1976) identified the importance of spiritual beliefs in the Hispanic population of the Bronx. To increase community engagement with their clinic, they recruited spiritual mediums (*espiritistas*), accepting referrals from them and referring cases back, in turn. Clinic staff actively outreached the community by visiting and making ethnographic observations at spiritual centers while also exchanging views with espiritistas and other spiritual authorities about explanatory models and treatment. Barrio (2000) similarly describes the importance of outreach to and engagement with the family and community through community support centers, which can bridge gaps between the community mental health center and the ethnically diverse populations they serve.

Using Systems to Aid Culturally Competent Services

In line with Barrio's description of creating systems linkages, another strategy is using access services, usually provided by community agencies that can provide language translation services. For example, Asian Pacific Community Counseling in Sacramento, California, provides language and culturally appropriate psychotherapy through the Transcultural Wellness Center (Asian Pacific Community Counseling 2013), and it also serves as a linkage for people to enter the county mental health system. Finally, another approach that has been helpful in linking ethnic minority patients from the community to mental health services has been the Bridges program at the Charles B. Wang Community Health Center. It capitalizes on systemic integration of physical health and mental health services. Chinese patients seen in primary care are referred to mental health professionals in the same building as their primary care colleagues, thus reducing the stigma they might experience if they were to be referred to a freestanding mental health clinic (Chen et al. 2003).

Ethnopsychopharmacology

Ethnopsychopharmacology is the study of how ethnicity affects the activity of psychoactive agents. Ng et al. (2008) and others discuss that there are many biological, environmental, and psychological reasons for the broad range of responses seen in different ethnic groups. The hepatic enzyme, cytochrome P450 (types CYP2D6, CYP3A4, CYP1A2, CYP2C19, and CYP2B6), is responsible for the metabolism of many psychotropic medications. Depending on the number of copies of genes coding for these enzymes, a person may be a slow metabolizer, where a small amount of a medication may have the same effect as a normal dose, which might bring on intolerable side effects for that patient. A person may be an ultra-fast metabolizer, when even a large dose of medication can be experienced as not taking anything at all. Constitutional factors such as gender and age as well as environmental factors such as diet and smoking also affect drug metabolism, sometimes inhibiting or accelerating its rate. Finally, the patient's expectation of how the drug will work may affect the perception of the actual effect or may cause an effect of its own ("the placebo effect") (Ninnemann 2012). For example, studies since the early 1980s have suggested that pharmacokinetic and pharmacodynamic profiles of various psychotropic medications may be different in Asians, leading to differences in dosage requirements and side effect profiles. While these variations appear to be largely determined by genetic predisposition, they are also influenced by other factors such as environment, social support, cultural perceptions, and physicians' prescribing habits (Wong and Pi 2012). Psychiatrists and primary care practitioners working with Asian Americans may consider prescribing an initial low dose and advance titration slowly in situations when the patient may be a slow metabolizer. In the future, it may be possible to measure the activity of a particular enzyme and adjusts dosages accordingly.

Culturally Competent Interventions at State and Local Levels

Clinicians need to have the support of their organization to provide culturally sensitive mental health services, as either seen by an application of the CLAS standards or other systematic cultural competence framework. California has an excellent example of a mental health-specific plan in its California Cultural Competence Plan (CCCP), which began in 1993 (Peifer 1997). Each of the 58 California counties had to assess the percentages of the languages spoken by their patients and providers and were required to provide services and brochures in any language spoken by 3000 Medi-Cal (California's version of Medicaid) members or 5% of the Medi-Cal population in that county. County agencies are to monitor their staff composition and ensure that their staff diversity mirrors the patient diversity. The cultural competence plan also requires training in cultural competence be provided for mental health clinicians on a continuing basis. Washington, California, Connecticut, New Jersey, and New Mexico all require continuing medical education courses including material on cultural competence or require cultural competence training as a condition of licensure (Like 2011).

Conclusions

US population projections show that the number of minorities will increase at a higher rate than the general population and in fact equal the majority population between 2040 and 2050. Community mental health providers will see most of these patients, as they are likely to be under or not insured, particularly if they are indigent or newly immigrants. The federal government, and many state mental health authorities, provides guidance on how to adapt our mental health services to meet the needs of the diverse populations they serve. On a clinical level, application of the DSM-5 OCF and CFI can inform the clinician's assessment and treatment planning using a culturally appropriate semi-structured interview. By taking a holistic, culturally, and linguistically competent and patient-centered approach, the community psychiatrist can deliver effective and culturally appropriate recovery-based mental healthcare.

References

Agency for Healthcare Research and Quality. (Content last reviewed July 2019). *What is cultural and linguistic competence?* https://www.ahrq.gov/ncepcr/tools/cultural-competence/definition.html

American Psychiatric Association. (1994). *Diagnostic and statistical manual of mental disorders (4th ed.). (DSM-IV).* American Psychiatric Association.

American Psychiatric Association (2013). *Diagnostic and statistical manual of mental disorders* (5th ed.). (DSM-5). American Psychiatric Association.

American Psychiatric Association. (2013b). *Supplementary modules to the core Cultural Formulation Interview (CFI).* https://www.psychiatry.org/File%20Library/Psychiatrists/Practice/DSM/APA_DSM5_Cultural-Formulation-Interview-Supplementary-Modules.pdf

Asian Pacific Community Counseling. (2013). http://apc-counseling.org/services

Barrio C. (2000). The cultural relevance of community support programs. *Psychiatric Services, (51),* 879–884.

Batalova J., Hanna M., & Levesque C. (2021, February 11). Frequently requested statistics on immigrants and immigration in the United States. *Migration Information Source.* https://www.migrationpolicy.org/article/frequently-requested-statistics-immigrants-and-immigration-united-states-2020

Chang D.F., Hsieh E., Somerville W.B., Dimond J., Thomas M., Nicasio A., Boiler M., & Lewis-Fernández R. (2021). Rethinking interpreter functions in mental health services. *Psychiatric Services, 72*(3), 353–357. https://doi.org/10.1176/appi.ps.202000085. Epub 2020 Sept. 29. PMID: 32988324.

Chen H., Kramer E.J., and Chen T. (2003). The Bridge Program: A model for reaching Asian Americans. *Psychiatric Services, (54),* 1411–1412.

Comas-Diaz L., & Jacobsen F.M. (1991). Ethnocultural transference and countertransference in the therapeutic dyad. *Am J Orthopsychiatry, 61*(3), 392–402.

Comas-Diaz, L. (2012). *Multicultural care: A clinician's guide to cultural competence.* American Psychological Association.

Compton M., & Shim R. (Eds.). (2015). *Social determinants of mental health.* American Psychiatric Publishing.

Cross T., Bazron B.J., Dennis K.W., & Isaacs M.R. (1989). *Towards a culturally competent system of care: A monograph on effective services for minority children who are severely emotionally disturbed.* CASSP Technical Assistance Center, Georgetown University Child Development Center, Washington, DC.

Hays P. (2022). *Addressing cultural complexities in counseling and clinical practice: An intersectional approach (4th ed.).* American Psychological Association.

Hinton D.E., & Otto M.W. (2006). Symptom presentation and symptom meaning among traumatized Cambodian refugees: Relevance to a somatically focused cognitive-behavior therapy. *Cogn Behav Pract., 13*(4), 249–260.

Ida D.J. (2007). Cultural competency and recovery within diverse populations. *Psychiatric Rehabilitation Journal, 31(1), 49–53.*

Kinzie J.D. (2001). Psychotherapy for massively traumatized refugees: The therapist variable. *Am J Psychother, 55*(4), 475–490.

Kinzie J.D. & Keepers G. (Eds.). (2020). *The psychiatric evaluation and treatment of refugees*. American Psychiatric Association Publishing.

Kirmayer L.J., Guzder J., & Rousseau C. (Eds.). (2013). *Cultural consultation: Encountering the other in mental health care.* Springer Publishing.

Kleinman A., Eisenberg L., & Good B. (1978). Culture, illness, and care: clinical lessons from anthropologic and cross-cultural research. *Ann Intern Med, 88*(2), 251–258.

Lewis-Fernandez R., Aggarwal N.K., Hinton L., Hinton D.E., & Kirmayer L.J. (Eds.). (2016). *DSM-5 handbook on the Cultural Formulation Interview*. American Psychiatric Publishing.

Like R.C. (2011). Educating clinicians about cultural competence and disparities in health and healthcare. *J Contin Educ Health Prof., 31*(3):196–206. https://doi.org/10.1002/chp.20127. PMID: 21953661.

Lim, R. (Ed.). (2015). *The clinical manual of cultural psychiatry* (2nd ed.). American Psychiatric Publishing.

McGoldrick M., Giordano J., & Garcia-Preto N. (Eds.). (2005). *Ethnicity and family therapy* (3rd ed.). Guilford Press.

Miranda J., Green B.L., & Krupnick J.L. (2006). One-year outcomes of a randomized clinical trial treating depression in low-income minority women. *J Consult Clin Psychol.*, (74), 99–111.

New Freedom Commission on Mental Health. (2003) *Achieving the promise: Transforming mental health care in America.* USDHHS Pub. No. SMA-03-3832. United States Department of Health and Human Services.

Ng, C.H., Lin, K.-M., Singh, B.S., & Chiu, E. (Eds.). (2008). *Ethno-psychopharmacology: Advances in current practice.* Cambridge University Press.

Ninnemann K.M. (2012). Variability in the efficacy of psychopharmaceuticals: contributions from pharmacogenomics, ethnopsychopharmacology, and psychological and psychiatric anthropologies. *Cult Med Psychiatry, 36*(1), 10–25.

Otto M.W., & Hinton D.E. (2006). Modifying exposure-based CBT for Cambodian refugees with Posttraumatic Stress Disorder. *Cogn Behav Pract., 13*(4), 261–270.

Peifer, K. L. (1997). *California medical managed mental health care plan: The issue of cultural competency* (Order No. AAM9703035). Available from APA PsycInfo®. (619256226; 1997-95004-366). Retrieved from https://www.proquest.com/dissertations-theses/california-medi-cal-managed-mental-health-care/docview/619256226/se-2?accountid=14505

Pinderhughes E. (1989). *Understanding race, ethnicity and power: The key to efficacy on clinical practice.* Free Press.

Ruiz P. & Langrod J. (1976). The role of folk healers in community mental health services. *Community Ment Health J, 12*(4), 392–398.

Ruiz P., & Primm A. (Eds.). (2010). *Disparities in psychiatric care: Clinical and cross-cultural perspectives.* Lippincott Williams & Wilkins.

Shim R. & Compton M.T. (2020). The social determinants of mental health: Psychiatrists' roles in addressing discrimination and food insecurity. *Focus, 18*(1), 25–30. https://doi.org/10.1176/appi.focus.20190035

Smedley B.D., Stith A.Y., & Nelson A.R. (2002). *Unequal treatment: What health care providers need to know about racial and ethnic disparities in healthcare.* National Academy Press. http://www.nap.edu/catalog/10260.html

Tervalon M., & Murray-García J. (1998). Cultural humility versus cultural competence: a critical distinction in defining physician training outcomes in multicultural education. *J Health Care Poor Underserved, 9(2),117–125.*

U.S. Census Bureau. (2019). *Fast facts*. https://www.census.gov/quickfacts/fact/table/US/PST045219

U.S. Dept. of Health and Human Services, Office of Civil Rights. (Content last reviewed on July 26, 2013). Guidance to Federal Financial Assistance Recipients Regarding Title VI Prohibition against National Origin Discrimination Affecting Limited English Proficient Persons. https://www.hhs.gov/civil-rights/for-providers/laws-regulations-guidance/guidance-federal-financial-assistance-title-vi/index.html

U.S. Dept. of Health and Human Services, Office of Minority Health. (2013). *National standards for CLAS in health and health care: A blueprint for advancing and sustaining CLAS policy and practice.* https://www.thinkculturalhealth.hhs.gov

U.S. Dept. of Health and Human Services, Office of the Surgeon General. (2001). *Mental health: Culture, race, and ethnicity: A supplement to Mental Health: A report of the Surgeon General.*

Vespa J., Medina L., & Armstrong D.M. (2020, February). *Demographic turning points for the United States: Population projections for 2020 to 2060.* https://www.census.gov/content/dam/Census/library/publications/2020/demo/p25-1144.pdf

Western Intercollegiate Commission for Higher Education. (1998). *Cultural competence standards in managed care mental health services: Four underserved/underrepresented racial/ethnic groups.* http://healthykansans2010.org/hk2010/cultural%20competency%20action%20coalition/references/culturalcompetenceManageCare.pdf

Wong F.K., Pi E.H. (2012). Ethnopsychopharmacology considerations for Asians and Asian Americans. *Asian J Psychiatr., 5*(1), 18–23.

Context-Specific Assessment

Stephen Mark Goldfinger
and Jacqueline Maus Feldman

Introduction

To appropriately evaluate people in their communities requires careful consideration of a panoply of contextual parameters. These include a welcoming and safe ambience; physical plant characteristics; the clinical setting (e.g., inpatient, outpatient, emergency room, homeless shelter or under a bridge, criminal justice location); whether the assessment is routine, urgent, emergent, or investigatory; the nature of the evaluation's expected product; the cultural attributes of the evaluator as well as the patient; and the social determinants impacting the patient. Consideration of all these contextual issues will expand the evaluator's capacity to establish a therapeutic alliance, to engage the patient in the assessment, and possibly to further treatment. Awareness of and responses to these contextual concerns will improve both the evaluative process and the evaluation product.

S. M. Goldfinger (✉)
Department of Psychiatry and Behavioral Sciences, SUNY Downstate Medical Center, Brooklyn, NY, USA

J. M. Feldman
Department of Psychiatry and Behavioral Neurobiology, University of Alabama at Birmingham, Birmingham, AL, USA
e-mail: jfeldman@uabmc.edu

Initial Considerations for an Assessment

Establishing the Interview Ambience

Approaching patients in a variety of settings is considered later in this chapter. However, establishing as comfortable and comforting a physical and emotional space as possible is the same, irrespective of setting and circumstance. As described in the chapter "Inspiring a Welcoming, Hopeful Culture", how people are made to feel when they enter a clinical enterprise can influence the process of their assessment. A return visit to a psychopharmacology ambulatory care clinic may arouse less discomfort, especially if protocols and staff members are consistent. Being greeted by a familiar clerk, sitting in a spacious waiting room with ready access to magazines, TV set on soft volume, toys for the kids, and being called back to a private office by a gracious nurse or a physician with whom one has worked for many years allow for relatively calm organized assessments. Disruption of protocols and expectations (new staff, a loud baby banging his pacifier, cramped clinic space packed with agitated patients with active psychosis, a rushed doctor, the fear of being unable to pay for one's medicines) may inhibit further assessment or make it more likely to be hurried, superficial, and incomplete. Clinic setting characteristics can be subtle and nuanced, but are important and significant

W. E. Sowers et al. (eds.), *Textbook of Community Psychiatry*,
https://doi.org/10.1007/978-3-031-10239-4_12

contextual considerations in whether the clinical setting is perceived as calm, warm and welcoming, or chaotic and inhospitable.

Hook et al. (2009), Segal et al. (2019), and Miller (2019) provide a detailed summary of parameters that must be considered when conducting mental health assessments. Each individual should be approached with respect, composure, empathy, and an appreciation of personal boundaries. Attention to language proficiency and the potential need for interpreters are imperative. Not every person who speaks a unique language will receive an on-site face-to-face interpreter, but telephonic interpretation services are often accessible. All interviews should begin with a personal introduction; initially addressing someone as Ms. or Mr. (or with other appropriate titles) reflects a more formal relationship and recognition that the patient is deserving of politeness and respect. Asking the individual how they would like to be addressed is another way of establishing that result.

Interviews used to begin with a handshake, but the onset of COVID mitigation processes (limited physical contact, social distancing, masks and other personal protective equipment, and the use of telemedicine) has led to an evolution in engagement (Sentell et al. 2021). See chapter "Telehealth and Technology" on Technology for further elaboration on tele-mental health assessment. Regardless, initiation of an interview that allows for some privacy and personal attention can make chances of a successful evaluation greater. Eye contact should be appropriate and empathic engagement practiced, and at all times interviewers should be mindful of nonverbal cues. Tempering one's word choices, though never in a patronizing fashion, to the perceived or actual educational or intellectual level of the patient will also facilitate communication (Andrews 2008).

Safety Issues/Physical Space

Safety and physical space in the age of COVID create challenges that must be addressed. If clinical enterprises are allowing face-to-face clinical practice, evidence-based practices of maintaining social distance and mask mitigation are important, as is consideration of mandating vaccinations of staff and patients. Liberalization of these practices may occur once the epidemic is controlled.

In addition to COVID-mitigating safety, until the patient and provider both perceive they are physically safe, it is difficult to establish the sense of psychological safety without which it is difficult for an assessment to proceed. Attention to a physical space that is welcoming, secure, and comfortable for someone with mental illness can prove to be a challenge, but it is well worth the time and effort (Hendricks et al. 2010). Setting up assessment space that ensures some privacy communicates recognition that boundaries and confidentiality are important. Patients with paranoia are often hypervigilant to boundary violations. They desire privacy but may also want sufficient space between them and the interviewer to minimize feeling physically threatened. Positioning of the examiner between patients and the door (e.g., not facilitating egress from the room) may make them feel trapped, which can inflame anxiety. The interview room/space should be furnished with an eye to minimizing objects that can be thrown or used for self-or-other injury. For example, psychiatric patients should not be placed in emergency department (ED) trauma rooms with access to needles or scalpels, emergency medicines, gauze, or inhalants. If at all possible, assessments should be conducted in areas of quiet and little traffic so as to minimize distractions and limit intrusions. It is important, however, to have security personnel rapidly accessible if the interviewer suspects or expects aggressive behavior (Hendricks et al. 2010).

The Nature of the Assessment and the Expected Product

The nature and process of the clinical assessment is also driven by the clinical or administrative/legal question (why is this person presenting?) and the expected product from the assessment. A leisurely three-session evaluation of a person who is concerned about sleep and anxiety differs vastly from an emergency room assessment of patients brought by the sheriff's office because they are aggressive and psychotic. The clinician might be wise to ask, "What are the goals of this assessment?" Answering this contextual question will guide the assessment process.

Every evaluation shares at least two initial goals, regardless of context: establishing rapport and developing as collaborative a doctor-patient relationship as the situation allows (Andrews 2008). The process and product of the rest of the assessment will be predicated, in part, on the clinical context: where is the evaluation occurring and under what circumstances (the clinical status of the patient and what clinical question is being asked and by whom). All medical evaluations are likely to involve feelings of anxiety, embarrassment, fear, or other negative feeling. Addressing these concerns from the start can greatly facilitate the ongoing evaluation process.

This is particularly true in psychiatric evaluations, which may be involuntary or simply misunderstood. Special attention must be paid to techniques of engagement when working with members of populations that have developed mistrust of systems of care. Thus, for example, engaging individuals who are homeless and mentally ill may involve multiple brief meetings focused on providing them with tangible help (food, vouchers) before any structured psychiatric evaluation can take place (Ross and Gholston 2006; Bond and Drake 2015). For other groups, particularly minorities with histories of negative experiences with medical or other organized or government agencies, exploration of these feelings and individual issues can be essential before other works can be accomplished.

Types of Assessments, Contextual Considerations

Routine Although routine evaluations can occur in places ranging from under a bridge to a homeless shelter, if the assessment is a prescheduled, voluntary, routine initial clinic visit to evaluate a proscribed complaint, the setting will typically be in an office where the person will probably hope to have a diagnosis and treatment plan by the end of the session. This applies regardless of whether the visit is an evaluation by a private sector provider or one working in a mental health center, Department of Veterans Affairs (VA) facility, or correctional setting. One or several assessment visits may ensue; the patient will be engaged, key information will be elicited, including old records or information from referring practitioners, and treatment, if necessary, will be recommended and follow-up established.

If the person is entering a system of care, education regarding confidentiality within the system should be made clear. For example, it is important to apprise patients that electronic health records are shared among all treatment team members in the VA or that the warden may read an inmate's chart. If appropriate, limits to the boundary of confidentiality (e.g., elder or child abuse, imminent homicide or suicide, threats to self or others) should be mentioned.

Investigation A one-time investigatory psychiatric assessment will be somewhat different. Examples of such assessments are referrals for disability determination, custody, competency, or other legal questions. These are also typically pre-scheduled, usually occur in an office setting, may be voluntary but are sometimes mandated, and often result in production of a report to the referring agency (e.g., Social Security Administration, public assistance authorities, child services, the court system). These issues may make engagement and establishing a consumer-provider alliance considerably more difficult. Individuals in these settings may be very symptomatic, exaggerating, minimizing, demanding, frightened, angry, or prevaricating, depending on the situation. Follow-up treatment is typically not a goal. The objective of these sessions is to do as thorough an evaluation as possible while making it as comfortable and supportive for the person as possible. The provider is ethically mandated to ensure the person is aware of the nature of the exam and should get consent for release of information to the referring agency.

Urgent Some individuals will present needing an urgent (needs to be seen today) evaluation. Perhaps their symptoms are of an acute, debilitating nature, or they have sustained an abrupt physical or emotional trauma. Some systems of care have the capacity to respond quickly to the need for rapid evaluations on-site, but most often these patients present to or are referred to emergency health-care providers. A brief triage evaluation to determine the urgency of need should take place at the site of presentation. Urgent evaluations will focus on the presenting clinical question (e.g., the patient is a victim of rape; the patient has missed his last three shots and is becoming increasingly psychotic and hostile; the patient has consumed three six-packs of beer and is now suicidal), and the evaluation may be tailored to spotlight the more salient issues while minimizing others. Concerns regarding affective lability, organicity, and impulsivity/unpredictability must be addressed. Safety is paramount, and establishing security protocols in advance can reduce the possibility of patient or staff injuries.

In the face of a confusing presentation that needs a rapid evaluation, collateral information and substantiation and/or organic workups are often overlooked, but may play a vital role in attempting to assess the nature of the acute presentation. Admitting to a psychiatric ward a confused and agitated patient with psychosis who is then found to have a fever of 103, pneumonia, and a pO2 of 42 reflects an incomplete urgent evaluation that places the patient, and the system of care, at risk. Hendricks et al. (2010) offer an excellent blueprint and review of approaches to patients and situations that need crisis intervention. Diamond (2002) offers an extensive review of medical illnesses that can have mental health presentations. Often, gathering information from sources other than the patient can be critical to making correct diagnostic and intervention decision.

Emergent Psychiatric patients do present who need to be evaluated quickly (not just today, but right now). Often, they are brought for evaluation by family or caregivers who report uncontrolled agitation or combativeness, suicidal or homicidal ideation with intent and/or plan, profound confusion, or some other acute clinical change or symptom onset. The evaluation may or may not be voluntary. Unless a mental health facility has access to emergent medical care, it is most prudent to move these patients to an emergency medical facility (by ambulance). Often these patients are grossly agitated, confused, or mute, and direct communication may be difficult, if not impossible. Setting a calm tone in the evaluation space (ED, office, jail cell, tent under the bridge) is imperative. Soft speech, slowed physical movements, and a relaxed demeanor help reduce anxiety in the person and the rest of the treatment team.

However, if these strategies have limited success, last-resort utilization of security methods, such as mechanical or chemical restraints, may be necessary. Explaining to the patient what will be occurring and describing what you are doing even while restraints are being applied or administered might feel like an exercise in futility. However, it is possible a person is aware of the situation and environment, and these explanations show humanism, personal respect, and procedural justice. They may prove reassuring and, in the end, helpful for eventual engagement. Certainly, processing the need for restraints after the event has resolved is important. Especially if this kind of presentation is new or different, or if the person is unknown and records/knowledgeable staff are unavailable, she/he should be medically evaluated for possible medical causes for said presentations. Glick et al. (2020) expand on these essentials of evidence-based practice of emergency psychiatry.

Key Information to Be Elicited in All Assessments

As noted above, depending on the situation and context, there are widely variable types of mental health assessments, but in all cases, core issues must be addressed in each assessment regardless of context. Additional information can be collected or deleted depending on the clinical situation, allocated time, and consumer capacity or willingness.

Demographics (Which Will Often Underscore Contributing Social Determinants of Mental Health and Resilience)

Getting a sense of the individual is imperative. It is essential to collect information of age, gender, sexual orientation, ethnicity, marital/relationship status, education status, employment status (working? job insecurity? underemployment?), housing situation (stability, location), food security, and capacity to access to medical and mental health care. There are other, more often overlooked questions; upon whom can the individual rely for support? Are they religious? Have they undergone racial or non-racial discrimination or trauma (sexual, physical, bullying, criminal justice)? Such information can give clues to potential sources of stressors, supports, and failures and successes that will play a useful role in figuring out what is impinging on the patient's life (Compton and Shim 2015).

Chief Complaint

Why is this person presenting at this point in his or her life? Is the presentation voluntary (routine med check), volitional (calling the taxi for a ride to the ED), mandated (disability determination or court-ordered), emergent (brought in by ambulance unconscious after an alleged overdose), or forced (brought by police after being caught breaking windows because of acute paranoia). A good way to ask this question and to make it present-focused is: what brings you here now?

Salient Mental and Medical Health Symptoms

What are they reporting? What is observed? What information is available from collateral sources? Each interview must assess for potential risk of harm to self or others. Information regarding sensory deficits such as sight or hearing, substance use, cognitive deficits, medical history (including recent trauma), and medications is important to elicit regardless of situation.

Who Else Is There?

Finding out who brought the patient in, who cares enough to stay, who hides out in the waiting room, who bolts or does not return phone calls, or who aggressively approaches the provider to offer imperative information regarding the consumer is contextual information that is helpful to ascertain. Knowledge about existing, or nonexistent, supports will help with diagnosis, treatment plan, and discharge planning.

Past Psychiatric History

Knowledge of prior inpatient and outpatient psychiatric interface can be helpful in establishing level of functioning, insight and judgment, and capacity for adherence. Eliciting past successful treatment modalities, as well as treatment failures, may help guide treatment planning and enhance the development of a therapeutic alliance. If one blithely suggests a treatment that has failed in the past, it indicates a lack of empathy or of inattention; the obverse – asking the patient what has worked, what are they willing to try – reflects concern and a willingness to work in partnership toward recovery. Similarly, asking who in their past encounters with the mental health system has been particularly helpful, or seen as useless, can give valuable clues to how to approach future treatment planning.

Past Medical History

Ascertaining this information is imperative. Multiple medical problems, including substance use, misuse, abuse, or dependence, can be the etiology of mental health presentations or can exacerbate patients' illnesses. Queries regarding present medications, including over-the-counter preparations, and adherence should be made, and the prescribers denoted so the treatment team can communicate with prior and present providers. Examining in as much detail as possible the patients tolerance and "likes and dislikes" about their prior psychiatric meds is essential, since no medication we prescribe will work if the patient doesn't take it. Surgical procedures, allergies, and prior physical trauma can inform possible differential diagnoses for a variety of mental health presentations.

Review of Systems

Taking the time to elicit how a patient feels physically reflects one's concern for the whole patient and may help the practitioner see more broadly how a mental health problem is touching the patient's life. If the patient is new to the mental health system, such review of medical systems can help the patient to feel more comfortable, as questions familiar to them from their internist's office are asked.

Family/Social/Developmental History: The Importance of Understanding Social Determinants

Hearing about one's upbringing and life circumstances from the patient's perspective can illustrate a more complete picture of the forces that had and have an influence on the patient. Developmental milestones, level of education and school performance, adverse childhood experiences, jobs held and lost, economic status, military service, arrests records, relationships gained, sustained and gone away or awry, physical or sexual trauma, and social injustice, all have a bearing on the patient's mental health; these social determinants should be elicited if possible. Any family history of mental health problems might help explain present illness, or a patient's desire to ignore symptoms. Understanding the patient's perception of successes and failures can be crucial in establishing strength-based, recovery-oriented, patient-centered treatment plans.

Mental Status Examination

Performing a formal mental status exam is helpful in painting a more complete picture of the patient's presentation. Serial assessments using such tools as the Beck Depression Inventory or Mini-Mental Status Exam can reflect response to treatment. Similarly, assessing for presence of symptoms of depression, including suicidal or homicidal ideation, intent or plan, or symptoms of mania, substance abuse, anxiety, psychosis, and confusion is important in establishing a diagnosis (or diagnoses) and viable treatment plan. If at all possible, performing a physical exam or obtaining the results of a recent physical exam with lab work is helpful in supporting or eliminating organic causes for a wide variety of mental health presentations.

All of this information should be garnered for a mental health assessment, regardless of clinical setting. Whether or not one is successful in getting all the information depends on the condition and capacity of the patient, the available time, the clinical setting, and if an alliance has been established that will facilitate a person's willingness to reveal his or her inner life. It is also important, process-wise, to embrace a patient-centered, strength-based, shared decision-making approach to the assessment and enable, encourage, anticipate, and feel comfortable with the patient establishing goals and treatment plan parameters (Maples et al. 2021).

Cultural Attributes and Structural Competence

The ability to garner information and establish an alliance may also be shaped by cultural considerations of the patient and the provider. Chapter "Cultural and Linguistic Competence" incorporates many of the considerations regarding how cultural attributes can impact patients with mental illness, but a brief review is necessary, especially focusing on context-specific assessments. Cultural predicates like race, ethnicity, socioeconomic-status, language, religion, customs, age, gender role, sexual orientation, sensory abilities (vision, hearing), perceived hierarchies in relationships, and levels of comfort (or discomfort) with physical boundary flexibility, all play a role in the context of an assessment.

Congruence between examiner and consumer can be helpful, but is not always easy to coordinate. "The greater the cultural differences existing between the provider and the consumer of mental health care, including socio-economics, gender, ethnicity, language and world views, the greater is the likelihood of misdiagnosis, inappropriate care or noncompliance with treatment" (Lindsey and Cuellar 2000, p 199). Matching patients with those of parallel race, sexual orientation, gender, religion, or personal experiences is challenging: presently while 13% and 15% of the general American population are, respectively, African American and Latino, only 3% of active psychiatrists are African American, and 5% of active psychiatrists are Latino; approximately 21% of mental health care comes from clinicians of diverse backgrounds (Feldman 2020). The CDC offers suggestions for a culturally competent evaluation (2014).

A wide variety of culturally driven coping styles and ways of communicating about illness have been observed, and the untrained, uninformed, or unemphatic provider might sabotage effective assessments by ignorance of cultural differences (Alegria et al. 2008). In addition, cultures vary vastly in the degree of stigma attached to mental illness, which can then impact on how the illness is perceived and understood (Nakash et al. 2010). This may affect how often different populations access mental health care and how accepting they will be of diagnostic and treatment regimens. The *Surgeon General's Report* (1999) endorses the use of culturally competent services that "incorporate respect for and understanding of ethnic and racial symptoms, as well as their histories, traditions, beliefs, and value systems." Working to increase communication, empathy, appreciation, insight, and comprehension for both the patient and the provider can but only help in culturally competent-driven assessment. Efforts to broaden understanding might ease levels of discomfort and encourage consumer engagement. Ruiz and Primm's text on Disparities in Psychiatric Care (Ruiz and Primm 2010) is replete with examples of the impact of cultural considerations on presentation and evaluation of mental illness; in this book, Nakash et al. (2010) have a brilliant chapter on the culturally sensitive evaluation that is a must-read for one who conducts psychiatric assessments with culturally diverse populations.

There is a growing literature on the need for clinicians to examine our own internal feelings about those different from us. This is particularly critical for mental health service providers, because our internal prejudices and biases can become powerful roadblocks to our ability to assess and treat those who are not "like us." We must thoughtfully, and critically, examine our stereotypes and conscious and preconscious feelings and be vigilant to how these impact our practice and interactions with those we serve, right from the first assessment.

In addition, more nuanced thinking, supported by a growing literature, has evolved vis-a-vis understanding the consequences of structural racism and the import of developing structural competency. Per Metzl and Hanson (2018):

> Whereas previous models such as cultural competency focus on identifying clinician bias and improving communication at moments of clinical encounter, structural competency encourages clinical practitioners to recognize how social, economic, and political conditions produce health inequalities in the first place. Structural competency calls on health care professionals to recognize ways that institutions, neighborhood conditions, market forces, public policies, and health care delivery systems shape symptoms and diseases, and to mobilize for correction of inequalities as they manifest both in physician patient interactions and beyond the clinic walls. (pg 115)

This means we must think more broadly and more deeply in our approach to contextual assessments, expanding our understanding and definitions of trauma, and how often un-addressed institutional inequalities can manifest in our patients' clinical presentations, capacity to engage, or ability to profit from treatment.

Conclusion

To embrace context-specific assessments in community psychiatry merits thoughtful consideration of many factors. While there are standard expectations of what information is necessary for any mental health assessment to be complete, the clinical status of a patient may interact with variable capacities of systems of care and unskilled providers, resulting in less than superior results. The ambience of a clinical setting can have a profound influence on how patients perceive their evaluation; maintaining a safe, welcoming contextual setting can make assessments more effective at gathering information and establishing therapeutic alliances. Gathering information on how social and structural determinants impact both patients and providers will prove invaluable in understanding the predicates of the presentation of the patient and help shape the treatment plan. Training staff to identify their own cultural attributes and prejudices, and those of patients, may work to mitigate stigma and confusion and to enhance understanding of mental health issues, allowing the provider and patient more effective communication, opportunities for shared-decision-making, and development of a healing partnership.

References

Alegria M, Nakash O, Lapatin S, Oddo V, et al (2008). How missing information in diagnoses can lead to disparities in the clinical encounter. J Public Health Management Practice, 14, 26–35.

Andrews LB (2008). The psychiatric interview and mental status examination. In Hales RE, Yudofsky SC, Gabbard, GO (eds.), The American Psychiatric Publishing Textbook of Psychiatry (5th edition). Arlington, VA: American Psychiatric Publishers, Inc. pp. 3–18.

Bond, GR, Drake, RE (2015) The critical ingredients of assertive community treatment. World Psychiatry, 14, 240–242. https://doi.org/10.1002/wps.20234.

Centers for Disease Control and Prevention (2014). Practical strategies for culturally competent evaluation. Atlanta, GA: US Department of Health and Human Services.

Compton, RT, Shim, RS (2015). The social determinants of mental health. FOCUS. https://doi.org/10.1176/appl.focus.20150017.

Diamond R (2002) Psychiatric presentation of medical illnesses. International Guide to the World of Alternative Mental Health. Available at: http://www.alternative-mentalhealth.com/articles/diamond.htm. Accessed 9/16/21.

Feldman, JM (2020). Achieving mental health equity: Community Psychiatry. In: Stewart, AJ, Shim, RS (eds) Achieving Mental Health Equity. Psychiatric Clinics of North America. 43. 511–524. https://doi.org/10.1016/j.psc.2020.06.002.

Glick, RL, Zeller, SL, Berlin, JS (eds) (2020). Emergency Psychiatry: Principles and Practice 2nd Edition. Philadelphia, PA: Lippincott Williams and Wilkins.

Hendricks JE, McKean J, Hendricks CG (2010). Crisis Intervention Skills. In Crisis Intervention (4th Edition): Contemporary Issues for On-Site Interveners. Springfield, IL: Charles C. Thomas. pp. 32–68.

Hook JN, Hodges EK, Segal DL, Coolidge FL (2009). Clinical interviews with adults. In Thomas JC, Hersen M (Eds.), Handbook of Clinical Psychology Competencies. New York, NY: Springer. pp. 195–208.

Lindsey ML, Cuellar (2000). Mental health assessments and treatment of African-Americans: A multicultural perspective. In Cuellar I., Paniagua FA (Eds.), Handbook if Multicultural Mental Health. San Diego, CA: Academic Press. Pp. 195–208.

Maples, NJ, Velligan, DI, Jones, EC, Espinosa, EM, Morgan, RO, Valerio-Shewmaker, MD (2021). Perspectives of patients and providers in using shared decision-making in psychiatry. Community Mental Health Journal. https://doi.org/10.1007/s10597-021-00856-z.

Metzl, JM, Hanson, H (2018). Structural competency and psychiatry. JAMA Psychiatry. 75(2), 115–116.

Miller, C. (2019). Interviewing strategies, rapport, and empathy. In: Segal, D (eds) Diagnostic Interviewing. Springer, New York, NY. https://doi.org/10.1007/978-1-4939_9127-3_1.

Nakash O, Rosen D, Alegria M (2010). The culturally sensitive evaluation. In Ruiz P, Primm AB (Eds.). Disparities in Psychiatric Care: Clinical and Cross-Cultural Perspectives. Baltimore, MD: Lippincott Williams & Wilkins, pp. 225–235.

Overview of cultural diversity and mental health services (1999) Mental Health: A Report of the Surgeon General. Available at: http://www.surgeongeneral.gov. Accessed 9/01/2021.

Ross J, Gholston JR (2006). We'll meet you on your bench: Developing a therapeutic alliance with the homeless mentally ill patient. In Rosenberg J, Rosenberg S (Eds.). Community Mental Health: Challenges for the 21st Century. New York, NY: Routledge, pp. 195–206.

Ruiz P, Primm AB (Eds.) (2010). Disparities in Psychiatric Care: Clinical and Cross-Cultural Perspectives. Baltimore, MD: Lippincott Williams & Wilkins.

Segal, DL, June, A, Pifer M (2019). Basics and beyond in clinical and diagnostic interviewing. In: Segal, D (eds) Diagnostic Interviewing. Springer, New York, NY. https://doi.org/10.1007/978-1-4939_9127-3_1.

Sentell, T, Foss-Durant, A, Patil, U, Taira, D, Paasche-Orlow, MK, Trinacty, CM (2021). Organized health literacy: Opportunities for patient-centered care in the wake of COVID-19. Quality Management in Health Care. https://doi.org/10.1097/QMH.0000000000000279.

Team Leadership: Promoting Diversity and Inclusion in the Aftermath of COVID-19

Juanita L. Redd and Hayward Suggs

Introduction

> Teamwork is the ability to work together toward a common vision. The ability to direct individual accomplishments toward organizational objectives. It is the fuel that allows common people to attain uncommon results.
> –Andrew Carnegie

This chapter is dedicated to our brilliant, esteemed, and world-renowned colleague Dr. Carl C. Bell who passed away in 2019 and was the principal author of this chapter when it appeared in the *Handbook of Community Psychiatry*.

Many have recognized the power of teams in various arenas. A sports team is a prime example where interdependence is apparent. For example, in a football team, each position has a set of skills and a knowledge base that accompanies it. Each position must depend and rely on the skills and knowledge base of the other positions to accomplish their collective goal successfully. This outlook can inform all teams, especially interdisciplinary administrative and clinical behavioral health teams, despite their complexity. Because of the strength of this model, this chapter focuses on team-based treatment in behavioral health. It places particular emphasis on a pertinent structure of community mental health centers (composed of administrative and clinical teams), the importance of multidisciplinary treatment teams in this context, the problems that multidisciplinary treatment teams often face, and possible solutions for teams to function effectively and possibly thrive.

This chapter is being written in what is hoped to be the waning of our so far 2-year COVID-19 pandemic, in the wake of multiple traumas caused by the pandemic as well as the national discussion of diversity inequity exposed by the pandemic. The chapter will outline how the development of each and the function of behavioral health teams can become protective factors for communities including efforts to combat diversity inequity and promote recovery from traumas such as of COVID-19.

The Trauma That Is COVID-19

Trauma is an emotional response to an extremely negative event. Traumatic events also referred to as traumatic stressors or negative events can take a significant toll emotionally and financially on communities. According to the American Psychiatric Association's Diagnostic and Statistical Manual, a traumatic stressor must be outside the range of normal human experience (American Psychiatric Association 2013).

J. L. Redd (✉)
J.L. Redd and Associates, Chicago, IL, USA

H. Suggs
Commonquest Consulting, Chicago, IL, USA
e-mail: Hayward@haywardsuggs.com

W. E. Sowers et al. (eds.), *Textbook of Community Psychiatry*,
https://doi.org/10.1007/978-3-031-10239-4_13

Traumatic events include, but are not limited to, natural or human disasters, war and violence, chronic or life-threatening medical conditions, community violence, the witnessing of traumatic events, physical abuse, sexual abuse, and other forms of interpersonal violence.

The National Alliance on Mental Health forecasted that the combination of mental health budget cuts, inadequate essential trauma-informed services, and climate-related disasters will dramatically escalate risk factors for stress-related disorders and lead to a mental health crisis the United States is not prepared to handle. This prediction was made well before the current and future trauma created in the wake of the worldwide COVID-19 pandemic.

As of March 2022, almost one million people have died in the United States from COVID-19. Almost 460 million people across the globe have contracted the virus. The worldwide death toll is over six million and climbing even after more than 11 billion doses of vaccinations have been administered in 184 countries with 64% of the world's population having received at least one dose. Millions and millions across the globe have experienced the loss of:

- Life
- Loved ones
- Health
- Homes
- Employment
- Opportunity
- Faith
- Income
- Will
- Sanity

Nearly the entire world has been traumatized, and the long-term impact as we know has the potential to be catastrophic. People are struggling greatly to deal with grief, anger, remorse, frustration, and fear. Global trauma risk factors have never been higher. As a result, the need for effective mental health treatment has never been greater and that need will persist.

Risk Factors, Predictive Factors, and Protective Factors

The available science suggests that the aforementioned trauma risk factors do not have to become predictive factors for communities exposed to trauma (Bell 2006). Predictive factors enable estimates of harm that are associated with the response or lack of response to a particular risk factor.

Protective factors are the conditions, characteristics, or attributes within an individual, their family, community, or culture that impact how they deal with stressful events (youth.gov, n.d.). Protective factors can either mitigate or eliminate risk factors in community exposure to trauma (Bell 2006).

Protective factors can be biological, psychological, social, and environmental. Biological attributes include intellectual ability, personality traits, temperamental traits, and toughness. As outlined by Bell et al. (2005), psychological attributes include intrapsychic, emotional, cognitive, spiritual, and posttraumatic growth. Social attributes include interpersonal skills, interpersonal relationships, connectedness, and social support. Lastly, environmental attributes include positive life events and socioeconomic status. It has also been argued that protective factors should be defined in relation to adverse experiences or risk factors (Griffin et al. 2011).

Trauma events are predictive factors for negative life outcomes (Breslau et al. 2006). The anticipated impact of the current trauma driven by COVID-19 would seem to forecast a severely challenging recovery. However, Bell et al. (2005) found that protective factors decrease the risk of being affected by a traumatic stressor and other disorders such as depression, suicide, and violent behavior. They argue that at-risk communities with well-developed protective factors do not experience the level of trauma-related disorders that would be predicted, based on their risk factors. In other words, the impact of risk factors was reduced when there were sufficient protective factors present in those communities exposed to trauma (Bell et al. 2002).

Behavioral health teams serve communities, yet are themselves micro-communities, with unique strengths, vulnerabilities, and functional capacities. Discussed next is how these micro-communities function and serve larger communities of people. This is followed by how behavioral health are affected by macro-environmental circumstances, such as challenges with COVID-19 and racial inequities.

The Value and Pitfalls of Multidisciplinary Teams in Community Mental Health Settings

A multidisciplinary team is necessary to deliver the complex array of services needed in community mental health settings – diagnostic services, prescribing medications, housing, securing benefits, teaching skills of daily living, teaching vocational skills, facilitating social interactions, conducting research, crisis and emergency work, hospitalization, psychosocial rehabilitation, care of physical illness, education, management, and leadership. A multidisciplinary team approach allows the transition from an individual and illness-focused conception of treatment to a broader view including the public health and prevention approach to services.

There are multiple models for running community mental health services. There is no right or wrong model as the success of an organization is dependent on multiple human factors involved in the work. Regardless of the objectives of the team (i.e., an administrative or a clinical team), persons trained in leadership and management, and even business, are often best equipped for cultivating a healthy multidisciplinary team.

The source of strength of multidisciplinary teams is also its source of weakness – diversity. While the diversity of multidisciplinary teams has its advantages in availing expertise in multiple domains, the difference in perspective of each professional and consumer/patient creates a tremendous potential for conflict in professional relationships. Covey (1989) points out the most valuable human resources are relationships. Weak relationships result in poor communication, disagreements, negative feelings (i.e., jealousy), and negative behaviors (i.e., backbiting and criticism). Unfortunately, work environments characterized by professional conflict and weak relationships drain time and energy that would be better used for personal growth and organizational success. Thus, the conflict potentially inherent in multidisciplinary teams, whether they are clinical, research, educational, or administrative teams, needs to be managed. The ability for a team to self-correct is essential for strong functioning. Part of self-correction is identifying behavior, skill, or attitudinal issues that influence outcomes.

Managing the Process of Conflicts on Multidisciplinary Treatment Teams

Goldsmith (2007) described several transactional team member behaviors that disrupt team functioning and lead to conflict, requiring monitoring and correction. The first is too much competition, such that the goal is winning and the team's mission is forgotten. This competition can manifest intellectually, as there are some team members that strive to display superior intelligence at the cost of listening to others. Related to this are individuals' tendencies to make destructive or negative comments that may be infused with sarcasm or derision. There may also be team naysayers who emphasize potential pitfalls instead of possible solutions. At times, there are others who are frequently angry and use their anger to control the team process. Another destructive dynamic on treatment teams is the withholding of information to gain personal advantage. Just as a team or person can express too much or too little criticism, a team can also have too much or too little praise. Some team members claim undeserved credit, make excuses, or blame others for disruptive behaviors. Team leaders may also contribute to derailment, by "playing favorites" and/or failing to assume responsibility for poor decisions.

In order to manage conflict in multidisciplinary treatment teams, the importance of mission has to be underscored. The qualities of functional teams mentioned above should be emphasized. As suggested earlier, the main mission of a multidisciplinary treatment team should be not only quality clinical care for mentally ill patients but also attention to issues of wellness (Keyes 2007). Whatever the details of a team's core mission principles, they must be worked out uniquely by each team. Consistent focus on principle-based mission-driven agendas generate interdependency and synergy, leading to the realization of targeted outcomes and even positive "side effects" (e.g., good relationships). Using mission and engagement effectively can smooth out and, in many cases, prevent conflicts. Attaining the team traits of interdependency and synergy is not easily achieved, and the team must understand that this is a process. Senge et al. (1994) indicate there will be times of frustration and even embarrassment, because while the idea of working together may not be new, the prospect of "learning together" for many is often new. In short, through effective leadership, a team is able to commit to its goal. A well-functioning team is conceptually unified about where they are going and that overall goal takes precedence over whatever conflict arises. DePree (1992) likens this quality of leadership to a jazz-band leader's aspiration of facilitating each player's opportunity to "do their own thing" while still maintaining harmony in the music the band plays.

There are several types of authority that leaders might use to manage a multidisciplinary team: (1) *legitimate authority* where there is a designated leader of the team who has the assigned power to reward and sanction various team behaviors; (2) *charismatic authority* where there is a person who has "winning ways" with people that encourages the team to follow their lead; and (3) *traditional authority* where there is a person who is the oldest or most experienced member of the team and who understands the history and process of the team (Bell 1974). Ideally, leaders will have elements of all three types; however, the type of authority is less important than the manner in which a person leads. This requires dedication to trusting others to carry out their responsibilities and have good judgment, being vulnerable and open, supporting self-reflection (i.e., being open to looking inward and evaluating oneself), assessing results, bolstering mutual accountability, and encouraging others.

In many ways the team is much like a family. When functioning poorly, it may be a source of distress and impede the progress of the people it is designed to help. When functioning well, it can accommodate and evolve when conflict arises. When this is the case, it provides a sense of home base for the team member, and a significant source of support, affiliation, and belonging. If the team fails to be coherent, it is unlikely that it will be successful in accomplishing its mission. It must work on its social and emotional team intelligence until an adequate level of cohesiveness can be achieved.

Team Leadership

Essentially, good leadership consists of the act of making a significant difference through people, which ultimately requires the effective execution of emotional and social skills. This process of excelling as a leader requires study of leadership and management and a true respect for humanity. Effective leadership requires connecting every day to your deepest and most enduring values, exemplifying integrity, caring for your loved ones, making a difference through your work, and inspiring hope within the people around you. Good multidisciplinary leaders follow their followers and tend to have an enduring sense of hope. Strong leaders are able to face the truth about their own weaknesses and help others see their weaknesses by having courage and compassion. Covey (1990) stated, "…to achieve that balance between courage and consideration, is the essence of real maturity…." Effective leaders believe in "creating" the future by cultivating "shared vision" on the team and facilitating movement toward that vision. They embody their values and motivate others through their example. In other words, effective leaders function in such a way so that when their team thinks of integrity, authenticity, enthusiasm, commitment, caring, and being on a mission, the team thinks of themselves.

With the right execution of good leadership and the application of guiding team principles and values, a healthy multidisciplinary team will emerge that embodies the following characteristics: (1) being proactive toward the mission, (2) engaging in collaboration instead of competition, (3) seeing the big picture instead of fragmentation, (4) seeking to understand patterns instead of cause-effect, (5) looking for deeper causes instead of surface symptoms, (6) engaging in ongoing learning instead of quick fixes, (7) studying process instead of events, (8) understanding "both/and" instead of "either/or," (9) making a point of seeing opportunities instead of threats, and (10) attempting to be anticipatory instead of being crisis-driven (Covey 1990). Successful teams recognize that conflict is healthy, even vital, for long-term success. Senge (1990) reiterated this point and asserted that a by-product of great teams is that conflict results in production of outcomes and free flow discussions that lead to better alternatives and discovery of new answers. Covey (1989) also supported healthy conflict and emphasized, "synergy means 1 + 1 may equal 8, 16, or even 1,600." Thus, synergy is worth the conflict because of the end result.

The Role of the Community Psychiatrist on Community Mental Health Teams

Community psychiatrists have to be collaborative when functioning on community mental health teams. There is inevitably a certain amount of blurring of roles: In addition to providing medical expertise, in recognition of their training, the psychiatrist may also be called upon to provide clinical leadership. In some instances the psychiatrist may even have formal leadership as program medical director (Ranz 1998). However, depending on the structure of the team itself, in exercising that clinical leadership, the psychiatrist defers on operational issues to a nonmedical team leader. This does not necessarily come as natural to early career psychiatrists, whose experience on teams in residency has usually been on hospital-based teams which are usually run by psychiatrists. In the same manner, psychiatrists may be part of executive teams in behavioral health organizations that are not led by physicians. Here, it is important for psychiatrists to exercise and capitalize on clinical expertise, yet collaborate with their peers on projects that are not strictly medical but still within the service mission of the organization (Eilenberg et al. 2000).

Leadership in the Wake of COVID-19

According to Greenleaf (2002), leadership is an act of service or servitude, while Collins (2001) notes how in his research, "great" leaders have a quality of selflessness. In response to the pandemic, we have seen the people on the front lines, including healthcare nurses, doctors, ambulance drivers, nutritionists, anesthesiologists, janitors, fire and police departments, teachers, support staff, epidemiologists, nursing home attendants, childcare workers, and many others, assume leadership roles. They are changing the behavior of the world by the wearing of masks, use of hand sanitizer, social distancing, crowd avoidance, and promoting vaccination. In the midst of turmoil, these micro-communities – our behavioral health teams have worked tirelessly for the health of our communities to ensure people are able to survive the pandemic. Behavioral health teams have been dealing with the burnout of those that have been caring for others, the fear of the community's economic devastation, and their pain and grief from so much traumatic loss in their communities and in their families. As a result of this ongoing stress, many healthcare workers have decided not to return to their jobs as the pandemic begins to show signs of possibly winding down in the United States. Yet the best treatment teams can have a leadership role in combatting this stress. They can lead by example, following seven basic field principles necessary for behavior change as a result of trauma (Greenleaf 2002).

1. Rebuilding the village
2. Providing access to healthcare
3. Improving bonding, attachment, connectedness dynamics, within the community and between stakeholders
4. Improving self-esteem
5. Increasing social skills for target recipients
6. Reestablishing the adult protective shield
7. Minimizing the residual effects of trauma

The individuals that lead behavioral health treatment teams in nonprofit hospitals and community organizations have often demonstrated unique impact of the mental health and social services provided to the communities they serve. They have a tremendous opportunity to impact those disproportionately exposed to COVID-19 trauma. But their success depends on having the right people in place. Collins (2001), in his book *Good to Great*, emphasizes the importance of getting the right people into an organization and into the right roles. Greenleaf (2002) refers to this as the "who" and "where." If an organization fails to successfully get the right people, and into the right roles, the organization's mission could be jeopardized. For nonprofit mental health and social service organizations which often have mission-critical work, Greenleaf's standpoint takes on particular importance. While sympathy is the act of feeling sorry or pity, empathy is having an understanding based on shared feelings or experiences. Greenleaf asserts that nonprofit mental health and social service leadership requires empathy, a major element of emotional intelligence.

Emotional Intelligence This includes self-control, zeal and persistence, and the ability to motivate oneself (Goleman 1996).

Empathy Goleman identifies three types of empathy; the first is "cognitive empathy" having mental awareness of how another person feels. Behavioral health treatment team leaders and members must have this level of empathy to be even marginally successful. Treatment providers must be able to relate to their clients in the same way leaders must relate at the intellectual level with their followers. The second is "emotional empathy" when a person feels what another person may be feeling. Different from sympathy, this allows the mental health practitioner to put on the shoes of the affected person without having to wear those shoes home. Leaders also must connect to the feelings of their followers, especially their sheer needs and urgency. The third and final level is "compassionate empathy" where a person recognizes what another is feeling, feels it to some extent themselves, and is compelled to act or help (Goleman 2007). Being compelled to do something on behalf of others is where one's body takes action. Moving beyond simply thinking about or feeling the problems of others, one is willing to do something about it. Effective leaders take action that leads to productive outcomes. By doing something, a leader provides opportunity for others to follow. When there is no action or movement, there is nothing to follow.

Compassion A feeling of deep sympathy and sorrow for another who is stricken by misfortune accompanied by a strong desire to alleviate the suffering

Heart Characteristics that cause a person to be firm in his or her beliefs and have the determination to accomplish their goals (Bell and Suggs 1998)

The willingness to help is essential in responding to trauma. Simply caring but not acting does little for many and nothing for most. True leadership is caring enough to take decisive action. Action taking and caring requires heart. Heart as exhibited by frontline nurses, doctors, and staff risking their lives and health. Or the first responders, contact tracers, and support staff of hospitals, ambulance drivers, case managers, mental health workers, daycare workers, bus drivers, clinical therapists, police, or schoolteachers who deal with the situations both first hand and over the long term. It takes a tremendous amount of heart to do work you know could kill you and kill those whom you love, especially when you see the realities of death on a daily basis among your patients, colleagues, and family. Yet that is what essential workers do; they risk their lives for the physical and mental health of others. With COVID-19 they know well the visible symptoms: the coughing, sneezing, mental confusion, and difficulty breathing that strikes fear. But mental health symptoms can be much more difficult to see. Lives are being risked to confront an invisible enemy. Yet everyday thousands of social workers, counselors, case aids, case managers, nurses and doctors, and mental health practitioners risk their lives for thousands more of strangers. We call these people leaders, and the pandemic has helped us redefine leadership. In mental health, we are a world full of heart, and we have compassionate leaders with heart at every level of our workforce.

How Behavioral Health Teams Can Redefine Community

A community is commonly defined as a group of people living in the same place or having a particular characteristic in common. By that definition, COVID-19 has now made the entire world a community. But we may not feel like one. Mental health centers, hospitals, schools, and several other institutions are all in unique positions to redefine community. When we think of communities, we often consider it as being all inclusive as if everyone is part of it. A helpful metaphor is that of a village. As such many would say now is the time to rebuild our village. As a major proponent of rebuilding the village, Dr. Carl Bell would have suggested it would also be a good time to "get rid of the rats." He often talked about the importance of not stopping at simply treating rat bites, but in a sense of true community, you have to get rid of the rats to solve the problem. While we may not be facing actual rats in our village rebuild, we are confronted by "mindbugs." Mindbugs are described by Professor Mahzarin Banaji (2016) as our hidden biases that keep us from fully embracing concepts and taking actions that we may know are right. These hidden biases are our blind spots. Our blind spots can stop us from welcoming "otherness," in the form of gender, race, sexual orientation, abilities, beliefs, thoughts, or any domain that may be "other" or different from us. When we exclude others from opportunities, services, processes, treatments, or rewards because they are different from us, we weaken the village.

Rebuilding the village provides a great opportunity for more inclusion of otherness in treatment efforts. Behavioral health teams must be able to bring people together in ways that are helpful, useful, meaningful, and credible. If your teams have been having conversations about diversity, inclusion, equity, and belonging, this is a time to reinforce those conversations with action. We all know people on teams who simply refuse to acknowledge they see color or gender, or sexual orientation, and thus seldom go out of their way to support action to combat disparities. This failure to see or act erodes team self-confidence and organization credibility, creating dysfunction.

Five Dysfunctions of a Team

As we consider the impact of discrimination and failures to address diversity, equity, inclusion, and belonging, Lencioni's work on the *Five Dysfunctions of a Team* has never been more relevant. Lencioni (2002) identifies the five dysfunctions of a team as (1) absence of trust, (2) fear of conflict, (3) lack of commitment, (4) avoidance of team accountability, and (5) inattention to team objectives.

What the pandemic has revealed is the potential for team members at every level to exert leadership, as has been seen on the front lines and behind the scenes. The opportunity to advance this important work puts us in the position where we can work collaboratively globally, locally, and every level in between. But trust is essential. Lencioni (2002) identifies the absence of trust as the first of the five dysfunctions of a team. The insecurities that many members of our society experience whether they are delivering care or receiving it are evident every day. From hiring processes to determining who gets what treatments and by whom, there are disparities. But the possibilities of change are unparalleled because the pandemic has allowed us to see how diversity and inclusion could ideally work to the benefit of all. Our vital work together has to begin by establishing the presence of trust.

The Absence of Trust

Dr. Stephen Covey (1990) talks about trust on two levels: competency and character. On the competency level, there are a number of professionals in the mental health environment who fail to see their own mindbugs. Certain institutions are notorious for failing to recognize their own mindbugs. When confronted with their failure to diversify, be inclusive, and create opportunities for equity and belonging, they often deny these behaviors.

Healthcare professionals who actually embrace diversity and develop partnerships to support the long-term success of people of color irrespective of gender or sexual orientation will have a more effective team. Yet competency-level trust is often absent because of the failure to even recognize our feelings as leaders of organizations where we struggle with diversity issues. This absence of awareness is equally as destructive as the character-level trust failures.

Character trust failures are typically anchored in intentional behaviors that can support destructive attitudes such as racism. We often acknowledge them yet fail to do anything about them. You may hear the phrase "I condemn racism." Yet, when a building is condemned, it is actually physically destroyed. But we seldom see the destruction of racism or even the disruption of racist activities following the phrase "I condemn racism." Unlike the demolished building, there is scarce evidence after the verbal condemnation of racism.

Leaders of teams who have the responsibility to act against racial injustice but fail to do so give silent permission to team members to mistreat others. This increases the lack of trust. Effective leadership requires high character and emotional intelligence to self-assess and self-manage and the self-awareness to find courage and take on the challenge of discrimination on your team. That is what is expected and needed from leaders. You also must be competent enough to understand that you will not have all the answers and be willing to ask for help. That help could come from internal support and/or external support. The bottom line is leaders must have the character and competence to earn the trust of people who do not look, act, or think like they do. And people have to feel they can be comfortably vulnerable within their organizations to take appropriate risks. Organizations that provide treatment have a responsibility to work with people who can help them identify and eliminate their blind spots and mindbugs.

Fear of Conflict

Many team members are aware of, and concerned about, disparate treatment of certain members of society, but they consider it someone else's job to combat such injustice. Sometimes they are reluctant to take action to combat injustice because they feel the organization will not back their position or action. There are other team members who embrace conflict, accept that disruption is part of doing business, and understand that you have to champion the rights of others to protect the rights of all. These people function as the conscience of their organizations. They understand the importance of social justice in a team-based environment. However, if those team leaders do not have the legitimate power of influence inside the organization, they may not be able to deliver the desired results.

When diversity efforts fail those who chose to duck the conflict may say something like "that's exactly why I didn't get involved." Those behaviors and actions can quickly become a reinforcing loop for others in the organization. In essence, *I see something; I do nothing, because I don't think the organization will support my efforts. I also watch others see something and do something, but I still see the organization fail to support their efforts. By doing nothing I am self-rewarded because I told you so.* The squeaky wheel may get the grease, but then it becomes much easier to slide that wheel out the door for rocking the boat.

Teams that are more diverse understand that conflict is part of why they're successful. Seeing things differently makes them stronger. They understand avoiding conflict is just delaying the inevitable. They also understand they see the world differently from their counterparts. The strongest team members welcome and celebrate differences. The best teams recognize that healthy conflict is an important strength. Strong teams understand that fake harmony only sounds good; it doesn't actually do good. Those teams celebrate the strength of others including the willingness to have conflicting views because they understand it is not the absence of conflict that makes a great team. But the absence of trust can make a great team mediocre. Effectively resolving or healthy acceptance of conflict can make all the difference in building trust.

Lack of Commitment

How many times have you participated in a diversity/inclusion/equity/belonging training? Everyone gathers together in the room; they are generally kind; the agenda is well laid out; it may be a person of color who opens up the event. Perhaps they even facilitate the event. And minutes into the diversity initiative someone will say "*I don't see color*." In that moment for many participants, the air has just been sucked out of the room. For a member of a team to tell a room full of participants that they do not see color speaks of the failure to commit to fixing a problem. If you can't commit to seeing color, how is it even possible you could commit to effectively addressing the problem? It is difficult, if not impossible, to solve problems we don't see.

As leaders, it is difficult to fix something that is invisible to us. It is helpful to see what we are working on. And it is hard for others to have to continue to spend their time proving to us that the problem even exists. Those are team leadership blind spots. However, in light of the nationwide discussion of structural racism, any leader who would tell you today that they do not see color in their organizations or outside of the organization is simply not committed or not in touch.

The organization's leader's responsibility in those moments is to address the issue. One of the most effective way we get around this barrier when we facilitate training on diversity, inclusion, equity, and belonging is to hold up colors or use color wheels. We have participants comment on the colors that they see in the room, including the articles of clothing that their counterparts are wearing. Of course, you will hear orange, yellow, pink, red, black, green, and blue, and every now and then someone says fuchsia or tangerine. However, by the time that exercise is over, it is clear that everybody in the room sees color. And that's where you can begin your work because you can secure a commitment by having other people acknowledge the current reality. And as Peter Drucker (1993) notes, that is a leader's first job, defining current reality. Nearly all of us see color. The question becomes: what do we do about it? For team leaders it is what we do that reflects our commitment. You will hear people say "I'm really on board with this whole diversity/inclusion thing. I think it's a great idea! But what action steps have they taken that reinforce their commitments? In essence, *we should always watch what our leaders say and listen to what they do*."

Simply saying something seldom gets the job done. Commitment takes a plan; it often takes training, meaningful conversations, and doing. Doing is what gets results; action provides the greatest clarity and is the truest evidence of commitment. You can tell the difference between teams that are committed and those that only talk about their commitment to valuing otherness. Commitment often begins with putting resources behind our words. Time, money, and intellectual capital are great investments that reflect the earnest intent of our commitment. Promises without the resources to achieve the outcomes often end as denied wishes demoralizing those who dared risk their hope.

Avoidance of Team Accountability

Bill Parcells, legendary NFL coach, said, *if playing the game didn't matter, they wouldn't be keeping score*. In the leadership world, someone must keep score. That's what accountability is; accountability is different than responsibility; accountability is where the buck stops. Leaders of great teams understand what is most important for their team to be successful. And they hold their team members and themselves accountable for the desired outcomes. If your leader says diversity, inclusion, equity, and belonging are important to the organization they cannot back away from the conversation simply because it makes some people uncomfortable. There has to be accountability. If no one is keeping score of the diversity work, it may not matter to the organization. When organizational leaders always tell you some mysterious team is working on something, you seldom see the benefits of the work because no one's keeping score. And worse, no one is truly accountable. Yes, someone may be responsible for the work, but they may as well be invisible because there's no true accountability scorecard. Many organizations have people who work there and have no measurable means of deciphering whether their work is winning or losing. Their behaviors may be disruptive, disturbing, and even dangerous. Yet the organization seems to ignore it. This results in creating emotional cancers that eat away at the organization's culture or social fabric. The culture begins to feel uncomfortable, scratchy, and prickly as it disintegrates. At some point the organization's culture becomes hard for many employees to wear. When wearing the culture becomes uncomfortable, some will leave, while others will stay until it becomes unbearable. That's when the difficult conversations start. When an organization has pain so deep, it has to talk, perhaps even scream. That is when true accountability starts but when mild discomfort suddenly turns to unbearable pain, it can also be too late.

You can tell a lot about an organization when you can identify what it is attempting to accomplish based on its true mission. Whatever results it is keeping score of are the things it expects to be held accountable for.

You can always tell when work is not celebrated or even recognized because no one is accountable; it is not really important to the organization, no matter what the newsletter says. And even in the midst of deep organizational pain, you may hear rallying cries about change and change champions, transparency, and accountability. But you can forecast the outcomes of the change based on the change champions. True change champions are hard to hide; they leave results wherever they work.

An organization that is accountable for diversity, inclusion, equity, and belonging will have a mandate. You will see that they don't simply talk about it; they have numbers that validate their mandate. You see diversity in the halls, in meetings, anywhere the work matters. Those organizations double check inequities. They don't assume that they are hiring diverse individuals. They trust but verify. When they look at who they are interviewing, they screen their training efforts to ensure that their implicit biases are not somehow keeping them from developing a diverse talent pool. They understand that accountability is about outcomes not just conversation. And when they don't see what they are looking for, they hold themselves and others accountable. And what are they looking for? Results, not more promises, just results.

Inattention to Team Objectives

Imagine a board of directors holding its executive director accountable for diversity in recruiting, hiring, promoting, and retention. Imagine that same person's compensation being linked to drivers that reflected diversity, inclusion, equity, and belonging. Now imagine the other managers and leaders of the same organization having the same expectations of them. All their compensation being partially linked to that organizational goal. That's accountability that cannot be avoided because it is focused on results. Just like in a sports arena; that result becomes a scoreboard people can see. The commitment is there because the buy-in occurs at the organization, team, and individual levels. Fear of conflicts is greatly diminished because the harmony is no longer artificial; it is tangible. Trust comes easier because the organization's espoused values are aligned with its actions.

Changes of this magnitude stick because they eliminate excuses such as we couldn't find any Black, Brown, or Asian candidate qualified for the role, but we tried. Or, being stuck on the disabilities a potential employee brings, instead of their abilities. We cannot lead or give people what we do not have or do not know. All of us can only work with what we have. But if not given a legitimate opportunity, we cannot work. Once there are legitimate consequences for failing to achieve desired results, the excuses disappear. Teams work to support the success of other teams and the success of the organization as a whole.

When organizations are allowed to escape the conversation as to why they can't find a gay person, women, or people of color to fill positions and fulfill dreams, it is often because the decision-makers do not really see the value being worth the effort. It is hard to maintain synergy when no one pays attention to the scoreboard. It's almost like no one knows what everyone else is really working on. That's exactly what happens in some organizations. Teams in those organizations go about their daily work, people meet, greet are basically nice to each other. Even though they set wonderful equity, inclusion, and diversity goals, like playing a sport where you don't keep score, they don't pay attention to the results.

The sad part is that science indicates that organizations that are diverse in most instances outperform their less diverse counterparts. Even if you disagree with the premise of team diversity, you can't argue with the business results. Diversity and inclusion aren't some things that are just nice to do or even "the right thing to do." For those who take it upon themselves to pay attention to the results, they are also effective business decisions that can create a sustainable competitive advantage.

To wit, many organizations seem to just be playing the game of diversity and not keeping score. Those organizations will be traumatized because, thanks to COVID-19, the world is becoming a working environment with a giant scoreboard of death versus survival, of economic productivity, and of broad societal well-being.

Among the traumas precipitated by the COVID-19 pandemic, a contemporaneous increase of attention to American racial inequities offers paradoxical hope. This hopeful glimmer can only be actualized if renewed efforts to combat racial inequities bear fruit, thus supporting societal resilience. This chapter has attempted to demonstrate that the seemingly prosaic functions of behavioral health team management will not only support the team's success but can be protective in combating community trauma.

References

American Psychiatric Association. (2013). Diagnostic and Statistical Manual of Mental Disorders (5th ed.). Arlington, VA: American Psychiatric Publishing.

Banaji, M. R. (2016). *Blindspot: Hidden Biases of Good People* (Reprint ed.). Bantam.

Bell, C. C. (1974). Analysis of the political sophistication of the black psychiatrist. Newsletter Black Psychiatrists of America, 3 (1), 5 & 7.

Bell, C. (2006). Exposure to a traumatic event does not automatically put a person on a path to develop PTSD: The importance of protective factors to promote resiliency. *PTSD Resources for Survivors and Caregivers.* Retrieved from http://www.giftfromwithin.org/html/promote.html#p2.

Bell, C., Flay, B. & Paikoff, R. (2002). *The Health Behavioral Change Imperative: Theory, Education, And Practice in Diverse Populations.* New York: Plenum Publishers.

Bell, C., Richardson J., & Blount, M. A. *Suicide prevention.* In Lutzker, L. R. (2005). *Preventing violence: Research and evidence-based intervention strategies.* Washington, DC: American Psychological

Bell, C. C., & Suggs, H. (1998). Using sports to strengthen resiliency in children: training heart. *Child and Adolescent Psychiatric Clinics*, *7*(4), 859–865. Association Press. 217–237.

Breslau, N., Lucia, V. C., & Alvarado, G. F. (2006). Intelligence and other predisposing factors in exposure to trauma and posttraumatic stress disorder; A follow-up study at age 17 years. *The Journal of the American Medical Association Psychiatry, 63*(11):1238–1245. https://doi.org/10.1001/archpsyc.63.11.1238

Collins, J. (2001). Good to Great. New York: HarperCollins Publications Inc

Covey, S. R. (1989). The 7 Habits of Highly Effective People. New York: Simon Schuster.

Covey, S.R. (1990). Principle Centered Leadership. New York:Simon Schuster.

DePree, M. (1992). Leadership Jazz. New York: Dell.

Drucker, P. (1993). The Effective Executive. Harper Collins Publisher, New York.

Eilenberg J, Townsend EJ, Oudens E (2000). Who's in charge here anyway? Managing the management split in mental health organizations. Administration & Policy in Mental Health 27(5), 287–297.

Goldsmith, M. (2007). What Got You Here Won't Get You There. New York: Hyperion.

Goleman, D. (1996). *Emotional intelligence; Why it can matter more than IQ.* Learning, 24(6), 49–50.

Goleman, D. (2007). *Social intelligence.* New York: Random house.

Greenleaf, R. K. (2002). *Servant Leadership.* New Jersey: Paulist Press.

Griffin, G., McEwen, E., Samuels, B. H., Suggs, H., Redd, J. L., & McClelland, G. M. (2011). Infusing protective factors for children in foster care. Psychiatric Clinics, development, reliability, and validity of the daily life stressors scale. *Journal of Child and Family Studies,* 2(4), 371–388.

Keyes, C. L. M. (2007). Promoting and protective mental health as flourishing. American Psychologist, 62 (2), 95–108.

Lencioni, P. (2002). San Francisco: Jossey-Bass. The Five Dysfunctions of a Team.

Ranz JM, Stueve A (1998). The role of the psychiatrist as program medical director. PsychiatricServices 49:1203–7.

Senge, P. (1990). The fifth discipline: The Art & Practice of the Learning Organization. New York: Doubleday.

Senge, P., Kleimer, A., Roberts, C., Ross, R., & Smith, B. (1994). The Fifth Discipline Fieldbook: Strategies And Tools for Building A Learning Organization. New York: Doubleday.

Youth.gov (n.d.). Retrieved from https://youth.gov/youth-topics/juvenile-justice/risk-and-protective-factors 59.

Community Education

Rachel M. Talley and Gary Belkin

There is a growing recognition that the environments in which individuals with mental health disorders live, learn, work, and play have a foundational influence on poor mental health outcomes (Compton and Shim 2015). As community mental health providers become increasingly aware of the importance of these upstream societal factors, it is critical to consider health education and health promotion, activities which extend beyond the exam room to touch the communities in which patients reside, as a necessary piece of the community psychiatrist's societal role. In the clinical environment, the teaching role has been historically identified as a key way in which the community psychiatrist can support patient care through cooperative relationships with staff, providing clinical background that can help non-medical staff to better understand treatment choices, provide information relevant to treatment decisions from their own observations, and contextualize patient trajectories (Diamond et al. 1991). Survey data indicates that community psychiatrists perceive clinical collaboration, including the provision of supervision, informal consultation, and formal training, as important to job satisfaction (Ranz et al. 2001). Beyond the clinical setting, there is a long-standing recognition of the role of the community psychiatrist not only consisting of direct patient care in the clinical context but also including macro-level health promotion in the larger community (Rosen 2006).

In taking on the community education role, how should community psychiatrists define a patient's community? We can assume that the individuals and institutions that define community will vary for each patient that the community psychiatrist serves; as such, there is a need to broadly consider a variety of settings and target audiences when attempting to assess the evidence base for community mental health education. Community education can include the micro-environment of a patient's closest family members and clinical providers and the macro-environments of institutions that impact a patient's daily life and functioning outside of the clinical setting.

There is a paucity of evidence in the literature specifically examining the role of the community psychiatrist in community mental health education efforts. However, community mental health education efforts more generally have been assessed for a few key stakeholders and entities that are highlight relevant to the community psychiatric work. The most established outcome

R. M. Talley (✉)
Perelman School of Medicine, University of Pennsylvania, Philadelphia, PA, USA
e-mail: Rachel.Talley@pennmedicine.upenn.edu

G. Belkin
Billion Minds Institute, New York City, NY, USA

Harvard TH Chan School of Public Health, Boston, MA, USA
e-mail: g@abillion.org

W. E. Sowers et al. (eds.), *Textbook of Community Psychiatry*,
https://doi.org/10.1007/978-3-031-10239-4_14

findings and conceptual commentary on the community psychiatrist role are available for mental health education targeted toward three audiences: (1) the patient's family members, (2) the law enforcement community, and (3) the patient's school community. Though these three realms are disparate in terms of target audience and setting, assessment of common themes and guiding principles across these forms of community education can inform the ways in which the community psychiatrist can most ideally approach this role. Despite evidence limitations, the community psychiatrist can consider extrapolating these common themes and approaches to new settings and modalities.

Family Psychoeducation

Family members of individuals with mental illness often form one of the most critical layers of a patient's community, making these stakeholders an important audience for the community psychiatrist's educational efforts. Family psychoeducation (FPE) emerged in the 1980s in recognition of the shortcomings of traditional family therapy to address the needs of families of individuals with serious mental illness; counter to the mindset of traditional family therapy, FPE interventions were formulated from a mindset of collaboration with family members, emphasizing the sharing of coping strategies and information on illness (McFarlane et al. 2003). Though one of FPE's eight core characteristics is that the intervention is created and led by a mental health professional (Lucksted et al. 2012), it has not been envisioned as specifically having to originate from a psychiatrist. That being said, the *Substance Abuse and Mental Health Services Administration* (SAMHSA) Evidence-Based Practices Kit for FPE provides examples of areas where the treating psychiatrist might specifically play a role in FPE, including providing content on the biology of mental health conditions and target participation in educational groups that focus on medication questions (SAMHSA 2020). In frontline practice, community psychiatrists frequently take on the role of family educator. FPE is a relevant arena from which to draw lessons for the community psychiatrist's educator role for two reasons: (1) FPE is a well-established evidence-based practice for which there are robust findings linking an educational effort to positive patient outcomes, and (2) FPE is a mental health education intervention for which there exists broad agreement on principles and goals to guide the educator, providing content from which to begin to draw a framework to guide community psychiatrists in other educational efforts.

Numerous controlled studies have validated the finding that FPE is associated with reduced rehospitalization rates and reduced symptom relapse for individuals with schizophrenia (McFarlane et al. 2003). This strong evidence base has driven the national recognition and dissemination of FPE as an evidence-based psychosocial intervention for the management of adults with schizophrenia (Dixon et al. 2009; SAMHSA 2020). More recent evidence has begun to build the case for the association between family intervention and these same outcomes for individuals with bipolar disorder, with more limited but emerging data exploring the role of family intervention in driving positive outcomes in other mental health disorders (Lucksted et al. 2012).

Literature from the above-cited reviews and treatment recommendations offers much guidance on key characteristics specific to optimal provision of FPE, including recommended length, inclusion as part of a treatment plan, being diagnosis-specific, etc. To draw more general lessons from FPE that might guide the community psychiatrist as an educator, it is worth taking a step back and considering some of FPE's broader guiding principles for success. Fifteen guiding principles have been envisioned as key to the success of clinicians in their work with families (Dixon et al. 2001). Principles most relevant to the education mission include paying attention to the social and clinical needs of the consumer; exploring family members' expectations of the treatment program and expectations for the consumer; providing relevant information for the consumer and his or her family at appropriate times; providing an explicit crisis plan and professional response; and providing training for the family in structured problem-solving techniques.

Extrapolating from these guiding principles, some key themes that the community psychiatrist can consider in approaching his/her community education role based on the lessons of FPE include:

1. *Alliance-building and the removal of hierarchy:* FPE's guiding principles emphasize a spirit of collaboration between the educator and the patient's family and specifically advise conceptualizing the patient's family as an equal partner in the treatment process.
2. *Bi-directional information exchange:* While FPE's guiding principles identify important information that the mental health educator should provide to families (including problem-solving techniques and crisis resources), several principles highlight the critical information that the family provides to the educator as part of the needs assessment process, including the family's expectations, concerns, strengths, and limitations.
3. *Broad target audience:* Per FPE's guiding principles, while patient outcomes are the primary target objective, a broader audience is relevant. Family outcomes including addressing family emotional distress and addressing loss are key.
4. *Flexibility:* One FPE guiding principle emphasizes flexibility in meeting family needs.

Community Education in Law Enforcement

Individuals with mental illness have substantial involvement with law enforcement, with data indicating that one in ten individuals with mental illness encounter the police as part of their pathway to mental healthcare and approximately 1% of police calls and encounters involve an individual with mental illness (Livingston 2016). The extent of this interface highlights the importance of law enforcement as a key target for community mental health education efforts.

Several models exist for collaboration between mental health and law enforcement. A recent review broadly examined the outcomes of mental health training for non-mental health professionals, with a primary focus on law enforcement learners, finding that the existing evidence base was not rigorous enough to inform recommended training format, content, delivery, etc. (Booth et al. 2017). Crisis intervention training (CIT) is described as a police-based specialized police response, consisting in part of self-selected law enforcement volunteers participating in a 40-hour training focused on the management of mental health crisis; training is typically conducted by a community health worker, patients, and patient advocates rather than psychiatrists (Compton et al. 2008). Compton et al.'s 2008 review of available literature on the effectiveness of CIT noted positive officer-level knowledge and attitude outcomes in post-survey and pre-/post-survey data but commented on the need for more rigorous evaluation. A more recent review of the CIT literature similarly found consistent post-survey and pre-/post-survey data supporting an association between CIT training and self-reported officer-level outcomes, including training satisfaction and self-perceived likelihood to use force; the available evidence was not adequate to fully support CIT's association with the desired outcome of actual reduced use of force in interactions between law enforcement and individuals with mental illness (Rogers et al. 2019).

The Council of State Governments has highlighted several other key models for partnership between law enforcement and mental health providers, including co-responder teams, in which a law enforcement officer has either in-person or remote support from a mental health worker in addressing a crisis; mobile crisis teams in which teams of mental health workers partner with law enforcement and the community to prevent unneeded hospitalization and incarceration of individuals with mental illness; and case management teams, in which follow-up and referral support is provided (The CSG Justice Center 2019). A recent review of co-responder interventions found a growing but still fairly limited evidence base, with no controlled trials (Puntis et al.

2018); implementation of co-responder teams was associated with reduced rates of police detention, less distress at police interactions among services users, and variable changes in psychiatric hospitalization. Puntis and colleagues made note of the considerable heterogeneity in models, making it challenging for on-the-ground providers to identify best practices from this literature.

In spite of some need to further develop the evidence base, initiatives aimed at training law enforcement professional to interface with individuals with mental illness have proliferated nationally, for example, approximately 2700 CIT programs existing in the United States as of 2019 (Rogers et al. 2019). Given the ubiquity of these initiatives and the favorable outcomes that have been noted, CIT and other law enforcement/mental health training models provide another ripe source from which community psychiatrists might extrapolate broad guiding principles for approaching community education.

The original "Memphis Model" of CIT included several core ongoing, operational, and sustaining elements. Core elements include partnership between law enforcement, advocates, and mental health providers; community ownership; the establishment of policies and procedures; etc. (Dupont et al. 2007). In a qualitative review of facilitators and barriers to effective mental health training as reported by non-mental health professionals (the majority of whom were law enforcement professionals), the learners emphasized the importance of the trainer's knowledge of unique aspects of their work environment and job role and tailoring of training content to fit their work setting, among other logistical and organizational factors (Scantlebury et al. 2018). In its framework to guide effective implementation of Police-Mental Health Collaborations, the CSG Justice Center suggests that quality mental health and stabilization training, a key feature of a successful police-mental health collaboration, should include provision of training to all staff; tailoring of training to the roles, interests, and experience of staff; provision of training not only from law enforcement and mental health professionals but also from individuals and families with lived experience; and evaluation of training (The CSG Justice Center 2019).

As with FPE's evidence base, literature on community education for law enforcement does not provide specific evidence-based guidelines on the role of the community psychiatrist in providing education to this population. However, core elements of evidence-based training (CIT), qualitative evidence from the relevant learners, and principles from the CSG Justice Center's framework further build on the key themes previously identified in this chapter as guiding principles to support the community psychiatrist in providing community education:

1. *Alliance-building and the removal of hierarchy:* CIT's core elements description implies a non-hierarchical partnership in which law enforcement, patients, advocates, mental health professionals, and the larger community are all stakeholders.
2. *Bi-directional information exchange:* CIT's core elements reference an information flow from several sources, including mental health providers, advocates, patients, and law enforcement. The qualitative data summarized above emphasizes the importance of the mental health provider acquiring knowledge of and familiarity with the unique work environment of a training's target audience to facilitate a successful training experience.
3. *Broad target audience:* As above, multiple stakeholders are identified as relevant to the success of training programs such as CIT. CIT's core elements include community ownership, emphasizing that while actual training content may be geared specifically toward law enforcement, the true target audience for the intervention is much broader. The CSG Justice Center encourages broad availability of mental health training to all law enforcement staff.
4. *Flexibility:* Both the above-describe qualitative results and the CSG Justice Center's framework emphasize the importance of adapting training content to the unique work environment, roles, and skills of different learners.

Community Education in Schools

Schools are a crucial part of the community environment in which individuals with mental illness grow, socialize, interact, and develop. Conceptually, the role of the child psychiatrist as a community consultant to institutions outside of the clinical context, including schools, has been described as foundational to the profession, with roots in the child guidance movement of the early twentieth century (Milam-Miller 2009). Milam-Miller describes the child psychiatrist consultant's role as involving a removal of hierarchy in which bi-directional knowledge is exchanged between the consultant and the system, highlighting the importance of the consultant's ability to align with the system, clearly identify the consultation questions, and measure intervention outcomes.

In terms of further conceptual framing of the community psychiatric consultant's role, Bostic and Bagnell propose a framework for approaching school consultation that incorporates five components, including clarifying confidentiality parameters; clarifying the consultation questions such that there is mutual agreement between consultant and consultee of the need; understanding the relevance and impact of the consultation question on different stakeholders in the system; considering legal and ethical issues relevant to addressing the child's needs in the context of the parental relationship; and formulating the question through the biopsychosocial lens (Bostic and Bagnell 2001). The authors further frame the importance of a sequential process of alliance-building with the client, a thorough focus on the assessing consultee needs which focuses on bridge-building and an understanding of the consultee's perspective and action in accordance with the needs assessment.

In terms of evidence specific to the community psychiatrist's consultation role in the school setting, Berkovitz's 2001 paper considers the outcome evidence from a select group of school-based consultation interventions as well as prior reviews of school consultation to highlight the importance of considering outcome evaluation when pursuing school consultation (Berkovitz 2001). Summarizing the findings, Berkovitz reports generally positive outcomes in terms of observed child behavior, child academic performance, administrator attitudes and perspectives, etc. However, it is challenging to derive global conclusions about key characteristics or most effective methods for school-based consultation from this report given the heterogeneity in terms of research design (e.g., use of control groups, outcomes measured, etc.) and content of intervention in the studies described, as well as limited information on these factors from the older reviews. A more recent review of mental health training for non-mental health professionals, which primarily aimed to assess interventions for police but ultimately broadened in focus, highlighted some positive changes in attitudes and knowledge of teachers and residential advisors in response to mental health training, including for interventions informed by the Mental Health First Aid model (Booth et al. 2017). However, the studies identified are few and heterogeneous in terms of target audience, training format, etc. Thus, the outcome data available argues for the need for more rigorous and standardized evaluation of the community psychiatrist's consultation role in schools.

Despite these limitations, prior conceptual framings of the community mental health consultant role in schools echo the key themes highlighted in regard community education for families and law enforcement:

5. *Alliance-building and the removal of hierarchy:* Milam-Miller's framing of the community psychiatric school consultant's role emphasizes the importance of reducing hierarchy as part of the alliance-building process needed for successful consultation.
6. *Bi-directional information exchange:* Milam-Miller cites bi-directional information exchange as important to alliance-building in school consultation, while Bostic and Bagnell highlight the importance of the consultant and consultee developing a mutual understanding of the need underlying the consultation question.

7. *Broad target audience:* Bostic and Bagnell highlight the importance of understanding the consultation question from the perspective of multiple stakeholders.
8. *Flexibility:* Milam-Miller describes a flexibility in interpreting the consultation question, with the consultant allowing for the possibility of the initial, surface consultation question revealing indirect system-level consultation asks that need to be solved.

Additional Target Audiences for the Community Psychiatrist Educator

Psychiatrist as Educator to Non-mental Health Providers

Integration of mental health services into non-mental health settings is increasingly viewed as furthering the treatment of individuals struggling with comorbid psychiatric and non-psychiatric health needs (Ramanuj et al. 2019). The emergence of the models suggests a role for community psychiatrist as educators in the non-psychiatric medical setting. Norfleet and colleagues conducted a mixed methods survey of a convenience sample of over 50 psychiatrists in integrated care roles to better understand their experiences. Beyond provision of information on diagnosis and medication choice, most surveyed psychiatrists (85%) identified education on specific topics as part of their consultation role. Qualitative results revealed the psychiatrist's role as educator to be one of four key themes encapsulating an overwhelmingly positive view of the integrated care role (Norfleet et al. 2016). Additional evidence is needed to better understand the key components and effectiveness of the psychiatrist as educator for clinical staff in non-mental health settings, as well as the impact of this education on learners and patients.

Psychiatrist as Educator to Other Mental Health Professionals

Interprofessional education in the healthcare setting has been described as having the potential to positively alter the attitudes and perceptions of healthcare professionals, including reducing negative stereotypes among professionals and fostering collaboration and common knowledge (Priest et al. 2008). There is a critical need to build the evidence base supporting the role of community psychiatrists in mental health interprofessional education. A recent Cochrane review of interprofessional education among healthcare professionals found that conclusions could not be drawn about key components or effectiveness of interprofessional education due to the poor quality of evidence (Reeves et al. 2013). Not unexpectedly given this, the evidence base for interprofessional education specific to the mental health setting is extremely limited. A 2001 systematic review of studies examining interprofessional education among mental health staff serving adults with mental illness yielded 19 studies, only 13 of which were rated "good" or "acceptable" in terms of quality of evidence (Reeves 2001). Reeves noted a lack of rigor in research design in addition to other methodologic shortfalls. Notably as regards the specific role of the psychiatrist, few studies specified the type of staff involved in the described interventions.

Psychiatrist as Educator on Social Media

As the use of social media applications and other online communication platforms flourishes, there has been increasing attention toward the use of these platforms to seek and/or exchange health information (Zhao and Zhang 2017). Particularly relevant to the community psychiatrist, emerging data reveal significant social media usage among patients with serious mental illness (SMI) (Miller et al. 2015). In one recent survey of community-dwelling individuals with SMI, a quarter of respondents reported using social media either for posting or seeking health information (Naslund et al. 2016). As the community psychiatrist's patients increasingly interface with the digital "communities," these platforms offer an exciting new avenue for community psychiatrists to educate both community patients and the public at large. In reviewing forms of social media and Internet communication, Peek and colleagues suggest modalities including traditional blogging, microblogging, and podcasts by which psychiatrists can combat stigma via educating the public (Peek et al. 2015).

The works of psychiatrists Dinah Miller, Steve Daviss, and Annette Hanson provide a compelling example of the power of social media engagement for the psychiatrist. These psychiatrists ran a popular blog for a broad audience, "Shrink Rap," for 12 years ("Shrink Rap" n.d.); this work blossomed into dozens of podcasts, a book intended to explain elements of mental health treatment to the lay public (Miller et al. 2011), and engagement with platforms including Facebook and Twitter. "Shrink Rap" includes over 2000 blog posts demonstrating unique contributions that psychiatrists can make to the social media dialogue, including nontechnical explanations of medication options and commentary combatting stigmatizing views of mental health and psychiatry in popular media. In reflecting on their social media experiences, the "Shrink Rap" psychiatrists highlight that as educators in the social media space, psychiatrists can play the unique role of demystifying and humanizing the psychiatric profession, as well as using lessons learned from the experiences of the lay public through bi-directional engagement to advocate for changes benefitting mental health patients (Daviss et al. 2015). In considering current and future roles for the psychiatrist on Twitter, Peters et al. (2015) similarly highlight a key role for psychiatrists in combatting disinformation about mental health and bi-directional information exchange for patient advocacy.

Psychiatrist as Educator in Mental Health Advocacy

Engagement with advocacy work has been noted as arena in which the physician can play a unique and powerful educator role, drawing on expert knowledge to translate technical medical concepts into a form that is understandable for the lay public and policymakers (Netherland 2019). The National Alliance on Mental Illness (NAMI) provides a notable example of this. NAMI's Chief Medical Officer, psychiatrist Kenneth Duckworth, utilizes the advocacy platform to educate the lay public through media engagement (NAMI 2020a), among a range of other activities; numerous physicians have provided educational content to benefit consumers and families through NAMI's "Ask the Expert" content (NAMI 2020b). Through partnership with NAMI, Dr. Duckworth and these clinicians draw on unique clinical expertise to provide practical, understandable, and accessible educational content.

Psychiatrist as Educator in Sharing Tasks and Power with Community Members

Finally, psychiatrists have yet untapped opportunity to explore and adopt a now formidable body of evidence and research often referred to as "task-sharing." This describes a range of skillsets that lay people of all walks of life can use to directly do steps in symptom reduction, illness prevention, and mental health promotion. In such an approach, clinicians can further extend their potential as coach and ongoing improvement partner beyond being clinical direct providers or consultants to also being part of an ecosystem where community mental health is largely done by community members.

Most of the early work in the evolution of task-sharing took place in the Global South. The appearance of work by Paul Bolton and colleagues and Vikram Patel is a good mark of its "launch." Bolton and his collaborators showed that residents of a rural village in Uganda could be taught the techniques of group interpersonal therapy for depression only with sustained outcomes (Bolton et al. 2003). Notably, this effort defined "depression," and the design of the group intervention itself, in collaboration with community members to reflect cultural meanings of experiences and behaviors the "depression" construct captured.

Patel's book *Where there is no Psychiatrist* first appeared in 2003 (Patel 2003). It broke down a range of skills in diagnosis, assessment, and care that could be picked up by community members. Patel's work also was part of a paradigm challenge in discrete-illness thinking, using similar methods to Bolton's in constructing a cultural-customized depression scale in the Shona language in Harare, Zimbabwe (Patel et al. 1997),

Both of these efforts capture key elements that defined a democratization of knowledge in which community members aren't just informed or coached to address an immediate need (such as supporting a family member) but actually shape how the work is defined and its aims while using sophisticated, clinical-science adapted, skill packages and protocols.

For addressing clinically significant and measured depression alone, some notable milestones in propelling this field include work such as that of Atif Rahman. His team showed how lay midwives in rural Pakistan could not only treat perinatal depression through CBT-derived counseling sessions, but doing so improved some birth outcomes (Rahman et al. 2008). Subsequent work by Patel included showing trained community members could educate, screen, and do early interventions for depression across villages in India that not only improved depression, but reduced suicide and closed care gaps at a scaled population level (Shidhaye et al. 2017).

There has been momentum toward growing such approaches in the United States, especially in the wake of the COVID-19 pandemic mental health crisis and increasing attention to strategies that meet escalated acute need while also addressing ongoing emotional resilience, durability, and connections, particularly in the face of racial and socioeconomic fault lines and the crisis of climate change.

Among the most robustly studied efforts, the Community Partners in Care (CPIC) initiative customized training across almost 100 community organizations in Los Angeles to tackle depression by embedding skills much closer to the ground across an array of trusted social supports and partners. It improved depression outcomes but also had impact upstream on social determinants such as reduced homelessness and its risk factors compared to usual care (Wells et al. 2013). Here too, the targets, methods, and desired skills were a co-created effort between clinician partners and community members. REACH-NOLA built on this operational know-how, along with the University of Washington's AIMS Center Collaborative Care model (http://aims.uw.edu), to apply that model beyond its initial application in primary care environments to entire neighborhoods flooded in New Orleans after Hurricane Katrina. As such, local residents worked together on recovery response also acted as home-visiting depression care managers (Wennerstrom et al. 2011).

This basic template of transferring effective care skillsets, and more contextually framed aims, has spread across disparate geographies to address a whole range of conditions beyond depression (Singla et al. 2018). So has attention to principles and practices to accelerate implementation and scale of task-shared work. This includes tools for better training and supervision of lay community volunteers or workers (Kohrt et al. 2015). The open-sourced learning platform EMPOWER has the potential to ease the way for any group of community health workers or community members to initiate self-directed learning and ongoing proficiency in use of skill packages for non-professionals tested by randomized control trials (https://mentalhealthforalllab.hms.harvard.edu/empower).

This work also more recently includes growing attention to the infrastructures, funding streams, governmental sectors, and tools to get to "new normal" levels of scale and mainstreamed adoption. *ThriveNYC* (Belkin and McCray 2019), for example, is to-date the largest investment by a local government in spreading task-share based. Across New York City agencies and community settings, this approach was spread to a wide array of otherwise unreached but high-risk populations such as in public day care settings, job training programs, youth drop-in programs, and homeless and intimate partner violence shelters and to teachers. It put skills in these hands not only for clinical or symptom defined help but to also deepen the reach of proven prevention and promotion interventions. *ThriveNYC* offered learning about the infrastructure needed to form a support system to lower the bar for ambitious spread of such work. But this effort also held lessons as to its newness and thus a fragility of political will to sustain and defend it and the need to build a professional voice to validate and help support it (Belkin 2020).

Conclusions

The role of community educator has long been viewed as a key responsibility of the community psychiatrist. Community psychiatrists should envision this role broadly, encompassing a variety of stakeholders and settings that are relevant not only to the community psychiatric patient's daily functioning and well-being, but to the entire community's functioning and well-being through a wider notion of who is a patient and who can be a provider. Though the formal evidence base regarding the specific role of the community psychiatrist in community education is limited, the guiding principles and conceptualizations of community mental health education in a variety of diverse settings share common themes which can guide a community psychiatrist's educational efforts, including removal of hierarchy, bi-directional information exchange, a broad target audience, and flexibility in interpreting and addressing education needs. Advances in task-sharing push that role further, including with tools and manuals ready to set the stage for scale, while understanding, too, that advocacy and action is needed to create reimbursement models and supports for training and implementation. As the range of audiences and settings for community education expands, it is critical for community psychiatry to further grow and actively use a rigorous evidence base to guide best practices for the community psychiatrist's role in community education.

References

Belkin, G. (2020, March 11). What would make ThriveNYC thrive? City & State New York. https://www.cityandstateny.com/opinion/2020/03/what-would-make-thrivenyc-thrive/176292/

Belkin, G., & McCray, C. (2019). ThriveNYC: Delivering on mental health. American Journal of Public Health, 109, S156–S163. https://doi.org/10.2105/AJPH.2019.305040

Berkovitz IH: Evaluations of Outcome in Mental Health Consultation in Schools. Child Adolesc Psychiatr Clin N Am 10: 93–103, 2001

Bolton, P., Bass, J., Neugebauer, R., Verdeli, H., Clougherty, K. F., Wickramaratne, P., Speelman, L., Ndogoni, L., & Weissman, M. (2003). Group Interpersonal Psychotherapy for Depression in Rural Uganda: A Randomized Controlled Trial. *JAMA*, *289*(23), 3117–3124. https://doi.org/10.1001/JAMA.289.23.3117

Booth A, Scantlebury A, Hughes-Morley A et al: Mental health training programmes for non-mental health trained professionals coming into contact with people with mental ill health: a systematic review of effectiveness. BMC Psychiatry 17:196–219, 2017

Bostic JQ, Bagnell A: Psychiatric School Consultation: An Organizing Framework and Empowering Techniques. Child Adolesc Psychiatr Clin N Am 10:1–12, 2001

Compton MT, Bahora M, Watson AC et al: A Comprehensive Review of Extant Research on Crisis Intervention Team (CIT) Programs. J Am Acad Psychiatry Law 36: 47–55, 2008

Compton MT, Shim RS (eds): The Social Determinants of Mental Health. Arlington, VA, American Psychiatric Publishing, 2015

Daviss S, Hanson A, Miller D: My three shrinks: Personal stories of social media exploration. Int Rev Psychiatry 27(2): 167–73, 2015.

Diamond RJ, Stein LI, Susser E: Essential and Nonessential Roles for Psychiatrists in Community Mental Health Centers. Hosp Community Psychiatry 42:187–9, 1991

Dixon L, McFarlane WR, Lefley H, et al: Evidence-Based Practices for Services to Families of People With Psychiatric Disabilities. Psychiatr Serv 52:903–910, 2001

Dixon LB, Dickerson F, Bellack AS et al: The 2009 schizophrenia PORT psychosocial treatment recommendations and summary statements. Schizophr Bull 36:47–70, 2009

Dupont R, Cochran MS, Pillsbury S: Crisis Intervention Team Core Elements. CIT International. September, 2007. Available at http://www.citinternational.org/

resources/Pictures/CoreElements.pdf Accessed November 29, 2020

Kohrt BA, Ramaiya MK, Rai S, Bhardwaj A, Jordans MJD: Development of a scoring system for non-specialist ratings of clinical competence in global mental health: a qualitative process evaluation of the Enhancing Assessment of Common Therapeutic Factors (ENACT) scale. Glob Ment Health (Camb) https://doi.org/10.1017/gmh.2015.21. Epub 2015 Dec 9. 2015;2:e23.

Livingston JD: Contact Between Police and People with Mental Disorders: A Review of Rates. Psychiatr Serv 67:850–7, 2016

Lucksted A, McFarlane W, Downing D et al: Recent Developments in Family Psychoeducation as an Evidence-Based Practice. J Marital Fam Ther 38:101–121, 2012

McFarlane WR, Dixon L, Lukens E, Lucksted A: Family Psychoeducation and Schizophrenia: A Review of the Literature. J Marital Fam Ther 29: 223–245, 2003

Milam-Miller S: The Psychiatrist as Consultant: Working Within Schools, the Courts, and Primary Care to Promote Children's Mental Health. Psychiatr Clin N Amer 32:165–176, 2009

Miller BJ, Stewart A, Schrimsher J, et al: How connected are people with schizophrenia? Cell phone, computer, email, and social media use. Psychiatry Res 225:458–63, 2015

Miller D, Hanson A, Daviss SR. *Shrink Rap: Three Psychiatrists Explain Their Work.* John Hopkins University Press, 2011

Naslund JA, Aschbrenner KA, Bartels SJ: How People with Serious Mental Illness Use Smartphones, Mobile Apps, and Social Media. Psychiatr Rehabil J 39:364–7, 2016

National Alliance on Mental Illness: Ken Duckworth interviewed for a segment on Mental Health and COVID-19. April 23, 2020a. Available at https://www.nami.org/Press-Media/In-The-News/2020/Ken-Duckworth-interviewed-for-a-segment-on-Mental-Health-and-COVID-19 Accessed January 3, 2020

National Alliance on Mental Illness: NAMI's Ask the Expert. Available at https://www.nami.org/Blogs/NAMI-s-Ask-the-Expert Accessed January 3, 2020b

Netherland J: Physicians as Policy Advocates: From the Clinic to the State House. In Structural Competency in Mental Health and Medicine. Edited by Hansen H and Metzle JM. New York, Springer, 2019, pp. 211–216

Norfleet KR, Ratzliff ADH, Chan YF et al: The Role of the Integrated Care Psychiatrist in Community Settings: A Survey of Psychiatrist's Perspectives. Psychiatr Serv 67:346–9, 2016

Patel, V. (2003). *Where There Is No Psychiatrist: A Mental Health Care Manual* (1st ed.). Royal College of Psychiatrists.

Patel, V., Simunyu, E., Gwanzura, F., Lewis, G., & Mann, A. (1997). The Shona Symptom Questionnaire: the development of an indigenous measure of common mental disorders in Harare. *Acta Psychiatrica Scandinavica*, *95*(6), 469–475. https://doi.org/10.1111/J.1600-0447.1997.TB10134.X

Peek HS, Richards M, Muir O, et al: Blogging and Social Media for Mental Health Education and Advocacy: a Review for Psychiatrists. Curr Psychiatr Rep 17:88, 2015.

Peters ME, Uible E, Chisolm MS: A Twitter Education: Why Psychiatrists Should Tweet. Curr Psychiatry Rep 17(12): 94, 2015

Priest HM, Roberts P, Dent H, et al: Interprofessional education and working in mental health: in search of the evidence base. J Nurs Manage 16: 474–85, 2008

Puntis S, Perfect D, Kirubarajan A, Bolton S, Davies F, Hayes A, Harriss E, Molodynski A: A systematic review of co-responder models of police mental health "street" triage. BMC Psychiatry 18(1): 256, 2018

Rahman, A., Malik, A., Sikander, S., Roberts, C., & Creed, F. (2008). Cognitive behaviour therapy-based intervention by community health workers for mothers with depression and their infants in rural Pakistan: a cluster-randomised controlled trial. *The Lancet*, *372*(9642), 902–909. https://doi.org/10.1016/S0140-6736(08)61400-2

Ramanuj P, Ferenchik E, Docherty M et al: Evolving Models of Integrated Behavioral Health and Primary Care. Cur Psychiatry Rep 21:4, 2019

Ranz J, Stueve A, McQuistion HL: The Role of the Psychiatrist: Job Satisfaction of Medical Directors and Staff Psychiatrists. Community Ment Health J 37:525–39, 2001

Reeves S: A systematic review of the effects of interprofessional education on staff involved in the care of adults with mental health problems. J Psychiatr Ment Health Nurs 8:533–42, 2001

Reeves S, Perrier L, Goldman J, et al: Interprofessional education: effects on professional practice and health-care outcomes. Cochrane Database of Systematic Reviews 2013, Issue 3. Art. No.: CD002213

Rogers MS, McNeil DE, Binder RL: Effectiveness of Police Crisis Intervention Training Programs. J Am Acad Psychiatry Law 47:414–421, 2019

Rosen A: The community psychiatrist of the future. Curr Opin Psychiatry 19:380–388, 2006.

Shidhaye, R., Murhar, V., Gangale, S., Aldridge, L., Shastri, R., Parikh, R., Shrivastava, R., Damle, S., Raja, T., Nadkarni, A., & Patel, V. (2017). The effect of VISHRAM, a grass-roots community-based mental health programme, on the treatment gap for depression in rural communities in India: a population-based study. *The Lancet Psychiatry*, *4*(2), 128–135. https://doi.org/10.1016/S2215-0366(16)30424-2

Singla, D. R., Raviola, G., & Patel, V. (2018). Scaling up psychological treatments for common mental disorders: a call to action. *World Psychiatry*, *17*(2), 226.

Substance Abuse and Mental Health Services Administration. Family Psychoeducation: Training Frontline Staff. HHS Pub. No. SMA-09-4422, Rockville, MD: Center for Mental Health Services, Substance Abuse and Mental Health Services

Administration, U.S. Department of Health and Human Services, 2009.

Scantlebury A, Parker A, Booth A: Implementing mental health training programmes for non-mental health trained professionals: a qualitative synthesis. PLoS One 13: e0199746, 2018

"Shrink Rap." Available at http://psychiatrist-blog.blogspot.com/. Accessed December 20, 2020

Substance Abuse and Mental Health Services Administration. Family psychoeducation: How to Use the Evidence-Based Practices KITs. Available at https://store.samhsa.gov/product/Family-Psychoeducation-Evidence-Based-Practices-EBP-KIT/SMA09-4422. Accessed November 29, 2020

The Council for State Governments Justice Center. Police-Mental Health Collaborations: A Framework for Implementing Effective Law Enforcement Responses for People Who Have Mental Health Needs. April, 2019. Available at https://csgjusticecenter.org/wp-content/uploads/2020/02/Police-Mental-Health-Collaborations-Framework.pdf. Accessed December 30, 2020

Wells, K. B., Jones, L., Chung, B., Dixon, E. L., Tang, L., Gilmore, J., Sherbourne, C., Ngo, V. K., Ong, M. K., Stockdale, S., Ramos, E., Belin, T. R., & Miranda, J. (2013). Community-partnered cluster-randomized comparative effectiveness trial of community engagement and planning or resources for services to address depression disparities. *Journal of General Internal Medicine*, *28*(10), 1268–1278.

Wennerstrom, A., Vannoy, S. D., Allen, C. E., Meyers, D., O'Toole, E., Wells, K. B., & Springgate, B. F. (2011). Community-Based Participatory Development of a Community Health Worker Mental Health Outreach Role to Extend Collaborative Care in Post-Katrina New Orleans. *Ethnicity & Disease*, *21*(3 0 1), S1. / pmc/articles/PMC3715302/

Zhao Y, Zhang J: Consumer health information seeking in social media: a literature review. Health Info Libr J 34: 268–283, 2017

Collaborative Medication Management and Discontinuation

Ronald J. Diamond and Wesley E. Sowers

Collaboration, Shared Decision-Making, and Using Medication to Support Recovery

Medication is considered a critical part of the treatment of people with serious mental illness. Most people with significant mental illness will have a more stable life, fewer relapses, and fewer hospitalizations if they consistently take appropriate medication (Gilmer et al. 2004; Lang et al. 2010). Despite this demonstrated effectiveness, many people with mental illness either refuse to take prescribed psychiatric medication or take it inconsistently (Fenton et al. 1997; Lacro et al. 2002; Velligan et al. 2010). Often, medication is considered not only important, but the critical element of treatment, especially for people with schizophrenia and bipolar disorder.

A person is labeled "treatment resistant," even if they are willing to accept all other recommended treatment except for the medication. Unfortunately, this attitude can lead to an adversarial relationship between clinician and the person in treatment, focused more on medication than on other important life issues. Inconsistent medication use is an issue not just with mental illness, but with all chronic illness. People with high blood pressure, diabetes, and other chronic illnesses also tend to be inconsistent with medication, despite clear benefit from following treatment recommendations (Yang et al. 2009; Mann et al. 2010). The issue is perceived as different for people with mental illness. Often there is an assumption that medication nonadherence is connected to impaired judgment that is part of the underlying illness (Cramer and Rosenheck 1998). Clinicians see their task as "convincing" a person to take prescribed medication and attempting to use coercion when medication is refused. The common approach is to overcome the patient's irrationality through exhortation, close supervision of medication use, or coercion.

This chapter suggests an alternative view of medication that can serve to reframe the problem and potentially lead to different kinds of solutions. The issue is not "compliance" or "adherence," but how medication can be used as effectively as possible in helping the person deal with some of the problems caused by the illness (Steiner and Earnest 2001). The key strategy is to work with the person to develop areas of common understanding of a problem and the potential role of medication in helping to decrease the distress caused by this problem. There is no need to agree about everything. Effective treatment only requires that there are some areas of agree-

R. J. Diamond (✉)
Professor Emeritus, University of Wisconsin
Department of Psychiatry, Madison, WI, USA
e-mail: diamond@wisc.edu

W. E. Sowers
Clinical Professor of Psychiatry, University of
Pittsburgh Medical Center, Pittsburgh, PA, USA
e-mail: sowerswe@upmc.edu

W. E. Sowers et al. (eds.), *Textbook of Community Psychiatry*,
https://doi.org/10.1007/978-3-031-10239-4_15

ment that can be addressed collaboratively by both client and clinician (Diamond and Scheifler 2007). Even the common focus on "insight" must be rethought. It is not important that the person agrees with the diagnosis. Rather, it is important that the client agrees that the medication is doing something useful in terms that are important for him. One of my clients adamantly denied that he had schizophrenia, but he did agree that the medication decreased the "sparks" that interfered with him going to work and that taking the medication helped him to keep his job. The focus is not on "medication compliance" but rather on the person's own goals, hopes, and beliefs about the problem and the solution. The most important clinical issue is not whether the person is taking medication as prescribed; it is whether the person's life is getting better in ways that are important to him or her and whether medication is being used as effectively as possible to support this improvement.

Medication is more likely to be used when both client and clinician can agree on the nature of the problem and can agree that this problem could be helped by medication.

Medication is a tool. As with any tool, it can help with some problems and not with others. It is not "good" or "bad." Rather it is either effective or ineffective. The goal of treatment is not to get a person to take prescribed medication; the goal of treatment is to help the person have a better life. Before we decide to use a tool, we have to understand what problem we want the tool to fix. An agreement on the problem is the first step to getting an agreement on the solution (Deegan 2005). This is more complicated than it might initially seem. The clinician may feel that frequent rehospitalizations or intrusive auditory hallucinations are the problem. The client may be more concerned about getting his own apartment or getting his driver's license back. If medication is seen as a tool to help a problem, it will be used when both client and clinician can agree on "target symptoms." Why is this medication being prescribed, and how will both clinician and the person taking it know if it is working? Target symptoms are most useful if they are observable behaviors that both client and clinician can track.

What is the problem that the medication is supposed to "fix" or help with?

A *clinician's problem list* for a person with a psychotic disorder might include (1) hearing voices; (2) having a delusional belief that a large amount of money has been stolen, leading to frequent calls to police and complaints that frighten neighbors; and (3) having a delusional belief that people on the street are plotting about him, talking about him, following him, and making him too afraid to leave his apartment. From the clinician's perspective, it would seem that antipsychotic medication would be a reasonable tool to help with all three of these problems. It seems clear that these significant problems are all symptoms of an illness. Antipsychotic medication is useful in the treatment of this illness. From this perspective, the need for medication becomes obvious, and a refusal to use medication is a sign of irrationality. Unfortunately, the client's problem list might look very different.

The client's problem list night include the following: (1) I want to get back to school, but I cannot concentrate enough to read my math books. I don't really mind the voices all that much, but they are distracting and make it even more difficult to concentrate. (2) A large amount of money has been stolen from my apartment and no one believes me. When I call the police, they just laugh at me. The more I try to convince people, the more they just think I am crazy. (3) I am very afraid I am being set up to be murdered. I am not sure by whom or why, but feeling this afraid is terrible. (4) People talk outside of my window or seem to follow me when I go out. I realize that they are probably not always talking about me, but I am so scared that I cannot always figure out when they are talking about me and when it is just people talking.

The role of medication with this problem list is much less obvious. The voices themselves are not that big of a problem, medication is not going to help get his stolen money back or even get people to believe him, and he is not sure how medication will help him figure out when to be frightened and when not.

The clinician may feel that the medication has been very effective since the patient is less bothered by voices and is not going back to the hospital. The person may feel that the medication is useless, because even when taking the medication, he still cannot concentrate enough to do his school work, is still upset that no one believes him about the money being stolen, and is still concerned that he is being talked about and followed.

A person is more likely to listen to and seriously consider a clinician's solution to a problem, if the clinician is willing to listen and seriously consider the client's understanding and solution to the problem.

Clinicians are often so convinced of their view of the problem that they dismiss the client's view as not worth serious consideration. Clinicians too often listen only enough to confirm a diagnosis. If I believe that something terrible has happened, I would be upset if no one believed me and still more upset if no one was willing to listen to me. If a friend told me about a catastrophe, I would be curious about the details, about when and what had occurred, who might have done what, or what else happened. I would not ask questions in an effort to disprove the event, but rather because I was interested in the details and in my friend's experience. This interest must be real. A fake interest is shallow and has an altogether different tone. Too often, when a person talks about something bad happening, it is treated very differently.

A real interest is not the same as passively waiting until the client gets finished telling about his or her delusions. A real interest does not require that we agree with all parts of what the person is saying and certainly does not mean that we should pretend to agree when we do not. It does require that we suspend disbelief enough to seriously consider what the person is saying, rather than automatically discounting the complaint as a fabrication caused by mental illness. If we consider the client's account seriously, we develop a respectful curiosity about the details of the story that we may otherwise have dismissed.

This "serious curiosity" is the basis of cognitive behavioral therapy (Wright et al. 2009). The goal is to understand the details of the story, not to collect evidence to prove the client wrong. Details allow for the experience to be looked at in new ways by both clinician and consumer.

Ambivalence about taking medication is the norm, not the exception. It may be necessary, but few people really like taking medication.

Few of us actually like the idea of taking medication. We may like feeling better, and we may feel that the medication is necessary. We may have learned to put our ambivalence away so that we do not continuously think about the risks and side effects and the dependency on our medication. Still, ambivalence is the norm, not the exception. A typical clinical response to client ambivalence is to try to overwhelm it with rationality, reason, and exhortation. Sometimes this works, but most often it does not. If we try to "push" on one side of the dilemma, we can inadvertently strengthen the person's natural tendency to think about all of the arguments on the other side. Instead of convincing someone to do something we feel is important, we can incite the person to muster all of the arguments against this decision. Our push to get the client to make the "right decision" can sometimes strengthen the client's inclination to make the opposite decision.

Motivational interviewing is an approach to behavioral change based on the idea that people are more likely to follow through with a decision if they feel it is theirs rather than someone else's (Miller and Rollnick 2002; Dobber et al. 2018). Helping the client to develop his or her own argument about why something should be done will be a more powerful way to induce behavioral change than telling the client to make this same change. A client is likely to come up with a better decision if the clinician listens to him rather than argues with him. Once the client's concern has been fully addressed, then attention can be gently directed to the potential benefit of the medication. There is a place for direct support that the medication is needed and is working, but this direct support will be much more effective after the client has had a chance to express his own concerns. Our issue is to guide the client into making those decisions that support his or her own life goals. It is the client's goals, and it is the client's behavior, that must change to support those goals. Our job is to help the client develop his or her own argument to support behavioral change.

P- *I am very worried about getting tardive dyskinesia. You told me about this risk, and now I look at myself in the mirror and think I see the beginning of it.*

Cl- *What do you see when you look in the mirror?*

P- *I am not sure, but I think I see my face twitch some time. I am not sure I have it, but the idea of it scares me.*

Cl- *So the idea that you might develop tardive dyskinesia is pretty scary, even if there is not much evidence that there are signs of it now. Do you think the medication is doing any good?*

P- *Well I am back in school and able to concentrate better, and I guess that is from the medication. I am also spending more time with friends and less worried about people talking about me, and that could be from the meds.*

Cl- *So on the one hand, taking the medication and the possible side effect of tardive dyskinesia is pretty scary, and on the other hand the medications seem to have helped you get back to school and has made it easier to spend time with friends.*

P- *I think that I need to keep taking it, but it still scares me….*

A person is more likely to take a medication from someone he likes and trusts and less likely to take a medication prescribed by someone who is more focused on the medication than on him.

We are all more likely to follow through with a suggestion made by someone we like and trust and less likely if we distrust the motives of the person making the suggestion. Coming up with a diagnosis and writing a prescription is not enough. An effective physician must work to engender a trusting relationship. Many people have had the experience of feeling disrespected, not listened to, and not taken seriously. They bring this historical experience when they meet with new physicians. Many clients are not at all clear if the physician is there "for them" or are there for some other more nebulous reason. Trust is something to be earned, and not assumed.

Medication decisions are just that: decisions. Dismissing a client's decision as "just part of the illness" interferes with the development of a dialogue and the chance to find shared understanding.

Most of us would not take a medication just because we are told to do so by our physician. While we are influenced by our physician, we weigh the potential benefits of the medication and the potential risks and side effects and come up with our own decision. The same is true for people with mental illness. If the client agrees with the physician or is inherently compliant, then all goes well, and they take the medication as prescribed, at least most of the time. At times, the client may weigh concerns differently than the prescriber and decide to stop a medication or take it differently than prescribed. Most clients have learned to avoid being too overt about their own views to avoid the inevitable pressure that would come if they openly disagreed.

It is important that the prescriber does everything possible to make the discussion about medication decisions overt rather than covert. The client should be encouraged to share his own views and decisions, and then not be punished for being honest. When I begin a dialogue with a client, I start by asking about how his job or his goal of exercising is going. After I first focus on the person's own goals and hopes, I ask how the medication is working and what he is taking. The answer is often a vague "it's going OK," and this begins the conversation rather than ends it. A response that "I am taking medication almost all of the time" leads to a query about what happens when he misses some of the pills, how long has he gone without taking it, and what has persuaded him to restart it. The tone is not an inquisition, but rather an open conversation and respectful curiosity about what decisions the consumer is making and the thinking behind these decisions. The issue is not to just persuade the person to take the medication more consistently. The goal is to understand the consumer's own ambivalence and thinking. If one assumes every refusal is just lack of insight connected to illness, then it becomes much more difficult to have a conversation that leads to the sharing of ideas that allows us to learn from each other.

Taking medication always has meaning, for the patient, for the family, and for the clinician.

One person experiences medication as something that controls his life. Another experiences taking medication as something he can do to take more control over his own illness and his own life. One person sees medication as one more proof that he is damaged and disabled and not able to work. Another person sees medication as a tool that can help him overcome his illness and get back to work. The meaning of medication can change over time.

The meaning that always accompanies medication is not unique to mental illness. Survivors of breast cancer are often required to take medication that decreases the risk of recurrence but comes with significant side effects. One person is reminded with every pill that the cancer may come back, while the self-talk for another person reinforces the message that taking medication is something she can actively do to prevent it from coming back.

Medication can increase, or decrease, the sense of personal power and control the person has over his own life. If I "medicate you," then I am doing something to you, and your personal power will feel diminished. If medication is a tool that you can use in your own recovery, the same medication can work to increase your sense of control over your own life. Many people with serious mental illness are struggling with issues of control. A client trying to assert control may connect taking medication with ceding power to others. Taking medication too often feels like a further loss of control and a further loss of personal power.

The prescriber can work to reinforce the idea that the consumer can use medication to take more control over his illness. For this to be effective, the locus of control must be with the individual. The client has no real control if he is only allowed to make decisions that agree with those of the psychiatrist. At times, this means the person may make decisions that disagree with what others think would be best. The disagreement between client and clinician can be minor, such as taking a slightly lower doses of medication or choosing a different but similar medication or major such as discontinuing all medications. The psychiatrist and support people do not need to be neutral about these decisions and in fact they should not be. They should be clear about what they think is best. There also needs to be acknowledgment of the client's right to disagree with clinician decisions. This conversation can lead to better decisions than might otherwise occur. A client may be adamant about stopping his medication because he does not really have schizophrenia and the voices have now stopped so medication is not needed. I may be ineffective about getting that person to continue the medication, but I may be able to encourage a slow taper rather than an abrupt discontinuation, or some shared behavioral targets about what to look for, both good and bad, that would suggest that the medication taper is helpful or not helpful.

In the presence of mental health commitment and legal coercion, finding areas of collaboration becomes much more complicated. Even when there is a court order forcing the use of medication, the goal is to support the person's own decisions as much as possible. It may matter less if a person takes 4 mg or 5 mg of risperidone, or ziprasidone instead of olanzapine, than if the client feels some legitimate say in his or her own treatment (Diamond 2008).

Medication decisions are, in part, social. They are influenced by the person's family, friends, people at work, and neighbors.

Medication also has meaning for other people in a person's life. Taking medication can be perceived as a sign that the person is improving, or the need for medication can be perceived that the person is getting worse. Family and even clinical staff often have unrealistic expectations of what medication could do if only the person would take it. Clinicians often feel the need to "do something" in the face of increasing distress. This translates into increasing the dose of medication or adding a new one, even if this is more likely to increase side effects than increase efficacy. Even mass media plays a part. If attractive, functional people are portrayed as using medication, we are more likely to be willing to take medication ourselves. If the only people taking psychiatric medication that we read about in magazines or see on TV are severely dysfunctional, then we get the message that we do not want to be doing what they are doing, we do not want our life to be like their life, and we certainly do not want to be taking psychiatric medication. We can get the message that medication is for "winners," or only for "losers," and this becomes part of our own conscious or unconscious decision-making process.

It can be useful, with the client's permission, to invite support people into the medication appointment. This is now a common part of the treatment of serious medical illnesses. Oncology and cardiology visits regularly include family members, but this is still unusual for visits with a psychiatrist. Family and friends should be invited, even if they are ambivalent or opposed to the use of medication. The close friend or brother who is opposed to the person's use of medication will exert this influence whether or not they are included in the psychiatric appointment. By including him, his concerns can be heard and perhaps addressed. Even if his views do not change, the client may be in a better position to balance the contrasting views of the people who support the use of a particular medication and those who are concerned. Speakerphones and video-conferencing platforms can be used to include support people even if they are not physically present in the office.

Side effects are real. Decreasing side effects can make it more likely that a person will continue taking medication.

We ask people to take medication that causes side effects that we would have great trouble tolerating. A minor side effect to the clinician may be perceived as a major life obstacle by the client. We ask these individuals to tolerate weight gain that we would find unacceptable or drooling that we would find very upsetting. We may not hear the distress caused by "minor" akathisia. We need to think about how we would react if we were experiencing the side effect reported by our clients. How upset would we be, and what would we want done? Sharing information and decision-making with the person can be an effective way of trying to address these problems. The New York State Office of Mental Health has developed some material to demonstrate constructive approaches to these conversations with clients and their families (NY State Office of Mental Health 2017).

Often the right course of action is not clear. Is weight gain more important than sexual side effects? Is maximum efficacy more important than some increase in long-term risk? Many of these are value decisions rather than medical decisions. Is it worth the risk of trying a new medication, or better to stay on a medication that is working but causing significant weight gain? We need to help decrease side effects as much as possible. Just as important, we need to involve the client in decisions so that together we come up with solutions that make sense for them. The decisions may not always work out, but that is true for many medical decisions. Some decisions are riskier than others, and some may have more chance of working than others. This does not mean that the prescriber must go along with every request made by the client. Some requests and some decisions lie outside of medical prudence. I may not agree to prescribe high-dose diazepam for someone who I know abuses alcohol. The goal is to strive for a set of decisions that are acceptable to both prescriber and consumer, even if both may feel that it is not what they would ideally choose.

Organization and structure can help. It is important to simplify the medication regimen, help connect medication taking to other structured activity, build in reminders to take medication, and consider the use of pillboxes or special packaging.

Make those changes that can help a person take medication more consistently. Be interested in the client's actual medication use and ask about barriers that make taking medication more difficult. Most psychiatric medications can be taken once a day, even if the package insert suggests twice a day. People may benefit from assistance that connects taking medication with some other consistent life activity. We do this so automatically in our own life that we may not realize that people with mental illness may need some concrete help to come up with these strategies. Does the person regularly brush their teeth, or eat breakfast, or have a morning cup of coffee, or have a nighttime pattern before going to bed. Some compromises on "ideal treatment" may improve actual outcome. I personally take medication that should ideally be taken in the morning, but my mornings are rushed and chaotic and I have found that I take my own medication more consistently if I take it before bed. Ideal management of diabetes often requires a complicated regimen of different medications at different times of day. Actual outcome is sometimes much better if the regimen is simplified to become practical rather than ideal. Some people are very sensitive to the "dose" of medication, and they prefer to take a medication with fewer milligrams even if this is explained as being an unimportant consideration. Other people are sensitive to the number of pills they are taking and would prefer taking one hundred milligrams tablets than three twenty-five milligram tablets even though the dose is higher with the one pill.

Help people use pillboxes and other packaging that assists in consistent medication use. At times, the pharmacy can set up assistive packaging, or perhaps a friend can help the person set up a pillbox system. Be aware of barriers to obtaining medication. Co-pays that seem small may still be enough to discourage medication use. Just getting to the pharmacy or the embarrassment of asking for a psychiatric medication at the pharmacy may all present barriers to obtaining medication. At times, clinicians may be only vaguely aware of insurance changes or prior authorization requirements that are overwhelming to our clients. A pharmacy's decision to change from one brand of medication to another may make a client uncomfortable about taking the new pill and lead to a decision to just stop taking it.

Long-acting injectable antipsychotic medications are underused. LAIs are not just a way of forcing patients to take medication under duress, but as a way of helping people use medication more effectively

In the United States, long-acting injectable medications (LAI) have commonly been associated with coercion, with court orders, and with non-compliant patients. This has interfered with using this medication delivery option with a much wider group of people who may find it effective. Very few people like the idea of a LAI, and even fewer agree the first time this option is brought up. No one likes injections; there is a sense of loss of control and legitimate concerns over side effects. If LAIs are discussed as an option as part of an ongoing discussion of what is likely to work best, many people will be willing to give them a try even if the initial reaction was negative. The data on the use of LAIs is mixed, with some studies showing that there is little difference on outcomes after 6 months, and other studies show very large and substantial differences (Rosenheck et al. 2011; Olivares et al. 2009). Some of the most interesting studies show the significant advantage of using LAIs on people early in their illness course with major improvements in outcomes (Subotnik et al. 2015).

While this is not part of the formal description, it seems that those studies that see LAIs as just a different medication are the ones that demonstrate little advantage in their use. What LAIs do is to convert a private event, the decision to take a pill, into a public event where some clinician knows if the person has had their injection. When medication is part of a person-focused service delivery system that is designed to help people get their life back and has shared goals and supports for work or school or relationships, if a missed injection is followed up by a call from a clinician well-known to the consumer and perceived as being on the consumer's side, then LAIs can be very effective. When the treatment is focused on "treating schizophrenia," if the person calling about a missed injection is a clerk not known to the patient, and if there are not clearly articulated shared treatment goals, then LAIs are probably effective only as long as there is coercion that reinforces their continued use.

LAIs can reinforce the powerlessness of the client. They can also make it impossible for the client to adjust dose to try to deal with side effects. Effective programs that use LAIs need to spend the time and the energy to make the medication as a true part of an ongoing, collaborative process, rather than as a way of forcing consistent medication use or trying to avoid difficult discussions. LAIs, besides their increased effectiveness with some people, can have other significant advantages. Pharmacologically, they can sometime decrease side effects. Psychologically, they eliminate the need for the person to make a daily, difficult, ambivalent decision about whether they are or are not going to take the pill. They can also change the focus of other discussions away from medication and onto issues much more important. With oral medication, many, if not most, conversations with the case manager or parents or other family members can be about whether the person is taking/has taken their medication. With the use of LAIs, those conversations can focus on how the new volunteer job is going, or how is school, or what kind of apartment are you thinking about. The conversations can change from one focused on medication to one focused on life.

Take a long-term point of view. The goal is not just to get the person to take medication today or next week. Consider the impact of what you are doing now on this person's willingness to use medication next year.

Almost everyone who needs a psychiatric medication is likely to continue to need it for a considerable period of time. The issue is not just to "get the person on meds," but rather to work to help the person come to an understanding of his problems and of the role of medication as a potential solution to these problems. There is pressure to "medicate the person rapidly." It is desirable to keep periods of acute distress as brief as possible, to shorten periods of psychotic relapse, to decrease risk, and to shorten periods of hospitalization. On the other hand, the pressure to get someone "medicated" rapidly often requires pressuring the person to take a medication before he has had time to consider and absorb the various options. The pressure to "medicate" a person reinforces the locus of control of medication onto the clinicians and "other people" and decreases the opportunity for the person to consider whether and how medication might be useful. Taking a longer-term point of view allows time for the consumer to actively be involved in the decision of the goals and targets of the medication, what medication to take, how much, and for how long. Most of us, faced with a decision about major surgery or treatment of cancer, need some time to think about the options. This is equally true of people with mental illness. I have talked about starting clozapine with many patients, and virtually none of them has agreed the first time I brought it up. This approach may take a bit longer for the person to get onto an effective medication. On the other hand, it may make it more likely that the person will continue to be on medication over time.

Not everyone with mental illness will benefit from medication. This means that when such a person says that the meds do not help, at least some of the time they are being objectively accurate.

While it is clear that groups of people with mental illness have fewer symptoms and fewer periods of relapse if they consistently take medication, this does not mean that every individual will benefit from these medications or benefit to the same extent. Some people with mental illness may get little or no benefit from medication. Others may find that the marginal benefit of medication is outweighed by the side effects.

The belief in the efficacy of medication has become so imbedded in our treatment programs and professional culture. It's as if we cannot seriously discuss the fact that it may not be effective. Many people who say that the medication does not help are thought to be misguided when *we see* that medication helps in very clear, objective ways based on history and changes in behavior. But on the other hand, we should at least listen and try to understand why they feel this way and how we can address their concerns. However, there are other situations where there is no evidence of positive changes related to medication use and we need to think about what we know about this person's response to medication in the past. If we pick up a chart that indicates the person has failed to have significant benefit from multiple trials of medication, is there reason to continue to prescribe more? The reason we rarely see such a question being asked is because of the clinician's irrational belief in the power of medication, our unwillingness to admit impotency, and the pressure on the larger system to continue to prescribe medication whether it is effective for a person or not.

Deprescribing and Discontinuation Assistance: More is usually not better, and simplification of medication regimens makes adherence more likely and reduces unwanted side effects

It is not uncommon for community psychiatrists to encounter clients who come to a new treatment setting on multiple medications that have had limited effectiveness. In the previous sections, the emphasis was on persons with severe mental illnesses, but public sector clinicians often work with people whose main concerns center around long-standing depressions, anxieties, and addictions of varying severity. Characterological disturbances resulting from trauma of various types often play a significant role in the development of these syndromes and their tenacity. Unfortunately, these individuals often have a slew of medications thrown at them in an effort to control their symptoms, often resulting in strange cocktails of medications with dubious benefit. Nonetheless, many clients may cling to a belief that they need all of these medications, even in the face of significant side effects and ongoing distress.

When encountering clients with ineffective polypharmacy regimens, the principles described in the foregoing sections are applicable and can be used to help people achieve their objectives more effectively with simplified and well-reasoned medication plans. A first step is to understand an individual's beliefs about medications and what role they may play in their recovery. An external locus of control is often observed in these individuals, particularly in clients with substance use issues. There may be an expectation/hope that medication should solve their problems and they often have a sense of helplessness and lack control over their recovery process (Sowers and Golden 1999). It will be important to gather information about the history and chronology of their prescriptions and the benefits and side effects they perceive of each and how they have been taking them.

When these tasks have been completed, the groundwork will be in place to provide the client with information about the evidence-based indications for each of their medications, appropriate dosages, and both short- and long-term adverse side effects. It is not unusual to find that they have been told very little in this regard and often have not retained very much of what they have been told. At this juncture, they can be engaged in a process of evaluation of the relative adverse effects and benefits of each of their medications, and it will be natural to raise the possibility of simplification and the rationale for considering it. Maintaining a neutral attitude while conveying a genuine concern for the client's well-being will be critical in helping them to identify possible targets for dosage reduction or discontinuation and a step-wise plan for doing so (CPSP 2021). Livingston (2012) and Groot and van Os (2020) offer guidance on how to safely withdraw psychotropic medication.

For the vast majority of people with mental illness, shared decision-making is not only possible, but leads to better outcomes.

Shared decision-making refers to having the client and the prescriber come together to collaboratively make decisions that best fit the client goals, values, and preferences. There is an explosion of interest in shared decision-making (Deegan and Drake 2006). Unfortunately, actually implementing it is surprisingly difficult. Shared decision-making is much more than just sharing information.

True participation in shared decision-making requires that all parties become educated about the range of treatment options. This means that the person needs a way to become educated about the various treatment options and that the prescriber becomes educated about the client's goals and values. Both sides of this education can be difficult. Historically, although clients have been provided with information about their medication, it is often overwhelming, incomplete, and inevitably biased by the preferences of the person providing the information. Written information is often lists of indications and side effects. While such information is a start and helps to at least open the conversation, it usually does not give a person enough information to become a true part of a shared decision process. Too often, this written information provides information that is only vaguely useful to the person trying to absorb and comprehend it all (Shrank and Avorn 2007).

Web sites are another typical source of information for individuals, but again these sites often organize information based on their own biases. It is difficult to know which web sites provide reliable information and which do not. Even the idea of "reliable information" is problematic. The authors of a web site or informational pamphlet will inevitably feel that medication is useful or that medication is dangerous. What one person sees as "reliable," another person will see as a polemic. Some information is much more reliable and balanced than others, but it can be difficult to sort this out.

These concerns have led to the development of "decisional aids," structured ways of presenting information starting with a person's own preferences, goals, and concerns. For example, is the person more interested in a medication that is most likely to help decrease voices or more likely to avoid weight gain? Is the person more concerned with feeling "drugged out" or more concerned about not sleeping? The information about options can then be filled in, within this structure. Education can be based on the persons own stated concerns (Kaar and et al. 2019). These decision aids are different than just an article or book about treatment options or medications and tend to help people work through complicated information to arrive at a decision that works for them. Some of the decision aids are on paper, while others involve computer technology that allows for better customization of the information flow to fit each consumer's needs. The better ones use concepts and language that are "person friendly." Most importantly, they provide information based on the person's own needs, so that it can be directly applicable to helping consumers to be true participants in the decision process. WRAP plans (Wellness Recovery Action Plans) are one form of a decisional aid (Copeland 1997).

Having information is necessary but not sufficient for having a true voice in decisions about one's own life. It requires that the prescribers and other formal decision-makers become willing to share power with their client, not just when the client's decision happens to agree with that of the prescriber. This in turn requires that the prescriber may need to support decisions that he or she would not necessarily choose. There is a range of such disagreement, from differences of opinion that can be easily tolerated and supported to those that appear particular self-defeating and dangerous. Part of the process of shared decision-making requires developing a process to discuss and arbitrate these disagreements, when prescribers disagree with consumers and when consumers disagree with prescribers. This also requires that both clients and prescribers receive training in the implementation of shared decision-making.

Shared decision-making is more than just another technique to convince a person to do the right thing. Rather, it is a way for re-establishing a more collaborative, less hierarchical relationship. The relationship between physician and their client is equal but asymmetrical. Patient and physician have different sources of information and different kinds of expertise. Shared decision-making requires that the physician relinquish certain kinds of control, even in the face of a variety of professional and societal pressure to maintain control. It requires that the client take on the burden of learning about his illness and treatment options in a serious way and then taking on the responsibility for his own decisions. It requires time to enter into this collaboration, and it requires the development of decision aids that can assist the process. Shared decision-making is not equally applicable in every situation, nor will it resolve all conflicts about medication decisions. At the same time, shared decision-making is an approach that is likely to allow more collaboration and less conflict and as a result lead to better outcome.

There is no way to ensure that the consumers will always agree with our view of the problem or our suggestions about treatment. Clients may decide to stop taking medications that we feel are extremely helpful and even necessary. We will, at times, attempt to use various kinds of pressure or even legal sanctions to force the use of medications, at times over the strident objections of the person whose life it is. There will be some situations where it will be difficult to find areas of common ground for an understanding of the problem or the solution. At the same time, without being naive about the difficulties that can ensue, it is imperative to try to understand the world from the client's point of view. It is important to look for areas where we can overlap with the person in a common view of the problem. It is useful to think of medication as a tool that the client can use to facilitate his or her own recovery journey. It is hoped that this reframing of the role of medication will lead to better long-term outcomes than more traditional ways of thinking about compliance and adherence. Our goal is not to get people to take their medication. Our goal is to help people get closer to their own recovery goals. Our job is to help consumers learn to use medication to facilitate this journey.

Acknowledgement My appreciation to Jon Berlin, Mark Ragins, Alan Rosen, David Katzelnick, and Cher Diamond for their comments on drafts of this chapter.

References

Copeland, M.E. (1997) *Wellness Recovery Action Plan*. Peach Press.

Center for Public Service Psychiatry (2021) Collaborative medication management and discontinuation assistance. Community Psychiatry Forum Video Seminar Series; Available at https://www.cpsp.pitt.edu/videoconferences-2020-2021/. Accessed on 2/26/2022

Cramer, J.A. & Rosenheck, R (1998) Compliance with medication regimens for mental and physical disorder. *Psychiatr Serv*, 49, 196–201.

Deegan, P.E. & Drake, R.E. (2006) Shared decision-making and medication management in the recovery process. *Psychiatr Serv*, 57, 11.

Deegan, P.E. (2005) The importance of personal medicine: A qualitative study of resilience in people with psychiatric disabilities. *J Public Health*, 33, 29–35

Diamond, R.J. & Scheifler, P.L. (2007) *Treatment Collaboration: Improving the Therapist, Prescriber, Client Relationship*. New York: WW Norton.

Diamond, R. (2008) Engaging the crisis patient around medication. In (Eds) Glick, R.L., Berlin, J.S., Fishkind, A., & Zeller, S. *Emergency Psychiatry: Principles and Practice*. Philidelphia: Lippincott Williams & Wilkins.

Dobber J et al (2018) Medication adherence in patients with schizophrenia: a qualitative study of the patient process in motivational interviewing. *BMC Psychiatry* 18: 135: 1274–9

Fenton, W.S., Blyler, C.R., Heinssen, R.K. (1997) Determinants of medication compliance in schizophrenia: Empirical and clinical findings. *Schizophre Bull*, 23, 637–651.

Gilmer, T.P., Dolder, C.R., Lacro, J.P., Folsom, D.P., Lindamer, L., Garcia, P., and Jeste, D.V. (2004) Adherence to treatment with antipsychotic medication and health care costs among Medicaid beneficiaries with schizophrenia. *Am J Psychiatry*, 161, 692–699.

Groot, PC., van Os. (2020). How user knowledge of psychotropic drug withdrawal resulted in the development of person-specific tapering medication. *Therapeutic Advances in Psychopharmacology*. 2000. 10, 1–13

Kaar S.J. et al. (2019) Making decisions about antipsychotics. a qualitative study of patient experiences and the development of a decision aid. *BMC Psychiatry* 19(1): 309

Lacro, J.P., Dunn, L.B., Dolder, C.R., Leckband, S.G., Jeste, D.V. (2002) Prevalence of and risk factors for medication nonadherence in patients with schizophrenia: A comprehensive review of recent literature. *J Clin Psychiat*, 63, 892–909.

Lang, K., Meyers, J.L., Korn, J.R., Lee, S., Sikirica, M., Crivera, C., Dirani, R., Menzin, J. (2010) Medication adherence and hospitalization among patients with schizophrenia treated with antipsychotics. *Psychiatr Serv*, 61, 1239–47.

Livingston, M (2012) Guide to when and how to safely withdraw antipsychotics. *Prescriber*. 23, 37–40.

Mann, D.M., Woodward, M., Muntner, P., Falzon, L., Kronish, I. (2010) Predictors of nonadherence to statins: A systematic review and meta-analysis. *Ann Pharmacother.* 44, 1410–21. Epub 2010 Aug 11.

Miller, W.R. & Rollnick, S. (2002) Motivational Interviewing: Preparing People for Change. New York: Guilford Press

New York State Office of Mental Health. (2017) Talking to patients and their families about Clozapine. Available https://www.thenationalcouncil.org/wp-content/uploads/2017/03/Talking-to-patients-and-their-families-about-Clozapine.pdf?daf+375ateTbd56 Accessed 05 January 2022.

Olivares J.M. et al.. (2009) Long-term outcomes in patients with schizophrenia treated with risperidone long-acting injection or oral antipsychotics in Spain: results from the Electronic schizophrenia Treatment Adherence Registry (eSTAR). *Eur Psychiatry* June, 24(5): 287–96

Rosenheck, R.A. et al. (2011) Long-acting risperidone and oral antipsychotics in unstable schizophrenia, *N Eng J Med* Mar 31; 364(13): 1281

Shrank, W.H. & Avorn, J. (2007) Educating patients about their medications: The potential and limitations of written drug information. *Health Affairs*, 26, 731–740.

Sowers W, Golden S (1999) Psychotropic medication management in persons with co-occurring psychiatric and substance use disorders. *Journal of Psychoactive Drugs*. January-March 31(1): 59–70.

Steiner J.F. and Earnest M.A. (2001) Lingua Medica: The Language of Medication-Taking. *Ann Intern Med* 132; 132: 926–930

Subotnik, K.L et al. (2015) Long-Acting Injectable Risperidone for Relapse Prevention and Control of Breakthrough Symptoms After a Recent First Episode of Schizophrnie. A Randomized Clinical Trial. *JAMA Psychiatry* Aug 72(8) 822–9

Velligan, D.I., Weiden, P.J., Sajotovic, M., Scott, J., Carpenter, D., Ross, R., & Docherty, J.P. (2010) Assessment of adherence problems in patients with serious and persistent mental illness: Recommendations from the expert consensus guidelines. *J of Psychiatric Prac,* 16, 32–45.

Wright, J.H., Turkington, D., Kingdon, D.G., & Basco, M.R. (2009) *Cognitive-Behavior Therapy for Severe Mental Illness: An Illustrated Guide.* Washington, DC: American Psychiatric Publishers, Inc.

Yang, Y., Thumula, V., Pace, P.F., Banahan, B.F. 3rd, Wilkin, N.E., Lobb, W.B. (2009) Predictors of medication non-adherence among patients with diabetes in Medicare Part D programs: A retrospective cohort study. *Clin Ther.,* 31, 2178–88; discussion 2150-1.

Traumatic Stress in the Community: Identification and Intervention

Paula G. Panzer, Preeya Desai, and Caroline Peacock

Introduction and Definitions

Descriptions of *trauma* – an experience that overwhelms an individual's ability to cope and elicits feelings of terror, helplessness, and/or out-of-control physiological arousal – have appeared in popular, historical, and medical texts for centuries. The relevance of *traumatization* (i.e., when "both internal and external resources are inadequate to cope with external threat") (van der Kolk 1989, p. 393) to normal and impaired functioning is described in greater detail in social, neuropsychological, and political texts. This chapter summarizes the current understanding of *traumatic stress* (i.e., the physical and emotional responses to events that threaten the physical or psychic integrity of an individual) and *traumatic stress disorders* and the evidence for effective intervention.

Within a clinical context, there are two broad categories of trauma: those that are "human-made," or caused by the actions of person(s), and those that are "natural," in which the source is out of human control. Some traumas can fall into either category, depending on the circumstances, such as fires, car accidents, and medical trauma.

Formal recognition of the psychological effects of trauma exposure and the distinct persistence of symptoms in some individuals did not occur until the 1980s. Historically, soldiers had experienced what was known as "shell shock" or "battle fatigue." In 1980, studies documenting a reliable pattern of symptoms (to traumas beyond combat exposure) led to the classification of these experiences as post-traumatic stress disorder (PTSD) (American Psychiatric Association 1980). PTSD is diagnosed 1 month after trauma exposure when accompanied by symptoms in four categories – intrusive thoughts/re-experiencing, avoidance/numbing, negative cognitions, and hyper-arousal – and the presence of clinically significant distress or impairment (American Psychiatric Association 2021).

Symptoms of PTSD can be seen in almost all people in the immediate aftermath of traumatic exposure (Yehuda and LeDoux 2007). They are the result of adaptive physiological and psychological processes that protect the organism from threat and danger. The normal process of recovery after exposure leads to spontaneous remission of all symptoms within 1–3 months. PTSD can be seen as an inability of the organism to recover from the physiological and psychological effects of trauma (Yehuda and LeDoux 2007).

In recent years, clinicians and researchers have recognized some diagnostic and therapeutic

P. G. Panzer (✉)
Systems and Traumatic Stress Disorders Consultant, New York, NY, USA; https://www.pgpanzermd.com

P. Desai
Long Island University, Brooklyn, NY, USA

C. Peacock
Director of Spiritual Health, Winship Cancer Institute, Emory Healthcare, Atlanta, GA, USA

W. E. Sowers et al. (eds.), *Textbook of Community Psychiatry*,
https://doi.org/10.1007/978-3-031-10239-4_16

limitations in the construct of PTSD, particularly for children and those exposed to ongoing or multiple traumas. An additional disorder, *Developmental Trauma Disorder*, may better explain the disruptions in multiple domains; studies on the accuracy and reliability of this profile are underway, and more data is needed to suggest this as a stand-alone diagnosis. At this moment, it is clinically useful after diagnosis for treatment planning and patient education. The disorder stems from trauma that is interpersonal in nature, such as child abuse, sexual abuse, or family violence (van der Kolk 2005). A range of somatic, affective, cognitive, and relational dysregulation occurs, leading to disruption in functioning in multiple domains, including education, peer relationships, and behavioral control.

Chronic stress is defined as a series of ongoing phenomena that cause distress, anxiety, and difficulty; examples include racism, poverty, and homophobia. *Chronic traumatization* is the experience of multiple traumatic events; for example, a person is exposed to domestic violence and neglected as a child, is involved in a car accident as a young adult, and then is exposed to combat. The effects of chronic trauma are cumulative, as events serve to remind the individual of prior trauma and reinforce the negative impact. Chronic stress with single trauma exposure, chronic trauma, or some combination may result in *complex trauma*. Complex trauma affects nearly every aspect of development and functioning, including problems with attachment.

Epidemiology

More than 75% of persons in the United States are exposed to at least one traumatic event in their lifetime, and approximately 6.8% of those persons will be diagnosed with PTSD (Breslau and Kessler 2001; Kessler et al. 2005). In a sample of older adults specifically, findings indicated that approximately 90% of individuals had experienced one or more events that may be traumatic (Ogle et al. 2013). While PTSD is defined in part by exposure to a traumatic event, only a small percentage of persons with traumatic exposure go on to develop the disorder. A metanalysis on PTSD in adults found that of types of trauma that may result in development of PTSD, sexual relationship violence such as rape, childhood sexual abuse, and intimate partner violence was most prominent at 33%. This was followed by interpersonal traumatic experiences (30%), defined by unexpected death of a loved one, life-threatening illness of a child, or other traumatic experiences related to a loved one (Sareen 2018).

The issue of racial and cultural disparities plays an important role in PTSD prevalence and treatment. However, of the great number of articles about the epidemiology and the efficacy of PTSD treatment in the past two decades, few have focused on racial and ethnic groups. Triffelman and Pole (2010) argue that this area of research must be greatly expanded to address the growing population of people of color in the United States. Research has shown that African American and Latinx individuals are at a higher likelihood to develop PTSD when compared to White adults (Himle et al. 2009; Marshall et al. 2009). Additional research has indicated that Asian American individuals are less likely to develop PTSD when compared to European American and Native American peers (Whealin et al. 2013). Similarly, findings from 34,653 adults who completed epidemiological surveys found that lifetime prevalence of PTSD was highest (8.7%) in Black Americans and lowest in Asian Americans (4.0%) (Roberts et al. 2011).

It should also be noted that issues of race, ethnicity, and culture could affect the course of PTSD. Traumatic events that include perceived racial discrimination, such as African American soldiers being given more severe combat duties than Whites, may result in more severe PTSD symptomatology (Pole et al. 2005). Further research has shown that the risk for developing PTSD in African Americans was prevalent throughout life, while White individuals were found to be less likely to develop PTSD after young adulthood (Himle et al. 2009). This parallels important findings that indicate that African American and Latinx adults experience more chronic PTSD. In a study of 139 Latinx and 152 African American individuals who have anxiety disorders, a 5-year follow-up showed that remission rates for PTSD were 0.15 and 0.35, respectively, suggesting that these individuals are at risk for recurring PTSD even after treatment (Sibrava et al. 2019). Additionally, research indicates that traumatic stress related to race and discrimination is connected to trauma symptoms, such as those associated with PTSD (Sibrava et al. 2019; Carter et al. 2020). This highlights the importance of considering the crucial factor of traumatic experiences related to racial discrimination and inequity when examining risk for future symptomatology. Research on children who were survivors of complex trauma found that Black children were more likely to endorse a greater number of trauma types, including community violence (Wamser-Nanney et al. 2018a), pointing to the early roots of trauma in certain populations.

There are treatment implications associated with race and ethnicity as well. One 2010 study (Lester et al. 2010) of CBT treatment outcomes among African American and White women with PTSD showed earlier dropout rates among African American women; however, it showed minimal difference in treatment outcome. The African American women might have experienced similar outcomes because they overcame social factors deterring them from treatment and thus might have been more motivated. This study raises the issues of clinician awareness of racial and cultural identity as well as structural racism and speaks to the importance of clinicians using a race lens in practice (Peacock et al. 2010, personal communication following formal presentation). In a meta-analysis on disparities in treatment for PTSD, McClendon et al. (2020) examined 23 studies from the past decade and found that across various settings, African American individuals were less likely to initiate treatment when compared to their White peers. Similarly, Black and Latinx veterans were found to be less likely to receive adequate care. The authors noted that across studies, culturally targeted treatments for individuals suffering from PTSD were efficacious and may improve retention (McClendon et al. 2020). However, additional research may be needed to determine wider implications for PTSD treatment of culturally diverse populations.

Additionally, social factors based on racial and cultural identity – such as community support, participation in faith communities, and extended family roles – need to be considered as elements that may decrease risk of PTSD and aid in recovery. Given the lack of significant and useful research, the clinician needs knowledge and skill in assessing both the impact of trauma and racism in the individual and formulating the diagnosis and treatment with this information.

Resilience and Risk Factors

A number of internal and external factors contribute to having risk for or inoculation against development of a trauma-related disorder. Event characteristics that affect trauma recovery include severity of the traumatic stressor and trauma type and event centrality (Wamser-Nanney et al. 2018b; Yehuda and LeDoux 2007), with rape, assault, and combat leading to PTSD more often than natural disasters or human-made accidents (Yehuda and LeDoux 2007; Kessler et al. 2017). Individual risk factors for PTSD include preexisting traits such as lower IQ, avoidant personality, and behavior problems, and pre- or post-traumatic life events, including childhood abuse, poor social support, and personal trauma history (Haglund et al. 2007; Yehuda and LeDoux 2007) and avoidant activities following trauma exposure, such as social withdrawal (Thompson et al. 2018). Factors associated with resilience in the face of post-traumatic stress include positive emotions, active coping style, cognitive flexibility, a moral compass, and adequate social support (Haglund et al. 2007; Banyard et al. 2017), capacity for self-regulation, positive religious coping and greater optimism (Yule et al. 2019), and the social context (Portnoy et al. 2018). Resilience programs, particularly for at risk populations with greater exposure to trauma, such as African

American women, may be protective (Holden et al. 2017), and those that incorporate creativity, such as expressive writing, may be especially helpful (Glass et al. 2019; Sayer et al. 2015). Exposure at a young age to manageable levels of stress also helps to inoculate the organism from the effects of future stressors (Haglund et al. 2007; Hulbert and Anderson 2018).

Table 1 Neurobiological factors

Endogenous agent/ brain structure	Hypothesized effect on risk/ resilience
Amygdala	Hyperactivity of the amygdala associated with PTSD
Medial prefrontal cortex (mPFC) and dopamine	PTSD associated with reduced activity of mPFC Decreased release of dopamine in mPFC may delay extinction of conditioned fears Resilience associated with reward systems that are hypersensitive to reward and resistant to change
Hippocampus	Small hippocampal volume/ decreased hippocampal function associated with increased risk for PTSD
Cortisol	Many studies have shown decreased levels of basal cortisol in people with PTSD Decreased levels of cortisol could place people at risk for developing PTSD
Corticotropin-releasing hormone (CRH)	Excessive stress in early life may result in increased CRH activity Resilience likely associated with effective regulation of CRH
Neuropeptide Y (NPY)	Counteracts anxiogenic effects of CRH Low levels of NPY associated with PTSD
Serotonin	Short allele for serotonin transporter protein results in less serotonin production than the long allele People with PTSD much more likely to have the short/short allele
DHEA	Enhances cognition and performance under stress High levels appear to be related to recovery from stress

Neurobiological Correlates

Recent research has elucidated known biologically based factors that influence an individual's response to traumatic exposure. Other risk and resiliency factors have been hypothesized based on current neurobiological research. A summary of these findings is presented in Table 1. Recent research has identified certain genes that may be related to the development of PTSD. Two epigenetic biotypes, G1 and G2, have been associated with 34 clinical features of PTSD. The G2 biotype was related to an increased risk of PTSD compared to healthy controls. These findings suggest the importance of examining biological risk factors for the development of PTSD (Yang et al. 2020). Additionally, other neurobiological correlates have been identified and mark areas for future research. Impaired coping of stress owing to decreased activity of the hypothalamic-pituitary-adrenal axis and the parasympathetic nervous system, combined with increased activity of the sympathetic nervous system, may be observed in those with PTSD. This may lead to increased proinflammatory cytokines, suggesting the possibility that chronic inflammation that may affect regions of the brain involved in controlling emotional behavior and regulating fear may be a biomarker for PTSD (Kim et al. 2019). Telomere length has also been identified as a marker for PTSD, with accelerated telomere shortening found in those who had PTSD (Kim et al. 2017). Future research will continue to expand on these findings to further identify neurobiological correlates of PTSD.

Assessment

A comprehensive assessment is one of the most important aspects of mental healthcare. All people seeking services should be assessed for trauma exposure, symptoms, disorders, and disruptions in functioning. Direct, trauma-specific assessment is crucial in providing effective trauma-related care. Assessment should be done after building an initial rapport and should be targeted and thorough, gathering information necessary to fully inform the most effective course of treatment without retraumatizing the individual. The latter is done by keeping the interview focused on symptoms after briefly (and succinctly) identifying the traumatic exposure. In this sense, imagine a one-page screening instrument with a very small box at the top describing the exposure (limited to three sentences). The goal, during assessment, is to identify the trauma without triggering symptoms.

Consequent assessment can be done through informal clinical interviewing, structured clinical interviewing, and the use of objective assessment measures. There are numerous empirically validated structured clinical interviews and objective assessment instruments. Table 2 displays some of the most widely used measures for PTSD, acute stress disorder, and dissociative identity disorder, the last of which is related to severe and persistent trauma, most commonly experienced in childhood.

Interventions

Trauma interventions occur on system and service levels. On a service level, a practitioner may use various interventions to treat PTSD. For example, trauma-focused cognitive behavioral therapy (TF-CBT) may be used in an outpatient treatment setting for children with PTSD. TF-CBT and eye movement desensitization and reprocessing (EMDR) have both been shown to be clinically effective in treating individuals who reported traumatic stress symptoms, especially those diagnosed with PTSD and acute stress disorder (Roberts et al. 2019). On a systems level, there are several evidence-based, trauma-informed models of care, such as the Sanctuary® Model (Rivard et al. 2003) and Trauma Systems Therapy (Saxe et al. 2007). These include a whole-system approach encompassing multiple layers of trauma understanding and intervention.

Trauma-informed care is not specifically designed to treat trauma-related symptoms or syndromes (Marsenich 2010). Rather, this type of system supports delivery of trauma-specific services (Hopper et al. 2010). All aspects of service in a trauma-informed system of care (TIC) are influenced by an understanding of the role of violence in the lives of people served by community agencies. Services accommodate the potential vulnerabilities of trauma survivors, thus avoiding inadvertent re-traumatization and facilitating consumer participation in treatment. TISCs also require collaborative relationships with service system partners, including child welfare, legal aid, and substance abuse agencies (Marsenich 2010). Recent literature has suggested that TISC take a resilience-focused approach, which emphasizes increased self-care and regulatory capacities in both patients and providers (Leitch 2017).

Intervention Selection

There is an extensive body of research consisting of large, methodologically sound randomized controlled trials examining the effectiveness of various treatment interventions for PTSD in adults. Meta-analyses of these individual studies indicate that cognitive behavioral approaches, including exposure therapy, TF-CBT, EMDR, and anxiety management, are all effective at treating PTSD (Bradley et al. 2005; Bisson and Cohen 2006; Cahill et al. 2006; Foa 2009).

Historically, research has indicated that no single cognitive behavioral approach is more effective than any other, and no combination of these approaches is more effective than any one cognitive behavioral treatment type alone (Bradley et al. 2005; Cahill et al. 2006; Foa 2009). In a recent study, however, Cloitre et al. (2010) found that combined skills training plus exposure therapy (STAIR/Exposure) was superior to supportive counseling plus exposure therapy in several domains, including attaining and maintaining PTSD-negative diagnostic status, reducing PTSD symptoms and anxiety, and improving emotion regulation, anger management, and interpersonal interactions. The authors postulate that exposure therapy may demonstrate its “maximum benefit” immediately following treatment, while combined therapies, such as skills training plus exposure therapy, continue to

Table 2 Assessment instruments

Instrument	General classification	Description	Population	Special considerations	Diagnostic category
The Clinician-Administered PTSD Scale (CAPS)	Structured clinical interview	Assessment of the 17 symptoms of PTSD derived from DSM-IV diagnostic criteria plus impact on social and occupational functioning, overall PTSD severity, and response validity	Adults	Considered the gold standard for adults, can take over an hour to administer	PTSD
The Structured Clinical Interview for DSM-IV (SCID) PTSD Module	Structured clinical interview	The PTSD module in the SCID-I assesses for symptoms of PTSD based on DSM-IV diagnostic criteria	Adults		PTSD
Post-traumatic Stress Diagnostic Scale (PDS)	Self-report	Assessment of the 17 symptoms of PTSD derived from DSM-IV diagnostic criteria plus level of symptom interference in daily Life	Adults	Not normed on general population, no T-scores	PTSD
PTSD Checklist-Civilian Version (PCL-C)	Self-report	Assessment of the 17 DSM-IV PTSD criteria during the last month, PCL-C refers subject to general trauma, PCL-S refers to a specific event	Adults	Military version (PCL-M) refers to combat related trauma	PTSD
Trauma Symptom Inventory (TSI)	Self-report	100-items, 3 validity scales, and 10 clinical scales, assess level of post-traumatic stress over previous 6-months	Adults	Often used to assess complex PTSD	PTSD
UCLA PTSD Index for DSM-IV (PTSD-RI)	Self-report	Screens for exposure to traumatic events and assesses for all DSM-IV PTSD symptoms	Children (ages 7–12) and adolescent (13 and up) versions	Parent version allows for assessment from another source	PTSD
Trauma Symptom Checklist for Children (TSCC)	Self-report	Assessment of trauma-related symptoms, 2 validity scales and 6 clinical scales	Children and adolescents (ages 7–17)	Comes in abbreviated or full-length form	PTSD
The Acute Stress Disorder Interview (ASDI)	Structured clinical interview	19 items assessing dissociation, reexperiencing, avoidance, and arousal	Adults	Brief administration time	Acute stress disorder (ASD)
Acute Stress Disorder Scale (ASDS)	Self-report	19 items assessing ASD symptoms that correlates with clusters measured by the ASDI	Adults		Acute stress disorder (ASD)

(continued)

Table 2 (continued)

Instrument	General classification	Description	Population	Special considerations	Diagnostic category
The Structured Clinical Interview for DSM-IV Dissociative Disorders-Revised (SCID-D)	Structured clinical interview	Assesses presence of 5 dissociative symptoms including, amnesia, depersonalization, derealization, identity confusion, and identity alteration	Adults		Dissociative identity disorder
Adolescent Dissociative Experiences Scale-II (A-DES)	Self-report	30 items assessing dissociative amnesia, depersonalization, derealization, dissociated identity, and dissociative relatedness	Adolescents ages 11–18	Brief administration time	Dissociative Identity Disorder

have an effect over time and lead to greater maintenance of symptom remission. When examining exposure therapy specifically, evidence is strongest for combined exposure: "imaginal" plus "in vivo" (Foa 2009).

Treatment of PTSD has been conceptualized as occurring in three phases: stabilization, resolution of traumatic memory, and integration. Phase One focuses on ensuring patient safety, providing psychoeducation, and actively assisting the patient in building skills for effectively coping with trauma-related symptoms. Phase Two consists of exposure to traumatic material through imaginal or in vivo exposure and often includes the writing of a trauma narrative. Cognitive processing is used to restructure trauma-related maladaptive thoughts and beliefs. A few trauma-focused treatments use prolonged gradual exposure throughout all three phases of treatment. Personality integration and rehabilitation are the focus of Phase Three. The goal is to help the patient return to fully functional daily living and enhance future safety (van der Hart et al. 2001).

Several trauma-focused treatment models have been developed for adults, adolescents, and children, all of which are grounded in cognitive behavioral techniques. These models follow the three-phase paradigm, though some emphasize a particular phase over others. Most of these models utilize individual therapy; relatively few studies have examined group protocols. The small body of research available on group treatment indicates that it is not more effective than individual therapy (Foa 2009). Research indicates that of all trauma types, combat-related PTSD is least responsive to treatment (Bradley et al. 2005). Little research exists on the effectiveness of treatment approaches not based on cognitive behavioral techniques, such as psychodynamic therapies and patient-centered/humanistic approaches. Some of the most widely studied and well-supported trauma-focused treatments are summarized in Table 3.

Treating PTSD and Comorbid Behavioral Health Disorders

If a person is diagnosed with PTSD, another mental health disorder co-occurs at a rate of approximately 80% (Foa 2009). PTSD most commonly co-occurs with depression, substance abuse, and other anxiety disorders (Bradley et al. 2005). The occurrence of PTSD is also high among patients with personality disorders and those with severe mental illnesses (SMI), including schizophrenia, bipolar disorder, and treatment refractory major depressive disorder. As cited by Bradley et al. (2005), one study reports a 35% lifetime prevalence rate of PTSD among patients diagnosed with Axis II disorders, and Mueser et al. (2008) report that rates of PTSD

Table 3 Trauma-focused therapies

Model	Population	Description	Modality
Exposure therapy: imaginal, in vivo, or Combined	Adults	Exposure to traumatic material, either through imaginal imagery, in vivo/real-life exposure to trauma reminders, or combination of the two	Individual
Cognitive processing therapy (CPT)	Adults	A formalized treatment for adult PTSD, comprised of CT and exposure in the form of a written "trauma account"	Individual
Stress inoculation training (SIT)	Adults	A form of anxiety management, support is especially strong for female victims of sexual assault, support for use with veterans is mixed	Individual
Cognitive therapy (CT)	Adults	Cognitive processing and restructuring of maladaptive trauma-related thoughts and beliefs	Individual
Eye movement desensitization reprocessing (EMDR)	Children, adolescents, and adults	An 8-stage treatment focused on assessment, desensitization, reprocessing, and replacement of cognitions	Individual
Trauma-focused cognitive behavior therapy (TF-CBT)	Children and adolescents	The most widely researched of all treatment interventions designed for use with children and adolescents, a component-based model that follows the 3-phase treatment paradigm, includes skill-building, CT, and a written trauma narrative	Individual, parent, and joint parent-child sessions
Trauma systems therapy (TST)	Children and adolescents	Focus on the social-environmental factors contributing to trauma-related problems, interventions focus on the family, school, and community	Individual and family therapy, office and community-based
Seeking safety (SS)	Adolescents and adults with comorbid substance abuse	Consists of 25 topics that can be addressed in any order, focused on establishing patient safety, no direct exposure components	Individual or group
Cognitive Behavioral Intervention for Trauma in Schools (CBITS)	Children and adolescents	Follows the 3-phase treatment paradigm, includes skill-building, CT, and exposure	School-based group modality, includes some individual and parent sessions

range between 29% and 48% in SMI populations.

In addition, trauma-related symptoms are associated with increased severity of co-occurring SMI diagnoses (Freuch et al. 2009; Mueser et al. 2002). Mueser et al. (2002) hypothesize that the core symptoms of PTSD have a direct effect on the severity and course of SMI; for example, avoidance of trauma-related stimuli may lead to increased social isolation, and re-experiencing of trauma-related memories can be seen as a chronic stressor. PTSD also frequently co-occurs with substance use disorders, as trauma survivors often use drugs and alcohol to avoid reminders of trauma. Substance use disorders have long been associated with negative outcomes in SMI populations, and substance abuse increases the likelihood of further trauma victimization.

Research on the concurrent treatment of PTSD with co-occurring disorders is limited. A meta-analysis on treatment of PTSD comorbid with substance abuse found that integrated treatments, such as seeking safety and CBT for PTSD, are effective at concurrently treating both diagnoses. Another treatment, referred to as *Concurrent Treatment of PTSD and Substance Use Disorders using Prolonged Exposure (COPE)*, was found to dually addresses symptoms of PTSD and substance abuse. Findings across a range of studies indicated that COPE is effective at significantly reducing PTSD and substance use severity (McCauley et al. 2012). When compared with a relapse prevention treatment, COPE led to greater remission of PTSD symptoms while maintaining comparable reduction of substance use severity (Back et al. 2019). Despite increasing research on treatment of disorders comorbid with PTSD, findings remain limited, and additional research is needed on more diverse high-risk populations (McCauley et al. 2012). Based on the limited information currently available, it is recommended that patients presenting with PTSD plus comorbid conditions be treated using an evidence-based trauma-focused approach while simultaneously integrating additional components targeting specific co-occurring diagnoses (Bradley et al. 2005; Foa 2009).

Debriefing

The effectiveness of individual Psychological Debriefing (PD) and group debriefing, including Critical Incident Stress Debriefing (CISD), has been debated for many years. Some research has indicated that individual PD is not effective at reducing symptoms of or preventing PTSD and therefore is not recommended for use following exposure to a traumatic event (Bisson and Cohen 2006; Foa 2009; National Institute for Clinical Excellence 2005). However, recent literature has suggested that several studies conducted on PD have shown efficacy as a group treatment for the original target population, namely, emergency personnel and first responders. Accordingly, it has been recommended that the effectiveness of PD for this target population be reassessed (Tamrakar et al. 2019). Much of the research on CISD is marked by flaws in study design and misuse of the CISD model (National Institute of Mental Health 2002; Robinson 2008; Elhart et al. 2019). A critical examination of all available studies indicates that group-based CISD is also likely not effective and not recommended for use following traumatic exposure (Foa 2009; National Institute for Clinical Excellence 2005).

Clinical guidelines for the treatment of PTSD by the National Institute for Clinical Excellence and the International Society for Traumatic Stress Studies (ISTSS) recommend that PTSD initially be treated with a course of trauma-focused cognitive behavioral therapy or EMDR. However, many clinicians have concerns about the enduring beneficial impact of EMDR and that issues lead to EMDR as a secondary treatment recommendation. The VA does not recommend EMDR as one of its preferred treatments. This exists despite a slowly emerging literature on the effectiveness of EMDR (Stanberry et al. 2020; Taylor et al. 2003; van Minnen et al. 2020). These guidelines do not recommend pharmacological interventions as first-line treatment; however, medications may be indicated for use when there is significant sleep disturbance, when severe and persistent hyperarousal or depression interferes with a person's ability to make gains in treatment, when they refuse to engage in therapy, and when therapy alone is not effective at reducing symptoms (Foa 2009; National Institute for Clinical Excellence 2005; U.S. Department of Veterans Affairs National Center for PTSD 2010). The clinical standards are not up to date, hence the differences seen between recommendations.

Pharmacological Treatment

Practice guidelines by the American Psychiatric Association (APA) conclude that pharmacological treatment as well as cognitive-behavioral and exposure-based psychotherapies has equal levels of empirical support. Additionally, the recommendation for EMDR and narrative exposure therapy (NET) was upgraded from suggested to recommended following a recent literature (American Psychological Association 2017). Numerous studies as well as practice guidelines from APA and ISTSS indicate that the SSRIs or SNRIs should be used as first-line pharmacological treatment. Risperidone or olanzapine are recommended as augmentation pharmacotherapy when an SSRI alone does not lead to significant symptom relief (American Psychiatric Association 2009; Berger et al. 2009; Foa 2009; Sullivan and Neria 2009). This recommendation, limited to certain medications, is based upon the limits of research study. Benzodiazepines are contraindicated in PTSD based upon some stud-

Table 4 Psychopharmacological agents used in PTSD

Medication	Recommendations for use
Selective serotonin reuptake inhibitors (SSRIs)	Considered first-line pharmacological intervention for non-combat-related PTSD Paroxetine and sertraline are most studied, most prescribed, and the only FDA-approved medications for treatment of PTSD Recent randomized controlled trials indicate that SSRIs may not be effective at treating combat related PTSD and suggest that pharmacological alternatives needs to be explored
Serotonin and norepinephrine reuptake inhibitors (SNRIs)	Venlafaxine ER is the only SNRI studied to date Results indicate that it is equally effective at treating PTSD as SSRIs
Antiadrenergic agents	Prazosin shown effective for improving quality of sleep and reducing nightmares Results on the prophylactic effects of propranolol are inconclusive, not enough current evidence to recommend it as an effective preventative treatment
Antipsychotics	Risperidone or olanzapine shown effective as augmentation therapy with SSRIs or SNRIs
Monoamine oxidase inhibitors (MAOI's)	Has been shown effective at reducing re-experiencing symptoms but has not been extensively tested
Anticonvulsants	Results have been varied and inconclusive Cannot be recommended for treatment at this time
Benzodiazepines	*They are contraindicated for PTSD treatment and should not be used* No evidence supporting the effectiveness of preventing or reducing the core symptoms of PTSD May reduce the effectiveness of CBT Have historically been frequently prescribed to prevent trauma-related symptoms or to reduce PTSD symptoms

ies – further examination is underway as studies have not distinguished recently traumatized individuals from PTSD. A further summary of current research on classes of medication and recommendations for their use is presented in Table 4.

The Patient's Role

PTSD is a disorder unlike any other. There is a known trigger (the trauma), and at the heart of the disorder is avoidance of talking about what happened. The clinician's role is to guide the patient through treatment while not forcing forward movement or becoming complicit in avoidance. For this reason, constant psychoeducation about the treatment process and the creation of a safe working environment are crucial. Trauma often causes feelings of powerlessness, since the individual was likely unable to stop the event from happening, either physically or emotionally. Regaining power, or a sense of mastery over the traumatic memory, is a part of recovery. Therefore, it is critical for the patient to feel *in control* in the treatment process. The patient must remain actively engaged and "drive the train" of treatment as the clinician helps to direct it. Clinicians should expect patient avoidance, which can manifest itself in missed sessions, unanswered phone calls, omission of trauma details, and non-completion of assignments between sessions (a common component of CBT-based trauma therapies). The clinician should acknowledge these forms of avoidance through open communication, so the patient can voice his or her fears and concerns in a safe environment and so that avoidance does not disrupt effective treatment.

Implementation Issues

There is a parallel between the symptoms of PTSD and the impact on implementation. Not only do patients experience avoidance as a part of PTSD, but often clinical staff and systems are complicit in avoiding trauma discussion. On a micro level, clinicians often worry about "re-traumatizing" patients by discussing the trauma. The clinician must have the skills to talk about the treatment process with the patient and to provide gradual exposure (TF-CBT web 2010). On a macro level, research over the past 20 years has greatly changed the face of trauma treatment. With treatment as usual, such as a patient-centered approach, the trauma may only be addressed as the patient raises it, and due to the nature of avoidance, this will likely be infrequent. Utilization of new methods, such as CBT, CPT (cognitive processing therapy), and EMDR, requires a shift in approach to the work. It takes time for clinics, hospitals, and other treatment centers to implement new models and practices, become trauma-informed systems of care, and utilize universal screening for trauma (Hodas 2006). This requires training and a different lens to be used each time a new patient enters the service setting. Utilization of new methods may also affect billing and insurance reimbursement. Examples of this include art, drama, and body-centered therapies that may be effective as a primary or supplementary method of treating PTSD. Despite implementation challenges, many clinical environments have successfully shifted services to become trauma-informed and offer more trauma-specific services.

Self-Care and Secondary Trauma Prevention

As defined by Osofsky et al. (2008), "vicarious traumatization (VT) or compassion fatigue (CF), also labeled secondary trauma, refers to the cumulative effect of working with survivors of traumatic life events…as part of everyday work" (p. 91). Pearlman (1995) refers to vicarious traumatization as "a process of change resulting from empathic engagement with trauma survivors. It can have an impact on the helper's sense of self, world view, spirituality, affect tolerance, interpersonal relationships, and imagery system of memory." Anyone working with trauma survivors is at risk of being affected by secondary trauma. Signs and symptoms can be similar to those of direct traumatization (Osofsky et al. 2008). Indirect exposure to trauma in helping professionals increases negative psychological responses, including vicarious trauma (VT), secondary traumatic stress (STS), and burnout (Cummings et al. 2018). Although the definitions of these three conditions are slightly different, much of the prevention and response is the same for systems and individuals. Anyone working with trauma survivors is at risk of being affected by VT, STS, and burnout.

Prevention of VT, STS, and burnout is a matter for both systems and individuals. Organizations may monitor their employees' wellness through regular inquiry and strategic response to issues of VT, STS, and burnout in their workforce. Self-assessment, which can be encouraged by organizations, of exposure to trauma-related material and symptoms of VT, STS, and burnout is an essential step in prevention. Individuals may aid in personal prevention through a variety of resilience-oriented activities (Ludick and Figley 2017). Personal self-care within the workplace should focus on pacing of work, building in time to engage in collegial support, utilizing supervision and crisis help, and managing and tolerating the strong affects raised by trauma-focused work without clinician or supervisory avoidance. It is equally essential that clinicians use personal self-care techniques within and outside the workplace. In the workplace, this can include taking breaks; eating lunch; going for walks; engaging in brief moments of stretching, breathing, or mindfulness; not answering every call immediately; and creating a soothing office environment. Techniques for personal self-care outside the workplace include practicing stress management through meditation, prayer, conscious relaxation, deep breathing, and exercise, obtaining emotional support from others, engaging in hobbies and enjoyed activities, getting adequate sleep, eating regularly, taking vacation, and developing a written plan focused on maintaining work-life balance (Quinn et al. 2019). It may also be helpful to consider seeking therapy for unresolved trauma given the potential activating effects of engaging in trauma-focused work.

On the systems level, there are steps that can be taken to prevent VT, STS, and burnout. Organizations may also work to emphasize the importance of prevention, using such strategies as quality supervisory relationships; higher salary; manageable caseload size (Quinn et al. 2019) with daily patient volume expectation tuned to the nature of the caseload; and education about trauma triggers (Taylor et al. 2019) to aid in prevention. Staff who engage in exposure to patients' traumatic stories can be helped through fostering an environment that is socially supportive through opportunities for cognitive processing of traumatic material (Ogińska-Bulik et al. 2020), support during crisis, encouraging open and supportive communication among employees, encouraging self-care, demonstrating explicit appreciation for work with traumatized patients, and providing variance within caseloads. Organizations may also help through acknowledgment of multiple layers and complexity of stress for clinicians, such as exposure to patients' traumatic stories, personal experiences with trauma exposure, and societal stressors, such as systemic racism.

Working with survivors of traumatic event(s) can be extraordinarily rewarding. In many ways, trauma work is arguably different than treating other disorders, and it takes tremendous focus, determination, and emotional self-care. The patient and clinician need to partner in a unique way. As patients gain healing from trauma, they can often enjoy life and function again, which can be enormously satisfying for the clinician who witnesses this transformation, contributing to a sense of purpose and meaning. This reality promotes hope and important antidote for both providers and consumers of service.

Acknowledgments Special thanks to Greg Sullivan, MD and the Jewish Board of Family & Children's Services MKSEI team for contributions and edits.

References

American Psychiatric Association. (1980). *Diagnostic and statistical manual of mental disorders* (3rd ed.). Washington, DC: Author.

American Psychiatric Association (2009). GUIDELINE WATCH (MARCH 2009): PRACTICE GUIDELINE FOR THE TREATMENT OF PATIENTS WITH ACUTE STRESS DISORDER AND POSTTRAUMATIC STRESS DISORDER. Available at https://psychiatryonline.org/pb/assets/raw/sitewide/practice_guidelines/guidelines/acutestressdisorderptsd-watch.pdf Accessed 8/19/22.

American Psychiatric Association. (2013). *Diagnostic and statistical manual of mental disorders* (5th ed., text revision). Washington, DC: Author.

American Psychiatric Association. (2021). *Diagnostic and statistical manual of mental disorders* (5th ed., Text Revision). Washington, DC: Author.

American Psychological Association. (2017). Clinical practice guideline for the treatment of posttraumatic stress disorder (PTSD) in adults.

Back, S. E., Killeen, T., Badour, C. L., Flanagan, J. C., Allan, N. P., Santa Ana, E., … & Brady, K. T. (2019). Concurrent treatment of substance use disorders and PTSD using prolonged exposure: A randomized clinical trial in military veterans. *Addictive behaviors, 90*, 369–377.

Banyard, V., Hamby, S., & Grych, J. (2017). Health effects of adverse childhood events: Identifying promising protective factors at the intersection of mental and physical well-being. *Child Abuse & Neglect, 65*, 88–98.

Beals, J., Manson, S. M., Shore, J. H., Friedman, M., Ashcraft, M., Fairbank, J. A., et al. (2002). The prevalence of posttraumatic stress disorder among American Indian Vietnam veterans: Disparities and context. *Journal of Traumatic Stress, 15*, 89–97.

Berger, W., Mendlowicz, M., Marques-Portella, C., Kinrys, G., Fontenelle, L., Marmar, C., & Figueira, I. (2009) Pharmacologic alternatives to antidepressants in posttraumatic stress disorder: A systematic review. *Progress in Neuro-Psychopharmacology & Biological Psychiatry, 33*, 169–180.

Bisson, J. I., & Cohen, J. A. (2006). Disseminating early interventions following trauma. *Journal of Traumatic Stress, 19*(5), 583–595.

Bradley, R., Greene, J., Russ, E., Dutra, L., & Westen, D. (2005). A multidimensional meta-analysis of psychotherapy for PTSD. *American Journal of Psychiatry, 162*(2), 214–227.

Breslau, N. & Kessler, R. C. (2001). The stressor criterion in DSM-IV posttraumatic stress disorder: An empirical investigation. *Biological Psychiatry, 50*, 699–704.

Cahill, S. P., Foa, E. B., Hembree, E. A., Marshall, R. D., & Nacash, N. (2006). Dissemination of exposure therapy in the treatment of posttraumatic stress disorder. *Journal of Traumatic Stress, 19*(5), 597–610.

Carter, R. T., Kirkinis, K., & Johnson, V. E. (2020). Relationships between trauma symptoms and race-based traumatic stress. *Traumatology, 26*(1), 11.

Cloitre, M., Stovall-McClough, K. C., Nooner, K., Zorbas, P., Cherry, S., Jackson, C. L., Gan, W., & Petkova, E. (2010). Treatment for PTSD related to childhood abuse: A randomized controlled trial. *American Journal of Psychiatry, 167*(8), 915–924.

Cummings, C., Singer, J., Hisaka, R., & Benuto, L. T. (2018). Compassion satisfaction to combat work-related burnout, vicarious trauma, and secondary traumatic stress. *Journal of Interpersonal Violence*, 0886260518799502.

Elhart, M. A., Dotson, J., & Smart, D. (2019). Psychological debriefing of hospital emergency personnel: review of critical incident stress debriefing. *International Journal of Nursing Student Scholarship, 6*, 37.

Foa, E. (2009). *Effective treatments for PTSD, second edition*. New York, NY: The Guilford Press.

Freuch, B. C., Grubaugh, A. L., Cusack, K. J., & Elhai, J. D. (2009). Disseminating evidence-based practices for adults with PTSD and severe mental illness in public sector mental health agencies. *Behavior Modification, 33*(1), 66–81.

Glass, O., Dreusicke, M., Evans, J., Bechard, E., & Wolever, R. Q. (2019). Expressive writing to improve resilience to trauma: A clinical feasibility trial. *Complementary Therapies in Clinical Practice, 34*, 240–246.

Haglund, M. E. M., Nestadt, P. S., Cooper, N. S., Southwick, S. M., & Charney, D. S. (2007). Psychobiological mechanisms of resilience: Relevance to prevention and treatment of stress-related psychopathology. *Development and Psychopathology, 19*, 889–920.

Himle, J. A., Baser, R. E., Taylor, R. J., Campbell, R. D., & Jackson, J. S. (2009). Anxiety disorders among African Americans, blacks of Caribbean descent, and non-Hispanic whites in the United States. *Journal of Anxiety Disorders, 23*(5), 578–590.

Hodas, G. R. (2006). *Responding to childhood trauma: The promise and practice of trauma*. Retrieved February 18, 2011, from http://www.nasmhpd.org/general_files/publications/ntac_pubs/Responding%20to%20Childhood%20Trauma%20-%20Hodas.pdf.

Holden, K. B., Hernandez, N. D., Wrenn, G. L., & Belton, A. S. (2017). Resilience: Protective Factors for Depression and Post Traumatic Stress Disorder among African American Women?. *Health, Culture and Society, 9*, 12–29.

Hopper, E. K., Bassuk, E. L., & Olivet, J. (2010). Shelter from the storm: Trauma-informed care in homelessness services settings. *The Open Health Services and Policy Journal,3*, 80–100.

Hulbert, J. C., & Anderson, M. C. (2018). What doesn't kill you makes you stronger: Psychological trauma and its relationship to enhanced memory control. *Journal of Experimental Psychology: General, 147*(12), 1931.

Ironson, G., Freund, B., Strauss, J. L., & Williams, J. (2002). Comparison of two treatments for traumatic stress: A community-based study of EMDR and prolonged exposure. *Journal of Clinical Psychology, 58*(1), 113–128.

Kessler, R. C., Aguilar-Gaxiola, S., Alonso, J., Benjet, C., Bromet, E. J., Cardoso, G., … & Koenen, K. C. (2017). Trauma and PTSD in the WHO world mental health surveys. *European Journal of Psychotraumatology, 8*(sup5), 1353383.

Kessler, R. C., Chiu, W. T., Demler, O., & Walters, E. E. (2005). Prevalence, severity, and comorbidity of twelve-month DSM-IV disorders in the National Comorbidity Survey Replication (NCS-R). *Archives of General Psychiatry, 62*, 617–627.

Kim, Y. K., Amidfar, M., & Won, E. (2019). A review on inflammatory cytokine-induced alterations of the brain as potential neural biomarkers in post-traumatic stress disorder. *Progress in Neuro-Psychopharmacology and Biological Psychiatry, 91*, 103–112.

Kim, T. Y., Kim, S. J., Choi, J. R., Lee, S. T., Kim, J., Hwang, I. S., … & Kang, J. I. (2017). The effect of trauma and PTSD on telomere length: An exploratory study in people exposed to combat trauma. *Scientific Reports, 7*(1), 1–7.

Lester, K., Resick, P., Young-Xu, Y., & Artz, C. (2010). Impact of race on early treatment termination and outcomes in posttraumatic stress disorder treatment. *Journal of Consulting and Clinical Psychology, 78*(4), 480–489.

Leitch, L. (2017). Action steps using ACEs and trauma-informed care: A resilience model. *Health & Justice, 5*(1), 1–10.

Ludick, M., & Figley, C. R. (2017). Toward a mechanism for secondary trauma induction and reduction: Reimagining a theory of secondary traumatic stress. *Traumatology, 23*(1), 112.

Marsenich, L. (2010). *Trauma informed care*. Retrieved February 18, 2010, from http://www.cacfs.org/materials/Alliance%20-%20trauma%20informed%20care.pdf.

Marshall, G. N., Schell, T. L., & Miles, J. N. (2009). Ethnic differences inposttraumatic distress: Hispanics' symptoms differ in kind and degree. *Journal of Consulting and Clinical Psychology*, 77, 1169–1178. Objective: This longitudinal study of physical injury survivors examined the degree to which Hispanic and non-Hispanic Caucasians reported similar PTSD symptoms.

McCauley, J. L., Killeen, T., Gros, D. F., Brady, K. T., & Back, S. E. (2012). Posttraumatic stress disorder and co-occurring substance use disorders: Advances in assessment and treatment. *Clinical Psychology: Science and Practice, 19*(3), 283–304.

McClendon, J., Dean, K. E., & Galovski, T. (2020). Addressing Diversity in PTSD Treatment: Disparities in Treatment Engagement and Outcome Among Patients of Color. *Current Treatment Options in Psychiatry, 7*, 275–290.

Mueser, K. T., Rosenberg, S. D., Goodman, L. A., & Trumbetta, S. L. (2002). Trauma, PTSD, and the course of severe mental illness: An interactive model. *Schizophrenia Research, 53*, 123–143.

Mueser, K. T., Rosenberg, S. D., Xie, H., Jankowski, M. K., Bolton, E. E., Lu, W., Hamblen, J. L., Rosenberg, H.J., McHugo, G. J., & Wolf, R. (2008). A randomized controlled trial of cognitive-behavioral treatment for posttraumatic stress disorder in severe mental illness. *Journal of Consulting and Clinical Psychology, 76*(2), 259–271.

National Institute for Clinical Excellence. (2005). *Post-traumatic stress disorder (PTSD): The management of PTSD in adults and children in primary and secondary care. Clinical Guideline 26*. London: Author.

National Institute of Mental Health. (2002). *Mental Health and Mass Violence: Evidence-Based Early Psychological Interventions for Victims/Survivors of Mass Violence. A Workshop to Reach Consensus on Best Practices*. NIH Publication No. 02-5138, Washington, D.C.: U.S. Government Printing Office.

Ogle, C. M., Rubin, D. C., Berntsen, D., & Siegler, I. C. (2013). The frequency and impact of exposure to potentially traumatic events over the life course. *Clinical Psychological Science, 1*(4), 426–434.

Ogińska-Bulik, N., Juczyński, Z., & Michalska, P. (2020). The Mediating Role of Cognitive Trauma Processing in the Relationship Between Empathy and Secondary Traumatic Stress Symptoms Among Female Professionals Working With Victims of Violence. *Journal of Interpersonal Violence*, 0886260520976211.

Osofsky, J. D., Putnam, F. W., & Lederman, C. S. (2008). How to maintain emotional health when working with trauma. *Juvenile and Family Court Journal, 59*(4), 91–102.

Peacock, C., Hardy, K., & Panzer, P. (2010). *Developing Training with a Racial Lens*. JBFCS. (personal correspondence after academic presentation).

Pearlman, L. A.. (1995). Self-care for trauma therapists: ameliorating vicarious traumatization. In B. H. Stamm (Ed.), *Secondary traumatic stress: Self-care issues for clinicians, researchers, and educators*, (pp. 51–64). Baltimore, MD, US: The Sidran Press.

Pole, N., Best, S. R., Metzler, T., & Marmar, C. R. (2005). Why are Hispanics at greater risk for PTSD? *Cultural Diversity and Ethnic Minority Psychology, 11*, 144–161.

Pole, N., Gone, JP, & Kulkarni, M. (2008). Posttraumatic stress disorder among ethnoracial minorities in the United States. *Clinical Psychology: Science and Practice, 15*(1), 35–61.

Portnoy, G. A., Relyea, M. R., Decker, S., Shamaskin-Garroway, A., Driscoll, M., Brandt, C. A., & Haskell, S. G. (2018). Understanding gender differences in resilience among veterans: Trauma history and social ecology. *Journal of Traumatic Stress, 31*(6), 845–855.

Quinn, A., Ji, P., & Nackerud, L. (2019). Predictors of secondary traumatic stress among social workers: Supervision, income, and caseload size. *Journal of Social Work, 19*(4), 504–528.

Rivard, J. C., Bloom, S. L., Abramovitz, R., Pasquale, L. E., Duncan, M., McCorkle, D., & Gelman, A. (2003). Assessing the implementation and effects of a trauma-focused intervention for youths. *Residential Treatment Psychiatric Quarterly, 74*(2), 137–154.

Roberts, A. L., Gilman, S. E., Breslau, J., Breslau, N., & Koenen, K. C. (2011). Race/ethnic differences in exposure to traumatic events, development of post-traumatic stress disorder, and treatment-seeking for post-traumatic stress disorder in the United States. *Psychological Medicine, 41*(1), 71.

Roberts, N. P., Kitchiner, N. J., Kenardy, J., Lewis, C. E., & Bisson, J. I. (2019). Early psychological intervention following recent trauma: A systematic review and meta-analysis. *European Journal of Psychotraumatology, 10*(1), 1695486.

Robinson R., (2008). Reflections on the debriefing debate. *International Journal of Emergency Mental Health, 10*(4), 253-260.

Sareen, J. (2018). Posttraumatic stress disorder in adults: Epidemiology, pathophysiology, clinical manifestations, course, assessment, and diagnosis. *Retrieved from UpToDate website:* https://www.uptodate.com/contents/posttraumatic-stress-disorder-in-adultsepidemiology-pathophysiology-clinical-manifestations-course-assessment-anddiagnosis.

Saxe, G. N., Ellis, H. B., & Kaplow, J. B. (2007). *Collaborative treatment of traumatized children and teens: The trauma-systems therapy approach*. New York: Guilford Press.

Sayer, N. A., Noorbaloochi, S., Frazier, P. A., Pennebaker, J. W., Orazem, R. J., Schnurr, P. P., … & Litz, B. T. (2015). Randomized controlled trial of online expressive writing to address readjustment difficulties among US Afghanistan and Iraq war veterans. *Journal of Traumatic Stress, 28*(5), 381–390.

Sibrava, N. J., Bjornsson, A. S., Pérez Benítez, A. C. I., Moitra, E., Weisberg, R. B., & Keller, M. B. (2019). Posttraumatic stress disorder in African American and Latinx adults: Clinical course and the role of racial and ethnic discrimination. *American Psychologist, 74*(1), 101.

Stanbury, T. M. M., Drummond, P. D., Laugharne, J., Kullack, C., & Lee, C. W. (2020). Comparative efficiency of EMDR and prolonged exposure in treating posttraumatic stress disorder: A randomized trial. *Journal of EMDR Practice and Research, 14*(1), 2–12.

Sullivan, G., & Neria, Y. (2009). Pharmacotherapy of PTSD: Current status and controversies. *Psychiatric Annals, 39*(6), 342–347. Retrieved June 6, 2009, from PsychiatricAnnalsOnline.com.

Tamrakar, T., Murphy, J., & Elklit, A. (2019). Was psychological debriefing dismissed too quickly? An assessment of the 2002 Cochrane review. *Crisis, Stress and Human Resilience: An International Journal, 1*(3), 146–155.

Taylor, A. K., Gregory, A., Feder, G., & Williamson, E. (2019). 'We're all wounded healers': A qualitative study to explore the well-being and needs of helpline workers supporting survivors of domestic violence and abuse. *Health & Social Care in the Community, 27*(4), 856–862.

Taylor, S., Thordarson, D. S., Maxfield, L., Fedoroff, I. C., Lovell, K., & Ogrodniczuk, J. (2003). Comparative efficacy, speed, and adverse effects of three PTSD treatments: exposure therapy, EMDR, and relaxation training. *Journal of Consulting and Clinical Psychology*, *71*(2), 330.

TF-CBT Web Trauma-Focused Cognitive Behavioral Therapy. (n.d.). Retrieved November 8, 2010, from http://tfcbt.musc.edu/.

Thompson, N. J., Fiorillo, D., Rothbaum, B. O., Ressler, K. J., & Michopoulos, V. (2018). Coping strategies as mediators in relation to resilience and posttraumatic stress disorder. *Journal of Affective Disorders*, *225*, 153–159.

Triffelman, E. G. & Pole, N. (2010). Future directions in studies of trauma among ethnoracial and sexual minority samples: Commentary. *Journal of Consulting and Clinical Psychology, 78*(4), 490–497.

U.S. Department of Veterans Affairs National Center for PTSD. (2010). Pharmacological treatment of acute stress reactions and PTSD. Retrieved February 2010, from www.ptsd.va.gov.

van der Hart, O., Steele, K., & Ford, J. D. (2001, Fall). Introducing issues in the treatment of complex PTSD. Traumatic Stress Points. Retrieved August 26, 2010, from http://www.istss.org/TraumaticStressPoints/2447.htm.

van der Kolk, B. A. (1989). The compulsion to repeat the trauma: Reenactment, revictimization, masochism. *Psychiatric Clinics of North America, Vol 12. Treatment of Victims of Sexual Abuse* (pp. 389–411). Philadelphia: W.B. Saunders.

van der Kolk, B. A. (2005). Developmental trauma disorder: Toward a rational diagnosis for children with complex trauma histories. *Psychiatric Annals, 35*(5), 401–408.

Van Minnen, A., Voorendonk, E. M., Rozendaal, L., & de Jongh, A. (2020). Sequence matters: Combining Prolonged Exposure and EMDR therapy for PTSD. *Psychiatry Research*, *290*, 113032

Wamser-Nanney, R., Cherry, K. E., Campbell, C., & Trombetta, E. (2018a). Racial Differences in Children's Trauma Symptoms Following Complex Trauma Exposure. *Journal of Interpersonal Violence*, 0886260518760019.

Wamser-Nanney, R., Howell, K. H., Schwartz, L. E., & Hasselle, A. J. (2018b). The moderating role of trauma type on the relationship between event centrality of the traumatic experience and mental health outcomes. *Psychological Trauma: Theory, Research, Practice, and Policy*, *10*(5), 499.

Whealin, J. M., Stotzer, R., Nelson, D., Li, F., Liu-Tom, H. T. T., & Pietrzak, R. H. (2013). Evaluating PTSD prevalence and resilience factors in a predominantly Asian American and Pacific Islander sample of Iraq and Afghanistan Veterans. *Journal of Affective Disorders*, *150*(3), 1062–1068.

Yang, R., Gautam, A., Getnet, D., Daigle, B. J., Miller, S., Misganaw, B., … & Jett, M. (2020). Epigenetic biotypes of post-traumatic stress disorder in war-zone exposed veteran and active duty males. *Molecular Psychiatry*, 1–15.

Yehuda, R., & LeDoux, J. (2007). Response variation following trauma: A translational neuroscience approach to understanding PTSD. *Neuron Review, 56*, 19–32.

Yule, K., Houston, J., & Grych, J. (2019). Resilience in children exposed to violence: A meta-analysis of protective factors across ecological contexts. *Clinical Child and Family Psychology Review*, *22*(3), 406–431.

Integrated Care and Community Psychiatry

John S. Kern and Patrick S. Runnels

Introduction

Integrated care as defined by a consensus publication from the Agency for Healthcare Research and Quality (AHRQ) is:

> The care that results from a practice team of primary care and behavioral health clinicians, working together with patients and families, using a systematic and cost-effective approach to provide patient-centered care for a defined population. This care may address mental health and substance abuse conditions, health behaviors (including their contribution to chronic medical illnesses), life stressors and crises, stress-related physical symptoms, and ineffective patterns of health care utilization. (Peek et al. 2013)

The authors note that definitions of integrated care are inclined to emphasize values and principles, "rather than functional specifics required for a particular implementation to count as 'the genuine article'." This chapter will focus on the specifics of implementation of integrated care to date, as opposed to why integrating is philosophically the right thing to do.

The integration of behavioral health with other medical care has been widely pursued over the last decade with the goal of addressing three intersecting issues:

1. Access to treatment of behavioral illness related to workforce shortages, which could be mitigated by primary care providers more effectively identifying and treating mild to moderate mental illness
2. Access to the treatment and prevention of chronic physical disease for individuals with chronic behavioral illness, whose lifespan is 1–2 decades shorter than that of the average individual
3. Increased recognition that effective management of chronic disease is contingent on effective management of co-occurring behavioral health issues

To address all three issues requires two things. First, broader healthcare systems must integrate behavioral health services into outpatient primary care and specialty settings in order to improve access to and engagement with psychiatric services. At the same time, those same systems must collaborate with communities to develop and deploy strategies that minimize the poor health outcomes of people living with serious mental illness through the integration

J. S. Kern (✉)
Department of Psychiatry and Behavioral Sciences, University of Washington School of Medicine, Seattle, WA, USA
e-mail: jkern2@uw.edu

P. S. Runnels
Case Western Reserve University School of Medicine, Population Health, University Hospitals, Shaker Heights, OH, USA
e-mail: patrick.runnels1@uhhospitals.org

W. E. Sowers et al. (eds.), *Textbook of Community Psychiatry*,
https://doi.org/10.1007/978-3-031-10239-4_17

of medical care, prevention, and care management services into community mental health settings.

Both efforts have become central to the provision of care in spaces occupied by community psychiatrists, as evidenced by the advent of Certified Community Behavioral Health Clinics, which create a platform to improve the monitoring and care of physical health conditions in people with serious mental illness, and the expansion of behavioral health care provision in primary care settings. In this chapter, we will focus on integration efforts most relevant to the work of the community psychiatrist.

Providing Behavioral Health Services in Primary Care Settings (BH in PC)

Attempts to establish the provision of behavioral health in primary care settings have a long history. Efforts to train primary care physicians to provide evidence-based psychiatric care have produced poor results (Unützer and Park 2012). Simple co-location – bringing a psychiatric provider on-site with a stand-alone schedule and workflow – is the most common form of integration, but also does not effectively increase access to services. Some clinics will augment co-location by having the psychiatric provider focus on short-term consultation and stabilization, with referral back to primary care for ongoing management of most cases. While this can increase psychiatric capacity by reducing long-term caseloads, significant gaps in care remain, while many primary care providers are uncomfortable taking on responsibility for even mild to moderate mental illness without more formal support from mental health professionals. The two most prominent models of true integration of behavioral health into primary care are Primary Care Behavioral Health and the Collaborative Care Model (described below), both of which are characterized by concerted efforts at integrating a behavioral health provider into the primary care workflow.

Primary Care Behavioral Health

The primary care behavioral health (PCBH) model "is a team-based, primary care approach to managing behavioral health problems and bio-psycho-socially influenced health conditions. The model's main goal is to enhance the primary care team's ability to manage and treat such problems/conditions, with resulting improvements in primary care services for the entire clinic population" (Reiter et al. 2018). An on-site behavioral health provider, often a psychologist, offers services "with the over-arching goal of improving primary care in general." This behavioral health provider, usually identified as a "behavioral health consultant" (BHC), functions as a generalist, working with patients of all ages and conditions, ideally on the day they are referred, as part of the clinic's routine team-based approach to care. Interventions by the BHC are focused and brief, directed at specific symptoms or functional improvement, and leans heavily on educating the primary care team to be able to manage mild to moderate mental health issues on their own.

The PCBH model does not include a role for a psychiatrist and is not designed to provide ongoing care for complex psychiatric disorders. Because of the high degree of responsiveness to PCP needs – e.g., immediate ability to engage with patients with acute needs in the clinic via a "warm handoff" to the behavioral health provider – these services are well-received by PCPs.

However, according to Reiter, who works in the PCBH model, it is "difficult to determine the extent to which (if at all) the addition of BHC [Behavioral Health Consultant] interventions improve outcomes relative to the usual PCP-only treatment" (Reiter et al. 2018).

Collaborative Care Model

The collaborative care model (CoCM) is a specific type of integrated care, developed at the University of Washington, that aims to identify and treat diagnosed psychiatric disorders, such as depression and anxiety. A team – including the PCP, a fully integrated behavioral health provider (typically a licensed social worker, counselor, therapist, or registered nurse), and a psychiatric consultant (usually remote and consulting by phone or video) – use a measurement-based strategy to provide psychiatric care. Following a caseload review, recommendations from the psychiatric consultant flow to the PCP through the behavioral health provider. The focus is on access to evidence-based psychiatric care where it is not otherwise available.

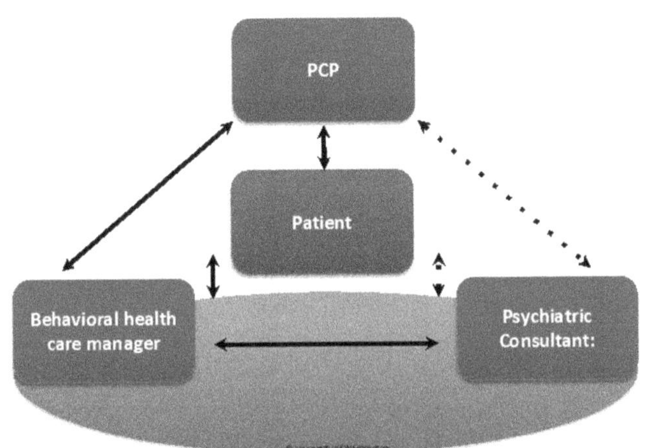

care for all patients seen in the clinic, not just those for which they are directly consulted.

Collaborative Care has been tested in more than 90 randomized, controlled trials in the USA and abroad. Several recent meta-analyses make it clear that Collaborative Care consistently improves care as usual (Archer et al. 2012; Gilbody et al. 2006; Woltmann et al. 2012). It leads to better patient outcomes, better patient and provider satisfaction, improved functioning, and reductions in healthcare costs (Levine et al. 2005; Schoenbaum et al. 2002; Unützer et al. 2008; Katon et al. 2002). Recent research has focused on expanding care to different populations and different conditions. Beyond depression, which was the initial focus of, Collaborative Care trials have shown efficacy for ADHD, anxiety disorders, PTSD, bipolar disorder, as well as efficacy in a number of different kinds of populations (e.g., children, general adults, and geriatric

Collaborative Care provides a number of opportunities for psychiatric consultants to impact care, including consultation for individual cases and the education of behavioral healthcare managers and other primary care staff, including the PCP. The development of treatment protocols for commonly encountered clinical situations can improve the confidence and competence of primary care staff, which reduces the need for psychiatrist input over time. An excellent psychiatric consultant will keep in mind means of improving populations) in the USA and internationally (Silverstein et al. 2015; Roy-Byrne et al. 2010; Fortney et al. 2021; Ng et al. 2020; Hu et al. 2020; Bowen et al. 2020). At least two studies have specifically addressed the difference in outcomes between organizations that include a formal *psychiatric caseload review process* and those that do not and found a significant, positive impact of this process on outcomes (Blackmore et al. 2018; Unützer et al. 2012).

A 2011 consensus conference identified five principles of Collaborative Care. These are widely cited but should be regarded as experience-tested guidelines for what might be most likely to work in providing psychiatric services in a behavioral health setting rather than evidence-based guidelines.

1. Population-Based Care: All patients treated and followed using a registry so that no patients are missed.
2. Measurement-Based Treatment to Target: Clinical screening and tracking measures are used to support treatment and treatment adjustments.
3. Patient-Centered Collaboration: A team of providers work together using a shared treatment plan, providing service that takes into account the needs and preferences of the patient.
4. Evidence-Based Care: Treatment that has been proven to work in the primary care setting is provided first, whether medication based or psychotherapy based, according to patient preference when appropriate.
5. Accountable Care: The team and the healthcare organization are responsible for patient populations as well as individual patients and conduct ongoing quality improvement efforts, making success in future value-based payment (see chapter "Financing Community Behavioral Health Services" on Financing for more information on value-based care) plans more likely.

Stepped Care a framework in which the simplest kind of care is offered first – is a concept that can apply to PCBH or, Collaborative Care, with more elaborate forms of care following if treatment is not effective. For example, this framework might recommend behavioral activation first for patient with mild depression before meds.

Real-World Considerations

Real-world implementation of behavioral health integration into primary care often includes aspects of both of these models. For example, a Collaborative Care team may also work to be as accessible as possible to immediate needs for PCP consultation and "warm handoffs," and to develop useful brief interventions to respond to immediate clinic needs.

At the individual level, few psychiatrists' practices consist entirely of work as a Collaborative Care psychiatric consultant, but physician satisfaction in a Collaborative Care setting is high (Levine et al. 2005). The attraction of Collaborative Care work derives from the ability to positively impact the care of an entire population, to work with an interesting primary care team, to be exposed to a wide range of psychiatric presentations, and to expand one's scope of expertise, as one inevitably is called upon to do. The range of disorders presenting to primary care includes just about everyone, and every psychiatric consultant requires ongoing self-education, often about parts of the specialty that the psychiatrist hasn't worked in before.

Workplace Culture Considerations

The implementation of a Collaborative Care program requires everyone involved – the PCP, the behavioral health provider, the psychiatric consultant, and, most importantly, the patient – to approach psychiatric care in a new way and to take on new duties. This can unfortunately sometimes be experienced by clinicians involved as risky, as new and additional work, or as an unwelcome expansion of scope. Studies of provider satisfaction with collaborative care have been very positive, but the transitional phase of implementation and accommodation can be quite challenging (Levine et al. 2005). To have the best chance of success, implementing organizations must identify the following five things:

1. *Leadership Support* – commitment from health system leadership overall (e.g., the CEO, CFO, and/or CMO) as well as from the leads for both the primary care service line and the behavioral health service line. Leadership needs to repeatedly share a positive vision for why this model is a necessary and important part of the future by (1) creating clear and consistent messaging that the system is culturally invested in a successful implementation and willing to see it through, even over many years; (2) aligning incentives across all stakeholders so that everyone is working together from the same script, including the clear identification of key metrics to assess program success; and (3) clearing space and resources to ensure success.
2. *Psychiatrist Champion* – In most settings, the psychiatric consultant will occupy the role of program champion, serving as both the cultural steward for the model and ambassador to primary care – particularly physicians – to do the hard work of securing buy-in to change.
3. *Primary Care Physician Champion* – this person serves both as a partner to the Psychiatrist Champion, including ownership of achieving results, and a cultural steward and ambassador while also providing primary care physicians with a resource who understands their practice and their concerns.
4. *Lead Behavioral Health Care Manager* – on the day-to-day level, the BHCMs do the hard work of driving implementation at the level of an individual practice. That work requires a temperament suited to change, but also support for managing practice and patient resistance, which can easily lead to BHCM burnout (and high turnover of BHCMs will sink CoCM). As systems expand beyond one practice, BHCMs will need to have someone supporting their work, holding term to account for adhering to the model, and maintaining a positive outlook when seemingly intractable difficulties are encountered.
5. *Investment in Team Culture* – as is necessary for any high-functioning team, the psychiatrist and BHCM must commit to spending direct time with the primary care team to ensure everyone agrees on and understands the roles and responsibilities of the primary care provider, the BHCM, and the consultant psychiatrist. In addition, they must have clear, agreed-upon channels of communication. While the tasks at hand can be accomplished remotely, building a new team culture entirely remotely can be a challenge. If the BHCM must operate remotely, team leads must be even more intentional about protecting intentional team-building time.

Financing Integrated Care

The model of team-based behavioral health in primary care, with a significant role for indirect consultation on the part of the psychiatric consultant, can be financially sustainable but doesn't fit well into a fee-for-service funding environment, which is organized around patient encounters. In just the past few years, CPT codes devised for collaborative care have been created and funded by Medicare, Medicaid in a growing number of states and many private insurers. These codes are time-based: paid according to the time spent by the behavioral healthcare manager in a calendar month for all activities related to the care of the patient. They include caseload review with the psychiatric consultant, contact with the primary care provider, face-to-face contact with the patient, or other activities on behalf of the patient. Among the collaborative care codes is a code for "general care management and BHI services" which has less stringent billing requirements than the collaborative care codes and will generally cover PCBH services if the time requirement is met.

Several facets of this unusual billing structure can create barriers to sustainability. Billing the

CoCM codes requires a means – preferably built into an electronic health record – to tally this expenditure of time for each patient to be billed. While some EMRs have an integrated registry available within the EMR, many providers will be forced to rely on a stand-alone registry, which invariably leads to duplicate documentation, reducing BHM time and efficiency. Furthermore, while the AIMS center has an Excel-based registry that is maintained and updated for CoCM, it comes at an additional cost.

Medicare and commercial payers also require cost sharing in the form of co-pays, or in high-deductible plans, responsibility for all or most of the cost until the deductible has been met. Patients can and will be confused by a service provided within the context of a primary care visit that is billed separately and adds unanticipated costs above what they may have expected. In order to prevent confusion, Medicare instituted a requirement that individuals give consent for the service before a bill can be submitted. However, the consent process itself often serves as a barrier to accepting care as people try to calculate the difference between a potential co-pay for a specialist appointment outside the CoCM environment compared to the risk of being responsible for most of the expense of the CoCM bill, which cannot be determined until the service is billed. Some non-Medicare payers do not require the co-pay and its attendant consent process.

Information about the codes and implementation recommendations were published in 2020 by the American Psychiatric Association, which has been a leader in advocacy for funding collaborative care services, and are available for free at https://www.psychiatry.org/psychiatrists/practice/professional-interests/integrated-care. (American Psychiatric Assocation 2020).

Primary Care in Behavioral Health (PC in BH)

Integration of medically focused services into behavioral health settings has generally focused on efforts to improve the excess mortality of people living with serious mental illness. Prescriber adherence to monitoring guidelines is poor for patients prescribed antipsychotic medication in general, certainly in adults, but alarmingly in children (Correll 2011; Mclaren et al. 2017). Nomenclature for this work can be challenging given the lack of an agreed-upon standard term. The following terms are used in various contexts:

- "Reverse Integration," based on the notion that integration is normally the provision of behavioral health services in primary care settings
- "Bidirectional Integration"
- "Whole Health"
- Primary Behavioral Health Care (obviously easy to confuse with "primary care behavioral health," discussed in the previous section)
- Medical Care Management
- Medical Care Management for people living with serious mental illness
- Behavioral Health Homes
- Integration of General Health

For the purposes of this chapter, with no attempt to name the work definitively, we will use the term Primary Care in Behavioral Health, abbreviated PC in BH.

Most PC in BH programs have a common behavioral health home approach in which teams may be constituted differently, but may include the individuals and responsibilities summarized in Table 1.

Table 1 Individuals and responsibilities in PC in BH programs

Team member	Activities
Psychiatric care providers	In order to effectively and safely treat patients, they should be responsible to: Diagnose and treat psychiatric disorders, usually including medication Prescribe psychopharmacological treatment that minimizes negative effects on medical conditions like obesity or diabetes Keep track of medical conditions that might impact the patient's medications and treatment. These conditions are usually (but not always) treated elsewhere Order, review, and respond to lab data Monitor and respond to information about physical measurements like blood pressure or weight Watch ALL the patient's medications (psychiatric and otherwise) for undesirable interactions. This includes medications the psychiatric care providers might not have prescribed Respond to patients concerns about medical care and physical symptoms Educate patients, their families, and clinic staff on medical information Function as a liaison with outside medical providers. There are times when this can significantly smooth out difficulties with those outside providers Coordinate care with outside medical agencies including clinics, pharmacies, medical equipment suppliers, labs, and more Lead the development of overall approach to physical health, including screening and management protocols Oversee and maintain a registry for tracking patients Make decisions about how to deploy case managers and other staff to best support patients in the program
Clinical support staff (e.g., medical assistants)	Play an important frontline role in the clinic. They are often the first to encounter a patient in clinic and help with the medical rooming process or intake process Collect patient weight, blood pressure, and lab samples May do much of what a nurse commonly does around lab work, care coordination and follow-up, and entering data in a registry of clients
Administrative support staff	Manage appointments Serve as frontline point of contact with the program for patients and other providers – this can be a pivotal role Troubleshoot issues with practical matters, like bills, transportation, needed documentation like work releases, disability paperwork, etc.
Nurse care managers	Focus on use of data in making decisions about how to deploy case managers and other staff to best support patients in the program Day-to-day overall management of the program and staff
Case managers	The behavioral health case manager, though they do not provide direct psychiatric or medical treatment, plays *a crucial role* in the support and coordination of medical care and in the support of healthier living for patients This is done in a number of ways: Direct personal contact and support The relationship the case manager has with the patient is maybe the most powerful driver of improvements in health behavior Coordination with medical system and with the social benefit system [e.g., Medicaid, disability, housing authorities, etc.] Support of healthy behaviors Support of adherence to medical treatment Shared decision-making with patients
Peers	Peers are individuals with lived experience of mental illness who can also work with patients in this setting to offer practical and emotional support and often tasks similar to those carried out by case manager
Family/ support system	Sadly, many of the individual with serious mental illness that we care for have been separated from their families, but when available, involved families can play a powerful role in supporting health, and their involvement should be encouraged
Mental health and substance use disorder providers	In most behavioral health organizations, therapists do not play a central role in supporting physical health. But their engagement and support of the care management team's efforts can help patients have a positive attitude toward the program

Examples to Date of PC in BH Programs

Primary Care Access, Referral, and Evaluation (PCARE)

In this program, nurse care managers communicate and advocate with medical providers on behalf of their patients, provided health education to patients, and supported patients to overcome barriers to accessing primary medical care. This improved the quality of medical care provided and reduced some measures of cardiovascular risk (Druss et al. 2010).

Primary Behavioral Health Care Initiative (PBHCI)

This program included a behavioral health organization partnering with primary care. It used a team approach where the PCP acted as a consultant, while the case manager coordinated a patient's care. Data was tracked and used to inform care. Several Washington State behavioral health agencies participated.

Behavioral Health Homes

The most successful approach to date has been the Medicaid Community Mental Health Center Behavioral Health Home program in Missouri, which designed its model with three distinctive features:

- A team that included case managers, nurse care managers, and PCP consultants
- Case managers for tasks including health education, support for positive health behaviors, and logistical support for medical care
- Data intensively to guide support and treatment to patients who were in need of more focused care or adjustment of care

This approach improved a number of health outcomes for patients and saved the state millions of dollars. However, it has been difficult to replicate in other states, where the needed administrative infrastructure and access to shared data has been less available and where patient selection may have been less focused. Still, the behavioral health home approach as outlined above serves as the model for most present-day programs.

Certified Community Behavioral Health Centers (CCBHCs)

This demonstration program, in 42 states as of 2022, was designed to support the creation of model systems that provide total, comprehensive care for people with serious mental illness (SMI). CCBHCs are required to provide a full range of high-quality services to community mental health populations. The funding for these additional services is provided by a prospective payment model similar to that found in Federally Qualified Health Centers. During the COVID epidemic, hundreds of "expansion" CCBHC grants in other states were awarded on a time-limited basis (2 years). CCBHCs have broadly been able to meet requirements and improve access to services, particularly crisis and medication-assisted treatment of substance use disorder. While some early cost information is available, data on impact of health utilization have not been published yet.

While managing medical illness in the behavioral health setting is not the primary aim of the CCBHC program, one of nine required services is "primary care screening and monitoring." To date, the prospective payment model represents the most sustainable platform for supporting novel, comprehensive, team-based approaches to the excess mortality of people with serious mental illness. While less has been reported or examined about how expansive CCBHCs have been in using the program to specifically impact long-term physical outcomes of this population, one leading example from Cascadia in Oregon, of which the authors of this chapter are familiar, shows what is possible. They used CCBHC funding to implement:

- Medication-assisted treatment for opioid use disorders
- Improvements in medical care coordination
- Integrated primary care services embedded with the behavioral health setting
- Construction of a population health infrastructure that enables them to carry out a risk stratification project reducing medical hospitalizations for their vulnerable SMI population

Evidence for the Effectiveness of PC in BH

Various behavioral health home programs have been able to show improvements in process metrics (e.g., an improved number of patients receiving recommended preventive services or a higher proportion of evidence-based services for cardiovascular conditions), and study patients were more likely to have a primary care provider (Druss et al. 2017). Significant improvements in outcome metrics, on the other hand, have been minimal, though a 2010 study did show improved scores on the Framingham Cardiovascular risk index. This circumstance is not unlike the equivocal or negative results seen in other attempts to address the needs of other health disparity groups, such as those of the Camden Coalition "hot-spotting" work with high-need, high-cost populations using a care management model (Finkelstein et al. 2020).

Barriers to effectiveness of health home programs include:

- The demands upon behavioral health agencies adding a significant physical health-related stream of work to their mission and learning to work in a measurement-based model
- The slow development of health information technology permitting a shared electronic medical record for partners
- The reluctance or inability of funders, such as Medicaid Managed Care Organizations, to share data
- The lack of readily available primary care partners willing to provide physician expertise for this population
- The profound impact of health behaviors and social determinants of health, independent of the presence of severe mental illness
- The lack of dependable financial support for this part of patient care in the behavioral health sector

Despite these barriers, most approaches to improving the health outcomes for people living with serious mental illness continue to be structured along behavioral health home lines:

> [Findings of the Druss et al HOME behavioral health home trial…] suggest a clear path for improving care and outcome: operationalization of the core principles of Collaborative Care including the implementation of evidence-based lifestyle modification interventions and pharmacotherapy; real integration of clinical pathways and data reporting between behavioral health and primary care providers; and a stepped care approach to tailoring treatment to the level of specific risk of individual patients. (Chwastiak and Fortney 2017)

Coordination of care and lifestyle modification may not be enough to optimize health outcomes in SMI populations, who carry a formidable burden of social determinants of health. As Druss says, "[…]it is possible, even under challenging real-world conditions, to improve quality of care for patients with serious mental illness and cardiovascular risk factors. Improving quality of medical care may be necessary, but not sufficient, to improve the full range of medical outcomes in this vulnerable population" (Druss et al. 2017). To that end, successful approaches to the health of SMI populations will likely overlap with more general societal efforts to address income and health access disparities, such as the Housing is Health movement (Taylor 2018).

Financial Barriers and Opportunities in PC in BH

Along with the challenge of implementing effective clinical approaches, to address the medical needs of individuals with serious mental illness is the challenge of financial sustainability. Reliable streams of funding to support this work suffer from siloed funding for the treatment of serious mental illness. Public entities with dollars allocated toward the treatment of individuals with severe mental illness have not traditionally included medically focused care management as part of their array of funded services, and as mental health funding is constantly under pressure, expanding the scope of care is challenging. While some Medicaid-managed care organizations have considered funding these efforts in the hope that this would offset other costs from acute care of serious physical illness in these populations, they have been reluctant to invest without clear demonstration that the cost would be offset by reduced utilization of medical services. We note here that some states have allowed for expansion of the scope of behavioral health clinical case management services to include activities related to managing chronic disease for individuals with severe mental illness. As of 2022, the dissemination and effectiveness of those changes had not been studied.

While grants (like the SAMHSA PBHCI grants and CCBHC expansion grants) can offset start-up costs, sustainability strategies are needed. As referenced above, CCBHCs augment FQHC funding with the goal of inducing traditional FQHCs to build programming that meets the comprehensive needs of those with severe mental illness. Yet, engaging primary care providers to consider SMI populations as an important project is challenging, especially for primary care providers serving populations with low rates of serious mental illness: in most primary care settings, people living with SMI just aren't a large enough percentage of the population to prompt the implementation of specialized services on their behalf.

Rather than waiting for hesitant FQHCs to move forward, however, many community mental health centers (CMHC) have elected to become FQHCs themselves. This path is neither simple nor quick: the application process alone takes about 2 years, and the intensity of FQHC regulatory and quality requirements stand can easily overwhelm CMHC leadership unaccustomed to such complex governance. Yet the trend is growing, and CMHCs on the other side of the process note that work was worth it, giving them direct control over designing care pathways to meet their patients' needs while providing a host of new funding streams that can buffer funding cuts on the behavioral health side. Furthermore, because their core identity was forged as community mental health providers, they do not need to worry about assimilating the culture of caring for the marginalized populations of individuals with severe mental illness and substance use disorders that traditional FQHCs might be resistant to serving.

The Role of the Psychiatrist in Integrated Care

Though integrated programs can be executed without psychiatrist involvement, in most settings psychiatric leadership can catalyze integration. A recent white paper describes the role of the fully deployed psychiatrist in a community mental health setting (National Council Medical Directors Institute 2021). A skillful psychiatric provider can add a great deal of value to the clinical enterprise of a behavioral health agency in the following ways:

- The psychiatric provider bears clinical license, leadership, and responsibility to make final care decisions, especially in complex cases. This responsibility extends to medicolegal decision-making.
- The psychiatric provider can contribute the broadest knowledge of psychiatric diagnosis and treatment, including pharmacological and psychosocial interventions. The responsibility for keeping the team up-to-date on developments in the field should rest with the psychiatric provider.
- The psychiatric provider can act as a role model for teams by demonstrating that boundaries between medical and psychosocial are illusory and must be integrated in the care of patients.
- The psychiatric provider has a special role in educating patients and families because of their in-depth familiarity with diagnoses and the range of available treatment and the cul-

tural sensitivities patients and families ascribe to both.

- The psychiatric provider can lead the team in integrated care and interagency collaboration. In a psychiatric setting that monitors and supports the physical health of people with SMI, the psychiatric provider can champion the agency's approach to these issues.
- Because serious mental disorders are biomedical conditions that require accurate diagnosis, medicolegal decisions, and pharmacological treatments, the role of the psychiatrist is of special importance on a mental health team.

The role of the psychiatric consultant in the Collaborative Care Model is even more central. A skillful consultant not only reviews and consults on primary care caseloads, but offers direct consult and curbside availability, helps create and improve workflows for behavioral health-related conditions and scenarios, and offers a continuing stream of education and practical training at the point of need. Examples of this might include assisting the primary care organization with its response to caring for patients with opioid use disorder or developing responses for managing patients with suicide risk effectively. It might also include educating primary care staff on the management of people living with SMI, who might otherwise be viewed as too challenging to engage with.

Finally, the physician's status as a consultant and subject matter expert in a scarcity specialty can lead to significant leverage in advocating within the primary care organization for change in services and policies that will improve psychiatric care and care overall in the clinic. For example, psychiatrists can advocate for rational development of clinic schedules for behavioral health managers or for reducing productivity pressure to make space for consultation time. Health system leadership benefits from regular reinforcement by psychiatrists of the value the program brings, including improved access to behavioral healthcare and the impact on primary care provider quality of life and retention, all for a remarkably small amount of psychiatric consultant time.

Conclusion

In the introduction to this chapter, we described three reasons for pursuing integrated models of care: addressing scarcity, improving efficacy, and addressing disparities in care. As we conclude, we return to answering those questions.

Regarding access, data on the number of patients seen in integrated settings is not readily available. We do know that CoCM has been implemented hundreds, if not thousands of times. On the other side of the coin, more than 400 CMHCs have been awarded CCBHC grants over the past decade, offering opportunities to integrate primary care into behavioral health settings.

Regarding efficacy, the evidence base for collaborative care powerfully supports a case for having improved the outcomes of treatment in primary care where it has been implemented, whereas programs addressing the support of medical outcomes in people living with serious mental illness have been less successful to date. Regarding disparities, BH in PH programs address issues of access to psychiatric services for people who are unable or unwilling to pursue care in formal behavioral health settings, while programs addressing behavioral health home approaches to medical outcomes for individuals with severe mental illness have shown improvement in the quality of medical care received, even if programs that have a sustained impact on physical health outcomes remain elusive.

This review of the integration of behavioral health and physical healthcare has focused on issues most germane to the work of the community psychiatrist. The particulars of how models of care are implemented and how they are funded can be expected to change quickly, but the practice of providing care in alternative settings and using new treatment models is here to stay, especially given the ongoing uptake of strategies such as collaborative care, the increasing demand for psychiatric services, and the insufficient supply of psychiatric practitioners to meet this demand using a traditional model of care.

Citations

American Psychiatric Assocation. (2020). Last accessed on January 1st, 2022 at https://www.psychiatry.org/psychiatrists/practice/professional-interests/integrated-care

Archer J, Bower P, Gilbody S, Lovell K, Richards D, Gask L, Dickens C, Coventry P. Collaborative care for depression and anxiety problems. Cochrane Database Syst Rev 2012;10:CD006525.

Blackmore M, Carleton K, Ricketts S, Patel U, Stein D, Mallow A, Deluca J, Chung H. (2018). Comparison of Collaborative Care and Colocation Treatment for Patients with Clinically Significant Depression Symptoms in Primary Care. Psychiatric Services 69. Appi.ps.2017005. Doi: https://doi.org/10.1176/appi.ps.201700569

Bowen DJ, Powers DM, Russo J, Arao R, LePoire E, Sutherland E, Ratzliff ADH. Implementing collaborative care to reduce depression for rural native American/Alaska native people. BMC Health Services Research (2020) 20:34. Doi: https://doi.org/10.1186/s12913-019-4875-6

Chung H, Smali E, Narasimhan V, Talley R, Goldman ML, Ingoglia C, Woodlock W, Pincus HA; Advancing Integration of General Health in Behavioral Health Settings A Continuum-based Framework. New York Community Trust, 2020.

Chwastiak L and Fortney J, Learning to Integrate Cardiometabolic Care in Serious Mental Illness: Am J Psychiatry 174:3, March 2017.

Correll CU. Safety and tolerability of antipsychotic treatment in young patients with schizophrenia. J Clin Psychiatry. 2011 Aug;72(8):e26. Doi: https://doi.org/10.4088/JCP.9101tx5c. PMID: 21899814.

Druss BG, Chwastiak L, Kern J, Parks JJ, Ward MC, Raney LE.. Psychiatry's Role in Improving the Physical Health of Patients With Serious Mental Illness: A Report From the American Psychiatric Association. Psychiatric Services 2018; 69:254–256; Doi: https://doi.org/10.1176/appi.ps.201700359

Druss BG, Esenwein S, Compton MT, Rask KJ, Zhao L, Parker RM. A Randomized Trial of Medical Care Management for Community Mental Health Settings: The Primary Care Access, Referral, and Evaluation (PCARE) Study. Am J Psychiatry 2010; 167: 151–159.

Druss BG, von Esenwein SA, Glick GE, Deubler E, Lally C, Ward MC, Rask KJ. Randomized trial of an integrated behavioral health home: the Health Outcomes Management and Evaluation (HOME) study. Am J Psychiatry 2017; 174: 246–255.

Finkelstein A, Zhou A, Taubman S, Doyle J. Health Care Hotspotting — A Randomized, Controlled Trial: N Engl J Med 2020; 382:152–162. Doi: https://doi.org/10.1056/NEJMsa1906848.

Fortney JC, Bauer AM, Cerimele JM, et al. Comparison of Teleintegrated Care and Telereferral Care for Treating Complex Psychiatric Disorders in Primary Care: A Pragmatic Randomized Comparative Effectiveness Trial. JAMA Psychiatry. 2021;78(11):1189–1199. Doi: https://doi.org/10.1001/jamapsychiatry.2021.2318.

Gilbody S, Bower P, Fletcher J, Richards D, Sutton AJ. Collaborative Care for Depression. A Cumulative Meta-analysis and Review of Longer-term Outcomes. Arch Intern Med. 2006;166:2314–2321.

https://www.psychiatry.org/psychiatrists/practice/professional-interests/integrated-care/get-paid accessed 01/15/2021.

Hu J, Wu T, Damodaran S, Tabb K, Bauer A, Huang H. The Effectiveness of Collaborative Care on Depression Outcomes for Racial/Ethnic Minority Populations in Primary Care: A Systematic Review. Psychosomatics, 2020 (6): 623–644.

Katon WJ, Roy-Byrne P, Russo J, Cowley D. 2002, op. cit. Cost-effectiveness and Cost Offset of a Collaborative Care Intervention for Primary Care Patients with Panic Disorder. Archives of General Psychiatry. December 2002;59(12):1098–1104.

Leading a Bold Shift in Mental Health & Substance Use Care: A CCBHC Impact Report, May 2021. National Council for Mental Wellbeing, Washington DC, 2021.

Levine S, Unützer J, Yip JY, Hoffing M, Leung M, Fan MY, Lin EH, Grypma L, Katon W, Harpole LH, Langston CA. Physicians' satisfaction with a collaborative disease management program for late-life depression in primary care. Gen Hosp Psychiatry. 2005 Nov–Dec;27(6):383–91. Doi: https://doi.org/10.1016/j.genhosppsych.2005.06.001. PMID: 16271652.

Mclaren J, Brunette MF, McHugo GJ, Drake RE, Daviss WB. Monitoring of Patients on Second-Generation Antipsychotics: A National Survey of Child Psychiatrists. Psychiatric Services 2017 68:9, 958–961.

National Council for Behavioral Health Medical Directors Institute: Optimizing the Psychiatric Workflow Within A Team-Based Framework, National Council for Behavioral Health, Washington DC, 2021.

Ng TP, Nyunt MSZ, Feng L, Kumar R, Fones CSL, Ko SM. Collaborative care for primary care treatment of late-life depression in Singapore: Randomized controlled trial. Int J Geriatr Psychiatry. 2020 Oct;35(10):1171–1180. Doi: https://doi.org/10.1002/gps.5353. Epub 2020 Jun 4. PMID: 32453449.

Peek CJ and the National Integration Academy Council. Lexicon for Behavioral Health and Primary Care Integration: Concepts and Definitions Developed by Expert Consensus. AHRQ Publication No.13-IP001-EF. Rockville, MD: Agency for Healthcare Research and Quality. 2013. Available at: http://integrationacademy.ahrq.gov/sites/default/files/Lexicon.pdf.

Reiter JT, Dobmeyer AC, Hunter CL. The Primary Care Behavioral Health (PCBH) Model: An Overview and Operational Definition. J Clin Psychol Med Settings. 2018 Jun;25(2):109–126. Doi: https://doi.org/10.1007/s10880-017-9531-x. PMID: 29480434.

Roy-Byrne P et al. Delivery of evidence-based treatment for multiple anxiety disorders in primary care: A randomized controlled trial. JAMA. 2010 May 19;303(19):1921–8.

Doi: https://doi.org/10.1001/jama.2010.608. PMID: 20483968; PMCID: PMC2928714.

Schoenbaum M, Unützer J, McCaffrey D, Duan N, Sherbourne C, Wells KB. The Effects of Primary Care Depression Treatment on Patients' Clinical Status and Employment. Health Services Research. October 2002;37(5):1145–1158.

Silverstein, M, et al. Collaborative Care for Children With ADHD Symptoms. Pediatrics 2015, 135, e858.

Taylor L. Housing and Health: An Overview of the Literature. Health Policy Brief, Health Affairs. 2018. Doi: https://doi.org/10.1377/hpb20180313.396577.

Unützer J, Chan YF, Hafer E, Knaster J, Shields A, Powers D, Veith RC. Quality improvement with pay-for-performance incentives in integrated behavioral health care. Am J Public Health. 2012 Jun;102(6): e41–5. Doi: https://doi.org/10.2105/AJPH.2011.300555. Epub 2012 Apr 19. PMID: 22515849; PMCID: PMC3483954.

Unützer J, Katon WJ, Fan MY, et al. Long-term Cost Effects of Collaborative Care for Late-life Depression. The American Journal of Managed Care. February 2008;14(2):95–100.

Unützer J, Park M. (2012). Strategies to improve the management of depression in primary care. *Primary care*, *39*(2), 415–431. https://doi.org/10.1016/j.pop.2012.03.010.

Woltmann E, Drogan-Kaylor A, Perron B, Georges H, Kilbourne AM, Bauer MS. Comparative Effectiveness of Collaborative Chronic Care Models for Mental Health Conditions Across Primary Specialty and behavioral health Care Settings: Systematic Review and Meta-Analysis. Am J Psychiatry 2012, 169; 790–804.

Group Appointments in Psychiatry+

Benjamin Crocker, Wesley E. Sowers, and Leslie Hartley Gise

Introduction

In recent decades, the demand for treatment with psychotropic medications has increased faster than psychiatric clinicians (psychiatrists, psychiatric nurse practitioners, and physician assistants) have been trained to properly prescribe their use. Primary care settings have stepped up to respond to some of this demand, but access to timely psychiatric and medication-assisted substance abuse treatment is strained even in urban areas of the USA where specialty clinicians tend to congregate. Group medical appointments for patients with mental illness or substance use problems are a powerful treatment vehicle for combining medical and psychosocial treatments in an efficient and accessible format. Group appointments were once widespread as the focus of treatment for persons with severe psychiatric illness as they were rapidly shifted from state hospitals to community mental health centers following the development of Medicare, Medicaid, and social security disability benefits. The availability of more effective medications for psychiatric disorders allowed longer tenure in the community for many of these individuals (Stone 1993). Despite significant clinical evidence for their effectiveness, few prescribers currently run groups for their patients. Today, group psychotherapy is rarely part of psychiatric education. Despite this, as economics and clinician shortages create pressure for systems change, group medical visits as an alternative to individual appointments will likely be encouraged. As medical providers are pressured by systems and patient demand to see patients for a steady stream of relatively brief appointments, burnout is a threat. Longer group sessions in partnership with another member of the treatment team can be a relieving change of pace. Likewise, as mental health and primary care systems converge, group treatments offer an attractive and efficient option for people seeking care outside traditional behavioral health settings.

History

In 1927 Pratt applied group treatment originally developed for tuberculosis patients in 1905 to patients with medically unexplained physical symptoms and found improved outcomes with

B. Crocker (✉)
Department of Psychiatry, Tufts University Medical School, Maine Medical Center, Portland, ME, USA
e-mail: benjamin.crocker@att.net

W. E. Sowers
University of Pittsburgh Medical Center, Pittsburgh, PA, USA
e-mail: sowerswe@upmc.edu

L. H. Gise
Department of Psychiatry, John A Burns School of Medicine, University of Hawai'i, Honolulu, HI, USA
e-mail: leslieg@maui.net

W. E. Sowers et al. (eds.), *Textbook of Community Psychiatry*,
https://doi.org/10.1007/978-3-031-10239-4_18

increased efficiency (Pratt 1953; Sabin 1990). Pratt incorporated a biopsychosocial model that included outreach, an interdisciplinary involvement, spirituality, relaxation, and meditation. Group psychotherapy became a prominent intervention in mental health services in England and the USA during World War II. In the period between the world wars, the effects of exposure to the traumas of war on both civilians and combatants came to be appreciated, and it was hoped that mental health services would reduce morbidity in both populations. However, the number of trained clinicians could not meet the demand for one to one treatment sessions, so group psychotherapy was attempted and proved to be helpful for many. After the war, theories of group psychotherapy reflected the overall dominance of psychoanalytic theory, but in psychiatric hospitals and within growing community mental health centers, the development of supportive and psychoeducational group therapy continued. In 1970 Yalom (1970) identified ten curative factors resulting from group therapy:

- Imparting of information
- Instillation of hope
- Universality
- Altruism
- The corrective recapitulation of the primary family group
- Development of socializing techniques
- Imitative behavior
- Interpersonal learning
- Group's cohesiveness
- Catharsis

Although there are a variety of formats used for group therapy, and some variability in structure and emphasis, most groups do incorporate some or all of these curative factors, including the medication management groups that will be the focus of discussion in this chapter.

Since the establishment of Alcoholics Anonymous (AA) in the 1930s, groups became increasingly important to persons attempting to recover from substance use problems. Although these group experiences initially developed independently of professional clinicians, since the middle of the twentieth century, they were increasingly incorporated into professionally run substance use treatment programs. With the reduction in long-term state hospital stays in the 1960s, outpatient group therapy for patients with severe mental illness was used in many community programs to treat patients now living in the community (Stone 1991; Abrahamson and Fellow-Smith 1991).

When clozapine began to be used in the USA in the early 1990s for patients with treatment-resistant psychotic or manic symptoms, treatment groups for patients taking this medication were developed to meet the demand for the special monitoring and psychoeducation required for recipients. Often a single doctor-nurse team would manage all the patients in a large clinic taking clozapine. A similar scenario was observed in the early days of lithium use. Groups were also developed for the treatment of anxiety and depression. Some of these grew out of marketing trials for antidepressant or anti-anxiety medications, which often offered treatment at little or no cost. The people who participated could access some ongoing services that were available with limited staff or expense. Groups that combined ongoing prescribing of medication with behavioral and cognitive therapy were often organized to manage these service users. Groups have been used for a variety of other special populations including medical patients, psychiatric patients in medical settings, personality disorders, trauma-induced disorders, substance use disorders, and premenstrual syndromes, to name a few (Gise 1989). Recently, group treatments have been used increasingly for patients receiving medication-assisted treatments (MAT) for substance use disorders, and shared medical visits have even been used for patients receiving the off-label use of sublingual ketamine for depression (Mcinnes 2020).

Efficacy

Reviews of psychotherapy for schizophrenia suggest that outpatient group treatment may improve social functioning and result in better outcomes

(Gise 1989; Mosher and Keith 1980; Schooler and Keith 1993; Stone 1997). A pilot study found reduction in suicide risk factors with a 20-week group intervention (Bergmans and Links 2009). Some data suggest better outcomes with group over individual treatment. In a study of patients discharged from a state hospital, group therapy patients were significantly less likely to be hospitalized than those receiving individual therapy (Bergmans and Links 2009). In a review of randomized controlled trials, group psychoeducation was more effective than individual psychoeducation at preventing relapse in patients with bipolar disorder (Bond and Anderson 2015).

With regard to medication adherence, group psychotherapy has been shown to maximize the benefit from psychopharmacology. For example, one study found higher, more stable serum lithium levels for patients with bipolar disorder (Abrahamson and Fellow-Smith 1991) among group participants. For patients with both mental illness and substance use disorders, better medication adherence and better outcomes, including less psychiatric hospitalization, have been reported with dual-focus self-help groups (Gise 1989). In a pilot study, group treatment was found to increase sobriety in bipolar substance-dependent patients (Mcinness 2020).

Several controlled trials of patients with schizophrenia have found better outcomes for group over individual treatment (Ward 1975), with fewer hospitalizations (Herz et al. 2000) and less frequent relapse (Colom et al. 2003a). Recent randomized controlled studies with 5-year follow-up have found group psychoeducation for patients with bipolar disorder to have a long-lasting prophylactic effect with an increase in adherence and retention and a decrease in recurrence, time acutely ill, number of days in the hospital, frequency of hospitalization, and cost (Colom et al. 2009; Scott et al. 2009; Barrowclough et al. 2006). Controlled trials of group treatment of patients with schizophrenia have found significant positive effects on auditory hallucinations, social functioning, self-esteem, self-assertion, and coping, with a reduction in hopelessness as compared to traditional care (Borras et al. 2009; Wykes et al. 2005). Barrowclough used group cognitive behavioral therapy for psychosis. Clinical evidence supports a positive association between group treatment and better outcomes including improved medication adherence, retention in treatment, less hospitalization, and shorter hospital stays (Bright et al. 1999).

While there is a great deal of evidence regarding the effectiveness of group treatment, relatively little research looks specifically at prescriber-led group treatment of psychiatric patients. As a result, definitive statements cannot be made regarding its effectiveness relative to other forms of medication management or therapy. Anecdotally, we know that this approach is more promising in its capacity to help people make social connections and in expanding the amount of contact prescribers have with their clients. More studies of groups which incorporate psychiatrists and other prescribers for medication management are needed to establish a sound evidence base for group medication visits.

Advantages of Psychiatric Group Medication Visits

Reduced Stigma and Balance of Power

Group expands the psychiatrist's knowledge of patients and their lives because of the potential for more frequent contacts and the opportunity to observe group members in a social context. Meeting in a group reduces the intensity of the therapist-patient relationship and the difference in power and status between the therapist and patient. Thus the leader becomes a member of the group, not only an authority figure. These dynamics serve to reduce the disparity in power in the therapist-patient relationship somewhat and reduce the social stigma and alienation associated with emotional problems. The group leader may begin to shift roles to some degree as they identify with their clients' struggles, recognizing their application of recovery principles in their personal lives. This identification process is quite distinct from the traditional role of prescribers.

Desmond is a middle-aged man with long-standing symptoms of schizophrenia, social anxiety disorder, mild intellectual disability, and a past history of polysubstance abuse. For years he said little in group, but one day when asked directly how he felt about the group, he says “I like that people say whatever they want. I feel like I can relax a little and like I'm more normal…not afraid. I listen to people and I understand them, and I don't feel so alone. I don't talk much, but I like to see everybody, and I feel better after group. Sometimes it helps me think about what I can do about my problems.” Groups members were surprised to hear him say so much and told him how glad they were to hear him speak and that he was part of the group. The psychiatrist noted that he “also feel(s) comfortable in the group and that it's nice for everyone to have a group of people they can feel comfortable with. It never feels good to be lonely.”

In group, content, emotions, interactions, and opportunities are expanded beyond those of the 1:1 dyad, broadening the perspective of the therapist. Because the leader has an interaction in group which is more egalitarian and active, an enriched experience results that allows a more profound knowledge of the individuals in the group. This interaction is satisfying and productive, bringing out the strengths of even the most disabled participants. Most groups develop a degree of solidarity that facilitates shared decision-making. Because groups with co-therapists or multiple clinical participants demonstrate aspects of team dynamics, they allow patients to see the psychiatric clinician in a social nexus and allow the clinician to demonstrate collaborative team interactions and mutual support.

Bertha, an elderly woman with persisting psychosis, faithfully attends group but speaks little. At the holiday party, she came to life leading all the singing with a great voice, knowing all the words. She had never told anyone that she was a choir leader when she was younger. Subsequently when asked about her church involvement, she eagerly belted out a favorite hymn. This made her feel good. She got a lot of praise, and others were encouraged to share their talents. In contrast, before joining the group, she shared that her periodic visits to her psychiatrist tended to be brief. There was seldom enough time for the psychiatrist to ask much about her life, and the focus of the visits was mainly on the status of her psychotic symptoms, suicidal ideation, and medication.

Focus on Rehabilitation, Recovery, and Psychosocial Issues

Group treatment facilitates recovery and addresses the task of reintegration into the community that confronts every patient after an episode of mental illness. In addition to independent living and employment, reintegration includes restoring and forming relationships, which are facilitated by group.

Audrey is bright, but quite depressed and sometimes psychotic with disorganized and disordered thought. Although she comes to group regularly, she does not seem to enjoy them and says she comes for her shots. In her 57 years, her paranoia has resulted in impulsive flight and moving every 2–5 years. For the past 11 years in group, she has stayed in one place in her independent housing, gone to school, and worked part-time. When pressed, she reluctantly admits that she likes being with the other group members and the staff, but she can't say why.

Psychiatry has recently been dominated by psychopharmacology with a disproportionate emphasis on medications in psychiatric training, continuing medical education, and the media. While medication can be invaluable in reducing symptoms, it is cognitive deficits and difficulties with interpersonal relations that interfere with recovery most. Both group cognitive behavior therapy and group psychoeducation have been found to improve quality of life in patients with schizophrenia (Bechdolf et al. 2010). Medication groups provide one opportunity to integrate psychosocial care with medication treatment. Such groups also reduce the problems associated with treatment split between psychiatrists, therapists, addiction counselors, and primary care providers.

Recent studies show that people with severe mental illness get worse medical care and have higher morbidity and mortality than the general population (NASMHPD 2006; Faglioni and Goracci 2009). In group, when a medical issue comes up, it provides an opportunity for the psychiatrist to address a variety of issues related to prevention and health management. The group can be polled about their health practices and their involvement with a primary care doctor. It is an opportunity to encourage regular primary care visits and the monitoring of important health indices. There is seldom enough time to address these issues as thoroughly in individual sessions. Screening, triage, and education can be accomplished more effectively in group, allowing the psychiatrist to do some basic medical monitoring, detection, and referral. Patients may both over- and under-use medical treatment and often communicate poorly with other medical providers. Group provides an opportunity for coaching effective self-advocacy and to rehearse the interaction with other providers.

Group work also provides an opportunity to integrate psychosocial rehabilitation and medication management. Activities may include social skills training, practicing assertiveness, vocational counseling, life skills training, problem-solving, role-playing, networking, linking patients to resources, and accessing multiple sources of support (Stone 2000). Psychoeducation is an important way to promote recovery and is done more efficiently in group (Liberman 2008). It also provides an opportunity to enhance members' understanding of the interaction of drug use with psychiatric symptoms and the common recovery principles that can be applied in overcoming both.

Socialization and Recovery

Social isolation is one of the hallmarks of severe mental illness. Psychiatric patients feel different and distressed by their isolation. Ignorance and fear of mental illness is prevalent in our society. People who hear voices or think about killing themselves feel alienated from friends and family and are reluctant to reveal these things. Sitting in a room with other people who have these symptoms and face the same stigma and exclusion may be the only place a person can talk about such symptoms and feelings. When people with mental illness hear others talk about side effects or disruptive symptoms, it makes it easier for them to share their own symptoms and face and accept their own illness, which they may have denied previously. Furthermore, participants feel good and are empowered when they are able to help their fellow group members. Group helps individuals feel like people, not just "patients." Many find the one-on-one therapy experience too intimidating and feel more comfortable and less threatened in group where they can gradually learn trust and build relationships.

Wendy, a woman with a history of depression and domestic abused said, "I didn't like the first meetings. But I listened to the other women with the same problems I was having, and I began to tell them things I'd never told anyone." As a person of color, she did not feel that what she said was being dismissed, as she often had in the past, and was glad that there were others in the group that she could identify with. "The therapist asked us questions to change how we thought, and I felt myself changing and getting stronger." After 2 months, Wendy got out of her abusive relationship and 2 months later, she got a job. (Solomon 2001).

An atmosphere develops which is like a family or a club with a great deal of mutual help. Members' concern and willingness to help each other is a revelation and makes both those receiving and those giving help feel better. Even people who are very impaired can be amazingly supportive and nonjudgmental, creating an atmosphere where members are appreciated and empowered. Sometimes the pain and despair of these chronic illnesses emerge clearly. In contrast to psychodynamically oriented groups where socializing outside of group is sometimes discouraged, just the opposite is usually the case in shared medication management groups. More often than not, members' socializing outside the group is beneficial and in no way undermines the goals of treatment (Stone 1996, 2000).

Ed and Jim are quite different but both socially awkward. Ed is older, often depressed, and has been drinking most of his life, but has been able to hold jobs nonetheless. Jim is a younger man with a diagnosis of bipolar disorder, frequently psychotic, who functions poorly and has had difficulty sticking with his treatment plan, especially psychotropic medication. Ed needs to lose weight and Jim needs to get out of the house. They live near one another, so after a year in group, members suggested that they start walking together. They agreed to try and after some fits and starts, they fell into a pattern of walking 3 days a week and rarely missed a day.

Treatment group experiences can prepare patients to join freestanding community support groups and otherwise participate in recovery activities that go beyond the realm of clinical services.

Improved Adherence to Medication Plan

Some people with mental illness don't take their medication because they do not believe that they are sick. Group can confront denial, increasing insight and easing the sting of acknowledging the presence of illness. Failure to adhere to medication plans is associated with poor outcomes and is the most common reason cited for hospital admissions (Ayuso-Guttierez and del Rio Vega 1997; Weiden and Glazer 1997; Weiden and Olfson 1995). A growing body of evidence indicates that psychosocial interventions can improve adherence and outcomes (Kane 1997). Group increases client investment in the plan through healthy engagement and by providing information, validation, and psychosocial support.

Scott was shocked when lithium was recommended for his mood problems. He refused to take it. He associated lithium with patients much sicker than he thought he was and was afraid of bad side effects. When Dennis said lithium was "good stuff" and that he had been helped by taking it, he reported few side effects and urged Scott to give it a try. After listening to Dennis, Scott said he would try it.

The give and take of the group that plays out place between the clinicians leading it and other group members support and demonstrate the process of shared decision-making, which improves adherence. Group fosters engagement and the establishment of long-term therapeutic relationships based on trust. Medication in the context of a positive and trusting relationship with the clinician has been found to be associated with better adherence to formulated plans (Beck 2001). Review of the literature shows three elements that are associated with good outcomes: (1) positive therapeutic relationships, (2) psychosocial rehabilitation, and (3) medication adherence. All three are facilitated by group treatment (Colom et al. 2003b).

Shared Group Leadership

Mental illness has a course that often lasts through life, like high blood pressure or diabetes, and is rarely cured in a few sessions. Thus continuity of care is an important factor in treatment. In addition, many people with mental illness are extremely sensitive to loss. Groups facilitate continuous healing relationships with individuals and with the institution. Shared group leadership provides continuity over time as clinicians come and go and allows the group to proceed if one therapist is absent. When one therapist is a trainee, shared leadership facilitates training. Other members of the clinical team such as nurses, psych techs, and medical assistants can also take the role of co-therapist. Clinical work in behavioral health can be stressful and co-therapists can provide emotional support for each other. When the co-therapists are from different disciplines, co-leadership provides a broader spectrum of experience. A co-therapist arrangement allows an opportunity to more effectively move beyond content issues and to discuss group process. This type of de-briefing fosters teamwork and the capacity to work effectively together. Finally, with two people, the tasks of leading the group, observing, making chart notes,

Table 1 Advantages of shared group leadership

Continuity
Training
Support
Feedback on process
Multidisciplinary teamwork

and writing prescriptions can be divided. In some instances, a scribe can attend the group to do most of the documentation, freeing the clinician to focus on the patients (Table 1).

Barriers and Limitations

Frequently billing rules regarding Medicaid are different for hospital-based and freestanding mental health clinics, and Medicare also has rules about the number of patients that can be treated in a group. A new billing code has been suggested to make psychiatrist-led group treatment more attractive financially, but since 2013 psychiatric providers have used the same E&M codes as other medical practitioners, and CMS has stated that these codes can be used in shared medical visits (Eisen 2017). In some instances the psychiatric practitioner can meet briefly with group participants individually during the group, but this detracts from their ability to follow the group process. In another model that avoids this distraction, the prescriber only meets with patients briefly after the group to manage their medications. In capitated or semi-capitated settings such as health homes or residential treatment settings, billing for group prescribing should not be a problem. With some imagination and flexibility, medication groups can be financially practical work despite current fee for service billing strictures.

Community and public psychiatry is often practiced in organizations in which the group format is unfamiliar, and thus not supported by administrative staff. The lack of suitable sized waiting and treatment rooms may be barriers to group treatment. Administrators need to be convinced of the advantages of group treatment, such as patient satisfaction, clinical care, increased productivity, and improved access. As traditional agencies face the challenges of competitive and capitated contracting with payers, they need the support of consumer and advocacy groups who appreciate the role of groups in supporting a recovery culture and access to services. Bringing medication groups into a clinic requires administrative as well as clinical champions.

Training in group psychotherapy is not a core part of psychiatric education today, and many other professionals working in mental health systems also have little training in group work. Some clinicians are better suited to this kind of work and are naturally drawn to it, i.e., those with a good capacity for multitasking, a high tolerance for ambiguity and chaos, and good social skills. These skills can be taught, but this is done most easily in the early part of a practitioner's career. In any case, direct participation in groups is the best way to train future group leaders. Trainees from various disciplines can observe experienced group leaders as they assist in the facilitation of treatment groups and as they make prescribing decisions with the patients. This approach provides opportunities for supervision and processing as well.

In small, rural clinics, confidentiality issues may limit patient's willingness to attend psychiatric groups. If patients are prescribed controlled substances, shared decision-making regarding these medications may be awkward in the group setting and should probably be avoided. In some cases, all the patients are prescribed the same medications, as in benzodiazepine discontinuation groups or buprenorphine (Sokol et al. 2018) groups.

How to Start a Group

Recruitment, Intake, and Preparation

Planning for shared medical visits involves first reviewing caseloads in the clinic for likely group participants. Many psychiatric clinics retain large numbers of stable patients who ideally could be referred to primary care for ongoing prescribing. However, patients often resist this, wanting to maintain a connection to the clinic. Offering patients participation in shared medical appointments as an alternative to referral to primary care can be a way to free up some clinician time to accommodate new acute patients. Transitions such as the redisposition of a caseload when a psychiatric clinician leaves and is not replaced, or when they reduce their time in the outpatient clinic due to other responsibilities, can be a good time to offer patients group visits. However, overall the group experience should not be presented as an inferior treatment, but rather as the best treatment available to the client. Sokol (2019) suggests six core components for groups in which patients are being prescribed buprenorphine. They are likely pertinent to planning any medication group: create clear expectations for patient conduct in group, regarding confidentiality and attendance. Group treatment should be part of a team-based approach, with clear plans for billing and adherence monitoring.

Patients who are new to group treatment should be interviewed before being invited to join a group (Stone 2000). When the patient is already being treated by the group leader, they may be invited directly into the group. In other cases, the prescribing clinician and co-therapist who is leading the group should do an intake. The intake assesses the patient's interest in group and their capacity to benefit from it. It is also an opportunity to point out the advantages of group treatment for the patient's individual concerns. Many individuals are resistant at first, some because they feel anxiety about talking in front of others. Others resist because they do not want others to know their problems. It may be helpful to reassure prospective members that when they start group, they don't necessarily have to talk. They can also be assured that what is said in group stays in group and the group will regularly be reminded of this rule. Some patients may benefit from coaching before starting group about how to use the group. It is sometimes helpful to note that people can discuss treatment and recovery issues without having to disclose sensitive personal issues. Over time, when their symptoms of anxiety, depression, and paranoia are reduced and they become more comfortable with the leader, some people who were initially resistant become more comfortable with group participation. Clinicians are more persuasive in getting clients to try groups if they themselves believe that groups are a superior modality, not a second-class alternative for people who function at a low level.

Those individuals referred from inpatient, partial hospital, and intensive outpatient programs that utilize group treatment may be more accustomed to groups and can more easily be encouraged to continue group work as outpatients. It is often helpful to discuss the advantages and disadvantages of group participation and to then allow people to make their own choice about participation. By simply asking, "Are you willing to try it once?" and promising "If you don't like it, you don't have to come any more," many people will be willing to start. In most cases, after they come once, feel the nonjudgmental atmosphere, and find that they are not forced to talk, they continue. Those who refuse should be seen individually, but the invitation to group can be repeated every 6–12 months, especially if the doctor-patient relationship is stronger and the individual's symptoms are reduced.

Once several patients indicate a willingness to try group visits, meetings can be initiated. Groups can range from 45 to 90 min depending on the number of participants and their level of tolerance and attention. An ideal group is 8–12 patients, but larger and smaller groups may function effectively. Some time should be allocated after each session for leaders to de-brief and review and for individual meetings with patients about issues that could not be resolved in the group.

Group Composition, Membership, Exclusionary Criteria

Most psychiatric patients are suitable for inclusion in shared medication management visits (Stone 2000). A few people who are especially needy or those with particular personality traits (such as mood instability, impulsivity, entitlement, distrustfulness) may have difficulty tolerating groups. They may refuse to participate or become too disruptive to continue. Individuals with a variety of psychiatric conditions can benefit from groups, however, including those with acute psychosis, suicidal ideation, substance problems, and cognitive deficits. Even group candidates who say that they only come to group because they are forced (e.g., the law and entitlements) often become engaged in the group over time and can definitely benefit from this treatment format. If space permits, a few patients who do not take psychotropic medication or who get their medication prescribed by their PCP may wish to attend in order to participate in the psychosocial aspects of the group.

Members are discouraged from bringing their children, but if child care is unavailable outside the treatment facility or within it, children can be accommodated on an "as needed" basis. Bringing children on a regular basis is generally discouraged, however, unless group members specifically approve it. Multifamily psychoeducation groups that include a psychiatric specialist have been shown helpful to recovery in psychotic disorders. In a small, rural settings, a highly heterogeneous group can be successful and may meet less frequently than would normally be the case. In centers that serve larger numbers of people, candidates can be invited to groups based on specific characteristics or experiences or based on the issues that will be addressed. Diagnostic categories and level of cognitive ability are also sometimes used for that purpose. In homogeneous groups, patients are more likely to form supportive relationship outside of group, while in heterogeneous groups, patients can appreciate the universality of human feelings and problems despite differences in background, diagnosis, and/or level of functioning. Homogeneous groups facilitate sharing, bonding, and cohesiveness, while heterogeneous groups promote tolerance, understanding, and sensitivity. These are generalizations though, and these characteristics are not mutually exclusive.

Acute Transition Groups

Acute stabilization groups can help provide frequent contact for patients stepping down from hospital or intermediate services or in situations where there is a delay in being assigned outpatient providers. These will generally be heterogeneous regarding diagnosis because of the need to accommodate a heterogeneous stream of patients seeking service. Patients should be encouraged to come weekly to acute groups with rolling admission until they can be picked up by individual providers or more homogeneous treatment groups that focus on a particular node of the diagnostic spectrum.

Flexibly Bound-Model

Many people have difficulty keeping regular appointments. The frequency of group meetings varies between weekly and monthly scheduling. Groups that meet frequently and have a fixed membership require the most discipline and commitment. Ultimately, the scheduling of groups sessions will depend on the resources available and the characteristics of group members. Some people may want to come to group weekly, but for others, irregular or infrequent attendance is the norm. Individuals who are more stable may prefer to come every few months. A "flexibly-bound model" empowers patients by allowing them to choose the frequency with which they attend (Stone 2000) and helps them learn to get help when they need it. Some groups may be flexible enough to permit some patients to come late and leave early. However, a certain minimum frequency of visits is usually required, along with limits on providing refills to persons who are not attending group. In large clinics with patients who often miss individual appointments, very open "refill groups" can offer frequent face-to-face opportunities for people to get their medications refilled without having to wait for an available individual appointment.

How to Run a Group

Content, Setting, and Duration

If the psychiatric clinician is billing E&M codes, they should make sure to address each member of the group individually about symptoms, medication adherence, and side effects, whether or not a prescription is actually written. In stable groups of patients, this may only take up half the allotted time, leaving time for psychoeducation, skills development, cognitive-behavioral treatment, support, and/or interpersonal process. Kanas suggests that groups should focus on the "here-and-now" and can be effective in helping patients cope with a variety of symptoms, including psychosis (Gise 2004; Kanas 1996). Groups may start with some socializing around "coffee and snacks," but informal pre-group contact may go on in the waiting room anyway.

Some groups have a specific agenda for each session, and some are time-limited and/or manualized. Although these groups are easier to study and require less improvisation and skill on the part of the leaders, there are advantages to ongoing groups with no set topics starting "where the patients are at" (Jensen et al. 2010). With ongoing groups, new members can be added at any time. With an open agenda, the leader can start with "Does anyone have anything special they would like to bring up before we start?" This lets members bring up something of special interest or concern and teaches them to prioritize urgent issues from routine ones. The leader can also initiate topics (e.g., psychoeducation on flu shots, disaster preparedness, relationship with spirituality). Since the distress and disability associated with many psychiatric diagnoses may persist, especially in populations with high social and economic stress, there are advantages to ongoing groups. Long-term treatment is required for many disabling psychiatric conditions, and today the treatment of people with a variety of psychiatric diagnoses involves medication. For disorders that tend to be more phasic, like some affective and anxiety disorders, flexibly bound groups offer long-term involvement in a familiar treatment setting.

Groups that combine psychotherapy and medication and which are more structured offer some advantages as well. Some examples of these include groups that combine cognitive behavior therapy (CBT) and medication for OCD or phobias, trauma-focused CBT, and medication for PTSD or groups using interpersonal therapy to address persistent depression.

A variety of formats may be used for groups focused on substance use. Because the use of medications in substance abuse treatment is open-ended and frequency of clinician contact is often mandated in the case of buprenorphine, prescribing groups fit in well with a variety of treatment plans. As community psychiatric clinics become behavioral health clinics, the group treatment culture of substance abuse treatment can be incorporated into the clinic style. Frequent, flexibly bound groups for substance use treatment can accommodate differing treatment intensity needs depending on the patient's stability (Eisen 2019).

Universalizing: Combating Stigma

Groups are de-stigmatizing. The group format allows the leader to poll the group, a technique called universalizing. For example, when a patient describes a problem, the leader can poll the group and ask who has had a similar problem, i.e., hearing voices, having suicidal thoughts, having a problem with alcohol or drugs, not taking medication, etc. When others indicate that they have had similar experiences, the member feels less stigmatized and less ashamed, and the stage is set for an open discussion of that problem. Various techniques for coping with auditory hallucinations are frequently shared, and the leader can offer alternatives to distraction and keeping busy such as talking back to the voices as if they were a nosey neighbor. A small randomized controlled trial found that group cognitive behavioral therapy reduces auditory hallucinations (McLeod et al. 2007). With a less intense relationship between members and the group leader, controlled staff disclosure is typically increased because it has less intense personal meaning than in a one-to-one session.

"Go Rounds"

By going around and checking in with each patient, the leader can address the problem of patients who don't talk and also of monopolizers who need to be contained (Stone 1997, 2000). But even with this format, feedback and discussion are encouraged. Patients don't have to talk at first and those who don't talk benefit from listening to others and feel encouraged to participate at their own pace. For groups with open attendance with little continuity in membership, starting the group by asking each participant to give a brief account of their lives can be a way to establish familiarity. It may be helpful for the clinician to start this process off with their own introduction to model self-disclosure and indicate their willingness to share. Members can be asked to provide information about their place of origin, significant people in their lives, activities that they enjoy, or other things that are important in their lives. Rather than focusing on problems at this point, asking clients to identify their best qualities or strengths can set a positive, nonjudgmental tone for the group.

Addressing Poor Adherence

In relatively acute medication groups much of the focus will be on adjusting medicines and monitoring treatment response. In more chronic, less frequent groups, unless a patient is having a problem, medication is only addressed when prescriptions need to be renewed or if new symptoms or side effects present. Using medication properly is usually more important than the medication itself. In a periodic review of medication use the leader can ask, "How many times in the last week did you forget to take your medication, one? two? three?". Asking the question in this way normalizes non-adherence and facilitates an honest response. After hearing other patients admit that they did not take their medication as prescribed, it is easier to have an open discussion of this problem. If a person has only forgotten to take medication once or twice during the week, they can be praised for taking it most of the time. When non-adherence is a problem, it can be broken down into forgetting or not wanting to take it. Forgetting can be addressed in a variety of ways such as medication boxes, notes, convenient placement of medication, etc. Group members can give suggestions and share their successes. Developing a willingness to keep open communications about medicine is a long-term process which is facilitated by an ongoing, open-ended, group format.

The second reason for non-adherence, not wanting to take medication, must be addressed in a nonjudgmental manner using motivational interviewing techniques and shared decision-making. Patients who have decided to stop taking medications can be encouraged to keep attending group so the outcome of this decision can be monitored and medication can be resumed quickly if need be. Group functions as a periodic wake-up call, reminding members that they need to take care of themselves. Many people with distressing symptoms need to work around their symptoms in their daily lives so that they can function. Conflicts and feelings may build up over time such that the outlet provided by the group can help them avoid becoming overwhelmed in their usual setting.

Individual Appointments

Group members should be told that they can have an individual appointment any time. They may rarely need to ask, but this availability can be reassuring. If they have something to say that is very personal and private, which they do not want to discuss in group, access to a more private outlet is appropriate. In many cases, however, when asked "Is there some reason you could not say that in group?", most will recognize that they actually could have raised it in group. Nevertheless, some patients prefer to discuss some things in private such as sexual problems, threatening thoughts or thoughts with otherwise disturbing content. Vagueness is a technique which can be used to discuss private material in group by using non-specific labels for these problems. For example, a high functioning man with bipolar disorder and a disturbing, disruptive addiction to Internet pornography may disclose this issue privately to the psychiatrist but does not want to mention it in group. However, he could be monitored in group without disclosing what his symptom was by posing the question "How have you been doing with your 'time management' this week?"

There will be instances in which a group member does not use the group well or is disruptive despite frequent interventions. In such cases, it is reasonable to suggest that the struggling individual take a vacation from group and refer them for individual treatment until they are better able to use the group format.

Conclusion

Group psychiatric appointments for patients across the spectrum of psychiatric disorders can be more efficient, more fun, more stimulating, and invigorating, for both therapists and patients, than individual treatment. Evidence suggests that group treatment is associated with better outcomes including retention in treatment, better medication adherence, fewer hospitalizations, and shorter hospital stays. Groups for psychiatric patients can provide psychotherapy, psychosocial rehabilitation, and medication management in a flexible, open, one-stop-shopping environment, which can enhance medication adherence and provide a safety net for persons with mental illness and substance use disorders living in the community. Better recovery outcomes have been associated with group treatment including improved social functioning, better self-esteem, more self-assertion, better coping, and less hopelessness. Group is an underutilized modality which supports recovery with clinical evidence of effectiveness and which deserves further development. Widespread participation of psychiatrists and other prescribers in group processes can only be accomplished if training programs provide adequate preparation for doing so.

References

Abrahamson D, Fellow-Smith E (1991), A combined group and individual long-term out-patient clinic. Psychiatric Bulletin 15:486–487

Ayuso-Guttierrez JL, del Rio Vega JM (1997), Factors influencing relapse in the long-term course of schizophrenia. Schizophr Res 28:199–206

Beck JS (2001), A cognitive therapy approach to medication compliance, in Integrated Psychiatric Treatment for Psychiatric Disorders. Edited by Kay J. Washington DC, American Psychiatric Press, pp 113–141

Barrowclough C, Haddock G, Lobban F et al. (2006), Group cognitive-behavioral therapy for schizophrenia: randomized controlled trial. Br J Psychiatry 198:527–532

Bechdolf A, Knost B, Nelson B et al. (2010), Randomized comparison of group cognitive behavior therapy and group psychoeducation in acute patients with schizophrenia: effects on subjective quality of life. Aust N Z J Psychiatry 44(2):144–150

Bergmans Y, Links PS (2009), Reducing potential risk factors for suicide-related behavior with a group intervention for clients with recurrent suicide-related behavior. Ann Clin Psychiatry 21 (1):17–25

Bond K, Anderson IM (2015), Psychoeducation for relapse prevention in bipolar disorder: a systematic review of efficacy in randomized controlled trials. Bipolar Disorders 17 (4) 349–62

Borras L, Boucherie M, Mohr S et al. (2009), Increasing self-esteem: efficacy of a group intervention for individuals with severe mental disorders. Eur Psychiatry 24(5):307–316

Bright JI, Baker KD, Neimeyer RA (1999), Professional and paraprofessional group treatments for depression: a comparison of cognitive-behavioral and mutual support interventions. J Consult Clin Psychol 67:491–501[A]

Colom F, Vieta E, Martinez-Aran A et al. (2003a), A randomized trial of the efficacy of group psychoeducation in the prophylaxis of recurrences in bipolar patients whose disease is in remission. Arch Gen Psychiatry 60:402–407

Colom F, Vieta E, Reinares M et al. (2003b), Psychoeducation efficacy in bipolar disorders: beyond compliance enhancement. J Clin Psychiatry 64(9):1101–1105

Colom F, Vieta E, Sanchez-Moreno J et al. (2009), Group psychoeducation for stabilized bipolar disorders: 5-year outcome of a randomized clinical trial. Br J Psychiatry 194 (3):260–265

Eisen, JC (2017), Group Psychopharmacology: Addressing Challenges in the Delivery of Outpatient Psychiatric Care. Grand Rounds Presentation, Maine Medical Center, October 24 2017 https://www.youtube.com/watch?v=EYZGgmjXZPs&t=9s

Faglioni A, Goracci A (2009), The effects of undertreated chronic medical illness in patients with severe mental disorders. J Clin Psychiatry 70 Suppl 3:22–29

Gise LH (1989), Group Approaches to the Diagnosis and Treatment of the Premenstrual Syndromes, in Group Psychodynamics: New Paradigms and New Perspectives, DA Halperin Ed, Chicago, Year Book Medical Publishers Inc, 139–155

Gise LH (2004), (unpublished report) American Psychiatric Association: Practice Guidelines for the treatment of patients with schizophrenia.

Herz MI, Lamberti JS, Mintz J et al. (2000), A program for relapse prevention in schizophrenia: a controlled study. Arch Gen Psychiatry 57 (3):277–283

Jensen HH, Mortensen EL, Lotz M (2010), Effectiveness of short-term psychodynamic group therapy in a public outpatient psychotherapy unit. Nord J Psychiatry 64(2):106–114

Kanas N (1996), Group Therapy for Schizophrenic Patients, Washington DC, APA Press

Kane JM (1997), What can we achieve by implementing a compliance-improvement program. Int Clin Psychopharmacol 12(suppl 1):S43–S46

Liberman, RP (2008), Recovery from Disability: Manual of Psychiatric Rehabilitation, Washington DC, APA Press

Mcinnes, LA (2020), presentation at Psych Congress 2020

McLeod T, Morris M, Birchwood M et al. (2007), Cognitive behavioral therapy group work with voice hearers. Br J Nurs 16(4):248–252

Mosher LR, Keith SJ (1980), Psychosocial treatment: individual, group, family and community support approaches. Schizophrenia Bulletin 6:10–41

NASMHPD (2006), (National Association of State Mental Health Program Directors), Thirteenth in a Series of Technical Reports, Morbidity and mortality in people with serious mental illness, Eds J Parks, D Svendsen, P Singer, ME Foti, B Mauer, October

Pratt JH (1953), The use of Dejerine's methods in the treatment of the common neuroses by group psychotherapy. Bull of New England Medical Center 15:1–9

Sabin JE (1990), Joseph Hersey Pratt's Cost-Effective Class Method and Its Contemporary Application: Some Problems in Biopsychosocial Innovation, Psychiatry 53:169–184

Schooler NR, Keith SJ (1993), The clinical research base for the treatment of schizophrenia, In Health Care Reform for Americans with severe mental illnesses: Report of the National Advisory Mental Health Council (US Dept of Health and Human Services, Washington DC, US Government Printing Office pp 22–30

Scott J, Colom F, Popova E et al. (2009), Long-term mental health resource utilization and cost of care following group psychoeducation or unstructured group support for bipolar disorders: a cost-benefit analysis. J Clin Psychiatry 70(3):378–386

Sokol R, LaVertu AE,Morrill D, Albanese C, Schuman-Oliver, Z (2018), Group-based treatment of opiate use disorder with buprenorphine: A systematic review. Journal of Substance Abuse Treatment 84:78–87

Sokol, R et al (2019), Building a group based opioid treatment (GBOT) blueprint: a qualitative study delineating GBOT implementation. Addiction Science in Clinical Practice 2019:14:47

Solomon A (2001), Case study: the depressed poor, location, Washington DC, a cure for poverty. NY Times Magazine 5/6/01 p 112

Stone WN (1991), Treatment of the chronically mentally Ill: an opportunity for the group therapist. Int J Group Psychother 41 (1) 11–22

Stone WN (1993), Group psychotherapy with the chronically mentally ill in Kaplan and Sadock. Comprehensive Group Therapy 418–429

Stone WN (1996), Group psychotherapy for people with chronic mental illness. New York: Guilford

Stone WN (1997), The model of the flexibly bound group: dynamic treatment for patients with chronic mental illness. Directions in Psychiatry, Lesson 9(17): 123–133

Stone WN (2000), Outpatient group treatment for persons with chronic mental illness. Directions in Psychiatry 20:337–349

Ward DJ (1975), Therapeutic groups and individual treatment in psychiatric out-patient clinics: a controlled study. Journal of the Irish Medical Association 68(19): 486–489

Weiden P, Glazer W (1997), Assessment and treatment selection for "revolving door" inpatients with schizophrenia. Psychiatr Q 68:377–392

Weiden PJ, Olfson M (1995), Cost of relapse in schizophrenia. Schizophr Bull 21:419–429

Wykes T, Hayward P, Thomas N et al (2005), What are the effects of group cognitive behaviour therapy for voices? A randomised control trial Schizophr Res 77(2–3):201–210

Yalom I (1970), The Theory and Practice of Group Psychotherapy, New York, Basic Books, p 5

Treatment Techniques for Co-occurring Substance Use and Mental Disorders

Richard N. Rosenthal

Introduction

This chapter focuses on a basic level of practice: basic techniques that underlie the common clinical approaches that community psychiatrists and other clinicians use in treating patients with COD. This focus does not describe new interventions for COD or describe standard treatment approaches, but offers a clinically oriented way for clinicians to think about them and facilitate their implementation. Chapter "Evidence-Based Practices for Co-occurring Addiction and Mental Illness" details the psychopharmacology and psychosocial evidence base for treating co-occurring mental illness and substance use disorders (COD).

Definitions

Skills are basic clinical abilities such as listening to patients, asking open-ended questions, assessing acute risk, maintaining professional boundaries, and developing differential diagnoses. Competence in these basic skills is prerequisite for clinicians wishing to treat COD. *Techniques* are clinical interventions within a conceptual hierarchy ranging from the basic skills through complex clinical strategies. They are how the clinician applies their skills to achieve a specific outcome, such as establishing a therapeutic alliance or managing intoxication.

Tactics are the clinical decisions about the method and timing to implement specific techniques, since patients are differentially receptive to techniques depending on various characteristics such as motivational stage, severity of psychopathology, cognitive functioning, and living environment. Tactics are therefore stage-specific and graded. For example, cognitive behavioral relapse prevention (CBRP) operates on the assumption that the person is motivated for change. If CBRP techniques are applied to someone in a pre-contemplation stage (not yet interested in changing behavior), they are likely to be less effectivethan if they were applied to a patient in a contemplation stage (thinking about changing) or preparation stage (hasdecided to change). In the case of an integrated approach to substance use disorders (SUD) and co-occurring posttraumatic stress disorder (PTSD), the evidence suggests that the tactic of first stabilizing the SUD through the teaching of sobriety skills with cognitive behavior therapy (CBT) improves outcomes of an exposure therapy later applied for PTSD (Back et al. 2009; Coffey et al. 2005).

Strategies employ tactics to achieve a specific clinical goal. Motivational interviewing (see

R. N. Rosenthal (✉)
Department of Psychiatry and Behavioral Health, Renaissance School of Medicine at Stony Brook University, Health Sciences Center, Stony Brook, NY, USA
e-mail: richard.rosenthal@stonybrookmedicine.edu

W. E. Sowers et al. (eds.), *Textbook of Community Psychiatry*,
https://doi.org/10.1007/978-3-031-10239-4_19

chapter "Motivational Interviewing as a Core Communication Style" is a clinical strategy to increase the patient's readiness to change his or her behavior. In MI the therapist uses various skills (i.e., asking open-ended questions or providing non-judgmental feedback) as part of the technique of reflective listening. *Strategies* are ways of employing tactics and techniques to achieve a specific clinical objective. A *treatment approach* codifies a set of clinical techniques, established through clinical trials, that organize tactics and strategies into a cohesive, internally consistent set of behavioral interventions for specific clinical problems. These are typically named "therapies" such as cognitive behavior therapy [CBT] or motivational enhancement therapy [MET] (Rosenthal et al. 2019).

Basic Concepts

Treatment Techniques Differ from Evidence: Or Consensus-Based Practices

Techniques are the main clinical procedures that clinicians use to conduct treatment (Table 1). In addition to those techniques used in evidence- and consensus-based approaches to COD, there are many techniques that are in use by clinicians for treating COD, which have not been formally examined through high-quality research or expert consensus panels. It is important to note that it is the approaches and strategies that are typically tested in clinical trials, not the core techniques. Nonetheless, many of these techniques are the content of day-to-day interactions that community psychiatrists treating COD should know. *Evidence-based practices* are those supported by research findings in making clinical and programmatic decisions about the care of patients (Rosenthal 2004). These practices typically rely upon a specific set of well-described techniques. The scope of evidence-based practices ranges from a single focused strategy or technical style (e.g., motivational interviewing, brief intervention) to a full program model that uses multiple techniques (e.g., assertive community treatment). *Consensus-based practices* are those that have clinical or expert consensus support but lack a well-documented scientific evidence base.

Engagement Strategies

Establishing and Maintaining a Therapeutic Alliance

The techniques that support the development and preservation of a therapeutic alliance are instrumental to the conduct of COD treatment (CSAT 2005). Without this alliance, which includes elements of trust, rapport, faith in the clinician's abilities, and agreement on treatment tasks and goals, it is more difficult for the clinician to obtain the most complete diagnostic and treatment-related information (Safran and Muran 2000). In general, an early and strong therapeutic alliance is predictive of a positive outcome in psychosocial treatment and decreased drug use in patients with substance use disorders (Winston and Winston 2002).

Specific clinical techniques that facilitate the development of a therapeutic or working alliance are maintaining a stance that is (1) respectful, (2) welcoming, (3) accepting, (4) warm, (5) empathic, (6) hope-inspiring, (7) confident, and (8) trustworthy. Setting appropriately frequent patient contacts, listening reflectively, setting appropriate limits, and being sensitive to the person's ethnic identity and cultural values and beliefs (Ackerman and Hilsenroth 2003; CSAT 2005; Misch 2000) are also important in building this alliance. Empathic attunement with the patient's internal state is affirmed when the clinician provides sensitive feedback and validation that enhances the patient's experience of being understood (Gabbard 2000). While these techniques are ideal, even simple interest in the patient helps build the therapeutic alliance and provide clinical benefits. In a study of recently detoxified primary care patients, care by clinicians who had more knowledge about the patient (medical history, home/work/school responsibilities, health concerns, and values and beliefs) predicted lower drug and alcohol severity on the

Table 1 Therapeutic approaches and related key techniques for COD patients

Approach	Core technique	Purpose
Motivational interviewing	Express empathy through reflective listening and acceptance	Demonstrates clinician's acceptance of patient's ambivalence to change
	Develop discrepancy between current behavior and patient's own goals	Shifts decisional balance towards change and healthier behavior
	Roll with the resistance by offering new information and perspectives	Supports the patient's autonomy and decision-making process.
	Support self-efficacy through engaging demonstration of patient's strengths and capacity to change	Supports patient empowerment to take responsibility for recovery process
Supportive psychotherapy	Form and enhance the therapeutic alliance through expression of interest, empathy and understanding, judicious self- disclosure, and purposive repair of misalliances	Increases treatment engagement and exposure through facilitated strengthening of the therapeutic alliance
	Enhance self-esteem through direct measures such as reassurance, praise, reframing, and encouragement	Decreases demoralization through improved self-efficacy and belief in possibility of change
	Improve adaptive skills through teaching, anticipatory guidance, modeling, and problem-solving	Increases personal and interpersonal functioning to improve quality of life and perceived competence
	Restore or improve psychological functioning by supporting adaptive defenses and reducing anxiety	Improves mechanisms for coping with stress, impulsivity or dysphoria and improves resilience
Cognitive behavioral relapse prevention	Conduct a functional analysis for each drug use episode to identify thoughts, feelings, and circumstances before and after drug use	Improves understanding of reasons for use and recognition of situations in which the patient is most likely to use, so the patient can avoid them when appropriate
	Provide skills training to unlearn drug abuse-associated habits and learn/relearn healthier skills (effective coping skills may never have been learned, may have decayed with reliance on substances for coping, or may have been weakened by co-occurring psychiatric disorders)	Improves patient's coping effectively with a range of substance-associated problems and behaviors
	Alter the contingencies of reinforcement. Since substance use excludes other experiences and rewards, identify and reduce drug-associated habits by substituting positive activities and rewards	Supports acquisition of healthy pleasures and movement toward more normative, socially reinforced behavior
	Teach techniques to recognize and cope with urges to use, a model for learning to tolerate other strong affects	Fosters overall management of painful affects
	Provide interpersonal skills training and strategies to help patients expand their social support networks and build enduring, drug-free relationships	Improves interpersonal functioning and enhance social supports

(continued)

Table 1 (continued)

Approach	Core technique	Purpose
Motivational enhancement therapy	Identify the patient's current stage of change	Allows therapist interventions to be *in synch* with the patient's motivational state, thus more likely to be effective
	Elicit self-motivational statements	Elicits the patient's intrinsic motivation to tip the decisional balance about change
	Use reframing to cast patient own statements about their behavior in a new light	Allows the patient to hear that problems are addressable and changeable
	Engage significant other in the recovery process by joining, normalizing, and eliciting feedback and support for the patient's intrinsic motivation for change	Allows the patient to obtain social support and collaboration for the work of recovery and promotes family cohesion
	Provide formative and summary feedback of patient statements during a session	Allows patient to hear reinforcing self-motivational statements several times during and at the end of a session
Substance abuse management module	Stop before a slip becomes a relapse; report a slip to a support person	Patient learns to practice damage control and reduce the abstinence violation effect
	Recognize warning signs and make U-turns; learn money management; remove triggers, ride out craving, and report side effects	Patient learns to avoid high-risk situations, including tolerating strong affects
	Model and role-play refusing drugs from an aggressive dealer, a friend, or relative	Patient learns to escape high-risk situations
	Identify healthy pleasures, and practice asking someone to join in	Patient learns to seek healthy pleasures, establish healthier habits and schedule, reinforce social connections
Contingency management	Arrange for regular, reliable, and valid assessment of a selected target behavior, e.g., testing for substances	Operationalizes to patient and clinician a specific and neutral means to measure behavior
	Find appropriate reinforcers and provide them after target behavior is demonstrated, e.g., sobriety, medication adherence. Add bonuses cumulatively	Applies behavioral principles in a way the patient finds rewarding, e.g., cash, vouchers, prizes, privileges
	Withhold incentives when target is missed, e.g., positive test for substance	Applies behavioral principles to shape behavior the patient agrees is unwanted
	Work with patient to establish alternative, non-risky behaviors	Expands behavioral repertoire, with positive impact on self-esteem

Twelve-step facilitation	Foster patient's acceptance of substance dependence as an illness characterized by loss of control and chronicity	Supports patient's adoption of a belief system conducive to engagement in twelve-step recovery
	Foster patient's surrender to some power outside of the self, since loss of control is a reality and 12-step fellowship has helped millions with the same problem	Supports the patient's exercise of a decision and commitment to accept external help and imparting of hope
	Foster commitment to AA: not only to show up at meetings but to engage in the AA program	Supports the patient's ability to engage in the active and intrinsically rewarding work of recovery
	Find and use meetings that the COD patient can feel a part of, the "right" meetings	Supports the COD patient to optimize the meetings attended so that resistance is lowered
	Identifying substance use relationship to patterns of thinking, feeling, and behavior	Patients learn to identify cognitive and emotional triggers to use and to use social contacts to support sobriety

Adapted from CSAT (2005), Higgins and Petry (1999), Miller et al. (1992), Miller and Rollnick (2002), Nowinski et al. (1992), Prochaska et al. (1992), Roberts et al. (1999), Rosenthal et al. (In Press)

Addiction Severity Index and decreased odds of future substance use (Kim et al. 2007).

A critical technique to reduce the risk of a rupture in the therapeutic alliance is management of countertransference, which can lead to argumentative interactions and evoke. resistance (Miller and Rollnick 2002). This will have a negative impact on therapeutic outcomes (Winston et al. 2020). Management of countertransference through self-awareness and identification of strong reactions and biases related to the patient will prevent interference with the therapeutic work. The clinician should obtain appropriate clinical supervision to troubleshoot specific issues, in addition to participating in periodic formal supervisions and team meetings to discuss general countertransference issues (CSAT 2005).

In addition, techniques to resolve conflicts between patient and clinician are also critical to maintaining the therapeutic alliance. These are:

- Addressing the problem practically in the context of the current situation
- Clarifying misunderstandings
- Expressing sincere regret at having unwittingly impugned or patronized the patient
- Supporting the patient's ability to express disagreements in the context of an ongoing therapeutic relationship
- Maintaining flexibility in one's position or on the current tasks when the patient is becoming angry or distant (Bond et al. 1998; Safran and Muran 2000)

If budding antagonisms are not resolved by approaching the patient's complaints and concerns with a practical discussion, then the clinician may move tactfully into a discussion of the therapeutic relationship and how it has evolved (Rosenthal et al. In Press).

At times, confrontation can be an appropriate technique to demonstrate to the patient the reality of his or her minimizing, evasive, blaming, rationalizing, or denying behavior, but it must be pursued with a strong awareness on the part of the clinician that the technique is not being propelled by the clinician's negative feelings (CSAT 2005; Rosenthal 2002). Confrontation is used to point out maladaptive behaviors but should not be harsh or accusatory (Rosenthal et al. In Press). However, confrontational or uncovering techniques may exacerbate symptoms in patients with psychotic disorders, so these may be less appropriate for COD patients with more severe mental disorders (Drake and Sederer 1986). The therapeutic task concerns how to balance using confrontative techniques without being punitive and using empathic, supportive techniques without being over-responsible (enabling) or fostering regressive, dependent behavior (Rosenthal 2013).

Engaging Significant Others and Families

It is often useful to involve patients' significant others when they give consent to contact them. Teaching the family about the nature of the patient's disorders can help stabilize the family around the patient in a way that is more supportive of recovery. Family psychoeducation is a treatment strategy that uses the techniques of empathic engagement, education, continuing support, increased clinical resources during periods of crisis, social network enhancement, and improving problem-solving and communication skills (McFarlane et al. 2003). Individuals with severe mental illness have lower rehospitalization rates and decreased psychotic symptoms when their families attend psychoeducation groups. Those with persistent symptoms have lower rates of relapse to psychosis when the family is engaged in multi-family rather than single-family psychoeducational groups (McFarlane et al. 1995). When family psychoeducation techniques are properly implemented, patients have reduced relapse rates and improved recovery and families have improved sense of well-being (McFarlane et al. 2003).

Engaging significant others and families also promotes better substance dependence treatment outcomes (Higgins et al. 1994). The techniques of engaging the patient's natural supports can range from enlisting families to join in the initial assessment process (offering supplemental information, another point of view, or relevant information unavailable to the patient), up to recruiting direct involvement of significant others or families in the ongoing treatment process. Significant others can participate in treatment by supporting adherence to program or medication schedules or as monitors of recovery behavior when they are permitted to communicate with the clinician (Galanter et al. 2002).

More specifically, therapeutic interventions with families and couples have significant positive impact upon recovery from SUD (Stanton and Shadish 1997). In cases where the patient lives or has daily contact with family or a significant other, behavioral couples therapy provides elements of increased social support for the patient's efforts to change and an incentive for sobriety. This can have a positive impact on substance use frequency and unwanted consequences of use (Powers et al. 2008). For example, in those who are being treated with disulfiram, a useful set of techniques is the creation of a contract between the patient and a significant other stating that (1) the significant other will observe the patient taking his daily dose of disulfiram; (2) record that action on a calendar; (3) the patient and spouse will then thank each other for their efforts; and (4) neither will argue or discuss the patient's drinking behavior (O'Farrell and Bayog 1986).

Facilitating Adherence to a Treatment Plan

Since COD treatment requires time, effort, and persistence on the part of the patient, understanding the rationale for treatment and having sufficient motivation to engage and continue in treatment is fundamental for a positive outcome. Education about mental illness and addictive disease is critical to that understanding. Teaching should include both the expected effects of recovery efforts and the negative social, behavioral, medical, and economic consequences of untreated disorders (see section "Providing Patient Education", below). When patients are uncertain about whether they want to make a change or doubt their ability to change, the techniques of motivational interviewing, such as reflective listening, developing perceived discrepancy between actual and ideal behavior, exploring patient's ambivalence (i.e., change talk and sustain talk), and avoiding argument (Miller and Rollnick 2013), can be used. There is significant evidence that MI is an effective intervention for SUD, especially for promoting entry to and engagement in more intensive substance abuse treatment, even when used by clinicians who are not addiction specialists (Dunn et al. 2001).

Another important adherence technique is for the clinician to assist the patient in formulating useful reminders for remembering treatment-related appointments or tasks, including medication schedules. The clinician directly addresses factors that may reduce adherence to prescribed medication, such as denial, complex medication dosing schedules, side effects, poor social support, as well as symptoms of mental illness (DiMatteo 2004; DiMatteo et al. 2000; Perkins 2002). The clinician should ask frequently about how patients are faring with medications, including beneficial effects, side effects, difficulties with the regimen, and whether they need to make adjustments with their physician (CSAT 2005).

Most people tend to have difficulty taking medications regularly, but this is especially true of patients with COD. Cognitive dysfunction, ambivalence, or a chaotic living environment all contribute, so using long-acting injectable (LAI) medications can be framed as an adherence strategy. Techniques that support the use of LAI encourage sound decision-making and include motivational interviewing, supportive skills-building interventions, giving advice, modeling adaptive behavior, and encouragement (Rosenthal et al. In Press). The following therapeutic interaction is an illustration of these:

Patient: "I don't much like taking the medications and I don't remember to take them a lot anyway. I'm usually focused on other things, but I'm getting the symptoms again, and I don't want to lose my good situation." *Expresses ambivalence about taking medications*

Clinician: "You know, we have a way for you to take the medicine in a long-acting form, so you would only need to get an injection after several weeks when you come here for visits. You won't even have to think about it! How does that sound?" *Psychoeducation, adaptive skills*

Patient: "Tell me more."

Clinician: "We know that if your system is exposed to the medication consistently, that greatly improves the benefits over starting and stopping—the long-acting medication is a good way for you to achieve that." *Psychoeducation,*

Patient: "Feels like I'm gonna be controlled if it's in me like that, I don't know…" *Expresses ambivalence*

Clinician: "You have concerns about not being able to stop it once it is in your body, but you also said you have concerns about what the symptoms coming back will do to your recovery" *Reflective listening*

Patient: "I don't want to end up back in the hospital again."

Clinician: "So this may be a way for you to control the decision, and you would be taking steps to further your recovery." *Encouragement, supporting adaptive behavior*

Patient: "I could stop it if I didn't like it and go back to taking pills next time?"

Clinician: "That can be your choice; we'll work together on this." *Reassurance*

Patient: "Ok, I can try it"

Clinician: "So you've decided to try the long-acting medication because your desire to stay healthy has outweighed your concerns about this form of the medicine. We can look at how you do after the first dose and discuss whether you wish to continue then. I think you've made a good choice. Now, let's talk more about side effects compared to the oral version." *Summarizing, reflective feedback, empowerment, praise.*

Currently there are several long-acting injectable forms of atypical antipsychotic agents as well as long-acting injectable naltrexone for alcohol and opioid use disorder (Garbutt et al. 2005). Long-acting subcutaneous and subdermal implant preparations of buprenorphine are available for opioid use disorder as well (Rosenthal 2019).

Maintaining Engagement in Treatment

People remain in treatment when they are motivated to do so and supported in their commitment. Motivation and support can be due to several factors:

- Strong affiliation to the provider, other patients, or the program
- Decisional balance that is tipped toward recovery
- Reduction in the negative effects of the co-occurring disorders
- External forces such as family involvement or court-mandated treatment

Thus, techniques that the clinician uses to further clinical engagement focus on continuously assessing the patient's current motivational state and providing accurate feedback in the context of MI (Miller and Rollnick 2013). Staying attuned to the patient's affective state and relatedness, tracking their ability to access healthy rewards and providing interventions matched to the patient's motivational stage are also important elements. Facilitating active use of self-help strategies and engaging significant others and/or families will improve treatment retention (Meichenbaum and Turk 1987). Supportive therapy techniques can be used to reinforce the therapeutic alliance (Rosenthal et al. In Press). Praising small gains is a supportive technique that clinicians can use to bolster the patient's self-esteem and provide impetus for continuing treatment engagement (Winston et al. 2020).

Maintaining Long-Term Care

Mental illness and substance use disorders are long-term illnesses; thus, the patient may need services indefinitely (CSAT 2005). Given the numerous environmental cues and stressors in the community that pull a person toward relapse, the patient needs support for recovery in the community that is synergistic with formal treatment. One technique that acknowledges this is assistance in developing a support network that espouses healthy behaviors and provides respect and acceptance. Examples include a 12-step home group and/or sponsor, engagement in a dual recovery mutual self-help group, and new friendships with persons in recovery. Such a network can support the continued development of a person's recovery, even when they are not receiving care from a provider or clinical program (CSAT 2005). However, it is important to recognize that these community support elements are not substitutes for treatment and clinical input is needed to optimize recovery.

Facilitating participation in mutual self-help groups is deemed a key technique for working with people with COD (CSAT 2005). Twelve-step facilitation (TSF) is an evidence-based clinical treatment approach designed to acquaint patients with the philosophy of AA and to encourage them to participate in this self-help activity (Nowinski et al. 1992). Research suggests that patients with alcohol dependence and low-level psychiatric severity have better outcomes with TSF than they do when treated with CBT (Project Match Research Group 1997). Techniques of TSF that support the recovery of COD patients are (1) encouraging patients to engage the programmatic aspects of AA in addition to attending meetings; (2) identifying meetings appropriate for the COD patient; (3) assistance with engagement in step work; and (4) identifying dysfunctional patterns of thinking and feeling (Nowinski et al. 1992).

COD patients may have symptoms such as social anxiety, suspiciousness, behavioral rigidity, or cognitive difficulties that will inhibit their ability to get to and engage in group meetings. The clinician should use techniques of anticipatory guidance and rehearsal to acquaint the patient with how the group works. Engagement of a significant other to accompany the patient to the group or writing down specific directions to get to the meeting can also be helpful. It will also be important to ensure that psychiatric symptoms are sufficiently stabilized to enable engagement with psychological support and motivational practices (CSAT 2005; Rosenthal 2002).

Psychosocial Treatment Strategies

Monitoring the Patient's Clinical Status

Clinicians can use subjective or objective clinical measures to monitor their patient's progress in treatment. The main areas of evaluation should be the person's motivational state, sobriety/abstinence, psychiatric symptoms, and his or her perceptions of the specificity and efficacy of the provided treatment (CSAT 2005). These assessments, whether informal or structured, should be performed with enough frequency that all progress that has a positive impact upon recovery is detected. Individualized care planning should address each person's unique characteristics. These may include genetic predisposition, addiction severity, severity of mental illness, stage of change for both mental, and substance use disorders. Culture, race, ethnicity, and living environment will also impact what the optimal combination of medications and psychosocial interventions should be. The technique of individualizing care for people with COD is also necessary to avoid a mismatch between the patient's beliefs and the clinician's interventions. The use of techniques inappropriate for the recovery stage will likely cause a highly stressed or ruptured therapeutic alliance and non-adherence to the treatment plan (Rosenthal 2013). Abstinence and sobriety should be monitored both through self-reports (e.g., checklists) and objective measures (toxicology screens, preferably random). All clinicians providing care to those with COD must know techniques to assess a person's mental status for changes in the severity of key psychiatric symptoms such suicidality (CSAT 2005). Finally, the patient's feedback about how they perceive the usefulness of treatment can provide essential information for adjusting the treatment plan. Feedback can take the form of a conversation in the context of a good therapeutic alliance or might be obtained from a standardized consumer satisfaction scale, especially as more of these service user-specific scales are developed (Greenwood et al. 2010).

Providing Patient Education

Educational techniques provide important cognitive restructuring for recovering COD patients and inform them about mental and substance use disorders, their sequelae, and treatment. For optimal impact, the clinician should understand the patient's capacity to make use of the information to support ego functioning and adaptive skills and formulate the educational plan accordingly. When a person with a substance use disorder learns that they have another, chronic mental illness, or vice versa, they may become demoralized. Imparting information along with supportive techniques, such as normalization and encouragement, can assist with the development of coping skills and improved self-efficacy (Rosenthal 2013). Typically, psychoeducation about substances focuses on different classes of drugs and their psychological and physical effects. The dangers of chronic use including pertinent medical problems and benefits of abstinence are also important topics. Current models of addiction and how drugs are used to address negative emotional states may also be included. Psychoeducation about mental disorders includes information about symptoms of relevance to the patient, their treatment, and natural history.

Psychoeducation should be framed in the context of a recovery perspective. This means active clinician-patient collaboration with person-centered planning that provides stage-specific interventions (see chapter "Person-Centered Recovery Planning as a Roadmap to Recovery. Outcomes of improved health, better self-care, increased independence, and improved self-esteem result from this process (CSAT 2005). The literature suggests that educating patients about their illness enhances the psychosocial rehabilitation of people with severe mental disorders and substance dependence (Goldman and Quinn 1988). In addition, a fact-based and non-judgmental accounting of the effects of drugs helps tip the decisional balance in favor of recovery. When teaching, the clinician must always take the patient's literacy level into account, as it may be lower than the readability level of treatment-related reading materials (Greenfield et al. 2005). In addition, since many people with COD may have cognitive or memory problems, it will be especially important for the therapist to briefly review the main points of the discussion frequently (CSAT 2005).

The cognitive behavior therapy relapse prevention technique of functional analysis uses teaching, exploration, and experiential learning. In this technique, for each substance use episode, the clinician helps the patient to identify their thoughts, feelings, and circumstances both before and after the substance use. In addition, the identification of relapse triggers is a CBT technique that helps the patient to identify sources of high risk for drug relapse from among potential high-risk situations, specific environmental cues, thought patterns, and emotions. Both the patient and the clinician learn the patient's reasons for use, whether it is to cope with interpersonal difficulties or to experience risk or euphoria.

Part of the recovery process for both substance use and mental disorders is learning new, more adaptive behavioral patterns and putting them into practice. The clinician teaches these skills, including relapse prevention skills derived from CBT (Kadden et al. 1992; Marlatt and Gordon 1985). Data from numerous clinical trials of CBT suggest a learning curve related to practice effects, so the efficacy of CBT tends to increase for some period of time after the therapeutic intervention.

Preventing Relapse

A corollary to the importance of learning new skills is that in order for them to be successful, a person must put them to use. An important technique in assisting the patient with skill acquisition is training through role-playing or rehearsal, where the clinician guides the patient through hypothetical, but typical, situations. This enables a person to practice recognizing which circumstances are high-risk and how to make U-turns away from them. Rehearsing drug refusal skills and steps to minimize the effects of a slip (quit early) can also be useful. These techniques are especially helpful to patients with severe

COD with limited social skills (Roberts et al. 1999).

Specific techniques that support relapse prevention include:

- Exploring negative consequences of continued substance use
- Enhancing the patient's ability to recognize drug cravings early on
- Identifying high-risk situations for use
- Helping the patient to develop coping strategies to avoid triggers and desires to use
- Identifying and developing activities that replace patient's needs otherwise satisfied by the substance use

Dysphoric mood is a frequently reported antecedent of relapse in people with COD, so relapse prevention techniques also focus on building adaptive skills for coping with the negative or painful mood states (Marlatt and Gordon 1985; Longabaugh et al. 1996). This may be especially helpful in patients with schizophrenia. For these individuals, abuse of substances, often stimulants, may be driven in part by negative symptoms. This is referred to as self-medication. In addition, techniques that help patients address negative thoughts are helpful, as they often accompany or trigger dysphoric states. The skills clinicians can teach patients for managing negative thoughts include thought stopping, positive self-talk, and substituting positive thoughts or feelings. CBT may hold particular promise in reduction in the severity of relapses when they occur (Kadden et al. 1992).

Medical Strategies

Managing Intoxication and Withdrawal States

Patients who are acutely intoxicated need a safe environment to sober up that also provides adequate medical monitoring of acute intoxication and withdrawal symptoms. The clinician needs to be able to understand what substances the patient has taken, in what amounts, and over what time. Depending upon the type and dose of the substance the person is intoxicated with, a treatment plan can be developed. Elements to consider include (1) level of stimulation (a low-light, low-sound environment), (2) need for reassurance, (3) safety precautions, (4) reality grounding, and (5) medical management (e.g., use of antagonists, gastric lavage, changing urinary pH, sedation).

Many patients who meet DSM-5 substance use disorder criteria will not develop physical symptoms of withdrawal after cessation of substance use (APA 2013). The substances that typically produce physical withdrawal symptoms in those with substance dependence are in the sedative-hypnotic group (e.g., alcohol, benzodiazepines, barbiturates) or the opioid group (e.g., prescription narcotics and heroin). Other substance groups (stimulants, cannabis) may produce withdrawal symptoms, but they produce fewer physiologic symptoms (e.g., blood pressure and heart rate). They are more likely to produce emotional arousal symptoms such as agitation, dysphoria, anxiety, and irritability. Medical personnel who work with COD patients must know the techniques of alleviating medical withdrawal from each class of substances and must recognize that COD may intensify the subjective symptoms of withdrawal.

Using Medication

Medications to treat traditional psychiatric illnesses are well-employed by psychiatrists, but the same is not true of the use of medications for the treatment of SUD, in spite of the fact that there are many evidence-based medications for SUD. These medications work best in combination with psychosocial approaches and are described in detail in chapter "Evidence-Based Practices for Co-occurring Addiction and Mental Illness". The text box below describes some key practical points that the community psychiatrist can use in employing pharmacology in COD.

1. Abstinence should not be a requirement to begin pharmacotherapy for a co-occurring Axis I disorder, unless there is a specific contraindication to that medicine for a particular intoxication or withdrawal state. For example, one generally shouldn't use medications during sedative-hypnotic withdrawal that lower the seizure threshold, such as antipsychotics or antidepressants.
2. Treat all treatable non-substance-related mental disorders, avoiding medications with a high abuse liability, if possible. The first choice for treating chronic anxiety shouldn't be a short-acting benzodiazepine. Try other, less risky strategies first.
3. Unless contraindicated, evidence-based medications for SUD should be used to treat SUD in patients with COD. Don't avoid treating SUD with pharmacotherapy in patients with mental disorders, as they may have an appropriate, even synergistic response (Petrakis et al. 2004).
4. Be careful in choosing and dosing medication, but don't undertreat. Cover as much ground with the fewest number of medications and minimize the schedule for dosing to once daily, if effective. Consider long-acting medication preparations for patients with high disorganization and poor social support, unstable living environments, or other chaotic elements lowering the likelihood of adherence to an oral regimen.
5. "Start low, go slow." Patients with co-occurring disorders may have increased initial sensitivity to medications and have difficulty tolerating side effects, but they may ultimately need a higher dose than patients without SUD (Kranzler et al. 1994).
6. It is best to use medications with a high safety index and low capacity for inducing delirium or seizures as those with COD may have a lower threshold for CNS side effects (Olivera et al. 1990).
7. Syndromes are less hazardous to treat than individual symptoms (e.g., insomnia, anxiety, dysphoria). When the patient communicates multiple complaints that may be independent of Axis I disorders, it is easier for the clinician to become uncertain about medication response.

Adapted from Rosenthal 2013

Reducing the Morbidity of Substance Use Disorders

New patients should have a medical screening examination in order to assess general health and to assess the medical impact of substance use. This is important because, in addition to substance-induced damage to different organ systems in the body, both patients with substance use disorders and those with severe mental disorders are less likely to engage in adequate self-care, including periodic medical examination (CSAT 2005). Because of impulsivity, and some dangerous routes of drug administration, people with COD are at high risk for sexually transmitted diseases and other infectious diseases such as HIV, hepatitis C, and COVID-19 (Wang et al. 2020). People coming to treatment are often demoralized and adopt a fatalistic posture due to the negative impact of substance abuse and mental illness (Winston et al. 2020). Treating clinicians can be supportive and use MI techniques to increase the possibility that patients will follow up with necessary medical care.

Implementing Techniques

Techniques to Convey Information to Patients

Supportive psychotherapy should always be the foundation of provider-to-patient communication since it is based on the factors common to all psychotherapies and there are relatively few circumstances where it is not indicated (Frank 1975). This is because the techniques of supportive psychotherapy are direct measures specifically geared to maintain, restore, or improve self-esteem, adaptive skills, and psychological functioning (Rosenthal et al. In Press). This enables even difficult information to be delivered to a patient in a respectful, direct, supportive, and alliance-building fashion.

Several component techniques of supportive therapy are specifically useful in engaging with people and promoting their self-efficacy. First, the therapist's empathic attitude of acceptance, respect, and interest allows the patient to feel welcomed and supported. Next, specific supportive techniques such as teaching, encouragement, reassurance, exhortation, modeling, and anticipatory guidance can be used to enhance motivation. *Exhortation* is the use of easily understood and remembered common phrases or slogans in order to convey important concepts to persons who may be cognitively impaired or frequently distracted by cravings or impulses (e.g., "Use HALT to remember your negative mood triggers—hungry, angry, lonely or tired!"). *Modeling* is where the provider serves as an exemplar of the adaptive behavior desired in the patient. *Anticipatory guidance* is the technique whereby the provider assists the patient in foreseeing obstacles to a proposed course of action and rehearsing behaviors successfully with those obstacles (Winston et al. 2020).

People often have negative self-evaluations about their own maladaptive behavior due to COD, typically worse with more severe disorders. Individuals coming from an environment in which they feel highly stigmatized are more likely to develop self-stigma, with attendant negative impact on role function, self-esteem, morale, social and treatment engagement, and symptom severity (Brohan et al. 2011; Yanos et al. 2008). Normalization is a supportive technique protective of the patient's self-esteem by reframing what the patient thinks of their own behavior or experience as a common experience of others. However, care must be taken to avoid conflict with the MI technique of developing discrepancy (Rosenthal et al. In Press). Techniques that support patients' experiences of self-efficacy should be implemented because empowerment and expanded areas of social contact are associated with lowered self-stigma (Brohan et al. 2010, 2011). These supportive techniques include (1) use of experience-based praise (finding and declaring something the patient will experience as praiseworthy) (Rosenthal et al. In Press); (2) reassurance and encouragement (Rosenthal et al. In Press); (3) identification of patients' strengths and capacity to change (Miller and Rollnick 2002); and (4) cognitive restructuring. This last technique comes from CBT in which clinician and patient examine and challenge the validity of self-stigmatizing beliefs that are due to cognitive distortions or dysfunctional attitudes (Yanos et al. 2008).

Within a supportive context, the techniques of MI (CSAT 1999; Miller and Rollnick 2013) should be implemented for people with COD to elicit change in cognitions and behaviors. Thus, while building a therapeutic alliance, the provider imparts information that is likely to motivate the patient toward healthier decisional process.

Increasing the Validity and Impact of Feedback Provided to Patients

In order to affect the decisional balance between a patient's tendency to continue to use substances and their countertendency to stop, accurate information must be supplied in a non-threatening and non-demeaning fashion. This will add to the patient's knowledge base and beliefs about the negative consequences of substance use. Therefore, the MI technique of providing feedback is useful, as valid information assists the patient in developing the discrepancy between present behavior and personal values or goals (Miller and Rollnick 2002). The highest quality information often takes the form of concrete personal measures generated by objective methods, which the patient can then read and discuss with the provider. These typically take the form of checklists, urine toxicity screens, and laboratory reports. For example, for those with severe COD, feedback consisting of graphical representations of their nicotine dependence and those in a control group of nonsmokers comparing expired breath carbon monoxide and money spent on cigarettes might be effective for engagement in smoking cessation treatment (Steinberg et al. 2004).

In addition, more general normative data about alcohol and substance abuse from national sources such as the federal Substance Abuse and Mental Health Services Administration (SAMHSA) can be used for more general feedback (SAMHSA.gov). For example, going online to the SAMHSA website, where five standard drinks at a sitting for men (four for women) is defined as an episode of "heavy drinking," can be a useful form of feedback. Conversely, hearsay and common myths tend not to have the same motivational impact, as they are more easily questioned and refuted. An additional source of useful feedback can be presented in the form of other patients' responses and stories related to their use of substances or non-adherence to medication. For example, a particular strength of mutual-help peer groups is that members get to hear others share the negative consequences of drinking and drug use in a supportive and like-minded group. Similarly, in a program-based recovery group, senior members, with clinical oversight, can offer new members information based on their own experience, about the whys and wherefores of early recovery (Rosenthal 2002).

Using Techniques to Help Address the Social Consequences of Co-occurring Illnesses

COD have direct effects on functioning that are the obvious foci for evaluating the efficacy of our treatments. However, there are also a range of negative social consequences of co-occurring disorders, including lowered self-esteem and motivation. There may also be disempowerment and alienation from families, the workforce, and systems of care. Clinical techniques must enable clinicians to evaluate the people in ecologically valid terms, not just in terms of symptoms and function in the clinic setting. There are techniques that support and empower people in the face of stigma, that help them better negotiate organizations, and those that address disenfranchisement. Techniques that improve the patient's safety are also important. For example, homelessness may be a mediator of risk for relapse to substance abuse, which in turn leads to exacerbation of mental illness (Boisvert et al. 2008; Kertesz et al. 2005). Interpersonal, teaching, and management skills can be used to defuse conflict between a client and a landlord who is threatening eviction, thus potentially reducing the risk of relapse.

Making an Appropriate and Effective Referral

In order to make "good referrals that stick," providers must implement techniques to properly assess the patient, to network with other agencies, and create alliances with other providers and provider groups.

A useful technique in creating a network of care for COD patients is the crafting and execution of a structured reciprocal agreement, which binds together the care of an identified patient between separate provider systems. Reciprocal agreements can be powerful networking tools for supporting interagency cooperation and flow of patients across treatment settings. These agreements create a pathway for patients to move between levels of care without the usual stress about placement out of one's domain. For example, a community service provider treating a patient with COD who frequently expresses suicidal ideation can enter into an agreement with a hospital-based program to assess patients for hospitalization on an as-needed basis, provided the community-based program agrees to take the patient back into treatment post-discharge. This may give the community provider greater security to work with higher-risk patients. Knowing that the hospital will easily accept the patients in crisis reduces apprehension of working with patients who have histories of instability. This anxiety-reducing agreement implemented at the institutional level fosters the formation of a working alliance between the provider systems.

Summary and Future Directions

Although infrequently studied, the individual treatment techniques underlying engagement, psychosocial, and medical treatment strategies are the basic and necessary clinical armamentarium for clinicians who wish to treat patients with COD. Most of the techniques described for engagement are generalizable to work with non-COD clinical populations. Similarly, techniques supporting strategies that focus on the transfer of clinical information are also more broadly generalizable. There are probably many effective techniques in use that will not gain wide dissemination unless packaged and tested to generate a proper evidence base. Future research should examine practice-based as well as hypothesis-driven designs to discover what clinical advances have been generated in the treatment setting.

References

APA. (2013). Diagnostic and Statistical Manual of Mental Disorders (DSM-5®), Fifth Edition Washington, DC, American Psychiatric Association.

Ackerman, S.J. and Hilsenroth, M.J. (2003). A review of therapist characteristics and techniques positively impacting the therapeutic alliance. *Clin Psychol Reviews* 23:1–33.

Back, S.E., Waldrop, A.E., Brady, K.T. (2009). Treatment challenges associated with comorbid substance use and posttraumatic stress disorder: clinicians' perspectives. *Am J Addictions*. 18:1, 15–20.

Boisvert RA, Martin LM, Grosek M, Clarie AJ. (2008). Effectiveness of a peer-support community in addiction recovery: participation as intervention. *Occup Ther Int*. 15:205–20.

Bond, M., Banon, E., Grenier, M. (1998). Differential effects of interventions on the therapeutic alliance with patients with personality disorders. *J Psychother Pract Res*, 7:301–318.

Brohan, E., Elgie, R., Sartorius, N., Thornicroft, G. (2010). Self-stigma, empowerment and perceived discrimination among people with schizophrenia in 14 European countries: The GAMIAN-Europe study. *Schizophrenia Research* 122: 232–238.

Brohan E, Gauci D, Sartorius N, Thornicroft G; GAMIAN-Europe Study Group. (2011). Self-stigma, empowerment and perceived discrimination among people with bipolar disorder or depression in 13 European countries: the GAMIAN-Europe study. *J Affect Disord* 129:56–63.

Center for Substance Abuse Treatment. (1999). *Enhancing Motivation for Change in Substance Abuse Treatment.* Treatment Improvement Protocol (TIP) Series, Number 35. (DHHS Pub. No. (SMA) 99-3354). Rockville, MD: Substance Abuse and Mental Health Services Administration.

Center for Substance Abuse Treatment. (2005). *Substance abuse treatment for persons with co-occurring disorders.* Treatment Improvement Protocol (TIP) Series No. 42 (DHHS Pub. No. SMA 05–39920). Rockville, MD: Substance Abuse and Mental Health Services Administration.

Coffey, S.F., Schumacher, J.A., Brimo, M.L., Brady, K.T. (2005). Exposure therapy for substance abusers with PTSD: translating research to practice. *Behav Modif* 29:10–38.

DiMatteo, M.R. (2004). Social support and patient adherence to medical treatment: a meta-analysis. *Health Psychol* 23:207–18.

DiMatteo, M.R., Lepper, H.S., Croghan, T.W. (2000). Depression is a risk factor for noncompliance with medical treatment: meta-analysis of the effects of anxiety and depression on patient adherence. *Arch Int Med* 160: 2101–2107.

Drake, R.E., Sederer, L.I. (1986). Inpatient psychosocial treatment of chronic schizophrenia: negative effects and current guidelines. *Hosp Community Psychiatry* 37: 897–901.

Dunn, C., Deroo, L., Rivara, F.P. (2001). The use of brief intervention adapted from motivational interviewing across behavioral domains: a systematic review. *Addiction* 96: 1725–1742.

Frank, J.D. (1975). General psychotherapy: the restoration of morale, in *American Handbook of Psychiatry*, 2nd Edition, Volume 5: Treatment. Edited by Freedman DX, Dyrud JE. New York, Basic Books, pp. 117–132.

Gabbard GO: Psychodynamic Psychiatry in Clinical Practice, 3rd ed. Washington, DC, American Psychiatric Press, 2000, pp. 97–98

Galanter, M.D., Dermatis, H., Keller, D., Trujillo, M. (2002). Network therapy for cocaine abuse: use of family and peer supports. *Am J Addictions* 11: 161–166.

Garbutt, J.C., Kranzler, H.R., O'Malley, S.S., Gastfriend, D.R., Pettinati, H.M., Silverman, B.L., Loewy, J.W., Ehrich, E.W; Vivitrex Study Group. (2005). Efficacy and tolerability of long-acting injectable naltrexone for alcohol dependence: a randomized controlled trial. *JAMA* 293:1617–1625.

Greenfield, S.F., Sugarman, D.E., Nargiso, J., Weiss, R.D. (2005). Readability of patient handout materials in a nationwide sample of alcohol and drug abuse treatment programs. *Am J Addictions* 14: 339–45.

Greenwood KE, Sweeney A, Williams S, Garety P, Kuipers E, Scott J, Peters E. (2010). CHoice of Outcome In Cbt for psychosEs (CHOICE): the development of a new service user-led outcome measure of CBT for psychosis. *Schizophr Bull.* 36:126–35. Epub 2009 Oct 30.

Goldman, C.R., Quinn, F.L. (1988). Effects of a patient education program in the treatment of schizophrenia. *Hosp Community Psychiatry* 39:282–286.

Higgins, S.T., Budney, A.J., Bickel, W.K., Badger, G.J. (1994). Participation of significant others in outpatient behavioral treatment predicts greater cocaine abstinence. *A J Drug Alcohol Abuse* 20:47–56.

Higgins, S.T., Petry, N.M. (1999). Contingency management: incentives for sobriety. *Alc Research Health* 23: 122–127.

Olivera, A.A., Kiefer, M.W., Manley, N.K. (1990). Tardive dyskinesia in psychiatric patients with substance abuse disorders. *Am J Drug Alcohol Abuse* 16: 57–66.

Kadden, R.M., Carroll, K., Donovan, D., Cooney, N., Monti, P., Abrams, D., Litt, M. & Hester, R. (Eds.) (1992). Cognitive-Behavioral Coping Skills Therapy Manual: A Clinical Research Guide for Therapists Treating Individuals with Alcohol Abuse and Dependence. Volume 4, Project MATCH Monograph Series. Rockville, MD: National Institute on Alcohol Abuse and Alcoholism. (DHHS Publication No. (ADM) 94-3724).

Kertesz SG, Larson MJ, Horton NJ, Winter M, Saitz R, Samet JH. (2005). Homeless chronicity and health-related quality of life trajectories among adults with addictions. Med Care 43:574–85.

Kim, T.W., Samet, J.H., Cheng, D.M., et al. (2007). Primary care quality and addiction severity: a prospective cohort study. *Health Serv Res*, 42:755–772.

Kranzler, H.R., Burleson, J.A., Del Boca, F.K., Babor, T.F., Korner, P., Brown, J., Bohn, M.J. (1994). Buspirone treatment of anxious alcoholics. A placebo-controlled trial. *Arch Gen Psychiatry* 51: 720–31.

Longabaugh, R., Rubin, A., Stout, R.L., Zywiak, W.H., Lowman, C. (1996). The reliability of Marlatt's taxonomy for classifying relapses. *Addiction* 91: S73–S88.

Marlatt, G.A., Gordon, J.R. (1985). *Relapse Prevention: Maintenance Strategies in the Treatment of Addictive Behaviors.* New York, Guilford Press.

McFarlane WR, Dixon L, Lukens E, Lucksted A. Family psychoeducation and schizophrenia: a review of the literature. *J Marital Fam Ther* 2003, 29:223–45.

McFarlane, W.R., Lukens, E., Link, B., Dushay, R., Deakins, S.A., Newmark, M., Dunne, E.J., Horen, B., Toran, J. (1995). Multiple-family groups and psychoeducation in the treatment of schizophrenia. *Arch Gen Psychiatry* 52:679–87.

Meichenbaum, D., and Turk, D.C. (1987). *Facilitating Treatment Adherence: A Practitioner's Handbook.* New York, Plenum Press.

Miller, W.R. and Rollnick, S. (2002). *Motivational interviewing: Preparing People for Change* (2nd ed.). New York, Guilford Press.

Miller, W.R. and Rollnick, S. (2013). *Motivational interviewing: Preparing People for Change* (3rd ed.). New York, Guilford Press.

Miller, W.R., Zweben, A., DiClemente, C.C., Rychtarik, R.G (1992). *Motivational Enhancement Therapy Manual: A Clinical Research Guide for Therapists Treating Individuals With Alcohol Abuse and Dependence.* Project MATCH Monograph Series. Vol. 2. NIH Pub. No. 94-3723. Washington, DC: Supt. of Docs., U.S. Gov. Print. Off.

Misch, D.A. (2000). Basic strategies of dynamic supportive therapy. *J Psychother Pract Res* 9: 173–189.

Nowinski, J., Baker, S., Carroll, K. (1992). *Twelve- Step Facilitation Therapy Manual: A Clinical Research Guide for Therapists Treating Individuals With Alcohol Abuse and Dependence.* Project MATCH Monograph Series Vol. 1. DHHS Publication No. (ADM)92–1893. Bethesda, MD: National Institute on Alcohol Abuse and Alcoholism.

O'Farrell, T.J., Bayog, R.D. (1986). Antabuse contracts for married alcoholics and their spouses: a method to maintain Antabuse ingestion and decrease conflict about drinking. *J Subst Abuse Treat* 3:1–8.

Perkins, D.O. (2002). Predictors of noncompliance in patients with schizophrenia. *J Clin Psychiatry* 63: 1121–1128.

Petrakis, I.L., O'Malley, S., Rounsaville, B., Poling, J., McHugh-Strong, C., Krystal, J.H. (2004). VA Naltrexone StudyCollaboration Group. Naltrexone augmentation of neuroleptic treatment in alcohol abusing patients with schizophrenia.*Psychopharmaco logy* (Berl) 172: 291–7.

Powers, M.B., Vedel, E., Emmelkamp, P.M. (2008). Behavioral couples therapy (BCT) for alcohol and drug use disorders: a meta-analysis. *Clin Psychol Rev*, 28:952–62. Epub 2008 Feb 16.

Prochaska, J.O., DiClemente, C.C. & Norcross, J.C. (1992). In search of how people change: Applications to addictive behaviors. *Am Psychologist* 47: 1102–1114.

Project Match Research Group. (1997). Matching alcoholism treatments to client heterogeneity: Project MATCH Posttreatment drinking outcomes. *J Studies Alc*, 58: 7–29.

Roberts, L.J., Shaner, A., Eckman, T. (1999). *Overcoming Addictions: Skills Training for People with Schizophrenia.* New York: W.W. Norton & Co.

Rosenthal, R.N. (2002). Group treatments for schizophrenic substance abusers, In: *The Group Psychotherapy of Substance Abuse*, eds. Brook, D.W., Spitz, H.I. The Haworth Press, Inc., New York.

Rosenthal, R.N. (2004). Concepts of Evidence Based Practice. In *Evidence-Based Practice Manual: Research and Outcome Measures in Health and Human Services,* eds. Roberts, A.R., Yeager, K.R. Oxford University Press, pp. 20–29.

Rosenthal, R.N. (2013). Treatment of persons with dual diagnoses of substance use disorder and other psychological problems. In: *Addictions: A Comprehensive*

Guidebook, McCrady, B.S., Epstein, E.E., eds. New York, Oxford University Press.

Rosenthal, R.N. (2019). Novel Formulations of Buprenorphine for Treatment of Opioid Use Disorder. *Focus* 17:104–109.

Rosenthal, R.N., Urmanche, A.A., Muran, J.C. (In Press). Techniques of Individual Supportive Psychotherapy, In: *The American Psychiatric Publishing Textbook of Psychotherapeutic Treatments in Psychiatry*, 2nd Edition, eds. Crisp, H., & Gabbard, G.O., Washington, DC, American Psychiatric Publishing, Inc.

Rosenthal, R.N., Zweben, J.E., Ries, R.K. (2019). Medical Management Techniques and Collaborative Care: Integrating Behavioral with Pharmacological Interventions in Addiction Treatment. In Eds. Miller SC, Fiellin D, Rosenthal RN, and Saitz R. *The ASAM Principles of Addiction Medicine, 6th Edition*, pp 1057–1072, Philadelphia, Lippincott, Williams & Wilkins.

Safran, J.D., Muran, J.C. (2000). *Negotiating the Therapeutic Alliance: A Relational Treatment Guide*. New York, Guilford, pp 11–15.

Stanton, M.D., Shadish, W.R. (1997). Outcome, attrition, and family-couple treatment for drug abuse: A meta-analysis and review of the controlled, comparative studies. *Psychol Bull* 122:170–191.

Steinberg, M.L., Ziedonis, D.M., Krejci, J.A., Brandon, T.H. (2004). Motivational interviewing with personalized feedback: a brief intervention for motivating smokers with schizophrenia to seek treatment for tobacco dependence. *J Consulting Clin Psychol* 72: 723–728.

Winston, A., Winston, B. (2002). *Handbook of Integrated Short-Term Psychotherapy*. Washington, DC, American Psychiatric Publishing, Inc.

Winston, A., Rosenthal, R.N., Roberts, L.W. (2020). *Learning Supportive Psychotherapy, Second Edition*. Washington, DC, American Psychiatric Association Publishing, Inc.

Wang, Q.Q., Kaelber, D.C., Xu, R., Volkow, N.D. (2020). COVID-19 risk and outcomes in patients with substance use disorders: analyses from electronic health records in the United States. *Mol Psychiatry*. https://doi.org/10.1038/s41380-020-00880-7

Yanos, PT, Roe, D, Markus, K, Lysaker, PH (2008). Pathways between internalized stigma and outcomes related to recovery in schizophrenia spectrum disorders. *Psych Svces* 59: 1437–1442.

Women's Mental Health: Core Concepts for Community Psychiatry

Sarah Nagle-Yang, Samantha Latorre, Sarah Quaratella, Riva Shah, Lana Weber, Rebekah Kanefsky, and Caitlin Hasser

Introduction

Women's mental health is a broad term that refers to the biological, psychological, and social aspects of mental health that differentially affect women. Discoveries in women's mental health span biological sex differences pertaining to psychiatric practice, the influence of female reproductive hormone fluctuations on psychiatric conditions, and the impact of societal influences on the mental health of women. The study of women's mental health has grown tremendously over the past four decades in the context of important policy and advocacy efforts within the medical scientific community and resulting mandates on the level of the National Institutes of Health (NIH) for inclusion of women in funded clinical research as well as for analysis of data by sex (Osborne et al. 2015). A sampling of important milestones includes the "postpartum onset specifier," first included in the DSM-IV. This was modified to the "perinatal onset specifier" in the DSM 5, an edition that also first formally acknowledged premenstrual dysphoric disorder (PMDD) as a distinct psychiatric diagnosis (American Psychiatric Association 2013). In 2015, in response to increased knowledge of how to understand potential risks of medications given during pregnancy, the Federal Drug Association (FDA) removed the misleading ABCDX categories and introduced a more comprehensive system to communicate reproductive safety data (Osborne et al. 2015). Finally, 2019 saw the first pharmacologic treatment approved specifically for postpartum depression, brexanolone (Powell et al. 2020).

While a full accounting of the field of women's mental health is beyond the scope of this textbook, this chapter aims to synthesize knowledge most applicable to the care of women living with severe mental illness (SMI) in a practical manner for community psychiatrists. The chapter is divided into two primary subsections. The first subsection covers aspects of women's mental health as they pertain to the reproductive lifespan, including sexual health, contraceptive care, preconception counseling,

S. Nagle-Yang (✉) · S. Quaratella
University of Colorado School of Medicine, Aurora, CO, USA
e-mail: Sarah.nagle-yang@cuanschutz.edu; Sarah.quaratella@cuanschutz.edu

S. Latorre
University of Maryland School of Medicine, Baltimore, MD, USA
e-mail: SLatorre@som.umaryland.edu

R. Shah · L. Weber
Oregon Health & Sciences University, Oregon, USA
e-mail: shahri@ohsu.edu; weberla@ohsu.edu

R. Kanefsky
University of Central Florida, Orlando, FL, USA
e-mail: Rebekah.kanefsky@Knights.ucf.edu

C. Hasser
VA Portland Health Care System, Portland, OR, USA
e-mail: Caitlin.Hasser@va.gov

W. E. Sowers et al. (eds.), *Textbook of Community Psychiatry*,
https://doi.org/10.1007/978-3-031-10239-4_20

perinatal care, and the perimenopause period. Each of these topics represents critical components of health with important considerations for women living with SMI. The second subsection covers three types of violence which disproportionately affect women and have pervasive effects on health: intimate partner violence, sexual assault, and sex trafficking. This section includes guidance on how to identify and respond to these experiences as encountered in clinical care.

A limitation of this chapter is that, while written to address the distinct needs of women within psychiatric treatment, the construct of "women's mental health" will not accurately capture many individuals who may be impacted by the outlined topics. Many people assigned female sex at birth do not identify as women, yet may experience pregnancy or menopause. Likewise, transgender females do not experience the same fluctuations in reproductive hormones as cisgender females. While a strong body of evidence exists to inform the critical need to reduce barriers and improve outcomes for LGBTQ+ individual across all domains of healthcare (Baptiste-Roberts et al. 2017), relatively little is known about the mental health impact of primary reproductive transitions for gender diverse populations (Hutner et al. 2021). While there is considerable momentum within the realm of women's health to move toward more gender-inclusive language (i.e., "reproductive and sexual health" rather than "women's health") (Stroumsa and Wu 2018), the implementation of this important concept has not been well-elucidated in women's mental health, which necessarily includes aspects of "womanhood" which are outside the domain of reproductive health. Nonetheless, it's likely that many of the subjects discussed in this chapter will be relevant to the care of individuals across the gender spectrum. For more information specifically on the clinical care of LGBT+ individuals, the reader may reference chapter "Clinical Issues and Programming for Sexual and Gender Minority Populations".

Women's Mental Health Across the Reproductive Lifespan

Sexual Health

According to the World Health Organization, sexual health "requires a positive and respectful approach to sexuality and sexual relationships, as well as the possibility of having pleasurable and safe sexual experiences, free of coercion, discrimination and violence" (World Health Organization 2021a). Across the female reproductive lifespan, fluctuations in reproductive hormones, psychological symptoms, relationship factors, and psychosocial issues may impact sexual health in critical ways. Furthermore, pharmacologic treatment for psychiatric conditions may impact sexuality. Clinicians often do not inquire about sexual health, yet research demonstrates that patients wish to discuss sexual health with their psychiatrist (Barker and Vigod 2020).

Individuals with serious mental illness (SMI), including schizophrenia, bipolar disorder, and major depressive disorder, have similar sexual needs to the general population, but may present with distinct challenges (Barker and Vigod 2020). For those living with psychotic disorders, positive and negative symptoms, cognitive deficits, and medication side effects impact the capacity for intimate relationships and sexual functioning. Depression and anxiety affect the sexual response at multiple levels, with lower levels of desire and incentives for sexual behavior and diminished capacity for psychological and physical arousal (Basson and Gilks 2018). Individuals with bipolar disorder may engage in higher-risk sexual behaviors during the manic phase (Dell'Osso et al. 2009). Further, sexual trauma has been identified as one of the most potent risk factors for adult sexual dysfunction in the general population, affecting arousal, desire, orgasm, and pain (Bigras et al. 2021).

Treating a woman's sexual dysfunction involves a multimodal approach including ensuring psychiatric stability, using lowest effective doses of agents with limited sexual side effects,

Table 1 Implications for sexual health by medication class

Medication/ class	Mechanism of action	Sexual dysfunction risk	Potential strategies for mitigating risk
SSRIs	Blocks 5HT reuptake	High	Exercise prior to sexual activity Dose reduction Switch to alternative with fewer sexual side effects (vortioxetine, vilazodone, bupropion, mirtazapine, or desvenlafaxine) Augmentation with bupropion, aripiprazole, or vortioxetine
Antipsychotics	Antagonism of D_2 antagonism of $5HT_{2A}$, variable effects at $5HT_{1a}$, a_1, a_2, H_1, M_1	Low-medium	Dose reduction Switch to alternative with fewer sexual side effects such as aripiprazole or quetiapine

Basson and Gilks (2018), de Boer et al. (2015), Keepers et al. (2020)

and optimizing medical comorbidities such as vulvovaginal atrophy, diabetes, obesity, and hypothyroidism (Barker and Vigod 2020). Psychotropic medications often compromise sexual health, resulting in side effects and sexual dysfunction. See Table 1 for a summary of the common sexual implications of major classes of medications.

Contraceptive Care

Contraceptive information and services are a critical component of health. Individuals with psychiatric illness may be at particular risk for inadequate contraception or nonadherence to methods which require daily use, such as oral contraceptive pills (Barker and Vigod 2020). Psychiatrists should be prepared to have informed discussions about contraception with all female patients of reproductive age. This involves engaging patients in discussion of reproductive health goals and preferences, having knowledge of available contraceptive options, and understanding interactions between contraceptives and psychotropic medications.

Approach to Contraceptive Counseling

Providers must consider that women with SMI may have limited knowledge about sexuality and reproduction and carry misperceptions about contraception. The following approaches should be utilized:

- *Timing:* Provide counseling when patients are not acutely experiencing symptoms that would affect their ability to attend to, comprehend, retain, or evaluate the information presented.
- *Presentation:* Present information in a way that is accurate, simple, and clear. Supplement verbal counseling with simple written educational materials.
- *Correct Use:* Emphasize method-specific effectiveness rates, many of which are dependent upon correct use. Explain how psychiatric illness may interfere with correct use of certain contraceptives (i.e., severe mood disorder or psychosis affecting one's ability to take oral contraceptive medication daily or attending regular appointments for a subcutaneous injection).
- *Partners:* Effective use of some methods, like condoms, relies upon partner cooperation and support. Because some women may have difficulties negotiating contraceptive use before or during sex, it is important for providers to screen for intimate partner violence (IPV) and discuss contraceptive methods which do not depend on partner cooperation. Engage partners in contraceptive counseling when appropriate (Guedes et al. 2009).

Contraceptive Methods and Considerations

The Medical Eligibility Criteria for Contraceptive Use developed by the Centers for Disease Control and Prevention is a comprehensive guide which rates contraceptive methods from most effective (Tier 1) to least effective (Tier 3) (Curtis et al. 2016). See Table 2 for a summary of contraceptive methods and ratings.

Psychotropic and Contraceptive Drug Interactions

Pharmacologic interactions between psychotropic drugs and contraceptives exist for hormonal contraceptives (HCs). See Table 3 for a review of said interactions.

Contraceptives and Mood Symptoms

The effect of contraceptives on mood symptoms remains unclear (McCloskey et al. 2021). Data from randomized placebo-controlled trials suggest that women with psychiatric illness who use hormonal contraception have equal or lower rates of mood symptoms compared to non-users (Lundin et al. 2017). However, contraceptive discontinuation rates from perceived mood symptoms have been reported from 14% to 21% (Robinson et al. 2004). It is important to counsel on possible emergence of mood symptoms and discuss options to switch to other effective contraceptive methods (i.e., formulations with lower hormonal dosages or non-hormonal options such as the copper IUD). Drospirenone-containing oral contraceptive pills have been approved by the FDA for the treatment of mood symptoms occurring during premenstrual dysphoric disorder and could be considered for women with mood and anxiety disorders (Lopez et al. 2012). If mood symptoms emerge during particular phases of the menstrual cycle, extended cycle regimen or continuous dosing could be considered (Edelman et al. 2014).

Preconception Counseling

Preconception planning is a critical component of psychiatric care for all women of reproductive age. Approximately 50% of pregnancies are unplanned and women living with SMI are likely to be at increased risk for unintended pregnancy (Barker and Vigod 2020). Pregnancy is likely to introduce additional risk for illness exacerbation, and medications prescribed for the treatment of psychiatric illness may be associated with obstetrical or neonatal risk at the earliest embryonic stages. The concept of preventative ethics, an aim to anticipate and prevent ethical dilemmas in the practice of healthcare, guides the psychiatrist to discuss family planning early in treatment and as a routine component of care during periods of illness stability (Miller 2009).

Psychiatrists should inquire about a patient's obstetrical history, plans for pregnancy, and contraceptive preferences and practices. Patients should be informed about potential risks of the underlying illness during the perinatal period, as well as the potential risks of prescribed medication to have teratogenic effects or increase obstetrical risk.

Impact of Psychiatric Illness on Fertility

While many patients may be concerned about how their psychiatric illness impacts their ability to conceive, current evidence suggests that the fertility rates of women with severe mental illness are equal to or approach that of the general population (Vigod et al. 2012). The exception to this general finding, however, is within the diagnostic domain of eating disorders. Anorexia and bulimia nervosa account for up to 60% of cases of anovulatory infertility (The ESHRE Capri Workshop Group 2006).

Pharmacologic Treatment Planning

Preconception treatment planning is best approached via a "risk-risk" analysis, in which the risks of potential pharmacologic treatments during pregnancy or lactation are weighed in conjunction with the risks of the underlying illness. This approach considers the potential for omission bias, defined as a discussion of the risks of commission (prescribing a medication) without a similar level of detail about the risks of omission (not prescribing a medication). In studies of medical decision-making, omission bias is common and likely to be based on an underlying belief on the part of a physician that introducing a risk is a stronger concern than failing to reduce a risk (Miller 2009).

Table 2 Medical and psychiatric considerations for contraceptives

	Typical use failure rate[a]	Administration	Medical considerations	Potential psychiatric drug interactions	Psychiatric considerations
Tier I					
IUDs[b] Copper Progestin	0.1–0.8%	Replace every 3–10 years	–		Few adherence issues and reversible, preferable for SMI Hormone action is local (with progestin-IUDs); copper IUD is non-hormonal and may be preferable for women who have experience adverse somatic or psychiatric effects with hormonal contraception. Irregular bleeding patterns possible Inconspicuous, preferable for IPV
Progestin subdermal implant[b]	0.1%	Replace every 3 years	–	Not recommended with TCAs, MAOIs, St. John's wort, mood stabilizers, antiepileptics	Few adherence issues and reversible, preferable for SMI Irregular bleeding patterns possible Inconspicuous, preferable for IPV
Permanent methods Female sterilization Vasectomy	0.15–0.5%	N/A – procedural			Present ethical concerns in women with SMI and cognitive impairment, especially in light of psychiatry's disturbing history in the eugenics movement (Roelcke 2019)
Tier II					
Medroxyprogesterone acetate injection	4%	Injection every 3 months	Monitor for weight gain, truncal fat deposit, and peripheral glucose intolerance		Irregular bleeding patterns possible Less invasive than IUDs, may be preferred in cases of cognitive impairment where ethical considerations arise Inconspicuous, preferable for IPV but requires frequent health service visits

(continued)

Table 2 (continued)

	Typical use failure rate[a]	Administration	Medical considerations	Potential psychiatric drug interactions	Psychiatric considerations
Progestin-only oral contraceptives	7%	Daily at the same time	Efficacy reduced with delayed or missed doses	Not recommended with TCAs, MAOIs, St. John's wort, mood stabilizers, antiepileptics	Daily dosing at the same time requires higher level of cognitive functioning
Combined oral contraceptives	7%	Daily	Efficacy reduced with missed doses Not recommended for women <1 month postpartum OR women with cardiovascular risk factors, age >35 years, smokers, and with other estrogen contraindications due to risk of VTE, MI, and stroke	Not recommended with TCAs, MAOIs, St. John's wort; not optimal with mood stabilizers, antiepileptics, may need to monitor drug levels and adjust dosages as necessary if other methods are not feasible Can cause increased drug levels of clozapine	Extended-cycle preparations may be preferable for women with somatic and mood symptoms that are sensitive to hormonal fluctuation Menstrual suppression for hygiene management may be requested by women with disabilities or their caretakers COCs may have therapeutic benefit for hyperprolactinemia Daily dosing requires higher level of cognitive functioning
Transdermal hormonal patch	7%	Weekly replacement			
Vaginal ring	7%	Monthly replacement			
Tier III					
Male condom	13%	Single use	Dual use of condoms plus more effective methods should be routinely encouraged to avoid STI	–	Significant adherence issues, high effort, high user failure rates, and need for partner compliance make these options not optimal as first-line contraceptives Condoms should be encouraged as dual use to protect against STIs Acceptable when all other effective options are not feasible
Female condom	21%	Single use		–	
Sponge, spermicide, diaphragm or cervical cap	14–27%	Variable	–	–	

[a]Estimates are provided of probabilities of failure during typical use (which includes both incorrect and inconsistent use) (Trussell 2011)
[b]IUDs and the progestin subdermal implant are long-acting reversible contraceptives (LARC)
Curtis et al. (2016)

Table 3 Psychotropic and contraceptive drug interactions

Effect of HCs on psychotropics
• *Clozapine concentrations* ***increase*** *when combined with HCs* because of reduced activity of hepatic CYP P450 1A2, 2C19, and 34A enzymes. Clozapine doses must parallel the contraceptive regimen and be reduced in the active hormone phase, during which clozapine plasma concentration may increase 2–3× compared to the non-hormonal phase (Bookholt and Bogers 2014). Intrauterine devices, subdermal implant, and depot-medroxyprogesterone acetate are preferred, as these do not undergo the first-pass hepatic metabolism of HCs.
• *Lamotrigine concentrations* ***decrease*** *when combined with HCs* as ethinyl estradiol is a potent inducer of the uridine diphosphate glucuronosyltransferase (UGT) system. Clinicians should consider an increase in the maintenance dose of lamotrigine prior to initiation of a combined oral contraceptive (OCP), with further increases if clinically indicated. A baseline serum level of lamotrigine obtained prior to OCP therapy can provide a useful baseline for comparison later (Christensen et al. 2007; Reddy 2010).
• *Valproic acid concentrations* ***decrease*** *when combined with HCs* in a similar mechanism to lamotrigine. Additionally, ethinyl estradiol increases clearance of valproic acid (Herzog et al. 2009). Without dose adjustment, this may lead to decreased mood stability. Valproic acid is generally not recommended for women of childbearing age unless combined with a high-efficacy long-acting reversible contraceptive (LARC) due to risk of teratogenicity and neurodevelopmental effects (Meador et al. 2009; Weston et al. 2016).
Effect of psychotropics on HCs
• *Carbamazepine* ***reduces*** *HC efficacy* by increasing the production of sex-hormone-binding globulin, which tightly binds and reduces the concentration of free progestin (Dutton and Foldvary-Schaefer 2008). Intrauterine devices and depot-medroxyprogesterone acetate are preferred.
• *Carbamazepine, oxcarbazepine, and St. John's wort* ***reduce*** *HC efficacy* by inducing the CYP3A4 system, which increases the clearance of contraceptive steroids (including progestin) (Berry-Bibee et al. 2016; Davis et al. 2011; Hlengwa et al. 2020). Intrauterine devices and depot-medroxyprogesterone acetate are preferred.
• *Lamotrigine* ***reduces*** *the blood concentration of progestin by approximately 20% in women taking HC;* however it has not been shown to reduce HC efficacy (Sidhu et al. 2006). Intrauterine devices and depot-medroxyprogesterone acetate may be preferred.

Risks of untreated psychiatric illness vary broadly by illness and severity, but generally include impaired functioning, risk of suicide and hospitalization, poor prenatal care, increased substance use, preterm birth, postpartum depression or psychosis, and problems with attachment (Fitelson et al. 2021). Understanding associated risk for illness recurrence or exacerbation during pregnancy and in the postpartum period for specific psychiatric conditions is critical. In the setting of long-standing mental illness and treatments, clinicians should carefully review all aspects of the patient's history to confirm current diagnoses and indicated treatments, particularly in the setting of traumatic experiences or substance use. Important considerations when evaluating risk of untreated psychiatric illness include the severity of a patient's previous illness episodes, degree of recurrence in her illness history, level of psychosocial and familial support, degree of insight into symptoms, and access to medical and psychiatric care (Fitelson et al. 2021).

In considering the risks of the medication, clinicians must consider several questions. The first is, "What is likely to work for this patient?" Introducing a medication that has a high level of reproductive safety is not helpful if it doesn't allow the patient to achieve or maintain illness stability. Once medications with likely efficacy are identified, one must consider the overall level of data ("how much is known"), as well as "what is known" about its associated risk of teratogenicity, spontaneous abortion, obstetrical complications, neonatal complications, and adverse developmental outcomes. Consideration of safety in lactation should be considered from the start to avoid the need to switch medications during a high-risk period. Purposefully selected medications should be utilized at the lowest effective dose and, when possible, polypharmacy should be avoided. These principles are summarized in Table 4. Ultimately, the goal is to develop a treatment plan that best balances risk with efficacy. By including the patient, her family, and her treatment team in discussions about treatment planning, providers can minimize miscommuni-

Table 4 General tenets perinatal psychiatry

Inquire about reproductive goals and contraceptive preferences as a component of routine care
Engage in preconception counseling with the goal of a treatment plan that best balances risk with efficacy
Confirm accuracy of historical diagnoses and indications for treatment
Engage patient in a risk-risk discussion which includes the risk of untreated/undertreated psychiatric illness vs. the risk of indicated medication
Consider risks associated with specific diagnoses
Consider severity of illness
Maximize non-pharmacologic treatments
Prioritize sleep
Consider the level of data when interpreting risk of medication
Utilize the lowest *effective* dose
Avoid polypharmacy when possible

cation and maximize the patient's treatment outcomes (Chisolm and Payne 2016).

It is important to note that a risk-risk analysis will almost always reveal elevated risk on both sides of the equation as treatment of illness during pregnancy is necessarily a situation with elevated risk. At times, this may lead to the false sense on either the part of the patient or the clinician that the well-being of the mother is at odds with the well-being of a developing fetus. In these circumstances, a helpful ethical construct to consider is that of relational ethics—the perspective that a mother's well-being and her baby's well-being are intertwined. Having a healthy and functioning mother is beneficial both for the developing fetus and future children; likewise a positive birth outcome, and a sense of security about the overall health and development of a child, is beneficial for mothers (Miller 2009).

Perinatal Psychiatry

As optimizing the treatment plan for women with psychiatric illness during the perinatal period is best accomplished in the preconception period, the general tenets of perinatal psychiatry are discussed in the preceding section. However, practically speaking, psychiatrists are likely to find themselves in the situation where a patient is seeking advice about the optimal treatment plan once already pregnant. In these instances, there are additional factors to consider. A patient currently taking an effective medication may inquire about switching to a medication that is "safer" in pregnancy. However, switching medication during pregnancy may potentially increase reproductive risk by increasing the number of exposures during a pregnancy as well as increasing the risk for recurrence of illness (Chisolm and Payne 2016). In this context, consideration should be given to continuing an effective medication that the patient has already taken during this pregnancy. The timing of reproductive risk should also be considered in the context of the patient's pregnancy. Switching a medication based on teratogenic risk would not be an effective strategy once organogenesis is complete.

Breastfeeding is associated with multiple well-established benefits for both mother and infant; thus many women prefer to breastfeed. Psychiatrists should discuss infant feeding preferences with patients early in the process of preconception planning or treatment during pregnancy. Considerations in this discussion should include the benefits of breastfeeding as well as the potential risks due to her underlying illness or indicated medications. Strategies to effectively prioritize sleep in the setting of breastfeeding are critical and may include entailing support persons to bring the infant to breastfeed during the night while attending to other aspects of infant nighttime care (changing diapers, settling back to sleep, etc.) (Nagle-Yang et al. 2021a). Women with very limited supports or severe symptoms may not be able to safely breastfeed. Likewise, in some instances, the risks of indicated medications or underlying illness outweigh the benefits of breastfeeding. Providing support to women in navigating this complex decision may be a powerful intervention at a stressful time. Finally, regardless of how a woman chooses to feed her infant, psychiatrists should exercise caution in prescribing sedating medications to a patient caring for a young infant. When such medications are required, psychiatrists should recommend additional supports during nighttime feedings and provide guidance on safe sleep practices, as sedating medications are known to further increase the risk for sudden infant death syndrome associated with parent-infant bed sharing (Task Force on Sudden Infant Death Syndrome 2016).

The field of perinatal psychiatry has grown tremendously over the past few decades and has translated to increased knowledge of the phenomenology of psychiatric illness as well as associated risks. While a full accounting of this field is beyond the scope of this chapter, a summary of diagnoses and treatments most relevant to community psychiatrists is provided below.

Schizophrenia

Prognosis in Perinatal Period

Current data suggests that pregnancy is not protective for women with schizophrenia. Preconception illness severity and choices surrounding medication management are correlated with risk of relapse. The postpartum period is a high-risk period with increased risk for hospitalization throughout the first 6 postpartum months (Taylor et al. 2018).

Risks of Not Treating

Women with schizophrenia are at increased risk for obstetric complications including antepartum hemorrhage, low birth weight, placental abruption, intrauterine growth restriction, and preterm delivery (Tosato et al. 2017). These risks are likely multifactorial in etiology, and associations are confounded by higher rates of medical comorbidities and substance use and lower rates of prenatal care among women with this illness (Møller-Olsen et al. 2018). Of note, one study found that controlling for various maternal factors reduced differences in adverse pregnancy outcomes between women with and without schizophrenia; however those with an acute episode of psychosis during pregnancy remained at elevated risk even after these adjustments (Nilsson et al. 2002).

Medication Treatments

- *Oral antipsychotics*: Increasing data on second-generation antipsychotics (SGAs) is largely reassuring and does not support a significant association with congenital malformations, although one study did find a slight increase in cardiac malformations with risperidone specifically (Nagle-Yang et al. 2021b). Patients taking SGAs during pregnancy should be monitored for gestational diabetes, excessive maternal weight gain, and abnormalities in fetal growth (Park et al. 2018). While quetiapine is often preferred due to low placental passage rate and low breast milk transmission, caution should be exercised in breastfeeding due to potential sedating qualities (Nagle-Yang et al. 2021b). Newer medications (i.e., lurasidone) should be avoided in pregnancy when possible due to overall lack of data. Among first-generation antipsychotics, haloperidol has the highest level of data, and available data suggest this medication is not a major teratogen (Einarson and Boskovic 2009). Use of first-generation antipsychotics during late pregnancy has been associated with transient extrapyramidal symptoms in exposed neonates (Kulkarni et al. 2014).
- *Clozapine*: Clozapine merits special consideration given its role in treatment of schizophrenia in treatment-resistant cases or instances where alternate medication side effects of intolerable (Warnez and Alessi-Severini 2014). A recent review article by Mehta and Van Lieshout (2017) discussed the limitations of evaluating the safety of clozapine during pregnancy, including difficulty establishing a control group, lack of ability to control for comorbidities, and the role of polypharmacy. Thus, careful consideration of risks and benefits of treatment must be considered in the treatment of pregnancy patients. Based on review of approximately 200 case reports, Larsen et al. (2015) report there is no clear pattern of congenital malformations identified (Larsen et al. 2015). Clozapine is often considered a contraindication to breastfeeding due to high concentration in breast milk and risk for agranulocytosis in infants (Mehta and Van Lieshout 2017).
- *Long-acting injectable antipsychotics*: While the benefits of long-acting injectable (LAI)

antipsychotics are well established, there is a paucity of literature on the reproductive safety profile during pregnancy (Orsolini et al. 2021). Available data is limited to case reports on individual long-acting agents, which have not reported associated malformations (Ballester-Gracia et al. 2019). Some, but not all, case reports have reported adverse obstetrical or neonatal outcomes (Clinebell et al. 2017). These case reports are difficult to interpret due concurrent polypharmacy or missing information regarding potential confounding factors. While the weak level of data for LAI antipsychotics suggests that a switch to oral formulations in anticipation of pregnancy may be indicated, psychiatrists must consider the individual patient's treatment history, disease course, and previous medication trials. In the setting of a patient with a history of nonadherence to oral medication and a severe disease course, continuing an LAI antipsychotic as a component of a comprehensive treatment plan may be the strategy that best balances the risk of the underlying illness vs. the risk of the indicated medication. As LAIs bypass first-pass hepatic metabolism, it is theorized that they are less effected by pharmacokinetic changes of pregnancy and may offer more stable blood levels as pregnancy progresses (Nagle-Yang et al. 2021b).

Depression

Prognosis in Perinatal Period

Perinatal depression is the most common complication of childbirth and affects 15–20% new mothers (Osborne and Birndorf 2021). For women with a history of major depressive disorder, pregnancy is not protective against recurrence, and the postpartum period can be particularly high risk (Osborne and Birndorf 2021). Discontinuing previously effective maintenance medication increases the likelihood of illness relapse (Cohen et al. 2006).

Of note, the DSM 5 provides a "peripartum onset" specifier that can be applied to depressive, manic, or hypomanic episodes with onset during pregnancy or within 4 weeks postpartum (Sharma and Mazmanian 2014). However, this time association remains controversial with evidence suggesting that mothers remain vulnerable to postpartum mental illness several months after delivery (Munk-Olsen et al. 2006a; Munk-Olsen et al. 2006b).

Risks of Not Treating

Left untreated, perinatal depression can have a pervasive impact on the health of the mother and her child. Depression during pregnancy is associated with adverse obstetrical outcomes such as preterm birth, low birth weight, operative delivery, and preeclampsia (Henshaw 2009). Depression during pregnancy also predicts postpartum depression, with well-established impact on parenting practices, infant and child development, and the mother-child relationship (McLearn et al. 2006).

Medication

SSRIs as a class have a high level of data to inform reproductive safety. Current data do not support associations with congenital malformations, although there is some mixed information specifically around paroxetine and cardiovascular malformations (Yonkers et al. 2014). SSRIs do show associations with a small increased risk for preterm delivery (as does untreated depression) and persistent pulmonary hypertension of the newborn (PPHN) (Grigoriadis et al. 2014). When used in the second half of pregnancy, they are associated with an increased risk for neonatal adaptation syndrome (Byatt et al. 2013). While sertraline is often considered first-line in the perinatal period due to the level of data available and its low breast milk transmission, all SSRIs are considered compatible with breastfeeding (Stewart and Vigod 2019).

Bipolar Disorder

Prognosis in Perinatal Period

Current research suggests pregnancy is not protective for women with bipolar disorder, and the postpartum period is particularly high risk (Di Florio et al. 2018). Women with bipolar disorder are 7x as likely to experience a first-time psychiatric admission and twice as likely to experience a psychiatric re-admission, for affective psychosis in the first postpartum month relative to postpartum healthy controls (Terp and Mortensen 1998). Data indicates that there is two times the risk of relapse in women who discontinue mood stabilizing medication during pregnancy compared to women who continued treatment (Viguera et al. 2007). Postpartum psychosis is a rare but serious condition that typically presents as a psychiatric emergency. While postpartum psychosis may occur outside of the setting of bipolar disorder, a personal or family history of bipolar disorder is one of the strongest risk factors for postpartum psychosis (Wesseloo et al. 2016).

Risks of Not Treating

Women with bipolar disorder are at increased risk for a variety of obstetrical and neonatal adverse outcomes including preeclampsia, placental abnormalities, intrauterine growth restriction, low birth weight, preterm birth, and small for gestational age infant and neonatal hypoglycemia (Nagle-Yang et al. 2021a). As in the setting of maternal schizophrenia, studies examining outcomes among women with bipolar are often confounded by higher rates of substance use and obesity and decreased rates of prenatal care among women with bipolar disorder relative to the general population.

Mood Stabilizers in Pregnancy

- *Lithium*: Associations between lithium and cardiac malformations, most notably Epstein's malformation, have been reported since the 1970s. However, beginning in the 1990s epidemiologic studies suggested that the initial reports of risk were likely overestimations (Cohen et al. 1994). In recent years, several large-scale studies have dramatically increased knowledge on this topic and suggest that while lithium may have an association with cardiac or overall malformations, this risk is occurring at rates much lower than previously suggested and may be dose-dependent (with stronger associations at doses at or greater than 900 mg/day) (Fornaro et al. 2020). As lithium is a highly effective treatment option for bipolar disorder, with increasing data to support its use for preventing postpartum mood episodes and postpartum psychosis in women with bipolar disorder, it is currently considered a viable option during the perinatal period for women when indicated.

- Physiologic changes in pregnancy which affect the pharmacokinetics of lithium include increased total body water content and increased glomerular filtration rate (GFR) (Pariente et al. 2016). Given the renal clearance of lithium (Oruch et al. 2014), changes in GFR can decrease lithium blood levels, making frequent serum monitoring important in assessing for adequate dosing and/or toxicity (Deligiannidis et al. 2014). Expert recommendations for lithium monitoring during the perinatal period are summarized in Fig. 1.
- *Lamotrigine*: Lamotrigine has a high level of largely reassuring data to inform reproductive risk (Nagle-Yang et al. 2021a). Thus, it is often considered a first-line approach to treatment of bipolar disorder in the perinatal period, particularly for women who have experienced a preponderance of depressive episodes. While earlier research by Holmes et al. (2008) of infants exposed to lamotrigine in the first trimester identified a small elevated risk of oral cleft palate or lip, a more recent large study incorporating data from over 10 million births did not identify an increased risk of cleft palate or overall malformation in infants with in utero exposure to lamotrigine (Dolk et al. 2016), and several international registries have reported no increase in risk for malformations with lamotrigine (Tomson et al. 2018).
- Increasing estrogen levels during pregnancy accelerate the metabolism of lamotrigine which correlates to decreased serum concentration of the medication (Clark et al. 2013). As there is not a clear consensus on the therapeutic level of lamotrigine for treatment of bipolar disorder, it is recommended to obtain a preconception therapeutic level in patients stabilized on lamotrigine. During pregnancy, some experts recommend monitoring monthly

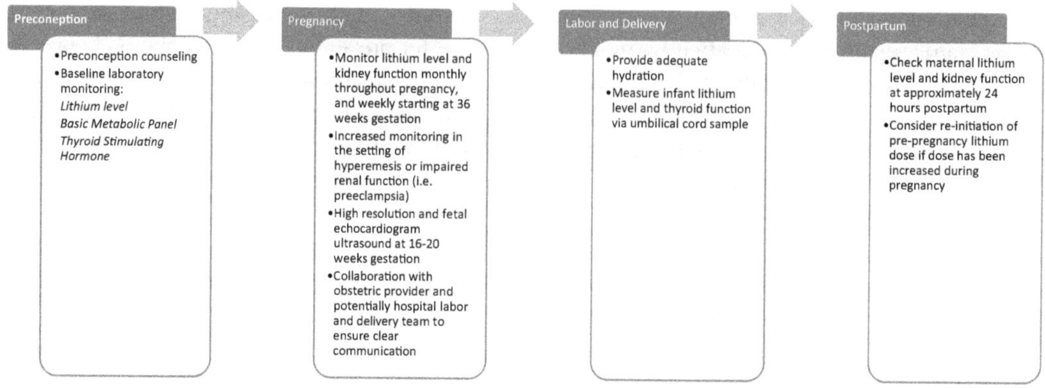

Fig. 1 Recommendations for lithium monitoring during the perinatal period (Nagle-Yang et al. 2021a; Wesseloo et al. 2017)

lamotrigine serum levels and, if clinically indicated, increasing the dose to maintain the patient's baseline therapeutic level (Clark et al. 2013). If the dose is increased during pregnancy, decreasing the dose by 25% after delivery is recommended to avoid toxicity, with subsequent decreases every 3–4 days until the patient is at preconception therapeutic dose (Clark and Wisner 2018).

- *Valproate*: Valproate is considered a human teratogen with a 10% overall risk of major malformations and clear association with adverse developmental outcomes in children exposed in utero including reduced IQ, autism spectrum disorders, impaired verbal acquisition, and behavioral disturbances (Wieck and Jones 2018). Psychiatrists should avoid use of valproate in women of reproductive age. If valproate is necessary for treatment of bipolar disorder that has been refractory to other treatment options, counseling on these risks and providing guidance on highly-effective contraception is recommended (Khan et al. 2016).

Parenting While Living with SMI

Recent data suggest that women living with SMI are as likely as women in the general population to become pregnant, and most will experience motherhood (Vigod et al. 2012). Motherhood is a normative experience of adulthood and one that, for most, is a central component of identity and purpose. For women living with severe mental illness, the role of motherhood may provide an increased sense of self-competence, meaning, and hopefulness or has the potential to reinforce feelings of stigma and shame (Hine et al. 2018). Despite the central role of parenthood in one's identity and connection to community, to date the experience of parenthood as a component of the mental health recovery model hasn't been well elucidated (Hine et al. 2018).

While many women living with SMI can successfully parent, mental illness is likely to have far-reaching impacts across domains of functioning, and as a group women with SMI demonstrate significant parenting challenges. Women with schizophrenia are more likely than healthy controls to display a passive or withdrawn parenting style, show interactional deficits with their infants, and lack knowledge of child development (Nagle-Yang et al. 2021b). Depressed mothers, relative to non-depressed mothers, are less likely to routinely talk with their child or adopt other age-appropriate safety and developmental practices such as using electric outlet covers, establishing daily routines, or limiting screen time (McLearn et al. 2006). Women who are experiencing sequelae of trauma may struggle with boundary distortions, difficulty with emotional regulation during parenting interactions, and diminished parenting supports (Noll et al. 2009). While there is a paucity of data regarding the parenting practices of mothers with bipolar disorder, children of parents with bipolar disorder are well-understood be at increased risk for mood disorders themselves (Axelson et al. 2015).

This risk is likely multifactorial and includes both genetic and environmental factors. Of note, families which include a parent with BD have been found to have lower levels of family cohesion and expressiveness and higher levels of conflict (Belardinelli et al. 2008).

When considering the care of mothers living with SMI, it is important to note that the rate of custody loss is high. Among women with mental illness, women with schizophrenia are at highest risk (Howard et al. 2003). Approximately half of women with this diagnosis will experience a period of custody loss, and fear of custody loss is a common experience in this population (Seeman 2012). Nonetheless, most women with SMI will raise or help to raise at least one child (Nicholson et al. 1998).

Support for parenting is a critical component of a comprehensive treatment plan for pregnant individuals and parents living with SMI. On the individual level, clinicians should acknowledge the centrality of the parenting role, even in situations in which a patient is not currently the primary parent. Positive, strength-based language balanced with acknowledgment of parenting challenges can move care toward a more person- and family-centered model (Hine et al. 2018). Parents living with SMI should be informed about psychiatric advanced directives as a potential mechanism to plan for childcare in the event of an acute illness episode (Atkinson et al. 2004). A focus on building family and community supports is vital to increasing protective factors (Abel et al. 2005). Of note, in a study of structured interviews completed with women living with SMI, participants identified several ideas to improve services for mentally ill mothers, including greater availability of parenting support workers, support groups for mentally ill mothers, childcare facilities within mental health treatment centers, dedicated space within psychiatric hospitals for visits with children, and the availability of respite centers for periods of intense treatment needs (Diaz-Caneja and Johnson 2004).

There is also emerging evidence to support parenting interventions directly offered within psychiatric or general health settings. Let's Talk About Children is an intervention designed to be implemented in adult mental health settings and has shown improvement in child, parent, and family well-being, as well as a reduction in referrals to child protective services (Allchin et al. 2020). While not studied specifically with parents with SMI, other evidence-based programs have integrated mother-infant treatment into home visiting programs and group-based parenting programs (Muzik et al. 2015; Renshaw and Wrigley 2015).

Perimenopause

What Is Perimenopause and Menopause?

The menopause transition, or perimenopause, typically begins in a woman's mid-40s and is defined as persistent variability in menstrual cycle length (Santoro et al. 2021). Female reproductive hormones fluctuate greatly, and menopausal symptoms are most intense during this period (Harlow et al. 2012). After 12 consecutive months of amenorrhea, a woman has officially entered menopause, the ovaries no longer produce estrogen, and there are no longer significant variations in hormone levels (Harlow et al. 2012). The average age of menopause is 51 years (ACOG 2018). Common menopausal symptoms include vasomotor symptoms, sexual complaints, insomnia, vaginal dryness, urinary changes, mood changes, and cognitive complaints (Santoro et al. 2015).

Depression During Perimenopause

Perimenopause is a period of increased risk for the development or recurrence of major depressive episodes. While women with a prior history of major depressive disorder are at highest risk for perimenopausal depression, women without any history of depression are two to four times as likely to develop depressive symptoms during perimenopause as compared to premenopausal periods (Gibbs and Kulkarni 2014). Depressive symptoms differ slightly during this period with more prominent irritability, anhedonia, and increased mood lability (Gibbs and Kulkarni

2014). Other more frequently reported symptoms include insomnia, impaired concentration, and memory complaints (Bromberger et al. 2007). As symptoms of depression can overlap with symptoms of menopause, the diagnosis of depression in this period can prove challenging.

As vasomotor symptoms are often a source of distress during this period, advising patients to speak with an ob-gyn about hormone therapy may also be appropriate. Of note, limited evidence suggests that estrogen therapy has antidepressant properties when utilized in perimenopausal, depressed women (Soares 2017). While not recommended as primary treatment of severe or recurrent depression, some experts recommend that women with mild depression and bothersome vasomotor symptoms may benefit from a brief trial of estrogen prior to determining need for antidepressant treatment (Soares 2017).

The first-line treatment for perimenopausal depression is pharmacotherapy with an antidepressant medication (Maki et al. 2018). While desvenlafaxine is the only antidepressant to be studied in large-scale RCTs in peri- or postmenopausal women with depression, available evidence supports the use of SSRIs, SNRIs, and vortioxetine for treatment of depression in the menopause transition (Maki et al. 2018, 2019). While not well-studied in perimenopausal women, bupropion and vortioxetine are sometimes preferred due to a reduced potential for weight gain and sexual side effects and positive effects on cognition (Freeman et al. 2017). Selection of medication can also be guided by the presence of comorbid VMS. In one study, paroxetine followed by venlafaxine and then by fluoxetine have been shown to have the greatest reduction in VMS between 45% and 63% (Joffe et al. 2003), and more recent data supports vortioxetine for reduction in VMS on a similar scale (Freeman et al. 2017). Gabapentin and clonidine have also been shown to help reduce vasomotor symptoms by 54% and 20–37%, respectively (Joffe et al. 2003), so they may be useful for women with comorbid anxiety symptoms. Of note, the efficacy of antidepressants in the treatment of VMS occurs at the lower end of the dose range for what is typical for treatment of depression, so titrating to a dose that adequately treats depression is likely to be effective for VMS as well (Santoro et al. 2015).

Perimenopause and Women Living with Severe Mental Illness (SMI)

While it is well-established that women with a history of recurrent depression are at high risk for recurrence during perimenopause, recent evidence also suggests women with bipolar disorder are at increased risk for perimenopausal depression (Marsh et al. 2015). The estrogen hypothesis of schizophrenia has been discussed since the 1990s and posits that estrogen is protective against psychosis and that psychosis itself can influence hormones and disrupt the function of the hypothalamic-pituitary-gonadal (HPG) axis (Riecher-Rössler and Häfner 1993). From a clinical perspective, significant changes in the phenomenology of the illness among women in mid-life coincide with the menopause transition and lend support for the estrogen hypothesis. Women experience a second peak of onset for schizophrenia in midlife, with twice as many women developing the disease after the age of 40 relative to men (Riecher-Rössler et al. 2018). Women with an established diagnosis of schizophrenia are also at risk for a worsening of psychotic symptoms, longer hospital admission, and a need for higher doses of antipsychotics later in life (Brzezinski et al. 2017).

Gender-Linked Violence

Intimate Partner Violence

An estimated 30% of women worldwide over the age of 15 have experienced physical and/or sexual intimate partner violence (IPV) in their lifetime (Devries et al. 2013). Prevalence of IPV is estimated to be as high as 50% in pregnant women and women living with SMI (Hellmuth et al. 2013). It is the leading cause of homicide globally. For women, IPV carries several detrimental short- and long-term health sequelae, including depression, anxiety, PTSD, suicidal behaviors, substance use disorder, detrimental pregnancy outcomes (i.e., low birth weight, miscarriage), economic hardship, and housing instability (Bacchus et al. 2018).

IPV includes physical violence, sexual violence, stalking behaviors, and psychological aggression by current or former partners. The cycle of IPV has been described as a pattern that begins with exerting control over the partner's activities which builds to an episode of violence (Beck 2016). A period of contrition and reconciliation follows the violence and defuses the tension, which produces hope in the person experiencing the violence and deters them from leaving. Violence may escalate over time and can involve coercive and threatening measures to keep the individual in the relationship or prohibit them from leaving. Other barriers to leaving the violent relationship include financial dependence, houselessness, childcare concerns, shame and guilt, real or perceived danger to self and children, isolation and lack of support, and past unsuccessful attempts at leaving.

The US Preventative Services Task Force (USPSTF) recommends that women of reproductive age be screened for IPV (Beck 2016). Reporting requirements vary by state, and clinicians should familiarize themselves with the laws in the areas in which they work. Evidence suggests that open, general survey questions, such as, "Have you been hit, kicked, punched, or otherwise hurt by someone within the past year? If so, by whom?" can appropriately identify up to 70% of women experiencing IPV (Beck 2016). The HITS screening tool (see Fig. 2) is well-established and demonstrates high sensitivity (30–100% with lower end of range for men) and specificity (86–99%) (Rabin et al. 2009). It is important to empathically provide an assessment without judgment, document carefully, and reinforce that the individual does not deserve the behavior and is not responsible for the violence (Beck 2016). Interventions for IPV include referral to appropriate resources (i.e., hotlines, shelter, financial, legal services) and establishing a plan for safety inclusive of barriers for leaving and regular follow-up. Clinicians are best equipped to understand risk and tailor treatment planning by learning nuanced aspects of the range of behaviors. Risks for lethality include use or presence of weapons, strangulation attempts, and attempts to leave the relationship. It is advised that psychiatrists avoid prescribing sedating medications (i.e., benzodiazepines, sedative-hypnotics) that would impair an individual's ability to act quickly to protect themselves (Beck 2016).

How often does your partner:

1. Physically hurt you?
2. Insult you or talk down to you?
3. Threaten you with harm?
4. Scream or curse at you?

Fig. 2 HITS screening tool. Scores are on a 5-point Likert scale: (1) never, (2) rarely, (3) sometimes, (4) fairly often, (5) frequently. Scores of >10.5 are positive. (Rabin et al. 2009)

Sexual Assault

Sexual assault is an umbrella term which encompasses multiple types of unwanted sexual contact such as rape, attempted rape, sexual touching, and forced oral sex (RAINN n.d.). Approximately 7.2% of women across the globe have experienced unwanted sexual contact (perpetrated by a non-partner) in their lifetime (Abrahams et al. 2014). A report by the World Health Organization found that 26% of women have experienced sexual violence by an intimate partner in their lifetime (WHO 2021b). Although sexual assault can be perpetrated by anyone, the majority of sexual assault is perpetrated by an individual known to the victim (Riggs et al. 2000).

Experiencing a sexual assault can have substantial impact on one's health. Survivors may develop posttraumatic stress disorder (PTSD), substance abuse, depression, and anxiety in the aftermath of sexual victimization (Ullman et al. 2013). Additionally, surviving a sexual assault is associated with an increased risk of developing a variety of psychopathologies including suicidality and disordered eating (Dworkin 2020).

Routine screening for sexual assault is recommended by the American College of Obstetricians and Gynecologists (Committee on Health Care for Underserved Women 2019). Barriers to disclosing sexual assault to clinicians include fear of being judged or blamed, perceived negative attitude of the provider, and lack of privacy. Conversely, factors that encourage disclosure of sexual assault include medical necessity of the disclosure, the positive attitude of the provider, perceived knowledge of the provider, and whether the provider directly queries about unwanted sexual experiences (Ahrens et al. 2009). Screening for sexual assault is crucial for clinicians to identify survivors and proceed with appropriate physical and mental health intervention or referral.

Sex Trafficking

The United Nations (UN) describes human trafficking as the recruitment and potential movement of vulnerable people using violence, deception, and/or threats for the purpose of exploitation (United Nations Office on Drugs and Crime 2000). The UN has reported that most human trafficking victims are women. Among more than 12,000 adult female victims of human trafficking, 77% were trafficked for sexual exploitation (United Nations Office on Drugs and Crime 2021).

Among sex trafficking victims, mental health concerns are prevalent. Approximately 37% of survivors have PTSD, 52% have depression, and 78% have clinically significant anxiety (Oram et al. 2012). Sex trafficking victims may also exhibit aggression, social withdrawal, decreased self-esteem, and substance misuse (Simkhada et al. 2018). Perpetrators can utilize drugs to maintain control over their victims, and most survivors utilize substances while being trafficked (Lederer and Wetzel 2014).

Victims of sex trafficking may present to healthcare facilities with a myriad of physical health issues that may have been a direct result of victimization (i.e., headaches, fatigue, abdominal or back pain) (Zimmerman et al. 2003). Additionally, sexual abuse experienced within the context of human trafficking has many implications for women's reproductive and gynecologic health. Survivors may face concerns such as sexually transmitted infections, unsafe abortions, and infertility (Zimmerman et al. 2003, 2008). Multiple studies of sex trafficked women have found a high prevalence of HIV and other STIs (Wirth et al. 2013). When sex trafficking victims visit healthcare facilities for treatment of physical health concerns, the opportunity for clinicians to provide social resources and mental health services appears. Figure 3 outlines red flags that may indicate a victim of sex trafficking within a healthcare encounter. Recommended strategies for examining sex trafficking victims include separating the victim from the individual who has accompanied them, communicating with the victim directly, and using questions designed to ask about the victim's safety without using words that could upset the victim (i.e., "Do the people you live with treat you with kindness?") (Chesnay 2013). Not all victims will be receptive to help escaping from the sex trafficking environment due to fear for their own safety, for the safety of

Fig. 3 Red flags that indicate a potential victim of sex trafficking (Shandro et al. 2016)

1) The individual accompanying the patient may appear reluctant to leave the patient alone with healthcare professionals.

2) The patient has an inconsistent medical history and/or medical history that does not match presenting complaints.

3) Patients may be irritable or anxious, demonstrate flat affect, or have difficulty making eye contact.

4) Patients may not know their home address or not be in possession of their own identification cards.

others, or distorted loyalty to perpetrators (Myths, Facts, and Statistics I Polaris 2018).

Conclusion

Women's mental health is a robust area of psychiatry that has emerged in recent decades. Given significant sex differences apparent in the phenomenology of psychiatric disorders and the impact of reproductive hormone transitions on psychiatric care, women's mental health is an area of importance to community psychiatry. Women living with SMI are likely to have unique needs around sexual health and contraceptive counseling, and most will become pregnant and engage in motherhood. Community psychiatrists, experts in person- and family-centered care, are well-positioned to take a primary role in the healthcare of women through these major reproductive events. Essential skills include providing psychoeducation on contraceptive options in the context of psychiatric care, engaging in preconception counseling as a component of routine care, and assisting the patient in a collaborative discussion weighing the risks of underlying disease against the risks of indicated treatment during pregnancy and lactation. Further, as trusted members of a patient's healthcare team, community psychiatrists are ideally situated to consider the impact of gender-linked trauma in the biopsychosocial formulation of illness. Routine and purposeful screening for traumatic events within psychiatric care can create a safe space for women to disclose IPV or sexual assault and allow clinicians to provide a more wholistic treatment plan that considers critical safety supports as well as psychosocial treatments. Finally, as victims of sex trafficking face many barriers to disclosing their abuse, community psychiatrists should be aware of red flags that indicate an individual is being trafficked, be comfortable with methods to sensitively screen potential victims, and provide care in a trauma-informed manner.

References

Abel, K. M., Webb, R. T., Salmon, M. P., Wan, M. W., & Appleby, L. (2005). Prevalence and predictors of parenting outcomes in a cohort of mothers with schizophrenia admitted for joint mother and baby psychiatric care in England. *J Clin Psychiatry*, *66*(6), 781–789.

Abrahams, N., Devries, K., Watts, C., Pallitto, C., Petzold, M., Shamu, S., & García-Moreno, C. (2014). Worldwide prevalence of non-partner sexual violence: A systematic review. *The Lancet*, *383*(9929), 1648–1654. https://doi.org/10.1016/S0140-6736(13)62243-6

ACOG. (2018). *The Menopause Years*. https://www.acog.org/womens-health/faqs/the-menopause-years

Ahrens, C. E., Cabral, G., & Abeling, S. (2009). Healing or Hurtful: Sexual Assault Survivors' Interpretations of Social Reactions from Support Providers. *Psychology of Women Quarterly*, *33*(1), 81–94. https://doi.org/10.1111/j.1471-6402.2008.01476.x

Allchin, B., O'Hanlon, B., Weimand, B. M., & Goodyear, M. (2020). Practitioners' application of Let's Talk about Children intervention in adult mental health services. *International Journal of Mental Health Nursing*, *29*(5), 899–907.

American Psychiatric Association (Ed.). (2013). *Diagnostic and statistical manual of mentaldisorders: –5*. American Psychiatric Association.

Atkinson, J. M., Garner, H. C., & Gilmour, W. H. (2004). Models of advance directives in mental health care. *Social Psychiatry and Psychiatric Epidemiology*, *39*(8), 673–680.

Axelson, D., Goldstein, B., Goldstein, T., Monk, K., Yu, H., Hickey, M. B., Sakolsky, D., Diler, R., Hafeman, D., & Merranko, J. (2015). Diagnostic precursors to bipolar disorder in offspring of parents with bipolar disorder: A longitudinal study. *American Journal of Psychiatry*, *172*(7), 638–646.

Bacchus, L. J., Ranganathan, M., Watts, C., & Devries, K. (2018). Recent intimate partner violence against women and health: A systematic review and meta-analysis of cohort studies. *BMJ Open*, *8*(7), e019995.

Ballester-Gracia, I., Pérez-Almarcha, M., Galvez-Llompart, A., & Hernandez-Viadel, M. (2019). Use of long-acting injectable aripiprazole before and through pregnancy in bipolar disorder: A case report. *BMC Pharmacology and Toxicology*, *20*(1), 1–4.

Baptiste-Roberts, K., Oranuba, E., Werts, N., & Edwards, L. V. (2017). Addressing Health Care Disparities Among Sexual Minorities. *Obstetrics and Gynecology Clinics of North America*, *44*(1), 71–80. https://doi.org/10.1016/j.ogc.2016.11.003

Barker, L. C., & Vigod, S. N. (2020). Sexual health of women with schizophrenia: A review. *Frontiers in Neuroendocrinology*, *57*, 100840.

Basson, R., & Gilks, T. (2018). Women's sexual dysfunction associated with psychiatric disorders and their treatment. *Women's Health, 14*, 1745506518762664.

Beck, BJ. (2016). Intimate Partner Violence. In *Massachusetts General Hospital Comprehensive Clinical Psychiatry* (Vol. 83, pp. 897–903). Elsevier Health Sciences.

Belardinelli, C., Hatch, J. P., Olvera, R. L., Fonseca, M., Caetano, S. C., Nicoletti, M., Pliszka, S., & Soares, J. C. (2008). Family environment patterns in families with bipolar children. *Journal of Affective Disorders, 107*(1–3), 299–305.

Berry-Bibee, E. N., Kim, M.-J., Tepper, N. K., Riley, H. E. M., & Curtis, K. M. (2016). Co-administration of St. John's wort and hormonal contraceptives: A systematic review.*Contraception, 94*(6), 668–677. https://doi.org/10.1016/j.contraception.2016.07.010

Bigras, N., Vaillancourt-Morel, M.-P., Nolin, M.-C., & Bergeron, S. (2021). Associations between childhood sexual abuse and sexual well-being in adulthood: A systematic literature review. *Journal of Child Sexual Abuse, 30*(3), 332–352.

Bookholt, D. E., & Bogers, J. P. A. M. (2014). Oral ContraceptivesRaisePlasmaClozapineConcentrations. *Journal of Clinical Psychopharmacology, 34*(3), 389–390. https://doi.org/10.1097/JCP.0000000000000074

Bromberger, J. T., Matthews, K. A., Schott, L. L., Brockwell, S., Avis, N. E., Kravitz, H. M., Everson-Rose, S. A., Gold, E. B., Sowers, M., & Randolph Jr, J. F. (2007). Depressive symptoms during the menopausal transition: The Study of Women's Health Across the Nation (SWAN). *Journal of Affective Disorders, 103*(1–3), 267–272.

Brzezinski, A., Brzezinski-Sinai, N. A., & Seeman, M. V. (2017). Treating schizophrenia during menopause. *Menopause, 24*(5), 582–588.

Byatt, N., Deligiannidis, K. M., & Freeman, M. P. (2013). Antidepressant use in pregnancy: A critical review focused on risks and controversies. *Acta Psychiatrica Scandinavica, 127*(2), 94–114.

Chesnay, M. (2013). Psychiatric-Mental Health Nurses and the Sex Trafficking Pandemic.*Issues in Mental Health Nursing, 34*(12), 901–907. https://doi.org/10.3109/01612840.2013.857200

Chisolm, M. S., & Payne, J. L. (2016). Management of psychotropic drugs during pregnancy. *BMJ*, h5918. https://doi.org/10.1136/bmj.h5918

Christensen, J., Petrenaite, V., Atterman, J., Sidenius, P., Öhman, I., Tomson, T., & Sabers, A. (2007). Oral Contraceptives Induce Lamotrigine Metabolism: Evidence from a Double-blind, Placebo-controlled Trial. *Epilepsia, 48*(3), 484–489.https://doi.org/10.1111/j.1528-1167.2007.00997.x

Clark, C. T., Klein, A. M., Perel, J. M., Helsel, J., & Wisner, K. L. (2013). Lamotrigine Dosing for Pregnant Patients With Bipolar Disorder. *American Journal of Psychiatry, 170*(11), 1240–1247. https://doi.org/10.1176/appi.ajp.2013.13010006

Clark, C. T., & Wisner, K. L. (2018). Treatment of Peripartum Bipolar Disorder. *Obstetrics andGynecology Clinics of North America, 45*(3), 403–417. https://doi.org/10.1016/j.ogc.2018.05.002

Clinebell, K., Gannon, J., Debrunner, S., & Roy Chengappa, K. N. (2017). Long-acting risperidone injections in a pregnant patient with bipolar disorder. *Bipolar Disorders 19*(7), 606–607.

Cohen, L. S., Altshuler, L. L., Harlow, B. L., Nonacs, R., Newport, D. J., Viguera, A. C., Suri, R., Burt, V. K., Hendrick, V., & Reminick, A. M. (2006). Relapse of major depression during pregnancy in women who maintain or discontinue antidepressant treatment. *Jama, 295*(5), 499–507.

Cohen, L. S., Friedman, J. M., Jefferson, J. W., Johnson, E. M., & Weiner, M. L. (1994). A reevaluation of risk of in utero exposure to lithium. *Jama, 271*(2), 146–150.

Committee on Health Care for Underserved Women. (2019). ACOG Committee Opinion Number 777 Sexual Assault. *Obstetrics & Gynecology, 133*(4), e296–e302.

Curtis, K. M., Tepper, N. K., Jatlaoui, T. C., Berry-Bibee, E., Horton, L. G., Zapata, L. B., Simmons, K. B., Pagano, H. P., Jamieson, D. J., & Whiteman, M. K. (2016). U.S. Medical Eligibility Criteria for Contraceptive Use, 2016. *MMWR. Recommendations and Reports, 65*(3), 1–103. https://doi.org/10.15585/mmwr.rr6503a1

Davis, A. R., Westhoff, C. L., & Stanczyk, F. Z. (2011). Carbamazepine coadministration withan oral contraceptive: Effects on steroid pharmacokinetics, ovulation, and bleeding:Carbamazepine and an Oral Contraceptive. *Epilepsia*, no-no. https://doi.org/10.1111/j.1528-1167.2010.02917.x

de Boer, M. K., Castelein, S., Wiersma, D., Schoevers, R. A., & Knegtering, H. (2015). The facts about sexual (Dys) function in schizophrenia: An overview of clinically relevant findings. *Schizophrenia Bulletin, 41*(3), 674–686.

Deligiannidis, K. M., Byatt, N., & Freeman, M. P. (2014). Pharmacotherapy for mood disorders in pregnancy: A review of pharmacokinetic changes and clinical recommendations for therapeutic drug monitoring. *Journal of Clinical Psychopharmacology, 34*(2), 244.

Dell'Osso, L., Carmassi, C., Carlini, M., Rucci, P., Torri, P., Cesari, D., Landi, P., Ciapparelli, A., & Maggi, M. (2009). Sexual dysfunctions and suicidality in patients with bipolar disorder and unipolar depression. *The Journal of Sexual Medicine, 6*(11), 3063–3070.

Devries, K. M., Mak, J. Y., Garcia-Moreno, C., Petzold, M., Child, J. C., Falder, G., Lim, S., Bacchus, L. J., Engell, R. E., & Rosenfeld, L. (2013). The global prevalence of intimate partner violence against women. *Science, 340*(6140), 1527–1528.

Di Florio, A., Gordon-Smith, K., Forty, L., Kosorok, M. R., Fraser, C., Perry, A., Bethell, A., Craddock, N., Jones, L., & Jones, I. (2018). Stratification of the risk of bipolar disorder recurrences in pregnancy and postpartum. *The British Journal of Psychiatry, 213*(3), 542–547.

Diaz-Caneja, A., & Johnson, S. (2004). The views and experiences of severely mentally ill mothers. *Social Psychiatry and Psychiatric Epidemiology*, *39*(6), 472–482.

Dolk, H., Wang, H., Loane, M., Morris, J., Garne, E., Addor, M.-C., Arriola, L., Bakker, M., Barisic, I., Doray, B., Gatt, M., Kallen, K., Khoshnood, B., Klungsoyr, K., LahesmaaKorpinen, A.-M., Latos-Bielenska, A., Mejnartowicz, J. P., Nelen, V., Neville, A., de Jong-van den Berg, L. T. W. (2016). Lamotrigine use in pregnancy and risk of orofacial cleft and other congenital anomalies. *Neurology*, *86*(18), 1716–1725. https://doi.org/10.1212/WNL.0000000000002540

Dutton, C., & Foldvary-Schaefer, N. (2008). Chapter 6 Contraception in Women with Epilepsy. In *International Review of Neurobiology* (Vol. 83, pp. 113–134). Elsevier. https://doi.org/10.1016/S0074-7742(08)00006-8

Dworkin, E. R. (2020). Risk for Mental Disorders Associated With Sexual Assault: A Meta-Analysis. *Trauma, Violence, & Abuse*, *21*(5), 1011–1028. https://doi.org/10.1177/1524838018813198

Edelman, A., Micks, E., Gallo, M. F., Jensen, J. T., & Grimes, D. A. (2014). Continuous or extended cycle vs. Cyclic use of combined hormonal contraceptives for contraception. *Cochrane Database of Systematic Reviews*. https://doi.org/10.1002/14651858.CD004695.pub3

Einarson, A., & Boskovic, R. (2009) Use and safety of antipsychotic drugs during pregnancy. *Journal of Psychiatric Practice*, 15, 183–192.

Fitelson, E., Osborne, L. M., & Payne, J. L. (2021). A Clinical Approach to Psychiatric Diagnosis and Treatment during Pregnancy. In L. A. Hutner, L. A. Catapano, S. Nagle-Yang, K. E. Williams, & L. M. Osborne (Eds.), *Textbook of Women's ReproductiveMental Health*. American Psychiatric Association.

Fornaro, M., Maritan, E., Ferranti, R., Zaninotto, L., Miola, A., Anastasia, A., Murru, A., Solé, E., Stubbs, B., & Carvalho, A. F. (2020). Lithium exposure during pregnancy and the postpartum period: A systematic review and meta-analysis of safety and efficacy outcomes. *American Journal of Psychiatry*, *177*(1), 76–92.

Freeman, M. P., Cheng, L. J., Moustafa, D., Davies, A., Sosinsky, A. Z., Wang, B., Petrillo, L. F., Hogan, C., & Cohen, L. S. (2017). Vortioxetine for major depressive disorder, vasomotor, and cognitive symptoms associated with the menopausal transition. *29*(4), 249–257.

Gibbs, Z., & Kulkarni, J. (2014). Risk Factors for Depression During Perimenopause. In D. L. Barnes (Ed.), *Women's Reproductive Mental Health Across the Lifespan* (pp. 215–233). Springer International Publishing.

Grigoriadis, S., VonderPorten, E. H., Mamisashvili, L., Tomlinson, G., Dennis, C.-L., Koren, G., Steiner, M., Mousmanis, P., Cheung, A., & Ross, L. E. (2014). Prenatal exposure to antidepressants and persistent pulmonary hypertension of the newborn: Systematic review and meta-analysis. *Bmj*, *348*.

Guedes, T. G., Moura, E. R. F., & de Almeida, P. C. (2009). Particularities of family planning in women with mental disorders. *Revista Latino-Americana de Enfermagem*, *17*(5), 639–644. https://doi.org/10.1590/S0104-11692009000500007

Harlow SD, Gass M, Hall JE, Lobo R, Maki P, Rebar RW, Sherman S, Sluss PM, de Villiers TJ, STRAW+10 Collaborative Group. (2012). Executive summary of the Stages of Reproductive Aging Workshop+ 10: Addressing the unfinished agenda of staging reproductive aging. *The Journal of Clinical Endocrinology & Metabolism*, *97*(4), 1159–1168.

Hellmuth, J. C., Gordon, K. C., Stuart, G. L., & Moore, T. M. (2013). Risk factors for intimate partner violence during pregnancy and postpartum. *Archives of Women's Mental Health*, *16*(1), 19–27.

Henshaw, C. (2009). *Modern management of perinatal psychiatric disorder*. RCPsych Publications.

Herzog, A. G., et al. (2009). Valproate and lamotrigine level variation with menstrual cycle phase and oral contraceptive use. *Neurology*, *72*(10), 911–914.

Hine, R. H., Maybery, D. J., & Goodyear, M. J. (2018). Identity in recovery for mothers with a mental illness: A literature review. *Psychiatric Rehabilitation Journal*, *41*(1), 16,

Hlengwa, N., Muller, C. J. F., Basson, A. K., Bowles, S., Louw, J., & Awortwe, C.(2020). Herbal supplements interactions with oral oestrogen-based contraceptive metabolism and transport. *Phytotherapy Research*, *34*(7), 1519–1529.10.1002/ptr.6623

Holmes, L. B., Baldwin, E. J., Smith, C. R., Habecker, E., Glassman, L., Wong, S. L., & Wyszynski, D. F. (2008). Increased frequency of isolated cleft palate in infants exposed to lamotrigine during pregnancy. *Neurology*, *70*(22 Part 2), 2152–2158.

Howard, L., Shah, N., Salmon, M., & Appleby, L. (2003). Predictors of social services supervision of babies of mothers with mental illness after admission to a psychiatric mother and baby unit. *Social Psychiatry and Psychiatric Epidemiology*, *38*(8), 450–455.

Hutner, L. A., Catapano, L. A., Erika, K., Kingsberg, S., Nagle-Yang, S., Williams, K. E., & Osborne, L. M. (2021). What's in a Name? Why We Use "Women's Reproductive Mental Health and Toward a Future of Different Names". In L. A. Hutner, L. A. Catapano, S. Nagle-Yang, K. E. Williams, & L. M. Osborne (Eds.), *Textbook of Women's Reproductive Mental Health*. American Psychiatric Association.

Joffe, H., Soares, C. N., & Cohen, L. S. (2003). Assessment and treatment of hot flushes and menopausal mood disturbance. *Psychiatric Clinics*, *26*(3), 563–580.

Keepers, G. A., Fochtmann, L. J., Anzia, J. M., Benjamin, S., Lyness, J. M., Mojtabai, R., Servis, M., Walaszek, A., Buckley, P., & Lenzenweger, M. F. (2020). The American Psychiatric Association practice guideline for the treatment of patients with schizophrenia. *American Journal of Psychiatry*, *177*(9), 868–872.

Khan, S. J., Fersh, M. E., Ernst, C., Klipstein, K., Albertini, E. S., & Lusskin, S. I. (2016). Bipolar Disorder in Pregnancy and Postpartum: Principles of Management. *Current Psychiatry Reports*, *18*(2), 13. https://doi.org/10.1007/s11920-015-0658-x

Kulkarni, J., Worsley, R., Gilbert, H., Gavrilidis, E., Van Rheenen, T. E., Wang, W., McCauley, K., & Fitzgerald, P. (2014). A prospective cohort study of antipsychotic medications in pregnancy: The first 147 pregnancies and 100 one year old babies. *PLoS One*, *9*(5), e94788.

Larsen, E. R., Damkier, P., Pedersen, L. H., Fenger-Gron, J., Mikkelsen, R. L., Nielsen, R. E., Linde, V. J., Knudsen, H. E. D., Skaarup, L., & Videbech, P. (2015). Use of psychotropic drugs during pregnancy and breast-feeding. *Acta Psychiatrica Scandinavica*, *132*, 1–28.

Lederer, L. J., & Wetzel, C. A. (2014). The health consequences of sex trafficking and their implications for identifying victims in healthcare facilities. *Annals Health L.*, *23*, 61.

Lopez, L. M., Kaptein, A. A., & Helmerhorst, F. M. (2012). Oral contraceptives containing drospirenone for premenstrual syndrome. *Cochrane Database of Systematic Reviews*. https://doi.org/10.1002/14651858.CD006586.pub4

Lundin, C., Danielsson, K. G., Bixo, M., Moby, L., Bengtsdotter, H., Jawad, I., Marions, L., Brynhildsen, J., Malmborg, A., Lindh, I., & Sundström Poromaa, I. (2017). Combined oral contraceptive use is associated with both improvement and worsening of mood in the different phases of the treatment cycle—A double-blind, placebo-controlled randomized trial. *Psychoneuroendocrinology*, *76*, 135–143. https://doi.org/10.1016/j.psyneuen.2016.11.033

Maki, P. M., Kornstein, S. G., Joffe, H., Bromberger, J. T., Freeman, E. W., Athappilly, G., Bobo, W. V., Rubin, L. H., Koleva, H. K., & Cohen, L. S. (2018). Guidelines for the evaluation and treatment of perimenopausal depression: Summary and recommendations. *Menopause*, *25*(10), 1069–1085.

Maki, P. M., Kornstein, S. G., Joffe, H., Bromberger, J. T., Freeman, E. W., Athappilly, G., Bobo, W. V., Rubin, L. H., Koleva, H. K., & Cohen, L. S. (2019). Guidelines for the evaluation and treatment of perimenopausal depression: Summary and recommendations. *Journal of Women's Health*, *28*(2), 117–134.

Marsh, W. K., Gershenson, B., & Rothschild, A. J. (2015). Symptom severity of bipolar disorder during the menopausal transition. *International Journal of Bipolar Disorders*, *3*(1), 1–9.

McCloskey, L. R., Wisner, K. L., Cattan, M. K., Betcher, H. K., Stika, C. S., & Kiley, J. W. (2021). Contraception for Women With Psychiatric Disorders. *American Journal of Psychiatry*, *178*(3), 247–255. https://doi.org/10.1176/appi.ajp.2020.20020154

McLearn, K. T., Minkovitz, C. S., Strobino, D. M., Marks, E., & Hou, W. (2006). The Timing of Maternal Depressive Symptoms and Mothers' Parenting Practices With Young Children: Implications for Pediatric Practice. *PEDIATRICS*, *118*(1), e174–e182. https://doi.org/10.1542/peds.2005-1551

Meador, K. J., Baker, G. A., Browning, N., Clayton-Smith, J., Combs-Cantrell, D. T., Cohen, M., Kalayjian, L. A., Kanner, A., Liporace, J. D., Pennell, P. B., Privitera, M., & Loring, D. W. (2009). Cognitive Function at 3 Years of Age after Fetal Exposure to AntiepilepticDrugs. *New England Journal of Medicine*, *360*(16), 1597–1605.https://doi.org/10.1056/NEJMoa0803531

Mehta, T. M., & Van Lieshout, R. J. (2017). A review of the safety of clozapine during pregnancy and lactation. *Archives of Women's Mental Health*, *20*(1), 1–9.

Miller, L. J. (2009). Ethical issues in perinatal mental health. *The Psychiatric Clinics of North America*, *32*(2), 259–270

Møller-Olsen, C., Friedman, S. H., Prakash, C., & North, A. (2018). Clinical characteristics of maternal mental health service users treated with mood stabilizing or antipsychotic medication. *Asia-Pacific Psychiatry*, *10*(2), e12304.

Munk-Olsen, T., Laursen, T. M., Pedersen, C. B., Mors, O., & Mortensen, P. B. (2006a). New parents and mental disorders: A population-based register study. *Jama*, *296*(21), 2582–2589.

Munk-Olsen, T., Laursen, T. M., Pedersen, C. B., Mors, O., & Mortensen, P. B. (2006b). New parents and mental disorders: A population-based register study. *JAMA*, *296*(21), 2582–2589. https://doi.org/10.1001/jama.296.21.2582

Muzik, M., Rosenblum, K. L., Alfafara, E. A., Schuster, M. M., Miller, N. M., Waddell, R. M., & Kohler, E. S. (2015). Mom Power: Preliminary outcomes of a group intervention to improve mental health and parenting among high-risk mothers. *Archives of Women's Mental Health*, *18*(3), 507–521. https://doi.org/10.1007/s00737-014-0490-z

Myths, Facts, and Statistics | Polaris. (2018, November 7). https://polarisproject.org/myths-facts-and-statistics/

Nagle-Yang, S., DeBrunner, S., Favini, A., Novick, A., Hasser, C., Prakash, C., & Nathan, M. (2021a). Bipolar Disorder and Related Disorders. In L. Hutner, L. Catapano, S. Nagle-Yang, K. Williams, & L. M. Osborne (Eds.), *Textbook of Women's Reproductive MentalHealth* (pp. 467–505). American Psychiatric Association.

Nagle-Yang, S., Hatters-Friedman, S., Hasser, C., Mulvihill, A., Novick, A., Jones, A., Reed, E., & Sabhapathy, S. (2021b). Schizophrenia and Related Disorders. In L. A. Hutner, L. A.Catapano, S. Nagle-Yang, K. E. Williams, & L. M. Osborne (Eds.), *Textbook of Women's Reproductive Mental Health* (pp. 521–561). American Psychiatric Association.

Nicholson, J., Sweeney, E. M., & Geller, J. L. (1998). Focus on women: Mothers with mental illness: I. The competing demands of parenting and living with mental illness. *Psychiatric Services*, *49*(5), 635–642.

Nilsson, E., Lichtenstein, P., Cnattingius, S., Murray, R. M., & Hultman, C. M. (2002). Women with schizophrenia: Pregnancy outcome and infant death among their offspring. *Schizophrenia Research*, *58*(2–3), 221–229.

Noll, J. G., Trickett, P. K., Harris, W. W., & Putnam, F. W. (2009). The cumulative burdenborne by offspring whose mothers were sexually abused as children: Descriptive results from a multigenerational study. *Journal of Interpersonal Violence*, *24*(3), 424–449.

Oram, S., Stöckl, H., Busza, J., Howard, L. M., & Zimmerman, C. (2012). Prevalence and Risk of Violence and the Physical, Mental, and Sexual Health Problems Associated with Human Trafficking: Systematic Review. *PLoS Medicine*, *9*(5), e1001224. https://doi.org/10.1371/journal.pmed.1001224

Orsolini, L., Sceusa, F., Pompili, S., Mauro, A., Salvi, V., & Volpe, U. (2021). Severe and persistent mental illness (SPMI) in pregnancy and breastfeeding: Focus on second-generation long-acting injectable antipsychotics. *Expert Opinion on Drug Safety*, *20*(10), 1207–1224. https://doi.org/10.1080/14740338.2021.1928634

Oruch, R., Elderbi, M. A., Khattab, H. A., Pryme, I. F., & Lund, A. (2014). Lithium: A review of pharmacology, clinical uses, and toxicity. *European Journal of Pharmacology*, *740*, 464–473. https://doi.org/10.1016/j.ejphar.2014.06.042

Osborne, L. M., & Birndorf, C. (2021). Depressive Disorders. In L. A. Hutner, L. A. Catapano, S. Nagle-Yang, K. E. Williams, & L. M. Osborne (Eds.), *Women's Reproductive Mental Health*. American Psychiatric Association.

Osborne, L. M., Hermann, A., Burt, V., Driscoll, K., Fitelson, E., Meltzer-Brody, S., Barzilay, E. M., Yang, S. N., Miller, L., & Health, N. T. F. on W. R. M. (2015). Reproductive psychiatry: The gap between clinical need and education. *American Journal of Psychiatry*, *172*(10), 946–948.

Pariente, G., Leibson, T., Carls, A., Adams-Webber, T., Ito, S., & Koren, G. (2016). Pregnancy-associated changes in pharmacokinetics: A systematic review. *PLoS Medicine*, *13*(11), e1002160.

Park, Y., Hernandez-Diaz, S., Bateman, B. T., Cohen, J. M., Desai, R. J., Patorno, E., Glynn, R. J., Cohen, L. S., Mogun, H., & Huybrechts, K. F. (2018). Continuation of atypical antipsychotic medication during early pregnancy and the risk of gestational diabetes. *American Journal of Psychiatry*, *175*(6), 564–574.

Powell, J. G., Garland, S., Preston, K., & Piszczatoski, C. (2020). Brexanolone (Zulresso): Finally, an FDA-Approved Treatment for Postpartum Depression. *Annals of Pharmacotherapy*, *54*(2), 157–163. https://doi.org/10.1177/1060028019873320

Rabin, R. F., Jennings, J. M., Campbell, J. C., & Bair-Merritt, M. H. (2009). Intimate partner violence screening tools: A systematic review. *American Journal of Preventive Medicine*, *36*(5), 439–445.

RAINN. (n.d.). *Sexual Assault*. Retrieved October 8, 2021, from https://www.rainn.org/articles/sexual-assault

Reddy, D. S. (2010). Clinical pharmacokinetic interactions between antiepileptic drugs and hormonal contraceptives. *Expert Review of Clinical Pharmacology*, *3*(2), 183–192. https://doi.org/10.1586/ecp.10.3

Renshaw, J., & Wrigley, Z. (2015). Service Evaluation of the Compassionate Minds Module of the Family Nurse Partnership programme. *Darlington Social Research*.

Riecher-Rössler, A., Butler, S., & Kulkarni, J. (2018). Sex and gender differences in schizophrenic psychoses—A critical review. *Archives of Women's Mental Health*, *21*(6),627–648.

Riecher-Rössler, A., & Häfner, H. (1993). Schizophrenia and oestrogens—Is there an association? *European Archives of Psychiatry and Clinical Neuroscience*, *242*(6), 323–328.

Riggs, N., Houry, D., Long, G., Markovchick, V., & Feldhaus, K. M. (2000). Analysis of 1,076 cases of sexual assault. *Annals of Emergency Medicine*, *35*(4), 358–362. https://doi.org/10.1016/S0196-0644(00)70054-0

Robinson, S. A., Dowell, M., Pedulla, D., & McCauley, L. (2004). Do the emotional side-effects of hormonal contraceptives come from pharmacologic or psychologicalmechanisms? *Medical Hypotheses*, *63*(2), 268–273. https://doi.org/10.1016/j.mehy.2004.02.013

Roelcke, V. (2019). Eugenic concerns, scientific practices: International relations in the establishment of psychiatric genetics in Germany, Britain, the USA and Scandinavia, *c*1910–60. *History of Psychiatry*, *30*(1), 19–37.https://doi.org/10.1177/0957154X18808666

Santoro, N., Epperson, C. N., & Mathews, S. B. (2015). Menopausal symptoms and their management. *Endocrinology and Metabolism Clinics of North America*, *44*(3), 497–515. https://doi.org/10.1016/j.ecl.2015.05.001

Santoro, N., Roeca, C., Peters, B. A., & Neal-Perry, G. (2021). The menopause transition: Signs, symptoms, and management options. *The Journal of Clinical Endocrinology & Metabolism*, *106*(1), 1–15. https://doi.org/10.1210/clinem/dgaa764

Seeman, M. V. (2012). Intervention to prevent child custody loss in mothers with schizophrenia. *Schizophrenia Research and Treatment*, 2012, Article ID 796763. https://doi.org/10.1155/2012/796763, 1–6.

Shandro, J., Chisolm-Straker, M., Duber, H. C., Findlay, S. L., Munoz, J., Schmitz, G., Stanzer, M., Stoklosa, H., Wiener, D. E., & Wingkun, N. (2016). Human Trafficking: A guide to identification and approach for the emergency physician. *Annals of Emergency Medicine*, *68*(4), 501–508.e1. https://doi.org/10.1016/j.annemergmed.2016.03.049

Sharma, V., & Mazmanian, D. (2014). The DSM-5 peripartum specifier: Prospects and pitfalls. *Archives of Women's Mental Health*, *17*(2), 171–173. https://doi.org/10.1007/s00737-013-0406-3

Sidhu, J., Job, S., Singh, S., & Philipson, R. (2006). The pharmacokinetic and pharmacodynamic consequences of the co-administration of lamotrigine and a combined oral contraceptive in healthy female subjects. *British Journal of Clinical Pharmacology*, *61*(2), 191–199. https://doi.org/10.1111/j.1365-2125.2005.02539.x

Simkhada, P., Van Teijlingen, E., Sharma, A., Bissell, P., Poobalan, A., & Wasti, S. P. (2018). Health consequences of sex trafficking: A systematic review. *Journal of Manmohan Memorial Institute of Health Sciences*, *4*(1), 130–150. https://doi.org/10.3126/jmmihs.v4i1.21150

Soares, C. N. (2017). Depression and menopause: Current knowledge and clinical recommendations for a critical window. *Psychiatric Clinics*, *40*(2), 239–254.

Stewart, D. E., & Vigod, S. N. (2019). Postpartum depression: Pathophysiology, treatment, and emerging therapeutics. *Annual Review of Medicine*, *70*, 183–196.

Stroumsa, D., & Wu, J. P. (2018). Welcoming transgender and nonbinary patients: Expanding the language of "women's health". *American Journal of Obstetrics and Gynecology*, *219*(6), 585.e1–585.e5. https://doi.org/10.1016/j.ajog.2018.09.018

Task Force on Sudden Infant Death Syndrome. (2016). SIDS and other sleep-related infant deaths: Updated 2016 recommendations for a safe infant sleeping environment. *Pediatrics*, *138*(5).

Taylor, C. L., Broadbent, M., Khondoker, M., Stewart, R. J., & Howard, L. M. (2018). Predictors of severe relapse in pregnant women with psychotic or bipolar disorders. *Journal of Psychiatric Research*, *104*, 100–107.https://doi.org/10.1002/14651858.CD003382.pub3

Terp, I. M., & Mortensen, P. B. (1998). Post-partum psychoses: Clinical diagnoses and relative risk of admission after parturition. *The British Journal of Psychiatry*, *172*(6), 521–526.

The ESHRE Capri Workshop Group. (2006). Nutrition and reproduction in women. *Human Reproduction Update*, *12*(3), 193–207. https://doi.org/10.1093/humupd/dmk003

Tomson, T., Battino, D., Bonizzoni, E., Craig, J., Lindhout, D., Perucca, E., Sabers, A., Thomas, S. V., Vajda, F., & Faravelli, F. (2018). Comparative risk of major congenital malformations with eight different antiepileptic drugs: A prospective cohort study of the EURAP registry. *The Lancet Neurology*, *17*(6), 530–538.

Tosato, S., Albert, U., Tomassi, S., Iasevoli, F., Carmassi, C., Ferrari, S., Nanni, M. G., Nivoli, A., Volpe, U., & Atti, A. R. (2017). A systematized review of atypical antipsychotics in pregnant women: Balancing between risks of untreated illness and risks of drug-related adverse effects. *The Journal of Clinical Psychiatry*, *78*(5), 0–0.

Trussell, J. (2011). Contraceptive failure in the United States. *Contraception*, *83*(5), 397–404. https://doi.org/10.1016/j.contraception.2011.01.021

Ullman, S. E., Relyea, M., Peter-Hagene, L., & Vasquez, A. L. (2013). Trauma histories, substance use coping, PTSD, and problem substance use among sexual assault victims. *Addictive Behaviors*, *38*(6), 2219–2223.

United Nations Office on Drugs and Crime. (2000). *UN Protocol to prevent, suppress and punish trafficking in persons, especially women and children*. https://www.unodc.org/res/human-trafficking/2021the-protocol-tip_html/TIP.pdf

United Nations Office on Drugs and Crime. (2021). *Global report on trafficking in persons 2020*. https://www.unodc.org/documents/data-and-analysis/tip/2021/GLOTiP_2020_15jan_web.pdf

Vigod, S. N., Seeman, M. V., Ray, J. G., Anderson, G. M., Dennis, C. L., Grigoriadis, S., Gruneir, A., Kurdyak, P. A., & Rochon, P. A. (2012). Temporal trends in general and age-specific fertility rates among women with schizophrenia (1996–2009): A population-based study in Ontario, Canada, *Schizophrenia Research*, *139*(1–3), 169–175.

Viguera, A. C., Whitfield, T., Baldessarini, R. J., Newport, D. J., Stowe, Z., Reminick, A., Zurick, A., & Cohen, L. S. (2007). Risk of recurrence in women with Bipolar Disorder during pregnancy: Prospective study of mood stabilizer discontinuation. *American Journal of Psychiatry*, *164*(12), 1817–1824. https://doi.org/10.1176/appi.ajp.2007.06101639

Warnez, S., & Alessi-Severini, S. (2014). Clozapine: A review of clinical practice guidelines and prescribing trends. *BMC Psychiatry*, *14*, 102. https://doi.org/10.1186/1471-244X-14-102

Wesseloo, R., Kamperman, A. M., Munk-Olsen, T., Pop, V. J., Kushner, S. A., & Bergink, V. (2016). Risk of postpartum relapse in bipolar disorder and postpartum psychosis: A systematic review and meta-analysis. *American Journal of Psychiatry*, *173*(2), 117–127.

Wesseloo, R., Liu, X., Clark, C. T., Kushner, S. A., Munk-Olsen, T., & Bergink, V. (2017). Risk of postpartum episodes in women with bipolar disorder after lamotrigine or lithium use during pregnancy: A population-based cohort study. *Journal of Affective Disorders*, *218*, 394–397.

Weston, J., Bromley, R., Jackson, C. F., Adab, N., Clayton-Smith, J., Greenhalgh, J., Hounsome, J., McKay, A. J., Tudur Smith, C., & Marson, A. G. (2016). Monotherapy treatment of epilepsy in pregnancy: Congenital malformation outcomes in the child. *Cochrane Database of Systematic Reviews*. https://doi.org/10.1002/14651858.CD010224.pub2

Wieck, A., & Jones, S. (2018). Dangers of valproate in pregnancy. *British Medical Journal*. https://doi.org/10.1136/bmj.k1609. PMID 29669728.

Wirth, K. E., Tchetgen Tchetgen, E. J., Silverman, J. G., & Murray, M. B. (2013). How does sex trafficking increase the risk of HIV infection? An observational study from southern India. *American Journal of Epidemiology*, *177*(3), 232–241. https://doi.org/10.1093/aje/kws338

World Health Organization. (2021a). *Defining Sexual Health*. https://www.who.int/health-topics/sexual-health#tab=tab_2

World Health Organization. (2021b) Violence against women; Prevalence estimates, 2018. https://www.who.int/publications/i/item/9789240022256

Yonkers, K. A., Blackwell, K. A., Glover, J., & Forray, A. (2014). Antidepressant use in pregnant and postpartum women. *Annual Review of Clinical Psychology*, *10*(1), 369–392. https://doi.org/10.1146/annurev-clinpsy-032813-153626

Zimmerman, C., Hossain, M., Yun, K., Gajdadziev, V., Guzun, N., Tchomarova, M., Ciarrocchi, R. A., Johansson, A., Kefurtova, A., Scodanibbio, S., Motus, M. N., Roche, B., Morison, L., & Watts, C. (2008). The Health of Trafficked Women: A survey of women entering post-trafficking services in Europe. *American Journal of Public Health*, *98*(1), 55–59. https://doi.org/10.2105/AJPH.2006.108357

Zimmerman, C., Yun, K., Shvab, I., Watts, C., Trappolin, L., Treppete, M., Bimbi, F., Adams, B., Jiraporn, S., & Beci, L. (2003). *The Health Risks and Consequences of trafficking in Women and Adolescents: Findings from a European Study*. London:London School of Hygiene & Tropical Medicine.

Part IV

Effective and Established Interventions

Developing, Evaluating and Implementing Evidence-Based Interventions in Real World Practice.

Kelly A. Aschbrenner and William C. Torrey

Introduction

Evidence-based interventions (EBIs) are practices or programs that have peer-reviewed, documented empirical evidence of effectiveness on a clinical outcome. Clinicians rely on the scientific evidence supporting EBIs to ensure they are delivering effective treatments for patients and their families. We assume that in order for a practice to be considered evidence-based, there must be an evidence base behind it. However, we often do not know and do not ask how the evidence was generated for a given intervention, which could cause problems transferring evidence when the research supporting an intervention was conducted in a specific setting with a specific population that differs from whom and where we intend to use the intervention. Interventions are often adapted from their original form when implemented in a new setting or with a new patient group to improve fit. However, changing the core components of an intervention could reduce its effectiveness. Drifting from fidelity to original intervention models is a source of tension in the field. This chapter will review how the evidence is generated for EBIs, discuss challenges that can arise when tested models do not fit into real-world practice settings, and present principles for guiding adaptations to intervention forms while maintaining the core functions that make them effective. Finally, it will provide a discussion of the overall merits and shortcomings of current approaches to generating EBIs and how we can encourage innovations in practice and discourage the use of interventions with limited support for their effectiveness.

Stages of Intervention Development

Intervention research establishes the evidence base for psychotherapeutic and behavioral treatments for mental and behavioral disorders. Interventions are developed and tested in phases, each phase with its own distinctive role and function in intervention development. There are various conceptualizations of phases or stages of intervention development (Czajkowski et al. 2015; Gitlin 2013; Onken 2019), with most stressing the importance of translating research

K. A. Aschbrenner (✉)
Geisel School of Medicine at Dartmouth College, Hanover, NH, USA
e-mail: Kelly.aschbrenner@dartmouth.edu

W. C. Torrey
The Dartmouth Institute, Lebanon, NH, USA
e-mail: william.c.torrey@hitchcock.org

W. E. Sowers et al. (eds.), *Textbook of Community Psychiatry*,
https://doi.org/10.1007/978-3-031-10239-4_21

into clinical practice quickly and efficiently with the engagement of patient and communities. The Stage Model for Behavioral Intervention Development advanced by the National Institutes of Health lays out six stages of intervention development: (Stage 0) basic research; (Stage 1) intervention generation and refinement; (Stage 2) "pure" efficacy testing; (Stage 3) "real-world" efficacy testing; (Stage 4) effectiveness research; and (Stage 5) implementation and dissemination (Onken 2019).

The NIH Stage Model emphasizes that research does not need to be done in any particular order as long as investigators justify the logic of their proposed sequence. For example, clinical and services researchers may choose to bypass Stage 2 "pure" efficacy testing of promising interventions conducted in highly controlled research settings to conduct Stage 3 "real-world" efficacy testing of interventions in community settings, or they may choose hybrid efficacy-effectiveness study designs that contain key elements drawn from both efficacy and effectiveness research (Carroll and Rounsaville 2003; Roy-Byrne et al. 2003). An advantage of an approach that blends critical components of efficacy research (e.g., random assignment of patients to treatment, objective use of outcomes measures, monitoring of treatments delivered, and specialized training of providers in delivering treatments) with elements of effectiveness trials that promote generalizability of study findings (e.g., care as usual comparison condition, few restrictions on patient participation, study interventionists drawn from the staff or performance sites) is that it maintains the scientific rigor that allows inferences to be made about causal relationships while increasing the extent to which study findings can be generalized to different providers, patients, and settings. Below we review the major types of research conducted during intervention development and discuss their role in and strengths and limitations for generating EBIs.

Pilot Trials

Pilot studies occur at an early phase of intervention development to examine the feasibility of interventions and the methods used to test them before conducting a full-scale definitive randomized clinical trial (RCT) (Bowen et al. 2009; El-Kotob and Giangregorio 2018; Kistin and Silverstein 2015). Pilot studies are designed to answer the overarching question "Can it work?" prior to examining "Does it work?". Pilot studies are designed to evaluate feasibility of recruitment, randomization, retention, and assessment procedures, as well as acceptability or the extent to which participants are satisfied with an intervention (Leon et al. 2011). Before conducting a larger-scale trial that requires a significant investment of time and resources, clinical researchers need to evaluate fundamental feasibility questions, including the following: *Can we recruit adequate numbers of patients? Can we deliver the intervention as intended? Will participants complete the assessments? Will participants be satisfied with the intervention?*

Pilot studies help researchers identify changes that need to be made to study procedures or interventions. They can also inform decisions about whether to proceed to more definitive studies. Although pilot studies are a critical step in the process of intervention development and testing, using pilot studies to test hypotheses about the effects of an intervention can lead to inaccurate estimations of true effectiveness, primarily because of small sample sizes resulting in lack of statistical power to detect an effect (Kraemer et al. 2006; Leon et al. 2011). Thus, using evidence generated from pilot studies to inform clinical practices is often inappropriate. The "Does it work?" question is best left to full-scale, definitive RCTs. Such trials can generate evidence of effectiveness of an intervention in real-world clinical practice settings along with patient values and preferences used to guide evidence-based practice.

Efficacy Trials

When pilot studies show that a larger, definitive trial is feasible, an RCT is conducted to examine the cause-effect relationship between an intervention and outcome (Torpy et al. 2010). The RCT is considered the gold standard for evaluating therapeutic treatment effects (Bauchner et al. 2019). The key methodological components of an RCT are (1) use of a control or comparison condition to which the experimental intervention is compared and (2) random assignment of participants to conditions. Multiple factors determine the generalizability or applicability of RCTs to routine clinical settings, including characteristics of the sample, the providers who delivered the treatment, and the setting in which the trial was conducted (Rothwell 2005). Efficacy trials are RCTs used to determine whether an intervention produces the expected result under ideal or highly controlled circumstances. Efficacy studies are designed to maximize internal validity (i.e., the ability to draw the conclusion that the intervention really did cause the change in outcome). However, the highly controlled conditions under which efficacy studies are conducted may involve substantial deviations from routine clinical practice, including a highly selective patient sample, control of provider actions, and implementation in a highly resourced academic or healthcare setting that limit generalizability (Shean 2012; Singal et al. 2014).

Effectiveness Trials

Effectiveness trials focus on maximizing external validity (i.e., the degree to which findings can be generalized to the people and settings the intervention is trying to help) (Marchand et al. 2011). Effectiveness trials are conducted in routine clinical settings and address practical questions about the risks, benefits, and costs of an intervention (Möller 2011). Because effectiveness studies take place in practice settings, they can produce results that are directly relevant to providers, patients, families, payers, healthcare administrators, and other relevant stakeholders. Given the focus of effectiveness research on practice-relevant questions, collaborations between academic researchers and clinical or community practice partners can strengthen the relevance of the research (Drake et al. 2009; Kilbourne et al. 2012).

McGurk and colleagues (2015) evaluated the effectiveness of cognitive enhancement treatment for people with mental illness who do not respond to supported employment. The supported employment model evaluated in the study followed the evidence-based Individual Placement and Support (IPS) model (Bond et al. 2012). Dr. McGuirk and colleagues enhanced IPS with a validated cognitive enhancement program and tested whether the intervention could improve work outcomes in people with serious mental illness who had not benefited from high-fidelity supported employment.

The study was conducted in real-world community mental health centers with broad inclusion criteria for participation. Participants continued to receive their usual mental health services throughout the study while being randomly assigned to either enhanced supported employment involving specialized cognitive training of employment specialists or enhanced supported employment plus the Thinking Skills for Work program, a standardized cognitive enhancement program. Thinking Skills for Work includes practice of computer cognitive exercises, strategy coaching, and teaching of coping and compensatory strategies delivered by employment specialists. Participants in the Thinking Skills for Work group improved more than those in the enhanced supported employment-only group on measures of cognitive functioning and had consistently better competitive employment outcomes during the follow-up period. Findings from this study suggest that cognitive enhancement interventions can reduce cognitive impairments that are obstacles to work, thereby increasing the number of people who can benefit from supported employment and competitive work. This study contributes relevant and generalizable information about the effectiveness of enhancements to a widely disseminated EBI in routine mental health settings.

Implementation Trials

Once the evidence supporting an intervention is generated through efficacy or effectiveness research, or a combination of both, it can take years to integrate research findings into real-world clinical practice (Morris et al. 2011). Many evidence-based practices never get disseminated in routine practice (Green 2014). The field of implementation science was developed to address the research to practice gap by studying methods to promote the uptake of research findings into clinical, organizational, or policy contexts (Eccles and Mittman 2006). Implementation research focuses developing and testing implementation strategies, defined as the methods and techniques used to promote the adoption, implementation, and sustainment of EBIs into routine practice in clinical or community settings (Powell et al. 2019; Proctor et al. 2013). Implementation strategies vary in complexity from single-component strategies, such as audit and feedback and technical assistance, to multifaceted, multi-level implementation strategies that combine strategies (Powell et al. 2015). Implementation studies evaluate the success of implementing a new EBI by examining implementation outcomes, which are distinct from clinical and service outcomes (Proctor et al. 2009). A widely used taxonomy of implementation outcomes focuses on acceptability, adoption, appropriateness, feasibility, fidelity, implementation cost, penetration, and sustainability of an EBI in routine practice settings (Proctor et al. 2011). In particular, implementation fidelity is viewed as critical to the successful translation of EBIs into practice (Carroll et al. 2007). Implementation strategies provide training and support for implementing an EBI with high fidelity to the protocol of the new innovation (Proctor et al. 2013).

Intervention Fidelity

Fidelity is defined as the degree to which an EBI adheres to specific model standards described by EBI developers in practice manuals or protocols (Bond et al. 2000). Mental health intervention researchers have long been concerned with providers' adherence to treatment in clinical trials (Moncher and Prinz 1991; Teague et al. 2012; Waltz et al. 1993). Fidelity to an EBI is typically evaluated by (1) adherence to the program protocol, (2) dose or amount of program delivered, and (3) quality of delivery and measured through self-report, review of clinical records, direct observation, and detailed ratings of taped interactions, though this technique is rarely feasible in real-world implementation (Bond and Drake 2020). Accordingly, there have been calls to use pragmatic measures of fidelity that are important to practice stakeholders and low burden with broad applicability (Breitenstein et al. 2010; Glasgow and Riley 2013).

Fidelity-Adaptation Tension

Despite imperatives to maintain strict adherence to treatment fidelity standards, EBIs are often adapted from their original designs when implemented in a new context as there may be mismatches between the original EBI and the characteristics of patients, implementing agency, and community (Aarons Gregory et al. 2012; Escoffery et al. 2018; Wiltsey Stirman et al. 2017). By forcing adherence to manualized intervention protocols that were originally developed and tested in other practice settings, research teams risk promoting an EBI that has poor fit in the local setting, cultural context, or population; low likelihood of sustainability; and high likelihood of alienating community partners and patients who are dissatisfied with an EBI. Striving for adherence to the "form" of an intervention (e.g., using the exact same education materials or delivery procedures at every site) may be counterproductive when tailoring to context might be more effective (e.g., allowing materials to be adapted to local cultural styles, literacy levels, or local delivery system characteristics) (Aschbrenner et al. 2020; Baumann et al. 2017). On the other hand, the effectiveness of an EBI may be threatened when implementers make inappropriate adaptations to EBIs that result in a loss of downstream participant benefits.

Balancing Adaptation and Fidelity

Balancing adaptation and fidelity is critical in EBI implementation. The development of theoretical guidance for how adaptations should be managed and documented is an emerging area of study within implementation science (Aarons et al. 2017; Kirk et al. 2019; Wiltsey Stirman et al. 2019). The Dynamic Sustainability Framework (DSF) embraces the theory that adaptations that do not deviate from the original core effective elements of an intervention are critical to long-term sustainment of EBPs (Chambers et al. 2013). Intervention core "functions" are the underlying purpose of an intervention and how the intervention works to produce a desired outcome (Perez Jolles et al. 2019) and thus should not be adapted as they make the intervention effective.

Developing and evaluating implementation models to guide organizations and clinicians in facilitating EBI delivery with appropriate adherence and competence while allowing for adaptations that do not interfere with EBI core functions is a priority for implementation research in mental health services. The fidelity to "function" approach focuses on assessing fidelity to underlying core intervention functions and allowing for adaptations to the forms (or strategies) to best meet the needs of patients in a given practice setting. Kirk et al. (2019) developed a step-by-step guide, including methods, tools, and recommendations for identifying core functions and forms which may be needed when an organization or clinician plan to implement a manualized EBI where core functions are not specified. Steps in this process include reviewing the original EBI protocol or consulting with EBI developers to identify core functions and forms; consulting with stakeholders (e.g., EBI developers and target audience of adapted EBI) to identify differences between old and new implementation context; making adaptations to form as necessary, but ensuring that adapted forms still fulfill core functions; and testing and evaluating outcomes of adapted EBI.

Similarly, Aaron and colleagues (2012) developed the Dynamic Adaptation Process (DAP), designed to guide EBI adaptation and system and organizational adaptations. The DAP is a collaborative, multi-stakeholder approach that involves identifying core functions and adaptable characteristics of an EBI and then supporting implementation with specific training on allowable adaptations to the model. The DAP involves iterative testing of planned adaptations using a continuous feedback loop to inform continued adaptation as needed. Core features of the DAP are collaboration of an implementation resource team (IRT) comprised of multiple stakeholders (e.g., academic researchers, intervention developers, administrators, clinicians), training and coaching in context-driven adaptation support, providing client feedback and the data based on client surveys to evaluate and inform adaptations, and making adaptation an explicit part of the implementation process.

In the absence of a formal implementation strategy, implementers can still make informed decisions when modifying an EBI from its original form by proactively and carefully thinking through the reasons and goals for the change and expected outcomes. This includes outlining the reasons for the adaptation (e.g., existing policies, service structure within the agency, provider training and skills, patient literacy and education) and proactively planning the process of modifying the EBI, including what is being modified (e.g., content itself, the way the program is delivered) and what is the nature of the modification (e.g., adding elements, removing/skipping elements, integrating another treatment) (Wiltsey Stirman et al. 2019). Careful consideration of the process, nature, and outcomes of change made to an EBI during the implementation process can help to promote adaptations that preserve the core effective elements of an intervention.

Summary

EBIs are practices or programs that have documented empirical evidence of effectiveness on a clinical outcome. The process of generating evidence supporting an intervention involves phases or stages of intervention development, with most stressing the importance of translating research into real-world clinical practice quickly and efficiently with the engagement of patients and communities. Efficacy trials can generate evidence with a high degree of internal validity to determine cause and effect relationships by eliminating other confounding variables with highly controlled study design and procedures. However, a limitation of most efficacy studies is the ability to generalize study findings to other providers, patients, and settings. Effectiveness studies are conducted in real-world settings with more flexible design and study procedures; however, the strength of the intervention effect may be compromised by confounding variables related to characteristics of the providers, patients, and/or setting. A common approach is to use core features of both efficacy and effectiveness trials to conduct scientifically rigorous research in real-world practice settings.

When research findings are translated to practice, EBIs are often adapted from their original form as they are implemented in a new setting or with a new patient group. However, changing the core components or functions of an intervention could reduce its effectiveness. Identifying the core functions and adaptable forms or activities of an EBI can guide implementers to modify an EBI without compromising its effectiveness. Understanding how, with whom, and where the research supporting an EBI was generated and identifying core functions and allowable adaptations of an EBI model can help organizations and clinicians make informed decisions about intervention implementation to ensure they are delivering effective treatments that are acceptable and beneficial for patients and their families.

References

Aarons, G. A., Sklar, M., Mustanski, B., Benbow, N., & Brown, C. H. (2017). "Scaling-out" evidence-based interventions to new populations or new health care delivery systems. *Implementation Science, 12*(1), 111. https://doi.org/10.1186/s13012-017-0640-6

Aarons Gregory, A., Miller Elizabeth, A., Green Amy, E., Perrott Jennifer, A., & Bradway, R. (2012). Adaptation happens: a qualitative case study of implementation of The Incredible Years evidence-based parent training programme in a residential substance abuse treatment programme. *Journal of Children's Services, 7*(4), 233–245. https://doi.org/10.1108/17466661211286463

Aschbrenner, K. A., Bond, G. R., Pratt, S. I., Jue, K., Williams, G., Banerjee, S., & Bartels, S. J. (2020). Evaluating agency-led adaptions to an evidence-based lifestyle intervention for adults with serious mental illness. *Implementation Research and Practice, 1*, 2633489520943200. https://doi.org/10.1177/2633489520943200

Bauchner, H., Golub, R. M., & Fontanarosa, P. B. (2019). Reporting and Interpretation of Randomized Clinical Trials. *JAMA, 322*(8), 732–735. https://doi.org/10.1001/jama.2019.12056

Baumann, A. A., Cabassa, L. J., & Stirman, S. W. (2017). Adaptation in dissemination and implementation science. In Dissemination and Implementation Research in Health: Translating Science to Practice, Second Edition (pp. 285–300). Oxford University Press. https://doi.org/10.1093/oso/9780190683214.003.0017

Bond, G. R., & Drake, R. E. (2020). Assessing the Fidelity of Evidence-Based Practices: History and Current Status of a Standardized Measurement Methodology. *Administration and Policy in Mental Health and Mental Health Services Research, 47*(6), 874–884. https://doi.org/10.1007/s10488-019-00991-6

Bond, G. R., Drake, R. E., & Becker, D. R. (2012). Generalizability of the Individual Placement and Support (IPS) model of supported employment outside the US. *World Psychiatry, 11*(1), 32–39. https://doi.org/10.1016/j.wpsyc.2012.01.005

Bond, G. R., Evans, L., Salyers, M. P., Williams, J., & Kim, H. W. (2000). Measurement of fidelity in psychiatric rehabilitation. *Ment Health Serv Res, 2*(2), 75–87. https://doi.org/10.1023/a:1010153020697

Bowen, D. J., Kreuter, M., Spring, B., Cofta-Woerpel, L., Linnan, L., Weiner, D., Bakken, S., Kaplan, C. P., Squiers, L., Fabrizio, C., & Fernandez, M. (2009). How we design feasibility studies. *American Journal of Preventive Medicine, 36*(5), 452–457. https://doi.org/10.1016/j.amepre.2009.02.002

Breitenstein, S. M., Gross, D., Garvey, C. A., Hill, C., Fogg, L., & Resnick, B. (2010). Implementation fidelity in community-based interventions. *Research in nursing & health, 33*(2), 164–173. https://doi.org/10.1002/nur.20373

Carroll, C., Patterson, M., Wood, S., Booth, A., Rick, J., & Balain, S. (2007). A conceptual framework for implementation fidelity. *Implementation Science, 2*(1), 40. https://doi.org/10.1186/1748-5908-2-40

Carroll, K. M., & Rounsaville, B. J. (2003). Bridging the Gap: A Hybrid Model to Link Efficacy and Effectiveness Research in Substance Abuse Treatment. *Psychiatric Services, 54*(3), 333–339. https://doi.org/10.1176/appi.ps.54.3.333

Chambers, D. A., Glasgow, R. E., & Stange, K. C. (2013). The dynamic sustainability framework: addressing the paradox of sustainment amid ongoing change. *Implementation Science, 8*(1), 117. https://doi.org/10.1186/1748-5908-8-117

Czajkowski, S. M., Powell, L. H., Adler, N., Naar-King, S., Reynolds, K. D., Hunter, C. M., Laraia, B., Olster, D. H., Perna, F. M., Peterson, J. C., Epel, E., Boyington, J. E., & Charlson, M. E. (2015). From ideas to efficacy: The ORBIT model for developing behavioral treatments for chronic diseases. *Health Psychol, 34*(10), 971–982. https://doi.org/10.1037/hea0000161

Drake, R. E., Wilkniss, S. M., Frounfelker, R. L., Whitley, R., Zipple, A. M., McHugo, G. J., & Bond, G. R. (2009). Public-Academic Partnerships: The Thresholds-Dartmouth Partnership and Research on Shared Decision Making. *Psychiatric Services, 60*(2), 142–144. https://doi.org/10.1176/ps.2009.60.2.142

Eccles, M. P., & Mittman, B. S. (2006). Welcome to Implementation Science. *Implementation Science, 1*(1), 1. https://doi.org/10.1186/1748-5908-1-1

El-Kotob, R., & Giangregorio, L. M. (2018). Pilot and feasibility studies in exercise, physical activity, or rehabilitation research. *Pilot and Feasibility Studies, 4*(1), 137. https://doi.org/10.1186/s40814-018-0326-0

Escoffery, C., Lebow-Skelley, E., Haardoerfer, R., Boing, E., Udelson, H., Wood, R., Hartman, M., Fernandez, M. E., & Mullen, P. D. (2018). A systematic review of adaptations of evidence-based public health interventions globally. *Implementation Science, 13*(1), 125. https://doi.org/10.1186/s13012-018-0815-9

Gitlin, L. N. (2013). Introducing a new intervention: an overview of research phases and common challenges. *The American journal of occupational therapy: official publication of the American Occupational Therapy Association, 67*(2), 177–184. https://doi.org/10.5014/ajot.2013.006742

Glasgow, R. E., & Riley, W. T. (2013). Pragmatic Measures: What They Are and Why We Need Them. *American Journal of Preventive Medicine, 45*(2), 237–243. https://doi.org/10.1016/j.amepre.2013.03.010

Green, L. W. (2014). Closing the chasm between research and practice: evidence of and for change. *Health Promotion Journal of Australia, 25*(1), 25–29. https://doi.org/10.1071/he13101

Kilbourne, A. M., Neumann, M. S., Waxmonsky, J., Bauer, M. S., Kim, H. M., Pincus, H. A., Hepburn, B., & Thomas, Marshall. (2012). Public-Academic Partnerships: Evidence-Based Implementation: The Role of Sustained Community-Based Practice and Research Partnerships. *Psychiatric Services, 63*(3), 205–207. https://doi.org/10.1176/appi.ps.201200032

Kirk, M., Haines, E. R., Rokoske, F. S., Powell, B., Weinberger, M., Hanson, L., & Birken, S. (2019). A case study of a theory-based method for identifying and reporting core functions and forms of evidence-based interventions. *Transl Behav Med.*

Kistin, C., & Silverstein, M. (2015). Pilot Studies: A Critical but Potentially Misused Component of Interventional Research. *JAMA, 314*(15), 1561–1562. https://doi.org/10.1001/jama.2015.10962

Kraemer, H. C., Mintz, J., Noda, A., Tinklenberg, J., & Yesavage, J. A. (2006). Caution regarding the use of pilot studies to guide power calculations for study proposals. *Arch Gen Psychiatry, 63*(5), 484–489. https://doi.org/10.1001/archpsyc.63.5.484

Leon, A. C., Davis, L. L., & Kraemer, H. C. (2011). The role and interpretation of pilot studies in clinical research. *Journal of psychiatric research, 45*(5), 626–629. https://doi.org/10.1016/j.jpsychires.2010.10.008

Marchand, E., Stice, E., Rohde, P., & Becker, C. B. (2011). Moving from efficacy to effectiveness trials in prevention research. *Behav Res Ther, 49*(1), 32–41. https://doi.org/10.1016/j.brat.2010.10.008

McGurk, S. R., Mueser, K. T., Xie, H., Welsh, J., Kaiser, S., Drake, R. E., Becker, D., Bailey, E., Fraser, G., Wolfe, R., & McHugo, G. J. (2015). Cognitive enhancement treatment for people with mental illness who do not respond to supported employment: A randomized controlled trial. *American Journal of Psychiatry, 172*(9), 852–861.

Möller, H.-J. (2011). Effectiveness studies: advantages and disadvantages. *Dialogues in clinical neuroscience, 13*(2), 199–207. https://pubmed.ncbi.nlm.nih.gov/21842617 https://www.ncbi.nlm.nih.gov/pmc/articles/PMC3181999/

Moncher, F. J., & Prinz, R. J. (1991). Treatment fidelity in outcome studies. *Clin Psychol Rev, 11*(3), 247–266. https://doi.org/10.1016/0272-7358(91)90103-2

Morris, Z. S., Wooding, S., & Grant, J. (2011). The answer is 17 years, what is the question: understanding time lags in translational research. *Journal of the Royal Society of Medicine, 104*(12), 510–520. https://doi.org/10.1258/jrsm.2011.110180

Onken, L. S. (2019). History and Evaluation of the NIH Stage Model: Overcoming hurdles to create behavioral interventions to improve public health. In S. Dimidjian (Ed.), *Evidence-based practice in action: bridging clinical science and intervention* (pp. 28–42). The Guilford Press.

Perez Jolles, M., Lengnick-Hall, R., & Mittman, B. S. (2019). Core Functions and Forms of Complex Health Interventions: a Patient-Centered Medical Home Illustration. *J Gen Intern Med, 34*(6), 1032–1038. https://doi.org/10.1007/s11606-018-4818-7

Powell, B. J., Garcia, K., & Fernandez, M. (2019). Implementation Strategies. In D. Chambers, C. Vinson, & W. Norton (Eds.), *Optimizing the Cancer Control*

Continuum: Advancing Implementation Research (pp. 98–120). Oxford University Press.

Powell, B. J., Waltz, T. J., Chinman, M. J., Damschroder, L. J., Smith, J. L., Matthieu, M. M., Proctor, E. K., & Kirchner, J. E. (2015). A refined compilation of implementation strategies: results from the Expert Recommendations for Implementing Change (ERIC) project. *Implementation Science, 10*(1), 21. https://doi.org/10.1186/s13012-015-0209-1

Proctor, E., Silmere, H., Raghavan, R., Hovmand, P., Aarons, G., Bunger, A., Griffey, R., & Hensley, M. (2011). Outcomes for implementation research: conceptual distinctions, measurement challenges, and research agenda. *Administration and policy in mental health, 38*(2), 65–76. https://doi.org/10.1007/s10488-010-0319-7

Proctor, E. K., Landsverk, J., Aarons, G., Chambers, D., Glisson, C., & Mittman, B. (2009). Implementation research in mental health services: an emerging science with conceptual, methodological, and training challenges. *Administration and policy in mental health, 36*(1), 24–34. https://doi.org/10.1007/s10488-008-0197-4

Proctor, E. K., Powell, B. J., & McMillen, J. C. (2013). Implementation strategies: recommendations for specifying and reporting. *Implementation science: IS, 8*, 139–139. https://doi.org/10.1186/1748-5908-8-139

Rothwell, P. M. (2005). External validity of randomised controlled trials: "to whom do the results of this trial apply?". *Lancet, 365*(9453), 82–93. https://doi.org/10.1016/s0140-6736(04)17670-8

Roy-Byrne, P. P., Sherbourne, C. D., Craske, M. G., Stein, M. B., Katon, W., Sullivan, G., Means-Christensen, A., & Bystritsky, A. (2003). Moving Treatment Research From Clinical Trials to the Real World. *Psychiatric Services, 54*(3), 327–332. https://doi.org/10.1176/appi.ps.54.3.327

Shean, G. D. (2012). Some Limitations on the External Validity of Psychotherapy Efficacy Studies and Suggestions for Future Research. *American Journal of Psychotherapy, 66*(3), 227–242. https://doi.org/10.1176/appi.psychotherapy.2012.66.3.227

Singal, A. G., Higgins, P. D. R., & Waljee, A. K. (2014). A primer on effectiveness and efficacy trials. *Clinical and translational gastroenterology, 5*(1), e45–e45. https://doi.org/10.1038/ctg.2013.13

Teague, G. B., Mueser, K. T., & Rapp, C. A. (2012). Advances in fidelity measurement for mental health services research: four measures. *Psychiatr Serv, 63*(8), 765–771. https://doi.org/10.1176/appi.ps.201100430

Torpy, J. M., Lynm, C., & Glass, R. M. (2010). Randomized Controlled Trials. *JAMA, 303*(12), 1216–1216. https://doi.org/10.1001/jama.303.12.1216

Waltz, J., Addis, M. E., Koerner, K., & Jacobson, N. S. (1993). Testing the integrity of a psychotherapy protocol: assessment of adherence and competence. *J Consult Clin Psychol, 61*(4), 620–630. https://doi.org/10.1037//0022-006x.61.4.620

Wiltsey Stirman, S., Baumann, A. A., & Miller, C. J. (2019). The FRAME: an expanded framework for reporting adaptations and modifications to evidence-based interventions. *Implementation Science, 14*(1), 58. https://doi.org/10.1186/s13012-019-0898-y

Wiltsey Stirman, S., Gamarra, J. M., Bartlett, B. A., Calloway, A., & Gutner, C. A. (2017). Empirical Examinations of Modifications and Adaptations to Evidence-Based Psychotherapies: Methodologies, Impact, and Future Directions. *Clinical Psychology: Science and Practice, 24*(4), 396–420. https://doi.org/10.1111/cpsp.12218

Cognitive Behavioral Therapy

Martha Page Burkholder

Cognitive behavioral therapy (CBT) is a well-studied and widely implemented psychological intervention for most of the diagnoses encountered in community mental health (CMH) settings (Beck 2019). It is an evidence-based practice recommended by a majority of regulatory and advisory bodies in the United States and around the world including the American Psychiatric Association, the American Association for Community Psychiatry, the American Psychological Association, the United Kingdom's National Institute for Health and Care Excellence Guidelines, the National Institute of Mental Health (NIMH), and the National Alliance on Mental Illness and one which is offered in most community mental health centers.

CBT draws upon principles from behaviorism and rational emotive behavior therapy and indeed from ancient texts on stoicism, mindfulness, and positive thinking (David et al. 2004). For example, the Yoga Sutra 2.33 states, "When negative thoughts present themselves cultivate and think the opposite thoughts with feeling." CBT is also recovery based, emphasizes improving functional capacity over diagnostic rigidity, requires active participation by both recipient and provider, is compatible with psychopharmacology and complementary interventions (mindfulness, exercise), and gives primary focus to individualized treatment planning and the encouragement of positive goals and hopefulness. It has also been amended and expanded to include mindfulness-based CBT (Segal et al. 2012), acceptance and commitment therapy (Hayes et al. 2016), dialectical behavior therapy (Linehan 2021), and applications to a multitude of psychological issues and diagnoses. There are now modifications of CBT treatment available online, through telehealth (Cuijpers et al. 2019) and with guided and self-guided formats that have been shown to be significantly more effective than treatment as usual or waiting lists (Lopez-Lopez et al. 2019).

In recent years, CBT has incorporated principles of mental health recovery orientation with a renewed emphasis on positive goals, hope, and health. Dr. Aaron T. Beck, the founder of CBT, describes "recovery oriented cognitive therapy (CT-R) as shifting from the initial emphasis of CBT on negative affect and dysfunctional thoughts to a focus on positive feelings, resilience, promoting empowerment and boosting self-esteem" (Beck et al. 2020). The addition of social skills training to CBT has also shown great promise (Granholm et al. 2016). This chapter gives an overview of the philosophy and building blocks of CBT followed by sections devoted to the primary diagnoses encountered in community settings. It will cover the treatment of mood disorders, anxiety disorders including panic

M. P. Burkholder (✉)
University of Arizona College of Medicine, COPE Community Services, Tucson, AZ, USA

W. E. Sowers et al. (eds.), *Textbook of Community Psychiatry*,
https://doi.org/10.1007/978-3-031-10239-4_22

disorder, psychotic disorders, sleep disorders, and suicide.

While psychologists and other independent licensed professionals are often the providers of CBT, the role of psychiatry is a crucial one. Prescribers are often the rate-limiting step in CMH settings due to cost and relative scarcity, but a CBT-informed formulation and treatment plan can augment the effectiveness of care and requires both collaboration with all team members and a mind and skill set ready to recommend and utilize CBT techniques.

Background and Core Concepts

Dr. Beck and his team at the University of Pennsylvania conceived CBT in the 1960s and 1970s (Beck et al. 1987; Beck et al. 1996). He noted that his patients with depressed moods consistently expressed negative and self-critical thoughts and beliefs, which he termed "dysfunctional" thoughts. Beck observed that these thoughts and beliefs influenced the emotional and behavioral responses to an occurrence or event more than the actual event itself and that those beliefs were amenable to examination and restructuring in collaboration with the patient. Examples of such irrational beliefs or distorted thinking can include "all or nothing thinking," "overgeneralizations," or thoughts and language full of "never, always, and should," as in "I should be able to do this perfectly every time" or "I never do anything right."

The therapeutic relationship is at the core of CBT for depression, emphasizing the Rogerian counseling skills of warmth, accuracy, empathy, and genuineness along with basic trust and rapport. It is individualized for each patient, grounded in collaboration on goals and the specific focus of each treatment. Cultural and individual characteristics of the patient are crucial in the formulation and treatment plan.

The stance of the therapist in CBT is engaged and interactive. Self-disclosure can be a powerful tool when used appropriately and moderated for each situation. It contributes to the collaborative nature of the sessions. For example, if the patient reports difficulty with procrastination and getting moving, the therapist can describe their own similar experience and how beginning with a 10-min walk in the mornings has really helped with energy, focus, and managing anxiety.

Basic CBT Tools

The ABC model is a good way to explain the basics of CBT to the patient while setting the stage for collaborative actions and interventions to manage depressed or anxious thoughts. The premise is that our beliefs and thoughts about events in our life powerfully influence our emotional and behavioral reactions. "A" is the activating event or perception (what happens), "B" is the belief or thoughts/cognitions about the event, and "C" is the consequence or feeling that results. By identifying and examining the beliefs and thoughts (Are they true? Are they useful? Are there any alternative explanations?), it is possible to change or modify the "B," thereby altering the "C" or emotional response.

For example, let's suppose you (the patient) are waiting at a restaurant table for your new "dream date" to arrive and they are over 15 min late. You check your watch, look hopefully and repeatedly at the door, and ask the server to stop asking if you are ready to order. These thoughts might arise: "I'll bet they're not coming. I've probably been stood up. I knew it was too good to be true. This kind of thing always happens to me. I might as well just give up on dating. I'll probably be alone for the rest of my life." Or, alternatively, as a patient with social phobia recently said to me, you may think, "Thank goodness, now I don't have to deal with a conversation with a new person!"

The therapist can ask, "How would that make you feel?" "Upset, sad, angry, disheartened, defeated" might be an answer (or "relieved" if you are the person with social phobia). The thera-

Activating event ⟶ Belief/thought ⟶ Consequence/feeling

pist would clarify the details of the event and pose any possible modifying or alternative explanations. Could the bus or subway be delayed? Did you forget to turn up the sound for your cell phone and might you have missed a message? Perhaps you got the date or time wrong? Would these alternative beliefs change your emotional reaction?

Another way to conceptualize this principle is the 3 C's: Catch It, Check It, and Change It (Granholm et al. 2016). The 3 C's suggest that patients can "catch" the thought or belief, "check" its validity (evidence for and against), and "change" it by looking at possible alternative explanations which can affect the emotional or functional outcome.

Importantly, CBT also looks at the behavioral or activating options for change, including setting goals and homework, behavioral experiments, mindful ways to manage anxiety and meaningful activities, and exercise to augment positive moods. The formulation which is developed collaboratively with the patient will include predisposing factors (e.g., childhood experiences), precipitating factors (life events and stresses), and perpetuating factors (social circumstances, unrealistic expectations) (Kingdon and Turkington 2002).

The basic structure of CBT therapy sessions is similar across diagnoses. Each session begins with a check-in and the measurement of symptoms including mood (Beck et al. 1996) and anxiety levels. The agenda is set in collaboration with the patient (Beck 2011), homework is reviewed, and goals are chosen for the session. Problems are clarified, problem-solving skills are rehearsed and discussed, and a goal and homework for the next session are set; all of this is done collaboratively. Role-playing and visualization of possible scenarios are used to practice possible responses. The mood and anxiety levels are re-checked to see if there has been a change, and the reasons for any changes are discussed. The number of visits is usually time limited, often 10–20 visits depending on the acuity and severity of symptoms. The interval between visits can be tapered toward the end of treatment with "brush-up" sessions scheduled if needed.

The remainder of the chapter is devoted to how CBT treatment has been adapted to the most prevalent diagnoses seen in community mental health.

Depression and Mood Disorders

Depression

Depression is a leading cause of disability worldwide and a major contributor to the overall global burden of disease (GBD 2020). There are also well-studied and effective treatments. Mild to moderate depression can be effectively treated with talk therapies (such as CBT or interpersonal psychotherapy) or with medications (Cipriani et al. 2018). Severe forms of depression respond best to a combination of medications and psychotherapy, although a recent study (Furokawa et al. 2017) found CBT alone to be effective in treating severe depression. The goal for future study will be a personalized treatment for adult depression, perhaps using multivariate equations to predict differential response (Kessler et al. 2017).

In his seminal publication, *Cognitive Therapy of Depression*, described a "negative triad" wherein a person's belief system involved automatic and negative thoughts about the self, the world (or environment), and the future. He found that people with depression think of themselves as faulty and defective and see the future as hopeless. He also described "cognitive distortions" or negative self-assessments. These can include:

*Selective abstraction or jumping to conclusions (decisions based on a limited part of a situation or limited evidence), for example, "The boss stayed late at work yesterday and his evaluations are due today. I'll bet he's going to fire me."

*Downplaying the positive and exaggerating the negative parts of an event.

*Overgeneralization (basing conclusions on a single fact or part of an event).

*Personalizing (assuming blame for things that aren't in a person's control).

*"Should" and "Always or Never" statements ("I should have known that would happen," "I'll never be able to finish anything!").

While explaining the ABC model as an initial part of therapy, the therapist can introduce the thought-processing distortions listed above and help the patient begin to "work backward" from a sad or uncomfortable emotion to the underlying thoughts and assumptions that led to their reaction. Noticing a shift in expression or affect, the therapist can investigate the underlying assumption or thought that went through the patient's mind as that was occurring (almost like seeing a ticker-tape notice run across their forehead!).

For example, during a group discussion about the ongoing stress of trying to move out of a women's shelter and find independent housing, a patient became initially frustrated and then sad, saying "And I don't have any friends either." The other group members quickly responded, asking, "Wait, what about me? What about us?" Slowly the first woman looked around the room and began to smile, "Yes, I know I have friends here. But when I realize I have to keep waiting for housing it feels like it will never end, and then I do get sad. It can make me forget you are my support and friends."

Another way to catch the "all or nothing" thinking is through the 3 C's (Catch It, Check It, Change It). The patient states, "I know my husband is going to leave me because I get sad." The therapist might use Socratic questioning here, asking to learn more about the origin of the thought and any evidence to support or refute it. "When you have that thought, how does it make you feel? Have you had that feeling in the past? What happened then? I remember you told me you both got through a time like this a few years ago when he lost his job. What helped then, how did you make it?"

Woven into the CBT approach is prioritizing positive goal setting and offering hopeful options (Beck 2011). Sharing your belief that the patient will get better is also therapeutic. An example of this is saying, "I remember you've mentioned things you can do that take your mind off the sad mood: walking in the mornings with your dogs, the calls to your kids and grandkids. The fact that you are calmer once you get home rather than at work is a good sign that the depression isn't there all the time. Let's talk about some rewarding things you could do this week. Would you be willing to set one or two as homework?"

It is also important to activate the behavioral part of CBT. This can be anything that gets the patient involved in exercise or projects. I usually suggest a 10-min walk in the morning, as most people will acknowledge that they think they can manage that. It not only gets them physically active; it helps reset the circadian rhythm and sleep pattern in helpful ways. Dancing to their favorite music while getting ready in the morning or to decompress after a difficult day is another option.

Tying up the sessions with a review of questions and setting a homework assignment geared toward overall goals is also an important part of each meeting. Rating scales of "before" and "after" mood can also be helpful.

Bipolar Disorder

Bipolar disorder affects about 45 million people worldwide. Effective treatments are available for both the acute phase and to prevent relapse. CBT can be adapted to the treatment of mood swings but needs to be grounded in psychoeducation and medication management as well (Chiang et al. 2017). CBT-R can lower the relapse rate and improve depressive symptoms, mania severity, and psychosocial functioning (Chatterton et al. 2017).

One way to conceptualize the way thoughts can influence behavior in bipolar disorder comes from a 2014 psychology and psychotherapy study (Jones et al. 2014). Extremely negative thoughts can bring on "descent behaviors" (like withdrawing from friends) associated with depression, while overly positive thoughts can lead to "ascent behaviors" (such as risk-taking) associated with mania. CBT can be a way to level out these extremes. Techniques include psychoeducation, too, to teach the signs, symptoms, and causes of the disorder. Diaries and journals are very helpful for monitoring moods and to evaluate what stressors, sleep issues, etc. can predict or foreshadow relapses.

As with CBT for depression, the therapy will work on identifying dysfunctional thoughts (Catch), evaluate their validity and usefulness (Check), and find problem-solving techniques to manage them (Change) in healthy ways. This could include finding healthy lifestyle choices to stabilize mood such as sleep and hygiene, limiting stress, and maximizing social supports.

Anxiety Disorders

Anxiety disorders are the most common mental health disorder in the United States, affecting 18.1% of adults (Carpenter et al. 2018; Locke et al. 2015). The category includes generalized anxiety disorder, panic disorder, agoraphobia, social anxiety disorder, and posttraumatic stress disorder (PTSD). CBT principles have been used in the treatment of all of these with adaptations specific to each. Please see chapter "Traumatic Stress in the Community: Identification and Intervention" for more specifics about PTSD.

The ABC model and identifying dysfunctional thoughts and beliefs are especially relevant for anxiety concerns (Zhang et al. 2019). The use of benzodiazepines to manage anxiety can lead to problematic outcomes for patients, owing to potential tolerance and dependence. CBT offers an alternative intervention that teaches tools the patient can use in many settings. Most patients can identify with feelings of worry or stress. Treatment begins by identifying presenting symptoms and then normalizing the physiological responses to stress. Discussing the "fight, flight, or freeze" paradigm and educating the patient on normal responses to threats allow the introduction of CBT as an intervention. For example, the rapid heart rate and breathing associated with stress are protective mechanisms intended to shield us from harm. The surge of adrenaline and its subsequent physiological response are intended to manage the perceived threat. But in our modern settings of work, family, etc., there is usually no "superhero" way to fight or flee, and repeated experiences of anxiety and panic become not only distressing but also harmful to long-term mental and physical health.

CBT postulates that there is a thought or belief that usually triggers or perpetuates the anxiety response. "Tomorrow is my test and I'm going to fail." "Everyone at the meeting will be looking at me and know how nervous I am." "My heart is racing and that means I'm having a heart attack." "I'm breathing fast and feel light-headed so I'm going to pass out or have a stroke."

Discovering the automatic thoughts that accompany the anxiety response, investigating their validity, testing more functional responses, and learning to use mindfulness techniques to manage the discomfort have been demonstrated to both guide the patient to an understanding of the causes of anxiety and provide relief from the episodes.

Often "safety behaviors" arise in response to ongoing anxiety. By avoiding the "threat," there is an initial relief of symptoms. "If I stay home and don't go out, I'll be safe from the stress that overwhelms me." Eventually, however, the "safe" situation becomes the problem, and the safety behavior reinforces dysfunctional thoughts and fears. CBT works to explain how confronting the fear through exposure is the path to recovery. Combined with mindfulness and relaxation techniques, graduated exposure or experiments to understand and then overcome unsubstantiated fears are key to behavioral change.

Panic Disorder

Panic attacks are a specific form of anxiety, usually lasting 10–15 min, also involving what can be frightening physiological experiences of rapid heart rate, shortness of breath, light-headedness, and/or tingling of the extremities. People initially often go to emergency departments, convinced they are close to dying. The person often distrusts the conclusion that this is a panic attack because the episodes can be so frightening. There is also a stigma to mental health, which will need to be addressed as part of the initial workup and treatment plan.

After establishing rapport and a therapeutic relationship and educating the patient about panic disorder and the fight or flight response begins the treatment. An initial option is to demonstrate how conclusions about the physical changes can lead to perpetuating panic attacks. In the office, after teaching mindfulness and relaxation techniques, a test can be offered to demonstrate these ideas. The patient will be asked to try rapid breathing while in the office with the expected results of setting off physiological responses that simulate a panic response. Hyperventilating on its own can induce many of the sensations of panic such as light-headedness, tingling of fingers and extremities, feeling of shortness of breath, and rapid heart rate.

Examining the thought "My heart is beating quickly so I'm having a heart attack" needs to be done carefully; generating other reasons for a fast heart rate and looking at previous episodes that led to negative workups can be of use. Learning breathing techniques to slow the heart rate and rate of respirations is also very helpful. People may be able to think, "If I were having a heart attack, I don't think I could slow my breathing like this. I am in a safe place."

Using collaboration and Socratic questioning, the therapist works to trace the possible thoughts or triggers that may set off a panic attack. Often, these are initially fleeting observations or thoughts, and the patient often report that the panic attacks come "out of the blue." Usually, there is a trigger, and once identified, it can be examined and its validity questioned or changed. For example, the thought "my teenage son left the house on an errand, and now I am hearing sirens coming from a few blocks away" could lead to worries that something had happened to the young man. There are, though, possible alternative beliefs: "This is a busy neighborhood and city, there are often sirens in the distance. He is a good driver and actually very cautious even if he is a teenager. He's only been away for 15 min and the pet store is at least a 10-min drive from here, so it's probable he only just now got to the store. I could text him to see." The goal is to discover the origin of the panic reaction and learn to manage the beliefs and sensations that accompany anxiety and panic. Incorporating information about exercise as an option when anxious (the quick 10-min walk) as well as mindfulness and breathing techniques offers immediate and practical interventions.

Outcome measures of CBT for anxiety are excellent, and there are self-help books and online resources for patients to use as well (Burns 2007; NIMH 2016).

Psychosis

Cognitive Therapy for Psychosis is an exciting addition to the treatment options for patients with serious mental illness. It combines well with the recovery model and offers a way to collaborate on goals and managing symptoms. For full details, please see chapter "Cognitive Behavior Therapy for Psychosis".

Insomnia

Reports of trouble with sleep are extremely common. Up to 50 percent of American adults will experience insomnia (difficulty falling asleep or staying asleep) at some point in their lives. The causes are multiple and include medical and psychiatric issues. Delineating and clarifying the specifics of the problem is key, as it is important to evaluate the presence of medical concerns like sleep apnea and restless leg syndrome in addition to promoting good sleep habits (Morin and Benca 2012; Bhaskar et al. 2016).

Asking for help with sleep is non-stigmatizing, and offering treatment for insomnia can be the window that allows patients to receive help they might otherwise avoid. The understanding and treatment of insomnia continue to evolve, and CBT for Insomnia (CBT-I) has strong evidence of efficacy (Wu et al. 2015). Once medical causes are ruled out or resolved, managing sleep disturbances can lead to the improvement, or even resolution, of a variety of psychiatric diagnoses.

CBT-I is a time-limited intervention for six to eight sessions. As with all CBT formulations, the first step is to collaborate with the patient and get a good history of the problem. While medications to help initiate sleep are commonly prescribed, sleep experts agree that ultimately good sleep hygiene helps to remediate the underlying problem and set up the tools for ongoing good sleep habits. CBTI can offer a means for tapering off hypnotic medications (Takaesu et al. 2019) and leads to more lasting healthy sleep habits. Booster sessions may later be required as the effectiveness of CBTI may decay with time.

Begin by educating patients on sleep hygiene tips from the American Sleep Association (Sateia 2014; Qaseem et al. 2016):

1. Set a regular sleep routine: Go to bed at the same time and (especially) wake up at the same time. Personalize it with what is relaxing: meditation, a shower or bath, music, or herbal teas.
2. Avoid daytime naps.
3. Learn to associate the bed with sleep. If you're in bed for more than 10 min without sleep, get out of bed, and sit in another quiet place. Do something calming (listen to music, herbal tea, read) until you are sleepy, and *then* get back in bed.
4. No "screens" (computers, phones) for at least an hour before bed.
5. Be careful about caffeine. It can fragment sleep. Try to use it before noon.
6. Avoid substances that interfere with sleep: tobacco, alcohol, and OTC medications.
7. Clean fresh air (crack open a window; use an air purifier).
8. Exercise (it promotes sleep) but aim for before 2 pm each day.
9. Quiet and comfortable bedroom and mattress.
10. Hide the clock.

Basics of CBT-I (Individual or Group)

1. A good health and sleep history, which should include the use of stimulants (caffeine, others) and hypnotics, alcohol and other substances, medical medications, over-the-counter meds, and current stressors.
2. Evaluate for trauma-based diagnoses and nightmares.
3. Housing specifics (i.e., work shifts, presence of a new baby in the home, possession of a bed, etc.). For example, a patient who is homeless or living in a shelter can certainly have more difficulty managing their sleep environment.
4. Sleep diary, including long-term concerns (how long has sleep been an issue), patterns and current specifics such as what time they like to go to bed and wake up, routines and work history (shift workers like nurses and EMTs can have a particularly difficult time setting sleep routines). It should preferably cover a month.
5. Beliefs about sleep (fact and myths). For example, an Army vet who could only fall asleep on a mat behind the couch, even though the rest of the family were in and out of the living room much of the night. He believed he had to be vigilant all night or something might happen to his family. His sleep was frequently disrupted, and his mood deteriorated. After elucidating the beliefs about why he slept there (having to be vigilant, protecting the family), the therapist was able to work through options that were more conducive to sleep. This was the first time he had dealt with ongoing issues related to his PTSD, which he was later able to address.
6. Automatic thoughts related to sleep issues ("This always happens, I am a terrible sleeper. Now I won't get enough sleep and I'll fail my job interview tomorrow"). Teach the ABC model and add "D," or "dispute negative thoughts about sleep."

CBT-I can be done in individual or group settings, and recent studies suggest that improvement of sleep can not only be the way into helping patients access therapy but it may also on its own provide relief from symptoms of mood and anxiety (Koffell et al. 2018; Chernyak 2019).

Suicide

Suicide rates in the United States have risen, which is of growing concern (Martinez-Ales and Keyes 2019). It is the tenth leading cause of death for adults and the second leading cause of death among young people 10–34. Between 2000 and 2018, the rate has increased by 35%. The risk for suicide increases with hopelessness, diminished problem-solving ability, and the addition of other diagnoses and issues (social isolation, decreased access to means, addictions, recent losses, pain, or medical problems). CBT targeted to suicidal ideation and behavior has a strong research base (Bryan et al. 2018; D'Anci et al. 2019). Targeting suicidality independent of the underlying diagnosis is key and can be initiated in many settings, including the emergency department. Safety planning (Stanley et al. 2018) led to a 30% reduction in attempts and is a critical part of all interventions.

The CBT approach to suicidality emphasizes that cognitions "rise to the surface" as automatic thoughts of hopelessness and despair. Problem-solving ability, which decreases with depression, shows cognitive constriction and limited attentional flexibility. Cognitions of suicidal patients often express core beliefs as automatic thoughts such as:

About self:	I'm worthless, unlovable, and a failure. I'll be abandoned and all alone; I'm incompetent and weak.
About others:	No one cares about me; they'd be better off without me.
The future:	Everything is hopeless, I'll never be happy; I'll always be in pain.
Distress:	It's unbearable, I cannot stand this pain, and it will only get worse.
Suicide:	There's nothing I can do to end this pain and no other way out.

These thoughts show reasoning biases and maintenance factors that include problem-solving deficits, trouble coping with strong emotion, perceived unbearableness of negative emotion, attentional bias, impulsivity, memory bias, pervasive avoidance, and maladaptive cognitions. The key is to manage hopelessness and may be measured by the Beck Hopelessness Scale with stronger findings than that of the BDI in suicidal patients.

The Treatment Outline

Session 1: Building Hope and Safety Plan
It is crucial to clarify and understand the current events and beliefs that led to suicidal thoughts. Once they are understood, it is easier to plan other actions and responses. Emphasize that people can learn new ways to solve problems and cope with negative emotions. Urges will fluctuate, so there can be planning for what to do with the ups and downs. Build hope, using recovery-oriented questions that ask about best or positive times of life. Ask about values and guide the patient to visualize aspirations. Identify reasons for living. Emphasize, "You will get better." Describe the treatment plan and collaborate on an action plan. Set specific and actionable goals. Record or write the conclusions for the patient to review daily. "What would you like to remember and what do you think you can do this week?"

Complete a safety plan (https://suicidepreventionlifeline.org/). In the safety plan, be specific and detailed. The goal is not to feel good immediately *but to get through.* Elicit likelihood of getting through and identify obstacles. Role-play possible scenarios, find ways to manage different stressors, and visualize successful outcomes.

Session 2
"Recall when you overcame difficulties, what resources did you use?" Ask about previous times when the patient overcame a difficult problem. Identify core beliefs about self, especially positive ones. Look at events and beliefs that create vulnerability, teach problem-solving skills, and practice visualization of change and role-plays. Identify maladaptive beliefs and evaluate the cognitive associations that come with hopelessness. Create a "hope box" (physical or virtual) for saving positive reminders. Discuss some of the things that could go in there (photos,

keepsakes), and remember to look inside when negative feelings and thoughts come up.

Session 3 and On

Reinforce positive coping skills and past successful responses. Review the safety plan; look for "reasons for living" (spiritual, family). Set specific goals and test the outcomes: exercise, the hope box, outreach to supports, and pets. Work on CBT techniques to Catch, Check, and Change dysfunctional thoughts and beliefs. Continue to measure hopelessness and reality test responses to negative or dysfunctional thoughts. Continue behavioral activation and relaxation techniques.

Booster and Check-In Sessions

Building from the safety plan, help the patient anticipate future fluctuations in moods and stressors, and role-play or write out specific interventions and crisis management options.

Conclusion

Cognitive behavioral therapy is a well-researched and evidence-based practice that offers practical mental health treatment options for the patients who seek services in community settings. It offers "tools" that can complement psychopharmacology and psychosocial interventions, and patients can continue to use those tools throughout their lives. The principles of CBT can be incorporated into recovery-focused care and provide practical interventions available to all members of the treatment team.

> Go to the people. Live with the people. Learn from them. Love them. Start with what they know. Build on what they have. When the task is finished, the people will say, 'we did it ourselves'. – Lao Tsu

References

Beck AT: A 60-year evolution of cognitive theory and therapy. Perspectives on Psychological Science 14:16-20, 2019

Beck AT, Grant P, Inverso E, et al: Recovery-Oriented Cognitive Therapy for Serious Mental Health Conditions, 1st Edition. New York, NY, The Guilford Press, 2020.

Beck AT, Rush AL, Shaw BF, et al: Cognitive Therapy of Depression. New York, NY, The Guilford Press, 1987

Beck AT, Steer RA, Brown GK: Beck Depression Inventory, 2nd Edition. San Antonio, TX, Psychological Corporation, 1996

Beck JS: Cognitive Behavior Therapy: Basics and Beyond, 2nd Edition. New York, NY, The Guilford Press, 2011

Bhaskar S, Hemavathy D, Prasad S: Prevalence of chronic insomnia in adult patients and its correlation with medical comorbidities. J Family Med Prim Care 5:780-784, 2016

Bryan CJ, Peterson AL, Rudd DM: Differential effects of brief CBT versus treatment as usual on posttreatment suicide attempts among groups of suicidal patients. Psychiatr Serv 69:703-709, 2018

Burns, DD: When Panic Attacks: The New Drug-Free Anxiety Therapy That Can Change Your Life. New York, NY, Harmony, 2007

Carpenter JK, Andrews LA, Witcraft SM, et al: Cognitive behavioral therapy for anxiety and related disorders: a meta-analysis of randomized placebo-controlled trials. Depress Anxiety 35:502-514, 2018

Chatterton ML, Stockings E, Berk M, et al 2017: Psychosocial therapies for the adjunctive treatment of bipolar disorder in adults: network meta-analysis. Br J Psychiatry 210:333-341

Chernyak Y: A practical application primer on cognitive behavioral therapy for insomnia for medical residents. MedEdPortal, 2019

Chiang KJ, Tsai JC, Dresses L, et al: Efficacy of cognitive-behavioral therapy in patients with bipolar disorder: A meta-analysis of randomized controlled trials. PLoS One 12:e0176849, 2017

Cipriani A, Furukawa TA, Salanti G, et al: Comparative efficacy and acceptability of 21 antidepressant drugs for the acute treatment of adults with major depressive disorder: a systematic review and network meta-analysis. Lancet 391:1357-1366, 2018

Cuijpers P, Noma H, Karyotaki E, et al: Effectiveness and acceptability of cognitive behavior therapy delivery formats in adults with depression: a network meta-analysis. Jama Psychiatry 76:700-707, 2019

D'Anci KE, Uhl S, Giradi G, et al: Treatments for the prevention and management of suicide: a systematic review. Ann Intern Med 171:334-342, 2019

David D, Kangas M, Schnur JB, et al: REBT depression manual; managing depression using rational emotive behavior therapy. Romania, Babes-Bolyai University, 2004

Furokawa TA, Weitz ES, et al: Initial severity of depression and efficacy of cognitive-behavioral therapy; individual-participant data meta-analysis of pill-placebo-controlled trials. Br J Psychiatry 210:190-196, 2017

GBD 2020 Diseases and Injuries Collaborators: Global burden of 369 diseases and injuries in 204 countries and territories, 1990-2019: a systematic analysis for the Global Burden of Disease Study 2019. Lancet 396:1204-1222

Granholm EL, McQuaid JR, Holden JL, et al: Cognitive-Behavioral Social Skills Training for Schizophrenia: A Practical Treatment Guide. New York, NY, The Guilford Press, 2016

Hayes SC, Strosahl KD, Wilson KG: Acceptance and Commitment Therapy, 2nd Edition. New York, NY, The Guilford Press, 2016

Jones SH, Smith G, Mulligan LD, et al: Recovery-focused cognitive-behavioural therapy for recent-onset bipolar disorder: randomised controlled pilot trial. Br J Psychiatry 206:58-66, 2014

Kingdon DG, Turkington D: The Case Study Guide to Cognitive Behavior Therapy of Psychosis. Chichester, West Sussex, England. 2002.

Koffell E, Bramoweth AD, Ulmer CS: Increasing access to and utilization of cognitive behavioral therapy for insomnia (CBT-I): a narrative review. J Gen Intern Med 33:955-962, 2018

Kessler RC, van Loo HM, Wardenaar KJ, et al: Using patient self-reports to study heterogeneity of treatment effects in major depressive disorder. Epidemiology and Psychiatric Sciences. 26:22-36, 2017

Linehan MM: DBT Skills Training Manual, 2nd Edition. New York, NY, The Guilford Press, 2021

Locke AB, Kirst N, Shultz CG: Diagnosis and management of generalized anxiety disorder and panic disorder in adults. Am Fam Physician 91:617-624, 2015

Lopez-Lopez JA, Davies SR, Caldwell DM, et al: The process and delivery of CBT for depression in adults: a systematic overview and network meta-analysis. Psychological Medicine 49:1937-1947, 2019

Martinez-Ales G, Keyes KM: Fatal and non-fatal self-injury in the USA: critical review of current trends and innovations in prevention. Current Psychiatry Reports 21, 2019

Morin CM, Benca R: Chronic insomnia. Lancet 379:1129-1141, 2012

NIMH: Panic disorder: when fear overwhelms (NIMH web site). 2016. Available at: https://www.nimh.nih.gov/health/publications/panic-disorder-when-fear-overwhelms/index.shtml

Qaseem A, Kansagara D, Forceia M, et al: Management of chronic insomnia disorder in adults: a clinical practice guideline from the american college of physicians. Ann Intern Med 165:125-133, 2016

Sateia MJ: International classification of sleep disorders third edition. Contemporary Reviews in Sleep Medicine 146:1387-1394, 2014

Segal SV, Williams JMG, Teasdale JD, et al: Mindfulness-Based Cognitive Therapy for Depression, 2nd Edition. New York, NY, The Guilford Press, 2012

Stanley B, Brown GK, Brenner LA, et al: Comparison of the safety planning intervention with follow-up vs. usual care of suicidal patients treated in the emergency department JAMA Psychiatry 75:894-900, 2018

Takaesu Y, Utsumi T, Okajima I, et al: Psychosocial intervention for discontinuing benzodiazepine hypnotics in patients with chronic insomnia: A systematic review and meta-analysis. Sleep Medicine Reviews 48, 2019

Wu JQ, Appleman ER, Salazar RD, et al: Cognitive behavioral therapy for insomnia comorbid with psychiatric and medical conditions: a meta-analysis. JAMA Intern Med 175:1461-1472, 2015

Zhang A, Franklin C, Jing S, et al: The effectiveness of four empirically supported psychotherapies for primary care depression and anxiety. Journal of Affective Disorders 245:1168-1186, 2019

Psychiatric Rehabilitation

Arundati Nagendra, Kim T. Mueser,
and Corinne Cather

Introduction

We define psychiatric rehabilitation as *nonpharmacological treatments aimed to improve the course of psychosocial functioning in individuals diagnosed with serious mental illnesses (SMI)* and, accordingly, conceptualize psychiatric rehabilitation and psychosocial treatments as interchangeable. This definition differs from some conceptualizations of the two as complementary but different parts of a recovery-oriented mental health system, in which psychiatric rehabilitation focuses on addressing psychosocial or functional needs (e.g., social and occupational functioning, independent living skills) and psychosocial treatment focuses on reducing symptoms and psychological distress (Farkas and Anthony 2010). The traditional distinction between psychiatric rehabilitation and psychosocial treatments is based on medical disorders or injuries, such as diabetes or spinal cord injury, in which symptoms and functioning can be easily separated. This distinction is less useful, however, when it comes to psychiatric disorders, for which both psychiatric symptoms and impaired psychosocial functioning are core defining features according to standard psychiatric diagnostic criteria. Moreover, distinguishing between efforts to target symptoms and functional impairments is problematic because their goals are often intertwined, with interventions frequently addressing both simultaneously. For example, individuals with SMI are often motivated to engage in treatments designed to improve illness management by their desire to achieve personally important goals such as improved social relationships, work, or independent living (Mueser et al. 2006). In this chapter, we provide an overview of the history of psychiatric rehabilitation, describe specific evidence-based psychosocial treatments for SMI,

A. Nagendra (✉)
Center of Excellence for Psychosocial and Systemic Research, Department of Psychiatry, Massachusetts General Hospital, Boston, MA, USA

Disparities Research Unit, Department of Psychiatry, Massachusetts General Hospital, Boston, MA, USA

Department of Psychiatry, Harvard Medical School, Boston, MA, USA
e-mail: anagendra@mgh.harvard.edu

K. T. Mueser
Center of Excellence for Psychosocial and Systemic Research, Department of Psychiatry, Massachusetts General Hospital, Boston, MA, USA

Center for Psychiatric Rehabilitation, Departments of Occupational Therapy and Psychological and Brain Science, Boston University, Boston, MA, USA
e-mail: mueser@bu.edu

C. Cather
Center of Excellence for Psychosocial and Systemic Research, Department of Psychiatry, Massachusetts General Hospital, Boston, MA, USA

Department of Psychiatry, Harvard Medical School, Boston, MA, USA
e-mail: ccather@mgh.harvard.edu

W. E. Sowers et al. (eds.), *Textbook of Community Psychiatry*,
https://doi.org/10.1007/978-3-031-10239-4_23

and summarize psychiatric rehabilitation interventions not covered elsewhere in this book.

Psychiatric rehabilitation has historical roots in the moral treatment and mental hygiene movements of the early 1900s (Corrigan et al. 2008). However, the field grew substantially following deinstitutionalization, which resulted in two-thirds of US psychiatric inpatients being discharged into the community between the 1950s and 1990s (Geller 2000). Due to the advent of psychotropic medications, proponents of deinstitutionalization envisioned that individuals with serious mental illnesses could manage their most severe symptoms outside of hospitals and consequently receive treatment in the community, where they would experience significantly improved quality of life (Geller 2000). However, it quickly became apparent that individuals with SMI discharged to the community often did not continue to take psychotropic medications as prescribed and were at high risk of substance misuse, incarceration, and unemployment (Lamb and Bachrach 2001). Many individuals with SMI ended up homeless, making their plight starkly visible to the public eye (Corrigan et al. 2008; Lamb and Bachrach 2001).

During the deinstitutionalization process, a number of efforts were made to address the needs of individuals with SMI. These included the 1963 Community Mental Health Act, which emphasized the importance of treating individuals with SMI in the "least restrictive environment" and led to funding for community mental health centers (Geller 2000). In parallel, the consumer movement highlighted the right of individuals with SMI to fully engage in mainstream society and demonstrated their capacity to lead self-determined, productive lives (Pulice and Miccio 2006). It was against this backdrop that researchers, providers, and consumers began to work in more earnest to develop programs to support and improve the psychosocial functioning of individuals with SMI, including psychosocial clubhouses, transitional living spaces, peer-led programs, and social and occupational skills training (Corrigan et al. 2008; McKay et al. 2018; Pulice and Miccio 2006).

These steps toward systematic and comprehensive treatment for individuals with SMI living in the community represent early iterations of psychiatric rehabilitation. In 1986, Anthony and Liberman proposed a formal conceptual framework for the field which posited that, like individuals with physical disabilities, those with psychiatric disabilities need a combination of *skills* and *environmental supports* to support their recovery. This conceptualization continues over three decades later such that within psychiatric rehabilitation, some treatments are primarily skills-based (e.g., social skills training), some primarily provide environmental support (e.g., family psychoeducation), and others integrate both approaches (e.g., supported employment).

Psychiatric rehabilitation services are flexible and can be implemented in a variety of settings and modalities, including community mental health centers, inpatient settings, and psychosocial rehabilitation centers, and through outreach services such as assertive community treatment teams. Psychiatric rehabilitation interventions can be categorized in terms of the primary domains they target: psychosocial functioning, core psychopathology, and comorbid conditions. Table 1 uses this framework to categorize psychiatric rehabilitation interventions while also understanding that many interventions have dual or multiple targets (e.g., illness management and recovery addresses both relapse prevention and functioning).

In this chapter, we focus on psychiatric rehabilitation services not discussed elsewhere in this book: social skills training, cognitive remediation, social cognitive training, and physical health management. For each intervention, we provide the rationale for the service, outline the intervention and how it is delivered, describe research on treatment outcomes for the treatment, and provide additional resources for providers interested in pursuing more information about how to implement these specific interventions.

Table 1 List of psychiatric rehabilitation interventions and their primary treatment targets

Psychosocial functioning	Core psychopathology	Comorbid conditions
Employment/education: Supported employment/education (covered in chapter "Supported Employment") Transitional employment (covered in chapter "Fountain House and the Clubhouse Movement") *Housing:* Supported housing (covered in chapter "Housing First and the Role of Psychiatry in Supported Housing") *Coordination of services*: Peer support (covered in chapter "Peer Service Providers as Colleagues") Health homes (covered in chapter "Service Coordination and Health Homes") *Interpersonal functioning:* Social skills training	*Symptoms:* CBT for psychosis (covered in chapter "Cognitive Behavior Therapy for Psychosis") *Impaired cognitive functioning:* Cognitive remediation Social cognitive training *Relapse prevention:* Family therapy (covered in chapter "Family Systems Care in Public Sector Settings") *Illness and wellness self-management:* Illness management and recovery; Wellness Action Recovery Program (covered in chapter "Health Self-Management: The Emerging Importance of Trauma and Resilience")	*Substance use:* Co-occurring substance use (covered in chapters "Treatment Techniques for Co-occurring Substance Use and Mental Disorders" and "Evidence-Based Practices for Co-occurring Addiction and Mental Illness") *Physical health management:* Smoking cessation programs Nutrition and fitness interventions Physical illness self-management *Trauma and post-traumatic stress disorder:* Trauma-focused treatments (covered in chapter "Traumatic Stress in the Community: Identification and Intervention")

Social Skills Training

Rationale for Social Skills Training

Individuals with SMI experience a breadth of challenges with social functioning. Despite reporting a desire for meaningful social relationships as well as feelings of loneliness, service users often struggle to develop and maintain relationships with friends and family members (Lim et al. 2018). Moreover, individuals with SMI experience difficulties with self-care, community living skills (e.g., household living skills, finances, use of transportation), and leisure activities (Granholm et al. 2020). These impairments reduce quality of life, self-esteem, optimism, and self-efficacy (Kopelowicz et al. 2006) and increase the likelihood of relapse and rehospitalization (Buck et al. 2019). Whereas pharmacological treatments do not directly affect social functioning in SMI (Veerman et al. 2017), psychosocial interventions such as social skills training can improve functioning and, thus, should be routinely offered.

Description of the Social Skills Training Approach

Social skills training (SST) is the treatment for social functioning in SMI with the most empirical support. Social skills are defined as the instrumental and affiliative behaviors necessary to navigate an array of interpersonal situations including everyday conversation, assertiveness, conflict management, expressing empathy, communal living, friendship, dating, health maintenance, and work (Bellack et al. 2004; Kopelowicz et al. 2006). The SST model theorizes that successful social interactions require the integration of five different components of social skills (Mueser et al. 2013): paralinguistic features (vocal characteristics of speech like tone and loudness), nonverbal skills (e.g., facial expressions, gestures), verbal content, interactive balance (e.g., making relevant statements, talking for relatively equal amounts of time), and social cognition (the ability to process social information). In recent years, there has been an increased awareness of the distinct role of training social cognitive skills specifically, which we will cover in a separate section within this chapter.

SST employs a behavioral approach to teaching participants social skills, based on the principles of social learning theory (learning social behaviors by watching others) and operant conditioning (learning how to socialize by experiencing positive consequences from socially skilled behaviors) (Bellack et al. 2004). The intervention can be delivered on an individual basis but is most frequently provided in a group context to capitalize on opportunities for roleplays and discussions of shared experiences and goals. It is recommended that social skills groups include between four and eight people, with sessions lasting between 45 and 90 min and conducted one or two times per week (Mueser et al. 2013).

Group social skills training is structured as follows: (1) Participants begin by discussing the rationale for the selected skill; (2) the therapist identifies and models the steps for the skill; (3) one group member practices the skill in a roleplay, after which the therapist provides both positive and constructive feedback to shape the targeted skill; (4) the same group member then practices the skill in the same situation at least one more time and receives additional feedback from the therapist and group; and (5) other group members then practice roleplays and receive feedback in a similar fashion. Toward the end of each group, individually tailored home assignments to practice the skill outside of the session are collaboratively set with each participant (Bellack et al. 2004). To facilitate generalization of social skills to real-world settings, participants are encouraged to practice with natural supporters, such as friends, peers, relatives, or residential staff, or take community trips to places like restaurants or grocery stores (Mueser et al. 2013).

Mental health practitioners can learn how to deliver SST from manuals or trainings, which provide specific skills, steps, and examples (e.g., Bellack et al. 2004). SST is a straightforward and flexible intervention that allows for teaching strategies to be adapted to individuals with a variety of needs in terms of symptoms and cognitive levels and can be delivered across a range of treatment settings (Kopelowicz et al. 2006). While social skills training is sometimes provided as a stand-alone intervention, it is often integrated into other psychiatric rehabilitation programs, such as illness management and recovery (Mueser et al. 2002), cognitive enhancement therapy (Eack et al. 2009), integrated psychological therapy (Roder et al. 2006), and cognitive behavioral therapy (Granholm et al. 2014).

Treatment Outcome Research for Social Skills Training

SST has substantial empirical support, especially in terms of improving social functioning and negative symptoms in schizophrenia spectrum disorders. A meta-analysis of post-treatment outcomes in 22 randomized controlled trials with 1521 participants revealed a large effect size for content learned in treatment and a medium effect size for performance-based measures of social and independent living skills (Kurtz and Mueser 2008). Notably, despite critiques that gains in social skills following SST do not generalize to improvements in real-world functioning, this meta-analysis also found a medium effect size for social functioning outcomes such as work performance and increased participation in social activities (Kurtz and Mueser 2008). A more recent meta-analysis of 27 randomized controlled trials with a total of 1437 participants showed SST is associated with a small to medium effect size on social functioning outcomes (Turner et al. 2018).

SST also improves negative symptoms, with a small to medium effect size (Kurtz and Mueser 2008; Turner et al. 2018). This finding is unsurprising, given that negative symptoms like social withdrawal, anhedonia, and low motivation overlap with social functioning (Kurtz and Mueser 2008). As such, SST may facilitate improvements in negative symptoms by teaching participants skills to engage in positive social interactions, providing structured social contact with peers, challenging defeatist thoughts like "This won't be fun, so why go?" (Granholm and Harvey 2018), and consequently increasing self-efficacy, social interest, and motivation to socialize, which may in turn improve negative symptoms (Granholm and Harvey 2018; Wright et al. 2020). Additionally,

SST participants are directly taught how to convey more affect in their tone of voice and facial expressions, which may reduce the affective blunting that is characteristic of individuals with negative symptoms of schizophrenia. The beneficial effects of SST on negative symptoms are promising, given that pharmacological treatments and other psychosocial treatments, such as cognitive behavioral therapy, show limited effects on negative symptoms (Fusar-Poli et al. 2015; Velthorst et al. 2015).

Unfortunately, available randomized controlled trials do not furnish adequate follow-up data to reliably evaluate the durability of these gains in social functioning over time (Kurtz and Mueser 2008; Turner et al. 2018). Available research does, however, suggest that group SST is a cost-effective (Kopelowicz et al. 2006) evidence-based practice that improves social skills, negative symptoms, and real-world functioning for individuals with SMI.

Cognitive Remediation

Rationale for Cognitive Remediation

Cognitive difficulties, in domains such as processing speed, attention, and memory, are often present in SMI, including schizophrenia, first-episode psychosis, bipolar disorder, and major depression (Bora et al. 2014; Bora and Pantelis 2015; Robinson and Ferrier 2006; Rock et al. 2014; Schaefer et al. 2013). These challenges interfere with day-to-day functioning, such as in work, interpersonal relationships, and daily living skills (Halverson et al. 2019). Moreover, cognitive impairments affect the ability of service users to benefit from psychiatric rehabilitation approaches like supported employment and social skills training due to the slower rate of learning new skills (Kurtz 2011). Consequently, improvements in cognition may help peoples' real-world functioning as well as facilitate their ability to benefit from other psychiatric rehabilitation services. At present, psychosocial but not psychopharmacologic approaches have been shown to improve cognition in individuals with serious mental illness (Goff et al. 2011; Marder 2006; Van Duin et al. 2019; Wykes et al. 2011).

Description of Cognitive Remediation

Cognitive remediation is a behavioral intervention designed to improve cognitive functioning in individuals with SMI, with the longer-term goal of translating into improved social, occupational, and daily living functioning. It is based on scientific principles of learning and consists of three primary approaches, which may be used separately or in combination (McGurk et al. 2013):

- *Restorative task practice* involves intensive and repeated completion of exercises that target different cognitive domains (e.g., attention, memory). These exercises are typically delivered via computer programs. Some computerized restorative task programs adapt to participants' performance, such that the difficulty of the task is adjusted to participants' performance and maintained at a specified level (e.g., 80% correct), while other programs gradually increase the difficulty of exercises over time. Research does not indicate one approach is superior to another, although increasing the difficulty of cognitive exercises over time may facilitate participants' sustained engagement in the task (Bowie et al. 2020).
- *Strategy coaching* involves teaching participants specific methods to improve their performance on cognitive exercises. Such interventions may include visualization strategies, repetition of key information, and reading the information aloud.
- *Cognitive self-management strategies* are behaviors intended to optimize cognitive performance in everyday life and to compensate for the effects of cognitive challenges (Allott et al. 2020). For example, a participant with memory difficulties could learn to establish "memory spots" in their home by placing important items in a specific location. These approaches were originally designed to bypass, rather than repair, cognitive impair-

ments. However, such strategies may also improve cognitive functioning in individuals with SMI (Allott et al. 2020).

The majority of CR programs employ restorative task practice, which is often substantially improved by strategic coaching with a trained staff member (Wykes et al. 2011). A cognitive coach teaches strategies for improving restorative task practice and also ensures that the cognitive exercises are linked to meaningful goals that the participant is pursuing (Bowie et al. 2020). Cognitive remediation interventions vary in terms of length and frequency, with experts recommending at least 20 h of treatment over at least 10 weeks (McGurk et al. 2013).

Cognitive remediation has the strongest impact on psychosocial functioning when integrated with other psychiatric rehabilitation practices such as supported employment or social skills training (McGurk et al. 2007, 2013, 2015; Van Duin et al. 2019; Wykes et al. 2011). In this context, cognitive remediation may augment the effects of psychiatric rehabilitation programs by facilitating peoples' ability to practice and apply cognitive skills relevant to their functional goals (McGurk et al. 2015; Van Duin et al. 2019; Wykes et al. 2011). For example, in the *Thinking Skills for Work* program, computerized restorative task exercises are combined with job searches that are informed by participant's cognitive strengths and weaknesses. Also, when a participant starts work, cognitive remediation methods are used to target specific cognitive skills that improve their work functioning. As such, *Thinking Skills for Work* is designed to optimize the translation of cognitive skills to work settings and to mitigate against negative effects of cognitive challenges on job performance (McGurk et al. 2015).

Treatment Outcome Research on Cognitive Remediation

Research demonstrates not only that cognitive remediation improves cognitive scores at both post-treatment and follow-up but also that it has the strongest impact on functional outcomes when used in combination with other psychiatric rehabilitation services rather than delivered as a stand-alone intervention. In a meta-analysis of 40 studies with 2104 participants, Wykes et al. (2011) found that the post-treatment effect size for a variety of functional outcomes was small for stand-alone cognitive remediation, medium when cognitive remediation was combined with psychiatric rehabilitation, and large when strategic coaching, restorative task practice, and psychiatric rehabilitation were used together. Recently, a meta-analysis of 23 studies with 1819 participants found that cognitive remediation enhanced psychiatric rehabilitation outcomes (Van Duin et al. 2019). Specifically, although there were no significant effects for relationships and community functioning outcomes, cognitive remediation significantly enhanced vocational outcomes with a small to medium effect size, as well as social skills with a small effect size (Van Duin et al. 2019). In summary, cognitive remediation is a well-supported intervention for improving cognition in SMI. However, for these gains to translate to improvements in real-world functioning, cognitive remediation should be integrated with other evidence-based psychiatric rehabilitation programs and delivered in the context of the pursuit of client-identified functional goals.

Social Cognitive Training

Rationale for Social Cognitive Training

Social cognition refers to the ability to interpret and process social information and includes skills such as recognizing facial expressions, detecting subtle hints during conversation, and generating plausible explanations for other's behavior (Green et al. 2019; Horan and Green 2019). Individuals with SMI demonstrate impairments in social cognition, which have been shown to emerge prior to the onset of illness during the prodromal period (Horan and Green 2019) and are associated with difficulties with independent living, employment, and interpersonal relationships (Halverson et al. 2019). In point of fact, social cognition has a stronger relationship to community functioning than neurocognition (Halverson et al. 2019). At present, existing psychopharmacological interventions do not effectively improve social cognitive impairments (Kucharska-Pietura and Mortimer 2013), suggesting a need for alternative approaches.

Description of Social Cognitive Training

In social cognitive training (SCT), participants learn social cognitive skills that fall into four domains (Pinkham et al. 2018). *Emotion perception* refers to identifying emotions in facial expressions, tone of voice, and nonverbal cues. For example, participants may be asked to verbalize how they can tell a face looks sad, angry, or happy. SCT also conceptualizes paranoia as an emotion, paving the way for participants to discuss how suspiciousness may lead them to misinterpret social interactions. *Social perception* involves an understanding of social knowledge, cues, goals, and relationships such as the balance of give or take in a social interaction. For example, SCT participants may be asked to generate guesses about how a person may behave in a given situation (e.g., sharing food or money) based on their past behavior. *Theory of mind*, also referred to as *mentalizing*, is the ability to understand the mental states of other people, such as possible thoughts, feelings, and motives or goals they may have, and may involve detecting subtle hints, white lies, or irony in a social interaction. *Attributional style* refers to how people explain the causes of positive and negative social situations. Individuals with SMI, especially those experiencing paranoia, tend to show a hostile attributional bias, such that ambiguous unpleasant situations are attributed to negative or hostile causes (e.g., assuming that an acquaintance who neglects to say hello in passing dislikes them; Buck et al. 2016). SCT teaches participants skills to consider alternative explanations to such situations (e.g., the acquaintance may have been distracted).

Generally speaking, there are two types of social cognitive training programs: broad-based interventions that train participants on skills across a variety of social cognitive domains and targeted interventions that focus only on one particular social cognitive domain, such as emotion recognition. Theoretically, broad-based interventions should be more effective at improving social functioning, given that social cognitive skills need to be combined with one another for a successful social interaction (Couture et al. 2006; Nijman et al. 2020). Specifically, individuals need to be able to identify emotions, contextualize them based on the person and setting (social perception), infer the mental state of the other person (theory of mind/attributional style), and respond accordingly (Couture et al. 2006; Nijman et al. 2020).

SCT is typically delivered in a group format using materials that depict social stimuli, such as still pictures of facial expressions and/or video clips of social interactions. Participants learn skills using a breadth of strategies including psychoeducation, guided problem-solving, and cognitive behavioral approaches such as Socratic questioning. Participants are also instructed to complete home assignments to practice using skills in real-life situations (Horan and Green 2019; Kurtz et al. 2016; Kurtz and Richardson 2012). These interventions vary in terms of length and frequency, commonly once or twice a week for approximately 6 months (Penn et al. 2007).

Treatment Outcomes Research on Social Cognitive Training

A 2012 meta-analysis of 19 studies with 692 participants examined the post-treatment effects of SCT on social cognition, symptoms, and community functioning (Kurtz and Richardson 2012). In 2018, this meta-analysis was updated and expanded to consider the effects of broad-based versus targeted SCT interventions, evaluate the extent to which cognitive remediation may enhance the effects of SCT, and assess the long-term effects of SCT (Nijman et al. 2020). The updated sample included 46 randomized controlled trials with 1979 participants.

Both meta-analyses found that SCT had medium to large effects on emotion recognition and small to medium effects on theory of mind at post-treatment. The findings on social perception were mixed: Kurtz and Richardson (2012) showed that SCT did not improve social perception, while Nijman et al. (2020) found both targeted and broad-based SCT resulted in large improvements in social perception. Both meta-analyses reported that SCT interventions did not have significant effects on changing attributional style (Nijman et al. 2020) and that cognitive remediation did not significantly enhance the effects of SCT on outcomes.

The evidence on whether SCT skills generalize to real-world functioning is unclear. Kurtz and Richardson (2012) found a medium to large effect of SCT on observer-rated community and institutional functioning, and Nijman et al. (2020) reported that broad-based SCT improved social functioning with medium to large effect size. However, many of the included studies employed broad-based SCT interventions in combination with other non-SCT therapies (e.g., integrated psychological therapy), which may have been responsible for the positive effects reported in this meta-analysis. Notably, while *targeted* SCT led to improvements in the targeted skill, these gains did not reliably generalize to improvements in social functioning (Nijman et al. 2020), highlighting the value of broad-based interventions. In Nijman et al. (2020), gains in social functioning from broad-based SCT were maintained during study follow-up with small effect sizes (Nijman et al. 2020).

Taken together, research suggests broad-based SCT is more effective than targeted SCT and gains from broad-based SCT are maintained over time. SCT reliably improves emotion recognition and theory of mind, with more mixed evidence for effects on social perception and no meaningful effects on attributional style.

Physical Health Management

Rationale for Physical Health Interventions

The life expectancy of individuals with schizophrenia and other serious mental illnesses is about 14 years lower than people without mental illness (Hjorthøj et al. 2017). This premature mortality results primarily from elevated rates of physical health problems, rather than unnatural causes such as accidents or suicide (Walker et al. 2015). In particular, individuals with SMI are at heightened risk for a variety of medical illnesses, most notably cardiovascular disease, but also including hepatitis A and B, HIV/AIDS, arthritis, irritable bowel syndrome, fibromyalgia, diabetes mellitus, obesity, hyperlipidemia, and hypertension (Firth et al. 2019; Walker et al. 2015).

Smoking cessation and improving fitness and nutrition are two important modifiable medical risk factors for people. Individuals with SMI have an estimated smoking prevalence rate of 59%, and smoking-related illnesses are the leading cause of morbidity and mortality for this group (Dickerson et al. 2013). Individuals with SMI also often have low rates of physical activity and eat an unhealthy diet, contributing to high rates of obesity and poor cardiovascular health (Firth et al. 2019), and weight gain and metabolic syndrome are common side effects of antipsychotic medication (Maayan and Correll 2010).

Health problems for individuals with SMI are often underrecognized and undertreated, as service users frequently experience obstacles to accessing quality healthcare, such as difficulty accessing medical services (e.g., due to low motivation or lack of appropriate referrals), challenges communicating effectively with healthcare providers, and being perceived by providers as less credible reporters of physical symptoms due to their mental illness. Thus, there is a need to teach people skills to improve communication and self-advocacy regarding their physical health, as well as ensure that they are connected to appropriate medical care.

Description of Physical Health Interventions

The psychosocial interventions for physical health with the most research support target smoking cessation, physical activity and nutrition, and self-management of physical illness.

Current recommendations suggest that providers advise all daily smokers to quit and offer to prescribe effective smoking cessation pharmacotherapy and refer to behavioral smoking cessation counselling (Evins et al. 2019a, b). Behavioral treatments for smoking cessation have been adapted to meet the needs of service users in a number of ways. These adaptations include discussing reasons that clients smoke and concerns about quitting in the context of their mental illness, coordinating care with psychiatric providers so that doses of antipsychotic medications can be adjusted in response to metabolic changes associated with quitting, exposure to peer models with SMI who have successfully quit smoking, and mitigating the effects of cognitive challenges by delivering information in small portions, using repetition, and modeling and practicing skills (Daumit et al. 2020; Evins et al. 2014). Of note, relapse prevention strategies, which consist of behavioral smoking cessation counselling in combination with maintenance smoking cessation medications, may need to be delivered over a significantly longer period following the successful attainment of abstinence for smokers with SMI (12–18 months) than for smokers without SMI (8–12 weeks; Evins et al. 2014). The role of pharmacotherapy for smoking cessation in SMI is especially important, as behavioral treatments are not as effective on their own (Evins et al. 2019a, b; Tsoi et al. 2013).

Psychosocial interventions for fitness and nutrition range from cognitive behavioral programs to exercise groups (McGinty et al. 2016). Across programs, there are several important common strategies. Practitioners can increase motivation for exercise by framing goals in terms of improving fitness rather than losing weight (Caemmerer et al. 2012; McGinty et al. 2016) and by choosing activities that participants find enjoyable (Firth et al. 2019). Additionally, dietary interventions for people with mental illness are more effective if they are delivered by specialist providers like nutritionists (Firth et al. 2015) and consider the needs of individuals with SMI such as buying and cooking food on a low budget. *In SHAPE* (Bartels et al. 2015) is an example of a fitness and nutrition intervention for overweight and obese individuals with SMI. This 12-month program includes a fitness club membership and a health promotion coach. Using shared goal setting, the interventionist helps participants develop individualized plans focused on fitness goals, reinforcement for activity, and education about healthy eating. At the end of 12 months, participants can transition to exercise activities without input from a coach.

A variety of different programs exist targeting physical illness self-management. Two well-known interventions are Integrated Illness Management and Recovery (I-IMR; Mueser et al. 2012) and the Health and Recovery Peer Program (HARP; Druss et al. 2010). These programs share several common elements. First, they provide psychoeducation focused on common medical disorders and how to take care of oneself (e.g., ensuring proper use and adherence to medications), the interaction between psychiatric and medical disorders (e.g., how stress can impact physical health), coping strategies (e.g., for chronic pain), and effective interactions with healthcare providers (e.g., scheduling and preparing for medical appointments, advocating to get one's needs met, and obtaining important medical information during appointments). Second, given that behavioral changes (e.g., regarding diet and exercise) are closely linked to health conditions, these programs also include interventions promoting healthy behaviors such as fitness and nutrition. Third, these programs employ staff whose primary role is to ensure coordination of care, such as by making referrals and appointments and accompanying clients to health visits. Fourth, these treatments tend to be cross-diagnostic rather than focusing on one health condition due to the high comorbidity of medical conditions in SMI, although information about specific medical diagnoses is provided in I-IMR. Lastly, these are both group-based interventions. The primary differences between the two programs is that HARP is always delivered by service users while I-IMR is usually delivered by mental health practitioners and that I-IMR is provided in weekly sessions for 8 months while HARP is delivered in weekly sessions for 6 weeks.

Treatment Outcome Research for Physical Health Interventions

Pharmacological treatments are safe and effective treatments for individuals with SMI who smoke. This was recently demonstrated in a randomized controlled trial of 8144 participants, 3268 of whom had SMI, who smoked daily and expressed an interest in quitting within the next 30 days (Anthenelli et al. 2016). Participants were randomly to receive 12 weeks of varenicline, bupropion, nicotine patches, or placebo together with brief (10 min) of weekly individual behavioral smoking cessation counselling. Quit rates were highest among those assigned to varenicline (Anthenelli et al. 2016). Individuals with schizophrenia in this study who received placebo plus behavioral treatment had quit rates of only 4% (Evins et al. 2020) as compared to 13–23% with smoking cessation pharmacotherapy plus behavioral treatment (Evins et al. 2020), paralleling prior research showing that medication is especially important to facilitate smoking cessation in this population (Tsoi et al. 2013).

Regarding weight loss interventions for overweight and obese adults with SMI, a meta-analysis of 17 exercise and nutrition intervention studies (including IN SHAPE) with a total of 1968 participants found small effect sizes for weight loss and cardiovascular risk reduction as compared to a variety of control conditions including usual care, waitlist groups, and informational classes (Naslund et al. 2017). Moreover, these gains were maintained with a small effect size at follow-up lengths for at least 1 year. Another meta-analysis of 20 studies of nutritional interventions found small to moderate post-treatment effects on weight loss, BMI, cardiovascular risk reduction, and blood glucose levels, although there were not enough data to determine if these gains were maintained at follow-up (Teasdale et al. 2017). Research also suggests that illness self-management interventions can improve health outcomes such as blood pressure and cardiovascular risk factors (McGinty et al. 2016). However, there are few studies of illness self-management interventions, and they vary in terms of sample, length of intervention, and other study characteristics. Consequently, there is a need for large-scale, longitudinal randomized controlled trials to draw substantive conclusions about the impact of illness self-management interventions (Kelly et al. 2014).

In summary, some evidence indicates that exercise and nutrition interventions are associated with small effect sizes for weight loss in SMI, although it is unclear if these gains are maintained at follow-up. Additionally, there is not enough data at present to draw solid conclusions about the efficacy of illness self-management interventions for health outcomes. However, there is substantial evidence for safe and effective approaches for smoking cessation for smokers with SMI who are interested in quitting in the next 30 days, and work is beginning to focus on approaches for those who express less or even no motivation to quit (Gilbody et al. 2019).

Summary

This chapter outlines evidence-based psychiatric rehabilitation practices that have been shown to significantly improve functioning for individuals with SMI when they are implemented effectively. While not covered in this chapter, there are several promising treatments with developing research evidence that may facilitate recovery for service users. These include metacognitive training as a way to increase participants' awareness of their own thinking patterns (such as the tendency to jump to conclusions; Moritz and Lysaker 2018), the integration of positive and mindfulness approaches into recovery frameworks (Gaiswinkler et al. 2020; Moran and Nemec 2013), and programs to prevent the development of medical comorbidities in first-episode psychosis (Curtis et al. 2016). While the field of psychiatric rehabilitation is still evolving, the services described in this chapter and throughout the book have the potential to provide substantial support individuals with SMI as they pursue their recovery-oriented goals.

Bibliography

Allott, K., Van-der-El, K., Bryce, S., Parrish, E. M., McGurk, S. R., Hetrick, S., Bowie, C. R., Kidd, S., Hamilton, M., Killackey, E., & Velligan, D. (2020). Compensatory interventions for cognitive impairments in psychosis: A systematic review and meta-analysis. *Schizophrenia Bulletin, 46*(4), 869–883.

Anthenelli, R. M., Benowitz, N. L., West, R., St Aubin, L., McRae, T., Lawrence, D., Ascher, J., Russ, C., Krishen, A., & Evins, A. E. (2016). Neuropsychiatric safety and efficacy of varenicline, bupropion, and nicotine patch in smokers with and without psychiatric disorders (EAGLES): A double-blind, randomised, placebo-controlled clinical trial. *The Lancet, 387*(10037), 2507–2520.

Bartels, S. J., Pratt, S. I., Aschbrenner, K. A., Barre, L. K., Naslund, J. A., Wolfe, R., Xie, H., McHugo, G. J., Jiminez, D. E., Jue, K., Feldman, J., & Bird, B. L. (2015). Pragmatic replication trial of health promotion coaching for obesity in serious mental illness and maintenance of outcomes. *The American Journal of Psychiatry, 172*, 344–352. https://doi.org/10.1176/appi.ajp.2014.14030357

Bellack, A. S., Mueser, K. T., Gingerich, S., & Agresta, J. (2004). *Social Skills Training for Schizophrenia: A Step-by-Step Guide* (2nd ed.). Guilford, New York City, USA.

Bora, E., Lin, A., Wood, S. J., Yung, A. R., Mcgorry, P. D., & Pantelis, C. (2014). Cognitive deficits in youth with familial and clinical high risk to psychosis: A systematic review and meta-analysis. *Acta Psychiatrica Scandinavica, 130*(1), 1–15.

Bora, E., & Pantelis, C. (2015). Meta-analysis of cognitive impairment in first-episode bipolar disorder: Comparison with first-episode schizophrenia and healthy controls. *Schizophrenia Bulletin, 41*(5), 1095–1104.

Bowie, C. R., Bell, M. D., Fiszdon, J. M., Johannesen, J. K., Lindenmayer, J. P., McGurk, S. R., Medalia, A. A., Penadés, R., Saperstein, A. M., Twamley, E. W., Ueland, T., & Wykes, T. (2020). Cognitive remediation for schizophrenia: An expert working group white paper on core techniques. *Schizophrenia Research, 215*, 49–53.

Buck, B. E., Pinkham, A. E., Harvey, P. D., & Penn, D. L. (2016). Revisiting the validity of measures of social cognitive bias in schizophrenia: Additional results from the Social Cognition Psychometric Evaluation (SCOPE) study. *British Journal of Clinical Psychology, 55*(4), 441–454.

Buck, B., Scherer, E., Brian, R., Wang, R., Wang, W., Campbell, A., Choudhury, T., Hauser, M., Kane, J. M., & Ben-Zeev, D. (2019). Relationships between smartphone social behavior and relapse in schizophrenia: A preliminary report. *Schizophrenia Research, 208*, 167–172.

Caemmerer, J., Correll, C. U., & Maayan, L. (2012). Acute and maintenance effects of non-pharmacologic interventions for antipsychotic associated weight gain and metabolic abnormalities: A meta-analytic comparison of randomized controlled trials. *Schizophrenia Research, 140*(1–3), 159–168.

Corrigan, P. W., Mueser, K. T., Bond, G. R., Drake, R. E., & Solomon, P. (2008). What is psychiatric rehabilitation? In *Principles and practices of psychiatric rehabilitation: An empirical approach.* (2nd ed.). Guilford Press, New York City, USA.

Couture, S. M., Penn, D. L., & Roberts, D. L. (2006). The functional significance of social cognition in schizophrenia: A review. *Schizophrenia Bulletin, 32*(S1), S44–S63.

Curtis, J., Watkins, A., Rosenbaum, S., Teasdale, S., Kalucy, M., Samaras, K., & Ward, P. B. (2016). Evaluating an individualized lifestyle and life skills intervention to prevent antipsychotic-induced weight gain in first-episode psychosis. *Early Intervention in Psychiatry, 10*(3), 267–276.

Daumit, G. L., Dalcin, A. T., Dickerson, F. B., Miller, E. R., Evins, A. E., Cather, C., Jerome, G. J., Young, D. R., Charleston, J. B., Gennusa, J. V., Goldsholl, S., Cook, C., Heller, A., McGinty, E. E., Crum, R. M., Appel, L. J., & Wang, N. Y. (2020). Effect of a comprehensive cardiovascular risk reduction intervention in persons with serious mental illness: A randomized clinical trial. *JAMA Network Open, 3*(6), e207247.

Dickerson, F., Stallings, C. R., Origoni, A. E., Vaughan, C., Khushalani, S., Schroeder, J., & Yolken, R. H. (2013). Cigarette smoking among persons with schizophrenia or bipolar disorder in routine clinical settings, 1999–2011. *Psychiatric Services, 64*(1), 44–50.

Druss, B. G., Zhao, L., von Esenwein, S. A., Bona, J. R., Fricks, L., Jenkins-Tucker, S., Sterling, E., DiClemente, R., & Lorig, K. (2010). The Health and Recovery Peer (HARP) Program: A peer-led intervention to improve medical self-management for persons with serious mental illness. *Schizophrenia Research, 118*(1–3), 264–270.

Eack, S. M., Hogarty, G. E., Cooley, S. J., DiBarry, A. L., Hogarty, S. S., Greenwald, D. P., Montrose, D. M., & Keshavan, M. S. (2009). Cognitive enhancement therapy for early course schizophrenia: Effects of a two-year randomized controlled trial. *Psychiatric Services, 60*(11), 1468–1476.

Evins, A. E., Benowitz, N. L., West, R., Russ, C., McRae, T., Lawrence, D., Krishen, A., St Aubin, L., Maravic, M. C., & Anthenelli, R. M. (2019a). Neuropsychiatric safety and efficacy of varenicline, bupropion, and nicotine patch in smokers with psychotic, anxiety, and mood disorders in the EAGLES Trial. *Journal of Clinical Psychopharmacology*, *39*(2), 108–116.

Evins, A. E., Cather, C., & Daumit, G. L. (2019b). Smoking cessation in people with serious mental illness. *The Lancet Psychiatry*, *6*(7), 563–564.

Evins, A. E., Cather, C., Pratt, S. A., Pachas, G. N., Hoeppner, S. S., Goff, D. C., Achtyes, E. D., Ayer, D., & Schoenfeld, D. A. (2014). Maintenance treatment with varenicline for smoking cessation in patients with schizophrenia and bipolar disorder: A randomized clinical trial. *JAMA - Journal of the American Medical Association*, *311*(2), 145–154.

Evins, A. E., West, R., Benowitz, N. L., Russ, C., Lawrence, D., McRae, T., Maravic, M. C., Heffner, J. L., & Anthenelli, R. M. (2020). Efficacy and safety of pharmacotherapeutic smoking cessation aids in schizophrenia spectrum disorders: Subgroup analysis of EAGLES. *Psychiatric Services (in Advance)*, appi.ps.2020000. https://doi.org/10.1176/appi.ps.202000032

Farkas, M., & Anthony, W. A. (2010). Psychiatric rehabilitation interventions: A review. *International Review of Psychiatry*, *22*(2), 114–129.

Firth, J., Cotter, J., Elliott, R., French, P., Yung, A. R. (2015). A systematic review and meta-analysis of exercise interventions in schizophrenia patients. *Psychological Medicine, 45*, 1343–1361. https://doi.org/10.1017/S0033291714003110.

Firth, J., Siddiqi, N., Koyanagi, A., Siskind, D., Rosenbaum, S., Galletly, C., Allan, S., Caneo, C., Carney, R., Carvalho, A. F., Chatterton, M. Lou, Correll, C. U., Curtis, J., Gaughran, F., Heald, A., Hoare, E., Jackson, S. E., Kisely, S., Lovell, K., … Stubbs, B. (2019). The Lancet Psychiatry Commission: A blueprint for protecting physical health in people with mental illness. *The Lancet Psychiatry*, *6*(8), 675–712.

Fusar-Poli, P., Papanastasiou, E., Stahl, D., Rocchetti, M., Carpenter, W., Shergill, S., & McGuire, P. (2015). Treatments of negative symptoms in schizophrenia: Meta-analysis of 168 randomized placebo-controlled trials. *Schizophrenia Bulletin*, *41*(4), 892–899.

Gaiswinkler, L., Kaufmann, P., Pollheimer, E., Ackermann, A., Holasek, S., Kapfhammer, H. P., & Unterrainer, H. F. (2020). Mindfulness and self-compassion in clinical psychiatric rehabilitation: A clinical trial. *Mindfulness*, *11*(2), 374–383.

Geller, J. L. (2000). The last half-century of psychiatric services as reflected in Psychiatric Services. *Psychiatric Services*, *51*(1), 41–67.

Gilbody, S., Peckham, E., Bailey, D., Arundel, C., Heron, P., Crosland, S., Fairhurst, C., Hewitt, C., Li, J., Parrott, S., Bradshaw, T., Horspool, M., Hughes, E., Hughes, T., Ker, S., Leahy, M., McCloud, T., Osborn, D., Reilly, J., … Vickers, C. (2019). Smoking cessation for people with severe mental illness (SCIMITAR+): a pragmatic randomised controlled trial. *The Lancet Psychiatry*, *6*(5), 379–390.

Goff, D. C., Hill, M., & Barch, D. (2011). The treatment of cognitive impairment in schizophrenia. *Pharmacology, Biochemistry and Behavior*, *99*(2), 245–253.

Granholm, E., & Harvey, P. D. (2018). Social Skills Training for Negative Symptoms of Schizophrenia. *Schizophrenia Bulletin*, *44*(3), 472–474.

Granholm, E., Holden, J. L., Mikhael, T., Link, P. C., Swendsen, J., Depp, C., Moore, R. C., & Harvey, P. D. (2020). What do people with schizophrenia do all day? Ecological momentary assessment of real-world functioning in schizophrenia. *Schizophrenia Bulletin*, *46*(2), 242–251.

Granholm, E., Holden, J., Link, P. C., & McQuaid, J. R. (2014). Randomized clinical trial of cognitive behavioral social skills training for schizophrenia: Improvement in functioning and experiential negative symptoms. *Journal of Consulting and Clinical Psychology*, *82*(6), 1173–1185.

Green, M. F., Horan, W. P., & Lee, J. (2019). Nonsocial and social cognition in schizophrenia: current evidence and future directions. *World Psychiatry*, *18*(2), 146–161.

Halverson, T. F., Orleans-Pobee, M., Merritt, C., Sheeran, P., Fett, A. K., & Penn, D. L. (2019). Pathways to functional outcomes in schizophrenia spectrum disorders: Meta-analysis of social cognitive and neurocognitive predictors. *Neuroscience and Biobehavioral Reviews*, *105*(April), 212–219.

Hjorthøj, C., Stürup, A. E., McGrath, J. J., & Nordentoft, M. (2017). Years of potential life lost and life expectancy in schizophrenia: A systematic review and meta-analysis. *The Lancet Psychiatry*, *4*(4), 295–301.

Horan, W. P., & Green, M. F. (2019). Treatment of social cognition in schizophrenia: Current status and future directions. *Schizophrenia Research*, *203*, 3–11.

Kelly, E. L., Fenwick, K. M., Barr, N., Cohen, H., & Brekke, J. S. (2014). A systematic review of self-management health care models for individuals with serious mental illnesses. *Psychiatric Services*, *65*(11), 1300–1310.

Kopelowicz, A., Liberman, R. P., & Zarate, R. (2006). Recent advances in social skills training for schizophrenia. *Schizophrenia Bulletin*, *32*(S1), 12–23.

Kucharska-Pietura, K., & Mortimer, A. (2013). Can antipsychotics improve social cognition in patients with schizophrenia? *CNS Drugs*, *27*(5), 335–343.

Kurtz, M. M. (2011). Neurocognition as a predictor of response to evidence-based psychosocial interventions in schizophrenia: What is the state of the evidence? *Clinical Psychology Review*, *31*(4), 663–672.

Kurtz, M. M., Gagen, E., Rocha, N. B. F., Machado, S., & Penn, D. L. (2016). Comprehensive treatments for social cognitive deficits in schizophrenia: A critical review and effect-size analysis of controlled studies. *Clinical Psychology Review*, *43*, 80–89.

Kurtz, M. M., & Mueser, K. T. (2008). A meta-analysis of controlled research on social skills training for schizophrenia. *Journal of Consulting and Clinical Psychology*, *76*(3), 491–504.

Kurtz, M. M., & Richardson, C. L. (2012). Social cognitive training for schizophrenia: A meta-analytic investigation of controlled research. *Schizophrenia Bulletin, 38*(5), 1092–1104.

Lamb, H. R., & Bachrach, L. L. (2001). Some perspectives on deinstitutionalization. *Psychiatric Services, 52*(8), 1039–1045.

Lim, M. H., Gleeson, J. F. M., Alvarez-Jimenez, M., & Penn, D. L. (2018). Loneliness in psychosis: A systematic review. *Social Psychiatry and Psychiatric Epidemiology, 53*(3), 221–238.

Maayan, L., & Correll, C. U. (2010). Management of antipsychotic-related weight gain. *Expert Review of Neurotherapeutics, 10*(7), 1175–1200. h

Marder, S. R. (2006). Drug initiatives to improve cognitive function. *Journal of Clinical Psychiatry, 67*(SUPPL. 9), 31–35.

McGinty, E. E., Baller, J., Azrin, S. T., Juliano-Bult, D., & Daumit, G. L. (2016). Interventions to address medical conditions and health-risk behaviors among persons with serious mental illness: A comprehensive review. *Schizophrenia Bulletin, 42*(1), 96–124.

McGurk, S. R., Mueser, K. T., Covell, N. H., Cicerone, K. D., Drake, R. E., Silverstein, S. M., Medialia, A., Myers, R., Bellack, A. S., Bell, M. D., & Essock, S. M. (2013). Mental health system funding of cognitive enhancement interventions for schizophrenia: Summary and update of the New York Office of Mental Health expert panel and stakeholder meeting. *Psychiatric Rehabilitation Journal, 36*(3), 133–145.

McGurk, S. R., Mueser, K. T., Xie, H., Welsh, J., Kaiser, S., Drake, R. E., Becker, D. R., Bailey, E., Fraser, G., Wolfe, R., & McHugo, G. J. (2015). Cognitive enhancement treatment for people with mental illness who do not respond to supported employment: A randomized controlled trial. *The American Journal of Psychiatry, 172*(9), 852–861.

McGurk, S. R., Twamley, E. W., Sitzer, D. I., McHugo, G. J., & Mueser, K. T. (2007). A meta-analysis of cognitive remediation in schizophrenia. *American Journal of Psychiatry, 164*(12), 1791–1802.

McKay, C., Nugent, K. L., Johnsen, M., Eaton, W. W., & Lidz, C. W. (2018). A systematic review of evidence for the clubhouse model of psychosocial rehabilitation. *Administration and Policy in Mental Health and Mental Health Services Research, 45*(1), 28–47.

Moran, G. S., & Nemec, P. B. (2013). Walking on the sunny side: What positive psychology can contribute to psychiatric rehabilitation concepts and practice. *Psychiatric Rehabilitation Journal, 36*(3), 202–208.

Moritz, S., & Lysaker, P. H. (2018). Metacognition – What did James H. Flavell really say and the implications for the conceptualization and design of metacognitive interventions. *Schizophrenia Research, 201*, 20–26.

Mueser, K. T., Corrigan, P. W., Hilton, D. W., Tanzman, B., Schaub, A., Gingerich, S., Essock, S. M., Tarrier, N., Morey, B., Vogel-Scibilia, S., & Herz, M. I. (2002). Illness Management and Recovery: a review of the research. *Psychiatric Services, 53*, 1272–1284.

Mueser, K. T., Bartels, S. J., Santos, M., Pratt, S. I., & Riera, E. G. (2012). Integrated Illness Management and Recovery: a program for integrating physical and psychiatric illness self-management in older persons with severe mental illness. *American Journal of Psychiatric Rehabilitation, 15*, 131–156. https://doi.org/10.1080/15487768.2012.679558.

Mueser, K. T., Gottlieb, J. D., & Gingerich, S. (2013). Social Skills and Problem-Solving Training. *The Wiley Handbook of Cognitive Behavioral Therapy*, 243–272.

Mueser, K. T., & McGurk, S. R. (2011). New tools for cognitive remediation and psychiatric rehabilitation of schizophrenia. *PsycCRITIQUES, 56*(16).

Mueser, K. T., Meyer, P. S., Penn, D. L., Clancy, R., Clancy, D. M., & Salyers, M. P. (2006). The Illness Management and Recovery program: Rationale, development, and preliminary findings. *Schizophrenia Bulletin, 32*(SUPPL.1), 32–43.

Naslund, J. A., Whiteman, K. L., McHugo, G. J., Aschbrenner, K. A., Marsch, L. A., & Bartels, S. J. (2017). Lifestyle interventions for weight loss among overweight and obese adults with serious mental illness: A systematic review and meta-analysis. *General Hospital Psychiatry, 47*(April), 83–102.

Nijman, S. A., Veling, W., van der Stouwe, E. C. D., & Pijnenborg, G. H. M. (2020). Social cognition training for people with a psychotic disorder: A network meta-analysis. *Schizophrenia Bulletin, 46*(5), 1086–1103.

Penn, D. L., Roberts, D. L., Comb, D., & Sterne, A. (2007). Best practices: the development of the Social Cognition and Interaction training program for schizophrenia spectrum disorders. *Psychiatric Services, 58*, 449–451.

Pinkham, A. E., Harvey, P. D., & Penn, D. L. (2018). Social cognition psychometric evaluation: Results of the final validation study. *Schizophrenia Bulletin, 44*, 737–748.

Pulice, R. T., & Miccio, S. (2006). Patient, client, consumer, survivor: The mental health consumer movement in the United States. In J. Rosenberg & S. Rosenberg (Eds.), *Community mental health: Challenges for the 21st century*. Routledge, Abingdon-on-Thames, UK.

Robinson, L. J., & Ferrier, I. N. (2006). Evolution of cognitive impairment in bipolar disorder: A systematic review of cross-sectional evidence. *Bipolar Disorders, 8*(2), 103–116.

Rock, P. L., Roiser, J. P., Riedel, W. J., & Blackwell, A. D. (2014). Cognitive impairment in depression: A systematic review and meta-analysis. *Psychological Medicine, 44*(10), 2029–2040.

Roder, V., Mueller, D. R., Mueser, K. T., & Brenner, H. D. (2006). Integrated psychological therapy (IPT) for schizophrenia: Is it effective? *Schizophrenia Bulletin, 32*(SUPPL.1).

Schaefer, J., Giangrande, E., Weinberger, D. R., & Dickinson, D. (2013). The global cognitive impairment in schizophrenia: Consistent over decades and around the world. *Schizophrenia Research, 150*(1), 42–50.

Teasdale, S. B., Ward, P. B., Rosenbaum, S., Samaras, K., & Stubbs, B. (2017). Solving a weighty problem: Systematic review and meta-analysis of nutrition interventions in severe mental illness. *British Journal of Psychiatry*, *210*(2), 110–118.

Tsoi, D. T., Porwal, M., & Webster, A. C. (2013). Interventions for smoking cessation and reduction in individuals with schizophrenia. *Cochrane Database of Systematic Reviews, 2017*(12). 3

Turner, D. T., McGlanaghy, E., Cuijpers, P., Van Der Gaag, M., Karyotaki, E., & MacBeth, A. (2018). A meta-analysis of social skills training and related interventions for psychosis. *Schizophrenia Bulletin*, *44*(3), 475–491.

Van Duin, D., De Winter, L., Oud, M., Kroon, H., Veling, W., & Van Weeghel, J. (2019). The effect of rehabilitation combined with cognitive remediation on functioning in persons with severe mental illness: Systematic review and meta-analysis. *Psychological Medicine*, *49*(9), 1414–1425.

Veerman, S. R. T., Schulte, P. F. J., & de Haan, L. (2017). Treatment for negative symptoms in schizophrenia: A comprehensive review. *Drugs*, *77*(13), 1423–1459. y

Velthorst, E., Koeter, M., Van Der Gaag, M., Nieman, D. H., Fett, A. K. J., Smit, F., Staring, A. B. P., Meijer, C., & De Haan, L. (2015). Adapted cognitive-behavioural therapy required for targeting negative symptoms in schizophrenia: Meta-analysis and meta-regression. *Psychological Medicine*, *45*(3), 453–465.

Walker, E. R., McGee, R. E., & Druss, B. G. (2015). Mortality in mental disorders and global disease burden implications a systematic review and meta-analysis. *JAMA Psychiatry*, *72*(4), 334–341.

Wright, A. C., Browne, J., Cather, C., Pratt, S. I., Bartels, S. J., & Mueser, K. T. (2020). Does self-efficacy predict functioning in older adults with schizophrenia? A cross-sectional and longitudinal mediation analysis. *Cognitive Therapy and Research*.

Wykes, T., Huddy, V., Cellard, C., McGurk, S. R., & Czobor, P. (2011). A meta-analysis of cognitive remediation for schizophrenia: Methodology and effect sizes. *American Journal of Psychiatry*, *168*(5), 472–485.

Family Systems Care in Public Sector Settings

Sarah A. Nguyen and Alison M. Heru

Introduction

Patients in public sector settings present with complex mental health and social needs, such as homelessness, substance abuse, immigration, poverty, and minority status. For these patients, a family-centered approach incorporating family psychoeducation provides a framework for understanding and including the individuals involved in their system of care. A family-centered approach may appear daunting because of the difficulty in bringing in family members or the clinician's lack of experience in dealing with family members, but family inclusion can begin by simply inviting the family into the conversation. This chapter uses case material to outline the current status of family-centered care and point to future directions. We weave in the knowledge base needed for family inclusion and evidence-based family interventions, focusing on family psychoeducation because of its evidence base, cultural adaptations, and efficiency.

Family-centered care encompasses multiple systems: the social support systems providing emotional, spiritual, and community life; the public system providing financial support (e.g., Medicaid, Medicare); and the healthcare system (Bamm and Rosenbaum 2008). In fact, patients and their families are supported by multiple individuals in these systems. A family-centered approach begins with collaborating with these individuals. All agencies can benefit from a comprehensive treatment plan which also includes information about advocacy organizations, such as the National Alliance on Mental Illness (NAMI), Mental Health America (MHA), and Depression and Bipolar Support Alliance (DBSA), as well as self-help organizations for alcoholism and substance abuse, such as Alcoholics Anonymous (AA), Narcotics Anonymous (NA), and Al-Anon (Alcoholics Anonymous support group for loved ones of alcoholics). Most important is our need to partner directly with families. We owe it to families to include them at all levels of care, especially decision-making and treatment planning and in ongoing treatment.

Many patients in the public sector setting have limited contact with their families. Despite this, family-centered approaches can still be utilized to provide stability and support. Staff members in different systems can become a patient's "family."

The case examples adopt the McMaster Approach to Family Assessment (Epstein et al. 1983). This model uses six dimensions of family functioning to guide assessment and treatment

S. A. Nguyen (✉)
Department of Psychiatry and Biobehavioral Sciences, David Geffen School of Medicine at UCLA, Los Angeles, CA, USA
e-mail: sanguyen@mednet.ucla.edu

A. M. Heru
University of Colorado, Denver, Denver, CO, USA

W. E. Sowers et al. (eds.), *Textbook of Community Psychiatry*,
https://doi.org/10.1007/978-3-031-10239-4_24

and has a comprehensive, time-efficient way to evaluate strengths and weaknesses in family functioning.

1. Problem-Solving: ability to resolve problems at a level that maintains effective family functioning.
2. Communication: exchange of information among family members.
3. Roles: established patterns of behavior for handling family functions, including provision of resources, support, and personal development.
4. Affective Responsiveness: extent to which individual family members experience appropriate affect and emotions.
5. Affective Involvement: extent to which family members are interested in and place value on each other's activities and concerns. A healthy family has an intermediate level of involvement, neither too little nor too much.
6. Behavioral Control: how a family expresses and maintains standards for the behavior of its members. Examples include patterns of control (flexible, rigid, chaotic, etc.).

Case Example #1

Ms. Smith is a 23-year-old single female who presents to establish care. Her past medical history includes chronic Lyme disease, fibromyalgia, irritable bowel disease, chronic pain previously on high-dose opioids, and a psychiatric history of hospitalizations for suicide attempts, depression with chronic suicidal ideation, anxiety, anorexia nervosa, and opioid and benzodiazepine dependence in full sustained remission. Her mother completed suicide by overdose 2 years ago, and her father has been absent from her life since her mother's death due to his inability to cope with his feelings of loss. Ms. Smith is an only child. She has remained sober from substances for 2 years after completing 9 months of residential treatment and ongoing connection with Alcoholics Anonymous (AA). Since attaining sobriety, her chronic suicidal ideation persisted, but she has had no suicide attempts. Her treatment team consists of her primary care doctor (eating disorders specialist), psychiatrist, DBT therapist, eating disorders program therapist, dietician, and support network including AA and her AA sponsor. Each clinician focuses on a single problem: her PCP, dietician, and eating disorders therapist focusing on her eating disorder; her DBT therapist and psychiatrist focusing on her chronic suicidal ideation and feelings of abandonment; and her AA sponsor on maintaining sobriety.

Family Assessment with Ms. Smith and Her Psychiatrist, Primary Care Doctor (PCP), DBT Therapist, Eating Disorders Program Therapist, Dietician, and AA Sponsor

Her psychiatrist scheduled a 1-hour meeting to develop a treatment plan. The first step is to clarify each person's understanding of the presenting problems.

Problem-Solving

Because of the instability in her family and housing, her treatment team and support network become her "family" and provide stability.

Communication

After the meeting, each clinician has a comprehensive understanding of how each of her symptoms is perpetuated and worsened by other symptoms. The plan is for all communication to go through her primary care physician.

Roles

The treatment team meeting allows each clinician to understand their role in Ms. Smith's care and agree that her symptoms need to be addressed as a whole.

Affective Responsiveness

Ms. Smith is angry that her mother died and her father left her. She used to spend time with her mother and misses her a great deal. These feelings trigger her urges to act impulsively. Her AA sponsor is scared when Ms. Smith is impulsive. Her psychiatrist and PCP feel overwhelmed because she is in constant crisis.

Affective Involvement

Each member of her treatment team is invested in her well-being and the need for consistent boundaries.

Behavior Control

Adequate when Ms. Smith is in control of her feelings.

Case Formulation

Ms. Smith's emotional balance (family stability) was disrupted by the loss of her parents and move to another state (family transitions). Early collaboration of care provided increased stability and understanding of all of Ms. Smith's needs from multiple perspectives. Everyone agreed that monthly check-in calls together as a cohesive treatment team allowed for the identification of triggers and earlier interventions to maintain remission and prevention of relapse. As she experiences feelings of abandonment and loss, the stability and consistency of her team helped her avoid acting on her suicidal ideation. The cohesiveness of her treatment team formed a "family" system that helped her navigate crises.

Learning Points

When patients do not have family, treatment team members and social and community support networks can become a "family." However, like any family system, ensuring consistent boundaries and limit-setting within the family, and, in this case, the treatment team, is crucial.

Family Inclusion

Involving families in assessment and treatment reduces risk for the patient and the provider. Good rapport with family members and good documentation provide a protective function against adverse provider outcomes such as lawsuits (Recupero 2007). By simply inviting and including family as part of the assessment, questions about family functioning (including adaptation to illness, the family narrative, caregiving concerns, family interactions) facilitate a solid working diagnosis (Heru 2015). Families provide information that increases the likelihood of an accurate diagnosis or early detection of harmful behaviors. Involving the family in decision-making about treatment and disposition is key to patient compliance and leads to more successful outcomes (Baird and Doherty 1990; Lang et al. 2002; McDaniel et al. 1990). Understanding family characteristics provides an understanding of how the psychosocial context influences the presenting symptoms. Listening to the family, taking their fears and concerns seriously, and teaching them how to help keep their loved one safe are steps in providing family-oriented patient care. A primary biomedical intervention may be sufficient to treat some presenting acute illnesses; most psychiatric problems require an understanding of the relational context for successful treatment.

This example demonstrates how inviting the family into the conversation allows for a broader understanding of the patient.

Case Example #2

Mrs. Nguyen is a 64-year-old, married, Vietnamese-speaking woman with obstructive sleep apnea, bilateral cataracts, recurrent urinary tract infections, and vaginal prolapse. She presents to the outpatient psychiatry clinic with severe anxiety and depression. She was previously a successful business owner, but in the past 2 years, she has progressively declined and become bed-ridden, isolative, and unable to work. She lives with her husband, and her family constellation includes a son and two adult daughters who live nearby and are involved in her care. She has had two prior extended inpatient hospitalizations of 2–3 months each, due to difficulty with discharge planning. When depressed, she is unable to care for herself independently and becomes extremely aggressive, prompting family to bring her to the emergency room for admission. This has been a repeated cycle every 6 months over the past 2 years. She has had many medication trials of antidepressants, benzodiazepines, antipsychotics, and mood stabilizers and biological trials of transcranial magnetic stimulation, electroconvulsive therapy, and ketamine infusions.

Inviting the family into the conversation Since she is accompanied by one of her daughters, the psychiatrist invites her to join the second half of the evaluation. The daughter is grateful to be included. The patient's husband joins by phone using a video conference interpreter service. The family provides information about an extensive trauma history: witnessing extensive violence and the patient herself is a victim of sexual abuse. Her daughter notes her strengths of being a good mother, raising three successful children, and maintaining a business for many years. It is revealed that in the last 2 years, her two daughters moved out of the home, married, and had children.

Shared decision-making between the professional, patient, and family Follow-up visits focus on collaborating with the family and validating the patient's trauma history. Consistent calls to both the husband and daughter, as well as connecting the patient with a Vietnamese-speaking therapist, allow the patient to become more engaged. The family members become aware of the patient's triggers and begin to understand how to manage her physical outbursts. They learn how to de-escalate the patient at home, rather than bringing her to the hospital. The patient's medication list is reduced, with emphasis on issues of adherence. Trauma-focused psychotherapy addresses years of repressed memories and feelings that were triggered by her two adult daughters leaving the home.

Case formulation The psychiatrist's discussion with Mrs. Nguyen's family helped place her symptoms in a larger relational context. The family's emotional balance (family stability) had been disrupted by the numerous changes such as her inability to work, her daughters leaving the home (family transitions), as well as a longstanding trauma history that was never previously discussed or addressed. The psychiatrist acknowledged the family's strengths and caring for one another and invited the family to explore how the family's functioning and involvement might play a part in Mrs. Nguyen's symptom presentation, her level of engagement, and ultimately her symptom alleviation (family as a system).

Learning points Including the family as members of the treatment team allowed both the psychiatrist and the family to identify the family's strengths as well as barriers to treatment: Mrs. Nguyen's unaddressed trauma and language and cultural barriers. Use of language interpreters helped Mrs. Nguyen feel more comfortable communicating with her entire treatment team and allowed for ongoing psychoeducation and collaboration throughout her hospitalization.

With family inclusion, the family is simply invited into the clinical setting (Heru 2015). Families are physicians' natural allies in caring for patients with chronic illness and can also uncover aspects of the patient that were not otherwise considered. Families can help with adhering to medication and watching for side effects, keeping appointments, promoting a healthy lifestyle, and providing positive emotional support. Patients need to know when they should be doing for themselves and when they can rely on family members. Families frequently need permission and guidance to carry out these functions. Clinicians should embrace the view that families are team members.

Barriers to Collaborating with Family Members and Incorporating Families into Their Work with Patients

Clinicians encounter multiple and interacting systemic barriers to routinely including family members of the people they treat even when their clients grant consent for them to do so. Other barriers include lack of confidence or expertise in collaborating with family members. In the past several decades, psychiatrists primarily focused on medication management in order to contain costs. Family and social systems work are often relegated to non-psychiatrists such as social workers or family advocacy groups, such as NAMI, which exist separately from behavioral health agencies (Mannion et al. 2012). Additional challenges include a lack of family-friendly policies and procedures and, in some instances, family members who are negative, critical, or hostile (Heru and Drury 2005). Lastly, even if family members want to be involved, coordinating a meeting time can be challenging.

For most clinicians, learning family-centered care skills requires additional training. Similarly, training in family skills in psychiatric residency programs has been challenging due to these conflicting theoretical paradigms. Currently, there is a lack of faculty and supervisors who can teach family-focused care, or supervisors who can demonstrate family interventions on a clinical rotation, providing a positive experience in involving family members in treatment (Mannion et al. 2012). Some ways to address these challenges in training include arranging community-based clinical services and consultation opportunities for trainees, engaging family support organizations for increased collaboration, including family members as faculty in trainee education, and increasing awareness and advocacy for family-centered care in training programs.

Family Assessment

Family assessment begins with the first visit and is a continuous process. Like the medical assessment, clinicians can assess the "anatomy," development, and functioning of a family over time. The family anatomy is understood by identifying the members of the nuclear family and who is part of the larger family system. Attending to family development means understanding the developmental stages of all family members. Family functioning is assessed by taking a history of the family, observing their interactions, and understanding the relational context of presenting symptoms. Table 1 outlines examples of

Table 1 Questions to help with family assessment

Family as a system
Who are the members of your family?
When it comes to daily support, who do you consider supportive?
Family stability
With all of the changes, how do you maintain a good family balance so everyone feels cared for?
If the illness progresses too quickly, what do you think might happen to your family?
Family transition
How have things changed now that your mother-in-law has moved in with you?
How are you, as a family, adjusting to your daughter starting high school?
Family world view (culture)
Do your parents generally feel that you are able to help each other out in crises?
How has it been when you've had to "fill in" for one another before?
How do family members let one another know when they need help?
Relational context of the symptom
How does a family member's symptoms influence everyone else in the family?
Have you noticed if there are things that you, as parents, do that make your son take more or less responsibility for his medications?

questions to ask both patients and available family to assess functioning.

Case Example #3

Mr. Cadie is a single, formerly incarcerated, homeless 50-year-old man living in a halfway house. He has diagnoses of bipolar disorder and alcohol dependence. Neighbors called police because he is outside yelling at midnight. He is admitted to a medical floor with uncontrolled diabetes, alcohol dependence, and metabolic syndrome. He is transferred to a psychiatric inpatient unit where he voices angry feelings toward his mother for betraying the memory of his father who died 4 years ago. A case manager and his 75-year-old mother, Mrs. Zabir, are his only social contacts. His mother is well, works part time, and recently remarried. She sees her son periodically but expresses fear about his impulsivity and anger since he recently threw his phone at her. The outpatient psychiatrist arranges to meet with Mrs. Zabir and the case manager to develop a treatment plan.

Family Assessment with Mr. Cadie and His Mother and Stepfather, Case Manager, and Psychiatrist

The meeting is scheduled for 1 hour and begins with the stated goal of developing a treatment plan for Mr. Cadie. Each family member is asked to identify problems. Mr. Cadie says that he does not want any contact with his mother. Mrs. Zabir says that she wants her son to have good medical care. Mr. Zabir says that he wants to be able to help Mr. Cadie in any way that he can. The case manager asks about medical problems and expresses concern about treatment compliance especially with his diabetic medication.

Problem-Solving

When sober, Mr. Cadie has good and adequate problem-solving, takes his medication reliably, and stays in the halfway house where he feels comfortable.

Communication

When sober, all agree that he communicates adequately.

Roles

His mother manages all his finances and all are happy with that role. In terms of other roles such as social contact, friendships, and relationships, all agree that Mr. Cadie has become isolated and socially less competent and now frequently abuses alcohol.

Affective Responsiveness

The patient is angry with his mother and sad about the loss of his father. Mr. Cadie used to spend time with his father and misses him a great deal. His mother is afraid of him; her new husband is unsure of the situation.

Affective Involvement

The patient is more isolated since his father died and his mother is more involved with her new husband.

Behavior Control

Adequate when Mr. Cadie is sober.

Case Formulation

All agreed with the assessment and the following problem list was generated.

Mr. Cadie has significant challenges getting his healthcare needs met.

Alcohol abuse is a result of his social isolation.

Mr. Cadie needs new social contacts.

Mrs. Zabir has a new life and wants to have less involvement with her son. She is afraid of him when he has been drinking.

Mr. Zabir is unsure how much he wants to be involved with Mr. Cadie.

The psychiatrist facilitates a family discussion about problem resolution and psychoeducation. The family decides that a good intervention is to have Mr. Zabir drive Mr. Cadie to AA meetings three times a week. Mrs. Zabir will wait to hear from her son when he next wants to talk with her. She will not visit him at his home. If her son wants to talk to her, they will meet in a neutral place such as Joe's Diner. (This place was chosen by Mr. Cadie as he had fond memories there as a child with his parents.) The case manager suggests that Mr. Cadie call his brother who is out of state to talk on the phone once a week. (The case manager has in mind a possible transfer of medical power of attorney to Mr. Cadie's brother.) A follow-up meeting is arranged for 1 month.

Learning Points

The family relationships have to change after Mr. Cadie threw a phone at his mother. A family approach allows the family members to renegotiate their own relationships with the guidance of professionals. This family assessment and intervention is proactive with the goal of preventing future deterioration of the patient, encouraging sobriety, and reducing isolation and allowing, if necessary, for a transition of power of attorney to another family member.

Homeless individuals and families are a diverse population. In addition to pragmatic issues created by poverty, homeless individuals exhibit a wide spectrum of serious psychiatric conditions including addiction, psychotic symptoms, anxiety, depression, personality disorders, and trauma symptoms. Relational symptoms such as domestic violence, separation and divorce, and alienation from family can be present.

Cultural Considerations to Family Assessment

In community settings, clinicians encounter patients from established ethnocultural communities and immigrants and refugees. Language barriers and cultural complexity may prevent adequate diagnosis and treatment for a significant number of patients, so it is essential to consider the cultural meaning of symptoms and explore the social context of distress. Various models have been developed to meet this clinical challenge, such as ethnospecific mental health services, mental health translators and culture brokers, and the training of clinicians in generic approaches to cultural competence (Kirmayer et al. 2003). Additionally, immigrants may report higher rates of mental disorders and lower levels of use of mental health service (Giammusso et al. 2018). The use of professional interpreters improves clinical care and raises the quality of care for limited English proficiency patients, approaching or equaling the outcome in patients without language barriers (Karliner et al. 2007). In the case example of Mrs. Nguyen, inviting the family into the conversation both provided a larger cultural context contributing to her illness and bridged the language barrier that was impeding her comprehension of care and collaboration with her family. Although these resources may not be as available in public sector settings, it is important to rely on family to help patients feel more at ease, secure, comfortable, and willing to communicate and share with the treatment team.

Healthcare redesign can incorporate family. Don Berwick, the Former Administrator for the Centers for Medicare & Medicaid Services, described Alaska's Southcentral Foundation Nuka System of Care as the "leading example of healthcare redesign in the nation, maybe the world" (https://scfnuka.com). The NUKA healthcare system incorporates family and cultural practices, creating a welcoming environment for patients and their families. The NUKA Native

Community emphasizes developing services that are built on relationships. One program, called the Family Wellness Warriors Initiative Program, addresses domestic violence, abuse, and neglect in the Alaska Native community.

Family-centered care does exist in mental health centers. A family-oriented recovery program for children called "wraparound" provides mental health and community services individualized to each child and family (Hinden and Wilder 2008). The wraparound process builds on family strengths with families and children setting their own goals. Frequently, there is a paid family support specialist from a similar cultural background as the family, which helps engage the family. Informal community supports include extended family, friends, the faith-based community, boys' and girls' clubs, teachers, and neighbors.

Despite these efforts, many people will not attend mental health clinics citing stigma and pathologizing labels. Such was the case with Bosnian and Kosovar refugees who ultimately benefited from a community-based family resilience approach. Families readily participated because it was held in a storefront in their neighborhood and tapped into cultural values. The 9-week treatment affirmed strengths, resources, and kinship networks and recognized the families' determination to rise above tragedy and forge a new life. Facilitators from the community were trained to co-lead the groups, thus fostering collaboration and the development of local resources (Walsh 2007). A family resilience perspective focuses on strengths and coping skills rather than deficits and psychopathology.

Afro-Caribbeans are sometimes labelled "hard-to-reach" by mainstream mental health services and are under-represented in research. However, a study using a "culturally adapted family interventions in schizophrenia model" demonstrated that Afro-Caribbeans were highly motivated to engage with providers and researchers (Edge and Grey 2018). Using an evidence-based model of family intervention with four focus groups, the English Afro-Caribbean participants recommended adding topics such as racism and discrimination and different models of mental health and illness to improve cultural appropriateness. Additionally, emphasis was placed on developing a new ethos of delivery, which participants called "shared learning." This approach explicitly acknowledges the power imbalances where delivery of interventions involves White therapists and Black patients. The therapists' cultural competence was considered fundamental for successful engagement.

While it is unfair to draw generalizations across cultures because this does not consider the within-group variation, some studies do suggest norms in specific cultural/ethnic settings. Historically, having high levels of expressed emotion (EE) within the family environment has generally been associated with poorer patient outcomes. However, high EE (high criticalness) in African-American families with a patient with schizophrenia was associated with better patient outcomes (Gurak and Weisman de Mamani 2017). On qualitative analysis, patients perceived high-EE family comments as "direct and expressive," supportive, and an expression of concern, whereas low-EE family comments were perceived as passive and uncertain.

Family Psychoeducation

Psychoeducation explores the meaning of the illness for each family member and helps develop a repertoire of coping skills. Psychoeducation can be delivered to individuals or to families either in single family sessions or in multifamily groups (MFPG) and is considered an evidence-based practice (McFarlane 2016). The skills needed to run a psychoeducational program can be taught in about 6 hours. This is done with didactic teaching about basic group principles and by becoming an observer/participant in a psychoeducational program. Training includes being able to handle family emotional reactions, such as feelings of anger, sadness, or frustration. Helping a family with these feelings facilitates the adjustment of the family to the presence of illness. McFarlane's online training workbook can be accessed here:

https://training.mccmh.net/Portals/0/training/MFG,FamPsychoEd_Workbook.pdf.

Family psychoeducation as a treatment for schizophrenia was developed over 40 years ago, and over 100 studies show the reduction in patient relapse rates by 50–60%, compared to treatment as usual (McFarlane 2016). Explicitly disavowing the assumptions that family pathology caused relapse and deterioration, family psychoeducation engages family members as partners in care, teaches them about the illness, and supports their struggles as a family. New iterations of MFPG are being applied to first episode and prodromal psychosis, internationally and nationally (McFarlane 2016). A qualitative study of an ethnoculturally specific MFPG allowed Chinese and Tamil participants to share experiences and support each other in their own language during and after sessions (Chow et al. 2010). The study found decreased hostility and conflict and better understanding among family members and patients. Communication skills training improved the family members' ability to handle disagreements. Increased knowledge about mental illness impacted positively on participants' beliefs about health maintenance, medication, and side effects. Family members learned to observe for signs and symptoms of relapse and seek help. Both patients and family members developed great trust toward staff, facilitating treatment.

In Mexican American families with a patient with schizophrenia (n = 174), Kopelowicz and colleagues successfully adapted MFPG, with the goal of supporting medication adherence (Kopelowicz et al. 2015). Before the intervention, a systematic assessment of each family enabled the clinical researchers to capture the cultural elements considered important for the adaptation. Family warmth and moderate family emotional over-involvement emerged as good prognostic factors.

Most MFPG research has focused on schizophrenia, but MFPG is also used for other psychiatric and medical illnesses. A group-based program that includes MFPG showed feasibility for patients with non-epileptic seizures and their families (Libbon et al. 2019). A program for Native Americans with substance use includes multifamily psychoeducational groups in which adolescents and their families learn together and celebrate the healing process in a Weekly Circle (Novins et al. 2012). A Weekly Circle (multifamily group) promotes sobriety and builds a community of healing. The Department of Veterans Affairs healthcare system's leadership has endorsed family involvement in veterans' mental healthcare as an important component of treatment. Evidence suggests that family interventions for PTSD improve veteran and family outcomes (Sherman et al. 2012).

Despite the consistent evidence demonstrating the effectiveness of family psychoeducation, it has been the least implemented of all of the evidence-based practices. According to the 2009 Community Mental Health Services Uniform Reporting System Output Tables, only 1.1% of providers nationally offer family psychoeducation, with only 19 states reporting any provision of this service (Mannion et al. 2012).

In contrast, NAMI's Family-to-Family (FTF) program has been widely implemented as an educational tool for family, significant others, and friends of people with mental health conditions. NAMI's FTF is a peer-led, self-help program. It includes a structured, 12-week curriculum, with participants attending weekly, for 2- or 3-hour sessions. The focus is on giving and receiving emotional support and to develop insight into their feelings about mental illness. This approach helps relatives who have unmet needs associated with their loved one's mental health concerns and care. Because of its time-limited approach and its inclusiveness of all family members, the program has had wider accessibility and utilization compared to family psychoeducation. A randomized controlled trial of FTF (n = 138) was conducted to assess the effectiveness of the program across a demographically diverse state in the USA. Compared to the 3-month wait-list control group, participants in FTF experienced improved coping, problem-solving, empowerment, and reduced anxiety and depression (Schiffman et al. 2015).

Other Family Considerations

In the next section, several non-traditional family roles are discussed.

Parenting as a Patient with Serious Mental Illness

Most parents who have mental illness do a great job of parenting their children; however, societal attitudes are stacked against mothers with mental illness. To support parents with mental illness, we can provide practical and emotional support, provide parenting classes, and discuss issues such as what to do if you become ill, who you trust to care for your child, and the implications of mental illness on questions of custody. The development of a care plan can be key in this regard. The care plan contains information for the care of a baby/child if the patient is unable to care for him/her due to illness or hospitalization. It can contain as much information as the parent wants, but usually contains the names of surrogate caregivers, medication information, vaccinations, feeding, and regular activities (http://www.copmi.net.au/parents/helping-my-child-and-family/care-plans).

The role of others in child-rearing must be considered, particularly for those women who are involved in multiple partner fertility unions. In these situations, the concept of "othermothering" is distinct from step-mothering and involves sharing parenting responsibilities with the children's biological parents. This can involve co-parenting children who are their romantic partners' children from previous or current relationships (Burton and Hardaway 2012). A study of 256 low-income mostly unmarried mothers (Latino, African American, and White) found that 78% of the mothers had been, or were involved, in multiple partner fertility relationships (Burton and Hardaway 2012). This study was carried out over a period of 6 years in economically disadvantaged neighborhoods in Boston, Chicago, and San Antonio to monitor the consequences of welfare reform for the well-being of families and children. "Othermothers" can be invited into the care of young adult patients who present in the clinic. The case that follows expands on the role of "othermothers."

Case Example #4

Ms. Talia is a 37-year-old, Hispanic woman with morbid obesity, obstructive sleep apnea, and asthma. She presents with anxiety and panic attacks. She has a past history of substance abuse and has been in prison for drug-related crimes. She is receiving disability. Her family constellation consists of four teenage sons in her mother's custody. Her sons live between her house and her mother's house. A young girl baby, who is the child of her niece, is living with the patient. The niece, who is actively using substances, sometimes stays with the patient and sometimes disappears for weeks. A boyfriend also sometimes stays with her. Ms. Talia wants custody of the baby girl and presents in the clinic asking for help with her psychiatric symptoms so that she can be well enough to go to court to get custody.

Family Assessment with Ms. Talia and Her Mother

The psychiatrist met with the patient and the mother and completed the family assessment over several routine visits. Medication management occurred in the treatment sessions.

Problem-Solving

Ms. Talia relies on her mother to help with all problems. She states that she would like to be more independent but does not know how. The mother supports her goal.

Communication

The mother and the daughter do everything together. Ms. Talia shares all her thoughts and feelings with her mother. The mother does not share her thoughts with the patient and says that she “just wants to help.” The mother is not critical and says, “It is my duty as a mother to help.”

Roles

The mother and the daughter spend most of their time caring for children, theirs and children of the extended family. The mother, although on a fixed income, provides as much financial support as possible for her daughter. Her daughter is also on a fixed income but gives away food and money to other family members and her boyfriend.

Affective Responsiveness

The patient is anxious most of the time. She experiences pleasure with her baby girl in the house, dressing her and changing her outfits many times a day. The mother thinks she is obsessed with the baby and she treats the baby like a doll. The patient cries and feels overwhelmed a lot and feels guilty because she depends on her mother for money and emotional support. The mother experiences a normal and full range of emotions.

Affective Involvement

There is over-involvement between the patient and her mother, with guilt on the part of the patient for depending on her mother. The mother accompanies her to all appointments, grocery shopping, etc. The mother acknowledges her over-involvement but says, “It is my duty to help.”

Behavioral Control

There are no house rules. It is unclear from appointment to appointment who is living in Ms. Talia’s house. She is thinking about setting rules about substance abuse and throwing her niece out of her house but is not able to because “there is nowhere for her to go.”

Case Formulation

Ms. Talia has generalized anxiety disorder, panic disorder, personality disorder with dependent and histrionic traits, and a significant past history of substance abuse. Her family assessment reveals an over-involved relationship with her mother and a chaotic living situation. Family strengths are caring of others and their self-identification as strong good mothers. Ms. Talia and her mother agree with the formulation. The mother and the patient agree that Ms. Talia needs to set limits with the niece and her boyfriend and tell them they cannot stay there if they are “high” or “crashing.” She agrees to tell family members that she can no longer give them money, when she herself does not have enough for groceries. She says that although she agrees and knows she needs to do this, she “feels bad for other people.” The mother, supported by the psychiatrist, takes the stance that while this is an admirable and valued family trait, she will not get better and thus will not be able to get custody of the baby girl unless she sets limits and controls her home environment. Ms. Talia asks for medications to help her. The psychiatrist agrees that medications are part of the plan but that the patient needs to do her part and set up house rules. The mother and the patient agree.

At each meeting, the plan is reviewed. Eventually, Ms. Talia puts out the freeloaders and sets family rules for those who remain in her house. Ms. Talia reports that her level of anxiety and panic has not changed but she is feeling better now that she has some control over her life. Monthly visits with the patient and her mother set goals such as the patient taking her citalopram 20 mg and keeping her medical appointments. She sets general health goals such as healthier eating and more exercise.

Learning Points

There are many potential interventions for Ms. Talia. The family assessment approach pinpointed family strengths that can be used in treatment: her relationship with her mother, strong mothering qualities, and her desire to care for the girl baby. The patient’s relationships have unsettling elements, e.g., dressing up the baby girl and over-involvement with her mother. Medication administration is incorporated into a larger contract with the patient and her mother. Without a family assessment, the strengths and weaknesses of the family system would not have been evident. The recommendations are framed in a family context with an emphasis on family strengths.

Children as Caregivers to Parents with Serious Mental Illness

Children are "invisible" to mental health professionals who provide care to adults, yet they are present in the home and participate in the care of their parents. It is estimated that 13% to 51% of adults attending psychiatric outpatient clinics have children (Maybery and Reupert 2018). In the development of one program, young adults who have lived experience of parents with mental illness and/or substance use problems were consulted to help with interventions (Reupert et al. 2019). The resulting intervention called mi.spot is an online intervention for groups of up to 20 young adults (aged 18–25), who have a parent with a mental illness and/or substance use problem. Mi.spot offers six, 1-hour, professionally facilitated psychoeducational modules using a private, online diary (called mi.thoughts.spot) for participants. There are opportunities for participants to chat informally with each other on threads initiated by a participant or facilitator. A lot of child care programs have been developed in the UK and Australia and could be implemented in the USA. In a book called *Building Children's Resilience in the Face of Parental Mental Illness* (Cooklin and Gorell Barnes 2020), Cooklin includes advice that young caregivers want to give to psychiatrists:

1. *Introduce yourself. Tell us who you are and what your job is.*
2. *Give us as much information as you can.*
3. *Tell us what is wrong with our parents.*
4. *Tell us what is going to happen next.*
5. *Talk to us and listen to us. Remember, it is not hard to speak to us; we are not aliens.*
6. *Ask us what we know and what we think. We live with our parents; we know how they have been behaving.*
7. *Tell us it is not our fault. We can feel really guilty if our mum or dad is ill. We need to know we are not to blame.*
8. *Please don't ignore us. Remember we are part of the family and we live there too.*
9. *Keep on talking to us and keep us informed. We need to know what is happening.*
10. *Tell us if there is anyone we can talk to. MAYBE IT COULD BE YOU.*

Lesbian, Gay, Bisexual, Transgender, Queer (LGBTQ) Families

Over the past few decades, lesbian, gay, bisexual, transgender, queer, questioning, and other sexual and gender minorities (LGBTQ) have become visible. LGBTQ youth may experience strained relationships with families due to the stigma related to their sexual orientation and/or gender identity (Newcomb et al. 2019). Family rejection is strongly associated with mental health problems, substance use, increased sexual risk, and higher prevalence of homeless youth (Bouris et al. 2010; Institute for Gender Health and Sexual Minority 2017; Simons et al. 2013). Additionally, LGBTQ youth are disproportionally represented in the foster care population and often face discrimination within the system (Fish et al. 2019).

For LGBTQ youth, having a strong, stable, supportive relationship with an adult, such as a parent, is one of the strongest predictors of long-term adjustment in the general adolescent population (Roe 2017). A study looking at the role of protective factors in suicidality of LGBTQ youth ($n = 2255$) found that family connectedness accounted for more variance than sexual orientation or the other protective factors. Despite the limited research and lack of randomized control trials on family-based interventions for LGBTQ youth, these findings suggest that improving relationships between LGBTQ youth and their parents is vital (Eisenberg and Resnick 2006). A study examining strategies for building stronger relationships between LGBTQ youth and their foster caregivers found that acceptance, support, and ensuring safety were important elements to include in programming aiming to improve placement stability and well-being (Salazar et al. 2018). The approach to LGBTQ families should start with rapport building to establish a sense of safety, support, and trust before exploring various factors that may contribute to feelings of rejection, isolation, and stigma. Assessment of families should include understanding these influences to better address the mental health needs of LGBTQ individuals.

Case Example # 5

Ms. Sharon presents with anxiety symptoms and requests benzodiazepines. She is new to the clinic and states that she has been treated in the past for PTSD and has had several hospitalizations. She lives with Ms. Anna whom she describes as her caregiver. You ask her to bring Ms. Anna to the next appointment. At the next few appointments, you find out that Ms. Anna has significant depressive symptoms and is Ms. Sharon's significant other but is afraid to acknowledge this out of fear of judgement, stigma, and rejection. Ms. Anna was disowned by her religious and conservative family. Both women express suicidal thoughts and want to support each other better.

Family Assessment with Ms. Sharon, Ms. Anna, the Psychiatrist, and the Social Worker

A 1-hour family assessment meeting is scheduled.

Problem-Solving

They each identify problems but do not communicate them to each other, nor do they try to solve them together.

Communication

There is poor communication due to fears of judgment and rejection and guilt of burdening each other.

Roles

They each contribute to the household income for rent and food. They are in an intimate and caring relationship that they both find satisfying. However, both are alienated from their families and only have each other to rely on.

Affective Responsiveness

They have warm caring feelings for each other but do not communicate these feelings. They each have intermittent suicidal ideation.

Affective Involvement

They spend most of their time together and have few friends. They both feel lonely and isolated.

Behavioral Control

They engage in secretive suicidal and self-injurious behaviors from time to time. They would like to change this.

Case Formulation

Both Ms. Anna and Ms. Sharon agree they want to work on improving their relationship. The psychiatrist is most concerned about their suicidal ideation and self-injurious behavior and works on developing a mutual safety plan. In the following appointments, the treatment team works on establishing rapport and fostering a supportive, accepting environment where they feel comfortable sharing with the clinicians and with each other. They work on spending quality time together, accepting that their relationship is strong, and feeling more comfortable with their sexual identities. They work on improving their communication, problem-solving, and sharing more positive feelings.

Learning Point

Although this couple cannot change the circumstances of their lives, they can reduce acting out behavior and improve the quality of their relationship.

Conclusion

A narrow approach to the treatment of psychiatric illness often does not yield optimal results. Although it may seem that one part of the family can exist in isolation from the rest of the family, the case examples demonstrate that family functioning cannot be fully understood by understanding each individual alone. Although there may be an assumption that involving families may increase conflict, the clinician can discuss strengths of the individual and the family and identify areas of agreement.

Starting with a family meeting is key to understanding the patient in their family context. When the patient says that the family cannot come to an appointment, clinicians can gently insist on meeting the family. "Thinking Family" is the first step. When families are difficult to understand or when the assessment process gets bogged down or when the psychiatrist feels unsure of what to do, then seeking supervision or a referral to an experienced family therapist is appropriate. Most families appreciate being involved and will work hard to help you help their family member (Heru 2015). "Thinking Family" means listening to family members when they call with a question, even if the patient has not signed a release. Confidentiality means stating that you cannot discuss patient specifics but that you can listen and provide general information on how to handle emergency situations.

Psychiatry in public sector settings can promote a clinic that is family-friendly, supporting connection and involvement, and include multifamily psychoeducational groups (Heru 2015). Educational literature can be offered in several languages. Resources may include a list of books written for families such as Michelle Sherman's *I'm Not Alone: A Teen's Guide to Living with a Parent Who Has a Mental Illness* (Sherman and Sherman 2006). The World Fellowship for Schizophrenia and Allied Disorders website (http://www.world-schizophrenia.org/resources/booklist.html) has a list of recommended books for patients and their families. Families can be given access to additional services such as transportation, parenting classes, learning English as a second language, etc. Psychiatry must recognize the important contribution that family members bring, allowing clinicians to understand the presenting symptoms and the orientation of the family and provide any needed family interventions.

References

Baird MA and Doherty WJ. (1990). Risks and benefits of a family systems approach to medical care. Fam Med. 22: 396–403.

Bamm EL and Rosenbaum P. (2008). Family-centered theory: origins, development, barriers, and supports to implementation in rehabilitation medicine. Archives of physical medicine and rehabilitation, 89(8), 1618–1624.

Bouris A, Guilamo-Ramos V, Pickard A, et al. (2010). A systematic review of parental influences on the health and well-being of lesbian, gay, and bisexual youth: time for a new public health research and practice agenda. The journal of primary prevention, 31(5–6), 273–309.

Burton LM and Hardaway CR. (2012). Low-income mothers as "othermothers" to their romantic partners' children: women's coparenting in multiple partner fertility relationships. Family process, 51(3), 343–359.

Chow W, Law S, Andermann L, et al. (2010). Multi-family psycho-education group for assertive community treatment clients and families of culturally diverse background: a pilot study. Community mental health journal, 46(4), 364–371.

Cooklin, A., Gorell Barnes, G. (Eds.). (2020). Building Children's Resilience in the Face of Parental Mental Illness. London: Routledge. https://doi.org/10.4324/9780429060731

Edge D and Grey P. (2018). An Assets-Based Approach to Co-Producing a Culturally Adapted Family Intervention (CaFI) with African Caribbeans Diagnosed with Schizophrenia and Their Families. Ethnicity & disease, 28(Suppl 2), 485–492.

Eisenberg ME and Resnick MD. (2006). Suicidality among gay, lesbian, and bisexual youth: The role of protective factors. Journal of Adolescent Health, 39, 662–668.

Epstein, NB, Baldwin LM and Bishop DS. (1983). The McMaster Family Assessment Device. Journal of Marital and Family Therapy. 9: 171– 180.

Fish JN, Baams L, Wojciak AS, et al. (2019). Are sexual minority youth overrepresented in foster care, child welfare, and out-of-home placement? Findings from nationally representative data. Child abuse & neglect, 89, 203–211.

Giammusso I, Casadei F, Catania N, et al. (2018). Immigrants Psychopathology: Emerging Phenomena and Adaptation of Mental Health Care Setting by Native Language. Clinical practice and epidemiology in mental health: CP & EMH, 14, 312–32.

Gurak K and Weisman de Mamani A. (2017). Caregiver Expressed Emotion and Psychiatric Symptoms in African-Americans with Schizophrenia: An Attempt to Understand the Paradoxical Relationship. Fam Process. 56(2):476–486.

Heru A. (2015). Family-centered Care in the Outpatient General Psychiatry Clinic. Journal of Psychiatric Practice: 21(5): 381–388.

Heru A. and Drury L. (2005). Overcoming Barriers in Working with Families. Acad Psychiatry 30, 379–384.

Hinden B and Wilder C. (2008). Family options: Supporting parents with mental illness and their children. Focal Point: Research, Policy, & Practice in Children's Mental Health, 22(2), 7–10.

Institute for Sexual and Gender Minority Health and Wellbeing: The State of LGBTQ Health and Wellbeing: Strengthening Schools and Families to Build Resilience. 2017. Available at https://cpb-us-e1.wpmucdn.com/sites.northwestern.edu/dist/3/817/files/2017/07/Working-Group-Historical-Record-2dytc7x.pdf. Accessed November 1, 2020.

Karliner LS, Jacobs EA, Chen AH, et al. (2007). Do professional interpreters improve clinical care for patients with limited English proficiency? A systematic review of the literature. Health services research, 42(2), 727–754.

Kirmayer KJ, Groleau D, Guzder J, et al. (2003). Cultural consultation: a model of mental health service for multicultural societies. Canadian journal of psychiatry. Revue canadienne de psychiatrie, 48(3), 145–153.

Kopelowicz A, Zarate R, Wallace CJ, et al. (2015). Using the theory of planned behavior to improve treatment adherence in Mexican Americans with schizophrenia. Journal of consulting and clinical psychology, 83(5), 985–993.

Lang F, Marvel K, Sanders D, et al. (2002). Interviewing when family members are present. American family physician, 65(7), 1351–1354.

Libbon R, Triana J, Heru A. et al. (2019). Family Skills for the Resident Toolbox: the 10-min Genogram, Ecomap, and Prescribing Homework. Acad Psychiatry 43: 435–439.

Mannion E., Marin R., Chapman P., et al. (2012). Overcoming Systemic Barriers to Family Inclusion in Community Psychiatry: The Pennsylvania Experience, American Journal of Psychiatric Rehabilitation, 15:1, 61–80.

Maybery D and Reupert AE. (2018). The number of parents who are patients attending adult psychiatric services. Current opinion in psychiatry, 31(4), 358–362.

McDaniel SH, Campbell TL, Seaburn DB. (1990). Family Oriented Primary Care: A Manual for Medical Providers. New York: Springer-Verlag.

McFarlane WR. (2016). Family Interventions for Schizophrenia and the Psychoses: A Review. Family process, 55(3), 460–482.

Miller I, Gabor C, Gabor K, et al. (2000). The McMaster Approach to Families: theory, assessment, treatment and research. Journal of Family Therapy, 22, 168–189.

Newcomb ME, LaSala MC, Bouris A, et al. (2019). The Influence of Families on LGBTQ Youth Health: A Call to Action for Innovation in Research and Intervention Development. LGBT health, 6(4), 139–145.

Novins DK, Boyd ML, Brotherton DT, et al. (2012). Walking on: celebrating the journeys of Native American adolescents with substance use problems on the winding road to healing. Journal of psychoactive drugs, 44(2), 153–159.

Recupero P. (2007). Risk management in the family. In: Heru AM, Drury LM, eds. Working with Families of Psychiatric Inpatients: A Guide for Clinicians (pp. 139–148). Baltimore: Johns Hopkins University Press.

Reupert A, Bartholomew C, Cuff R, et al. (2019). An Online Intervention to Promote Mental Health and Wellbeing for Young Adults Whose Parents Have Mental Illness and/or Substance Use Problems: Theoretical Basis and Intervention Description. Frontiers in psychiatry, 10, 59.

Roe S. (2017). "Family Support Would Have Been Like Amazing": LGBTQ Youth Experiences With Parental and Family Support. The Family Journal, 25(1), 55–62.

Salazar AM, McCowan KJ, Cole JJ, et al. (2018). Developing Relationship-Building Tools for Foster Families Caring for Teens who are LGBTQ2S. Child welfare, 96(2), 75–97.

Schiffman, J., Reeves, G. M., Kline, E., Medoff, D. R., Lucksted, A., Hoagwood, K., Fang, L. J., & Dixon, L. B. (2015). Outcomes of a Family Peer Education Program for Families of Youth and Adults with Mental Illness. International journal of mental health, 44(4): 303–315.

Sherman MD and Sherman DM. (2006). I'm Not Alone: A Teen's Guide to Living with a Parent Who Has a Mental Illness, Beaver Pond Publishing.

Sherman MD, Perlick DA, Straits-Tröster K. (2012). Adapting the multifamily group model for treating veterans with posttraumatic stress disorder. Psychological Services, 9(4), 349–360.

Simons L, Schrager SM, Clark LF et al. (2013). Parental support and mental health among transgender adolescents. The Journal of adolescent health: official publication of the Society for Adolescent Medicine, 53(6), 791–793.

Walsh F. (2007). Traumatic loss and major disasters: strengthening family and community resilience. Family process, 46(2), 207–227.

Evidence-Based Practices for Co-occurring Addiction and Mental Illness

Christine Yuodelis-Flores, Matthew Iles-Shih, and Richard K. Ries

Introduction

Development of an integrated co-occurring disorder program in the community mental health center is essential for comprehensive care. Addiction is a chronic relapsing and remitting disorder that severely impacts the course, treatment, and prognosis of mental and physical disorders and presents complex challenges for providers. Conversely, severe and chronic mental illness also impacts the course and treatment of the substance use disorder (SUD). Providers are in need of adequate training and supervision to work with this population, and careful treatment planning with coordinated interventions is essential for success. Clinicians unprepared to treat addictive disorders may avoid treating the co-occurring disorder (COD) patient, referring the individual to another treatment program, or alternatively make treatment demands that the individual cannot achieve. Better outcomes are possible and rewarding for both the participants and the providers by organizing effective interventions through practical evidence-based clinical approaches.

COD patients have been shown to do poorly in traditional addiction treatment without some emphasis on their comorbid SMI. Thus, there has been concerted effort nationally to transition toward an evidenced-based model of integrated treatment, in which providers knowledgeable about both conditions treat SMI and SUD concurrently in the same program (Minkoff and Cline 2004). This chapter discusses the prognosis and complications of co-occurring disorders, provides an overview of integrated treatment, and delineates the role of evidence-based psychiatric and psychosocial treatment, treatment teams, group therapies, and ancillary services such as self-help groups, peer support, medical services, and vocational and housing support commonly used in co-occurring treatment programs.

Scope of Co-occurring Disorders (COD) in the Community

Results from the Epidemiological Catchment Area (ECA) survey (Regier et al. 1990) showed greater than 60% lifetime prevalence rate for

C. Yuodelis-Flores (✉)
Department of Psychiatry and Behavioral Sciences, University of Washington, Harborview Addiction and Rehabilitation Programs, Harborview Medical Center, Seattle, WA, USA
e-mail: floresc@uw.edu

M. Iles-Shih
Department of Psychiatry and Behavioral Sciences, University of Washington, Harborview Medical Center, Seattle, WA, USA
e-mail: mattiles@uw.edu

R. K. Ries
Division of Addictions, Department of Psychiatry and Behavioral Sciences, University of Washington, Harborview Medical Center, Seattle, WA, USA
e-mail: rries@uw.edu

W. E. Sowers et al. (eds.), *Textbook of Community Psychiatry*,
https://doi.org/10.1007/978-3-031-10239-4_25

SUD in those diagnosed with bipolar disorder. In those diagnosed with schizophrenia, nearly half have a lifetime diagnosis of an alcohol or drug use disorder. The ECA survey also found that one third of individuals with a mood disorder had a lifetime history of a comorbid SUD. A more recent study, the National Epidemiologic Survey on Alcohol and Related Conditions (NESARC) (Grant et al. 2004), reported that of those with drug use disorders (DUD) who sought treatment over the past 12 months, 60% had an accompanying mood disorder and 43% had an anxiety disorder. Forty-one percent of those with alcohol use disorders (AUD) presenting for treatment had a mood disorder, and 33% had an anxiety disorder. Poly-substance use is more common than not in those with DUD.

There is a significant association of SUD with Axis II disorders. Among those in the NESARC study with current AUD, 29% had a personality disorder diagnosis, and among those with DUD, 48% had that diagnosis. Antisocial personality disorder holds the distinction of being the most common comorbid psychiatric illness in patients with addictive disorders, followed by borderline personality disorder.

Prognosis and Complications of Comorbid Disorders

Addiction alone predicts an increase in completed suicides for the non-psychiatrically ill. Murphy and Wetzel estimated the risk for suicide in people with AUD was between 60 and 120 times that of the general population (Murphy and Wetzel 1990). For other drugs of abuse, association with suicide is even more compelling. A meta-analysis of worldwide suicide studies (Harris and Barraclough 1997) reported that suicide risk is 14 times that expected for those with opioid dependence. It is 17 times more likely for persons with mixed drug abuse, 20 times more likely for those with prescription drug abuse, and 44 times more likely for those with combined prescription and illicit drug abuse. Although men have a higher rate of completed suicide, the association of suicide with SUD is markedly stronger for women (Wilcox et al. 2004).

Depression has a significant adverse effect on the course of substance dependence, predicting poor treatment response, increased risk of suicide, and higher rates of relapse (Murphy and Wetzel 1990). One year of sobriety from alcohol is associated with a threefold reduction in risk of depression (Agosti and Levin 2006). However, the rate of current depressive disorders in people with AUD abstinent for greater than a year is still four times that of the general population (Hasin and Grant 2002). Subjects with co-occurring major depressive disorder (MDD) and AUD report more previous depressive episodes, suicide attempts, and recent adverse life events as compared to subjects with MDD alone (Sher et al. 2008). Substance-induced depressive disorders also increase the risk of suicidal behavior. Ries and colleagues studied acutely suicidal psychiatric inpatients with substance-induced psychiatric disorders and found that this subgroup had higher severity of suicidal ideation but improved more quickly than other patients and tended to have shorter lengths of stay (Ries et al. 2009).

It can be very difficult to differentiate between substance-induced and independent depressive disorders, and the diagnosis may change if the patient is followed over time. Nunes et al. (2006) studied depressive disorders in patients with alcoholism admitted to an inpatient psychiatric unit and found that about half of patients were given a diagnosis of substance-induced depression. However, after following them for a 1-year period, one third of those with that diagnosis were reclassified as having a major depression independent of substance use.

More than a third of panic disorder patients have a lifetime history of SUD (Regier et al. 1990). Among people with AUD, preexisting anxiety disorders (in particular social phobia and panic disorder) predict a significant increase in relapse rates (Driessen et al. 2001). Patients with post-traumatic stress disorder (PTSD) have increased risk for DUD and AUD which is two to four times greater than non-PTSD patients (Kessler et al. 1995). Rates of PTSD among female opiate- and cocaine-dependent patients were ten times that of the general population using ECA data (Cottler et al. 1992). Addiction treatment outcomes in these women can be highly dependent on the availability of supportive and trauma-informed psychosocial and psychiatric care (Najavits et al. 1997).

Substance abuse worsens the course of illness and treatment outcome in bipolar disorder and is associated with increased violence against self and others. Those with bipolar and addictive disorders are less adherent to treatment (Strakowski et al. 1998), have more frequent and more prolonged affective episodes (Tohen et al. 2003), and have lower overall quality of life (Weiss et al. 2005) in comparison to non-substance-using patients with bipolar disorder. Around 30% of individuals with bipolar disorder will attempt suicide, but the presence of SUD appears to double the risk for suicide attempts (Comtois et al. 2004).

Comorbid addiction and schizophrenia increase the likelihood of homelessness, legal problems, violence and victimization, treatment noncompliance, multiple medical problems, frequent emergency visits, frequent hospitalizations, and suicidal behavior (Mueser et al. 1992; Ziedonis et al. 2004). It predicts poor prognosis, vulnerability to social dysfunction, suicide attempts, and more problems with housing and finances (Drake et al. 1990).

Stimulant-induced psychotic disorder is very common during intoxication and withdrawal. In chronic methamphetamine use, the presence and duration of psychotic symptoms increase with severity and length of use and are particularly associated with long-term intravenous use. Chronic intravenous methamphetamine-dependent patients can present with long-term psychotic symptoms that appear almost identical to paranoid schizophrenia. In the US population, the abuse of smokable methamphetamine also known as "crank," "ice," or "crystal" is more common than intravenous methamphetamine use. Chronic use of this drug is associated with longer duration of psychotic symptoms (up to several months) compared to psychotic symptoms observed in smokers of crack cocaine. Individuals with schizophrenia who use stimulants would be expected to experience marked intensification of psychotic symptoms that last longer than the psychotic experiences of those who do not have an independent psychotic disorder.

Screening and Assessment of Substance Use Disorders in Community Mental Health

All people presenting for mental health treatment should be screened for past and present SUD and related medical problems. Individuals should also be screened for acute safety risk related to intoxication, potential for overdose, withdrawal, and suicidality. Positive screening should be followed up with a more detailed assessment. A variety of screening tests are in use for the detection of SUD. One clinically useful screening tool is the Global Appraisal of Individual Needs – Short Screener (GAIN-SS) (Dennis et al. 2006), a very brief instrument designed to identify individuals who are likely to have a mental health and/or substance use disorder and who should be referred for further assessment or treatment. It is used to place individuals into one of the four quadrants of care to determine the level of integrated treatment (see Text Box 1).

Text Box 1 Four-Quadrant Model for Level of Care*

QUADRANT I MENTAL ILLNESS – LOW SEVERITY SUD – LOW SEVERITY Mild psychiatric illness with substance dependence (*Clients served by primary care clinics*)	QUADRANT II MENTAL ILLNESS – HIGH SEVERITY SUD – LOW SEVERITY Serious and persistent mental illness with substance abuse (*Clients served primarily by community mental health clinics*)
QUADRANT III MENTAL ILLNESS – LOW SEVERITY SUD – HIGH SEVERITY Psychiatrically complicated substance dependence (*Clients served primarily by addiction treatment programs*)	QUADRANT IV MENTAL ILLNESS – HIGH SEVERITY SUD – HIGH SEVERITY Serious and persistent mental illness and substance dependence (*Clients served by community mental health clinics with integrated co-occurring disorder programs*)

*Source: Center for Substance Abuse Treatment (2005).

Laboratory screening including a urine toxicology screen, complete blood count and differential, metabolic panel, and hepatic function tests should also be done on anyone with a past or present SUD if it has not already been done by their primary care provider. For individuals with recent intravenous drug use, a hepatitis screen and HIV testing should also be done if there are no recent results. If an individual presenting with mental illness screens positive for a SUD, the next step will be assessment of the severity of the SUD and its temporal relationship to the mental illness, which is important for diagnosis and treatment planning (see Text Box 2).

Text Box 2 Assessment of SUD and Relationship to Mental Illness

1. Document timeline: History of substance use, treatment, relapse and recovery, and onset of SUD in relation to onset of mental illness.
2. Assessment of negative consequences of SUD (psychiatric, social, and medical).
3. Determination of mental health and addiction symptom severity and placement in one of the four quadrants of care (GAIN-SS).
4. Assessment of motivation (stage of change).
5. Develop treatment plan: detoxification, treatment setting, individual and group therapy, case management, and pharmacological management.

Patients at significant risk for suicide may need management of their treatment in an inpatient psychiatric facility where clinical safety can be intensively monitored. Indicators of such risk include active suicidal ideation, severe mood symptoms, and a history of past suicide attempts.

The American Society of Addiction Medicine (ASAM) has designed patient placement criteria (Gastfriend and Mee-Lee 2004) to guide clinicians in determining a patient's level of need and matching them to an appropriate setting. The placement criteria distinguish between five major levels of care, and patients move between levels as the severity of their addictive disorder changes. Similarly, the American Association of Community Psychiatry (AACP) considers the impact of comorbid disorders, such as substance misuse and physical illnesses, on mental health in its validated LOCUS (Level of Care Utilization System for Psychiatric and Addiction Services). Further information regarding these tools is available in chapter "Creating Value: Resource and Quality Management"..

Principles of Integrated Treatment

The goal of integrated treatment is to provide comprehensive, continuous care emphasizing recovery principles and focusing on individualized treatment plans. The Comprehensive Continuous Integrated System of Care (CCISC) (Minkoff and Cline 2004) includes a multidisciplinary team approach with providers trained in both addiction and mental health. Integrated programs also include a variety of evidence-based psychosocial treatments, pharmacological treatment including both psychiatric and addiction medication, case management, and comprehensive support services such as vocational and housing assistance as well as peer support services. Principles for the care and treatment of persons with COD and principles of a comprehensive and integrated system of care are summarized in Text Box 3.

Text Box 3 Principles of Integrated Treatment*

1. *Common treatment philosophy.* Both addiction and mental illness have a similar chronic relapse/recovery course which necessitates client and family participation, consumer support, education about illness and adherence, relapse prevention skill training, continuity of care, and tailored, flexible treatment planning with motivational approaches to combat shame, denial, and demoralization.
2. *Motivational approach.* Many patients with severe mental illness do not recog-

nize that substance abuse is a problem and are not motivated to maintain abstinence. Thus, it is important to foster a client-focused therapeutic alliance, utilize harm reduction techniques, and incorporate motivational interventions in a stage-wise manner that correspond to a patient's stage of recovery.

3. *Coordinated treatment interventions at each phase of care*. Treatment interventions for persons with COD should be matched according to the diagnosis of each disorder, the phase of treatment and recovery for each disorder, and the acuity, severity, disability, and motivation for the treatment of each disorder at any point in time.
4. *Individualized treatment.* Treatment should be tailored to individual need and strive to provide each consumer with a balance of appropriate case management, care, and empathic detachment. Integrated programs include components of assertive outreach, case management, group interventions, individual counseling, and family interventions.
5. *Continuity*. Continuous integrated treatment relationships should be maintained over time, through multiple episodes of acute and subacute treatment and which are independent of any particular setting or locus of care.
6. *Optimism and recovery*. People with COD become demoralized with successive failures to achieve recovery, and this attitude is sometimes perpetuated by their treatment team. Pessimistic attitudes about people with COD represent a major barrier to successful system change and to effective treatment interventions. Every person with COD is considered to have potential to achieve dual recovery.
7. *Acceptance and accessibility*. In an accessible system for persons with COD, crisis services are available to provide welcoming, empathetic, culturally sensitive, and competent assessment and intervention for psychiatric and addictive disorders without barriers or waiting lists. They do not require such patients to self-define as either "psychiatric," "substance abuse," or "dual" in order to be accepted for evaluation and treatment.

*Adapted from the American Association of Community Psychiatrists online publication: *Principles for the Care and Treatment of Persons with Co-Occurring Psychiatric and Substance Disorders* (2/26/2000) website: http://www.communitypsychiatry.org/

Critical Components of an Integrated Co-occurring Disorder Program

1. *Treatment Team.* The multidisciplinary treatment management team is an important component of an integrated treatment approach. The team provides mental health and addiction interventions by the case manager, addiction specialist, psychiatric nurse, and prescriber. Additional team members may include a psychologist, pharmacist, and medical provider as well as vocational, housing, and peer specialists. Cross-training of the treatment team through continuing education on co-occurring disorders is important for basic COD treatment capability. The role of the community psychiatrist on this team is to assess the patient's mental illness and degree of addiction and their relationship to each other, stabilize the patient with psychiatric medications, and appropriately integrate addiction medication when indicated. The psychiatrist's role is also to participate in the education of team members and ensure that there is a shared vision of the impact of COD on patients' clinical status and the interventions needed for a person-centered treatment plan. For example, a case manager or addic-

tion specialist may not be able to identify or assess the limited cognitive abilities or impairment of insight in some patients with severe mental illness and unable to modify interventions accordingly. A psychiatrist or psychologist can clarify these issues and identify modifications necessary to help the person succeed in treatment.

2. *Phased Treatment.* Coordinated treatment interventions should be based on the stage of change and level of engagement. Readiness for treatment for psychiatric and substance use disorders often differ, and persons may be more or less ready for the treatment of one disorder and not at the same stage of change for the other disorder. (See Text Box 4)
3. *Comprehensive Services.* Supportive services should include 24-h crisis care and inpatient referral; residential, vocational, and parenting supports; living and social skills training; physical health assessment and referral; and peer support networking, such as 12-step groups and peer support specialists.

Text Box 4 Integrated Treatment Phases Based on Readiness for Treatment and Level of Engagement*

Phase 1. Acute Stabilization – Short-term focused intervention to stabilize the acute manifestation of the disorder.

Phase 2. Engagement/Motivational Enhancement – Interventions designed to establish a primary clinical relationship and to facilitate the person's ability and motivation to initiate and maintain participation in a program of stabilizing treatment. Harm reduction treatment.

Phase 3. Active Treatment/Maintenance – Interventions of any type designed to stabilize the symptoms of the disorder, prevent relapse, and help persons to maintain a stable baseline and optimal level of functioning.

Phase 4. Rehabilitation and Recovery – Interventions designed to help develop new skills, reacquire old skills, and achieve personal growth and serenity, once prolonged stabilization has been consistently established.

*Adapted from the American Association of Community Psychiatrists online publication: *Principles for the Care and Treatment of Persons with Co-Occurring Psychiatric and Substance Disorders* (2/26/2000) website: http://www.communitypsychiatry.org/

Evidence-Based Psychosocial Treatments for Co-occurring Addiction and Mental Illness

Evidence-based treatments available for the treatment of COD include motivational interviewing, relapse prevention therapy (Marlatt and Gordon 1985), 12-step facilitation (Ries et al. 2008), and contingency management therapy (Rawson et al. 2005). These non-pharmacologic interventions are described by Richard Rosenthal in chapter. "Treatment Techniques for Co-occuring Substance Use and Mental Disorders". Assertive outreach and intensive case management are also essential in COD programs for those patients with severe mental illnesses (SMI). All these interventions are modified for those with SMI who may have challenges with reality testing, motivation and self-efficacy, interpersonal skills, and cognitive deficits. The COD treatment approach is more flexible than traditional addiction treatments and emphasizes decreased confrontation, greater sensitivity to individual differences, and more direct affirmation for achievements. Demoralization is a common problem in patients with co-occurring SMI and SUD, and this is addressed by utilizing empathy, affirmation of individual strengths, offering alternative perspectives, and pointing out discrepancies in self-defeating statements while maintaining that successful change is always possible.

Case

Carl is middle-aged man with bipolar disorder and a long history of heroin, cocaine, and cannabis dependence who attained stable remission from his SUD by means of buprenorphine treatment and his COD mental health program. He was initially served by a parallel addiction program for buprenorphine but soon dropped out due to frequent relapses on cocaine, combined with a feeling that his addiction counselor disapproved of his relapses and doubted his sincerity and commitment to recovery. His buprenorphine treatment was consequently taken over by his COD program, and he quickly regained sobriety and re-engaged with his co-occurring group. During the following year, he attended a COD group with relapse prevention and supportive group therapy modified for patients with severe mental illness. He also attended a dual recovery 12-step group and had a mental health case manager experienced with co-occurring disorders, and his psychiatrist maintained him on his psychotropic medications as well as his buprenorphine-naloxone. He attained 6 months of sobriety from all substances but then relapsed for a week-long period on cocaine. Because of a strong therapeutic alliance with his case manager, he was able to be honest about his use, analyze the triggers leading to his relapse, reaffirm his commitment to recovery, and continue his COD treatment again, achieving a long period of sobriety. He revealed to his psychiatrist that a strong motivating factor was when his case manager told him that she still viewed him as "clean and sober" despite his recent lapse. He felt honored by this simple affirmation indicating that she had faith that he would be able to resume his recovery based on his long sober period before the relapse. By "normalizing" the relapse, reassuring Carl that his treatment team did not view his relapse as a permanent setback nor as evidence that he was failing, and supportively encouraging him to continue in treatment and 12-step groups, he was able to re-achieve a long period of sobriety. Over the course of the next 3 years, Carl would relapse on cocaine for short 1–2-day periods about every 6–9 months but he never relapsed on heroin and he continued to attend his recovery groups, take his medications, and attend 12-step meetings.

Abstinence Support Groups

Support groups should be modified for those with SMI, emphasizing behavioral techniques over cognitive therapy, problem-solving skills, and incorporating social skills training. Dual Recovery Anonymous (DRA) meetings may be particularly helpful for clients with SMI and co-occurring addictive disorders as they may not be able to tolerate more traditional AA meetings or 12-step therapy. DRA meetings are smaller and more private and less confrontational, and they emphasize peer support and insight enhancement by addressing recovery both from severe mental illnesses and from addiction. DRA groups are often led by peer support specialists at hospitals and community mental health clinics.

Evidence-Based Psychopharmacological Treatment of COD

Pharmacotherapy can be both safe and effective in patients with CODs. This is especially true when used in conjunction with psychosocial treatments as part of an integrated treatment plan. In the context of COD, particular attention is paid to minimizing potential interactions between prescribed medications and non-prescribed substances, identifying opportunities for therapeutic synergy among multiple treatments, and considering alternatives to medications that may be reinforcing, be misused, or lead to dependence.

The selection of medications in the treatment of CODs can vary according to the specific combination of co-occurring disorders. Thus, an early goal in treatment is diagnostic clarity. If accomplished in a timely manner, this facilitates appropriate treatment, enhances retention, and advances recovery. However, with the potential for overlapping symptomatology and the often complex interactions between substance use and other psychiatric disorders, the presence of CODs can create certain diagnostic challenges. For example, many symptoms characteristic of acute intoxication, withdrawal, and sequelae of chronic substance use can also be seen as part of primary affective, anxiety, psychotic, attentional, and other disorders. Therefore, whenever possible, it is important obtain clinical data and patient history that facilitate diagnostic clarity. For example, the order of onset, time course, composition, and severity of symptoms, together with family history, response to prior treatments, and data from laboratory and clinical exams, can help the clinician distinguish between a substance-induced affective disorder and a primary affective disorder that is comorbid with a substance use disorder. In this way, the presence of significant psychiatric symptoms prior to the development of an SUD or psychiatric symptoms atypical for intoxication or withdrawal from a particular substance (i.e., psychosis or mania in the setting of isolated opioid use disorder) is suggestive of a separate psychiatric condition rather than one that is substance-induced. Early pharmacological treatment is recommended in these cases, as well as when life-threatening or severely disabling symptoms such as active suicidal ideation or acute psychosis occur.

Without early intervention for severe psychiatric symptoms, treatment retention and remission of the SUD are unlikely to occur. For example, untreated depression in the setting of alcohol (Greenfield et al. 1998), cocaine (McKay et al. 2002), and opioid use disorders (Kosten et al. 1986) has been shown to lead to poorer addiction treatment outcomes. However, in the absence of significant suicidality or clearly disabling symptoms, clinicians may withhold pharmacological treatment of mood or anxiety symptoms until the diagnosis can be clarified. For example, while subacute withdrawal symptoms and sleep disturbances may have a lengthy and variable course, alcohol-induced depression often remits within 2–4 weeks of abstinence, and cocaine-induced depression is often far shorter.

Even beyond the challenges posed by their core symptoms, addiction and mental health disorders tend to be highly stigmatized conditions. This often presents a barrier to seeking and fully engaging in treatment. Working to understand the individual patient's perspective, showing empathy and building mutual trust, nurturing a strong therapeutic alliance over time, and developing and adjusting a treatment plan collaboratively will improve treatment engagement, retention, and outcomes. It is important to strive to meet an individual "where they're at" and try to understand and value their goals and concerns. Person-centered interventions are important. This includes shared decision-making, which emphasizes freedom of choice and individually defined reasonable risk taking, and openly discussing the persons' goals and fears regarding medication and addiction treatment. Use of motivational interviewing techniques can help to identify areas of ambivalence and clarify the connections between an individual's experiences, behaviors, and psychosocial context and the potential role of different treatment strategies in aligning these with their values and goals.

Pharmacotherapy for Affective Disorders with Co-occurring Addiction

Unipolar Major Depression Selective serotonin reuptake inhibitors (SSRIs) and tricyclic antidepressants (TCAs) are commonly prescribed in major depressive disorder (MDD) with and without co-occurring substance use disorders. Still, evidence for benefit in populations with COD remains of only low to moderate quality. In several studies, TCAs (McGrath et al. 1996) and SSRIs (Carpenter et al. 2004) have been shown to be modestly effective in MDD in the setting of comorbid AUD although with variable reported impact on alcohol consumption and abstinence. Elsewhere, SSRIs have not been shown to consistently reduce depressive symptoms with comorbid cocaine or opioid use disorders although tricyclics have shown more promise (Hassan et al. 2017; McDowell et al. 2005). A recent systematic review and meta-analysis found that, among individuals with MDD and co-occurring SUDs, pharmacological therapy with imipramine was more effective than placebo for reducing depressive symptoms, whereas SSRIs had no statistically significant effect. In aggregate, MDD pharmacotherapy did increase rates of abstinence (though not consumption rates) from alcohol without significantly impacting opioid use (Stokes et al. 2020). In the setting of co-occurring MDD and amphetamine/methamphetamine use disorder, it would be reasonable to consider whether mirtazapine or bupropion would be warranted in light of modest evidence of benefit from these atypical antidepressants (Coffin et al. 2020; Lee et al. 2018b). In practice, SSRIs and SNRIs are still the most often prescribed treatment for depressive and anxiety disorders in COD clients. This is likely due to their improved tolerability and lower toxicity compared to tricyclic antidepressants, although monitoring for serotonin syndrome is warranted when serotonergic agent is taken in conjunction with stimulants or methadone.

Evidence for the impact of medications for AUD on depressive symptoms are generally mixed (Hillemacher 2019). There is some evidence, however, for improving outcomes for both disorders by combining SUD and MDD therapies, such as in a double-blind placebo-controlled study in which sertraline combined with naltrexone and CBT for the treatment of co-occurring depression and alcohol dependence produced *double* the abstinence rate compared to sertraline, naltrexone, and/or CBT alone (Pettinati et al. 2010).

Bipolar Disorder Valproic acid, lithium, antipsychotics (e.g., quetiapine), and carbamazepine are all commonly utilized treatments for co-occurring bipolar disorder as well as prophylaxis of mania in patients with addictive disorders, although patients with SUD may have a less robust response to lithium monotherapy than those without (Bowden 1995; Yatham et al. 2018). In the context of co-occurring AUD, valproic acid may be advantageous for co-occurring bipolar disorder because of the favorable side effect profile and benefit in reducing anxiety and withdrawal effects (Brady et al. 1995). Further support is provided by one study in which a combination of divalproex and lithium significantly reduced percentage of heavy drinking days (i.e., the percent of days in which women and men, respectively, consume greater than three and four standard drinks) and number of drinks per day relative to lithium alone (Kemp et al. 2009). Divalproex and lithium have demonstrated some efficacy in reducing cocaine in one study, while lamotrigine's benefits were not clear (Yatham et al. 2018). Further consideration regarding use of lithium, particularly in the setting of AUD, involves potential electrolyte imbalances and lithium toxicity. Severe, acute, or chronic hepatic dysfunction may be relevant for the use of valproic acid and other agents (Kemp et al. 2009).

Antipsychotics are another mainstay of treatment for individuals with bipolar disorder, although there is limited high-quality research regarding their effectiveness for co-occurring bipolar and substance use disorders. It has been noted that relative to placebo, treatment with quetiapine significantly improved manic symptoms but not bipolar depression symptoms or alcohol use (Stokes et al. 2020) and is therefore generally considered inferior to divalproex in co-occurring AUD. There is some evidence, however, for benefit from quetiapine and risperidone in co-occurring bipolar and stimulant use disorders (Yatham et al. 2018). Given the reinforcing nature and high misuse potential of benzodiazepines, these are not recommended as a first-line treatment for mania outside of acute care settings.

The approach to the use of other medications for AUD among individuals with bipolar disorder is largely unchanged from other populations, though at this time there is better evidence of benefit for naltrexone than other agents. There is some research indicating no significant benefit from acamprosate and worse outcomes (relative to placebo) for topiramate (Salloum and Brown 2017). While evidence is limited, gabapentin is a potentially useful medication for mild acute and subacute alcohol and benzodiazepine withdrawal management and maintenance therapy. The role of other medications, such as baclofen, is not established in this population (Agabio 2018).

Pharmacotherapy for Anxiety Disorders with Co-occurring Addiction

SSRIs and SNRIs remain the mainstay of pharmacotherapy in treating co-occurring anxiety disorders and SUDs, though high-quality research on this constellation of CODs is limited (Gimeno et al. 2017). These medications are most often utilized, in conjunction with evidence-based psychotherapy (CBT), when anxiety symptoms are persistent, severe, and/or comorbid with MDD. TCAs and antipsychotics are also utilized in clinical practice though their side effect profiles may be disadvantageous. Buspirone has no significant abuse potential and has shown modest success in patients with anxiety disorders and alcohol dependence (Modesto-Lowe 1999). Limited evidence also suggests potential benefit from N-acetylcysteine and topiramate in the context of PTSD (Back et al. 2016; Batki et al. 2014). Other medications that could offer more rapid anxiolytic effect include α- or β-blockers such as prazosin, clonidine, or propranolol, anticonvulsants, and antihistamines although research in COD is limited ((CSAT) 2009; Brady et al. 1995).

Benzodiazepines in COD remain controversial (Saitz 2017) and are not often recommended because of their side effect profile, their potential for interaction with other medications and nonprescribed substances, and their potential for dependence and misuse. In selecting among such agents, it may be helpful to consider the specific anxiety and substance use disorder pair being treated. For example, pregabalin or gabapentin may be especially helpful for those with generalized anxiety and co-occurring alcohol and cannabis use disorders, while clonidine may be particularly beneficial for an individual undergoing induction on an opioid agonist therapy.

Pharmacotherapy for Schizophrenia/Psychotic Disorders

Individuals experiencing co-occurring addictions and schizophrenia tend to suffer worse psychosocial, general medical, psychiatric, and addiction-related outcomes than those with either condition alone. These disorders often interact in deleterious ways. For example, substance use may directly exacerbate a co-occurring primary psychotic disorder. At the same time, cognitive deficits, delusional thought content, and perceptual disturbances may increase difficulty with treatment engagement, retention, and adherence. Thus, such individuals are likely to benefit from a more intensively resourced and fully integrated treatment (Musser et al. 2003).

For most individuals with co-occurring SMI and SUD, a cornerstone of integrated treatment is the use of antipsychotic medications. Research in this population remains limited and has not yet yielded clear evidence-based treatment hierarchies. Still, several smaller studies and subgroup analyses have suggested possible differences in treatment efficacy, such as improved psychiatric and addiction-related outcomes with clozapine (Brunette et al. 2006; Jones et al. 2011). Given the need to consider the significant variability in side effect profiles and individual response to medications, there is not yet a clear rationale for antipsychotic choice based primarily on co-occurring SUD. Similarly, evidence is lacking as to whether specific formulations may be superior to others, although individuals struggling to consistently take medication may benefit from long-acting injectable formulations.

When treating SUDs in this population, most standard treatment approaches are appropriate. Still, considering the potential for additive side effects or medication interactions is always warranted. For example, while the actual risk of new or exacerbated psychiatric symptoms appears small, in the setting of current or recent history of suicidal ideation, it may be appropriate to initially treat tobacco use disorder with nicotine replacement and behavioral therapies, reserving bupropion or varenicline for cases where nicotine replacement and psychosocial therapy have not yielded cessation. In addition, it is worth considering that smoking tobacco products increases hepatic metabolism of many antipsychotic medications. Thus, higher doses may be required for stabilization, while the individual is actively smoking, with consideration for dose reduction with tobacco cessation. Similarly, for an individual with AUD, in most cases, naltrexone would be preferable to disulfiram. This will avoid the potential challenges related to treatment compliance as well as the small potential risk of neuropsychiatric side effects with disulfiram.

Pharmacotherapy for Select Other Disorders with Co-occurring Addiction

Substance-Induced Psychiatric Disturbances Substance-induced psychiatric symptoms and signs can be variable, corresponding to the specific effects of substances, their different intoxication and withdrawal syndromes, and their longer-term sequelae. The interaction of these and any co-occurring psychiatric disorders may introduce additional variability in timing and severity of symptoms. In general, the initial treatment involves addressing the underlying cause of the disturbance. This may include supporting cessation of the causative substance and management of intoxication and withdrawal syndromes according to best practices for the specific substance involved and clinical circumstances. This is usually done without reliance on antipsychotic medications (outside of treatment of co-occurring primary psychotic disorders). They are best avoided because there is little evidence for their efficacy and their potential for increasing the risk of seizure, arrhythmia, and rhabdomyolysis during withdrawal or intoxication. For example, supportive treatment and benzodiazepines are the first choice for stimulant-associated agitation, before employing antipsychotics (these may be required in some cases for the management of residual psychotic symptoms).

Attention Deficit Hyperactivity Disorder (ADHD) ADHD increases the risk of developing of a SUD and can subsequently interfere with its treatment (Charach et al. 2011). There is evidence that treating ADHD in youth, including with prescribed stimulants, does not impart increased risk (Humphreys et al. 2013) and may actually reduce risk of developing SUDs (Groenman et al. 2013). Moreover, there is evidence that pharmacotherapy for adults with co-occurring ADHD-SUDS can improve ADHD symptoms (Cunill et al. 2015) and, potentially, the clinical course of some SUDs (Konstenius et al. 2014; Levin et al. 2015). Further research providing guidance for specific SUDs, COD symptom severities, and patient populations is needed (De Crescenzo et al. 2016). In the interim, while attending to the usual medical contraindications and following optimization of other COD treatments, it is reasonable to utilize standard ADHD treatment protocols in some individuals with SUDs. This may include the use of prescribed stimulants in individuals with stimulant use disorders – perhaps with a preference for the treatment of individuals with more severe ADHD symptomatology and heavier stimulant use, utilization of long-acting formulations at robust doses, and concurrent use of evidence-based psychosocial treatments (Konstenius et al. 2014; Levin et al. 2015).

Use of Addiction Pharmacotherapy in Patients with Psychiatric Illness

In general, medications for relapse prevention and withdrawal management are used similarly in individuals with or without co-occurring psychiatric conditions. The subsections below outline common evidence-based treatments for SUDs and highlight opportunities, where they exist, to optimize treatment in light of co-occurring disorders.

Pharmacotherapy for Alcohol Use Disorder

There are currently four FDA-approved medications (including two formulations of naltrexone) for the treatment of chronic alcohol use disorder.

Pharmacotherapy is generally most effective when combined with robust psychosocial treatments, as described above.

1. *Naltrexone*. Originally developed to treat opioid use disorder, the opioid receptor antagonist naltrexone decreases the reinforcing effects of alcohol and has been shown to delay relapse to alcohol and reduce the percentage of drinking days (Kranzler and Van Kirk 2001). It generally appears efficacious compared to placebo in reducing relapse to heavy drinking (Mann 2004) as long as adherence is good. It has also been shown to be even more effective when combined with sertraline for co-occurring depression and alcoholism (Pettinati et al. 2010). Naltrexone also comes in an extended-release injectable formulation which is administered monthly as a 360 mg gluteal injection, potentially reducing nonadherence. It has been shown to be effective compared to placebo in reducing heavy drinking (Garbutt et al. 2005). This is also the FDA-approved naltrexone formulation for the treatment of opioid use disorder and can be used in individuals with comorbid AUD and OUD. Additional advantages of long-acting intramuscular naltrexone include less risk of hepatotoxicity and less nausea.
2. *Acamprosate.* Chronic alcohol use leads to compensatory upregulation of the brain's major excitatory system (glutamate) and downregulation of its major inhibitory system (GABA) as the CNS attempts to maintain homeostasis.

   Cessation of chronic alcohol use leads to withdrawal, characterized by glutamatergic hyperactivity and GABA hypoactivity. This imbalance can take several months to dissipate, leading to prolonged subsyndromal symptoms of alcohol withdrawal such as insomnia, dysphoria, anxiety, and restlessness.

   Acamprosate is believed to help restore the balance between the glutamate and GABA systems, decreasing subsequent cravings and risk of relapse in early recovery. It also diminishes the amount of alcohol consumed by patients in treatment who do experience relapse and leads to higher total abstinence rates and longer time to relapse (Chick et al. 2003). Acamprosate's efficacy has been established in multiple randomized controlled European studies (Chick et al. 2003) though it has failed to do so in others (Jonas et al. 2014). This medication is started after a short period of abstinence has been achieved, but there are no safety issues if the patient relapses on alcohol, and acamprosate should be continued if relapse occurs. There is some indication that it is less effective for individuals with bipolar disorder, so it is generally not used as a first-line agent in this population (Salloum and Brown 2017). This does not limit its use with other co-occurring disorders, but all patients started on acamprosate should be monitored for suicidal thoughts since such thoughts occurred more frequently among acamprosate-treated patients than among placebo-treated patients in clinical trials.
3. *Disulfiram.* By inhibiting aldehyde dehydrogenase, disulfiram causes accumulation of acetaldehyde after alcohol ingestion. An "alcohol-disulfiram reaction" is characterized by diaphoresis, flushing, nausea and vomiting, tachycardia, and headache. This aversive reaction motivates patients to abstain from alcohol but can also lead to hesitation to adhere with pharmacotherapy. Disulfiram has greater benefit with monitoring of medication administration. There have been reports suggesting that disulfiram, especially at high doses, may exacerbate mania and psychosis (Li and Shen 2008) and so should be used with care in individuals with poorly managed bipolar disorder or schizophrenia.
4. *Other treatment options (non-FDA approved)*: Gabapentin, which is thought to stabilize the inhibitory GABAergic system, is a potentially useful medication for mild acute and subacute withdrawal management where it compares favorably to lorazepam (Myrick et al. 2009). Moreover, there is growing evidence for its role in maintenance treatment, with reduction

in percentage of heavy drinking days (Kranzler et al. 2019). Among heavy drinkers, statistically significant differences in percentage of heavy drinking days and total abstinence are observed (Anton et al. 2020). Other antiepileptics have been found to be effective for withdrawal management and maintenance treatment. For example, valproic acid and carbamazepine have been used successfully in withdrawal management and maintenance therapies (Jonas et al. 2014). Topiramate, as a maintenance therapy, has been found to decrease the amount, frequency, and percentage of heavy drinking days in some studies (Johanson et al. 2007).

Pharmacotherapy for Opioid Use Disorder

Pharmacotherapy is the mainstay of treatment of opioid use disorder (OUD). Four well-studied, highly efficacious, FDA-approved medications for opioid use disorder (MOUD) are available in the United States. Of note, long-term treatment with MOUD of patients with moderate to severe OUD is strongly indicated over short-term withdrawal management or other MOUD taper, as continuous MOUD treatment is associated with reduced risk of return to opioid use and associated morbidity and mortality (Ma et al. 2019). In selecting treatment, clinicians should value patient preference and consider any relevant medical comorbidities, CODs, and any practical concerns relating to treatments and treatment settings (e.g., feasibility of accessing a methadone clinic). In addition, patients experiencing significant psychosocial instability or increased psychiatric comorbidity may benefit from clinical settings offering more intensive treatment.

1. *Methadone:* The objective of opioid agonist treatment is to reduce non-prescribed opioid use and the negative effects on patients' physical health, mental health, and interpersonal and occupational functioning. Methadone, a long-acting μ opioid agonist, has been an effective life-saving treatment with far better retention and clinical outcomes than psychosocial treatment alone (Mattick et al. 2009). Under US federal law, only physicians working in federally regulated methadone programs can legally prescribe methadone for the treatment of opioid dependence outside of an acute care setting. Treatment in a methadone program may provide increased structure, support, and monitoring of patients than is treatment in many office-based settings. However, as a long-acting full agonist, relative to other MOUD, methadone has elevated risks of intoxication, sedation, respiratory suppression, and death by overdose when used in combination with other sedating substances or when rapidly titrated.
2. *Buprenorphine:* Buprenorphine is a long-acting partial μ agonist with very high μ receptor affinity and demonstrated efficacy for withdrawal management and maintenance treatment of opioid use disorder (Mattick et al. 2014). At therapeutic doses, it blocks the euphoric effects of misused opioids while relieving cravings through partial stimulation of the receptor. Due to its partial agonism, it has a ceiling effect for CNS respiratory depression – making it far safer than other opioids in overdose. However, concomitant use of high doses of benzodiazepines, alcohol, or other sedating or respiration-suppressing substances can pose risks of intoxication, sedation, and, rarely, death. Buprenorphine can be used to treat opioid use disorder in a variety of clinical settings, including primary care and community mental health clinics. It is most commonly administered sublingually as a combination agent with the opiate antagonist naloxone in a ratio of 4 mg buprenorphine:1 mg naloxone. Because naloxone is systemically available when inhaled or injected (though only minimally taken sublingually or orally), it has been added to buprenorphine in an effort to deter its injection or nasal inhalation. There is also an efficacious long-acting subcutaneous injectable formulation of buprenorphine that can be

administered monthly (Haight et al. 2019). Care is warranted with buprenorphine induction given the medication's partial agonism and high μ receptor affinity, which can precipitate withdrawal by displacing competing full μ agonist. Traditionally, buprenorphine is delayed until a patient is abstinent from full μ agonists and in moderate withdrawal (e.g., last use of a short-acting opioid 8–12 h prior to induction while scoring 10–12 on the Clinical Opioid Withdrawal Scale). The duration of abstinence is prolonged further in the setting of use of longer-acting full μ agonist, which can be challenging for patients. Development of "microdosing" protocols has be helpful in facilitating a more comfortable and effective transition in such contexts or in the setting of ongoing pain management with full agonists in acute care settings, allowing for buprenorphine induction while continuing treatment with a full μ agonist (Klaire et al. 2019; Terasaki et al. 2019).

3. *Extended-Release Naltrexone.* This long-acting formulation is administered in a 360 mg monthly gluteal injection and can be an effective treatment for OUD for select patients and is also shown to reduce heavy drinking in individuals with AUD (Garbutt et al. 2005). The duration of action alleviates the problem of non-adherence to daily dosing; however, follow-up for monthly injections may remain a challenge, and treatment initiation in individuals with active opioid use requires an extended period of abstinence which is often challenging to complete (Lee et al. 2018a).
4. *Naloxone.* In addition to the medications above, the short-acting opioid antagonist, naloxone, is available in "rescue kits" for opioid reversal (Boyer 2012). Formulations involving administration by nasal inhalation and intramuscular injections are both available, though the former is easier for most people to use. Naloxone rescue kits should be offered to those who use prescribed or non-prescribed opioids or who are likely to encounter individuals at risk of opioid overdose.

Pharmacotherapy for Stimulant Use Disorders

In contrast to OUD, there are no FDA-approved medication for the treatment of stimulant use disorders and no strong, consistent evidence of reduced use, abstinence, or treatment retention for specific medications or classes of medications. However, several medications have shown initial promise and may be incorporated into an individual's integrated treatment plan, taking into account the person's co-occurring disorders, addiction severity, treatment history, medical comorbidities, treatment preferences, and other variables (Brandt et al. 2020; Tardelli et al. 2020). In the setting of cocaine use disorder, psychostimulants (including modafinil, methylphenidate, and amphetamines at robust doses), bupropion (Elkashef et al. 2008), and topiramate (Johnson et al. 2013) have all shown some promise in promoting abstinence (Chan et al. 2019b). Of these medications, the most robust responses are found with psychostimulants and, in particular, higher-dose amphetamines. This finding persists in studies including individuals with co-occurring opioid use disorder as well (Tardelli et al. 2020). Limited evidence suggests disulfiram (Dackis et al. 2005) may assist with lapse prevention, though both it and modafinil may not be effective in the setting of co-occurring alcohol use disorder, where topiramate may be a better option. Antipsychotic medications, as a class, are associated with increased retention, while results for antidepressants are mixed. There is evidence that SSRIs may be helpful in lapse/relapse prevention in individuals already abstinent from cocaine, while other classes of antidepressants potentially improve retention regardless of baseline use status (Chan et al. 2019b).

One recent large multisite, randomized, double-blinded, placebo-controlled clinical trial of treatment-seeking individuals with methamphetamine use disorder found that a combination of bupropion and extended-release injectable naltrexone reduced methamphetamine use and cravings compared to placebo (Trivedi et al. 2021). Other clinical trials have thus far offered less robust evidence for the benefit of pharmacotherapy in amphetamine/methamphetamine use disorder than in cocaine use disorder. Still, there is some evidence that topiramate may be helpful in reducing use and reducing relapse among those who are abstinent before beginning treatment (Elkashef et al. 2012). Though additional research is needed, emerging evidence suggests higher-dose psychostimulants may hold promise, perhaps even among those with more severe use patterns (Ling et al. 2014). There have been double-blind placebo-controlled trials examining monotherapy with other medications, including bupropion, modafinil (McElhiney et al. 2009), atomoxetine, naltrexone (Jayaram-Lindstrom et al. 2008), and mirtazapine (Coffin et al. 2020), that, in the aggregate, have shown either inconsistent results or small effect sizes (Chan et al. 2019a, b). Existing data indicates no clear benefit for anticonvulsants, antidepressants, or antipsychotics, though use of these medication classes in specific COD populations is poorly studied.

Pharmacotherapy for Tobacco Dependence in People with Co-occurring Disorders

The overall tobacco abstinence rates in both psychiatric and substance abuse treatment populations are lower than the rate in the general population, and efforts to integrate smoking treatment into COD programs are lacking. De Leon and colleagues (De Leon et al. 2005) reported that among people with co-occurring SUD and SMI, the cessation rate for alcohol and drugs was around 45%, while the cessation rate for smoking was 10%. Fortunately, this can be improved with clinical attention and provision of appropriate treatment. For example, one double-blind placebo-controlled trial using a combination pharmacotherapy (nicotine replacement therapy plus bupropion) and CBT for tobacco cessation among people with schizophrenia demonstrated a quit rate of 50% (Evins et al. 2007). Varenicline, an alpha4beta2 nicotinic acetylcholine receptor partial agonist, approved by the US FDA in 2006 for smoking cessation demonstrates improved success rates over nicotine replacement therapy and bupropion in the general population (Hall 2009) and among smokers with mental illness (Evins et al. 2007). Earlier concerns regarding an increased rate of psychiatric symptoms in people with mental illness with varenicline have not been demonstrated in subsequent research (Purvis et al. 2009), although it is often used with some caution among individuals with SMI.

Conclusions

Integrated substance abuse treatment in the mental health center is essential given the prevalence of co-occurring addictive disorders in community psychiatry clients. Principles of integrated treatment are delineated on the AACP website, and the Substance Abuse and Mental Health Services Administration (SAMHSA) website also has a publication site which includes the Center for Substance Abuse Treatment (CSAT) (www.csat.samhsa.gov) page where Treatment Improvement Protocol (TIP) publications can be ordered at no cost. The authors recommend the TIP 42 publication entitled *Substance Abuse Treatment for Persons with Co-occurring Disorders* ((*Ed.*), 2005) which is an evidence-based best practice guideline and provides a wealth of information from consensus panels of nationally known substance use disorder experts and professionals in related areas of mental health, primary care, and social services.

References

(CSAT), C. f. S. A. T. (2009). *Addressing Suicidal thoughts and Behaviors in Substance Abuse Treatment*. (HHS Publication No. (SMA) 09-4381). Rockville, MD: SAMHSA.

(Ed.), C. f. S. A. T. (2005). *Substance abuse treatment for persons with co-occurring disorders*. Rockville, MD: Substance Abuse and Mental Health Services Administration.

Agabio R., L. L. (2018). Baclofen in the Treatment of Patients with Alcohol Use Disorder and Other Mental Health Disorders. *Front. Psychiatry, 29*(9), 464. doi: https://doi.org/10.3389/fpsyt.2018.00464/fpsyt.2018.00464

Agosti, V., & Levin, F. R. (2006). One-year follow-up study of suicide attempters treated for drug dependence. *Am J Addict, 15*(4), 293–296.

Anton RF, L. P., Voronin K, Book S, Hoffman M, Prisciandaro J, Bristol E. (2020). Efficacy of gabapentin for the treatment of alcohol use disorder in patients with alcohol withdrawal symptoms: A randomized clinical trial. *JAMA Intern Med, 180*(5), 728–736.

Back SE, M. J., Korte KJ, et al. (2016). A Double-Blind, Randomized, Controlled Pilot Trial of N-Acetylcysteine in Veterans With Posttraumatic Stress Disorder and Substance Use Disorders. *J Clin Psychiatry, 77*, e1439.

Batki S.L., P. D. L., Lasher B., et al. . (2014). Topiramate treatment of alcohol use disorder in veterans with posttraumatic stress disorder: a randomized controlled pilot trial. *Alcohol Clin Exp Res, 38*, 2169.

Bowden, C. L. (1995). Predictors of response to divalproex and lithium *J Clin Psychiatry, 56*(Suppl 3), 25–30.

Boyer, E. W. (2012). Management of opioid analgesic overdose *N Engl J Med, 367*(2), 146–155.

Brady, K. T., Sonne, S.C., Anton, R., Ballenger, J.C. (1995). Valproate in the treatment of acute bipolar affective episodes complicated by substance abuse. *J Clin Psychiatry, 56*(3), 118–121.

Brandt L, C. T., Comer SD, Levin FR. (2020). Pharmacotherapeutic strategies for treating cocaine use disorder-what do we have to offer?. *Addiction*. doi: https://doi.org/10.1111/add.15242

Brunette MF, D. R., Xie H, McHugo GJ, Green AI. (2006). Clozapine use and relapses of substance use disorder among patients with co-occurring schizophrenia and substance use disorders. *Schizophr Bull, 32*(4), 637–643.

Carpenter KM, B. A., Vosburg SK, Nunes EV. (2004). The effect of sertraline and environmental context on treating depression and illicit substance use among methadone maintained opiate dependent patient: a controlled clinical trial. *Drug Alcohol Depend, 74*(2), 123–134.

Chan B, F. M., Kondo K, Ayers C, Montgomery J, Paynter R, et al. (2019a). Pharmacotherapy for methamphetamine/amphetamine use disorder-a systematic review and meta-analysis. *Addiction, 114*(12), 2122–2136.

Chan, B., Kondo, K., Freeman, M., Ayers, C., Montgomery, J., Kansagara, D. (2019b). Pharmacotherapy for Cocaine Use Disorder-a Systematic Review and Meta-analysis. *J Gen Intern Med, 34*(12), 2858–2873.

Charach A., Y. E., Climans T., Lillie E. (2011). Childhood attention-deficit/ hyperactivity disorder and future substance use disorders: comparative meta-analyses. *J Am Acad Child Adolesc Psychiatry, 50*, 9–21.

Chick J, L. O., Landron F. (2003). Does acamprosate improve reduction of drinking as well as aiding abstinence? *J Psychopharmacol, 17*(4), 397–402.

Coffin PO, S. G.-M., Hern J, Vittinghoff E, Walker JE, Matheson T, et al. (2020). Effects of mirtazapine for methamphetamine use disorder among cisgender men and transgender women who have sex with men: A placebo-controlled randomized clinical trial *JAMA Psychiatry, 77*(3), 246–255.

Comtois, K. A., Russo, J. E., Roy-Byrne, P., & Ries, R. K. (2004). Clinicians' assessments of bipolar disorder and substance abuse as predictors of suicidal behavior in acutely hospitalized psychiatric inpatients. *Biol Psychiatry, 56*(10), 757–763.

Cottler, L. B., Compton, W. M., 3rd, Mager, D., Spitznagel, E. L., & Janca, A. (1992). Posttraumatic stress disorder among substance users from the general population. *Am J Psychiatry, 149*(5), 664–670.

Cunill R, C. X., Tobias A, et al. (2015). Pharmacological treatment of attention deficit hyperactivity disorder with co-morbid drug dependence. *J Psychopharmacol (Oxford), 29*, 15–23.

Dackis CA, K. K., Lynch KG, Pettinati HM, O'Brien CP. (2005). A double-blind, placebo-controlled trial of modafinil for cocaine dependence. *Neuropsychopharmacology, 30*, 205–211.

De Crescenzo F., C. S., Adamo N., Janiri L. (2016). Pharmacological and non-pharmacological treatment of adults with ADHD: a meta-review. *Evid Based Ment Health, 20*(1), 4–11.

De Leon J, S. M., Diaz FJ, Rendon DM, Velásquez DM. (2005). Variables associated with alcohol, drug, and daily smoking cessation in patients with severe mental illnesses. *J Clin Psychiatry, 66*(11), 1447–1455.

Dennis, M. L., Chan, Y. F., & Funk, R. R. (2006). Development and validation of the GAIN Short Screener (GAIN-SS) for psychopathology and crime/violence among adolescents and adults. *American Journal on Addictions, 15*(supplement 1), 80–91.

Drake, R. E., Osher, F. C., Noordsy, D. L., Hurlbut, S. C., Teague, G. B., & Beaudett, M. S. (1990). Diagnosis of alcohol use disorders in schizophrenia. *Schizophr Bull, 16*(1), 57–67.

Driessen, M., Meier, S., Hill, A., Wetterling, T., Lange, W., & Junghanns, K. (2001). The course of anxiety, depression, and drinking behaviours after completed detoxification in alcoholics with and without comorbid anxiety and depressive disorders. *Alcohol and Alcoholism, 36*(3), 249–255.

Elkashef A, K. R., Yu E, Iturriaga E, Li SH, Anderson A, et al. (2012). Topiramate for the treatment of methamphetamine addiction: a multi-center placebo-controlled trial. . *Addiction, 107*(7), 1297–1306.

Elkashef AM, R. R., Anderson AL, Li SH, Holmes T, Smith EV, et al. (2008). Bupropion for the treatment of methamphetamine dependence. *Neuropsychopharmacology, 33*(5), 1162–1170.

Evins AE, C. C., Culhane MA, Birnbaum A, Horowitz J, Hsieh E, et al. (2007). A 12-week double-blind, placebo-controlled study of bupropion sr added to high-dose dual nicotine replacement therapy for smoking cessation or reduction in schizophrenia. *J Clin Psychopharmacol, 27*(4), 380–386.

Garbutt JC, K. H., O'Malley SS, Gastfriend DR, Pettinati HM, Silverman BL, et al. (2005). Efficacy and tolerability of long-acting injectable naltrexone for alcohol dependence: a randomized controlled trial. *JAMA, 293*(13), 1617–1625.

Gastfriend, D., Mee-Lee, D (2004). The ASAM Patient Placement Criteria. *J Addic Dis, 22*(S1), 1–8. doi: https://doi.org/10.1300/J069v22S01_01

Gimeno C, Dorado ML, Roncero C., Szerman N., Vega P., Balanzá- Martínez V. et al. (2017). Treatment of Comorbid Alcohol Dependence and Anxiety Disorder: Review of the Scientific Evidence and Recommendations for Treatment *Front Psychiatry, 8*(173).

Grant, B. F., Stinson, F. S., Dawson, D. A., Chou, S. P., Dufour, M. C., Compton, W., … Kaplan, K. (2004). Prevalence and co-occurrence of substance use disorders and independent mood and anxiety disorders: results from the National Epidemiologic Survey on Alcohol and Related Conditions. *Arch Gen Psychiatry, 61*(8), 807–816.

Greenfield SF, W. R., Muenz LR, Vagge LM, Kelly JF, et al. (1998). The effect of depression on return to drinking: a prospective study. *Arch Gen Psychiatry, 55*(3), 259–265.

Groenman AP, O. J., Rommelse NJ, Franke B, Greven CU, et al. (2013). Stimulant treatment for attention-deficit hyperactivity disorder and risk of developing substance use disorder. *Br J Psychiatry, 203*(2), 112–119.

Haight, B. R., Learned, S.M., Laffont, C.M., Fudala, P.J., Zhao, Y., et al. (2019). Efficacy and safety of a monthly buprenorphine depot injection for opioid use disorder: a multicentre, randomised, double-blind, placebo-controlled, phase 3 trial *Lancet, 393*(10173), 778–790.

Hall SM, P. J. (2009). Treatment of smokers with co-occurring disorders: emphasis on integration in mental health and addiction treatment settings. *Annu Rev Clin Psychol, 5*, 409–431.

Harris EC, & Barraclough, B. (1997). Suicide as an outcome for mental disorders. *Br J Psychiatry, 170*, 205–228.

Hasin, D. S., & Grant, B. F. (2002). Major depression in 6050 former drinkers: association with past alcohol dependence. *Arch Gen Psychiatry, 59*(9), 794–800.

Hassan AN, H. A., Samokhvalov AV, Le Foll B, George TP (2017). Management of mood and anxiety disorders in patients receiving opioid agonist therapy: review and meta-analysis. *Am J Addict, 26*(6), 551–563. doi: https://doi.org/10.1111/ajad.12581

Hillemacher T, F. H. (2019). Pharmacotherapeutic options for co-morbid depression and alcohol dependence. . *Expert Opin Pharmacother, 20*(5), 547–569. doi: https://doi.org/10.1080/14656566.2018.1561870

Humphreys, K. L., Eng, T., Lee, S.S. (2013). Stimulant medication and substance use outcomes: a meta-analysis. *JAMA Psychiatry, 70*(7), 740–749.

Jayaram-Lindstrom N, H. A., Beck O, Franck J. (2008). Naltrexone for the treatment of amphetamine dependence: a randomized placebo-controlled trial. *Am J Psychiatry, 165*, 1142–1148.

Johanson BA, R. N., Capece, JA, Wiegand F, et al. (2007). Topiramate for treating alcohol dependence: a randomized controlled trial *JAMA, 298*(14), 1641–1651.

Johnson, B. A., Ait-Daoud, N., Wang, X.Q., Penberthy, J.K., Javors, M.A., Seneviratne, C., Liu, L. (2013). Topiramate for the treatment of cocaine addiction: a randomized clinical trial. *JAMA Psychiatry, 70*(12), 1338–1346.

Jonas DE, A. H., Feltner C, Bobashev G, Thomas K, Wines R, et al. . (2014). Pharmacotherapy for adults with alcohol use disorders in outpatient settings: a systematic review and meta-analysis *JAMA, 311*(18), 1889–1900.

Jones RM, L. P., Grann M, Långström N, Fazel S. (2011). Alcohol use disorders in schizophrenia: a national cohort study of 12,653 patients. *J Clin Psychiatry, 72*(6), 775–779.

Kemp DE, G. K., Ganocy SJ, Elhaj O, Bilali SR, Conroy C, et al. (2009). A 6-month, double-blind, maintenance trial of lithium monotherapy versus the combination of lithium and divalproex for rapid-cycling bipolar disorder and co-occurring substance abuse or dependence. *J Clin Psychiatry, 70*(1), 113–121. doi: https://doi.org/10.4088/jcp.07m04022

Kessler, R. C., Sonnega, A., Bromet, E., Hughes, M., & Nelson, C. B. (1995). Posttraumatic stress disorder in the National Comorbidity Survey. *Arch Gen Psychiatry, 52*(12), 1048–1060.

Klaire, S., Zivanovic, R., Barbic, S.P., Sandhu, R., Mathew, N., Azar, P. (2019). Rapid micro-induction of buprenorphine/naloxone for opioid use disorder in an inpatient setting: A case series *Am J Addict, 28*(4), 262–265.

Konstenius M, J.-L. N., Guterstam J, Beck O, Philips B, Franck J, et al. (2014). Methylphenidate for attention deficit hyper-activity disorder and drug relapse in criminal offenders with substance dependence: a 24-week randomized placebo-controlled trial. *Addiction, 109*(3), 440–449.

Kosten TR, R. B., Kleber HD. (1986). A 2.5 year follow-up of depression, life crises, and treatment effects on abstinence among opioid addicts. *Arch Gen Psychiatry, 43*(8), 733–738.

Kranzler HR, F. R., Morris P, Hartwell EE. (2019). A meta-analysis of the efficacy of gabapentin for treating alcohol use disorder *Addiction, 114*(9), 1547–1555. doi: https://doi.org/10.1111/add.14655

Kranzler, H. R., Van Kirk, J. . (2001). Efficacy of naltrexone and acamprosate for alcoholism treatment. *Alcohol Clin Exp Res, 25*(9), 1335–1341.

Lee, J. D., Nunes, E.V., Novo, P., Bachrach, K., Bailey, G.L., Bhatt, S., et al. (2018a). Comparative effectiveness of extended-release naltrexone versus buprenorphine-naloxone for opioid relapse prevention (X:BOT): a multicentre, open-label, randomised controlled trial *Lancet, 391*(10118), 309–318.

Lee NK, J. L., Harney A, Cameron J. (2018b). Pharmacotherapy for amphetamine dependence: A systematic review. *Drug Alcohol Depend, 191*, 309–337.

Levin FR, M. J., Specker S, Mooney M, Mahony A, Brooks DL, et al. (2015). Extended-Release Mixed Amphetamine Salts vs Placebo for Comorbid Adult Attention-Deficit/Hyperactivity Disorder and Cocaine Use Disorder: A Randomized Clinical Trial. *JAMA Psychiatry, 72*(2), 593–602.

Li, M. Y., Shen, Y.C. (2008). Manic episode with psychosis following a lower than recommended dosage regimen of disulfiram. *Prog Neuropsychopharmacol Biol Psychiatry, 32*(1), 311–312.

Ling W, C. L., Hillhouse M, Ang A, Striebel J, Jenkins J, et al. (2014). Sustained-release methylphenidate in a randomized trial of treatment of methamphetamine use disorder. *Addiction, 109*(9), 1489–1500.

Ma, J., Bao, Y.P., Wang, R.J., Su, M.F., Liu, M.X., Li, J.Q., et al. (2019). Effects of medication-assisted treatment on mortality among opioids users: a systematic review and meta-analysis *Mol Psychiatry, 24*(12), 1868–1883.

Mann, K. (2004). Pharmacotherapy of alcohol dependence: a review of the clinical data. *CNS Drugs, 18*(8), 485–504.

Marlatt, G. A., & Gordon, J. R. (1985). *Relapse Prevention: Maintenance Strategies in the Treatment of Addictive Behaviors.* New York: Guilford Publications.

Mattick RP, B. C., Kimber J, Davoli M. (2014). Buprenorphine maintenance versus placebo or methadone maintenance for opioid dependence. *Cochrane Database Syst Rev, 2014*(2), CD002207.

Mattick RP, B. C., Kimber J, Davoli M. (2009). Methadone maintenance therapy versus no opioid replacement therapy for opioid dependence. *Cochrane Database Syst Rev, 2009*(3), CD002209.

McDowell D, N. E., Seracine AM, Rothenberg J, Vosburg SK, Ma GJ, et al. (2005). Desipramine treatment of cocaine-dependent patients with depression: a placebo-controlled trial. *Drug Alcohol Depend, 80*(2), 209–221.

McElhiney MC, R. J., Rabkin R, Nunes EV. (2009). Provigil (modafinil) plus cognitive behavioral therapy for methamphetamine use in HIV+ gay men: a piolet study. *Am J Drug Alcohol Abuse, 35*(1), 34–37.

McGrath PJ, N. E., Stewart JW, Goldman D, Agosti V, Ocepek-Welikson K, et al. (1996). Imipramine treatment of alcoholics with primary depression: A placebo-controlled clinical trial. *Arch Gen Psychiatry, 53*(3), 232–240.

McKay JR, P. H., Morrison R, Feeley M, Mulvaney FD, Gallop R. (2002). Relation of depression diagnoses to 2-year outcomes in cocaine-dependent patients in a randomizing continuing care study. *Psychol Addict Behav, 16*(3), 225–235.

Minkoff, K., Cline, CA. (2004). Changing the world: the design and implementation of comprehensive continuous integrated systems of care for individuals with co-occurring disorders *Psychatr Clin N Am, 27*, 727–743.

Modesto-Lowe V, K. H. (1999). Diagnosis and treatment of alcohol-dependent patients with co-morbid substance use disorders. *Alcohol Res Health, 23*(2), 144–149.

Mueser, K. T., Bellack, A. S., & Blanchard, J. J. (1992). Comorbidity of schizophrenia and substance abuse: implications for treatment. *J Consult Clin Psychol, 60*(6), 845–856.

Murphy, G. E., & Wetzel, R. D. (1990). The lifetime risk of suicide in alcoholism. *Arch Gen Psychiatry, 47*, 383–392.

Musser KT, N. D., Drake RE, Flox L. (2003). *Integrated Treatment for Dual Disorders. A Guide to Effective Practice.* New York: Guilford Press.

Myrick H, M. R., Randall PK, Boyle E, Anton RF, Becker HC, Randall CL. (2009). A double-blind trial of gabapentin versus lorazepam in the treatment of alcohol withdrawal. *Alcohol Clin Exp Res, 33*(9), 1582–1588.

Najavits, L. M., Weiss, R. D., & Shaw, S. R. (1997). The link between substance abuse and posttraumatic stress disorder in women. A research review. *Am J Addict., 6*(4), 273–283.

Nunes, E. V., Liu, X., Samet, S., Matseoane, K., & Hasin, D. (2006). Independent versus substance-induced major depressive disorder in substance-dependent patients: observational study of course during follow-up. *Journal of Clinical Psychiatry, 67*(10), 1561–1567.

Pettinati HM, O. D., Kanmpman KM, Dundon WD, Xie H, Gallis TL, et al. (2010). A double-blind, placebo-controlled trial combining sertraline and naltrexone for treating co-occurring depression and alcohol dependence. *Am J Psychiatr, 167*(6), 668–675.

Purvis TL, M. S., Balvanz TM, Magallon HE, Pham RH. (2009). Safety and effectiveness of varenicline in a veteran population with a high prevalence of mental illness. *Ann Pharmacother, 43*, 862–867.

Rawson, R. A., McCann, M. J., Flammino, F., Shoptaw, S., Miotto, K., Reiber, C., & Ling, W. (2005). A comparison of contingency management and cognitive-behavioral approaches for stimulant -dependent individuals. *Addiction, 101*, 267–274.

Regier, D. A., Farmer, M. E., Rae, D. S., Locke, B. Z., Keith, S. J., Judd, L. L., & Goodwin, F. K. (1990). Comorbidity of mental disorders with alcohol and other drug abuse. Results from the Epidemiologic Catchment Area (ECA) Study. *Jama, 264*(19), 2511–2518.

Ries, R. K., Galanter, M., & Tonnigan, J. S. (2008). Twelve Step Facilitation: an adaptation for psychiatric practitioners and patients. In M. Galanter & H. Kleber (Eds.), *Textbook of Substance Abuse Treatment* (4th ed.). Arlington: American Psychiatric Publishing, Inc.

Ries, R. K., Yuodelis-Flores, C., Roy-Byrne, P., Nilsson, O., & Russo, J. E. (2009). Addiction and Suicidal Behavior in Acute Psychiatric Inpatients. *J. Compr Psychiatry, 50*(2), 93–99.

Saitz, R. (2017). Should Benzodiazepines Be Used to Treat Anxiety in People With Substance Use Disorders? Contentious Debate With Similar Conclusions. *Journal of Addiction Medicine, 11*(2), 83.

Salloum, I. M., Brown, E.S. (2017). Management of comorbid bipolar disorder and substance use disorders. *Am J Drug Alcohol Abuse, 43*(4), 366–376. doi: https://doi.org/10.1080/00952990.2017.1292279

Sher L, Stanley BH, et al. (2008). Depressed patients with co-occurring alcohol-use disorders: a unique patient population. *J Clin Psychiatry, 69*, 907–915.

Stokes PRA, J. T., Amawi S, Quereshi M, et al. (2020). Pharmacological Treatment of Mood Disorders and Comorbid Addictions: A Systematic Review and Meta-Analysis. *Can J Psychiatry, 65*(11), 749–769. doi: https://doi.org/10.1177/0706743720915420

Strakowski, S. M., Keck, P. E., Jr., McElroy, S. L., West, S. A., Sax, K. W., Hawkins, J. M., ... Bourne, M. L. (1998). Twelve-month outcome after a first hospitalization for affective psychosis. *Arch Gen Psychiatry, 55*(1), 49–55.

Tardelli VS, B. A., Arcadepani FB, Gerra G, Levin FR, et al. (2020). Prescription psychostimulants for the treatment of stimulant use disorder: a systematic review and meta-analysis *Psychopharmacology (Berl), 237*(8), 2233–2255. doi: https://doi.org/10.1007/s00213-020-05563-3

Terasaki, D., Smith, C., Calcaterra, S.L. . (2019). Transitioning Hospitalized Patients with Opioid Use Disorder from Methadone to Buprenorphine without a Period of Opioid Abstinence Using a Microdosing Protocol. *Pharmacotherapy, 39*(10), 1023–1029.

Tohen, M., Zarate, C. A., Jr., Hennen, J., Khalsa, H. M., Strakowski, S. M., Gebre-Medhin, P., ... Baldessarini, R. J. (2003). The McLean-Harvard First-Episode Mania Study: prediction of recovery and first recurrence. *Am J Psychiatry, 160*(12), 2099–2107.

Trivedi MH, W. R., Ling W, Dela Cruz A, Sharma G, et al. (2021). Bupropion and Naltrexone in Methamphetamine Use Disorder. *N Engl J Med, 384*(2), 140–153.

Weiss, R. D., Ostacher, M. J., Otto, M. W., Calabrese, J. R., Fossey, M., Wisniewski, S. R., ... Sachs, G. S. (2005). Does recovery from substance use disorder matter in patients with bipolar disorder? *J Clin Psychiatry, 66*(6), 730–735; quiz 808-739.

Wilcox HC, Conner KR, & ED., C. (2004). Association of alcohol and drug use disorders and completed suicide: an empirical review of cohort studies. *Drug and Alcohol Dependence, 76*(S), S11–S19.

Yatham LN, K. S., Parikh SV, et al. (2018). Canadian Network for Mood and Anxiety Treatments (CANMAT) and International Society for Bipolar Disorders (ISBD) 2018 guidelines for the management of patients with bipolar disorder. *Bipolar Disord, 20*(2), 97–170. doi: https://doi.org/10.1111/bdi.12609

Ziedonis, D. M., Steinberg, M. L., D'Avanzo, K., & Smelson, D. (2004). Co--Occurring Schizophrenia and Addiction. In H. R. Kranzler & B. Rounsaville (Eds.), *Dual Diagnosis and Psychiatric Treatment: Substance Abuse and Comorbid Disorders* (2nd ed., pp. 387–436). New York: Marcel Drecker.

Case Management and Assertive Community Treatment

Richard J. Goscha, Lorna Moser, and Maria Monroe-Devita

Introduction

Case management has been a core component of the mental health service delivery system since the 1960s. While the term has remained constant in the vernacular to the present time, there has been confusion about what the term means and what it entails. Case management has evolved since its original conceptualization of helping individuals to navigate and access the fragmented array of programs and services developed following the Community Mental Health Act of 1963. The evolution of case management has been shaped by multiple factors including cost containment efforts associated with the advent of managed care and the rise of the peer movement associated with the paradigm shift of mental health recovery. The populations targeted to receive case management services have also shifted over the years with wide variation in levels of functioning and complexity of need. Initially, case management focused on the needs of individuals with serious mental illnesses being discharged from inpatient settings. Since that time, case management services have been used in diverse behavioral health settings to support specialized populations including those with co-occurring substance use disorders, chronic health conditions, criminal justice diversion, homelessness, children and youth, and older adults.

The evolution of various case management models that differ widely in their structure, function, and scope of service has further compounded the ambiguity around the term. While there are common core elements shared across these models including functions related to assessment, planning, referrals, linkage to services, monitoring, and advocacy, the manner in which these functions are carried out and the role of the case manager related to provision of any direct behavioral health services vary substantially. The variability in approaches to case management services creates one of the many direct impacts on decision-making for program administrators and policy makers when deciding which form of case management to implement to best respond to the unique needs of the population being served.

In this chapter, we trace the history of case management in behavioral health services specifically as it applies to persons diagnosed with serious mental illness, review the evidence for

R. J. Goscha (✉)
Strengths Model Inc., Cameron Park, CA, USA
e-mail: rick@strengthsmodel.com

L. Moser
University of North Carolina at Chapel Hill, Department of Psychiatry, Chapel Hill, NC, USA
e-mail: lorna_moser@med.unc.edu

M. Monroe-Devita
University of Washington, Department of Psychiatry and Behavioral Sciences, Seattle, WA, USA
e-mail: mmdv@uw.edu

W. E. Sowers et al. (eds.), *Textbook of Community Psychiatry*,
https://doi.org/10.1007/978-3-031-10239-4_26

specific models of case management, outline key elements that distinguish each of the major models, enumerate general principles of effective case management, and discuss current challenges as case management continues to evolve in a rapidly changing behavioral health environment.

History

During the era when people with a mental illness spent considerable periods of their lives in asylums and psychiatric hospitals, available services were all under one roof. The era of deinstitutionalization, which began in the 1950s, seemingly created opportunities for people to live and receive care within the community. In reality, however, available and accessible community-based services and resources were significantly lacking to achieve the support people needed. Despite the aims of the Community Mental Health Act to establish local mental health service agencies throughout the United States, the number of agencies built was far fewer than originally envisioned, and only a limited array of services, such as counseling, partial hospitalization/day treatment, and medication management, were made available to people in need. Furthermore, these agencies, under the authority of local agencies and communities, focused on the care of people with common mental disorders rather than people with serious mental illnesses, which had been under the purview of state agencies. Many people with serious mental illnesses (SMI) discharged from the hospital lived in inadequate living conditions or with overwhelmed families. Furthermore, people living in the community were often poor and isolated, lacked decent and affordable housing, and had few opportunities for meaningful activity (Draine et al. 2002). The narrow range of supports was clearly insufficient to sustain a person in the community, and the "revolving door" of psychiatric hospitalization became the de facto course of treatment for many.

The Community Support Program (CSP), initiated by the National Institute of Mental Health (NIMH) in 1977, sought to address some noticeable gaps left by the Community Mental Health Act enacted 15 years earlier. CSP recommended and helped establish a wide range of support services, including crisis stabilization services, vocational services, various forms of housing, daytime and evening activities, support to families, and assistance in accessing entitlements. This range of services, while desperately needed, added considerable complexity for clients and families to access and coordinate care from multiple organizations and service providers. As such, case management was included in CSP to assure the continuous availability of individualized assistance to navigate this growingly complex terrain (Turner and Ten Hoor 1978).

This initial model of case management, frequently termed "broker" case management, sought to coordinate care by linking clients to resources and services based on an assessment of need. These case managers often had high caseloads and served as an administrative, rather than a clinical, function (Intagliata 1982). The assumption was that once people had access to services and resources (e.g., housing, food, benefits, medications, recreational services, clinical services), they would then be able to live more independently and their quality of life would improve. Unsurprisingly, this model fell short of such achievements given the faulty premise that adequate community resources and services existed and simply needed to be accessed. Furthermore, the services that were available were ineffective in meeting the full range of needs of people with the most serious mental illnesses. Evidence-based practices, interventions with the most robust empirical support, were not implemented in most settings then and are inconsistently available today (Bruns et al. 2016).

Over the next four decades, the concept, role, and functions of case management transformed to recognize several realities in the field. First, people with SMI want what many of us want – including success with school and employment, independent housing, social connections, and community involvement (Tabak et al. 2015) – and are indeed capable of such achievements

(Thomas et al. 2018). Second, research on best practice interventions continues to deepen our understanding of how to effectively meet these recovery-oriented aspirations (Chester et al. 2016). Third, there is evidence that services that address multiple co-occurring challenges (e.g., chronic health conditions, substance use disorder, homelessness, poverty) together rather than in parallel or sequentially improve outcomes (Drake et al. 2004). Fourth, use of shared decision-making throughout service provision activates, empowers, and embraces the client as an expert in their own care and is essential to good outcomes (Shay and Lafata 2015). Fifth, the system of care, which now includes even more stakeholders given the broader attention to client preferences and needs, continues to be disjointed and fragmented, therefore making clinical care coordination essential to best practices (Isaacs et al. 2019).

Various models of case management emerged along the way of this evolution. An intermediary case management model that emerged from the original broker model is what is often broadly referred to as "clinical case management." Clinical case management addressed some of the obvious shortcomings of the broker model, especially as it related to serving people with more serious impairments and complex needs, by blending direct service delivery (e.g., counseling, living skills training, and psychoeducation) and linkage to other services and providers (Walsh 2000). In addition to conducting needs assessment, and developing person-centered plans, clinical case managers often provided rehabilitative interventions and held primary responsibility for continuity of care and coordinating services. Clinical case management models vary in their service intensity, community focus, specialization, and use of a multidisciplinary team approach to providing care.

Intensive Case Management arose as yet another iteration of this model. Although there may not be a linear relationship between intensity of service and outcomes, such as reduced hospital use, there appears to be a minimal threshold of service intensity to achieve as an average (Dietzen and Bond 1993). The next section will provide an overview of ICM while also highlighting two well-studied models in particular: Assertive Community Treatment (ACT) and the Strengths Model. ACT teams operate with highly integrated care coordination using a multidisciplinary team approach. The Strengths Model puts the client at the forefront and center of care. Both models focus on delivering community-based services that include rehabilitative supports. Recognizing that service engagement can be difficult with many people experiencing SMI, which then can be a significant barrier to effective treatment and outcomes (Kreyenbuhl et al. 2009), both models are also tasked with using creative assertive outreach and engagement strategies.

Intensive Case Management

A lingering problem in the ICM literature has been a lack of clear defining characteristics, in particular what separates ICM from less intensive, standard, broker models, as well as what distinguishes it from more comprehensive, well-defined models like ACT that include but also extend beyond the provision of case management. Although the focus and intention of these models were originally to reduce the extent to which individuals accessed more costly inpatient and emergency services (Surles and McGurrin 1987), all evolved to embrace the core focus on supporting individuals' independence and recovery. To that end, there are various iterations of ICM models with differing practice approaches (e.g., housing first principles) and staffing (e.g., inclusion of peer support specialists).

Despite no universally agreed-upon definition, ICM models tend to have the following characteristics, which distinguish them from broker models and standard clinical case management: (1) a combination of both direct and linked services; (2) individual caseloads; (3) small caseloads; and (4) use of more assertive, community-based outreach (Schaedle and Epstein 2000). Intensive case managers often operate as part of a larger team and provide support to each other while having individual caseloads. That is, they assume primary responsibility for a set group of individuals receiving services and do not formally share caseloads or operate within a multidisciplinary team using a "team approach." ICM teams can vary greatly in size, with anywhere from 3 to 15 staff and varying caseload sizes of 10 to 25 clients per staff. Intensive case managers provide direct, face-to-face psychosocial support as well as connect to other providers who can meet individuals' more specialized needs. Direct services are offered in natural, community settings (vs. office-based). Such in vivo work allows workers to help people navigate complex social and environmental interactions necessary to achieve the goals they desire, which may include working with property managers, employers, family members, teachers, and other community agencies.

Individuals typically eligible for ICM services will exhibit at least moderately severe psychiatric symptoms and challenges in more independent, community participation and functioning. Co-occurring physical health conditions, substance use disorder, and histories of trauma are common for individuals served by an ICM team. ICM is equipped to serve a more heterogeneous clinical population that needs access to a broad array of services rather than a self-contained bundle of services delivered by a single team. Hence, ICM service is appropriate when a person's clinical and rehabilitation needs would be better served by multiple providers available in the community, along with the intensive follow-up and care coordination offered by a single case manager. Because intensive case managers provide direct services and serve individuals with higher needs, they generally have higher credentialing requirements (i.e., a bachelor's or master's degree in a rehabilitation or behavioral health field) than case managers operating in a service broker capacity only. Below, we highlight both ACT and the Strengths Model as two stand-alone service models in their own right that build on and integrate key components of ICM, noting a few important and overlapping enhancements reflected in each model.

Assertive Community Treatment (ACT)

Since its inception, ACT has grown from a single, experimental research treatment program (Stein and Test 1980) to an essential element within the service continuum of most public mental health systems for people with SMI (Dixon et al. 2010). ACT was designed to address the needs of individuals with the most serious mental illnesses, with priority to those with schizophrenia spectrum disorders and bipolar disorder, who exhibit significant impairments with independent living activities (e.g., homelessness, chronic unemployment) and significant continuous high service needs (e.g., high rates of crisis service use, incarceration, and hospitalization).

As a fixed point of responsibility to meet a range of biopsychosocial service needs, ACT uses a multidisciplinary team-based approach to service delivery. When implemented with high fidelity, typical staffing includes a psychiatric care provider (i.e., psychiatrist or psychiatric nurse practitioner), nurses, a co-occurring substance use disorder specialist, an employment specialist, a peer specialist, a program assistant, and a mix of social workers and therapists, one of whom serves as the team leader. This multidisciplinary team works in close collaboration meeting daily to review client needs and service contact assignments and offers a full array of comprehensive, community-based services inclusive of treatment, rehabilitation, and case management support. From a client's perspective, they may be seen multiple times per week, even daily, by several ACT team members who are best suited to meet their unique needs as opposed to working exclusively with one case manager. To provide intensive, all-inclusive services, large ACT teams operate with caseload caps of 100–120 clients, with a staff-to-client ratio no higher than 1:10. ACT teams are designed to attend to the many barriers that impede service engagement (e.g., lack of insight into having a mental illness; cultural norms, distrust of the mental health system; disorganized behaviors), while being assertive in their treatment efforts, exhausting all options in the engagement process. As part of a broader continuum of care, ACT is one of the most intensive community-based models and as such has been deemed as a "least restrictive alternative" to many other institutional settings. As an all-inclusive, 365-day-per-year service, ACT provides a full breadth of care and biopsychosocial supports to address issues that may result in crisis episodes.

Over the past four decades, its recognition as a psychosocial evidence-based practice for people with SMI has grown (Kreyenbuhl et al. 2010). ACT continues to be vigorously advocated by the National Alliance on Mental Illness (NAMI) (Allness and Knoedler 2003), and there have been more recent demands for expanding ACT capacity to meet service system needs across the United States (Spivak et al. 2019).

Strengths Model

The Strengths Model emerged in the mid-1980s in response to traditional deficit-based approaches to care. These approaches often held low expectations for what people with mental illnesses could achieve in their life and frequently used stabilization and maintenance as measures of success. The Strengths Model viewed that the focus of case managers should be on helping people build or rebuild lives in the community around life goals that anyone else in the community pursued: housing, employment, education, supportive relationships, and community involvement. While case managers often need to respond to immediate life concerns and challenges related to symptoms, health, substance use, legal, transportation, food insecurity, and poverty, there was an emphasis on not losing sight of the person's overall recovery journey.

The Strengths Model introduced two practice tools (the Strengths Assessment and the Personal Recovery Plan) and a method of group supervision to keep the team focused on client-centered, recovery-oriented goals and then identify and mobilize the person's unique array of personal and environmental strengths to make movement toward these goals (Goscha 2020; Rapp and Goscha 2012). Structural features of the Strengths Model included caseload sizes not to exceed 20:1; low supervisor-to-staff ratio to allow for skill building, review and feedback on use of tools, and field mentoring; weekly group supervision using a prescribed case presentation format; and community-based service delivery. Clinical components included specific tools and methods to help clients identify and achieve recovery goals, use of naturally occurring resources over formal supports when possible, and an emphasis on choice and autonomy. The Strengths Model centers around the relationship between the individual case manager and the person receiving services, which work within a team under a single supervisor. The Strengths Model does not prescribe the composition of staff on the team, like ACT, though some Strengths Model teams have included clinicians, peer support, employment specialists, substance abuse counselors, and nursing staff depending on the unique needs and service intensity required by the population served. Even when the Strengths Model has been implemented within multidisciplinary team structures, the individual case manager still holds responsibility for service delivery, using specific practice tools, and overall care coordination.

Research on Case Management

Research on the broker model, or sometimes referred to as "standard case management" or "targeted case management," typically did not yield encouraging findings. At least nine experimental or quasi-experimental studies of the broker model have been published (Bigelow and Young 1991; Curtis et al. 1992; Edwards et al. 1991; Franklin et al. 1987; Hornstra et al. 1993; Jerrell and Ridgely 1995; Lehman et al. 1994; Muller 1981; Rossler et al. 1992). These studies have generally found increased use of psychiatric hospitalization (Curtis et al. 1992; Franklin et al. 1987) and no differences in quality of life (Curtis et al. 1992; Lehman et al. 1994). While these results are disappointing on the surface, they point to the need for better research on case management and the fact that the effectiveness of broker case management is dependent on the availability and quality of external resources and services, which remain inadequate today (Lake and Turner 2017). Further, recognizing that both individual and system factors can influence outcomes, case management research would be strengthened by measuring and accounting for moderators and mediators (Kenny et al. 2004). Moderators, or characteristics or experiences of a research subject that precede a treatment intervention, may include race and ethnicity, gender identification, age, homeless history, trauma history, diagnosis, substance use status, and personality disorder status. Mediators, or intervening variables that can help explain *how* research participants achieve (or not) hypothesized outcomes, may include access to housing subsidies, frequency of contacts, nature of services rendered or accessed, or prevalence of staff turnover.

ICM research studies, where ICM was compared to less intensive (typically broker) case management models, yielded positive outcomes, albeit still mixed. In addition to sharing the methodological concerns cited above, some reviewers have used ICM as a broader rubric to include ACT as well as other variants of ICM (Dieterich et al. 2017). There is no existing ICM fidelity measure (i.e., assessment of the extent to which key structural and process ingredients have been implemented as intended). There are several such ACT fidelity measures, some of which have been used within studies of ICM. To our knowledge, no review has expressly examined non-ACT ICM studies as a subcategory. Moreover, no rigorous head-to-head comparisons between ACT and ICM have been reported in the literature.

Despite a lack of explicit definition of ICM and a related measure of fidelity, the following appear to be well-designed studies of ICM. In a randomized control trial (RCT) of ICM compared to usual care. Harrison-Read et al. (2002) found that there were no between-group differences in any of the main outcome measures, but did find that ICM had a marked impact on hospital use and related healthcare costs when only looking at the top 25% heaviest users of psychiatric beds. Issakidis et al. (1999) also conducted a RCT of ICM compared to standard case management and found that ICM was associated with improved social functioning, fewer psychiatric hospital admissions involving police, and increased likelihood to engage and remain in treatment compared to standard case management. The groups did not differ in hospital bed days or admissions. Another RCT of ICM compared to usual care (Holloway and Carson 1998) found that there were no between-group differences in hospital bed utilization, symptoms, social behavior, or social functioning. ICM was associated with improved quality of life, higher satisfaction with services, and better engagement and maintenance of contact with clients.

Assertive Community Treatment

ACT is the most extensively studied community-based psychosocial program, with over 25 randomized controlled trials (Bond et al. 2001) and multiple systematic reviews and review papers (Burns et al. 2007; Coldwell and Bender 2007; Corrigan et al. 2008; McDonagh et al. 2017; Nelson et al. 2007; Smith and Newton 2007), some of which have focused specifically on ACT, whereas others have broadened their focus to include any ICM model. Despite this heterogeneity, several key findings are consistent.

First, ACT increases community tenure for clients with extensive psychiatric hospitalizations. Second, ACT improves housing outcomes, though the specific measures in this domain have been diverse and have included reductions in homelessness, residential stability, independence of living arrangement, and other indicators. ACT is particularly effective for clients with the highest rates of hospitalization (Burns et al. 2007; Cuddeback et al. 2013) and for those who have been homeless (Coldwell and Bender 2007). Third, ACT sustains engagement in treatment (Bond et al. 1995). Fourth, ACT clients and their families express higher satisfaction with services (Mueser et al. 1998). The evidence for ACT is more mixed in the areas of psychiatric symptoms, substance use, employment, criminal justice involvement, and social functioning, with some studies showing no improvement and/or significant differences with the comparison (McDonagh et al. 2017).

Mixed findings may be a consequence of inadequate implementation of the model, referred to as "program fidelity," and/or unaddressed service needs of special populations. With regard to ACT program fidelity, two measures in highest use include the Dartmouth Assertive Community Treatment Scale (DACTS; Teague et al. 1998) and the more contemporary Tool for Measurement of ACT (TMACT; Monroe-DeVita et al. 2011). Despite the availability of an ACT fidelity measure for nearly 25 years, relatively few studies have included fidelity measurement in the study design. Of those that have, findings are generally positive in favor of higher-fidelity teams yielding improved outcomes (McHugo et al. 1999; Cuddeback et al. 2013; Monroe-DeVita et al. 2015). These fidelity measures, in turn, influence training and implementation efforts to reinforce the importance of using each multidisciplinary team member in spearheading delivery of evidence-based interventions specific to these domains. For example, to address co-occurring substance use disorders, the ACT co-occurring disorders specialist should take the lead in implementing integrated treatment for co-occurring substance use disorders (Drake et al. 2008) and cross-training other team members in the principles and practices to support substance use disorder outcomes in the work they do with the same clients. Similarly, ACT employment specialists should incorporate the Individual Placement and Support (IPS) model of supported employment (see chapter "Supported Employment") to improve employment outcomes (Bond et al. 2008). Similar work is being done to integrate interventions that focus on improving health outcomes (Guérin et al. 2019) and integrating Illness Management and Recovery (IMR) (Monroe-DeVita et al. 2018) and other psychiatric rehabilitation practices to improve psychosocial functioning.

Yet another effort to address mixed outcomes is to adapt ACT to better address the service needs of special populations. For example, because increasing numbers of clients with psychiatric disabilities are now involved in correctional systems, ACT has been used to serve this population and to reduce criminal justice recidivism. As described above, earlier ACT studies have generally found no impact in this area. To address these unmet needs, a forensic ACT (FACT) model has been developed (Lamberti et al. 2004; Morrissey et al. 2007). Of the handful of evaluations conducted to date, FACT has been shown to reduce hospital use, improve quality of life, and reduce homelessness, recidivism, and probation/parole technical violations (Cuddeback et al. 2020). Recent work has also focused on adapting ACT to serve other subpopulations with high service needs, including veterans (Rosenheck et al. 2010; McCarthy et al. 2019), people using substances (Penzenstadler et al. 2019), adolescents (Mantzouranis et al. 2019; Schmidt et al. 2018), the elderly (Klug et al. 2019), and individuals with intellectual disabilities (Neijmeijer et al. 2018). In contrast to the original ACT model, which was designed to address the needs across these subpopulations, specialized ACT teams typically give greater weight to respective eligibility criteria (e.g., requirement of criminal justice involvement) and ramp up relevant resources and staffing to align with those criteria (e.g., FACT teams may include a probation officer or specialty court liaison).

ACT is cost-effective compared to standard case management (Latimer 1999; Weisbrod et al. 1980; Wolff et al. 1997) and has been widely disseminated. While a current national study is underway to determine the number of ACT and ICM programs nationally, it is estimated there are more than 600 ACT programs across the United States. Despite this, analyses have shown that ACT can be challenging to fund and can be vulnerable to disruption (Rochefort 2019), often facing significant and disproportionate budget cuts in times of financial distress (Aron et al. 2009).

After success in the United States, ACT spread internationally (Rochefort 2019), with countries like the Netherlands (van Veldhuizen 2007), Norway (Odden et al. 2019), South Africa (Hering et al. 2008), Japan (Ito et al. 2009), and others drawing from the existing research base to implement their own programs. The spread of ACT to other countries has necessitated the adaptation of ACT to different sociopolitical contexts. For example, the Netherlands pioneered a new approach called Flexible ACT to serve lower population density areas. These teams offer full ACT services to individuals who require it but also lower-intensity case management, with the flexibility to switch individuals between levels of care based on need (Van Veldhuizen and Bähler 2013). This approach is spreading to similarly populated counties (Nugter et al. 2016; Svensson et al. 2018).

Unresolved is the larger question of length of stay within an ACT team. The intention of the core principle of "time-unlimited services" within ACT is to ensure that there are no arbitrary time limits within the program, given what can be an unpredictable and changing course of illness for this population. Efforts have been made to determine how long an individual should stay within ACT (Huz et al. 2017), but these decisions can be largely dependent on external factors such as availability of step-down programs and housing. While the question remains about a specific length of stay within ACT as a result, there is wide consensus on the need to routinely assess for readiness to transition to less intensive services using measurement-based care to inform those next steps (Donahue et al. 2012).

Strengths Model

Besides ACT, the most widely studied case management approach is the Strengths Model. Eleven studies have tested the effectiveness of the Strengths Model with people who have SMI. Four of the studies employed experimental or quasi-experimental designs (Modrcin et al. 1988; Macias et al. 1994, 1997; Stanard 1999), and seven used non-experimental methods (Rapp and Chamberlain 1985; Rapp and Wintersteen 1989; Ryan et al. 1994; Kisthardt 1993; Barry et al. 2003; Fukui et al. 2012; Tsoi et al. 2018). These studies collectively produced positive outcomes in the areas of hospitalization, housing, employment, reduced symptoms, leisure time, social support, and family burden.

In the four experimental studies, positive outcomes were reported far more often than those with no significant difference. In none of the studies did clients who received services through Strengths Model case management do worse. The results have also been remarkably consistent across settings and within studies. Three of the studies had multiple sites with different case managers, supervisors, and affiliations, with a total of 15 different agencies.

The two outcome areas in which results have been consistently positive are reduction in symptoms and enhanced quality of community life. All three studies assessing symptom outcomes reported statistically significant differences favoring the Strengths Model. This included findings that people receiving Strengths Model case management reported fewer problems with mood and thoughts and greater stress tolerance and psychological well-being than the control groups. In one study that compared ACT and the Strengths Model, no differences were found in hospitalization and social functioning, but statistically significant differences favoring the Strengths Model were found for symptomatology (Barry et al. 2003).

Although the studies used a variety of measures (e.g., increased competitive employment, increased post-secondary education, increased leisure time in the community, enhanced skills for successful community living, increased social supports, decreased social isolation, achievement of goals, and increased quality of life), people receiving Strengths Model case management had enhanced levels of competence and involvement in community living. Ten of the 11 studies using these types of measures reported statistically significant positive outcomes.

More specific outcomes that seem to be strong indicators of the effectiveness of Strengths Model case management include reduced hospitalization (four out of seven studies showing positive outcomes when this was measured), vocational (four out of four showing positive outcomes where this was measured), and housing (three out of three showing positive outcomes where this was measured).

Research on Strengths Model case management is suggestive of its effectiveness. On the downside, the research is limited to two experimental, two quasi-experimental, and seven non-experimental studies. The size of the samples in three of the experimental studies was small. The measures used across studies varied, and questions have been raised about many of these measures (Chamberlain and Rapp 1991). Also, only the two most recent studies on the Strengths Model (Tsoi et al. 2018; Fukui et al. 2012) used the Strengths Model fidelity scale, which was not developed until 2004, adding questions to the degree of adherence to the model for the intervention group.

Optimizing Key Elements of Effective Case Management

A lack of best practice fidelity measures continues to be problematic for interpreting case management research findings (Dixon and Swartz 2014). Where fidelity is measured, results indicate that the probability of generating desired outcomes increases when the practice is implemented with higher fidelity (Fukui et al. 2012; Cuddeback et al. 2013; Monroe-DeVita et al. 2015). For a variety of reasons, evidence-based practices, such as ACT and the Strengths Model, may only be partially implemented, sometimes under a different program name (e.g., Community Support Program (CSP) in Wisconsin and Full Service Partnership (FSP) in California). Likewise, there is a clear need for more comprehensive fidelity measurement and data to guide ACT implementation and service delivery (Moser and Monroe-DeVita 2019). Although not every fidelity element carries equal importance, certain elements of Intensive Case Management likely contribute to improved outcomes. We list several in Table 1 and describe further below.

Many people with SMI have difficulty navigating the large array of supports they may need and vary in their ability and, sometimes, interest in seeking out office-based services. System fragmentation becomes problematic when a person requires support across multiple life domains (e.g., housing, employment, health, addictions, life skills, symptom management), while providers offering support in these areas operate independently and at times at cross-purposes. Direct service delivery within community settings is fundamental to high-quality Intensive Case Management and is a defining feature of the Strengths Model and ACT.

By way of person-centered treatment planning, case managers attend to clients' strengths and needs that cut across these life domains and are well positioned to meet needs more directly. In providing direct services, case managers may operate as generalists, carrying the "case manager" title, or in a specialty role (e.g., employment, housing), the latter of which has been shown to produce desired outcomes (Gold et al. 2006). In addition to providing specialized services, case managers reinforce and support the work of others with whom they coordinate. For example, while we do not expect case managers to prescribe or offer advice regarding psychiatric medications, they could still have a role when a client has a goal to find a medication that offers relief from distressing voices. Case manager roles might include assisting the client to write questions they have for their doctor, helping the client list specific side effects they find uncomfortable, and accessing information on non-pharmaceutical methods of managing voices.

Direct service delivery within the community, rather than the office, more effectively addresses challenges associated with access and engagement (Bond et al. 1995; Marty et al. 2001) and is the preference for most clients (Rapp and Goscha 2012). Clients are more satisfied with their care (Huxley and Warners 1992), and hospitalizations decrease (Bond et al. 1990) when they are offered more practical assistance with community-based needs. Teaching and practicing skills in the settings in which they will be used are more effective than teaching in artificial settings which then require a transfer of learning (Bellack 2004). Further, we gather more valid assessment data on what is helping and hindering client wellness during community visits. For example, community-based psychiatrists often remark how much more they learn about a client when they

Table 1 Optimizing key elements of effective case management

Element	Description
Direct service delivery	Direct service delivery helps address the challenges of a fragmented and under-resourced service system. Case managers provide services to meet clients' service needs across a range of life domains. Care coordination with other providers may also be present, especially as it relates to medical care. Some community mental health providers may specialize in a service area (e.g., employment, housing, co-occurring substance use disorder treatment), but also provide case management services
Community-based service delivery	Case managers provide services within clients' natural environments rather than expect clients to participate in office-based meetings. Community-based services allow for greater assistance with everyday challenges, reduce problems with transfer of learning across environments, and create greater opportunity for engagement and more accurate assessment
Community inclusion	Case managers direct services in a manner that facilitates' client participation and involvement within their local community, which includes building up a supportive network of natural supports. Such relationships may include family of birth, family of choice, friends, neighbors, landlords, employers, and religious leaders. Emphasizing community inclusion is essential to recovery-oriented care that seeks to harness self-determination and independence
Choice and person-driven care	Case managers operate within a shared decision-making framework, which includes seeking to understand and respect clients' values, preferences, experiences, and personal goals. Relatedly, case managers guide and teach clients to make their own informed choices, along with developing advocacy skills. Optimizing choice and person-driven care is central to all psychosocial evidence-based practices
Supervision	Case managers' training and qualifications may range from being a new graduate with a bachelor's degree to a more seasoned master's level clinician. Supervision is critical for services of sufficient quality to be delivered while also balancing the delivery of case management tasks with other direct services. Case managers are often underpaid and experience high turnover; consistently delivered, higher-quality supervision can compensate for such system shortcomings
Small caseloads	Case managers operate with manageable caseload sizes so that clients with SMI get a sufficient level of direct support. Caseload sizes range from 1:12 to 1:20 with the strengths Model and no more than 1:10 within ACT. Small caseloads are critical for providing direct care in the community for individuals with higher needs. In addition to the time invested in direct care, case managers spend considerable time in indirect work (e.g., travel to the community, participation in team meetings)
Reimbursement	Unlike fee-for-service reimbursement, bundled case rates account for a range of services with one billing code. Rate setting with the bundle should also consider the investment of indirect time that otherwise goes unreimbursed. The reimbursement unit is likely more supportive to best practice delivery when larger than a 15-minute unit

can observe their environment (e.g., a client's increased distress is more likely due to the very thin walls, loud neighbors, and bug infestation, rather than inconsistent medication adherence). Supporting people around their personal goals often entails supporting their participation and inclusion in their larger community, as opposed to the limited segregation of clients within a community of other people with SMI. As such, case managers are oriented to helping clients identify and build a network of natural supports (e.g., employers, neighbors, friends, faith leaders, landlords) and supportive family. The primacy of natural community resources is consistent with notions of recovery that emphasize building a life apart from the mental health system (Kaplan et al. 2012; Ridgway 2001) and is emphasized in both the Strengths Model and ACT fidelity scales (Rapp and Goscha 2012, Teague et al. 1998; Monroe-DeVita et al. 2013).

People not only want a true connection and sense of belonging; they want to be independent, be self-determined, and have choice (Hamann et al. 2006; Adams et al. 2007). Research has shown how optimizing choice yields improved outcomes (Chinman et al. 1999; Gowdy et al. 2003; Mueser et al. 2001; Ridgway and Rapp 1997). The importance of choice is also seen in motivational interviewing strategies (Drake et al. 2001; Miller and Rollnick 2002) and resounds from the hundreds of first-person accounts of recovery.

To optimize the previously described elements, reliable delivery of clinical supervision to support those providing case management is needed, but unfortunately often lacking. Case managers vary in their education, training, and background experience. In the United States, it is common for case management positions to be filled by bachelors-level staff who are underpaid, are prone to burnout, and experience high staff turnover. Reliable, competent supervision from a seasoned professional can bolster staff in these roles. Role clarity is important to know points of education and supervision. The Strengths Model prescribes a list of behaviors and competencies to be performed in order to achieve high fidelity (Rapp and Goscha 2012) and attends to the availability and quality of supervision in the fidelity scale (Rapp and Goscha 2012). Staff are able to attain the skills to achieve proficiency in the model through structured teaching methods employed by the supervisor (Carlson et al. 2016).

Intensive case managers operate with small caseloads to effectively have sufficient time to provide individualized, person-centered, Intensive Case Management services, which entails both direct time (service provision) and a significant amount of indirect time (travel, team meetings, supervision, working with natural supports). The importance of low ratios received virtuously unanimous agreement among ACT experts (McGrew and Bond 1995).

Despite having smaller caseloads, case managers' number one source of stress can be pressure to meet productivity demands. Fee-for-service reimbursement models (i.e., each delivered service has an associated billable service code and reimbursement rate), in particular, often create stressful productivity expectations that can undermine the provision of higher-quality care. In contrast, bundled case rates account for a range of services, but can also be problematic if the reimbursement unit remains small (e.g., 15-minute unit). The quality of case management services, as described in the previous elements, is optimized when reimbursement is bundled, of a larger reimbursement unit, and of a sufficient rate that accounts for indirect time.

A common element of ACT fidelity measures (Monroe-DeVita et al. 2011; Teague et al. 1998), but with less agreement by experts (McGrew and Bond 1995), is on the importance of full-time access to services. Once referred to the "hospital without walls," ACT is designed to provide around-the-clock supports in terms of both extended planned service hours that include early mornings and early evenings and planned supports on the holidays and weekends. The assumption is that ACT serves individuals whose needs do not necessarily subside outside of typical weekday business hours and person-centered service delivery will result in evening and weekend services. Relatedly, ACT is designed to provide crisis supports by way of operating their own crisis hotline while being positioned to respond to crises in person, when necessary. Although ICM teams may vary in their adoption of this element, we recommend teams schedule services with some flexibility to accommodate clients' needs and preferences. We also recommend that ICM teams network closely with local crisis service providers to assist with crisis stabilization and diversion efforts. The effectiveness of crisis services is enhanced by in-person or phone access to staff who have familiarity and a relationship with the person and are committed to avoiding hospital care when possible (Carlson et al. 1998).

Level of Care Supports (Finding a Good Fit)

As noted throughout this chapter, it is critical that individuals have access to not only high-quality services but also the right level of services and supports. To this end, it is important that local service systems create options so a good-fit case management service and support is available (Giesler and Hodge 1998). What determines goodness of fit when it comes to case management? Often in consideration are the complexity of needs and severity of impairments.

At one end of the continuum would be people who are acutely psychotic, are dangerous to themselves and others, and/or are not lucid. People in this group often have high levels of need in multiple areas and frequently live in "survival mode" from day to day. A middle group is in the process of recovering their lives and has goals where symptoms of mental illness impact progress. The other end of the continuum contains people who are stable, but still require some behavioral health support.

In light of healthcare changes in the United States, it remains an open question how to allocate resources to staff such tiered services and whether to incorporate step-down mechanisms and hybrid models established to respond to fluctuating needs (van Veldhuizen 2007). Several states have entered into legal settlements with the federal department of justice as a result of gross violations of the US Supreme Court Olmstead v. L.C., 527 U.S. 581 (1999). In short, these states did not create opportunities for individuals to receive services in the least restrictive alternative, and in most cases, individuals are instead institutionalized (e.g., hospital, assisted living facilities, group homes) in lieu of receiving opportunities for community-based supports.

Environmental factors (e.g., poverty, social alienation, lack of transportation, unemployment, institutionalized living) can substantially impact presenting problems and must be given equal or greater consideration when determining level of support. An individual with relatively moderate psychiatric symptoms can present as more impaired when living in poverty, alienated from supportive relationships (e.g., family, friends), unable to access transportation, and unemployed. For example, a person living in a restrictive group home, which was initially intended to be a brief 6-month transition from a state hospital, resulted in a longer-term stay due to iatrogenic effects related to the placement. Another example is an individual who receives only minimal case management services, is often at risk of homelessness while managing to hold down a part-time job, and finds themselves hospitalized for an undertreated severe anxiety disorder and possible manic episodes. Hospital stays are typically very brief due to a lack of sufficient hospital and crisis respite beds in the area. This person, on paper, may appear to be appropriate for ACT, but with slightly more intensive, higher-quality supports, such as through a Strengths Model case management team, a more expensive ACT option likely isn't necessary.

Because of the many factors that can affect case management scaling decisions, many service areas are inadequately resourced, which has historically been a problem (Wang et al. 2002). Budget constraints have led to the de facto adoption of less expensive but also less effective models with high caseloads (Rapp and Goscha 2004). As Moser and Monroe-DeVita (2019) stated, "ACT cannot be clinically effective or cost-effective when used as a panacea for all outreach and community-based service needs; thus, examining the availability of alternative services surrounding a given ACT team is also important" (p. 261).

Specifically, both ICM and ACT are not cost-effective if provided to clients with SMI without regard to service need (Burns et al. 2007; Harrison-Read et al. 2002; Latimer 2001). Two basic questions, then, are as follows: What proportion of the SMI population should receive ICM or ACT? What kind of case management services should be provided to clients not receiving ICM or ACT? Available estimates for ACT, in particular, have appeared to be rather inflated (Cuddeback et al. 2006; van Veldhuizen 2007) when relying solely on hospitalization criteria. These estimates are based on a generally outdated premise that ACT teams are designed primarily to serve frequent users of psychiatric hospitals, which was the primary mission for ACT in the 1980s (Bond et al. 1995; Mowbray et al. 1997). Because of deinstitutionalization, far fewer clients are hospitalized, and inpatient stays are now much shorter in the United States (Lamb and Bachrach 2001). Thus, the original mission for ACT has been largely eclipsed, except in countries like Japan, where deinstitutionalization has not yet occurred (Ito et al. 2009). A primary source for ACT funding is Medicaid, and in turn, measures of ACT cost-effectiveness are limited to Medicaid expenses, such as hospital and crisis and emergency services. Not accounted for are cost-savings associated with reduced homelessness, increased employment and related decreased use of social security, increased preventative health management practices, and increased criminal justice diversion. Of late, US states are paying greater attention to the need for braiding and blending funds to promote social determinants of health, thereby addressing problems associated with current siloed department budgets (Butler et al. 2020).

As illustrated by the earlier example, another complicating factor in ACT eligibility estimation is that ACT services do not exist in a vacuum. Inadequate basic mental health services (e.g., housing, other community support services, crisis services) may lead to clients' deterioration and increased need for ACT. Since people often stay on ACT teams for prolonged periods of time, ACT services become unavailable for new clients. So, this begs the question: what should case management services look like for the remainder of the SMI population?

The Strengths Model was primarily designed for those individuals with a mental illness who experience significant barriers and challenges to goal achievement, but do not require the intensity of services like ACT. While Strengths Model philosophies, tools, and methods can be used within Intensive Case Management services, the model is most applicable to the middle group mentioned above. Using data from the two studies above (Cuddeback et al. 2006; van Veldhuizen 2007), 50–80% of all people in a service area could benefit from Strengths Model case management. Clients served by Strengths Model case management teams in the research conform to the parameters of this middle group described earlier.

Another consideration with finding good-fit care options is the timing of service delivery given the course of the illness. In the past decade, there has been greater attention directed at prevention of disability through early intervention with clients experiencing early and first episode of psychosis (Killackey et al. 2006). The duration of untreated psychosis is negatively associated with outcomes (Marshall et al., 2005) (see chapter "Early Psychosis and the Prevention and Mitigation of Serious Mental Illness").

Conclusions

Case management has been a central feature of community mental healthcare for people with SMI for nearly 50 years. An accumulated evidence base strongly supports the effectiveness of specific models of case management and of several foundational elements of case management, including direct delivery of services, small caseloads, and services delivered in the community. Even with the plethora of evidence available, the use of ineffective models or hybrids of models continues to dominate the behavioral health landscape. Even when researched models are used, there is often little consideration given to its fit with the specific population being served and the level of care coordination needed to meet their needs.

Case management will continue to evolve, as behavioral health systems continue to find effective solutions to address the high numbers of people with mental illnesses who are homeless, are involved in criminal justice systems, are experiencing co-occurring substance use disorders, have chronic healthcare conditions, and are disadvantaged due to racial inequities. Effective models like ACT have taught us the importance of team-based approaches to integrated, coordinated care where case management is but one of the several necessary components. Strengths Model case management has taught us the importance of aligning our services with the recovery-oriented aspirations people desire and raising our expectations for what people with SMI can accomplish. The lessons of the past 50 years should critically inform the reconstruction process.

References

Adams, J. R., Drake, R. E., & Wolford, G. L. (2007). Shared decision-making preferences of people with severe mental illness. Psychiatric Services, 58(9), 1219–1221.

Allness, D. J., & Knoedler, W. H. (2003). The PACT model of community-based treatment for persons with severe and persistent mental illness: A manual for PACT start-up (2nd ed.). Arlington, VA: NAMI.

Aron L, Honberg R, Duckworth K, et al. Grading the States 2009: A Report on America's Health Care System for Adults with Serious Mental Illness. Arlington, VA: National Alliance on Mental Illness; 2009.

Barry, K. L., Zeber, J. E., Blow, F. C., & Valenstein, M. (2003). Effect of strengths model versus assertive community treatment model on participant outcomes and utilization: Two-year follow-up. Psychiatric Rehabilitation Journal, 26(3), 268–277.

Bellack, A. S. (2004). Skills training for people with mental illness. Psychiatric Rehabilitation Journal, 27(4), 375–391.

Bigelow, D. A., & Young, D. J. (1991). Effectiveness of a case management program. Community Mental Health Journal, 27,115–133.

Bond GR, Drake RE, Becker DR. An update on randomized controlled trials of evidence-based supported employment. Psychiatric Rehabilitation Journal. 2008 Spring;31(4):280–90.

Bond, G. R., Drake, R. E., Mueser, K. T., & Latimer, E. (2001). Assertive community treatment for people with severe mental illness: Critical ingredients and impact on patients. Disease Management & Health Outcomes, 9, 141–159.

Bond, G. R., McGrew, J. H., & Fekete, D. M. (1995). Assertive outreach for frequent users of psychiatric hospitals: A meta-analysis. Journal of Mental Health Administration, 22, 4–16.

Bond, G. R., Witheridge, T. F., Dincin, J., Wasmer, D., Webb, J., & De Graaf-Kaser, R. (1990). Assertive community treatment for frequent users of psychiatric hospitals in a large city. American Journal of Community Psychology, 18, 865–891.

Bruns, E. J., Kerns, S. E., Pullmann, M. D., Hensley, S. W., Lutterman, T., & Hoagwood, K. E. (2016). Research, data, and evidence-based treatment use in state behavioral health systems, 2001–2012. Psychiatric Services, 67(5), 496–503.

Burns, T., Catty, J., Dash, M., Roberts, C., Lockwood, A., & Marshall, M. (2007). Use of intensive case management to reduce time in hospital in people with severe mental illness: systematic review and meta-regression. British Medical Journal, 335, 336–340.

Butler, S., Higashi, T., & Cabello, M. (2020). Budgeting to promote social objectives—a primer on braiding and blending. The Brookings Institution. https://www.brookings.edu/wp-content/uploads/2020/04/BraidingAndBlending20200403.pdf

Carlson, L., Goscha, R., & Rapp, C. (2016). Field Mentoring: An Important Strategy for Evidence-Based Practice Implementation. Best Practices in Mental Health, 12(2), 1–13.

Carlson, L., Gowdy, E., & Rapp, C. A. (1998). Best practice in reducing hospitalization. Lawrence, KS: University of Kansas School of Social Welfare.

Chamberlain, R., & Rapp, C. A. (1991). A decade of case management: A methodological review of outcome research. Community Mental Health Journal, 27(3), 171–188.

Chester, P., Ehrlich, C., Warburton, L., Baker, D., Kendall, E., & Crompton, D. (2016). What is the work of recovery oriented practice? A systematic literature review. International Journal of Mental Health Nursing, 25(4), 270–285.

Chinman, M. J., Allende, M., Weingarten, R., Steiner, J., Tworkowski, S., & Davidson, L. (1999). On the Road to Collaborative Treatment Planning: Consumer and Provider Perspectives. The Journal of Behavioral Health Services and Research, 26(2), 211–218.

Coldwell, C. M., & Bender, W. S. (2007). The effectiveness of assertive community treatment for homeless populations with severe mental illness: A meta-analysis. American Journal of Psychiatry, 164, 393–399.

Corrigan, P. W., Mueser, K. T., Bond, G. R., Drake, R. E., & Solomon, P. (2008). Principles and practice of psychiatric rehabilitation: An empirical approach. New York: Guilford Press.

Cuddeback GS, Morrissey JP, Domino ME, Monroe-DeVita M, Teague GB, Moser LL. (2013). Fidelity to Recovery-Oriented ACT Practices and Consumer Outcomes. Psychiatric Services, 64(4), 318–323.

Cuddeback, G. S., Morrissey, J. P., & Meyer, P. S. (2006). How many assertive community treatment teams do we need? Psychiatric Services, 57, 1803–1806.

Cuddeback, G.S., Simpson, J.M., & Wu, J.C. (2020) A comprehensive literature review of Forensic Assertive Community Treatment (FACT): Directions for practice, policy and research, International Journal of Mental Health, 49(2), 106–127.

Curtis, D. L., Millman, E. J., Struening, E., & D'Ercole, A. (1992). Effect of case management on rehospitalization and utilization of ambulatory care services. Hospital and Community Psychiatry, 43, 895–899.

Dieterich, M., Irving, C. B., Bergman, H., Khokhar, M. A., Park, B., & Marshall, M. (2017). Intensive case management for severe mental illness. The Cochrane database of systematic reviews.

Dietzen, L. L., & Bond, G. R. (1993). Relationship between case manager contact and outcome for frequently hospitalized psychiatric clients. Hospital and Community Psychiatry, 44, 839–843.

Dixon LB, Dickerson F, Bellack AS, et al. (2010). The 2009 schizophrenia PORT psychosocial treatment recommendations and summary statements. Schizophrenia Bulletin, 36, 48–70.

Dixon L, & Swartz E. (2014). Fifty years of progress in community mental health in the US: the growth of Evidence based practice. Epidemiology and Psychiatric Sciences, 23, 5–9.

Donahue SA, Manuel JI, Herman DB, et al. (2012). Development and use of a transition readiness scale to help manage ACT team capacity. Psychiatric Services, 63, 223–229.

Draine, J., Salzer, M. S., Culhane, D. P., & Hadley, T. R. (2002). Role of social disadvantage in crime, joblessness, and homelessness among persons with serious mental illness. Psychiatric Services, 53, 565–573.

Drake, R. E., Essock, S. M., Shaner, A., Carey, K., Minkoff, K., & Kola, L. (2001). Implementing dual diagnosis services for recipients with severe mental illness. Psychiatric Services, 52(4), 69–76.

Drake, R. E., Mueser, K. T., Brunette, M. F., & McHugo, G. J. (2004). A review of treatments for people with severe mental illnesses and co-occurring substance use disorders. Psychiatric rehabilitation journal, 27(4), 360.

Drake, R. E., O'Neal, E. L., & Wallach, M. A. (2008). A systematic review of psychosocial research on psychosocial interventions for people with co-occurring severe mental and substance use disorders. Journal of Substance Abuse Treatment, 34, 123–138.

Edwards, D. V., Nikkel, B., & Coiner, B. (1991). Final report of the National Institute of Mental Health Young Adult Dual Diagnosis Oregon Demonstration Project. Unpublished manuscript, Oregon Mental Health and Developmental Disability Division.

Franklin, J. L., Solovitz, B., Mason, M., Clemons, J. R., & Miller, G. E. (1987). An evaluation of case management. American Journal of Public Health, 77, 674–678.

Fukui, S., Goscha, R., Rapp, C. A., Mabry, A., Liddy, P., & Marty, D. (2012). Strengths Model Case management fidelity scores and client outcomes. Psychiatric Services, 63(7), 708–711.

Giesler, L. J., & Hodge, M. (1998). Case management in behavioral health care. International Journal of Mental Health, 27, 26–40.

Gold, P. B., Meisler, N., Santos, A. B., Carnemolla, M. A., Williams, O. H., & Kelleher, J. (2006). Randomized trial of supported employment integrated with assertive community treatment for rural adults with severe mental illness. Schizophrenia Bulletin, 32, 378–395.

Goscha, R. J. (2020). Strengths Model Case Management: Moving Strengths from Concept to Action. University of Kansas Libraries

Gowdy, E., Carlson, L., & Rapp, C. A. (2003). Practices differentiating high performing from low performing supported employment programs. Psychiatric Rehabilitation Journal, 26(3), 232–239.

Guérin, E., Dupuis, J. P., Jacob, J. D., & Prud'homme, D. (2019). Incorporating a physical activity program into an assertive community treatment team: impact and strategies. Community Mental Health Journal, *55*(8), 1293–1297.

Hamann, J., Langer, B., Winkler, V., Busch, R., Cohen, R., Leucht, S., et al. (2006). Shared decision making for in-patients with schizophrenia. Acta Psychiatrica Scandinavia, 114(4), 265–273.

Harrison-Read P, Lucas B, Tyrer P, et al. (2002). Heavy users of acute psychiatric beds: Randomized controlled trial of enhanced community management in an outer. London borough. Psychological Medicine 32, 403–416.

Hering, L., Koen, L., Joska, J., Botha, U., & Oosthuizen, P. (2008). Assertive community treatment in the South African context. African Journal of Psychiatry, 11(4), 272–275.

Holloway F, Carson J (1998). Intensive case management for the severely mentally ill. Controlled trial. British Journal of Psychiatry, 172, 19–22.

Hornstra, R. K., Bruce-Wolfe, V., Sagduyu, K., & Riffle, D. W. (1993). The effect of intensive case management on hospitalization of patients with schizophrenia. Hospital and Community Psychiatry, 44, 844–847.

Huz, S., Thorning, H., White, C. N., Fang, L., Tran Smith, B., Radigan, M., Dixon, L. B. (2017). Time in assertive community treatment: A statewide quality improvement initiative to reduce length of participation. Psychiatric Services, 68 (6), 539–541.

Huxley, P. J., & Warner, R. (1992). Case management for long term psychiatric patients: A study of quality of life. Hospital and Community Psychiatry, 43(8), 799–802.

Intagliata, J. (1982). Improving the quality of community care for the chronically mentally disabled: The role of case management. Schizophrenia Bulletin, 8(4), 655–674.

Isaacs, A., Beauchamp, A., Sutton, K., & Kocaali, N. (2019). Care coordination can reduce unmet needs of persons with severe and persistent mental illness. Frontiers in Psychiatry, 10, 563.

Issakidis C, Sanderson K, Teesson M, et al. (1999). Intensive case management in Australia: a randomized controlled trial. Acta Psychiatrica Scandinavica, 99, 360–367.

Ito, J., Oshima, I., Nishio, M., & Kuno, E. (2009). Initiative to build a community-based mental health system including assertive community treatment for people with severe mental illness in Japan. American Journal of Psychiatric Rehabilitation, 12, 247–260.

Jerrell, J., & Ridgely, M. S. (1995). Comparative effectiveness of three approaches to serving people with severe mental illness and substance abuse disorders. Journal of Nervous and Mental Disease, 183, 566–576.

Kaplan, K., Salzer, M. S., & Brusilovskiy, E. (2012). Community participation as a predictor of recovery-oriented outcomes among emerging and mature adults with mental illnesses. Psychiatric Rehabilitation Journal, *35*(3), 219–229.

Kenny, D. A., Calsyn, R. J., Morse, G. A., Klinkenberg, W. D., Winter, J. P., & Trusty, M. L. (2004). Evaluation of Treatment Programs for Persons with Severe Mental Illness: Moderator and Mediator Effects. *Evaluation Review*, *28*(4), 294–324. https://doi.org/10.1177/0193841X04264701

Killackey, E. J., Jackson, H. J., Gleeson, J., Hickie, I. B., & McGorry, P. D. (2006). Exciting career opportunity beckons! Early intervention and vocational rehabilitation in first-episode psychosis: employing cautious optimism. Australian and New Zealand Journal of Psychiatry, 40, 951–962.

Kisthardt, W. (1993). The impact of the strengths model of case management from the consumer perspective. In M. Harris & H. Bergman (Eds.), *Case management: Theory and practice* (pp. 165–82). Washington, DC: American Psychiatric Association.

Klug G, Gallunder M, Hermann G, et al. (2019). Effectiveness of multidisciplinary psychiatric home treatment for elderly patients with mental illness: a systematic review of empirical studies. BMC Psychiatry, 19:382.

Kreyenbuhl, J., Nossel, I. R., & Dixon, L. B. (2009). Disengagement from mental health treatment among individuals with schizophrenia and strategies for facilitating connections to care: A review of the literature. Schizophrenia Bulletin, 35, 696–703.

Kreyenbuhl, J., Buchanan, R. W., Dickerson, F. B., & Dixon, L. B. (2010). The Schizophrenia Patient Outcomes Research Team (PORT): Updated treatment recommendations 2009. Schizophrenia Bulletin, 36, 94–103.

Lake, J., & Turner, M. S. (2017). Urgent Need for Improved Mental Health Care and a More Collaborative Model of Care. The Permanente journal, 21, 17–024.

Lamb, H. R., & Bachrach, L. L. (2001). Some perspectives on deinstitutionalization. Psychiatric Services, 52(8), 1039–1045.

Lamberti, J. S., Weisman, R. L., & Faden, D. I. (2004). Forensic Assertive Community Treatment (FACT): An emerging model for preventing incarceration of severely mentally ill adults. Psychiatric Services, 55, 1285–1293.

Latimer, E. A. (2001). Economic impacts of supported employment for the severely mentally ill. Canadian Journal of Psychiatry, 46, 496–505.

Latimer, E. (1999). Economic impacts of assertive community treatment: A review of the literature. Canadian Journal of Psychiatry, 44, 443–454.

Lehman, A. F., Postrado, L. T., McNary, S. W., & Goldman, H. H. (1994). Continuity of care and client outcomes in the Robert Wood Johnson Foundation program on chronic mental illness. Milbank Quarterly, 72, 105–122.

Mantzouranis G, Baier V, Holzer L, et al. (2019). Clinical significance of assertive community treatment among adolescents. Social Psychiatry and Psychiatric Epidemiology, 54, 445–453.

Macias, C., Farley, O. W. et al. (1997). Case management in the context of capitation financing: An evaluation of the strengths model. Administration and Policy in Mental Health, 24(6), 535–543.

Macias, C., Kinney, R., Parley, O. W., Jackson, R., & Vos, B. (1994). The role of case management within a community support system: Partnership with psychosocial rehabilitation. Community Mental Health Journal, 30(4), 323–339.

Marshall, M., Lewis, S., Lockwood, A., Drake, R., Jones, P., & Croudace, T. (2005). Association between duration of untreated psychosis and outcome in cohorts of first-episode patients. Archives of General Psychiatry, 62, 975–983.

Marty, D., Rapp, C. A., & Carlson, L. (2001). The experts speak: The critical ingredients of Strengths Model case management. Psychiatric Rehabilitation Journal, 24(3), 214–221.

McCarthy JF, Valenstein M, Dixon L, et al. (2019). Initiation of assertive community treatment among veterans with serious mental illness: client and program factors. Psychiatric Services, 60:196–201.

McDonagh M., Dana, T., Cantor, A., Selph, S., Monroe-DeVita, M., Kopelovich S., Devine, B., Blazina, I., Bougatsos, C., Grusing, S., Fu, R., Haupt, D. (2017). Treatments for adults with schizophrenia: A systematic review (AHRQ Publication No. 17(18)-EHC031-EF). Rockville, MD: Agency for Healthcare Research and Quality. Retrieved from www.effectivehealthcare.ahrq.gov/reports/final.cfm.

McGrew, J. H., & Bond, G. R. (1995). Critical ingredients of assertive community treatment: Judgments of the experts. Journal of Mental Health Administration, 22, 113–125.

Miller, W. R., & Rollnick, S. (2002). Motivational interviewing: Preparing people for change (second ed.). New York: Guilford Press.

McHugo GJ, Drake RE, Teague GB, et al (1999). Fidelity to assertive community treatment and client outcomes in the New Hampshire dual disorders study. Psychiatric Services, 50, 818–824.

Modrcin, M., Rapp, C. A., & Poertner, J. (1988). The evaluation of case management services with the chronically mentally ill. Evaluation and Program Planning, 11, 307–314.

Monroe-DeVita, M., Morse, G., Mueser, K., McHugo, G. J., Xie, H., Hallgren, K., Peterson, R., Miller, J., Akiba, C., York, M. M., Gingerich, S., & Stiles, B. (2018). Implementing illness management and recovery within assertive community treatment: A pilot trial of feasibility and effectiveness. Psychiatric Services, 69, 562–71.

Monroe-DeVita M, Teague GB, Moser LL. (2011). The TMACT: a new tool for measuring fidelity to assertive community treatment. Journal of the American Psychiatric Nurses Association, 17, 17–29.

Monroe-DeVita, M., Moser, L.L. & Teague, G.B. (2013). The tool for measurement of assertive community treatment (TMACT). In M. P. McGovern, G. J. McHugo, R. E.

Monroe-DeVita M, Moser L, Teague G, Heirvang K, Odden S. (June 2015) Implementation and evaluation of ACT using the tool for measurement of ACT (TMACT): Current findings and perspectives in Norway and the U.S. Symposium presented at the 3rd Biennial European Congress on Assertive Outreach, Oslo, Norway.

Morrissey, J., Meyer, P., & Cuddeback, G. (2007). Extending assertive community treatment to criminal justice settings: Origins, current evidence, and future directions. Community Mental Health Journal, 43, 527–544.

Moser L, Monroe-DeVita M. (2019). A call for better data to guide ACT policy and programs. Psychiatric Services, 70:261.

Mowbray, C. T., Plum, T. B., & Masterton, T. (1997). Harbinger II: Deployment and evolution of assertive community treatment in Michigan. Administration and Policy in Mental Health, 25, 125–139.

Mueser, K. T., Bond, G. R., Drake, R. E., & Resnick, S. G. (1998). Models of community care for severe mental illness: A review of research on case management. Schizophrenia Bulletin, 24, 37–74.

Mueser, K. T., Becker, D. R., & Wolfe, R. (2001). Supported employment, job preferences, and job tenure and satisfaction. Journal of Mental Health, 10, 411–417.

Muller, J. (1981). Alabama community support project evaluation of the implementation and initial outcomes of a model case manager system. Community Support System Journal, 4, 1–4.

Neijmeijer LJ, Didden R, Nijman HL, Kroon H. (2018). Assertive community treatment for people with mild intellectual disability or borderline intellectual functioning and mental health problems or challenging behavior: state of the art and implementation in the Netherlands. Journal of Policy and Pract in Intellectual Disabilities, 15, 329–342.

Nelson, G., Aubry, T., & Lafrance, A. (2007). Review of the literature on the effectiveness of housing and support, assertive community treatment, and intensive case management interventions for persons with mental illness who have been homeless. American Journal of Orthopsychiatry, 77, 350–361.

Nugter MA, Engelsbel F, Bähler M, et al. (2016). Outcomes of FLEXIBLE assertive community treatment (FACT) implementation: a prospective real life study. Community Mental Health Journal, 52, 898–907.

Odden, S., Landheim, A., Clausen, H. *et al.* (2019). Model fidelity and team members' experiences of assertive community treatment in Norway: a sequential mixed-methods study. International Journal of Mental Health Systems, 13, 65.

Olmstead v. L. C., 527 U. S. 581 (1999).

Penzenstadler L, Soares C, Anci E, et al. (2019). Effect of assertive community treatment for patients with substance use disorder: a systematic review. European Addiction Research, 25, 56–67.

Rapp, C. A., & Chamberlain, R. (1985). Case management services for the chronically mentally ill. Social Work, 30(5), 417–422.

Rapp, C. A., & Goscha, R. J. (2012). The strengths model: A recovery-oriented approach to mental health services (3rd ed.). New York: Oxford University Press

Rapp, C. A., & Goscha, R. J. (2004). The principles of effective case management of mental health services. Psychiatric Rehabilitation Journal, 27, 319–333.

Rapp, C. A., & Wintersteen, R. (1989). The Strengths Model of case management: Results from twelve demonstrations. Psychosocial Rehabilitation Journal, 23(1), 23–32.

Ridgway, P. (2001). Re-storying psychiatric disability: Learning from first person narrative accounts of recovery. Psychiatric Rehabilitation Journal, 24(4), 335–343.

Ridgway, P., & Rapp, C. A. (1997). The active ingredients of effective supported housing: A research synthesis. Lawrence, KS: University of Kansas School of Social Welfare

Rochefort, D. A. (2019). Innovation and its discontents: pathways and barriers in the diffusion of assertive community treatment. The Milbank Quarterly, 97(4), 1151–1199.

Rosenheck RA, Neale MS, Mohamed S. (2010). Transition to low intensity case management in a VA assertive community treatment model program. Psychiatric Rehabilitation Journal, 33(4), 288–96.

Rossler, W., Loffler, W., Fatkenheuer, B., & Riecher-Rossler, A. (1992). Does case management reduce the hospitalization rate? Acta Psychiatrica Scandinavica, 86, 445–449.

Ryan, C. S., Sherman, P. S., & Judd, C. M. (1994). Accounting for case management effects in the evaluation of mental health services. Journal of Consulting and Clinical Psychology, 62(5), 965–74.

Schaedle, R., & Epstein, I. (2000). Specifying intensive case management: A multiple stakeholder approach. Mental Health Services Research, 2, 95–105.

Schmidt, S.J., Lange, M., Schöttle, D., et al. (2018). Negative symptoms, anxiety, and depression as mechanisms of change of a 12-month trial of assertive community treatment as part of integrated care in patients with first-and multiepisode schizophrenia spectrum disorders (ACCESS I trial). European Archives of Psychiatry and Clinical Neuroscience, 268, 593–602.

Shay, L. A., & Lafata, J. E. (2015). Where is the evidence? A systematic review of shared decision making and patient outcomes. Medical Decision Making, 35(1), 114–131.

Smith, L., & Newton, R. (2007). Systematic review of case management. Australian and New Zealand Journal of Psychiatry, 41, 2–9.

Spivak, S., Cullen, B. A., Green, C., Firth, T., Sater, H., & Mojtabai, R. (2019). Availability of assertive community treatment in the United States: 2010 to 2016. Psychiatric services, 70(10), 948–951.

Stanard, R. P. (1999). The effect of training in a strengths model of case management on outcomes in a community mental health center. Community Mental Health Journal 35(2), 169–179.

Surles, R., & McGurrin, M. (1987). Increased use of psychiatric emergency services by young chronic mentally ill patients. Hospital and Community Psychiatry, 38, 401–405.

Stein, L., & Test, M. A. (1980). Alternative to mental hospital treatment I. Conceptual model, treatment program, and clinical evaluation. Archives of General Psychiatry, *37*(4), 392–397. doi:https://doi.org/10.1001/archpsyc.1980.01780170034003.

Svensson, B., Hansson, L., Lexén, A. (2018). Outcomes of clients in need of intensive team care in Flexible Assertive Community Treatment in Sweden. Nordic Journal of Psychiatry, 72(3), 226–231.

Tabak, N. T., Link, P. C., Holden, J., & Granholm, E. (2015). Goal attainment scaling: tracking goal achievement in consumers with serious mental illness. American Journal of Psychiatric Rehabilitation, 18(2), 173–186.

Teague, G. B., Bond, G. R., & Drake, R. E. (1998). Program fidelity in assertive community treatment: Development and use of a measure. American Journal of Orthopsychiatry, 68, 216–232.

Thomas, E. C., Despeaux, K. E., Drapalski, A. L., & Bennett, M. (2018). Person-oriented recovery of individuals with serious mental illnesses: A review and meta-analysis of longitudinal findings. Psychiatric services, 69(3), 259–267.

Tsoi, E. W. S., Tse, S., Yu, C., Chan, S., Wan, E., Wong, S., & Liu, L. (2018). A nonrandomized controlled trial of strengths model case management in Hong Kong. Research on Social Work Practice, 29(5), 540–554.

Turner, J. C., & TenHoor, W. J. (1978). The NIMH community support program: Pilot approach to a needed social reform. Schizophrenia Bulletin, 4, 319–348.

van Veldhuizen, J. R. (2007). A Dutch version of ACT. Community Mental Health Journal, 43, 421–423.

van Veldhuizen, J. R., & Bähler, M. (2013). Manual flexible ACT, vision, model, practice and organization. www.factfacts.nl

Walsh, J. (2000). Clinical case management with persons having mental illness. A relationship-based practice. Florence, KY: Cengage Learning.

Wang, P. S., Demler, O., & Kessler, R. C. (2002). Adequacy of treatment for serious mental illness in the United States. American Journal of Public Health, 92, 92–98.

Weisbrod, B.A., Test, M.A., Stein, L.I. (1980). Alternative to mental hospital treatment. II. Economic benefit-cost analysis. Archives of General Psychiatry, 37(4), 400–5.

Wolff, N., et al., (1997). Cost-effectiveness evaluation of three approaches to case management for homeless mentally ill clients. American Journal of Psychiatry, 154(3), 341–8.

Crisis and Emergency Services

Margaret E. Balfour and Matthew L. Goldman

Introduction

How a community responds to behavioral health emergencies is both a public health and social justice issue. Unfortunately, our healthcare system is often ill-equipped to address the needs of individuals experiencing a behavioral health crisis. While there are nationwide standards and expectations for medical emergencies, the response to behavioral emergencies varies widely and rarely delivers comparable quality and experience of care.

This disparity begins the moment a person asks for help. While a 911 call for chest pain results in an ambulance response with emergency medicine technicians, a call for suicidal ideation often triggers an armed law enforcement response. With police as the default first responders, individuals in behavioral health crisis account for a quarter of police shootings and over 2 million jail bookings per year. Explicit and implicit bias magnify these problems for people of color. At the emergency department (ED), the chest pain patient receives rapid assessment, treatment, and, if needed, admission to an inpatient bed upstairs. The person with the behavioral health emergency has a much different experience. Most EDs lack the capability to provide psychiatric assessment and treatment. Instead, an individual can "board" for hours, even days, awaiting transfer to an outside facility for inpatient psychiatric admission. In addition to the poor experience for the person in crisis, this creates significant operational and financial burdens on the healthcare system.

However, a confluence of multiple developments has created an unprecedented opportunity for a much-needed transformation of behavioral health crisis care on a potentially massive scale. Implementation of the new nationwide 988 mental health hotline has prompted federal and state policymakers to focus attention on creating the crisis services callers will need. Police reform movements like Black Lives Matter are causing communities to seek alternatives to law enforcement as the default first responders for behavioral health emergencies. At the same time, the COVID-19 pandemic has raised awareness of the widespread need to increase access to behavioral health services and given rise to relief packages containing the funding to do so. It is an exciting time for the crisis field!

M. E. Balfour (✉)
Connections Health Solutions, Tucson, AZ, USA

Department of Psychiatry, University of Arizona, Tucson, AZ, USA
e-mail: margie.balfour@connectionshs.com

M. L. Goldman
Comprehensive Crisis Services, San Francisco Department of Public Health, San Francisco, CA, USA

Department of Psychiatry and Behavioral Sciences, UCSF, San Francisco, CA, USA
e-mail: matthew.goldman@ucsf.edu

W. E. Sowers et al. (eds.), *Textbook of Community Psychiatry*,
https://doi.org/10.1007/978-3-031-10239-4_27

This chapter will provide an overview of the rapidly evolving landscape of crisis services while highlighting opportunities for leadership, advocacy, and strategies for creating a well-coordinated crisis system that meets the needs of the community.

Defining Crisis Services

A common thread throughout this chapter is the wide variability in crisis services. Even the definition of "crisis" seems to vary widely. Some focus on risk of harm, while others defer to the individual to determine for themselves what constitutes a crisis. Systems are increasingly adopting the latter self-defined approach. The term "crisis" itself possibly perpetuates the stigma and disparities attached to mental health. Why use separate terminology to distinguish mental health and substance use emergencies from other types of health emergencies? Does this distinction make it easier to accept a lesser standard of care for behavioral health emergencies? This chapter conforms to the current usage of behavioral health crisis interchangeably with behavioral health emergency and is inclusive of both mental health and substance use-related emergencies.

Because crisis services are typically funded and regulated at the state or local level, there is substantial regional variation in terms of program definitions, financing, licensure, accessibility, and quality. Comprehensive national standards are needed, but progress has been made during the several years leading up to 988 implementation.

Crisis Now: Transforming Services Is Within Our Reach (National Action Alliance for Suicide Prevention: Crisis Services Task Force 2016) is based on successful models in Arizona and outlines the essential components of a crisis system as crisis lines with "air traffic control" capability, mobile crisis teams, and crisis stabilization facilities.

National Guidelines for Crisis Care: A Best Practice Toolkit (Substance Abuse and Mental Health Services Administration 2020) adopts Crisis Now core services into its "someone to call, someone to respond, somewhere to go" rubric and provides more detailed guidelines for each component.

Roadmap to the Ideal Crisis System: Essential Elements, Measurable Standards and Best Practices for Behavioral Health Crisis Response (Group for the Advancement of Psychiatry 2021) builds on Crisis Now and the SAMHSA guidelines to also address the governance, financing, and oversight needed to support a high-performing crisis system. The Roadmap also expands the continuum to include post-crisis services, which are needed for continued stabilization, successful transition to routine community-based care, and prevention of repeated crisis episodes.

The Crisis Continuum

On the surface, it may seem that access to care problems like ED boarding can be solved by building more inpatient psychiatric beds. However, this approach is contrary to the Supreme Court's *Olmstead* decision, which affirms the rights of people with mental health disabilities to receive the care they need in the most community-integrated (i.e., least restrictive) setting possible. Rather, a system of care is needed with services spanning a continuum of intensity and restrictiveness (Pinals and Fuller 2017). The more robust the continuum, the more the options to meet the person's needs without resorting to EDs, hospitals, or jails. SAMHSA defines a core continuum consisting of three types of services: someone to talk to (crisis lines), someone to respond (mobile crisis), and somewhere to go (crisis facilities). The continuum should include options for individuals who are under involuntary commitment and/or highly agitated because they are the most in need of specialized psychiatric care in lieu of the ED. It is also important to ensure a smooth transition to community-based care so that individuals remain stable after the crisis.

Someone to Call: Crisis Lines, 988, and "Care Traffic Control"

Crisis lines are often the first entry point to crisis services, providing support 24 hours a day, 7 days a week via phone, text, or chat. They vary widely in terms of scope, funding, and staffing. Suicide hotlines often include a mix of clinical professionals and/or volunteers, while warm lines focus on emotional support and are often staffed by peers. In some communities, crisis calls are handled by nonemergency information lines such as 211 and 311. The National Suicide Prevention Lifeline was created by the Substance Abuse and Mental Health Services Administration (SAMHSA) in 2005 to improve access via a single toll-free number (1-800-273-TALK) and promote standardization via a common set of guidelines, training, performance standards, and infrastructure. Studies of Lifeline call centers have found that callers have significantly decreased suicidality during the course of the call (Gould et al. 2007), a third are successfully connected with mental health referrals (Kalafat et al. 2007), and less than a quarter result in law enforcement or EMS being sent without the caller's collaboration (Gould et al. 2016). Implementation of Applied Suicide Intervention Skills Training (ASIST) resulted in callers feeling less depressed, less suicidal, less overwhelmed, and more hopeful by the end of calls handled by ASIST-trained counselors (Gould et al. 2013). The Lifeline chat function has also been shown to be effective at reducing suicidal distress (Gould et al. 2021).

Today, the Lifeline consists of a network of nearly 200 locally operated and funded crisis lines and is linked to the Veterans Crisis Line, with SAMHSA providing oversight via a single administrator, Vibrant Emotional Health. The 2022 implementation of a new universal three-digit crisis hotline number (988) is expected to catalyze even more growth. In addition to increased call volumes as public awareness grows and more crisis lines join the 988/Lifeline network, many crisis lines are expanding their scope beyond suicide counseling to include "care traffic control" functions such as dispatching mobile crisis teams, making outpatient appointments, and bed placement. A growing number of communities are integrating crisis lines into local 911 call centers so that behavioral health calls can be diverted to the crisis line in lieu of a police response.

Someone to Respond: Mobile Crisis Teams (MCTs)

MCTs are typically one- or two-person teams that meet the person where they are—in the ED, at home, or on the street—obviating the need to transport them to a more restrictive level of care for evaluation. MCTs are composed of clinical staff (in contrast to co-responder teams that pair clinicians and law enforcement). MCTs can be staffed by any combination of clinical staff including masters-level clinicians, behavioral health technicians, peers, nurses, paramedics, or emergency medical technicians. Some localities have established centralized dispatch for MCTs, often within crisis call centers, aided by technology such as GPS-enabled mobile apps for location tracking and transmission of clinical information. Studies of MCTs have demonstrated reduction of psychiatric hospitalization and ED utilization (Scott 2000; Guo et al. 2001; Fendrich et al. 2019; Vakkalanka et al. 2021) although additional studies are needed to better define clinical best practices for MCTs.

Somewhere to Go: Specialized Crisis Facilities

Crisis facilities can serve as a safe and therapeutic alternative to hospital EDs, inpatient psychiatric units, and jails. However, crisis programs vary widely in scope, capability, and populations served. Some are designed for low acuity individuals who primarily need peer support and a safe place to spend the night, while others can treat the highest acuity individuals presenting with suicidal behaviors, acute agitation, and substance intoxication. When coupled with the lack of standardized nomenclature, this variation can create confusion and unsafe situations unless expectations are clearly articulated and understood. The Level of Care Utilization System (LOCUS), described in more detail in chapter "Creating Value: Resource and Quality Management", is a useful tool to ensure that the facility capabilities are matched to the individual's clinical needs. A brief description of different types of facilities is outlined below and summarized in Table 1.

Crisis Receiving and Stabilization Facilities (LOCUS Level 6) accept any individual regardless of behavioral acuity or involuntary legal status, including those who may be actively suicidal, acutely agitated, intoxicated, or in withdrawal, arriving directly from the field via law enforcement. To incentivize the police to bring people for treatment, the center must have 24/7 availability, faster drop-off times than jail (10 minutes or less), and a "no wrong door" policy of never turning officers away (Dupont et al. 2007a). They are typically staffed with an interdisciplinary team of psychiatrists and other psychiatric providers, nurses, social workers, behavioral health technicians, and peers, and they may be freestanding or part of an ED or hospital. With rapid assessment, early intervention, and proactive discharge planning, most individuals can be stabilized and discharged to community-based care within 24 hours. This level of crisis care is associated with reduced rates of inpatient psychiatric hospitalization (Little-Upah et al. 2013), ED boarding (Zeller et al. 2014), and arrest (Steadman et al. 2001). Other terms for these programs sometimes include 23-hour observation, Psychiatric Emergency Services (PES), Crisis Stabilization Units (CSU), or EmPATH (Emergency Psychiatric Assessment, Treatment, and Healing) units.

Living Rooms, detoxification centers, and sobering centers (LOCUS Level 5) provide 24/7 alternatives for less acute needs and often accept police drop-offs for those who meet their admission criteria. They are typically unlocked and serve individuals who are voluntary, non-violent, and motivated for help. Living Rooms offer a home-like environment with couches and artwork and are staffed predominantly by peer specialists, with limited coverage by a psychiatrist or other provider. They are especially helpful if psychosocial stressors are the main precipitants of the crisis. Detoxification centers provide medically supervised detoxification services, while sobering centers employ primarily psychosocial and peer support.

Crisis residential, crisis respite, and peer respite (LOCUS Level 5) facilities offer longer-term (days to weeks) stabilization in a residential setting. They are often used as step-down from inpatient or acute crisis care. Some programs may accept low acuity individuals directly from law enforcement.

Crisis clinics or mental health urgent care centers (LOCUS Level 4 and below) offer same-day or walk-in access for outpatient assessment, crisis counseling, medication management, care coordination, and bridge services until the person is connected to appropriate outpatient care.

After the Crisis: Post-Crisis Care

A variety of models have been developed to facilitate the successful transition to community-based care. These range from pre-discharge interventions such as psychoeducation and structured discharge planning, post-discharge interventions such as follow-up phone calls and case management, and transitional interventions that engage with people prior to discharge and continue for some period of time after discharge. These services can be provided by nurses, social workers, case managers, or peers. Small study sizes and the wide variability in program elements, intensity, and duration make comparative research between different models difficult, and effects on readmission rates are often mixed or inconclusive (Bruffaerts et al. 2005). Earlier appointments (within 3 days) are associated with higher attendance and longer community tenure (McCullumsmith et al. 2015). A number of studies focus specifically on suicide-related outcomes, and there is promising evidence that follow-up calls and "caring contacts" (e.g., letters, postcards, text messages, phone calls) decrease repeat suicide attempts (Shand et al.

Table 1 Facility-based crisis services

Model	Description	Level of care	Acuity	Locked	Police drops	Use of peers
Crisis Receiving Center or 23 hour observation	Short-term (<24 hours) assessment and stabilization with hospital-level staffing and safety protocols	LOCUS 6 "Medically Managed" Residential with 24/7 nursing and medical coverage	Can take both low and high acuity/violent patients	Yes	Yes	Yes
Subacute	Short-term (3–5 days) inpatient-like care. Can be reimbursed as crisis via MHBG/SABG				Sometimes	Yes
Living Rooms	Short-term (<24 hours) stabilization in a home-like environment with mostly peer staffing	LOCUS 5 "Medically Monitored" Residential with medical/nursing staff available but not on-site 24/7	Lower acuity patients not at imminent risk of harm to self/other, not agitated or violent	No	Sometimes	Yes
Sobering centers and "Social Detox"	Short-term (<24 hours) stabilization for patients with substance use needs, typically not using meds			No	Sometimes	Yes
Crisis residential	Intermediate-term (days to a couple weeks) crisis stabilization in a residential setting			No	Usually not	Yes

Examples of facility-based crisis services and how they differ in terms of intensity, population served, and LOCUS level of care. Without national standards, any of these different programs might be called a "crisis stabilization unit" depending on state and local regulations

2019) and are cost-effective (Hegedüs et al. 2020).

Intersection with Law Enforcement

The Sequential Intercept Model (SIM) is a well-established framework for mental health/justice system collaboration and service design (Munetz and Griffin 2006). It describes the typical pathway through criminal justice system for a person with behavioral health needs and identifies opportunities for the healthcare system to intervene, with Intercept 1 focused on law enforcement collaboration. An additional Intercept 0 was later added to capture the opportunity for crisis systems to intervene even earlier and prevent law enforcement involvement altogether. In this framework, crisis services are considered a means of "pre-arrest diversion" from the justice system, meaning that the person is connected to care instead of being arrested and charged. SIM is discussed in more detail in chapter "Collaborative Reduction of Criminal Justice Involvement for Persons with Mental Illness".

In recent years, social justice and policing reform movements like Black Lives Matter have increased the momentum for rethinking and reducing law enforcement's role in responding to behavioral emergencies. Ideally, behavioral health emergencies should be routed to clinical interventions such as telephonic crisis counseling, MCTs, or facility-based crisis care. Law enforcement involvement is unlikely to be completely eliminated, however, as some situations may pose an unacceptable amount of safety risk to civilian clinicians while other behavioral health emergencies may not become apparent until after officers are on scene for another issue. Even if clinical crisis care options exist, civil commitment laws often require law enforcement to transport individuals to treatment facilities. (However, a survey of law enforcement agencies estimated that 65% of these transports did not pose a risk of harm to others and could be completed by another entity (Treatment Advocacy Center 2019). Many of these laws were written decades ago and should be updated to include earlier interventions and alternative crisis responses rather than relying so heavily on police.)

Collaboration between law enforcement and the crisis system is needed to create the optimal response for each situation, and the responders—whether law enforcement officers or clinicians—require appropriate training and a behavioral health crisis system that can quickly accept individuals in crisis and provide the care they need in the safest and least restrictive setting possible.

The Crisis Intervention Team (CIT) Model

CIT provides law enforcement with tools to recognize individuals experiencing a behavioral health crisis, de-escalate them, and divert them to treatment instead of jail. CIT began in the late 1980s in Memphis, Tennessee, in response to a police shooting involving a Black man with mental illness. Its centerpiece is a 40-hour training that involves scenario-based exercises and participation of community stakeholders including behavioral health clinicians, treatment agencies, people with lived experience of mental illness, families, and advocacy groups. (Volunteering to help with CIT training is an excellent way for psychiatrists to develop partnerships with local law enforcement.)

The National Council for Mental Wellbeing and CIT International both recommend that 100% of a department's uniformed patrol officers receive a basic 8-hour training such as Mental Health First Aid for Public Safety, while the 40-hour CIT training is voluntarily undertaken by a subset of officers large enough to ensure 24/7 availability of trained officers to respond to calls for service. 911 personnel should also receive training to help them dispatch CIT-trained officers when needed. This approach ensures both a basic level of competency among all officers and 24/7 availability of a specialized CIT response (Margiotta and Gibb 2016).

While CIT is often thought of as a police training program, its creators continue to underscore that training is only one piece of a more comprehensive approach. Once officers are trained to identify a person in crisis and divert them to treatment, their first question is often "divert to what?" Thus, the full CIT model recommends a crisis system with quick and easy access and 24/7 availability (Dupont et al. 2007b).

CIT encourages communities to adapt the model to its needs, allowing departments to develop their own curricula and tailor processes to work with local mental health systems. While pragmatic, this approach creates research challenges (Watson et al. 2019). Without a standard implementation or fidelity tool to measure variability across programs, comparative research is difficult, and studies are often mixed or inconclusive. There is strong evidence that CIT training improves officers' knowledge, attitudes about mental illness and treatment, and self-efficacy for interacting with someone suicidal or psychotic (Compton et al. 2014a). When comparing the behavior of CIT-trained versus non-trained officers in the field, CIT-trained officers are more likely to report verbal de-escalation as the highest level of force used (Compton et al. 2014b), use less force with more resistant subjects (Angell et al. 2012), and refer or transport to mental health treatment, but the effect on arrests is mixed (Compton et al. 2014b; Watson et al. 2010, 2011). Similarly, system-level studies of outcomes pre-post-implementation show increases in transports to mental health facilities (Kubiak et al. 2017) but contradictory results in overall cost-effectiveness (Cowell et al. 2004; El-Mallakh et al. 2014). Some of this variability may be related to officer selection. Newer research demonstrates that compared to officers mandated to receive CIT training, voluntarily trained officers demonstrate better self-efficacy, de-escalation skills, and referral decisions. Even when physical force was documented, voluntarily trained CIT officers were more likely to refer to treatment services and less likely to make an arrest (T. Compton et al. 2017). Another potential source of variation may be the availability of mental health crisis services available in a given community (Steadman et al. 2000).

Co-responder Models

A variety of co-responder models are emerging in which officers respond to crisis calls with a clinician, peer, or other social services staff. Teams may ride and respond together, arrive separately, or involve the clinician via phone or video. There is no consensus on which model is most effective, and programs should be adapted to the local needs, such as geography and service availability. Qualitative research indicates that most people prefer MCT or co-responder teams to police-only teams (Boscarato 2014). In particular, they value responders with mental health knowledge and verbal de-escalation skills and a compassionate, empowering, and non-criminalizing approach (Lamanna et al. 2018). Studies of other outcomes have been mixed (Watson et al. 2019). A review of police and mental health co-responder programs concluded that these programs decreased arrests and the amount of time officers spent handling mental health calls, but evidence was limited for other impacts (Shapiro et al. 2015). Furthermore, many programs are limited in hours or operation or geographical area served. In particular, programs experience difficulty when there is a lack of community mental health resources.

911 Integration

Integration of crisis line functions with 911 systems is an emerging area of innovation. By identifying behavioral health emergencies as early as possible, callers can be triaged to the clinical intervention, such as telephonic crisis counseling or dispatch of an MCT to the person's location, without the need for law enforcement involvement. Strategies include protocols for call triage and transfer to the crisis line, physical co-location of crisis line staff within 911, and virtual co-location via shared access to computer-aided dispatch systems.

Putting it All Together: Crisis System Versus Crisis Services

While each of the individual programs described in this chapter may improve outcomes, the impact is multiplied when a robust continuum of programs and services work together as a coordinated system to achieve common goals (Balfour et al. 2021). This approach is illustrated in Fig. 1. In this model, based on the crisis system in Tucson, Arizona, healthcare and law enforcement stakeholders agree on a common goal of preventing avoidable jail, ED, and hospital use by providing care in the least restrictive setting that can safely meet the needs of an individual experiencing a crisis. Because less restrictive settings tend to be less costly, clinical and financial goals are aligned as well. The crisis continuum is composed of an array of services organized along a continuum of intensity, restrictiveness, and cost. At all points along the continuum, easy access for law enforcement (e.g., 911 co-location, co-responder teams, "no wrong door" policies) facilitates connection to treatment instead of arrest.

Governance and accountability are key to ensuring that crisis services operate as an organized and coordinated system. In the Arizona model, the Regional Behavioral Health Authority (RBHA) serves as the "accountable entity" via its role as the single payer and regulator for the crisis system. The RBHA contracts with multiple service providers to create the crisis continuum and set expectations for system performance that are aligned with overarching system goals. Contracts confer a "preferred customer" status to law enforcement, so that, for example, response time targets for MCTs are faster for calls that involve law enforcement. The RBHA is financed via braided funding from a variety of sources (e.g., Medicaid, SAMHSA block grants, state and local funds) and accountable to the state for both clinical and fiscal outcomes.

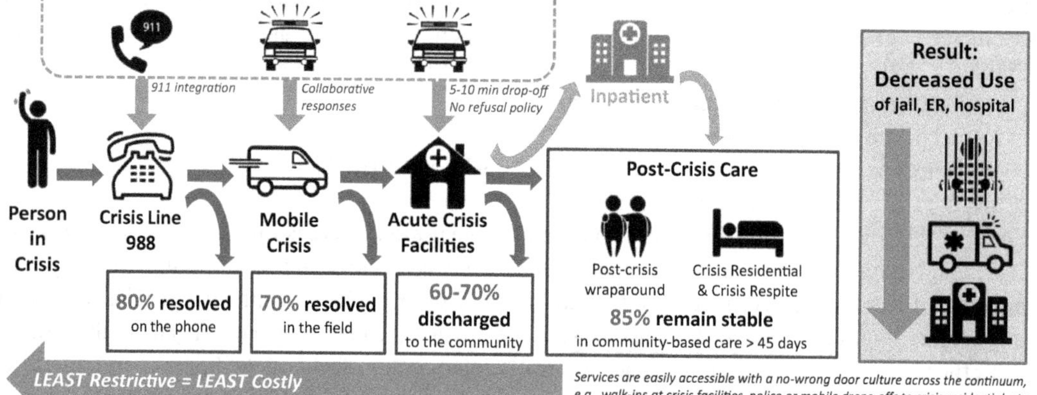

Fig. 1 Alignment of crisis services toward a common goal. In a high-functioning system, the individual services in the continuum work together to achieve a common goal, in this case, stabilization in the least restrictive (which is also the least costly) level of care. Data is provided courtesy of Johnnie Gasper at Arizona Complete Health/Centene and applies to the southern Arizona geographical service area for 2019 (Cochise, Graham, Greenlee, La Paz, Pima, Pinal, Santa Cruz, and Yuma counties). Crisis line resolved calls is the percentage of calls resolved without dispatching MCT, LE, or EMS. MCT resolved cases is the percentage of face-to-face encounters resolved without the need for transport to a higher level of care. Crisis facilities community disposition is the percentage of discharges to levels of care other than hospital, ED, or jail. Continued stabilization is the percentage of individuals with an MCT or crisis facility encounter who did not have a subsequent ED visit or hospitalization within 45 days

Cost Savings Across Systems

The power of a systems approach becomes apparent when considering the impact across multiple silos. For example, an analysis of the crisis system in Maricopa County, Arizona, which includes many of the elements described in this chapter, estimated that a $100 million investment in crisis care resulted in savings of $260 million in psychiatric inpatient spending, $37 million in ED costs, 45 years of ED psychiatric boarding hours, and 37 full-time equivalents (FTEs) of police officer time and salary (Crisis Tech 360 2018).

Financing

Crisis financing models are rapidly evolving, vary widely by state, and often draw upon multiple funding sources. From a parity standpoint, the cost of providing crisis care can and should be primarily financed via Medicaid and other healthcare payers, as is care for other health emergencies. Supplemental funds are needed for nonbillable services such as admin, infrastructure maintenance, caring for the uninsured, and the idle capacity needed to staff to a "firehouse model" that ensures services are always available (Shaw 2020). State general funds, local funds, and federal block grants are often used for this purpose, and SAMHSA added an annual crisis "set aside" to the Mental Health Block Grant in 2021. Medicaid 1115, 1915(b), or 1915(c) waivers provide states a powerful tool to braid together multiple funding streams, maximizing efficiency and accessibility by pooling resources to create a common safety net crisis infrastructure that can serve anyone in need, regardless of payer (Substance Abuse and Mental Health Services Administration 2014).

The 988 implementation has been an impetus for states to bolster crisis infrastructure via federal planning grants, telecom fees, and new appropriations of state funds for crisis services. Emerging financing models such as value-based payments provide additional mechanisms to invest in crisis and other social services (Hogan and Goldman 2021).

In contrast, Medicare and most private health plans provide little or no coverage for crisis services, and oftentimes the care for their members is financed by the safety net mechanisms described above. These payers must be held accountable to provide parity coverage for behavioral health emergency care. The Centers for Medicare & Medicaid Services (CMS) Emergency Triage, Treat, and Transport (ET3) demonstration program provides parity Medicare reimbursement for EMS to transport to "alternative" destinations other than the ED, including crisis facilities. Models like this are a step in the right direction.

Data and Quality Improvement

At the individual level, data sharing can help law enforcement agencies and behavioral health providers coordinate care. For example, knowing that someone is receiving behavioral health services can help officers choose the right intervention. Conversely, law enforcement often has information about past interactions and psychosocial factors that can aid clinicians in their assessment. The Health Insurance Portability and Accountability Act (HIPAA) is often seen as a barrier but does allow data sharing in emergencies. Data can also be shared via Business Associate Agreements (BAA) or by obtaining consent from the individual receiving services. When developing protocols, it is important to reach consensus regarding relevant state and federal laws and to include input from stakeholders with lived experience so that concerns about privacy and other potential negative consequences of data sharing can be addressed.

At the system level, data is a powerful tool for quality improvement (Balfour et al. 2018) and will also be increasingly tied to financing as alternative payment models evolve. However, very few quality measurement standards exist for crisis services. Some standard measures are in use by crisis call centers (Wireline Competition Bureau and Office of Economics and Analytics 2019), and a measure set for crisis facilities has been proposed (Balfour et al. 2016). Reporting through SAMHSA's Uniform Reporting System may be expanded to include crisis metrics as a condition of the new MHBG crisis services set aside (Hogan and Goldman 2021). In the meantime, communities can choose metrics that guide their system toward common goals. For example, in Fig. 1, the various system components report the percentage of individuals stabilized without the need for a higher level of care. Each of these measures is one facet of the overarching goal of crisis stabilization in the least restrictive setting possible.

Data is an important tool in addressing disparities and racial bias. Stratifying outcomes by race, gender, socioeconomic status, and other demographic characteristics can reveal inequities in access to quality care. Disparities in key law enforcement outcomes such as use of force, arrest, and connection to care can reveal implicit bias in policing (Council of State Governments 2019). Openly and transparently sharing such data with the public is an important first step toward gaining trust and implementing policies to address these problems.

Research Considerations

As crisis services rapidly expand across the nation, there is an urgent need to deepen the evidence base. Established clinical standards are needed to guide program implementation, set quality benchmarks, justify financing, and ensure that equity and justice diversion goals are truly being achieved. Current quality measurement in crisis services tends to focus on descriptive structure measures (e.g., how many teams, how many beds) and simple process measures (e.g., response times, call and visit duration). To expand the evidence base for these services, programs will need to collect more sophisticated outcome measures (e.g., suicide rate, overdose rate, symptom reduction, client satisfaction). Equity analyses that stratify measures by race and ethnicity are needed to examine impact on disparities for all of these measures.

Researchers and stakeholders must come together to develop a research agenda for crisis services, with direct involvement of people with lived experience. Federal funding of mental health services research is needed both from the National Institute of Mental Health to develop clinical models and from federal agencies such as SAMHSA to promote evaluation in a "services to science" paradigm. Technical assistance to programs can promote best practices for obtaining, linking, and analyzing complex multi-sector data for both quality and research purposes. Advocates can support this work by including mandates and funding for rigorous evaluation in crisis legislation. By bridging entrenched silos between health officials and academic partners, learning communities can be built to support and sustain these efforts.

Addressing Racism and Inequity via a "Health-First" Approach

The crisis system has been called "a cauldron of the intersection of the criminal legal system with the health care system, both of which have well-documented histories of disproportionately negative outcomes for Black, Indigenous, and People of Color (BIPOC)" (Fountain House 2021). This history underscores the importance of involving communities of color and people with lived experience in the design, delivery, and oversight of crisis services. While each community will have its own unique experiences and priorities, initiatives like the Front End Project have begun to define a unifying set of principles and strategies based on input from a diverse convening of cross-sector subject matter experts, many of whom with lived experience as recipients of crisis services. The resulting report *From Harm to Health: Centering Racial Equity and Lived Experience in Mental Health Crisis Response* envisions a "health-first" approach that is centered around public health rather than public safety. A public health framing shifts the focus away from law enforcement in favor of clinical services centered on crisis response, recovery, and prevention. Social determinants of health and systemic racism are framed as upstream risk factors for future crisis and thus become targets for ongoing prevention efforts after the acute crisis. Other key principles include significant involvement of peers, self-determination and autonomy through the use of Psychiatric Advance Directives, and use of alternatives to emergency departments.

Improving Crisis Care in Your Community via Stakeholder Engagement

Strong partnerships are critical to generating the enthusiasm and political will to design, fund, and implement crisis systems and ensure they function effectively on an ongoing basis. Potential stakeholders include state and local governmental agencies, payers, law enforcement, 911, behavioral health providers, social service agencies, advocacy groups, and individuals with lived experience of a behavioral health crisis. It is critical that these processes actively engage and incorporate input from community members with lived experience of receiving crisis services.

How to begin largely depends on the dynamics of each local community. Momentum may be driven by county leadership seeking to reduce the jail population, hospital leaders strained by ED boarding, or community leaders advocating for policing reform. Collaborative groups can be built upon existing organizational infrastructure (e.g., a county task force or CIT steering committee) or created de novo. For communities just beginning to organize, data collection can be a good first step. Data helps to engage stakeholders, build the business case for investing in crisis services, and garner trust and legitimacy via transparency. Most localities already have at least some components of a crisis system, and system mapping exercises such as Sequential Intercept Mapping serve as a process to both ensure understanding of the existing context and engage additional stakeholders. The Stepping Up Initiative (stepuptogether.org) challenges counties to sign a resolution pledging to reduce the prevalence of mental illness in jails and includes a framework for engaging stakeholders, setting goals, and learning from the over 500 counties who have made the pledge thus far.

Successful collaborations are iterative and longitudinal and may begin with small, simple improvements that require no additional resources (e.g., setting up a process for partners to communicate with one another). By building on the success of these "easy wins," partners can progress to more sophisticated solutions. Eventually, the collaborative is no longer building a crisis system but rather monitoring and improving the system they built.

Role of Psychiatrists

Crisis care is nuanced and complex, in terms of both clinical assessment and intervention at the individual patient level and coordination of care across the multiple systems involved in crisis response. With such complexity come significant risks for negative outcomes and the need for clinical expertise and leadership. Psychiatrists are an integral part of the interdisciplinary care team and can provide clinical care in a variety of settings ranging from direct in-person care at a crisis stabilization facility to as-needed telepsychiatry support to MCTs in the field. Psychiatrists often play a key role in civil commitment processes as well. As the medical director of a crisis program, psychiatrists ensure that clinical activities, policies, and procedures meet the standard of care and are appropriate and effective in responding to crises.

As crisis services grow, new opportunities are emerging for psychiatrists to provide medical leadership at the system level. Similar to how emergency medical services have system-wide medical directors, a crisis services medical director can be uniquely positioned to provide direction and oversight of administrative, operational, educational, and clinical activities related to crisis care (National Council for Mental Wellbeing 2022). Even if not in a formal medical director role, psychiatrists can serve as effective advocates and educators, for example, volunteering to give a lecture for CIT training. Opportunities for psychiatrists will only increase as the field continues to evolve. It is an exciting time for the crisis field!

References

Angell, B., Morabito, M. S., Kerr, A. N., Watson, A., Draine, J., & Ottati, V. (2012). Crisis Intervention Teams and People With Mental Illness: Exploring. *Crime & Delinquency*, *58*(1), 57–77.

Balfour, M. E., Hahn Stephenson, A., Delany-Brumsey, A., Winsky, J., & Goldman, M. L. (2021). Cops, Clinicians, or Both? Collaborative Approaches to Responding to Behavioral Health Emergencies. *Psychiatric Services*, appi.ps.202000721. https://doi.org/10.1176/appi.ps.202000721

Balfour, M. E., Tanner, K., Jurica, P. J., Rhoads, R., & Carson, C. A. (2016). Crisis Reliability Indicators Supporting Emergency Services (CRISES): A Framework for Developing Performance Measures for Behavioral Health Crisis and Psychiatric Emergency Programs. *Community Mental Health Journal*, *52*(1), 1–9. https://doi.org/10.1007/s10597-015-9954-5

Balfour, M. E., Zinn, T. E., Cason, K., Fox, J., Morales, M., Berdeja, C., & Gray, J. (2018). Provider-Payer Partnerships as an Engine for Continuous Quality Improvement. *Psychiatric Services (Washington, D.C.)*, *69*(6), 623–625. https://doi.org/10.1176/appi.ps.201700533

Boscarato, K. L. S. (2014). *Consumer experience of formal crisis-response services and preferred methods of crisis intervention*. *4*, 287–295.

Bruffaerts, R., Sabbe, M., & Demyttenaere, K. (2005). Predicting community tenure in patients with recurrent utilization of a psychiatric emergency service. *General Hospital Psychiatry*, *27*(4), 269–274.

Compton, M. T., Bakeman, R., Broussard, B., Hankerson-Dyson, D., Husbands, L., Krishan, S., Stewart-Hutto, T., D'Orio, B. M., Oliva, J. R., Thompson, N. J., & Watson, A. C. (2014a). The Police-Based Crisis Intervention Team (CIT) Model: I. Effects on Officers' Knowledge, Attitudes, and Skills. *Psychiatric Services*, *65*(4), 517–522. https://doi.org/10.1176/appi.ps.201300107

Compton, M. T., Bakeman, R., Broussard, B., Hankerson-Dyson, D., Husbands, L., Krishan, S., Stewart-Hutto, T., D'Orio, B. M., Oliva, J. R., Thompson, N. J., & Watson, A. C. (2014b). The Police-Based Crisis Intervention Team (CIT) Model: II. Effects on Level of Force and Resolution, Referral, and Arrest. *Psychiatric Services*, *65*(4), 523–529. https://doi.org/10.1176/appi.ps.201300108

Council of State Governments. (2019). *Police-Mental Health Collaborations: A Framework for Implementing Effective Law Enforcement Responses for People Who Have Mental Health Needs*. https://csgjusticecenter.org/publications/police-mental-health-collaborations-a-framework-for-implementing-effective-law-enforcement-responses-for-people-who-have-mental-health-needs/

Cowell, A. J., Broner, N., & Dupont, R. (2004). The cost-effectiveness of criminal justice diversion programs for people with serious mental illness co-occurring with substance abuse: Four case studies. *Journal of Contemporary Criminal Justice*, *20*(3), 292–314.

Crisis Tech 360. (2018). *Business Case: The Crisis Now Model*. https://crisisnow.com/wp-content/uploads/2020/02/CrisisNow-BusinessCase.pdf

Dupont R, Cochran S, & Pillsbury S. (2007a). *Crisis Intervention Team core elements. The University of Memphis School of Urban Affairs and Public Policy, Department of Criminology and Criminal*. The University of Memphis School of Urban Affairs and Public Policy, Department of Criminology and Criminal.

Dupont Randolph, Cochran Sam, & Pillsbury Sarah. (2007b). *Crisis Intervention Team Core Elements Randolph Dupont, PhD University of Memphis Major Sam Cochran, MS Memphis Police Services Sarah Pillsbury, MA University of Memphis 2*. The University of Memphis School of Urban Affairs and Public Policy Department of Criminology and Criminal Justice CIT Center. http://cit.memphis.edu/CoreElements.pdf

El-Mallakh, P. L., Kiran, K., & El-Mallakh, R. S. (2014). Costs and savings associated with implementation of a police crisis intervention team. *Southern Medical Journal*, *107*(6), 391–395.

Fendrich, M., Ives, M., Kurz, B., Becker, J., Vanderploeg, J., Bory, C., Lin, H.-J., & Plant, R. (2019). Impact of Mobile Crisis Services on Emergency Department Use Among Youths With Behavioral Health Service Needs. *Psychiatric Services*, appi.ps.201800450. https://doi.org/10.1176/appi.ps.201800450

Fountain House. (2021). *From Harm to Health: Centering Racial Equity and Lived Experience in Mental Health Crisis Response*. https://www.fountainhouse.org/assets/From-Harm-to-Health-2021.pdf

Gould, M. S., Chowdhury, S., Lake, A. M., Galfalvy, H., Kleinman, M., Kuchuk, M., & McKeon, R. (2021). National Suicide Prevention Lifeline crisis chat interventions: Evaluation of chatters' perceptions of effectiveness. *Suicide and Life-Threatening Behavior*, *n/a*(n/a). https://doi.org/10.1111/sltb.12795

Gould, M. S., Cross, W., Pisani, A. R., Munfakh, J. L., & Kleinman, M. (2013). Impact of Applied Suicide Intervention Skills Training on the National Suicide Prevention Lifeline. *Suicide & Life-Threatening Behavior*, *43*(6), 676–691. https://doi.org/10.1111/sltb.12049

Gould MS, Kalafat J, Harrismunfakh JL, & Kleinman M. (2007). *An evaluation of crisis hotline outcomes. Part 2: Suicidal callers* (No. 3). *37*(3), 338–352.

Gould MS, Lake AM, & Munfakh JLH. (2016). *Helping callers to the national suicide prevention lifeline who are at imminent risk of suicide: Evaluation of caller risk profiles and interventions implemented* (No. 2). *46*(2), 172–190.

Group for the Advancement of Psychiatry. (2021). *Roadmap to the Ideal Crisis System: Essential Elements. Measurable Standards and Best Practices for Behavioral Health Crisis Response*. National Council for Mental Wellbeing. https://www.crisis-roadmap.com

Guo, S., Biegel, D. E., Johnsen, J. A., & Dyches, H. (2001). Assessing the Impact of Community-Based Mobile Crisis Services on Preventing Hospitalization. *Psychiatric Services, 52*(2), 223–228. https://doi.org/10.1176/appi.ps.52.2.223

Hegedüs, A., Kozel, B., Richter, D., & Behrens, J. (2020). Effectiveness of transitional interventions in improving patient outcomes and service use after discharge from psychiatric inpatient care: A systematic review and meta-analysis. *Frontiers in Psychiatry, 10*, 969.

Hogan, M. F., & Goldman, M. L. (2021). New Opportunities to Improve Mental Health Crisis Systems. *Psychiatric Services, 72*(2):169-173. doi: https://doi.org/10.1176/appi.ps.202000114. Epub 2020 Sep 29.

Kalafat J, Gould MS, Munfakh JLH, & Kleinman M. (2007). *An evaluation of crisis hotline outcomes. Part 1: Nonsuicidal crisis callers* (No. 3). *37*(3), 322–337.

Kubiak, S., Comartin, E., Milanovic, E., Bybee, D., Tillander, E., Rabaut, C., Bisson, H., Dunn, L. M., Bouchard, M. J., & Hill, T. (2017). Countywide implementation of crisis intervention teams: Multiple methods, measures and sustained outcomes. *Behavioral Sciences & the Law, 35*(5–6), 456–469.

Lamanna, D., Shapiro, G. K., Kirst, M., Matheson, F. I., Nakhost, A., & Stergiopoulos, V. (2018). Co-responding police-mental health programmes: Service user experiences and outcomes in a large urban centre. *International Journal of Mental Health Nursing, 27*(2), 891–900. https://doi.org/10.1111/inm.12384

Little-Upah, P., et al. (2013). *The Banner psychiatric center: A model for providing psychiatric crisis care to the community while easing behavioral health holds in emergency departments. 17*(1), 45–49.

Margiotta, N., & Gibb, B. (2016). *Mental Health First Aid or CIT: What Should Law Enforcement Do?* National Council for Mental Wellbeing. https://perma.cc/9TPC-DMHS

McCullumsmith, C., Clark, B., Blair, C., Cropsey, K., & Shelton, R. (2015). Rapid follow-up for patients after psychiatric crisis. *Community Mental Health Journal, 51*(2), 139–144. https://doi.org/10.1007/s10597-014-9782-z

Munetz MR & Griffin PA. (2006). *Use of the sequential intercept model as an approach to decriminalization of people with mental illness. 57*, 544–549.

National Action Alliance for Suicide Prevention: Crisis Services Task Force. (2016). *Crisis Now: Transforming Services is Within Our Reach.* Education Development Center, Inc. https://theactionalliance.org/sites/default/files/inline-files/CrisisNow%5B1%5D.pdf

National Council for Mental Wellbeing. (2022). *Psychiatric Leadership in Crisis Systems: The Role of the Crisis Services Medical Director.* https://www.thenationalcouncil.org/wp-content/uploads/2022/01/22.01.25_MDI-Psychiatric-Leadership-in-Crisis-Systems-FINAL.pdf?daf=375ateTbd56

Pinals, D. A., & Fuller, D. A. (2017). *Beyond Beds: The Vital Role of a Full Continuum of Psychiatric Care.* National Association of State Mental Health Program Directors. https://www.nasmhpd.org/sites/default/files/TAC.Paper_.1Beyond_Beds.pdf

Scott RL. (2000). *Evaluation of a mobile crisis program: Effectiveness, efficiency, and consumer satisfaction.* (No. 9). *51*(9), 1153–1156.

Shand, F., Woodward, A., McGill, K., et al. (2019). *Suicide Aftercare Services: An Evidence Check Rapid Review.* The Sax Institute. https://www.saxinstitute.org.au/wp-content/uploads/2019_Suicide-Aftercare-Services-Report.pdf

Shapiro GK, Cusi A, Kirst M, O'Campo P, Nakhost A, & Stergiopoulos V. (2015). *Co-responding police-mental health programs: A review* (No. 5). *42*(5), 606–620.

Shaw, R. (2020). *Financing Mental Health Crisis Services.* National Association of Mental Health Program Directors. https://www.nasmhpd.org/sites/default/files/2020paper7.pdf

Steadman, H. J., Deane, M. W., Borum, R., & Morrissey, J. P. (2000). Comparing outcomes of major models of police responses to mental health emergencies. *Psychiatric Services (Washington, D.C.), 51*(5), 645–649. https://doi.org/10.1176/appi.ps.51.5.645

Steadman, H. J., Stainbrook, K. A., Griffin, P., Draine, J., Dupont, R., & Horey, C. (2001). A specialized crisis response site as a core element of police-based diversion programs. *Psychiatric Services (Washington, D.C.), 52*(2), 219–222. https://doi.org/10.1176/appi.ps.52.2.219

Substance Abuse and Mental Health Services Administration. (2014). *Crisis Services: Effectiveness, Cost- Effectiveness, and Funding Strategies* (HHS Publication No. (SMA)-14-4848). Substance Abuse and Mental Health Services Administration. https://store.samhsa.gov/system/files/sma14-4848.pdf

Substance Abuse and Mental Health Services Administration. (2020). *National Guidelines for Behavioral Health Crisis Care—Best Practice Toolkit.* https://www.samhsa.gov/sites/default/files/national-guidelines-for-behavioral-health-crisis-care-02242020.pdf

T. Compton, M., Bakeman, R., Broussard, B., D'Orio, B., & C. Watson, A. (2017). Police officers' volunteering for (rather than being assigned to) Crisis Intervention Team (CIT) training: Evidence for a beneficial self-selection effect. *Behavioral Sciences & the Law, 35*(5–6), 470–479.

Treatment Advocacy Center. (2019). *The Road Runners: The Role and Impact of Law Enforcement in Transporting Individuals with Severe Mental Illness.* https://www.treatmentadvocacycenter.org/road-runners

Vakkalanka, J. P., Neuhas, R. A., Harland, K. K., Clemsen, L., Himadi, E., & Lee, S. (2021). Mobile Crisis Outreach and Emergency Department Utilization: A Propensity Score-matched Analysis. *Western Journal of Emergency Medicine: Integrating Emergency Care with Population Health*, *22*(5). https://doi.org/10.5811/westjem.2021.6.52276

Watson, A. C., Ottati, V. C., Draine, J., & Morabito, M. (2011). CIT in context: The impact of mental health resource availability and district saturation on call dispositions. *International Journal of Law and Psychiatry*, *34*(4), 287–294.

Watson, A. C., Ottati, V. C., Morabito, M., Draine, J., Kerr, A. N., & Angell, B. (2010). Outcomes of police contacts with persons with mental illness: The impact of CIT. *Administration and Policy in Mental Health and Mental Health Services Research*, *37*(4), 302–317.

Watson AC, Compton MT, & Pope LT. (2019). *Crisis Response Services for People with Mental Illnesses or Intellectual and Developmental Disabilities: A Review of the Literature on Police-based and Other First Response Models*. Vera Institute of Justice.

Wireline Competition Bureau & Office of Economics and Analytics. (2019, August 14). *Report on the National Suicide Hotline Improvement Act of 2018*. Federal Communications Commission. https://docs.fcc.gov/public/attachments/DOC-359095A1.pdf

Zeller, S., Calma, N., & Stone, A. (2014). Effects of a dedicated regional psychiatric emergency service on boarding of psychiatric patients in area emergency departments. *The Western Journal of Emergency Medicine*, *15*(1), 1–6. https://doi.org/10.5811/westjem.2013.6.17848

Part V

Creating Healthy Communities

Epidemiology in Community Psychiatry

Andrew Wooyoung Kim and Ezra Susser

Psychiatric epidemiology has played a central role in shaping the development of psychiatric care in the community over a period of 150 years. Signal developments in the evolution of community psychiatry emerged in tandem with psychiatric epidemiology in the mid-nineteenth century and again in the mid-twentieth century (Susser et al. 2010). In the current era, this close relationship continues, especially in the effort to "close the mental health gap," that is, give the same priority to mental as to other health conditions in national as well as global health initiatives.

In this chapter, we offer an introduction to two central topics in psychiatric epidemiology: (1) observational studies of incidence and prevalence and (2) observational studies of causes. These concepts are then exemplified in a case study from South Africa, which examines the mental health impacts of the 2019 coronavirus (COVID-19) pandemic in Soweto, a major urban township located southwest of Johannesburg. We omit key research areas that emerged from psychiatric epidemiology before branching out as partially separate disciplines that are still closely related to epidemiology: randomized clinical trials (especially preventive trials), mental health services research, and cross-cultural psychiatric research. For more in-depth discussion and a wider range of topics, see this chapter's references (Bhattacharya et al. 2010; Frank and Glied 2006; Susser et al. 2006; Thornicroft and Tansella 2009; Tsuang et al. 2011). For more on services research, also see chapter "Mental Health Services Research and Informatics".

Incidence and Prevalence

It is useful to distinguish between two measures of disease/disorder occurrence, prevalence, and incidence, as they serve distinct purposes for community psychiatry. *Prevalence* is the number of cases of disease or disorder in a given population at a particular time or during a particular time frame. Prevalence includes both new and existing cases. Prevalence is useful to determine the burden of disease and helps to determine the demand for care and services. *Incidence* is the occurrence of new cases of disease or disorder over a specified period of time in a given population. Thus, incidence times duration is equal to prevalence. Incidence is expressed as a rate, reflecting the change in cases of disease over

A. W. Kim
Department of Anthropology, University of California, Berkeley, Berkeley, CA, United States
e-mail: awkim@berkeley.edu

E. Susser (✉)
Departments of Epidemiology and Psychiatry, Mailman School of Public Health, Columbia University, New York State Psychiatric Institute, New York, NY, USA
e-mail: ess8@columbia.edu

W. E. Sowers et al. (eds.), *Textbook of Community Psychiatry*,
https://doi.org/10.1007/978-3-031-10239-4_28

time. In community psychiatry, incidence is particularly useful in surveillance (i.e., is the number of new cases per year of autism on the rise in the United States?) for determining causes of disease (i.e., why is the number of new cases per year of autism on the rise? Is it because the distribution of some risk factor has shifted such that it is more common?). We discuss studies that use these measures of disease occurrence and their utility in depth below.

Prevalence of Common Mental Disorders

Cross-sectional studies that measured prevalence of common mental disorders in adults comprise a large swath of the observational epidemiologic studies informing community psychiatry. Such studies have for decades cataloged the burden of various mental disorders, thereby determining the need for services. In tandem, these studies often have examined patterns of service use, thus providing a critical epidemiologic frame for the distribution and provision of psychiatric care in the community. Such studies have both a fundamental utility and a rich history that has transcended shifting notions of what causes mental illness over time. This section of the chapter highlights the context, contributions, and limitations of key cross-sectional studies over time to community psychiatry, with special attention to the United States. These studies, which have been related integrally to public health policy, have established primarily that mental disorders are common and disabling and that there is a need to reconcile gaps in service use with disorder burden.

The Burden of Proof: The Midtown Manhattan and Stirling County Studies

Severe shortages in psychiatric services during World War II formed an advocacy platform for leading psychiatrists in the United States and cemented the foundation for critical policy shifts in the postwar years. The community became the focus of renewed attention generated by the interplay between the field of psychiatry and policymakers in the United States. The National Mental Health Act of 1946 initiated a cascade of funding for psychiatric education and research that resulted in the establishment of the National Institute of Mental Health in 1949 and financial support for epidemiologic research in service of community psychiatry. Over the ensuing decades, an institutional and research context took shape in which the dynamic between community psychiatry and public policy would play out. Generations of key cross-sectional studies, which we examine here, were born of this marriage.

One of the earliest community-based cross-sectional studies conducted in the context of policy shifts and blossoming psychiatric research and education was the Midtown Manhattan Study (Srole et al. 1962). The purpose of the Midtown Study, initiated in 1952, was tripartite: to canvas the community for variations in mental health, to examine sociocultural determinants of mental health, and to establish the need for psychiatric services in the community. The Midtown Study examined mental health in 1660 adults culled from 1911 Midtown dwellings, selected as a probability sample. All participants were white, ethnically heterogeneous, and similar in age and sex to the Midtown population, comprising approximately 100,000 adults. The outcomes of Midtown were framed and defined in terms of health. Among several sources of data, interviewers collected data about symptoms and described systematically their observations.

One or more psychiatrists evaluated all of the components for each participant to arrive at an ecologically informed global judgment, which ranged from extremes of "symptom-free" to "incapacitated," and included intermediate grades of symptom severity. Impairment in one or more areas of social functioning was chosen, according to the investigators, as the "arbitrary benchmark of morbidity" (Srole et al. 1962). By and large, the same ecological approach and set of methods employed by the Midtown Manhattan Study were used by Alexander Leighton, himself a Midtown investigator, in the non-urban context of Stirling County, Nova Scotia. It reflected the recognition that the specificity of the context necessarily influenced the specific distribution of psychopathology—a hallmark of early epidemiologic studies informing community psychiatry. The Stirling County study also collected information on disorders as defined by the first edition of the *Diagnostic and Statistical Manual* (DSM-I) (Association 1952; Leighton 1959; Leighton et al. 1963a, b).

Importantly, because of the pitfalls of measuring lifetime disorders, Midtown and Stirling County investigators studied the point prevalence of psychiatric morbidity, which would become a standard metric in the major psychiatric epidemiologic studies that would follow. Over 80% of those surveyed, chosen to reflect the ethnic heterogeneity of Midtown, had some form of psychopathology. About a quarter (23.4%) were classified as impaired, signifying the presence of marked, severe, or incapacitating symptoms—mostly anxiety. Moreover, about three quarters of those who were impaired had never sought help for their symptoms (Srole et al. 1962). In Stirling County, lifetime prevalence of any DSM-I mental disorder was about 57%; point prevalence was estimated at 90% of the lifetime prevalence, and like Midtown, significant impairment was found in about 24% of participants (Leighton 1959; Leighton et al. 1963a, b).

Most in the scientific community found these rates shocking. However, the Midtown and Stirling County investigators believed the results were reasonable, given the composition and context of the community. Despite social status, members of these communities were burdened with a range of mental problems, and the availability of mental health services was, quite simply, inadequate.

The Proof of Burden: The Next Generation of Epidemiologic Studies

As controversial as they were, the results of these key studies highlighted important differences from previous studies, such as the Baltimore Morbidity Study (Illness 1957), which found rates of mental disorder in the community to be about half that of the Midtown Manhattan and Stirling County Studies, and set the stage for increasingly sophisticated contemporary psychiatric epidemiology studies. In conjunction with major advances in diagnostic criteria and nomenclature, the 1961 Joint Commission on Mental Illness and Health and a cascade of other shifts that prioritized systematic data collection in service of community psychiatry gave rise to a new era of community-based epidemiologic studies.

The Epidemiologic Catchment Area Study

The Epidemiologic Catchment Area (ECA) study was a signal study of this new era. The ECA was initiated in response to the 1977 Report of the President's Commission on Mental Health, which described the state of American mental health research and services (Grob 2005). NIMH needed to provide descriptive psychiatric epidemiologic data to the President's Commission, since the clinical picture of community mental health was incomplete (Regier et al. 1978; Robins 1978). The ECA, therefore, sought to address the gaps identified in the President's commission report (Robins and Regier 1991).

The ECA was done in five US communities: Baltimore, New Haven, St. Louis, Durham, and Los Angeles. Each site was a defined "catchment area" accessible to a skilled research team. Investigators collected data on a common set of core questions and sample characteristics and sampled over 3000 community residents and 500 institutionalized residents. Together, the 5-site ECA collected diagnostic and service need and use data on 20,861 adults, aged 18 and over. The ECA used the lay-administered NIMH Diagnostic Interview Schedule (DIS), Version III, and the newly issued third edition of the DSM (Association 1980) for diagnostic classification (Robins and Regier 1991). The ECA was the first study to document the prevalence of DSM-III disorders. Overall, the ECA found a somewhat similar burden of mental illness documented by the Midtown Manhattan and Stirling County studies; lifetime diagnoses of anxiety disorders were reported in nearly a third of respondents, compared to mood disorders in about 8% (Table 1).

The ECA was critical in determining the prevalence of specific psychiatric disorders, as well as service needs and use patterns in the five communities studied. The study once again supported

Table 1 Prevalence estimates from contemporary psychiatric epidemiology surveys

	Study %			
	ECA	NCS	NCS-R	World Mental Health Surveys
Mood disorders				
12-month	3.7	11.3	9.5	0.8–19.6
Lifetime	7.8	19.3	20.8	3.3–21.4
Anxiety disorders				
12-month	18.1	17.2	18.1	2.4–18.2
Lifetime	28.8	24.9	28.8	4.8–31.0
Psychotic disorders				
12-month		0.5	–	–
Lifetime	1.4	0.7	–	–

the notion that services were inadequate relative to need; under 20% of respondents with recent mental disorders accessed services in the year prior to study participation (Regier et al. 1993; Robins and Regier 1991). However, because the samples in the ECA were not collected to be nationally representative, there was an imperative to address epidemiologic gaps regarding the prevalence and distribution of psychiatric disorders in the United States. Moreover, the ECA could only provide basic information regarding the comorbidity of psychiatric disorders; it was, therefore, necessary to determine patterns of comorbidity and the complexities of the affiliated need for and use of services.

The National Comorbidity Surveys and the Collaborative Psychiatric Epidemiology Surveys

Some of the limitations of the ECA influenced deeply the National Comorbidity Survey (NCS), a study of the prevalence, causes, and consequences of comorbidity between psychiatric and substance use disorders (Kessler 1994). The NCS, which began in 1990, was the first survey of mental and substance use disorders in the United States to use a completely structured diagnostic interview, the Composite International Diagnostic Interview (CIDI), to determine the prevalence and correlates of DSM-III-R disorders in a nationally representative sample of 8098 individuals, aged 18–54. The prevalence estimates of lay-administered CIDI-diagnosed psychiatric disorders were higher than those reported by the ECA, with the exception of psychotic disorders and lifetime anxiety disorders (Table 1). Almost half of those surveyed reported at least one lifetime disorder, and about 30% endorsed a psychiatric disorder within the past year. Notably, over 50% of all lifetime disorders occurred in a small proportion of the respondents with a history of three or more comorbid disorders (Kessler et al. 1994). Like the ECA, the NCS reported underuse of mental health services—about 13% of respondents accessed outpatient services in the prior 12 months. One of the most striking findings of the NCS indicated a problem with "met unneed"—that is, people with low levels of need had a higher probability of accessing treatment (Kessler et al. 1997; Mojtabai et al. 2002), with implications for policies affecting the distribution of community-based mental health services.

Similar prevalences of DSM-IV (Association 1994) disorders and service use patterns were observed in the NCS Replication (NCS-R), conducted about a decade later in a nationally representative sample of 9282 respondents, aged 18–54 (Table 1) (Kessler et al. 2005a, b). Harkening to the results of the Midtown Manhattan Study, 26.2% of respondents reported a past-year psychiatric disorder; nearly a quarter those with a past-year psychiatric disorder were classified as serious (Kessler et al. 2005b). As in the NCS, comorbidity was common; nearly 30% of the people surveyed had two disorders, and almost 20% had three (Kessler et al. 2005a, b). Likewise, significant unmet need for services was observed in the NCS-R; nearly 60% of those endorsing a past-year psychiatric disorder remained untreated. Racial/ethnic minorities, low SES individuals, elderly persons, the uninsured, and rural residents were least likely to receive services (Wang et al. 2005). Moreover, the "met unneed" assessed originally in the NCS showed that the bulk of services for psychiatric or substance use problems are delivered to people with indicators of need, including past year diagnoses, and that those without indicators of need are in care delivered outside of the formal healthcare system (Druss et al. 2007).

Along with the NCS-R, two other cross-sectional studies examining the prevalence and correlates of psychiatric disorders and rates of service utilization among specific racial/ethnic groups in the United States—the National Survey of American Life (NSAL) and the National Latino and Asian American Study (NLAAS)—comprised the Collaborative Psychiatric Epidemiology Surveys (CPES). Together, these studies indicate that the prevalence of common mental disorders is higher in non-Hispanic white Americans than in other racial/ethnic groups except Puerto Ricans (Alegria et al. 2007; Kessler et al. 2005a, b; Williams et al. 2007), although this has been the subject of much debate. Critically, despite a purported lower prevalence of common mental disorders among most racial/ethnic minority groups, the course of disorder is more chronic, disabling, and more likely to remain untreated.

In the United States, therefore, community psychiatry faces particular and historically enduring challenges of meeting the complex needs of those with psychiatric disorders, particularly those that are more common. The burden of common mental illness, and the relative lack of services for those most in need, has been well documented, with increasing diagnostic precision and methodological advances—albeit not without growing pains—over the postwar decades. The "proof" of the burden of mental illness demonstrated by cross-sectional epidemiologic studies carries with it directives to those responsible for shaping policies allocating the requisite resources for community psychiatry. Unfortunately, the response is somewhat diffuse and insufficient, underscoring the need for continued and expanded advocacy in this arena.

World Mental Health Surveys

Efforts to determine the burden of mental illness in communities across the world have been plagued by diagnostic difficulties; specifically, cross-national studies prior to the ECA and NCS eras lacked a common format. Structured diagnostic instruments facilitated the conduct of large psychiatric epidemiology surveys across settings. In the 1980s and the 1990s, cross-national epidemiologic surveys were conducted using the DIS (as in the ECA) and the CIDI (as in the NCS and NCS-R). However, while these instruments provided a means of obtaining comparable prevalence estimates, they did not adequately assess severity, impairment, or treatment. Thus, in 1998, the World Health Organization established the World Mental Health (WMH) Survey Consortium in 1998 to create a diagnostic instrument that would fill these gaps (Consortium 2004). After extensive cross-national piloting, the WHO Composite International Diagnostic Interview (CIDI) was ready for use (Consortium 2004).

The WMH surveys, which spanned 14 countries ranging in development status, were based on the NCS model. Face-to-face community interviews were conducted with 60,343 adults. The WMH surveys estimated the prevalence of mental disorders worldwide to be approximately 30% (Consortium 2004). Moreover, mental disorders account for nearly 40% of healthy years lost from disease and are the leading cause of disability worldwide, even in low- and middle-income countries, where the burden of other communicable and non-communicable diseases is substantially greater than in high-income countries (Wang et al. 2007).

Limitations of Cross-Sectional Studies of Common Mental Disorders

While the strengths of cross-sectional studies have been extremely useful, especially for informing community psychiatric care, it is important to keep in mind their limitations. First, cross-sectional studies are restricted in their ability to identify causes. That is because cross-sectional studies are unable to establish temporality or the temporal ordering of exposure and outcome. It is also because prevalence, the metric of burden established by cross-sectional studies, reflects both incidence, or the occurrence of new cases over a given period of time, and duration of illness (Susser et al. 2006). Second, with few exceptions (Phillips et al. 2009), these studies only provide good estimates of common disorders and have not proved useful for studying the prevalence of severe but less common disorders such as schizophrenia. Third, they have focused largely on young and middle-aged adults, leaving a gap for information on mental disorders in childhood and later life. Fourth, faced with limited resources and the need to apply the same procedures across settings, they have in general not given sufficient attention to cross-cultural differences in the expression and measurement of mental disorders, although there are some exceptions (Kim et al. 2011). Finally, these cross-sectional studies perform much better for estimates of current prevalence (whether the individual had the disorder over the past 3 or 12 months) than for estimates of lifetime prevalence (whether the individual ever had the disorder) (Susser and Shrout 2009). In public and policy forums, however, the far less reliable lifetime prevalences tend to be used; when there is a need to make sweeping statements about needs and services to policymakers and the public, lifetime prevalences are elusively simple and more likely to engage the audience.

Incidence Studies

For severe mental disorders that often persist over a long period, such as schizophrenia, incidence studies have provided more information than cross-sectional community surveys. We use examples of incidence studies of schizophrenia, where incidence studies have provided vital information on the occurrence of disease across time and place and thereby have provided key information regarding paths to pursue to understand causes (see the next section).

In the 1960s, the International Pilot Study of Schizophrenia (IPSS), sponsored by the WHO, set out to determine if it was feasible to engage in large-scale epidemiologic research of psychiatric disorders, specifically schizophrenia, with comparable methods across different contexts and to determine what, if any, differences existed in the incidence of schizophrenia across contexts (Sartorius et al. 1974). Indeed, the IPSS, which included 1202 participants in its initial assessment, showed that this type of study was feasible. The IPSS also demonstrated that what schizophrenia was, both broadly and narrowly defined as a construct with extensively tested instruments, was fairly consistent across contexts (Sartorius et al. 1974).

Later, the WHO sponsored the Determinants of Severe Mental Disorders (DOSMeD), also known as the Ten-Country Study, which built on the work of the IPSS to study the variation in incidence and course of severe mental illness, particularly schizophrenia, across 13 sites in 10 countries. The DOSMeD found that that narrowly defined schizophrenia arose at about the same rate across the countries; more broadly defined schizophrenia was far more variable, ranging from 1.5 to 4.2 per 100,000 persons aged 15–54. In addition, the DOSMeD showed a better course of schizophrenia in developing versus developed countries over a period of 2 years (Jablensky et al. 1992), which gave rise to a long debate over the potential factual and artifactual explanations (Hopper and Wanderling 2000). These findings have recently been challenged (Saha et al. 2006), and a new study is underway to examine whether they hold in contemporary societies (Morgan et al. 2015).

As demonstrated by the IPSS and WHO Ten-Country Study, incidence studies across contexts can show uniformity in rates of a given outcome—here, schizophrenia. A meta-analysis by McGrath shows considerable variation in schizophrenia across population and context (McGrath et al. 2004). Some of the most interesting studies of schizophrenia incidence, which integrate both population and context, are the studies of migrants. Elevated rates of schizophrenia have been shown among migrants since the 1930s (Cantor-Graae and Selten 2005; Kirkbride et al. 2006; Ødegaard 1932; Veling et al. 2006). More recent studies of schizophrenia incidence have examined rates in migrants to Holland in a first-contact study in The Hague compared to those in the native Dutch (Veling et al. 2006) and a study of schizophrenia rates in African Caribbean migrants compared to native British in Southeast London (Kirkbride et al. 2006). Rates are considerably higher among migrants in these studies. That variation of incidence rates exists among these populations indicates that a potential social mechanism is at play. For instance, discrimination has been shown to be related to elevated rates among migrants in The Hague (Veling et al. 2006). In addition, other community-level factors, such as social fragmentation, have been shown to be related to the elevated rates among African Caribbean people in Southeast London (Kirkbride et al. 2006). Other studies have examined race/ethnicity pursuant to these findings and have found, for example, variation between blacks and whites in the United States (Bresnahan et al. 2007).

Some of the most compelling avenues to pursue involve studying the cascades of social factors that may produce variation in rates of schizophrenia across place and population (March et al. 2008). Upstream social factors, such as poverty or structural discrimination, are by themselves insufficient to cause disease or disorder. However, these upstream risk factors either shape or work in conjunction with other, risk factors more proximate to the individual that accumulate to produce illness (Susser et al. 2006). By studying these multilevel factors, we can work to identify multiple levels of intervention for illnesses like schizophrenia.

Limitations of Incidence Studies

While incidence studies can help to address some of the limitations of prevalence studies and can permit the examination of underlying causes, should variation exist, they also have limitations. For example, incidence studies are often first-contact studies or studies that rely necessarily on the incident cases presenting to services for ascertainment. Therefore, in contexts that do not have coordinated or linked health service records, incidence studies prove quite challenging. Increasingly, psychiatric registries are used to determine incidence rates in given populations (e.g., Denmark, Sweden, and Finland), although these also have similar limitations because they require cases to present to services.

Observational Studies of Causes

Natural Experiments

Natural experiments constitute the strongest observational design. Natural experiments capitalize on external circumstances (whether naturally occurring or, on some level, human-made) that select people into groups that are exposed or unexposed to a risk factor for disease in order to study causes. In natural experiments, the population under study has little or no control over the circumstances that render them either exposed or unexposed to a risk factor or set of risk factors for a particular outcome of interest. Because people often have the ability to shape their exposure to a given set of risk factors for disease (e.g., individual dietary choices, smoking habits, etc.), and because those choices are often linked (e.g., people who eat high-fat foods tend to exercise less), those who are exposed or unexposed to a particular risk factor are likely to differ on many other factors that may influence a particular outcome of interest. That is, the association between exposure and outcome may be confounded by other factors that are related to both the exposure and the outcome. Isolating the effect of the cause, therefore, may prove difficult. Natural experiments, however, help to isolate the causal effect of the risk factor of interest by removing from consideration other factors that may influence the association between exposure and outcome (Susser et al. 2006).

Many examples of natural experiments exist (Susser et al. 2006), but we will focus on two instances that help elucidate the association between prenatal exposure to famine and adult schizophrenia here. The first natural experiment we highlight here is the Dutch Famine Study, a study of prenatal exposure to famine in Holland during the Dutch Hunger Winter of 1944–1945. A Nazi blockade of Western Holland at the end of World War II gave rise to a severe famine that had a clear beginning and end in a particular location. In the cities that experienced the famine, the birth cohort in gestation during the famine period was nutritionally deficient during gestation. Birth cohorts before and after the Nazi blockade were not nutritionally deficient during gestation, and neither were the birth cohorts in cities that were not subject to the Nazi blockade. Rates of schizophrenia during adulthood were twice as high among the birth cohorts exposed to prenatal nutritional deficiency than those that were not (Susser et al. 2006; Susser and Lin 1992).

Another natural experiment in China obtained similar results. During the Great Leap Forward in China in the 1950s and 1960s, the collectivization of agriculture, adoption of poor agricultural practices, and reduction of cultivated land contributed to a famine that affected the entire country. However, certain provinces in China were more profoundly affected than others. Anhui province was one of the most severely affected. By the spring of 1959, people in Anhui were starving and began dying in masses. In early 1961, the famine had receded, whereas it continued in other provinces in China throughout the year—circumstances that were beyond the control of those exposed or unexposed. As in the Dutch Famine Study, researchers capitalized on this natural experiment to examine the rates of adult schizophrenia among those exposed to famine in utero. And, as in the Dutch Famine Study, rates of schizophrenia were twice as high among the people in provinces exposed to famine during gestation as those who were not exposed to famine during gestation (St Clair et al. 2005). Both studies provided robust evidence in the context of a string design consisting of naturally occurring (albeit man-made) experiments indicating that prenatal nutritional deficiency was associated with increased risk of schizophrenia during adulthood.

Limitations of Natural Experiments

While natural experiments assess conditions that are arguably the most reflective of everyday life because of the high ecological validity of the study design, these studies are not without limitations. First, natural experiments are difficult to replicate in the same form as they derive from conditions uncontrolled by study investigators. For example, the famines in the Netherlands and in China affected different kinds of societies for different lengths of time. Nonetheless, these differences resulted in complementary results, lending strength to the inference that early prenatal maternal famine was linked to schizophrenia in offspring. Natural experiments can be biased by unadjusted confounding, because investigators typically conduct these studies retrospectively and opportunistically and are unable to fully assess potential differences between exposed and unexposed populations. Finally, in some natural experiments, follow-up data may be subject to recall bias affected by memory, emotional states, and an awareness of the study's goals.

Cohort Studies

Cohort studies, which are longitudinal observational studies of subjects with a shared characteristic (e.g., birth date) or experience (e.g., military service), can grapple with the issue of temporality and distinguish between cause and effect. One of the most notable cohort studies with real relevance to community psychiatry is the British 1946 birth cohort study, known formally as the National Survey of Health and Development (NSHD). This particular study is the oldest—now in its 65th year (Pearson 2011)—among the British birth cohort studies, which include samples from 1946 (Wadsworth et al. 2006), 1958 (Power and Elliott 2006), 1970 (Elliott and Shepherd 2006), and 2000 (Parkinson et al. 2011), and the longest ongoing birth cohort study in the world (Council 2011). The NSHD comprises a cohort of 5362 children born in the England, Scotland, and Wales in the same week of March 1946, which has been assessed 22 times to date. The 5362 cohort members were culled from an original sample of 13,867 children born to 91% of all British mothers giving birth during the weeklong time frame. Like the cross-sectional studies described in the previous section, the NSHD was initiated in response to a set of social contextual concerns—poverty, employment, housing, declining birth rates, and health—and in service of shaping policies that might make a difference in the health and lives of a generation coming up in a dramatically changed postwar Britain (Council 2011).

The architect of the study, physician James Douglas, wove an interest in mental health and wellbeing into the study, undertaken originally to examine the quality of maternity services across social class, very early on. As a result, cohort assessments during childhood included maternal and teacher questions regarding children's behavior and mental wellbeing. Over the course of the entire study—during some childhood assessments and all assessments during adulthood, cohort members have been surveyed on their thoughts and emotions (Council 2011) using a variety of validated instruments for surveying symptoms of mental disorders. With implications for prevention, assessments of cognitive functioning, and aspects of physical health, the NSHD offers a trove of epidemiological information regarding how these illnesses unfold over time together with the types of exposures that are particularly important.

The NSHD has provided some key information regarding mental health over the life course, including early determinants of mental health, the course of mental disorders over the life span, the role of reproductive issues in the mental health of women, and treatment use. For example, researchers have documented long-term psychiatric effects of child and adolescent psychological conditions 40 to 60 years later (Colman et al. 2007; Stafford et al. 2015) as well as strong associations between vascular risk, cognitive function, and brain function in older adults (Lane et al. 2019, 2020).

Over time, new cohort studies of psychiatric epidemiology have emerged to examine trends among diverse study samples (e.g., National Latino and Asian American Study) and extend well-known, existing studies through follow-up data collection waves (e.g., National Epidemiologic Survey of Alcohol and Related Conditions I–III) (Grant and Dawson 2006). Large population birth cohorts have been launched with mental disorders as a central outcome of interest and biological as well as questionnaire data (Fraser et al. 2013; Magnus et al. 2006; Olsen et al. 2001). Additionally, studies have increasingly utilized electronic medical records and medical registries as rich sources of psychiatric epidemiological data and have also incorporated the collection of a wide range of genetic and biological data to better assess the physiological correlates and underlying molecular mechanisms of psychiatric disease (e.g., iPSYCH) (Pedersen et al. 2018).

Strengths and Limitations of Cohort Studies

Perhaps the most notable strength, cohort studies permit an assessment of a causal relation between exposure and outcome, because they satisfy the hallmark criterion for causality—that the exposure preceded the outcome. Cohort studies also permit the examination of the relations among a variety of exposures and outcomes, as they unfold over the life course. The major drawbacks to cohort studies are the investments required, in terms of financial and temporal commitments. Two factors underlying the marked success of the NSHD, for example, are the virtually continuous stream of funding and the continuity of investigators and research personnel.

Case-Control Studies

Case-control studies, which examine exposure to a given risk factor of interest among pre-defined outcome groups (e.g., one with the disorder of interest and one without), can be used to answer a question more efficiently than a cohort study, particularly for outcomes that occur in less than 10% of the population. The efficiency offered by a case-control study outweighs the potential for bias, although steps can be taken to minimize bias. There are also many other advantages and disadvantages to the use of each of these designs, elaborated elsewhere (Rothman et al. 2008; Susser et al. 2006).

One way to conceptualize a case-control study is as an efficient way of sampling an underlying cohort of exposed and unexposed people, some of whom develop the disease of interest (Rothman et al. 2008; Susser et al. 2006). This is most clearly seen in the context of a *nested case-control study* where the underlying cohort is enumerated, though the same logic applies to all case-control studies. A good example of a nested case-control study is the ABC study of autism within a large Norwegian birth cohort, which drew both the autism cases and the controls from the same source population, i.e., the large research cohort (Stoltenberg et al. 2010).

The goal of a case-control study is to obtain the result that one would have obtained in a perfect cohort study, but using far fewer respondents. The validity of the case-control study depends on two critical steps regarding selection of controls: (1) selecting controls from the same source population that gave rise to the cases and (2) selecting controls independent of exposure status. When these two principles are applied, the controls will represent the ratio of exposed to unexposed in the population from which the cases were derived.

Under these conditions, other things being equal (e.g., control of confounding, validity of exposure data), the odds of exposure for cases versus noncases (exposure odds ratio from a case-control study) is equal to the odds of disease for exposed versus unexposed (disease odds ratio from a cohort study based in the same source population). This equality of the exposure odds ratio in a case-control study and the disease odds ratio in the underlying cohort can be demonstrated algebraically. Thus, the relation of exposure to disease, in the form of an odds ratio, can be obtained from a case-control study. In a nested case-control study, when the underlying cohort can be fully enumerated, one can select controls from the source population (i.e., the underlying cohort) independent of exposure status and thereby obtain the same odds ratio in a case-control study as one would have obtained in a cohort study, but at much less cost and in a much shorter time.

The majority of case-control studies, however, are not nested in a fully enumerated cohort. One has to conceptualize and then sample the source population that gave rise to the cases. This introduces potential for bias, because there is generally some uncertainty about the source population and the best approach to sample it. In many though not all scenarios, this potential bias can be minimized by a thoughtful design, and case-control studies will produce valid results. Like cohort studies, there are numerous variations of the case-control design, but they are all based on the premise that the (exposure) odds ratio from the case-control study will approximate the (disease) odds ratio that would have been obtained from a cohort study of the source population.

Here, we use the example of a case-control study that examined the contribution of heavy alcohol use to the increase in adult mortality rates in Russia in the 1990s (Zaridze et al. 2009). By the year 2000, in Russia, the probability that a 15-year-old man would die before age 35 was 10% and that a 35-year-old man would die before age 55 was 27%; in Western Europe, these probabilities were only 2% and 6%, respectively (Zaridze et al. 2009). This reflected a dramatic increase in mortality that was unprecedented for an industrialized society, except in the context of war. Researchers hypothesized that the increase in mortality could be related to increased alcohol consumption in the context of the social upheaval that accompanied the dissolution of the Soviet Union.

The investigators studied three industrial cities in western Siberia with 2002 census populations of 0.5 million, 0.7 million, and 0.2 million and principally European Russian populations. In these cities, both the overall mortality rates and the distribution of certified causes of death were similar to those in the whole of Russia and fluctuated in a similar way, with a sudden large increase in mortality from 1992 to 1994 (Men et al. 2003). The cases and controls were selected from 200,000 residents of these 3 cities who died age 15–74 years between 1990 and 2001. In addition to name, age, sex, and cause of death (recoded to ICD by the investigators), the address of the deceased was recorded on death records. The investigators culled information about alcohol use by the deceased by visiting their addresses in death records and conducting proxy interviews with family members. Cases were defined as persons who died from causes suspected beforehand to be related to alcohol or tobacco. Controls were persons who died from any other cause.

We call attention to three key results of this study. First, the authors inferred that there was a causal relation between heavy alcohol use and mortality. Further, they estimated that alcohol was responsible for about one half of deaths among men and one quarter of deaths among women in the age group 35–54 and was also a major cause of death among men and women in the age group 55–74. Second, the largest contributors to alcohol-associated excess mortality were accidents and violence.

Third, after their case-control data suggested that the association between heavy alcohol use and mortality was likely to be causal, the authors turned to another approach to help rule out alternative explanations. They examined the ecological relationship between alcohol use and mortality in the 1980s in Russia, the period prior to the social upheaval that accompanied the collapse of communism. They showed that between 1985 and 1987, following a short-lived 1985 restriction placed on alcohol use under the Gorbachev regime, both alcohol use and mortality declined suddenly and sharply. This suggested that other effects of the social upheaval of 1991 were less viable explanations for the increased mortality of the 1990s and supported the view that increased mortality was mediated by increased alcohol consumption, as suggested by their case-control study. This finding is also remarkable for the closeness in timing of the fluctuations in alcohol use and mortality, again suggesting that immediate behavioral effects of alcohol mediated much of the relationship to mortality. It provides an informative contrast with cigarette smoking, for which mortality is mainly related to long-term effects on disease risk later in life.

Case Study: Evaluating the Mental Health Impacts of the COVID-19 Pandemic During the First Six Weeks of the National Lockdown in Soweto, South Africa

In this section, we provide a case study to illustrate some of the concepts explored in this chapter using a prolonged global health catastrophe that has highlighted the importance of psychiatric epidemiology worldwide: the coronavirus (COVID-19) pandemic. COVID-19 began in December 2019 originating in Wuhan, China. COVID-19 quickly traveled out of its initial epicenter to affect the rest of the world. The first confirmed case of severe acute respiratory syndrome coronavirus 2 (SARS-CoV-2) infection in South Africa appeared on March 5, 2020. South Africa quickly became a site of international interest for the public health community as the pathophysiological sequelae of the novel virus among those with pre-existing chronic conditions and broader societal impact of the COVID-19 pandemic in low- and middle-income countries (LMIC)—with exception to China—were unknown at the time. The country's high prevalence of disease morbidity (including HIV/AIDS and tuberculosis) and socioeconomic constraints posed major concerns for the country's public health infrastructure.

Similar to other LMICs, South Africa already faced high rates of psychiatric morbidity and low mental healthcare access and usage (Docrat et al. 2019; Williams et al. 2008). The rapid onset of the pandemic and its drastic societal consequences, including the national lockdown and its harsh enforcement, introduced new adversities to existing problems. Evidence on COVID-19 reported that forced quarantine and its secondary impacts, including social isolation, psychological distress, and household socioeconomic damages, have had widespread psychiatric consequences among affected communities (Kim et al. 2020).

Soon after President Cyril Ramaphosa commenced the national lockdown on March 27, 2020, the first author and colleagues quickly shifted an ongoing survey to examine the mental health impacts of the COVID-19 pandemic in

Soweto, a major urban city located southwest of Johannesburg. Soweto was a major site of political resistance in the anti-apartheid movement and is now a diverse African township comprised of many communities from various ethnic, linguistic, and socioeconomic backgrounds. The prevalence of infectious and non-communicable diseases is also quite high among residents (Hopkins et al. 2019). During this time, the epidemiological literature on COVID-19 lacked sufficient data from studies with longitudinal designs and was thus limited to cross-sectional analyses. Furthermore, many of these studies utilized online surveys to collect data on COVID-19 experiences, excluding hard-to-reach and other marginalized communities with little to no access to the internet, computers, and other electronic devices. Thus, using a community-based epidemiological study, our study team combined pre-existing data with telephonic follow-up survey data on COVID-19 and mental illness risk to understand experiences during lockdown and the mental health impacts of living through the pandemic. Our follow-up interviews extended what was initially a cross-sectional survey into a longitudinal cohort study among those who participated in our COVID-19 study.

We reported that higher perceived risk of COVID-19 infection predicted greater depressive symptoms ($p < 0.001$; Fig. 1). This cross-sectional association was stronger among adults who reported worse histories of childhood trauma, assessed through the adverse childhood experiences (ACEs) survey, though after adjusting for covariates this effect was marginally significant ($p = 0.063$; Fig. 2). The strong association between perceived COVID-19 risk and depressive symptomatology remained after controlling for a suite of demographic, socio-environmental, and psychological data that came from the first wave of data collection of the study before the onset of the pandemic, which allowed us to rule out the possibility that pre-pandemic mental health status and social circumstances confounded the relationship between COVID-19 risk perceptions and depressive symptoms. These variables included recent psychiatric risk (assessed by the General Health Questionnaire-28), perceived quality of life, social stress, coping behaviors, and demographic factors, all of which were assessed during the first wave of data collection, and COVID-19 knowledge. We also found that childhood traumatic events were common in our sample as the average number of ACEs was 3.5 events. Furthermore, 14.5% of participants exhibited symptoms of major depressive disorder, which was assessed using the Center for Epidemiologic Studies-Depression 10-item screener. Depressive risk was determined if participants surpassed the cutoff score of 10.

Notably, our study only assessed the psychological impacts of the pandemic during the first 6 weeks of the national lockdown, which is when rates of COVID-19 infection were still quite low in Soweto relative to the initial origin sites in the wealthier, white northern suburbs of Johannesburg, where many travelers from Europe resided and were understood to have brought COVID-19 to the country. Outbreaks of COVID-19 were most severe during the first peak of the pandemic during July–August 2020, which likely led to greater psychological and social burdens in Soweto. As we are continuing to survey individuals in this study, we aim to continue tracing the mental health impacts throughout the course of pandemic. In summary, our results highlight the compounding effects of past traumatic histories and recent stress exposures from the COVID-19 pandemic on exacerbating the severity of depressive symptoms among adults living in urban South Africa.

Since the completion of this analysis, the course of the COVID-19 pandemic in South Africa rapidly shifted after several key events occurred: the introduction of new viral variants, a second wave of COVID-19 cases, the successful development of several vaccines, subsequent global inequities in vaccine availability and distribution, and the limited efficacy of early vaccines. The South African public saw temporary relief from the daily adversities and elevated risk of infection stemming from the first wave for a few months after peak levels substantially declined in September 2020. Yet millions of families were left to face the ongoing consequences

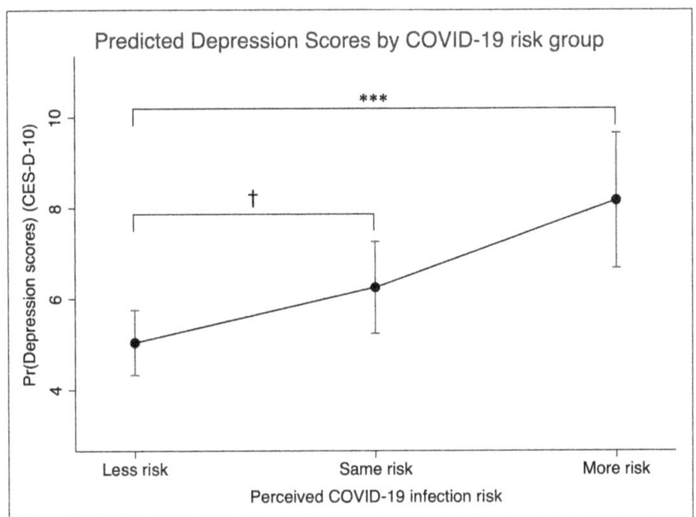

Fig. 1 Predicted depression scores by perceived COVID-19 risk group. *Note:* Greater perceived risk of COVID-19 infection corresponds with greater depression symptomatology in adults living in Soweto. The effect of being in the "More risk" group is highly significant ($p = <0.001$) relative to being at "Less risk," while the effect of perceiving that one is at the "Same risk" of COVID-19 infection relative to other individuals living in Soweto on depression symptoms is marginally significant ($p = 0.088$). The respective predicted CES-D-10 scores for each group are as provided

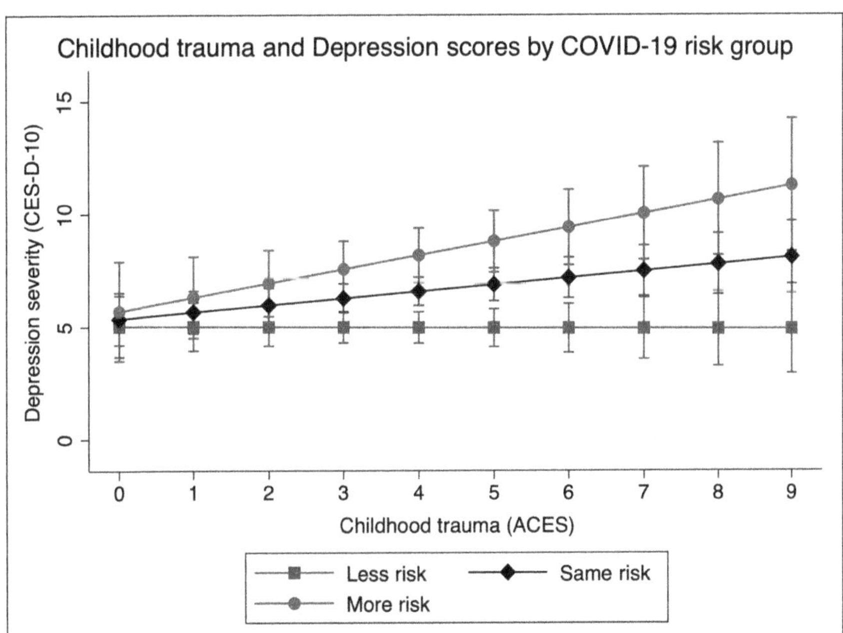

Fig. 2 Childhood trauma (ACEs) and depression scores (CESD) by COVID-19 risk group. *Note:* Greater childhood trauma (ACEs) potentiates the positive relationship between greater perceived COVID-19 risk and the severity of depressive symptomatology. The effect of the interaction between childhood trauma and perceived COVID-19 risk on depression is marginally significant ($F[1, 208] = 3.51$, $p = 0.0625$)

of the pandemic and lockdown, including intense economic insecurity, the physical and psychosocial effects of the prolonged quarantine, and, for some who contracted COVID-19, the lingering effects of the relatively unknown disease and its side effects.

Conclusion

In this chapter, we have covered epidemiological terrain with particular relevance to community psychiatry. We have focused and anchored historically our discussion on two key areas: observational studies of incidence and prevalence and observational studies of causes. In examining first observational studies of incidence and prevalence, we have provided basic information on the measures of disease occurrence and their practical uses. We have sketched the epidemiology of mental disorders in the United States through select surveys, presented the key results of an important cross-national survey, and addressed their implications for public policy and the allocation of resources for prevention and treatment.

In subsequent discussions of observational studies of causes, we have covered in-depth natural experiments, cohort studies, and case-control studies by use of examples that highlight the connection between epidemiology and community psychiatry and indicate how useful methodologically sound epidemiologic studies can be for the purposes of undertaking studies of causes in the broad range of outcomes with which community psychiatry concerns itself.

Psychiatric epidemiology is needed to track mental health profiles of population, especially during public health emergencies and pandemics like COVID-19. In our case study in Soweto, we illustrated the numerous barriers that limited resources settings faced for effective sampling strategies, especially during COVID-19.

In closing, epidemiology and its armamentarium of methods provide a set of tools that can be put to good use in community psychiatry. Epidemiology helps provide an evidence base for community psychiatry, with an eye, ultimately, toward intervention. Indeed, epidemiologic studies have contributed much to the evidence base policymakers leverage to allocate funding for interventions, services, models of treatment provision, and directions in what treatments work best for people in a given circumstance. Finally, we propose that professionals in community psychiatry and the people they hope to serve should be actively involved in determining the most important questions to which epidemiology should be applied in the coming era. New methods might be needed, but these should be driven by new as well as still unresolved questions.

References

Alegria M, Mulvaney-Day N, Torres M, Polo A, Cao Z, Canino G (2007). Prevalence of Psychiatric Disorders Across Latino Subgroups in the United States. Am J Public Health 97(1):68–75.

Association AP (1980). Diagnostic and Statistical Manual of Mental Disorders, Third Edition. Washington, DC: American Psychiatric Association.

Association AP (1994). Diagnostic and statistical manual of mental disorders (4th Edition). Washington, DC: American Psychiatric Association.

Association TCoNaSotAP (1952). Diagnostic and Statistical Manual. Washington, DC: American Psychiatric Association.

Bhattacharya R, Cross S, Bhugra D, editors (2010). Clinical Topics in Cultural Psychiatry. London: The Royal College of Psychiatrists.

Bresnahan M, Begg MD, Brown A, Schaefer C, Sohler N, et al (2007). Race and risk of schizophrenia in a US birth cohort: another example of health disparity? International Journal of Epidemiology 36(4):751–758.

Cantor-Graae E, Selten J-P (2005). Schizophrenia and migration: A meta-analysis and review. Am J Psychiatry 162(1):12–24.

Colman I, Wadsworth ME, Croudace TJ, Jones P (2007). Forty-year psychiatric outcomes following assessment for internalizing disorder in adolescence. American Journal of Psychiatry, 164(1), 126–133.

Consortium TWWMHS (2004). Prevalence, Severity, and Unmet Need for Treatment of Mental Disorders in the World Health Organization World Mental Health Surveys. JAMA: The Journal of the American Medical Association 291(21):2581–2590.

Council MR (2011). National Survey of Health and Development, 1946–2011: Celebrating 65 years of research into the health and lives of British people. London: Medical Research Council.

Docrat S, Besada D, Cleary S, Daviaud E, Lund C (2019). Mental health system costs, resources and constraints in South Africa: a national survey. Health Policy Plan 34(9):706–719.

Druss BG, Wang PS, Sampson NA, Olfson M, Pincus HA, et al (2007). Understanding Mental Health Treatment in Persons Without Mental Diagnoses: Results From the National Comorbidity Survey Replication. Arch Gen Psychiatry 64(10):1196–1203.

Elliott J, Shepherd P (2006). Cohort Profile: 1970 British Birth Cohort (BCS70). International Journal of Epidemiology 35(4):836–843.

Frank RG, Glied SA. (2006). Better But Not Well: Mental Health Policy in the United States since 1950. Baltimore: Johns Hopkins University Press.

Fraser A, Macdonald-Wallis C, Tilling K, Boyd A, Golding J, et al (2013). Cohort Profile: the Avon Longitudinal Study of Parents and Children: ALSPAC mothers cohort. Int J Epidemiol 42(1):97–110.

Grant BF, Dawson DA (2006). Introduction to the national epidemiologic survey on alcohol and related conditions. Alcohol Research & Health 29(2):74.

Grob GN (2005). Public Policy and Mental Illnesses: Jimmy Carter's Presidential Commission on Mental Health. Milbank Quarterly 83(3):425–456.

Hopkins KL, Hlongwane K, Otwombe K, Dietrich J, Cheyip M, et al (2019). Demographics and health profile on precursors of non-communicable diseases in adults testing for HIV in Soweto, South Africa: a cross-sectional study. BMJ Open 9(12):e030701.

Hopper K, Wanderling J. (2000). Revisiting the Developed Versus Developing Country Distinction in Course and Outcome in Schizophrenia: Results From ISoS, the WHO Collaborative Followup Project. Schizophrenia Bulletin 26(4):835–846.

Illness CoC (1957). Chronic Illness in the United States, Vol. III, Chronic Illness in a Large City: The Baltimore Study. Cambridge, MA: Harvard University Press.

Jablensky A, Sartorius N, Ernberg G, Anker M, Korten A, et al (1992). Schizophrenia: manifestations, incidence and course in different cultures. A World Health Organization ten-country study. Psychol Med Monogr Suppl 20:1 - 97.

Kessler RC. (1994). Building on the ECA: The National Comorbidity Survey and the Children's ECA. International Journal of Methods in Psychiatric Research 4(2):81–94.

Kessler RC, Berglund P, Demler O, Jin R, Merikangas KR, Walters EE (2005a). Lifetime Prevalence and Age-of-Onset Distributions of DSM-IV Disorders in the National Comorbidity Survey Replication. Arch Gen Psychiatry 62(6):593–602.

Kessler RC, Chiu WT, Demler O, Walters EE (2005b). Prevalence, Severity, and Comorbidity of 12-Month DSM-IV Disorders in the National Comorbidity Survey Replication. Arch Gen Psychiatry 62(6):617–627.

Kessler RC, Frank RG, Edlund M, Katz SJ, Lin E, Leaf P (1997). Differences in the Use of Psychiatric Outpatient Services between the United States and Ontario. New England Journal of Medicine 336(8):551–557.

Kessler RC, McGonagle KA, Zhao S, Nelson CB, Hughes M, et al (1994). Lifetime and 12-month prevalence of DSM-III-R psychiatric disorders in the United States: Results from the National Comorbidity Survey. Archives of General Psychiatry 51(1):8–19.

Kim AW, Nyengerai T, Mendenhall E (2020). Evaluating the mental health impacts of the COVID-19 pandemic: perceived risk of COVID-19 infection and childhood trauma predict adult depressive symptoms in urban South Africa. Psychol Med:1–13.

Kim YS, Leventhal BL, Koh Y-J, Fombonne E, Laska E, et al (2011). Prevalence of Autism Spectrum Disorders in a Total Population Sample. Am J Psychiatry:appi.ajp.2011.10101532.

Kirkbride JB, Fearon P, Morgan C, Dazzan P, Morgan K, et al (2006). Heterogeneity in incidence rates of schizophrenia and other psychotic syndromes: findings from the 3-center AeSOP study. Arch Gen Psychiatry 63(3):250–258.

Lane CA, Barnes J, Nicholas JM, Sudre CH, Cash DM, et al (2019). Associations between blood pressure across adulthood and late-life brain structure and pathology in the neuroscience substudy of the 1946 British birth cohort (Insight 46): an epidemiological study. The Lancet Neurology, 18(10), 942–952.

Lane CA, Barnes J, Nicholas JM, Sudre CH, Cash DM, et al (2020). Associations between vascular risk across adulthood and brain pathology in late life: evidence from a British birth cohort. JAMA neurology, 77(2), 175–183.

Leighton AH. (1959). My Name is Legion. Foundations for a Theory of Man in Relation to Culture. New York: Basic Books.

Leighton DC, Harding JS, Macklin D, Hughes CC, and Leighton AH (1963a). Psychiatric findings of the Stirling County Study. American Journal of Psychiatry 119(11):1021–1026.

Leighton DC, Harding JS, Macklin D, Macmillan A, and Leighton AH (1963b). The Character of Danger: Psychiatric Symptoms in Selected Communities. New York: Basic Books.

Magnus P, Irgens LM, Haug K, Nystad W, Skjaerven R, et al (2006). Cohort profile: the Norwegian Mother and Child Cohort Study (MoBa). Int J Epidemiol 35(5):1146–1150.

March D, Hatch SL, Morgan C, Kirkbride JB, Bresnahan M, et al (2008). Psychosis and place. Epidemiologic Reviews 30(1):84–100.

McGrath J, Saha S, Welham J, El Saadi O, MacCauley C, Chant D (2004). A systematic review of the incidence of schizophrenia: the distribution of rates and the influence of sex, urbanicity, migrant status and methodology. BMC Medicine 2(1):13.

Men T, Brennan P, Boffetta P, Zaridze D (2003). Russian mortality trends for 1991–2001: analysis by cause and region. BMJ 327(7421):964.

Mojtabai R, Olfson M, Mechanic D (2002). Perceived Need and Help-Seeking in Adults With Mood, Anxiety, or Substance Use Disorders. Arch Gen Psychiatry 59(1):77–84.

Morgan C, Hibben M, Esan O, John S, Patel V, er al. (2015). Searching for psychosis: INTREPID (1): systems for detecting untreated and first-episode cases of psychosis in diverse settings. Soc Psychiatry Psychiatr Epidemiol 50(6):879–893.

Ødegaard Ø. (1932). Emigration and insanity. Acta Psychiatr Neurol Scand Suppl 4:1–206.

Olsen J, Melbye M, Olsen SF, Sørensen TI, Aaby P, Nybo Andersen AM, Søndergaard C. (2001).The Danish National Birth Cohort-its background, structure and aim. Scandinavian journal of public health 29(4):300–307.

Parkinson KN, Pearce MS, Dale A, Reilly JJ, Drewett RF, et al (2011). Cohort Profile: The Gateshead Millennium Study. International Journal of Epidemiology 40(2):308–317.

Pearson H. (2011). Study of a Lifetime. Nature 471:20–24.

Pedersen CB, Bybjerg-Grauholm J, Pedersen MG, Grove J, Agerbo E, et al (2018). The iPSYCH2012 case–cohort sample: new directions for unravelling genetic and environmental architectures of severe mental disorders. Molecular psychiatry 23(1):6–14.

Phillips MR, Zhang J, Shi Q, Song Z, Ding Z, et al (2009). Prevalence, treatment, and associated disability of mental disorders in four provinces in China during 2001?05: an epidemiological survey. The Lancet 373(9680):2041–2053.

Power C, Elliott J. (2006). Cohort profile: 1958 British birth cohort (National Child Development Study). International Journal of Epidemiology 35(1):34–41.

Regier DA, Goldberg ID, Taube CA (1978). The De Facto US Mental Health Services System. Archives of General Psychiatry 35:685–693.

Regier DA, Narrow WE, Rae DS, Manderscheid RW, Locke BZ, Goodwin FK (1993). The de Facto US Mental and Addictive Disorders Service System: Epidemiologic Catchment Area Prospective 1-Year Prevalence Rates of Disorders and Services. Arch Gen Psychiatry 50(2):85–94.

Robins LN (1978). Psychiatric Epidemiology. Archives of General Psychiatry 35:697–702.

Robins LN, Regier DA, editors (1991). Psychiatric Disorders in America: The Epidemiologic Catchment Area Study. New York: The Free Press.

Rothman K, Greenland S, Lash T. (2008). Modern Epidemiology, Third Edition. Philadelphia: Lippincott, Williams & Wilkins.

Saha S, Welham J, Chant D, McGrath J. (2006). Incidence of schizophrenia does not vary with economic status of the country. Social Psychiatry and Psychiatric Epidemiology 41(5):338–340.

Sartorius N, Shapiro R, Jablensky A (1974). The International Pilot Study of Schizophrenia. Schizophrenia Bulletin 1(11):21–34.

Srole L, Langner TS, Michael ST, Opler ST, Rennie TAC (1962). Mental Health in the Metropolis: The Midtown Manhattan Study. New York: McGraw-Hill.

Stafford M, Gale CR, Mishra G, Richards M, Black S, Kuh DL (2015). Childhood environment and mental wellbeing at age 60–64 years: prospective evidence from the MRC National Survey of Health and Development. PLoS One, 10(6), e0126683.

St Clair D, Xu M, Wang P, Yu Y, Fang Y, et al (2005). Rates of Adult Schizophrenia Following Prenatal Exposure to the Chinese Famine of 1959–1961. JAMA: TheJournal of the American Medical Association 294(5):557–562.

Stoltenberg C, Schjølberg S, Bresnahan M, Hornig M, Hirtz D, et al (2010). The Autism Birth Cohort: a paradigm for gene–environment–timing research. Molecular Psychiatry 15, 676–680

Susser E, Baumgartner JN, Stein Z (2010). Commentary: Sir Arthur Mitchell: pioneer of psychiatric epidemiology and of community care. International Journal of Epidemiology 39(6):1417–1425.

Susser E, Schwartz S, Morabia A, Bromet EJ (2006). Psychiatric Epidemiology: Searching for the Causes of Mental Disorders. New York: Oxford University Press.

Susser E, Shrout PE (2009). Two plus two equals three? Do we need to rethink lifetime prevalence? Psychological Medicine 40(06):895–897.

Susser ES, Lin SP. (1992). Schizophrenia After Prenatal Exposure to the Dutch Hunger Winter of 1944–1945. Arch Gen Psychiatry 49(12):983–988.

Thornicroft G, Tansella M. (2009). Better Mental Health Care. Cambridge: Cambridge University Press.

Tsuang MT, Tohen M, Jones PB, editors. (2011). Textbook of Psychiatric Epidemiology, Third Edition. New York: John Wiley & Sons.

Veling W, Selten J-P, Veen N, Laan W, Blom JD, Hoek HW (2006). Incidence of schizophrenia among ethnic minorities in the Netherlands: A four-year first-contact study. Schizophrenia Research 86(1–3):189–193.

Wadsworth M, Kuh D, Richards M, Hardy R. (2006). Cohort Profile: The 1946 National Birth Cohort (MRC National Survey of Health and Development). International Journal of Epidemiology 35(1):49–54.

Wang PS, Aguilar-Gaxiola S, Alonso J, Angermeyer MC, Borges G, et al (2007). Use of mental health services for anxiety, mood, and substance disorders in 17 countries in the WHO world mental health surveys. The Lancet 370(9590):841–850.

Wang PS, Lane M, Olfson M, Pincus HA, Wells KB, and Kessler RC (2005). Twelve-Month Use of Mental Health Services in the United States: Results From the National Comorbidity Survey Replication. Arch Gen Psychiatry 62(6):629–640.

Williams DR, Haile R, Gonzalez HM, Neighbors H, Baser R, Jackson JS (2007). The Mental Health of Black Caribbean Immigrants: Results from the National Survey of American Life. Am J Public Health 97(1):52–59.

Williams DR, Herman A, Stein DJ, Heeringa SG, Jackson PB, et al (2008). Twelve-month mental disorders in South Africa: prevalence, service use and demographic correlates in the population-based South African Stress and Health Study. Psychol Med 38(2):211–220.

Zaridze D, Brennan P, Boreham J, Boroda A, Karpov R, et al (2009). Alcohol and cause-specific mortality in Russia: a retrospective case?control study of 48?557 adult deaths. The Lancet 373(9682):2201–2214.

Social and Political Determinants of Health and Mental Health

Ruth S. Shim and Monica Taylor-Desir

Introduction

The rise of the Community Mental Health Movement in the early 1960s, bolstered by the Civil Rights Movement, brought the biopsychosocial model to the center of mental health care, resulting in a greater acknowledgment that biological, psychological, and social factors interact to create poor mental health outcomes. At the same time, deinstitutionalization, coupled with inadequate and underfunded community mental health services, led to an exacerbation of mental health inequities among marginalized populations with serious mental illness and substance use disorders. These marginalized populations were most susceptible to the damaging effects of the social and political determinants of health and mental health. The World Health Organization (WHO) defines the social determinants of health as "the conditions in which people are born, grow, work, live, and age, and the wider set of forces and systems shaping the conditions of daily life" (World Health Organization 2020). The WHO goes on to implicate the social determinants of health as the major cause of health inequities worldwide. When considering community psychiatry in the modern era, one cannot begin to consider mental health disparities and inequities without accounting for the social determinants of mental health. While not distinctly different from the social determinants of health, the social determinants of *mental health* deserve special emphasis because they may lead more robustly to poor mental health outcomes and mental health inequities seen in society.

With increased attention to the social determinants of health and mental health over time, community psychiatrists have a greater understanding of its importance. Much awareness was gained with the release of the seminal report, *Closing the Gap in a Generation*, written by the WHO's Commission on Social Determinants of Health (2008). This report assembled the data on the role of the social determinants of health in perpetuating social injustice and inequities in health outcomes, leading to a significant increase in publications and initiatives focusing on these issues. Healthy People 2020 emphasized five social determinant areas: economic stability, education, social and community context, health and health care, and neighborhood and built environment. Healthy People 2030 builds on this work, identifying the social determinants of health as one of its five overarching goals (US Department of Health and Human Services 2020).

R. S. Shim (✉)
Department of Psychiatry & Behavioral Services, University of California, Davis School of Medicine, Sacramento, CA, USA
e-mail: rshim@ucdavis.edu

M. Taylor-Desir
Department of Psychiatry and Psychology, Mayo Clinic, Rochester, MN, USA
e-mail: taylor-desir.monica@mayo.edu

W. E. Sowers et al. (eds.), *Textbook of Community Psychiatry*,
https://doi.org/10.1007/978-3-031-10239-4_29

Additionally, over the years, there have been calls to action to address the social determinants of mental health within the behavioral health field (Shim and Compton 2018). This chapter discusses the importance of the social determinants of mental health, presents evidence highlighting specific social determinants, and identifies intervention points to illustrate how community psychiatrists can combat structural racism by addressing the social and political determinants of mental health, leading to more equitable and improved mental health outcomes.

Framework for the Social Determinants of Mental Health

In considering the social determinants of mental health, a conceptualization (see Fig. 1) is helpful to enhance understanding of multiple contextual factors (Shim and Compton 2020).

The top of the figure represents poor mental health outcomes (and mental health inequities). Moving down the figure, underlying poor mental health outcomes are risk factors for mental illnesses and substance use disorders. Risk factors are defined as characteristics that precede a disorder and are statistically associated with the development of the disorder. These include physiological stress responses, psychological stress, behavioral risk factors, "poor choices," and reduced options. Psychiatry places a great deal of emphasis on the identification and stratification of risk factors, especially when conducting suicide risk assessments. However, when considering the social determinants of mental health, it becomes increasingly clear that if one is intervening at the level of the risk factor (i.e., at the level that directly precedes the development of disease), the intervention may be too late. Rather, research on the social determinants of health advocates moving "upstream" to address "the causes of the causes" (Marmot 2007). Moving upstream (or down the figure) leads to the social determinants of mental health. These are grouped into four categories in Fig. 1: (1) *pervasive US societal problems* (adverse early life experiences, discrimination and racism, exposure to violence, and interaction with the criminal justice system), (2) *opportunities for accruing wealth* (low edu-

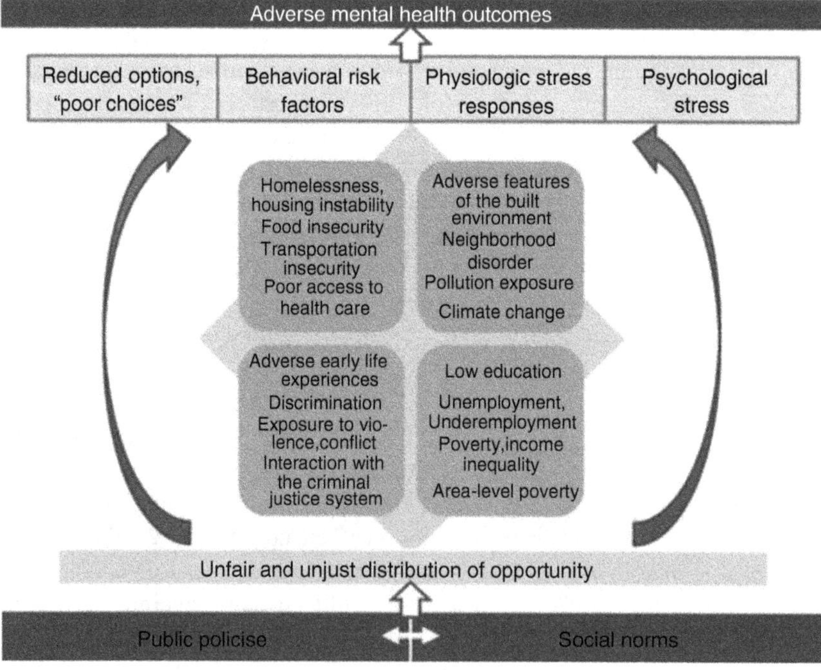

Fig. 1 A conceptualization of the social determinants of mental health

cation, unemployment and underemployment, poverty and income inequality, and area-level poverty), (3) *basic needs* (housing instability, food insecurity, transportation insecurity, and poor access to health care), and (4) *the physical environment* (adverse features of the built environment, neighborhood disorder, exposure to pollution, and climate change) (Compton and Shim 2020). This is not meant to be a complete list of social determinants of mental health, but it should serve as a starting point for considering the upstream "causes of the causes" of poor mental health outcomes.

In further examining the conceptualization, beneath these social determinants of mental health are the unfair and unjust distribution of opportunity – a concept defined as *social injustice*. The driving forces behind injustice in society are the public policies and social norms that govern that society. Public policies are the laws, policies, ordinances, and rules (both written and unwritten) that regulate institutions, communities, and governments. The political determinants of health describe these public policies which influence relationship structures, resource distribution, and the administration of power. These elements influence one another to tip the balance of health equity and health inequities (Dawes 2020). Social norms are the values that we intrinsically place on population groups – specifically, those groups we choose to value as a society and those groups we choose to diminish or devalue. Throughout history, people with serious mental illnesses and substance use disorders have been consistently stigmatized, devalued, and oppressed. Social norms include beliefs that people with mental health problems and substance use disorders are morally and spiritually deficient, make poor decisions, or are emotionally weak. As a result, society passes laws and creates policies to reflect these values. For example, the policy that creates a lack of insurance parity for mental health and substance use disorders ensures that people with mental illnesses and substance use disorders have less access to services compared to people with physical health conditions. Similarly, other damaging policies have led to people with mental health problems and substance use disorders being criminalized, resulting in disproportionate levels of interaction with the carceral system (Dvoskin et al. 2020).

The Social Determinants of Mental Health Evidence Base

Social determinants of mental health are important contributors to poor mental health outcomes and mental health inequities. This chapter will highlight evidence that demonstrates how the social determinants of mental health impact the lives of individuals and their communities. We will highlight the importance of addressing the social determinants of mental health in developing prevention, treatment, and research strategies.

Exposure to Violence

Violence is an expressed form of oppression, meaning that commonly oppressed groups (minoritized populations, people of lower socioeconomic status) are at risk for being victims of physical and structural violence (Young 1990). Recent studies have estimated the prevalence of US children's exposure to community violence ranging from a shocking level of 50–75%, and one study found that the number of indirect violence exposures was significantly associated with any adverse mental health outcome, especially posttraumatic stress disorder (PTSD) and depression (Gollub et al. 2019). The National Survey on Children's Exposure to Violence surveyed children of various races, gender, socioeconomic status, family structure, region, and developmental stage of the child, noting that most children in the United States have experienced direct or indirect exposure to violence within the previous year, with 10% reporting five or more violent exposures within the previous year (Finkelhor et al. 2013). Additionally, among North American Indigenous youth populations, Hautala and Sittner (2018) found an association between direct and indirect violence exposure and increased risk of substance use disorders.

Unemployment and Job Insecurity

The mental health impacts associated with employment have been exposed in the wake of the coronavirus disease 2019 (COVID-19) pandemic, in which a significant portion of the US population has lost their jobs or have been deemed "essential workers," requiring them to take significant risks to their health to maintain employment. During the COVID-19 pandemic, job insecurity was associated with an increase in anxiety symptoms (Wilson et al. 2020). Unemployment is associated with poor mental health, and, in Norway, one study found a direct association with increased prescriptions of psychotropic drugs at times of unemployment compared to times when individuals were employed (Kaspersen et al. 2016; Øverland 2016).

Homelessness and Housing Instability

Housing instability and homelessness is a major contributor to poor health outcomes for children, adults, and families. While it is difficult at times to determine causality, data suggests that serious mental illness is not the main contributor to homelessness in the United States (Substance Abuse and Mental Health Services Administration 2011). The United States Conference of Mayors conducts an annual survey of hunger and homelessness which has consistently showed the dearth of affordable housing is the leading cause of homelessness. The other top contributors to homelessness include unemployment, poverty, and low wages (National Law Center on Homelessness and Poverty, 2018). However, evidence does support that being homeless does contribute to worse mental health outcomes, including suicidal ideation, trauma, and substance misuse (Padgett 2020). Similarly, a systematic review of people under threat of eviction found associated poor mental health outcomes, including depression, anxiety, and psychological distress (Vásquez-Vera et al. 2017).

Climate Change

The most recent United Nations (UN) Climate Report sounded the alarm for a concerted global effort to address climate change. The UN noted that a rise in global temperatures of 1.5 °C could lead to the displacement of millions of people, rising sea levels, decreased production of critical crops, forest fires, and pandemics (World Meteorological Organization 2020). Nevertheless, it is challenging to attribute climate change to adverse mental health outcomes for several reasons, including lack of data on premorbid mental health problems, associated transient stress responses associated with weather-related disasters, and interaction with various other social determinants of mental health (Hayes et al. 2018). That said, data on the aftermath of Hurricane Katrina found sustained, elevated rates of PTSD over time. These findings have persisted across many other extreme weather events, including floods and drought (Rataj et al. 2016). The impact of climate change as a social determinant of mental health is still an emerging area of research and investigation (see chapter "Climate Change: Impact on Community Mental Health").

Points of Intervention to Address the Social Determinants of Mental Health

Discrimination and Racism

The Aspen Institute defines structural racism as "a system in which public policies, institutional practices, cultural representations, and other norms work in various, often reinforcing ways to perpetuate racial group inequity" (The Aspen Institute 2016). These racial group inequities are often expressed in actions as discrimination. Structural racism contributes to the unjust and unfair distribution of opportunity in society, which leads to the creation of the various social determinants of mental health. As racial inequities are baked into the structures of society (through policies and institutional practices), they cannot be easily undone by changing individual interpersonal interactions. Dismantling structural racism involves ending old, racist policies and creating new, anti-racist policies. For example, in 2018, the majority of Black (69%) and Latinx (67%) people with mental illnesses reported not receiving treatment, compared to 51% of White people (Substance Abuse and Mental Health Services Administration 2019). For people with serious mental illnesses, the numbers were equally concerning, with 42% of Black and 44% of Latinx people not receiving treatment, compared to 33% of White people with serious mental illnesses (Substance Abuse and Mental Health Services Administration 2019). If these numbers are considered through the lens of patient-level factors, it is easy to conclude that Black and Latinx people do not access or receive treatment due to stigma, lack of insight about illness, and poor adherence to treatment recommendations (Nadeem et al. 2007). However, recent studies have determined that cost and lack of insurance are the most common cause given for those that report unmet need, almost twice as often as minimization of symptoms and nearly five times as often as perceived stigma (Alang 2019; Walker et al. 2015). Thus, structural forces, not individual patient preference, are the main drivers of poor access to mental health care.

Another factor contributing to the significant lack of access to mental health services of minoritized populations includes the low numbers of psychiatrists that accept insurance compared with physicians in other specialties (Bishop et al. 2014). In 2009–2010, only 55% of psychiatrists accepted private, noncapitated insurance, and only 43% accepted Medicaid (compared to 88% and 73% of physicians in other specialties). There are many explanations for this inequity in insurance acceptance, including lower reimbursement rates, coupled with longer visits needed to provide psychotherapy. However, the shortage of psychiatrists and general high demand for mental health care services mean that psychiatrists have the power to dictate how they interface with the mental health care system. For those psychiatrists without a background or interest in community psychiatry, the desire to provide psychotherapy to patients of a higher socioeconomic status (patients that are of similar backgrounds and experiences) may be very strong. Similarly, psychiatrists who have implicit bias and discriminatory beliefs toward Black, Indigenous, and other People of Color, operating a solo private practice that takes cash only can ensure less interaction with these populations.

Lack of equitable insurance access is the result of discrimination and structural racism – policies that promoted desegregation of the health care system in the United States were often coupled with pushes for universal health care coverage (Hoffman 2008). During these efforts, the American Medical Association was strongly opposed to expanding health care coverage to all Americans, leading to widening gaps in access. Efforts to expand Medicaid and decrease uninsurance rates in the United States (including the Affordable Care Act) continue to be met with significant opposition that ensures the persistence of racial and other inequities in health care coverage (Lantz and Rosenbaum 2020).

Thus, in considering improving mental health treatment outcomes and closing the gap of mental health inequities, greater attention should be paid to ensuring that everyone has access to health insurance at rates that cover mental health and substance use disorders at the same level as physical health conditions. Further, policies must ensure that mental health professionals can provide services to all sectors of the population, not just those people with access to insurance or with income levels that enable people to pay out-of-pocket for treatment services.

The point of intervention involves changing existing policies and laws that regulate mental health care insurance access. This requires electing public officials with a commitment to advocate for more racially equitable policies that support greater access to mental health services and incentivize training mental health workers with an interest in providing services in community settings. Thus, laws and policies that impede or suppress voting result in perpetuating the status quo. Because of policies and laws that have criminalized mental illness, many people with substance use disorders and mental illnesses access mental health services after they have been arrested or served time in criminal justice settings. As a result, some of the very people who could vote to improve policies for people with serious mental illnesses and substance use disorders (people with lived experiences of substance use disorders and serious mental illnesses) have been marginalized in society and unable to vote. Thus, policies need to focus on improving community power and political voice for oppressed and marginalized communities.

Adverse Early Life Experiences

Childhood trauma is a powerful social determinant of mental health. Previous studies (utilizing the Adverse Childhood Experience [ACE] study) have found correlations between early childhood trauma and a host of poor health and mental health outcomes, including increased behavioral risk factors (e.g., early age of initiation of sexual activity and cigarette smoking), increased suicide attempts, and early mortality (Felitti et al. 1998). These findings are remarkably consistent, but also made more concerning in light of newer findings that show that the original ACE study did not include many common traumatic experiences that are more often experienced by children of color, including interaction with the foster care system, experiencing racism, and witnessing violence in neighborhoods (Cronholm et al. 2015). Additionally, the concept of complex posttraumatic stress disorder (C-PTSD), recognized as a mental illness internationally, but not in the United States, highlights the unique risk that children and adolescents who are unable to remove themselves from traumatic circumstances face when they have the potential to be re-traumatized in their social environments (Kazlauskas et al. 2020). Thus, unfair and unjust distribution of opportunity is a major contributor to differential experiences of childhood trauma that exist in society. Public policies and social norms drive these differential and inequitable opportunities. Children of lower socioeconomic status or of minoritized groups are often not valued (or given the same opportunities to achieve healthy lives) as children from higher socioeconomic status. As a result, these children often experience greater incidence and prevalence of adverse childhood experiences.

The intervention point for addressing the social determinant of adverse childhood experiences involves taking action to change public policies and social norms. If the societal norms dictate that some children are not worthy of the same legal protections and support as other children, then policies are implemented to support this claim – as evidenced by higher rates of discipline of Black, Latinx, and Indigenous children in school compared to White children (Welsh and Little 2018). Therefore, the intervention involves undoing inequitable policies that disadvantage students of color. Investments in early childhood education programs (e.g., those programs modeled after Head Start) demonstrate significantly improved outcomes and lower societal costs due to less criminal activity and less reliance on social welfare programs (Belfield et al. 2006). Similarly, the Nurse-Family Partnership program, which sends nurses out on home visits to pregnant mothers, has shown significantly lower rates of child mistreatment compared to usual care over the long term (Eckenrode et al. 2017). These interventions require monetary and human capital investments in children and families of color in order to reap rewards 10–20 years in the future, far beyond a standard election cycle.

The Moral Determinants of Mental Health

Berwick (2020) calls on health professionals to embrace the *moral determinants of health,* in which investment in human well-being takes precedent, and solidarity and shared responsibility are embraced above other values. Berwick lists several recommendations to take action to address the moral determinants of health, which equally apply to determinants of mental health, including ratification of human rights treaties and conventions, ensuring universal health care, leadership in reversing climate change, reforming the

US carceral system, reforming immigration laws to protect families and reduce trauma, ending food and housing insecurity/homelessness in the United States, and resisting voter suppression tactics so that all voters have a voice in political institutions. These goals are simultaneously lofty, but also achievable with a clear plan of action that is bolstered by community empowerment and leadership that enacts policies that promote creating equitable opportunities for people to achieve health.

As previously discussed, action on the moral determinants of health involves interventions in public policies and social norms. From a public policy perspective, both global and local interventions are necessary. Psychiatrists and other mental health professionals must advocate for people with serious mental illnesses and substance use disorders, both by working to empower oppressed communities and by leveraging privilege to effect change with those political actors that hold power. Many examples of organizations that develop and sustain community power exist across sectors. To address multiple social determinants, including housing insecurity, area-level poverty, exposure to violence, and poor education, Purpose Built Communities has redesigned and transformed neighborhoods, leading to increased employment, decreased violent crime, and dramatically increased school performance (Franklin and Edwards 2012). To tackle the social determinants of discrimination, unemployment, and poverty, the National Domestic Workers Alliance has organized domestic workers and helped to pass bills of rights in various states and cities, guaranteeing basic employment rights to minimum wage and overtime pay (National Domestic Workers Alliance 2020). Color of Change has worked to empower communities to address multiple social determinants of health, including, but not limited to, discrimination, interaction with the carceral system, unemployment, poverty, and neighborhood disorder (Color of Change 2020). These examples demonstrate how effective organization to build community power can lead to lasting changes in outcomes. The main question becomes, "How do community psychiatrists and other mental health professionals contribute to this work?" These organizations are just some examples of community-based organizations that are making positive change in addressing social determinants of mental health. Community psychiatrists must partner with these and other organizations in their communities to implement and effect change in their local communities. Additionally, community psychiatrists must also develop strategic relationships with lawmakers. This simultaneous top-down and bottom-up approach can lead to lasting improvements in addressing the social, political, and moral determinants of health.

To address the social norms that lead to harmful policies, community psychiatrists and other community mental health professionals have a responsibility to increase their knowledge of the above noted inequities that are often not incorporated in medical or professional school curricula. Scholarly work informed by critical race theory, feminist theory, and queer theory, to name a few, helps to increase understanding of how systems of oppression and structural violence are perpetuated in the assessment, diagnosis, and treatment of serious mental illnesses and substance use disorders. Once armed with additional information, community psychiatrists and other mental health professionals have a moral responsibility to speak up when witnessing and observing injustice occurring. Existing social norms have made it acceptable to express discriminatory or exclusionary thoughts, in the form of off-color jokes, microaggressions, and racial abuse. This cannot be tolerated in backrooms where power is being expressed, and it cannot be allowed to invade policies that occur in the open. Thus, racial equity impact assessments must be conducted on all proposed policies to address the social determinants of mental health.

There are challenges and threats to taking action to address the social determinants of mental health. First, many community psychiatrists and other mental health professionals have made sacrifices (monetary, geographic, etc.) to work in the public sector. Often, their schedules are overloaded due to the demand for providers. Committing to additional work is challenging and working with communities is time-consuming. Furthermore, this work is far outside of most providers' level of expertise, and a lack of mastery in this space might lead to frustration or disillusionment for those providers that are used to appearing competent and fully knowledgeable. Finally, the scope of work to be done may seem insurmountable as there is much injustice in the world and people with serious mental illness and substance use disorders are suffering. For all of these valid concerns, it is important to consider the words of Nobel Laureate Elie Wiesel, who said:

> But where was I to start? The world is so vast, I shall start with the country I know best, my own. But my country is so very large. I had better start with my town. But my town too, is large. I had best start with my street. No: my home. No: my family. Never mind, I shall start with myself! (Weisel 1982, p. 135)

Community psychiatrists and community mental health professionals must begin with a deep self-inventory and then translate that investment outward into their communities and work settings.

Conclusion

The social and political determinants of mental health are primarily responsible for the vast differences in mental health outcomes that are observed among gender, race and ethnicity, and other demographic groups. Prior tendencies toward individuation have led us to attribute personal responsibility and choices to these differences in outcomes, rather than examine the unjust and unfair policies and practices that set the context for the social determinants of mental health. When community psychiatrists are better able to understand the driving factors that create mental health inequities, they are better able to design and execute effective interventions to begin to address the social determinants of mental health and improve outcomes for people with mental illness and substance use disorders. By intervening upstream at the level of social norms and public policies, community psychiatrists can effectively prevent a host of poor outcomes that routinely and characteristically occur downstream. Effective models exist that can help guide our efforts. There are many barriers to action, but everyone must start somewhere if we are to make lasting and sustainable change.

References

Alang, S. M. (2019). Mental health care among blacks in America: Confronting racism and constructing solutions. *Health Services Research, 54*(2), 346–355.

Belfield, C. R., Nores, M., Barnett, S., & Schweinhart, L. (2006). The High/Scope Perry Preschool Program Cost–Benefit Analysis Using Data from the Age-40 Followup. *Journal of Human Resources, XLI*(1), 162–190.

Berwick, D. M. (2020). The Moral Determinants of Health. *JAMA, 324*(3), 225.

Bishop, T. F., Press, M. J., Keyhani, S., & Pincus, H. A. (2014). Acceptance of Insurance by Psychiatrists and the Implications for Access to Mental Health Care. *JAMA Psychiatry, 71*(2), 176.

Color of Change. (2020). About Color of Change. Retrieved on 1 November, 2020 at https://colorofchange.org/about/

Commission on Social Determinants of Health. (2008). Closing the Gap in a Generation: Health Equity Through Action on the Social Determinants of Health: Final Report of the Commission on Social Determinants of Health. World Health Organization.

Compton, M. T., & Shim, R. S. (2020). Why Employers Must Focus on the Social Determinants of Mental Health. *American Journal of Health Promotion, 34*(2), 215–219.

Cronholm, P. F., Forke, C. M., Wade, R., Bair-Merritt, M. H., Davis, M., Harkins-Schwarz, M., Pachter, L. M., & Fein, J. A. (2015). Adverse Childhood Experiences: Expanding the Concept of Adversity. *American Journal of Preventive Medicine, 49*(3), 354–361.

Dawes, D. (2020). *The Political Determinants of Health.* Baltimore: Johns Hopkins University Press.

Dvoskin, J. A., Knoll, J. L., & Silva, M. (2020). A brief history of the criminalization of mental illness. *CNS Spectrums, 25*(5), 638–650.

Eckenrode, J., Campa, M. I., Morris, P. A., Henderson, C. R., Bolger, K. E., Kitzman, H., & Olds, D. L. (2017). The Prevention of Child Maltreatment Through the Nurse Family Partnership Program: Mediating Effects in a Long-Term Follow-Up Study. *Child Maltreatment, 22*(2), 92–99.

Felitti, V. J., Anda, R. F., Nordenberg, D., Williamson, D. F., Spitz, A. M., Edwards, V., Koss, M. P., & Marks, J. S. (1998). Relationship of Childhood Abuse and Household Dysfunction to Many of the Leading

Causes of Death in Adults: The Adverse Childhood Experiences (ACE) Study. *American Journal of Preventive Medicine*, *14*(4), 245–258.

Finkelhor, D., Turner, H.A., Shattuck, A., & Hanby, S. L. (2013). Violence, Crime, and Abuse Exposure in a National Sample of Children and Youth. An Update. *Journal of American Medical Association Pediatrics*, 167(7), 614–621.

Franklin, S., & Edwards, D. (2012). It takes a neighborhood: Purpose built communities and neighborhood transformation. Investing in What Works for America's Communities, 170–183.

Gollub, E. L., Green, J., Richardson, L., Kaplan, I., & Shervington, D. (2019). Indirect violence exposure and mental health symptoms among an urban public-school population: Prevalence and correlates. *PLOS ONE*, *14*(11), e0224499.

Hautala, D., & Sittner, K. (2018). Moderators of the Association Between Exposure to Violence in Community, Family, and Dating Contexts and Substance Use Disorder Risk Among North American Indigenous Adolescents. *Journal of Interpersonal Violence*, 0886260518792255.

Hayes, K., Blashki, G., Wiseman, J., Burke, S., & Reifels, L. (2018). Climate change and mental health: Risks, impacts and priority actions. *International Journal of Mental Health Systems*, *12*(1), 28.

Hoffman, B. (2008). Health Care Reform and Social Movements in the United States. *American Journal of Public Health*, *98*(Supplement_1), S69–S79.

Kaspersen, S. L., Pape, K., Ose, S. O., Gunnell, D., & Bjørngaard, J. H. (2016). Unemployment and initiation of psychotropic medication: A case-crossover study of 2 348 552 Norwegian employees. *Occupational and Environmental Medicine*, *73*(11), 719–726.

Kazlauskas, E., Zelviene, P., Daniunaite, I., Hyland, P., Kvedaraite, M., Shevlin, M., & Cloitre, M. (2020). The structure of ICD-11 PTSD and Complex PTSD in adolescents exposed to potentially traumatic experiences. *Journal of Affective Disorders*, *265*, 169–174.

Lantz, P. M., & Rosenbaum, S. (2020). The Potential and Realized Impact of the Affordable Care Act on Health Equity. *Journal of Health Politics, Policy and Law*, *45*(5), 831–845.

Marmot, M. (2007). Achieving health equity: From root causes to fair outcomes. *The Lancet*, *370*(9593), 1153–1163.

Nadeem, E., Lange, J. M., Edge, D., Fongwa, M., Belin, T., & Miranda, J. (2007). Does Stigma Keep Poor Young Immigrant and U.S.-Born Black and Latina Women From Seeking Mental Health Care? *Psychiatric Services*, *58*(12), 8.

National Domestic Workers Alliance. (2020). Raising Standards. Retrieved 1 November, 2020 from https://www.domesticworkers.org/raising-standards

National Law Center on Homelessness and Poverty. (2018). Homelessness in America: Overview of Data and Causes. Retrieved 2 February, 2021 from https://nlchp.org/wp-content/uploads/2018/10/Homeless_Stats_Fact_Sheet.pdf

Øverland, S. (2016). Unemployment and mental health. *Occupational and Environmental Medicine*, *73*(11), 717–718.

Padgett, D. K. (2020). Homelessness, housing instability and mental health: Making the connections. *BJPsych Bulletin*, *44*(5), 197–201.

Rataj, E., Kunzweiler, K., & Garthus-Niegel, S. (2016). Extreme weather events in developing countries and related injuries and mental health disorders—A systematic review. *BMC Public Health*, *16*(1), 1020.

Shim, R. S., & Compton, M. T. (2018). Addressing the Social Determinants of Mental Health: If Not Now, When? If Not Us, Who? *Psychiatric Services*, *69*(8), 844–846.

Shim, R. S., & Compton, M. T. (2020). The Social Determinants of Mental Health: Psychiatrists' Roles in Addressing Discrimination and Food Insecurity. *FOCUS*, *18*(1), 25–30.

Substance Abuse and Mental Health Services Administration. (2011). Current Statistics on the Prevalence and Characteristics of People Experiencing Homelessness in the United States. Retrieved on 1 November, 2020 from https://www.samhsa.gov/sites/default/files/programs_campaigns/homelessness_programs_resources/hrc-factsheet-current-statistics-prevalence-characteristics-homelessness.pdf

Substance Abuse and Mental Health Services Administration. (2019). Key Substance Use and Mental Health Indicators in the United States: Results from the 2018 National Survey on Drug Use and Health.

The Aspen Institute. (2016). 11 Terms You Should Know to Better Understand Structural Racism. Retrieved 1 November, 2020 from https://www.aspeninstitute.org/blog-posts/structural-racism-definition/

U.S. Department of Health and Human Services. (2020). Healthy People 2030. Retrieved 1 November, 2020 from https://www.who.int/health-topics/social-determinants-of-health#tab=tab_1

Vásquez-Vera, H., Palència, L., Magna, I., Mena, C., Neira, J., & Borrell, C. (2017). The threat of home eviction and its effects on health through the equity lens: A systematic review. *Social Science & Medicine*, *175*, 199–208.

Walker, E. R., Cummings, J. R., Hockenberry, J. M., & Druss, B. G. (2015). Insurance Status, Use of Mental Health Services, and Unmet Need for Mental Health Care in the United States. *Psychiatric Services*, *66*(6), 578–584.

Weisel, E. (1982). Souls on Fire: Portraits of Legends of Hasidic Masters. New York, Simon & Schuster.

Welsh, R. O., & Little, S. (2018). The School Discipline Dilemma: A Comprehensive Review of Disparities and Alternative Approaches. *Review of Educational Research*, *88*(5), 752–794.

Wilson, J. M., Lee, J., Fitzgerald, H. N., Oosterhoff, B., Sevi, B., & Shook, N. J. (2020). Job Insecurity and Financial Concern During the COVID-19 Pandemic Are Associated With Worse Mental Health. *Journal of Occupational and Environmental Medicine*, *62*(9), 686–691.

World Health Organization. (2020). The Social Determinants of Health. Retrieved 1 November, 2020 from https://www.who.int/health-topics/social-determinants-of-health#tab=tab_1

World Meteorological Organization. (2020). WMO Statement on the State of the Global Climate in 2019. Retrieved 2 February, 2021 from https://library.wmo.int/doc_num.php?explnum_id=10211

Young, I. M. (1990). Five Faces of Oppression, in Justice and the Politics of Different. Princeton, Princeton University Press, pp. 39–65.

Mental Health Services Research and Community Psychiatry

Nichole Goodsmith and Mario Cruz

Introduction

Whether you are a mental health care administrator, a medical director of a clinic, or a clinician, you likely find yourself asking questions about the quality, cost, reach, and value of your services. Do our services aid service users in their recovery and in acquiring the ability to bounce back from life's typical stressors or traumatic events? How do we identify gaps within our service array? How do we decide what services would fill those gaps? And how do we implement those services in the most cost-effective and sustainable way?

N. Goodsmith (✉)
Center for the Study of Healthcare Innovation, Implementation & Policy, Greater Los Angeles VA Medical System, Los Angeles, CA, USA

Department of Psychiatry and Biobehavioral Sciences, David Geffen School of Medicine, University of California, Los Angeles, CA, USA
e-mail: Nichole.Goodsmith@va.gov

M. Cruz
Department of Psychiatry and Behavioral Health Sciences, University of New Mexico School of Medicine, Albuquerque, NM, USA

Health Information Management, University of New Mexico Health System, Albuquerque, NM, USA

American Board of Preventive Medicine, Albuquerque, NM, USA

Department of Psychiatry, MSC09 5030, University of New Mexico, Albuquerque, NM, USA
e-mail: MaCruz@salud.unm.edu

Mental health services research is a means of asking and answering questions like these—questions about service delivery at the policy, system, clinic, provider, and consumer levels. To answer these questions, we need high-quality data on service use and quality measures. To make decisions on how to improve our services, we need results from well-designed studies that compare the effectiveness and costs of specific interventions in care settings similar to our own. Finally, we need evidence-based implementation strategies to ensure that any new interventions are effective and sustainable within our system. Addressing these issues is vital to our work as community psychiatrists.

This chapter will introduce the reader to the core features of mental health services research that are salient to the needs of community psychiatrists. In the first section, "Defining Health Services Research," we explain what we mean by services research and provide an overview of different areas within the field. Next, in "Putting Research into Practice," we highlight the significant gap between research supporting a new practice and the widespread uptake of that practice. We then discuss how health services research is evolving to close that gap. In the third section, "Mental Health Services Research: Examples and Impact," we guide you through a range of approaches and topics encompassed by mental health services research, illustrated by specific highly impactful studies. In the fourth section,

W. E. Sowers et al. (eds.), *Textbook of Community Psychiatry*,
https://doi.org/10.1007/978-3-031-10239-4_30

we introduce the rapidly growing field of informatics and explain how it applies to health services research and to the work of community psychiatrists.

We approach this chapter from the view that research can help to improve the work of all community psychiatrists, and likewise, that all community psychiatrists can help to improve health services research. Whether you are a clinician, administrator, policymaker, or trainee, we hope this chapter will leave you with the following:

- A basic understanding of the principles, vocabulary, and subfields of mental health services research.
- An appreciation for how services research can apply to your practice, clinic, or system.
- An understanding of the important role clinicians and administrators can play on research teams.
- Curiosity and enthusiasm for mental health services research.

Defining Health Services Research

> Health services research is the multidisciplinary field of scientific investigation that studies how social factors, financing systems, organizational structures and processes, health technologies, and personal behaviors affect access to health care, the quality and cost of health care, and ultimately our health and well-being. Its research domains are individuals, families, organizations, institutions, communities, and populations. (Lohr and Steinwachs 2002).

In 2001, the Institute of Medicine published a landmark report, *Crossing the Quality Chasm: A New Health System for the twenty-first Century*, which outlined six major domains of quality in health services (Institute of Medicine Committee on Quality of Health Care in America 2001). These domains included (1) patient safety, (2) effectiveness, (3) timeliness, (4) patient-centeredness, (5) efficiency, and (6) equity. The objective of mental health services research is to use a scientific approach to improve care in these domains. The 2020 Strategic Plan of the National Institute of Mental Health highlights the potential for mental health services research in "optimizing the organization and sustained delivery of evidence-based prevention and treatment intervention, speeding the implementation of research-informed innovations in community settings, and ultimately ensuring optimal outcomes for all affected individuals, including those from underrepresented and underserved communities" (National Institute of Mental Health Strategic Plan for Research 2020). Mental health services research draws approaches and expertise from a range of disciplines, including biostatistics, epidemiology, behavioral economics, sociology, and psychology, among others. Mental health services research has been instrumental to changing how we think, how we practice, and how we allocate resources.

Health services research differs from clinical research in both the questions asked and settings in which the research takes place. In contrast to clinical research, which focuses on addressing the etiology and treatment of disease, mental health services research asks questions related to the cost, quality, usability, and effectiveness of services. Whereas clinical research tests hypotheses in controlled settings, health services research takes place in the real world. For example, a clinical research study on cognitive behavioral therapy (CBT) for treating panic disorder might examine the impact of CBT on symptoms, with therapy delivered by specially trained research staff in a controlled research setting. In contrast, a mental health services study might examine the effectiveness of CBT versus usual care when implemented in a particular health system under real-world conditions. The mental health services version of this study might also assess cost, fidelity, feasibility, and/or acceptability of implementing the CBT intervention, rather than focusing solely on patient-level outcomes (e.g., reduction in panic symptoms). Another mental health services study might look at demographic factors affecting access to CBT programs, or the impact of a health policy on access to anxiety treatment nationwide. Thus, services research goes beyond the question of, "Does treatment X work?" to address a broad set of questions around access, cost, quality, effectiveness, and implementation in the real world.

Health services researchers devote their attention to understanding how to provide effective services in an efficient, economical, and equitable manner. Topics in mental health services research range widely from the impact of policy changes to system organization, financing, and management, to implementation of evidence-based practices. Topics with particular relevance to community psychiatrists include the following:

- Identifying the nature and scope of local service needs.
- Identifying the core features of treatment interventions that must be applied uniformly across service settings and all service users to achieve optimal impact.
- Identifying demographic, socioeconomic, or geographic factors associated with receiving a diagnosis, or accessing treatment.
- Developing the best strategies to implement and sustain evidence-based treatments.
- Allocating financial resources so that service users and providers have proper incentives to use services appropriately.
- Implementing statutory procedures such as civil commitment, consumer's rights, informed consent, and confidentiality.
- Measuring the impact of an intervention on improving or worsening disparities in mental health care.

In Box 1 below, we define key terms in health services research that will be used throughout the chapter.

Box 1 Key Terms in Health Services Research

Quantitative research uses numerical data and statistical methods to test hypotheses. Quantitative research may utilize *primary data* collected expressly for the purpose of a given study, such as ratings or symptom scores measured for study participants at different time points. Quantitative research may also include analysis of preexisting *secondary data* obtained from state- or nationwide surveys, databases of healthcare utilization and expenditures, or other sources.

Qualitative research uses non-numerical data to deepen our understanding of an issue and generate theories and hypotheses. Common qualitative methods include interviews with key stakeholders, focus groups, document analysis, and observation (Palinkas 2014).

Mixed-methods research is just what the name implies: research using a combination of qualitative and quantitative approaches in a complementary fashion to understand different dimensions of a single topic.

Quality improvement is a field that often overlaps with health services research. The main distinctions between the two are in scope and generalizability: quality improvement aims to characterize and solve a specific problem in a specific setting, while health services research aims to generate knowledge that can be applied more broadly.

Efficacy is a measure of how well an intervention or treatment works under ideal, controlled research conditions. This contrasts with *effectiveness,* a measure of how well an intervention works in real-world settings (Hohmann and Shear 2002).

Dissemination in health care is the targeted distribution of information on evidence-based health interventions. An example of this is an educational presentation about new treatment guidelines, shared at a medical conference.

Diffusion is the spread and use of new ideas, behaviors, practices, or organizational forms in an unintended or spontaneous manner. An example is the use of assertive community treatment (ACT) teams to deliver services to populations for which ACT does not yet have a significant evidence base, such as individuals with borderline personality disorder or developmental disabilities.

Implementation is the translation and application of innovations, recommended practices, and policies. An example of successful implementation would be executing a new ACT program with a high level of fidelity to the evidence-based ACT model.

Implementation science is a field of research examining the processes and strategies that move or integrate evidence-based treatments into real-world settings (Bauer et al. 2015). An example is a study of barriers and facilitators to implementing an evidence-based collaborative care depression treatment program in a new setting.

Putting Research into Practice

The Science-to-Practice Gap

The so-called science-to-practice gap is well recognized, with an estimated 17-year delay before original research translates into changes in patient care (Balas and Boren 2000). Early theories suggested a "pipeline" model of research dissemination, beginning with research funding priorities, funneled through peer review and publication, progressing to release of guidelines for evidence-based practice, and finally, making it to practitioners, who implement the intervention. This model implied that roadblocks or acceleration at one of these points would be key to influencing the duration of the science-to-practice gap.

Critics including Lawrence Green have suggested the pipeline model presupposes that the provider is an empty vessel waiting for new knowledge (Green 2008). In reality, the qualities of the intervention are not the only—or even the primary—drivers of adoption. Mental health organizations and providers typically react quickly to changes in mental health care financing and reimbursement, the political landscape that impacts the sustainability of any new intervention, and an ever-increasing demand for a diverse array of services. Adoption may be influenced by local contextual factors, such as the organizational climate (e.g., staff attitudes toward the work environment and job satisfaction), perceived support for quality improvement, or dimensions of organizational culture such as shared beliefs on how to deliver quality care and the services that are considered valuable (Greenhalgh et al. 2004).

Together, these contextual factors call into question the pipeline model's assumption of a passively waiting provider and suggest that it takes more than knowledge of an effective intervention for that intervention to be implemented widely. For example, despite extensive evidence and agreement on effective mental health practices and interventions for persons with severe mental illness, many of these practices, such as supported employment and ACT, are not employed in typical mental health care settings (Drake et al. 2009). Health services research seeks to minimize the science-to-practice gap, so that we can ensure that important services reach those who need them most.

Barriers to Success of Evidence-Based Practices

Widespread implementation is only one barrier to the success of evidence-based practices. Even when evidence-based practices are implemented, they may fail to have the anticipated impact. Many promising interventions in controlled environment trials fail to be as effective in real-world settings. One reason for this failure in effectiveness is that many clinical studies exclude service users who have difficulty accessing or adhering to care. The characteristics of the excluded service users may be more consistent with the population we serve than those who were included in the intervention trial. Other reasons for the ineffectiveness of controlled trial interventions in real-world settings are the costs associated with implementing and sustaining a new intervention, the incapacity of organizations to negotiate change, or difficulty in implementing with high fidelity to key components of the original intervention.

In light of these reasons behind the science-to-practice gap, changes are occurring in the research and development process. Specifically, it is becoming increasingly common for researchers to collaborate with clinicians and other stakeholders in all aspects of the research process, from defining the questions that are asked to developing details of the study design, to brainstorming implementation models and strategies (Green 2008; Sullivan et al. 2005). The involvement of key stakeholders, including clinicians and administrators as well as service users, has the potential to dramatically improve the relevance and effectiveness of research studies and findings. This partnered approach is exemplified by community-based participatory research (CBPR), discussed below.

Community-Based Participatory Research

With growing recognition of the gross inequities both in access to treatment and in outcomes, policymakers, communities, providers, and researchers alike have recognized the need for inclusive and community-informed research. Community-based participatory research (CBPR) meets this need through a collaborative approach that equitably involves researchers and community stakeholders, recognizing the unique strengths that each brings to the research endeavor (Israel et al. 2008; Jones and Wells 2007; Wallerstein et al. 2018). In CBPR, academic and community partners collaborate in the development of the questions asked, the methods employed to address the question, the interventions developed, and the kinds of outcomes desired, valued, and measured.

CBPR is participatory and cooperative, grounded in a two-way exchange of knowledge in which researchers and community stakeholders learn from one another. The approach involves systems development and local community capacity building, thereby achieving a balance between research and action. For community psychiatrists, CBPR affords an orientation to research that allows for their direct involvement in the research process as well as the development and tailoring of research interventions that take into consideration the unique features of the setting in which they work.

Although CBPR is often referred to as a research method, it is actually an orientation to research. What is new is not the use of unique research methods or study designs. Rather, the uniqueness lies in the attitudes of the researchers, which in turn determines how research is conceptualized and conducted. The location of power and control over the research process is another distinctive factor. CBPR ensures that relevant stakeholders share power in the research process, rather than the traditional unidirectional model in which researchers develop, implement, and analyze the study in relative isolation. Community partners give their knowledge and experience to the formulation of research questions and to many other aspects of the research process. As a consequence of this change in location of power and control over the research process, CBPR strengthens the awareness of community members' own capabilities as researchers while providing a depth and relevance to the research that might otherwise be lacking.

Mental Health Services Research: Examples and Impact

Mental health services research serves many varied purposes. In this section, we discuss some of these purposes, using examples of studies to highlight the potential impact of this work. We focus on six key areas: policy impact, service utilization, disparities, costs, practice patterns, and implementation. These topic areas are not intended to comprise an exhaustive list, but rather, to provide a glimpse of some of the many forms mental health services research can take. For each area, we provide context and relevance to community psychiatrists, accompanied by a case study to illustrate the approach and potential impact. We hope these cases will spark curiosity and help you to see how mental health services research can apply to your work—and how your work can be a part of mental health services research.

Understanding the Impact of Policies

Policies at the national, state, and local levels can have major impacts on access, utilization, and cost of mental health services, as well as clinical outcomes. Policies with a significant impact on mental health services include national initiatives such as the Community Mental Health Act of 1963, which spurred deinstitutionalization in favor of community-based care. The Affordable Care Act (ACA) of 2010, which expanded insurance coverage and requirements for mental health parity, is another example. State initiatives such as the California Mental Health Services Act of 2004, designed to increase funding for a broad expansion of behavioral health services, can also have a significant impact. Studies examining the impact of policy changes are typically *quantitative* analyses (see Box 1), drawing on data sources such as large national surveys and insurance databases and applying sophisticated statistical methods.

An example of policy-related mental health services research is a 2011 study by Rachel Garfield and colleagues looking at the anticipated impact of the ACA on mental health service use (Garfield et al. 2011). The passage of the ACA spurred the authors to ask how the new policies might affect health coverage for individuals with serious mental illness (SMI). Aiming to estimate the impact well before it could be measured, they used data from the Medical Expenditure Panel Surveys (MEPS) from 2004 to 2006. MEPS is a large, extensive national survey conducted annually, collecting demographic data as well as information on sources of health care coverage. They compared individuals with and without a diagnosis of SMI, looking at insurance coverage and use of mental health services.

The authors highlighted several findings with potential to shift the landscape of mental health services. First, they showed that people with SMI were less likely to have insurance coverage than those without SMI. Second, they found that among people with SMI, those with insurance were much more likely to use mental health services than those without insurance coverage. Using MEPS data, they predicted the scale of new enrollment, and the expected increase in service use, under the ACA. Because people with SMI were overrepresented among the uninsured prior to the ACA, they predicted that they would represent a disproportionate amount of increased demand under the ACA. These estimates had major implications for allocation of scarce resources and raised questions of what changes to incentives and payment structures might be needed to ensure that increased demand was appropriately met, particularly for the patients with the greatest need (Essock and Hogan 2011).

Policy-related research like this is important to community psychiatrists at all levels. For policymakers, understanding the impact of policy changes is crucial to guide decisions. For clinicians, understanding the effects of policies on your patients and the treatment you offer can allow you to help them navigate complex systems. Additionally, understanding policy repercussions helps you to advocate for equitable policies in the future.

Understanding Service Utilization

To identify problems in care and potential intervention strategies to improve care, we need data on the current state of care provision. Whether you are a State Behavioral Health Medical Director charged with offering recommendations to improve the care of the seriously mentally ill, or a clinician in a community-based mental health center concerned about no-show rates, you need information that can direct you to potential solutions to the problem at hand. Mental health services research that intends to inform funding decisions at the federal, state, local, or program level uses utilization data collected within defined periods.

To highlight the use of utilization data in mental health services research, we can look at the development of the movement to enhance mental health services in primary care practice settings. The White House Executive Order of February 17, 1977, established the President's Commission on Mental Health. As a first priority, the White House requested that the Commission seek to identify how the mentally ill were being served, to what extent they were being underserved, and who was affected by such underservice. At that point, a few studies had shown that primary care clinics were screening and treating a large percentage of mental health service users. However, it was unclear how essential primary care clinics were to mental health service delivery.

Regier and colleagues turned these potential policy-driving questions into study objectives. They sought to, first, produce the best available estimates of the number of individuals in the population who have mental disorders and, second, determine the number of people identified and/or treated within specified sectors of the mental health and health services system in a single year (Regier 1978). They defined the mental health system as a largely unorganized and "de facto" system comprised of four major sectors: specialty mental health, general hospital inpatient/nursing home, primary care/outpatient medical, and not in treatment/other. They combined several epidemiological datasets to assess the national prevalence of psychiatric disorders, integrated with another dataset to assess service utilization.

Their results revealed that 54% of all mental health screening and treatment took place in primary care, compared to 15% in the specialty mental health sector. In addition, depression was more often treated in primary care than specialty mental health settings. The impact of this work was substantial, with considerable subsequent research focused on improving the detection and treatment of mental disorders in primary care settings (Gilbody 2006). This research effort has resulted in the successful development and testing of several evidence-based interventions for the treatment of depression in primary care settings.

Understanding Inequities

Eliminating racial and ethnic disparities in diagnosis, access to treatment, and outcomes is a national priority (McGuire and Miranda 2008). Increasingly, the academic community recognizes that such disparities are not driven by individual-level differences, but, rather, result from a history of structural racism (Ford and Airhihenbuwa 2010; Thomas et al. 2011). Mental health services research has the potential to help identify the extent of these inequities and, more importantly, to suggest approaches to build a more equitable system of care.

A classic example of research in this area is the work to understand racial inequities in psychiatric diagnoses. By the early 1980s, psychiatrists raised concerns about the overdiagnosis of Black patients, particularly Black men, with psychosis (Bell and Mehta 1980). It was observed that Black men were far more likely to receive a diagnosis of schizophrenia, when their white counterparts might be diagnosed with affective psychosis (i.e., bipolar disorder). The Epidemiologic Catchment Area was a landmark national study that used lay interviewers to survey participants with standardized diagnostic questionnaires based on the DSM-III criteria (Robbins and Regier 1991). With data collected from approximately 20,000 individuals in the late 1970s and early 1980s, this study provided invaluable estimates of the prevalence of different psychiatric disorders and demonstrated conclusively that no significant racial difference existed in the prevalence of schizophrenia when using clear diagnostic criteria.

Numerous subsequent studies have affirmed trends in the misdiagnosis of schizophrenia for Black men with affective psychosis, showing race as the strongest predictor of receiving a diagnosis of schizophrenia (Schwartz and Blankenship 2014). For the community psychiatrist, they encourage us not only to examine our own diagnostic choices, but also to examine how the systems in which we work may be promoting racially biased and harmful decision-making.

Understanding Costs

For policymakers, administrators, and clinicians alike, cost has a major impact on care delivery. Even the most impactful intervention will fail in the real world if it cannot be implemented in a cost-effective manner. Thus, mental health services studies to examine costs of innovative services are crucial to assist with planning of what to implement and how to allocate resources. Cost-effectiveness studies may involve complex statistical modeling techniques to estimate both cost of implementation and potential savings due to improved outcomes and reduced use of other services.

To look at cost-effectiveness, we use the example of the ACT, or assertive community treatment, model. Created in 1974, ACT has evolved and expanded over the years, gaining popularity in a range of settings (Dixon 2000). ACT teams include a multidisciplinary staff, working together to provide wraparound services and close contact with high-needs clients. Given the staff and labor involved, ACT teams are not inexpensive to operate. Several studies have sought to determine the cost-effectiveness of the approach. The earliest of these found promising results, with an overall cost savings to the system despite increased outpatient costs (Weisbrod et al. 1980). A more recent study utilizing data from the Veterans' Administration ACT program participants found that cost savings were most strongly correlated with reduction in inpatient hospitalizations, concluding that basing eligibility criteria on prior hospitalizations would increase cost-effectiveness (Slade et al. 2013). This reflects prior research supporting cost-effectiveness for patients with frequent or extended inpatient admissions (Latimer 1999).

While costs cannot be viewed independently of corresponding clinical outcomes, cost-effectiveness studies help administrators and policymakers to understand how to allocate resources and funding. In the case of the ACT model, cost-effectiveness research helps us to understand how to best focus efforts to ensure sustainability and how funding streams and incentives might need to be modified in order to respond to the shift from inpatient to outpatient costs. Administrators may also consider whether cost-effectiveness might differ when the same intervention is applied in a special population, such as individuals experiencing homelessness or with concurrent substance use.

Understanding Practice Patterns

Psychiatry has changed dramatically over the past several decades. Prior to the 1990s, psychiatrists provided both pharmacotherapy and psychotherapy in longer and more frequent appointments. With the inception of managed behavioral care organizations, coupled with the rise in new pharmacologic treatments, there has been a significant shift in the role psychiatrists play in care. Since the 1990s, many psychiatrists principally function as pharmacotherapists, i.e., psychiatrists who solely prescribe medications in brief and infrequent appointments.

Though many felt the impact of these changes, it was not known if this was a national or local trend. Olfson and colleagues performed an analysis of psychiatrist-reported practice pattern data from the 1985 and 1995 National Ambulatory Care Surveys, an annually conducted survey by the National Center for Health Statistics (Olfson et al. 1999). In this survey, physicians, or their office staff, completed a one-page data form for each visit during a specified one-week period within a year. Olfson and colleagues extracted information on the characteristics of psychiatric visits in both survey years to estimate changes in practice patterns over time. Compared to 1985, the 1995 survey revealed a significantly greater proportion of psychiatric visits by older individuals, individuals of color, publically insured individuals, and individuals who paid for their care through a managed care organization. In addition, there was a significantly higher rate of prescriptions and the appointment length was significantly shorter. More recent analyses by Olfson and colleagues show the trend toward psychiatrists practicing solely as pharmacotherapists continues (Olfson et al. 2002; Olfson and Marcus 2009). This research helped us to better understand changes in workforce practice that suggest a need to reassess workforce training and education (Cruz and Pincus 2002) and call for further studies to determine the impact of psychiatrists' role changes on treatment outcomes.

Understanding Effective Implementation

As discussed above in "Putting Research into Practice," many interventions that are effective in controlled research settings fail to show the same impact in the real world. Implementation science is a relatively young field of research that seeks to address this failure by looking not only at characteristics of intervention themselves, but also at contextual factors that might impact implementation success (Bauer et al. 2015).

Implementation science research asks questions about acceptability, feasibility, and sustainability of an evidence-based intervention in a new setting. Instead of asking, "Does the intervention work?" implementation research might ask, "What is helping it to work? What is getting in the way?" Implementation researchers often apply a *mixed-methods* approach (see Box 1), using both quantitative and qualitative data (Palinkas 2014). Quantitative data might include structured surveys or administrative data, while qualitative data obtained from interviews or focus groups with key stakeholders, such as administrators or providers, can help to provide a fuller picture.

Implementation strategies can be broadly categorized as "top-down" or "bottom-up" approaches. Top-down implementation strategies originate from system or clinical administrators. Bottom-up implementation strategies intend to engage clinicians and office staff in the process of changing how they provide care. Top-down strategies include evidence-based practice tool kits and algorithms, practice guidelines, system and organizational interventions from management science, and economic, fiscal, and regulatory incentive and disincentive strategies. Bottom-up strategies include quality improvement interventions and techniques that engage practitioners and clinical staff in the process of improving care such as the Plan-Do-Study-Act (PDSA) cycle.

Proctor and colleagues developed a useful conceptual model to describe the process of translating evidence-based practices into service delivery systems (Proctor et al. 2009). This model incorporates theories of implementation, dissemination, and diffusion of innovation and includes ways to assess the effectiveness of the implementation strategies used. The model presupposes three distinct types of outcomes: *implementation*, *service*, and *client* outcomes (Fig. 1). Considering this range of outcomes, Proctor's model captures involvement of stakeholders at different levels

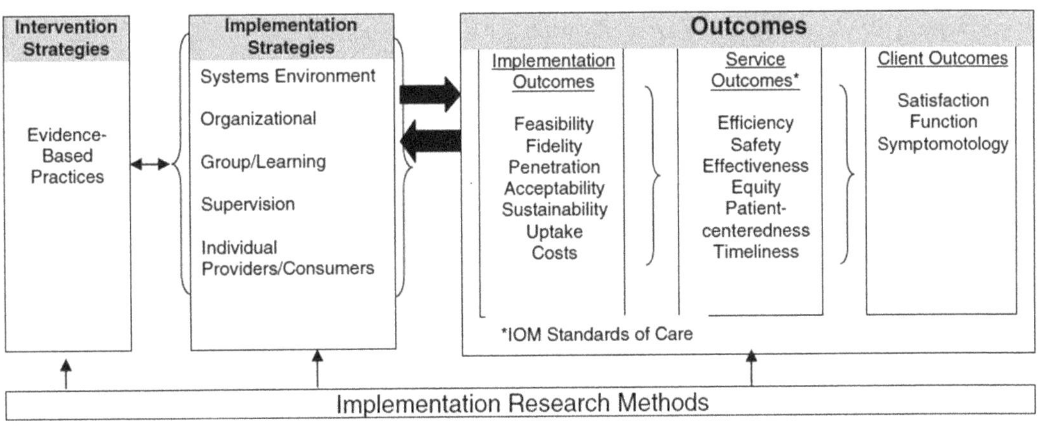

Fig. 1 Proctor and colleagues' conceptual model of implementation research

within a system of care including payers, clinical administrators, providers, and patients.

Implementation studies look at the process of introducing and sustaining an evidence-based intervention in a real-world setting. The scale of such studies can vary widely, from implementation of a specific intervention at a single site to large studies taking place at dozens of sites nationwide. An example of the latter is the National Implementing Evidence-Based Practices Project, carried out at 53 sites across eight states beginning in 2002. Prior work showed that key interventions for people with SMI were underutilized, despite ample evidence of efficacy. In this study, researchers examined the use of toolkits to assist with implementation of five evidence-based interventions for people with SMI: ACT, family psycho-education, illness management and recovery, integrated dual disorder treatment, and supported employment. Each participating site implemented one of these practices. Taking a mixed-methods approach, researchers collected a range of implementation data—including information about fidelity, sustainability, implementation challenges, and contextual factors—from a range of sources, including surveys and interviews with patients and administrators, observation of meetings, and chart review. This mixed-methods design allowed for a depth and breadth of understanding of the barriers and facilitators to effective implementation and for the evaluation of uptake, fidelity, and other implementation measures.

The rich data obtained in the National Implementing Evidence-Based Practices Project led to numerous important analyses. In one, researchers examined program fidelity to established evidence-based models. They found that over half of the sites implemented programs with high fidelity, with an increase in fidelity over the first 12 months before leveling off (McHugo et al. 2007). In another analysis, researchers looked at sustainability, finding that 80% of sites maintained the programs 4 years after initiation (Swain et al. 2010). Qualitative and quantitative survey assessment allowed identification of factors that differentiated sustaining from non-sustaining sites, including financing, training, fidelity, leadership, and degree of local adaptation. Implementation research such as this has potential to bridge the research-to-practice gap by helping us to see not just *what* works, but how it works (or does not work) and how to make it work better.

New Directions in Health Services Research: Informatics and Machine Learning

Despite a century of progress in our understanding of the underlying factors associated with mental illnesses, diagnoses are still unclear (Freedman et al. 2013; Hirschfeld et al. 2003), psychotherapeutic or pharmaceutical treatments are often effective in only 30–50% of patients (Hofmann et al. 2012; Rush et al. 2006; Wong et al. 2010), and prognoses remain uncertain (Wunderink et al. 2009). Treatment choices are often guided by recommendations based on broad symptom classifications, such as current guidelines for treating depression, anxiety, and psychosis. Without personalized data to guide treatment decisions, determining the optimal treatment often requires sequential trials, leading to unnecessary suffering and increased health care costs (Rush et al. 2006; Wong et al. 2010).

The field of informatics (Box 2) introduces promising approaches to address the clinical decision support needs of the community psychiatrist. Informatics research employs machine learning, a subfield of artificial intelligence which aims to uncover general principles underlying a series of observations without explicit instructions or hypotheses (Bzdok and Meyer-Lindenberg 2018; Breiman 2001; Goodfellow et al. 2016). Compared to traditional research, machine learning takes a markedly different analytic approach. Traditional research methods are hypothesis driven, limit analysis to a particular study sample, and employ a combination of statistical techniques that assess the significance of results, which are then generalized. The traditional research method approach is now being scrutinized due to issues with reproducibility

(Ioannidis 2005; Schooler 2014) and lack of clinical significance (Ioannidis 2016).

Box 2 Areas of Informatics

Informatics is a broad field encompassing many different topics and approaches. *Public health informatics*, also known as *population health informatics*, applies informatics approaches to problems of population-wide importance. *Translational bioinformatics* involves the development of storage, analytic, and interpretive methods to optimize the transformation of increasingly voluminous biomedical and genomic data. *Clinical research informatics* applies informatics to the discovery and management of new knowledge relating to health and disease. *Clinical informatics* relates to the delivery of healthcare services. Finally, *consumer health informatics* takes a consumer-focused (rather than provider-focused) approach, integrating multiple consumer and patient views.

Unlike traditional research methods, machine learning is neither hypothesis driven nor does it routinely require random sampling. Instead, machine learning seeks to find patterns of relationships within very large datasets. These patterns can then be tested for reproducibility, accuracy, and generalizability with subsequent data sets (i.e., cross-validation procedures) (Shalev-Shwartz and Ben-David 2014). Models are refined over time as more data sets are processed. Machine learning has been used in psychiatry to identify characteristics of individuals with mental illness (e.g., genetic biomarkers, structural and functional brain imaging, psychological testing findings, symptom and diagnostic assessment tools, demographic and social assessments) that predict treatment response and prognosis in depression (Chekroud et al. 2016; Etkin et al. 2015; Khodayari-Rostamabad et al. 2013), schizophrenia (Khodayari-Rostamabad et al. 2010), and anxiety (Ball et al. 2014; Doehrmann et al. 2013; Hahn et al. 2015; Whitfield-Gabrieli et al. 2016). Machine learning has also been used to identify data-derived subgroups of patients that can predict treatment outcomes with greater accuracy than the DSM-V diagnostic classification system (Bzdok and Meyer-Lindenberg 2018; Insel et al. 2010).

Machine learning can also be applied to the analysis of narrative electronic health record (EHR) data. Widespread use of EHRs provides opportunities for research using large data sets from real-world data (Friedman et al. 2010). However, human-generated text—like the narrative text comprising much of EHR data—can be challenging to analyze. Natural language processing (NLP) is a method used to derive meaning from human-generated text, allowing for differentiation between very similar text phrases with different meanings. When coupled with machine learning algorithms, NLP can be powerful. For example, NLP with machine learning has been used with EHR data to identify trauma patients at risk for future alcohol misuse (Afshar et al. 2019) and obsessive compulsive symptoms in patients with schizophrenia, schizoaffective, and bipolar disorders (Chandran et al. 2019).

Machine learning has several advantages compared to traditional research methods (Perna et al. 2018). First, the development of treatment strategies is not dependent upon a full understanding of complex disease mechanisms. Therefore, machine learning research may be less expensive and reduce the time it takes for discoveries to be translated into practice. Second, the discovered predictive models are translated into algorithms that can be used to develop decision support tools to aid community psychiatrists in making diagnoses and treatment decisions. Third, machine learning methods are naturally applicable to prospective clinical predictions on the single subject level as opposed to traditional research methods where predictions are based on group-level averages that may not be appropriate for the individual patient in front of you. Machine learning could thus be helpful in personalizing treatment. Fourth, machine learning algorithms can be used to automate the analysis of electronic health record (EHR) data.

Machine learning research has the potential to reduce the time for translating research into practice, improve the specificity of mental health diagnoses, and personalize treatment decisions and the prediction of the future course of illness. NLP paired with machine learning algorithms can automate the extraction and analysis of EHR-derived real-world data to further our understanding of illnesses, their treatment, and prognosis. The translation of these algorithms into decision support tools has the potential to improve clinical outcomes.

Summary

Unlike other psychiatric subspecialties, community psychiatry embraces the complexity of mental health service systems and organizations and their impact on how treatment must be altered or changed to improve the quality, cost, and outcomes of care. In addition, community psychiatry focuses attention on community-based factors that impede individuals' access to care and the outcomes from the care they provide. We seek to employ evidence-based practices that are implementable and sustainable and aid service users in their recovery in real-world settings. To achieve these goals, community psychiatrists must have a sound appreciation of mental health services research methods, the strengths and weaknesses of interventions developed in the traditional pipeline research strategy, and the contextual factors that influence the dissemination, implementation, and sustainability of traditionally developed evidence-based research interventions. To provide services that are valuable to recovery, we must be involved in all aspects of intervention development— from the questions addressed, the methods used, and the analysis, interpretation, and application of study findings. Inclusive approaches to research such as CBPR provide a roadmap to how we can be more active in the creation of the interventions we employ.

References

Afshar, M., Phillips, A., Karnik, N., Mueller, J., To, D., Gonzalez, R., Price, R., Cooper, R., Joyce, C., & Dligach, D. (2019). Natural language processing and machine learning to identify alcohol misuse from the electronic health record in trauma patients: Development and internal validation. *Journal of the American Medical Informatics Association: JAMIA*, *26*(3), 254–261. https://doi.org/10.1093/jamia/ocy166

Balas, E. A., & Boren, S. A. (2000). Managing Clinical Knowledge for Health Care Improvement. *Yearbook of Medical Informatics*, *1*, 65–70.

Ball, T. M., Stein, M. B., Ramsawh, H. J., Campbell-Sills, L., & Paulus, M. P. (2014). Single-Subject Anxiety Treatment Outcome Prediction using Functional Neuroimaging. *Neuropsychopharmacology*, *39*(5), 1254–1261. https://doi.org/10.1038/npp.2013.328

Bauer, M. S., Damschroder, L., Hagedorn, H., Smith, J., & Kilbourne, A. M. (2015). An introduction to implementation science for the non-specialist. *BMC Psychology*, *3*(1). https://doi.org/10.1186/s40359-015-0089-9

Bell, C. C., & Mehta, H. (1980). The Misdiagnosis of Black Patients with Manic Depressive Illness. *Journal of the National Medical Association*, *72*(2), 141–145.

Breiman, L. (2001). Statistical modeling: The two cultures (with comments and a rejoinder by the author). *Statistical Science*, *16*(3), 199–231.

Bzdok, D., & Meyer-Lindenberg, A. (2018). Machine Learning for Precision Psychiatry: Opportunities and Challenges. *Biological Psychiatry. Cognitive Neuroscience and Neuroimaging*, *3*(3), 223–230. https://doi.org/10.1016/j.bpsc.2017.11.007

Chandran, D., Robbins, D. A., Chang, C.-K., Shetty, H., Sanyal, J., Downs, J., Fok, M., Ball, M., Jackson, R., Stewart, R., Cohen, H., Vermeulen, J. M., Schirmbeck, F., de Haan, L., & Hayes, R. (2019). Use of Natural Language Processing to identify Obsessive Compulsive Symptoms in patients with schizophrenia, schizoaffective disorder or bipolar disorder. *Scientific Reports*, *9*(1), 14146. https://doi.org/10.1038/s41598-019-49165-2

Chekroud, A. M., Zotti, R. J., Shehzad, Z., Gueorguieva, R., Johnson, M. K., Trivedi, M. H., Cannon, T. D., Krystal, J. H., & Corlett, P. R. (2016). Cross-trial prediction of treatment outcome in depression: A machine learning approach. *The Lancet Psychiatry*, *3*(3), 243–250. https://doi.org/10.1016/S2215-0366(15)00471-X

Cruz, M., & Pincus, H. A. (2002). Research on the influence that communication in psychiatric encounters has on treatment. *Psychiatric Services (Washington, D.C.)*, *53*(10), 1253–1265. https://doi.org/10.1176/appi.ps.53.10.1253

Dixon, L. (2000). Assertive Community Treatment: Twenty-Five Years of Gold. *Psychiatric Services*,

51(6), 759–765. https://doi.org/10.1176/appi.ps.51.6.759

Doehrmann, O., Ghosh, S. S., Polli, F. E., Reynolds, G. O., Horn, F., Keshavan, A., Triantafyllou, C., Saygin, Z. M., Whitfield-Gabrieli, S., Hofmann, S. G., Pollack, M., & Gabrieli, J. D. (2013). Predicting Treatment Response in Social Anxiety Disorder From Functional Magnetic Resonance Imaging. *JAMA Psychiatry*, *70*(1), 87. https://doi.org/10.1001/2013.jamapsychiatry.5

Drake, R. E., Bond, G. R., & Essock, S. M. (2009). Implementing Evidence-Based Practices for People With Schizophrenia. *Schizophrenia Bulletin*, *35*(4), 704–713. https://doi.org/10.1093/schbul/sbp041

Essock, S. M., & Hogan, M. F. (2011). Looking Into the Health Reform Crystal Ball: Seeing More Constructive, Less Expensive Management Scenarios. *American Journal of Psychiatry*, *168*(5), 449–451. https://doi.org/10.1176/appi.ajp.2011.11020205

Etkin, A., Patenaude, B., Song, Y. J. C., Usherwood, T., Rekshan, W., Schatzberg, A. F., Rush, A. J., & Williams, L. M. (2015). A Cognitive–Emotional Biomarker for Predicting Remission with Antidepressant Medications: A Report from the iSPOT-D Trial. *Neuropsychopharmacology*, *40*(6), 1332–1342. https://doi.org/10.1038/npp.2014.333

Ford, C. L., & Airhihenbuwa, C. O. (2010). Critical Race Theory, Race Equity, and Public Health: Toward Antiracism Praxis. *American Journal of Public Health*, *100*(S1), S30–S35. https://doi.org/10.2105/AJPH.2009.171058

Freedman, R., Lewis, D. A., Michels, R., Pine, D. S., Schultz, S. K., Tamminga, C. A., Gabbard, G. O., Gau, S. S.-F., Javitt, D. C., Oquendo, M. A., Shrout, P. E., Vieta, E., & Yager, J. (2013). The Initial Field Trials of DSM-5: New Blooms and Old Thorns. *American Journal of Psychiatry*, *170*(1), 1–5. https://doi.org/10.1176/appi.ajp.2012.12091189

Friedman, C. P., Wong, A. K., & Blumenthal, D. (2010). Achieving a nationwide learning health system. *Science Translational Medicine*, *2*(57), 57cm29. https://doi.org/10.1126/scitranslmed.3001456

Garfield, R. L., Zuvekas, S. H., Lave, J. R., & Donohue, J. M. (2011). The Impact of National Health Care Reform on Adults With Severe Mental Disorders. *American Journal of Psychiatry*, *168*(5), 486–494. https://doi.org/10.1176/appi.ajp.2010.10060792

Gilbody, S. (2006). Collaborative Care for Depression: A Cumulative Meta-analysis and Review of Longer-term Outcomes. *Archives of Internal Medicine*, *166*(21), 2314. https://doi.org/10.1001/archinte.166.21.2314

Goodfellow, I. J., Bengio, Y., & Courville, A. C. (2016). *Deep Learning, ser. Adaptive computation and machine learning*. MIT Press.

Green, L. W. (2008). Making research relevant: If it is an evidence-based practice, where's the practice-based evidence? *Family Practice*, *25 Suppl 1*, i20-24. https://doi.org/10.1093/fampra/cmn055

Greenhalgh, T., Robert, G., Macfarlane, F., Bate, P., & Kyriakidou, O. (2004). Diffusion of Innovations in Service Organizations: Systematic Review and Recommendations. *The Milbank Quarterly*, *82*(4), 581–629. https://doi.org/10.1111/j.0887-378X.2004.00325.x

Hahn, T., Kircher, T., Straube, B., Wittchen, H.-U., Konrad, C., Ströhle, A., Wittmann, A., Pfleiderer, B., Reif, A., Arolt, V., & Lueken, U. (2015). Predicting Treatment Response to Cognitive Behavioral Therapy in Panic Disorder With Agoraphobia by Integrating Local Neural Information. *JAMA Psychiatry*, *72*(1), 68. https://doi.org/10.1001/jamapsychiatry.2014.1741

Hirschfeld, R. M. A., Lewis, L., & Vornik, L. A. (2003). Perceptions and Impact of Bipolar Disorder: How Far Have We Really Come? Results of the National Depressive and Manic-Depressive Association 2000 Survey of Individuals With Bipolar Disorder. *The Journal of Clinical Psychiatry*, *64*(2), 161–174. https://doi.org/10.4088/JCP.v64n0209

Hofmann, S. G., Asnaani, A., Vonk, I. J. J., Sawyer, A. T., & Fang, A. (2012). The Efficacy of Cognitive Behavioral Therapy: A Review of Meta-analyses. *Cognitive Therapy and Research*, *36*(5), 427–440. https://doi.org/10.1007/s10608-012-9476-1

Hohmann, A. A., & Shear, M. K. (2002). Community-Based Intervention Research: Coping With the "Noise" of Real Life in Study Design. *American Journal of Psychiatry*, *159*(2), 201–207. https://doi.org/10.1176/appi.ajp.159.2.201

Insel, T., Cuthbert, B., Garvey, M., Heinssen, R., Pine, D. S., Quinn, K., Sanislow, C., & Wang, P. (2010). Research Domain Criteria (RDoC): Toward a New Classification Framework for Research on Mental Disorders. *American Journal of Psychiatry*, *167*(7), 748–751. https://doi.org/10.1176/appi.ajp.2010.09091379

Institute of Medicine Committee on Quality of Health Care in America. (2001). *Crossing the Quality Chasm: A New Health System for the 21st Century*. National Academies Press (US).

Ioannidis, J. P. A. (2005). Why most published research findings are false. *PLoS Medicine*, *2*(8), e124. https://doi.org/10.1371/journal.pmed.0020124

Ioannidis, J. P. A. (2016). Why Most Clinical Research Is Not Useful. *PLoS Medicine*, *13*(6), e1002049. https://doi.org/10.1371/journal.pmed.1002049

Israel, B. A., Schulz, A. J., Parker, E., Becker, A., Allen, A. J., & Guzman, R. (2008). Critical issues in developing and following CBPR principles. *Community-Based Participatory Research for Health: From Process to Outcomes*, 47–66.

Jones, L., & Wells, K. (2007). Strategies for academic and clinician engagement in community-participatory partnered research. *JAMA*, *297*(4), 407–410. https://doi.org/10.1001/jama.297.4.407

Khodayari-Rostamabad, A., Hasey, G. M., MacCrimmon, D. J., Reilly, J. P., & de Bruin, H. (2010). A pilot study to determine whether machine learning methodologies using pre-treatment electroencephalography can predict the symptomatic response to clozapine therapy. *Clinical Neurophysiology*, *121*(12), 1998–2006. https://doi.org/10.1016/j.clinph.2010.05.009

Khodayari-Rostamabad, A., Reilly, J. P., Hasey, G. M., de Bruin, H., & MacCrimmon, D. J. (2013). A machine learning approach using EEG data to predict response to SSRI treatment for major depressive disorder. *Clinical Neurophysiology*, *124*(10), 1975–1985. https://doi.org/10.1016/j.clinph.2013.04.010

Latimer, E. A. (1999). Economic Impacts of Assertive Community Treatment: A Review of the Literature. *The Canadian Journal of Psychiatry*, *44*(5), 443–454. https://doi.org/10.1177/070674379904400504

Lohr, K. N., & Steinwachs, D. M. (2002). Health Services Research: An Evolving Definition of the Field. *Health Services Research*, *37*(1), 15–17. https://doi.org/10.1111/1475-6773.01020

McGuire, T. G., & Miranda, J. (2008). New Evidence Regarding Racial And Ethnic Disparities In Mental Health: Policy Implications. *Health Affairs*, *27*(2), 393–403. https://doi.org/10.1377/hlthaff.27.2.393

McHugo, G. J., Drake, R. E., Whitley, R., Bond, G. R., Campbell, K., Rapp, C. A., Goldman, H. H., Lutz, W. J., & Finnerty, M. T. (2007). Fidelity Outcomes in the National Implementing Evidence-Based Practices Project. *Psychiatric Services*, *58*(10), 1279–1284. https://doi.org/10.1176/ps.2007.58.10.1279

National Institute of Mental Health Strategic Plan for Research (NIH Publication Number: 20-MH-8096; p. 48). (2020). https://www.nimh.nih.gov/about/strategic-planning-reports/goal-4-strengthen-the-public-health-impact-of-nimh-supported-research.shtml

Olfson, M., & Marcus, S. C. (2009). National Patterns in Antidepressant Medication Treatment. *Archives of General Psychiatry*, *66*(8), 848. https://doi.org/10.1001/archgenpsychiatry.2009.81

Olfson, M., Marcus, S. C., Druss, B., Elinson, L., Tanielian, T., & Pincus, H. A. (2002). National trends in the outpatient treatment of depression. *JAMA*, *287*(2), 203–209. https://doi.org/10.1001/jama.287.2.203

Olfson, M., Marcus, S. C., & Pincus, H. A. (1999). Trends in Office-Based Psychiatric Practice. *American Journal of Psychiatry*, *156*(3), 451–457. https://doi.org/10.1176/ajp.156.3.451

Palinkas, L. A. (2014). Qualitative and Mixed Methods in Mental Health Services and Implementation Research. *Journal of Clinical Child & Adolescent Psychology*, *43*(6), 851–861. https://doi.org/10.1080/15374416.2014.910791

Perna, G., Grassi, M., Caldirola, D., & Nemeroff, C. B. (2018). The revolution of personalized psychiatry: Will technology make it happen sooner? *Psychological Medicine*, *48*(5), 705–713. https://doi.org/10.1017/S0033291717002859

Proctor, E. K., Landsverk, J., Aarons, G., Chambers, D., Glisson, C., & Mittman, B. (2009). Implementation Research in Mental Health Services: An Emerging Science with Conceptual, Methodological, and Training challenges. *Administration and Policy in Mental Health and Mental Health Services Research*, *36*(1), 24–34. https://doi.org/10.1007/s10488-008-0197-4

Regier, D. A. (1978). The De Facto US Mental Health Services System: A Public Health Perspective. *Archives of General Psychiatry*, *35*(6), 685. https://doi.org/10.1001/archpsyc.1978.01770300027002

Robbins, L., & Regier, D. A. (1991). *Psychiatric Disorders in America: How to Take Immediate Control of Your Mental, Emotional, Physical and Financial*. Simon & Schuster.

Rush, A. J., Trivedi, M. H., Wisniewski, S. R., Nierenberg, A. A., Stewart, J. W., Warden, D., Niederehe, G., Thase, M. E., Lavori, P. W., Lebowitz, B. D., McGrath, P. J., Rosenbaum, J. F., & Sackeim, H. A. (2006). Acute and Longer-Term Outcomes in Depressed Outpatients Requiring One or Several Treatment Steps: A STAR*D Report. *Am J Psychiatry*, 13.

Schooler, J. W. (2014). Metascience could rescue the 'replication crisis.' *Nature*, *515*(7525), 9–9.

Schwartz, R. C., & Blankenship, D. M. (2014). Racial disparities in psychotic disorder diagnosis: A review of empirical literature. *World Journal of Psychiatry*, *4*(4), 133–140. https://doi.org/10.5498/wjp.v4.i4.133

Shalev-Shwartz, S., & Ben-David, S. (2014). *Understanding machine learning: From theory to algorithms*. Cambridge University Press.

Slade, E. P., McCarthy, J. F., Valenstein, M., Visnic, S., & Dixon, L. B. (2013). Cost Savings from Assertive Community Treatment Services in an Era of Declining Psychiatric Inpatient Use. *Health Services Research*, *48*(1), 195–217. https://doi.org/10.1111/j.1475-6773.2012.01420.x

Sullivan, G., Duan, N., Mukherjee, S., Kirchner, J., Perry, D., & Henderson, K. (2005). The Role of Services Researchers in Facilitating Intervention Research. *Psychiatric Services*, *56*(5), 537–542. https://doi.org/10.1176/appi.ps.56.5.537

Swain, K., Whitley, R., McHugo, G. J., & Drake, R. E. (2010). The Sustainability of Evidence-Based Practices in Routine Mental Health Agencies. *Community Mental Health Journal*, *46*(2), 119–129. https://doi.org/10.1007/s10597-009-9202-y

Thomas, S. B., Quinn, S. C., Butler, J., Fryer, C. S., & Garza, M. A. (2011). Toward a Fourth Generation of Disparities Research to Achieve Health Equity. *Annual Review of Public Health*, *32*(1), 399–416. https://doi.org/10.1146/annurev-publhealth-031210-101136

Wallerstein, N., Duran, B., Oetzel, J. G., & Minkler, M. (Eds.). (2018). *Community-based participatory research for health: Advancing social and health equity* (Third edition). Jossey-Bass.

Weisbrod, B. A., Test, M. A., & Stein, L. I. (1980). Alternative to mental hospital treatment. II. Economic benefit-cost analysis. *Archives of General Psychiatry*, *37*(4), 400–405. https://doi.org/10.1001/archpsyc.1980.01780170042004

Whitfield-Gabrieli, S., Ghosh, S. S., Nieto-Castanon, A., Saygin, Z., Doehrmann, O., Chai, X. J., Reynolds,

G. O., Hofmann, S. G., Pollack, M. H., & Gabrieli, J. D. E. (2016). Brain connectomics predict response to treatment in social anxiety disorder. *Molecular Psychiatry, 21*(5), 680–685. https://doi.org/10.1038/mp.2015.109

Wong, E. H. F., Yocca, F., Smith, M. A., & Lee, C.-M. (2010). Challenges and opportunities for drug discovery in psychiatric disorders: The drug hunters' perspective. *The International Journal of Neuropsychopharmacology, 13*(09), 1269–1284. https://doi.org/10.1017/S1461145710000866

Wunderink, L., Sytema, S., Nienhuis, F. J., & Wiersma, D. (2009). Clinical Recovery in First-Episode Psychosis. *Schizophrenia Bulletin, 35*(2), 362–369. https://doi.org/10.1093/schbul/sbn143

Climate Change: Implications for Community Mental Health

John Sullenbarger, Emily Schutzenhofer, and Elizabeth Haase

Introduction

The term climate change encompasses all the planetary systems disrupted as a result of greenhouse gas emissions. The most notable impacts due to rising atmospheric greenhouse gases include increased ambient temperatures, more acidic and warmer oceans, rising sea levels, extreme weather, poor air quality, and loss of biodiversity. These impacts, otherwise known as "climate drivers" or "exposure pathways," directly interface with communities to harm human health. Respiratory illnesses, cardiovascular deaths, allergies, kidney injuries, neurodevelopmental impairment, preterm and low-weight births, food nutritional content, access to safe water, and neuropsychiatric illnesses are all seeing depreciated outcomes in relation to these exposure pathways. Consequently, climate change has been labeled "the single biggest health threat facing humanity" by the World Health Organization (WHO 2021).

Climate psychiatry has been defined as "that psychiatry which draws on an understanding of the direct and indirect links between climate change and mental health and wellbeing to transform psychiatric practice. It enables psychiatrists to better and more equitably support patients and families, to communicate suffering from climate effects, and to contribute toward positive climate change adaptation and mitigation. The practice of climate psychiatry broadly includes, but is not limited to, clinical, educational, public health and systems, research, and advocacy work (Coverdale et al. 2018) and the related roles for the psychiatrist of clinician, public health officer, mental health advocate, activist, researcher, community leader, and policy advisor" (Haase et al. In press).

Community psychiatrists are both obliged and uniquely positioned to embrace climate psychiatry as part of their practice. Pernicious implications for public health affect every area with which community psychiatry is particularly concerned: social equity, local prevalence of psychiatric illnesses and psychological distress, communal cohesion, and more. Thus, climate change undoubtedly impedes the mission of community psychiatry to "promote health, recovery, and resilience in people, families, and commu-

J. Sullenbarger (✉)
Wright State University Boonshoft School of Medicine, Department of Psychiatry, Dayton, OH, USA
e-mail: john.sullenbarger@wright.edu

E. Schutzenhofer
George Washington University School of Medicine and Health Sciences, Department of Psychiatry and Behavioral Sciences, Washington, DC, USA
e-mail: emschutzenhofer@gwu.edu

E. Haase
Carson Tahoe Regional Medical Center, Carson City, NV, USA

University of Nevada School of Medicine, Reno, NV, USA
e-mail: ehaase@me.com

W. E. Sowers et al. (eds.), *Textbook of Community Psychiatry*,
https://doi.org/10.1007/978-3-031-10239-4_31

nity" (AACP Mission Statement). The interdependent connections of community psychiatrists, community mental health centers, local populations, and broader health systems fit well into models of optimal engagement with "wicked problems" like climate change, where solutions in one area tend to impact other parts of the system in mixed ways (Crowley and Head 2017). These connections can serve to simultaneously distribute centralized information and resources and act as a conduit for community input to larger interventions so that solutions can be tested and adjusted at multiple levels. Consequently, it is of critical importance that community psychiatrists familiarize themselves with the literature of climate change impacts on mental health and vulnerable populations and champion the numerous potential interventions available for community and all other psychiatrists to implement—actions this chapter strives to aid.

Climate Change and Mental Health

The effects of climate change on mental health are categorized into two broad areas: (1) direct and indirect impacts and (2) psychological responses to climate distress. Both of these are briefly reviewed within this chapter, along with their particular impacts on vulnerable populations, before exploring the role of community psychiatry in the climate crisis given these effects on mental health.

Direct and Indirect Impacts

Direct impacts on mental health from climate change refer to the neurobiologic and psychiatric symptom responses to exposure to climate drivers. For example, the anticipation of climate disasters can trigger significant distress, while the traumatic experience of a climate disaster and the associated losses are associated with increased rates of psychological distress, depression, anxiety, PTSD, cognitive impairment, substance use, psychiatric hospitalizations, suicides, and overall mortality in populations with mental illness (Charlson et al. 2021). The indirect impacts of the array of climate drivers, however, lead to more pervasive and long-lasting mental health consequences through significant economic losses, mass migrations, diminished natural resources and related conflicts, and environmental injustice. The impacts of the climate crisis are not shared equitably, which is why climate change is considered to be a "threat multiplier" of social determinants of health.

Heat

As a result of increasing levels of greenhouse gases and their warming potential, the average ambient temperature has increased to 1.07 °C (1.97 °F) since the start of the industrial revolution, with the hottest years ever recorded increasing in frequency since 2005 and the rate of temperature increase per decade escalating more rapidly than in any period observed in geological studies (Masson-Delmotte et al. 2021). This temperature elevation and further anticipated increases in extreme heat have been associated with the following mental health ramifications in recent studies:

- A predicted nine to forty thousand additional suicides in the United States and Mexico by 2050 attributable to temperature increase under current emission trajectories (Burke et al. 2018), and increases in suicide rates of 1% for every one-degree increase in temperature over previous ambient means (Dumont et al. 2020).
- A 3.61 (95% CI 1.3–9.8) increased odds of heat-related death for those with preexisting mental illness, particularly those with psychotic illness (Bouchama et al. 2007).
- Disruption of dopaminergic, adrenergic, and serotonergic function in thermoregulation placing those on psychotropics at 1.9 (95% CI 1.3–2.8) increased odds for heat-related death (Bouchama et al. 2007), particularly those on antipsychotics and anticholinergics.
- A 3.9% increase in interpersonal violence and 13.6% increase in intergroup violence per

standard deviation increase in temperature (Hsiang et al. 2013).
- Reduction in measured working memory, reaction times, and attention during heat waves (Schlader et al. 2015).
- Elevated rates of heat stroke that will particularly affect those who are lacking housing or other protective resources commonly inadequate in a community psychiatry population (Lõhmus 2018).
- An increased risk of stroke by 5–20% and myocardial infarction by 20–40%, with their attendant psychiatric complications of disability, depression, and cognitive impairment (Li et al. 2018).
- Loss of sleep quality and days of physical activity with elevated temperatures, with implications for depression, anxiety, bipolar disorder, and more (Obradovich and Fowler 2017).

Air Pollution

Climate change increases air pollution through increased dust, wildfires, ozone levels, and pollen in addition to the release of particulate matter (PM 2.5 μm, PM 10 μm, and ultrafine particles 0.1 μm), nitric oxide compounds, and other gases when fossil fuels are combusted. Because 90% of the world's population is affected by poor air quality, air pollution has been identified as the greatest global cause of lost life years—causing a loss of 4.2 years per person on average in recent decades (Cohen et al. 2017).

Many air pollutants, but especially particulate matter, can transmit systemically via alveoli and the olfactory tract, causing neuroinflammation and cerebral oxidative stress with corresponding neuropsychiatric impacts. Neuropsychiatric risks include:

- Increased risk of dementia (OR 1.16, 95% CI 1.07–1.26), Parkinson's disease (OR 1.34, 95% CI 1.04–1.7), and Alzheimer's disease in particular (OR 3.26, 95% 0.84–12.74) with prolonged exposure to PM 2.5 μm and other particulates (Fu et al. 2019).
- Elevated rates of ADHD, behavioral disorders, reduced IQ, and developmental delay in children (Perera 2017).
- Increased risk for autism spectrum disorders (OR 1.02–1.68) (Fu et al. 2019).
- Increased odds of depression (OR 1.1–1.19) and suicide (RR 1.02, OR 1.05) (Gu et al. 2019).
- Increased rates of violence of 1.1% per each 10 μm^2 increase in PM 2.5 μm and a 0.6% increase on days with high ozone levels (Berman et al. 2019).

Wildfires and Extreme Weather Events

Climate-related disasters, such as wildfires and severe storms, are occurring in escalating frequency and severity. A warming climate intensifies both precipitation events and drought (Masson-Delmotte et al. 2021), and climate change doubled the forest fire area in the western United States between 1984 and 2016 (Abatzoglou and Williams 2016) with dramatic consequences. The direct trauma of such events has a wide array of mental health outcomes, including prolonged indirect effects on mental health from economic, housing, and other losses. Specific impacts include:

- Individuals exposed to extreme weather events are approximately 90% more likely to experience psychological impairments such as hyperarousal, insomnia, concentration difficulties, depression, anxiety, PTSD, and substance use (Chique et al. 2021).
- Flood survivors experience depression at rates of 16.5–20%, anxiety at rates of 20.6–28.3%, and PTSD at rates of 13.1–36% (Chique et al. 2021).
- Severe storms (e.g., hurricanes and derechos) have been associated with prevalence rates of 21.2% for depression, 13.7% for anxiety, and 17.8% for PTSD (Chique et al. 2021).
- The population affected by Hurricane Katrina experienced a doubling of the prevalence of any mental illness from 15% to 31% and "serious" mental illness from 6.1% to 11.3% ($p < 0.001$) (Kessler et al. 2006).

- Direct exposure to wildfires has resulted in rates of 31–33% for major depressive disorder and 24–37% for PTSD (Chique et al. 2021).
- In 2020 alone, there were approximately 30 million people displaced by climate-related disasters (Internal Displacement Monitoring Centre 2021), with hundreds of millions more predicted (Masson-Delmotte et al. 2021).

Droughts

While extreme weather events have become more frequent in some areas of the world, droughts have also grown more frequent and intense with higher temperatures and longer periods between precipitation (Masson-Delmotte et al. 2021). Groups more dependent on the land, such as farmers and indigenous peoples, are particularly susceptible to mental health effects during droughts given their reliance on the land's productivity for economic stability, identity, and social cohesion. These indirect impacts of drought will likely be the most detrimental long term. Repercussions include:

- When drought conditions worsened from first to third quartile, rural middle-aged males had a 15% increased risk (95% CI 8–22%) of suicide (Hanigan et al. 2012), a finding supported by other studies (Parida et al. 2018).
- Drought has been associated with a wide range of negative mental health outcomes, including increased anxiety, depression, and domestic violence and adverse effects on spousal, interpersonal, and community conflicts (Vins et al. 2015).

Vector-Borne Diseases

Vector-borne neuro-encephalitic diseases will also increase with climate change. Modeling these changes can be difficult due to the complex and variable interactions between CO_2 concentrations, higher temperatures, precipitation, shifting host and vector species' niches, and seasonal changes. However, recent trends correlated with climate change show mosquito- and tick-related diseases tripling between 2004 and 2016 in the United States (Rosenberg et al. 2018), with clear neuropsychiatric implications related to the acute and chronic complications of diseases like Lyme disease, tick paralysis, and Zika virus. These diseases add to the direct and indirect impacts of infectious waterborne diseases following extreme weather events. The penetrance of neuropsychiatric symptoms in such diseases include:

- 40% incidence of developmental delays and 60% incidence of later seizures in infants affected by Zika virus (Souza et al. 2019).
- 60% incidence of at least one neurological symptom in those affected by malaria (Singh et al. 2016).
- Permanent neurologic sequelae in up to 70% of cases of equine encephalitic diseases (Simon et al. 2020).
- Neurologic symptoms in up to 40% of Lyme disease patients (Fallon and Nields 1994).
- 50% incidence of neurological impairment following Powassan disease, a viral tick-borne illness that has increased in prevalence in the midwest and northeastern United States by 671% between 1997 and 2017 (Fatmi et al. 2017).
- Neuropsychiatric symptoms in 20% of cases of ehrlichiosis, which has increased by 200% in eastern and central United States between 1990 and 2010 (Ismail et al. 2010).

Nutrition and Water Security

Food and water insecurity, as well as malnutrition, are increasing under current climate change trajectories, with estimates that one billion people worldwide will experience increasing water scarcity (Masson-Delmotte et al. 2021) and 80% of populations living within areas vulnerable to environmental degradation will see threats to their food supply (Sova et al. 2019) over this century. Food staples like wheat, maize, rice, and soybeans will see deficiencies in micronutrients such as iron, zinc, and protein as carbon dioxide concentrations continue to increase to 555 ppm, the current projection for 2050 (Smith and Myers 2018). These effects would result in 122 million additional people having protein deficiency and 175 million more people having zinc deficiency worldwide, while 1.4 billion young women and children would be located in areas at high risk for iron deficiency (Smith and Myers 2018). Other effects include:

- Cognitive development, attention, depression, externalizing behaviors, stress, worry, sadness, and anger have all been positively correlated with food insecurity (Jones 2017).
- Iron deficiency has been associated with a 5.6-fold increase of bipolar disorder in women and two- to threefold increases in autism, tic disorder, anxiety, and neurodevelopmental delay (Chen et al. 2013).
- Zinc deficiency has serious negative impacts on major depression, immune function, and neurodevelopment (Wang et al. 2018).

Psychological Effects

"Psychoterratic syndromes" is a term meant to encompass all the fear, grief, and other emotions derived from the innumerable losses, threats, uncertainties, and instability of the climate crisis (Albrecht 2011). The terms ecological grief and ecoanxiety further refer to psychological responses to that which has been lost and that which will be lost without intervention, respectively. As people directly and indirectly experience the effects of climate change, the necessity for a shared language to describe psychological responses unique to climate change and the associated environmental degradation has become clear. Solastalgia is one such term, capturing the emotional pain experienced from the loss of solace in one's home or cherished environments (Albrecht et al. 2007). These responses to the climate crisis should not be treated as pathological, but as normal responses to a difficult reality requiring creative interventions to bolster individual and community resilience as described later in this chapter.

While these terms have not been studied adequately to have construct validity, they do serve to fill gaps within the lexicon of mental wellness and psychiatric symptoms. A 2021 survey on climate emotions showed that 70% of the public in the United States are worried about global warming, with 35% of that group identifying as having great worry (Leiserowitz et al. 2021). In a study of 10,000 youth in ten countries, 84% reported at least moderate anxiety with 45% noting a negative impact in their daily lives and functioning (Hickman et al. 2021). These high levels of distress are likely to only increase, as the full effects of climate change are expected to intensify over this century on the current emissions trajectory.

Subpopulations Most Vulnerable in the Context of Climate Change

The direct and indirect effects of climate change touch all individuals, warranting community psychiatrists' intervention. However, climate change is most urgently and devastatingly affecting the health of individuals in underserved and marginalized communities. Those of higher social vulnerability experience magnified effects due to disproportionately increased exposure to natural hazards, decreased resources to mitigate the effects of climate change, and uneven burdens imposed by policies, which constitute social determinants of equity. This next section examines what is known about the unique climate-driven challenges posed to various vulnerable populations, especially highlighting aspects critical for community psychiatrists providing their mental healthcare to consider.

Individuals Experiencing Homelessness

Individuals experiencing homelessness are regularly exposed to harsh natural elements and climate drivers likely to negatively impact health such as heat and air pollution. Most notably, extreme temperatures put them at higher risk for hyperthermia or hypothermia than non-homeless individuals (Bezgrebelna et al. 2021). Beyond the lack of reliable temperature-controlled shelter, health conditions such as mental illness, chronic diseases, and abuse of substances and alcohol—all highly prevalent among those experiencing homelessness—increase an individual's vulnerability to heat events (Gronlund et al. 2018). Due to alterations in perception, cognition, and physical abilities, these health conditions may limit an individual's ability to take precautionary measures against environmental conditions and adapt to protect themselves. Furthermore, individuals experiencing homelessness are less likely to receive communication on heat advisories because the media does not adequately target warning messages to them (Bassil and Cole 2010). Homelessness in urban areas carries two additional distinctive risks relative to extreme heat. Urban areas are at increased risk of heat waves due to the "heat island effect," a phenomenon often worsened by coincident entrapment of heat by higher air pollution. Meanwhile, urban areas often lack greenspace, which can be protective against heat waves and air and noise pollution while also reducing the mental fatigue, stress, depression, aggression, and anxiety that climate drivers like high temperatures exacerbate (Beyer et al. 2014).

In addition to disproportionately affecting those who are already experiencing homelessness, climate drivers increase homelessness through a variety of means of displacement and will increasingly do so without climate mitigation. As just one example, energy bills increase as people seek to cool or warm their homes in response to extreme temperatures and natural disasters, and failure to pay these bills results in utility shutoffs and evictions (Bezgrebelna et al. 2021; Jessel et al. 2019). Damage to homes from natural disasters and the erosion of habitable land increasingly leads to the displacement of people across both rural and urban areas. This migration further strains already low housing resources, contributing to homelessness. Finally, inability to afford to move to new areas after climate damage to homes contributes to homelessness or drives individuals to remain in hazardous conditions as their only alternative (Bezgrebelna et al. 2021).

Children and Adolescents

Many of the aforementioned impacts of climate change have outsize impacts on youth, including increased rates of malnutrition, neurodevelopmental disorders, infectious diseases, ecoanxiety, and overall mortality. Exposure to various climate drivers during pregnancy is associated with lower birth weight, stillbirth, and preterm births (Hellden et al. 2021). Children's higher exposure to pollution per unit body weight, greater time outdoors, rapid growth, and developmental windows, as well as their immature physiology, all place children at greater risk of adverse outcomes from environmental insults (Sheffield and Landrigan 2011). Documented worsening of interpersonal violence with droughts and elevated temperatures includes increased rates of child abuse (Seddighi et al. 2019) and gender-based violence (Gearhart et al. 2018) within families, as well. Additional evidence points to the negative impacts of climate change on economics and social stability leading to increased rates of childhood marriage as a means to alleviate financial concerns (Asadullah et al. 2020). To this point, there is no data on how this increase in adverse childhood events linked to climate change will burden future population physical and mental health. With over 88% of the known burden of climate change-related diseases falling on children born in the twenty-first century (Zhang et al. 2007), few should be surprised that climate-related anxiety is higher in youth populations overall (Hickman et al. 2021) or that it is spurring documented phenomena like many youth and young adults developing hesitance to bear children of their own.

Older Adults

Climate change is known to both exacerbate and create vulnerabilities for older persons, particularly those with mental illness, leading to disproportionate rates of climate-related mortality among this population. Older persons with mental health conditions tend to suffer disproportionately from social isolation, which serves as a barrier for both adapting to climate change and protecting their own safety during climate disasters (Ayalon et al. 2021). Older persons experience a disproportionate amount of heat-related adverse medication effects and heat mortality due to changes in body composition and the thermoregulatory system; in fact, heat stroke occurs in individuals over age 65 years at rates up to 23 times higher than in other age groups (Gamble et al. 2013). This must be taken into special account when working with older adults with mental illness. Higher rates of chronic medical comorbidities, such as cardiovascular disease and diabetes, among older adults with mental illness further exacerbate their sensitivity to extreme heat.

Beyond temperature changes and heat events, several climate drivers, such as air pollution and loss of green spaces, demonstrate detrimental effects on the mental capacities of older persons, leading to increased rates of cognitive decline and increased risk of dementia (Cianconi et al. 2021; Béjot et al. 2018). Disasters such as droughts have been linked with increased suicidality among older persons (Sena et al. 2018). Finally, unique causes of psychological distress related to climate change—such as survivor's guilt among the elderly who have lost younger loved ones due to climate change and internalized ageism from the villainization of older adults for contributing to greenhouse gas emissions—take a toll on older persons' mental health (Ayalon et al. 2021).

Ethnic/Racial Minorities

Hazardous waste sites and fossil fuel pollution output have been disproportionately located in neighborhoods of ethnic and/or racial minorities. For instance, African American populations in counties with oil refineries range from 16% to 54% compared with 13% of the total US population comprised by African Americans in 2010 (Fleischman and Franklin 2017). Redlined communities, demarcated by a racist convention of limiting financial support to minority communities as a form of segregation, have been associated with higher rates of air pollution exposure from traffic sources, diminished green spaces, greater risk of floods, and exposure to higher temperatures as a result of urban heat-island effect (Tessum et al. 2021; Katz 2021). In fact, compared to non-Hispanic Whites, the likelihood of residing in areas with elevated heat-related risks has been shown to be 52% higher for African Americans, 32% higher for Asians, and 21% higher for Hispanics (Jesdale et al. 2013), while African Americans and Hispanics also have experienced 56% and 63% excess exposure to particulate matter air pollution, respectively (Tessum et al. 2019). All of these factors contribute to the greater impact of climate change on ethnic and racial minorities' health, along with the obligation of psychiatrists to understand and address racial injustices pertaining to environmental and social determinants of health.

Rural Communities

Rural communities rely upon agriculture for economic stability. Because the geographic location of these communities puts them in closer proximity to flood and wildfire-prone areas, they are vulnerable to climate disasters that destroy crops and devastate local economies while making access to crisis resources more difficult. Additionally, the dependency on and close relationship with the land and landscape of rural people increases their risk of psychological distress and mental illness compared to urban populations when climate-driven disasters disrupt that relationship (OBrien et al. 2014), as evidenced by the increased risk of suicide by farmers during periods of drought (Vins et al. 2015). The difficulty in responding to these vulnerabilities is compounded by the higher rates of poverty and lower emphasis on planning capacity in rural communities when compared to urban areas, exemplified by their much lower likelihood of having a land-use planner compared to metropolitan counties (NCA 2014).

Indigenous Peoples

Many Indigenous populations live subsistence lifestyles in deep connection with the land. Similar to rural communities, this greater identification with nature and landscapes confers a greater risk of negative mental health impacts by climate change, magnified by the unjust exploitation of natural resources by non-Indigenous populations (Middleton et al. 2021). Meanwhile, similar to other ethnic minorities, discriminatory practices expose them to further risk related to fossil fuel consumption. As wildfires, deforestation, drought, and flooding damage crops and disrupt animal reproductive and migration patterns, risks of food insecurity and poverty—already overrepresented in Indigenous populations worldwide—are multiplied. For example, Inuit communities' mental health and livelihood have been threatened by sea-ice instability, which disrupts whale and other hunting activities that make up the backbone of their cultural tradition and sustenance. This disruption is reflected by increased rates of substance abuse, mental disorders, and suicidal thoughts (Middleton et al. 2021). For Yolngu Aboriginal peoples, self-concept includes a literal understanding of the relation of one's footprints (djalkiri) to the footprints of one's ancestors and the footprints of the land, and social networks (gurrutu) are intimately defined by the sustainable use of a set of natural resources (Christie and Greatorex 2004). Ultimately, these climate changes and environmental injustices jeopardize the social connections, spiritual practices, traditional foods, mental health, and ancestral culture of Indigenous groups (Durkalec et al. 2015).

Community Psychiatry, Climate Change, and Social Justice

As discussed above, the effects of climate change fall disproportionately across the population. The ethical practice of both community psychiatry and climate psychiatry, therefore, requires a foundational engagement in social justice and health equity. In enacting these core values to serve underserved and marginalized communities who often face a plethora of challenges related to basic human needs and social justice, community psychiatrists have to consider how to prioritize attention to climate change and related mental health effects in the context of other important, urgent psychosocial forces affecting their patients. Yet efforts that drive policies to counteract climate change, design a more sustainable future, and enable a just transition will inherently also create economic opportunity and promote equity across races, genders, cultures, and socioeconomic backgrounds. In this way, climate action unites other movements for social justice and health equity.

This relationship is not unidirectional; policies to promote social justice also empower climate-vulnerable populations and often promote a more sustainable future. In contrast, ambivalence in climate action permits continued harm to health as well as to community resources such as food, water, and shelter which will, in turn, only worsen psychological and psychosocial conditions. For these reasons, engagement in addressing climate change by community-focused psychiatrists is not only morally imperative, but well aligned with the values and other goals core to the practice of community psychiatry.

Solutions designed to both protect mental health and decrease disparities exacerbated by the effects of climate disruption on health are fortunately also well aligned with five core skill sets of the community psychiatrist. Recovery and person-centered care, contributions to population health and preventive efforts, community leadership and collaboration with local departments and organizations for collective action, skilled advocacy and social justice efforts, and expertise in navigating and driving systems toward a just transition and sustainable future will all be critical components of the response by psychiatrists to address climate change in their communities. Here, we outline examples of climate-related interventions that are practical for the community psychiatrist, set in the foundation of these five pillars of community psychiatry.

Recovery and Person-Centered Care

The emotional responses and mental health implications of climate change for each individual vary, and the community psychiatrist may best be prepared to address individual responses by adapting the framework of person-centered care and recovery. Emotional reactions in the context of climate change depend on how one makes sense of what is happening and how one frames their own response. Mental health promotion in this context requires mental health providers to help patients realistically understand how climate change affects them and what actions they can take on both individual and collective levels (Fritze et al. 2008).

Using person-centered communication—such as noting the need to prepare for heat waves in order to protect their families or in recognizing a pattern of experiencing more frequent asthma attacks as being related to increasing pollen counts and air pollution—may be the most effective way for psychiatrists to frame educational messages about the health risks of climate change for each individual and also ultimately have the broadest community impact (Senay et al. 2021). Effective climate communication skills rely significantly on respect for, responsiveness to, and empowerment of patient preferences, needs, and values—principles that are also core to person-centered care (Stanhope et al. 2021).

The community psychiatrist's additional therapeutic role is also to normalize the emotional response of patients confronting the frightening reality of the climate crisis. First, because psychiatrists are equal stakeholders in our behavior-driven planetary crisis, it may be particularly helpful to highlight that the psychiatrist and the patient are in a shared circumstance as related to climate disruption. Personal sharing—which overlaps with the concepts of intersubjective "metaphorizing empathy" and "narrative empathy" often used in person-centered care—can be a tool for empowering the patient through identification with the capabilities and strength of the physician and through demonstrating how to build a supportive community (Mezzich et al. 2016). Second, psychiatrists can help individuals leverage their unique strengths to enter a phase of adaptation and transformation parallel to the journey of the recovery model. This process will utilize positive psychology to redirect anxieties and despair toward hope and resilience through collective action (Fritze et al. 2008; Baudon and Jachens 2021). Finally, psychiatrists may use social prescriptions for sustainability-oriented activities and/or education on what can be done toward collective action, which has powerful healing benefits for the individual while also galvanizing community collaborative efforts and transformation. Further recovery-oriented activities include:

- Educating oneself and other mental health professionals about the local effects of climate change on overall health and mental health, as well as the mental health benefits of a transition to a clean economy for local businesses and workers.
- Educating patients and the community on local climate-related risks and how to protect themselves (e.g., heat impacts on psychiatric medications, air pollution and air filtration, fires and "go kits," tornado and in-ground shelter).
- Educating oneself and one's patients about local sustainability initiatives affecting their health.
- Issuing social prescriptions to patients to spend time in nature or connect with nature, including animal life (Dean et al. 2018).
- Issuing social prescriptions to participate in local collaborative action on sustainable habitat improvement, which can include sustainability efforts such as community gardening, or air, water, and land advocacy efforts (Hayes et al. 2020).
- Referring patients to group therapy oriented toward addressing climate distress through shared experiences of recovery (Mark and Lewis 2020).
- Adapting current methods of psychotherapy to address climate psychological issues. ACT, feminist therapy, ecotherapy, and dialectical techniques may be particularly helpful (Baudon and Jachens 2021; Lewis et al. 2020).
- Adapting existing person-centered treatment planning instruments to ensure long-term

patient goals are sustainable in the face of likely climate disruption (Stanhope et al. 2021).

Population Health and Prevention

Mental health promotion in the context of climate change extends beyond care of the individual and presents an opportunity for community psychiatrists to practice prevention and health promotion at the level of their community. First, in order to detect and track the effects that climate change is having on the health of any given community, surveillance and needs assessments must be conducted to ensure that communities are equipped with resources to adapt. Community psychiatrists with close exposure to the challenges faced by their patients can aid these assessments by collecting data on and reporting prevalence of health effects to health department officials and local organizations providing services in their area (Hayes et al. 2020) and assessing the adequacy of local health services to address local climate challenges. Second, community psychiatrists may examine the adequacy of health system responsiveness to regional climate needs through health services research which may be used to direct adaptive measures (Haase 2020). This research should be used to inform policymakers, who otherwise may not have regionally specific understanding of how to prioritize health services development to provide the most regionally responsive adaptive and preventive services. Most importantly, contributions by community psychiatrists to encourage groups of patients, health systems, local organizations, and policymakers to engage in strategies to mitigate climate change ultimately serve the purpose of prevention of its varied health sequelae. Psychiatrists' knowledge of theories of psychology, behavior change, and trauma and fear responses, as well as their abilities with processing difficult emotions at the group and individual level, are critical to enhancing capacities for social change and helping communities articulate new self-defining narratives under evolving circumstances, particularly under the conditions of ongoing personal and collective trauma that climate change will bring.

Additional activities include:

- Screening patients for climate-related psychological distress; useful scales may include the Environmental Distress Scale (Higginbotham et al. 2006), the Solastalgia Scale (Eisenman et al. 2015), and the Kessler Psychological Distress Scale.
- Screening patients for their degree of climate awareness in order to prompt and personalize discussion; for example, the SASSY scale developed by Yale Climate Communications can be used to categorize an individual's climate attitudes and suggest data-driven, effective communication strategies (Leiserowitz et al. 2020).
- Screening patients for access to protective measures, such as cooling centers during extreme heat, and protective factors, such as neighborhood greenness and sense of connectedness to nature (Beyer et al. 2014; Dean et al. 2018).
- Participating in general community needs assessments to promote intentional inclusion of climate-based behavioral and mental health needs.
- Contributing expertise on community mental health to aid regional health officials in conducting formal Health Impact Assessments, which assess and manage the community health risks of intended local development projects or actions, particularly when those actions have environmental implications (Bell 2011).
- Conducting community-based participatory research with members of vulnerable populations, so that they can provide nuanced feedback on how climate change is differentially affecting them in a local context (Bell 2011).
- Developing community-based climate change resilience plans, to address psychosocial well-being, that include measures of mitigation (increased greenspace, availability of public transportation, decreased food waste, insurance of family planning, incentives for clean energy) and adaptation and resilience (disaster

response, clean water and water rights protections) (Masson-Delmotte et al. 2021).

- Educating about climate health risks through public service messages targeted to the most vulnerable populations.
- Spreading the word about the health harms of climate change through public health marketing campaigns, which help make the personal impact of climate change more relevant for individuals and inspire adaptive and mitigative behaviors on a population level (Krygsman and Speiser 2016).

Leadership and Collaboration

Broad interventions to address climate change must be rooted in local knowledge and culture in order to meet the needs of those affected. Yet organizational hierarchy can create barriers to local voices being heard during pivotal decisions. Community psychiatrists and mental health centers are optimally positioned to serve as a primary channel between the local populace and national organizations since they are prominent members of both. Community psychiatrists fill numerous leadership roles, including education of future healthcare providers and leadership of both national organizations and community mental health systems. As healthcare transforms to paying for value rather than just volume, psychiatrists must expand their leadership roles to address issues that affect wellness, like climate change, as outlined below through:

- Partnering with other community and national organizations to reflect the interconnectedness of the climate crisis and mental health in order to build solidarity around calls for change, such as ceasing use of and divestment from fossil fuels.
- Forming consortiums to ensure that all communal decisions and messaging include climate equity, including for infrastructure projects, legislation, land planning, and more (Climate Health Action Recommendations 2021).
- Promoting climate health literacy by expanding health professional curricula to include this material, with particular emphasis on adequate climate mental health didactics (Pollack and Haase 2022).
- Including time and funding in community psychiatry leadership positions to participate in local initiatives and governance on communal wellness plans, such as land planning for green spaces that have co-benefits for social connectedness and mental and physical health while providing buffers to climate drivers (Engemann et al. 2019).
- Introducing community mental health adaptation strategies to climate change, such as transformational resilience practices (Doppelt 2016) and emerging group support networks responsive to the unique qualities of the climate crisis, like Climate Cafes and the Deep Adaptation and Good Grief Networks (Mark and Lewis 2020).

Advocacy and Social Justice

The American Association of Community Psychiatry's (AACP) strategic plan includes "influenc[ing] health and social policies to develop and sustain coordinated public health and clinical delivery systems… guided by social justice and evidence informed clinical practices…" (AACP Strategic Plan). The mounting known harms from climate change present a moral imperative to include advocacy for climate mitigation, justice, and community resilience in all such efforts. Furthermore, expanding healthcare provider support for climate action is pivotal in growing public messaging, as health professionals are among the most trusted messengers (Maibach et al. 2021). Further actions include:

- Lobbying policymakers through organizational and established channels to adopt climate mitigation and adaptation legislation as a matter for public health.

- Educating the public regarding the implications that climate change has on health through marketing campaigns and local op-ed publications.
- Vocalizing and implementing the need for carbon footprint reduction within the healthcare sector, which currently emits 10% of US greenhouse gas emissions (Lenzen et al. 2020).
- Reducing the carbon footprint of psychiatric practice through measures including transitions to zero carbon energy sources; office sharing; hospital bed reduction through use of mobile mental health teams; extension of telemedicine; geographically distributed care and collaborative care; reductions in overprescribing, low-yield prescriptions, and polypharmacy; and video-based attendance at CME events and conferences (Yarlagadda et al. 2014).
- Demanding strategies aimed at ending carbon emissions that incorporate "Just Transition" principles, ensuring resources and employment are distributed to frontline workers and fenceline communities that have suffered more climate impacts and are more at stake during the transition to sustainable energy (Krawchenko and Gordon 2021).
- Expanding programs such as the EPA's Environmental Justice Screening Tool, CalEnviroScreen, to ensure that health investments are targeted to those most vulnerable and exposed to adverse climate impacts (Climate Health Action Recommendations 2021).
- Correcting research practices, such as those used to estimate mortality from air pollution, that underestimate effects on minority and underrepresented populations (Spiller et al. 2021).

Integrated and Comprehensive Systems

Although locally based work is vitally important to ensure a just and smooth transition for communities, the breadth of climate change makes systematic improvements critical to maintain a healthy living environment. Comprehensive mental health systems are increasingly integrated into broader health systems along with longstanding integration into the communities in which individuals live. Solutions that address climate change must be integrated into these systems, and community psychiatrists must integrate them into the continuum of services provided. As with prior global health risks, climate change requires we increase the flexibility, responsiveness, and interactive feedback loops between centralized coordinating agencies and local convening bodies, as well as improve communication to patients (Overton et al. 2021). The Intergovernmental Panel on Climate Change (IPCC) recommends that policy initiatives perform three broad things: (1) promote decisions that produce decent outcomes under a wide variety of scenarios, mathematical decision-making models, and institutional stability; (2) propagate credible, legitimate, actionable, and salient information; and (3) engage stakeholders in ongoing education to solve their own problems over time (Masson-Delmotte et al. 2021). Specific actions include:

- Ensuring mental health impacts of climate change be prioritized in all national and local climate legislations, policies, and strategies, such as inclusion in the National Health Security Strategy (Climate Health Action Recommendations 2021).
- Conducting adequate research to define how the mental health impacts of climate change intersect with known psychiatric symptoms and disease.
- Advocating that all community mental health funding meet sustainability, decarbonization, and social determinants of health goals.
- Incentivizing healthcare system carbon footprint reduction by incorporating sustainability benchmarks into reimbursement metrics, such as increasing reimbursement amounts when clinics achieve higher efficiency certifications, and creating funds for smaller and rural healthcare systems to meet these metrics (Salas et al. 2020).

- Mapping community assets to identify gaps in resources as well as coordinate adaptation to climate change and preparation for climate emergencies (Hayes et al. 2019).
- Building national surveillance and notification tools for climate-related health risks, such as alerts about vector-borne disease outbreaks or heat waves that include resources and evidence-based recommendations for both providers and patients (Salas et al. 2020).
- Adding capability at community mental health centers to act as hubs for climate-related disasters— for example, using these centers as cooling centers for those experiencing homelessness.

Conclusion

Climate change is an existential threat to humans with far-reaching consequences for community healthcare, particularly mental health. Increasing temperatures, heat waves, extreme weather events, droughts, air pollution, vector-borne diseases, and nutritional scarcity all stand to directly impact mental health by exacerbating current illness and increasing the incidence of mental illness. Furthermore, mounting financial, communal, housing, and personal losses indirectly influence local population health, lasting long beyond any of the direct impacts and multiplying inequities in social determinants of health. The worst of these effects can be addressed with collaborative interventions between local, national, and international governance. Community psychiatrists have a responsibility to safeguard the health, recovery, and resilience of the populations they serve and have a large and compelling role to play in developing and enacting these creative solutions as prominent members of their local and broader communities.

References

Abatzoglou, J.T., Williams, A.P. (2016). Impact of anthropogenic climate change on wildfire across western US forests. *PNAS*, 113(42), 11770–75.

Albrecht, G. (2011). Chronic environmental change: Emerging 'psychoterratic' syndromes. In *Climate change and human wellbeing*. Springer.

Albrecht, G., Sartore, G.M., Connor, L., et al. (2007). Solastalgia: the distress caused by environmental change, *Australas Psychiatry* 15(S1):S95–98.

Asadullah, M.N., Islam, K.M.M., & Wahhaj, Z. (2020). Child marriage, climate vulnerability and natural disasters in coastal Bangladesh. *J Biosoc Sci*, 1–20.

Ayalon, L., Keating, N., Pillemer, K., & Rabheru, K. (2021). Climate Change and Mental Health of Older Persons: A Human Rights Imperative. *Am J Geriatr Psychiatry*, 29(10), 1038–40.

Bassil, K.L., & Cole, D.C. (2010). Effectiveness of Public Health Interventions in Reducing Morbidity and Mortality during Heat Episodes: A Structured Review. *Int J Environ*, 7, 991–1001.

Baudon, P., & Jachens, L. (2021). A Scoping Review of Interventions for the Treatment of Eco-Anxiety. *Int J Environ*, 18(18), 9836.

Béjot, Y., Reis, J., Giroud, M., Feigin, V. (2018). A review of epidemiological research on stroke and dementia and exposure to air pollution. *Int J Stroke*, 13, 687–695.

Bell, E. Readying health services for climate change: a policy framework for regional development. *Am J Public Health*, 101(5):804–813, 2011

Berman, J. D., Burkhardt, J., Bayham, J., et al. (2019). Acute Air Pollution Exposure and the Risk of Violent Behavior in the United States. *Epidemiology* (Cambridge, Mass.), 30(6), 799–806.

Beyer, K.M.M., Kaltenbach, A., Szabo, A., et al. (2014). Exposure to neighborhood green space and mental health: Evidence from the survey of the health of wisconsin. *Int J Environ*, 11(3), 3453–72.

Bezgrebelna, M., McKenzie, K., Wells, S., et al. (2021). Climate Change, Weather, Housing Precarity, and Homelessness: A Systematic Review of Reviews. *Int J Environ*, 18, 5812.

Bouchama, A., Dehbi, M., Mohamed, G., et al. (2007). Prognostic factors in heat wave related deaths: a meta-analysis. *Arch Intern Med*, *167*(20), 2170–76.

Burke, M., Gonzalez, F., Baylis, P., et al. (2018). Higher temperatures increase suicide rates in the United States and Mexico. *Nat Clim Change*, 8, 723–279.

Charlson, F., Ali, S., Benmarhnia, T., et al. (2021). Climate change and mental health: a scoping review. *Int J Environ*, 18(9), 4486.

Chen, M.H., Su, T.P., Chen, Y.S., et al. (2013). Association between psychiatric disorders and iron deficiency anemia among children and adolescents: a nationwide population-based study. *BMC Psychiatry*, 13, 161.

Chique, C., Hynds, P., Nyhan, M.M., et al. (2021). Psychological impairment and extreme weather event (EWE) exposure, 1980-2020: A global pooled analysis integrating mental health and well-being metrics. *Int J Hyg Environ Health*, 238, 113840.

Christie, M. & Greatorex, J. (2004). Yolngu Life in the Northern Territory of Australia: The Significance of Community and Social Capital. *Asia Pac J Public Adm*, 26(1), 55–69.

Cianconi, P., Betro, S., Grillo, F., et al. (2021). Climate shift and mental health adjustment. *CNS Spectrums*, 26(1), 5–6.

Climate Health Action Recommendations. (2021). Climate change, health and equity at the department of Health and Human Services. Call to action signed by health groups.

Cohen, A.J., Brauer, M., Burnett, R., et al. (2017). Estimates and 25-year trends of the global burden of disease attributable to ambient air pollution: an analysis of data from the Global Burden of Diseases Study 2015. *Lancet*, 389(10082), 1907–18.

Coverdale, J., Balon, R., Beresin, E., et al. (2018). Climate change: A call to action for the psychiatric profession. *Acad Psychiatry*, 42, 317–323.

Crowley, K. & Head, B. (2017). The enduring challenge of 'wicked problems': revisiting Rittel and Webber. *Policy Sci*, 50(5).

Dean, J.H., Shanahan, D.F., Bush, R., et al. (2018). Is Nature Relatedness Associated with Better Mental and Physical Health? *Int J Environ*, 15(7), 1371.

Doppelt, B. (2016). Transformational Resilience: How Building Human Resilience to Climate Disruption Can Safeguard Society and Increase Wellbeing. *Greenleaf Publishing*.

Dumont, C., Haase, E., Dolber, T., et al. (2020). Climate Change and Risk of Completed Suicide. *J Nerv Ment Dis*, 208(7), 559–565.

Durkalec, A., Frugal, C., Skinner, M.W., Sheldton, T. (2015). Climate change influences on environment as a determinant of Indigenous health: Relationships to place, sea ice, and health in an Inuit community. *Soc Sci Med*, 136–137 (17–26).

Eisenman, D., McCaffrey, S., Donatello, I., & Marshal, G. (2015). An Ecosystems and Vulnerable Populations Perspective on Solastalgia and Psychological Distress After a Wildfire. *EcoHealth*, 12(4), 602–610.

Engemann, K., Pederson, C.B., Arge, L., et al. (2019). Residential green space in childhood is associated with lower risk of psychiatric disorder from adolescence into adulthood. *PNAS*, 116(11), 5188–93.

Fallon, B.A., Nields, J.A. (1994). Lyme disease: a neuropsychiatric illness. *Am J Psychiatry*, 151(11), 1571–83.

Fatmi, S. S., Zehra, R., & Carpenter, D.O. (2017). Powassan Virus-A New Re-emerging Tick-Borne Disease. *Front Public Health*, 5, 342.

Fleischman, L., Franklin, M. (2017). Fumes across the fence-line: the health impacts of air pollution from oil & gas facilities on african american communities. *Clean Air Task Force* 2017. Available at www.naacp.org/climate-justice-resources/fumes-across-the-fence-line. Accessed on January 22, 2021

Fritze, J.G., Blashki, G.A., Burke, S., Wiseman, J. (2008). Hope, despair and transformation: Climate change and the promotion of mental health and wellbeing. *Int J Ment Health Syst*, 2(13).

Fu, P., Guo, X, Cheung, F.M.H, & Yung, K.K.L. (2019). The association between PM2.5 exposure and neurological disorders: A systematic review and meta-analysis. *Sci Total Environ*, 655, 1240–48.

Gamble, J.L., Hurley, B.J., Schultz, P.A., et al. (2013). Climate change and older Americans: state of the science. *Environ Health Perspect*, 121(1), 15–22.

Gearhart, S., Perez-Patron, M., Hammond, T.A., et al. (2018). The Impact of Natural Disasters on Domestic Violence: An Analysis of Reports of Simple Assault in Florida (1999–2007). *Violence Gend*, *5*(2), 87–92.

Gronlund, C.J., Sullivan, K.P., Kefelegn, Y., et al. (2018). Climate change and temperature extremes: A review of heat- and cold-related morbidity and mortality concerns of municipalities. *Maturitas*, 114, 54–59.

Gu, X., Liu, Q., Deng, F., et al. (2019). Association between particular matter air pollution and risk of depression and suicide: Systematic review and meta-analysis. *Br J Psychiatry*, 215, 456–67.

Haase E. (2020). Finding value in the psychiatric response to climate change. In W. Sowers & J. Ranz. (Eds.) Seeking value: balancing cost and quality in psychiatric care (1st ed, pp. 461–490). Washington, DC: *American Psychiatric Publishing*.

Haase, E., Augustinavicius, J., Hayes, K. (In press). Climate change and psychiatry. In Tasman, A. et al. (Ed.), Tasman's psychiatry (5th ed.). Cham, Switzerland: Springer.

Hanigan, I.C., Butler, C.D., Kokic, P.N., & Hutchinson, M.F. (2012). Suicide and drought in new South Wales, Australia, 1970–2007. *PNAS*, 109(35), 13950–55.

Hayes, K., Berry, P., & Ebi, K. L. (2019). Factors Influencing the Mental Health Consequences of Climate Change in Canada. *Int J Environ, 16*(9), 1583.

Hayes, K., Poland, B., Cole, D., Agic, B. (2020). Psychosocial adaptation to climate change in High River, Alberta: implications for policy and practice. *Can J Public Health*, 111(6), 880–89.

Hellden, D., Andersson, C., Nilsson, M., et al. (2021). Climate change and child health: a scoping review and an expanded conceptual framework. *Lancet Planet Health*, 5, e164–175.

Hickman, C., Marks, E., Pihkala, P., et al. (2021). Young people's voice on climate anxiety, governmental betrayal and moral injury: a global phenomenon. Available at SSRN: https://ssrn.com/abstract=3918955

Higginbotham, N.H.. Connor, C., Albrecht, G., et al. (2006). Validation of an environmental distress scale. *EcoHealth*, 3, 245–54.

Hsiang, S.M., Burke, M., Miguel, E. (2013). Quantifying the influence of climate on human conflict. *Science*, 341, 6151.

Internal Displacement Monitoring Centre. Global Report on Internal Displacement 2021. https://www.internal--displacement.org/global-report/grid2021/. Accessed January 6, 2022

Ismail, N., Bloch, K.C., & McBride, J.W. (2010). Human ehrlichiosis and anaplasmosis. *Clin Lab*, 30(1), 261–92.

Jesdale, B.M., Morello-Frosch, R., Cushing, L. (2013). The racial/ethnic distribution of heat risk-related land cover in relation to residential segregation. *Environ Health Perspect*, 121(7), 811–17.

Jessel, S., Sawyer, S., Hernández, D. (2019). Energy, Poverty, and Health in Climate Change: A Comprehensive Review of an Emerging Literature. *Frontiers Pub Health*, 7, 357.

Jones A. D. (2017). Food insecurity and mental health status: A global analysis of 149 countries. *Am J Prev Med*, *53*(2), 264–73.

Katz, L. (2021). A racist past, a flooded future: formerly redlined areas have $107 billion worth of homes facing high flood risk - 25% more than non-redlined areas. *Redfin News*. Accessed January 22, 2022

Kessler, R. C., Galea, S., Jones, R. T., & Parker, H. A. (2006). Mental illness and suicidality after Hurricane Katrina. *Bull World Health Organ*, 84, 930–39.

Krawchenko, T.A., Gordon, M. (2021). How Do We Manage a Just Transition? A Comparative Review of National and Regional Just Transition Initiatives. *Sustainability*, 13(11), 6070.

Krygsman, K., Speiser, M. (2016). ecoAmerica. Let's talk health and climate: Communication guidance for health professionals. *Climate for Health*, Washington, DC.

Leiserowitz, A., Maibach, E., Rosenthal, S., et al. (2021). Climate change in the American mind: March 2021. Yale University and George Mason University. *Yale Program on Climate Change Communication*.

Leiserowitz, A., Marlon, J., Wang, X., et al. (2020). Global warming's six americas in 2020. Yale Program on Climate Change Communication. Available at https://climatecommunication.yale.edu/publications/global-warmings-six-americas-in-2020/. Accessed January 19, 2022.

Lenzen, M., Malik, A., Li, M., et al. (2020). The environmental footprint of health care: a global assessment. *Lancet Planet Health*, 4(7), e271–279.

Lewis, J., Haase, E., & Trope, A. (2020). Climate dialectics in psychotherapy: Holding open the space between abyss and advance. *Psychodyn Psychiatry*, 48(3).

Li, T., Horton, R.M., Bader, D.A., et al. (2018). Long-term projections of temperature-related mortality risks for ischemic stroke, hemorrhagic stroke, and acute ischemic heart disease under changing climate in Beijing, China. *Environ Int*, 112, 1–9.

Lõhmus M. (2018). Possible biological mechanisms linking mental health and heat - A contemplative review. *Int J Environ*, *15*(7), 1515.

Maibach, E., Frumkin, H., Ahdoot, S. (2021). Health Professionals and the Climate Crisis: Trusted Voices, Essential Roles. *World Med Health Policy*, 13(1), 137–45.

Mark, B. & Lewis, J. (2020). Group interventions for climate change distress. *Psychiatric Times*. Available at https://www.psychiatrictimes.com/view/group-interventions-climate-change-distress. Accessed on January 28, 2022.

Masson-Delmotte, V., Zhai, P., Pirani, A., et al. (2021). Climate change 2021: The physical science basis. *Contribution of Working Group I to the Sixth Assessment Report of the Intergovernmental Panel on Climate Change*. IPCC. Available at https://www.ipcc.ch/report/ar6/wg1/downloads/report/IPCC_AR6_WGI_Full_Report.pdf. Accessed January 5, 2022.

Mezzich, J.E., Botbol, M., Christodoulou, G.N., et al. (2016). Person Centered Psychiatry. *Switzerland: Springer International Publishing*.

Middleton, J., Cunsolo, A., Pollock, N., et al. (2021). Temperature and place associations with Inuit mental health in the context of climate change. *Environ Research*, 198, 111166.

National Climate Assessment: Rural communities. (2014). *U.S. Global Change Research Program*, 2014. Available at https://nca2014.globalchange.gov/report/sectors/rural-communities. Accessed January 24, 2022

Obradovich, N. & Fowler, J.H. (2017). Climate change may alter human physical activity patterns. *Nat Hum Behav*, 1(5), 97.

Obrien, L.V., Berry, H.L., Coleman, C., Hanigan, I.C. (2014). Drought as a mental health exposure. *Environ Research*, 131, 181–87.

Overton, D., Ramkeesoon, S.A., Kirkpatrick, et al. (2021). Lessons from the COVID-19 crisis on executing communications and engagement at the community level during a health crisis. *The National Academies of Sciences, Engineering, Medicine*.

Parida, Y., Dash, D.P., Bhardwaj, P., & Chowdhury, J.R. (2018). Effects of drought and flood on farmer suicides in Indian states: an empirical analysis. *Economics of Disasters and Climate Change*, 2(2), 159–80.

Perera, F.P. (2017). Multiple Threats to Child Health from Fossil Fuel Combustion: Impacts of Air Pollution and Climate Change, *Environ Health Perspect*, 125(3), 141–48.

Pollack, D. & Haase, E. (2022). Climate and health curriculum development: mental health impacts and responses. *Transformational Times*. Accessed January 20, 2022. Available at https://files.constantcontact.com/adf622bd601/1e2f02f2-ac34-4170-8a04-746ca2186a1b.pdf

Rosenberg, R., Lindsey, N.P., Fischer, M., et al. (2018). Vital signs: trends in reported vector borne disease cases – United States and Territories, 2004–2016, MMWR. *Centers for Disease Control*, 67(17), 496–591.

Salas, R., Friend, T.H., Bernstein, A., Jha, A.K. (2020). Adding a climate lens to health policy in the United States. *Health Affairs*, 39(12), 2063–70.

Schlader, Z.J., Gagnon, D., Adams, A., et al. (2015). Cognitive and perceptual responses during passive heat stress in younger and older adults. *American J Physiol Regul Integr Comp Physiol*, 308, 847–54.

Seddighi, H., Salmani, I., Javadi, M. H., & Seddighi, S. (2019). Child abuse in natural disasters and conflicts: A systematic review. *Trauma Violence Abuse*, 1524838019835973.

Sena, A., Freitas, C., Feitosa Souza, P., et al. (2018). Drought in the Semiarid Region of Brazil: Exposure, Vulnerabilities and Health Impacts from the Perspectives of Local Actors. *PLOS Currents*, 10, 1–29.

Senay, E., Sarfaty, M., & Rice, M.B. (2021). Strategies for Clinical Discussions About Climate Change. *Ann Intern Med*, 174(3), 417–18.

Sheffield, P.E. & Landrigan, P.L. (2011). Global Climate Change and Children's Health: Threats and Strategies for Prevention. *Environ Health*, 119(3).

Simon, L.V., Coffey, R., Fischer, M.A. (2020). Western Equine Encephalitis. In: StatPearls [Internet]. *StatPearls Publishing*. Available at https://www.ncbi.nlm.nih.gov/books/NBK470228/

Singh, V. B., Kumar, H., Meena, B. L., et al. (2016). Neuropsychiatric Profile in Malaria: An Overview. *J Clinical Diagn*, 10(7), OC24–OC28.

Smith, M.R., Myers, S.S. (2018). Impact of anthropogenic CO2 emissions on global human nutrition. *Nat Clim Change*, 8, 834–839.

Souza, I., Barros-Aragão, F., Frost, P. S., et al. (2019). Late Neurological Consequences of Zika Virus Infection: Risk Factors and Pharmaceutical Approaches. *Pharmaceuticals*, *12*(2), 60.

Sova, C., Flowers, K., & Man, C. (2019). Climate change and food security: A test of U.S. leadership in a fragile world. *Center for Strategic and International Studies*. Available at https://www.csis.org/analysis/climate-change-and-food-security-test-us-leadership-fragile-world

Spiller, E., Proville, J., Roy, A., & Muller, N. (2021). Mortality risk from PM2.5: A comparison of modeling approaches to identify disparities across racial/ethnic groups in policy outcomes. *Environ Health*, 129, 12.

Stanhope, V., Baslock, D., Tondora, J., et al. (2021). Developing a Tool to Measure Person-Centered Care in Service Planning. *Front Psychiatry*, 12, 681597.

Tessum, C.W., Apte, J.S., Goodkind, A.L., et al. (2019). Inequity in consumption of goods and services adds to racial-ethnic disparities in air pollution exposure. *PNAS*, 116(13), 6001–6.

Tessum, C.W., Paolella, D.A., Chambliss, S.E., et al. (2021). 2.5 polluters disproportionately and systemically affect people of color in the United States. *Sci Adv*, 7(18).

Vins, H., Bell, J., Saha, S., & Hess, J.J. (2015). The Mental Health Outcomes of Drought: A Systematic Review and Causal Process Diagram. *Int J Environ*, *12*(10), 13251–75.

Wang, J., Um, P., Dickerman, B.A., & Liu, J. (2018). Zinc, magnesium, selenium and depression: A review of the evidence, potential mechanisms and implications. *Nutrients*, 10(5), 584.

World Health Organization. (2021). Climate change and health. Available at https://www.who.int/news-room/fact-sheets/detail/climate-change-and-health. Accessed January 6, 2022

Yarlagadda, S., Maughan, D., Lingwood, S., & Davison, P. (2014). Sustainable psychiatry in the UK. *Psychiatri Bull*, 38(6), 285–90.

Zhang, Y., Bi, P., & Hiller, J.E. (2007). Climate change and disability-adjusted life years. *J Environ Health*, 70(3), 32–36.

Disaster Victims and the Response to Trauma

Matthew N. Goldenberg, David Benedek, and Robert J. Ursano

Disasters are common and widespread. As this textbook chapter is being written, the United States and much of the world have been in the throes of the COVID-19 pandemic for more than two years. Not since the Spanish Flu of the 1918 has the world witnessed such profound devastation to life, economies, and threats to social values. Much of the psychological impact of the pandemic remains to be studied, yet early data suggest a profound toll and a robust need for enhanced prevention and treatment resources. The scope, longevity, and nature of the pandemic distinguish it from more proscribed disaster events. In this chapter, we review elements common to all disasters and specifically address the COVID-19 pandemic.

M. N. Goldenberg (✉)
Department of Psychiatry, Yale University School of Medicine, New Haven, CT, USA
e-mail: matthew.goldenberg@yale.edu

D. Benedek
Department of Psychiatry, Uniformed Services University of the Health Sciences, Bethesda, MD, USA
e-mail: dbenedek@usuhs.mil

R. J. Ursano
Center for the Study of Traumatic Stress, Department of Psychiatry, Uniformed Services University of the Health Sciences, Bethesda, MD, USA
e-mail: rursano@usuhs.mil

Introduction

In his 2020 memoir *A Promised Land*, former President Barack Obama cites the devastation of Hurricane Katrina, particularly the inadequate government preparation and response, as pivotal factors in his decision to seek the presidency (Obama 2020). In late August of 2005, just over a year into his first term as a U.S. Senator, Obama watched with sadness and dismay as Hurricane Katrina roared ashore on the Gulf Coast of the southern United States, leaving in its wake large swaths of physical destruction and human tragedy. The storm resulted in the deaths of nearly 2000 people, most of them residents of New Orleans, where the storm's water surge breached nearby levees and flooded nearly 80% of the city. Coastal communities in Mississippi and Alabama were also ravaged by the hurricane. During and immediately following the storm, many residents experienced extreme adversity—life threats, physical injury, and lack of appropriate food, water, sanitation, or shelter. Some had to walk long distances through flood waters, while others were rescued from the rooftops of their homes by boat or helicopter. Many locals, including a disproportionate number of poor and Black residents, were left homeless and unemployed, coping with the deaths of loved ones, the separation from family members, and the loss of important social institutions such as churches, medical clinics and hospitals, and community centers.

W. E. Sowers et al. (eds.), *Textbook of Community Psychiatry*,
https://doi.org/10.1007/978-3-031-10239-4_32

The storm created a large diaspora, with thousands of Gulf Coast residents relocating to cities such as Houston and Chicago. Property damage due to the storm was estimated at over $80 billion, with the total economic cost estimated at up to $150 billion (Tate 2010).

Because of the destructive toll of Hurricane Katrina, much attention has been paid to the storm from a variety of perspectives. The psychological impact of the storm on the residents of New Orleans and other affected regions has been the focus of significant interest among mental health and public policy professionals. The American Psychiatric Association held its 2010 annual meeting in New Orleans in part to focus on important questions that Hurricane Katrina raised about the psychiatric dimensions of disaster (American Psychiatric Association 2010). What are the psychological and behavioral effects of disaster or other traumatic events? What are the trajectories of such effects? Who is at risk for significant problems? To what extent and by what means can the adverse sequelae of disaster be prevented or mitigated? How can psychiatrists and other mental health professionals assist in disaster preparedness and response? This chapter will address these issues, especially highlighting the important roles that community psychiatrists and other mental health professionals can play in the pre-, peri-, and post-disaster setting.

Defining the Problem

Disasters

While the COVID-19 pandemic has undoubtedly been one of the great tragedies in American history (and a hugely devastating event around the world), it is hardly the only disaster that has or will befall the nation's communities or citizens. By definition, disasters are events that overwhelm personal and/or social coping resources (Ursano et al. 2007). Disasters are classically characterized in a variety of ways, differing in terms of type, intent of agent, and scale. Disasters can be natural (e.g., tornado) or man-made (e.g., terrorist attack), though the distinction blurs somewhat in instances like the COVID-19 pandemic or Hurricane Katrina where a natural event (a virus or hurricane) combined with human factors (deficient public health policy/practice or inadequate levee construction) lead to such devastation. Disasters can result from intentional acts (e.g., bombing) or accidents (e.g., industrial spill). Disasters can affect a few individuals, a small community, an entire nation, or even large numbers of people in various countries simultaneously as in the COVID-19 pandemic or the Indian Ocean tsunami of 2004.

Worldwide between 1994 and 2013, nearly 218 million people per year were directly affected by disasters, including natural events such as hurricanes or earthquakes (Centre for Research on the Epidemiology of Disasters, 2015). Man-made disasters such as terrorism and war inflict a heavy burden in many parts of the world. In 2017, more than 49 armed conflicts raged in 34 countries (Project Ploughshares 2008). Millions of people have been forced to migrate as refugees as a result of conflicts. The US military has been at war with Afghanistan and Iraq for much of the last two decades. As of 2019, nearly 7000 American service members and 8000 contractors had died in country, there had been over 50,000 officially counted as wounded in action, with many of those individuals having suffered head injuries and/or amputations (Watson Institute for International and Public Affairs 2020).

As was the case with Hurricane Katrina, disasters disproportionately affect the world's poor. Over 90% of deaths due to natural disasters occur in poor countries (McMahon 2007). Even in developed countries, poor citizens are most affected by disasters including the COVID-19 pandemic in the United States. An event of similar physical magnitude is likely to cause more deaths in a developing country than in a developed country. The disparity in disaster outcomes between rich and poor can be understood as a function of both pre-event vulnerability and post-event response. Factors such as geography, personal resources, community infrastructure, and political stability all impact the occurrence and consequences of natural disasters. Large disparities in the distribution of wealth and income may also lead to differential health outcomes.

The Mental Health Effects of Disasters

In the immediate aftermath of many disasters, affected communities often respond with an increased sense of cohesion and commitment to a common purpose. On an individual level, most people exposed to a disaster actually respond quite well—resilience in the face of adversity is the rule, not the exception. But many are not as fortunate. Some of those exposed to a disaster develop psychiatric disorders such as posttraumatic stress disorder (PTSD) or depression. Others experience reactions that, while not reaching a diagnostic threshold, are quite distressing, including feelings of grief, social withdrawal, sleep problems, or decreased concentration. Still others may change their health risk behaviors, including increasing their cigarette or alcohol use or altering their driving patterns (Hamaoka et al. 2007). Many disaster victims grow angry, resentful, or distrusting of those they deem either responsible for the disaster (e.g., industry in a chemical spill) or unhelpful in the response (e.g., government).

Distinguishing a "normal" reaction from a more problematic condition following a traumatic event continues to be a somewhat controversial issue. Transient psychological reactions such as fear, sadness, helplessness, grief, or anger in the aftermath of trauma are common and often referred to as acute stress reactions (ASRs). ASRs could be considered to be psychiatry's common cold—widely distributed, but minimally disabling and with expected full recovery, often without significant intervention. Although the DSM-5 does not include ASR as a diagnosable mental disorder, the international classification system (ICD) does. Unfortunately, the posttraumatic reaction for a subset of the population seems more like a pneumonia or chronic bronchitis, with a more severe, protracted course. It is this prolonged symptomatology and significant functional impairment that distinguish more pathological responses such as PTSD or acute stress disorder (ASD) from less severe ASR.

Posttraumatic stress disorder is the psychiatric condition most often associated with disasters, and it is often the primary focus of the post-disaster mental health response. PTSD is rare among mental disorders in that an external event is etiologically necessary for the diagnosis. Posttraumatic stress disorder is characterized by the development, after exposure to a traumatic event, of symptoms of (1) intrusion, reexperiencing of the event, often through involuntary thoughts, flashbacks, and/or nightmares; (2) avoidance of reminders of the event; (3) alterations in mood or cognition, inability to recall aspects of the event, exaggerated blame of self or others, or anhedonia; and (4) alterations in arousal or reactivity, such as hypervigilance, increased startle, poor sleep, irritability or aggression, and risk behavior. PTSD requires the presence of symptoms at least 1 month after the event and, like all mental disorders, impairment in psychosocial functioning. DSM-5 added a specifier for patients experiencing dissociation, but eliminated the distinction between "acute" and "chronic" phases. PTSD is classified as "delayed expression" if criteria for the disorder are not met until at least 6 months after the event (American Psychiatric Association 2013).

Acute stress disorder (ASD) has similar clinical characteristics as PTSD, differing only in time course. ASD may be diagnosed anywhere from 3 to 30 days post-event, whereas PTSD may only be diagnosed after 30 days or more. ASD is characterized by the same symptom domains as PTSD. In prior iterations of the DSM, a diagnosis of ASD required the presence of dissociation—such as time distortion or feeling detached or outside oneself—at the time of the event (American Psychiatric Association 2013), but this requirement was removed in the DSM-5. Initially, the presence of ASD was thought to be the predictor of subsequent PTSD. Most current data support the finding that many but not all people with ASD go on to develop PTSD. And many of those who do not meet the criteria for ASD are later diagnosed with PTSD. ASD is neither necessary nor sufficient for the diagnosis of PTSD (Bryant et al. 2008a). At present the best predictor of PTSD may well be high levels of PTSD symptoms in the first month.

Although ASD and PTSD are the most recognized disorders in the wake of the disaster, they may not even be the most common. Other psychiatric conditions may also occur either independently or comorbidly with PTSD. Major depressive disorder (MDD) frequently develops following a traumatic event, and those with a history of depression may experience a recurrence of their symptoms in the post-disaster setting. Anxiety disorders including panic disorder and certain phobias may also emerge or be exacerbated following a disaster. Some individuals may experience severe grief or adjustment reactions that cause significant distress but do not meet criteria for a specific disorder such as PTSD or MDD. There have been multiple studies that indicate that substance use rises in the post-disaster setting, but it is not clear that the incidence of substance use disorders increases. While overall substance use may rise somewhat, research indicates that most of the increased substance use occurs in individuals with preexisting substance use disorders.

Depending on the nature of the disaster, some victims may present with psychological and behavioral symptoms as a direct result of physical injury or illness. Disaster victims with head injuries may suffer neuropsychological symptoms as a direct result of traumatic brain injuries. Those who sustain injuries or develop illnesses may present confused or agitated as a result of delirium. Some people who are dependent on medication or other substances (including alcohol or illicit drugs) may experience withdrawal symptoms if there is an interruption in their supply chain. Persons who experience more serious physical disabilities as a result of injury may experience psychological distress due to the loss of prior function.

Vulnerable Populations

Not all of those who experience a disaster are equally likely to develop psychological distress and/or psychiatric illness in its wake. Those with prior trauma exposure including adverse childhood experiences, those with premorbid psychiatric illness, females, children, the elderly, and the physically disabled are at increased risk of PTSD after traumatic events, including disasters (Hamaoka et al. 2007). In addition to the direct victims of disasters, first responders such as paramedics, firefighters, police officers, soldiers, and other disaster workers are also at risk for the development of PTSD and other posttrauma psychiatric disorders (Benedek et al. 2007). Rates of posttraumatic psychiatric illness vary depending on the type of trauma. Multiple studies (mostly focused on non-disaster-related trauma) have suggested that interpersonal violence such as rape or assault results in higher rates of PTSD than noncrime trauma (Breslau et al. 1998; Kelley et al. 2009). Combat exposure is the trauma most associated with PTSD development in men (Kessler et al. 1995). Human-made disasters seem to be associated with higher rates of PTSD than natural disasters. It may be that the meaning of interpersonal trauma—where another person has intentionally harmed another—impacts the development of symptoms.

Persons with serious and persistent mental illness may be particularly vulnerable to disasters. Like much of the population, they often respond quite ably to assist themselves and others in a time of great need. But evidence suggests that they are less likely to have an emergency plan in place or appropriate access to supplies in the event of a disaster. They may be more reliant on others to assist them to evacuate or take other precautions prior to a disaster. Those with a history of mental illness may also be more likely to develop stress-related symptoms or a relapse of prior symptoms following a disaster. Those with prior diagnosis of PTSD may be particularly vulnerable to an exacerbation of symptoms due to an association of the current disaster and response (e.g., sirens) to their prior trauma (Center for the Study of Traumatic Stress 2011; Frieden 2006). Post-disaster disruptions in mental health care (including hospitals, physicians, and pharmacies) and other social services (including financial assistance, supported housing, and public transportation) may greatly affect the seriously mentally ill. Persons with chronic, severe mental health problems are often cared for by family members who may be injured or killed or have their attention otherwise diverted during and after a disaster. Because overall demand for mental health services often increases in the wake of a disaster due to the mass trauma exposure, diversion of resources away from care for the chronically mentally ill may result.

The Mental Health Interventions in the Disaster Setting

Prevention

ASD and PTSD are rare among psychiatric conditions in that a necessary etiologic element for the diagnosis is exposure to a specific traumatic event, including disaster. As a result, these disorders offer clinicians and policy makers the specific opportunity to focus on prevention. Prior to or following a disaster, interventions may be designed to reduce the likelihood of a disorder (primary prevention). It may also be possible to identify persons with early symptoms in order to mitigate their suffering and prevent progression to a more chronic condition (secondary prevention). Among those who develop an illness such as PTSD, treatment of the disorder can reduce the negative impact of the illness and avert negative outcomes such as suicide (tertiary prevention). Tertiary prevention can be seen as synonymous with standard psychiatric treatment and rehabilitation.

Preventive interventions are often subdivided into three categories: (1) universal prevention, (2) selective prevention, and (3) indicated prevention. Universal interventions target the entire affected population. Psychological first aid (PFA), discussed in more detail below, is a universal intervention that can be employed for all affected individuals following a traumatic event. Selective interventions focus on groups or individuals whose risk for developing PTSD or other long-term problems may be particularly high. Provision of additional support to all first responders is a selective intervention. This may take the forms of psychoeducation, stress management, and self-care tips and resources, provided via web-based outreach or embedded providers within response teams, and must target not only frontline response workers, but also their leadership (Wynn et al. 2020). Indicated interventions identify and treat persons who are already experiencing some distress in order to prevent a worsening of symptoms. Providing prolonged exposure therapy to people with ASD to prevent PTSD is an indicated intervention (Bryant et al. 2008b).

Before the Event

Given that, by definition, posttraumatic syndromes develop after a horrible event, prevention of the event itself could be an effective way to limit psychological distress. Cessation of war would reduce the amount of property damage, lower the number of displaced persons, limit the injuries and deaths of civilians and soldiers, and lessen the psychological sequelae of battle. Securing the levees in New Orleans or developing a more effective evacuation strategy may have reduced the scope of the disaster and prevented much physical and psychological suffering. In 2020, developing and implementing more effective public health measures to limit COVID-19 spread could have saved lives, livelihoods, and psyches. These interventions are undoubtedly valuable in their own right, but they have traditionally been seen as beyond the scope of mental health professionals' practice. Increasingly, though, extraclinical advocacy around issues that directly and indirectly affect our patients' lives are viewed to be within our professional purview. At both the individual and community levels, in both the clinic and outside its walls, clinicians and especially public health practitioners can take action in anticipation of a disaster in order to prevent disasters and post-event distress.

Planning at both the individual and community levels in anticipation of a disaster is vital to an appropriate, organized response once an event occurs. For individuals and families, preparedness includes the creation of a disaster plan, including storage of at least two days of food and water, a flashlight, a portable radio and spare batteries, emergency phone numbers, and a meeting place for family members should evacuation be necessary. A large national survey suggested that nearly two-thirds of respondents had not formulated a basic family emergency plan (National Center for Disaster Preparedness 2004). Public education campaigns can increase preparedness among families and potentially lower disaster-related distress. Because patients with severe and persistent mental illness are even less likely to appropriately plan for disaster, they may benefit from assistance in preparation from their mental health treatment team.

At the community level, pre-disaster preparedness involves ensuring that appropriately trained human resources (e.g., police, firefighters, military, and health care providers), adequate physical resources (e.g., food supply, shelters), and a functioning communications system are available when needed. Role definition and coordination of activities among various government and other community agencies is very important and can best be accomplished if organized in advance of a traumatic event. Gaining an understanding of why some people do not heed protective warnings, such as social distancing or mask wearing during the COVID-19 pandemic or evacuation in the face of Hurricane Katrina, may help limit these maladaptive disaster behaviors and reduce traumatic exposure in the future. Pre-event identification of those who may be most vulnerable to disaster—for example, knowing the location of nursing homes, group homes, or hospitals—can help prioritize the response and prevent later distress. Health care facilities, including psychiatric units or hospitals, should make appropriate preparations in the anticipation of disasters, including keeping emergency provisions on hand and developing appropriate staffing and evacuation plans.

Another concept of pre-trauma prevention of PTSD or other posttraumatic psychological distress is the "inoculation" of people who may later be exposed. The related notions of enhancing resistance to psychological injury and building the capacity for resilience in the face of injury have led to a variety of policies and programs aimed at preventing adverse psychological sequelae. Current U.S. military policies encourage training in simulated combat environments at least in part to reduce the likelihood of development of stress-related symptoms after genuine combat exposure. Such training decreases novelty of combat (and, therefore, the associated anxiety), increases self-efficacy and social support skills, and directly decreases the risk of injury. A school-based, universal, or selective intervention that teaches cognitive-behavioral and social problem-solving skills to children has been shown to lower rates of depressive symptoms, though results have been inconsistent (Gillham et al. 2008). The U.S. Army has begun a program known as Comprehensive Soldier Fitness, a set of universal interventions addressing physical (e.g., sleep, exercise, nutrition), emotional, and spiritual aspects of a service member's life, which seeks to enhance soldiers' psychological resilience in the face of war (Cornum 2009). It is not yet known whether this program will have a positive impact on soldiers' mental health including rates of PTSD or, by extension, whether even broader-based initiatives in resistance- and resilience-building may be helpful in averting adverse outcomes following a disaster.

It is difficult to measure the value of preventive interventions, but the cost of inadequate preparation transcends the burden of the diseases such as PTSD or depression. Distress-related absenteeism and presenteeism (e.g., "at work but distracted by symptoms so not productive") and work missed to attend to the care needs of children affected also need to be factored into the cost. The financing of disaster preparedness and response is shared by federal, state, and local governments as well as private citizens and businesses. Emergency and disaster management agencies at the national and local levels are charged with the planning and execution of prevention and response efforts. Mental health professionals can become involved in larger-scale planning efforts through involvement with those agencies or through the Medical Response Corps, a volunteer division of the Office of the Surgeon General. Preparedness at the level of the physician office, clinic, or business is also important. Training is an essential element of budgets for most industries (including health care), so preparedness efforts should be factored into faculty/staff training and education budgets. Professional training of teachers, clergy, law enforcement, physicians, and other community leaders that includes concepts of psychological first aid (see below) may prove to lower disease/distress burden and even be cost-effective.

During or Soon After the Event: Psychological First Aid and Primary Prevention

Since distress reactions—even in those without prior psychiatric illness—are common in the aftermath of trauma, emphasis should be placed not only on identifying and treating psychiatric illness, but also on sustaining the mental health of the broader population. Vulnerable populations, including those physically injured in the event, first responders, and those with a history of mental illness, require planned intervention. A combination of universal and selective approaches may be the best approach, though specific evidence-based interventions are lacking and have proven difficult to research in traditional randomized controlled trials in the immediate aftermath of disaster. Using a combination of broad-based interventions for many and specific interventions for a few may optimize the care provided and efficiently utilize available resources.

Psychological first aid (PFA) is a set of evidence-informed, guiding principles that are recommended as a first-line intervention for all individuals following traumatic events, prior to the development of any disorders (Hobfoll et al. 2007). PFA principles include (1) safety, (2) calming, (3) connectedness to both instrumental and emotional support, (4) self-efficacy (both the belief one can do what is needed and has the skills to do so), and (5) optimism/hope. Mental health professionals familiar with these principles can advocate for their inclusion in any disaster response.

Establishing a sense of *safety* is paramount to the initiation of recovery. Until a person feels safe from an immediate threat—an earthquake aftershock, rising floodwaters, crime, spreading infection—fear may persist, and it is difficult to restore a sense of healthfulness. Transporting victims to higher ground, out of the crossfire, toward stable structures, or otherwise away from danger are important first steps. Providing appropriate security is another initial intervention that can yield benefits. Ensuring safety can go a long way in addressing the second component of psychological first aid—*calming*. Anxiety and physiologic hyperarousal are normal and, often, adaptive responses to a stressful event. Acknowledging, normalizing, and validating these reactions are helpful for many, as is assisting in positively channeling increased energy. Community leaders are critical in promoting public calm in the face of a crisis by modeling a calm approach, delivering clear, accurate risk assessments, and providing explicit directions (Bushnell 2003). Mental health practitioners can assist other community leaders by emphasizing the importance of calm and clear information delivery. Clinicians, in caring directly for a recently traumatized patient, can be helpful in establishing a sense of safety and calm by providing appropriate direction and reassurance. The nature of COVID-19—unseen, widespread transmission and highly variable but sometimes lethal course—along with the inconsistent and at times inaccurate communication from leadership has challenged feelings of the safety and calmness during the pandemic.

Another important element in a posttraumatic response is the promotion of *connectedness*. Social support is a relatively robust protective factor for psychiatric illness including PTSD (Brewin et al. 2000; Butler et al. 2009; Pietrzak et al. 2009). In the wake of a mass trauma, social and community structures may be compromised, especially if a population is geographically displaced or families are separated. Interventions that encourage reconnecting with friends, family, or others in one's social network can relieve both short-term distress and longer-term problems. Providing access to communication tools such as a telephone or email is helpful. Encouraging, as much as possible, geographic unification of families and/or friends is extremely beneficial. As a result of social distancing to minimize viral spread, enhancing social connectedness has been particularly challenging during the COVID-19 pandemic. Use of distanced communication (phone, video chat) has been increasingly employed to help connect loved ones, friends, colleagues, and health care providers.

One of the effects of a traumatic event is that people often feel they lack control—over the event itself as well as over their post-event life. Restoring *self-efficacy*—a sense of control and an ability to affect positive change—and instilling *hope* for the future are major goals of a successful response (Flatten et al. 2008). Only with hope do disaster and trauma victims begin to think of a future, perform work to care for themselves and others, and begin to rebuild a future. Encouraging a widespread return to work and school when possible is one good approach. Enlisting the population in key decisions and recovery projects is important to restoring a sense of self- and collective efficacy while also strengthening social ties. For individuals, cognitive-behavioral therapy may be able to assist in restoring that sense of control over one's life.

Operationalizing these five PFA principles is the challenge for disaster planners and clinicians who work with disaster and trauma victims. Ideal interventions in the posttrauma setting must be flexible and adaptable but also be able to be delivered on a broad scale by laypersons who may not have a background in mental health. More research is needed to establish evidence for specific programmatic elements, but there is increasing support for using these five principles in the development of population-based, posttrauma interventions.

Certain psychotherapeutic interventions should be used with caution or avoided in the acute setting. Once the standard of care following various traumatic exposures, universal, individual psychological debriefing (often referred to as critical incident stress debriefing, or CISD) has not proven to be helpful either in the relief of short-term psychological distress or in the prevention of PTSD (Rose et al. 2002). It is not clear why this is the case, but it may be that requiring people to discuss their recent traumatic experience in a prescribed fashion serves to activate rather than calm them. A more selective approach may more appropriately target those who could benefit from psychotherapy.

One Week to One Month After Traumatic Events: Acute Stress Disorder and Secondary Prevention

Those people whose adverse psychological responses are more severe or prolonged warrant special attention and monitoring. Most who are experiencing significant distress following a traumatic event visit a primary care provider—not a psychiatrist or psychologist—so screening for psychiatric disorders such as ASD may be more appropriate in that setting (Benedek and Wynn 2011). Recent studies have examined the use of short screening forms to identify PTSD in primary care (Gore et al. 2008). Regardless of diagnosis, most posttrauma care is accomplished in the primary care setting. This environment may also be less stigmatizing to many patients than the specialized mental health care clinic. Primary care providers often have longitudinal relationships with patients so they can provide additional support. Furthermore, in the wake of a trauma, many patient complaints are physical in nature, and primary care physicians are often skilled at determining how to evaluate and treat such symptoms (Engel et al. 2003). Supportive psychotherapeutic techniques including helping a patient to problem-solve can also be accomplished in the primary care setting. Primary care providers can also monitor their patients' clinical status and can screen for psychiatric conditions including ASD, PTSD, and depression.

Pharmacologic intervention to reduce acute posttraumatic distress may seem intuitive, but there is scant evidence that medication is particularly beneficial. There is little or no evidence that benzodiazepines are helpful in the prevention of or treatment of PTSD (D. Benedek and Wynn 2011). Though widely used and theoretically helpful—they are useful in the treatment of generalized anxiety disorder—benzodiazepines have shown little efficacy in treating the core symptoms of PTSD except for some hyperarousal symptoms. Risks also include rebound anxiety when stopping the medication and dependence. There is also some evidence that early treatment with a benzodiazepine may lead to increased incidence of PTSD at 1 and 6 months (Gelpin et al. 1996). There had been initial suggestions that beta-blockers used in the hours and days after the traumatic event might mitigate acute symptoms and prevent the development of PTSD. Despite some signs that beta-blockers reduced exposure-related physiologic arousal, a more recent placebo-controlled study failed to demonstrate superior efficacy of propranolol (Stein et al. 2007). Presently there is interest in determining whether other classes of medication often administered in the trauma setting, such as opiates, might be helpful in preventing PTSD (Bryant et al. 2009; Zatzick and Roy-Byrne 2006).

Psychotherapeutic interventions that target patients with ASD have been shown to have some efficacy in the prevention of the development of PTSD. Data on ASD is somewhat limited, largely because enrollment in a research study during the acute posttraumatic phase (less than one month) can be difficult. Cognitive-behavioral therapy in patients with ASD has been effective in reducing rates of PTSD when compared with supportive therapy (Bryant et al. 1999). Prolonged exposure is thought to be an important component of that therapy.

Months After the Trauma: Treatment of PTSD and Tertiary Prevention

Much more is known about treatment once a diagnosis of PTSD has been made. Perhaps no intervention for the treatment of PTSD has as much evidence of its utility as exposure-based cognitive-behavioral therapies (EBCBTs). There is no consensus on the appropriate categorization of the many varied psychotherapeutic interventions for PTSD. But the Institute of Medicine and the APA have both utilized EBCBTs as a broad, inclusive designation for therapeutic approaches and techniques that share, as the name suggests, common elements of exposure as well as cognitive reprocessing and/or behavioral modification (D. Benedek and Wynn 2011). Multiple clinical trials have demonstrated the efficacy of these psychotherapies.

Eye movement desensitization and reprocessing (EMDR) is a psychotherapeutic technique that combines elements of cognitive-behavioral therapy, exposure therapy, and prescribed attention to eye movements of the patient. While there have been a number of studies that seem to suggest a benefit of EMDR, it is clear that the benefit is not due to the focus on eye movements. Instead, evidence suggests that the therapeutic benefit is related to the elements of exposure therapy and CBT—sharing the trauma experience and reprocessing its emotional content (Ursano et al. 2004).

The APA guidelines note the lack of formal, randomized controlled trial data to support the efficacy of psychodynamic psychotherapy. As with the study of psychodynamic therapy for other problems, data is limited due to challenges in study design. However, the conclusion reached by the APA leaves open the use of this psychotherapy for addressing the long-term personality elements of trauma exposure. Based on clinical consensus, the guidelines state that "a psychodynamic approach is useful in helping the patient integrate past traumatic experience(s) into a more adaptive or constructive schema of risk, safety, prevention, and protection, thereby reducing core symptoms of PTSD" (Benedek et al. 2009).

Psychopharmacologic therapy is a mainstay in the clinical management of PTSD, and evidence supports a role for medication in treatment. There is substantial evidence that selective serotonin reuptake inhibitors (SSRIs) are efficacious in the treatment of PTSD, especially in women with the disorder who have been exposed to civilian trauma including physical or sexual assault and motor vehicle accidents. There is less data to suggest that combat-related PTSD is as responsive to

SSRI therapy, and their use is recommended with less confidence in treating that disorder (Benedek et al. 2009). There is some evidence that SNRIs, particularly venlafaxine, are efficacious in the treatment of PTSD. Other classes of antidepressants that include bupropion, mirtazapine, and nefazodone have not demonstrated significant efficacy. Tricyclic antidepressants and monoamine oxidase inhibitors, though less widely studied than SSRIs, have also been demonstrated to be effective in the treatment of PTSD (Ursano et al. 2004). However, concern about safety often leads to physicians' reluctance to prescribe those classes of medication. Of interest, a small study of pediatric burn patients with ASD suggested that tricyclic antidepressants quickly, dramatically, and effectively reduced symptoms for most children compared to those who received chloral hydrate, though no follow-up was performed to determine longer-term outcome (Robert et al. 1999).

One of the most encouraging recent discoveries in the treatment of PTSD is that the alpha-adrenergic antagonist prazosin, in a number of placebo-controlled trials, reduced trauma-related nightmares and sleep disruption (Raskind et al. 2007; Taylor et al. 2008). There is some evidence that second-generation antipsychotic medications (SGAs) may lessen intrusive and hyperarousal symptoms, but more research is needed to establish whether or not SGAs are useful and safe in the treatment of PTSD (Benedek et al. 2009). Caution about side effects including weight gain and metabolic syndrome is required.

There are other emerging somatic treatments including ketamine and stellate ganglion block that show early promise but require further study to clarify their efficacy and determine in which populations they might be effective (Liriano et al. 2019; Odosso and Petta 2020). The FDA also recently approved a nightmare-disrupting watch (U.S. Food and Drug Administration 2020).

COVID-19 Pandemic

As of early August 2022, the virus had killed over six million people around the world, including over 1 million in the United States. A large majority of Americans had been infected, including a subset whose symptoms persist. The nation's economy experienced its worst crisis since the Great Depression, with tens of millions of people having lost their jobs and millions newly facing housing and food insecurity. Virus-related precautions upended the ways of life for many as people were encouraged to limit travel and limit in-person social contacts. The families of the dying were often unable to be with their loved ones or mourn their loss with traditional rites. Governments at various levels have come under criticism for failures in planning, messaging, and responding to the crisis.

In the face of such loss and uncertainty, traditional sources of support have been compromised. Engaging the practices of psychological first aid have therefore been particularly challenged. To reduce risk of contagion, many people went more than a year without socializing with family or close friends outside their immediate households. Workplaces, schools, houses of worship, stores, restaurants, gyms, and social and cultural organizations were forced to change their practices, in some cases shuttering their doors. Health care providers, including psychiatrists and other mental health care professionals, have also changed their practices, with many moving their care to online platforms as much as possible. Social service agencies such as shelters, job training centers, and food pantries were forced to change accessibility. Supply chains for goods including certain pharmaceuticals were impacted.

Much is still unknown about the ultimate trajectory and lasting effects of the pandemic. It appears that people with preexisting mental health and substance use disorders were at increased risk for contracting COVID-19. As a result of diminished cognitive status or risk awareness, people with serious mental illness may have been less likely to adhere to infection control practices. The increased risk may also have been conveyed through social factors—people with severe mental illness have less access to health care and other resources and are more likely to live in congregate settings such as group homes, nursing homes, shelters, or prisons. Psychiatric facilities themselves were sites of several viral outbreaks. High rates of medical comorbidities such as smoking, obesity, and diabetes increased the risk of poor outcomes if patients did contract the virus.

Several studies have suggested significant mental health effects of the pandemic. In population surveys, a large percentage of the population reports mental distress. People with preexisting mental disorders are more likely to report difficulty coping. Early in the pandemic in the United States, emergency department psychiatric visits, like all medical visits, decreased. But as the pandemic has continued, studies have suggested that there was a substantial increase in children's visits to emergency departments for psychiatric or behavioral problems. Though respiratory symptoms are most strongly associated with the virus, many patients also experience neuropsychiatric symptoms due to their infections. Long-term sequelae remain unknown.

Around the world as well as in the United States, health care workers including first responders and hospital-based professionals may be at particular risk for developing mental health problems due to the stress of their work tempo, their first-hand care of critically ill and dying patients, societal stigmatization related to fear of contagion, their own fears of contracting the virus and/or passing it to their family, and their frustration over inadequate policies of their governments or irresponsible behavior of their fellow citizens (Shigemura et al. 2020). Other essential workers including grocery employees, food distributors, truck drivers, funeral directors, and teachers may also be particularly vulnerable to operational and exposure-related stress.

Ending the pandemic and limiting its further physical and psychological toll will likely require the widespread uptake of an effective vaccine. Supply and logistical challenges may result in anger, frustration, and anxiety related to delays in vaccination or real or perceived inequalities in vaccination delivery. Fear of vaccines and mistrust of scientists and/or government actors have also resulted in significant vaccine hesitancy. Health workers, including those involved in mental health care, will have a role in disseminating accurate information about vaccine safety to individual patients and to the broader public.

Conclusion

Unfortunately, even after the sustained rapid and widespread transmission of COVID-19 illness and death around the world was suppressed, the longer-term consequences of the pandemic have persisted. At present much remains to be learned about the long-term health consequences for the many who recover from acute COVID-19. Persistent physical, cognitive, and emotional symptoms have been documented in as many as 20% of patients months after recovery. Moreover, the impact of unanticipated loss of friends and family members, particularly under circumstances where traditional final goodbyes, burials, and funeral services have not been feasible, is difficult to estimate. The possibility of the emergence of a viral strain resistant to rapidly developed therapeutics or vaccinations, or the emergence of entirely new virus capable of similar devastation may leave many in a state of persistent hypervigilance, distress, or fatigue. Even if none of these come to pass, various new disasters will surely continue to plague human beings around the globe. Climate change will doubtless contribute to more natural disasters, human displacement, and associated suffering (see chapter "Climate Change: Impact on Community Mental Health"). In the aftermath of such events, some people will experience adverse psychological reactions and behavioral changes. The majority of exposed individuals will exhibit resilience in the face of such trauma, while some will experience transient distress and still others will develop more debilitating disorders such as PTSD. Appropriate preparation and a preventive approach by policy makers, disaster responders, and mental health practitioners may lead to a significant reduction of long-term psychiatric illness and disability. More research is needed to better understand the risk and protective factors associated with the development of significant psychiatric illness following a disaster. Mental health practitioners can be helpful in delivering the effective treatments that are available for ASD, PTSD, and other post-disaster problems.

References

American Psychiatric Association. (2010). Annual Meeting Highlights. *Psychiatric News, 45*(4), 36.

American Psychiatric Association. (2013). *Diagnostic and Statistical Manual of Mental Disorders, Fifth Edition*. Washington, DC: American Psychiatric Association.

Benedek, D., & Wynn, G. (Eds.). (2011). *Clinical Manual for Management of PTSD* (First ed.). Washington, DC: American Psychiatric Publishing, Inc.

Benedek, D. M., Friedman, M.J., Zatzick, D., Ursano, R.J. (2009). *Guideline Watch (March 2009): Practice Guideline for the Treatment of Patients with Acute Stress Disorder and Posttraumatic Stress Disorder.*: American Psychiatric Association.

Benedek, D. M., Fullerton, C., & Ursano, R. J. (2007). First responders: mental health consequences of natural and human-made disasters for public health and public safety workers. *Annu Rev Public Health, 28*, 55–68.

Benedek, D. M., & Wynn, G. H. *Clinical manual for management of PTSD* (1st ed.). Washington D.C.: American Psychiatric Pub.

Breslau, N., Kessler, R. C., Chilcoat, H. D., Schultz, L. R., Davis, G. C., & Andreski, P. (1998). Trauma and posttraumatic stress disorder in the community: the 1996 Detroit Area Survey of Trauma. *Arch Gen Psychiatry, 55*(7), 626–632.

Brewin, C. R., Andrews, B., & Valentine, J. D. (2000). Meta-analysis of risk factors for posttraumatic stress disorder in trauma-exposed adults. *J Consult Clin Psychol, 68*(5), 748–766.

Bryant, R. A., Creamer, M., O'Donnell, M., Silove, D., & McFarlane, A. C. (2009). A study of the protective function of acute morphine administration on subsequent posttraumatic stress disorder. *Biol Psychiatry, 65*(5), 438–440.

Bryant, R. A., Creamer, M., O'Donnell, M. L., Silove, D., & McFarlane, A. C. (2008a). A multisite study of the capacity of acute stress disorder diagnosis to predict posttraumatic stress disorder. *J Clin Psychiatry, 69*(6), 923–929. doi: ej07m03605 [pii]

Bryant, R. A., Mastrodomenico, J., Felmingham, K. L., Hopwood, S., Kenny, L., Kandris, E., . . . Creamer, M. (2008b). Treatment of acute stress disorder: a randomized controlled trial. *Arch Gen Psychiatry, 65*(6), 659–667.

Bryant, R. A., Sackville, T., Dang, S. T., Moulds, M., & Guthrie, R. (1999). Treating acute stress disorder: an evaluation of cognitive behavior therapy and supportive counseling techniques. *Am J Psychiatry, 156*(11), 1780–1786.

Bushnell, P. (2003). Leadership in the wake of disaster. In R. J. Ursano, C. Fullerton, & A. Norwood (Eds.), *Terrorism and disaster : individual and community mental health interventions*. Cambridge, UK; New York: Cambridge University Press.

Butler, L. D., Koopman, C., Azarow, J., Blasey, C. M., Magdalene, J. C., DiMiceli, S., . . . Spiegel, D. (2009). Psychosocial predictors of resilience after the September 11, 2001 terrorist attacks. *J Nerv Ment Dis, 197*(4), 266–273.

Center for the Study of Traumatic Stress. Addressing the Needs of the Seriously Mentally Ill in Disaster. January 4, 2011, from http://www.centerforthestudyoftraumaticstress.org/csts_items/CSTS_Seriously_Mentally_Ill.pdf.

Centre for Research on the Epidemiology of Disasters. (2015). The Human Cost of Natural Disasters.

Cornum, R. L. (2009). Comprehensive Soldier Fitness Program Helps Soldiers Build Resilience. *Army Aviation*, 56–57.

Engel, C. C., Jaffer, A., Adkins, J., Sheliga, V., Cowan, D., Katon, W.J. (2003). Population-based health care: A model for restoring community health and productivity following terrorist attack. In R. J. Ursano, Fullerton, C.S., Norwood, A.E. (Ed.), *Terrorism and Disaster: Individual and Community Mental Health Interventions* (pp. 287–307). Cambridge: Cambridge University Press.

Flatten, G., Walte, D., & Perlitz, V. (2008). Self-efficacy in acutely traumatized patients and the risk of developing a posttraumatic stress syndrome. *Psychosoc Med, 5*, Doc05.

Frieden, L. (2006). The Needs of People with Psychiatric Disabilities during and after Hurricanes Katrina and Rita: Position Paper and Recommendations. In National Council on Disability (Ed.). Washington, DC.

Gelpin, E., Bonne, O., Peri, T., Brandes, D., & Shalev, A. Y. (1996). Treatment of recent trauma survivors with benzodiazepines: a prospective study. *J Clin Psychiatry, 57*(9), 390–394.

Gillham, J. E., Brunwasser, S.M., & Freres, D.R. (2008). Preventing depression early in adolescence: The Penn Resiliency Program. In J. R. Z. A. B. L. Hankin (Ed.), *Depression in children and adolescents: Causes, treatment and prevention.* (pp. 309–332). New York: Guilford Press.

Gore, K. L., Engel, C. C., Freed, M. C., Liu, X., & Armstrong, D. W., 3rd. (2008). Test of a single-item posttraumatic stress disorder screener in a military primary care setting. *Gen Hosp Psychiatry, 30*(5), 391–397.

Hamaoka, D., Benedek, D., Grieger, T., Ursano, R.J. (2007). Crisis Intervention *Encyclopedia of Stress.* (Second ed., Vol. I, pp. 662–667): Elsevier.

Hobfoll, S. et al. (2007). Five Essential Elements of Immediate and Mid-Term Mass Trauma Intervention: Empirical Evidence. *Psychiatry, 70*(4), 283–315.

Kelley, L. P., Weathers, F. W., McDevitt-Murphy, M. E., Eakin, D. E., & Flood, A. M. (2009). A comparison of PTSD symptom patterns in three types of civilian trauma. *J Trauma Stress, 22*(3), 227–235.

Kessler, R. C., Sennega, A., Bromet, E., Hughes, M., Nelson, C.B. (1995). Posttraumatic Stress Disorder in the National Comorbidity Survey. *Archives of General Psychiatry, 52*(12), 1048–1060.

Liriano, F., Hatten, C., & Schwartz, T. L. (2019). Ketamine as treatment for post-traumatic stress disorder: a review. *Drugs Context, 8*, 212305.

McMahon, M. M. (2007). Disasters and poverty. *Disaster Manag Response, 5*(4), 95–97.

National Center for Disaster Preparedness. (2004). How Americans Feel About Terrorism and Security: Three Years After September 11. New York: Columbia University Mailman School of Public Health.

Obama, B. (2020). *A Promised Land*. New York: Crown.

Odosso, R. J., & Petta, L. (2020). The Efficacy of the Stellate Ganglion Block as a Treatment Modality for Posttraumatic Stress Disorder Among Active Duty Combat Veterans: A Pilot Program Evaluation. *Mil Med*.

Pietrzak, R. H., Johnson, D. C., Goldstein, M. B., Malley, J. C., Rivers, A. J., Morgan, C. A., & Southwick, S. M. (2009). Psychosocial buffers of traumatic stress, depressive symptoms, and psychosocial difficulties in veterans of Operations Enduring Freedom and Iraqi Freedom: the role of resilience, unit support, and post-deployment social support. *J Spec Oper Med, 9*(3), 74–78.

Project Ploughshares. (2008). Armed Conflicts Report Summary 2009. Waterloo, Ontario, Canada.

Raskind, M. A., Peskind, E. R., Hoff, D. J., Hart, K. L., Holmes, H. A., Warren, D., . . . McFall, M. E. (2007). A parallel group placebo controlled study of prazosin for trauma nightmares and sleep disturbance in combat veterans with post-traumatic stress disorder. *Biol Psychiatry, 61*(8), 928–934.

Robert, R., Blakeney, P. E., Villarreal, C., Rosenberg, L., & Meyer, W. J., 3rd. (1999). Imipramine treatment in pediatric burn patients with symptoms of acute stress disorder: a pilot study. *J Am Acad Child Adolesc Psychiatry, 38*(7), 873–882.

Rose, S. C., Bisson, J., Churchill, R., Wessely, S. (2002). Psychological debriefing for preventing post traumatic stress disorder (PTSD). *Cochrane Database of Systematic Reviews, 2002*(2).

Shigemura, J., Ursano, R. J., Morganstein, J. C., Kurosawa, M., & Benedek, D. M. (2020). Public responses to the novel 2019 coronavirus (2019-nCoV) in Japan: Mental health consequences and target populations. *Psychiatry Clin Neurosci, 74*(4), 281–282.

Stein, M. B., Kerridge, C., Dimsdale, J. E., & Hoyt, D. B. (2007). Pharmacotherapy to prevent PTSD: Results from a randomized controlled proof-of-concept trial in physically injured patients. *J Trauma Stress, 20*(6), 923–932.

Tate, K. (2010). Hurricane Katrina History and Numbers. Retrieved November 15, 2010, from http://www.livescience.com/environment/hurricane-katrina-new-orleans-aftermath-infographic-100824.html

Taylor, F. B., Martin, P., Thompson, C., Williams, J., Mellman, T. A., Gross, C., . . . Raskind, M. A. (2008). Prazosin effects on objective sleep measures and clinical symptoms in civilian trauma

U.S. Food and Drug Administration. (2020). FDA Permits Marketing of New Device Designed to Reduce Sleep Disturbance Related to Nightmares in Certain Adults [Press release]. Retrieved from https://www.fda.gov/news-events/press-announcements/fda-permits-marketing-new-device-designed-reduce-sleep-disturbance-related-nightmares-certain-adults

Ursano, R. J., Bell, C., Eth, S., Friedman, M., Norwood, A., Pfefferbaum, B., . . . Yager, J. (2004). Practice guideline for the treatment of patients with acute stress disorder and posttraumatic stress disorder. *Am J Psychiatry, 161*(11 Suppl), 3–31.

Ursano, R. J., Fullerton, C., Weisaeth, L., & Raphael, B. (2007). *Textbook of disaster psychiatry*. Cambridge; New York: Cambridge University Press.

Watson Institute for International and Public Affairs. (2020). The Costs of War. Retrieved January 5, 2021, from https://watson.brown.edu/costsofwar/costs/human/military/killed-:~:text=Over%207%2C000%20US%20service%20members,wars%20in%20Iraq%20and%20Afghanistan

Wynn, G., Morganstein, J., Jetly, R., Ford, S., Vance, M., Meyer, E., . . . Ursano, R. J. (2020). Military mental health and COVID-19. *Journal of Military, Veteran and Family Health., 6*(3).

Zatzick, D., & Roy-Byrne, P. P. (2006). From bedside to bench: how the epidemiology of clinical practice can inform the secondary prevention of PTSD. *Psychiatr Serv, 57*(12), 1726–1730.

The Role of the Psychiatrist in Community Consultation and Collaboration

Altha J. Stewart and Mary K. Smith

Introduction

Much has changed in the field of community psychiatry since the publication of the original Handbook of Community Psychiatry almost a decade ago, including this follow-up volume being elevated to textbook status (McQuiston et al. 2012). This acknowledges the updated text to be a formal and acceptable compendium of knowledge, to be used in the training of professionals entering the field, as well as a refresher to update knowledge and skill in more experienced professionals.

In addition to the notable changes in mental health delivery systems and the definitions of community and community psychiatry, the role of mental health consultation and collaboration with the community has changed significantly as well. Since its beginning in the mid-twentieth century, there has been a consistent growth in the interest and practice of community psychiatry. Many of today's leaders in the field have decades of experience and some of the leaders in training and innovation in the area are still hard at work today. From the early days of catchment area-designated treatment settings and mandated outpatient treatment continuums of the 1970s to the current recovery models of assertive community treatment, intensive outpatient programs, and peer-directed support, much has been achieved that has elevated community psychiatry to a place of significance in the system of psychiatric treatment services available for this nation's citizens. For those most vulnerable that depend on publicly funded services, the evolution and progress seen shows significant, though insufficient, movement towards improvement in the quality and access to care. With each successive external challenge, the stress on an already overwhelmed system displays the absolute inadequacy of a system with no real safety net, resulting in more people falling through the cracks. Psychiatrists that work in this system care primarily for those with the most serious illnesses, but also must respond to the needs of those with situational distress, mental disorders related to co-occurring medical conditions, and those with accompanying and often complex social issues that complicate their care. Today, that includes working on issues due to the impact of a global pandemic on the world's population. This places community psychiatrists on the frontline of ignoring the advice of Goldfarb in his 2019 WSJ Op-Ed piece to "stay in their lane" (Goldfarb 2019).

Training in community psychiatry prepares the psychiatrist to utilize a range of skills essential for creating and managing effective community-based treatment and support pro-

A. J. Stewart (✉)
University of Tennessee Health Science Center, Memphis, TN, USA
e-mail: astewa59@uthsc.edu

M. K. Smith
Sylvania, OH, USA

W. E. Sowers et al. (eds.), *Textbook of Community Psychiatry*,
https://doi.org/10.1007/978-3-031-10239-4_33

grams. However, working in community psychiatry and addressing social determinants of mental health must now also include attention to climate change, natural disasters, pandemics, and structural racism. Community psychiatrists are routinely called upon to assist not only with challenges and distress affecting those with diagnosed mental illness, but with those being impacted by these issues and experiencing psychological distress as a result. This has created a new perspective for defining community consultation and collaboration that is the focus of this chapter. Building on the central pillars of community psychiatry, epidemiology, public health and prevention, financing, advocacy, and recovery and person-centeredness, this chapter will address how community psychiatrists can incorporate these new consultation and collaboration practices into their work no matter the practice setting.

It is important that the psychiatrist who aspires to work in a community-based setting recognize their role as consultant and collaborator, in addition to providing direct services. Having an understanding of the "community" and those issues that impact a community's overall health requires active outreach and engagement beyond the health care delivery system. There is no one way to serve in this role but there is consensus among those in the field regarding several essential steps in performing this work. All physicians have a long-recognized responsibility to participate in activities to protect and promote the health of the public. This includes mental health and requires psychiatrists to balance dual responsibilities in order to promote the welfare and confidentiality of their individual patients and, simultaneously, to protect public safety.

The World Health Organization defines health promotion and encourages physicians to promote health through a "collaborative, patient-centered process that promotes trust." It challenges physicians to "[a]dvocate for community resources designed to promote health and provide access to preventive services" (World Health Organization 2016).

The American Medical Association (AMA) Code of Ethics and its nine *Principles of Medical Ethics* form the foundation of the Code of Ethics by articulating the standards of conduct expected of physicians. Chapter "Inspiring a Welcoming, Hopeful Culture" expands those responsibilities to include prevention of disease and promotion of health at the community level:

> A physician shall recognize a responsibility to participate in activities contributing to the improvement of the community and the betterment of public health.

In addition, the supporting document for this opinion requires that physicians "be aware of how individual patient circumstances may impact the effectiveness of health promotion efforts," thereby highlighting the social determinants of health (American Medical Association 1980).

These social determinants of health include factors such as education, employment and economic status, the safety of the neighborhood in which one lives, availability of healthy food, and access to health and mental health care. In other words, all physicians have an ethical responsibility to promote public health and to improve the communities in which they live and work in addition to fulfilling obligations to individual patients, colleagues, and themselves. While the AMA appears to stop shy of stating directly that physicians should address all that is now called social determinants, the principle uses verbs such as educate, recommend, encourage, delegate, consider, advocate, and promote in stating what physicians should do in keeping with their commitment to health promotion for their patients and communities.

Addressing social determinants of health that impact mental health is an essential component of the work performed in most community-based mental health programs. The challenges and barriers persons with mental illness in our systems of care face represent the underlying factors described by Wendy Ellis and colleagues at the Center for Community Resilience as "adverse community environments" (Ellis and Dietz 2017). In their work to address the many challenges facing underresourced and vulnerable (especially racial and ethnic) communities, they identified a common root cause: trauma and toxic stress. These stressors include much of what is now described as social determinants of health. In cities and neighborhoods with high levels of poverty, violence, food and housing insecurity, and other health-related adversities, high levels of mental illness and addiction disorders are found without the level of services or infrastructure to adequately address them. It is in these environments that many community psychiatrists practice and where their consultation and collaboration skills are very much needed.

Brief History of Consultation and Collaboration in Community Psychiatry

In 1959, Dr. Victor J. Freeman wrote of the emerging dual roles of psychiatric consultants in the community as they assumed greater responsibility, stating:

> With this rapid expansion of the 'mental health' movement into the area of health promotion, communities are discovering that their already overtaxed psychiatric facilities are unable to meet the new demands. Consequently, pressures are placed on the psychiatrist to yield the priority of clinical treatment to psychiatrically nontraditional professional functions. (Freeman 1959)

In the early 1960s, there was no agreement on the definition of "community psychiatry" which led to the interchangeable use of several terms still in use today. In addition to community psychiatry, these include "public psychiatry," "social psychiatry," and "community mental health" and all focused on the operational definition, i.e., what it does, not what it is (Barclay 1968).

Caplan is credited with developing the role for a psychiatrist as a community consultant. He defined community psychiatry as being "based upon the acceptance by psychiatrists of responsibility for dealing with all mentally-disordered persons within the confines of the community." He believed that "the only legitimate limitation of the population facing the community psychiatrist is the boundary of his community." He noted that in addition to the clinical and administrative issues on which they might work with a provider organization, there was also the potential for involvement with larger systems to assist in the design, improvement, and evaluation of services, or to manage a crisis, develop public health and prevention policies, or provide needed mental health education in the community (Caplan 1964).

Bernard wrote that although social and community psychiatry were often used interchangeably, there was a difference – "we think that community psychiatry tends to signify greater emphasis on applied practice at the community level while social psychiatry has come to connote a more exclusive emphasis on theory and research rather than practice." She described community psychiatry as "the practice of the art and social psychiatry as research into the theoretical underpinnings of the art" (Bernard 1964).

Many major psychiatric reforms over the last two centuries were based on reforms spearheaded in part by the global psychiatric community (Uchtenhagen 2008; Chibanda et al. 2016; Smith 2020). The need to address new challenges due to changes in society overall has led to new struggles with definitions and roles in order to operationalize what is expected of psychiatrists working in community-based organizations, publicly funded and regulated systems, or other settings where care for patients is based on the framework first established in what is known as the Community Mental Health Act of 1964 (Public Law 88-164 1963). In proposing the CMHC model as the major reform of mental health services ever undertaken, President Kennedy created a model that is still reflected in the framework used by most jurisdictions today. He called it a "bold new approach to the problems of mental illness and mental health" and the principles included then remain embedded in our work in communities today:

- *Comprehensive* because a complete range of services is to be provided under a single administrative structure.
- *Community* because this is a grassroots approach. Patients are to be treated close to their own homes and their regional community services are to be small and personalized,

with close links between the treatment personnel and the population they serve.

- *Mental health* because the program is to extend beyond direct treatment into the field of primary prevention.

Early on psychiatry was challenged by the importance of balancing advocacy on behalf of persons with mental illness with assuring provision of the best quality care with the limited resources available. At the time the Act was passed, the service dichotomy was essentially mental hospitals (mostly state-run) and community services (not well organized or funded and offering very little continuum of care).

Moreover, the Act made no formal mention of a role for the lead clinical professional (i.e., psychiatrist) to serve as consultant or collaborator in the implementation of this new system, but structurally the early CMHCs created significant roles for psychiatrists in leading the treatment teams, even if they were not head of the organization. Early community psychiatry programs reflected another dichotomy as well. In the traditional model of psychiatric treatment, the individual psychiatrist assumed responsibility for those patients that sought them out for treatment. With the advent of the field of community psychiatry, psychiatrists working in community settings had responsibility for members in a bounded geographic area (initially called catchment areas) needing mental health care. And much like the experience of psychiatrists working in hospital-based settings, those community psychiatrists worked with other disciplines to achieve each patient's treatment goals. In fact, over time it was community psychiatrists who led the way in incorporating nonphysician mental health professionals into the community mental health workforce to meet the increased needs of patients in the community as state hospitals reduced capacity and community mental health centers saw a rise in patients needing the services they now offered. Community psychiatrists embraced professionals from other disciplines as team members, as well as new practice models which drove a shift from institutionalized care systems to recovery-focused, person-centered, and peer-supported system of care in the community.

The original CMHC Act listed "mental health consultation" as one of five basic services to be provided by all community mental health centers. This chapter suggests the conceptualization of consultation now goes beyond what was envisioned in the CMHC Act.

Brown et al. defined community psychiatry as "a branch of psychiatry which emphasizes the integration of social and environmental factors with the biological and psychological components of mental health and mental illness… also a significant component of … community medicine which focuses broadly on the prevention and treatment of illness for all individuals in a given community" (Brown et al. 1993).

Feiner described consultation in community psychiatry settings as "more focused than supervision and …often centered on a particular clinical or administrative problem" (Feiner 2012). More recently, Rosen et al. described components to inform the future design, development, sustenance, and monitoring of community mental health services to emphasize skills of public advocacy, working with consumers, families, and the media, and involvement in social movements to improve the mental health and well-being of regional and local communities (Rosen et al. 2020).

Finally, a review of recent textbooks in psychiatry shows that there is still little to no attention given to this increasingly more important subspecialty area in psychiatric medicine. In fact, the American Psychiatric Publishing Textbook of Psychiatry Seventh Edition added seven new chapters, yet did not include a specific chapter dedicated to this area. It is praised as "outstanding," "an indispensable tool and reference to inform practice, lifelong learning and shared decision-making," and "comprehensive in scope, this volume reflects .. behavioral sciences that have continued to evolve." Yet the term *community psychiatry* does not appear in the table of contents as a separate topic and is not listed in the index as a topic or under "settings" (Roberts 2019). There are references to sports-related concussions, complementary medicine, integrated care models, and other more recent topics in the practice of psychiatry, however, not a single discussion of community psychiatry as a specialized topic area in the field of psychiatry. This speaks volumes considering how far community psychiatry has really progressed as a field regarding our understanding of the importance of the psychiatrist's role in settings where the majority of patients currently receive their treatment and how critical it is that those psychiatrists working in that setting understand the many facets to their work beyond the clinical treatment role. That absence is also significant because it is now understood that the biopsychosocial model which came to prominence in community-based treatment settings serves as the framework for much of the work in clinical practice today. Many of the treatments now recognized as highly effective began in the community-based treatment setting: integrated care and collaborative care models, complementary medicine, multidisciplinary teams in recovery practices, and the understanding about how effective and appropriate treatments grew out of the creative necessity that comes with limited resources and restrictive regulatory policies. Growing awareness and understanding of the impact of how social determinants of health impact on manifestations and outcomes in persons with mental illness helps reframe the role of the psychiatrist in community-based service systems and led our colleagues, Compton and Shim, to remind us that these societal, environmental, and economic conditions influence a population's mental health and should not be underestimated (Compton and Shim 2015).

Community Psychiatry for the Twenty-First Century and Beyond

The work of Feiner and Rosen provides ideal transitional points in our understanding of the definition of community psychiatry and its role in the twenty-first century and beyond. Many psychiatrists today acknowledge that their roles in the community have expanded beyond that which can be neatly divided into clinical treatment or "nontraditional" professional functions; for most their role and identity still focuses heavily on provision of clinical care. That is changing, however, as models of disease and illness are beginning to recognize the contribution of preventable factors that negatively impact individuals in their communities and contribute to poor health and mental health outcomes. Psychiatrists working in the community must now be prepared to address how to incorporate consultation and collaboration approaches into effective community mental health practices.

At the forefront of the work of psychiatrists in community settings is the concept of "community engagement." In the academic setting, engagement is defined as "connecting the rich resources of the university to our most pressing social, civic, and ethical problems" (Boyer 1996). Community engagement, as it relates to psychiatry, establishes the framework for all community planning regarding adequate and appropriate mental health services, as well as a community's overall health and well-being. It is the process through which community involvement and input regarding needs assessment, planning, governance, and implementation of service and support programs occur and establish the basis for an effective and sustained relationship between a community and those providing the services, as well as alignment with other local health priorities. To be effective and trusted, community engagement, for purposes of improving overall psychological health and well-being, requires mutual respect, transparency, and accountability. The psychiatrist working in that setting plays a significant role in developing resources and communication channels that encourage the type of community feedback that strengthens the relationship between treatment systems and community residents that use the services. Community engagement is not unique to the United States, and various models are used around the world as a tool for change through empowerment (World Health Organization 2016).

Community engagement is also one method being adopted to conduct needed work to reduce and eliminate mental health disparities in racially diverse, historically marginalized populations.

Government agencies as well as philanthropic organizations are now recognizing the importance of funding efforts in this area, the effectiveness of these strategies to achieving desired outcomes in these communities, and how communities can create the types of programs that work best for them. Recognizing the health and life span disparities that exist between those with psychiatric disorder and their peers without psychiatric disorders, it is clear that psychiatrists can and must play a role in the design and implementation of such programs to assure they include best practice and evidence-based components in treating mental disorders and other medical conditions, especially for those individuals with serious mental illness. This level of engagement with communities which are outside the institutions and organizations providing health and mental health care serves as the basis for a foundation of mutual respect in collaboration and consultation to create goals and shared authority in deciding how to address community health issues, share information, and establish directions for the future.

Reimagining Community Consultation and Collaboration

What might happen if individuals living with a persistent psychiatric illness or other behavioral health issue were more involved in activities beyond those offered by social services and mental health systems? What direct and indirect benefits might be realized if community psychiatrists were able to spend a bit more of their time promoting mental health by partnering with others to help create, implement, or simply contribute to community-based initiatives? Reimagining psychiatric consultation and collaboration in communities allows for consideration of creative answers to those questions. And how we approach this reimagined consultation and collaboration means we can incorporate discussions of racism, sexism, and other social justice issues and their impact on the psychological health and well-being in historically marginalized communities. This also allows for a different approach to creating collaborative partnerships in our communities when the culture of health and medicine, and our systems in general, is impacted by racism, discrimination, and mistrust. Well-documented stories of harm from the scientific and health care communities have been passed down through many generations in these communities, and we have come to acknowledge the growing scientific evidence that these issues continue to impact our systems and culture of health and medicine. The resulting distrust is exacerbated further when health care institutions and organizations fail to prioritize transparency and trustworthiness as they approach working with these communities.

In addition to understanding these issues and demonstrating competency in the clinical care areas, psychiatrists and other mental health professionals of the future working in community settings will need to be well trained in the general management skills and infrastructures required to take responsibility for the mental health and well-being of these former "catchment area" communities and provide leadership in service planning, management, and continuing revision based on rigorous evaluation. These approaches should be at the core of all training in psychiatry and other mental health disciplines.

The Psychiatrist as Consultant and Collaborator

Out of necessity, community psychiatrists frequently find themselves engaging across the private, public, and social sectors when addressing the needs of individuals for whom they provide health care. Though their primary subject matter expertise typically is grounded in psychiatric medicine, the capacity to understand other sectors' underlying mission and principles and apply them when addressing cross-sector issues often develops over time. When motivated by a deep sense of mission and purpose, community psychiatrists appear well positioned to help promote health and wellness in local communities, in addition to providing health care to the individuals living there. This is especially true when they are able to tap into cross-sector networks to identify existing opportunities or convene people from diverse groups to create opportunities to address a community's mental health needs.

There is also a role for psychiatrists as consultants to communities through work with national organizations. At an American Psychiatric Association-sponsored meeting on mental health in Appalachia, one of the authors stated in her remarks: "Poverty begins a process that ends up in poor health. Rural America has unique challenges that will have to be dealt with uniquely." She proposed moving towards what she called "place-based care," "informed by a deep understanding of the history, geography, and culture of a specific location and how that culture shapes the social determinants of health and ultimately determines the outcomes." She ended with encouraging that psychiatrists work within their professional organizations on these issues to "further collaboration and attention to the social determinants of health .... to better serve the population there" (Moran 2018). The American Association of Community Psychiatry (AACP) also works at the organizational level to create new models of care and provide opportunities for community psychiatrists to serve as consultants in work with communities through its training and mentoring programs.

It is recognized that these two roles – consultation and collaboration – are integral to community psychiatry in the twenty-first century. While defined from time to time across the history of community psychiatry, today we must clarify these roles to provide a framework for the next generation of psychiatrist-leaders to work effectively in community behavioral health settings. Creating a definition for the twenty-first century means that many of our colleagues working from a social justice perspective, already leaders in community psychiatry, can help to shape the basic curriculum for training psychiatrists to get "upstream" in this work with the community and create structures and systems that will address existing mental health disparities; integrate aspects of culture, ethnicity, language, equity, and social justice; and organize services to address social determinants of mental health as part of the comprehensive community behavioral health treatment system.

Today's psychiatrist can move beyond current conceptualizations of public sector, community-based mental health care delivery to envision changes that might lead to improved health and psychological wellness in the communities in which they work. The opportunity exists to reimagine the roles of psychiatrists and other mental health professionals and *how* they interact, consult, and collaborate within these communities. Rather than limiting themselves to roles as health care providers, they can explore barriers to health care access and improve health by listening to the people living in local communities. Instead of compartmentalizing individuals into those with a chronic mental illness or other behavioral health problem and those without, they can forge collaborative partnerships with individuals and community organizations to identify effective prevention and intervention strategies and utilize the strengths of *all* individuals in achieving the common goal of improved psychological health and well-being to mitigate or eliminate negative health outcomes. And rather than assuming that other systems can, and will, address structural barriers to good health upon referral, twenty-first-century psychiatrists in consultation and collaboration with communities can create opportunities to help improve overall health and well-being in neighborhoods that are disproportionately impacted by the preventable factors that lead to poor health and mental health outcomes.

In 2019, the combination of the coronavirus disease (COVID-19) pandemic, racial unrest and social injustice, and acknowledged health inequities represents a new *syndemic* in the United States and globally. Working to understand and address the impact of COVID-19, mental health inequities, and structural racism on persons with mental illness and to improve our systems of care represents an opportunity to finally address the significant disparities and the social determinants of mental health (Gravlee 2020; Poteat et al. 2020). In order to meet the challenging needs of those in these systems, opportunities must be embraced to expand mechanisms to encourage, solicit, and respond to community members' concerns, suggestions, and needs. This will mean including more activities to encourage engagement, such as community health committees, community advisory boards, patient and family advisory councils, community meetings, and other feedback forums in collaboration with treatment providers and programs.

The Psychiatrist as Consultant

As physicians specializing in psychiatry, for some, the term consultant brings to mind how that function may be defined in the pure clinical setting – consulting on a clinical case at the request of a colleague to identify a likely cause for "X" symptom that may be within the scope of the consultant's specialty. The consultant in that case will examine the patient, review the history of the presenting illness, and offer recommendations for etiology and treatment to the patient's primary provider. Previously this would have likely been a hospital-based encounter, and unless asked for more in terms of maintenance or follow-up, the psychiatrist moved on to the next case. Today, however, psychiatrists may also perform this in a community-based setting where a system of collaborative or integrated care is in place.

For the community psychiatrist, however, the term consultant can have a different meaning. When working in the community in addition to the expert clinical skills the psychiatrists may bring, it is the knowledge and skills in effective communication and messaging, utilizing community engagement strategies and establishing collaborative relationships that is the most useful. When considering areas to engage with the community in a consultative role, the psychiatrist should consider how the primary service delivery system can support health promotion, address a community's social determinant risk factors, and relate to the community in a culturally sensitive and responsive manner to empower them to achieve the changes and improvements they desire in health outcomes. Psychiatrists are trained in interpersonal and group dynamics, as well as effective communication and should learn to use those skills outside of the clinical setting in order to be good consultants for the communities with whom they work. Learning the critical issues facing the population served is key to any successful consultation. Whether the issue is health literacy, advocacy for more or different services, changes in funding or legislation, or issues that promote equity and community empowerment, the psychiatrist-consultant works to communicate, educate, and empower a community to work together to obtain the type and quality of mental health services they need and desire. And while there is no single best way to engage communities, a range of methods are available for health systems to facilitate community engagement. This continuum includes simple, passive mechanisms to solicit feedback such as suggestion boxes or complaint lines, as well as more active methods such as community buy-in and ownership, sign-off, and decision-making. The requests for psychiatric consultation may come from many directions – general community, targeted groups within the community, or those external to the service system but critical to the service delivery availability and access, i.e., legislators, policymakers, and funders.

In these settings critical consultation tasks include:

1. Introduction of the potential areas for consultation with the program and team (including any community governance bodies)
2. Development of a community engagement strategy with buy-in from the program team and including identification of key stakeholders, champions, and allies with whom to initiate the work (related to local social justice and other social determinant of mental health issues)
3. Establishing task priorities with timelines, responsibilities, and measurable outcomes
4. Alignment of skills with community needs and determining how the community program resources can be most effectively used

Examples of this are provided in Table 1.

Table 1 Examples of critical consultation tasks

Consultation area	Purpose/activity	Consultant role	Example(s)
Media/communication	MH month – anti-stigma campaign activities	Psychiatrist as speaker as subject matter expert (SME)	Co-author Op-Ed; local TV/radio appearances alongside community stakeholders
Local consumer/family groups	Participation in community support and governance groups	Serve on governance boards as SME	Promotion of recovery activities; coordinate participation in service improvement activities; liaison with academic medical centers
Academic medical center linkage to community clinics (clinical services, training, and research/evaluation activities)	Workforce development (including employment opportunities for consumers and families)	Provide professional development and training; participate in community-based participatory research	Trainee lectures and community MH education sessions; trainee supervision; facilitate and coordinate funding and advocacy activities

The Psychiatrist as Collaborator

In the role of collaborator, the psychiatrist requires a strong organizational structure, community trust in the organization (or at least a measure of credibility as trust is built), and a strong champion and ally base. There must be community organizations and providers willing to work with the psychiatrist as a collaborative partner to address a broad range of health activities including treatment and prevention strategies, health education, and other activities to address the social determinants of mental health, as well as health as a social justice issue. Collaboration requires establishing a platform for understanding the voices, opinions, and expertise of service providers, residents, and consumers to support the design and planning of mental health services appropriate and accessible to the communities served.

Essential steps in effective collaboration include:

1. Community engagement – this important first step allows the psychiatrist to develop relationships to work with community leaders and stakeholders to address health and mental health issues and achieve positive health outcomes. Community engagement is critical in planning and delivering person-centered care and meeting community-responsive needs. Stakeholders bring multiple perspectives (community members, patients, health professionals, policymakers, and others) and are often called on to speak on behalf of their community regarding health and mental health matters.
2. Local priority setting – as a collaborator, the psychiatrist works to assist community leaders/stakeholders frame local actions in response to national or regional policies based on needs and preferences of a community regarding its concerns (e.g., use of CBG funds by state mental health authority).
3. Community governance bodies – these regularly scheduled meetings serve to identify issues and review actions and offer updates on work of the team or community to resolve known or identify new areas of concern. Active ongoing review ensures that responsibility for and attention to these matters is continuously monitored to reduce the likelihood of important concerns "falling through the cracks." Members of this group may be called upon to present concerns to local or state bodies with oversight for health and mental health and are supported by the psychiatrist-consultant in being prepared to do so.
4. Proactive community outreach – the psychiatrist reaches out to communities to provide health and mental health information and also encourage proactive use of available service options (i.e., crisis stabilization and support, ACT teams, homeless mental health outreach,

Table 2 Examples of effective collaboration

Collaboration area	Purpose/activity	Role	Example(s)
Advocacy	Upcoming legislative or regulatory changes	Testify at local/state hearings; support community, consumer, and family groups prepared to advocate	Presentations at legislative meetings sponsored by community advocacy organizations
Community education	Locally sponsored community meetings on health promotion, governmental health planning meetings, and media campaigns to destigmatize mental health	Subject matter expert (SME) in mental health-related issues in the community	Speaker at a community, educational or faith organization-sponsored meeting; media appearances
Sustainability or funding request opportunity	Community-expressed interest in grant proposal being developed by community-based organization	Assist in preparation of proposal; provide letter of support for organization; serves as community liaison to academic medical center in implementation of the program if funded	Funding opportunity to develop and/or implement a needed community mental health service component (SOC for children's MH, AOT program, MH, or drug court)

community corrections mental health services).

Examples of this are provided in Table 2.

Conclusion

One of the lessons we have learned about a reimagined community psychiatry is that it is now understood that the breadth of opportunity for system improvement available when traditional psychiatric system service models and treatment approaches are visualized through the lens of the community and recipients of service is limited only by our ability to innovate and creatively use the knowledge, skills, and tools available today.

Moving forward, community psychiatrists will continue to experience systemic social and economic barriers that are inconsistent with the stated ideals, vision, and goals of community psychiatry. Combined with the stigma of mental illness, lack of a culturally diverse behavioral health workforce, language challenges, and a mental health system that have historically not provided adequate treatment to marginalized and socioeconomically depressed populations with significant social determinant of mental health risks means opportunities are created to continue efforts to improve our work in the evolving area of community psychiatry (Torres Stone et al. 2020). This is the behavioral health system in which future community psychiatrists will work. And it is our hope that this chapter will provide insight into some of the new roles and responsibilities for which future community psychiatrists must be prepared.

References

American Medical Association. (1980). Code of Medical Ethics, Principles of Medical Ethics, Chapter 8: Opinion 8.11, Ethics for Physicians and the Health of the Community. https://www.ama-assn.org/system/files/2020-12/code-of-medical-ethics-chapter-8.pdf retrieved: 3/2/2022.

Barclay WA. (1968). Community Psychiatry. *Australian & New Zealand Journal of Psychiatry*. 2(3),122–127. DOI:https://doi.org/10.3109/00048676809159229

Bernard, Viola W. (1964). Education for community psychiatry in a university medical center. In L. Bellak (Ed.), *Handbook of Community Psychiatry and Community Mental Health*. New York: Grune & Stratton.

Boyer E. (1996). The scholarship of engagement. *Bulletin of the American Academy of Arts and Sciences*, 49(7),18–33.

Brown DB, Goldman CR, Thompson KS, Cutler DL. (1993). Training residents for community psychiatric practice. *Community Mental Health Journal*, 29, 271–283.

Caplan, G. (1964). Community Psychiatry – Introduction and Overview. In Stephen and Goldstein (Ed.),

Concepts of *Community Psychiatry*. US. Public Health Service Publication No. 1319.

Chibanda D, Weiss HA, Verhey R, et al. (2016). Effect of a Primary Care–Based Psychological Intervention on Symptoms of Common Mental Disorders in Zimbabwe: A Randomized Clinical Trial. *JAMA*. 316(24):2618–2626. DOI:https://doi.org/10.1001/jama.2016.19102

Compton MT, Shim RS (Eds). (2015). The Social Determinants of Mental Health. Washington, DC. American Psychiatric Publishing.

Ellis W and Dietz W. (2017). A New Framework for Addressing Adverse Childhood and Community Experiences: The Building Community Resilience (BCR) Model. *Academic Pediatrics*. 17, pp. S86–93. DOI: https://doi.org/10.1016/j.cap.2016.12.011 http://ccr.publichealth.gwu.edu/ retrieved March 3, 2022.

Feiner JS. (2012). Mentoring, Supervision, and Consultation in Community Mental Health. In McQuiston HL, Sowers WE, Ranz JM & Feldman JM (Eds.), *Handbook of Community Psychiatry*, Springer, New York, 2012.

Freeman VJ. (1959). Dual Role of the Psychiatric Consultant in the Community. *AMA Arch Gen Psychiatry*. 1(6):561–564. DOI:https://doi.org/10.1001/archpsyc.1959.03590060023001

Goldfarb S. (2019 September 15). Take Two Aspirin and Call Me By My Pronouns. *Wall Street Journal*, Opinion/Commentary. https://www.wsj.com/articles/take-two-aspirin-and-call-me-by-my-pronouns-11568325291?reflink=desktopwebshare_permalink retrieved: October 28, 2021.

Gravlee CC. (2020). Systemic racism, chronic health inequities, and COVID-19: A syndemic in the making? *Am J Hum Biol* 32: e23482.

McQuistion HL, Sowers WE, Ranz JM, & Feldman JM (eds). (2012). *Handbook of Community Psychiatry*, Springer, New York, NY.

Moran M. (2018, Dec 4). APA Collaborates to Promote Mental Health in Appalachia. *Psychiatric News*, Published Online: psychnews.psychiatryonline.org/doi/10.1176/appi.pn.2018.12a11 retrieved: 3/3/2022.

Poteat T, Millett GA, Nelson LE & Beyrer C. (2020, July). Understanding COVID-19 risks and vulnerabilities among black communities in America: the lethal force of syndemics. *Ann Epidemiol.* 47:1–3. DOI: https://doi.org/10.1016/j.annepidem.2020.05.004

PUBLIC LAW 88-164-OCT. 31, 1963. Mental Retardation Facilities and *Community Mental Health* Centers Construction *Act* of *1963, pp. 282-299.* https://www.govinfo.gov/content/pkg/STATUTE-77/pdf/STATUTE-77-Pg282.pdf retrieved: 3/2/2022.

Roberts LW (ed). (2019). The American Psychiatric Association Publishing *Textbook of Psychiatry Seventh Edition*. American Psychiatric Association Publishing. Washington, D.C.

Rosen A, Gill NS, Salvador-Carulla L. (2020, July). The future of community psychiatry And community mental health services. *Curr Opin Psychiatry*, 33:(4):375–390. DOI:https://doi.org/10.1097/YCO.0000000000000620

Smith B. (2020, August 2). Harnessing the power of grandmothers to treat depression and anxiety. *The Brilliant*, Case Studies. https://thebrilliant.com.au/case-studies/dixon-chibanda/ retrieved: 3/2/2022.

Torres Stone RA, Cardemil EV, Keefe K, Bik P, Dyer Z, Clark KE. (2020, July). A Community Mental Health Needs Assessment of a Racially and Ethnically Diverse Population in New England: Narratives from Community Stakeholders. *Community Ment Health J.* 6(5):947–958. DOI: https://doi.org/10.1007/s10597-020-00562-2. Epub 2020 Jan 31. PMID: 32006294.

Uchtenhagen AA. (2008, December). Which future for social psychiatry? *Int Rev Psychiatry*. 20(6):535--9. DOI: https://doi.org/10.1080/09540260802565471

World Health Organization. Community Engagement, Module B5. 2016. https://www.who.int/risk-communication/training/Module-B5.pdf retrieved: 3/2/2022.

Collaborative Reduction of Criminal Justice Involvement for Persons with Mental Illness

Michelle Joy and Fred C. Osher

> I am dismayed to be "forced to authorize the confinement of persons with mental illness in the Williamsburg jail, against both my conscience and the law" because of lack of appropriate services. (Deutsch 1937)

Introduction and Background

Through mass incarceration, the United States has a higher number and rate of people incarcerated than anywhere else in the world. At their bloated peaks, 4.7 million people were on probation in 2008; in 2018, there were upwards of 875,000 people on parole; in 2010, there were more than 2.3 million people behind bars (Barboriak 2017). Persons with mental illnesses are vastly overrepresented in the criminal justice system (Wilson et al. 2020). Estimates vary by definitions, time, and mode of inquiry. Researchers have documented mental health problems in upwards half of inmates in federal and state prisons as well as in local jails – the highest proportion being 73% of women in state prisons (James and Glaze 2006). Serious mental illness has been reported in 14.5% of male jail inmates and 31% of female jail inmates in Maryland and New York (Steadman et al. 2009), which are approximately three to six times the rates found in the general population (Pratt et al. 2006). Schizophrenia, bipolar disorder, and major depressive disorder are themselves two to three times more prevalent in jails than the community (Dvoskin et al. 2003). Conservative estimates indicate that 10–15% of people would benefit from treatment of a primary mental health problem and that 7–9% of persons on probation or parole have serious mental illness (Pinals 2017). The presence of so many people with mental illnesses in criminal justice settings represents an enormous burden on correctional and behavioral health systems of care, communities, families, and those with mental illnesses. There are many factors that contribute to this problem, and understanding these factors is crucial to providing relief throughout the system.

The majority of individuals with mental illnesses who wind up in jails have committed nonviolent misdemeanors (Ventura et al. 1998). The crimes of persons with mental health problems are often related to undertreatment (Allison et al. 2017), which is the basis of the concept of *criminalization* of mental illness. Nonetheless, even adequate treatment would not significantly prevent crime, and it is also important to be mindful that people with mental illnesses will commit crimes for which legal remedies are appropriate (Draine et al. 2010; JLI 2010). Safety must

M. Joy (✉)
Department of Psychiatry, Perelman School of Medicine, Philadelphia, PA, USA

F. C. Osher
Charleston Community Mental Health Center, Charleston, SC, USA

W. E. Sowers et al. (eds.), *Textbook of Community Psychiatry*,
https://doi.org/10.1007/978-3-031-10239-4_34

remain emphasized. Persons with mental illnesses who commit crimes can be held responsible for their actions while relevant effects of illness on their behavior are simultaneously taken into account. In fact, appropriate intervention for persons with mental illness also seeks to reduce characteristics of criminality, as will be later discussed.

For individuals with mental illnesses, contact with the criminal justice system often begins a cycle of arrest, incarceration, release, supervision, and rearrest that can pose nearly insurmountable challenges to recover. However, jail and prison environments are not the best setting for individuals with mental illnesses and in fact may worsen many symptoms and outcomes (Anestis and Carbonell 2014). This chapter focuses on integrations between components of mental health and criminal justice systems in an effort to reduce the prevalence of persons with mental illnesses behind bars and under supervision. The following pages focus on the factors that increase the risk of incarceration for persons with mental illnesses and the role of community psychiatry providers in mediating that risk by participating in comprehensive care coordination.

The incarceration of high numbers of persons with mental illnesses has been taking place in the context of expanding incarcerated populations in general. Until 2008, the nation's prison and jail population continued to skyrocket to an all-time high of over two million people incarcerated and over five million under some form of correctional supervision (Kaeble et al. 2016). Around that time, the United States reached the dubious landmark of having over 1 in every 100 adults in the nation behind bars (Rich et al. 2011). Beyond the considerable human cost, correctional spending is also important to recognize. Although the correctional population decreased between 2007 and 2016 (Kaeble and Cowhig 2018), state spending on corrections accounted for 2.9% of expenditures in 2020, amounting to $65.9 billion – an increase of $20 billion annually since the first edition of this chapter was published (2012). Continued reduction of the number of persons with mental illnesses under correctional supervision should be a shared goal for behavioral health and criminal justice systems, as well as anyone who cares about human dignity.

Involvement in the criminal justice system should be a public health opportunity rather than the setback it often becomes. Jails and prisons are obligated to provide general and mental health care (Cohen 2008); in fact, incarcerated individuals are the only US citizens with constitutionally protected access to health care. The US Supreme Court, in *Estelle v. Gamble* [*429 U.S. 97 (1976)*], found that deliberate indifference to prisoners with "serious medical needs" constitutes a violation of the 8th Amendment of the Constitution and is thus cruel and unusual punishment. In *Estelle v. Ruiz* [503 F.Supp. 1265 (S.D. Tex. 1980)] and subsequent cases, "serious medical needs" were extended to include mental illness by the Fifth Circuit. The American Psychiatric Association (Weinstein et al. 2000), the National Commission on Correctional Health Care (Care 2008), and the National Institute of Correction (Hills et al. 2004) have all recommended that all jails provide the following, at a minimum: (a) mental health screening, referral, and evaluation, (b) crisis intervention and short-term treatment (most often medication), and (c) discharge and prerelease planning.

There have been concerted efforts by criminal justice systems to identify persons with mental illnesses at the earliest possible moments and to develop mechanisms to leverage legal authority to improve their connection to treatment. Innovative police-based responses, specialty courts, and jail, prison, and community corrections programs have been developed for persons with psychiatric problems. The shared goal for all systems is to reduce the frequency of contacts and absolute numbers of justice-involved persons with mental illnesses in criminal justice settings. At the heart of this approach lies the continuity of effective mental health care in the community and in corrections.

Why Are There So Many People with Mental Illnesses in Jail and Prison?

To develop appropriate interventions, it is important to understand the various factors that contribute the presence of persons with mental illness behind bars. A public misconception is that people who struggle with mental illness are inherently violent (Rozel and Mulvey 2017). Most crime is instead related to socioeconomic circumstances intersecting with demographics (Stuart 2003). For example, due to social determinants and structural factors including institutional racism, young, poor, Black men are much more likely to be incarcerated than other populations (Massoglia and Remster 2019). By disrupting these communities and families with incarceration, they are often pushed further into poverty, increasing odds of future arrest in a multigenerational manner.

It is critical to acknowledge that most people with mental illnesses are not violent, and most people who commit violent crimes do not have mental illnesses. Only about 4% of criminal violence can be linked to individuals with mental health problems (Rozel and Mulvey 2017). People with mental illnesses who are in fact violent often have untreated symptoms of psychosis and/or co-occurring substance use disorders, with stimulant abuse being particularly problematic (Miles et al. 2003). Furthermore, people with mental illness are three times more likely to be the victims of crime than perpetrators (Rozel and Mulvey 2017), and those with serious mental illness (SMI) are 11 times more likely to be victims of crime than the general population (Teplin et al. 2005). Nonetheless, while hard to predict and relatively infrequent, psychiatric symptoms do at times contribute to the commission of criminal offenses (Skeem et al. 2014). The risk of violence by persons with mental illness increases with being a previous victim or perpetrator of crime, lack of treatment, poverty, and unstable housing, as well as substance use, which is discussed below (Swanson et al. 2015).

There is an established link between substance abuse and crime, including violence (Rozel and Mulvey 2017). As a consequence of the failed War on Drugs, rates of substance use disorders are overrepresented in correctional settings – rates in the community are around 9% and prisons around 50% (including 20% with a history of injection drug use) – and affect nearly two-thirds of persons in jail (Peters et al. 2015; Rich et al. 2011). As the number of people incarcerated in the United States quadrupled between 1982 and 2007 (Swanson et al. 2013), drug-related arrests also tripled – nearly half of which were for marijuana (Mauer and King 2007). In general, people with substance use disorders also have a mental health diagnosis around 40–50% of the time (Kessler 2004). So it stands that incarcerating people with substance use problems will also lead to imprisonment of those with other psychiatric difficulties.

There are layered interrelationships between mental health problems, poverty, substance abuse, trauma, housing instability, and arrest (Osher 2013; Swanson et al. 2015). Being homeless and some symptoms of serious mental illness each make a person visible in the community and frequently result in calls to law enforcement; they can also make treatment engagement difficult. Recent homelessness is very common among incarcerated people; in fact, it is 7.5–11.3 times more common than in the general population (Greenberg and Rosenheck 2008). In addition, incarcerated persons with mental illness are more likely to have been homeless at the time of their arrest than those without mental illness. In jails, 30.3% of inmates with mental illness were homeless in the year prior to arrest compared to 17.3% of other inmates (Stephan 2001). This relationship has been tied to the closure of state hospitals beginning in the 1970s, leaving people without structured housing and treatment. The same population then ended up incarcerated through a process called *trans-institutionalization* (Lamb and Weinberger 2017). On the other hand, not having a stable place to live severely complicates the reentry of a person with mental illness following release from prison. In fact, a detailed home plan is required for supervised release through parole, and absence of an adequate residence can effectively lengthen time behind bars.

A third factor that contributes to the incarceration of people with mental illness is harsh correctional conditions that can have harmful effects on a person's mental health. Compounding past histories of extensive trauma, the overcrowding, witnessed violence, and sexual and violent victimization behind bars often make the experience of incarceration a prolonged distressing event (Sindicich et al. 2014). The deleterious effects of these circumstances on persons with serious mental illnesses are predictable: despair, worsened symptoms, and acting out. There is also an association between experiencing trauma and having a mental illness in this population (Karlsson and Zielinski 2020).

Most – but not all – studies find that people with mental illness tend to be incarcerated for longer periods of time and are less likely to be placed on probation or parole than others charged with similar offenses (Leifman and Coffey 2020). Inmates who have psychotic illnesses are often profoundly impacted by these timelines. Parole board members may lack knowledge about community resources for individuals with mental illnesses, have misconceptions about their risk, or fear negative public reactions; prisoners with MI are also more likely to forgo parole and "max out" their sentences (Matejkowski and Ostermann 2020). As a result, people with mental illness have their releases delayed and more frequently serve the maximum sentence allowed by law (2002). The trend also worsens overcrowding, destabilizes the milieu, and increases the potential for violence overall (Houser and Welsh 2014).

Fifth, once released, former incarcerees with mental illnesses are significantly more likely to recidivate, with serious mental illness, substance use disorders, and lack of treatment associated with higher levels of risk for return to incarceration (Zgoba et al. 2020). Cuts in mental health services have an impact on the prevalence of mental illnesses in jails and prisons insofar as they make it more difficult for treatment providers to dedicate resources to this population. Compared to their counterparts, probationers and parolees with mental illness are significantly more likely to have their probation or parole term suspended or revoked, resulting in reincarceration (Meredith et al. 2020). Stigma of supervision officers should be considered to be a potential factor in these trends (Eno Louden et al. 2018).

What Can Be Done to Reduce the Likelihood that They Will End Up There?

There are programmatic responses that can identify persons with mental illnesses in the criminal justice system, divert them from jail and prison, and reduce the likelihood of return. All of these programmatic efforts are dependent upon communication and integration between the mental health and criminal justice systems. Both linkage to effective treatment in the community and reverse communication with providers in incarceration settings are important (Lamberti 2016). The next section discusses evidence-based practices (EBPs) and program models intended to reduce criminal engagement of persons struggling with mental health problems.

The broad set of responses to behavioral needs of citizens within a community is shaped by local, state, and federal regulations and policy. When this focus is narrowed to a specific target population defined by its participation in criminal activity, the need for mental health leadership to incorporate the perspectives of law enforcement, courts, and local and state corrections personnel is imperative, as is the perspective of individuals with lived experience in these systems. Clarity in the goals and objectives for initiatives is critical to determine the range, format, and intensity of partnerships. At the outset, stakeholders may be convened as a strategic planning committee, but more collaborative partners will emerge as goals are formulated. Additional partners may include other treatment providers, housing officials, private funders, elected officials, peer supports, crime victims, family members, academic partners, advocates, or other community representatives.

The *sequential intercept model* (SIM) creates a framework around which to organize responses to assist justice-involved individuals with mental illnesses (Munetz and Griffin 2006). The model diagrams the various stages at which an individual may come in contact with the criminal justice system. The five intercept points identified in the model are: (1) law enforcement, (2) initial detention and hearings, (3) jails/courts, (4) reentry from jail or prison, and (5) community corrections. The US Substance Abuse and Mental Health Services Administration (SAMHSA) offers SIM training for communities (Center 2020a). See Fig. 1.

The SIM focuses on a series of intercepts where interventions can prevent individuals from penetrating further into the criminal justice system. At each of these intercept points, there is an opportunity to develop programs tailored to the needs of persons with mental illnesses and subpopulations within this group. The hope is that the further upstream a person can be redirected, the fewer legal consequences will obstruct their path to recovery. The ultimate and most effective intercept has been described as accessible, comprehensive, and effective community-based services (Munetz and Griffin 2006).

At the first three intercepts, the processes are referred to as *jail diversion* which is defined as:

> A community-based, collaborative criminal justice-mental health response for justice-involved people with mental illnesses where jail time is reduced or avoided, and the individual is linked to comprehensive and appropriate services. (JLI 2010)

Police-Based Responses

The earliest and most prevalent prebooking diversion programs exist within the community and often rely on law enforcement officers interacting with people in psychiatric crisis. Law enforcement officers have become the de facto first-line responders to deal with persons with mental health emergencies or criminal activity. How law enforcement personnel react to these individuals can have a huge impact on their outcomes and determine whether a person is linked to treatment and/or enters the criminal justice system (see chapter "Community Education"). A well-recognized program is the Crisis Intervention Team (CIT) through which officers receive training in how to recognize mental health problems and deescalate crises. CITs are associated with increased confidence and decreased stigma in law enforcement as well as more referrals to treatment (Pinals 2017). Another intervention relies on mental health specialists who provide consultation to law enforcement and often located within the department. A third prebooking approach is a specialized community mental health response, which includes mental health mobile crisis teams that work in partnership with police to deescalate emergencies and link individuals to services. Appropriate recognition of mental health crises, with deescalation and other nonaggressive techniques, also works towards decreasing the risk of violence in police encounters (Watson et al. 2008).

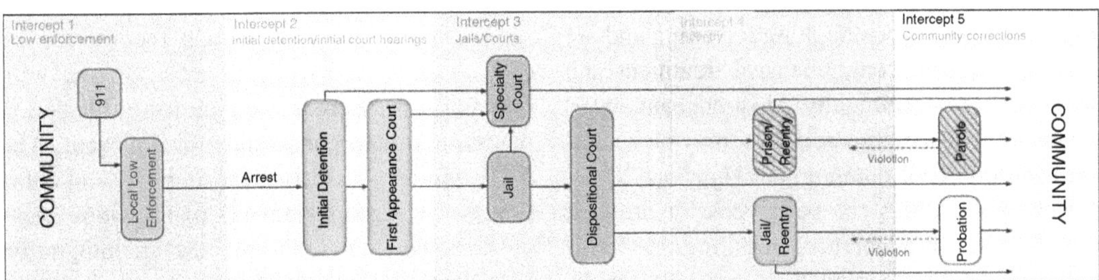

Fig. 1 Sequential intercept model (SAMHSA 2021)

Jail- and Court-Based Strategies

Postbooking diversion programs at intercept 2 involve jail- and court-based strategies. In these programs, individuals identified as having mental health needs are linked to treatment with leveraged conditions of release. These interventions may consist of teams of mental health providers that operate within the jail and are available to assess individuals and to provide recommendations on diagnoses, treatment needs, and the possibility of alternative dispositions in the community. Identification of arrested persons with mental illnesses in some communities has been improved by the matching of jail rosters to public mental health rosters. A one-way flow of information is then generated to the mental health provider informing them that their client is in custody. The mental health provider can then attempt to engage their client and coordinate care within the jail, helping to promote alternatives to incarceration.

Specialized Courts

At intercept 3, specialized courts have been developed in jurisdictions across the country. Broadly characterized, mental health courts have been shown to reduce recidivism (Loong et al. 2019). The Honorable Steve Leifman established the foundation for the Miami Model in 2000, which continues to successfully function in its aims to divert individuals with serious mental illness away from the courts and into a full spectrum of treatment options (Leifman and Coffey 2020). Participants are identified by CIT-trained officers as well as postbooking screening and are then linked with comprehensive treatment and supports in the community. Most engagement is voluntary, but some participation may be actualized through civil commitment (Iglehart 2016). Legal consequences can be lowered or dropped with treatment adherence, resulting in fewer incarcerated people with SMI, reduced recidivism, cost savings, improved health and safety, and less homelessness (Leifman and Coffey 2020).

Transition Planning

With the constitutional obligation to provide health care comes an opportunity to identify and begin treatment for mental illnesses within jails and prisons. Despite chronic staffing shortages and limited formularies, critical treatment can take place behind bars. Assuring continuity from the community to the jail or prison and back to the community is imperative for effective mental health care. Almost all jail inmates, including those with mental illnesses will leave correctional settings and return to the community. Thoughtful transition planning from jails and prisons can reduce the possibility of return to criminal justice systems (Skeem et al. 2011).

At intercept 4, inadequate transition planning can put individuals who entered jail in a crisis state back on the street in the middle of the same crisis. Individuals were often released without Medicaid benefits or medical insurance (though this improved somewhat with that passage of the Affordable Care Act in 2010) (Heiss et al. 2016). Enrollment in Medicaid should be a focus of intervention. Inadequate treatment upon release increases the risks for repeat offenses, psychiatric instability, hospitalization, homelessness, rearrest, and death from overdose (Binswanger et al. 2007). We follow the suggestion of the American Association of Community Psychiatrists (AACP) by using the term *transition planning*, rather than *discharge planning* or *reentry planning*, in order to imply bidirectional responsibility and collaboration among providers (Sowers and Rohland 2004). It is understood that some ex-offenders will return to custody and as such reentry can be seen as part of a cycle of care, though with attempts to decrease recidivism. Transition planning is a process and not an event. The APIC model – assess, plan, identify, and coordinate – describes elements of transition planning associated with successful integration back into the community (Osher et al. 2003). The model pays attention to biopsychosocial strengths and needs, short- and long-term projections, and coordination of support. Such planning can serve as an investment in public health by reducing future costs associated with reincarceration (Wolff 2005).

Specialized Community Supervision

At intercept 5, there are significant opportunities to reduce the prevalence of persons with mental illnesses in jail and prison. The number of people with mental illness under correctional supervision reached unprecedented levels in the mid-aughts, with the vast majority of persons supervised in the community (Glaze and Bonczar 2010). Probation and parole officers are often left with revocation to jail or prison as a punishment for failing to meet conditions of release. These *technical violations*, where a new crime has not been committed, are a principal contributor to ballooning correctional populations (White et al. 2011). In this context, specialized community caseloads have been developed to improve outcomes for persons with mental illnesses under community correctional supervision. The key features of such programs are closer supervision and support of persons with mental illness, officer training on psychiatric issues, and collaboration with community-based providers (Prins and Draper 2009). Studies support this model as effective in improving the well-being and reducing the reincarceration risk of people with mental illness on probation and parole (Skeem and Louden 2006). However, with states facing the grim reality of enormous budget constraints, the resources to fund effective, specialized transition resources are difficult to come by.

Comprehensive, Effective Community-Based Care: The Ultimate Intercept

It has been said that any effort to keep people with mental illnesses out of the criminal justice system will only be as good as the community treatment and supports available – the ultimate intercept. Towards that end, this chapter now discusses linkage to community treatment. There are several EBPs that have the potential to reduce jail days for persons with mental illnesses. In discussing justice-involved persons with mental illnesses, it is important to keep in mind the heterogeneity of this group. They differ in terms of the seriousness of their mental illnesses, charge levels, criminogenic risks, demographics, and access to community supports. Unfortunately, many inmates are un- or undertreated at the time of their arrests (Wilper et al. 2009). The community mental health system also rarely assesses the nature of criminal justice involvement or criminogenic risk. Almost one-half of the clients seen for the first time at community mental health centers have had contact with the criminal justice system and that nearly one-third of them had been sentenced to jail (Theriot and Segal 2005). Lumping justice-involved persons with mental illnesses into a single class does not allow for prioritization of scarce resources to those with highest need or who might benefit most. There is a great need for valid, reliable screening and assessment processes that can drive the development of effective, integrated treatment and supervision plans. What follows are recommended services to reduce criminal justice involvement in persons with mental illnesses.

Integrated Mental Health and Substance Use Services

Since the majority of justice-involved persons with mental illnesses will have co-occurring addictive disorders, effective and integrated treatments must be available. The structure of services as well as the treatments themselves can be integrated. There are a number of evidence-based, integrated practices for correctional implementation, though gaps in service delivery remain (Peters et al. 2017). These interventions include integrated dual disorder treatment (IDDT), cognitive-behavioral therapy (CBT), modified therapeutic community (MTC), and the risk-need-responsivity (RNR) model. Integrated treatment for justice-involved persons has been associated with improved criminal justice and mental health outcomes, including reduced criminal activity, substance abuse, arrest, and reincarceration (Osher 2013; see chapters "Integrated Care and Community Psychiatry", and "Social and Political Determinants of Health and Mental Health", for more detailed discussion). Given the high correlation of substance use disorders with crime, they should be the primary target of treatment. It is also associated with significant cost-saving for correctional systems (BEM 2009).

Supportive Housing

High rates of homelessness among justice-involved persons with mental illnesses must be considered in comprehensive treatment planning (Osher and Steadman 2007). Housing needs range from owning their own homes or living in independent rental units to institutional care. Supportive housing can significantly decrease the chance of recidivism as well as time spent in shelters or hospitals and is less costly on a daily basis than time spent in institutions (Salem et al. 2015). Supportive housing includes a variety of residential settings with on-site or easily accessible services, including case management, peer support, medical care, mental health and substance abuse treatment, vocational training, cognitive skills groups, and assistance in obtaining income supports and entitlements. Unfortunately, affordable housing is in short supply in many communities, and persons with criminal records often have trouble accessing public housing assistance (For greater detail, please refer to chapters "Psychiatric Care for People Experiencing Homelessness" concerning homelessness and "Housing First and the Role of Psychiatry in Supported Housing" for a discussion of housing).

Trauma Interventions

Incarceration is closely linked with trauma in myriad ways. Almost all categories of adverse childhood experiences (ACEs) are associated with future incarceration, as well as with later victimization, drug use, and homelessness (Eaves et al. 2020). Evidence also indicates that treatment for those with a history of ACEs may need to be substantially different than for those without such experiences. Rates of physical and sexual abuse in jail and prison populations have been found to be at least twice as high as in the general population (Teplin et al. 1996) and are associated with having a mental illness (Karlsson and Zielinski 2020). Among some inmate populations, such as previously homeless women with co-occurring mental and substance use disorders, histories of violent victimization are extremely high (Anderson et al. 2016). Studies indicate that posttraumatic stress disorder (PTSD) may exist in nearly 50% of inmates, as compared to less than 10% of the general population (Anderson et al. 2016). Moreover, the very experience of incarceration is one of trauma, coercion, injury, invasiveness, violence, and dehumanization (Piper and Berle 2019). In particular, solitary confinement is highly associated with the development of PTSD. Having posttraumatic stress disorder is then associated with negative post-release experiences including self-harm and suicide, additional trauma, homelessness, and reincarceration (Piper and Berle 2019).

Because of the pervasiveness and profound consequences of trauma, criminal justice system programs must integrate sensitivity to trauma into service delivery (Levenson and Willis 2019) (a detailed discussion of trauma-informed care is present in chapter "Traumatic Stress in the Community: Identificationand Intervention"). Training correctional treatment staff in this approach can work towards creating a calmer and safer environment for inmates as well as employees. Both rehabilitative efforts (intended to reduce criminality) and mental health treatment (framed for diagnoses and symptoms) can specifically address trauma. SAMHSA offers training for trauma-informed responses to court personnel, law enforcement, community corrections, and providers (Center 2020a, b). Trauma-focused models that fit the correctional setting focus on the present, use cognitive behavioral approaches, provide education, and emphasize coping skills; one example would be the seeking safety approach (Miller and Najavits 2012). Various models have been shown to reduce violence and recidivism in youth and adolescents, including trauma-focused cognitive-behavioral therapy (TF-CBT), family functional therapy (FFT), and multisystemic therapy (MST), though more research is needed for these and other populations (Zettler 2020).

Supported Employment

Given that some criminal activity is driven by the need for money, successful employment is expected to mitigate contact with the criminal justice system. In fact, many studies have shown that employment of returning citizens is associated with lower chances of recidivism (Bunting et al. 2019). As detailed in chapter "Supported Employment", over the past 30 years, supported employment has become an important tool for improving the well-being of persons with serious mental illness (Drake et al. 2016). Such programs should be modified to accommodate conditions of release, allowing community correctional obligations to exist concurrently with employment responsibilities. A number of successful community reintegration programs include supported employment, but more research is needed on the efficacy of this component in reducing recidivism (Leifman and Coffey 2020). Individual placement and support (IPS) is an employment model that may be particularly effective for justice-involved individuals with serious mental illness, particularly when coupled with dual diagnosis treatment (Bond 2013).

Illness Management and Recovery

Illness management and recovery comprise a group of EBPs that teach skills required to manage a person's own mental illness in collaboration with health care professionals and other supports (see chapter "Health Self-Management: The Emerging Importance of Trauma and Resilience" for details). These EBPs have been demonstrated to promote recovery in functional, personal, and clinical domains (Roosenschoon et al. 2019). There are several illness management and recovery programs, including the Wellness Recovery and Action Plan (WRAP) and Social and Independent Living Skills (SILS).

When these programs have been implemented for persons with mental illnesses and co-occurring disorders within correctional settings, they produce the expected social and coping skill gains (Black et al. 2019). The common application of psychoeducational and cognitive components within illness management and recovery programs makes them well-suited for adaptations that could address criminogenic thinking and antisocial tendencies. Using WRAP with homeless individuals has been shown to reduce recidivism (Listwan et al. 2018), but more evidence is needed.

Case Management and Forensic Assertive Community Treatment

Access to case management services is important for individuals with complex mental health and legal needs. Assertive community treatment (ACT) is a well-validated EBP that combines treatment, rehabilitation, and support services within a multidisciplinary team (Dixon 2000). It is a high-intensity, high-cost package that is typically reserved for the topmost utilizers of acute and emergency mental health services (see chapter "Case Management and Assertive Community Treatment" for a detailed discussion). Particularly when combined with the provision of low-demand housing, it has been associated with less criminal justice involvement (Hirschtritt and Binder 2017).

More recently, ACT services have been augmented by specifically focusing on justice-involved populations and training team members to be responsive to criminal justice partners (Weisman et al. 2004). These forensic ACT teams, also known as *FACT teams*, aim to specifically reduce recidivism, are integrated into the legal system, and include additional forms of supervision; substance use treatment is highly recommended for their success (Kelly et al.

2017). Some studies show FACT involvement to be associated with reduced time spent behind bars, yet to effectively realize such goals, the teams should be part of an overall forensic continuum of care (Cuddeback et al. 2020).

The development of forensic intensive case management (FICM) teams is another effort to coordinate criminal justice and treatment services. FICM focuses on arranging access to services rather than direct provision of care and, without requiring a large team, is less costly to implement (Lee and Cain 2020). The bottom line for many justice-involved persons with mental illness is that any case management team must have a sound understanding of legal issues. With "criminal justice savvy" case management, teams can be expected to reduce recidivism and have been found to have better success than regular ACT teams (Cuddeback et al. 2020).

Cognitive-Behavioral Interventions

Critical to a more complete understanding of these patterns of incarceration are the concepts of *criminogenic risk factors* and *criminogenic needs*. *Criminogenic risk factors* are those associated with criminal conduct and arrest. According to the risk-need-responsivity (RNR) model, the primary risk factors are antisocial personality, substance use, antisocial behavior, family circumstances, low levels of employment and education, antisocial peers, antisocial cognition, and how one spends leisure time (Wilson et al. 2020). While originally describing a more general population, studies have shown that the same factors are associated with criminal recidivism in those with mental illness (Wilson et al. 2020). In our support of and advocacy for persons with mental illness, we cannot overlook the (often times, even higher) levels of criminogenic risk factors present in people with mental illness who are justice-involved (Wilson et al. 2020); to do so would be a missed opportunity for intervention. The intensity of mental health symptoms covaries with higher criminogenic risk (Van Deinse et al. 2021), though shared criminogenic risk factors largely predict recidivism independently of mental illness (Skeem et al. 2014).

The four risk factors that are often portrayed to be the most amenable to improvement are a person's criminal thinking, behavior, personality, and associates (Abracen et al. 2016). Cognitive-based correctional programming tends to target antisocial personality and behavior and focuses more on interpersonal expression than, as typical, on individual distress (Rotter and Carr 2010). Unfortunately, relatively simple approaches for substance use and other risk factors are often neglected. *Criminogenic needs* are individual characteristics associated with risk factors; those associated with criminal personality and behavior include risk-taking, hostility, anger, irritability, and cold-heartedness. While a time-limited correctional program may address anger in a meaningful way, other needs such as emotional callousness might be harder to intervene upon. Furthermore, research has found inmates with serious mental illness to have low levels of employment and education, substance abuse, and maladaptive recreational endeavors, which are usually not addressed by the justice system (Wilson et al. 2020). Unfortunately, incarceration can also increase contact with criminal- minded peers and call for certain behaviors intended to protect oneself, in effect working against a stated goal of criminal rehabilitation.

The more criminogenic needs that are addressed by treatment and supports in general, the bigger the expected impact on recidivism (Latessa and Lowenkamp 2005). Addressing the criminogenic needs of incarcerated or formerly incarcerated people with SMI can be specifically adapted to increase chances of success (Wilson et al. 2018). Given the prevalence of social and neurocognitive difficulties, effective programs will include actively involved staff who frequently repeat and summarize information using concrete language. The format should allow for accessible participation.

Accessible and Appropriate Medication

Psychiatric medication is a critical tool, and for many individuals, treatment is disrupted when they enter and exit the criminal justice system. Having access to appropriate medication at suitable doses, for sufficient lengths of time, is imperative. It is clear that effective psychopharmacology is important for the personal recovery of many people as well as for fulfillment of criminal justice requirements (by being able to function better with a reduced symptom burden) (Skeem et al. 2014).

Research points towards more specific associations, as well. Some findings indicate that mood stabilizers and antipsychotic medications (particularly long-acting injectables) are associated with reduced violent crime (Fazel et al. 2014), and data indicates that medication nonadherence, in concert with substance use, is associated with increased rates of violence in those with SMI (Swartz et al. 1998). Populations with attention-deficit hyperactivity disorder (ADHD) are also less likely to engage in crime when appropriately medicated (Lichtenstein et al. 2012). On the other hand, population-level prescriptions of selective serotonin reuptake inhibitors (SSRIs) or serotonin-norepinephrine reuptake inhibitors (SNRIs) have been recently associated with having no effect on violent crime (Osler et al. 2019) as well as with an increased risk of violent crime in past offenders and youth (Lengvenyte and Vieta 2020).

Conclusion

As for other persons with serious mental illnesses, access to prescribers, funding for medications, supports for adherence, and fluid continuity across systems are challenges for those involved in the criminal justice system. These programs are components of a comprehensive strategy to reduce the overrepresentation of persons with mental illnesses in the justice system. Few communities have all components and none have sufficient capacity, yet inroads are being made. Financing these EBPs relies on a patchwork of block grant funding, public and private insurance, and uncompensated care. Advocacy for investments in these services is essential. At the time of publication of the previous edition of this chapter, the passage of the Patient Protection and Affordable Care and Health Care and Education Reconciliation Acts held promise for this population. Ten years later, however, significantly increased insurance coverage has not been associated with improved access to mental health care for formerly incarcerated patients, reinforcing that there are no simple solutions for addressing the complex needs of this population (Howell et al. 2019).

Community psychiatrists are working, and will continue to work, with persons who have criminal justice histories. They should develop familiarity with the system and how it intersects with their patient's lives and future trajectories. Recovery-oriented practices are as germane to justice-involved persons as any. Community psychiatrists must understand the literature and work with their patients towards a vision of what is likely to work, for whom, and under what circumstances. Gaining this expertise can be achieved through formal training (such as a forensic and/or community psychiatry fellowship program) as well as through other routine methods of lifelong learning. If we are to avoid being a society where punishment inappropriately substitutes for care, a shared commitment to our patients' dignity and our communities' safety is of paramount importance.

References

(2002) *Criminal Justice/Mental Health Consensus Project Report*. New York, NY, Council of State Governments Justice Center.

(2008) *One in 100: Behind bars in America 2008*. Washington, DC, Pew Center on the States.

(2020) *State Expenditure Report* (Fiscal 2018-2020 Data). Washington, DC, National Association of State Budget Officers.

Abracen, J., Gallo, A., Looman, J. & , Goodwill, A. (2016). Individual community-based treatment of offenders with mental illness: Relationship to recidivism. *Journal of Interpersonal Violence,* 31(10), 1842–1858.

Allison, S., Bastiampillai, T., & Fuller, D. A. (2017). Mass incarceration and severe mental illness in the USA. *The Lancet*, 390(10089), 25.

Anderson, R. E., Geier, T. J., & Cahil, S. P. (2016). Epidemiological associations between posttraumatic stress disorder and incarceration in the National Survey of American Life. *Criminal Behaviour and Mental Health,* 26(2), 110–123.

Anestis, J. C., & Carbonell, J.L. (2014). Stopping the revolving door: Effectiveness of mental health court in reducing recidivism by mentally ill offenders. *Psychiatric Services,* 65(9), 1105–1112.

Barboriak, P.N. (2017). The history of correctional psychiatry in the United States. *Principles and Practice of Forensic Psychiatry, 3rd edition*. Edited by Rosner R, Scott CL, New York, CRC Press. 511–520.

BEM, M. D. F. (2009*). Providing chemical dependency treatment to low-income adults results in significant public safety benefits*, Olympia (WA), Washington State Department of Social and Health Services.

Binswanger, I. A., Stern, M. F., Deyo, R. A., Heagerty, P. J., Cheadle, A., Elmore, J. G. & , Koepsell, T.D. (2007). Release from prison--a high risk of death for former inmates. *N Engl J Med,* 356(2), 157–165.

Black, A et al. (2019). *The treatment of people with mental illness in the criminal justice system: The example of Oneida County*, New York, Clinton, NY, Levitt Center for Public Affairs, Hamilton College. https://digitalcommons.hamilton.edu/student_scholarship/6/.

Bond, G.R. (2013). *Supported employment for justice-involved people with mental illness.* SAHSA GAINS Center for Behavioral Health and Justice Transformation. http://gainscenter.samhsa.gov.

Bunting, A.M., Staton, M., Winston, E., & Pangburn, K. (2019). Beyond the employment dichotomy: An examination of recidivism and days remaining in the community by post-release employment status. *International Journal of Offender Therapy and Comparative Criminology,*. 63(5), 12–733.

Care, N. (2008). *Standards for Mental Health Services in Correctional Facilities.* National Commission on Correctional Health Care.

Center, S. (2020a). Training Opportunities. Retrieved 12/20/2020, from https://www.samhsa.gov/gains-center/trauma-training-criminal-justice-professionals/training-opportunities.

Center, S. (2020b). Trauma Training for Criminal Justice Professionals. Retrieved 12/20/2020, from https://www.samhsa.gov/gains-center/trauma-training-criminal-justice-professionals.

Cohen, F. (2008). *The Mentally Disordered Inmate and the Law: Cumulative Supplement.* Kingston, NJ, Civic Research Institute, Inc.

Cuddeback, G. S., Simpson, J.M., & Wu, J. C. (2020). A comprehensive literature review of Forensic Assertive Community Treatment (FACT): Directions for practice, policy and research. *International Journal of Mental Health,* 49, 106–127.

Deutsch, A. (1937). *Mental Illness in America: A History of Their Care and Treatment from Colonial Times.* New York, Columbia University Press.

Dixon, L. (2000). Assertive community treatment: Twenty-five years of gold. *Psychiatric Service,* 51(6), 759–765.

Draine, J., A. Blank Wilson, S. Metraux, T. Hadley & A. C. Evans (2010). The impact of mental illness status on the length of jail detention and the legal mechanism of jail release. *Psychiatric Services*, 61(5), 458–462.

Drake, R. E., Bond, G. R., Goldman, H. H., Hogan, M. F., & Karakus, K. M. (2016). Individual placement and support services boost employment for people with serious mental illnesses, but funding is lacking. *Health Affairs,* 35(6), 1098–1105.

Dvoskin, J. A., Spiers, E. M., Metzner, J. L., & Pitt, SE. (2003). The structure of correctional mental health services. In *Principles and Practice of Forensic Psychiatry, 2Ed.* Boca Raton, FL, CRC Press, 511–526.

Eaves, E. R., Camplain, R.L., Lininge, M.R., & Trotter II, R. T. (2020). Adverse childhood experiences in relation to drug and alcohol use in 30 days prior to incarceration in a county jail. *International Journal of Prisoner Health,* 17, 142–155.

Eno Louden, J., Manchak, S. M., Ricks, E. P., & Kennealy, P. K. (2018). The role of stigma toward mental illness in probation officers' perceptions of risk and case management decisions. *Criminal Justice and Behavior,* 45(5), 573–588.

Fazel, S., Zetterqvist, J., Larsson, H., Långström, N., & Lichtenstein, P. (2014). Antipsychotics, mood stabilisers, and risk of violent crime. *The Lancet*, 384(9949), 1206–1214.

Glaze, L. E. & Bonczar, T. P. (2010). *Probation and parole in the United States, 2006.* Washington, DC, Bureau of Justice Statistics.

Greenberg, G. A. & Rosenheck, R. A. (2008). Jail incarceration, homelessness, and mental health: A national study. *Psychiatric services*, 59(2), 170–177.

Heiss, C., Somers, S. A., & Larson, M. (2016). *Coordinating Access to Services for Justice-Involved Populations*. Center for Health Care Strategies. New York, Milbank Memorial Fund. 1–21.

Hills, H., Sigfried, C., & Ickowitz, A. (2004). *Effective prison mental health services: Guidelines to expand and improve treatment.* Washington, DC, US Department of Justice, National Institute of Corrections.

Hirschtritt, M. E., & Binder, R. L. (2017). Interrupting the mental illness–incarceration-recidivism cycle. *Jama,* 317(7), 695–696.

Houser, K. A., & Welsh, W. (2014). Examining the association between co-occurring disorders and seriousness of misconduct by female prison inmates. *Criminal Justice and Behavior,* 41(5), 650–666.

Howell, B. A., Wang, E. A., & Winkelman, T. N. (2019). Mental health treatment among individuals involved in the criminal justice system after implementation of the Affordable Care Act. *Psychiatric Services,* 70(9), 765–771.

Iglehart, J. K. (2016). Decriminalizing mental illness—the Miami model. *New England Journal of Medicine*, 374(18), 1701–1703.

James, D. J. and L. E. Glaze (2006). *Mental health problems of prison and jail inmates*. US Department of Justice/Office of Justice Programs. Washington, DC, Bureau of Statistics.

JLI (Judges' Criminal Justice/Mental Health Leadership Initiative). (2010). *Judges' guide to mental health diversion: A reference for justice system practitioners*. Delmar, NY, Policy Research Associates, CMHS National GAINS Center.

Kaeble, D., Glaze, L., Tsoutis, A., & Minton, T. (2016). *Correctional populations in the United States, 2014*. Washington, DC, Bureau of Justice Statistics, 1–19.

Kaeble, D. and M. Cowhig (2018). *Correctional Populations in the United States, 2016*. Washington, DC, Bureau of Justice Statistics, 1–13.

Karlsson, M. E., & Zielinski, M. J. (2020). Sexual victimization and mental illness prevalence rates among incarcerated women: A literature review. *Trauma, Violence, & Abuse*, 21(2), 326–349.

Kelly, B. L., Barrenger, S. L., Watson, A. C., & Angell, B. (2017). Forensic assertive community treatment: Recidivism, hospitalization, and the role of housing and support. *Social Work in Mental Health*, 15(5), 567–587.

Kessler, R. C. (2004). The epidemiology of dual diagnosis. *Biological Psychiatry*, 56(10), 730–737.

Lamb, H. R., & Weinberger, L.E. (2017). Understanding and treating offenders with serious mental illness in public sector mental health. *Behavioral Sciences & the Law*, 35(4), 303–318.

Lamberti, J. S. (2016). Preventing criminal recidivism through mental health and criminal justice collaboration. *Psychiatric Services*, 67(11), 1206–1212.

Latessa, E. J., & Lowenkamp, J. (2005). What are criminogenic needs and why are they important. *For the Record*, 4, 15–16.

Lee, L. H., & Cain, D. S. (2020). Mental Health Policy for Justice-Involved Persons: Exploring History, Perspectives, and Models in the United States. *Best Practices in Mental Health*, 16(2), 55–68.

Leifman, S., & Coffey, T. (2020). Jail diversion: the Miami model. In *Decriminalizing Mental Illness*, K. Warburton and S. Stahl (eds), Cambridge, UK, Cambridge University Press, 97–105.

Lengvenyte, A., & Vieta, E. (2020). Association between selective serotonin reuptake inhibitors and violent crime - could underlying psychopathology be the cause? *Eur Neuropsychopharmacol* 36, 151–153.

Levenson, J. S., & Willis, G. M. (2019). Implementing trauma-informed care in correctional treatment and supervision. *Journal of Aggression, Maltreatment & Trauma*, 28(4), 481–501.

Lichtenstein, P., Halldner, L., Zetterqvist, J., Sjölander,A., Serlachius, E., Fazel, S., Långström, N., & Larsson, H. (2012). Medication for attention deficit–hyperactivity disorder and criminality. *New England Journal of Medicine*, 367(21), 2006–2014.

Listwan, S. J., Hartman, J. L., & LaCourse, A. (2018). Impact of the MeckFUSE Pilot Project: Recidivism among the chronically homeless. *Justice Evaluation Journal*, 1(1), 96–108.

Loong, D., Bonato,S., Barnsley, J., & Dewa, C. S. (2019). The effectiveness of mental health courts in reducing recidivism and police contact: a systematic review. *Community Mental Health Journal*, 55(7), 1073–1098.

Massoglia, M., & Remster, B. (2019). Linkages between incarceration and health. *Public Health Reports*, 134(1_suppl), 8S–14S.

Matejkowski, J., & Ostermann, M. (2020). The Waiving of Parole Consideration by Inmates With Mental Illness and Recidivism Outcomes. *Criminal Justice and Behavior*, 48 (8), 1052–1071.

Mauer, M., & King, R. K. (2007). *25-Year Quagmire: The "War On Drugs" and Its Impact on American Society*, Washington, DC, Sentencing Project.

Meredith, T., Hawk, S. R., Johnson, S., Prevost, J. P., & Braucht, G. (2020). What Happens in Home Visits? Examining a Key Parole Activity. *Criminal Justice and Behavior* 47(5), 601–623.

Miles, H., Johnson, S., Amponsah-Afuwape, S., Finch, E., Leese, M., & Thornicroft, G. (2003). Characteristics of subgroups of individuals with psychotic illness and a comorbid substance use disorder. *Psychiatric Services*, 54(4), 554–561.

Miller, N. A., & Najavits, L. M. (2012). Creating trauma-informed correctional care: A balance of goals and environment. *European Journal of Psychotraumatology*, 3(1), 17246, https://doi.org/10.3402/ejpt.v3i0.17246.

Munetz, M. R., & P. A. Griffin (2006). Use of the sequential intercept model as an approach to decriminalization of people with serious mental illness. *Psychiatric Services*, 57(4), 544–549.

Osher, F., Steadman, H. J., & Barr, H. (2003). A best practice approach to community reentry from jails for inmates with co-occurring disorders: The APIC model. *Crime & Delinquency*, 49(1), 79–96.

Osher, F. C. (2013). *Integrating mental health and substance abuse services for justice-involved persons with co-occurring disorders*. Delmar, NY: SAMHSA's GAINS Center for Behavioral Health and Justice Transformation.

Osher, F. C., & Steadman, H. J. (2007). Adapting evidence-based practices for persons with mental illness involved with the criminal justice system. *Psychiatric Services* 58(11), 1472–1478.

Osler, M., Wium-Andersen, M. K., Wium-Andersen, I. K., Gronemann, F. S., Jørgensen, M. B., & Rozing, M. P. (2019). Incidence of suicidal behaviour and violent crime following antidepressant medication: a Danish cohort study. *Acta Psychiatrica Scandinavica*, 140(6), 522–531.

Peters, R. H., Wexler, H. K., & Lurigio, A. J. (2015). Co-occurring substance use and mental disorders in the criminal justice system: A new frontier of clinical practice and research. *Psychiatric Rehabilitation Journal*, 38(1), 1–6.

Peters, R. H., Young, M. S., Rojas, E. C., & Gorey, C. M. (2017). Evidence-based treatment and supervision practices for co-occurring mental and substance use disorders in the criminal justice system. *The American Journal of Drug and Alcohol Abuse,* 43(4), 475–488.

Pinals, D. A. (2017). Jail diversion, specialty court, and reentry services: Partnerships between behavioral health and justice systems. Principles and Practice of Forensic Psychiatry, 3rd edition. Edited by Rosner R., Scott C. L., New York, CRC Press, 237–246.

Piper, A., Berle, D. (2019). The association between trauma experienced during incarceration and PTSD outcomes:A systematic review and meta-analysis. *J Forensic Psychiatry & Psychology,* 30(5), 854–875.

Pratt, S. I., Mueser, K. T., Driscoll, M. R., et al. (2006). Medication nonadherence in older people with serious mental illness: Prevalence and correlates. *Psychiatric Rehab J* 29(4), 299–310.

Prins, S. J., & Draper, L (2009). *Improving Outcomes For People with Mental Illness Under Community Corrections Supervision: A Guide to Research-Informed Policy and Practice*. New York City, NY, Council of State Governments Justice Center.

Rich, J. D., Wakeman, S. E., Dickman, S. L. (2011). Medicine and the epidemic of incarceration in the United States. *NEJM*, 364(22), 2081–2083.

Roosenschoon, B. J., Kamperman, A. M., Deen, M. L., van Weeeghel, J., et al. (2019). Determinants of clinical, functional and personal recovery for people with schizophrenia and other severe mental illnesses: A cross-sectional analysis. *PloS One* 14(9), e0222378.

Rotter, M., & Carr, C. (2010). *Targeting criminal recidivism in justice-involved people with mental illness: structured clinical approaches.* Rockville, Md, Substance Abuse and Mental Health Services Administration, GAINS Center for Behavioral Health and Justice Transformation.

Rozel, J.S., & Mulvey, E. P. (2017). The link between mental illness and firearm violence: implications for social policy and clinical practice. *Ann Rev Clin Psychol,* 13, 445–469.

Salem, L., Crocker, A. G., Charette, Y., et al. (2015). Supportive housing and forensic patient outcomes. *Law Hum Behav*, 39(3), 311–320.

Substance Abuse and Mental Health Services Administration (2021). The Sequential Intercept Model. Available at https://www.samhsa.gov/criminal-juvenile-justice/sim-overview. Accessed 20 March, 2022.

Sindicich, N., Mills, K. L., Barrett, E. L., et al. (2014). Offenders as victims: Post-traumatic stress disorder and substance use disorder among male prisoners. *J Forensic Psychiatry & Psychology,* 25(1), 44–60.

Skeem, J. L., & Louden, J. E. (2006). Toward evidence-based practice for probationers and parolees mandated to mental health treatment. *Psy Services,* 57(3), 333–342.

Skeem, J. L., Manchak, S., Peterson, J. K. (2011). Correctional policy for offenders with mental illness: Creating a new paradigm for recidivism reduction. *Law Hum Behav* 35(2), 110–126.

Skeem, J. L., Winter, E., Kennealy, P. J., et al. (2014). Offenders with mental illness have criminogenic needs, too: Toward recidivism reduction. *Law Hum Behav*, 38(3), 212–224.

Sowers, W. E., & Rohland, B. (2004). American Association of Community Psychiatrists' principles for managing transitions in behavioral health services. *Psy Services*, 55(11), 1271–1275.

Steadman, H. J., Osher, F. C., Robbins, P. C., et al. (2009). Prevalence of serious mental illness among jail inmates. *Psy Services*, 60(6), 761–765.

Stephan, J. J. (2001). *Census of Jails, 1999.* Washington, D. C., Bureau of Justice Statistics.

Stuart, H. (2003). Violence and mental illness: An overview. *World Psychiatry,* 2(2), 121–124

Swanson, J. W., Frisman, L. K., Robertson, A. G., et al. (2013). Costs of criminal justice involvement among persons with serious mental illness in Connecticut. *Psy Services*, 64(7), 630–637.

Swanson, J. W., McGinty, E.E., Fazel, S., Mays, V. M. (2015). Mental illness and reduction of gun violence and suicide: Bringing epidemiologic research to policy. *Ann Epidemiology*, 25(5), 366–376.

Swartz, M. S., Swanson, J. W., Hiday, V. A., et al. (1998). Violence and severe mental illness: the effects of substance abuse and nonadherence to medication. *Am J Psychiatry,* 155(2), 226–231.

Teplin, L. A., Abram, K. M., McClelland, G. M. (1996). Prevalence of psychiatric disorders among incarcerated women: I. Pretrial jail detainees. *Arch Gen Psychiatry*, 53(6), 505–512.

Teplin, L. A., McClelland, G. M., Abram, K. M., Weiner, D.A. (2005). Crime victimization in adults with severe mental illness: Comparison with the National Crime Victimization Survey. *Arch Gen Psychiatry,* 62(8), 911–921.

Theriot, M. T., & Segal, S. P. (2005). Involvement with the criminal justice system among new clients at outpatient mental health agencies. *Psy Services,* 56(2), 179–185.

Van Deinse, T. B., Cuddeback, G. S., Wilson, A. B., Eswards, D., Jr., et al. (2021). Variation in criminogenic risks by mental health symptom severity: Implications for mental health services and research. *Psychiatric Q*, 92(1), 73–84.

Ventura, L. A., Cassel, C. A., Jacoby, J. E., Huang, B. (1998). Case management and recidivism of mentally ill persons released from jail. *Psy Services,* 49(10), 1330–1337.

Watson, A. C., Morabito, M. S., Draine, J., Ottati, V. (2008). Improving police response to persons with mental illness: A multi-level conceptualization of CIT. *Int J Law Psychiatry*, 31(4), 359–368.

Weinstein, H. C., Burns, K. A., Newkirk, C. S., Zil, J. S., Dvorkin, J. A., Steadman, H. J. (2000). *Psychiatric Services in Jails and Prisons: A Task Force Report of the American Psychiatric*

Association, 2nd Edition. Arlington, VA, American Psychiatric Publishing, Inc.

Weisman, R. L., Lamberti, J., Price, N. (2004). Integrating criminal justice, community healthcare, and support services for adults with severe mental disorders. *Psy Quarterly*, 75(1), 71–85.

White, M. D., Mellow, J., Englander, K., Ruffinengo, M. (2011). Halfway back: An alternative to revocation for technical parole violators. *Crim Justice Policy Rev*, 22(2), 140–166.

Wilper, A. P., Woolhandler, S., Boyd, J. W., et al. (2009). The health and health care of US prisoners: Results of a nationwide survey. *Am J Public Health*, 99(4), 666–672.

Wilson, A. B., Farkas, K., Bonfine, N., Duda-Banwar, J. (2018). Interventions that target criminogenic needs for justice-involved persons with serious mental illnesses: A targeted service delivery approach. *Internatl J Offender Therapy Compar Criminol*, 62(7), 1838–1853.

Wilson, A. B., Ishler, K. J., Morgan, R., et al. (2020). Examining criminogenic risk levels among people with mental illness incarcerated in U.S. jails and prisons. *J Behav Hlth Services & Resch*, 1–16 (online). https://doi.org/10.1007/s11414-020-09737-x

Wolff, N. (2005). Community reintegration of prisoners with mental illness: a social investment perspective. *Internatl J Law Psychiatry*, 28(1), 43–58.

Zettler, H. R. (2020). Much to do about trauma: a systematic review of existing trauma-informed treatments on youth violence and recidivism. *Youth Violence Juv Justice*, 19(1), 113–134.

Zgoba, K. M., Reeves, R., Tamburello, A., Debilio, L. (2020). Criminal recidivism in Inmates with mental illness and substance use disorders. *J Am Acad Psychiatry Law*, 48(2), 209–215.

Part VI

Supportive Services for Community Living

Housing First and the Role of Psychiatry in Supported Housing

Van Yu

Introduction

Permanent Supportive Housing provides housing assistance and support services to people living with disabilities including serious mental illness and substance use disorders. The 1987 McKinney-Vento Act, the first-ever federal legislation addressing homelessness and mental illness, established funding within the Federal Department of Housing and Urban Development (HUD) for the development of Permanent Supportive Housing for people who are "chronically homeless." The HUD definition of chronic homelessness is:

> A homeless individual or head of household with a disability that meets the HUD definition of a disability who (a) lives in a place not meant for human habitation, a safe haven, or in an emergency shelter; AND (b) has been homeless and living in one of these places continuously for at least 12 months OR on at least 4 separate occasions in the last 3 years, as long as the combined occasions equal at least 12 months…. (Department of Housing and Urban Development 2015, 80 FR 75791)

"Supported Housing" is an evidence-based practice that is a form of Permanent Supportive Housing based on a "Housing First" philosophy. Other forms of Permanent Supportive Housing serve as part of a continuum model of housing to be described below. Housing development based on a Housing First philosophy has been the predominant strategy for moving people who are homeless and living with serious mental illness out of chronic homelessness for the past three decades. Since serious mental illness and substance use disorders are qualifying "disabilities" for admission into Permanent Supportive Housing, mental health care is one of the support services offered in many Supported Housing programs.

The aim of Supported Housing is not only to provide housing, but also to help integrate people into the community as much as possible. Homes are lease-based with the consumer as the leaseholder. Tenancy is contingent on paying rent and abiding by the same tenancy rules governing other renters in the community. Accessing services and participating in treatment are voluntary. Other models of housing for people living with serious mental illness are more structured with programs instead of tenants owning or leasing units and with service and treatment being mandatory. Since the development of the first Supported Housing programs in the 1980s, several studies have demonstrated that the model is both effective at housing retention and also cost-effective (Rog 2004; Rosenheck et al. 2003). Mental health care is a crucial support service that helps many tenants of Supported Housing both to remain stably housed and to be able to work towards recovery. The delivery of mental

V. Yu (✉)
Center for Urban Community Services, New York, NY, USA
e-mail: van.yu@janianmed.org

W. E. Sowers et al. (eds.), *Textbook of Community Psychiatry*,
https://doi.org/10.1007/978-3-031-10239-4_35

health care in Supported Housing deviates in some ways from care in more traditional brick-and-mortar clinics with advantages and disadvantages described below.

The Need for a New Model of Housing

A significant proportion of single adults who are homeless are living with serious mental illness or substance use disorder or both with estimates ranging from 1/5 to 2/3 (Fazel et al. 2008; Koegel et al. 1988; Roberts 1992; Susser et al. 1993), and serious mental illness is both a cause of homelessness and a factor that causes people to remain homeless (Shelton et al. 2009; Susser et al. 1993).

For the first half of the twentieth century, people living with serious mental illness lived in institutional settings, mainly state hospitals, often involuntarily. In the 1950s and 1960s, two dynamics coincided to trigger a process referred to as "deinstitutionalization" that led to a drastic reduction of this infrastructure. First, the civil rights and antipsychiatry movements spawned a concern about the legitimacy of involuntary institutionalization, especially in the face of some well-publicized abuses at state hospitals (Grob 1980). Second, major changes in the health care economy, including the creation of Medicaid and Medicare, encouraged states to shift some of the cost of care to the federal government (Yohanna 2013). As a result, tens of thousands of people living in institutions were discharged to live independently with family or in "community residences" and were to be served by a community mental health system (Yohanna 2013). Early models of community residences included halfway houses and family foster care but no organized model for residential services for formerly institutionalized people beyond these limited options developed in the first years of deinstitutionalization (Ridgway and Zipple 1990). Over time, community residences became the first step in a "continuum" model which was developed to move people in stepwise fashion from more to less structured and restrictive settings towards the goal of becoming "housing-ready." A person is proved housing-ready by demonstrating insight into their mental illness, compliance with behavioral health treatment, and abstinence from drugs and alcohol.

Operating a residential system based on a continuum model, however, required resources that were never adequate to the need and set a high bar for people to move into less expensive independent housing (Ridgway and Zipple 1990). Moreover, the 1970s and 1980s saw a rise of single, adult homelessness, especially in cities, among people living with serious mental illness with inadequate care or no care at all (Bassuk and Lamb 1986; Cooper and O'Hara 2002; Kushel et al. 2001). Furthermore, people of color have been disproportionately affected by these forces resulting in their overrepresentation among people who are homeless (Fusaro et al. 2018; Uehara 1994). This increase of homelessness in the 1970s and 1980s put pressure on the system to create a different kind of housing.

Coinciding with this increase in homelessness, the mental health community was developing recovery-oriented models of psychiatric care encompassing concepts of consumer choice, harm reduction, and strengths focusing. Out of this confluence rose a "Housing First" philosophy of targeting homelessness. Housing First turned the continuum philosophy on its head proposing that having a home makes it possible for a person to effectively address their mental health conditions which in turn will help a person be successful in housing. The development of Supported Housing, with its emphasis on client choice and community integration, is a logical outcome of this Housing First philosophy and a recovery orientation in general. The prototype of Housing First was a program developed in the 1990s called Pathways to Housing in New York City which placed people in scatter-site apartments with support services delivered by Assertive Community Treatment (ACT) teams (Tsemberis and Eisenberg 2000). Initially there was concern that Supported Housing would not be able to provide adequate support to people who are homeless and living with serious mental illness (Siegel et al. 2006), but numerous studies have since shown Supported Housing programs to be both effective at providing housing and services and cost-effective (Lipton et al. 2000; Padgett et al. 2016; Rog et al. 2014; Rosenheck et al. 2003; Tsemberis and Eisenberg 2000).

The 1999 Olmstead decision further hastened the expansion of Supported Housing. In 1995, two women living with serious mental illness sued the state of Georgia (Tommy Olmstead was the Commissioner of the State Department of Human Resources) because the women were confined in institutional settings even after being assessed to be better-suited for services in the community. The case made it to the United States Supreme Court which ruled that under the Americans with Disabilities Act, people living with serious mental illness should be cared for in the least restrictive setting possible (Olmstead v L.C. 527 U.S. 581). In the aftermath of Olmstead, jurisdictions have been increasingly looking to Supported Housing to be a "least restrictive setting" for providing housing and care to people who are chronically homeless (Whitley and Henwood 2014).

This chapter focuses on single adults who are homeless. Family homelessness is more often the result of socioeconomic factors like underemployment and domestic violence. Although originally and predominately a practice targeting single, adult homelessness, Supported Housing has been increasingly utilized for families. In 1993, HUD began funding Supportive Housing for families with an adult member living with a disability, and since 2003 HUD funding for families has also been limited to people who meet the chronic homelessness criteria (Gewirtz 2007). Although not yet as widely studied as single-adult Supported Housing, family Supportive Housing does seem to improve housing stability and even reduce emergency department usage among families with an adult living with a disability (Lim et al. 2018).

Permanent Supportive Housing programs are funded in a variety of different ways with some funding coming directly through government contracts and other monies coming from tenant resources. Several different government entities fund housing programs and many programs cobble together contracts from different sources. For example, in New York City, government funders of Permanent Supportive Housing include the federal Department of Housing and Urban Development, the state Office of Mental Health, the city Departments of Health and Mental Hygiene, Housing Preservation and Development, and Homeless Services, and the city HIV AIDS Services Administration. Tenants contribute by paying rent, and there are various ways tenants are supported in making rent including by using Section 8 vouchers or a portion of Supplemental Security Income (SSI) or Public Assistance.

Two Approaches to Supported Housing

Although most Americans who are living with serious mental illness are *not* homeless, an American who has experienced homelessness and is living with serious mental illness often requires housing support, income support, and specialized physical and behavioral health care to remain housed and integrated into the community. As a Housing First model, Supported Housing presumes not only that housing ought to precede other services and interventions, but furthermore that rapidly housing a person in a system where tenancy is not contingent on service participation is a necessary first step towards community integration, psychiatric recovery, and improved physical health. Studies have demonstrated that housing itself is treatment as multiple clinical conditions tend to improve after people are housed even if there is not an accompanying increase in health care utilization (Henwood et al. 2013).

Various features common to all Supported Housing models reinforce housing as foremost above other care and services. Tenancy is contingent on the same laws that apply to any landlord and tenant in the community. There are no curfews. There are few if any limitations on visitors including overnight visitors. Social services, psychiatric care, and sometimes medical care are offered, but there is no obligation to access these services. To support this, having different agencies manage tenancy issues (e.g., rent collection, building maintenance) and service provision is a common arrangement—the landlord works for a different agency than the social worker.

With all of these features in common, two models of Supported Housing have emerged—scatter-site and congregate (also called single-site or project-based). In scatter-site Supported Housing, a tenant rents an apartment in the community and is offered support services including services that can be offered at home or at an off-site location. In congregate Supported Housing, some portion of apartments in a single building is set aside for consumers, and service providers are often based in the same building. Such buildings typically include units of affordable housing interspersed with apartments for people who are living with an identified disability. There are advantages and disadvantages to each model.

The scatter-site model greatly resembles "normal" housing and offers people more choice. Living in ordinary housing can be a substantial first step towards community integration and sidesteps some sources of stigma. People have more freedom to control their environment and develop their social network, although some report struggling with isolation (Parsell et al. 2015). Start-up and operating costs are lower compared to congregate models as apartments that already exist are utilized instead of needing to manage, or even build, whole buildings. However, scatter-site programs are more vulnerable to the vagaries of the local housing market including fluctuations in supply and rent. An advantage of scatter-site housing for families is the opportunity to locate based on school district (Collins et al. 2016).

The congregate model is more "institutional" and can limit choice, feel restrictive, and contribute to stigmatization (Parsell et al. 2015). Moreover, start-up is expensive and complicated, generally involving building renovation or construction and a cobbling together of multiple funding sources. On the other hand, services are more accessible and easier to provide. On-site project staff can offer social services and psychiatric and medical care to people who might struggle to access these supports independently. A congregate setting allows opportunities for mutual support and community building among tenants living with similar challenges (Dickenson-Gomez et al. 2017; Parsell et al. 2015). Ongoing costs, including rents, can be easier to control. In addition, there can be benefits to the surrounding community. Buildings in disrepair are renovated or empty lots are developed. Programs provide low-income units to the community at large and services to the tenants of those units. The properties sometimes provide storefronts or greens-paces. Program staff patronizes local businesses.

Practicing Psychiatry in Supported Housing

As indicated earlier, many single adults who are homeless or formerly homeless suffer from serious mental illness while at the same time facing many barriers to access effective psychiatric care. Furthermore, serious mental illness often impairs a person's ability to seek and maintain housing. Because of this, many programs serving people who are homeless or formerly homeless place psychiatrists in the field to improve access to care—in drop-in centers, shelters, food pantries, housing programs, and even the streets. As described below, psychiatrists in these settings engage in a lot of activity that is not billable to health insurers, and billable patient encounters do not generate enough revenue to support on-site psychiatry. So, on-site psychiatry practice at programs that serve people with lived experience of homelessness is typically directly funded through the contracts that fund other support services at these programs.

Practicing psychiatry in the field is different from practicing in more traditional clinical settings and there are advantages and disadvantages to practicing in these settings.

Role and Activities of an On-Site Psychiatrist in Supported Housing

A psychiatrist serving a Supported Housing program has a more varied role compared to a psychiatrist at a clinic or other more traditional treatment setting. A Supported Housing psychiatrist is not only a provider of evaluation and treatment, but can also provide outreach, training, consultation, and technical assistance to help a program's clinical operations. Understanding the different scope of this role ideally enables a Supported Housing psychiatrist to determine how best to harness their expertise to not only deliver state-of-the-art psychiatric evaluation and treatment to this underserved population, but also to influence the processes and culture of program sites.

Outreach and Engagement

People with lived experience of homelessness are often unable or unwilling to access traditional psychiatric services. For example, some people who are formerly homeless, although often eligible for Medicaid or Medicare, still face obstacles to obtaining medical insurance and therefore have no way to pay for psychiatric treatment. Also, many people with lived experience of homelessness are apprehensive about or frankly suspicious of psychiatrists and therefore actively avoid contact with traditional treatment settings. Many people experience offers of services as condescending and believe services available to them to be of low quality (Hopper et al. 1997) or are frankly mistrustful of outreach workers (Kryda and Comptom 2009). Overcrowding at clinics and having to change psychiatrists annually at many clinics also deters people from community mental health clinics. Experience has shown that many people with lived experience of homelessness, however, are more open to contact with a psychiatrist in familiar settings.

Outreach to people with lived experience of homelessness requires a psychiatrist to have a flexible clinical approach and to be able to address people's low expectations about the quality of services offered to them. There is a famous story of a psychiatrist running a bingo game at a shelter that exemplifies the kind of activity a psychiatrist may engage in to build trust among a community of tenants in Supported Housing. Supported Housing tenants who are unwilling to travel to see the psychiatrist, even in congregate programs where the psychiatrist sees patients in the building, may be more receptive to being visited in their apartment. People value their autonomy and so outreach and engagement approaches that respect a person's "expertise concerning his/her situation" have been shown to increase trust of service providers (Piat et al. 2020). People want to be offered services that are professional, expert, and respectful. When people believe this is the case and even begin to expect it, effective working relationships form.

Evaluation

There are significant advantages to performing psychiatric evaluations in Supported Housing settings. Housing staff know tenants very well and are a rich source of information. Interacting in a familiar setting often helps people be more forthcoming with a psychiatrist. Even if a person refuses to meet with a psychiatrist, a fairly comprehensive evaluation is possible based on staff knowledge and psychiatrist observation.

When evaluating a person with lived experience of homelessness, attention to social history can be an invaluable source of insight. Investigating the circumstances that resulted in and maintained a person's homelessness often provides clues about a person's psychiatric condition. For example, a person who denies having paranoid ideas will sometimes speak in great detail about an elaborate conspiracy that led to eviction. Homelessness and unemployment can be conceptualized as symptoms like depression or psychosis that may provide clues to psychiatric conditions. For example, a person who does not complain about depression may reveal periods of anergia and amotivation leading to unemployment. People with lived experience of homelessness also frequently have histories of trauma, education difficulties, and legal troubles that may be clues to psychiatric illness.

Treatment

There are advantages and challenges to providing psychiatric care in Supported Housing. Supported Housing programs offer more support of psychiatric treatment than a home without supports, but less than a hospital. A psychiatrist who is flexible about the frame of treatment can mitigate the challenges and take advantage of opportunities that are unique to this setting.

In clinics and hospitals, the psychiatrist has a lot of influence or leverage. Most patients either have demonstrated a motivation for treatment by virtue of coming to the office or are involuntarily engaged in treatment. In Supported Housing, on the other hand, where participating in services including psychiatric treatment is voluntary, the psychiatrist must rely more on their ability to convince a person to participate in treatment. This challenge naturally lends itself to a more "person-centered" approach to practice which conceptualizes a patient as a more active consumer of services rather than a passive recipient of treatment. A person-centered approach assumes that people are more likely to participate in, and benefit from, the opportunity to be a partner in care.

Even though most Supported Housing tenants take their own medication, many programs offer medication monitoring to help tenants take medications as prescribed when needed. This has the added benefit of tracking medication usage. Housing staff, however, are generally social service professionals with no training in handling medication, so some programs hire nurses to administer medications.

Most Supported Housing programs do not have blood-drawing capability and many people will refuse to go for blood tests in the community. So prescribing medications requiring blood monitoring is challenging.

Many people may be willing to engage in some kind of treatment but are unwilling to take medication or are only willing to take doses of medication that may be inadequate for therapeutic effect. Because of this, psychotherapy becomes a primary treatment more frequently and for more indications than in other, more traditional settings.

Treatment of psychiatric symptoms is often not a primary concern of Supported Housing tenants. Many people, understandably, identify poverty or unemployment, not psychiatric illness, as their primary problem and attribute this to primarily social, economic, and even political circumstances. Because of this, the extent to which a psychiatrist can convince a person that psychiatric treatment can help a person move towards income and employment often determines how much treatment a person is willing to accept.

Consultation

In addition to having expertise in treating mental illness, psychiatrists also ideally have some expertise in advising social service staff how to effectively work with Supported Housing tenants—psychiatrists are not only treaters of individual "patients" but also are behavioral consultants and system analysts. Thus, a social service team may have difficulty working with a tenant because of some systemic practice that exacerbates that tenant's symptoms. The psychiatrist, not only by virtue of being a behavioral expert, but also by being able to consider a situation from a somewhat outside, objective perspective, may be able to offer valuable insight and advice. For example, a case management team might have difficulty engaging people with schizophrenia because of rigidity about keeping appointments. The psychiatrist might identify this and offer possible ways for the team to be more flexible about scheduling.

Individual case managers also frequently consult with psychiatrists about engagement with individual tenants. These "curbside" consults can be opportunities for the Supported Housing psychiatrist to learn more about the program and its tenants, to contribute to the overall care of tenants, and to provide education.

Liaison

The Supported Housing psychiatrist can be quite valuable in serving as a link between the Supported Housing staff and a tenant's other medical providers in the community. A psychiatrist can often be more successful at making contact with other physicians to begin with and are often more effective at communicating a program's observations and concerns and at interpreting the information provided by off-site providers. Since the Supported Housing psychiatrist is familiar with the limitations of the program, they may also be able to work with an off-site provider to adjust treatment plans to take this into account, for example, to schedule evening medications earlier in the day when staff are available to assist. The Supported Housing psychiatrist can also be quite effective at advocating for benefits. For example, a Supported Housing psychiatrist is often instrumental in securing Supplemental Security Income (SSI) or Social Security Disability (SSD). A psychiatrist can also coach housing staff about advocating for tenants and coach tenants about advocating for themselves.

Tenant and Staff Education

Offering education can be quite effective at helping both tenants and housing staff to be better able to recognize and manage psychiatric symptoms. For example, education-based programs like Wellness Self-Management (see chapter "Health Self-Management: The Emerging Importance of Trauma and Resilience") have been shown to improve a variety of outcomes. A psychiatrist has multiple options for education including staff meetings, case conferences, lectures, informal consultations for staff and groups, community meetings and individual consultations. A Supported Housing psychiatrist should also try to identify training needs in an ongoing way.

Technical Assistance

Unlike hospitals and clinics, Supported Housing programs are not primarily providers of psychiatric or medical treatment and are therefore usually not experienced at developing or maintaining systems that manage clinical processes. As mentioned previously, although many program sites can "monitor medications" (but are not allowed to "dispense medications"), the policies and procedures in place that govern this activity are not as robust as in hospitals and this can lead to errors in dosing and scheduling of medications and medication changes. A psychiatrist can be very helpful in adjusting medication monitoring policies and in trouble-shooting inconsistencies in medication monitoring procedures. A psychiatrist can also help identify staffing needs including determining how much psychiatry time a program needs.

Coordinating the Work of an On-Site Psychiatrist

The activities of the psychiatrist working for a Supported Housing program described above must be effectively coordinated with housing staff if the psychiatrist's efforts are to be optimally utilized. The usual mechanisms in place in more traditional treatment settings to ensure appropriate scheduling and effective communication between clinicians and housing staff are different or absent from these social service programs. The particular needs and characteristics of this population and the structure of Supported Housing necessitate a careful consideration and planning about how to transform the traditional practice and role of psychiatrists to function effectively in Supported Housing. A psychiatrist typically visits a housing program from a half day per week to two days per week. Attention and planning about how the psychiatrist's time will be utilized and how they will communicate with housing staff will go a long way towards creating an environment that will allow the psychiatrist to be as effective as possible in this limited time. The goal in addressing these process issues then—scheduling the psychiatrist's time and managing communication between psychiatrist and housing staff—is to optimally integrate the psychiatrist into the activity and culture of the Supported Housing program so that a psychiatrist can be as effective and productive as possible.

The Schedule

A system for scheduling is necessary to ensure optimal use of the psychiatrist's time. There are many ways to effectively create and maintain a schedule. At some programs, social service staff maintains the schedule, at others the psychiatrist maintains the schedule, and at still others both program staff and psychiatrists collaborate to maintain a schedule. Not only should tenant encounters be scheduled, but there should also be time set aside for a psychiatrist's other activities such as meeting with staff.

Even a well-conceived system of scheduling will be ineffective if there is not also a system in place to ensure that scheduled activities happen in a timely manner—having a session scheduled is moot if the tenant does not show up. Again, there are many strategies to effectively use time. At some programs housing staff reminds tenants a day before appointments and then tries to contact tenants who have not shown for their appointments. At some programs housing staff escorts tenants to their appointments.

Although attention to the time management of the psychiatrist is essential, there is a risk of becoming too rigid about scheduling in an attempt to make optimal use of a psychiatrist's time. Some tenants cannot tolerate more than few minutes with the psychiatrist, while others may require more of a time commitment. Some tenants are unwilling or unable to cooperate with scheduled appointments but are instead quite happy to interact with the psychiatrist in a more informal, catch-as-catch-can manner. Also, psychiatrists themselves will individually be more or less comfortable and effective with systems of scheduling of varying flexibility. Part of the circumstance that resulted in consumers (and psychiatrists!) ending up participating in psychiatric treatment in nontraditional treatment settings in the first place is often an unwillingness or inability to tolerate the tightly scheduled structure of traditional treatment settings. Utilizing a psychiatrist's time requires a balance between being flexible enough to accommodate those who cannot tolerate too much structure and paying enough attention to scheduling to prevent ineffective, empty time.

Communication with the Psychiatrist

Information makes psychiatric evaluation and treatment possible. Housing staff's knowledge about a consumer is invaluable to the psychiatrist and the psychiatrist's access to this knowledge is probably the most significant advantage a Supported Housing psychiatrist has over a clinic- or office-based psychiatrist. Furthermore, a Supported Housing staff's access to the psychiatrist can be invaluable to a housing staff's understanding of a tenant and their treatment.

Psychiatrists must also effectively communicate orders and recommendations. Some communications are about *orders*, for example, about medication changes and follow-up appointments. The psychiatrist may also make *recommendations* about other issues, for example, about appropriate housing placement or about money management. Of course the expectation is that orders are executed faithfully, while recommendations may or may not be accepted. There are multiple strategies a program staff and psychiatrist can employ to ensure effective communication:

1. *Sign In and Sign Out*

A housing program should identify a liaison between housing staff and psychiatrist who meets with the psychiatrist regularly, preferably each time the psychiatrist is working for the program. This meeting might be a sign-in or sign-out meeting and preferably both happen. The sign in is most useful for the psychiatrist to learn about what has been going on with tenants since the psychiatrist's last visit. The sign in can also be a time to review the day's schedule and strategize about the day's appointments and other activities. For example, the sign in is often a good time to strategize about outreaching to a tenant who frequently misses appointments. The sign out is most useful for the program staff to understand the psychiatrist's treatment decisions. A very important aspect of this is communication about the timing of medication changes. A psychiatrist may make a decision and document this decision about a medication change early in the day while the sign out, when communication about this change happens, may not happen until the end of the day. At sign out, then, the psychiatrist and liaison should decide when the medication change should take effect taking into account the time that might be needed to obtain new medications from a pharmacy. Obviously, if the psychiatrist decides a medication change should occur immediately, they should not wait for the regularly scheduled sign out or for housing staff to read about the medication change in the sign-out note.

Sign-in and sign-out meetings need not only be with one liaison. On the contrary, especially the sign-out meeting is probably even more effective as a staff meeting.

2. *Staff Meetings*

Periodic staff meetings with the psychiatrist can be a very valuable adjunct to the regular meeting between the program liaison and psychiatrist. Staff meetings similar to hospital clinical rounds help a housing staff and psychiatrist collaborate to formulate, understand, and plan for the execution of treatment and service plans. There is also the opportunity to assess the effectiveness of treatment plans already in place. Case conferencing allows a housing staff to collaborate more thoroughly with the psychiatrist about particularly complicated or difficult clinical situations. Housing staffs should also consider inviting the psychiatrist to give trainings or lectures about psychiatric evaluation and treatment.

3. *Phone Calls*

The Supported Housing psychiatrist should be available by phone to consult about emergent or urgent issues that arise at times when the psychiatrist is not on site. Examples of situations to call the psychiatrist include consulting about missed or improperly taken medication doses, consulting about emerging or changing side effects, requesting that the psychiatrist contact the emergency room to communicate about a tenant who has been taken there, or consulting about a tenant's suicidal, dangerous, or nuisance behavior. Calling the psychiatrist, however, is not a replacement for calling 911. Some emergent situations, for example, when a tenant is violent, require that 911 be called and housing staff should not call the site psychiatrist in lieu of this. Also, care should be taken to prevent an overwhelming number of calls to the psychiatrist. Having the liaison be the single point of contact can help streamline these communications.

4. *Clinical Charting*

A system is required to keep medical records that are complete, accessible to the psychiatrist and other staff involved in the tenant's care, and inaccessible to unauthorized staff and other consumers. Psychiatrists will document treatment and interventions that are meant to be acted upon in a timely manner and therefore appropriate staff, e.g., the liaison to the psychiatrist or the tenant's case managers should read and appreciate clinical notes the same day the psychiatrist writes them. The psychiatrist must be mindful of time-sensitive data, for example, medication changes, and should decide if they must communicate with housing staff prior to their reading of clinical notes. The psychiatrist and housing staff are often charting in different electronic records with varying levels of connectivity, including no connectivity, between these records. Therefore, the psychiatrist and housing staff should develop a system to ensure timely delivery of treatment records to housing staff (e.g., by e-mailed PDFs through a secure e-mail system, or even providing hard copies).

Making the Team Approach Work: Managing the Collaboration

Psychiatric practice in a clinic or medical center is typically a one-to-one endeavor with psychiatrist and patient making up a dyadic treatment team with little influence from others. A psychiatrist at a Supported Housing program, however, is part of a service team and the psychiatrist's treatment is one of multiple services that are offered to tenants.

A team approach to service provision is associated with multiple advantages. As mentioned above, team members have access to different information about tenants providing more data about people than any one service provider would have access to individually. For example, an employment specialist may know about symptoms a person experiences at work that the person does not express to their psychiatrist. Team members can coordinate services and ensure that these services are not at cross-purposes with each other. A psychiatrist and social worker can make sure they share a consistent psychological understanding of a person that promotes similar psychotherapeutic interventions. Team members can support each other's practice. Social work staff monitors medications prescribed by psychiatrists. Psychiatrists liaison between social service staff and medical providers.

A hazard of the team approach, however, is the risk of blurring boundaries between professional roles. Is deciding what frequency of medication monitoring a person ought to have a clinical issue or a case management issue? If it is a little of both, who ought to decide if there is disagreement between psychiatrist, medical provider, and social service staff? Is deciding if a person ought to be on money management a clinical or case management issue? The Social Security Administration requires that a physician sign off on involuntary money management of disability benefits, but is not bill paying less of a clinical issue than medication taking? Even a role as clearly medical as medication prescribing is also partly a case management issue. A tenant in a Supported Housing program is not only a patient of a psychiatrist but is also a member of a community that is affected by the behavior of its members. Housing staff may seek pharmacologic intervention, among other interventions, to address disruptive or dangerous behavior.

In the midst of this potential blurriness, systematic, crystal-clear communication and disciplined, consistent spheres of responsibility are necessary for optimal functioning. Psychiatrists have final say on medication treatment, but also have a responsibility to ensure that other team members understand medication decisions. Housing staff faces management decisions when the psychiatrist is not working for the program, but also have a responsibility to consult with their psychiatrist if these decisions can affect tenants clinically (e.g., changes in medication monitoring). There should be an effective process for addressing disagreements between team members. For example, if a psychiatrist and social worker disagree about a medication treatment, that psychiatrist and social worker could present this disagreement as a team to a supervisor. The psychiatrist is ultimately responsible for medication decisions, but consulting a supervisor may result in alternative solutions or help either party change their opinion. Similarly, if there is a disagreement about the frequency of medication monitoring, consulting with a supervisor might yield alternative solutions.

Co-locating a psychiatrist and a social worker does not make a team. Teamwork requires clear, frank communications, mutual respect and understanding of roles, and separate, defined spheres of responsibility. Team leaders should support and nurture this kind of teamwork while at the same time keeping a clear eye on how decisions ultimately get made, executed, and communicated about.

Psychiatry in Supported Housing: Community Psychiatry in Action

What is the value of a house call versus care in a clinic, office, or medical center? Office-based settings offer access to medical technologies and procedures that cannot be replicated in a home, but the processes and structures of office-based practice can be a barrier to ongoing, productive engagement in psychiatric care. And more than other branches of medicine, psychiatric care is often suboptimal or even ineffective without effective engagement between provider and patient—the relationship is the treatment. That community psychiatry exists in the first place is due to opportunities to nurture provider-patient relationships in the community that are difficult to sustain in more traditional treatment facilities. Furthermore, practicing psychiatry in the community promotes collaboration with other service providers that also supports networks of engagement—true interdisciplinary practice is easier in community settings. Practicing psychiatry in Supported Housing offers both clinician and patient an opportunity to benefit from these possibilities of community psychiatry. The psychiatrist comes to the patient and joins their circle of care, and there is an opportunity for integration into the community. In today's health care environment, this kind of on-site care offers an accessible, effective resource to pursue meaningful recovery to an underserved and often disenfranchised population.

References

Bassuk E, Lamb R (1986). Homelessness and the implementation of deinstitutionalization. In Bassuk E (Ed.) The Mental Health Needs of the Homeless. San Francisco: Jossey-Bass.

Collins C, D'Andrea R, Dean K, Crampton D. (2016). Service providers' perspectives on permanent supportive housing for families. Families in Society: The Journal of Contemporary Social Services, 97(3), 243–252.

Cooper E, O'Hara A(2002). Priced out in 2002: Housing crisis worsens for people with psychiatric disabilities. Boston, MA: Technical Assistance Collaborative.

Department of Housing and Urban Development. (2015). Homeless Emergency Assistance and Rapid Transition to Housing: Defining "Chronically Homeless." Federal Register. 80, 75791–75806.

Dickenson-Gomez J, Quinn K, Bendixen A, Johnson A, Nowicki K, Ko Ko T, Galletly C. (2017). Identifying variability in permanent supportive housing: a comparative effectiveness approach to measuring health outcomes. The American Journal of Orthopsychiatry, 87(4), 414–424.

Fazel S, Khosla V, Doll H & Geddes J. (2008). The prevalence of mental disorders among the homeless in western countries: systematic review and meta-regression analysis. PLoS Medicine / Public Library of Science, 5, e225. https://doi.org/10.1371/journal.pmed.0050225

Fusaro, VA, Levy, HG, Shaefer, HL. Racial and Ethnic Disparities in the Lifetime Prevalence of Homelessness in the United States. Demography 55, 2119–2128 (2018). https://doi.org/10.1007/s13524-018-0717-0

Gewirtz AH. (2007). Promoting children's mental health in family supportive housing: a community-university partnership for formerly homeless children and families. J Primary Prevention. 28:359–374.

Grob GN. (1980). Abuse in American mental hospitals in historical perspective: myth and reality. International Journal of Law & Psychiatry, 3, 295–310. https://doi.org/10.1016/0160-2527(80)90009-6

Henwood BF, Cabassa LJ, Craig CM, Padgett DK. (2013). Permanent Supportive Housing: Addressing Homelessness and Health Disparities? American Journal of Public Health, 103, S188–S192. https://doi.org/10.2105/AJPH.2013.301490

Hopper, K., Jost, J., Hay, T., Welber, S., Haugland, G. (1997). Homelessness, severe mental illness, and the institutional circuit. Psychiatric Services, 48, 659–665.

Koegel P, Burnam MA & Farr RK. (1988). The prevalence of specific psychiatric disorders among homeless individuals in the inner city of Los Angeles. Archives of General Psychiatry, 45, 1085–92. https://doi.org/10.1001/archpsyc.1988.01800360033005

Kryda, A. D., & Comptom, M. T. (2009). Mistrust of outreach workers and lack of confidence in available services among individuals who are chronically street homeless. Community Ment Health J, 45, 144–150.

Kushel MB, Vittinghoff E, Haas JS. (2001). Factors Associated With the Health Care Utilization of Homeless Persons. JAMA. 285(2):200–206. https://doi.org/10.1001/jama.285.2.200

Lim S, Singh TP, Hall G, Walters S, Gould LH. (2018). Impact of a New York City supportive housing program on housing stability and preventable health care among homeless families. Health Services Research. 53:5,Part I;3437–3454. https://doi.org/10.1111/1475-6773.12849

Lipton FR, Siegel C, Hannigan A. (2000). Tenure in supportive housing for homeless persons with severe mental illness. Psychiatric Services. 51:479–486.

Padgett DK, Henwood BF, Tsemberis SJ. (2016) Housing First: Ending Homelessness, Transforming Systems, and Changing Lives. New York: Oxford University Press.

Parsell C, Petersen M, Moutou O. (2015). Single-site supportive housing: tenant perspectives. Housing Studies, 30(8), 1–21.

Piat M, Seida K & Padgett D. (2020). Choice and personal recovery for people with serious mental illness living in supported housing. Journal of Mental Health, 29, 306–313. https://doi.org/10.1080/09638237.2019.1581338

Ridgway P, Zipple, AM. (1990). The paradigm shift in residential services: From the linear continuum to supported housing approaches. Psychosocial Rehabilitation Journal, 13(4), 11–31. https://doi.org/10.1037/h0099479

Roberts, M. (1992). The prevalence of mental disorder among the homeless: A review of the empirical literature. In Janiel R. (Ed). Homelessness: A Prevention-Oriented Approach. Baltimore, MD: Johns Hopkins University Press.

Rog DJ. (2004). The evidence on supportive housing. Psychiatric Rehabilitation Journal. 27:334–344.

Rog DJ, Marshall T, Dougherty RH, George P, Daniels AS, Ghose SS, et al. (2014). Permanent supportive housing: assessing the evidence. Psychiatric Services, 65, 287–94. https://doi.org/10.1176/appi.ps.201300261

Rosenheck R, Kasprow W, Frisman L & Liu-Mares W. (2003). Cost-effectiveness of supported housing for homeless persons with mental illness. Archives of General Psychiatry, 60, 940–51. https://doi.org/10.1001/archpsyc.60.9.940

Shelton, K, Taylor, P, Bonner, A & van den Bree, M. (2009). Risk Factors for Homelessness: Evidence From a Population-Based Study. Psychiatric Services, 60(4), 465–472. Retrieved from http://ovidsp.ovid.com/ovidweb.cgi?T=JS&PAGE=reference&D=ovftj&NEWS=N&AN=00042727-200904000-00011.

Siegel CE, Samuels J, Tang DI, Berg I, Jones K & Hopper K. (2006). Tenant outcomes in supported housing and community residences in New York City. Psychiatric Services, 57, 982–91. https://doi.org/10.1176/ps.2006.57.7.982

Susser E, Moore R & Link B. (1993). Risk factors for homelessness. Epidemiologic Reviews, 15, 546–

56. https://doi.org/10.1093/oxfordjournals.epirev.a036133

Tsemberis S & Eisenberg RF. (2000). Pathways to housing: supported housing for street-dwelling homeless individuals with psychiatric disabilities. Psychiatric Services, 51, 487–93. https://doi.org/10.1176/appi.ps.51.4.487

Uehara, ES (1994). Race, gender, and housing inequality: An exploration of correlates of low-quality housing among clients diagnosed with severe and persistent mental illness. J Health and Social Behavior. 35, 309–321.

Whitley R, Henwood BF. (2014). Life, liberty, and the pursuit of happiness: reframing inequities experienced by people with severe mental illness. Psychiatric Rehabilitation Journal, 37, 68–70. https://doi.org/10.1037/prj0000053

Yohanna D. (2013). Deinstitutionalization of People with Mental Illness: Causes and Consequences. Virtual Mentor, 15(10), 886–891. https://doi.org/10.1001/virtualmentor.2013.15.10.mhst1-131

Health Self-Management: The Emerging Importance of Trauma and Resilience

Anthony J. Salerno and Paul J. Margolies

Introduction

In addition to its traditional focus on acute illnesses and injuries, our health care system has increasingly focused on enduring, serious conditions (Wagner et al. 2001). With this shift in focus has come a shift in the role for users of these services. Acute, non-enduring problems do not typically require patients/consumers to acquire knowledge and skills to self-manage their situations, though in the age of person-centered care, they are encouraged to know and choose among their options, when appropriate. This changes considerably when the focus shifts to enduring conditions. The term "chronic" is customarily used in the medical community to describe enduring conditions, while the behavioral health system typically uses the term "serious mental illness." Both terms are used throughout this chapter to describe those non-acute conditions that are long-lasting, associated with functional difficulties and require ongoing care.

The concept of health self-management has been employed widely in the treatment of chronic physical health problems (Lorig et al. 1993; Anderson et al. 1995; Boulware et al. 2001). In the last two decades, there has been considerable interest in applying and expanding the principles of health self-management to behavioral health problems. The focus has been on assisting adults with behavioral health problems to gain the knowledge and learn the skills to self-manage enduring mental health and substance use issues as well as associated physical health problems.

For adults with serious mental health and/or substance use problems, *behavioral and physical health self-management* refers to the integration of recovery principles such as self-direction, empowerment, hope, autonomy, and goal orientation with interventions that enhance an individual's ability to self-manage behavioral and physical health symptoms and problems. Important recovery principles include person-centeredness in treatment, an emphasis on strengths, holistic care, and hopefulness about the future. The term *behavioral and physical health self-management* is meant to emphasize the importance of an active and involved patient/consumer in managing enduring health problems and also recognizes the interdependence of behavioral and physical health issues. Each influences and is influenced by the other.

A. J. Salerno (✉)
McSilver Institute for Poverty Policy and Research, Silver School of Social Work, New York University, New York, NY, USA
e-mail: anthony.salerno@nyu.edu

P. J. Margolies
Department of Psychiatry, Columbia University Vagelos College of Physicians and Surgeons, New York, NY, USA

Center for Practice Innovations, New York State Psychiatric Institute, New York, NY, USA
e-mail: Paul.Margolies@nyspi.columbia.edu

W. E. Sowers et al. (eds.), *Textbook of Community Psychiatry*,
https://doi.org/10.1007/978-3-031-10239-4_36

Behavioral health-focused self-management programs such as Illness Management and Recovery (Mueser et al. 2002), Wellness Self-Management (Salerno et al. 2011), and Wellness Recovery Action Planning (Cook et al. 2009) represent efforts to create resources to support and guide consumers and practitioners in enhancing self-management capabilities through the use of structured and curriculum-based tools.

Beginning a generation ago (Felitti et al. 1998) and continuing to the present day (SAMHSA 2019), there has been a recognition of the impact of significant adversities and psychological trauma, especially childhood trauma, on an individual's behavioral and physical health conditions and outcomes. In addition to the behavioral and physical health risks associated with trauma, there has been a growing interest in the study of resilience and protective factors in mitigating the impact of adversity and promoting health and growth (Traub and Boynton-Jarrett 2017).

This recognition of the importance of the influence of trauma and the development of resilience was not highlighted in the first generation of behavioral health self-management programs. As our knowledge has evolved, it has become important to design the next generation of self-management programs that incorporate this perspective. This includes the specific role that a person's exposure to significant adverse events and conditions of living, trauma-related difficulties and the presence or absence of resilience factors might play in the self-management of chronic behavioral health conditions. A truly comprehensive self-management approach is one that integrates a number of key principles and practices designed to address trauma and strengthen resilience.

The purpose of this chapter is to:

- Update the findings on behavioral health self-management programs since the 2012 first edition of the Handbook (now Textbook) of Community Psychiatry
- Revisit the first-generation self-management programs and make the case for a next generation that integrates the principles and practices of trauma-informed care and resilience-building approaches
- Describe an updated conceptual framework for self-management approaches, which emphasizes the importance of trauma and resilience in the development of behavioral and other health difficulties
- Illustrate an example of an innovative resilience-oriented program that includes topics that may be integrated into existing self-management programs
- Discuss the implications of a trauma and resilience perspective for the role of psychiatrists and other healthcare providers engaged in supporting consumers to self-manage behavioral and physical health problems

Key Self-Management Behavioral Health Programs in Use Today

Behavioral health self-management programs share the common goal of enhancing an individual's active participation in and responsibility for treatment outcomes and quality of life improvements. They involve imparting information and assisting participants to make informed decisions and to actively increase self-management capabilities. These programs tend to differ on the range of issues covered, which aspects of self-management are emphasized and the specific methods and resources employed.

The challenge is to develop resources, tools, and practical approaches that support behavioral healthcare practitioners, provider organizations, and consumers to achieve successful treatment, rehabilitation, and recovery outcomes.

Illness Management and Recovery (IMR)

IMR is recognized by the Substance Abuse and Mental Health Services Administration (SAMHSA) as an evidence-based practice and was one focus of SAMHSA's national Evidence Based Practices dissemination project in 2002–2005 (McHugo et al. 2007). It is a curriculum-based treatment that utilizes research-informed psychosocial approaches. It empowers consumers to manage their illnesses, develop their own goals for recovery, and make informed decisions about their treatment. Topics include recovery strategies, practical facts on mental illness, stress vulnerability model and treatment strategies, building social support, using medication effectively, drug and alcohol use, reducing relapses, coping with stress, coping with persistent symptoms, and getting your needs met in the mental health system. Interventions provided by practitioners include psychoeducation, behavioral tailoring of medication, coping skills training, and relapse prevention.

The IMR resource kit (SAMHSA 2010) includes promotional materials for a variety of stakeholders, informational handouts for consumers, and a comprehensive practitioner's manual. IMR can be employed in individual and group meetings. Its intervention components have been found to contribute to positive symptom and functional outcomes (Mueser et al. 2002). The effectiveness of the IMR package has been examined, with positive effects found on hospitalization rates, symptoms, hopefulness, and psychosocial functioning (Salyers et al. 2010; Levitt et al. 2009; Mueser et al. 2006), implementation within Assertive Community Treatment teams (Monroe-DeVita et al. 2018), and internationally (Daass-Iraqi et al. 2020; Egeland et al. 2017; Tan et al. 2016).

McGuire and colleagues (2014) reviewed the existing literature concerning IMR consisting of 26 studies (9 measuring outcomes, 16 examining implementation and adaptation of IMR, and one a qualitative follow-up of a prior study). The authors noted that "The RCTs found that consumers receiving IMR reported significantly more improved scores on the IMR Scale (IMRS) than consumers who received treatment as usual. IMRS ratings by clinicians and ratings of psychiatric symptoms by independent observers were also more improved for the IMR consumers. Implementation studies (N = 16) identified several important barriers to and facilitators of IMR, including supervision and agency support. Implementation outcomes, such as participation rates and fidelity, varied widely" and concluded "IMR shows promise for improving some consumer-level outcomes." Recently, an enhanced Illness Management and Recovery (E-IMR) manual was developed for individuals diagnosed with both mental health and substance use disorders by combining Integrated Dual Disorder Treatment (IDDT) with IMR (Gingerich et al. 2018).

Wellness Self-Management (WSM)

WSM (Salerno et al. 2007) is an adaptation of IMR which was developed by the New York State Office of Mental Health. In WSM, the entire curriculum, consisting of 57 lessons, is organized into a bound workbook that belongs to the participant. The workbook was designed to emphasize and reinforce the principles of recovery such as shared decision-making, choice, and hope, recognize the role of cultural beliefs and values, highlight the connection between mental and physical health, and address the challenges of providing WSM services in a group modality. The topics covered in the WSM program are designed to provide participants with the knowledge and skills that promote informed decision making and self-management competency.

The WSM program is most often delivered in a group format, although it can be utilized in individual treatment as well. WSM sessions are held a minimum of once weekly and variations including back-to-back sessions and multiple sessions per week have been reported. While the duration of the WSM program varies, it typically takes a year or more to complete the entire curriculum. Programs with shorter lengths of stay such as inpatient hospitals select specific lessons that most closely match the needs of consumers at that time.

Optimally, WSM groups are closed groups in order to provide members with a secure environment in which they can build a sense of trust and camaraderie. However, when this is not possible, WSM programs have been successfully conducted in open groups. The use of the workbook facilitates the entry of individuals at various points throughout the program. Each group ideally consists of eight to ten members and is led by two group facilitators. Peer facilitation is strongly encouraged. WSM also assists individuals to consider involving family and friends who may be able to support their work by assisting with action steps, giving encouragement, providing needed information, and discussing topics of interest.

WSM has been successfully implemented in over 120 agencies involving over 5000 consumers across numerous program types, clinical conditions, and cultural populations. Participants report substantial gains in accomplishing personally meaningful goals which are substantiated by their treating clinicians (Salerno et al. 2011). The workbook is currently available in English, Spanish, Korean, and Chinese. In 2010, the Center for Practice Innovations at Columbia Psychiatry was awarded a SAMHSA Science and Service award for the development of WSM.

The National Council for Behavioral Health (recently renamed the National Council for Mental Wellbeing) worked with member behavioral healthcare agencies to implement WSM in two projects. In 2010–2011, ten agencies across the United States implemented the WSM over a 6-month period with adults diagnosed with schizophrenia in a variety of settings including clinics, residential programs, ACT teams, intensive treatment programs, rehabilitative day programs, peer-run groups, case-management services, and day-treatment programs. Using the Daily Living Activities (DLA-20) functional assessment scale, they found that participants in six of the ten centers showed modest but steady improvements from the baseline assessment to the final DLA assessment, and three centers experienced minor gains or flat scores. The DLA-20 subscales with the most consistent statistically significant improvements were communications, interaction with one's social network, and coping skills.

In 2013, ten agencies across the United States implemented WSM over a 6-month period with adults diagnosed with bipolar disorder, also using the DLA-20 functional assessment scale. Overall outcomes included statistically significant improvements in all 20 DLA-20 areas of functioning as well as in the overall estimated Global Assessment of Functioning. The subscales with the most consistent statistically significant improvements within individual organizations included productivity, social networking, coping skills, health practices, communication, managing money, problem solving, and leisure. Nine of the organizations had statistically significant improvements in overall estimated GAF.

In Italy, Landi et al. (2018) implemented an abbreviated Italian version of the WSM over a period of 4 weeks in a day hospital setting, using a randomized controlled trial. Compared to controls, at immediate post-intervention, WSM participants reported significant improvement in processing speed, psychopathology, neurocognitive, and personal resources and real-life functioning.

One important adaptation to the WSM is the Wellness Self-Management Plus (WSM+) workbook, designed for adults with both serious mental illness and substance use issues. Originally developed in 2010 (Salerno et al. 2010), the WSM+ workbook has been revised and updated in 2020 (Salerno et al. 2020). It is available in English and Spanish. It is currently (2020–2021) being implemented in a New York statewide learning collaborative with approximately 20 community psychiatric rehabilitation programs.

As of September 2020, over 10,000 WSM and WSM+ workbooks have been downloaded or purchased. An online training module, teaching practitioners about WSM and WSM+ and focusing on group implementation, is available through the Center for Practice Innovations at Columbia Psychiatry. Through September 2020, over 5500 learners have completed this module. Further information about the WSM can be found at the Center for Practice Innovations website (Center for Practice Innovations n.d.).

Wellness Recovery Action Planning (WRAP)

Mary Ellen Copeland (2018) designed WRAP plans to help individuals diagnosed with mental illness to take an active role in maintaining personal mental health wellness. Goals include decreasing/preventing symptoms, increasing personal empowerment, improving quality of life, and helping the individual to achieve personal goals. The individual works with trained peers to develop a detailed wellness plan. Elements of the plan include maintaining daily wellness, identifying and dealing with triggers, identifying and dealing with early warning signs, identifying when things are breaking down and what to do, and developing detailed crisis plans. Cook et al. (2009) found that use of WRAP resulted in significant improvements in self-reported symptoms, recovery, hopefulness, self-advocacy, and physical health. Canacott et al. (2019), in a systematic review and meta-analysis, found that relative to inactive control conditions, WRAP was superior for promoting self-perceived recovery outcomes, but not superior for reducing clinical symptomatology. They also noted that improvements were not sustained over time.

These three approaches share some similarities and also differ in a number of ways. All three approaches empower consumers to proactively take control over their experiences, providing them with information and tools to do so. They are all designed to be provided in individual or group meetings. IMR and WSM place greater emphasis on psychoeducation than does WRAP and offer adapted versions focusing on co-occurring mental health and substance use problems (E-IMR and WSM+). There are differences in who provides these services with WRAP provided by peer specialists and IMR and WSM provided by clinicians with or without the assistance of peer specialists. Duration also differs, with the typical WRAP experience lasting 2–3 months, IMR 9–10 months, and WSM approximately a year. Also, IMR emphasizes homework assignments between meetings, whereas WSM recommends voluntary action steps.

Trauma and Overall Health Self-Management

SAMHSA notes that "Individual trauma results from an event, series of events, or set of circumstances that is experienced by an individual as physically or emotionally harmful or life threatening and that has lasting adverse effects on the individual's functioning and mental, physical, social, emotional, or spiritual well-being" (SAMHSA 2014).

There are three types of trauma:

- Natural events such as floods and tornadoes
- Human-caused accidents such as airplane crashes and train derailments
- Human-caused intentional acts such as abuse, neglect, arson, rape, and torture

One important category of traumatic events is "adverse childhood experiences" (ACEs). These occur between birth and age 17 years and involve experiencing violence, abuse, or neglect, witnessing violence, living in a household with members experiencing mental health and/or substance use problems, and being separated from caregivers.

An early study of ACEs (Felitti et al. 1998) found a high level of ACEs among respondents (more than half had experienced at least one ACE and one-fourth had experienced two or more ACEs) and a graded relationship between the number of categories of childhood exposure and each of the adult health risk behaviors and diseases that were studied. "Persons who had experienced four or more categories of childhood exposure, compared to those who had experienced none, had 4- to 12-fold increased health risks for alcoholism, drug abuse, depression, and suicide attempt; a 2- to 4-fold increase in smoking, poor self-rated health, ≥50 sexual intercourse partners, and sexually transmitted disease; and a 1.4- to 1.6-fold increase in physical inactivity and severe obesity. The number of categories of adverse childhood exposures showed a graded relationship to the presence of adult diseases including ischemic heart disease, cancer, chronic lung disease, skeletal fractures, and liver disease. The seven categories of adverse childhood experiences were strongly interrelated and persons with multiple categories of childhood exposure were likely to have multiple health risk factors later in life."

Related findings have been reported in the years since this groundbreaking study. SAMHSA notes that "Research has shown that traumatic experiences are associated with both behavioral health and chronic physical health conditions, especially those traumatic events that occur during childhood. Substance use (e.g., smoking, excessive alcohol use, and taking drugs), mental health conditions (e.g., depression, anxiety, or PTSD), and other risky behaviors (e.g., self-injury and risky sexual encounters) have been linked with traumatic experiences" (SAMHSA 2019).

According to the Centers for Disease Control and Prevention, about 61% of adults surveyed reported experiencing at least one ACE, and nearly one in six reported experiencing four or more types of ACEs. The CDC estimates that up to 1.9 million cases of heart disease and 21 million cases of depression could have been potentially avoided by preventing ACEs (Centers for Disease Control and Prevention 2020).

The importance of integrating a trauma-informed approach in behavioral health self-management programs is related to the prevalence of trauma in adults with serious mental illness. In a review of the literature, Mauritz et al. (2013) found that "Prevalence rates of interpersonal trauma and trauma-related disorders were significantly higher in SMI than in the general population." They found that "Population-weighted mean prevalence rates in SMI were physical abuse 47% (range 25–72%), sexual abuse 37% (range 24–49%), and posttraumatic stress disorder (PTSD) 30% (range 20–47%). Compared to men, women showed a higher prevalence of sexual abuse in schizophrenia spectrum disorder, bipolar disorder, and mixed diagnosis groups labelled as having SMI."

Although the findings demonstrating the significant impact of adversities on numerous physical and behavioral health problems have been dominating the conversation for several decades, the protective and recovery-supporting role of resilience is now more fully understood. Our understanding of the critical factors contributing to the well-being and recovery for individuals with persisting behavioral health and physical health problems is advancing towards a conceptual framework that integrates trauma-informed and resilience-building approaches.

Resilience: A Holistic Perspective

Among the varying definitions of resilience, we prefer the approach taken by researchers (Kent et al. 2014) who describe resilience as a "combination of three core elements: resilience as a sustained adaptive effort that prevails despite challenge, as a bouncing back and recovery from a challenge, and as a process of learning and growth that expands understanding, new knowledge, and new skills" (Kent et al. 2014, page xii). Furthermore, in contrast to conceptualizations of resilience as the innate strengths, grit, and hardiness of an individual (Maddi 2004), current researchers emphasize the multilevel dimensions involved in successful adaptations that include "a host of biological, psychological, social and cultural factors that interact with one another to determine how one responds to stressful experiences" Southwick et al. 2014, p. 3).

We have learned a great deal about the personal factors associated with resilience reflected in ways of thinking, perceiving, and behaving that increase the likelihood that a person will cope more effectively with past and current adversity and more effectively manage challenges related to behavioral health and physical health problems. For example, resilient individuals are generally optimistic, self-confident, and cognitively flexible, find meaning in adversity, regulate negative affect, have an internal locus of control, and engage in active problem solving (Windle et al. 2011).

In addition to these personal characteristics, the presence of environmental factors such as reliable and accessible social, community, and cultural supports plays an instrumental role in facilitating effective coping. Key resiliency-supporting environmental resources include access to stable housing, education, safety net programs, general healthcare, transportation, and social services. The role of these social determinants on one's overall health suggests that self-management programs must take into account the importance of a person's contextual realities as instrumental factors affecting an individual's overall health and well-being (Adler and Stewart 2010; Sanchez-Jankowski 2008). Unfortunately, these supports may be particularly challenging for many individuals served by the public healthcare system (see chapter "Social and Political Determinants of Health and Mental Health").

The combination of a supportive environment and accessible resources along with a person's ability to utilize those resources offers the most effective response to adversity. Self-management resources, available through the behavioral healthcare system, are one such environmental support that offers individuals the opportunity to gain the knowledge and information needed to engage in informed decision making and problem solving, two key characteristics of resilience (Windle et al. 2011).

What Does Science Tells Us About the Relationship Between Resilience and Overall Health?

Research on the relationship between resilience and a number of positive psychological and health indicators includes findings that adults with higher resilience were less likely to experience depression and negative health status and more likely to report that they exercised, ate nutritiously, and were more likely to report less use of tobacco products (Wagnild 2015); less likely to report fatigue, insomnia, pain, and depressive symptoms after traumatic brain injury (Losoi et al. 2014); more likely to report positive concepts such as perceived meaning in life, satisfaction with life, and reduced indexes of psychological distress (e.g., depression, anxiety, stress, and posttraumatic stress) (Aiena et al. 2014); and more likely to report intrinsic religiosity associated with reduced suicide risk (Mosqueiro et al. 2015).

Learning to Be Resilient: Features of Resilience-Building Programs

The literature on resilience-building approaches summarized by Southwick and Charney (2012) points to the importance of cognitive behavioral strategies and strengthening social supports. Other common elements of resilience training include mindfulness, emotional regulation, proactive psychoeducation about trauma and resilience, and the importance of maintaining a healthy lifestyle (i.e., sleep, nutrition, physical activity, and de-stressing relaxation) to increase energy for effortful coping and stress management. Some approaches emphasize meaning making as a key element to resilience (i.e., finding meaning in adversity and exploring ways in which the experience of adversity may promote personal growth). This is similar to the concept of posttraumatic growth as described by Tedeschi et al. (2018). A review of resilience-building programs generally includes many of the following components (Southwick and Charney 2012):

- Emotional regulation training to recognize and manage reactivity and impulsivity
- Cognitive behavioral approaches to reframe thought processes that are self-defeating and increase hopeful and health-promoting beliefs and expectations
- Physical health information on exercise, nutrition, sleep, and relaxation to increase protective behavior
- Social support to build connections to family, peers, and mentors to increase protective factors
- A neurobiological component, such as mindfulness-based stress reduction to increase the ability to manage tension and stress
- Education on trauma and resilience designed to support thoughtful decision making and develop greater insight into one's motivations and current disappointments

Resilience-focused interventions have been employed to address the needs of individuals with behavioral health and physical health problems. For example, a resilience-based self-management program designed to address the needs of African Americans with type 2 diabetes demonstrated improvement in disease self-management behaviors and blood glucose levels (Steinhardt et al. 2015). An intervention focusing on tics found that a resilience-oriented approach decreased tic-related impairment and improved quality of life and self-concept for children and youth (Storch et al. 2012). A study of the impact of a resilience-focused programs for youth at risk for substance use revealed a reduction in the prevalence of alcohol, marijuana, and smoking use among participants (Hodder et al. 2011). The direct impact of a resilience-focused approach on trauma-specific symptoms has also demonstrated significant benefit to veterans with PTSD. Veterans completing the 12-week program experienced significant reductions in PTSD symptom severity and improvements in positive emotional health and cognitive functioning compared to the control condition (Kent et al. 2011).

The increasing emphasis on resilience has also been proposed as an integral part of trauma-specific treatment. For example, Kent and Davis (2010) focus their treatment on the individual's personal and social strengths and have individuals identify and focus on positive experiences before trauma-related issues are explored and addressed. Their approach, Building Resilience for Change (BRC), places the emphasis throughout the program on rebuilding social engagement and personal competence. The strength-focused approach emphasizes the very characteristics that resilient individuals exhibit: positive thinking, social connections, flexible thinking, focusing on positive experiences, successful coping, and personal capacities and accomplishments. This stands in contrast to most trauma-specific approaches that directly address the trauma-related issues throughout treatment. Research comparing the BRC model with a waiting list control group indicated that the BRC group reported reduction in PTSD and depression symptoms as well as showing improved performance on measures of memory, attention, and mental flexibility. The control group, in contrast, remained unchanged in symptoms and cognitive functioning.

In the absence of studies comparing the advantages and disadvantages of the BRC approach in comparison to traditional interventions, we are not in a position to recommend one approach over another. The key research question for future research is not which approach is superior but which individuals are more likely to benefit from a resilience-building phase prior to addressing trauma directly. The BRC may be most helpful for individuals who are particularly vulnerable, emotionally fragile, disorganized, and highly anxious. Beginning with resilience strengths may help such individuals build confidence and emotional readiness to address trauma. For individuals who are less vulnerable and display resiliency strengths, addressing trauma immediately may be appropriate and effective.

Next Generation of Self-Management Programs: The Brite Program

As noted previously, the first generation of behavioral health self-management programs did not fully incorporate findings from the field of trauma and resilience. This raises a number of questions: What trauma- and resiliency-related topics should be added to self-management programs to ensure that consumers have the information, knowledge, and skills to better self-manage behavioral health and physical health problems? How do we integrate our understanding of trauma and resilience into the structure, process, and content of the next generation of self-management programs?

An example of one such next-generation self-management program is called BRITE (Building Resilience for Individuals thru Trauma Education) (Salerno 2019). This 24-lesson curriculum was designed to integrate the knowledge reflected in the trauma and resilience literature into a curriculum-based resource. It was designed to be consistent with the purpose, values, structure, process, and content of self-management programs and most closely modeled after the WSM framework that has been well received by consumers, practitioners, and behavioral health organizations (Salerno et al. 2011; Landi et al. 2018).

Similar to wellness self-management, BRITE consists of individual lessons that typically require 45 minutes to complete, applicable to individual and group modalities, and flexibly adapted to align with time limitations, treatment setting realities, and consumer preferences. Providers may focus on a subset of lessons or complete the entire 24-lesson program in sequence. BRITE represents one of the first attempts to assist and empower adults with serious behavioral health challenges to explore the relationship between adversity and current difficulties, to recognize and expand resilience-related strengths as an integral component of overall behavioral health self-management, and to improve problem-solving skills and informed decision-making.

A core aspect of BRITE involves psychoeducation, a common element across self-management programs. Psychoeducation provides consumers with information to better understand the nature of their behavioral health problems, potential causes, treatments, and strategies to effectively manage symptoms and functional problems. This educational approach assists individuals to view challenges as problems to be solved through information and action, a core characteristic of resilient individuals (Wagnild 2015). The support for emphasizing psychoeducation has been demonstrated across a number of behavioral and physical health problem areas including relapse reduction in individuals with bipolar disorder (D'Souza et al. 2010), increasing medication adherence (Eker and Harkın 2012), posttreatment adaptation to breast cancer (Jones et al. 2013), and increasing substance abuse abstinence (Campbell et al. 2014). As a psychoeducational resource, BRITE provides individuals with information related to key foundational topics that describe (1) the impact of adversity on a person's mental health, physical health, substance use risks, and daily functioning problems; (2) the meaning of resilience, why it is important, and what steps a person may take to increase their resilience; and (3) the benefits of recognizing and building on one's strengths to manage one's overall health and well-being.

Since BRITE is a very new resource, data on its benefits has been collected as part of initial field testing with 30 consumers with serious mental illness, many of whom struggle with significant substance use problems and 11 group facilitators across three behavioral health programs in New York City including residential, shelter, and day program settings. The aim of the field test was to determine the degree to which practitioners and consumers who completed the BRITE program in a group modality found the material clear, helpful, and practical to implement and to use that feedback to improve the curriculum and the training process.

Survey measures were created to assess each consumer's (1) perception of benefit over the course of the program and (2) the overall helpfulness and relevance of the program. The perception of benefit following the completion of the program was assessed using a 20-item 5-point Likert scale created by the author (Salerno 2019). Participants were asked to indicate the degree to which they improved on each of 20 resilience-related statements since the start of the program. For example, participants were asked to indicate if they perceived themselves to be much better, better, the same, worse, or much worse on statements such as the following:"Being confident that I will achieve many of my life goals"

"Being aware of how very stressful experiences have affected my overall wellbeing"

"Recognizing that I have many personal strengths"

"Knowing how to calm down when I feel stressed out"

"Feeling safe and in control of my life"

"Being confident that I can manage future stressful experiences"

"Generally feeling stronger as a person"

Scores ranging from 1 to 5 for each item were calculated for the 30 participants. The aggregate scores ranged from 3.9 for the item "Being confident that I will achieve many of my life goals" to 4.6 for the item "Generally feeling stronger as a person." The average score for all items was 4.26, suggesting that participants experienced the program as contributing to a perception of improved resilience. Responses to the 5-item helpfulness scale also revealed that participants overwhelmingly found the program helpful and relevant to their needs (mean score of 4.7 out of a maximum positive score of 5).

One of the critical factors associated with sustainable adoption and implementation of an innovative practice such as BRITE is the degree to which the practitioners experience the program as positive for consumers, practical, and professionally rewarding such as enhancing clinical knowledge and skills (Fixsen et al. 2005). A 10-item 5-point Likert scale was designed by the author (Salerno 2019) to assess the experience of group facilitators on these factors. Results revealed an overall mean score of 4.6 for the 10 items out of a maximum positive score of 5 suggesting that group facilitators found the BRITE program as very helpful to consumers (mean score of 4.9), easy to use (mean score of 4.7), and contributing to their professional development (mean score of 4.5).

Qualitative findings from focus groups with participants and group facilitators suggested that the value of a resilience-focused program such as BRITE was based on having a workbook that included a predictable format that was clear and easy to use, addressed relevant topics, and focused on strengths rather than deficiencies. Focus group participants also indicated that the language was nonjudgmental, non-stigmatizing, and respected each person's autonomy and self-directed approach to learning. As one group facilitator mentioned, "consumers have expressed that they are beginning to not feel stigmatized or shamed by the trauma they have experienced; understanding that most people have experienced some sort of trauma in their lives." A frequent comment from group facilitators was that many consumers in the BRITE program revealed critical aspects of their lives that were previously unknown to practitioners. As a group facilitator from a women's shelter stated, "We have had consumers share trauma experiences that they had never disclosed prior to the BRITE group and has helped individuals with insight into their mental health." One consumer mentioned how the positive nature of the program was also helpful. "I found it very helpful to see how my past traumatic events have influenced my current life and how to better talk about my issues. I really liked the positive message at the end of each lesson and really focused on hope and being a capable person."

These initial findings from BRITE suggest that adding trauma and resilience lessons to self-management programs will likely be well received by consumers and staff alike. BRITE may also serve as a starting point to answer a number of key questions critical to develop a next-generation comprehensive self-management resource for adults with complex and persisting mental health, substance use, and related health problems. For example, What topics should a behavioral health self-management program incorporate to address trauma and resilience as an important component of a comprehensive self-management program? In what way may the BRITE approach provide the field with a helpful starting point to develop such a comprehensive model?

The BRITE program curriculum consists of three categories with a related set of lessons corresponding to each of the bullet points in Table 1.

As the field considers a next generation of self-management approaches, the trauma- and resilience-focused topics listed in Table 1 may serve as a resource that provides specific examples and options. The goal is to ensure that adults with serious behavioral health challenges are offered the opportunity to explore, understand, and address the impact of adversity on their overall health and well-being and to recognize, develop, and build on resilience-supporting strengths.

Conclusion

Research on adverse life events, trauma, and resilience has clearly demonstrated their role in the overall health and well-being of individuals. The high prevalence of adversity and trauma among people with serious behavioral and physical health problems requires us to consider

Table 1 The BRITE program curriculum

Category 1: understanding adversity, stress, and Trauma	Category 2: understanding and building resilience	Category 3: empowering knowledge and strategies
Basic information about trauma and stress Exploring your adverse life experiences Exploring and identifying the relationship between adverse life experiences and physical health and behavioral health challenges including symptoms of mental illness and substance use Understanding stress and coping with adverse life experiences Understanding the relationship between positive and negative thinking and trauma	Basic information about the meaning of resilience Identifying and using your personal and environmental resilience strengths Building resilience through mindfulness Strengthening resilience through social supports and healthy relationships Creating a personalized resilience-focused wellness plan	Understanding your rights as a survivor of adversities Learning about trauma-specific services Identifying goals related to trauma and resilience Making current services work for you Speaking up in ways that supports your resilience Deciding if leadership, advocacy, and helping others are right for you

including these factors as part of a comprehensive overall health self-management approach to care. Research on trauma, the characteristics of resilient individuals, the environmental conditions which facilitate resilience, and the valuable role of psychoeducation provides us with the conceptual and empirical guidance to integrate these topics as part of a behavioral health self-management curriculum.

The implications for the role and training of practitioners and community psychiatrists include developing a multidimensional professional lens that recognizes and engages consumers in three critical areas: (1) providing traditional basic self-management approaches to symptom reduction and relapse prevention, (2) assisting individuals to explore the presence and impact of adverse life experiences on both physical and behavioral health problems, and (3) assisting individuals to explore, recognize, identify, and utilize personal and environmental resilience strengths and resources to promote recovery. Recent efforts to operationalize and create resilience-focused tools and resources provide the field with concrete guidance concerning the creation of a truly comprehensive health self-management approach supporting the recovery of individuals challenged by mental health, addictions, and related health problems.

References

Adler, N.E., & Stewart, J, editors (2010). The biology of disadvantage: Socioeconomic status and health. New York: John Wiley & Sons.

Aiena, B.J., Baczwaski, B.J., Schulenberg, S.E., & Buchanan, E. (2014). Measuring Resilience with the RS-14: A Tale of Two Samples. *Journal of Personality Assessment, 97*, 291–300. https://doi.org/10.1080/00223891.2014.951445

Anderson, R.M., Funnell, M.M., Butler, P.M., Arnold, M.S., Fitzgerald, J.T., & Feste, C.C. (1995). Patient empowerment. Results of a randomized controlled trial. *Diabetes Care, 18*, 943–949. https://doi.org/10.2337/diacare.18.7.943

Boulware, L.E., Daumit, G.L., Frick, K.D., Minkovitz, C.S., Lawrence, R.S., & Powe, N.R. (2001). An evidence-based review of patient-centered behavioral interventions for hypertension. *American Journal of Preventive Medicine, 21*, 221–32. https://doi.org/10.1016/S0749-3797(01)00356-7

Campbell, A. N., Nunes, E. V., Matthews, A. G., Stitzer, M., Miele, G. M., Polsky, D., & Wahle, A. (2014). Internet-delivered treatment for substance abuse: A multisite randomized controlled trial. *American Journal of Psychiatry, 171*, 683–690. https://doi.org/10.1176/appi.ajp.2014.13081055

Canacott, L., Moghaddam, N., & Tickle, A. (2019). Is the Wellness Recovery Action Plan (WRAP) efficacious for improving personal and clinical recovery outcomes? A systematic review and meta-analysis. *Psychiatric Rehabilitation Journal, 42*(4), 372–381. https://doi.org/10.1037/prj0000368

Center for Practice Innovation. (n.d.). Resources for wellness self-management. Retrieved from https://practiceinnovations.org/Initiatives/WSMWellnessSelf-Management

Centers for Disease Control and Prevention. (2020). Retrieved February 14, 2021 https://www.cdc.gov/violenceprevention/aces/fastfact.html?CDC_AA_refVal=https%3A %2F%2Fwww.cdc.gov%2Fviolenceprevention%2Facestudy%2Ffastfact.html

Cook, J.A., Copeland, M.E., Hamilton, M.A., Jonikas, J.A., Razzano, L.A., Floyd, C.B., Hudson, W.B.,

Macfarlane, R.T., & Grey, D.D. (2009). Initial outcomes of a mental illness self-management program based on wellness recovery action planning. *Psychiatric Services, 60,* 246–249. https://doi.org/10.1176/ps.2009.60.2.246

Copeland, M.E. (2018). Wellness Recovery Action Planning Resources. Retrieved January 18, 2021. https://mentalhealthrecovery.com

Daass-Iraqi, S., Mashiach-Eizenberg, M., Garber-Epstein, P., & Roe, D. (2020). Impact of a culturally adapted version of Illness Management and Recovery on Israeli Arabs with serious mental illness. *Psychiatric Services, 71,* 951–954. https://doi.org/10.1176/appi.ps.201900424

D'Souza, R., Piskulic, D., & Sundram, S. (2010). A brief dyadic group based psychoeducation program improves relapse rates in recently remitted bipolar disorder: a pilot randomized controlled trial. *Journal of Affective Disorders*, 120(1), 272–276.

Egeland, K.M., Ruud, T., Ogden, T. et al. (2017) How to implement Illness Management and Recovery (IMR) in mental health service settings: evaluation of the implementation strategy. *Int J Ment Health Syst* 11, 13. https://doi.org/10.1186/s13033-017-0120-z

Eker, F., & Harkın, S. (2012). Effectiveness of six-week psychoeducation program on adherence of patients with bipolar affective disorder. *Journal of Affective Disorders*, 138(3), 409–416.

Felitti V.J., Anda, R.F., Nordenberg, D., Williamson, D.F., Spitz, A.M., Edwards, V., Koss M.P., & Marks, J.S. (1998) Relationship of childhood abuse and household dysfunction to many of the leading causes of death in adults. The Adverse Childhood Experiences (ACE) *Study. Am J Prev Med.* May;14(4):245–258. https://doi.org/10.1016/s0749-3797(98)00017-8

Fixsen, D. L., Naoom, S. F., Blase, K. A., Friedman, R. M. & Wallace, F. (2005). Implementation Research: A Synthesis of the Literature. Tampa, FL: University of South Florida, Louis de la Parte Florida Mental Health Institute, *The National Implementation Research Network* (FMHI Publication #231).

Gingerich, S., Mueser, K.T., Fox-Smith, M., Meyer-Kalos, P.S., Freedland, T. (2018) Enhanced Illness Management and Recovery. Center for Practice Transformation, University of Minnesota. Retrieved December 28, 2021. https://practicetransformation.umn.edu/wp-content/uploads/2020/02/Pages-from-Preview-for-Web.pdf

Hodder, R. K., Daly, J., Freund, M., Bowman, J., Hazell, T., & Wiggers, J. (2011). A school-based resilience intervention to decrease tobacco, alcohol and marijuana use in high school students. *BMC Public Health*, 11(1), 1.

Jones, J. M., Cheng, T., Jackman, M., Walton, T., Haines, S., Rodin, G., & Catton, P. (2013). Getting back on track: evaluation of a brief group psychoeducation intervention for women completing primary treatment for breast cancer. *Psycho-Oncology*, 22(1), 117–124. https://doi.org/10.1002/pon.2060

Kent, M., Davis, M. C., Stark, S. L., & Stewart, L. A. (2011). A resilience-oriented treatment for posttraumatic stress disorder: Results of a preliminary randomized clinical trial. *Journal of Traumatic Stress*, 24(5), 591–595.

Kent, M., & Davis, M.C. (2010). The emergence of capacity-building programs and models of resilience. In J. W. Reich, A. J. Zautra, & J. S. Hall (Eds.), *Handbook of Adult Resilience* (p. 427–449). The Guilford Press.

Kent, M., Davis, M.C., & Reich, J.W. (2014). *The resilience handbook: approaches to stress and trauma*, New York, NY: Routledge, Taylor & Francis Group.

Landi, S., Palumbo, D., Margolies, P., Salerno, A.J., Cleek, A., Castaldo, E., & Mucci, A. (2018). Implementation of a wellness self-management program for individuals with severe mental illness in an Italian Day Hospital setting: a pilot study. *Journal of Psychopathology, 24,* 3–9.

Levitt, A.J, Mueser, K.T., Degenova, J., Lorenzo J., Bradford-Watt, D., Barbosa A., Karlin, M., & Chernick, M. (2009). Randomized controlled trial of illness management and recovery in multiple-unit supportive housing. *Psychiatric Services, 60,* 1629–1636. https://doi.org/10.1176/ps.2009.60.12.1629

Lorig, K.R., Mazonson, P.D., & Holman, H.R. (1993). Evidence suggesting that health education for self-management in patients with chronic arthritis has sustained health benefits while reducing health care costs. *Arthritis Rheum, 36,* 439–446. https://doi.org/10.1002/art.1780360403

Losoi, H., Waljas, M., Turunen, S., Brander, A., Helminen, M., Luoto, T.M., Rosti-Otajarvi, E., Julkunen, J., & Ohman, J. (2014). Resilience associated with fatigue after mild traumatic brain injury. *Journal of Head and Trauma Rehabilitation, 30,* E24–E32. https://doi.org/10.1097/HTR.0000000000000055

Maddi, S. R. (2004). Hardiness: An operationalization of existential courage. *Journal of Humanistic Psychology, 44,* 279–298. https://doi.org/10.1177/0022167804266101

Mauritz, M. W., Goossens, P. J. J., Draijer, N., Van Achterberg, T. (2013). Prevalence of Interpersonal trauma exposure and trauma-related disorders in severe mental illness. *European Journal of Psychotraumatology, 4.* https://doi.org/10.3402/ejpt.v4i0.19985. Epub Apr 8.

McGuire, A.B., Kukla, M., Green, A., Gilbride, D., Mueser, K.T., & Salyers, M.P. (2014). Illness Management and Recovery: A Review of the Literature. *Psychiatric Services,* 65,171–179. https://doi.org/10.1176/appi.ps.201200274

McHugo, G.J., Drake, R.E., Whitley, R., Bond, G.R., Campbell, K., Rapp, C.A., Goldman, H.H., Lutz, W.J., & Finnerty, M.D. (2007) Fidelity outcomes in the national implementing of evidence-based practices. *Psychiatric Services, 58,* 1279–1284. https://doi.org/10.1176/ps.2007.58.10.1279

Monroe-DeVita, M., Morse, G., Mueser, K.T., McHugo, G.J., Xie, H., Hallgren, K.A., Peterson, R., Miller, J., Akiba, C., York, M., Gingerich, S., & Stiles, B. (2018). *Psychiatric Services, 69,* 562–571. https://doi.org/10.1176/appi.ps.201700124

Mosqueiro, B.P., da Rocha NS, de Almeida Fleck, M.P. (2015). Intrinsic religiosity, resilience, quality of life, and suicide risk in depressed inpatients. *Journal of Affective Disorders* 179: 128–133. https://doi.org/10.1016/j.jad.2015.03.022

Mueser, K.T., Corrigan, P.W., Hilton, D.W., Tanzman, B., Schaub, A., Gingerich, S., Essock, S.M., Tarrier, N., Morey, B., Vogel-Scibilia, S., & Herz, M.I. (2002). Illness Management and Recovery: A Review of the Research. *Psychiatric Services, 53*, 1272–1284. https://doi.org/10.1176/appi.ps.53.10.1272

Mueser, K.T., Meyer, P.S., Penn, D.L., Clancy R., Clancy, D.M., & Salyers, M.P. (2006). The illness management and recovery program: rationale, development, and preliminary findings, *Schizophrenia Bull., 32,* Suppl 1:S32–S43. https://doi.org/10.1093/schbul/sbl022

Sanchez-Jankowski, M. (2008). *Cracks in the Pavement: Social Change and Resilience in Poor Neighborhoods.* Los Angeles, CA: University of California Press.

Salerno, A., Margolies, P., & Cleek, A. (2007). *Wellness Self-Management:Personal Workbook.* Albany, NY: New York State Office of Mental Health.

Salerno, A., Margolies P., Cleek A., Pollock M., Gopolan G., & Jackson C. (2011) Wellness Self-Management: An Adaptation of the Illness Management and Recovery Practice in New York State. *Psychiatric Services, 62,* 456–458.

Salerno, A., Margolies, P., Kipnis, S., Bonneau, P., Marnell, S., & Killar, B. (2010). *Wellness Self-Management Plus: Personal Workbook.* Albany, NY: New York State Office of Mental Health.

Salerno, A., Margolies, P., Kipnis, S., Bonneau, P., Marnell, S., Killar, B., Foster, F., Covell, N., Lipton, N., Lincout, P., Cooper, R., Olsen, D., & Huntley, T. (2020). *Wellness Self-Management Plus: Personal Workbook – 2020 Revision.* Albany, NY: New York State Office of Mental Health. https://doi.org/10.1176/ps.62.5.pss6205_0456

Salerno, A. (2019). Building Resilience for Individuals thru Trauma Education. Retrieved February 16, 2021. www.briteresources.com

Salyers, M.P., McGuire, A.B., Rollins, A.L., Bond, G.R., Mueser, K.T., & Macy, V.R. (2010). Integrating assertive community treatment and illness management and recovery for consumers with severe mental illness. *Community Mental Health Journal, 46,* 319–329. https://doi.org/10.1007/s10597-009-9284-6

SAMHSA. (2019). Impact of trauma on individuals, families and Communities. Retrieved November 30, 2021. https://www.samhsa.gov/trauma-violence

SAMHSA. (2010). Illness-management and recovery evidence based practice kit. Retrieved January 18, 2021. https://store.samhsa.gov/product/Illness-Management-and-Recovery-Evidence-Based-Practices-EBP-KIT/SMA09-4462

SAMHSA. (2014). SAMHSA's Trauma and Justice Strategic Initiative. Retrieved January 6, 2021. https://ncsacw.samhsa.gov/userfiles/files/SAMHSA_Trauma.pdf

Southwick, S. M., & Charney, D. (2012). The science of resilience: Implications for the prevention and treatment of depression. *Science*, 338(6103), 79–82. https://doi.org/10.1017/CBO9781139013857

Southwick, S.M., Bonanno, G.A., Masten A.S., Brick, C.P., Yehuda, R. (2014). Resilience definitions, theory, and challenges: interdisciplinary perspectives. *European Journal of Psychotraumatology,* 5, 1. https://doi.org/10.3402/ejpt.v5.25338

Steinhardt, M.A., Brown, S.A., Dubois, S.K., Harrison Jr, L., Lehrer, H.M., & Jaggars, S.S. (2015). A Resilience Intervention in African-American Adults with Type 2 Diabetes. *American Journal of Health Behavior,* 39(4), 507–518. https://doi.org/10.5993/AJHB.39.4.7

Storch, E.A., Morgan, J.E., Caporino, N. E., Brauer, L., Lewin, A.B., Piacentini, J., & Murphy, T.K. (2012). Psychosocial treatment to improve resilience and reduce impairment in youth with tics: an intervention case series of eight youth. *Journal of Cognitive Psychotherapy,* 26(1), 57–70. https://doi.org/10.1891/0889-8391.26.1.57

Tan, C.H.S., Ishak, R.B., Lim, T.X.G., Marimuthusamy, P., Kaurss, K., & Leong, J.J. (2016). Illness management and recovery program for mental health problems: Reducing symptoms and increasing social functioning. *Journal of Clinical Nursing, 26,* 3471–3485. https://doi.org/10.1111/jocn.13712

Tedeschi, R. G., Shakespeare-Finch, J., Taku, K., & Calhoun, L.G. (2018). *Posttraumatic growth: Theory, research, and applications.* New York: Routledge.

Traub, F., & Boynton-Jarrett, R. (2017). Modifiable Resilience Factors to Childhood Adversity for Clinical Pediatric Practice. *Pediatrics.*139(5): e20162569. https://doi.org/10.1542/peds.2016-2569

Wagner, E.H., Austin, B.T., Davis, C., Hindmarsh, M., Schaefer, J., & Bonomi, A. (2001). Improving Chronic Illness Care: translating evidence into action. *Health Affairs. 20,* 64–78. https://doi.org/10.1377/hlthaff.20.6.64

Wagnild, G. (2015) Resilience, self-reported depression and health. Resilience Scale User's Guide, Worden, M.T.

Windle, G., Bennett, K.M., & Noyes, J. (2011). A methodological review of resilience measurement scales. *Health and Quality of Life Outcomes* 9:8. https://doi.org/10.1186/1477-7525-9-8

Supported Employment

Gary R. Bond and Kim T. Mueser

Introduction

Worldwide, many surveys show that most people with severe mental illnesses (SMI) such as schizophrenia and treatment refractory major mood disorders want to work (Bond et al. 2020a) but only a small fraction are employed at any time after their initial diagnosis – for example, less than 15% of people with schizophrenia (Hakulinen et al. 2020). For most people with SMI, employment is a goal because working is a normal adult role and it provides meaning, social contact, community integration, self-esteem, increased income, and better quality of life (Luciano et al. 2014; Modini et al. 2016a). Moreover, more than two-thirds of people with SMI live in poverty (Draine et al. 2002). Employment income can help reduce this source of misery.

People with SMI are often demoralized but fearful about the consequences of working. Yet most yearn to lead normal lives, to be part of general society, and to be productive (Maslow 1970). A job is a place where you are *needed*; if no one depends on you showing up, then why even bother getting up in the morning? (Beard et al. 1982).

Among the many different vocational approaches described in the literature, few have been adequately described, and, until the turn of the century, none had a systematic body of rigorous research showing effectiveness in increasing competitive employment rates (Bond 1992; Bond et al. 1999; Lehman 1995). Vocational approaches that enjoyed widespread adoption include various skills training approaches (Wallace et al. 1999), the clubhouse model (McKay et al. 2018), the job club (Corrigan et al. 1995), and the Boston University choose-get-keep model (Rogers et al. 2006). More recently, customized employment has gained popularity as a promising approach (Riesen et al. 2015). However, in most cases these approaches have not been systematically studied using randomized controlled trials; among those that have been subjected to rigorous research, the findings have been disappointing or lacking replication. In this chapter we describe individual placement and support (IPS), the one program that has demonstrated effectiveness in helping clients with SMI gain competitive employment.

G. R. Bond (✉)
Westat, Rivermill Commercial Center, Lebanon, NH, USA
e-mail: GaryBond@westat.com

K. T. Mueser
Center for Psychiatric Rehabilitation, Departments of Occupational Therapy and Psychological and Brain Sciences, Boston University, Georgetown, ME, USA

W. E. Sowers et al. (eds.), *Textbook of Community Psychiatry*,
https://doi.org/10.1007/978-3-031-10239-4_37

Principles of Individual Placement and Support

IPS is a well-defined model of supported employment for people with SMI. It was first described in a manual in 1993 (Becker and Drake 1993) and further delineated a decade later (Becker and Drake 2003). IPS is defined by a core set of principles: zero exclusion criteria, focus on competitive employment, integration of vocational and clinical services, individualized benefits counseling, attention to client preferences, rapid job search, targeted job development, and provision of long-term follow-along supports. These principles are all supported by empirical research (Drake et al. 2012). IPS researchers have developed a fidelity scale, called the IPS-25, to measure adherence to IPS principles (Bond et al. 2012b). Numerous studies have documented that the IPS-25 is psychometrically sound, and state and local mental health administrators and IPS team leaders frequently use it as a quality improvement tool in routine practice.

Zero Exclusion Criteria

Neither clinicians nor researchers can accurately predict which persons with SMI can obtain competitive work (Anthony and Jansen 1984). Therefore, not excluding any client who wants to work improves the likelihood that IPS will be available to the greatest number of clients who may potentially benefit from it. For clients with SMI, the only criterion for admission to an IPS program is the expressed desire to work in a competitive job. Thus, IPS programs do not use the many criteria that traditional vocational programs use to exclude clients, such as substance abuse, clinical instability, medication nonadherence, cognitive impairment, or time since the most recent hospitalization.

Focus on Competitive Work

Most people with SMI specifically seek to work competitive jobs, defined as regular jobs in community settings paying at least minimum wage and not set aside for people with disabilities (Bond and Drake 2014). IPS honors this preference by focusing only on competitive work, in contrast to other vocational approaches, which may emphasize sheltered work as a steppingstone to competitive work, or transitional employment, in which individuals work at jobs in the community that have been secured by the agency providing the vocational services and are owned by that agency, in order to develop their work experience and resumés before moving onto competitive jobs. Thus, unlike traditional vocational approaches that followed a "train-place" model in which clients receive training before placement into a competitive job, IPS follows the "place-train" approach in which consumers receive any necessary training following attainment of a competitive job (Wehman and Moon 1988). When on-the-job training is needed, it is most often provided by the employer, but it can also be provided by the IPS specialist, whereas any training conducted off the job site is given by the IPS specialist. In practice, people with serious mental illness typically receive little formal on-the-job coaching from IPS specialists.

Integration of Vocational and Clinical Services

Clients enrolled in vocational services benefit more if they also receive appropriate mental health treatment services (Cook et al. 2005). As first documented in a pioneering work by Stein and Test (1980), treatment and rehabilitation programs are most effective when practitioners addressing different aspects of a client's treatment plan collaborate closely. This holds true for vocational services, for several reasons (Drake et al. 2003): First, the integration of IPS with mental health treatment maximizes the chances that the client's clinical treatment providers will support the client in pursuing his or her vocational goals. Second, issues pertinent to the clinical management of the client's psychiatric disorder may become apparent to the IPS specialist in the process of working with the individual (e.g., medication side effects, disruptive or distressing symptoms), and communicating these problems to the treatment team may lead to effective solutions that both address the clinical problems and increase the client's ability to work. Third, clinicians involved in the treatment of the client's psychiatric disorder may have valuable suggestions for job leads. Fourth, clinicians may help address problems that interfere with work, such as inadequate coping, relapses, substance abuse, and limited interpersonal skills by providing these treatments directly or referring clients to appropriate services. For example, cognitive behavioral therapy for psychosis (Kukla et al. 2020), integrated treatment for co-occurring substance use disorders (Becker et al. 2005), and teaching illness self-management skills (Gingerich and Mueser 2010, 2011) are evidence-based practices that can be effective at addressing these problems.

The integration of vocational and clinical services occurs most effectively when the IPS specialist collaborates closely with the client's clinical treatment team, attending weekly team meetings and interacting frequently with the client's case manager and other clinicians. Integration is most easily attained when the IPS program and the clinical treatment team are located within the same agency and ideally have offices in close proximity to each other. IPS programs typically collaborate with multiple mental health treatment teams. In order to foster strongly working relationships, it is preferable for each IPS specialist's caseload to be limited to one or two treatment teams. Unlike in the assertive community model, however, the IPS specialist is usually not a formal member of a specific treatment team.

Benefits Counseling

People with SMI have often suffered a long and arduous process of applying for and obtaining disability benefits. After this struggle to obtain benefits, it is understandable that many clients are concerned about the effects of work on their benefits (Livermore and Bardos 2017). Benefits counseling is aimed at helping clients understand the impact of returning to work on their benefits, including how much they can work before experiencing a reduction in their financial benefits and the potential loss of their health insurance. Clients with psychiatric disabilities who receive personalized counseling on the impact of earnings on their benefits accrue more earnings from employment (Tremblay et al. 2006).

Client Preferences

Respect for individual client preferences is an important defining characteristic of supported employment. Client preferences for the type of work desired can inform the job search. Research shows that clients who obtain jobs that match the expressed interests have significantly longer job tenures than clients who obtain jobs outside of their areas of interest (Becker et al. 1996; Mueser et al. 2001). Client preferences also have a significant bearing on the type of supports provided by the IPS specialist. Typically half or more of clients opt to disclose their psychiatric disability to a prospective employer (DeTore et al. 2019; Jones and Bond 2007), thereby enabling IPS specialists to play an active role in helping them obtain the job and keep it through direct contacts with the employer. For example, IPS specialists can join discussions with the employer to help clients negotiate any needed reasonable accommodations, as protected by the Americans with Disabilities Act. Other clients prefer not to disclose their psychiatric disability, in which case the IPS specialist plays a "behind-the-scenes" role in helping the client achieve his or her employment goals.

Targeted Job Development

To help clients find jobs matching their preferences, IPS specialists must network with employers. The job-finding process takes several forms: sometimes clients meet employers alone with the IPS specialist coaching behind the scenes; other times the IPS specialist and client together have an introductory meeting with a prospective employer. The job match is often made through individualized job searches but can also draw on a pool of prospective employers that IPS specialists are continuously building. The process of contacting employers and cultivating relationships is called job development. It entails IPS specialists who make multiple contacts with individual employers over a period of time, usually well before any client makes contact. The IPS job development approach is inspired by the metaphor of "three cups of tea" ("The first time you share tea with a stranger, you are a stranger. The second time you take tea, you are an honored guest. The third time you share a cup of tea, you become family.") (Mortenson and Relin 2006). Through this process, IPS specialists are successful in finding (or creating) jobs openings (Carlson et al. 2018). Job development increases the likelihood of obtaining competitive employment (Leff et al. 2005).

Rapid Job Search

The process of helping clients find a job begins soon after a client enrolls in an IPS program, with the first face-to-face employer contacts usually occurring within 1 month. This is in contrast to other vocational approaches, which may require prevocational skills training and/or extensive workplace assessments that involve extensive periods of time to complete. Research suggests that when clients receive prevocational preparation prior to beginning a job search, they often become habituated to prevocational settings and never seek competitive employment; they also tend to lose interest and drop out of vocational services (Bond 2004). Therefore, rapid job search is one of the most defining characteristics of IPS.

Follow-Along Supports

Historically, vocational rehabilitation was deemed successful when a client obtained competitive employment and remained in that job for a period of a few months, at which point funding and follow-along support were discontinued. In contrast, IPS continues to provide follow-along supports without a predetermined time period. IPS specialists provide a wide variety of follow-along supports. These include helping the client learn job-related tasks, providing on-site or off-site support to the client, negotiating reasonable accommodations with an employer, and facilitating the transition to new job responsibilities, or, if a client loses a job, helping them find a new job. Provision of follow-along supports for a year or more after a client obtains a job is associated with longer job tenure (Bond and Kukla 2011). Some research suggests that face-to-face contact is more strongly associated with job tenure (Bond and Kukla 2011), though more recent research suggests promising new approaches to long-term support through videoconferencing, texting, and other forms of telehealth (Drake 2020a).

Other Features of IPS Programs

In addition to the principles described above that guide the provision of IPS, several key features distinguish IPS from other approaches to vocational rehabilitation. Work is a normalizing activity that takes place in the community, and therefore most IPS services are provided in the community rather than the mental health center or rehabilitation agency. IPS specialists meet with clients in settings that are convenient and comfortable for them and often spend time together walking around the community, exploring possible jobs, and talking to prospective employers.

IPS is also recovery-oriented and strengths-based. The consumer movement has argued successfully for a redefinition of recovery that is not based on the absence of psychopathology (as in traditional medical definitions) but rather defined in terms of individual consumers' hopes and dreams (Jaiswal et al. 2020). Thus, recovery has been defined as "the development of new meaning and purpose in one's life as one grows beyond the catastrophic effects of mental illness" (Anthony 1993). Another definition of recovery is "the process in which people are able to live, work, learn, and participate fully in their communities" (New Freedom Commission on Mental Health 2003). As work is a common personal recovery goal for many clients (Provencher et al. 2002), the emphasis in IPS on community-based services, competitive employment, zero eligibility exclusion criteria, and respect for client self-determination is all compatible with the philosophy of recovery.

Also consistent with recovery is the emphasis in IPS on client strengths rather than deficits and viewing the community as a potential resource rather than a barrier to the client's employment goals (Rapp and Goscha 2011). The identification of client strengths plays an important role in building up clients' self-confidence and helping them sell themselves to prospective employers. IPS specialists are always on the lookout to engage natural supports for the client in the community, including both in the workplace (e.g., supervisor, coworkers) and at home (e.g., family or friends), in addition to the client's treatment team. Capitalizing on natural supports in the client's environment takes advantage of the spontaneous opportunities these individuals may have to help the client, often at times when the IPS specialist cannot be available, thereby avoiding unnecessary dependence on the IPS specialist for providing all the needed supports.

Although IPS specialists provide a full range of vocational services, such as job development and follow-along supports, they often may be involved in helping clients manage their psychiatric disorder more effectively and improving their interpersonal skills. For example, cognitive difficulties may make it difficult for some clients to achieve their vocational goals (McGurk and Mueser 2004), and IPS specialists are often actively involved in helping clients use coping strategies for managing or minimizing their cognitive difficulties (McGurk and Mueser 2006).

The Organization of IPS Services

Except in very rural areas, IPS programs usually consist of a team staffed by at least one part-time team leader and two full-time IPS specialists. To remain grounded in the everyday realities of helping clients find and keep jobs, the IPS team leader carries a reduced caseload of clients. The team leader provides weekly supervision to the IPS specialists and serves as a liaison for the program or other teams and programs, both within the agency and at other agencies. IPS specialists focus exclusively on providing vocational services; they do not have clinical responsibilities, such as case management, leading skills training groups, or providing psychotherapy. This clear delineation of job duties ensures that IPS specialists need not decide whether to provide vocational services or some other service to clients on their caseload.

In addition, every IPS specialist provides the full range of vocational services for each client, as described above (e.g., assessments, job development, and provision of follow-along supports). This is in contrast to the division of labor found in some vocational programs in which services such as job development and follow-along supports are provided by different individuals. By ensuring that a single practitioner provides the entire range of vocational services, IPS programs avoid requiring clients to develop relationships with multiple vocational service providers as they progress through the employment process. By having all IPS specialists involved in job development rather than just one or two specialists, the team is able collectively to identify a much broader range of jobs. While job development is primarily aimed at finding a job matched for a specific client, IPS specialists also identify jobs that may not be suitable for the jobseeker for which the search was intended but which can be shared with other IPS specialists to the benefit of other clients in the program.

Research on the Effectiveness of Supported Employment

Numerous reviews conclude that IPS is effective in helping clients achieve competitive employment (Brinchmann et al. 2020; Frederick and VanderWeele 2019; Modini et al. 2016b). The IPS evidence base includes quasi-experimental studies examining conversion of day treatment services to IPS (Bond 2004) and randomized controlled trials (RCTs) of well-implemented IPS programs (Bond et al. 2020a). Since RCTs are the gold standard in evaluating the effectiveness of an intervention, we will focus primarily on this body of research. We also briefly summarize the findings from four long-term follow-up studies.

Randomized Controlled Trials

The most recent compilation of RCTs of IPS for people with serious mental illness identified 28 studies (including 7 multisite studies) with a total of 3187 IPS clients and 3281 control clients (Bond et al. 2020a). Although the initial studies were conducted in the USA, increasingly other countries have also conducted RCTs of IPS. These RCTs included 12 conducted in the USA and 16 conducted in 12 countries outside the USA. Study sites ranged widely geographically and included mostly large and midsized cities and a few rural communities. Most studies recruited unemployed clients receiving services from a community mental health center, though some studies enrolled other target groups (e.g., young adults with early psychosis, disability beneficiaries, and veterans with posttraumatic stress disorder). The control groups were usually offered services as usual (whatever vocational rehabilitation services were available in the community), but in some studies the control group received well-regarded vocational programs that followed a different service model, typically a train-place model or, in some cases, multiple vocational models. (For the list of studies and more methodological details, go to *Evidence for IPS* at https://ipsworks.org/index.php/library/.)

In 60% of the studies, the follow-up period was 18 months or longer. All 28 RCTs found that employment outcomes significantly favored IPS, usually with large differences. Averaging across studies, 55% of IPS participants worked in a competitive job during follow-up, compared to 25% of control participants. The findings from the USA generalize well outside the USA: RCTs in 11 countries and 4 continents have found that IPS participants had significantly better competitive employment outcomes than control participants. The IPS competitive employment rate in these RCTs is similar in North America, Asia, and Australia, though somewhat lower in Europe (Drake et al. 2019).

Controlled trials of IPS consistently show its effectiveness across a wide range of employment outcomes. For example, one meta-analysis combining results from four RCTs found that, compared to control participants, IPS participants gained employment faster, maintained employment four times longer during follow-up, earned three times the amount from employment, and were three times as likely to work 20 hours or more per week (Bond et al. 2012a).

Long-Term Outcome Studies

Long-term follow-up studies are important for assessing the permanence of the impact of an intervention. In IPS studies, the general standard is to measure the percentage of the sample who are "steady workers" (employed at least 50% of the follow-up period). In a 10-year follow-up study of IPS, 86% of former IPS clients reported working during follow-up and 33% were steady workers (Salyers et al. 2004). In a second study, 100% had worked at some time during follow-up 8–12 years after enrollment, and 71% were steady workers (Becker et al. 2007). A Swiss RCT examined outcomes 5 years after enrollment and found that the percentage of steady workers was much higher for IPS than for the control group (44% versus 11%) (Hoffmann et al. 2014). A follow-up study of a large, multisite trial examined earned income reported to the Internal Revenue Service and found significantly higher annual earnings for IPS clients compared to controls which persisted over a 5-year period after the initial 2-year follow-up study had ended (Baller et al. 2020).

The implications of this research are especially significant in light of two general findings. First, as noted earlier, the competitive employment rate for individuals with SMI in the public mental health system is 15% or less. Therefore, a steady employment rate of 50% or more in this population is far above the norm. Second, these findings are in stark contrast to the attenuation effects found for many psychosocial interventions once the active intervention has been discontinued (e.g., Stein and Test 1980). Once IPS clients begin working, the natural reinforcers of work (a paycheck, making a meaningful contribution to society, social connectedness) may provide incentives to continuing to work. In any case, the "yo-yo effect" of diminishing gains following treatment cessation for weight loss and exercise programs has not been found for IPS. These findings suggest that IPS promotes a life trajectory that differs from that of patienthood and dependence.

Growth of IPS

The effectiveness of IPS has been well established for two decades. Throughout the USA, state leaders show great interest in implementing IPS, and many states now offer IPS services statewide. According to a 2019 telephone survey of state mental health and vocational rehabilitation (VR) leaders, 80% of states in the USA have implemented IPS services, with over 850 IPS programs nationwide (Pogue et al., 2022). Yet the total number of people receiving IPS is only a fraction of the total population of unemployed Americans with serious mental illness. Clearly, the key question is no longer whether IPS works, but rather, as for other evidence-based psychosocial practices, how to close the gap between the known population of those who want and need these evidence-based services and those who have access. According to over a dozen surveys, 60% of people with serious mental illness want to work (https://ipsworks.org/index.php/evidence-for-ips/), but only about 2% have access to IPS (Bruns et al. 2016).

The paramount obstacles to adequate access to IPS include the failure of policymakers to understand the connection between work and general health and the lack of political will. Government leaders often do not recognize that employment is a critical mental health intervention (Drake and Wallach 2020). At the practical level, the primary barriers have been inadequate funding and the lack of an evidence-based methodology for widescale expansion (Drake et al. 2016). Inadequate funding for employment services is a worldwide problem, though some countries, such as England and the Netherlands, have made national commitments to fund IPS access (Becker and Bond 2020). The second ingredient is a strategy to facilitate adoption, high-fidelity implementation, and sustainment of IPS. One strategy that has borne fruit is a "learning community." Since 2002, the IPS Employment Center has led an international learning community that coordinates education, training, technical assistance, fidelity and outcome monitoring, and regular communications through newsletters, bimonthly calls, and an annual meeting (Drake et al. 2020a).

In the USA, IPS programs participating in the learning community continuously monitor employment rates and report them to the IPS Employment Center every 3 months, a process that has been maintained over 18 years. The quarterly employment rate for the US states in the learning community has not declined below 40%, even during the Great Recession of 2007–2009 and during the COVID pandemic (as of October 2020). The learning community has facilitated sustainment of IPS services over time: one prospective study found that 96% of 129 IPS programs were sustained over 2 years (Bond et al. 2016). The number of IPS programs has expanded steadily, with a mean annual growth rate of 26% in the number of IPS programs in the USA. The learning community has helped to initiate and maintain over 450 IPS programs, including 366 in the USA and 100 outside the USA, most at high fidelity with good employment outcomes (Drake and Wallach 2020).

While the learning community has had a catalytic effect on IPS expansion, another mechanism that has independently (and in some case synergistically) promoted the spread of IPS in the USA has been class action lawsuits. In 2009, the US Department of Justice began to enforce the Supreme Court's decision in *Olmstead v. L.C.*, requiring states to ensure that persons with disabilities should have the opportunity to live like people without disabilities and to receive services in the most integrated setting appropriate to their needs (Burnim 2015). As part of furthering community integration, Olmstead settlements in numerous states have included the mandated expansion of supported employment services for people with serious mental illness. These class-action lawsuits have promoted IPS services in a dozen states over the last decade, some with considerable success (Bond et al. 2021; Johnson-Kwochka et al. 2017).

IPS has expanded worldwide, with IPS programs in 19 countries (Australia, Belgium, Canada, China, Czech Republic, Denmark, France, Germany, Iceland, Ireland, Italy, Japan, New Zealand, the Netherlands, Norway, Spain, Sweden, Switzerland, and the UK) (Drake 2020b). Factors that have promoted its international growth include unique features of the IPS model that make its adoption attractive and its implementation feasible, local champions, local research studies demonstrating the effectiveness of IPS, the development of technical assistance centers, and national initiatives (Bond et al. 2020b).

Costs of IPS

Several studies have estimated an average annual cost of IPS of approximately 5000–8000 USD per client, though these estimates vary widely depending on estimation methods, assumptions, and caseload size (Salkever 2013). Cost-benefit and cost-effectiveness analyses of IPS are rare. The most rigorous IPS cost-benefit analysis was a large multinational randomized controlled trial in Europe, which concluded that IPS yielded better employment and health outcomes than alternative vocational services at lower cost overall to the health and social care systems. The major cost savings were in reduced hospitalizations for IPS (Knapp et al. 2013). A 5-year follow-up RCT of IPS reported substantially greater return on investment for IPS compared to usual vocational services ($0.54 vs. $0.18 per dollar invested) (Hoffmann et al. 2014). A recent cost-effectiveness study of IPS has found that IPS was less costly and more effective than services as usual (Christensen et al. 2021). An early study found that service agencies converting their day treatment programs to IPS reduced service costs by 29% (Clark 1998). A promising area for cost savings concerns young adults who are experiencing early psychosis. If IPS can help young adults gain steady employment and thereby avert or at least delay entry into the disability system, the savings would be enormous (Drake et al. 2020b). One Norwegian study suggests that such a strategy may be viable (Sveinsdottir et al. 2020).

Conclusions and Future Directions

Abundant research shows that the IPS is effective at improving employment outcomes for persons with SMI. In addition to the clinical efficacy of the IPS model, research has demonstrated that IPS can be implemented and sustained in routine community settings. Furthermore, economic analyses suggest that IPS can be implemented and sustained as relatively modest cost (compared to many mental health services) and that the costs of IPS may be potentially offset by decreases in the use of other mental health services.

The success of the IPS model has led to several other avenues of research, including efforts to identify ancillary services designed to target client characteristics thought to interfere with achieving positive vocational outcomes. One fruitful area has been augmenting IPS with cognitive remediation for people with impaired cognitive functioning or who do not respond to standard IPS (McGurk et al. 2007, 2015). Another important area of research concerns the impact of IPS on young adults with mental health conditions, especially young adults with a first episode of psychosis (Bond et al. 2015). As the early onset of psychosis often curtails individuals' educational attainment (Kessler et al. 1995), which has negative repercussions in the labor market, there has been a growing interest in supported education, or helping clients achieve educational goals such as receiving a high school diploma, pursuing an associate's or bachelor's degree, or completing a certificate program (Manthey et al. 2012). The principles of supported education parallel those for IPS (Bond et al. 2019; Swanson et al. 2017). Many IPS programs, especially those serving young adults, now integrate supported employment with supported education. Coordinated specialty care programs for first episode psychosis (Heinssen et al. 2014) often include an intervention that provides both supported employment and education, depending on the client's goals (Nuechterlein et al. 2020; Rosenheck et al. 2017). However, the impact of supported education, or programs that provide both supported employment and education, on educational outcomes has not yet been convincingly demonstrated in randomized controlled trials, and at present it cannot be considered an evidence-based practice (Ringelsen et al. 2017). More work is needed to address the impact of IPS on the first episode psychosis population and to establish standardized guidelines for providing supported education.

The rehabilitation field has made important strides in improving employment outcomes for people with SMI over the past two decades. The IPS model of supported employment is an evidence-based practice for vocational rehabilitation. An important priority is to increase the access of persons with SMI to IPS programs, which have the potential to enhance quality of life by improving the economic standing of clients, giving them something meaningful and rewarding to do with their time, and promoting their integration into their communities.

References

Anthony, W. A. (1993). Recovery from mental illness: The guiding vision of the mental health service system in the 1990s. *Psychosocial Rehabilitation Journal, 16*(4), 11–23.

Anthony, W. A., & Jansen, M. A. (1984). Predicting the vocational capacity of the chronically mentally ill: Research and implications. *American Psychologist, 39*, 537–544.

Baller, J., Blyler, C., Bronnikov, S., Xie, H., Bond, G. R., Filion, K., & Hale, T. (2020). Long-term follow-up of a randomized trial of supported employment for Social Security disability beneficiaries with mental illness. *Psychiatric Services, 71*, 243–249.

Beard, J. H., Propst, R. N., & Malamud, T. J. (1982). The Fountain House model of psychiatric rehabilitation. *Psychosocial Rehabilitation Journal, 5*(1), 47–53.

Becker, D. R., & Bond, G. R. (2020). Commentary on special issue on IPS International. *Psychiatric Rehabilitation Journal, 43*, 79–82.

Becker, D. R., Drake, R., & Naughton, W. J. (2005). Supported employment for people with co-occurring disorders. *Psychiatric Rehabilitation Journal, 28*, 332–338.

Becker, D. R., & Drake, R. E. (1993). *A working life: The Individual Placement and Support (IPS) Program*. Concord, NH: New Hampshire-Dartmouth Psychiatric Research Center.

Becker, D. R., & Drake, R. E. (2003). *A working life for people with severe mental illness*. New York: Oxford University Press.

Becker, D. R., Drake, R. E., Farabaugh, A., & Bond, G. R. (1996). Job preferences of clients with severe psychiatric disorders participating in supported employment programs. *Psychiatric Services, 47*, 1223–1226. https://doi.org/10.1176/ps.47.11.1223

Becker, D. R., Whitley, R., Bailey, E. L., & Drake, R. E. (2007). Long-term employment trajectories among participants with severe mental illness in supported employment. *Psychiatric Services, 58*, 922–928. https://doi.org/10.1176/ps.2007.58.7.922

Bond, G. R. (1992). Vocational rehabilitation. In R. P. Liberman (Ed.), *Handbook of psychiatric rehabilitation* (pp. 244–275). New York: Macmillan.

Bond, G. R. (2004). Supported employment: Evidence for an evidence-based practice. *Psychiatric Rehabilitation Journal, 27*, 345–359.

Bond, G. R., Campbell, K., & Drake, R. E. (2012a). Standardizing measures in four domains of employment outcome for Individual Placement and Support. *Psychiatric Services, 63*, 751–757. https://doi.org/10.1176/appi.ps.201100270

Bond, G. R., & Drake, R. E. (2014). Making the case for IPS supported employment. *Administration and Policy in Mental Health and Mental Health Services Research, 41*, 69–73. https://doi.org/10.1007/s10488-012-0444-6

Bond, G. R., Drake, R. E., & Becker, D. R. (2020a). An update on Individual Placement and Support. *World Psychiatry, 19*, 390–391. https://doi.org/10.1002/wps.20784

Bond, G. R., Drake, R. E., Becker, D. R., & Mueser, K. T. (1999). Effectiveness of psychiatric rehabilitation approaches for employment of people with severe mental illness. *Journal of Disability Policy Studies, 10*, 18–52. https://doi.org/10.1177/104420739901000104

Bond, G. R., Drake, R. E., Becker, D. R., & Noel, V. A. (2016). The IPS Learning Community: a longitudinal study of sustainment, quality, and outcome. *Psychiatric Services, 67*, 864–869.

Bond, G. R., Drake, R. E., & Luciano, A. E. (2015). Employment and educational outcomes in early intervention programmes for early psychosis: a systematic review. *Epidemiology and Psychiatric Sciences, 24*, 446–457. https://doi.org/10.1017/S2045796014000419

Bond, G. R., Johnson-Kwochka, A. V., Pogue, J. A., Langfitt-Reese, S., Becker, D. R., & Drake, R. E. (2021). A tale of four states: factors influencing the statewide adoption of IPS. *Administration and Policy in Mental Health and Mental Health Services Research, 48*, 528–538. https://doi.org/10.1007/s10488-020-01087-2

Bond, G. R., & Kukla, M. (2011). Impact of follow-along support on job tenure in the Individual Placement and Support model. *Journal of Nervous and Mental Disease, 199*, 150–155.

Bond, G. R., Lockett, H., & van Weeghel, J. (2020b). International growth of Individual Placement and Support. *Epidemiology and Psychiatric Sciences, 29*, e183, 181–183. https://doi.org/10.1017/S2045796020000955.

Bond, G. R., Peterson, A. E., Becker, D. R., & Drake, R. E. (2012b). Validation of the revised Individual Placement and Support Fidelity Scale (IPS-25). *Psychiatric Services, 63*, 758–763. https://doi.org/10.1176/appi.ps.201100476

Bond, G. R., Swanson, S. J., Becker, D. R., Ellison, M. L., & Reeder, K. E. (2019). The IPS-Y: IPS Fidelity Scale for Young Adults. *American Journal of Psychiatric Rehabilitation, 22*, 239–255. https://www.muse.jhu.edu/article/797612

Brinchmann, B., Widding-Havneraas, T., Modini, M., Rinaldi, M., Moe, C. F., McDaid, D., … Mykletun, A. (2020). A meta-regression of the impact of policy on the efficacy of Individual Placement and Support. *Acta Psychiatrica Scandinavica, 141*, 206–220. https://doi.org/10.1111/acps.13129

Bruns, E. J., Kerns, S. E., Pullmann, M. D., Hensley, S. W., Lutterman, T., & Hoagwood, K. E. (2016). Research, data, and evidence-based treatment use in state behavioral health systems, 2001–2012. *Psychiatric Services, 67*, 496–503. https://doi.org/10.1176/appi.ps.201500014

Burnim, I. (2015). The promise of the Americans with Disabilities Act for people with mental illness. *Journal of the American Medical Association, 313*, 2223–2224.

Carlson, L., Smith, G., Mariscal, E. S., Rapp, C. A., Holter, M. C., Ko, E., … Fukui, S. (2018). The comparative effectiveness of a model of job development versus treatment as usual. *Best Practices in Mental Health, 14*, 21–31.

Christensen, T. N., Kruse, M., Hellström, L., & Eplov, L. F. (2021). Cost-utility and cost-effectiveness of Individual Placement Support and cognitive remediation in people with severe mental illness: Results from a randomised clinical trial. *European Psychiatry*, https://doi.org/10.1192/j.eurpsy.2020.111.

Clark, R. E. (1998). Supported employment and managed care: Can they coexist? *Psychiatric Rehabilitation Journal, 22*(1), 62–68.

Cook, J. A., Lehman, A. F., Drake, R., McFarlane, W. R., Gold, P. B., Leff, H. S., … Grey, D. D. (2005). Integration of psychiatric and vocational services: A multisite randomized, controlled trial of supported employment. *American Journal of Psychiatry, 162*, 1948–1956. https://doi.org/10.1176/appi.ajp.162.10.1948

Corrigan, P. W., Reedy, P., Thadani, D., & Ganet, M. (1995). Correlates of participation and completion in a job club for clients with psychiatric disability. *Rehabilitation Counseling Bulletin, 39*, 42–53.

DeTore, N. R., Hintz, K., Khare, C., & Mueser, K. T. (2019). Disclosure of mental illness to prospective employers: clinical, psychosocial, and work correlates in persons receiving supported employment. *Psychiatry Research, 273*, 312–317.

Draine, J., Salzer, M. S., Culhane, D. P., & Hadley, T. R. (2002). Role of social disadvantage in crime, joblessness, and homelessness among persons with serious mental illness. *Psychiatric Services, 53*, 565–573.

Drake, R. E. (2020a). Mental health technology tools: two alternative approaches. *Epidemiology and Psychiatric Sciences, 29*, e99, 91–91.

Drake, R. E. (2020b). Special Issue: International Implementation of Individual Placement and Support. *Psychiatric Rehabilitation Journal, 43*(1), 1–82.

Drake, R. E., Becker, D. R., & Bond, G. R. (2019). Introducing Individual Placement and Support (IPS) supported employment in Japan. *Psychiatry and Clinical Neurosciences, 73*, 47–49.

Drake, R. E., Becker, D. R., & Bond, G. R. (2020a). The growth and sustainment of Individual Placement and Support. *Psychiatric Services, 71*, 1075–1077.

Drake, R. E., Becker, D. R., Bond, G. R., & Mueser, K. T. (2003). A process analysis of integrated and non-integrated approaches to supported employment. *Journal of Vocational Rehabilitation, 18*, 51–58.

Drake, R. E., Bond, G. R., & Becker, D. R. (2012). *Individual Placement and Support: An evidence-based approach to supported employment*. New York: Oxford University Press.

Drake, R. E., Bond, G. R., Goldman, H. H., Hogan, M. F., & Karakus, M. (2016). Individual Placement and Support services boost employment for people with serious mental illness, but funding is lacking. *Health Affairs, 35*, 1098–1105. https://doi.org/10.1377/hlthaff.2016.0001

Drake, R. E., Meara, E. R., & Bond, G. R. (2020b). Policy issues regarding employment for people with serious mental illness. In H. H. Goldman, R. G. Frank, & J. P. Morrissey (Eds.), *The Palgrave Handbook of American Mental Health Policy* (pp. 449–470). New York: Palgrave Macmillan.

Drake, R. E., & Wallach, M. A. (2020). Employment is a critical mental health intervention. *Epidemiology and Psychiatric Sciences, 29*, e178, 171–173. https://doi.org/10.1017/S2045796020000906.

Frederick, D. E., & VanderWeele, T. J. (2019). Supported employment: Meta-analysis and review of randomized controlled trials of individual placement and support. *PLOS ONE, 14*(2), e0212208. https://doi.org/10.1371/journal.pone.0212208

Gingerich, S., & Mueser, K. T. (2010). *Illness Management and Recovery Implementation Resource Kit* (Revised ed.). Rockville, MD: Center for Mental Health Services, Substance Abuse and Mental Health Services Administration.

Gingerich, S., & Mueser, K. T. (2011). *Illness management and recovery: Personalized skills and strategies for those with mental illness* (3rd ed.). Center City, MN: Hazelden.

Hakulinen, C., Elovainio, M., Arffman, M., Lumme, S., Suokas, K., Pirkola, S., … Böckerman, P. (2020). Employment status and personal income before and after onset of a severe mental disorder: a case-control study. *Psychiatric Services, 71*, 250–255. https://doi.org/10.1176/appi.ps.201900239

Heinssen, R. K., Goldstein, A. B., & Azrin, S. T. (2014). *Evidence-based treatments for first episode psychosis: Components of coordinated specialty care*. Rockville, MD: NIMH.

Hoffmann, H., Jäckel, D., Glauser, S., Mueser, K. T., & Kupper, Z. (2014). Long-term effectiveness of supported employment: five-year follow-up of a randomized controlled trial. *American Journal of Psychiatry, 171*, 1183–1190.

Jaiswal, A., Carmichael, K., Gupta, S., Siemens, T., Crowley, P., Carlsson, A., … Brown, N. (2020). Essential elements that contribute to the recovery of persons with severe mental illness: a systematic scoping study. *Frontiers in Psychiatry,* https://doi.org/10.3389/fpsyt.2020.586230.

Johnson-Kwochka, A. V., Bond, G. R., Drake, R. E., Becker, D. R., & Greene, M. A. (2017). Prevalence and quality of Individual Placement and Support (IPS) supported employment in the United States. *Administration and Policy in Mental Health and Mental Health Services Research, 44*, 311–319.

Jones, A. M., & Bond, G. R. (2007). Disclosure of severe mental illness in the workplace. *Schizophrenia Bulletin, 33*, 593.

Kessler, R. C., Foster, C. L., Saunders, W. B., & Stang, P. E. (1995). Social consequences of psychiatric disorders I.: Educational attainment. *American Journal of Psychiatry, 152*, 1026–1052. https://doi.org/10.1176/ajp.152.7.1026

Knapp, M., Patel, A., Curran, C., Latimer, E., Catty, J., Becker, T., … Burns, T. (2013). Supported employment: cost-effectiveness across six European sites. *World Psychiatry, 12*, 60–68.

Kukla, M., Strasburger, A. M., Salyers, M. P., Rollins, A. L., & Lysaker, P. H. (2020). Psychosocial outcomes of a pilot study of work-tailored cognitive behavioral therapy intervention for adults with serious mental illness. *Journal of Clinical Psychology,* https://doi.org/10.1002/jclp.23048.

Leff, H. S., Cook, J. A., Gold, P. B., Toprac, M., Blyler, C., Goldberg, R. W., … Raab, B. (2005). Effects of job development and job support on competitive employment of persons with severe mental illness. *Psychiatric Services, 56*, 1237–1244.

Lehman, A. F. (1995). Vocational rehabilitation in schizophrenia. *Schizophrenia Bulletin, 21*(4), 645–656.

Livermore, G. A., & Bardos, M. (2017). Characteristics of adults with psychiatric disabilities participating in the federal disability programs. *Psychiatric Rehabilitation Journal, 40*, 153–162. https://doi.org/10.1037/prj0000239

Luciano, A. E., Bond, G. R., & Drake, R. E. (2014). Does employment alter the course and outcome of schizophrenia and other severe mental illnesses? A systematic review of longitudinal research. *Schizophrenia Research, 159*, 312–321. https://doi.org/10.1016/j.schres.2014.09.010

Manthey, T. J., Holter, M., Rapp, C. A., Davis, J. K., & Carlson, L. (2012). The perceived importance of integrated supported education and employment services. *Journal of Rehabilitation, 78*, 16–24.

Maslow, A. H. (1970). *Motivation and personality* (2nd ed.): Harper & Row.

McGurk, S. R., & Mueser, K. T. (2004). Cognitive functioning, symptoms, and work in supported employment: A review and heuristic model. *Schizophrenia Research, 70*, 147–173.

McGurk, S. R., & Mueser, K. T. (2006). Strategies for coping with cognitive impairment in supported employment. *Psychiatric Services, 57*, 1421–1429.

McGurk, S. R., Mueser, K. T., Feldman, K., Wolfe, R., & Pascaris, A. (2007). Cognitive training for supported employment: 2–3 year outcomes of a randomized controlled trial. *American Journal of Psychiatry, 164*, 437–441.

McGurk, S. R., Mueser, K. T., Xie, H., Welsh, J., Kaiser, S., Drake, R. E., … McHugo, G. J. (2015). Cognitive enhancement treatment for people with mental illness who do not respond to supported employment: a randomized controlled trial. *American Journal of Psychiatry, 172*, 852–861.

McKay, C., Nugent, K. L., Johnsen, M., Eaton, W. W., & Lidz, C. W. (2018). A systematic review of evidence for the clubhouse model of psychosocial rehabilitation. *Administration and Policy in Mental Health and Mental Health Services Research, 45*, 28–47.

Modini, M., Joyce, S., Mykletun, A., Christensen, H., Bryant, R. A., Mitchell, P. B., & Harvey, S. B. (2016a). The mental health benefits of employment: results of a systematic meta-review. *Australasian Psychiatry 24*, 331–336. https://doi.org/10.1177/1039856215618523

Modini, M., Tan, L., Brinchmann, B., Wang, M., Killackey, E., Glozier, N., … Harvey, S. B. (2016b). Supported employment for people with severe mental illness: a systematic review and meta-analysis of the international evidence. *British Journal of Psychiatry, 209*, 14–22. https://doi.org/10.1192/bjp.bp.115.165092

Mortenson, G., & Relin, D. O. (2006). *Three cups of tea: one man's mission to fight terrorism and build nations...one school at a time*. New York: Penguin Press.

Mueser, K. T., Becker, D. R., & Wolfe, R. S. (2001). Supported employment, job preferences, job tenure and satisfaction. *Journal of Mental Health, 10*, 411-417.

New Freedom Commission on Mental Health. (2003). *Achieving the promise: Transforming mental health care in America. Final Report. DHHS Pub. No. SMA-03-3832*. Rockville, MD: Substance Abuse and Mental Health Services Administration.

Nuechterlein, K. H., Subotnik, K. L., Ventura, J., Turner, L. R., Gitlin, M. J., Gretchen-Doorly, D., … Liberman, R. P. (2020). Enhancing return to work or school after a first episode of schizophrenia: the UCLA RCT of Individual Placement and Support and Workplace Fundamentals Module training. *Psychological Medicine, 50*, 20–28.

Pogue, J. A., Bond, G, R., Drake, R. E., Becker, D. R., Logsdon, S. M. (2022). Growth of IPS Supported Employment Programs in the United States: An Update. Psychiatric Services 73(5):533-538. https://doi.org/10.1176/appi.ps.202100199

Provencher, H. L., Gregg, R., Mead, S., & Mueser, K. T. (2002). The role of work in the recovery of persons with psychiatric disabilities. *Psychiatric Rehabilitation Journal, 26*, 132–144.

Rapp, C. A., & Goscha, R. J. (2011). *The strengths model: a recovery-oriented approach to mental health services* (2nd ed.). New York: Oxford.

Riesen, T., Morgan, R. L., & Griffin, C. (2015). Customized employment: A review of the literature. *Journal of Vocational Rehabilitation, 43*, 183–193.

Ringelsen, H., Ellison, M. L., Ryder-Burge, A., Biebel, K., Alikhan, S., & Jones, E. (2017). Supported education for individuals with psychiatric disabilities: state of the practice and policy implications. *Psychiatric Rehabilitation Journal, 40*, 197–206.

Rogers, E. S., Anthony, W. A., Lyass, A., & Penk, W. E. (2006). A randomized clinical trial of vocational rehabilitation for people with psychiatric disabilities. *Rehabilitation Counseling Bulletin, 49*, 143–156.

Rosenheck, R. A., Mueser, K. T., Sint, K., Lin, H., Lynde, D. W., Glynn, S. M., … Kane, J. M. (2017). Supported employment and education in comprehensive, integrated care for first episode psychosis: Effects on work, school, and disability income. *Schizophrenia Research, 182*, 120–128. https://doi.org/10.1016/j.schres.2016.09.024

Salkever, D. S. (2013). Social costs of expanding access to evidence-based supported employment: concepts and interpretive review of evidence. *Psychiatric Services, 64*, 111–119.

Salyers, M. P., Becker, D. R., Drake, R. E., Torrey, W. C., & Wyzik, P. F. (2004). Ten-year follow-up of clients in a supported employment program. *Psychiatric Services, 55*, 302–308. https://doi.org/10.1176/appi.ps.55.3.302

Stein, L. I., & Test, M. A. (1980). An alternative to mental health treatment. I: Conceptual model, treatment program, and clinical evaluation. *Archives of General Psychiatry, 37*, 392–397.

Sveinsdottir, V., Lie, S. A., Bond, G. R., Eriksen, H. R., Tveito, T. H., Grasdal, A., & Reme, S. E. (2020). Individual placement and support for young adults at risk of early work disability (the SEED trial). A randomized controlled trial. *Scandinavian Journal of Work, Environment and Health, 46*, 50–59. https://doi.org/10.5271/sjweh.383

Swanson, S. J., Becker, D. R., Bond, G. R., & Drake, R. E. (2017). *The IPS supported employment approach to help young people with work and school: a practitioner's guide*. Rockville, MD: IPS Employment Center, Westat.

Tremblay, T., Smith, J., Xie, H., & Drake, R. E. (2006). Effect of benefits counseling services on employment outcomes for people with psychiatric disabilities. *Psychiatric Services, 57*, 816–821.

Wallace, C. J., Tauber, R., & Wilde, J. (1999). Teaching fundamental workplace skills to persons with serious mental illness. *Psychiatric Services, 50*, 1147–1149, 1153.

Wehman, P., & Moon, M. S. (Eds.). (1988). *Vocational rehabilitation and supported employment*. Baltimore: Paul Brookes.

Peer Service Providers as Colleagues

Paolo del Vecchio

Introduction

The inclusion of peer providers – individuals in recovery from mental health problems as service providers – is now a common practice across mental and behavioral healthcare settings. Known by various titles (e.g., peer specialists, consumer providers, recovery coaches, family support providers), these individuals use their lived experiences to assist others to cope with mental illnesses and to navigate highly complex behavioral health, primary care, and associated social service systems.

This chapter will review the development of this profession, the evidence for peer-provided services, and the roles and settings where such services are provided. A major focus will be on how community psychiatrists work with peer providers to promote recovery from mental illnesses. Finally, challenges and solutions to successfully implementing peer specialist initiatives will be addressed.

Peers as behavioral health service providers grew out of the mental health consumer self-help movement. This movement began in the United States in the late 1960s and early 1970s when small groups of ex-patients or consumers of mental health services began to meet in major eastern and western coast cities. It grew from the civil and human rights movements of people of color, women, and other groups to improve their social standing, protect rights, and bring the needs and desires of their members to the forefront (Pulice and Miccio 2006). Local mental health self-help groups formed for three primary reasons: (1) mutual support, providing reciprocal emotional support and encouragement based on common experiences; (2) information and social learning, educating members on coping strategies and services available in their local and state communities; and (3) advocacy, participating in both individual case advocacy (to assist members with service access and rights protection) and systems advocacy. The latter was useful to foster needed reforms including the need to address the stigma and discrimination experienced by people with mental illnesses (Van Tosh and del Vecchio 2001). Over time, the number of these groups expanded, including the development of state and national consumer organizations as well as publications, annual conferences, and other efforts. Starting in the late 1970s, the Federal government, through the National Institute for Mental Health's Community Support Program, began to endorse the benefits of these activities and to fund consumer-led organizations.

One of this movement's significant accomplishments has been the development of

P. del Vecchio (✉)
Office of Management, Technology, and Operations, Substance Abuse and Mental Health Services Administration, U.S. Department of Health and Human Services, Rockville, MD, USA
e-mail: Paolo.delvecchio@samhsa.hhs.gov

W. E. Sowers et al. (eds.), *Textbook of Community Psychiatry*,
https://doi.org/10.1007/978-3-031-10239-4_38

consumer-operated service programs. These are services that are primarily planned, developed, and evaluated by mental health service consumers – although some models use traditional mental health professionals for certain aspects of their services. In essence, mental health consumers expanded their role from simply being passive recipients of care to actually providing care themselves. Recovery, Incorporated was formed as a self-help program in the late 1930s by neuropsychiatrist Abraham Low. Fountain House, a well-known psychiatric rehabilitation program in New York City, was initially developed in the 1940s as a consumer-operated service. Over time, Fountain House became the model for the clubhouse movement and incorporated professional staff in 1955.

Promoting an approach of full consumer control, ex-patient advocate and author Judi Chamberlin's 1978 book "On Our Own: Patient Controlled Alternatives to the Mental Health System" (Chamberlin 1978) was a landmark work, documenting the development of peer-provided service programs. Consumer-provided services are now a well-established model that includes drop-in centers, housing programs, homeless services, crisis response, benefits acquisition, public education, employment, research, and much more.

Again, the Federal government played a key role in promoting such approaches including funding national technical assistance centers to help grow such models and research to examine and document their value (Clay 2005).

The above peer service models were developed in parallel to the traditional mental health system. In distinction, one of the outgrowths of the development of consumer-operated services has been the use of peers as providers in traditional mental health treatment settings. This paradigm shift has seen the role of peer-delivered services moving from its position as solely an alternative to the mental health system to one in which it is now working in partnership with treatment professionals.

An early model for such efforts was the Colorado Consumer Case Management Aid Program that begun in 1986. It consisted of training and employing people with serious mental illnesses to provide case management services to other consumers in the state's public mental health system. In 1991, it was a finalist for the prestigious Harvard Kennedy School's Innovations in American Government Award (Government Innovators Network 1991).

Since that time, we have seen the growth of such approaches, and now virtually all states have developed or are implementing peer specialist programs, often with extensive training and certification initiatives (Daniels et al. 2009). Currently, it is estimated that over 25,000 individuals are working as peer specialists (Cook and Jonikas 2020). In 2004, the National Association of Peer Specialists, a national trade organization for this specialty profession, formed with representatives from all of the states (National Association of Peer Specialists 2010). The Veterans Health Administration, which has embraced this approach, employs over 1100 peer specialists across their services (Chinman et al. 2017).

The growth in peer specialist services is driven by several factors. First, as highlighted in the next section, there is growing recognition of the efficacy of these approaches in promoting recovery from mental illnesses. Peer-delivered services and approaches have been cited by the US Surgeon General (US Department of Health and Human Services 1999), the President's New Freedom Commission on Mental Health (New Freedom Commission on Mental Health 2003), and the Institute of Medicine (Institute of Medicine 2006). Financing is another key driver in promoting the use of peer specialists. The use of peer providers can be an efficient and cost-effective way of providing care. An August 2007, the Center for Medicare and Medicaid Services' (CMS) letter to State Medicaid Directors was another milestone in the development of peer-provided services (Smith 2007). This correspondence provided guidance to states on how they can bill Medicaid for peer-delivered services while noting, "CMS recognizes that the experiences of peer support providers, as consumers of mental health and substance use services, can be an important component in a State's delivery of effective treatment." Finally, peer specialists can assist in meeting the shortage of mental health providers in many parts of the United States including to assist in increasing access to the full range of recovery-oriented services such as supported employment, housing, peer services, and more (Myrick and del Vecchio 2016).

Evidence for Peer-Provided Services

There is a well-established body of evidence that document the benefits and efficacy of peer-operated services. These studies have shown that peer-provided services have the following impacts: reduced symptoms, improved well-being, reduced hospitalizations, enhanced empowerment, expanded social supports, increased self-efficacy, and greater consumer knowledge (Van Tosh and del Vecchio 2001; Myrick and del Vecchio 2016).

The federal Substance Abuse and Mental Health Services Administration (SAMHSA) completed the largest multi-site-controlled trial study of consumer-operated services. The 5-year, $20 million effort examined such services as an adjunct to traditional services and determined that consumer-operated services enhanced the well-being – as measured by scales that assessed hope, empowerment, meaning of life, self-efficacy, and goal attainment – of recipients as compared to services as usual (Rogers et al. 2007). Based on these findings, SAMHSA released an evidence-based practice toolkit to increase the adoption of such models (Substance Abuse and Mental Health Services Administration 2011).

Research has also documented that the use of peer specialists in traditional service settings has positive results. In 2013, a meta-analysis of randomized controlled trials conducted by Cochrane identified that consumers were as effective as other professionals employed in similar roles (Pitt et al. 2013). Other studies have replicated these findings and shown additional positive outcomes including increased engagement of people into care, reduced emergency room and hospital use, diminished substance use, decreased re-incarceration rates, and reduced overall treatment costs (Davidson et al. 2012; Bellamy et al. 2019).

Roles and Settings for Peer Providers

Peer specialists provide the following fundamental services to recipients: (1) offering social support, (2) sharing experiential knowledge, and (3) and brokering the needs of consumers. These reflect the self-help foundations of the consumer movement. Further, peer providers assist consumers by increasing the outreach and engagement of individuals served into treatment and other services, acting as powerful sources of motivation, and serving as mentors and role models (Solomon 2004; Chinman et al. 2008). They also help recipients navigate often-fragmented services, assist with transportation and other life skills development, act as liaisons and mediators between staff and recipients, augment overburdened clinical staff, and help challenge the often-unacknowledged stigma and discrimination faced by people with mental illnesses (Chinman et al. 2008). Finally, peer providers assist treatment providers by encouraging the adoption of recovery-based principles and approaches such as holistic and integrated services, person-centered planning, and trauma-informed care (Substance Abuse and Mental Health Services Administration 2012) (see Table 1 for definition of recovery and recovery-based principles).

Table 1 Recovery definition and principles

Definition: A process of change through which individuals improve their health and wellness, live a self-directed life, and strive to reach their full potential. Four major dimensions support a life in recovery: health, home, purpose, and community	
Principles:	
Emerges from hope	Relational
Person-driven	Culturally based
Occurs via multiple pathways	Addresses trauma
Holistic	Focuses on strengths and responsibilities
Support by peers and allies	Based on respect

From SAMHSA's Working Definition of Recovery (2012)

An added benefit of working in the role of a peer specialist is that these individuals also help themselves by helping others. The "helper-therapy principle" – something traditional providers experience as well – results in the helper experiencing a heightened sense of self-mastery, competency, and self-esteem (Solomon 2004).

Peer specialists are found in an increasingly large array of service settings including outpatient clinics, inpatient settings, assertive community treatment teams, residential settings, psychosocial programs, vocational initiatives, and others. They are working with a variety of populations including individuals across the life span, those involved in criminal justice settings, persons who experience homelessness, trauma survivors, and individuals with addictions and/or co-occurring substance use problems. Given the high rates of early mortality and comorbidities experienced by people with mental illnesses, key areas with which peer specialists can assist recipients with co-occurring physical health conditions: (1) access primary care, (2) practice self-management for chronic illnesses, and (3) smoking cessation (Daniels et al. 2009; University of California, San Francisco 2010; Druss et al. 2018).

Working with Peer Providers

Peer specialists are a valuable asset and partner for the community psychiatrist. The following section reviews how peer specialists assist clinicians in promoting recovery, the administrative issues in establishing and sustaining such efforts, and the challenges and suggested solutions with such approaches.

Peer Specialists in Clinical Treatment

Peers play key roles in conducting outreach and engagement of consumers into clinical services. Through sharing common experiences, peers can often establish rapport and trust more quickly than traditional mental health treatment providers. This skill is particularly evident for those considered "most alienated from the healthcare service system" (Sells et al. 2006). Having "been there," peers are also often able to conduct outreach in naturalistic settings – on the streets, in home, and community-based settings (Solomon 2004). On a highly practical level, peer specialists help consumers attend their treatment appointments by giving them reminders or assisting with transportation (Chinman et al. 2008). Further, as noted above, peer specialists provide an important role model that motivates consumers to engage in recovery and mental health services. Importantly, peer specialists bring the essential message of hope and the possibility of improving one's life, which acts as a catalyst for people to begin their journeys of recovery (Substance Abuse and Mental Health Services Administration 2012).

Both the Institute of Medicine (Institute of Medicine 2006) and the President's New Freedom Commission on Mental Health (New Freedom Commission on Mental Health 2003) cite the imperative for consumers to be actively involved in their own treatment as a means to improve systems outcomes. Peer specialists play an important role in teaching mental health literacy to those they serve. Research revealed that the information provided by peer specialists is often viewed as more credible than those provided by mental health treatment providers (Woodhouse and Vincent 2006). Further, peer specialists promote a whole healthcare approach that addresses the social determinants of health and mental health. This includes providing information on how to access crucial supportive services and benefits – including Medicaid, Social Security, housing, employment, and others.

Decision Support

Through shared decision-making approaches, peer specialists assist consumers to work with their clinicians to make informed treatment decisions. SAMHSA has developed decision aids to assist consumers to collaborate with providers to make decisions about anti-psychotic medications and other issues (Substance Abuse and Mental Health Services Administration 2020b). Peer specialists assist consumers in weighing the benefits and costs of treatment options prior to having a treatment encounter with a clinician. Such approaches can improve clinician efficiency, increase consumer engagement in services, and enhance consumer satisfaction with services. Additionally, peer specialists assist consumers in identifying personal goals and objectives that can help clinicians and consumers in developing person-centered treatment or recovery plans (Chinman et al. 2006).

Information Access

A peer specialist acts as a communication liaison between a consumer and the treating clinicians to translate clinical terminology as well as relay consumer concerns. Regarding the former, jargon and terminology used by clinical staff may be alien to and even antagonize service recipients. Peer specialists use lay language to increase consumer understanding. Further, for a number of reasons, consumers may be reticent to actively voice their dissatisfaction with service provision. Peer specialists help provide that voice to make sure that consumer needs and preferences are heard and met. As such, it is important for peer specialists to be active and equal members of the treatment team (Substance Abuse and Mental Health Services Administration 2015). In addition to peer specialist involvement on the treatment team, it is also important that the consumer who is being served also fully participates on the team.

Advocacy and Quality Improvement

Peer specialists address discrimination and other rights violations that may impact clinical care. This ranges from ensuring parity compliance to attending to breaches of confidentiality to addressing abuses related to the use of such practices as seclusion and restraints. Peer specialists act as monitors and ombudspersons to ensure that consumer rights are protected and respected in clinical treatment and other settings (Substance Abuse and Mental Health Services Administration 2015).

Peer specialists can also assist with improving the quality of treatment by collecting, analyzing, and reporting measures of consumer feedback and satisfaction. This can include operating consumer satisfaction teams, administering surveys, and developing consumer advisory boards (Wallcraft et al. 2009).

Administrative Issues

Several administrative issues are important to address when establishing and sustaining peer specialist initiatives. The financing of peer specialists in public mental health systems is critical and can be realized from various sources. As noted earlier, most states are billing Medicaid for this allowable service (Chinman et al. 2017). Often, this funding is combined with SAMHSA Mental Health Services Block Grant awards and other state general revenue funds. A majority is contracting for this service via managed behavioral health care organizations. The State Mental Health Authority and in particular, if one exists, the Office of Consumer Affairs within that entity can be good sources of information on financing options. No matter what source, individuals should be compensated at a fair standard of wages comparable to similar positions. There should also be opportunities for career advancement – including supervisory and managerial positions – so that these positions offer growth and do not become stagnant jobs (Silver and Nemec 2016).

The recruitment and hiring of peer specialists are conducted through various approaches. External consumer advocacy and support organizations, which exist in virtually all states, can be an excellent source. If individuals are recruited from within an organization, it is generally recommended that the person is employed in a different organization from where they receive their

Table 2 Behavioral health peer worker core competencies

1. Engages peers in collaborative and caring relationships
2. Provides support
3. Shares lived experiences of recovery
4. Personalizes peer support
5. Supports recovery planning
6. Links to resources, services, and supports
7. Provides information about skills related to health, wellness, and recovery
8. Helps peers to manage crises
9. Values communication
10. Supports collaboration and teamwork
11. Promotes leadership and advocacy
12. Promotes growth and development

From SAMHSA's Core Competencies for Peer Workers in Behavioral Health Services (2015)

mental health services whenever possible to avoid any potential conflicts. (Chinman et al. 2017).

Peer specialists should undergo comprehensive training and continuing education and skill development and receive a certification to ensure they possess the essential knowledge and abilities to perform required duties. Training and certification programs for peer specialists are state-specific and are a requirement for Medicaid billing. Training is based on the critical competencies required for such positions (see Table 2 for peer worker core competencies). Training content also addresses the values, philosophies, ethics, and standards of peer support services and provides the competencies – including on culturally competent, trauma-informed, whole healthcare – for peer specialists (Chinman et al. 2008; Substance Abuse and Mental Health Services Administration 2015). SAMHSA recently compiled a state-by-state directory of peer recovery coaching training and certification programs (Substance Abuse and Mental Health Services Administration 2020a).

Peer specialists should be treated on par with all other staff of the organization and subject to all of the benefits and requirements associated with an organization's personnel policies. This includes reasonable accommodations for those who so request it. Most accommodations for people with mental illnesses – such as having flexible schedules or taking time off for appointments – are very low cost and easily implemented (Job Accommodation Network 2010). As is important for all care providers, efforts should be implemented to promote the well-being – including health and mental healthcare – of peer specialists (Silver and Nemec 2016).

Challenges and Solutions

Stigma

One of the largest challenges that peer specialists face is the degree of acceptance – or lack thereof – they experience from other staff members. Issues of stigma, misperception, and lack of staff knowledge can fuel these experiences. Attitudes and behaviors can be difficult to change as peer specialists modify their role from patient to colleague. To help address this, it is important for all levels of staff to be educated on the roles and responsibilities – and the value of such – of peer specialists. At the same time, peer specialists should be educated on the roles and responsibilities of other staff members. It is also important for leadership to act as champions of peer specialists and continually reaffirm their support for these efforts (Daniels et al. 2009; Chinman et al. 2008; Gates and Akabas 2007). It is important that staff do not patronize or act paternalistically toward peer specialists. They should have the same performance expectations as any other staff member.

Relationship to the Team

Mental health recovery – and high-quality treatment – is predicated on honest, trust-based relationships. The same is true of the relationships between peer specialists and traditional mental health providers – including psychiatrists. The absence of such relationships is detrimental to building an effective, collaborative, interdisciplinary team to assist the consumer who is being served. As noted above, stigma and misperceptions can be barriers to effective relationships (Jones et al. 2019). While the preceding focused on the stigma that peers may face, peer specialists themselves may also harbor unknowing misperceptions about traditional providers, in particular psychiatrists. The key to breaking down these barriers and building effective relationships is open and transparent interpersonal communication. Peer specialists and traditional providers should invest time in engaging in dialogue with one another about their values, roles, challenges, and goals. Such dialogue can both be formal – through facilitated roundtable meetings (Substance Abuse and Mental Health Services Administration 2020c) or during staff meetings – and informal conversations over a cup of coffee or at lunch.

Self-disclosure is an important aspect in the provision of peer specialist services. The ability of an individual to share their own history can be a powerful tool in establishing trusting clinical and professional relationships. Disclosure, however, can bring risks in terms of stigma and discrimination. It is important for peer specialists to own their own histories and for them to determine when and how they choose to disclose. A good practice is for peer specialists to conduct a cost/benefit analysis when choosing whether and how to disclose.

It can be challenging for a single individual to be the only person to staff such a role within a treatment organization. To avoid the potential isolation that this brings, it is suggested that a minimum of two peer specialists be hired for any clinical team. Allowing opportunities for peer specialists to participate in peer support groups can also be helpful (Chinman et al. 2008).

If there is insufficient clarity on roles and responsibilities, peer specialists and other staff members can experience role conflict and confusion. For example, without these clarifications, peer specialists can be relegated to ancillary positions such as drivers, data entry staff, and administrative support personnel. It is important, as with any job, that clearly defined, formal position description be developed and communicated to avoid this pitfall (Daniels et al. 2009; Chinman et al. 2008).

Professionalization of Peer Specialists

The formalization of peer support brings the potential of unintended consequences of reinforcing social inequalities of lower social roles, income, and power as related to other professional team members (Adams 2020). A national survey of peer providers found that peer specialists are significantly satisfied with their work but they perceive a lack of recognition for their roles (Cronise et al. 2016).

While well established in many communities, the peer specialist workforce is still in its formative stage. There continues to be the need for improved training and awareness among many groups and individuals. This includes behavioral as well as primary health providers, payers, other service providers, policy officials, and the general public as well (Daniels et al. 2017). As earlier noted, living wage pay scales and advancement opportunities are critical to elevating the worth of the peer specialist profession. Organizational preparation is essential to successfully integrating peer specialists into service delivery (Gates and Akabas 2007).

Technology

The use of information technologies in health and behavioral health is transforming how care is delivered. Online behavioral healthcare and software applications are increasingly common tools to increase access, deliver quality care, and manage costs. Peer support is based on the premise that trust-based relationships are central to recovery. Similar to traditional clinicians, establishing such relationships can be challenging in a digital environment. Can peer specialist services be provided in a digital environment? Findings from a review of published research indicate that digital peer support shows promise in improving mental health symptoms, self-management skills, social functioning, hope, and empowerment (Fortuna et al. 2019).

Special Populations

The need to serve a highly diverse population is essential in community mental health. Disparities in access and quality of care are great challenges to be overcome. Peer specialists are shown to be effective in assisting people with mental illness. Can peer specialists also be effective with diverse populations? The use of peer specialists is known to reduce service use disparities among African American and Latinx youth populations (Ojeda et al. 2020). Peer specialists have been cited as a promising model of care in serving older adults (Joo et al. 2016). Peer specialists have also been shown to increase housing stability among formerly homeless veterans with co-occurring mental health and substance use conditions (Ellison et al. 2020). For families of children and adults with mental health problems, a review of randomized studies shows that peer-delivered services were associated with significant improvements in family functioning, knowledge about mental illness, and parenting skills (Acri et al. 2016). Further, research has shown that peer advocates for rural LGBTQ people with mental health problems offer an affirmative, community-based strategy (Willging et al. 2016). Finally, forensic peer specialists are known to contribute to positive recovery-based outcomes for individuals with mental illness who have criminal justice involvement (Berrenger et al. 2019).

Over-identification with "Provider" Role

A final challenge is the possibility that peer specialists over-assimilate and take on the values, beliefs, and practices of traditional mental health services that may reinforce stigma and inequities. Via socialization, individuals can take on the norms and operating practices of those that surround them. Taking on traditional provider norms is counter to the very purpose of these positions – for individuals to use their lived experiences of mental illnesses to assist others in a nontraditional way of peer support, information, and advocacy. To prevent this, clear job descriptions and codes of ethics should be put into practice. Supervision and ongoing training can also reinforce the unique roles of peer specialists (Jones et al. 2019).

Conclusion

Peer specialists have emerged as a valuable asset to community psychiatry. The initiation and growth of this innovative approach is testament itself to the resiliency and strengths of people with mental illnesses to overcome obstacles and become productive, contributing members to our communities. This is the essence of recovery.

This development also speaks to the collective growth and maturity of the mental health consumer movement. From its origins as an alternative to traditional mental health services, the consumer movement is now working in close partnership with providers.

Community psychiatrists have recognized the value that this new profession brings to their work. They are encouraging the expansion of peer specialists by supporting and championing peer specialists within their organizations and treatment settings. In the future, we will see peer specialists working in partnership with clinicians in all treatment settings throughout our communities – together striving for a common goal: to facilitate mental health recovery for those we serve.

References

Acri M, et al (2016). Peer models in mental health for caregivers and families, Community Mental Health Journal, 53:241–249.

Adams W (2020). Unintended consequences of institutionalizing peer support work in mental healthcare. Social Science & Medicine 262.

Bellamy C, et al (2019). Peer support on the "inside and outside": building lives and reducing recidivism for people with mental illness returning from jail. Journal of Public Mental Health, 18(3):188–198.

Berrenger, S, et al (2019). Enacting lived experiences: Peer specialists with criminal justice histories. Psychiatric Rehabilitation Journal, 42(1):9–16.

Chamberlin J: (1978). On Our Own: Patient-controlled alternatives to the mental health system, New York City, McGraw-Hill.

Chinman, M, Young, AS, Hassell, J, Davidson L (2006). Toward the implementation of mental health consumer provider services. Journal of Behavioral Health Services & Research 33(2):176–195.

Chinman M, Hamilton A, Butler B et al (2008). Mental Health Consumer Providers: A Guide for Clinical Staff, Santa Monica, CA, Rand Corporation.

Chinman M. et al (2017). Establishing a research agenda for understanding the role and impact of mental health peer specialists. Psychiatric Services. 68(9): 955–957.

Clay S (ed) (2005). On Our Own, Together, Nashville, TN, Vanderbilt University Press.

Cook J, Jonikas J (2020). The importance of psychiatric rehabilitation services during and after the COVID-19 pandemic. Psychiatric Services 71(9):883–884.

Cronise R, et al (2016). The peer support workforce: Results of a national survey. Psychiatric Rehabilitation Journal 39(3):211–221.

Daniels A, Daniels A., Grant E, Filson B, Powell, I., et al (2009). Pillars of Peer Support: Transforming mental health systems of care through peer support services. Available at www.pillarsofpeersupport.org. Accessed August 26, 2020.

Daniels A, et al (2017). Defining peer roles and status among community health workers and peer support specialists in integrated systems of care. Psychiatric Services 68(12):1296–1298.

Davidson L, et al (2012). Peer support among persons with severe mental illnesses: A review of evidence and experience. World Psychiatry 11(2):123–128.

Druss B, et al (2018). Peer-led self-management of general medical conditions for patients with serious mental illnesses: A randomized trial. Psychiatric Services 69(5):529–535.

Ellison M, et al (2020). Impact of peer specialist services on residential stability and behavioral health status among formerly homeless veterans with co-occurring mental health and substance use conditions. Medical Care 58(4):307–313.

Fortuna K, et al (2019). The future of peer support in digital psychiatry: Promise, progress, and opportunities. Current Treatment Options in Psychiatry 6:221–231.

Gates LB, Akabas SH (2007). Developing Strategies to Integrate Peer Providers into the Staff of Mental Health Agencies. Administration and Policy in Mental Health and Mental Health Services Research, 34:293–306.

Government Innovators Network, Harvard Kennedy School (1991). Consumer Case Management Aid Program. Available at https://www.innovations.harvard.edu/consumer-case-manager-aide-program. Accessed August 26, 2020.

Institute of Medicine (2006). Improving the Quality of Health Care for Mental and Substance Use Conditions, National Academies Press: Washington, DC.

Job Accommodation Network (2010). Job Accommodations for People with Mental Health Impairments. Washington, D.C., U.S. Department of Labor.

Jones N, et al (2019). Peer specialists in community mental health: Ongoing challenges of inclusion. Psychiatric Services 70(12).

Joo J, et al (2016). An innovative model of depression care delivery: Peer mentors in collaboration with a mental health professional to relieve depression in older adults. The American Journal of Geriatric Psychiatry 42(5):407–416.

Myrick K, del Vecchio P (2016). Peer support services in the behavioral healthcare workforce: state of the field. Psychiatric Rehabilitation Journal, 39(3):197–203

National Association of Peer Specialists (2010). Available at https://www.inaops.org/. Accessed August 26, 2020.

New Freedom Commission on Mental Health (2003). Achieving the Promise: Transforming Mental Health Care in America. Final Report (DHHS Pub. No. SMA-03-3832), Rockville, MD.

Ojeda V, et al (2020). The availability of peer support and disparities in outpatient mental health service use among minority youth with serious mental illness. Administration and Policy in Mental Health and Mental Health Services Research, July 29.

Pitt V, et al (2013). Consumer-providers of care for adults clients of statutory mental health services. Cochrane Database of Systematic Reviews, Issue 3, Art. No: CD004807. Available at https://www.cochranelibrary.com/cdsr/doi/10.1002/14651858.CD004807.pub2/information. Acccessed August 26, 2020.

Pulice, Richard T, Miccio, S (2006). Patient, client, consumer, survivor: The mental health consumer movement in the United States in Community Mental Health: Challenges for the 21st Century Edited by Rosenberg J, Rosenberg S, Routledge, pp. 7–14.

Rogers ES, et al (2007). Effects of Participation in consumer-operated service programs on both personal and organizationally mediate empowerment: Results of multisite study. Journal of Rehabilitation Research and Development, 44:785–800.

Sells D, Davidson L, Jewell, C et al (2006). The Treatment Relationship in Peer-based and Regular Case Management for Clients with Severe Mental Illness. Psychiatric Services, 57:1179–1184.

Silver, J, Nemec P (2016). The role of the peer specialists: Unanswered questions. Psychiatric Rehabilitation Journal 39(3):289–291.

Smith, D (2007). State Medicaid Director Letter # 07-011. Baltimore, MD, Centers for Medicaid and Medicare Services. Available at https://downloads.cms.gov/cmsgov/archived-downloads/SMDL/downloads/SMD081507A.pdf. Accessed August 26, 2020.

Solomon P (2004). Peer Support/Peer-provided Services: Underlying processes, benefits, and critical ingredients. Psychiatric Rehabilitation Journal, 27(4):392–402.

Substance Abuse and Mental Health Services Administration (2011). Consumer-Operated Services Evidence-Based Practices (EBP) Kit. Rockville, MD, SAMHSA. Available at https://store.samhsa.gov/product/Consumer-Operated-Services-Evidence-Based-Practices-EBP-KIT/SMA11-4633. Accessed August 26, 2020.

Substance Abuse and Mental Health Services Administration (2012). National Consensus Statement on Mental Health Recovery. Rockville, MD, SAMHSA,

Substance Abuse and Mental Health Services Administration (2015). *Core competencies for peer workers in behavioral health services.* Rockville, MD, SAMHSA. Available at https://www.samhsa.gov/sites/default/files/programs_campaigns/brss_tacs/core-competencies_508_12_13_18.pdf. Accessed August 26, 2020.

Substance Abuse and Mental Health Services Administration (2020a). State-by-State Directory of Peer Recovery Coaching Training and Certification Programs, Rockville, MD: SAMHSA. Available at https://c4innovates.com/brsstacs/BRSS-TACS_State-by-State-Directory-of-Peer-Recovery-Coaching-Training-and-Certification-Programs_8_26_2020.pdf. Accessed by September 3, 2020.

Substance Abuse and Mental Health Services Administration (2020b). Shared Decision Making Tools. Rockville, MD, SAMHSA. Available at: https://www.samhsa.gov/brss-tacs/recovery-support-tools/shared-decision-making. Accessed August 26, 2020.

Substance Abuse and Mental Health Services Administration (2020c). Participatory Dialogues. SAMHSA: Rockville, MD. Available at https://www.theweb.ngo/history/Docs/SAMHSADialogue.pdf. Accessed August 31, 2020.

University of California, San Francisco (2010). Rx for Change: for mental health peer counselors. Available at: http://rxforchange.ucsf.edu/about.php. Accessed August 26, 2020.

US Department of Health and Human Services: Mental Health (1999). A Report of the Surgeon General. Rockville, MD, Substance Abuse and Mental Health Services Administration.

Van Tosh, L, del Vecchio P (2001). Consumer/Survivor-Operated Service Programs: A Technical Report, Rockville, MD, Substance Abuse and Mental Health Services Administration.

Wallcraft J, Schrank B, Amering, M (2009). Handbook of Service User Involvement in Mental Health Research, West Sussex, UK, Wiley-Blackwell.

Willging C, et al. (2016). Coaching mental health peer advocates for rural LGBTQ people, Journal of Gay & Lesbian Mental Health 20(3):214–236.

Woodhouse A, Vincent A (2006). Mental health delivery plan—development of peer specialist roles: A literature scoping exercise. Edinburgh, Scotland, Scottish Recovery Network and the Scottish Development Centre for Mental Health.

Fountain House and the Clubhouse Movement

Francesca Pernice, Lori D'Angelo, Kenn Dudek, Amber Michon, and Ralph Aquila

Prior to the 1960s, people suffering from a serious mental illness (SMI), such as schizophrenia, major depression, and other conditions, lived in state institutions and asylum wards. Although these asylums for the mentally ill evolved from a caring, therapeutic approach of the moral treatment,[1] by the mid-twentieth century these institutions had become overcrowded, underfunded, and hardly reflective of the humane values upon which they were originally based. With the passage of President Kennedy's Community Mental Health Centers Act of 1963, a new initiative ushered in approaches to the care and treatment of people suffering from mental illness to receive treatment within their community. Community mental health centers originally focused on patients with common mental disorders and thus did not treat people with serious mental illness until decades later. Deinstitutionalization emerged as one of the largest social experiments in American history in which nearly one-half million people moved out of these institutions and back into their communities (Grob 2005). This occurred regardless of sufficient consideration of the effects that inadequate social supports, the lack of federal housing support, unemployment, and drug addiction would have in the lives of people struggling with mental illness. Furthermore, former patients were expected to live communities where the stigma associated with mental illness caused them to be viewed with both fear and suspicion. Five decades later, policy makers and practitioners, commenting on the challenges facing mental health care in the community (Rosenberg and Rosenberg 2006), found a "fragmented system" (p. 3). This is also reflected in the President's New Freedom Commission on Mental Health (2003) report describing the system as "crisis oriented" and "in disarray" (Executive Summary, p. 4). There remain few no consistent approaches to community treatment, and the funding system remains ill-suited to the demands of those with the greatest need. The goal of deinstitutionalization—namely, that people suffering from serious mental

[1] *Traitement morale*, or the moral treatment, was a psychological treatment for people suffering from mental illness developed by the renowned French physician Philippe Pinel in the late eighteenth century. It emphasized therapeutic observations and discussions and an environment conducive to a humane, caring approach to mental illness.

F. Pernice (✉) · A. Michon
Wayne State University, Detroit, MI, USA
e-mail: Francesca.Pernice@wayne.edu; Amber.Michon@wayne.edu

L. D'Angelo
Magnolia Clubhouse, Cleveland, OH, USA
e-mail: lori@magnoliaclubhouse.org

K. Dudek
President of Fountain House (1992-2019), Present Mental Health Consultant, New York, NY, USA

R. Aquila
Horizon House, Philadelphia, PA, USA

W. E. Sowers et al. (eds.), *Textbook of Community Psychiatry*,
https://doi.org/10.1007/978-3-031-10239-4_39

illness can live and function in society—is a book whose final chapter has yet to be written. This chapter will review the origins of one of the earliest approaches to this problem, Fountain House. This solution emerged from the transformation of a method of psychiatric treatment referred to as activity group therapy (AGT) into a normalized approach predicated on building a community through social relationships, meaningful work, and activities which subsequently result in shared meaning and purpose through membership.

The story of Fountain House, a *working community*[2] (Doyle et al. 2013) for people living with mental illness, relates a different narrative concerning the treatment of mental illness. While society relegates those leaving mental hospitals to the periphery, Fountain House welcomes them on West 47th Street to find meaning in their lives and invites them to demonstrate their productive talents in the heart of New York City. Fountain House embodies a fundamental understanding of the destructive nature of mental illness and offers a comprehensive approach to help its members regain their lives. It has endorsed choice and empowerment for people with serious mental illness and has done so long before they became standard mental health practices. The approach offers an "intentional therapeutic community" utilizing needed work, done in partnership by members and professional staff, as the vehicle for furthering the development of connection to others, community, and recovery. The tenets of this *working community*, and more recently, the further articulation of a process, named "Social Practice," rely on the building of Albert Bandura's psychological concept of self-efficacy. The building of self-efficacy through meaningful and equitable relationships, work, and activity is the foundation of methods of Social Practice at Fountain House. As such, Fountain House consistently held employment, decent housing, and school/educational success to be the measures of its effectiveness in promoting psychiatric recovery. These inherent ideas and a philosophy grounded in humane and equitable power attracted, and continue to attract, widespread imitation around the world and have become known as the Clubhouse Model. Fountain House is regarded as a pioneer in community mental health practice, which fostered the goal of social integration a decade before the onset of the deinstitutionalization movement.

Its approach to mental health recovery, however, was not achieved without allies; foremost among them are *community psychiatrists*. It was often seen as an anti-psychiatry model but in reality always had significant connections with the psychiatric world. Fountain House and community psychiatry both came of age during the latter half of the twentieth century, sharing the same goal: supporting people who suffer from mental illness to live and thrive in their community. Community psychiatrists provided the initial conceptual and programmatic framework for Fountain House. Additionally, faculty members of major universities, as well as past presidents of the American Psychiatric Association, have served on its Board of Directors and Advisory Councils.

The Beginnings of Fountain House

Fountain House was founded in 1948. It grew out of the enterprise of a self-help group of patients that formed in Rockland State Hospital, located in a suburban community just north of New York City. The group had been organized in the early 1940s by Dr. Hiram Johnson, a supervising psychiatrist, and Elizabeth Schermerhorn, a volunteer from a prominent New York family. Dr. Johnson sought to apply the emerging self-help approach of the Alcoholics Anonymous (AA) movement for these patients (it is speculated that the Director of Rockland State Hospital's, Dr. Russell Blaisdell, connection to the newly emerging AA movement influenced Dr. Johnson).

Thus, Dr. Johnson became one of the first psychiatrists to lead an AA group in the hospital (Karlsson 2013). He envisioned patients assisting each other in returning to society by replacing relationships that were lost or destroyed as a

[2]The term *working community* ™ was introduced by Fountain House to describe its signature approach to supporting its members in recovery from mental illness and more recently augmented by further articulation of the approach defined as *Social Practice* by Fountain House.

consequence of the mental illness with newly found friendships formed in the hospital. The self-help approach serves to mobilize members to cope with the challenges of hospital discharge, such as in finding housing and jobs.[3] By 1944, the members of the group called themselves the We Are Not Alone Society (W.A.N.A.) and continued to reach out to ex-patients of Rockland State.

W.A.N.A, although loosely organized, functioned for several years in New York City but then floundered and disappeared. The importance of the group to people leaving mental institutions, however, was not lost on Michael Obolensky, an ex-patient, and Elizabeth Schermerhorn, one of the original founders. By 1948, Schermerhorn supported a nearby "settlement house," called Hartley House, to buy a brownstone at 412 West 47th Street in Manhattan, in order to reorganize W.A.N.A. and create a *place* for its members. The name Fountain House was inspired by the brownstone's architecture, which included a fountain located on the patio. It was decided that this new *social club*, which would be known as the Fountain House Foundation, would be financially led by an outside board of directors and operationally by the Fountain House Fellowship, involving ex-patients. Although a Board of Directors are now a requirement for all nonprofit organizations, establishing a foundation was the only way to establish a board at that time.

Fountain House operated much like a settlement house, that is, it was situated in the community and offered social and educational programs to support its membership after long-term psychiatric hospitalization. It immediately attracted public attention as a viable framework for helping patients successfully leave the institution. A professional advisory committee including Dr. Lawrence Kubie, a prominent psychiatrist from Columbia University, and Dr. Russell Blaisdell, the Director of Rockland State, guided Fountain House to open a series of occupational training programs to support social integration and reentry. In 1949, additional funding from the National Mental Health Act of 1946 funded the first professional staff at Fountain House. However, these early formative years of establishing a viable organization and training programs were tumultuous and, by 1955, proved unworkable. Public funding was lost, and staff began resigning. This emerged as a critical turning point in Fountain House's history and one that has led the model to what it is known for today: inspiring ongoing research, practice, and human rights for people living with serious mental illnesses.

At that time, John Beard, soon to become the Executive Director of Fountain House, arrived in New York to present his work from the Eloise Asylum, located in Detroit, Michigan. Most patients with schizophrenia and psychosis at Eloise were assigned a grave prognosis and considered "chronic" with no hope of recovery. John Beard's contributions, however, focused on the individual's ego strengths, which animated the rest of his career and approaches at Fountain House.

Beard was enthralled by the methods of a young psychiatrist, Dr. Arthur Pearce, at Eloise. Pearce and other mental health reformers of the time were appalled by the conditions of people housed in the nation's asylums. They observed that, despite their illnesses, these patients were functioning and engaging in daily work; patients went out into the fields to pick vegetables, and they staffed hospital laundry rooms and kitchens. They hypothesized that normal group activities done on the ward would support the patient regaining ego strength, which they referred to as rehabilitation and is now referred to as recovery. Accordingly, Beard introduced ordinary activities such as painting, woodworking, play-acting, mathematics lessons, and even popcorn-making onto the ward. Pearce and his team found that even though most of the patients were withdrawn, they were still eager to engage in these activities. This perceptible change in the patients compelled the attendants and nurses to alter their attitudes; they saw their patients as capable and the patients, in turn, felt better about themselves. This form of *milieu therapy*

[3] Mandiberg (2010) notes the importance of such relationships, which are currently overlooked in hospital discharge planning for psychiatric patients.

could be enlisted to contribute to the recovery of people with mental illness.[4] The team wanted to demonstrate that what they called activity group therapy (AGT; Beard et al. 1958) could be applied to even the most withdrawn patients who rarely, if ever, left the ward. By linking the attendant staff and even the other patients together in normal human activities on the ward, the team found that such group efforts were constructive, empowering, and ultimately transformative. They concluded that participation in AGT resulted in varying degrees of patient improvement and broadly summarized their success in a paper (Beard et al. 1958) noting that "the patient's new experience in participation with others on a basic reality level seems to promote a process of reinstituting lost ego capacities; and 'AGT' can play an important part in facilitating adjustment in the community, thereby potentially lessening the probability of re-hospitalization" (p. 136).

Beard and other psychiatrists learned that despite the illness, patients still possessed within themselves the resiliency to take control of their lives. Participation in ordinary human endeavors contributed to their recovery and staff played a crucial role. These insights acquired amidst the desolate conditions of a custodial mental hospital ward in 1950–1951 accompanied Beard for the rest of his professional career and resulted in his recasting of the foundations of Fountain House. While not denying their illness, Beard believed (as have many practitioners) that patients who engaged in purposeful everyday activities felt better and were able to move on with their lives. It is the main reason why members come to a Clubhouse regularly (Rice et al., 2020); the non-judgmental social environment provides members with a sense of community where they engage in something from which they derive pride, accomplishment, and personal satisfaction.

[4]A similar movement was taking place in England with the *therapeutic community* of Maxwell Jones (1953) that involved the entire hospital community in contributing to the recovery process.

Fountain House Today

John Beard concluded that the framework of a workday organized around meaningful daily activities such as preparing food for peers, answering the phone, or helping each other secure New York city housing post-hospitalization would be the organizational scaffolding around which the members and staff at Fountain House would join together. These practices are what constitute the elements of the *work-ordered day* in Social Practice and continue to be the primary influence for positive recovery experiences among members today (Tanaka and Davidson 2015). As there is nothing unusual about going to work, the notion of designing an AGT environment around these 9-to-5 h, as is common for most everyone in society, was natural. Thus, the day program (as it was referred to at the time) would feature work as its programmatic center. Work at Fountain House became a therapeutic application of group activities that supported member recovery. It provides as well the rationale for referring to Fountain House as a "working community" (Goertzel et al. 1960).

Transformative Design Fountain House today differs from its inception mainly in size and diversity, not in its central themes and purpose. The House conveys an attractive and desirable appearance to anyone entering its front doors: with a grand staircase, wood-paneled walls, dignified spaces, and state-of-the-art technology. The design and appearance, dignified and respectful, are deliberately contrived to challenge the expectations of most people upon entering a mental health setting.

The Structure The activities of the House are organized around a normal 9-to-5 work day with an after-hours program in the evenings and on weekends and holidays. During weekdays, members and staff collaborate on activities that are needed to support members in psychiatric recovery. Various work activities are organized into groups, called units or departments. Some units directly address the interests of members in returning to society through education and employment. Fountain House has always addressed the social determinants of health by offering stable housing and promoting health and wellness while helping people get jobs and develop careers. The organization also bridges the internal and external communities by supporting employment and education through engaging in advocacy and community education, as well as social activities. Units sustain the operation of the *working community,* providing member enrollment and orientation, culinary operations, horticulture, and research and development. Fountain House incorporates members into its accounting, fundraising, technology, and human resources departments. Fountain House also developed methods to address specific population needs to better attract and serve young adults, seniors, and those who are deaf or hearing impaired.[5]

Members and staff work together in partnership, known in the field as "side by side" in the daily routines of the House. The membership shares with staff the responsibility and the acknowledgment, for its smooth running. While member participation in the tasks or activities at hand is essential, members are free to choose if and how they will participate. Staff are expected to reach out and support member involvement by engaging members and demonstrating confidence in the members' abilities, structuring the environment with opportunities for meaningful involvement, supporting members in taking risks, and recognizing their achievements. The real integration of members in as many activities as possible creates one of the most unique attributes of Fountain House. The *need to be needed* and having *choice* within a *collaborative* environment give Fountain House its programmatic and structural identity as well as its therapeutic punch. Core ethical and quality standards reflect collegiality, respect, human rights, and equity. Stripped of a medical surrounding and a preoccupation with illness, the workday at Fountain House provides an ordinary setting for social interaction and personal contributions in which the collaboration of staff and members in everyday activities becomes a transformative event that aids in the process of mental health recovery.

Fountain House is run by the Executive Director, who holds the ultimate responsibility for all community operations, and the Board of Directors, who exercise fiduciary responsibility and provide access to broader resources in the community to ensure the organization's long-term sustainability. In addition, as a social agency deeply committed to the health and welfare of its members, as well as to people suffering from the stigma of mental illness worldwide, Fountain House attracts numerous individuals who volunteer their time to work within its community or provide financial support as donors. Today, Fountain House has become a large social service agency with approximately 1200 active members annually and over 70 staff, referred to as social practitioners.[6]

Goals Gainful, competitive employment continues to be the ultimate goal for Fountain House members. However, it was initially recognized that development of personal capacity was simply not enough. Fountain House recognized that for many, long-term hospitalization, no recent job experiences, and fear and insecurities prevented many from seeking jobs. Thus, John Beard drew upon his practice of securing employment for his patients at Eloise Hospital to connect with local businesses, allowing for the development of a unique method of vocational rehabilitation. The vast potential of local establishments in New York City resulted in the development of *transitional employment*[7] in 1958 at

[5]Additionally, Fountain House operates an international training institute, a professional art gallery for member artists to sell their paintings, and a rural farm in northern New Jersey, providing services for hearing-impaired adults and serving young adults with mental illness and college re-entry.

[6]Figures do not include the number of staff separately employed in the Fountain House housing program.

[7]Transitional employment was an innovation wherein Fountain House partnered with employers in establishing a temporary position for its members to test out their abili-

Fountain House. Transitional Employment is a method of supporting employment, whereby members of Fountain House become employees of partnering businesses for 6–9 months. Fountain House provides all the training and support and coverage by other members or staff, if necessary. A variety of entry-level positions are developed, and this highly supported opportunity allows members to build their confidence and skills prior to obtaining competitive employment, if they so desire. Fountain House offers a full range of employment options including transitional and supported employment, member-owned businesses, and independent social enterprises. The latter two are independent entities incorporated under New York law. At any one time, Clubhouses report that 35% of their membership holds positions of paid employment. Employment continues to be a marker of success for Fountain House and other Clubhouses, as it represents an ongoing testament to the capabilities of people to hold down competitive employment despite their illness.

The lack of affordable or available housing stock in the USA is a major cause of homelessness crises among people with serious mental illness (see chapter "Psychiatric Care for People Experiencing Homelessness"). During the 1950s, apartments for members were only affordable if they had multiple roommates, and many others were forced to live in dangerous single-room occupancy (SRO) motels. Keenly aware of the lack of affordable housing or the isolation of living alone in SRO motels, Fountain House responded by expanding into the New York housing market in 1958 and became one of the first mental health programs to provide housing when it was considered beyond the mission of departments of mental health in New York City. Representatives of the organization negotiated with landlords and signed leases to apartments in various locations around the city. Today, Fountain House provides residences and partners with housing organizations serving over 500 members a year through various levels of supported housing. The program ensures that every member has a stable living environment, whether in Fountain House residences, independent apartment, and/or family and friends.

By 1960, under John Beard's leadership, Fountain House established the essential framework providing inroads into the larger society via employment, housing, education, and the daily work of operating the organization. In this model, each component was integral to the others within the context of a *working community* setting.

Foundational Elements of a Fountain House Community Although Fountain House established itself around the construct of AGT and designed itself around the cultural and societal notions of a *workplace*, it is not a conventional setting. There is no manufacturing, market product, or service for the general public. For those who have often lost personal and professional relationships as a consequence of their illness (Beard et al. 1958), Fountain House is a *working community*, a *place* where members can engage in meaningful activities and regain their sense of self and sense of community (Carolan et al. 2011; Sarason 1974); it is the treatment that counteracts social isolation and idleness. With staff and members as partners in the process, Fountain House recreates a social ecology supportive of member recovery (Doyle et al. 2013).

Several key principles operationalize such an outcome. Fountain House features a normalized work environment in which the need for member participation (the *need to be needed*) becomes the catalyst that operationalizes the collaborative nature of the endeavor and empowers its members to participate in their own recoveries. At the same time, Fountain House is wholly built upon member choice and creates a concrete setting wherein the fundamental insights of such theorists as Deci and Ryan (1985) into the power of personal choice in fostering self-identity and self-actualization are substantiated. As Deci (1995) has described:

> The main thing about choice is that it engenders willingness. It encourages people to fully endorse what they are doing; pulls them into the activity

---

ties and establish a work history.

> and allows them to feel a greater sense of volition; it decreases their alienation. (p. 34)

In effect, Fountain House shifts the focus of treatment of those with mental illness from patient pathologies and recipients of care and services to individuals with their own agency and an identity beyond that of their illness. Finally, Fountain House calls for a shift in the power arrangements between the professionals and patients, requiring those with power to join on an equal footing, *side by side*, with those who are systematically denied such status. It expects mental health staff workers who are accustomed to working arrangements based on hierarchy and specialization to shift to a framework based on mutuality and collaboration. In this respect, as a *working community* in which recovery is the result of normalized staff and member relationships, Fountain House offers a professional alternative to the more typical caretaking or patriarchal role more often the norm in the treatment of mental illness, that is, members and staff of Fountain House engage in the operations of the House in partnership, working side by side.

Replicating Fountain House Fountain House is the essence of John Beard's original approach to mental health advocacy. It held a powerful demonstrative payoff and presented a visible statement of the inherent worth and health of people suffering from mental illness. If the members of Fountain House were perceived as doing normal things, then society would be forced to acknowledge they were not just "sick." By its very existence, Fountain House would challenge the prejudices and stigmas associated with mental illness and demand a reevaluation of how people with mental illness were perceived and treated.

However, a demonstration approach to widespread diffusion proved insufficient. Despite its national reputation and hundreds of visitors annually, Fountain House remained practically alone in its way of working (a handful of places modeled after its design were started by former employees), until 1977. At that time Beard responded to a proposal from the National Institute of Mental Health (NIMH) to develop a training program for those seeking to improve the lives of the mentally ill in the community. Training was centered on the principles and standards of developing and operating a Fountain House Clubhouse Model, thus began what became at the time the most successful training effort ever underwritten by NIMH (Propst 1997). The diffusion of the model entered into a new phase in 1987 when Fountain House, in collaboration with Clubhouses throughout the world, defined a set of International Clubhouse Model Standards (1990) that codified the practice of the model after Fountain House's innovative insights. Teams of Clubhouse members and staff comprised accreditation review teams. Accreditation was designed to ensure the standardization of the model and quality assurance. These efforts were initially funded through grants and foundation supports, and the process includes a self-study, onsite visit by a faculty review team, preliminary report, and final determination made by the accrediting body, Clubhouse International. Within 20 years of the initial training grant, over 300 programs were accredited throughout the world.

Many individuals with serious mental illness continue to live in isolation (Dell et al. 2019; Prince et al. 2018), are overrepresented in homelessness statistics (Kuno et al. 2000) and incarcerations (DeMartini et al. 2020; Huxter 2013), and have well-established lower life expectancy rates than the general population (Hayes et al. 2012). In 2016, the World Health Organization in collaboration with Fountain House increased awareness on the excessive mortality rates among this population, emphasizing that people with severe mental disorders on average tend to die 10–25 years earlier than the general population and do not receive the same quality of physical care as the general population (WHO 2016). Employment, a criterion of success, continues as a major barrier to social integration with unemployment running seven to eight times higher among people suffering from serious mental illness than the rest of the population (Marwaha and Johnson 2004; Mechanic et al. 2002;

Milazzo-Sayre et al. 2001). There is also emerging evidence supporting that programs meeting health and social service needs are more effective than programs aimed at improving cognitive functioning among serious mental illness populations (Gabrielian et al. 2020). Therefore, Fountain House Clubhouse models offer solutions for this disparity and support the collaboration between physicians and Clubhouse social practitioners to advance community mental health. Many of the leading causes of death among this population are modifiable (Dickerson et al. 2018).

Yet, funding for mental health continues to represent a bifurcated system where funding for general hospitals comes at the expense of community-based treatment programs. The problem is further exacerbated by the fact that patients must travel to a variety of agencies in order to get the help they need and, all too often, get lost in the process. What is missing is an adequate and flexible funding stream from both national governments and local municipalities. In America, traditional funding of medical services provided by Medicaid or Medicare is structured at its heart for hospital and medical treatment and not community-based services which encompass a much more comprehensive approach.

The Void in the Community Mental Health Service System

For those who do receive treatment, it primarily consists of psychiatric services and case management, covered by Medicaid and commercial insurance. The vast majority of people suffering from some form of serious mental illness meet with their psychiatrist once a month or less, primarily for medication review. This state of affairs is no different from the concerns of 45 years ago, when a federal report called for improvements in community-based supports for people discharged from mental hospitals (US Comptroller General 1977; US Accounting Office, 1977). Despite the intervening decades, society offers only limited support in managing the illness to those living outside of a mental health hospital. Case management (Rubin 1991) seeks to link "the client to the maze of direct service providers" (p. 5). The linkage is primarily to disability and medical benefits, housing, medical and psychiatric services, and vocational specialists. This linkage is necessary, but not sufficient (see chapter "Case Management and Assertive Community Treatment").

Fountain House combines aspects of both the case management and self-help models in psychiatric rehabilitation services while offering a choice to people who are regularly denied entry into the job market, reflecting the basis of empowerment within the consumer movement. It features a clear professional role as a "social practitioner" that fuses staff collaboration with member empowerment (see section "Future Implications") in creating a *community of psychiatric rehabilitation and recovery.* Most importantly, Fountain House combats the fragmentation in services that has resulted from deinstitutionalization by providing a comprehensive and holistic social framework within which all the services needed that directly address the major stumbling blocks to success in deinstitutionalization—homelessness, unemployment, and school failure—with the availability of general and mental health treatment as described later in this chapter.

Model Effectiveness

Early Fountain House studies were mostly anecdotal with transcriptions of conference event speeches and shared lived experiences solidifying a movement called recovery. The effectiveness of Fountain House as psychiatric rehabilitation is empirically grounded in supporting gainful employment among people living with mental illness. The employment model is characterized by a three-tiered developmental approach: transitional employment, supported employment, and competitive (independent) employment. Using a team-based (social practitioner, psychiatrist, vocational sites) approach, it supports member-driven interest toward full employment independence. Overall, randomized controlled studies in employment approaches for serious mental illness reveal similarities and differences between various approaches to employment outcomes—each with their own strengths and weaknesses. While supported employment was deemed a standalone evidenced-based practice (see chapter "Supported Employment") long before Fountain House achieved the same status, the Clubhouse employment model allows people to experience various employment supports including job coverage and transitional and supported employment. Furthermore, outcome studies consistently demonstrate that members of Clubhouse earn more money, have greater job tenure (Macias et al. 2006), and report higher quality of life in social and financial domains of their life when compared to consumers in Assertive Community Treatment (ACT) models.

Fountain House and other accredited Clubhouse programs continue to demonstrate robust employment outcomes as a measure of social integration among people living with serious mental illness (Gold et al., 2016). In addition, randomized control trials demonstrated reductions in hospitalization recidivism rates as compared to other community models (Di Masso et al. 2001). With the widespread adoption of the Fountain House model of psychosocial rehabilitation in many US states and countries, the model became a beacon of hope for both practitioners and consumers alike. Program costs compared favorably to those of partial hospitalization programs, with lower Medicaid costs and better clinical outcomes (Plotnick and Salzer 2008; Solís-Román and Knickman 2016).

Apart from the early studies focused on employment and rehospitalization, researchers examining aspects of the model from a recovery perspective find effectiveness of the model impacting many psychosocial domains. People value recovery-oriented services that recognize capabilities and strengths and offer a place to go (Rice et al., 2020).

Over the course of 20 years, the study of Clubhouse models has been subject to empirical inquiry and fall within the following outcome domains: (1) employment; (2) hospitalization, (3) education, (4) housing, (5) social support, (6) mental health recovery, and (7) utilization. For example, among the social support domain, Clubhouse members with psychosis spectrum disorders generally report more people in their support network than what is reported in other studies (Pernice-Duca 2008). Given the international standards on accreditation, cross-cultural studies also serve as important markers of evidence. For instance, interpersonal relationships and perceived stigma were assessed between a "Clubhouse" in South Korea and a "Skills Only" training psychiatric rehabilitation program. Participants in the Clubhouse group reported significantly lower perceived stigma and significantly higher quality of life and interpersonal relationship scores than did the recipients of the rehabilitation skills training model (Jung and Kim 2012).

Taken together, these studies demonstrate the effectiveness of the model, yet more research is needed. The early studies constitute the basis for expansion, with some of the greatest adopters located in Scandinavia, Korea, Canada, and Italy. In a recent review, McKay et al. (2018) examined outcomes among all studies to be associated with methodological rigor. Randomized control studies support the efficacy of the model by promoting employment, reducing psychiatric hospitalization, and improving quality of life; quasi-experimental and observational studies offer moderate support in educational outcomes and in improving the quality of social relationships and the number of social connections. In another methodological review, Battin et al. (2016) synthesized studies that affirm moderate effect sizes for quality of life, employment, and re-hospitalization rates but lower effect sizes for studies examining symptomology or social functioning.

Future Implications

Fountain House has adopted new language to reflect the practice of supporting member recovery in the Clubhouse environment. Social Practice defines the method used in the Clubhouse setting to create enriching opportunities and recovery experiences through an ongoing partnership between the social practitioner and the member.

Social Practice uses elements of the environment and qualities of the interpersonal relationship to support goals, personal understanding, and recovery (Rice et al., 2020). The social practitioner role denotes a professional partnership between staff and the member to cultivate a rich social and meaningful experience.

Fountain House has a long history of inviting ongoing academic endeavors with educational institutions. A curriculum to educate emerging community psychiatrists and other healthcare providers on the philosophy of Fountain House and the Clubhouse Model, the methods, and the outcomes is in the late stages of development. The aim of this project is to diffuse the Clubhouse model to professionals in hopes of partnering and raising awareness to address the ongoing crisis in mental health treatment.

Clubhouses Working with Community Psychiatry

Due to the disproportionate numbers of health and mental health comorbidities, such as diabetes, hypertension, obesity, and cellulitis, there was an urgency to incorporate a primary care physician. During the 1990s, Fountain House developed a relationship with a local community hospital on the westside of Manhattan to deliver onsite psychiatric services for a new type of residence for formerly homeless men and women with serious mental illness. Psychiatrists recognized the disproportionate number of health and mental health comorbidities. By the late 1990s, the Fountain House Medical Director, Dr. Ralph Aquila (Aquila et al. 1999), formed a relationship between Fountain House and community psychiatrists, leading to the initiation of the first integrated care clinic known as the "Store-Front" or "Health Home," and then later referred to as the "Rehabilitation Alliance."

The Rehabilitation Alliance integrated both psychiatry and primary care with the Fountain House community, adopting a truly "patient centric" culture and focusing on the social determinants of health (e.g., housing, employment, integration) long before these priorities became commonly encouraged. The clinic evolved into the Sydney Baer Clinic by 2011 and touted by the then New York State's Health Commissioner, Nirav Shah, as "on the leading edge of innovation."[8] A team involving psychiatry, primary care, and Clubhouse community members as a whole oversees the goals of employment, wellness, housing, and education as mutually supportive and vital to the long-term health and recovery of the member. In most instances Fountain House social practitioners (e.g., staff, social workers) who see members on a daily basis are in a unique position to collaborate with doctors to support improvements in members' health and well-being and likely to signal signs of physical health conditions. This alliance has resulted in the timely detection and treatment or prevention of major medical conditions, such as diabetes and heart disease. In addition, the Clubhouse community promotes the health and wellness of each member in various ways, including supporting weight management, smoking cessation, better nutrition, and exercise (McKay and Pelletier 2007). This model affords benefits to both members and medical professionals. Attracting medical professionals and general practitioners to devote a portion of their practice to serving people with serious mental illness, Fountain House's emphasis on recovering in a *community* is strength-based, values autonomy and choice and is situated in a safe environment (Herman et al. 2005). This collaboration nested in a community of professional and peer support honors the legacy of the role of psychiatry and importance of peer community in the endeavor of integrating the whole person.

Yet for wider adoption of these Fountain House programs, a consistent and extensive funding stream must be developed. Funding for Fountain House has relied on a combination of state and city contracts, along with some and private funds. Other Clubhouses in the USA are either nearly 100% Medicaid funded, 100% state contract funded, or, in few cases, almost com-

[8]Nirav Shah Shah, N. R., MD, 2011. From a transcript of remarks at the opening of the Sidney Baer Center at Fountain House New York, June 14, 2011

pletely privately funded. Each of these approaches limits the scope of necessary activities. For instance, medical and vocational services overlap, as well as a myriad of other interventions (e.g., housing, social interventions); thus, Fountain House programs do not fit neatly into a US Medicaid/Medicare funding stream. Programs that creatively use this medical funding can be limited in their scope of services, which leads them to provide additional services for free or not at all. In contrast, Scandinavian countries (Norway, Sweden, Denmark, and Finland) receive ongoing national and city contracts from the social funds to primarily fund programs.

The authors propose a modest funding formula for effective Clubhouse programs, a combination of both state and city contracts to support base operations, complemented by limited Medicaid and private grant funding. This combination connects the program to the community by tying funds to local city and state governments to address social issues such as homelessness, food insecurity, and employment. Private and grant funding connect these models to business and philanthropic communities to support the mental health of their larger community. Clubhouses in mid-size cities such as Cleveland (Magnolia House) and Worcester serve as models of blended funding streams with large budgets. If the approach is to become a major part of the community mental health system in the future, it will take this level and type of financial commitment from the city, state, and federal governments.

Conclusion

Fountain House began with a belief in the fundamental resiliency of the human spirit. It continues to operate under this belief. At Fountain House, recovery is translated into living in a permanent home, finding and keeping a job, and enjoying friends and peers. The hope, self-efficacy, empowerment, and supportive relationships that define the recovery-oriented approach are all integrated into the *working community* through relationships with peers and social practitioners. Empirical studies in the core elements, methods, and outcomes of Clubhouse programs worldwide emphasize robust employment and socialization outcomes (Carolan et al. 2011; Battin et al. 2016; Gold et al. 2016), reduced hospitalization rates (Di Masso et al. 2001), improved quality of life (Jung and Kim 2012; McKay et al. 2018), and proved that sense of community is an essential method in the Clubhouse milieu (Herman et al. 2005). People come to the Clubhouse for structure, activity, and ultimately for meaning (Rice et al., 2020). Harnessing this motivation is crucial to meeting each person *where they are at* and offering ways to partner with them and others to support psychosocial goals (Kinn et al. 2018).

Fountain House achieved this framework with therapeutic pioneers who inspired its constituent structures. It expresses in practice the person-centered, strengths-based approaches of modern architects of positive psychology such as Rogers (1986) and Maslow (1943) and prefigures by decades the critical importance of Deci and Ryan's self-determination theory (1985) in a recovery paradigm. Ultimately, the first executive director, John Beard, applied these therapeutic approaches into a framework that can be easily embedded in the structure of society in the USA and worldwide.

References

Aquila, R. MD, Santos, G., Malamud, T. J. & McCrory, D. MD (1999, Summer). The rehabilitation alliance in practice: The Clubhouse connection. *Psychiatric Rehabilitation Journal*, *23* (1), 19-23.

Battin, C., Bouvet, C., & Hatala, C. (2016). A systematic review of the effectiveness of the clubhouse model. *Psychiatric Rehabilitation Journal, 39*(4), 305–312. https://doi.org/10.1037/prj0000227

Beard, J. H., Goertzel, V., & Pearce, A. J. (1958). The effectiveness of activity group therapy with chronically regressed adult schizophrenics. *International Journal of Group Psychotherapy*, *8* (2), 123-136.

Carolan, M., Onaga, E., Pernice-Duca, F., & Jimenez, T. (2011). A place to be: The role of clubhouses in facilitating social support. *Psychiatric Rehabilitation Journal, 35*(2), 125–132. https://doi.org/10.2975/35.2.2011.125.132

Deci, E. L., & Ryan, R. M. (1985). *Intrinsic motivation and self determination in human behavior.* New York: Plenum Press.

Deci, E. L., with R. Flaste (1995). *Why we do what we do: Understanding self- motivation*. New York: Penguin Books.

Dell, N. A., Pelham, M., & Murphy, A. M. (2019). Loneliness and depressive symptoms in middle aged and older adults experiencing serious mental illness. *Psychiatric Rehabilitation Journal, 42*(2), 113–120. https://doi.org/10.1037/prj0000347

DeMartini, L., Mizock, L., Drob, S., Nelson, A., & Fisher, W. (2020). The barriers and facilitators to serious mental illness: Recovery post incarceration. *Psychological Services*. https://doi.org/10.1037/ser0000431

Dickerson, F., Origoni, A., Schroeder, J., Adamos, M., Katsafanas, E., Khushalani, S., Savage, C. L. G., Schweinfurth, L. A. B., Stallings, C., Sweeney, K., & Yolken, R. (2018). Natural cause mortality in persons with serious mental illness. *Acta Psychiatrica Scandinavica, 137*(5), 371–379. https://doi.org/10.1111/acps.12880

Di Masso, J., Avi-Itzhak, T., & Obler, D. R. (2001). The Clubhouse model: An outcome study on attendance, work attainment and status, and hospitalization recidivism. *Work: Journal of Prevention, Assessment & Rehabilitation, 17*(1), 23–30.

Doyle, A., Lanoil, J. & Dudek, K. (2013). *Need to be needed: Community as social practice in mental health*. New York: Columbia University Press.

Gabrielian, S., Hellemann, G., Koosis, E. R., Green, M. F., & Young, A. S. (2020). Do cognition and other person-level characteristics determine housing outcomes among homeless-experienced adults with serious mental illness? *Psychiatric Rehabilitation Journal*. https://doi.org/10.1037/prj0000457

General Accounting Office. (1977). Returning the mentally disabled to the community: Government needs to do more. (HRD-76-152) Washington D.C.

Goertzel, V., Beard, J.H. and Pilnick, S. (1960), Fountain House Foundation: Case Study Of An Expatient's Club. Journal of Social Issues, 16: 54-61. doi:https://doi.org/10.1111/j.1540-4560.1960.tb00949.x

Gold, P. B., Macias, C., & Rodican, C. F. (2016). Does competitive work improve quality of life for adults with severe mental illness? Evidence from a randomized trial of supported employment. *The Journal of Behavioral Health Services & Research, 43*(2), 155–171. https://doi.org/10.1007/s11414-014-9392-0

Grob, G. N. (2005). Public policy and mental illnesses: Jimmy carter's presidential commission on mental health. *The Milbank Quarterly, 83*(3), 425–456.

Hayes, R. D., Chang, C.-K., Fernandes, A. C., Begum, A., To, D., Broadbent, M., Hotopf, M., & Stewart, R. (2012). Functional status and all-cause mortality in serious mental illness. *PLoS ONE, 7*(9). https://doi.org/10.1371/journal.pone.0044613

Herman, S. E., Onaga, E., Pernice-Duca, F., Oh, S., & Ferguson, C. (2005). Sense of Community in Clubhouse Programs: Member and Staff Concepts. *American Journal of Community Psychology, 36*(3-4), 343-356. doi:https://doi.org/10.1007/s10464-005-8630-2

Huxter, M. J. (2013). Prisons: The psychiatric institution of last resort? Journal of Psychiatric and Mental Health Nursing, 20,735–743. https://doi.org/10.1111/jpm.12010

Jones, M. (1953). *The therapeutic community*. New York: Basic Books.

Jung, S. H., & Kim, H. J. (2012). Perceived stigma and quality of life of individuals diagnosed with schizophrenia and receiving psychiatric rehabilitation services: A comparison between the Clubhouse model and a rehabilitation skills training model in South Korea. *Psychiatric Rehabilitation Journal, 35*(6), 460–465. https://doi.org/10.1037/h0094580

Karlsson, M. (2013). Introduction to Mental Health Clubhouses: How the Fountain House Became an International Model. *International Journal of Self-Help & Self Care*, 7(1).

Kinn, L. G., Tanaka, K., Bellamy, C., & Davidson, L. (2018). "Pushing the Boat Out": A meta-synthesis of how members staff and family experience the clubhouse model. *Community Mental Health Journal, 54*(8), 1199–1211. https://doi.org/10.1007/s10597-018-0257-5

Kuno, E., Rothbard, A. B., Averyt, J., & Culhane, D. (2000). Homelessness among persons with serious mental illness in an enhanced community-8GABRIELIAN, HELLEMANN, KOOSIS, GREEN, AND YOUNG based mental health system. Psychiatric Services, 51,1012–1016. https://doi.org/10.1176/appi.ps.51.8.1012

Macias, C., Rodican, C. F., Hargreaves, W. A., Jones, D. R., Barreira, P. J., & Wang, Q. (2006). Supported employment outcomes of a randomized controlled trial of ACT and clubhouse models. *Psychiatric Services, 57*(10), 1406–1415. https://doi.org/10.1176/ps.2006.57.10.1406

Mandiberg, J. M. (2010). Another way: Enclave communities for people with mental Illness. *American Journal of Orthopsychiatry, 80* (2), 167-173.

Marwaha, S. & Johnson, S. (2004). Schizophrenia and employment: A review. *Social Psychiatry and Psychiatric Epidemiology, 39*, 337-349.

Maslow A.H (1943). A Theory of Human Motivation. *Psychological Review* 50(4), 370.

McKay, C. E., & Pelletier, J. R. (2007). Health promotion in clubhouse programs: Needs, barriers, and current and planned activities. *Psychiatric Rehabilitation Journal, 31*(2), 155–159. https://doi.org/10.2975/31.2.2007.155.159

McKay, C., Nugent, K. L., Johnsen, M., Eaton, W. W., & Lidz, C. W. (2018). A Systematic Review of Evidence for the Clubhouse Model of Psychosocial Rehabilitation. *Administration and Policy in Mental Health and Mental Health Services Research; New York, 45*(1), 28–47. https://doi.org/10.1007/s10488-016-0760-3

Mechanic D., Blider, S. & McAlpine, D. D. (2002). Employing persons with serious mental illness. *Health Affairs, 21* (5), 242–253.

Milazzo-Sayre L. J., Henderson, M.J., Manderscheid, R.W. et al. (2001). Persons treated in specialty mental health care programs in the United States, 1997. In R. W.

Pernice-Duca, F. M. (2008). The structure and quality of social network support among mental health consumers of Clubhouse programs. *Journal of Community Psychology, 36*(7), 929–946. https://doi.org/10.1002/jcop.20265

Plotnick, D. F., & Salzer, M. S. (2008). Clubhouse costs and implications for policy analysis in the context of system transformation initiatives. *Psychiatric Rehabilitation Journal, 32*(2), 128–131. https://doi.org/10.2975/32.2.2008.128.131

President's New Freedom Commission on Mental Health. (2003). Achieving the promise: Transforming Mental Health Care in America. Final Report. July 22, 2003. Retrieved from http://www.mentalhealthcommission.gov/reports/FinalReport/FullReport.htm

Prince, J. D., Oyo A., Mora, O, Wyka K, Schonebaum AD (2018). Loneliness among persons with severe mental illness. *The Journal of Nervous and Mental Disease*, 206(2), 136-14. doi: https://doi.org/10.1097/NMD.0000000000000768.

Propst, R. N. (1997). Stages in realizing the international diffusion of a single way of working: The Clubhouse model. *New Directions in Mental Health Services, 74,* 53-66.

Rice, K., Pernice, F., & Michon, A. (2020). Metacognition and the clubhouse model in treating severe mental illness. *Psychiatric Rehabilitation Journal, 43*(4), 284–289. https://doi.org/10.1037/prj0000464

Rogers, C. R. (1986). Carl Rogers on the development of the person-centered approach. *Person-Centered Review, 1*(3), 257–259.

Rosenberg, J., & Rosenberg, S.J. (2006). Introduction: Conceptualizing the challenges in community mental health. In J. Rosenberg, & S. J. Rosenberg (Eds.), *Community mental health: Challenges for the 21st century* (pp. 1-3). New York: Routledge.

Rubin, A. (1991). Case management. In S. Rose (Ed.), *Case management and social work practice* (pp. 5-20). White Plains, NY: Longman.

Sarason, S. B. (1974). The psychological sense of community: Prospects for a community psychology. San Francisco: Jossey-Bass.

Solís-Román, C., & Knickman, J. (2016). Project to evaluate the impact of Fountain House programs on Medicaid utilization and expenditures. Report for the Health Evaluation and Analytics Lab: New York University.

Tanaka, K., Davidson, L. (2015). Meanings Associated with the Core Component of Clubhouse Life: The Work-Ordered Day. *Psychiatric Quarterly* 86, 269–2 https://doi.org/10.1007/s11126-014-9330-6

US Comptroller General (1977). Annual Report of Comptroller General, United States Accounting Office. Retrieved from https://www.gao.gov/assets/b-119600-091264.pdf

World Health Organization (2016). Report on the Excess Mortality in Persons with Severe Mental Disorder. Geneva, Switzerland. WHO Reference No.WHO/MSD/MER/16.5

Service Coordination and Health Homes

Joseph J. Parks

Introduction

Care coordination and care management are necessary due to the poor health outcomes and subsequent increased mortality, morbidity, and costs that occur in its absence. During the past 10–15 years, there has been a steady accumulation of data that indicates that individuals with more serious mental health conditions are at more risk for comorbidities, have higher rates of morbidity and mortality (Colton and Manderscheid 2006; Parks et al. 2006; Lutterman et al. 2003; Daumit et al. 2010), and have higher costs and poorer outcomes than individuals with either no mental illness or less serious mental illnesses. Individuals with serious mental illness have a high lifetime prevalence of co-occurring substance use disorder (SUD), which is additive to risk of poor health. Over half of these individuals have other physical illnesses in addition to their mental health concerns (Jones et al. 2004; Sokal et al. 2004). While primary care has been referred to as the "de facto mental health system" in the United States (Fondow et al. 2015), literature examining visit patterns for this vulnerable group suggests individuals with SMI are less likely than the general population to use traditional primary medical care even if they have access to it (Mental Health America 2007; Morden et al. 2009). Clearly, these poor outcomes related not only to the simple presence of comorbid conditions but also to lack of access to and participation in receiving effective health care for these conditions. Based on all of the above, it is fair to say that co-occurring health conditions are an expectation, not an exception, in the population of individuals with serious mental illness (SMI).

The population of individuals with serious mental illness is overrepresented among the highest-cost utilizers of health dollars in two different ways. First, the general medical health (not behavioral health) costs for the population of individuals with serious mental illness are dramatically higher than those of their non-seriously mentally ill peers (Melek et al. 2018). This is due to both the prevalence of comorbidity and the greater likelihood of receiving health services in emergency rooms and hospital settings rather than in less costly and more effective primary care settings. Comorbid serious mental illness is overrepresented in the high health utilizer population in a general health population (particularly Medicaid), with some studies reporting that 75–80% of individuals who are Medicaid "high utilizers" have a co-occurring SMI, most commonly depression (because it is the serious mental illness with the highest population prevalence)

J. J. Parks (✉)
National Council on Mental Wellbeing, Washington, DC, USA

Missouri Institute of Mental Health, University of Missouri, St. Louis, St. Louis, MO, USA
e-mail: joep@thenationalcouncil.org

W. E. Sowers et al. (eds.), *Textbook of Community Psychiatry*,
https://doi.org/10.1007/978-3-031-10239-4_40

(Ford et al. 2004; Bartels et al. 2003). Second, individuals with the most serious mental illnesses are more likely to experience adverse social conditions (e.g., homelessness) that also negatively impact health outcomes and costs.

There are several major features in care as usual that must be addressed in order to make significant progress (Parks et al. 2006):

1. *No locus of accountability for health and behavioral health costs and outcomes for the whole individual across all health conditions.* The current finance system design generally has separate administrative structures, for planning, evaluating, and improving health services and behavioral health services both at the state and local levels. In many state and local systems, substance abuse service accountability and mental health services accountability are also disconnected (Parks and Minkov 2015). Subsequently individual providers are not held responsible and are incentivized to be accountable for care and outcomes for the whole individual across all health outcomes.
2. *Difficult access to primary care for individuals with behavioral health conditions.* Individuals with SMI (particularly those who have co-occurring substance use conditions) are not usually viewed as priority patients to be welcomed into primary care settings, even those which concentrate on serving public sector populations (such as federally qualified health centers, rural health centers, or community health centers). Individuals with significant psychiatric disabilities and/or those whose illness results in challenging symptoms or behaviors (e.g., people with persistent psychotic conditions) are often labeled as "misfits" in primary health settings because they exhibit "difficult" behavior in the waiting room or in interaction with medical personnel. For this reason, primary health settings may not make the extra effort to facilitate access and engagement for the individuals with more serious combinations of health and behavioral health conditions, which need that access the most.
3. *Challenges participating in care.* Even when individuals with behavioral health conditions, particularly those with associated psychiatric disabilities, have access to care, they have significant challenges in participating in their behavioral health and general medical care. These challenges may range from failure to keep appointments, to difficulty attending to routine preventive health recommendations (e.g., colonoscopies, PAP smears), to difficulty adhering to medical recommendations for the treatment of chronic disease. In addition, research from the Adverse Childhood Experiences Survey (ACES) data on the impact of early life trauma on the onset of both chronic medical conditions and chronic mental illnesses indicates the likelihood that many individuals with SMI have traumatic histories that further contribute to poor outcomes, as well as creating challenges in developing trusting and successful relationships with their caregivers. Finally, individuals with SMI are at higher risk for having challenges in other domains—"the social determinants of health." They are more likely to be homeless, impoverished, incarcerated, and in "unhealthy" living environments, all of which can make attending to medical recommendations particularly challenging.
4. *Lack of routine coordination and partnership between SMI BH settings and primary health providers.* Specific examples of lack of coordination may include one or more of the following: no routine protocol for insuring all SMI clients have a primary care provider, that they have signed a release of information, and/or that there has been direct communication between mental health prescribers and primary health providers to discuss coordination of care; lack of routine transmission of records of primary care visits to behavioral health providers; and/or lack of easy access to behavioral health telephone consultation for the primary care provider to ask questions or to problem-solve regarding a challenging shared patient (which would be more routine with other specialties) (Parks and Pollack 2004).

Care coordination and care management are the major tools currently available for addressing the discontinuities described above in treatment as usual care.

Care coordination has no consensus definition. A recent systematic review identified over 40 definitions of "care coordination." The systematic review authors combined the common elements from many definitions to develop one working definition for use in identifying reviews of interventions in the vicinity of care coordination and, as a result, developed a purposely broad definition: "Care coordination is the deliberate organization of patient care activities between two or more participants (including the patient) involved in a patient's care to facilitate the appropriate delivery of health care services. Organizing care involves the marshalling of personnel and other resources needed to carry out all required patient care activities and is often managed by the exchange of information among participants responsible for different aspects of care" (McDonald et al. 2007).

Care management has no consensus definition. Care management is inclusive of care coordination but also has the goals of providing cost-effective and non-duplicative services. Care management activities include identification, stratification, and prioritization of health risks, interdisciplinary team-based care, patient engagement, and utilization of guidelines to implement evidence-based practices. Care management commonly focuses decreasing on underutilization of high value, low-cost interventions (Center for Health Care Strategies 2007).

Care management is a relatively resource-intensive strategy that is most effective when used with particularly complex patients with chronic conditions. The care manager uses data to select patients with high utilization of avoidable services, such as emergency room visits and inpatient hospital admissions, and uses data to determine actionable care gaps to reduce this level of intervention in the future. The program enrollees are analyzed as a population to identify their common characteristics (e.g., particular diagnoses, comorbid mental health and substance use conditions, chronic pain, polypharmacy), which allows for identification of patient-specific actionable issues. Care management typically includes a health risk assessment, followed by educating patients about their conditions and how to manage them, and recommended best treatments. The main work in care management consists of identifying care gaps and remediating them (Parks 2015).

Both managed care companies/payers and healthcare provider organizations undertake care coordination and care management activities. When performed by a payer, care coordination and care management are usually done by a group of clinicians and their assistance who are separate from the utilization management team and function. The interventions more frequently involve interaction with providers than directly with the patient and only very rarely involve an ongoing in-person interaction with the patient and staff providing care coordination/care management.

In addition, behavioral healthcare management and care coordination are often combined with community mental health case management which identifies and addresses social determinants of health impacting the cost of care. Community mental health case management (CMHCM) is an ongoing individual relationship between a (usually) bachelor's-level case manager providing primarily direct face-to-face assistance in home or in various community settings and the patient. The case manager assists with maintaining housing, eligibility for various benefits, activities of daily living, and adherence to medication, as well as coordinating care between healthcare providers and attending clinic visits resulting in substantial reductions in the total cost of care (Parks et al. 2010).

When provided by payers, the cost of the internal teams providing the services is funded by a portion of their capitation rate or premiums. When healthcare providers are performing care coordination and care management, there is a broad array of payment methodologies including per member per month (PMPM) capitated payments for specific care management services, perspective payments (PPS), and fee-for-service bundled payments.

Healthcare screening and the management of chronic medical illness have gotten little attention for individuals with SMI inside BH care settings. As we shall discuss below, the past 5 years has seen steady growth and development in primary care capacity within behavioral health settings serving individuals with SMI. The SAMHSA-HRSA PHBHI grantee program has funded nearly 100 such programs over this time period, and many more programs have been developed without such grant funding (see SAMHSA PBHCI Program, http://www.integration.samhsa.gov/about-us/pbhci). Some states, like Missouri (see below), have developed incentives and funding for the development of certified behavioral health homes in mental health centers statewide (Parks 2015; Townley and Takach 2012). While this movement is growing, embedding primary care where individuals with SMI receive BH services is still the exception rather than the rule.

Collaboration and Information Sharing

The more that primary care (PC) and behavioral health (BH) providers work together in a true collaboration with the patient at the center, the more likely the care will be successful. Information sharing is an important starting place, and electronic health record platforms may facilitate that sharing. However, if the information in the record is not reviewed, and if the practitioners don't talk to each other to coordinate efforts and provide consistent messaging to the patient, electronic information sharing alone will not be productive. Further, care coordination means more than just taking people to appointments. Care coordination requires PC and BH practitioners to communicate about both sets of issues and to work as partners to help the patient and family understand recommendations and participate successfully in care, in the face of significant challenges of all kinds (which—as noted above—are more likely to be present in individuals with SMI). When this coordination happens in a *person-centered* or *patient-centered* fashion, the outcomes are much more successful (SAMHSA-HRSA 2012. HHS publication number pending 2012 – Resource Guide for Person-Centered Planning).

Information Sharing Technology and Confidentiality

Sharing information across multiple healthcare providers is the backbone intervention of care coordination. The most common barrier is incorrect and inappropriately restrictive interpretations of the confidentiality requirements of HIPAA and 42 CFR part 2. Absent specific state regulations to the contrary, the Federal HIPAA requirements allow not only sharing information between treatment providers without patient consent but even over patient objections unless the agency has adopted a policy to honor such objections (45 CFR 164.522(a)).

In July 2020, the substance abuse confidentiality rules under 42 CFR part 2 were amended in a new final rule. While patient consent is still required to share treatment information, that consent no longer has to be specific to a particular individual and can include organizations or even broad categories of healthcare providers. Re-disclosure of information obtained from a part 2-covered entity but now part of another medical record is no longer prohibited. Effective and efficient care coordination requires that healthcare organizations and individual treatment providers do not operationalize HIPAA and 42CFR part 2 regulations in a manner that is more restrictive than the regulation's actual requirements.

More people are harmed by failure to exchange information to coordinate care than are harmed by an inappropriate release of information. Jessica Grubb died in 2016 at age 30 from an overdose of oxycodone after being prescribed the medication at discharge from a hospital following surgery. Despite letting doctors know she was in recovery from opioid addiction, the information was not listed on her chart. The Protecting Jessica Grubb's Legacy Act was passed as part of the Coronavirus Aid, Relief, and Economic Security Act (CARES Act) and became law on March 27, 2020. The Legacy Act modifies 42 U.S.C. § 290dd-2, the statute on which the 42 CFR part 2 substance use treatment privacy rule is based, aligning it more closely with the privacy and security regulations under the Health Insurance Portability and Accountability Act (HIPAA). It also supports the ultimate goal of consent—that any person be able to easily share his or her health data with their healthcare providers if they so desire. The Legacy Act also includes heightened privacy restrictions on use of SUD data in legal, administrative, and legislative proceedings and an unprecedented set of antidiscrimination protections related to SUD health records. The new legislation substantially modifies current 42 CFR part 2 requirements as follows:

A patient may, if they choose to do so, sign a consent to allow their SUD treatment to be used or disclosed records for the purposes of Treatment, Payment and Health Care Operations (TPO) under HIPAA. This permits the redisclosure of part 2 health data, in accordance with HIPAA

- Heightened prohibitions on use of part 2 data in criminal and civil proceedings
- Stronger anti-discrimination protections
- More stringent penalties and violation enforcement under HIPAA

At the time of this publication, SAMHSA has not yet promulgated rules implementing the changes 42 CFR part 2 in the CARES act. These changes when implemented should substantially improve coordination of care for persons with SUD while simultaneously strengthening the protections against misuse of SUD treatment information.

Population Management Data and Tracking

An advanced approach to care coordination involves collecting good population management data and having the capacity to track the population, whether through disease-specific registries (for basic monitoring) or capturing cost and utilization for more complex populations, as referenced above. Care coordination and care management are much more labor intensive and inefficient without the use of disease registries or data analytics. For individuals with SMI, a basic step is to track how many individuals served have a primary care provider, have seen the provider, and have a chronic health condition requiring ongoing integrated attention (regardless of diagnosis). This core data in a BH setting serving the SMI provides a "baseline" for developing care coordination and care management capacity throughout the organization. Further, it is important to recognize that unmet or under-met BH needs are a key contributor of poor health outcomes, including high utilizers of medical ER and inpatient services. Most of these individuals have SMI. Therefore, tracking health utilization costs across the SMI population provides a valuable database for population management within any clinic, as well as providing an opportunity to demonstrate cost-effectiveness of integrated wraparound interventions targeted to that population.

Advanced Models of Care Coordination

The medical/health home model was originally proposed by pediatricians and family medicine physician groups. In 1967, the American Academy of Pediatrics' (AAP) standards of child health care proposed the medical home as "one central source of a child's pediatric records to resolve duplication and gaps in services that occur as a result of lack of communication and coordination." The American Academy of Family Physicians (AAFP), American College of Physicians (ACP), American Academy of Pediatrics (AAP), and American Osteopathic Association wrote the Joint Principles of the Patient-Centered Medical Home, stating that patient-centered medical homes (PCMH) should have seven characteristics:

1. A personal physician
2. Physician-directed medical practice
3. Whole-person orientation
4. Coordinated care
5. Quality and safety
6. Enhanced access
7. Adequate payment

In 2008, the Department of Health and Human Services (HHS) developed a conceptual model of the medical home, including service domains, training requirements, financing, policy, and research. It intended for the model to lower health care costs, increase quality, reduce health disparities, produce better outcomes, lower utilization rates, improve compliance with recommended care, and coordinate medical and social services required by the individual across the lifespan. The National Committee for Quality Assurance used this model to develop its medical home recognition program (Centers for Medicare and Medicaid Services 2010).

Since then, several major payment mechanisms for provider-based care coordination and care management have been implemented presented in the date order they became available.

Primary Care Case Management (PCCM)

In 1981, the 97th session of Congress enacted the Omnibus Budget Reconciliation Act (OBRA) which allowed state Medicaid programs to implement risk-based managed care programs as well as PCCM, pending HCFA (now known as CMS) waiver approval. The state had to meet two requirements in order to be granted HCFA approval. The case management restrictions must not "substantially impair access" to primary care services of "adequate quality where medically necessary"; and the case management restrictions must be "cost-effective." PCCM incorporates aspects of both managed care and FFS.

In a PCCM program, each enrollee is assigned to a designated primary care provider (PCP) who is paid a monthly case management fee to assume responsibility for care management and coordination. Individual providers are not at financial risk and continue to be paid on an FFS basis for covered services. States can determine which types of providers can serve as PCPs, for example, a general practitioner, family physician, internist, obstetrician gynecologist, pediatrician, or, at state option, physician assistant, nurse practitioner, or certified nurse-midwife. Many states use PCCM as an alternative to comprehensive managed care in areas where plans do not operate (e.g., rural areas) or for Medicaid populations with complex healthcare needs. In 2020, 12 states have PCCM programs making PMPM payments for care coordination and care management.

State Medicaid programs have implemented delivery systems expanding on traditional primary care case management programs, many focusing on high-cost, high-user beneficiaries (not limited to specific diagnoses). While many of these models are physician-based, there is a growing movement toward interdisciplinary, team-based approaches. Services such as care coordination and follow-up, linkages to social services, and medication compliance are

reimbursed through a "per member per month" structure. Prior to the ACA, states have already been using the authority in other sections of the Social Security Act, such as section 1932(a) of the Act and full-risk managed care plans and demonstrations approved under section 1115 of the Act to implement their medical homes.

Health Homes for Chronic Conditions (Section 2703 of ACA)

On January 1, 2011, the state option to provide health home services to Medicaid beneficiaries with chronic conditions became effective. This option offers the opportunity for behavioral health provider organizations to become health homes for the people they serve. Federal health home guidance lays out service requirements stemming from the ACA and "well-established chronic care models". The required services include:

- Each patient must have a comprehensive care plan.
- Services must be quality-driven, cost-effective, culturally appropriate, person- and family-centered, and evidence-based.
- Services must include prevention and health promotion, health care, mental health and substance use, and long-term care services, as well as linkages to community supports and resources.
- Service delivery must involve continuing care strategies, including care management, care coordination, and transitional care from the hospital to the community.
- Health home providers do not need to provide all the required services themselves but must ensure that the full array of services is available and coordinated.
- Providers must be able to use health information technology (HIT) to facilitate the health home's work and establish quality improvement efforts to ensure that the work is effective at the individual and population level.

Selecting Patients: Eligibility and Enrollment

Individuals who are eligible for health home services must have one of the following:

1. Two chronic conditions
2. One chronic condition and the risk of having a second
3. One serious and persistent mental health condition

"Chronic conditions" as defined by statute include mental health conditions, substance use disorders, asthma, diabetes, heart disease, and obesity with a body mass index over 25. CMS can authorize additional chronic conditions for incorporation into health home models (CMS 2022). CMS can also authorize state-proposed definitions of conditions and situations that constitute merely a risk of having a second chronic condition. The eligibility criteria are so potentially broad as to be able to cover almost all clients in a state's public mental health system.

Regardless of which conditions states select for focus, states must address mental health and substance use disorders, prevention, and treatment services and consult with the Substance Abuse and Mental Health Services Administration (SAMHSA) on how they propose to provide these services. States may apply to have their Medicaid state plan amended to include health homes, either in primary care, behavioral health specialty care, or both.

Health Home Service Definitions

Section 1945(h)(4) of the Act lists six required health home services. CMS has not provided definitions of the six services but instead requires states to define each service, describe which team members are responsible for that service, and describe how health information technology (HIT) will be used to deliver and support each service. States have broad flexibility to determine how to use health information technology in their health home models. The six services are:

1. Comprehensive care management
2. Care coordination
3. Health promotion
4. Comprehensive transitional care from inpatient to other settings, including follow-up
5. Individual and family support, which includes authorized representatives
6. Referral to community and social support services, if relevant

As of November 2020, Medicaid had approved 65 health home programs in 19 states specifically targeting behavioral health conditions through payment of PMPM for care coordination, care management, and other health home services. An independent federally funded evaluation by the Urban Institute of the first 13 health home programs approved in 11 states found the health home approach resulted in better quality of care for enrollees, including improvements in care coordination and management, greater integration of behavioral and primary care, increased rates of transitional care (including follow-up after emergency department visits or hospitalizations), and improved access to social services and community-based supports (Spillman and Allen 2017). In addition, CHMC enrollees who had longer and more stable health home exposure showed significant reductions in overall Medicaid spending, suggesting that the ability of health homes to gain and maintain enrollee engagement is a key factor in health home performance (Spillman and Allen 2017). Missouri behavioral health homes have reported improvements in chronic care performance indicator treatment of chronic disease and net savings of $32.98 PMPM in the total cost of care for their participants (Parks and Minkov 2015).

Certified Community Mental Health Centers

In 2014, Section 223 of the Protecting Access to Medicare Act (PAMA) was enacted, authorizing the Certified Community Behavioral Health Clinic (CCBHC) demonstration to allow states to test new strategies for delivering and reimbursing services provided in community mental health centers (CMHCs). The CCBHC demonstration aims to improve the availability, quality, and outcomes of ambulatory services provided in CMHCs and other providers by establishing a standard definition and criteria for CCBHCs and developing a new payment system that accounts for the total cost of providing comprehensive services to all individuals who seek care. The payment methodology is very similar to the perspective payment methodology that supports Federally Qualified Health Centers. Perspective payments are a bundled payment with the rate set individually for each organization based on its cost report. This assures that the payment rate is adequate to actually cover the cost of providing the services. The service bundle can include the costs of care and interventions that do not have specific fee-for-service billing codes available. Many of the evidence-based components of care coordination and care management do not have specific fee-for-service codes available. CCBHCs are paid either daily or monthly based on their annual cost reports. CCBHCs are required to coordinate care across the spectrum of health services, including physical and behavioral health and other social services. CCBHCs are required to conduct population health management, for quality improvement, for reducing disparities, and for research and outreach. The demonstration also aims to provide coordinated care that addresses both behavioral and physical health conditions. CCBHCs have certification requirements (SAMHSA 2016) in six important areas: (1) staffing; (2) availability and accessibility of services; (3) care coordination; (4) scope of services; (5) quality and reporting; and (6) organizational authority.

Partnerships or care coordination agreements required with:

- FQHCs/rural health clinics
- Inpatient psychiatry and detoxification
- Post-detoxification step-down services
- Residential programs
- Other social services providers, including schools, child welfare agencies, juvenile and criminal justice agencies and facilities, Indian Health Service Youth Regional Treatment centers, child placing agencies for therapeutic foster care service
- Department of Veterans Affairs facilities
- Inpatient acute care hospitals and hospital outpatient clinics

Reporting of quality metrics hold CCBHCs accountable for follow-up after hospitalization or ER department use and readmissions. Independent evaluation by Mathematica found that CCBHCs have used a variety of strategies to improve care coordination, including adding various provider types to treatment teams and expanding targeted care coordination strategies to different populations and service lines (Wishon-Siegwarth et al. 2020). In the early stages of the demonstration, improvements to electronic health records (EHR) and health information technology aided clinics in their care coordination efforts, in some cases permitting CCBHCs to integrate care plans more fully, connect with external providers, and receive alerts about clients' care transitions. As the demonstration progressed, clinics implemented additional strategies and initiated collaboration with various external organizations to facilitate coordinated care. For example, some clinics partnered with first responders and law enforcement officials on strategies to intervene in crisis situations and divert those in crisis from the criminal justice system.

Medicare Care Management Bundled Payments

In 2015, Medicare began paying separately for chronic care management (CCM) services furnished to Medicare patients with multiple chronic conditions under the Medicare Physician Fee Schedule (PFS). Medicare offers three levels of payment to healthcare providers for care management services: chronic care management (CCM), complex CCM, and principal care management (PCM). The CCM service includes structured recording of patient health information, maintaining a comprehensive electronic care plan, managing transitions of care and other care management services, and coordinating and sharing patient health information timely within and outside the practice. CCM services are typically provided outside of face-to-face patient visits and focus on characteristics of advanced care such as a continuous relationship with a designated member of the care team; patient support for chronic diseases to achieve health goals; 24/7 patient access to care and health information; receipt of preventive care; patient and caregiver engagement; a comprehensive care plan; management of care transitions; and timely sharing and use of health information (Center for Medicare and Medicaid Services, 2019).

Both CCM and complex CCM require:

- Multiple (two or more) chronic conditions expected to last at least 12 months, or until the death of the patient.
- Chronic conditions place the patient at significant risk of death, acute exacerbation/decompensation, or functional decline.
- Comprehensive care plan established, implemented, revised, or monitored.
- Complex CCM also requires moderate or high complexity medical decision-making.

Principal care management requires (Clements 2020):

- One complex chronic condition lasting at least 3 months, which is the focus of the care plan.
- The condition is of sufficient severity to place patient at risk of hospitalization or has been the cause of a recent hospitalization.
- The condition requires development or revision of disease-specific care plan.
- The condition requires frequent adjustments in the medication regimen, and/or the management of the condition is unusually complex due to comorbidities.

The eligible provider for all three is a physician or other qualified healthcare professionals. Payment is by monthly bundled rates.

Service and provider	Code	Minutes/Month	
CCM by Qualified Provider	CPT 99490	20	
CCM –Other Clinic Staff	CPT 99491	30	
Complex CCM Other Clinic Staff	CPT 99487	First 60	
Complex CCM –Other Clinic Staff	CPT 99489	Each additional 30	
PCM by Qualified Provider	HCPCS code G2064	30	
PCM –Other Clinic Staff	HCPCS code G2065	30	

A qualified provider is a physician, nurse practitioner, or physician assistant.

Conclusion

Care coordination and care management are essential for persons with multiple conditions receiving care from multiple providers to receive high-quality care that results in reduced morbidity, mortality, and costs. The majority of persons with behavioral health conditions have multiple conditions both behavioral and general medical. Interactions with these patients constitute the majority of visits of most healthcare providers. Both behavioral health, general medical providers, and payers of health care cannot meet the expected standards of care without actively implementing in participating in care coordination and care management.

Portions of this chapter were adapted from an article previously published in the Community Mental Health Journal (32) and Parks, J. J. Health Homes. In Raney, L. (ed.), 2015 pp 193–216; Integrated Care: Working at the Interface of Primary Care and Behavioral Health (pp.193–216). Washington, DC: American Psychiatric Press, Inc.

References

Bartels SJ, Clark RE, Peacock WJ, et al. (2003). Medicare and Medicaid costs for schizophrenia patients by age cohort compared with costs for depression, dementia, and medically ill patients. American Journal of Geriatric Psychiatry, 11(6), 648–657.

Center for Health Care Strategies, Inc. (2007). Care Management Framework. Last accessed on April 5th, 2022 at: https://www.chcs.org/media/Care_Management_Framework.pdf

Centers for Medicare and Medicaid Services. (2010). SMDL# 10-024 ACA# 12. Re: Health Homes for Enrollees with Chronic Conditions.

Centers for Medicare and Medicaid Services. (2022). https://www.medicaid.gov/medicaid/long-term-services-supports/healthhomes/index.html#:~:text=Chronic%20conditions%20listed%20in%20the,target%20health%20home%20services%20geographically

Center for Medicare and Medicaid Services Medicare Learning Network (2019). Chronic Care Management Services. Accessed on April 5th, 2022 at: https://www.cms.gov/outreach-and-education/medicare-learning-network-mln/mlnproducts/downloads/chroniccare-management.pdf

Clements J. (2020). Learn About Billing Medicare's New Principal Care Management Codes. Outsource Strategies International. Accessed on April 5th, 2022 at: https://www.outsourcestrategies.com/blog/learn-about-billing-medicares-new-principal-care-management-codes.html

Colton, CW & Manderscheid RW (2006). Congruencies in increased mortality rates, years of potential life lost, and causes of death among public mental health clients in eight states. Preventing Chronic Disease: Public Health Research, Practice, & Policy, 3(2), 1–14.

Daumit GL, Anthony CB, Ford DE, et al. (2010). Pattern of mortality in a sample of Maryland residents with severe mental illness. Psychiatry Research, 176(2–3), 242–245.

Fondow M, Pandhi N, Ricco J, et al. (2015). Visit Patterns for Severe Mental Illness with Implementation of Integrated Care: A Pilot Retrospective Cohort Study AIMS Public Health; 2(4): 821–831.

Ford JD, Trestman RL, Steinberg K, et al. (2004). Prospective association of anxiety, depressive, and addictive disorders with high utilization of primary, specialty and emergency medical care. Social Science & Medicine, 58(11), 2145–2148.

Jones DR, Macias C, Barreira PJ, et al. (2004). Prevalence, severity, and co-occurrence of chronic physical health problems of persons with serious mental illness. Psychiatric Services; 55:1250–1257.

Lutterman T, Ganju V, Schacht L & Monihan K (2003). Sixteen State Study on Mental Health Performance Measures. DHHS Publication No. (SMA) 03-3835. Rockville, MD: Center for Mental Health Services, Substance Abuse and Mental Health Services Administration.

McDonald KM, Sundaram V, Bravata DM, et al. (2007). Care coordination. In: Shojania KG, McDonald KM, Wachter RM, and Owens DK, eds. Closing the quality gap: A critical analysis of quality improvement strategies. Technical Review 9 (Prepared by Stanford-UCSF Evidence-Based Practice Center under contract No. 290-02-0017). Vol. 7. Rockville, MD: Agency for Healthcare Research and Quality. AHRQ Publicatioen No. 04(07)-0051-7.

Melek SP, Norris DT & Paulus J et al. (2018). Milliman American Psychiatric Association Report; Potential economic impact of integrated medical-behavioral healthcare. Retrieved on April 4th, 2022 at: https://www.psychiatry.org/File%20Library/Psychiatrists/Practice/Professional-Topics/Integrated-Care/Milliman-Report-Economic-Impact-Integrated-Implications-Psychiatry.pdf

Mental Health America, Alexandria; VA, Mental Health America (2007). Communicating About Health: A Mental Health America Survey of People with Schizophrenia and Providers.

Morden NE, Mistler LA, Weeks WB, et al. (2009). Health care for patients with serious mental illness: family medicine's role. J Am Board Family Med; 22:187–195.

Parks JJ (2015). Health Homes. In Raney, L. (ed.), Integrated Care: Working at the Interface of Primary Care and Behavioral Health (pp.193–216). Washington, DC: American Psychiatric Press, Inc.

Parks JJ & Minkov K (2015). Primary Health-Behavioral Health Integration for the Population of Individuals with Serious Mental Illness. In O'Donohue. W.T. (ed.), Integrated Primary and Behavioral Care: Role in Medical Homes and Chronic Disease Management (pp.171–199). New York, NY: Springer Publishing.

Parks JJ, & Pollack D (2004). Integrating behavioral health and primary care services: Opportunities and challenges for state mental health authorities: Eleventh in a series of technical reports. Alexandria, VA: National Association of State Mental Health Program Directors. Retrieved from http://www.nasmhpd.org/general_files/publications/med_directors_pubs/Final%20Technical%20Report%20on%20Primary%20Care%20%20Behavioral%20Health%20Integration.final.pdf

Parks JJ, Swinfard T and Stuve P (2010). Mental Health Community Case Management and Its Effect on Healthcare Expenditures. Psychiatric Annals, 40 (8); pp. 415–419.

Parks JJ, Svendsen D, Singer P, & Foti ME (eds.) (2006). Morbidity and mortality in people with serious mental illness: Thirteenth in a series of technical reports. Alexandria, VA: National Association of State Mental Health Program Directors Council. Retrieved from http://www.nasmhpd.org/general_files/publications/med_directors_pubs/Technical%20Report%20on%20Morbidity%20and%20Mortaility%20-%20Final%2011-06.pdf

SAMHSA-HRSA. (2012). Behavioral Health Homes for People With Mental Health & Substance Use Conditions – The Core Clinical Features"; SAMHSA-HRSA Center for Integrated Health Solutions; Available at HYPERLINK "https://urldefense.com/v3/__https:/www.thenationalcouncil.org/wp-content/uploads/2021/04/CIHS_Health_Homes_Core_Clinical_Features.pdf__;!!NHLzug!MlgRl1XxBMKNFay9pZslm8PsdA15IAtYZoCAf1YoZVxHYfnYxOL1DcdbN44ByOViwQuHNIzgenTRt97I1iXvIds$" https://www.thenationalcouncil.org/wp-content/uploads/2021/04/CIHS_Health_Homes_Core_Clinical_Features.pdf, Accessed September, 2022.

Sokal J, Messias E, Dickerson FB, et al. (2004) Comorbidity of medical illnesses among adults with serious mental illness who are receiving community psychiatric services. J Nervous Mental Disease; 192:421–427.

Spillman BC, Allen EH (2017). Evaluation of the Medicaid Health home option for Beneficiaries with Chronic Conditions: Evaluation of Outcomes of Selected Health Home Program, Annual Report – Year Five. Urban Institute.

Substance Abuse and Mental Health Services Administration (2016). Criteria for the Demonstration Program to Improve Community Mental Health Centers and to Establish Certified Community Behavioral Health Clinics. Rockville, MD: SAMHSA

Townley C & Takach M (2012). Developing and implementing the Section 2703 health home state option: state strategies to address key issues. http://nashp.org/sites/default/files/health.home_.state_.option.strategies.section.2703.pdf

Wishon-Siegwarth A, Miller R Little J, et. al. (2020). Implementation Findings from the National Evaluation of the Certified Community Behavioral Health Clinics Demonstration-September 2020. Mathematica Policy Research, Prepared for Office of Behavioral Health, Disability, and Aging Policy Office of the Assistant Secretary for Planning and Evaluation U.S. Department of Health and Human Services Contract #HHSP233201600017I

Part VII

Special Populations

Community-Based Psychiatric Care for Individuals with Intellectual and Developmental Disabilities

Jennifer D. Bellegarde, Amelia Polzella, Thomas Scheidemantel, and Stephen L. Ruedrich

Most individuals with IDD and comorbid psychiatric illness and/or behavioral issues are cared for by general psychiatrists in community settings. This can be quite challenging given that the mental health needs of individuals with intellectual and developmental disabilities (IDD) receive little attention in either medical school or residency training. This chapter offers an overview of the concept of IDD, the history that has led to current treatment needs in the community, and the systems of care involved. We discuss the presentation and care of persons with IDD in outpatient, emergency, and psychiatric inpatient settings while highlighting the implications this has for community psychiatry. We end by offering ideas for improving education and training of mental health professionals to better care for this challenging patient population.

J. D. Bellegarde (✉) · T. Scheidemantel · S. L. Ruedrich
Case Western Reserve University School of Medicine, University Hospitals – Cleveland Medical Center, Cleveland, OH, USA
e-mail: Jennifer.Bellegarde@UHhospitals.org; Thomas.Scheidemantel@UHhospitals.org; Stephen.Ruedrich@UHhospitals.org

A. Polzella
Department of Psychiatry, University Hospitals – Cleveland Medical Center, Cleveland, OH, USA
e-mail: Amelia.Polzella@UHhospitals.org

Terminology, Classification, and Epidemiology

Intellectual and developmental disabilities (IDDs) refer to disorders with onset during the developmental period (prior to age 22 years) which are characterized by deficits in both intellectual and adaptive functioning. Compared to previous versions, the DSM-5 places less emphasis on intelligence (as measured by IQ) and more focus on adaptive functioning and continues to classify IDD by severity of impairment (mild, moderate, severe, profound). IDD affects about 1% of the population, with men more likely to be affected than women (Hales, 2016). The majority (85%) of persons with IDD have disability in the mild range (DSM-5; American Psychiatric Association 2013).

The Concept of Dual Diagnosis

Through the first half of the twentieth century, it was unusual for individuals with IDD in the USA to seek or receive mental health services in community settings (Menolascino 1968). In fact, prior to 1960, most behavioral or psychiatric symptomatology exhibited by persons with IDD was ascribed to the IDD itself, a phenomenon described as "diagnostic overshadowing" (Reiss et al. 1982). This began to change with increasing recognition that persons with IDD can also have co-occurring

W. E. Sowers et al. (eds.), *Textbook of Community Psychiatry*,
https://doi.org/10.1007/978-3-031-10239-4_41

psychiatric disorders, a term characterized as the original "dual diagnosis" (Menolascino 1968). Since then, this dual diagnosis has been well-studied across a variety of clinical and nonclinical groups and treatment settings (Munir 2009). Today, it is generally agreed that 25–40% of all persons with IDD have a co-occurring psychiatric and/or behavioral disorder (Mazza et al. 2020).

It is also well-recognized that arriving at an accurate psychiatric diagnosis in many individuals with IDD is challenging, as these patients often have difficulty expressing emotions, describing internal feelings, and with communication in general (Harris 2006). To address this dilemma, some clinical organizations have offered extrapolated or modified diagnostic systems adapted to persons with IDD (Royal College of Psychiatrists 2001; Barnhill et al. 2017). Compared to the DSM or ICD, use of these modified diagnostic systems improves diagnostic accuracy of dual diagnoses (Cooper et al. 2007).

History: Past, Present, and Future

Much like their counterparts with mental illness, the initial psychiatric treatment of persons with IDD took place in large residential settings. At its peak in the mid-1960s, nearly 200,000 persons with IDD in the USA were residing in large institutions, often numbering in the hundreds or thousands of beds (National Council on Disability 2012). At the time, this represented nearly 10% of persons with IDD. The institutionalization of individuals with IDD in the USA occurred for a variety of reasons, including stigma, fear, and lack of community resources. Unfortunately, many states also engaged in the involuntary sterilization of persons with IDD, as part of a eugenics movement which presaged some of the atrocities of the Nazi era (Harris 2006).

With the establishment of the President's Panel on Mental Retardation in the early 1960s, persons with IDD began to move from large state institutions to community settings (Harris 2006). Subsequent legislation, such as the Americans with Disabilities Act of 1990 (Americans with Disabilities Act, 1990), and legal cases such as Olmstead v. L.C. (1999) have strengthened the rights of individuals with IDD to live and work in the community. Substantial de-institutionalization has resulted. Today, fewer than 60,000 persons with IDD continue to reside in "congregate settings," defined as a living abode housing at least 16 persons. In contrast, the majority (72%) of persons with IDD reside with their families, while over 1.4 million individuals live alone or with a single roommate (Braddock et al. 2017). An increasingly alarming trend is that nearly a quarter of those living with family reside with elderly caregivers (AAIDD, 2016). Most states have significant waiting lists for residential placement of adults with IDD currently living with aging parents (United Cerebral Palsy Association 2020).

Systems of Care

Evolution of Treatment Settings

As needs of persons with IDD and mental health (MH) began to be seen in community settings, they faced significant treatment challenges. First was coordinating care across IDD and MH services (Menolascino et al. 1986). When many individuals with dual diagnoses were living in large institutions, it was typical to "import" psychiatry into the institution, in the form of psychiatric consultants who could advise the medical team or provide care directly. This model became impractical once most individuals were living in the community. Second, most American states have separate state-run agencies responsible for IDD and MH services, with separate budgets, leadership, regulatory provisions, and agendas. The former mostly focuses on residential and vocational services for individuals with IDD, whereas the latter provides MH services primarily for persons with severe and persistent mental illness. Specifically, as recently as 2017, 41 of the 50 states had separate state departments overseeing IDD and MH services (Pinals et al. 2017).

Dueling Systems of Care

Traditionally, state departments coordinating IDD services suggested that MH care was not their mandate, and MH services similarly stated that they could not absorb MH care for persons with IDD, which should be the responsibility of the IDD agencies (Pinals et al. 2017). As a result, it was not uncommon for persons with IDD and dual diagnoses to fall through treatment cracks. A recent review of best practices for community treatment of individuals with dual diagnoses noted that evidence-based practices (EBP) frequently used in IDD settings (such as communication training and positive behavioral supports) are rarely utilized for persons with dual diagnoses seen in psychiatric settings. Conversely, EBP with pharmacotherapy and psychotherapy exist for persons with IDD and behavioral challenges, but these persons often have limited access to psychiatric treatment settings (Constantino et al. 2020).

The situation has improved in recent years, with the increasing recognition that dual diagnoses occur in up to a third of individuals with IDD, so that service needs alone justify improved coordination of care between IDD and MH agencies. This integrated care can take the form of dual diagnosis programs/clinics within mainstream psychiatric treatment settings, or at least the designation of either the IDD or MH system as having the primary responsibility for care of persons with a dual diagnosis.

Outpatient Care

The lack of adequate outpatient MH services for persons with IDD is long-standing (Holingue et al. 2020). Besides the separate funding of systems which disagree about responsibility for care, there are also barriers to access within existing MH systems and often a basic lack of financial resources and health care personnel (Constantino et al. 2020). As a result, outpatient psychiatric services for persons with dual diagnoses tend to be uneven in their quality and in some locations do not exist at all (Munir 2009). A recent review of Medicaid waiver services for individuals with IDD noted significant variance across states in projected spending and actual reimbursement for MH services. It also noted an apparent lack of most states' commitment to providing (or at least funding) mental and behavioral services for persons with IDD using this waiver (Friedman et al. 2015).

This struggle with access to MH services is particularly true for individuals with IDD at two critical times of transition. The first is when adolescents or young adults with IDD must transition from child/adolescent services, which are typically better developed, to adult services whose availability is often limited (Nathenson and Zablosky 2017). The second occurs when adults with IDD enter their senior years, where both medical and MH services for these individuals are often lacking (Heller et al. 2010). Additionally, irrespective of age, individuals with IDD in the severe/profound range encounter barriers accessing care in general psychiatric settings (Chaplin 2009).

Best Practices and Model Programs

There are multiple examples of outpatient psychiatric care which exemplify best practices for persons with dual diagnoses. Hackerman et al. (2006) described a special needs clinic for adults with IDD and dual diagnoses within a larger Baltimore community mental health center (CMHC). Over 5 years, the program evaluated over 200 patients, providing initial assessments, ongoing medication management, psychotherapy, and for some, psychoeducational programs addressing life skills, health and wellness, work adjustment, and communication. The authors attributed elements of their success to their location within a larger CMHC, strong liaisons to primary medical care, and formal relationships with local developmental disability agencies and facilities.

START (systemic, therapeutic, assessment, resources, and treatment) is another model program. It offers multidisciplinary treatment, education, and research coordinated by the Center for START Services at the University of New Hampshire Institute on Disability. START programs, currently located in 15 states, provide dual diagnosis treatment, consultation services, crisis intervention, and other services (Center for START Services 2019). In a recent study, the START program produced significant improvement in mental health symptoms and service experience, as well as significant decreases in both emergency department visits and psychiatric hospitalizations (Kalb et al. 2019).

Assertive Community Treatment (ACT) has been adapted for use in individuals with IDD and co-occurring psychiatric and behavioral disorders (Burns 2010). ACT programs provide multidisciplinary teams with around-the-clock availability, often with outreach services addressing both routine and crisis care. Although the ACT approach makes intuitive sense as an optimal model for delivering outpatient care to persons with dual diagnoses, there is thus far limited research demonstrating benefit of this model over treatment as usual (Martin et al. 2005; Balogh et al. 2016).

Coordinating Care Across Different Systems

As previously discussed, the common lack of coordination between MH and IDD services for persons with dual diagnoses often extends into the ambulatory care setting. Recent reviews of this area found few empirically sound studies comparing integrated vs separate systems (Chaplin 2009), or the use of outreach systems (Balogh et al. 2016). Chaplin (2009) found that while persons with more severe IDD have reduced access to general MH services, those with borderline intellectual functioning tend to do well in mainstream outpatient psychiatric care. Additionally, the advent of community-based IDD teams improved the care of those treated in inpatient settings. Similarly, Hassiotis et al. (2009), in a randomized controlled trial in the UK comparing the addition of a specialist behavior therapy team to treatment as usual, demonstrated that the addition of this specialized service was more effective in addressing challenging behavior in persons with IDD and was more cost-effective. Most authors have supported attempting to integrate ambulatory MH care for persons with dual diagnoses within mainstream MH service systems and recognized that those receiving IDD support were more likely to be able to access MH care (Hemmings et al. 2014; Lewis et al. 2020).

Special Populations Within a Special Population

Among persons with IDD and dual diagnoses in ambulatory settings, three special populations merit mention: those with co-occurring substance use disorders, individuals with autism spectrum disorder (ASD), and forensically involved individuals.

Substance use disorders are common in persons with IDD. This "triple diagnosis" primarily affects those with mild ID and borderline intellectual functioning (Didden et al. 2020). Psychiatric comorbidities such as anxiety and depression are common and complicate ambulatory treatment, which requires care coordination, agency collaboration, and tailored therapeutic approaches for success (Van Duijenbode and Vander 2019).

Children with ASD utilize emergency services more than peers without ASD. Their ED visits are more likely to be for psychiatric and/or behavioral problems and more likely to result in psychiatric hospitalization (Lytle et al. 2018). A recent review suggests that investing in ambulatory services for children with ASD reduces the likelihood of psychiatric hospitalization but not that of ED visits (Mandell et al. 2019).

Finally, persons with IDD and dual diagnosis who have been arrested or incarcerated have been particularly difficult to connect successfully with adequate ambulatory psychiatric care (Glaser and Floria 2004). These individuals are typically male, with mild ID or borderline intellectual functioning and often with long-standing chronic behavioral disturbances regardless of psychiatric comorbidity. Their ambulatory care is often poorly coordinated across multiple agencies, resulting in fragmented contact and frequent recidivism (Glaser and Floria 2004). In a recent study of the care of this population within mainstream mental health courts, it appeared that having IDD did not change the likelihood of termination from the MH court but did reduce the likelihood of re-arrest for a year after leaving the MH court. The authors concluded that offenders with IDD should be included in this treatment setting, which have often excluded persons with IDD in the past (Linhorst et al. 2018).

Clinical Pearls: General Precepts and Outpatient Care

Interact directly with the patient, at whatever level of communication is possible. Avoid speaking only with family/caregivers

Limited communication abilities and the need for informants to provide history add significant evaluation time. Plan for longer appointment duration

Always begin by ruling out a medical etiology for psychiatric and behavioral symptoms

The goal of initial and subsequent visits should be to establish a psychiatric diagnosis or diagnostic hypothesis. Revisit the diagnostic hypothesis at each visit. Consider using a recognized diagnostic system modified for use in IDD such as the Diagnostic Manual-Intellectual Disability (DM-ID-2)

Consider nonpharmacologic treatment approaches (e.g., psychosocial therapies, behavioral interventions), both in lieu of and in combination with medication

When prescribing, explain risks, benefits, alternatives, and off-label use. Obtain informed consent from the patient and/or guardian before initiating medication. Obtain assent if patient unable to provide informed consent

Minimize polypharmacy, particularly intraclass polypharmacy. Avoid frequent drug and dose changes. Make only one change at a time. Minimize use of PRN medication, especially benzodiazepines

Individuals with IDD are at elevated risk for medication adverse events (AEs) and may not have the ability to report side effects. Educate family/caregivers about their recognition and systematically screen for AEs at every visit. Rating scales may be useful to assess both treatment response and AEs

Deb et al. (2009) and University of Toronto (2002)

Care in the Emergency Department

As a group, individuals with IDD are frequent utilizers of emergency department (ED) services. They visit the ED more often than persons without IDD, especially for conditions more appropriately managed in an outpatient setting (Balogh et al. 2010). In the USA, the limited number of general psychiatrists in many settings makes it challenging to find a community provider willing and able to manage behavioral concerns in patients with IDD. Given limited options, families and caregivers often have no choice but to seek help in an ED in times of crisis (Cheng et al. 2017). Unfortunately, most EDs are poorly suited to address behavioral issues in patients with IDD, and ED providers typically have little to no training in caring for this complex patient population. Clinicians and support staff often resort to use of chemical and/or physical restraints in ED settings (Lunsky et al. 2014), which place patients at risk of serious injury and psychological trauma (Wilkins 2012).

Barriers to Quality Care in the ED

An ED visit for someone with IDD can be frightening and anxiety-provoking due to difficulty coping with the loud, busy, unfamiliar setting, and long wait times. To make matters worse, the care provided to individuals with IDD in the ED is often of poor quality (Iacono et al. 2014). ED staff report a general lack of knowledge about persons with IDD and feel ill-prepared to care for them (Lunsky et al. 2008). Patients note feeling disrespected by providers (Lunsky and Gracey 2009), while families/caregivers report feeling dismissed (Weiss et al. 2009). Additional barriers are listed in the Table 1.

Patterns of ED Utilization

Reasons for ED utilization by persons with IDD can generally be classified as either medical or psychiatric/behavioral. The most common medical presentation is injury, whereas the most common psychiatric/behavioral presentation is

Table 1 Barriers to quality care of individuals with IDD in the ED

Barriers
Staff feel ill-prepared to care for individuals with IDD
Staff lack training/knowledge of IDD population
Staff not aware patients are at risk for certain medical conditions (e.g., epilepsy)
Perceived lack of caring from staff
Staff acting disrespectfully
Discrimination
Diagnostic overshadowing
Delay/omission of diagnostic procedures
Failure to identify/adequately treat pain
Little or no attempts at communicating with patient
Poor communication with family/caregiver
Inability to adjust communication/environment for patient's needs
Long wait times/loud waiting rooms
Lack of discharge planning/poor continuity of care

aggression. Retrospective review often reveals an ambulatory care-sensitive condition, i.e., a preventable issue more appropriate for outpatient management (Balogh et al. 2010). ED visit costs and resource use are higher in patients with IDD (Lindgren et al. 2020). Factors predictive of ED utilization by individuals with IDD are summarized in Table 2.

Of the predictors of ED use by individuals with IDD, recent life events are common critical predictors. Persons with IDD often have limited coping skills for dealing with stress and difficulty adapting to new situations. Significant life events are commonly associated with emotional, psychological, and behavioral problems (Owen et al. 2004). Common life events for persons with IDD include changes in staffing and/or housing, conflict with peers or family, and bereavement, all of which may precipitate an ED visit. Failure to recognize these factors can lead to inappropriate treatment and unnecessary use of medication.

Table 2 Predictors of emergency department utilization in individuals with IDD

Predictor	Findings
History of ED use	Past year history of ED visit is the strongest predictor of future ED use. Adults with one prior visit are nine times more likely to have additional visits
Demographics	Mixed findings for age, gender, income
IDD/ASD severity	Milder severity of IDD predicts likelihood of psychiatric/behavioral ED visits, whereas greater severity predicts ED visits for medical concerns
Medication	Use of medication is associated with increased ED utilization. The number of medications increases likelihood of hospitalization
Psychiatric issues	Individuals with IDD and comorbid psychiatric disorders were more likely to and frequently visit the ED than individuals without mental health issues. Behavioral issues, aggression, and externalizing problems are associated with greater ED utilization
Life events	Past year history of certain life events increases likelihood of ED visits. Life events include moving residence, conflict with family/caregiver, being unemployed, having issues with police, substance abuse, and recent trauma/abuse
Crisis planning	In Canada, where crisis planning is emphasized in primary care guidelines, individuals without crisis plans are twice as likely to visit the ED when experiencing a mental health/behavioral crisis
Family	Family distress is a predictor of ED utilization. Qualitative research suggests that families present to the ED when feeling poorly supported and unable to cope with IDD patient at home
Living arrangements	Individuals living with family are four times more likely than those living in a group home to visit the ED when experiencing a psychiatric/behavioral crisis
Healthcare access	While lack of primary care predicts ED use, simply having access to primary care does not decrease ED utilization. Individuals with IDD who have continuity of care with the same PCP/specialist over time have fewer ED visits, suggesting that continuity of care may have a greater impact than access to care

Weiss (2011), Lunsky and Elserafi (2011), Lunsky et al. (2012), and Lunsky et al. (2017)

Outcomes Associated with ED Visits

Besides frequent visits, individuals with IDD also have prolonged lengths of stay in the ED compared to individuals without IDD. They are also more likely to be boarded when needing psychiatric hospitalization (Wharff et al. 2011), often lasting several days. Difficulty finding a psychiatric unit willing to admit an individual with IDD is the most common cause of delay. During prolonged boarding, the busy unfamiliar surroundings, absence of usual supports, and frequent failure to continue scheduled home medications are associated with symptom exacerbation leading to use of restraints, injury, and elopement (Wilkins 2012). ED boarding also consumes ED resources unnecessarily, contributes to ED overcrowding, and increases costs (Joint Commission 2015). Lastly, individuals with IDD, both with and without comorbid psychiatric disorders, have higher ED readmission rates (Durbin et al. 2019).

Interventions to Decrease ED Utilization and Improve Patient Care

Multiple policy-level interventions have been piloted for persons with IDD in ED settings, in an attempt to improve quality outcomes and reduce ED-related costs. Early reports support the use of patient-centered medical homes (PCMHs) and accountable care organization (ACO) models. The use of Medicaid managed care has been found to reduce ED use and inpatient hospitalization (Yamaki et al. 2019), but not necessarily cost savings (Yamaki et al. 2018). The previously discussed START model has been shown to decrease ED utilization (Kalb et al. 2019), but it is unclear which components of the complex model produce that effect. Additional interventions with intuitive support but lacking a firm evidence base include the use of telepsychiatry, 24-hour nursing hotlines, and improved training for ED providers in the care of individuals with IDD (Wachob and Pesci 2017).

Clinical Pearls: Emergency Department Management

Allow the presence of family/caregiver at the bedside. They may provide comfort and valuable information. Provide consistent staffing

Before assessing a patient, obtain the following information: Reason for ED visit (both explicit and implicit), communication abilities and use of adaptive communication tools, the patient's psychiatric and behavioral baseline, living environment (including safety precautions, need for assistance with ADLs, usual level of supervision)

Optimize communication. Explain and re-explain in very simple language what you are doing and why. Make use of picture cards to describe procedures. Have family or a caregiver help you communicate with the patient in a way that they are familiar

Begin by ruling out a medical etiology for any behavioral change. Common causes include constipation, dental pain, GERD, and seizures. Patients may be unable to communicate symptoms or indicate when they are in pain. Obtain comprehensive workup including physical exam, imaging, and labs

In the absence of serious side effects, significant medication changes during a brief ED visit should be avoided. Instead, consider small adjustments to target specific symptoms such as sleep, anxiety, psychomotor agitation

Complete and document a thorough risk assessment that includes both acute and chronic degree of risk to self and others. Take into consideration current level and adequacy of supervision, safety precautions in place at home, prior history, and magnitude of change from patient's baseline

Deb et al. (2009) and University of Toronto (2002)

Inpatient Psychiatric Hospitalization

Utilization, Presentation, and Risk Factors for Admission

In the USA, individuals with IDD requiring psychiatric hospitalization are typically admitted to general inpatient psychiatric units, to general or free-standing psychiatric hospitals, and rarely to state-operated psychiatric hospitals. Few IDD-specialized psychiatric inpatient units exist, especially for adults with dual diagnoses. The most common reason for admission is challenging behavior, such as agitation, aggression, and/or self-injurious behavior. The next most common are exacerbation of known psychiatric disorders and "social" admissions (Oxley et al. 2013). A notable finding from retrospective analysis is that a significant number of patients psychiatrically hospitalized for challenging behavior actually had a treatable medical condition (e.g., seizures, dental pain) which was the primary cause of their behavioral challenges. In some samples, a medical etiology has been found in up to 50% of admissions, highlighting the critical need to rule out organic causes of challenging behavior (Guinchat et al. 2015).

Risk factors for inpatient psychiatric hospitalization include male gender, mild intellectual disability, psychosis, and history of prior admission (Sheehan et al. 2021). That those with mild ID are more likely to be admitted than those with more significant impairment may reflect the reluctance of psychiatric units to accept patients with severe or profound IDD (Bouras and Holt 2001). There is also a commonly held belief that patients with severe ID do not benefit from inpatient psychiatry and that general psychiatric units may not be an appropriate treatment setting for them.

Quality of Care and Stakeholder Experiences

The experiences of patients, family, caregivers, and hospital staff suggest that patients with IDD receive suboptimal care in the psychiatric hospital. Common experiences include failure to order or complete adequate diagnostic procedures, to identify and treat pain, and to make necessary treatment adjustments to accommodate individual patient's needs. There is also a perception that inpatient staff lack the training and experience necessary to care for individuals with IDD, exhibit negative attitudes toward patients, communicate poorly, and are unable to appropriately deal with challenging behavior. Patients able to self-report describe frustration, boredom, lack of choice, and a variety of fears with hospitalization (Iacono et al. 2014).

Hospital Course

Most studies report length of stay (LOS) in general inpatient psychiatric units to be longer for individuals with IDD compared to those without. Hospitalization in specialized IDD psychiatric units tends to be longer than that of general psychiatric units (Oxley et al. 2013). In both cases, patients who can be discharged to their previous residential setting tend to have shorter stays than patients discharged elsewhere, which likely reflects a delay in discharge associated with securing new housing (Saeed et al. 2003; Lunsky and Balogh 2010). Indeed, the LOS for persons with IDD is often longer than clinically indicated, with delayed discharge rates as high as 50%. In most cases, delays reflect the need to secure appropriate placement or funding for additional supports (Oxley et al. 2013).

The hospital course of patients with IDD is often characterized by poor outcomes and negative experiences (Iacono et al. 2014). Patients with IDD have higher rates of complications than patients without IDD who are hospitalized for the same reason, including greater likelihood of experiencing an adverse medication event (Erickson et al. 2020) or being placed in restraints or seclusion (Way and Banks 1990). Finally, individuals with IDD are more likely to have multiple repeat hospitalizations for psychiatric/behavioral complaints compared to those without IDD (Lunsky and Balogh 2010). Table 3 highlights the

Table 3 Risks, challenges, and limitations of psychiatric hospitalization

Risks of psychiatric hospitalization
Overall poor outcomes
Inadequate and/or inappropriate treatment
Patients with IDD are more likely to be restrained or placed in seclusion (Way and Banks 1990)
Patients with IDD are more likely to exhibit aggression towards others on the unit (Saeed et al. 2003; Tardiff and Sweillam 1982)
Absence of familiar caregivers may be distressing to patients
Individuals with IDD are vulnerable to exploitation and/or abuse by peers and staff
Prolonged length of stay/delayed discharge
Many individuals with IDD do not benefit from psychiatric hospitalization
Challenges associated with psychiatric hospitalization
Staff lack training/experience in caring for individuals with IDD
Communication barriers
Patients with IDD are often more sensitive to environmental factors and may not cope well with unfamiliar surroundings, limited access to preferred objects/activities, and other unit rules. They may be easily upset by the behavior of peers
Patients with IDD utilize more resources, commonly require supervision and/or assistance with ADLs, and are more likely to require one-to-one staffing (Lohrer et al. 2002)
Securing placement upon discharge can be difficult and often leads to delayed discharges
IDD patients' prolonged length of stay limits bed availability and exacerbates boarding of patients needing psychiatric admission
Patients and families/caregivers commonly report negative experiences with hospitalization
Limitations of psychiatric hospitalization
Available activities/therapeutic interventions may not be appropriate for individuals with IDD
Severity of IDD often limits patients' ability to participate in groups and therapeutic programming
Few general psychiatric units are able and/or willing to accept patients with IDD, which limits psychiatric bed availability and exacerbates boarding of IDD patients needing admission
Assessments (e.g., rating scales) may not be valid when used with individuals with IDD; particularly self-reported measures

risks, challenges, and limitations of psychiatric hospitalization of persons with IDD.

Specialized Versus Generic Psychiatric Units

The challenges outlined in Table 3 makes the concept of specialized IDD inpatient units appealing. They remain rare in the USA, particularly for adults. Specialized units are specifically designed for individuals with IDD and co-occurring psychiatric and behavioral disorders. Advantages include staff expertise, adapted therapeutic programming, and environmental features promoting a calmer and safer setting (Day 2008). Disadvantages primarily derive from limited availability (e.g., long-distance travel to nearest unit) and the potential for perpetuating stigma and marginalization. Although promising, there is currently little evidence that specialized units provide superior care compared to general psychiatric units or reduce costs (Siegel et al. 2012).

Improving Inpatient Psychiatric Care

Inpatient specialist units are unlikely to become widespread in the USA. Therefore, quality improvement efforts are best focused on enhancing the care of IDD patients treated in general psychiatric units. Promising strategies involve staff education/training, minimizing communication barriers, addressing delayed discharges with proactive discharge planning, and coordinating care with ambulatory MH and IDD services (Backer et al. 2009; Hall et al. 2006).

Clinical Pearls: Psychiatric Hospitalization

Strive for familiarity. Allow a patient to keep a preferred object or picture. Provide consistent staffing from day to day. Work with family/caregivers to adapt hospital routines to replicate a patient's home routines

Patients may become easily overstimulated. Attend to the physical environment to ensure safety of patients and staff. Minimize noise, lights, large groups of people

Optimize communication with use of picture cards, scripted phrases, and communication devices. Family/caregivers can provide useful information about patient's means of communication and can assist with interpretation when patient has limited communication abilities

Remember that patients may be unable to communicate their needs. They may also require substantial supervision and prompting with everyday tasks. Adjust staffing as necessary

Communicate with community mental health providers and Board of Developmental Disabilities staff to facilitate discharge planning

Deb et al. (2009) and University of Toronto (2002)

Impact of Ideological Factors on Community Psychiatry

Since the 1970s, grassroots advocacy by individuals with IDD and their families has made strides in promoting the rights of persons with IDD, which has helped transform practices, policies, and legislation. It is now accepted that exercising one's right to self-determination enables individuals with IDD to become valued and included members of the community. Person-centered planning recognizes the needs of the individual and provides individualized services that support them in expressing their preferences.

In most states, developmental disabilities agencies and intermediate care facilities have a human rights committee (HRC) to provide independent oversight. Comprised of professionals and community volunteers, their mandate is to safeguard the rights of individuals with IDD and protect them from harm. Importantly, HRCs review, approve, and monitor the use of restrictive treatment measures. This process is of particular interest to community psychiatrists as they often prescribe restrictive measures such as use of pro re nata (PRN) (i.e., as needed) psychotropics for challenging behavior. To facilitate approval, psychiatrists should document which less-restrictive methods previously failed, provide a specific definition of the targeted behavior, and define a threshold for its use. Such documentation helps families/caregiver safely and appropriately utilize PRN medication. Other restrictive measures include prescribed diet and exercise regimens, behavioral strategies such as a loss of privileges surrounding challenging behavior, safety features such as door alarms, and one-to-one supervision. Such interventions must be justified, individualized, clearly defined, and include a plan for its termination when the challenging behavior has been successfully addressed.

Educating and Training a Skilled Psychiatric Workforce

There are too few subspecialty trained and experienced psychiatrists and advanced practice nurses (APNs) in the USA to address the mental health of persons with IDD and dual diagnoses (NADD 2007; APNA 2019). This task falls upon community psychiatrists and APNs, most of whom have had little education to prepare them for these complex patients. Their care requires more time and effort (due to communication challenges, medical comorbidities, social concerns, polypharmacy, and the need to collaborate with multiple caregivers). Much of this additional work is not reimbursed by insurance; additionally, many clinicians may have negative attitudes and perceptions about working with this patient population.

Most medical and nursing schools in the USA do not provide adequate preclinical or clinical education regarding individuals with IDD (USPHS 2001). Similarly, many psychiatric residency programs fail to include didactic or clinical experiences caring for individuals with IDD and comorbid psychiatric or behavioral issues. Currently, the ACGME has no requirement for IDD-related education in general psychiatry residency training. Although the ACGME does require education about ASD and IDD during Child and Adolescent Psychiatry (CAP) fellowships, the average fellow receives less than 5 annual lecture hours and evaluates/treats only one to five patients with IDD per year (Marrus et al. 2014). And, although some residency and fellowship programs do offer elective opportunities in IDD, such rotations are usually optional and underutilized.

There are currently no accredited post-residency fellowships in the psychiatry of intellectual disability in the USA and no formalized route for psychiatrists to pursue this training. The closest specialist equivalent is neurodevelopmental disabilities, a 6-year program combining pediatrics with child neurology. In contrast, the UK mandates IDD training as a component of psychiatric residency education and offers post-residency specialty training in the psychiatry of intellectual disability.

Providing quality medical and psychiatric care for individuals with IDD must begin with education about these patients in medical and nursing school curricula, perhaps as part of basic education schools now provide on diversity, culture, and health disparities. Multiple didactic and clinical modalities have demonstrated success for improving attitudes and increasing knowledge, skills, and confidence in caring for patients with IDD (Jones et al. 2015). Increasing exposure to IDD during residencies (by establishing mandatory minimum requirements akin to those for geriatric and addiction psychiatry) would also help. More enriched IDD learning tracks could include training in related fields of genetics and neurology. Ultimately, the American Board of Psychiatry and Neurology could establish an accredited subspecialty in the Psychiatry of Intellectual Disability.

Conclusion

The recognition of co-occurring mental health and/or behavior disorders in individuals with IDD has become widely accepted, yet systems of care continue to struggle to meet the needs of these patients. Specialist IDD care in the USA is quite limited. As such, the majority of individuals with IDD are cared for by community psychiatrists, who often feel ill-equipped to manage such patients. Dedicated learning and exposure to this vulnerable patient population during training is essential to improving the quality of care for these persons. Harnessing telepsychiatry to make consultation with IDD specialists more widely available to community psychiatrists would also be beneficial.

References

American Association on Intellectual and Developmental Disabilities (2016). *Position Statement: Community living and participation for people with intellectual and developmental disabilities.* https://www.aaidd.org/news-policy/policy/position-statements

American Psychiatric Association. (2013). *Diagnostic and statistical manual of mental disorders (5th ed).* Arlington, VA: American Psychiatric Publishing.

American Psychiatric Nurses Association (2019). *Report – Expanding Mental Health Care Services in America: the Pivotal Role of Psychiatric-Mental Health Nurses.*

Americans With Disabilities Act (1990). *Pub. L. No. 101-336*, 104 Stat. 328.

Backer C., Chapman M., Mitchell D. (2009). Access to Secondary Healthcare for People with Intellectual Disabilities: A Review of the Literature. *Journal of Applied Research in Intellectual Disabilities, 22*, 514-525.

Balogh R., Brownell M., Ouellette-Kuntz H., Colantonio A. (2010). Hospitalisation rates for ambulatory care sensitive conditions for persons with and without an intellectual disability: a population perspective. *Journal of Intellectual Disability Research, 54* (9), 820-832.

Balogh, R., McMorris, C.A., Lunsky, Y., Ouellette-Kuntz, H. et al. (2016). Organising healthcare services for persons with an intellectual disability. *Cochrane Database Syst Rev, 11* (4).

Barnhill J., Fletcher R.J., Cooper SA. (2017). *Diagnostic Manual - Intellectual Disability 2 (DM-ID): A Textbook of Diagnosis of Mental Disorders in Persons with Intellectual Disability.* New York, N.Y. NADD Press.

Bouras N. and Holt G. (2001). Psychiatric treatment in community care. In A. Dosen & K. Day (Eds.), *Treating mental illness and behavior disorders in children and adults with mental retardation* (pp. 493–502). Washington, DC: American Psychiatric Press.

Braddock, D.L., Hemp, R.E., Tanis, E.S., Wu, J. & Haffer, L. (2017). The State of the States in Intellectual and Developmental Disabilities. *Coleman Institute for Cognitive Disabilities.* Boulder, CO.

Burns T. (2010). The rise and fall of assertive community treatment. *International Review of Psychiatry, 22 (2),* 130-7.

Center for START Services (2019). *Annual program report.* https://www.centerforstartservices.org/regional-start-program-annual-evaluations

Chaplin R. (2009). New research into general psychiatric services for adults with intellectual disability and mental illness. *J Intellectual Disability Research, 53* (3), 189-99.

Cheng C., Chan C.W., Gula C.A., Parker M.D. (2017). Effects of outpatient aftercare on psychiatric rehospitalization among children and emerging adults in Alberta, Canada. *Psychiatric Services, 68* (7), 696–703.

Constantino J., Strom S., Bunis M., Nadler C., et al. (2020). Toward Actionable Practice Parameters for Dual Diagnosis: Principles of Assessment and Management for Co-occurring Psychiatric and Intellectual/Developmental Disability. *Current Psychiatry Rep, 22* (2).

Cooper S.A., Smiley E., Morrison J., Williamson A., Allan L. (2007). Mental ill-health in adults with intellectual disabilities: prevalence and associated factors. *Br J Psychiatry, 190,* 27-35.

Day K.A. (2008). Mental health services for people with mental retardation: a framework for the future. *Journal of Intellectual Disability Research, 37,* 7-16.

Deb S., Kwok H., et al. (2009). International guide to prescribing psychotropic medication for the management of problem behaviours in adults with intellectual disabilities. World Psychiatry, 8(3), 181-86.

Didden R., VanDerNagel J., Delforterie M., Van Duijvenbode N. (2020). Substance use disorders in people with intellectual disability. *Current Opinion in Psychiatry, 33* (2), 124-129.

Durbin A., Balogh R., Lin E., Wilton A., et al. (2019). Repeat emergency department visits for individuals with intellectual disabilities and psychiatric disorders. *American Journal of Developmental Disabilities, 124* (3), 206-19.

Erickson S.R., Kamdar N., Wu C.H. (2020). Adverse Medication Events Related to Hospitalization in the United States: A Comparison Between Adults With Intellectual and Developmental Disabilities and Those Without. *Am J Intellect Dev Disabil, 125* (1), 37-48.

Friedman C., Lulinski A., Rizzolo M.C. (2015) Mental/Behavioral Health Services: Medicaid Home and Community-Based Services 1915(c) Waiver Allocation for People with Intellectual and Developmental Disabilities. *Intellectual and Developmental Disabilities, 53* (4), 257-70.

Glaser W. & Floria D. (2004). Beyond specialist programmes: a study of the needs of offenders with intellectual disability requiring psychiatric attention. *J Intellectual Disability Research, 48* (6), 591-602.

Guinchat V., Cravero C., Diaz L., Périsse D., et al. (2015). Acute behavioral crises in psychiatric inpatients with autism spectrum disorder (ASD): recognition of concomitant medical or non-ASD psychiatric conditions predicts enhanced improvement. *Res Dev Disabil, 38,* 242-55.

Hackerman F., Schmidt C.W., Dyson C.D., Hovermale L., Gallucci G. (2006). Developing a model psychiatric treatment program for patients with intellectual disability in a community mental health center. *Community Ment Health J, 42* (1), 13-24.

Hales, R. (2016). *Neurodevelopmental Disorders: DSM-5 Selections.* Arlington, VA. American Psychiatric Association.

Hall I., Parkes C., Samuels S., & Hassiotis A. (2006). Working across boundaries: clinical outcomes for an integrated mental health service for people with intellectual disabilities. *J Intellectual Disabilities Research, 50* (8), 598-607.

Harris J. (2006). *Intellectual Disability: Understanding its developmental causes, classification, evaluation, and treatment* (pp. 11-41). New York, NY. Oxford University Press.

Hassiotis A., Robotham D., Canagasabey A., Romeo R., et al. (2009). Randomized, single-blind, controlled trial of a specialist behavior therapy team for challenging behavior in adults with intellectual disabilities. *Am J Psychiatry, 166* (11), 1278-85.

Heller T., Stafford P., Davis L.A., Sedlezky L., & Gaylord V. (2010). People with intellectual and developmental disabilities growing old: an overview. *Impact: Feature Issue on Aging and People with Intellectual and Developmental Disabilities, 23* (1), 22-23.

Hemmings C., Bouras N., Craig T. (2014). How should community mental health of intellectual disability services evolve? *International Journal of Environmental Research in Public Health, 11* (9), 8624-31.

Holingue C., Kalb L.G., Klein A., Beasley J.B. (2020). Experiences with the Mental Health Service System of Family Caregivers of Individuals with an Intellectual/Developmental Disability Referred to START. *Intellect Dev Disabil, 58* (5), 379-92.

Iacono T., Bigby C., Unsworth C., Douglas J., Fitzpatrick P. (2014). A systematic review of hospital experiences of people with intellectual disability. *BMC Health Serv Res, 14,* 505.

Jones J., McQueen M., Lowe S., Minnes P., Rischke, A.E. (2015). Interprofessional Education in

Canada: Addressing Knowledge, Skills, and Attitudes Concerning Intellectual Disability for Future Healthcare Professionals. *Journal of Policy and Practice in Intellectual Disabilities, 12*, 172-180.

Kalb L.G., Beasley J., Caoili A., Klein A. (2019). Improvement in Mental Health Outcomes and Caregiver Service Experiences Associated with the START Program. *Am J Intellect Dev Disabil, 124* (1), 25-34.

Lewis S., Florio T., Srasuebkul P., Trollor J. (2020). Impact of disability services on mental health service utilization in adults with intellectual disability. *J Appl Res Intellect Disabil, 33*, 1357-67.

Lindgren S., Lauer E., Momany E., Cope T., ET AL. (2020). Disability, Hospital Care, and Cost: Utilization of Emergency and Inpatient Care by a Cohort of Children with Intellectual and Developmental Disabilities. *Journal of Pediatrics, in press.*

Linhorst D.M., Loux T.M., Dirks-Linhorst P.A., Riley S.E. (2018). Characteristics and Outcomes of People with Intellectual and Developmental Disabilities Participating in a Mental Health Court. *Am J Intellect Dev Disabil, 123* (4), 359-70.

Lohrer S.P., Greene E., Browning C.J., Lesser M.S. (2002). Dual diagnosis: examination of service use and length of stay during psychiatric hospitalization. *Journal of Developmental and Physical Disabilities, 14*, 143-158.

Lunsky Y. & Balogh R. (2010). Dual diagnosis: A national study of psychiatric hospitalization patterns of people with developmental disability. *Can J Psychiatry, 55* (11), 721-8.

Lunsky Y., Balogh R., Cairney J. (2012). Predictors of emergency department visits by persons with intellectual disability experiencing a psychiatric crisis. *Psychiatr Serv, 63* (3), 287-90.

Lunsky Y. & Elserafi J. (2011). Life events and emergency department visits in response to crisis in individuals with intellectual disabilities. *Journal of Intellectual Disability Research, 55*, 714-18.

Lunsky Y., Gracey C. (2009). The reported experience of four women with intellectual disabilities receiving emergency psychiatric services in Canada: a qualitative study. *J Intellect Disabil, 13* (2), 87-98.

Lunsky Y., Gracey C., Gelfand S. (2008). Emergency psychiatric services for individuals with intellectual disabilities: perspectives of hospital staff. *Intellectual and Developmental Disabilities, 46* (6), 446-55.

Lunsky, Y., Paquette-Smith, M., Weiss, J., & Lee, J. (2014). Predictors of emergency service use in adolescents and adults with autism spectrum disorder living with family. *Emergency Medicine Journal, 32* (10), 787-92.

Lunsky Y., Weiss J.A., Paquette-Smith M., et al. (2017). Predictors of emergency department use by adolescents and adults with autism spectrum disorder: a prospective cohort study. *BMJ Open, 7*, e017377.

Lytle S., Hunt A., Moratschek S., Hall-Mennes M., Sajatovic M. (2018). Youth with Autism Spectrum Disorder in the Emergency Department. *J Clin Pyschiatry, 79* (3), p17r11506.

Mandell D., Candon M., Zie M., Marcus S., et al. (2019). Effect of Outpatient Service Utilization on Hospitalizations and Emergency Visits among Youths with Autism Spectrum Disorder. *Psychiatr Serv, 70* (10), 888-93.

Marrus N., Veenstra-Vanderweele J., Hellings J.A., Stigler K.A., et al. (2014). Training of child and adolescent psychiatry fellows in autism and intellectual disability. *Autism, 18* (4), 471-5.

Martin G., Costello H., Leese M., Slade M., Bouras N., Higgins S. and Holt G. (2005). An exploratory study of assertive community treatment for people with intellectual disability and psychiatric disorders: conceptual, clinical, and service issues. *Journal of Intellectual Disability Research, 49*, 516-24.

Mazza M.G., Rossetti A., Crespi G., Clerici M. (2020). Prevalence of co-occurring psychiatric disorders in adults and adolescents with intellectual disability: A systematic review and meta-analysis. *J Appl Res Intellect Disabil, 33* (2), 126-138.

Menolascino F.J. (1968). Emotional disturbances in mentally retarded children: diagnostic and treatment aspects. *Archives of General Psychiatry, 19* (4), 456-64.

Menolascino F.J., Gilson F., Levitas A. (1986). Issues in the treatment of mentally retarded patients in the community mental health system. *Community Mental Health Journal, 22* (4), 314-27.

Munir K. (2009). Psychiatry of Intellectual and Developmental Disability in the US: Time for a New Beginning. *Psychiatry, 8* (11), 448-52.

National Association for the Dually Diagnosed (NADD; 2007). http://www.thenadd.org (last accessed January 2020).

Nathenson R.A. & Zablosky B. (2017). The transition to the adult health care system among youths with autism spectrum disorder. *Psychiatric Services, 68*, 735-38.

National Council on Disability (2012). *Policy Toolkit Companion Paper – De-institutionalization: Unfinished Business.* https://ncd.gov/publications/2012/Sept192012

Olmstead v. L. C., 527 U.S. 581 (1999).

Oxley C., Sathanandan S., Gazizova D., Fitzgerald B. et al. (2013). A comparative review of admissions to an intellectual disability inpatient service over a 10-year period. *British Journal of Medical Practitioners*, 6.

Owen D.M., Hastings R.P., Noone S.J., Chinn J., et al. (2004). Life events as correlates of problem behavior and mental health in a residential population of adults with developmental disabilities. *Res Dev Disabil, 25* (4), 309-320.

Pinals D., Hovermale L., Mauch D., Anacker L. and the National Association of State Mental Health Program Directors (2017). Assessment #7. The Vital Role of Specialized Approaches: Persons with Intellectual and Developmental Disabilities in the Mental Health System. Proceedings of the third in a series of ten briefs addressing: What is the inpatient bed needs if you have a Best Practice Continuum of Care? Held in August 2017 in Alexandria VA. https://www.nasmhpd.org/site/default/file/TAC.Paper.7.IDD.Final.pdf

Reiss S., Levitan G.W., Szyszko J. (1982). Emotional disturbance and mental retardation: diagnostic overshadowing. *Am J Ment Defic, 86* (6), 567-74.

Royal College of Psychiatrists (2001). *DC-LD: diagnostic criteria for psychiatric disorders for use with adults with learning disabilities/mental retardation*. London, UK. Gaskell.

Saeed H., Oullette-Kuntz H., Stuart H., Burge P. (2003). Length of stay for psychiatric inpatient services: a comparison of admissions of people with and without developmental disabilities. *Journal of Behavioural Health Services and Research, 30*, 406-417.

Sheehan R., Mutch J., Marston L., Osborn D., Hassiotis A. (2021). Risk factors for in-patient admission among adults with intellectual disability and autism: Investigation of electronic clinical records. *BJPsych Open, 7* (1), E5.

Siegel M., Doyle K., Chemelski B., Payne D., et al. (2012). Specialized inpatient psychiatry units for children with autism and developmental disorders: a United States survey. *J Autism Dev Disord, 42* (9), 1863-9.

Siegel M., Milligan B., Chemelski B., et al. (2014). Specialized Inpatient Psychiatry for Serious Behavioral Disturbance in Autism and Intellectual Disability. *J Autism Dev Disord, 44*, 3026–3032.

Tardiff K. and Sweillam A. (1982). Assaultative behaviour among chronic inpatients. *Am J Psychiatry, 139*, 212-215.

The Joint Commission (2015). Alleviating ED boarding of psychiatric patients. *Quick Safety, 19*, p. 1-3.

United Cerebral Palsy Association (2020). *Annual Report: The case for inclusion*. https://caseforinclusion.org/

University of Toronto, Centre for Addiction and Mental Health (2002). Guidelines for managing the patient with intellectual disability in accident and emergency. http://www.intellectualdisability.info/how-to-guides

U.S. Public Health Service (2001). Closing the Gap: A National Blueprint for Improving the Health of Individuals with Mental Retardation. *Report of the Surgeon General's Conference on Health Disparities and Mental Retardation*. Washington, D.C.

Van Duijenbode N. & Vander Nagel J. (2019). A Systematic Review of Substance Use Disorder in Individuals with Mild to Borderline Intellectual Disability. *European Addiction Research, 25* (6), 263-82.

Wachob D., Pesci L.J. (2017). Brief Report: Knowledge and Confidence of Emergency Medical Service Personnel Involving Treatment of an Individual with Autism Spectrum Disorder. *J Autism Dev Disord, 47* (3), 887-891.

Way B.B. and Banks S.M. (1990). Use of seclusion and restraint in public psychiatric hospitals: patient characteristics and facility effects. *Hospital and Community Psychiatry, 41*, 75-81.

Weiss J.A., Lunsky Y., Gracey C., Canrinus M., Morris S. (2009). Emergency Psychiatric Services for Individuals with Intellectual Disabilities: Caregivers' Perspectives. *Journal of Applied Research in Intellectual Disabilities 22*(4), 354-362 https://doi.org/10.1111/j.1468-3148.2008.00468.x

Weiss J.A., Slusarczyk M., Lunsky Y. (2011). Individuals With Intellectual Disabilities Who Live With Family and Experience Psychiatric Crisis: Who Uses the Emergency Department and Who Stays Home?. *Journal of Mental Health Research in Intellectual Disabilities 4*(3), 158-171 3 https://doi.org/10.1080/19315864.2011.599013

Wharff, E.A., Ginnis, K.B., Ross, A.M., Blood, E.A. (2011). Predictors of psychiatric boarding in the pediatric emergency department: Implications for emergency care. *Pediatric Emergency Care, 27* (6), 483–89.

Wilkins, D. (2012). Ethical dilemmas in social work practice with disabled people: the use of physical restraint. *Journal of Intellectual Disabilities, 16* (2), 127–133.

Yamaki K., Wing C., Mitchell D., Owen R., Heller T. (2018). Impact of Medicaid Managed Care on Illinois's Acute Health Services Expenditures for Adults with Intellectual and Developmental Disabilities. *Intellect Dev Disabil, 56* (2), 133-146.

Yamaki K., Wing C., Mitchell D., Owen R., Heller T. (2019). The Impact of Medicaid Managed Care on Health Service Utilization among Adults with Intellectual and Developmental Disabilities. *Intellect Dev Disabil, 57* (4), 289-306.

Psychiatric Care for People Experiencing Homelessness

Tony Carino and Hunter L. McQuistion

The core of community psychiatry is the caring, therapeutic relationship. This relationship is an essential part of the engagement and long-term recovery of those experiencing homelessness and mental health conditions. This chapter outlines the current landscape of services, suggests a guidance model, and offers useful interventions to support the individuals' transition from the street to home.

Contemporary Homelessness

Epidemiology

Estimates of homeless individuals in the USA range from 550,000 to 1.5 million people. Though an underestimate (US Government Accountability Office 2020), the US Department of Housing and Urban Development (2021) estimated that 580,466 people experienced homelessness in the USA on a single day in January 2020. More than 226,000 slept outdoors or in a location not made for human habitation. Compared to the previous year, overall homelessness increased by 2.2 percent. This marked the fourth consecutive year of increased numbers of people experiencing homelessness in America.

It is reliably estimated that as many as 8,000,000 Americans, or 3% of the population, will have at least one episode of homelessness during the past 5 years of their lives (Culhane et al. 1994). Although 80% of those secure housing within weeks, ten percent remain homeless for more than a year. In comparison to some European countries, one study has shown that lifetime homeless prevalence rates in the USA are almost twice those found in Belgium, Germany, and Italy (Fazel et al. 2008).

While recent trends indicate improvements among some subpopulations, general trends are concerning. Since 2016, homelessness increased each consecutive year. This increase is largely due to an increase in the number of single adults experiencing homelessness. From 2009 to 2019, single adults experiencing homelessness has increased by 11%. Over the same decade, there has been a decline in homelessness among veterans by 50%, and people in families experiencing homelessness declined by 29% (US Government Accountability Office 2020). Climate change and the COVID 19 epidemic threatened to increase rates of homelessness even further at the time of this writing.

A causative relationship between substance misuse and homelessness is far from clear. At

T. Carino
Columbia University Vagelos College of Physicians and Surgeons,
New York, NY, USA

Janian Medical Care, New York, NY, USA

H. L. McQuistion (✉)
New York University Grossman School of Medicine | NYU Langone Health, New York, NY, USA

W. E. Sowers et al. (eds.), *Textbook of Community Psychiatry*,
https://doi.org/10.1007/978-3-031-10239-4_42

least one study was unable to establish it as a risk in a sample of single adults with recurrent homelessness, emerging only if clustered with other factors (McQuistion et al. 2013). Regardless, Fazel et al.' (2008) rigorous meta-analysis of international studies between 1966 and 2007 derived pooled prevalence rates among homeless individuals of 37.9% for alcohol use disorder and 24.4% for other substance use disorders. Surveys of single adults in different American Midwestern communities have also shown high prevalence of lifetime substance use disorders. North et al. (2004) identified rates of 84% and 58%, and other researchers uncovered rates of 77% and 55%, respectively, for men and women (Forney et al. 2007).

Mental health conditions are more prevalent for those experiencing homelessness than the general population. The prevalence of mental health conditions is significantly higher for those who experience more than a year of homelessness than other types of homelessness. For example, a point-in-time count of those experiencing chronic homelessness in Los Angeles and San Francisco estimated 70% have a mental health condition (US Interagency Council on Homelessness 2018). There has been an upward trend in the size of this subpopulation since 2016, increasing by 15% between 2019 and 2020 alone, reaching its highest estimate (110,528) since 2009, with the single largest population living in Los Angeles (23,000) (US Department of Housing and Urban Development 2021).

Studies that include those experiencing shelter-based homelessness estimate rates of mental illness in adult homeless populations of between a third and a half (Roth and Bean 1986). Fazel et al. (2008) pooled prevalence estimates for psychotic disorders at rates of 12.7%, major depression of 11.4%, and personality disorders (predominantly DSM IV TR cluster C) of 23.1%.

Another subpopulation of concern is families. In 2020, 29.6% of all people identified as homeless were members of family units (US Department of Housing and Urban Development (2021). Fortunately, most families have just a single and relatively brief episode of homelessness. In 2020, New York City had the highest number of people in family units, estimated at over 41,500. As discussed below, preventing family homelessness may have long-term positive implications.

Basic Causes

Economic trends, systemic racism, and lack of any affordable housing are powerful forces that drive homelessness in the USA. The macroeconomic transition from manufacturing to service economies coupled with a loss of affordable housing is an important factor that has given rise to contemporary homelessness. This economic shift began after the 1960s with a relative transition in manufacturing jobs away from most western countries, including the USA, to less expensive labor markets (Lee and Mather 2008). Massive job losses led to defaulted rental payments, leading landlords in poor communities to neglect and abandon property for want of rental income. This yielded a significant expansion in the homeless population (Culhane et al. 1996).

Simultaneously, availability of affordable housing plummeted. In many urban areas, substandard housing was removed, gentrified, or converted to commercial real estate. In New York City, it was estimated that there were 129,000 single-room occupancy units in 1960, whereas by 1979, only 25,000 remained (Sullivan and Burke 2013). One unintended consequence of structural economic shifts became apparent by the beginning of the 1980s with dramatic increases in homelessness, particularly during periods of recession. The increasing income disparity between the poor and affluent in the USA since the 1980s has also perpetuated this phenomenon. Groups with higher incomes drive the types of new housing being constructed and acquired (Culhane et al. 1994). In 2017, eight of the top ten states with the highest rates of homelessness were also the most expensive states by median price of housing. Median rent increases of $100 a month were associated with a 9% increase in homelessness in these states (US Government Accountability Office 2020).

Racism continues to be a major driver of homelessness. Structural racism has directly led a disproportionate number of black, indigenous, and people of color (BIPOC) to experience homelessness in America. An important example of these discriminatory practices is *redlining*. Historically, government-funded entities would mark communities of color on housing maps in red and label these locations as poor financial investments. This practice limited access to financial loans and home ownership to people of color. This, in combination with many other racist policies and practices, has contributed to the disproportionately high rate of homelessness among black people in America. Black people comprise 39.8% of people experiencing homelessness, though they make up only 13.4% of the total population. Pacific Islanders and Native Americans are most likely to be homeless in America when compared to all other racial or ethnic groups. One hundred sixty per 10,000 people who self-identify as Pacific Islander or Native American experience homelessness compared to the national average of 17 out of every 10,000. Latinx people comprise 22% of people experiencing homelessness and comprise 18% of the population (Corporation for Supported Housing 2021).

BIPOC communities experience the consequences of these racist practices today. Black households pay more for mortgages and rent relative to white households. In 2016, in California, more than 60% of black renters paid more than 30% of their income in rent (Khouri 2020). Given the disproportionate health and economic impact of COVID-19 on BIPOC communities, it was predicted that homelessness would increase for individuals living in them (The Atlantic 2021). People who self-identify as lesbian, gay, bisexual, transgender, questioning (LGBTQ+) are overrepresented among homeless populations. Among homeless youth, up to 20–40% may identify as LGBTQ+ (Ray 2006).

Homelessness can become intergenerational and cyclical. Adverse childhood experiences are risk factors for homelessness. Up to 25% of children experiencing homelessness are separated from their parents (Susser et al. 1991). Findings from a national survey show that lack of parental care, combined with childhood physical or sexual abuse, was associated with an increased risk of adult homelessness by a factor of 26 (Herman et al. 1997). Children in foster care, who are at risk for future homelessness, appear to be more likely to have biological parents who have experienced homelessness (Zlotnick et al. 1998).

There is a robust and bidirectional relationship between psychiatric disorders and homelessness. Mental health conditions preceded homelessness in almost 2/3 of instances of homelessness in one study (Sullivan et al. 2000). Homelessness has been associated with poorer mental health outcomes and lower perceived levels of recovery from serious mental illness (Castellow et al. 2015). Most people with serious mental illnesses experiencing homelessness will accept safe, secure, and accessible housing (Larimer 2009). However, direct clinical experience makes it clear that there are some individuals whose untreated mental health symptoms create a barrier to accepting housing and prolong their homeless experience. For example, some individuals experience untreated paranoid delusions that specifically lead to an inability to accept secure and safe housing and continued homelessness.

Homelessness has multiple, heterogeneous causes that interact with one another. Many of these causes are structural and disproportionately impact BIPOC communities and those individuals with behavioral health conditions and traumatic experiences. Multiple clinical approaches are necessary to support a person's efforts to exit homelessness, which we will now discuss.

The Development of Services

Homeless support services evolved from a crisis-driven patchwork to elaborated systems in many urban areas offering outreach, shelter, housing, and clinical interventions (McQuistion et al. 2008). In 1987, the landmark McKinney-Vento Act was signed and created an ongoing, federal funding stream for homelessness relief, prevention, and research (National Coalition for the Homeless 2006). In 2001, the federal government made a commitment to encourage localities to set up 10-year plans to end chronic homelessness.

In 2004, the federal Substance Abuse and Mental Health Services Administration (SAMHSA) issued its Blueprint for Change (Backer et al. 2007), outlining best practices for localities to set up services for people with homelessness and psychiatric disorders.

In this context, there have been consistent efforts to improve services based on increasingly rigorous epidemiological studies and services research. If there are adequate and accessible community resources, successful movement out of homelessness is an attainable goal for many. In fact, Larimer (2009) found that most episodes of homelessness are brief and not repeated. However, as noted above, there are subpopulations with increased risk of repeated or chronic homelessness; among them are people with behavioral health disabilities.

Evidence-based practices (EBPs) specifically focused on homelessness, and mental health conditions have been developed. Other EBPs for housed individuals with mental health conditions have been adapted. EBPs are complemented by promising interventions as well as day-to-day work and outreach to people experiencing homelessness. It is useful to employ a frame in which these practices may be provided. The next section describes a clinical compass for working with people with homelessness and behavioral health disorders.

A Compass for Work with People Experiencing Homelessness

The community psychiatrist has the potential to offer a caring, therapeutic relationship to individuals experiencing homelessness and mental health conditions. Given the marginalization faced by people experiencing homelessness and the resultant distrust of support services, welcoming, empowering relationships are essential. Timing therapeutic interventions in the context of the relationship is equally critical.

A psychotherapeutic maxim dictates that the timing of an intervention is everything. It is useful to have a structure for implementing interventions that reflects an understanding of where a person is in their trajectory from homelessness. The resultant approach must necessarily be recovery-oriented or "person-centered." Person-centeredness focuses on the recognition that specific therapeutic interventions and services "must be constructed to meet the needs of individuals and that individuals should not be expected to benefit from programs or treatments designed for stereotypic patients with preconceived needs" (see the chapter "Recovery and Person-Centered Care: Empowerment, Collaboration and Integration"). People are constantly developing in terms of their needs and goals, and supports should be tailored to individual needs as they change over time.

A Phasic Model

This model offers a phase-like transit through the condition of homelessness for those with behavioral health problems. It incorporates three complementary dimensions. Two dimensions specifically focus on the person's internal state, while a third dimension describes clinical behaviors of support teams. These dimensional phases are schematically described in Fig. 1.

First Dimension: Stages of Change

The first dimension was borrowed from the literature concerned with substance use disorders. Prochaska and colleagues' (1992) transtheoretical model describes *stages of change* that represent a continuum of psychological states referring to relative readiness for behavioral change over the course of a person's healing process, spanning a "precontemplation" of problematic behaviors progressing through "relapse prevention." These stages of readiness also apply to the acceptance of, and readiness to manage, mental wellness. Progress is not unidirectional and it is usual for a person to shift among stages. Because of this, a smooth progression toward change is not an expectation. Supportive interventions may be calibrated according to a person's stage of change. These may range from questions about managing the extremes of weather while sleeping "rough" during "precontemplation" to the

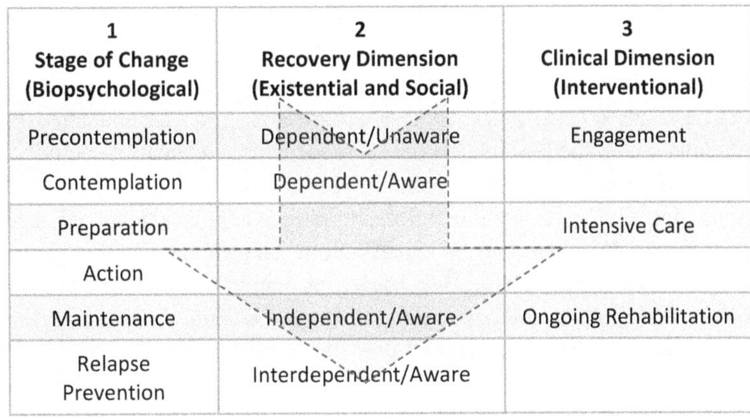

1 Stage of Change (Biopsychological)	2 Recovery Dimension (Existential and Social)	3 Clinical Dimension (Interventional)
Precontemplation	Dependent/Unaware	Engagement
Contemplation	Dependent/Aware	
Preparation		Intensive Care
Action		
Maintenance	Independent/Aware	Ongoing Rehabilitation
Relapse Prevention	Interdependent/Aware	

Fig. 1 Phasic model of work with homelessness. (McQuistion 2007; Prochaska et al. 1992; Townsend et al. 2000)

engagement with self-help supports in supportive housing during "relapse prevention" at the other end of the continuum.

Second Dimension: Recovery

A second parallel dimension describes an important aspect of *personal recovery*. Recovery is a process that is paradoxically both nonlinear and progressive (see chapter "Recovery and Person-Centered Care: Empowerment, Collaboration and Integration"). In other words, a person will not necessarily follow an uninterrupted or direct path toward recovery, but progress toward recovery relies on incremental growth as a person. Townsend, Boyd, and Griffin (Townsend et al. 2000) presented important aspects of recovery in a stage-related framework, focusing also on aspects of social inclusion or connectedness (Aron et al. 1992). Their characterization described movement from a "dependent and unaware" state to a fully socially integrated position within the community. In a dependent and unaware state, a person is surviving and has minimal awareness of how they are dependent on formal social institutions (e.g., shelters, jails, hospitals) to manage on a day-to-day basis. In this sense, they may suffer from the quintessential homeless experience of disaffiliation. This develops from an increased realization of personal challenges and awareness of dependency on others. This evolves toward an increasing independence from these supports and finally a sense of interdependence. Interdependence is a point of personal development marked by optimal understanding of one's self and how one depends on others and vice versa.

Third Dimension: Clinical Behavior

After appreciating the phasic aspects of readiness for change regarding psychiatric conditions and then in personal recovery, clinicians are able to time interventions accordingly. The third dimension therefore defines stages of *clinical behavior* within the two preceding parallel processes (McQuistion and Gillig 2006). While this dimension is applicable to other populations with serious psychiatric disorders, those with homelessness typically require this systematic approach because of the complexity of their problems.

Engagement

The clinician starts with a simple encounter and builds an engagement in which they begin to encourage hope and a foundation of a meaningful relationship with another person. Engagement often occurs in shelters and public spaces but can also occur when a person is "in-reached" during a hospitalization or if incarcerated. It is important to underscore that behavioral health care is usually a low priority for the person experiencing homelessness. The priority is often daily survival practicalities. The community psychiatrist focuses on a person's manifest or declared survival needs to build trust. It can often be helpful to provide concrete support (such as clothing, food, offer of support with benefits) and engage the person around their strengths. Embracing harm reduction is particularly important in this stage, and motivational interviewing techniques are particularly useful in this stage and throughout all stages of change. As there is progression into this phase, the psychiatrist may provide care for the person through harm reduction interventions such as education about naloxone, fentanyl test strips, and clean syringe distribution. The eventual engaged relationship develops and serves both patient and psychiatrist through the vicissitudes of the next stage, called intensive care.

Forming and nurturing relationships with people experiencing homelessness is labor-intensive and requires patience and a focus on the person's strengths. At times, lifesaving care may require time-limited, involuntary interventions. Clinicians occasionally implement involuntary measures, such as transport to an emergency room when there is imminent risk to self or others. This is determined on a case-by-case and encounter-by-encounter basis, bearing in mind the following important factors: (1) risk and protective factors, (2) the opportunities for subsequent observations and assessment, (3) the degree to which an established relationship with the person in distress can help negotiate voluntary interventions, and (4) risk of harm of implementing the involuntary transport. Care must be taken in light of extremely high rates of physical and sexual trauma in the histories of people experiencing homelessness (Foster et al. 2009). Re-traumatization is often associated with involuntary measures. Physical injury or death is a possibility from police-facilitated transport of individuals with mental health conditions or homeless and especially those who are BIPOC. Community psychiatrists must be active to minimize the risk of a bad outcome if involuntary transport is implemented. The use of civilian mental health teams and being present and communicative during emergencies will increase the likelihood of safe transport to medical care. Coercive measures should be avoided if at all possible as they are not only traumatizing but often fracture the relationship that clinician has worked so hard to build.

Intensive Care

If there is successful engagement, the clinical intervention transitions to a higher level of activity, termed intensive care. The sequencing and intensity of activity is determined by the person's individual goals and needs. Housing is often the touchstone and accessing it can include layers of treatment for mental health, substance use, and physical health conditions, the securing of benefits, and the beginnings of vocational/educational rehabilitation. The team of people working with the person can include housing specialists, vocational/educational counselors, social workers, primary care clinicians, and mental health professionals. Psychiatrists typically become more actively involved during this stage as they are positioned to provide direct psychiatric care, advocate for housing, and provide a bridge to the larger medical care system. Some individuals benefit from assertive community treatment or intensive mobile treatment models of support during this phase. The community psychiatrist should be aware of these models, initiate treatment, and refer individuals to more intensive mobile treatment teams when indicated. Community psychiatrists use a full range of biopsychosocial skills to coordinate interventions and support the expertise of other team members so that the person receives optimal care and support.

Ongoing Rehabilitation

Intensive care segues to an open-ended third stage of ongoing rehabilitation. This stage synchronizes with movement toward Townsend's "interdependence" and is related to Prochaska and colleagues' (1992) "relapse prevention" and "maintenance." During this stage a person gradually sheds an identity of homelessness while continuing to pursue personal recovery goals with increased agency. At this stage, people are nearly always housed. They may be pursuing work or vocational/educational rehabilitation, re-establishing ties with family, forming other supportive relationships, and pursuing broader social and/or spiritual concerns with faith-based or other community institutions. Psychiatrists work with these formerly homeless people through psychoeducation and supportive psychotherapy. These practices enhance their awareness of triggers that might exacerbate their illness or lead to substance use relapse and solidify their problem-solving skills.

On an individual level, while transitioning through the phases of intensive care and ongoing rehabilitation, a homeless person often confronts the phenomenological challenge of "internalized homelessness," persisting after permanent housing is obtained. Past homelessness is associated with higher levels of psychiatric distress and trauma than those who have never had such experience (Castellow et al. 2015). These individuals are also less likely to feel secure in their recovery. Many of these individuals have continued housing instability and demonstrate behaviors and decisions consistent with the belief they may lose their housing at any moment despite months to years of permanent housing. People may collect belongings necessary for survival on the street, rapidly consume high volumes of highly caloric food, avoid utilization of banks, avoid social interactions with peers, or even sleep in locations other than a bed in an apartment. It is a potential barrier for individuals to fully accept supports and engage in community re-integration and a personal recovery journey. Psychiatric practitioners must be aware of this and educate their support teams. They can provide a sense of normalization to their clients and connect them to peer-based and other supportive services.

Some Key Principles

Augmenting this methodology are some basic service principles articulated over the past three decades. They include the following watchwords, which are also listed in Table 1 (Osher 2001; SAMHSA 2021).

Housing access as bulwark: Achieving housing stability for people with behavioral health disorders requires more than housing itself. However, without permanent housing, a solution to homelessness is obviously impossible. Supportive housing is discussed in detail in the chapter "Housing First and the Role of Psychiatry in Supported Housing".

Income stability as key: In order to manage day-to-day living, there must be a stable source of income. Unfortunately, public assistance is notoriously unstable and inadequate. If eligible and unable to work in the short term, the use of federal disability insurance would be the best springboard to financial stability. However, the social security disability determination process is lengthy and inaccessible to many experiencing homelessness, and decisions seem arbitrary in many instances, so this is not an easy solution either. As a result, establishing financial stability is a significant challenge in most states. When available, this benefit must be evaluated in an ongoing manner and/or coupled with supported employment. Advocacy and support around people's access to benefits is an integral part of the clinical care a community psychiatrist provides.

Using active, persistent, yet flexible techniques: Clinical behavior must be flexible and patiently assertive. Trust is hard-won, especially with those who have had lifelong exposure to the criminal incarceration system, structural racism,

Table 1 Key principles in clinical work with homeless populations

Access housing *The first order of business*
Enable income stability *Employment or federal disability insurance without delay*
Be active, persistent, yet flexible *Trust is hard-won and respect is necessary*
Maintain optimism and think longitudinally *Culture the relationship, be a real object, setbacks are natural*
Connect to natural support network *Extended family, peer supports, community institutions*
Focus on cultural competence *Ethnicity, race, gender, sexual orientation affect the experience of homelessness*
Integrate services *Teamwork and careful attention to biopsychosocial complexity*

traumatizing human service systems, and childhood experience with domestic violence or other traumas.

Being optimistic, having a longitudinal perspective, and recognizing "the long game": The road from homelessness can be a very long one with setbacks and rewards. In the pursuit of mutual respect and engagement – and the building of personal agency – even acceptance of decisions that may have suboptimal outcomes may be necessary. Understanding that people remain in a recovery process, regardless of setbacks, is critical. Clinician-driven urges to be overly assertive or coercive to gain rapid results can fracture the relationship. A community psychiatrist should not over prioritize a single medication decision or the acceptance of a particular type of shelter over the caring relationship. However, it is often appropriate to use the alliance that emerges from the relationship to make recommendations to help the person achieve their goals. Examples range from suggesting a person accepts a medication dose change to observing limits on disruptive behaviors (e.g., not using substances on shelter premises). The reciprocity implied in this process helps other transference-countertransference events and assists a clinician in advocating for and supporting the patient.

Using natural support networks: Whenever possible, it is helpful to reach out to extended family, develop peer support, and link people with community institutions, such as faith-based organizations. These efforts will help counter the isolation and alienation that many homeless people experience. This support may be particularly helpful in preventing a recurrence of homelessness for adults precariously housed with family.

Integrating services: Social, psychological, vocational, substance use, and physical health complexity is the rule and not the exception for people experiencing homelessness. It is an absolute requirement that effective care is integrated. This integration occurs at many levels and includes psychiatry, addictions care, primary care, housing, case management, peer, vocational, and educational supports. As noted in the discussion of stages of clinical care, teamwork is key – with communication that is regular, methodical, and non-crisis driven.

Relationship building: A variety of treatment approaches have developed to support and provide care to those experiencing homelessness. No matter what intervention is offered, it is important to consider that the person experiencing homelessness is likely to mistrust medical personnel and human resource institutions. This should be expected given the fragmentation, authoritarian, and racist structures in place that cause and perpetuate homelessness and racial inequities. As such, it is important to initiate the relationship with active listening, self-esteem building, and fostering empowerment around decision-making whenever possible. The relationship is the core of treatment. Establishing optimal collaboration with the person struggling to emerge from homelessness will ultimately yield high rewards for clinicians, too.

Teamwork: We have also found that given the fragmentation of services designed to support people who have behavioral health conditions and homelessness, it is often helpful for psychiatric practitioners to work together to create a continuum of support. Group practices that embed psychiatrists as part of a team operating across multiple systems, such as outreach teams, shelter, ACT, food pantries, and permanent housing, can be effective at providing continuity of care to individuals as they transition from the street to home.

Effective Interventions

Street Psychiatry or Homeless Outreach

Targeted case management by outreach teams is often effective for developing an understanding of the specific clinical needs a person may have (Rowe et al. 2015). Outreach is the archetypal engagement phase activity. For people experiencing street homelessness outreach, teams can coordinate with psychiatrists to literally meet people where they are. A highly effective model involves integrating the psychiatrist within the street outreach team. The street psychiatrist visits with people living on the street or in other public spaces, constructs psychiatric assessments (typically over a series of unobtrusive visits), and consults with the team on optimal approaches to engage and support people on their recovery path. They also provide leadership during behavioral or physical health crises. These psychiatrists may provide psychotherapy and pharmacotherapy with people while they are staying on the street. As with the "housing first" model, needed services should not be withheld or delayed because individuals are unable to access traditional services. These interventions lower behavioral health barriers in the transition to housing, transitional shelters, safe havens, or other benefits. Additionally, considering the high rates of physical health challenges experienced among this population, an extremely important psychiatric role is to collaborate with street medicine teams, linking people "sleeping rough" to primary care.

Critical Time Intervention (CTI)

CTI is an evidence-based intervention specifically tailored to assist people who are homeless and have mental illnesses during transitions. First developed in a men's shelter setting, its original iteration's goal was to help assure successful transition from that setting to housing (Valencia et al. 1996). The intervention's evidence base is primarily derived from an adult homeless sample (Susser et al. 1997) and has been applied to veteran subpopulations, to homeless families headed by young single mothers, and as a mechanism to facilitate movement from relatively costly ACT to less intensive services (criticaltime.org 2021).

CTI's time-limited model is divided into three phases of decreasing intensity of service guided by individualized service planning according to Rowe et al. (2015). The first is engagement with the case manager who acts as collaborator and advocate while evaluating the individual's strengths, needs, and community supports. The second phase involves arranging and monitoring various supports, allowing the person experiencing homelessness to try them out. The final phase is fine-tuning supportive elements, gradually transferring care to involved community providers and termination of the CTI services. CTI often initiates in the earliest precontemplation/engagement stages and most logically begins to terminate during a later action/intensive care stage as a person reunites with family or transitions to a range of community providers. So, while CTI addresses the practical challenge of housing stability, it also helps in a process of social connectedness by actively prioritizing the establishment and renewal of relationships, both services-related and personal. Among homeless adults there is evidence of a decrease in negative symptoms in those with schizophrenia (Herman et al. 2000) and overall cost-effectiveness in general (Jones et al. 2003).

Assertive Community Treatment (ACT)

Assertive community treatment provides mobile and comprehensive community-based care and case management for people with serious psychiatric disorders. Its proactive and continuous approach is a good fit for the needs of people who are homeless and have mental illnesses (Morse et al. 2017). ACT's flexibility enables it to be implemented during the stage of precontemplation when individuals are dependent-unaware and not fully engaged. ACT can continue to the clinical stage of intensive care, transitioning to stages of relapse prevention/independent-aware/ongoing rehabilitation. ACT has been adapted to homeless populations for over 45 years, with evidence of improved housing stability. ACT programs decrease hospitalization rates, emergency room visits, and criminal justice involvement

(Philips et al. 2001). Program modifications more closely meeting a homeless person's needs are often desirable. These include (1) the creation of drop-in centers; (2) subdividing the team into mini-teams to improve engagement capacities; (3) using time-limited service to encourage transition to less intensive care; (4) hiring peer workers to diminish stigma within the team; and (5) a family outreach coordinator to help rebuild those relationships (Hackman and Dixon 2006). For a full description of ACT, please see the chapter "Case Management and Assertive Community Treatment".

Pathways to Housing

The "housing first" model was pioneered by Pathways to Housing (Tsemberis and Eisenberg 2000). Although housing literature suffers from significant methodological issues (Rog 2004), this model has strong evidence supporting its effectiveness when compared to the traditional "housing continuum" approach. This approach relies on the loose criteria of "housing readiness" and concentrates on a gradual movement of people, for example, from the streets, to drop-in centers and shelters, then to congregate housing, and finally to independent housing only after they have demonstrated success at the previous step.

Conversely, the Pathways' technique offers housing to people as soon as benefits or other means for rent have been obtained. A key element to success is combining Pathways' scattered site supported housing with an ACT team. Although access to ACT's support can be restricted by payer funding and/or regulatory restrictions, it has the capacity to supply a range of treatment and rehabilitation supports. A prospective random assignment study showed 79% retention in Pathways, as opposed to 27% for a traditional control group using a continuum of care model of housing (Aubry et al. 2015). Because of its use of ACT, the Pathways model has the capacity to serve people through clinical dimension stages of engagement and intensive care, only terminating at the point of ongoing rehabilitation, when a person is at least independent/aware and involved in relapse prevention or maintenance.

Pharmacotherapeutic Approaches

One of the aims of pharmacotherapy for people experiencing homelessness is to provide an accessible path for medication from a caring clinician. If individuals are open to clinically indicated pharmacotherapy, treatment should *not* be withheld or delayed due to housing status. Many people experiencing homelessness respond to such treatment, and the community psychiatrist must consider ways to provide access and support adherence. More than 70% of people diagnosed with schizophrenia do not adhere to medications (Fenton et al. 1997). For those experiencing schizophrenia and homelessness, nonadherence rates are even higher.

Effective strategies to support adherence include offering long-acting injectable (LAI) medications, the use of medications that have long half-lives (such as extended-release preparations), and co-mingling pills in blister packs. Co-mingling pills involves the pharmacy dispensing different pills to be taken at the same time in discrete packaging that can be handed off to people at regular intervals while in shelter or the streets. The combination of LAI antipsychotics with psychoeducation is associated with significant improvements in LAI adherence (76% at 6 months) in addition to improvements in oral medication adherence (Sajatovic et al. 2013).

Medication-assisted treatment (MAT) is often indicated for co-occurring substance use and mental health conditions. People may be in the precontemplation stage with regard to acceptance of medication for their mental health conditions, yet simultaneously in action stage regarding treatment for their substance use disorders. For those experiencing street homelessness who are open to MAT, long-acting injectable preparations of naltrexone or buprenorphine are often helpful for alcohol use disorder and opioid use disorders. Recent studies have demonstrated that LAI naltrexone combined with harm reduction counseling for people experiencing homelessness was associated with decreased alcohol use, alcohol-related harm, and improved physical health (Collins et al. 2021). Clinical experience has been that having a low threshold for inducing someone on buprenorphine while they are street homeless or in shelter can be highly effective during engagement and intensive care. This approach supports reductions in opioid misuse, decreases overdose risk, and often leads to engagement in more comprehensive support.

There is a clear role for clozapine in treatment refractory schizophrenia among people who are homeless, particularly those with suicidal ideation. Despite challenges in adherence and accessing laboratory testing, community psychiatrists who are part of team-based care systems benefit from developing processes to deliver clozapine and monitor absolute neutrophil counts (ANCs). Strategies may include transport to lab centers, visits by street medicine teams, or point-of-care ANC testing devices. Blister packs that include clozapine co-mingled with other pills are additional tools.

It is essential to consider how homelessness impacts medication decisions. Explicit conversations about how sedating medications may affect the person given their sleeping environment and how they will access pills should be initiated by the clinician. Shared decision-making is the guide. Medications should be discussed in a context and manner that lines up with a person's level of motivation and stage of change. For example, people who are staying in shelter may prefer to avoid psychiatric medications that may result in drowsiness, given the physical risks of those environments. For some, regular lab monitoring may be inaccessible. The practitioner may consider medications that require less frequent monitoring or may initiate medications without recent labwork if the benefits of treatment outweigh the risk. Lower dosing while the person is on the street may be suggested until lab work is accessible and upward dosage adjustment practical (Table 2).

Employment and Education: Supported and Transitional

Supported employment, such as individual placement and support (IPS) (see the chapter "Supported Employment")), and transitional employment (see the chapter "Fountain House and the Clubhouse Movement") are EBPs that have gained wide recognition in general populations with serious psychiatric disorders, many of whom might have had histories of homelessness. Vocational or educational rehabilitation most frequently begins during intensive care or ongoing rehabilitation. Because work is practical, associated with positive clinical outcomes and frequently improves self-esteem, efforts must be made to offer vocational or educational rehabilitation opportunities to homeless people who are at all stages of engagement and recovery. Access to these supports should not be withheld due to housing status. For individuals motivated to work, access to supported employment can be a helpful engagement tool for people staying in shelter or the streets. Clinical experience is that there are benefits to integrating accessible supported employment into supportive housing for those who are further along on their recovery journey.

Integrated Dual Disorder Treatment

Clinicians recognize that rates of co-occurring mental illness and substance use are elevated among people experiencing homelessness, with estimates in the literature have been as high as 85% (Joseph & Langrod 2004). This reality helped inspire efforts to develop interventions for these co-occurring disorders for all clinical popu-

Table 2 Pharmacotherapy principles for those experiencing homelessness

Utilize shared decision-making *Promote collaboration, emphasize personal choice, and the long-term relationship is primary to any one medication decision*
Offer medications for mental health conditions *Do not withhold indicated psychiatric medications, consider risk/benefit of initiating medications if lab results are initially inaccessible, clozapine and lithium may be indicated and are not contraindicated for people experiencing homelessness*
Offer addictions medications for substance use conditions *Co-occurring disorders are often responsive to MAT and psychotropic medications*
Consider practical measures to support adherence *Consider offering long-acting injectable medications in a trauma-informed way, co-mingle blister packing of medications, and offer medications with long half-lives*

lations. Integrated dual disorder treatment (IDDT) demonstrated benefit for people experiencing homelessness with co-occurring disorders. Systems of care that deliver services to those experiencing homelessness may deliver IDDT as part of supportive housing or homeless ACT models (Pringle et al. 2017).

Modified Therapeutic Communities (MTCs)

MTCs offer an intervention that is grounded in intensive care (action/dependent-aware) and has been shown to be effective in homeless populations with co-occurring disorders (Sacks et al. 2008). MTCs are associated with improved measures of abstinence, psychiatric symptoms, and housing. Compared with classic therapeutic communities, MTCs are less confrontational and incorporate treatment for mental health. This modification makes it easier to engage individuals so that they may benefit from treatment. However, whatever gains they achieve can be lost without continuous aftercare, resulting in high relapse rates and setbacks in progress toward ongoing rehabilitation. One MTC evidenced comparably less substance use and greater housing stability with inclusion of aftercare groups and case management. These interventions support sobriety and create a bridge to the community, building on the social connectedness established in the MTC (Sacks et al. 2003).

Peer Workers

In the 1980s, prescient homelessness outreach programs pioneered the inclusion of peer workers. These formerly homeless people, who were often in recovery from addictive or mental health disorders, enhanced the effectiveness of engaging people who were on the street. Peer workers reinforce hope, are role models, enhance credibility, and offer day-to-day education for professional staff about a culture many have only glimpsed. In addition to street outreach, peer counselors have been used in a variety of homeless subgroups throughout the stages of clinical care, such as youth and veteran populations, ACT team clients (Dixon et al. 1997), adults with forensic histories (Rotter et al. 2005), and people in therapeutic communities.

Promising Practices

Intensive Mobile Treatment (IMT)

IMT is an innovative model aiming to support and continue to treat people with very high behavioral health needs who were in frequent contact with homelessness, mental health, substance use, and criminal justice systems. This model began in New York City in 2016 to serve people as they move among street locations, shelters, and institutions (NYC Department of Health and Mental Hygiene 2017). The IMT team actively outreaches to people who experience homelessness and also can provide office-based support and care. IMT includes community psychiatrists, peer specialists, mental health professionals, and community nurses and provides care to 27 individuals with very high staff to participant ratios. IMT has demonstrated capacity to rapidly accept referrals for service, maintain service connection, and improve overall engagement. The psychiatrist assesses, coordinates basic primary care, and provides psychotherapy, pharmacotherapy, and psychiatric leadership within the team. IMT has a higher staff to patient ratio than ACT. It is much more flexible than ACT models in a way that is helpful for many people experiencing homelessness. For example, traditional ACT teams are often pressured to limit office-based drop in visits to people experiencing homelessness by auditing bodies. These office-based visits are extraordinarily helpful to engage people experiencing street homelessness. ACT teams also depend on managed care organization billing and authorization for services. These payer systems are not always supportive of the continuity of care and the flexible engagement patterns necessary to provide support to people experiencing homelessness. Finally, given its staffing capacity, IMT teams are able to provide relationship building and intensive psychotherapy to people who would benefit or are not yet ready to accept pharmacotherapy for their conditions.

Trauma-Informed Services and Treatment

Many people experiencing homelessness have suffered from multiple and repeated traumas throughout their lives (see the chapter "Traumatic Stress in the Community: Identification and Intervention"). Trauma-informed services have been applied to homeless populations and focus on an individual's strengths to regain a sense of control and emphasize psychological and physical safety. This reduces the threat of re-traumatization and increases access to services (Hopper et al. 2010). Given the high burden of trauma for those experiencing homelessness, it is recommended that all organizations that provide homelessness support services implement services that assess for trauma and its sequelae and provide services appropriate to people with trauma histories (Hayes et al. 2010). According to Hayes, the provision of supportive housing alone is inadequate to address the consequences of trauma for individuals experiencing homelessness. Specific treatments for trauma show modest but encouraging results when applied to homeless populations with co-occurring mental illness and substance abuse (Desai et al. 2008; Magwood et al. 2019). Seeking safety is a helpful therapeutic intervention for individuals experiencing homelessness, trauma, substance use, and/or PTSD. Clinical experience indicates that it is helpful to integrate these programs into shelter, drop-in, supportive housing, or ACT teams.

Primary Care Behavioral Health Integration (PCBHI)

Integrated treatment of co-occurring disorders has become widely accepted in behavioral health circles over the past decade (see the chapter "Integrated Care and Community Psychiatry"). However, PCBHI has been practiced in varying degrees by programs serving homeless populations long before that. The need to serve people who are homeless, and who frequently present with extreme clinical and social complexity, has motivated this practice. Boston Health Care for the Homeless Program's medical respite service is an iconic example and provides short-term residential medical care for people unable to manage on the streets or in shelters (O'Connell et al. 2010). Janian Medical Care in New York City practices a model that embeds a psychiatrist into outreach teams that collaborate with street medicine teams. By teaming psychiatric and primary care clinicians, especially within the same organization, integrated care may continue for years, even after a person gains housing. These programs developed by community-based organizations provide models on which to build.

Conclusion

Working with individuals experiencing homelessness offers challenges and rewarding clinical opportunities for community psychiatrists and hope for the people with whom they work. At the time of writing of this chapter, the COVID-19 pandemic disproportionately threatened the physical and behavioral health of those experiencing homelessness and probably contributed to an increase in homelessness. Similarly, dislocations due to climate change create surges in homelessness, disproportionately affecting marginalized people with mental illnesses. While awaiting research and policy initiatives addressing social and natural calamities such as these, psychiatric services need to rapidly respond and adapt. In this chapter we have discussed some interventions that are likely to reduce the impact of homelessness, but many challenges and threats remain. Community psychiatrists will need the skills described here to meet future needs as they develop.

References

Advisory: *Behavioral Health Services for People Who Are Homeless*. (March 2021) Publication ID PEP20-06-04-003. Substance Abuse and Mental Health Services Administration. Accessed from: https://store.samhsa.gov/product/advisory-behavioral-health-services-people-who-are-homeless/

Aron A, Aron EN, Smollan D (1992). Inclusion of other in the self scale and the structure of interpersonal closeness. Journal of Personality and Social Psychology, 63(4), 596-612.

Aubry T, Nelson G, Tsemberis S (2015). Housing first for people with severe mental illness who are

Homeless: A review of the research and findings from the at Home—Chez soi demonstration project. The Canadian Journal of Psychiatry, 60(11), 467-474.

Backer, TE Howard EA, Moran GE. (2007). The role of effective discharge planning in preventing homelessness. The Journal of Primary Prevention, 28(3-4), 229-243.

Castellow J, Kloos B, Townley G (2015). Previous homelessness as a risk factor for recovery from serious mental illnesses. Community Mental Health Journal, 51(6), 674-684.

Collins S, Duncan MH, Saxon AJ, Taylor EM, Mayberry N, et al. (2021). Combining behavioral harm-reduction treatment And Extended-release Naltrexone for people experiencing homelessness and alcohol use disorder in the USA: a randomised clinical trial. The Lancet Psychiatry, 8(4), 287-300.

Corporation for Supported Housing (2021). Racial disparities and disproportionality index. Available at https://www.csh.org/supportive-housing-101/data/#RDDI. (Retrieved 3/20/2021).

Critical Time Intervention. Training & Consultation. (n.d.). Retrieved March 29, 2021, from http://www.criticaltime.org/training/

Culhane DP, Dejowski EF, Ibañez, J, Needham E, Macchia, I. (1994). Public shelter admission rates in Philadelphia and New York city: The implications of turnover for sheltered population counts. *Housing Policy Debate, 5*(2), 107-140.

Culhane, DP, Lee, C, Wachter SM. (1996). Where the homeless come from: a study of the prior address distribution of families admitted to public shelters in New York City and Philadelphia. Housing Policy Debate, 7(2), 327-365.

Desai RA, Harpaz-Rotem I, Najavits LM, Rosenheck, RA. (2008). Impact of the seeking safety program on clinical outcomes among homeless female veterans with psychiatric disorders. Psychiatric Services, 59(9), 996-1003.

Dixon L, Hackman A, Lehman A (1997). Administration and Policy in Mental Health, 25(2), 199-208.

Fazel S, Khosla V, Doll H, Geddes J (2008) The prevalence of mental disorders among the homeless in Western countries: systematic review and meta-regression analysis. *PLoS Medicine* (www.plosmedicine.org) 5: 0001-0012.

Fenton WS, Blyler CR, Heinssen RK (1997). Determinants of medication compliance in schizophrenia: Empirical and clinical findings. Schizophrenia Bulletin, 23(4), 637-651.

Forney JC, Lombardo S, Toro PA (2007). Diagnostic and other correlates of HIV risk behaviors in a probability sample of homeless adults. Psychiatric Services, 58(1), 92-99.

Foster S, LeFauve C, Kresky-Wolff M, Rickards LD (2009). Services and supports for individuals with co-occurring disorders and long-term homelessness. The Journal of Behavioral Health Services & Research, 37(2), 239-251.

Hackman A, Dixon L. Assertive community treatment. In Clinical Guide to the Treatment of the Mentally Ill Homeless Person. (2006). Eds. Gillig PM, McQuistion HL. American Psychiatric Press, Inc., Washington, DC

Hayes M, Zonneville M, Bassuk E. (2010) The SHIFT Study: Services and Housing Interventions for Families in Transition. American Institutes for Research.

Herman DB, Susser, ES, Struening EL, Link BL (1997). Adverse childhood experiences: Are they risk factors for adult homelessness? American Journal of Public Health, 87(2), 249-255.

Herman D, Opler L, Felix A, Valencia E, Wyatt RJ, Susser E (2000). A critical time intervention with mentally iii homeless men. The Journal of Nervous and Mental Disease, 188(3), 135-140.

Hopper EK, Bassuk EL, Olivet J (2010). Shelter from the storm: Trauma-informed care in homelessness services settings. The Open Health Services and Policy Journal, 3(2), 80-100.

Intensive Mobile Treatment Team Concept Paper. (June 2017) NYC Department of Health and Mental Hygiene https://www1.nyc.gov/assets/doh/downloads/pdf/acco/2017/intensive-mobile-treatment-concept-paper.pdf

Jones K, Colson PW, Holter MC, Lin, S, Valencia, E, et al. (2003). Cost-effectiveness of critical time intervention to reduce homelessness among persons with mental illness. Psychiatric Services, 54(6), 884-890.

Joseph H, Langrod JG. (2004). The homeless Substance abuse: A Comprehensive Text- Book (4th ed.; pp. 1141–1168). Eds. Lowinson JH, Ruiz P, Millman RB, Langrod JG. Lippincott, Williams, & Wilkins, Philadelphia.

Khouri, A (2020, July 19) Amid the coronavirus pandemic, a Black housing crisis gets worse. Los Angeles Times. https://www.latimes.com/homeless-housing/story/2020-07-19/amid-coronavirus-pandemic-black-housing-crisis-gets-worse

Larimer ME (2009). Health care and public service use and costs before and After provision of housing for chronically homeless persons with severe alcohol problems. JAMA, 301(13), 1349.

Lee, M. A., Mather, M. (2008). US labor force trends, Population Bulletin 63:1-16.

Magwood O, Leki VY, Kpade V, Saad A, Alkhateeb Q, et al (2019). Common trust and personal safety issues: A systematic review on the acceptability of health and social interventions for persons with lived experience of homelessness. PLOS ONE, 14(12).

McQuistion HL (2007, October 12). Services for mentally ill homeless people: The quest for best practices. (Symposium presentation) APA Institute for Psychiatric Services, New Orleans, LA.

McQuistion HL, Felix A, Samuels, J (2008). Serving people who have mental illness and homelessness. Tasman A, Lieberman J, Kay J (eds), *Psychiatry,* 3rd Ed. John Wiley & Sons, London.

McQuistion HL, Gillig PM. (2006). Introduction: Mental illness, homelessness, and clinical practice. In Gillig

PM, McQuistion HL (eds), The American Association of Community Psychiatrists Clinical Manual in Treating Mentally Ill Homeless People. American Psychiatric Press, Washington, DC.

McQuistion HL, Gorroochurn P, Hsu E, Caton CL (2013). Risk factors associated with recurrent homelessness after a first homeless episode. Community Mental Health Journal, 50(5), 505-513.

Morse GA, York MM, Dell N, Blanco J, Birchmier C. (2017). Improving outcomes for homeless people with alcohol disorders: A multi-program community-based approach. *Journal of mental health*, 6, 684-691.

National Coalition for the Homeless (2006). McKinney-Vento Act. Available at http://www.nationalhomeless.org/publications/facts/McKinney.pdf. Accessed July 21, 2022.

North, C. S., Eyrich, K. M., Pollio, D. E., & Spitznagel, E.L. (2004). Are rates of psychiatric disorders in the homeless population changing? American Journal of Public Health, 94, 103–108

O'Connell JJ, Oppenheimer SC, Judge CM, Taube RL, Blanchfield BB, et al (2010). The Boston health care for the Homeless program: a public health framework. American Journal of Public Health, 100(8), 1400-1408.

Osher FC (2001). Co-occurring addictive and mental disorders. In RW Manderscheid & MJ Henderson (Eds.). Center for Mental Health Services, Mental Health, United States 2000. DHHS Pub No (SMA))1-3537. Washington, DC: Superintendant of Doscuments, US Government Printing Office, 91–98.

Philips SD, Burns BJ, Edgar ER, Mueser KT, Linkins KW, et al (2001). Moving assertive community treatment into standard practice. Psychiatric Services, 52 (6): 771-779.

Pringle J, Grasso K, Lederer L (2017). Integrating the Integrated: Merging integrated Dual Diagnosis Treatment (IDDT) with Housing First. Community Mental Health Journal, 53(6), 672-678.

Prochaska JO, DiClemente CC, Norcross JC (1992). In search of how people change: Applications to addictive behaviors. American Psychologist, 47(9), 1102-1114.

Ray N. (2006). Lesbian, gay, bisexual and transgender youth: An epidemic of homelessness. New York: National Gay and Lesbian Task Force Policy Institute and the National Coalition for the Homeless.

Rog D J (2004). The evidence on Supported Housing. Psychiatric Rehabilitation Journal, 27(4), 334-344.

Roth D, Bean J (1986). The Ohio study: A comprehensive look at homelessness. Psychosocial Rehabilitation Journal, 9(4), 31-38.

Rotter M, McQuistion HL, Broner N, Steinbacher M (2005). Best practices: The impact of the "incarceration culture" on reentry for adults with mental illness: A training and group treatment model. Psychiatric Services, 56(3), 265-267.

Rowe M, Styron T, David DH (2015). Mental health outreach to persons who are homeless: implications for practice from a Statewide Study. Community Mental Health Journal, 52(1), 56-65.

Sacks S, DeLeon G, Sacks JY, et al.: TC-oriented supported housing for homeless MICAs. *J Psychoactive Drugs* 35: 355-366, 2003

Sacks S, Banks S, McKendrick K, Sacks JY (2008). Modified therapeutic community for co-occurring disorders: A summary of four studies. Journal of Substance Abuse Treatment, 34(1), 112-122.

Sajatovic M, Levin J, Ramirez LF, Hahn DY, Tatsuoka C, et al (2013). Prospective trial of customized adherence enhancement plus long-acting injectable antipsychotic medication in homeless or recently homeless individuals with schizophrenia or schizoaffective disorder. The Journal of Clinical Psychiatry, 74(12), 1249-1255.

Sullivan BJ, Burke J (2013). Single-Room occupancy housing in New York city: The origins and dimensions of a crisis. CUNY Law Review, 17(01), 113.

Sullivan, G, Burnam A, Koegel P (2000). Pathways to homelessness among the mentally ill. Social Psychiatry and Psychiatric Epidemiology, 35(10), 444-450.

Susser, E, Struening EL, Conover S, Lin SP (1991). Childhood antecedents of homelessness in psychiatric patients. American Journal of Psychiatry, 148(8), 1026-1030.

Susser E, Valencia E, Conover S, Felix A, Tsai WY, Wyatt, RJ (1997). Preventing recurrent homelessness among mentally ill men: A "critical time" intervention after discharge from a shelter. American Journal of Public Health, 87(2), 256-262.

The COVID Tracking Project at The Atlantic. (2021, March 20) https://covidtracking.com/race

Townsend W, Boyd S, Griffin G. (2000). *Emerging Best Practices in Mental Health Recovery.* Columbus, Ohio: Ohio Department of Mental Health, Office of Consumer Services.

Tsemberis S, Eisenberg RF (2000). Pathways to housing: Supported housing for street-dwelling homeless individuals with psychiatric disabilities. Psychiatric Services, 51(4), 487-493.

U.S. Department of Housing and Urban Development (2021). 2020 AHAR: Part 1 - PIT Estimates of Homelessness in the U.S. https://www.huduser.gov/portal/sites/default/files/pdf/2020-AHAR-Part-1.pdf

U.S. Government Accountability Office. July 2020 Homelessness. More HUD oversight of data collection would improve the estimates of homeless population. https://www.gao.gov/assets/gao-20-433.pdf

U.S. Interagency Council on Homelessness (2018) https://www.usich.gov/resources/uploads/asset_library/Homelessness-in-America-Focus-on-chronic.pdf.

Valencia E, Susser ES, McQuistion HL (1996). Critical time points in the clinical care of homeless mentally ill individuals. J. Vaccaro, G. Clark (Eds.), Practicing psychiatry in the community: A manual (pp. 259–276). American Psychiatric Press, Washington, DC.

Zlotnick C, Kronstadt D, Klee L (1998). Foster care children and family homelessness. American Journal of Public Health, 88(9), 1368-1370.

Early Psychosis and the Prevention and Mitigation of Serious Mental Illness

Iruma Bello, Ilana Nossel, and Lisa B. Dixon

Schizophrenia spectrum disorders are psychiatric illnesses with a lifetime prevalence near 1%; they can cause extensive functional impairment and have for too long carried low expectations for recovery (Lieberman et al. 2013). This group of disorders typically includes schizophrenia, schizoaffective disorder, delusional disorder, and schizophreniform disorder. Hallucinations, delusions, and disorganized behavior constitute the hallmark symptoms of these disorders. In 2013, excess total costs of schizophrenia in the United States were estimated at $155.7 billion, including significant direct health care costs but mostly indirect costs related to losses to the labor market (Cloutier et al. 2013).

Specialized early treatment services for first-episode psychosis (FEP), now referred to as coordinated specialty care (CSC) in the United States, emerged during the last 25 years internationally and have proven effective for engaging clients in treatment and improving short-term and possibly longer-term outcomes. CSC can lead to improvements in symptoms, social functioning, quality of life, and treatment satisfaction (Dixon et al. 2018). In this chapter, we will discuss the scientific foundations for CSC, including describing the association between longer duration of untreated psychosis (DUP) and worse short-term and long-term outcomes. We will also describe the essential components of evidence-based CSC treatment and policy factors that led to the unusually rapid dissemination of FEP treatment throughout the United States.

Relationship Between DUP and Outcomes

DUP is defined as the time from onset of psychotic symptoms to effective treatment and is measured in months to years across psychotic spectrum disorders (Kessler et al. 2005). In the United States, schizophrenia-related disorders have an average DUP of over a year (Addington et al. 2015). Longer DUP has been robustly associated with poor outcomes across health-care systems (Howes et al. 2021; Marshall et al. 2005); however, there is not enough evidence to support causality.

Several meta-analyses have consistently indicated the negative relationship between longer DUP and outcomes. A meta-analysis conducted by Marshall et al. (2005) evaluated the relationship between DUP and a range of outcomes including depression, anxiety, social functioning, overall functioning, quality of life, positive symptoms, negative symptoms, rates of remission, time

I. Bello (✉) · I. Nossel · L. B. Dixon
New York State Psychiatric Institute, Columbia University Vagelos College of Physicians and Surgeons, New York, NY, USA
e-mail: Iruma.Bello@nyspi.columbia.edu; Ilana.Nossel@nyspi.columbia.edu; Lisa.Dixon@nyspi.columbia.edu

W. E. Sowers et al. (eds.), *Textbook of Community Psychiatry*,
https://doi.org/10.1007/978-3-031-10239-4_43

to remission, and relapse at baseline, 6, 12, and 24 months. The meta-analysis reviewed 26 studies with 4490 people over the age of 16 but under 60 with FEP. DUP was defined as the time from psychosis onset to neuroleptic treatment or hospital admission. The mean DUP for all studies was 124 weeks. There were limited significant correlations between DUP and outcomes at baseline (e.g., depression and anxiety, and quality of life); however, at follow-up time points, there were consistent negative correlations between DUP and an array of outcomes which support the idea that longer DUP is associated with worse outcomes. For example, at 6 months' follow-up, longer DUP was significantly correlated with greater levels of positive symptoms, negative symptoms, depression, and anxiety, as well as reduced overall and social functioning, and lower rates of achieving remission. At 12 months' follow-up, longer DUP was significantly correlated with more positive, negative, depressive, and anxiety symptoms, lower quality of life, and lower overall functioning, and individuals with longer DUP were not as likely to be in remission and took longer to achieve remission. While only two studies followed patients for 24 months, the link between longer DUP and greater positive symptoms, poorer quality of life, and overall functioning persisted (Marshall et al. 2005).

Results of the recent National Institute of Mental Health (NIMH) Recovery After an Initial Schizophrenia Episode Early Treatment Program (RAISE ETP) study provide information on the impact of DUP in a US-based early psychosis sample. In this study, DUP was defined as the time between psychosis onset and first-time antipsychotic medication treatment. The study included 404 individuals with first-episode nonaffective psychosis between 15 and 40 years of age with a mean DUP of 193.5 weeks and a median DUP of 74 weeks. Using a cluster randomized design, outcomes of 223 participants receiving "NAVIGATE," the CSC program, were compared to 181 individuals receiving usual care after 2 years of treatment. Notably, DUP moderated the effects of NAVIGATE such that individuals with a DUP less than 74 weeks benefitted significantly more on quality of life and symptom measures compared to those with a DUP greater than 74 weeks (Kane et al. 2015).

One of the most recent meta-analyses, which also included an umbrella review of available meta-analyses, examined the strength of the evidence supporting this proposition (Howes et al. 2021). They included 13 meta-analyses derived from 129 studies with a total sample of 25,657 individuals. Across the studies, the relationship between DUP and individual outcomes was classified as convincing, highly suggestive, suggestive, weak, or nonsignificant. Howes et al. (2021) found suggestive evidence for a relationship between longer DUP and more severe negative symptoms and greater chance of previous self-harm. At follow-up, they found highly suggestive evidence for a relationship between longer DUP and more severe positive symptoms, more severe negative symptoms, and lower chance of remission. There was suggestive evidence for a relationship between longer DUP and poorer overall functioning and more severe global psychopathology. Importantly, the effect sizes found in this meta-analysis were clinically meaningful. Using statistical analyses, the researchers were able to create a predictive model which calculated that a DUP of 4 weeks predicted >20% more severe symptoms at follow-up relative to a DUP of 1 week. This suggests that delaying treatment by 3 weeks would be associated with symptom outcomes that are 20% worse, and as the delay in treatment increases, so does the worsening of the outcomes.

One longitudinal study (Jonas et al. 2020) analyzed 20-year follow-up data for a cohort of individuals diagnosed with schizophrenia spectrum disorders. In their data, individuals, in general, had markedly deteriorating functioning either before or after hospitalization or treatment; DUP did not impact longer-term outcomes. The study has been critiqued because of the limited nature of the sample as well as the lack of adequate treatment provided after admission (Woods et al. 2020). Further investigation is needed.

Notwithstanding the study conducted by Jonas et al. (2020), evidence for the association between DUP and outcome is robust. At the same time, as mentioned before, a causal linkage has not been firmly established, and it is clear that more studies are necessary to fully understand the extent of any causal relationship between DUP and outcomes. In addition to understanding the causal relationship between DUP and outcomes, the ability to intervene early and reduce DUP is of paramount importance. In FEP, these delays to care can have detrimental consequences. Not only do they occur during periods of highest risk for self-harm and aggression, but even in the most stable circumstances, navigating the fragmented US mental health system and experiencing delayed access to the right treatment lead to increased suffering, trauma, and despair for youth and families who are trying to make sense of and cope with these experiences (Dixon et al. 2018). There is also evidence that the impact of social inequities and scarcity of resources for some groups compounds these delays.

Impact of Social Determinants of Mental Health Care on Pathways to Care in Psychosis

Many studies have attempted to elucidate the pathways to care for individuals with early psychosis. Cabassa et al. (2018) conducted a qualitative study to specifically examine pathways to care from symptom onset to CSC in individuals with nonaffective psychosis in the RAISE-Implementation and Evaluation Study (RAISE-IES). They were able to identify factors that shaped facilitators and barriers to care along the pathway. Their model illustrates the relationship between family, client, and health-care system factors and how these factors impact help-seeking decision-making and in turn may contribute to shortened or lengthened pathways to care. During the emergence of psychotic symptoms, the ways in which clients and families make sense of symptoms, level of stigma experienced, and ideas about self-reliance influenced help-seeking behaviors particularly, given the uncertainty that permeates all aspects of the experience. For example, during this initial phase, individuals and families are unfamiliar with symptoms, therefore making it difficult to accurately recognize them and the effects they are having on the young person's life. Individuals and their families also lack information and clarity about where and when to seek help, all of which can serve to delay engagement with treatment. Even when individuals and families connect with mental health services, Cabassa's model suggests that the pathway can be delayed if individuals and families have negative experiences and receive poor care, which is characterized as receiving poor treatment marked by inaccurate evaluations, feeling trapped in a hospital, receiving little information about treatment options and side effects, families feeling ignored or alienated during the process, not being referred to expert providers, and poor care transitions particularly from inpatient to outpatient settings (Cabassa et al. 2018). All of these experiences can be traumatizing and prevent the person and family from engaging further with mental health services.

The relationship between risk for psychosis, social determinants of health, and DUP is complex and worth examining. In communities of color, henceforth referred to as BIPOC (Black, Indigenous, and People of Color), pathways to care are delayed even more due to social and environmental inequities experienced across the life span conceptualized as social determinants of health. Social determinants are defined as community and population-level economic and social conditions that negatively impact people's behaviors, limit help-seeking, and are associated with poor access to care (Compton and Shim 2014). At the societal level, they can include prejudice, discrimination, and social exclusion based on race, ethnicity, and sexual orientation. At the environmental level, they can include factors such as unemployment, housing instability, and food insecurity. Elevated risk factors experienced by BIPOC communities are typically associated with increased risk of mental illness and a worsened, more persistent illness course (Compton and Shim 2014).

At the neighborhood level, disparities create increased stress as individuals in BIPOC communities struggle to meet basic needs and have limited access to opportunities. This environmental stress may be a driver for increased risk of psychosis; particularly given the established association between stress, adverse childhood events, and schizophrenia (Rosenberg et al. 2007). For instance, studies have found that immigrant communities are at greater risk of developing schizophrenia and other psychotic disorders compared to native-born communities possibly due to socio-environmental factors, such as urbanicity, discrimination, or socioeconomic deprivation (Bourque et al. 2011). Narita et al. (2020) examined the relationship between social stressors in the neighborhood setting as a risk factor for psychotic experiences in a general population sample of individuals residing in New York City and Baltimore. They specifically focused on perceived neighborhood disruption and gentrification. Results indicated that individuals who perceived greater neighborhood disruptions (i.e., characterized as feeling pushed out of the neighborhood, perceiving a disruption of social ties and neighborhood connections, and observing changes to the sense of community in the neighborhood) tended to endorse psychotic-like experiences more often than other members of the community. However, they did not find significant differences for the gentrification construct. Anglin et al. (2020) examined whether perceived ethnic density from childhood was associated with psychotic-like symptoms in a sample of young urban adults. Results indicated that individuals from racial and ethnic minority groups raised in neighborhoods perceived as primarily racially or ethnically different from their identity tended to report higher rates of psychotic-like experiences compared to individuals raised in White, mixed, or racially concordant neighborhoods.

In terms of diagnosis of psychosis, there is evidence that individuals from Black and Latinx communities are disproportionately diagnosed with psychosis, and this is in part due to clinicians misinterpreting and misattributing the clinical presentation (Schwartz and Blackenship 2014). We use Latinx as a gender-neutral term to describe the heterogenous group of people living in the United States of Latin American origin or decent. In the United States, BIPOC communities which have faced sustained systemic racism are under-resourced, segregated, and disenfranchised. Community members live under stressful conditions that limit their ability to overcome poverty and have limited access to stable housing, health care, and education. Frequently they experience increased discrimination and are exposed to higher rates of violence, all of which are associated with decreased access to care and poorer health outcomes (Feagin and Bennefield 2014). Studies have found structural disparities experienced by racial and ethnic minoritized groups such as limited access to care, lack of insurance coverage, and experiences of implicit bias when engaging in care (Alegría et al. 2007). As such, it is probable that all of these disadvantages and stressors serve to increase risk for psychosis while complicating and delaying pathways to care.

Ku et al. (2020) examined the relationship between neighborhood-level characteristics and age at onset of psychosis and DUP. The study included 143 participants between the ages of 18 and 30 diagnosed with a schizophrenia spectrum disorder; 86% of the sample was African American. In addition to collecting individual-level data, they characterized the neighborhood using census tract-level data. Of the neighborhood-level factors they examined, they found that neighborhood-level residential instability was associated with earlier age of onset of psychosis even when controlling for individual-level residential instability. They also found that perceived neighborhood disorder, measured by the Neighborhood Disorder Scale, was associated with longer DUP. The Neighborhood Disorder Scale asks individuals to rate 15 statements related to how much they perceive the presence of several neighborhood qualities such as drugs, crime, noise, graffiti, etc. This study potentially points to the increased distress that individuals living in these communities might experience and how this impacts their ability to access supports and mental health care.

Studies conducted in Latinx communities consistently support the notion that social determinants of mental health impact recognition and help-seeking in racial and ethnic minoritized communities. There is evidence that poor Latinx groups, for instance, tend to access specialized mental health services at a disproportionately lower rate than non-Latinx White individuals, possibly due to language fluency, a cultural value placed on access to affordable services in their neighborhoods, differences in recognition of mental health problems, and lower quality of mental health care (Alegría et al. 2007). López and colleagues (2018) studied psychosis literacy among Latinos, primarily of Mexican origin, with FEP and their caregivers and found that young people with FEP had generally low psychosis literacy. Their caregivers had significantly better levels of literacy but still demonstrated significant gaps in knowledge which likely directly impacts help-seeking. A qualitative analysis of a sub-sample of this cohort indicated that stronger family relationships characterized by open communication and disclosure of symptoms that facilitated awareness and direct action by family caregivers were associated with shorter DUP (Hernandez et al. 2019). When considering DUP, it therefore becomes important to contextualize the pathway to care and to take into account the unique barriers and facilitators present across communities. Although national studies provide information on aggregate-level delays, they do not provide a detailed perspective on the unique issues that BIPOC communities face and specific cultural and neighborhood-level factors that need to be considered and targeted to reduce DUP.

Strategies for Reducing DUP

Internationally, efforts have been made to reduce DUP using a variety of strategies. The Treatment Intervention in Psychosis Study (TIPS) conducted in Norway demonstrated that a multipronged public information campaign focused on building community awareness and providing clear instructions on how to access specialized services was able to reduce DUP by 50% in a large sector of the community (Friis et al. 2005). Lloyd-Evans et al. (2011) evaluated 11 DUP intervention studies to determine strategies for effective reduction of DUP. They included eight interventions which targeted increasing early detection of psychosis and connecting people to treatment. Three of the interventions included education campaigns for general practitioners to identify early signs of psychosis and encourage timely referral to care; the remaining initiatives involved a multi-intervention approach. These multi-element interventions included large-scale public service announcements across various media outlets, outreach to schools, face-to-face and written contact with general practitioners and other health care providers, and a telephone line for the public to call for advice. They concluded that the most effective way of reducing DUP consisted of taking a multi-focused approach which targeted multiple audiences through diverse modes of communication.

In the United States, several studies have focused on identifying strategies to shorten DUP by improving early detection and referral pathways. Srihari and colleagues (2020) used a quasi-experimental design to examine the impact of a 4-year early detection (ED) campaign (Mindmap), adapted from the Scandinavian TIPS approach, across ten towns in Connecticut. They used mass and social media messaging, professional detailing, and rapid triage of referrals and measured DUP as the time between the onset of psychosis and initiation of antipsychotic treatment and CSC. The comparison DUP group was derived from a CSC program in Boston during the same time period as the campaign. Results indicated a reduction in DUP at specific timepoints, measured in quartiles. For example, a time-series analysis revealed a cumulative effect of the campaign over time, i.e., for each year of campaigning, a 46-day reduction was achieved for connecting with their CSC program (Srihari et al. 2020). However, there are limitations to these findings since the overall differences between groups were not significant.

Other projects have focused on testing a variety of strategies for different populations. For instance, Kane and Birnbaum (2017) developed Internet-based strategies to reach young people through social media and concluded that young people with psychosis use the Internet and social media platforms such as Facebook frequently throughout the day and indicated that they would be okay with proactive outreach via the Internet as symptoms emerged. Additionally, the researchers found that their algorithm was able to accurately differentiate between psychotic disorder, mood disorders, and healthy controls 67% of the time (Kane and Birnbaum 2017). New York City has taken a public health approach and now requires all individuals hospitalized with first-episode psychosis to be identified and reported; the city also offers a critical time intervention model staffed by a peer and a professional, called NYC START, aimed at enhancing optimal follow-up care and facilitating connection with appropriate services 3 months post-discharge from an inpatient unit.

A significant limitation of current attempts to reduce DUP is that, for the most part, they lack attention to how social determinants of mental health limit access to care in BIPOC neighborhoods. Employing generalized population-level strategies for reducing DUP may prove insufficient, as these population-level strategies do not address the differential limitations that some communities experience when accessing health care and fail to account for the lack of capacity of current CSC programs to meet the population-based need for CSC services. A public health campaign that raises awareness about psychosis without considering and changing neighborhood-level deprivation, discrimination, and inequities that delay pathways to care will likely have limited effectiveness for a heterogenous group. Furthermore, if there is limited availability of CSC programs in a given area, then increasing awareness without providing adequate services could compound frustrations and mistrust toward the mental health system. More research is needed to understand whether engaging communities using individualized messages and strategies that have cultural resonance and that work to address disparities can more effectively reduce DUP in BIPOC communities. Overall, more work is needed to develop approaches to shorten DUP, to clarify the relationship between DUP and outcomes across various groups, and to consider the actual resources available to provide treatment. It is important that young people be connected to evidence-based treatment services as quickly as possible after developing psychotic symptoms to increase the probability of recovery and building a meaningful life; a more individualized, culturally informed approach might be more effective for achieving this goal.

Evidence for the Early Treatment for Early Psychosis

Early intervention services (EIS) for FEP have been supported by a combination of international research studies and implementation efforts carried out during the past 20 years. EIS have been broadly implemented in Australia, the United Kingdom, Scandinavia, and Canada (Heinssen et al. 2014). Studies have focused on specific treatment components (i.e., single-element studies), as well as multi-element team-based approaches. Multi-element services that combine each of the single elements (e.g., medications, supported employment and education services, cognitive behavioral therapy for psychosis, family therapy) have consistently demonstrated better short-term outcomes (Dixon et al. 2015; Craig et al. 2004; Petersen et al. 2008; Srihari et al. 2015). The most recent studies conducted in the United States have led to the creation of the label, "coordinated specialty care" (CSC) to represent these team-based approaches which encompass a package of evidence-based treatment modalities. We will review the literature that has established the evidence base for EIS services, focusing on describing foundational studies.

A study conducted in Denmark was the first randomized control trial (RCT) of multi-element care for early psychosis (Petersen et al. 2008). It recruited 547 individuals ages 18–45 with psychosis who had no more than 12 weeks of exposure to antipsychotic medications and randomly assigned them to either multi-element care (named OPUS) or treatment as usual (TAU). Individuals randomized to OPUS received services for 2 years based on the assertive community treatment model, which included individualized case management; family groups; low-dose antipsychotic medications and, when indicated, cognitive behavioral therapy (CBT); and social skills training. OPUS clinicians preferred to see individuals at their homes, and the client to staff ratio was 10:1. In contrast, individuals in the TAU group had monthly meetings with a psychiatric nurse in a community mental health center, consultations with a social worker, and medication when indicated. Home visits were infrequent, and participants consulted psychiatric emergency departments for care after office hours. In this group, the client to staff ratio was 25:1. OPUS participants had lower levels of positive and negative symptoms of psychosis, reductions in substance use, and increased engagement in, and satisfaction with, treatment compared to individuals in the control group (Petersen et al. 2008).

In the United Kingdom, the Lambeth Early Onset (LEO) study was the second RCT to test the impact of multi-element care for early psychosis. It included 144 individuals living in London, ages between 16 and 40, diagnosed with non-affective psychosis who had sought mental health services less than two times prior to study enrollment (Craig et al. 2004). Individuals randomized to multi-element care received atypical antipsychotic medications at low doses, CBT, family therapy, and vocational services for 18 months. Individuals randomized to standard care were treated by teams untrained in specialized services for early psychosis at a local community mental health center in the Lambeth section of London. Individuals who received the specialized intervention had fewer hospital readmissions, better medication adherence, and better occupational functioning and quality of life compared to those in standard care and were more likely to stay in the study (Craig et al. 2004).

The largest multi-element study to date was conducted across ten clinical sites in China by Guo et al. (2010). The study enrolled 1268 individuals aged 16–50 with an onset of psychosis within 5 years. Participants were randomly assigned to the control condition which focused on antipsychotic medication management or specialized treatment which included monthly visits consisting of medication management coupled with 4 straight hours of psychosocial groups, which covered individual and family psychoeducation and support, skills training, and CBT for 12 months. In total, 406 individuals received the multi-element intervention and 338 individuals received medication alone. After 1 year, individuals who received the psychosocial interventions had significantly greater improvement in insight, social functioning, obtaining employment or education, activities of daily living, and quality of life in addition to lower rates of "clinical relapse," which was defined by worsening symptoms, hospitalization, need for increased level of psychiatric treatment, self-harming behaviors, or violent behaviors (Guo et al. 2010).

In the United States, Srihari et al. (2015) compared their comprehensive early psychosis program (STEP) in Connecticut, which included antipsychotic medications, CBT, family education, and case management to help individuals access education and employment supports. Treatment received in the TAU condition varied because it was determined by the participant's current provider or by an outside treatment provider to whom they were referred. The sample included 120 individuals who had an onset of psychosis of less than 5 years before entry into the study and fewer than 12 weeks of exposure to antipsychotic medications. After 1 year of treatment, STEP participants had fewer total hospital admissions, fewer hospital days, and a greater likelihood of being employed or in school (Srihari et al. 2015).

Additionally, the National Institute of Mental Health (NIMH) funded the Recovery After an Initial Schizophrenia Episode (RAISE) initiative. Launched in 2008, RAISE aimed to develop and test a treatment model to reduce relapse and long-term disability for individuals experiencing early schizophrenia. NIMH required that the model be ready for rapid deployment if found effective (Heinssen et al. 2014; Bello et al. 2017). Two RAISE studies, the RAISE Early Treatment Program (ETP) and the RAISE-IES, laid the groundwork for larger-scale implementation of CSC programs (Dixon et al. 2015; Kane et al. 2015). The RAISE ETP study, a cluster-randomized control trial, enrolled 404 individuals who were between 15 and 40 years of age, diagnosed with non-affective psychosis, who had only experienced one episode of psychosis and were treated with antipsychotic medications for less than 6 months. The study was conducted across the United States in 34 clinics, half of which were randomized to the NAVIGATE condition and the other half to TAU. The NAVIGATE multi-element treatment was comprised of evidence-based prescribing of antipsychotic medications, family psychoeducation, and supported employment and education services. The individual therapy component entitled Individual Resiliency Training consisted of CBT-based strategies for symptom management, skills training, and substance abuse treatment utilizing shared decision-making with a focus on promoting individual resilience, recovery, and goal attainment. TAU included available community services as determined by clinicians within community clinics. Individuals receiving NAVIGATE remained in treatment longer, had more improvement on quality of life measures, were more likely to have a job or be in school, and experienced greater symptom reduction compared to participants in the TAU clinics after 2 years of treatment (Kane et al. 2015).

The RAISE-IES study (Dixon et al. 2015) focused on developing training materials for rapid deployment and implementation of CSC. The study recruited 65 participants at two sites, in Baltimore and New York City. Participants received multi-element treatment for up to 2 years which consisted of evidence-based pharmacology, case management, supported employment and education, family support and education, and a flexible CBT-based psychotherapy approach which offered psychoeducation, social skills training, substance use treatment, and an emphasis on reducing suicide risk. The model was delivered using the principles of cultural competency, shared decision-making, and with an emphasis on individualized recovery trajectories which were guided by a person's strengths and goals. Results indicated high retention rates in the program; 91% of individuals stayed in services for as long as they were offered. Study participants also demonstrated improved social and occupational functioning, decreased symptoms, decreased rates of hospitalization, and increased rates of remission. Furthermore, they found significant increased participation in competitive employment and degree granting educational programs (Dixon et al. 2015). The materials developed by the RAISE-IES study were later adapted to the OnTrackNY model. OnTrackNY and NAVIGATE are two of the leading models used in the United States to train specialized teams on the implementation of CSC.

Evidence-Based Treatment for Early Psychosis

In the United States, coordinated specialty care (CSC) became the umbrella term to describe multi-element approaches for delivering evidence-based early intervention treatment for young adults experiencing early psychosis. As described in the literature review above, the multi-disciplinary CSC team approach encompasses a suite of evidence-based practices that have been shown to reduce relapse and improve outcomes for individuals experiencing schizophrenia spectrum disorders. The services are recovery-oriented and emphasize shared decision-making, assertive outreach and engagement, and cultural competency in an effort to effectively engage young people and their supports. Furthermore, CSC is offered utilizing a person-centered, collaborative, and youth-oriented framework, to help people achieve meaningful goals and reduce disability. The CSC team strives to convey hope for recovery and views the person diagnosed with early psychosis as the central member of the team's efforts. Individuals' life goals, aspirations, and ambitions drive treatment planning; therefore, none of the treatment components are mandatory. In general, CSC teams have low client to staff ratios typically in the range of 10:1 (Heinssen et al. 2014).

Evidence-based treatments provided by CSC programs include (1) evidence-based psychopharmacology which emphasizes prescribing the lowest effective dose of antipsychotic medications with the fewest side effects; (2) health, wellness, and primary care coordination meant to address cardiometabolic factors associated with antipsychotic medications by providing education on nutrition and exercise, assessing health with routine lab work, and coordinating with other medical professionals; (3) case management aimed at helping individuals and families meet concrete needs and connect to outside resources; (4) psychotherapy that is generally supportive, focused on engagement, collaboration, and enhancing resiliency coupled with cognitive behavioral treatments to target symptoms of psychosis and related comorbidities; (5) family support and education consistent with individual and family preferences, to promote family involvement across all treatment components and address family needs; (6) supported education and employment using the individual placement and support model to assess work and school interest, facilitate rapid placement, and provide supports as needed; and (7) peer support services which are also included in some programs to help enhance engagement, peer connections, and promote self-advocacy (Heinssen et al. 2014).

These services are provided in a flexible, developmentally sensitive way for an average of 2 years – although sometimes much longer. Within the CSC model, participants are not required to engage in any of the interventions in order to maintain enrollment, although everyone is connected to a primary provider who serves as the point person for the participant and family member. It is the participant's and family's ability to engage with the team in a flexible way that allows the interventions to be tailored specifically to each individual and his/her set of circumstances to promote achievement of school, work, and relationship goals. Similarly, families have access to the team of providers and receive individualized services to help them navigate this precarious time and support the young person in their recovery journey.

At the outset of treatment, teams focus on forging highly collaborative and engaging alliances with participants and family members through the use of specific assertive outreach and engagement strategies (Bennett and Bellack 2017). For instance, successful teams are able to remain proactive in connecting with participants and family members throughout all phases of treatment, and this might include the use of various forms of communication (phone, texting, email, and in-person meetings). The time and location of sessions are flexible and responsive to the needs and preferences of the participants and family members (e.g., in the home, community, or clinic with increased or decreased frequency, as needed). Considerations of transportation, work schedules, and other caregiving are critical, as well. Especially in areas that are geographically spread out where public transportation may not be readily available, the flexibility of team members to be creative in communication and scheduling is critical to developing a solid working alliance. Teams typically have the flexibility to keep the participant's file open in the program for longer periods of time than in traditional clinical settings, even when there is little contact with the participant.

Teams are also able to provide important information for participants to consider all relevant treatment choices rather than dictating treatment recommendations and, therefore, ensure that treatment decisions are guided by pressing concerns expressed by participants and family members – not the priorities of the team. Providers maintain a flexible and consistent stance toward treatment, which allows them to respond sensitively and practically to the range of situations that might arise on an as-needed basis. At the same time, they focus on demonstrating to the participant and family members that the team will remain a consistent presence by behaving in a reliable manner and offering support, empathy, and trustworthiness (Bennett and Bellack 2017). This therapeutic alliance usually serves to ensure treatment engagement remains across time and serves as the foundation for introducing and delivering the pharmacological, psychosocial, and other treatments offered.

National Expansion of Coordinated Specialty Care

The creation and dissemination of CSC programs across the United States and the contribution of the RAISE projects can be understood as the intersection of trends in both science and policy that converged to create the foundation for changes in care and care delivery (Dixon 2017a, 2017b). In 2014, House of Representatives Bill 3547 provided an increase of 5% to the Community Mental Health Block Grant program, an allocation targeted at evidence-based programs for individuals experiencing early psychosis. The funds were maintained in 2015 and doubled in 2016. This funding allowed for the widespread national implementation of CSC programs (Heinssen et al. 2014; Bello et al. 2017). At this point, every state has at least one CSC program. However, many challenges remain. First, there is no standard CSC program and no well-validated measure of fidelity, although some researchers are developing this process (Addington et al. 2016). This complicates the ability to train the workforce and the financial sustainability of CSC continues to be a challenge (Dixon 2017a). Furthermore, the fragmented US health-care system has contributed to a variety of experiences regarding how to implement CSC programs across diverse contexts.

As the implementation of CSC programs has been expanding throughout the United States, the differences across implementation efforts have become more evident. Decisions regarding specific implementation practices appear to be influenced by population density and incidence of FEP, community-based needs, available workforce, involvement of state-level leadership and coordination efforts, and financial circumstances. Even though clinical trials have demonstrated the effectiveness of CSC treatment for individuals aged 15–25 diagnosed with non-organic, non-affective, non-substance-induced psychotic disorders, who have started experiencing symptoms within 5 years of receiving care, some programs try to reach a broader sector of the population. Some programs have decided to expand the age range and others to focus on any transition aged youth demonstrating high levels of service use, and others have broadened the diagnostic criteria for program inclusion. One important permutation is the expansion of the eligibility criteria to include individuals experiencing affective psychosis, as a way of addressing the real-world needs of participants in certain communities and enhance the sustainability of the programs. It is yet to be determined whether these adaptations and permutations will preserve the effectiveness of CSC models. However, it is evident that there needs to be a balance between maintaining fidelity to the key elements of the model and being able to deploy a program that is responsive to the needs of the population in a given community.

There needs to be further consideration of community-level factors that impact the ways in which individuals and families relate to and utilize CSC programs. One way to do this might be to systematically include the conceptualization of the impact of social determinants of mental health into the fabric of the CSC interventions. CSC models need to go beyond delivering culturally competent care. They should explicitly incorporate a focus on social justice that encompasses an anti-racist framework. This is fundamental to being able to really alter the short- and long-term outcomes of young people diagnosed with psychosis across communities. At this time, there is limited guidance within these models on how to conceptualize the impacts of population-level economic and social conditions that negatively impact people's behaviors.

OnTrackNY developed a guide for delivering culturally competent care to individuals with early psychosis (Lewis-Fernandez et al. 2018). This guide describes key concepts and principles, best practices, and case examples to help individuals with FEP; their supports and providers work together to implement culturally competent early intervention services. Specifically, it guides teams on how to think about and work with areas such as religion and spirituality, family culture, language barriers, gender and sexuality, youth culture, and the team's own culture. At the individual level, these are important things to consider and incorporate particularly if they are salient to the individual and family. However, teams also need to be able to consider the impacts of the broader systemic, structural racism associated with significant disparities in most aspects of life in the US for BIPOC individuals. Individuals cannot be separated from their skin color, backgrounds, or the systemic oppression that these characteristics guarantee in society. CSC providers would benefit from training on a model that includes a specific understanding of the effects of discrimination, social exclusion, and neighborhood-level disadvantage that their BIPOC participants experience. Furthermore, training on delivering evidence-based interventions that are adapted to include and respond to the effects of discrimination, stigma, and community-level disenfranchisement would benefit young people and their families and likely have long-standing effects. Failure to address these barriers in treatment limits the team's ability to truly understand, connect, and help the individuals they serve. For example, understanding that certain communities have been harmed by mental health systems and acknowledging the well-founded level of mistrust that participants and families might have toward the team from the outset could help build a more genuine, stronger relationship. Recognizing that some BIPOC participants live in communities where their friends in families experience police brutality, are disproportionally incarcerated, and face food insecurity could help shape where providers focus their interventions and modify the way they work with participant and family members, as well as communities.

It is insufficient to deliver a high-fidelity CSC intervention that does not acknowledge and address the disparities that people face in their daily lives and lack of resources they and their families have for meeting basic needs due to their race or ethnic background. The flexibility and time afforded within the CSC model provide a unique opportunity to deliver care that is able to meet unique individual needs while at the same time work toward dismantling racism. As a field, we have achieved a great deal in a relatively short amount of time by continuing to study and develop strategies for reducing DUP and providing evidence-based CSC treatments to young people as quickly as possible. More work remains to be done to make these programs responsive to the specific needs faced across communities and understand how these programs could be shaped to provide improved long-term outcomes and even have an impact on changing policies to create systemic change.

References

Addington J., Heinssen R. K., Robinson D. G., Schooler N. R., & Marcy P. et al. (2015). Duration of untreated psychosis in community treatment settings in the United States. *Psychiatric services, 66*(7), 753–56. https://doi.org/10.1176/appi.ps.201400124

Addington D. E., Norman R., Bond G. R., Sale T., Melton R., et al. (2016). Development and testing of the First-Episode Psychosis Services Fidelity Scale. *Psychiatric Services, 67*(9), 1023–25. https://doi-org.ezproxy.cul.columbia.edu/10.1176/appi.ps.201500398

Alegría, M., Mulvaney-Day, N., Woo, M., Torres, M., Gao, S., & Oddo, V. (2007). Correlates of past-year mental health service use among Latinos: results from the National Latino and Asian American Study. *American journal of public health, 97*(1), 76–83. https://doi.org/10.2105/AJPH.2006.087197

Anglin D. M., Lui F., Schneider M., Ellman L. M. (2020). Changes in perceived neighborhood ethnic density among racial and ethnic minorities over time and psychotic-like experiences. *Schizophrenia research, 216*, 330–8. https://doi.org/10.1016/j.schres.2019.11.034

Bello I., Lee R., Malinovsky I., Watkins L., Nossel I., et al. (2017). OnTrackNY: the development of a coordinated specialty care program for individuals experiencing early psychosis. *Psychiatric services, 68*(4), 318–20. https://doi.org/10.1176/appi.ps.201600512

Bennett, M. E., & Bellack, A. S. (2017). OnTrackNY: Recovery coach manual. Retrieved from http://www.ontrackny.org/portals/1/Files/Resources/RecoveryCoach_2015.01.21.pdf

Bourque, F., van der Ven, E., Malla A. (2011). A meta-analysis of the risk for psychotic disorders among first- and second-generation immigrants. *Psychological medicine, 41*(5), 897–910. https://doi.org/10.1017/S0033291710001406

Cabassa, L. J., Piscitelli, S., Haselden, M., Lee, R. J., Essock, S. M., & Dixon, L. B. (2018). Understanding Pathways to Care of Individuals Entering a Specialized Early Intervention Service for First-Episode Psychosis. *Psychiatric services, 69*(6), 648-656. https://doi.org/10.1176/appi.ps.201700018

Cloutier M., Aigbogun, M. S., Guerin, A., Nitulescu, R., Ramanakumar, A. V., et al. (2013). The economic burden of schizophrenia in the United States in 2013.

Journal of clinical psychiatry 77(6):764–71. https://doi.org/10.4088/JCP.15m10278

Compton, Michael T, M.D., M.P.H., & Shim, Ruth, M.D., M.P.H. (2014). This issue: The Social Determinants of Mental Health. *Psychiatric annals, 44*(1), 17–20. https://doi.org/10.3928/00485713-20140108-03

Craig, T.K., Garety, P,. Power, P., Rahaman, N., Colbert, S., et al. (2004). The Lambeth Early Onset (LEO) team: randomised controlled trial of the effectiveness of specialised care for early psychosis. *BMJ, 329*, 1067–72. https://doi.org/10.1136/bmj.38246.594873.7C

Dixon, L. (2017a). What it will take to make coordinated specialty care available to anyone experiencing early schizophrenia: getting over the hump. *JAMA psychiatry, 74*(1), 7–8. https://doi.org/10.1001/jamapsychiatry.2016.2665

Dixon, L. (2017b). Coordinated specialty care for first-episode psychosis: an example of financing for specialty programs. Philadelphia: Scattergood Found. http://www.scattergoodfoundation.org/sites/default/files/%20Coordinated_Specialty_Care_for_First-Episode_Psychosis.pdf.

Dixon, L. B., Goldman, H. H, Bennett, M. E, et al. (2015). Implementing coordinated specialty care for early psychosis: The RAISE connection program. *Psychiatric services, 66(7*), 691-698. https://doi.org/10.1176/appi.ps.201400281

Dixon, L. B., Goldman, H. H, Srihari, V., & Kane, J. (2018). Transforming the treatment of schizophrenia in the United States: the RAISE initiative. *Annual review of clinical psychology, 14,* 237-258. https://doi.org/10.1146/annurev-clinpsy-050817-084934

Feagin, J., & Bennefield, Z. (2014). Systemic racism and U.S. health care. *Soc sci med., 103*, 7–14. https://doi.org/10.1016/j.socscimed.2013.09.006

Friis, S., Vaglum, P., Haahr, U., Johannessen, J. O., Larsen, T. K, et al. (2005). Effect of an early detection programme on duration of untreated psychosis: part of the Scandinavian TIPS study. *British journal of psychiatry 48*(Suppl.), S29–32. https://doi.org/10.1192/bjp.187.48.s29

Guo, X., Zhai, J., Liu, Z., et al. (2010). Effect of antipsychotic medication alone vs combined with psychosocial intervention on outcomes of early-stage schizophrenia: a randomized, 1-year study. *Arch general psychiatry, 67*(9), 895-904. https://doi.org/10.1001/archgenpsychiatry.2010.105

Heinssen, R. K., Goldstein, A. B., & Azrin, S. T. (2014). Evidence-based treatment for first-episode psychosis: Components of coordinated specialty care. Available at http://www.nimh.nih.gov/health/topics/schizophrenia/raise/coordinated-specialty-care-for-first-episode-psychosis-resources.shtml.

Hernandez, M., Hernandez, M. Y., Lopez, D., Barrio, C., Gamez, D., & López, S. R. (2019). Family processes and duration of untreated psychosis among US Latinos. *Early intervention in psychiatry, 13*(6), 389–1395. https://doi.org/10.1111/eip.12779

Howes, O. D., Whitehurst, T., Shatalina, E., Townsend, L., Onwordi, E.C., Mak, T.L.A., Arumuham, A., O'Brien, O., Lobo, M., Vano, L., Zahid, U., Butler, E. and Osugo, M. (2021), The clinical significance of duration of untreated psychosis: an umbrella review and random-effects meta-analysis. *World psychiatry, 20*, 75-95. https://doi.org/10.1002/wps.20822

Jonas, K. G., Fochtmann, L. J., Perlman, G., Tian, Y., Kane, J. M., Bromet, E. J., & Kotov, R. (2020). Lead-Time Bias Confounds Association Between Duration of Untreated Psychosis and Illness Course in Schizophrenia. *The American journal of psychiatry, 177*(4), 327–334. https://doi.org/10.1176/appi.ajp.2019.19030324

Kane, J. M., Robinson, D. G., Schooler, N. R., et al. (2015). Comprehensive versus usual community care for first-episode psychosis: 2-year outcomes from the NIMH RAISE early treatment program. *American journal of psychiatry, 173*(4), 362-372. https://doi.org/10.1176/appi.ajp.2015.15050632.

Kane, J., & Birnbaum, M. (2017). 178.2 Developing Strategies to Reduce DUP in the Age of Social Media and the Internet. *Schizophrenia bulletin, 43*(Suppl 1), S94–S95. https://doi.org/10.1093/schbul/sbx021.254

Kessler, R. C., Demler, O., Frank, R. G., Olfson, M., Pincus, H. A., Walters, E. E., Wang, P., Wells, K. B., & Zaslavsky, A. M. (2005). Prevalence and treatment of mental disorders, 1990 to 2003. *The New England journal of medicine, 352*(24), 2515–2523. https://doi.org/10.1056/NEJMsa043266

Ku, B. S., Pauselli, L., Manseau, M., & Compton, M. T. (2020). Neighborhood-level predictors of age at onset and duration of untreated psychosis in first-episode psychotic disorders. *Schizophrenia research, 218,* 247–254. https://doi.org/10.1016/j.schres.2019.12.036

Lewis-Fernandez, R., Jiménez-Solomon, O., Diaz, S., Bello, I., Malinovsky, I. et al., (2018). OnTrackNY: Delivering Competent Care in FEP. Retrieved from https://ontrackny.org/Portals/1/Files/Resources/OnTrackNY%20Cultural%20Competency%20Guide_%20Final%205.29.18.pdf?ver=2018-06-07-11044

Lieberman J. A., Dixon L. B., Goldman H. H. (2013). Early detection and intervention in schizophrenia: a new therapeutic model. *JAMA, 310*(7), 689–90. https://doi.org/10.1001/jama.2013.8804

Lloyd-Evans, B., Crosby, M., Stockton, S., Pilling, S., Hobbs, L., Hinton, M., & Johnson, S. (2011). Initiatives to shorten duration of untreated psychosis: systematic review. *The British journal of psychiatry: the journal of mental science, 198*(4), 256–263. https://doi.org/10.1192/bjp.bp.109.075622

López, S. R., Gamez, D., Mejia, Y., Calderon, V., Lopez, D., Ullman, J. B., & Kopelowicz, A. (2018). Psychosis Literacy Among Latinos With First-Episode Psychosis and Their Caregivers. *Psychiatric services, 69*(11), 1153–1159. https://doi.org/10.1176/appi.ps.201700400

Marshall, M., Lewis, S., Lockwood, A., Drake, R., Jones, P., & Croudace, T. (2005). Association between duration of untreated psychosis and outcome in cohorts of first-episode patients: a systematic review. *Archives of general psychiatry, 62*(9), 975–983. https://doi.org/10.1001/archpsyc.62.9.975

Narita, Z., Knowles, K., Fedina, L., Oh, H., Stickley, A., Kelleher, I., & DeVylder, J. (2020). Neighborhood change and psychotic experiences in a general population sample. *Schizophrenia research, 216*, 316–321. https://doi.org/10.1016/j.schres.2019.11.036

Petersen, L., Thorup, A., Øqhlenschlaeger, J., Christensen, T. Ø., Jeppesen, P., Krarup, G., Jørrgensen, P., Mortensen, E. L., & Nordentoft, M. (2008). Predictors of remission and recovery in a first-episode schizophrenia spectrum disorder sample: 2-year follow-up of the OPUS trial. *Canadian journal of psychiatry. Revue canadienne de psychiatrie, 53*(10), 660–670. https://doi.org/10.1177/070674370805301005

Rosenberg, S. D., Lu, W., Mueser, K. T., Jankowski, M. K., & Cournos, F. (2007). Correlates of adverse childhood events among adults with schizophrenia spectrum disorders. *Psychiatric services, 58*(2), 245–253. https://doi.org/10.1176/ps.2007.58.2.245

Schwartz, R. C., & Blankenship, D. M. (2014). Racial disparities in psychotic disorder diagnosis: A review of empirical literature. *World J Psychiatry, 4*(4),133–140. https://doi.org/10.5498/wjp.v4.i4.133. PMID: 25540728. PMCID: PMC4274585.

Srihari, V. H., Tek, C., Kucukgoncu, S., Phutane, V. H., Breitborde, N. J., Pollard, J., Ozkan, B., Saksa, J., Walsh, B. C., & Woods, S. W. (2015). First-Episode Services for Psychotic Disorders in the U.S. Public Sector: A Pragmatic Randomized Controlled Trial. *Psychiatric services, 66*(7), 705–712. https://doi.org/10.1176/appi.ps.201400236

Srihari, V. H., Ferrara, M., Li, F., Kline, E., Gülöksüz, S., Pollard, K. M., Cahill, J. D., Mathis, W. S., Sykes, L. Y., Walsh, B. C., McDermott, G., Seidman, L. J., Gueorguieva, R., Woods, S. W., Tek, C., Keshavan, M. S. (2022). Reducing the Duration of Untreated Psychosis (DUP) in a US Community: A quasi-experimental trial. *Schizophrenia Bulletin Open, 3*(1), sgab057. https://doi.org/10.1093/schizbullopen/sgab057

Woods, S. W., Yung, A. R., McGorry, P. D., & McGlashan, T. H. (2020). Duration of Untreated Psychosis: Getting Both the Timing and the Sample Right. The American journal of psychiatry, 177(12), 1183. https://doi.org/10.1176/appi.ajp.2020.20040389

Cognitive Behavior Therapy for Psychosis

David Kingdon and Douglas Turkington

Psychological approaches to psychosis have a long history, but it is only in the past couple of decades that experimental studies have shown that specific ways of working can be effective. However, there has always been, and to some extent remains, a degree of skepticism about how such approaches can effectively reduce distress from hallucinations or improve insight into delusions. By their very nature, delusions have traditionally been viewed as not being amenable to reason, and so reasoning approaches seem inherently doomed to failure. There is also a more general perspective that psychosis has been shown to be associated with biological changes, and therefore the implication can be drawn that biological methods are needed to rectify these problems.

Perhaps the latter issue is the most straightforward to address. A disorder which has demonstrable biological origins, such as stroke, can still benefit from psychosocial methods in adaptation, motivation, and rehabilitation. In this instance, treatment of associated depression and use of occupational and physiotherapies may play the major part in moving the individual toward recovery. Jaspers (1997) postulated that delusions were non-amenable to reason; this may be the case on an initial assessment, but this may not be a permanent state; and more refined and newly developed methods of reasoning may benefit the individual – just as medication can have beneficial effects. Again, it may well be that the person can also benefit, in the short- and particularly the long term, from being able to manage and live with delusions or hallucinations and their consequences or implications. It may still be possible to regain a more meaningful and less distressing and disabling existence.

D. Kingdon (✉)
Mental Health Care Delivery, University of Southampton, Southampton, UK
e-mail: dgk@soton.ac.uk

D. Turkington
Psychosocial Psychiatry, University of Newcastle, Newcastle upon Tyne, UK

Evidence

The most important is that there is now an abundance of evidence that cognitive behavior therapy for psychosis (CBTP) adds value to medication and in one specific, yet to be replicated, study has had beneficial effects when medication is refused (Morrison et al. 2014b). There has been debate about the studies involved, in particular when these have been meta-analyzed. The recent article by McKenna and colleagues (McKenna et al. 2019) clarifies the issues regarding outcomes and inclusion criteria, and its conclusion was unequivocal – that CBTP is effective against positive symptoms. Thus, for patients with such persistent symptoms, CBTP has a beneficial effect over and above medication and given the potential severity of the illness is now recommended by

W. E. Sowers et al. (eds.), *Textbook of Community Psychiatry*,
https://doi.org/10.1007/978-3-031-10239-4_44

international guidelines including those from the APA (Keepers et al. 2020), PORT (Kreyenbuhl et al. 2010), and NICE (NICE 2014) in the UK.

Most studies have used CBTP courses of 16–20 individual sessions with a dedicated trained therapist. There have also been successful studies which have been longer, for example, up to 50 sessions for patients with predominantly negative symptoms (Grant et al. 2012), and shorter, 6–10 where mental health staff have had training to supplement their clinical skills (Turkington et al. 2006). Brief targeted interventions have also been used: mindfulness groups for voices (Chadwick et al. 2016) and use of an intervention for paranoia targeted at worry (Freeman et al. 2015) are examples. They have also been employed by case management (Turkington et al. 2014) and early intervention teams (Morrison et al. 2012), and some of the techniques were included in the US RAISE study (Kane et al. 2016).

Psychosis is a term covering a very broad group of presentations and specific problems that can be challenging. Substance misuse is a common complication, and there has been limited investigation of its effect on the success of CBTP. The one major study of CBTP with motivational interviewing did not show a positive result (Barrowclough et al. 2010) although it recruited very well and seemed very acceptable to patients. Interestingly, an earlier pilot that incorporated family work as well as individual work did have benefits.

Moreover, it does seem that low levels of substance misuse are not incompatible with progress (Naeem et al. 2005). Childhood and later-life trauma is also frequently a major issue in psychosis. Trauma-focused CBTP, eye movement desensitization and reprocessing (EMDR), and prolonged exposure have been used successfully in these circumstances (van den Berg et al. 2015), and further studies are ongoing.

A brief needs assessment instrument (DIALOG) has been evaluated with community mental health teams. It systematically elicits individuals' satisfaction with various domains of experience in their lives and then uses a solution-focused approach (DIALOG+) to address those issues. It has also been shown to improve quality of life, is cost-effective, and has other benefits (Priebe et al. 2015). Similarly brief training in improving communication with people with psychosis using, in part, CBTP has been shown to improve the therapeutic relationship as experienced by the psychiatrists receiving the training and the individuals with whom they work (McCabe et al. 2016).

Finally, CBTP has been developed and seems most effective with broader service approaches, e.g., integrated with community, rehabilitation, and recovery approaches. It is potentially useful with the open dialogue (OD) model with its emphasis on the therapeutic relationship (currently OD is being evaluated in a randomized controlled trial).

CBTP in Practice

Cognitive behavior therapy for psychosis builds on general clinical skills (Wright et al. 2009; Kingdon and Turkington 2004) and the fundamentals of CBT. These primarily involve eliciting linkages between thoughts, feelings, and behavior (see chapter "Cognitive Behavioral Therapy"). A good mental health assessment helps clinicians understand how specific symptoms have developed and provides good background information that can lead to understanding of how and why specific beliefs or perceptions have arisen. The process of exploration and guided discovery is a key part of the approach. It helps to unravel issues which may have occurred many years ago but still affect current beliefs about the world and those around the individual. An understanding of paranoia, for example, is clarified when the history reveals events that have eroded trust and have seriously damaged a person's sense of security. Associated disparaging auditory hallucinations experienced by involved individuals begin to make sense. Negative symptoms can also become understandable as ways of avoiding uncomfortable situations which repeatedly cause distress and fear, resulting in demoralization or "self-defeating" beliefs (Beck et al. 2013).

Gathering information is essential to moving forward but it does need to make sense and be well formulated. Predisposing, precipitating, perpetuating, and protective factors can be linked to current and underlying concerns, physical issues, and the cognitive triad – thoughts, emotions, and behaviors. Diagrams can be helpful where the interactions are complex and can clarify connections. However verbal summarization of specific mutual conclusions may be an alternative. This process can lessen the confusion about which area to focus on and the therapeutic plan to be developed. Usually, the specific concerns that the individual has will need to be addressed as priority. For example, voices may be causing considerable distress and interfering with daily living, or there may be social issues which interfere with progress.

Although studies have tended to focus on individual work, there have been a small number which have included families and shown very clearly that this can enhance recovery. Even small numbers of joint (or, if necessary, separate) sessions can allow collaborative development and sharing of the formulation and development of individual coping strategies. Group work on specific topics, e.g., understanding voices or paranoia or improving motivation can be useful, but the nature of psychotic symptoms is such that some individual work always seems to be necessary.

Therapy develops through engagement which is a continuing process and will occur alongside assessment, formulation, and symptom work.

Engagement

Engagement is key to any therapeutic interaction although it has often been thought to be challenging with people with psychosis. Frequently the problem is that the person will say that they have not felt that their concerns are understood or taken seriously. Therefore, simply listening, using a normalizing perspective, and addressing issues related to the voices or delusions in a direct and open way can lead to excellent engagement. If the person feels their paranoia is being investigated and their safety taken seriously, they're much more likely to work well with a mental health practitioner. It may well be that, after assessment, the beliefs that they have are not supported by evidence but attempting to understand why they feel the way they do can enhance the therapeutic relationship – and often there is some logic in the beliefs themselves. It becomes possible to understand why they believe what they do.

In some circumstances, symptoms may be minimized by other professionals. Voices may be described as "pseudo-hallucinations," not "real voices" or "just thoughts or dissociation". This is particularly common when there is comorbid borderline personality disorder (Kingdon et al. 2010). However, these experiences – voices as perceived by the individual – can be very distressing and insight variable. Working with these individuals can reduce that distress and helping them to cope can be very engaging. Normalizing symptoms in a way which helps them become understandable is helpful. For example, discussing how voices can occur with sleep deprivation, trauma, or bereavement can help the person to recognize that the approach being taken is one which is accepting and non-judgmental.

Engagement is a continuous process which may fluctuate and needs monitoring. Difficult periods can develop when discussing traumatic events or when the therapist is challenged by the individual (e.g., whether the therapist believes what the person is telling them). It is sometimes necessary to "agree to differ," which is a tactic that can work very well in defusing tension and allowing a refocusing on the impacts of beliefs. It doesn't involve collusion or confrontation and respects the individual's perspective while not endorsing it.

Working with Voices

It is very important to get a good understanding of how voices are affecting the individual, considering frequency, volume, pattern, level, and amount of distressing content as well as their beliefs about the experiences. Psychosis rating scales (Beck et al. 2013) provide a useful and systematic way of assessing these processes. It is very important to gain an understanding of who the patient thinks is speaking, whether they are identifiable, and what are they saying. Sometimes what is being said is so unpleasant and personal that the individual finds it very difficult to convey. In those circumstances it can be sufficient and advisable to simply suggest that it may be too unpleasant to disclose this material, but nevertheless, meaningful work on the associated effects – and beliefs – can be done. Voices can sometimes be positive rather than negative and can be quite supportive. It is their negative effects that usually need addressing.

It may be helpful to characterize what the person is experiencing and assuring them that you understand and care about their concerns. Questions that help characterize the experience such as: "Is it just like me speaking to you now, or perhaps louder?" or "Why can't the originator of the speech be seen?" may accomplish this. There may be different explanations for them which need to be explored: it may be that the sounds heard are coming through the walls from neighbors or are from God or the devil or other supernatural sources. Sometimes there may be a technological reason that speech is projected to the individual only. Securing these explanations is very important if they exist. However, the individual is often uncertain about the origin of the voices. Sometimes it is worth appraising why the individual thinks that other people, including the practitioner, can't hear their voices. It may be the case that the individual has doubts about their explanation and it can be worth testing in session. Asking them to let the practitioner know when they're hearing voices can allow assessment of what is happening at the time. Sometimes there may be an explanation in terms of distortion of sounds that they're hearing. Sometimes suggesting that attempting to record experiences of voices on a phone or other voice recorder can allow identification of misinterpretations, e.g., of noises from machinery, or confirm recognition that voices are not being heard in conventional ways – clarifying that this is not normal speech but something different.

In these situations, developing explanations is the way to understand the experience. Any explanation that they have come to themselves can be explored, understood, and discussed. They may well have already reached an understanding that the voices are something unique to themselves which relates to their past experiences and to the mental health problems that they have. Sometimes the beliefs are delusional and paranoid relating to persecution by people or agencies that they will specify, and it will be important to work with these as you would with delusional belief (see later in this chapter).

Often there is the opportunity to explain what is known about hallucinations. For example, when people hear voices, the area of the brain that is involved in speech (Broca's area) is active so there is, in a very literal sense, inner speech occurring – what "sounds" external is occurring in the brain. It can also be very helpful to describe situations in which hallucinations occur in the absence of psychosis, for example, sleep deprivation, bereavement, delirium, and even when going off or waking up from sleep. An explanation that many patients find helpful is related to sleep – when we are asleep and we hear speech, we just think of this as dreams, and when you wake up, they generally stop. Hallucinations have been described many times, including by Freud, as "dreaming awake" or even a "waking nightmare." The fact that the person is hearing someone else's voice can be taken, erroneously, to mean that it's not from their own mind.

Memories, especially where the originating experience has been a particularly emotional and disturbing one, may be the source of these perceptual experiences. Memories of events like a car crash, or a wedding, are usually much more vivid than everyday experience and can be recalled easily. Sometimes it's important to understand the origin of the statements which may have come from relationships in childhood. There may be particular phrases used by key individuals or related to specific instances of childhood trauma or bullying.

Although hallucinations are often related to emotional experiences, this is not always the case. Sometimes they can present as muddled, jumbled thoughts which seem to have no particular meaning and may not be distressing but are puzzling. An explanation of how automatic thoughts are generated can be helpful as the experience being described is often one of externalizing such thoughts and the failure to recognize them as the individual's own. Having clarified the nature of the voices, it is usually important to address the content. If it is neutral or positive, it may well be that the content is unimportant or may be a support for the individual. Although it can still be helpful to agree on an explanation for the phenomena, the voices may be enlisted as allies rather than a problem to deal with. Where the content is negative, each statement from the voice often takes the form of negative comments about the person, e.g., "you're useless" (or usually more venomous and vulgar), and work with these statements can be managed in a very similar way to that which is used in cognitive therapy for depression. The evidence for and against the statements can be weighed and, importantly, some conclusion established, which is often along the lines of "I'm not that bad" or "I'm trying my best." Key issues about the power relationship with the voices can be addressed by weighing up why and why not the statements made should be believed. This may mean questioning the authority of the originator of them. It may be part of therapeutic work which addresses the specific issues related to trauma or relationships. Specific phrases can sometimes be valuable, often using those that have come from the conclusions drawn. "I'm doing my best" might be an example – sometimes qualifying this, with a short list of the reasons why we believe this, can be helpful. Thinking it, or even saying it aloud when in an appropriate setting to the voices, can sometimes be a useful approach.

It is always worth exploring the ways that the individual has already developed in addressing voices. In general, heightened emotion including anger tends to lead to exacerbation, but this can be an individual response. Some people do find that cursing and swearing at the voice reinforces their power over it, but most find that this just leads to greater aggravation. Using different approaches to explore which works best can produce better coping. This can be in concert with approaches such as mindfulness, distraction, or socialization. Again, it is important to establish and reinforce those approaches that help.

Working with Delusions

Delusional beliefs may be very accessible to discussion as they are usually the major concern that the individual has. However, in some circumstances time and patience may be needed to elicit these concerns. This may be because they involve paranoid beliefs, which are essentially about lack of trust, and it may take time to build up sufficient trust for the individual to feel that the practitioner is not part of the conspiracy. At least they need to feel that the therapist can be trusted to listen to them, even if they don't believe the individual can help. Frequently they have expressed their beliefs and not felt believed by practitioners or, more specifically, not felt that their beliefs are taken seriously. Assessing frequency, volume, pattern, degree of conviction, and level of distress gives a dimensional understanding that can be helpful as with voices (Haddock et al. 1999).

Delusional beliefs have origins and understanding how they began (i.e., what was happening in the period leading up to the belief presenting and what has happened to reinforce it since) can be a very helpful process to the practitioner. It can also allow the individual to systematically examine their explanation of the beliefs themselves. It would be very unusual for someone to go through this process and then concur that they may have got it all wrong, but it is quite frequent for this process to begin to sow seeds of internal doubts. The process of exploring the delusion takes time: for most this is a question of minutes, but just occasionally, especially with systematized delusions, it takes longer. The process can be explored over the course of a few sessions. Exploring the circumstances from start to finish can provide a continuity which enables the individual to feel they are listened to and accepted and also feel prepared to consider alternative approaches to their problems, even if not alternative explanations.

Fully exploring these issues can lead to specific plans and problem-solving, leading to an action, e.g., this might involve writing a letter or complaint to the police or a government official. In practice, such a letter or complaint is often not sent, and any implications of sending it need to be discussed although most official departments are very familiar with unusual letters and complaints. The process enables the individual to assemble and inevitably review the evidence for their belief, and frequently this allows the person to move their life forward. Their beliefs may differ with the practitioner, but they can accept that there are limits to what they can do about their situation and its domination of their life. Sometimes an inference chaining approach, e.g., "what is it about people believing that you are the inventor of the Internet that is important to you?" can elicit material which can be worked on directly. For example, a discussion about self-esteem may allow the therapeutic relationship to move forward.

An alternative, or complementary approach, has recently been subject to specific evaluation. After initially establishing the relationship and assessing symptomatology, a "worry intervention" can be offered. This is similar to that used in CBT for generalized anxiety disorder, focusing on the premise that spending all day ruminating about the belief may not be helpful. Although the worry involved can have positive value in problem-solving and possibly maintaining safety, it is leaving them little time in their life to do anything else. The belief itself is not challenged, but it is suggested that using a "worry period" regularly once or twice a day may be a way of concentrating on that concern for a set period but then leaving time free to do the normal day-to-day activities of life. The evidence is that this can then allow the individual to take control of worry, a manifestation of their paranoia. This may have a positive impact on the worry, quality of life, and perhaps the delusional conviction (Freeman et al. 2015).

The aim of each of these approaches is not to convince the individual that they are wrong but to understand why they believe what they believe and what the impacts are on their and other's lives and then assist them to manage these more productively and with less associated distress.

Negative Symptoms

Although many CBTP studies have focused on positive symptoms, some have been broader in scope and reported success (Grant et al. 2012; Sensky et al. 2000; Turkington et al. 2006). Essentially the cognitive-behavioral conceptualization of negative symptoms considers possible individual psychosocial explanations (e.g., blunted affect can be a response to trauma or institutionalization, low motivation can be due to demoralization or self-defeating beliefs, poverty of speech from isolation). They generally involve protection – by avoidance – against stressful circumstances which can cause social and general anxiety and worsen ideas of reference and hallucinations. They can be addressed through CBTP approaches used for anticipated positive symptoms, management of stress, and behavioral activation. Mastery and pleasure diaries and graded target setting can be effective over time in putting the gains made through these tactics into an improved quality of life and movement toward recovery.

Relapse Prevention and Medication Management

Developing lasting change and recovery can occur through understanding, anticipation, and resilience. Recognizing the emergence of anxiety and positive symptoms as possible signs of stress allows them to be used as signals that social and psychological issues need to be addressed. This can often be done by problem-solving and sometimes enlisting support of family for encouragement. An understanding can be developed that the use of medication is a coping strategy which can assist with resilience and reduce chances of relapse and which can be adapted to circumstances. This does not necessitate an acceptance of illness or even that hallucinations and delusions are "not real," just that medication, for whatever reason, (such as its effects on sleep or stress) can be helpful.

The Third Wave of CBT Interventions

If the first wave of therapeutic interventions for psychosis was behavior therapy and the second wave was cognitive therapy, the third wave is the emergence of new directions in CBT, which have been based on modifications of the original cognitive model. These new directions have tended to be transdiagnostic, e.g., voices or paranoia, rather than developed for specific mental disorders. These include (1) metacognitive therapy, (2) acceptance and commitment therapy (ACT), (3) mindfulness training, (4) positive psychology interventions, (5) imagery modification, method of levels (MoL), (6) compassion-focused therapy (CFT), and (7) dialectical behavior therapy (Wright et al. 2014). The third wave interventions have a less robust evidence base for implementation in the treatment of psychosis, but all have found their place within the current psychosocial repertoire.

Metacognitive therapy for psychosis (Morrison et al. 2014a) was adapted from Wells (Wells 2011) model for anxiety and depression. The shift here is from working with the content of thoughts and beliefs and linked cognitive distortions toward the style of thinking. This is based on the cognitive attentional state derived from the self-referencing executive function model and postulates that emotional distress is driven by a ruminative thinking style. Rumination can be depressive or angry and worry tends to be threat related. Worry or rumination postponement through set worry periods allows time for other hobbies and activities. Meta-beliefs drive the thinking style. These styles might include "paranoia will keep me alert and worry will keep me safe," or "voices are supernatural…they are dangerous and can harm me." The approach in metacognitive therapy is to reduce these ruminative styles by showing that they aren't efficient and to change frightening over-arching beliefs. Once accomplished, this should allow a reduction in attention to voices and delusions and the beginnings of recovery. Metacognitive therapy can also tackle the mistaken belief that unpleasant intrusive thoughts should or can be suppressed. Suppressed intrusions bounce back with increased force leading to feelings of escalating anxiety which worsens psychosis. Metacognitive therapy has mostly been tested, as discussed above, with paranoid delusions (Freeman et al. 2015).

Acceptance and commitment therapy (ACT) relies on the cognitive model of Hayes (Hayes et al. 1999). This centralizes the importance of group work, awareness, cognitive flexibility, use of metaphor, mindfulness practice, valued goals, and metacognitive coping style of acceptance. ACT has mostly been tested in the treatment of auditory hallucinations with some evidence of benefit, but it was not significantly more effective than a befriending control (Shawyer et al. 2017).

Mindfulness training for people with psychosis in group format has been described and evaluated by Chadwick et al. (2016) as being both safe and therapeutic. However, it seems likely that prolonged periods of mindfulness are not indicated, but rather certain mindfulness techniques such as the mindful breath, mindful walking, and mindful eating might be useful (Wright et al. 2014). In particular the body scan might unlock somatic memories of trauma which need specific therapy.

Positive psychology interventions might include using techniques to activate pleasant emotions of joy, serenity, and happiness. This could be done by practicing with positive memories and activating the linked affects. Triggers for positive moods can be explored including particular pieces of music or pictures of events or locations. Research has not clarified the best symptoms for this intervention, but the anhedonia and blunting of negative symptoms would seem to be good targets.

Imagery modification has been used for auditory hallucinations as part of an avatar approach where a therapist works to modify negative beliefs through a computer construction of the "voice" (Leff et al. 2013) and also as part of positive memory training approach (Steel et al. 2020) by identifying the main emotion linked to distressing voice hearing, e.g., sadness, and then activating an image linked to the opposite emotional state, for example, the euphoria of scoring a goal for your local soccer team and then practicing with the image and linked emotion. Images linked to voice hearing triggered by unprocessed traumatic memories can also be modified during the process of CBT.

Method of levels for psychosis (Tai 2009) works by focusing attention on unresolved goal conflicts which have been described in the pre-psychotic periods leading to voice hearing and delusion emergence. A series of questions is used within a conversational therapeutic style to allow goal conflicts to be resolved. This approach has the advantage of not needing the classical CBT process of therapy including goal setting and homework exercises.

Compassion-focused therapy for psychosis (Wright et al. 2014) has principally been tested in a case series of clients with treatment-resistant critical hallucinations. The approach is based on the model that the self-nurturing system has switched off in many clients with psychosis but can be reactivated using a series of exercises. These include compassionate self-talk, compassionate meditation, and work with a compassionate image.

Dialectical behavioral therapy for psychosis is increasingly being used for clients at the traumatic end of the psychosis spectrum (dissociative disorder with psychosis, complex PTSD with psychosis, dissociative identity disorder with psychosis, and emotionally unstable personality disorder (borderline with psychosis). Here DBT techniques are very useful as a prelude to CBT or EMDR as a means of stabilizing mood and reducing self-harm and dissociation.

Summary

CBT for psychosis has now established itself as an evidence-based treatment alongside medication and other interventions (e.g., employment and case management) endorsed by clinical guidelines. It is continuing to develop and research needs to keep pace with the newer third wave approaches. However, availability of evidence-based CBT for psychosis remains a problem internationally. Full training is available now in many countries, and services do need to consider how to access this to provide the expertise for application, teaching, and supervision. It is also possible to use the techniques described in clinical practice with peer support and using teaching materials available (McCabe et al. 2016; Kingdon and Turkington 2004; Hazell et al. 2018). These interventions have great promise for the future of treatment for psychosis.

References

Barrowclough C, Haddock G, Wykes T, Beardmore R, Conrod P, Craig T, et al. (2010) Integrated motivational interviewing and cognitive behavioural therapy for people with psychosis and comorbid substance misuse: randomised controlled trial. BMJ. 341: c6325.

Beck AT, Grant PM, Huh GA, Perivoliotis D, Chang NA. (2013) Dysfunctional attitudes and expectancies in deficit syndrome schizophrenia. Schizophr Bull. 39(1): 43-51.

Chadwick P, Strauss C, Jones AM, Kingdon D, Ellett L, Dannahy L, et al. (2016) Group mindfulness-based intervention for distressing voices: A pragmatic randomised controlled trial. Schizophr Res. 175(1-3): 168-73.

Freeman D, Dunn G, Startup H, Pugh K, Cordwell J, Mander H, et al. (2015) Effects of cognitive behaviour therapy for worry on persecutory delusions in patients with psychosis (WIT): a parallel, single-blind, randomised controlled trial with a mediation analysis. Lancet Psychiatry. 2(4): 305-13.

Grant PM, Huh GA, Perivoliotis D, Stolar NM, Beck AT. (2012) Randomized trial to evaluate the efficacy of cognitive therapy for low-functioning patients with schizophrenia. Arch Gen Psychiatry. 69(2): 121-7.

Haddock G, McCarron J, Tarrier N, Faragher EB. (1999) Scales to measure dimensions of hallucinations and delusions: the psychotic symptom rating scales (PSYRATS). Psychol Med. 29(4): 879-89.

Hayes SC, Strosahl KD, Wilson KG. (1999) Acceptance and commitment therapy: An experiential approach to behavior change. Guilford Press, New York City, NY.

Hazell C, Hayward M, Strauss C, Kingdon D. (2018) An introduction to self-help for distressing voices. Robinson, London.

Jaspers K. (1997) General psychopathology. JHU Press; Nov 27. P.95.

Kane JM, Robinson DG, Schooler NR, Mueser KT, Penn DL, Rosenheck RA, et al. (2016) Comprehensive Versus Usual Community Care for First-Episode Psychosis: 2-Year Outcomes From the NIMH RAISE

Early Treatment Program. Am J Psychiatry. 173(4): 362-72.

Keepers GA, Fochtmann LJ, Anzia JM, Benjamin S, Lyness JM, Mojtabai R, et al. (2020) The American Psychiatric Association Practice Guideline for the Treatment of Patients With Schizophrenia. American Journal of Psychiatry. 177(9): 868-72.

Kingdon DG, Ashcroft K, Bhandari B, Gleeson S, Warikoo N, Symons M, et al. (2010) Schizophrenia and borderline personality disorder: similarities and differences in the experience of auditory hallucinations, paranoia, and childhood trauma. J Nerv Ment Dis. 198(6): 399-403.

Kingdon D, Turkington D. (2004) Cognitive therapy of schizophrenia. Guilford

Kreyenbuhl J, Buchanan RW, Dickerson FB, Dixon LB. (2010) The schizophrenia patient outcomes research team (PORT): updated treatment recommendations 2009. Schizophrenia Bulletin. 36(1): 94-103.

Leff J, Williams G, Huckvale MA, Arbuthnot M, Leff AP. (2013) Computer-assisted therapy for medication-resistant auditory hallucinations: proof-of-concept study. Br J Psychiatry. 202: 428-33.

McCabe R, John P, Dooley J, Healey P, Cushing A, Kingdon D, et al. (2016) Training to enhance psychiatrist communication with patients with psychosis (TEMPO): cluster randomised controlled trial. Br J Psychiatry. 209(6): 517-24.

McKenna P, Leucht S, Jauhar S, Laws K, Bighelli I. (2019) The controversy about cognitive behavioural therapy for schizophrenia. World Psychiatry. 18(2): 235-6.

Morrison AP, French P, Stewart SL, Birchwood M, Fowler D, Gumley AI, et al. (2012) Early detection and intervention evaluation for people at risk of psychosis: multisite randomised controlled trial. BMJ. 344: e2233.

Morrison AP, Pyle M, Chapman N, French P, Parker SK, Wells A. (2014a) Metacognitive therapy in people with a schizophrenia spectrum diagnosis and medication resistant symptoms: a feasibility study. Journal of Behavior Therapy and Experimental Psychiatry. 45(2): 280-4.

Morrison AP, Turkington D, Pyle M, Spencer H, Brabban A, Dunn G, et al. (2014b) Cognitive therapy for people with schizophrenia spectrum disorders not taking antipsychotic drugs: a single-blind randomised controlled trial. Lancet. 383: 1395-1403

Naeem F, Kingdon D, Turkington D. (2005) Cognitive behavior therapy for schizophrenia in patients with mild to moderate substance misuse problems. Cogn Behav Ther. 34(4): 207-15.

NICE. (2014) Psychosis and schizophrenia in adults: prevention and management. NICE

Priebe S, Kelley L, Omer S, Golden E, Walsh S, Khanom H, et al. (2015) The Effectiveness of a Patient-Centred Assessment with a Solution-Focused Approach (DIALOG+) for Patients with Psychosis: A Pragmatic Cluster-Randomised Controlled Trial in Community Care. Psychother Psychosom. 84(5): 304-13.

Sensky T, Turkington D, Kingdon D, Scott JL, Scott J, Siddle R, et al. (2000) A randomized controlled trial of cognitive-behavioral therapy for persistent symptoms in schizophrenia resistant to medication. Arch Gen Psychiatry. 57(2): 165-72.

Shawyer F, Farhall J, Thomas N, Hayes SC, Gallop R, Copolov D, et al. (2017) Acceptance and commitment therapy for psychosis: randomised controlled trial. Br J Psychiatry. 210(2): 140-8.

Steel C, Korrelboom K, Fazil Baksh M, Kingdon D, Simon J, Wykes T, et al. (2020) Positive memory training for the treatment of depression in schizophrenia: A randomised controlled trial. Behav Res Ther. 135: 103734.

Tai SJ. (2009) Using Perceptual Control Theory and the Method of Levels to work with people who experience psychosis. The Cognitive Behaviour Therapist. 2(3): 227-42.

Turkington D, Munetz M, Pelton J, Montesano V, Sivec H, Nausheen B, et al. (2014) High-yield cognitive behavioral techniques for psychosis delivered by case managers to their clients with persistent psychotic symptoms: an exploratory trial. J Nerv Ment Dis. 202(1): 30-4.

Turkington D, Kingdon D, Rathod S, Hammond K, Pelton J, Mehta R. (2006) Outcomes of an effectiveness trial of cognitive-behavioural intervention by mental health nurses in schizophrenia. The British Journal of Psychiatry. 189(1): 36-40.

van den Berg DP, de Bont PA, van der Vleugel BM, de Roos C, de Jongh A, Van Minnen A, et al. (2015) Prolonged exposure vs eye movement desensitization and reprocessing vs waiting list for posttraumatic stress disorder in patients with a psychotic disorder: a randomized clinical trial. JAMA Psychiatry. 72(3):259-67.

Wells A. (2011) Metacognitive therapy for anxiety and depression. Guilford Press, New York City, NY.

Wright N, Turkington D, Kelly O, Davies D, Jacobs A, Hopton J. (2014) Treating Psychosis: A Clinician's Guide to Integrating Acceptance and Commitment Therapy, Compassion-Focused Therapy, and Mindfulness Approaches within the Cognitive Behavioral Therapy Tradition. 2014. New Harbinger Publications, Oakland, CA.

Wright JH, Turkington D, Kingdon DG, Basco MR. (2009) Cognitive-behavior Therapy for Severe Mental Illness: An Illustrated Guide. American Psychiatric Publishers, Inc, Washington, DC.

Veterans' Services

Liliya Gershengoren, Pantea Farahmand, and Adam Wolkin

Introduction

The US Department of Veterans Affairs (officially "DVA" but still widely referred to as "VA") is a Cabinet-level agency that is directed by the Secretary of Veterans Affairs. Integrity, commitment, advocacy, respect, and excellence (iCARE) are the core values of the VA. The largest component within VA is the Veterans Health Administration (VHA), responsible for healthcare and related services (the other divisions include Veterans Benefits Administration and National Cemetery Administration). The identified missions of VHA include an emphasis on *clinical care*, advancement in *medical research*, upholding the *educational efforts* of medical training programs, as well as *assistance during national medical emergencies* (US Department of Veterans Affairs 2020a).

VA endeavors to meet the medical, surgical, and mental health needs of veterans who have been discharged from the military under honorable conditions. Increasingly over recent decades, VA has prioritized mental health care and recognized that mental health is an essential element of overall health and well-being. VA strives to consistently integrate mental health services, including substance use-associated conditions, with the other components of health care. This creates the foundation for a comprehensive and progressive healthcare system and is the basis by which mental health care for military veterans has evolved in the quality and the breadth of the multitude of services offered by the VA.

The "Uniform Mental Health Services" Handbook (Department of Veterans Affairs 2008) exemplifies the principle that mental health concerns are essential and impact the physical wellness and quality of life of veterans. It establishes the minimum mental health program requirements that are to be executed across all VA facilities in order to increase access to mental health care. The implementation of the healthcare programs is facilitated through the operation of multiple VA medical centers (VAMC), community-based outpatient clinics (CBOC), and VA community living centers (VA nursing home). Medical services continue to be expanded as there has also been a longstanding initiative to shift care from inpatient facilities to the community. In addition to the clinical services provided, VA recognizes the impact of mental health stigma on adherence with mental health care. Systematic study of the enduring effects of combat trauma in veterans along with possible effective treatments

L. Gershengoren · A. Wolkin (✉)
VA NY Harbor Healthcare System, NYU Grossman School of Medicine, New York, NY, USA
e-mail: liliya.gershengoren@va.gov; Adam.Wolkin@va.gov

P. Farahmand
NYU Grossman School of Medicine, New York, NY, USA
e-mail: Pantea.farahmand@nyulangone.org

W. E. Sowers et al. (eds.), *Textbook of Community Psychiatry*,
https://doi.org/10.1007/978-3-031-10239-4_45

has been a research focus with wide-reaching implications. Consideration of what we now identify as post-traumatic stress disorder (PTSD) was initially shaped by the experiences of Vietnamese veterans and is now a widely recognized implication of combat. In addition to PTSD, there have been notable contributions in the areas of traumatic brain injury research as well as substance use disorders.

This chapter provides an in-depth look at the ways that VA strives to realize its four missions for the benefit of veterans, caregivers, and their communities.

History and Evolution of the VA

Caring for military veterans is a viewed as a societal imperative throughout the world and the United States has one of the most comprehensive systems of any other nation. Going back as far as the Plymouth Colony in 1636, disabled soldiers were provided with much needed support by the colony. Later on, the Continental Congress of 1776 offered pensions to the disabled soldiers of the Revolutionary War. Initially, states and communities were tasked with providing medical and hospital care to veterans (US Department of Veterans Affairs 2020a). However, during the nineteenth century, the federal government authorized the first military veterans medical facility and expanded the program to include benefits and pensions to veterans as well as their widows and dependents:

> …to care for him who shall have borne the battle and for his widow and his orphan. (Abraham Lincoln, second inaugural address)

During the post-World War I era, Congress combined all the veterans programs including disability compensation, insurance, and vocational rehabilitation, to create the Veterans Bureau. During this time, as the nature of the war and weapon utilization began to change, it became apparent that soldiers who were exposed to various chemicals and fumes during their service would require specialized medical care. As a result, specialized medical hospitals, such as tuberculosis and neuropsychiatric hospitals, were created to better service the needs of veterans. Furthermore, veteran benefits were also extended to cover the medical and mental health needs of veterans that were not considered to be service-related. In 1930, President Hoover created the Veterans Administration elevating it to a federal administration position.

Over the years and with each subsequent military conflict, the VA has continued to evolve to the present-day Department of Veteran Affairs, which continues to emphasize ambulatory care and community access. Over time, VA healthcare system has increased from 54 hospitals in 1930 to over 1500 healthcare facilities including 144 VA medical centers serving about nine million enrolled veterans each year.

The VA Maintaining Internal Systems and Strengthening Integrated Outside Networks Act of 2018 (MISSION Act) fundamentally transformed the VA's healthcare system as it established a new veterans community service program. Veterans are empowered to seek medical care in VA healthcare facilities as well as in the community. Consequently, Veterans can continue to receive efficient, timely, and quality medical services which are covered by their VA benefits.

Patient Demographics

When the United States eliminated the draft in 1973, the military force transitioned from those drafted to an all-volunteer force. As a result, the military became a more selective experience and far less common for Americans. The veteran population declined from 26 million to 18 million, and presently about 1 in 8 adult men and 1 in 100 adult women have ever served in the military. Close to 62% of veterans who served in Operation Enduring Freedom (OEF), Operation Iraqi Freedom (OIF), or Operation New Dawn (OND) from 2003 through 2017 have utilized VA health care since 2001. The most common diagnoses include musculoskeletal disorder (62%), conditions that do not appear to have an immediate obvious cause (59%), and mental disorders

(58%). Many veterans have multiple diagnoses. About five million veterans live in rural areas making accessibility to health care a priority for the VA (US Department of Veterans Affairs 2017).

Women became part of the military with the creation of the Army Nurse Corp in 1901, although in addition to nurses, women served as cooks, spies, and soldiers. Since 1973, when the draft ended, women have been able to enlist, occupy many different roles in all the branches of the military, and take part in combat. The number of women in the military has been steadily increasing, and today they comprise 20% of new recruits. About 9% (1.7 million) of all veterans are women. Of all the post-9/11 veterans, 17% are women. This is a substantial increase from the Vietnam War era when women made up 4% of all veterans. When compared to the general population of women, female veterans are more likely to have a college degree and earn a higher salary during full-time employment. In fact, a greater portion of today's veterans, both men and women, have completed higher levels of education than those from older periods such as the Vietnam War era (US Department of Veterans Affairs 2017).

Clinical Services: Mental Health

Clinical Services: Inpatient Psychiatric Care

VA is the largest integrated healthcare systems in the United States and perhaps, most notably, boasts a universal electronic medical record system, which allows for better coordination of care, patient follow-up, and patient safety efforts (Marcus et al. 2018). Veterans with acute emotional and behavioral symptoms and those who may pose a risk to self or others require a higher level of care such as inpatient psychiatric hospitalization, focusing on stabilization. VA inpatient services follow the recovery paradigm and provide evidence-based psychiatric care specifically tailored to the needs of each veteran. Each facility provides safe and private rooms for women veterans that include locking bedrooms and bathrooms. As the number of women joining the military service continues to increase, the inpatient psychiatric units have undergone remodeling to accommodate their growing number. There are on average more than 100,000 discharges from inpatient units annually (True et al. 2017).

Clinical Services: Residential Rehabilitation and Treatment Programs

Residential rehabilitation and treatment programs (RRTPs) treat veterans with a wide range of illnesses and rehabilitative needs (Department of Veterans Affairs VHA Handbook 2010; Department of Veterans Affairs VHA Handbook 2008). Programs includes medical, psychiatric, educational, vocational, substance use disorder, and homelessness, among other rehabilitative services. Programs specific to mental health are identified as MH-RRTP and include psychosocial rehabilitative treatment programs, post-traumatic stress disorder programs, substance abuse residential rehabilitative treatment programs, compensated work therapy, transitional residence, and domiciliary care for homeless veterans. Veterans in need of specialized, 24/7 structure, due to mental health or substance use MH-RRTPs, can seek treatment at 1 of 97 programs in the nation (Ellerbe et al. 2017). Evidence-based psychosocial services are the required treatment modalities provided at the MH-RRTPs—such as Seeking Safety, motivational interviewing for recovery-based programs. All VA medical centers are required to provide access to MH-RRTP services and can be met on local and regional basis through service agreements with other VA hospitals. Each must have programs with full capacity to serve veterans, including women, who suffer from serious mental illnesses, with trauma syndromes, and with substance and alcohol use disorders. These embrace subpopulations with homelessness and/or co-occurring mental illness and substance misuse. They also provide ongoing monitoring and case management referral ability (Department of

Veterans Affairs VHA Handbook 2010; Department of Veterans Affairs VHA Handbook 2008). To routinely monitor the performance of all mental health services including residential treatment programs, the Office of Mental Health Operations developed the mental health information system, using up to 15 required metrics to assess access and quality of services, including average lengths of stay, and access to treatment measures (Trafton et al. 2013; Ellerbe et al. 2017).

Clinical Services: Ambulatory Care

All new patients referred to mental health services are expected to receive an initial evaluation within 24 hours and are screened for urgent concerns such as hospitalization or immediate outpatient needs. The initial evaluation can be conducted by primary care or other referring licensed independent providers. More comprehensive diagnostic and treatment planning is expected within 30 days of the initial screen. Referrals to any service are expected to be completed within 30 days of the patient's desired appointment. Ambulatory care services include particular focus on issues such as PTSD, MST, homelessness, and specialty substance use treatment services (Department of Veterans Affairs VHA Handbook 2008).

One way the VA has increased access to ambulatory care services is through telemental health. Telemental health services require a qualified mental health professional at VA facility and support staff at the distal end to arrange the appropriate times, technical support, and space for the veteran. As a result of expansion in telemental health technologies, VA undertook initiatives to expand this service nationally. From 2003 to 2011, telemental health services expanded tenfold and continue to grow to address mental health needs across the United States (Godleski et al. 2012).

Ambulatory care settings offer comprehensive evaluation, individual and group psychotherapy (emphasizing evidence-based treatments), neuropsychological testing, family education, and case management supports (Department of Veterans Affairs VHA Handbook 2008). For individuals with severe mental illnesses and challenges with adherence to treatment, community outreach is conducted via the Mental Health Intensive Case Management (MHICM) program. MHICM consists of a multidisciplinary team which includes prescribing professionals, social workers, and visiting nurses. They provide services to patients within a 50 mile radius of a VA facility. Their services include crisis intervention, socialization skills, budget management, client advocacy (comparable to ACT teams in the community, medication management, and family/caregiver support). Their objectives are to minimize the need for hospitalization and improve function in the community (Mohamed et al. 2009).

Clinical Services: Minority-Specific Programs

According to the US Department of Veterans Affairs, minority veterans are identified as African Americans, Asian American/Pacific Islander, Hispanic, Native American/Alaska Native, and Native Hawaiian. Women veterans and lesbian, gay, bisexual, and transgender (LGBT) veterans are the two other groups who are now also identified as minority veterans. According to recent VA data analysis, minority veterans were more likely to have been diagnosed with post-traumatic stress disorder (PTSD) than non-minority veterans. This is often attributed to the reality that minority groups in the military are most likely to be exposed to trauma. Furthermore, Black and Latinx veterans are more likely to lack primary care physicians and adhere to treatment as compared to White veterans (Saha et al. 2008). In 1994, the Center for Minority Veterans was established to ascertain and address the healthcare needs of minority veterans. On a local level, each VA regional office is expected to have a minority veterans outreach coordinator to assist with benefits available to minority veterans. The Office of Health Equity was established in 2012 in order to further address the ongoing health disparities for veterans despite the progress that has already been made over the years. It offers training to healthcare providers on topics such as unconscious bias and cultural competence.

VA facilities offer the services of women veterans program managers to assist and advocate for women veterans. Specially designated women's health clinics at VA hospitals provide medical and mental health care suitable to their particular needs. Runnals et al. (2014) noted in their systematic review of the literature on veterans' mental health that the rates of depression and non-PTSD anxiety disorders are higher for women veterans as compared with male veterans. Women veterans also have higher rates of comorbidity of PTSD and depression. There are also higher rates of depression that is comorbid with medical conditions such as diabetes (Runnals et al. 2014). Women veterans show higher rates of health and functional impairments which is in part attributed to the availability of "gender-sensitive mental health services" (Runnals et al. 2014). An increasing number of VA hospitals are also developing special programs for women veterans which include services for homeless women veterans and those have been victims of domestic violence (US Department of Veterans Affairs 2015a).

There are more than one million veterans who identify as LGBT and are eligible for health care through the VA (Puntasecca et al. 2019). During their military service and upon returning to civilian life, LGBT veterans have encountered stigma, discrimination, and harassment.

Historically, military ethos has led to anti-LGBT sentiment and excluded LGBT people from military service. They were faced with the possibility of a dishonorable discharge and being court martialed if suspected of acts of sodomy (Byne and Wise 2020). It was not until the Department of Defense policy 1304.26 in 1993, also known as "Don't Ask, Don't Tell" (DADT), that the harassment of LGB service members became prohibited. Of note, transgender military members were not included in the policy since it covered only sexual orientation and not gender identity. Homosexuality in the military was still not legalized and military personnel were expected to conform to gender norms. The DADT policy was repealed in 2011 and there has since been increased awareness and openness for LGBT people in the military (Wise 2019). Nevertheless, LGBT individuals continue to experience greater frequency of harassment and assault as compared to their heterosexual and cisgender counterparts in the military.

The VA now recognizes LGBT veterans as individuals with "unique healthcare needs" (Sherman et al. 2014). There has been an increase in research examining the mental health impact of discrimination and harassment in the military. LGBT veterans are at an increased risk of suicide, depression, and substance abuse (Cochran et al. 2013). Furthermore, transgender veterans incur a risk of suicide that is 20 times higher than that for the veteran population (Blosnich et al. 2013). In order to better address the needs of the LGBT veterans, VA hospitals have supported a number of interventions and programs. Many of the VA hospitals have LGBT care coordinators and support outreach initiatives. Transgender Education Workgroup within the larger Office of Patient Care Services has been tasked with developing online resources as well as delivering webinars about the transgender healthcare resources. As of 2011, clinical services available to LGBT veterans include medical and mental health care, hormone therapy, preoperative evaluation for sex reassignment surgery, and medically necessary postoperative care (Mattocks et al. 2014).

Clinical Services: Post-traumatic Stress Disorder Programs

The relationship between psychological trauma and military service was first documented in 490 B.C, with early warriors reporting symptoms similar to those noted in recent history (Swartz 2014; Abdul-Hamid and Hughes 2014). In the United States, the American Civil War (1861–1865) had the first documented efforts to provide formal medical treatment for the psychological effects of war (Da Costa 1871). Shortness of breath, rapid pulse, and fatigue were given the name "irritable heart" or "Da Costa's syndrome"—named after the physician who researched the PTSD-like disorder—which was noted in soldiers during times of fear and stress. Though over the years additional names were given to describe the disorder (i.e., "shell shock," "battle fatigue," "post-Vietnam syndrome"), the diagnosis of PTSD was not adopted until the 1970s and officially in 1980 in the DSM III (APA 1980; Reisman 2016).

Prevalence of PTSD varies among veterans across wars. Estimates of lifetime prevalence of combat-related PTSD across all US veterans ranges between 6% and 31%. Estimates of point prevalence rates ranges from 2.2% to 15.2% during the Vietnam War, 1.9% to 13.2% during the Persian Gulf War, and 4% to17% during the Afghanistan/Iraq War (Richardson et al. 2010). Often PTSD is comorbid with other conditions, and high rates of comorbidity are seen in military veterans. Most commonly, major depression is noted to be three to five times more likely in individuals with PTSD (Rytwinski et al. 2013). Anxiety and substance use disorders are also commonly co-occurring (Hoge et al. 2006; Milliken et al. 2007; Richardson et al. 2010). Estimates of comorbid PTSD and substance or alcohol use are as high as 76% (Seal et al. 2011; McCauley et al. 2012).

To address the long-lasting wounds of service, in 1989, the National Center for PTSD—consisting of seven VA academic centers of excellence—was created within the Department of Veterans Affairs. The center provides leadership in research and development of evidence-based treatments, dissemination of best practices, and consultative services for the treatment of PTSD. The center has become a leader in research and education on PTSD as it exists in all forms—civilian and military assault, rape, child abuse, disaster, etc. (National Center of PTSD, 2020a). Access to evidence-based PTSD treatment including cognitive processing therapy (CPT) or prolonged exposure therapy is widely available at VA sites throughout the United States. These services are offered in person or via telehealth modalities to reach veterans throughout the country. Similarly, PTSD with comorbid substance use disorders, pain, or other psychiatric conditions are provided evidence-based and validated treatments such as seeking safety, psychopharmacology, etc. Levels of care can vary from individual outpatient treatment, PTSD groups, and inpatient or residential treatment services. To augment PTSD care and allow for reentry into the community, veterans are also provided psychosocial supports such as help with housing, vocational support, and programs for veterans leaving state or federal prisons (Department of Veterans Affairs VHA Handbook 2008). The VHA also provides funding for innovative and leading PTSD research. Some of the most impactful strides made in PTSD care are promoted and transmitted by the veterans themselves who are each other's greatest supports as comrades in service.

Clinical Services: Military Sexual Trauma Treatment

Military sexual trauma (MST) refers to sexual assault or harassment that occurs during military service. VA offers a wide range of services for victims of MST as part of their treatment and recovery (Johnson et al. 2015). Veterans who have suffered MST can receive medical and mental health care related to their experience at no cost. VA's national screening program revealed that 1 in 3 women and 1 in 50 men reported experiencing MST during the screening (Military Sexual Trauma 2020). MST is not in itself a diagnosis and can affect veterans in different ways. It is often associated with poor medical and mental health care, increased chronic health issues, and a decreased quality of life. Women veterans who experienced MST are more likely to be diagnosed with PTSD compared with male veteran survivors of MST. Male survivors are more likely to present with somatic symptoms and medical conditions as well as depression and PTSD as compared to male veterans who did not experience sexual assault.

MST-related services include outpatient clinic-based therapy as well as inpatient and residential programs for those veterans who require more intense treatment. There are mixed-gender inpatient and residential programs that provide separate sleeping areas for their women and men veterans. Residential programs available specifically to women veterans are also offered. A crucial component of MST treatment is risk-reduction interventions and an integrated treatment approach that considers co-occurring disorders such as PTSD, depression, or substance use disorders. The first stage of treatment is focused on coping skills followed by the second stage which then involves trauma processing. Dialectical behavior therapy is used to help develop distress tolerance and emotion regulation skills in order to prepare the patient for the second stage of treatment. Acceptance and commitment therapy (ACT) is also often implemented for the treatment of PTSD symptoms. Many VA centers will deliberately place their MST clinics within primary care in order to offer privacy and an environment of safety and support. Increased efforts to identify MST survivors, diagnose associated mental health conditions, and offer evidence-based treatment continue on local and national levels (Vantage Point 2016).

Clinical Services: Suicide Prevention Programs

Since 2001, veteran suicides increased 32 percent compared with a 23 percent for the US adult population. Veteran suicide rate is 1.5 times higher than rate of suicide for the civilian population. Furthermore, approximately two-thirds of veterans who died by suicide had not utilized VA services (Vantage Point 2016; Warren and Smithkors 2020). Factors such as mental health conditions, substance use conditions, and access to lethal means increase the likelihood of suicide.

Suicide prevention strategies mandated by the VA include decreasing access to or securing firearms, increasing suicide risk screening, and further enhancement of the suicide prevention program. One such program is the Recovery Engagement and Coordination for Health-Veterans Enhanced Treatment (REACH-VET) which is a novel predictive model that analyzes veterans' health records in order to identify them at an elevated risk for adverse outcomes such as suicide. Upon identification, the veteran then is closely followed by VA mental health specialists and clinicians. REACH-VET initiative was fully implemented in 2017 and at the time of this writing data analysis remains ongoing. However the data from the initial 6 months, from March to May 2017, indicated that the REACH-VET program helped facilitate more healthcare appointments, increased suicide prevention safety plans, and decreased all-cause mortality (US Department of Veterans Affairs 2020b).

Each VA hospital has designated suicide prevention coordinators (SPC) whose responsibilities include working with the identified High Risk for Suicide List (HRL) patients. Veterans on the high-risk list have a "flag" placed in their medical chart to increase awareness of the elevated suicide risk, thus prompting suicide risk assessments during their appointments. Furthermore, HRL patients are required to have increased contact with their mental health providers (Warren and Smithkors 2020). Another suicide prevention resource is the Veterans Crisis Line (988 PRESS 1), a free and confidential support offered to veterans in crisis adding another layer of assistance and access to care. Of course, no amount of available resources will be enough without ongoing efforts to address stigma of mental illness and suicide. Together with Veterans (TWV) is one such initiative which supports efforts to decrease stigma in rural communities in order to prevent suicide (Warren and Smithkors 2020). There are numerous ongoing efforts to provide education, support, and resources to ultimately prevent veteran suicide.

Clinical Services: Substance Use Treatment Programs

Alcohol, nicotine, and illicit substance use are associated with numerous social and health consequences. Despite progress, the use of these substances remains a leading cause of preventable death in the United States (Wilson et al. 2020). The 2018 National Survey on Drug Use and Health found that among veterans, 300,000 had a substance use disorder, 800,000 had alcohol use disorder, and 78,000 had both an alcohol and substance use disorder (SAMSHA 2020). Substance use disorder among veterans is complicated by high rates of co-occurring mental health conditions, pain, traumatic brain injuries, and suicide (Hankin et al. 1999; Kaplan et al. 2007; Hoge et al. 2008; Tanielian and Jaycox 2008). VA's approach to treating alcohol, nicotine, and substance-related disorders is multilayered and involves both innovations in research, clinical care, and management of co-occurring psychiatric conditions and psychosocial supports. Veterans have access to substance use treatments in a variety of settings at VA including telehealth, outpatient, 12-step group, motivational enhanced treatment, intensive outpatient, residential treatment, and inpatient levels of care. If services are not accessible at a VA facility closest to the veteran, arrangements are made for community care access. As a result of implementation of specialized, evidence-based treatments in VA, rates of treatment response are considerably higher in veterans compared with the general population. Though the need to reach more veterans is apparent, initiatives and goals of VA are to continually expand and develop new ways for addressing these diseases (Dalton et al. 2012).

VA addresses alcohol use disorders by integrating screening and treatment in primary care and specialty care settings (Hagedorn et al. 2016). The use of FDA-approved medications for alcohol use disorder, such as naltrexone and acamprosate, is published in VA Department of Defense Clinical Practice Guidelines for Management of Substance Use disorders updated in 2015 and recommended for use across setting for the treatment of alcohol use disorder (Department of Veterans Affairs, Department of Defense 2015).

Innovation in addressing nicotine use disorders has been spearheaded in VA by programs and research that focus on improving delivery and access to treatments. Services include 24-hour access to an on-call counselor, individual counseling, and use of FDA-approved medications (Sherman et al. 2007; Sherman 2008; Rogers et al. 2018). Referrals are facilitated through a telephone care coordination program, with resultant increased cessation rates (18% versus 11% in control group) (Sherman et al. 2018).

Efforts to prevent and reduce opioid related harms among veterans are a priority for VHA and have been a focus of policy initiatives and research (Frank et al. 2020). Major comorbidities that contribute to opioid addiction and overdose are acute and chronic pain and co-occurring mental health illness. In 2019, the VA hosted a state-of-the-art conference to address management of pain and addiction. Consensus was reached in three areas: (1) managing opioid use disorders, (2) long-term opioid therapy and opioid tapering, and (3) managing co-occurring pain and substance use disorders. Some key recommendations from the conference included increasing access to medication for opioid use disorders (MOUD)—such as buprenorphine, naltrexone, and methadone—improving fidelity to evidence-based models of MOUD, increasing provider comfort with MOUD prescribing, providing wide access to team-based care, and improving access to evidence-based non-pharmacologic treatments for pain (Frank et al. 2020).

Clinical Services: Social Determinants of Mental Health

The VA has numerous programs that provide wrap-around veteran services that enable veterans to reintegrate into the workplace and adjust back into their families after military service, including caregiver and family supports, vocational training, homelessness programs, and legal services. In order to be eligible for many of the services, the veteran must be within 12 years from the date of separation from active military service. While in the program, veterans may qualify for a monthly payment or a monthly subsistence allowance. The payments are based on attendance rates, number of dependents, and type of training. In this section we discuss vocational support, homelessness programs, and incarcerated veteran programs.

Vocation Support: The Veteran Readiness and Employment (VR&E) program provides job training, employment accommodations, resumé development, job coaching, and personalized counseling to help guide veterans through their career paths. Additional services help veterans start their own careers or provide independent living services for those who are severely disabled and unable to work (US Department of Veterans Affairs 2020c).

Homelessness Programs: On a single night in January 2018, nearly 38,000 veterans were found experiencing homelessness according to a report by the Department of Housing and Urban Development (HUD). In 2010, that number was 74,000 (The US Department of Housing and Urban Development 2018). Though the overall trend shows declines in homelessness, housing remains a significant concern for many veterans. The National Center on Homelessness among veterans conducts and supports research assessing the effectiveness of programs, identifies and disseminates best practices, and integrates these practices into policies, programs, and services for homeless veterans or veterans at risk. Currently there are over 30 researchers affiliated with the center and are investigating issues related to veteran homelessness in four areas: population-based studies, physical and mental health, program evaluation, and function and flourishing. These four areas identify the contributing causes of veteran homelessness, focus on mental and physical illnesses that disproportionately affect homeless veteran populations, determine how to help veterans flourish beyond housing and into vocational supports, and investigate existing or new models to improve care for veterans (VA National Center on Homeless Among Veternas 2020). A notable program is HUD's VA Supportive Housing (HUD-VASH) program. This provides housing vouchers with VA supportive services to help veterans and their families find and sustain permanent housing. VA case managers, as part of the program, connect veterans to heath care, mental health treatment, substance use counseling, and vocational training. Nationwide, HUD-VASH currently works with 90,000 veterans.

Incarcerated Veterans: Evidence supports specialty treatment courts for individuals at risk for incarceration with co-occurring substance or mental health issues for their reduction in recidivism (Huddleston III et al. 2008; Marlowe 2010; Sarteschi et al. 2011). In 2007, 10% of the people incarcerated in the United States were military veterans, with the highest percentage being from Vietnam War era service (36% state and 39% federal prison) (Noonan and Mumola 2007). Of those veterans incarcerated, 87% are reported to have experienced traumatic events and 31% have been formally diagnosed with PTSD (Saxon et al. 2001). The Veterans Justice Outreach (VJO) program connects veterans in jails, courts, or in contact with law enforcement to mental health and substance use treatment (Finlay et al. 2016). Veteran treatment courts operate independently of the VA but are supported by the VJO. They are modeled after mental health or drug treatment courts (US Department of Veterans Affairs 2015). They supervise veterans with charges to ensure adherence to treatment and can result in reduced or expunged charges following completion of treatment (Cavanaugh 2010; Clark et al. 2010). Veterans who completed the program have been found to have reduced recidivism, improved mental health outcomes, and improved employment and housing relative to those veterans who did not complete the program (Tsai and Rosenheck 2016; Knudsen and Wingenfeld 2016; Tsai et al. 2018). Of those rearrested, substance use, property offenses, and probation violence were noted (Tsai et al. 2018). Those who committed property offenses and probation have been speculated to have greater financial hardship post-incarceration (Motivans 2015). Those rearrested due to addiction illustrate both the psychosocial challenges and consequences of substance use disorders among veterans and underscore the importance of mandated addiction treatment.

Medical Research

The Office of Research and Development (ORD) is the research and development branch of VA. It was established in 1947 and is a congressionally mandated research program focused on veteran health. It is the only federally funded research program that is directly tied to a fully integrated healthcare system. In 2019, the ORD budget was 1.3 billion dollars with 119.1 million and 33 million allocated to mental health and substance use research, respectively (Congressional Research Service 2020). ORD has been a leader in veteran and American healthcare innovation for over 60 years. VA investigators have been awarded Nobel Prizes, Lasker Awards, and other distinctions. All the while VA research remains closely tied to clinical work, with 70 percent of researchers providing direct patient care. ORD promotes programs for veterans via ties to federal agencies, nonprofit organizations, and private industries (US Department of Veterans Affairs, 2020).

Within ORD there are several research services. Clinical sciences R&D involves clinical trials, comparing existing therapies, and improving clinical practice. The clinical sciences section also oversees VA's Cooperative Studies Program, which is responsible for multisite clinical trials and epidemiological research on health issues in veteran populations. Rehabilitation R&D supports research focusing on restoring limbs lost due to traumatic amputations, central nervous system injuries, loss of sight or hearing, and restoring other physical and cognitive impairments. Health sciences R&D supports healthcare system and patient outcomes level research. This includes quality improvement, increasing access, measuring outcomes, and reducing wasteful healthcare spending.

The VA launched a major restructuring effort in the 1990s (1995–2000) in which the VA transitioned from a tertiary/specialty and inpatient-based care system delivering care in a traditional model to one that focuses on primary, outpatient-based, team, and evidence-based management practice. The goals of providing industry-leading quality and performance measured services subsequently led to multiple systematic evaluations affirming the high quality of care in VA (Jha et al. 2003; Ashton et al. 2003; Committee on Quality of Health Care in America 2001; McQueen et al. 2004). In an effort to further systematically study and enhance VA clinical programs, the VA Quality Enhancement Research Initiative (QUERI) was created in 1998.

QUERI is a large-scale, multidisciplinary, quality improvement initiative that spans clinical services including inpatient, outpatient, and long-term care settings (McQueen et al. 2004). QUERI coordinating centers are staffed by teams of researchers and clinical leaders who conduct research and evaluation activities that identify practices with strong evidence base in clinical care and work to implement these practices across the VA. QUERI centers exist for mental health and substance use disorder analysis, as well as medical conditions such as colorectal cancers, HIV/AIDS, diabetes, etc. (McQueen et al. 2004). In 1 year QUERI-funded programs implemented 50 evidence-based practices for a wide range of conditions across VAs nationally.

Some of the successful outcomes and findings of QUERI initiatives have concerned antipsychotic medication management and use of opioid agonist therapies (McQueen et al. 2004). In both, there have been measurable improvements in clinician adherence to best practice recommendations (Willenbring et al. 2004).

Education

> To educate for VA and for the Nation (Mission of the Office of Academic Affiliations 2019).

In accordance with its mission to uphold the educational efforts for the benefit of veterans, DVA supports education and training programs for medical, nursing, and allied health professionals (Mission of the Office of Academic Affiliations 2019). Many VA hospitals are affiliated with academic medical centers and coordinate training as part of their training efforts. This unique collaboration was implemented following World War II under the leadership of General Omar Bradley, Administrator of VA at the time, in order to address the national shortage of physicians. VA strives to support and train new health professionals in order to continue to provide hig-quality health care to the veterans and the nation.

VA works in collaboration with 144 out of 152 accredited medical schools and is affiliated with more than 40 other health professional institutions. It is estimated that over 60% of medical trainees and about 50% of psychologists spend a portion of their training at VA hospitals (Mission of the Office of Academic Affiliations 2019). Nationally recognized specialties such as geriatrics, spinal cord injury medicine, and addiction psychiatry have grown and continue to develop in part due to the VA's educational efforts. As a result of VA-led initiatives and training programs, pain management is now accepted as a significant healthcare concern. Consequently, the VA is a valuable resource in the national educational efforts of future health professionals.

Disaster Preparedness: "Fourth Mission"

VA's "Fourth Mission" includes humanitarian support and national disaster preparedness in the event of war, national emergencies, and natural disasters (Veterans Affairs Fourth Mission Summary 2020). The Emergency Management Strategic Healthcare Group is tasked with developing comprehensive emergency management plans (Koenig 2003). Its purpose is to ensure continued service to veterans as well as civilians in support of local emergency efforts.

Over the years, VA has offered support and crucial medical as well as mental health resources in the wake of floods, tornadoes, and hurricanes. During the unprecedented and devastating COVID-19 pandemic, VA pledged to make 1500 medical beds available to non-veteran patients including those living in community nursing homes across the country. VA employees were also reassigned and deployed to COVID-19 hot spots to assist with clinical care (Massarweh et al. 2020). While the VA has traditionally provided care only to veterans, its "Fourth Mission" allows it to extend its resources and personnel for the benefit of the entire nation (Motivans 2015; Tsai et al. 2018).

Conclusion

The overarching mission of the Department of Veterans Affairs has always been to care for and honor military veterans. It is the largest integrated healthcare system in this country with over a thousand healthcare centers, serving close to nine million veterans each year. Overtime, VA has evolved and expanded; however, the spirit of its purpose has not changed: serving those who served remains the very foundation of its mission. Clinical services, education, research, and disaster preparedness are the four missions that inspire its growth and ongoing improvement.

References

Abdul-Hamid, W.K., Hughes, J.H. Nothing new under the sun: post-traumatic stress disorders in the ancient world. Early Sci Med. 2014;19:–557.

American Psychiatric Association. Diagnostic and Statistical Manual of Mental Disorders. 3rd ed. Washington, D.C.: American Psychiatric Association; 1980.

Ashton, C.M., Souchek, J., Petersen, N.J., et al. Hospital use and survival among Veterans Affairs beneficiaries. N Engl J Med 2003; 349:1637–46.

Blosnich, J. R., Brown, G. R., Shipherd, P. J., Kauth, M., Piegari, R. I., & Bossarte, R. M. (2013). Prevalence of Gender Identity Disorder and Suicide Risk Among Transgender Veterans Utilizing Veterans Health Administration Care. *American Journal of Public Health, 103*(10). doi:https://doi.org/10.2105/ajph.2013.301507

Byne, W., & Wise, J. (2020). Toward Optimizing Mental Health Care for Sexual and Gender Minority Veterans. *Focus, 18*(3), 289-295. doi:https://doi.org/10.1176/appi.focus.20200009

Cavanaugh, J.M. (2010). Helping those who serve: Veterans treatment courts foster rehabilitation and reduce recidivism for offending combat veterans. New England Law Review, 45, 463–487.

Clark, S.C., McGuire, J., & Blue-Howells, J. (2010). Development of veterans treatment courts: Local and legislative initiatives. Drug Court Review, 7, 171–208

Cochran, B. N., Balsam, K., Flentje, A., Malte, C. A., & Simpson, T. (2013). Mental Health Characteristics of Sexual Minority Veterans. *Journal of Homosexuality,*

60(2–3), 419-435. doi:https://doi.org/10.1080/00918369.2013.744932

Congressional Research Service. Federal Research and Development (R&D) Funding: FY 2020. Updated March 18th, 2020. Retrieved 11/11/2020 from https://fas.org/sgp/crs/misc/R45715.pdf.

Committee on Quality of Health Care in America. Crossing the Quality Chasm: A New Health System for the 21st Century. Washington, DC: National Academy Press, 2001.

Da Costa, J.M. On irritable heart: A clinical study of a form of functional cardiac disorder and its consequences. Am J Med Sci. 1871;61:17–52.

Dalton, A., Oliva, E., Harris, A., Trafton, J. Health services for VA patients with substance use disorders: comparison of utilization in fiscal years 2011, 2010, and 2002. Palo Alto: Program Evaluation and Resource Center; 2012.

Department of Veterans Affairs, Department of Defense (2015). Clinical Practice Guideline for the Management of Substance Use Disorders. Version 3.0. Retrieved 11/6/2020 from https://www.healthquality.va.gov/guidelines/MH/sud/VADoDSUDCPGRevised22216.pdf

Department of Veterans Affairs, V.H.A. VHA handbook 1162.02: Mental Health Residential Rehabilitation Treatment Program (MH RRTP) Washington, DC: Author; 2010.

Department of Veterans Affairs, V.H.A. VHA handbook 1160.01: Uniform Mental Health Services in VA Medical Centers and Clinics. Washington, DC: Author; 2008.

Ellerbe, L. S., Manfredi, L., Gupta, S., Phelps, T. E., Bowe, T. R., Rubinsky, A. D., Burden, J. L., & Harris, A. H. (2017). VA residential substance use disorder treatment program providers' perceptions of facilitators and barriers to performance on pre-admission processes. Addiction science & clinical practice, 12(1), 10. https://doi.org/10.1186/s13722-017-0075-z

Frank, J. W., Bohnert, A., Sandbrink, F., McGuire, M., & Drexler, K. (2020). Implementation and Policy Recommendations from the VHA State-of-the-Art Conference on Strategies to Improve Opioid Safety. Journal of general internal medicine, 1–5. Advance online publication. https://doi.org/10.1007/s11606-020-06295-y

Finlay, A. K., Smelson, D., Sawh, L., McGuire, J., Rosenthal, J., Blue-Howells, J., Timko, C., Binswanger, I., Frayne, S. M., Blodgett, J. C., Bowe, T., Clark, S. C., & Harris, A. (2016). U.S. Department of Veterans Affairs Veterans Justice Outreach Program: Connecting Justice-Involved Veterans with Mental Health and Substance Use Disorder Treatment. Criminal justice policy review, 27(2), https://doi.org/10.1177/0887403414562601

Godleski, L., Darkins, A., Peters, J. Outcomes of 98,609 U.S. Department of Veterans Affairs patients enrolled in telemental health services, 2006–2010. Psychiatr Serv. 2012 Apr;63(4):383-5. doi: https://doi.org/10.1176/appi.ps.201100206.

Hagedorn, H. J., Brown, R., Dawes, M., Dieperink, E., Myrick, D. H., Oliva, E. M., Wagner, T. H., Wisdom, J. P., & Harris, A. H. (2016). Enhancing access to alcohol use disorder pharmacotherapy and treatment in primary care settings: ADaPT-PC. Implementation science : IS, 11, 64. https://doi.org/10.1186/s13012-016-0431-5

Hankin, C.S., Spiro, A., I II, Miller, D.R., Kazis, L. Mental disorders and mental health treatment among U.S. Department of Veterans Affairs outpatients: The Veterans Health Study. American Journal of Psychiatry. 1999;156:1924–1930.

Hoge, C.W., Auchterlonie, J.L., Milliken, C.S. Mental health problems, use of mental health services, and attrition from military service after returning from deployment to Iraq or Afghanistan. JAMA. 2006;295(9):1023–1032.

Hoge, C.W., McGurk, D., Thomas, J.L., Cox, A.L., Engel, C.C., Castro, C.A. Mild traumatic brain injury in U.S. Soldiers returning from Iraq. New England Journal of Medicine. 2008;358:453–463.

Huddleston, C.W. III, Marlowe, D.B., & Casebolt, R. (2008). Painting the current picture: A national report card on drug courts and other problem-solving court programs in the United States Volume II, Number 1. Washington, DC: National Drug Court Institute

Jha, A.K., Perlin, J.B., Kizer, K.W., Dudley, R.A. Effect of the transformation of the Veterans Affairs health care system on the quality of care. N Engl J Med. 2003;348:2218–27.

Johnson, N. L., Robinett, S., Smith, L. M., & Cardin, S. (2015). Establishing a new military sexual trauma treatment program: Issues and recommendations for design and implementation. *Psychological Services, 12*(4), 435-442. doi:https://doi.org/10.1037/ser0000061

Kaplan, M.S., Huguet, N., McFarland, B.H., Newsom, J.T. Suicide among male veterans: A prospective population-based study. Journal of Epidemiological Community Health. 2007;61(7):619–624.

Knudsen, K.J., Wingenfeld, S. A specialized treatment court for veterans with trauma exposure: Implications for the field. Community Mental Health Journal. 2016;52(2):127–135.

Koenig, K. L. (2003). Homeland Security and Public Health: Role of the Department of Veterans Affairs, the US Department of Homeland Security, and Implications for the Public Health Community. *Prehospital and Disaster Medicine, 18*(4), 327-333. doi:https://doi.org/10.1017/s1049023x0000128x

Marcus, S. C., Hermann, R. C., Frankel, M. R., & Cullen, S. W. (2018). Safety of Psychiatric Inpatients at the Veterans Health Administration. *Psychiatric Services, 69*(2), 204-210. doi:https://doi.org/10.1176/appi.ps.201700224

Marlowe, D.B. (2010). Research update on adult drug courts. Alexandria, VA: National Association of Drug Court Professionals.

Massarweh, N. N., Itani, K. M., & Tsai, T. C. (2020). Maximizing the US Department of Veterans Affairs'

Reserve Role in National Health Care Emergency Preparedness—The Fourth Mission. *JAMA Surgery, 155*(10), 913. doi:https://doi.org/10.1001/jamasurg.2020.4153

Mattocks, K. M., Kauth, M. R., Sandfort, T., Matza, A. R., Sullivan, J. C., & Shipherd, J. C. (2014). Understanding Health-Care Needs of Sexual and Gender Minority Veterans: How Targeted Research and Policy Can Improve Health. *LGBT Health, 1*(1), 50-57. doi:https://doi.org/10.1089/lgbt.2013.0003

McCauley, J.L., Killeen, T., Gros, D.F., et al. Posttraumatic stress disorder and co-occurring substance use disorders: advances in assessment and treatment. Clin Psychol Sci Prac. 2012;19:283–304.

McQueen, L., Mittman, B.S., Demakis, J.G. Overview of the Veterans Health Administration (VHA) Quality Enhancement Research Initiative (QUERI), Journal of the American Medical Informatics Association. 2004; 11(5):339-343. https://doi.org/10.1197/jamia.M1499

Military Sexual Trauma (2020). Retrieved 11/22/2020, from https://www.mentalhealth.va.gov/docs/mst_general_factsheet.pdf

Milliken, C.S., Auchterlonie, J.L., Hoge, C.W.Longitudinal assessment of mental health problems among active and reserve component soldiers returning from the Iraq war. JAMA. 2007;298:2141–2148.

Mission of the Office of Academic Affiliations. (2019). Retrieved 11/22/2020, from https://www.va.gov/oaa/oaa_mission.asp

Mohamed, S., Neale, M. & Rosenheck, R. (2009). VA Intensive Mental Health Case Management in Urban and Rural Areas: Veteran Characteristics and Service Delivery. Psychiatric services (Washington, D.C.). 60. 914-21. https://doi.org/10.1176/appi.ps.60.7.914.

Motivans, M.A. Federal Justice Statistics, 2012-Statistical Tables. 2015 Retrieved 11/6/2020 from Washington, DC: http://www.bjs.gov/index.cfm?ty=pbdetail&iid=5217.

National Center for PTSD (2020a). History of the National Center for PTSD. Retrieved 11/12/2020 from https://www.ptsd.va.gov/about/work/ncptsd_history.asp

Noonan, M.E., & Mumola, C.J. (2007). Veterans in state and federal prison, 2004. Retrieved 11/6/2020 from http://bjs.gov/content/pub/pdf/vsfp04.pdf

Puntasecca, C., Hall, E. A., & Ware, J. (2019). Serving All Who Served: An Analysis of the VA's Visual and Digital Rhetorics for Welcoming Sexual and Gender Minority Veterans into VA Care. *World Medical & Health Policy, 11*(4), 440-463. doi:https://doi.org/10.1002/wmh3.321

Reisman, M. (2016). PTSD Treatment for Veterans: What's Working, What's New, and What's Next. P & T: a peer-reviewed journal for formulary management, 41(10), 623–634. https://www.ncbi.nlm.nih.gov/pmc/articles/PMC5047000/

Richardson, L.K., Frueh, B.C., Acierno, R. Prevalence estimates of combat-related post-traumatic stress disorder: critical review. Aust N Z J Psychiatry. 2010;44:4-19 https://doi.org/10.3109/00048670903393597

Rogers, E.S., Fu, S.S., Krebs, P., Noorbaloochi, S., Nugent, S.M., Gravely, A., Sherman, S.E. Proactive tobacco treatment for smokers using VA mental health clinics: a randomized controlled trial. Am J Prev Med. 2018 May; 54(5): 620-9.

Runnals, J. J., Garovoy, N., McCutcheon, S. J., Robbins, A. T., Mann-Wrobel, M. C., Elliott, A., & Strauss, J. L. (2014). Systematic Review of Women Veterans' Mental Health. *Women's Health Issues, 24*(5), 485-502. doi:https://doi.org/10.1016/j.whi.2014.06.012

Rytwinski, N.K., Scur, M.D., Feeny, N.C., et al. The co-occurrence of major depressive disorder among individuals with posttraumatic stress disorder: a meta-analysis. J Trauma Stress. 2013;26:299–309.

Saha, S., Freeman, M., Toure, J., Tippens, K. M., Weeks, C., & Ibrahim, S. (2008). Racial and ethnic disparities in the VA health care system: a systematic review. *Journal of general internal medicine, 23*(5), 654–671. https://doi.org/10.1007/s11606-008-0521-4

SAMSHA (2020). 2018 National Survey on Drug Use and Health: Veterans. Retrieved 11/6/2020 from https://www.samhsa.gov/data/report/2018-nsduh-veterans.

Sarteschi, C.M., Vaughn, M.G., & Kim, K. (2011). Assessing the effectiveness of mental health courts: A quantitative review. Journal of Criminal Justice, 39, 12–20. doi: https://doi.org/10.1016/j.crimjus.2010.11.003

Saxon, A.J., Davis, T.M., Sloan, K.L., McKnight, K.M., McFall, M.E., Kivlahan, D.R. Trauma, symptoms of posttraumatic stress disorder, and associated problems among incarcerated veterans. Psychiatric Services. 2001;52(7):959–964.

Seal, K.H., Cohen, G., Waldrop, A., et al. Substance use disorders in Iraq and Afghanistan veterans in VA healthcare, 2001–2010: implications for screening, diagnosis and treatment. Drug Alcohol Depend. 2011;116:93–101.

Sherman, S.E. A Framework for Tobacco Control: Lessons learnt from Veterans Health Administration. BMJ, 2008; 336: 1016-9. PMCID: PMC2364861

Sherman, S.E., Estrada, M., Lanto, A.B., Farmer, M.M., Aldana, I. Effectiveness of an on-call counselor at increasing smoking treatment. J Gen Intern Med., 2007; 22: 1125-31. PMCID: PMC2305728

Sherman, M. D., Kauth, M. R., Ridener, L., Shipherd, J. C., Bratkovich, K., & Beaulieu, G. (2014). An empirical investigation of challenges and recommendations for welcoming sexual and gender minority veterans into VA care. *Professional Psychology: Research and Practice, 45*(6), 433-442. doi:https://doi.org/10.1037/a0034826

Sherman, S.E., Krebs, P., York, L.S., Cummins, S.E., Kuschner, W., Guvenc-Tuncturk, S., Zhu, S.H. Telephone care co-ordination for tobacco cessation: randomized trials testing proactive versus reactive models. Tob Control. 2018 Jan; 27(1): 78-82.

Sherman, S.E., Takahashi, N., Kalra, P., Gifford, E., Finney, J., Canfield, J., Kelly, J., Joseph, G., Kuschner, W. Care coordination to increase referrals to smoking cessation telephone counseling: A demonstration project. Am J Managed Care., 2008; 14: 141-8. PMID: 18333706

Swartz, M.H. Textbook of Physical Diagnosis: History and Examination. 7th ed. Philadelphia, Pennsylvania: Elsevier; 2014.

Tanielian, T.L., Jaycox, L. Invisible wounds of war: Psychological and cognitive injuries, their consequences, and services to assist recovery. Santa Monica, CA: Rand Corporation; 2008.

Trafton, J.A., Greenberg, G., Harris, A.H., Tavakoli, S., Kearney, L., McCarthy, J., Blow, F., Hoff, R., Schohn, M. VHA mental health information system: applying health information technology to monitor and facilitate implementation of VHA Uniform Mental Health Services Handbook requirements. Med Care. 2013 Mar;51(3 Suppl 1):S29-36. doi: https://doi.org/10.1097/MLR.0b013e31827da836.

True, G., Frasso, R., Cullen, S. W., Hermann, R. C., & Marcus, S. C. (2017). Adverse events in veterans' affairs inpatient psychiatric units: Staff perspectives on contributing and protective factors. *General Hospital Psychiatry, 48*, 65-71. doi:https://doi.org/10.1016/j.genhosppsych.2017.07.001

Tsai, J., Finlay, A., Flatley, B., Kasprow, W. J., & Clark, S. (2018). A National Study of Veterans Treatment Court Participants: Who Benefits and Who Recidivates. Administration and policy in mental health, 45(2), 236–244. https://doi.org/10.1007/s10488-017-0816-z

Tsai, J., Rosenheck, R.A. Psychosis, lack of job skills, and criminal history: Associations with employment in two samples of homeless men. Psychiatric Services. 2016;67(6):671–675.

The US Department of Housing and Urban Development, Office of Community Planning and Development (2018). The 2018 Annual Homeless Assessment report (AHAR) to Congress. Retrieved 11/11/2020 from https://www.hudexchange.info/resource/5783/2018-ahar-part-1-pit-estimates-of-homelessness-in-the-us/

US Department of Veterans Affairs (2020a). About Veterans Affairs. Retrieved 11/22/2020 from https://www.va.gov/about_va/

U.S. Department of Veterans Affairs (2015). Veterans justice outreach. Retrieved 11/6/2020 from http://www.va.gov/homeless/vjo.asp.

US Department of Veterans Affairs (2015a). Women Veterans Health Care. Retrieved 11/22/2020 from https://www.womenshealth.va.gov/WOMENSHEALTH/healthcare.asp

VAntage Point, July 2016. VA conducts nation's largest analysis of veteran suicide. Retrieved 10/20/20 from https://www.blogs.va.gov/VAntage/28983/va-conductsnations-largest-analysis-veteran-suicide.

US Department of Veterans Affairs (2020). Office of Research and Development. Retrieved 11/11/2020 from https://www.research.va.gov/about/.

US Department of Veterans Affairs (2020b). Office of Research and Development. Retrieved 12/17/2020 from https://www.hsrd.research.va.gov/for_researchers/cyber_seminars/archives/video_archive.cfm?SessionID=3527&Seriesid=78

US Department of Veterans Affairs. Profile of Veteran: 2017 Highlights. Retrieved 11/22/2020 from https://www.va.gov/vetdata/Quick_Facts.asp

US Department of Veterans Affairs (2020c). Veteran Readiness and Employment. Retrieved 11/15/2020 from https://www.benefits.va.gov/vocrehab/

VA National Center on Homelessness Among Veterans (2020). Veterans Experiencing Homelessness. Retrieved 5/15/2020 from https://www.va.gov/homeless/nchav/research/index.asp.

Veterans Affairs Fourth Mission Summary (2020). Retrieved November 22, 2020, from https://www.va.gov/health/coronavirus/statesupport.asp

Warren, M. B., & Smithkors, L. A. (2020). Suicide Prevention in the U.S. Department of Veterans Affairs: Using the Evidence Without Losing the Narrative. *Psychiatric Services, 71*(4), 398-400. doi:https://doi.org/10.1176/appi.ps.201900482

Wise, J. E. (2019). Loss of moral high-ground: The transgender ban, a military psychiatrist's perspective and call to action. *Journal of Gay & Lesbian Mental Health, 23*(2), 114-116. doi:https://doi.org/10.1080/19359705.2019.1579037

Willenbring, M.L., Hagedorn, H., Postier, A., Kenny, M. Variations in evidence-based clinical practices in nine VA opioid agonist therapy clinics. Drug Alcohol Depend. 2004;75:97–106.

Wilson, N., Kariisa, M., Seth, P., Smith, H. IV, Davis, N.L. Drug and Opioid-Involved Overdose Deaths — United States, 2017–2018. MMWR Morb Mortal Wkly Rep 2020;69:290–297.

Child and Adolescent Psychiatric Services

J. Rebecca Weis and Schuyler Henderson

Introduction

The provenance of the proverb "It takes a village to raise a child" is unclear, with some tracing its origin to assorted cultures within Africa. It became a popular saying in the 1990s, however, because it succinctly encapsulates an important concept in any child-focused endeavor – that children are integrally related to and products of their environment. Psychologist Urie Bronfenbrenner provided one useful structure for thinking about the layers of environmental influences that surround children from the microsystem level all the way up to the macrosystem. More recently the recognition of how culture cuts across all these levels is influencing Bronfenbrenner's conceptualization with a multiplicity of intersecting influences of co-occurring cultural influences, even at the microlevel (Vélez-Agosto et al. 2017). Together with the effect of culture, a child's growth and social-emotional well-being are impacted by a number of factors including the family in which they live, the school they attend, the peers they increasingly value as essential, the setting where they receive pediatric care, the neighborhood in which they are raised, and the public systems that provide a safety net for nutrition and care. So, too, any attempt to provide mental health intervention for children and adolescents may be viewed as inherently "community psychiatry" since the child and adolescent (C&A) psychiatrist must keep all of these factors in mind when working with youth and their families.

The scope of child and adolescent mental health is broad. According to recent US data, between the ages of 2 and 17, 9.4% (6.1 million) have diagnosed ADHD, and between 3 and 17, 7.4% (4.5 million) have a diagnosed behavior problem, 7.1% (4.4 million) have diagnosed anxiety, and 3.2% (1.9 million) have diagnosed depression (Ghandour et al. 2019). Many children develop mental, behavioral, or developmental health diagnoses early in life. One in 6 children age 2–8 can be diagnosed with at least one of these (Cree et al. 2018), although on a broader scale, one might consider infant mental health beginning during pregnancy, given emerging research about fetal brain development and how it can be impacted by maternal stress (Van den Bergh et al. 2020). One may also consider child

J. R. Weis (✉)
Bellevue Hospital Center, New York, NY, USA

Department of Child and Adolescent Psychiatry, NYU Grossman School of Medicine, New York, NY, USA

NYC H+H/NYU Public Psychiatry Leadership Program, New York, NY, USA
e-mail: rebecca.weis@nyulangone.org

S. Henderson
Bellevue Hospital Center, New York, NY, USA

Department of Child and Adolescent Psychiatry, NYU Grossman School of Medicine, New York, NY, USA

W. E. Sowers et al. (eds.), *Textbook of Community Psychiatry*,
https://doi.org/10.1007/978-3-031-10239-4_46

and adolescent mental health to extend through young adulthood. Because not all children receive treatment, with only 53.5% of children diagnosed with a behavioral or conduct problem receiving mental health treatment or counseling in the past year (Ghandour et al. 2019), mental health practitioners with a community focus may find that innovative primary and secondary prevention programs are just as an important piece of the puzzle as treatment of more chronic mental health problems in children and adolescents.

In the remainder of this chapter, we will explore examples of primary, secondary, and tertiary preventive mental health interventions in which C&A psychiatrists may become involved as treatment provider, consultant, supervisor, educator, developer, leader, and advocate. Psychiatrists who have not completed specialty training in C&A psychiatry also at times become engaged on some level in work that affects children and adolescents, so this chapter is helpful to any psychiatrist dedicated to the cause of improving the social and emotional development of our next generation.

Primary Prevention

Psychiatrists have traditionally been less involved in primary prevention of mental illness, typically becoming involved when symptoms have become evident; however, psychiatrists along with other mental health providers and advocates have exciting opportunities to support true preventive interventions. These interventions can be especially effective when structured to provide support to those most at risk and implemented in settings where children are already an established presence. This approach recognizes that it takes a village and helps those who are already caring for children.

As an example, one program that has attempted to prevent child mental health problems is Healthy Steps. This program, focused on children aged 0–3 and based in pediatric primary care, promotes screening for child development (including social-emotional development) as well as parent mental health, provides enhanced resources for pediatricians to use with families who may encounter problems, and embeds psychologists and/or social workers in pediatric clinics to work with children and families with substantial risk factors for adverse social-emotional developmental outcomes (Briggs 2016). Among other positive outcomes, the program has improved outcomes for social-emotional development in families with parent histories of childhood trauma, thereby potentially interrupting cycles of intergenerational transmission of trauma that every psychiatrist knows all too well as connected to child and adolescent mental health problems (Healthy Steps Evidence Summary 2017). Although psychiatrists are not the clinicians providing direct service in this program within pediatrics, they can perform a valuable function in advocating for such programs in their communities and health systems and by partnering with pediatric colleagues to implement such programs, such as by providing supervision and support to mental health providers in the practice when more challenging mental health issues come up with specific families. C&A psychiatrists may here be able to have even more impact, given their experience in dealing with child, adolescent, and adult mental health. They are uniquely qualified to be part of the treatment team when parent mental health challenges are identified, assuring that parents receive mental health services they need while maintaining a strong family-centered perspective connected to the ultimate goal of supporting social-emotional development in young children.

Part of the reason Healthy Steps has succeeded as a preventive program is that it takes advantage of meeting children where they are already – parents of young children are highly motivated to adhere to pediatric well-visits, so most make it to these clinic visits.

As children age, their pediatric visits typically decrease significantly, and almost all are by then spending time at school, so school-based mental health prevention programs gain increasing traction. Programs have been developed for implementation at various grade levels, and while some have been targeted for socioeconomically disadvantaged school settings that tend to serve more at-risk populations, others are intended to be universal in their spread. These programs focus on helping children and adolescents learn problem-solving, interpersonal, and goal-setting skills as well as encouraging resilience with coping skills, stress management, mindfulness, self-care, and help-seeking behaviors. Additionally, some include education about specific mental health and related issues, with the goal of decreasing stigma around seeking assistance for those experiencing symptoms. This verges into secondary prevention territory since these activities enable identification and treatment of mental health problems before they reach a crisis state.

These programs have been successful in a variety of settings, although the impact for at-risk youth may be viewed as most notable (Fenwick-Smith et al. 2018). Questions remain about how and to what degree parent involvement plays a role in these programs (Bradshaw et al. 2021; Shucksmith et al. 2010; Stormshak et al. 2005); however, psychiatrists can certainly play an important role. As noted with preventive efforts in pediatrics with Healthy Steps, psychiatrists may be involved at various levels in these programs: advocating for school systems to implement such curricula, assisting in the implementation by providing consultation to school systems and specific schools to assist teachers and other school personnel, and volunteering to provide time to the schools directly interacting with groups of students to provide information through educational sessions. Psychiatrists may also help schools create plans for managing when these types of programs draw out existing mental health problems among students, creating referral pathways to ease access to care.

Although working within the pediatric and school environments provides robust opportunities for primary preventive services in which psychiatrists may be involved, there are other settings as well where C&A psychiatrists might contribute on either systems or direct care levels such as in family shelters, child welfare services, and community service organizations. Innovative platforms leveraging social media and other online platforms may increase reach even beyond these traditional in-person settings. Hopefully, the examples presented here can help activate creative thoughts for other opportunities in various communities.

Although long overdue, one of the most important fronts in primary prevention for C&A community psychiatry is addressing and changing the systemic racism and discrimination that have plagued communities and healthcare for far too long, impacting the lives of many racial and ethnic minority children. C&A psychiatrists can participate in antiracist initiatives that promote well-being in communities targeted by racism. Although it will take time, they can hope to contribute to an even deeper level of prevention – primordial prevention – eliminating the risk factors that predispose minority children to higher rates of mental health challenges by ensuring every person in these communities is treated with respect and guaranteed societal safety.

At the healthcare level, C&A psychiatrists can also work to make their organizations places of healing where all children and families feel comfortable seeking the help they need. For instance, they can support recruiting and retention practices to ensure diversity among mental health providers in their organizations. They can also consider other ways to support development of an antiracist environment in their setting such as participating in dialogues about important concepts such as microaggressions and privilege, exploring how they factor into mental health challenges, and treatment for minority populations. Although not strictly primary prevention work, assuring the healthcare system is racially and culturally sensitive is of crucial importance.

Secondary Prevention

From a public health perspective, screening for depression, anxiety, attentional and behavioral symptoms, and substance use problems has received increased attention in the past several years. Screenings usually again take advantage of settings where children and adolescents are already present. However, screenings alone are not enough. Treatment must be acceptable and quickly accessible to prevent any further progression of symptoms already present.

One exciting model of service delivery meeting that need is the collaborative care model (see chapter "Integrated Care and Community Psychiatry"). The AIMS Center at the University of Washington has been especially active in defining and codifying approaches that are effective for integrated behavioral health services in primary care (AIMS Center: Advancing Integrated Mental Health Solutions 2021), with initial efforts focused on adult services but then rapidly expanding to include pediatric primary care (Richardson et al. 2014; Yonek et al. 2020). Emerging research also points to elements of collaborative care that are most effective (Silverstein et al. 2015; Yonek et al. 2020) and to the inclusion of tele-mental health services as an exciting augmentation strategy to improve access and symptoms in areas where direct access to mental health services is most severely limited, such as outside of metropolitan areas (Myers et al. 2015). Additional benefits of collaborative care programs and similar psychiatric consultative services to primary care pediatric settings may include decreases in mental health care costs (Yu et al. 2017) and decreases in the prescribing of antipsychotics by primary care providers (Barclay et al. 2017; Baum et al. 2019).

C&A psychiatrists are typically connected to pediatric collaborative care efforts through providing consultation in the background to mental health clinicians (often social workers) integrated into primary care and to pediatricians/family medicine providers; however, emerging models including session/time-limited tele-mental health or in-person direct psychiatric consultation services allow a modicum of increased involvement with patients and may further improve outcomes (Myers et al. 2015). Psychiatric education and consultation roles to pediatric primary care providers can also be of great value, even if a practice is unable to integrate direct mental health providers (ProjectTEACH: Training and Education for the Advancement of Children's Health; Van Cleave et al. 2018).

Regardless of the exact role of the psychiatrist in assisting the spread of mental health care to primary care, their span of influence is greatly increased for treatment of mild to moderate mental health disorders, those for which patients might not otherwise come to treatment until symptoms have become much more pronounced. With these services, many more children may get early treatment for mental health problems, decreasing risk that these become chronic problems as a result of waiting too long for care.

Similar programs implementing treatment for mild to moderate mental health problems in schools, in community social service agencies, or online could be potential additional avenues for psychiatrists to become involved in secondary prevention efforts.

Tertiary Prevention

Although the goals of preventing mental health problems or solving them early on are certainly appealing and may be accomplished with a relatively small chunk of the psychiatrist workweek, most C&A psychiatrists will continue to find that most of their efforts in community psychiatry will serve those youth who are already displaying a considerable level of mental health symptomatology, often also combined with social and familial adversities. All too often, children and adolescents diagnosed with one mental health disorder also meet criteria for another comorbid disorder. This starts early: in the preschool years, epidemiologic diagnostic studies have found that between 25% and 50% of preschoolers with one mental health diagnosis met the criteria for at least one more diagnosis (Egger and Angold 2006). Add the compounding risks created by having symptoms early in life, and the accumulation of diagnoses may become even higher. The special expertise of C&A psychiatry clinicians is crucial to meeting the complex needs of many children and adolescents, and beyond treatment, these children need psychiatrists to participate in the development of rational systems of care as well as coordination with various government and educational systems in which they are involved.

Providing Treatment

For the C&A psychiatrist intending to practice using a community psychiatry lens, finding the best practice setting to maximize these efforts is the first step. In the first edition of this textbook, Charles Huffine presented that although some might not initially consider private practice to be a setting for the practice of community psychiatry, there are definite opportunities even in a non-public setting (Huffine 2012). To quote:

> The irony is that because remuneration tends to be better in private practice then in agency work, it may be possible in that setting to absorb some lower paid hours devoting them to a more active community psychiatry style of practice; visiting schools to deal with the social and academic problems of one's patients, helping families deal with juvenile courts, addressing parenting issues that can avert marital tensions and domestic violence.

Many psychiatrists interested in practicing community psychiatry, though, will choose to spend at least a portion of their career working in a community or public mental health clinic or agency (Ranz et al. 2006). In such settings, psychiatrists may find that they need to advocate not only for patients and families but also for themselves to avoid being forced into compromised positions, boiled down to only short visits with patients for the purpose of prescribing. C&A psychiatrists can and do shape their practices in agencies so that they can carry out the critical functions of a complete evaluation of a child, together with their family context, by developing either formal or informal leadership roles in their agencies. They take interest in administrative problems and use their creativity to collaborate in developing a more effective and efficient treatment system (AACP Guidelines for Psychiatric Leadership in Organized Delivery Systems for the Treatment of Psychiatric and Substance Disorders 2010). They may learn to do this in alliance with the other mental health professionals in their workplace, especially if they have not had prior experience with certain realities of caring for service users in public agencies. Joining with line staff in such agencies will very likely provide an education in community factors critical to their patients. We cannot overemphasize the importance of seeking out mentorship and connecting with psychiatrist peers with similar interests and goals. Post-graduate leadership training programs for physicians, such as public psychiatry fellowships or quality management training institutes, although requiring an investment of time in the short term, help psychiatrists develop skills not adequately focused on in traditional medical training. These are skills that are helpful, if not crucial, to thriving in systems that are often under-resourced but indispensable in the treatment of vulnerable populations.

Additional challenges often faced in any community health setting include dissemination of best practices at the community level and retention of quality mental health providers. Children and adolescents struggling with mental health problems deserve continuity and the best possible treatment, but unfortunately services often fail to provide these basic elements to the most vulnerable children. Psychiatrists can again use their position of expertise and collaborative skills to try to guide the clinics and agencies in which they work to address these issues. Utilizing professional organizations and connections from the academic institutions in which they trained may help them connect clinics to training resources for evidence-based treatments. Connections to researchers particularly interested in implementation science of mental health treatments may be particularly fruitful. Although at times academic centers may be viewed as "ivory towers," dispersing best practices to all people, including those in public health systems, is a social justice imperative (Cristofalo 2013). Standardized clinical decision support systems may be another mechanism for disseminating best practices to the community level (Røst et al. 2020), and psychiatrists can play a role in helping to monitor whether this is an approach that might ultimately be of use for their own setting. C&A psychiatrists may also develop opportunities to provide training themselves within their organizations and provide supervision in collaboration with other disciplines within the multidisciplinary team. Fostering an environment of multidisciplinary collaboration may be one component that is important to retention of staff within community settings (Hayashi et al. 2009), although certainly much more research is needed to fully understand how to best address the frequent turnover of staff members in these settings.

Systems Serving Special Populations and Needs

As was discussed at the beginning of this chapter, child and adolescent development and wellness are always embedded in multiple systems, and this is particularly true for those with more serious mental health issues. At a minimum, these youth are often involved in the special education system and frequently also connected in some way to the child welfare system and/or, as they age, to the juvenile justice system. A relatively large overlap exists between those impacted with mental health problems and those who require services for intellectual developmental delays or serious medical problems (Glasson et al. 2020; Hysing et al. 2007). Finally, numerous other youth need services that are tailored to their life and situations, such as those who have experienced trauma; are dealing with issues related to immigration; are homeless; have been the subject of discrimination because of their race, religion, sexuality, or gender; have required forensic evaluation; or are struggling with substance use disorders. In-depth discussion of each of these crucial populations and the role of C&A psychiatrists in serving them is beyond the scope of this chapter, so we will cover only a few of the most common concepts.

First, C&A psychiatrists need to be informed about, and up to date with, changes within the educational system. Individualized education plans, the Individuals with Disabilities Act, and Section 504 of the Americans with Disabilities Act all play very important roles in work with children and adolescents. At the individual level, C&A psychiatrists may need to advocate for patients to receive appropriate neuropsychological evaluations to support requests for needed services. Knowledge of special education resources available to children in the community is also crucial and in some larger cities requires close relationships with other professionals who specialize in keeping up-to-date with the entire spectrum of both public and private education services and settings available to students. C&A psychiatrists may also provide direct treatment or assistance with supervision/planning in school-based mental health clinics that enable children and adolescents to function in less restrictive educational settings despite their mental health problems or, if needed, to get the best education possible in settings specifically designed to also address their mental health treatment needs. Similarly, psychiatrists may provide both direct service and leadership of services for children in foster care, juvenile justice, and public mental health residential settings – all of these pursuits fall squarely within the practice of community psychiatry given the emphasis on working across and maximizing effectiveness of service systems in the best interests of the child.

Second, trauma-informed care also deserves special mention as a specialized type of care, for which a substantial body of evidence exists. On a primary prevention level, C&A psychiatrists may influence how society views the impact of child trauma and advocate for policies and programs known to decrease adversities and traumas for children, such as availability of high-quality daycare for all young children. In clinical settings, though, one often finds that children have already experienced one or more situations qualifying as "an event, series of events, or set of circumstances that is experienced by an individual as physically or emotionally harmful or life threatening and that has lasting adverse effects on the individual's functioning and mental, physical, social, emotional, or spiritual well-being" (Menschner 2016). These events are unfortunately highly prevalent; using the Adverse Childhood Experiences (ACE) questionnaire, studies have found that between 38% and 56% of the population between the ages 0 and 17 in the Unite States have been exposed to one ACE, and those who have one ACE are likely to have had exposure to another. Being poor or black increases the risk for exposure to ACEs (Adverse Childhood Experiences Among US Children 2017). Some events, such as physical or sexual abuse, are clear-cut traumata based on traditional psychiatric definitions, but other less clear-cut traumatic events nevertheless frequently place children in toxic stress situations in the absence of buffering supportive adult relationships. Mechanisms through which trauma and toxic exposure impact on mental (and medical) health in children include potential long-term alterations in the hormonal stress response system as well as changes in brain development (Shonkoff and Garner 2012). Studies using the ACEs questionnaire also likely underestimate the prevalence of trauma exposure given that the questionnaire does not account for community exposure to violence, cumulative exposures to systemic racism and discrimination, or both man-made and natural disasters, as well as numerous other common sources of traumatic exposure. Also, the child is rarely the only member of a family who has been the victim of trauma, with parents often carrying the effects of trauma from their own childhoods as well as more recent trauma. In some troubled situations, the parent may even have played a role in the exposure to trauma by being abusive or being unable to address interpersonal violence in the home to protect the child.

Understanding the scope and nature of child trauma and adversity informs the practice of C&A community psychiatry. Trauma is unfortunately nearly ubiquitous, and psychiatrists must try to understand specific adversities impacting the population they serve at both the individual, family, and community level to be able to address this effectively in treatment. This means continuing to understand, and be open to, developments in society, especially ones that are youth-driven and that-involve changing concepts of identity and disclosures of trauma that are too often hidden, suppressed, or ignored.

At a more systemic level, each community mental health setting must strive to create an environment that is conducive to healing through trauma-informed practices. Psychiatrists can play a pivotal role in developing both the organizational and clinical structures needed to address trauma most effectively. Clinically, in addition to screening for exposure and providing trauma-specific treatments, treatment should include the goals of promoting resilience skills and empowering parents to be involved in addressing the trauma and adversity they and their children have endured/are still enduring (Menschner 2016), thus strengthening a protective buffer that may at least bring adversities that cannot be quickly ameliorated back into the tolerable range of effect on the child.

The Systems of Care Concept

The "village" raising children includes many places specifically designed for youth. The educational, child welfare, and mental health agencies already mentioned in this chapter, when combined along with other elements, form a system of care. In the past three decades, there has been great emphasis on understanding how the system of care works for children, adolescents, and their families. There are important questions to consider in evaluating whether a system of care is as functional as it should be: Is it fragmented into silos, or are services coordinated? Must a family having difficulties with their child manage multiple meetings each week with different agencies while often getting contradictory advice, or can they participate with all involved professionals as a full member of a team to create a single cohesive plan for their child? C&A psychiatrists with understanding of systems can be a source of support for families by assuring collaboration between the agencies involved in getting a troubled youth back on track.

Fragmentation in human services for children led to the System of Care movement. The context for development of this concept can be traced to the early 1900s, but especially during the 1960s as the federal government under the Kennedy administration began making changes within the previously established public mental healthcare system, which had been focused to a large degree on institutionalization of adults with chronic mental illness. The creation of a community mental healthcare clinic system provided a possible foundation for services for children and adolescents; however, by 1982, the Children's Defense Fund highlighted that there were still many deficits in the realm of children's mental health in an important monograph titled *Unclaimed Children: The Failure of Public Responsibility to Children and Adolescents in Need of Mental Health Services* (Knitzer 1982).

At the same time, families who were furious with fragmented care joined together, first in communities and then nationally. The National Federation of Families for Children's Mental Health emerged in 1989 through the efforts of parents demanding coherent services for their children. Ira Lourie, a C&A psychiatrist directing the NIMH in the early 1980s, demanded federal attention to fragmented care for multisystem involved children and youth. He is credited with initiating the Child and Adolescent Service System Program (CASSP). Stoul and Friedman (1986) wrote the CASSP monograph that defined the term System of Care and created the values and principles statement widely credited for influencing many communities in the United States to adopt System of Care concepts as a "value-based practice" (Winters and Terrell 2003).

In 1993, CASSP evolved into the Comprehensive Community Mental Health for Children and Their Families grant program (often called System of Care grants). Between 1993 and 2015, the federal Center for Mental Health Services funded a total of 300 grants in states, territories, counties, and federally recognized tribal entities. Grantees used their funding to create and/or expand systems of care that serve children and adolescents with serious emotional disturbances and their families, establishing a coordinated network of community-based services and supports organized to meet the challenges of children, adolescents, and their families. Table 1 shows the important components/concepts of System of Care services.

Table 1 Important components/concepts of System of Care services

Family driven
Individualized, strengths based, and evidence informed
Youth guided
Culturally and linguistically competent
Provided in the least restrictive environment
Community based
Accessible
Collaborative and coordinated across an interagency network

These programs ultimately led to a new philosophy in planning treatment: the wraparound process, which emphasizes that parents (and older youth) should be in charge of planning for the care they receive for behavioral health problems, supported by experienced parents and professional care managers who enable them to meaningfully collaborate with the professionals involved. Wraparound's chief innovation is in mobilizing communities to help a family through inviting extended families, neighbors, community leaders, and other natural support groups (Pumariega and Winters 2003).

Within adult community mental health circles, especially those serving populations with more chronic and severe mental health challenges, concepts akin to some of the tenets of systems of care have emerged in the recovery paradigm. In particular, patient-centered and patient-driven approaches to planning for treatment and other services and the emphasis on building on strengths (not just addressing problems) play roles in each model. One important conceptual difference, though, is that children and adolescents are not trying to regain losses secondary to mental illness to "recover" but rather may be trying to find their way back to a developmental trajectory disrupted by the struggles they are facing. Getting back to the most functional trajectory ideally initiates a virtuous cycle, with each success then setting the stage for the next success. Depending on developmental level, children and adolescents may not yet be able to imagine long-term outcomes based on here and now decisions, reinforcing the need for parents and other supports to help develop the optimal course.

In some instances, children and adolescents will have access to an already established wraparound team, but in others they will not. In these instances, C&A psychiatrists can play a vital role in helping to assess needs and engage other providers, services, and community resources to build a team that will effectively assist the patient and family in reaching the best outcome, utilizing systems of care and recovery concepts as guidance.

Although systems of care has typically focused on the web of different agencies serving children and adolescents, the internal system of care within the mental health system is another opportunity for the C&A psychiatrist to have an organizing influence to improve patient care and outcomes, especially for patients with higher-level mental health needs. Transitions between emergency room visits, inpatient care, acute outpatient care, and standard clinic care can be tremendously disruptive, resulting in dropping out of care or frustration with uncoordinated services. Whenever possible, having strong lines of communication between services at these different levels makes the transitions safer and simpler, and C&A psychiatrists may assist in building connections and communicating with leadership in relevant programs.

Connections to adult services as youth "age out" of adolescent services is another point of transition that may be especially difficult when long-term mental health challenges have interfered with youth developing skills for navigating systems that they now must engage with as "adults." Psychiatrists will often find themselves helping these youth through the transition, so building and maintaining connections with the adult mental health services in the same community is important. Some programs have been developed that specifically recognize this challenge, such as those that serve patients with early onset of psychosis in the teen years (see chapter "Early Psychosis and the Prevention and Mitigation of Serious Mental Illness"). Such models might be worth considering for other youth and other mental health disorders to improve continuity of care across what is already an enormous transition in life.

Empowerment Programs for Families

The peer support movement in adult psychiatry is mirrored in C&A community psychiatry by parent advocates working within the mental health system. Parents with lived experience parenting children with mental health challenges offer practical knowledge that can be extremely useful to other families. They also may be able to help bridge connections between families who find it hard to trust the mental health system and mental health providers. There are, though, some unfortunate barriers to broader involvement of parents in the mental health system as advocates. First, many systems do not provide employment positions for parent advocates. While there are some formal employment positions for this work with clearly defined responsibilities on wraparound teams, reimbursement pathways through health insurance have not been well developed to support employment in most settings. Realistically, most parents are not able to become advocates if doing so means having to volunteer significant chunks of time while still working to support their own families. Additionally, there is no current standardized training for parent advocates, as compared to the professional norm in the mental health field, including an expanding cohort of adult peer counselors. Some states have developed special training to assure that parent advocates have solid basic knowledge in mental health, but of course training usually also requires funds. An organized approach to train and support volunteer parent advocates has been developed in Ohio in partnership with the National Alliance for Mental Illness (Davis et al. 2010), and such partnerships can increase availability of quality training at lower costs.

Although the current state of affairs for parent advocates is not ideal, C&A community psychiatrists should recognize how valuable a resource parents as advocates can be and seek to become aware of available parent advocate resources, whether available at their place of work or through outside resources. Additionally, they may advocate at an organizational level as well as more broadly for further development and availability of this type of resource. Psychiatrists may also serve as a source of support by being available when parent advocates are occasionally overwhelmed with the depth of problems they must face as they work with other families who are in need of support.

Balancing the Many Roles of the Child and Adolescent Community Psychiatrist

Throughout this chapter, we have covered numerous ways that C&A psychiatrists can operate utilizing a community focus. In many cases, these roles are dependent on strong collaborative skills so the psychiatrist can smoothly and effectively interact with the many other influences that are important in the life of patients they serve. Being able to partner with other care providers and service organizations, as well as with families, can require a great deal of diplomacy, patience, and effort to ensure true understanding of what partners mean, need, and want. It also requires a clear understanding of the administrative structure of programs, the rules and regulations governing them, and the culture of an array of community resources. Although not discussed above, it is also important to maintain understanding of the financing strategies that keep the child and adolescent mental health system functioning, as expectations sometimes must be calibrated to resources (or matched with creative discovery of new resources).

Although collaboration and practicality are necessary, they are not always enough and should never replace the C&A psychiatrist's commitment to take a stand when the situation demands. This may occur on an individual level for a patient when the psychiatrist sees a misunderstanding of diagnosis or of the social situation interfering with the most appropriate treatment plan. Perhaps even more importantly, it occurs at the level of leadership and advocacy. In community mental health settings, psychiatrists may need to advocate strongly for change within systems that are resistant to such change, especially when the system has become entrenched in providing care in a way that ill-serves children and adolescents. There are also times when a psychiatrist's knowledge and ethics lead them to contest a social or community issue in the interest of children and adolescents; in such situations, respectfully engaging in thoughtful discussion can sometimes sway opinion or at least may move some to consider loosening ties to certain tightly held but unhelpful or outmoded beliefs. As an example, C&A psychiatrists are occasionally called upon to address child and adolescent issues more globally, especially in the case of disruptive behavior. Within a system or community, such behaviors are difficult for others to tolerate, but punitive approaches frequently employed are not effective in changing the behavior in troubled youth. By bringing a developmental and trauma-informed perspective to the discussion, psychiatrists can hope to influence adoption of much more effective approaches and policies.

In all of the situations noted, child and adolescent psychiatrists must develop a finely honed knowledge of their communities, how children are functioning and treated in those communities, and the balance of social crosscurrents and cultures within the mental health system and in other child-serving systems. Those armed with such understanding will stand the best chance of succeeding as clinician, collaborator, leader, and advocate.

References

American Association for Community Psychiatry (2010). AACP Guidelines for Psychiatric Leadership in Organized Delivery Systems for the Treatment of Psychiatric and Substance Disorders.. Retrieved from https://drive.google.com/file/d/0B89glzXJnn4cVG1JNzJRY0JReGM/view

Adverse Childhood Experiences Among US Children. (2017, October 2017). Retrieved from https://www.cahmi.org/wp-content/uploads/2018/05/aces_fact_sheet.pdf

AIMS Center: Advancing Integrated Mental Health Solutions. (2021). Retrieved from https://aims.uw.edu/collaborative-care

Barclay, R. P., Penfold, R. B., Sullivan, D., Boydston, L., Wignall, J., & Hilt, R. J. (2017). Decrease in Statewide Antipsychotic Prescribing after Implementation of Child and Adolescent Psychiatry Consultation Services. *Health Serv Res, 52*(2), 561-578. doi:https://doi.org/10.1111/1475-6773.12539

Baum, R. A., King, M. A., & Wissow, L. S. (2019). Outcomes of a Statewide Learning Collaborative to Implement Mental Health Services in Pediatric Primary Care. *Psychiatr Serv, 70*(2), 123-129. doi:https://doi.org/10.1176/appi.ps.201800163

Bradshaw, M., Gericke, H., Coetzee, B. J., Stallard, P., Human, S., & Loades, M. (2021). Universal school-based mental health programmes in low- and middle-income countries: A systematic review and narrative synthesis. *Prev Med, 143*, 106317. doi:https://doi.org/10.1016/j.ypmed.2020.106317

Briggs, R. D. (Ed.) (2016). *Integrated Early Childhood Behavioral Health in Primary Care: A Guide to Implementation and Evaluation*. Switzerland: Springer International Publishing.

Cree, R. A., Bitsko, R. H., Robinson, L. R., Holbrook, J. R., Danielson, M. L., Smith, C., . . . Peacock, G. (2018). Health Care, Family, and Community Factors Associated with Mental, Behavioral, and Developmental Disorders and Poverty Among Children Aged 2–8 Years – United States, 2016. *MMWR Morb Mortal Wkly Rep, 67*(50), 1377–1383. doi:https://doi.org/10.15585/mmwr.mm6750a1

Cristofalo, M. A. (2013). Implementation of health and mental health evidence-based practices in safety net settings. *Soc Work Health Care, 52*(8), 728-740. doi:https://doi.org/10.1080/00981389.2013.813003

Davis, T. S., Scheer, S. D., Gavazzi, S. M., & Uppal, R. (2010). Parent advocates in children's mental health: program implementation processes and considerations. *Adm Policy Ment Health, 37*(6), 468-483. doi:https://doi.org/10.1007/s10488-010-0288-x

Egger, H. L., & Angold, A. (2006). Common emotional and behavioral disorders in preschool children: presentation, nosology, and epidemiology. *J Child Psychol Psychiatry, 47*(3-4), 313-337. doi:https://doi.org/10.1111/j.1469-7610.2006.01618.x

Fenwick-Smith, A., Dahlberg, E. E., & Thompson, S. C. (2018). Systematic review of resilience-enhancing, universal, primary school-based mental health promotion programs. *BMC Psychol, 6*(1), 30. doi:https://doi.org/10.1186/s40359-018-0242-3

Ghandour, R. M., Sherman, L. J., Vladutiu, C. J., Ali, M. M., Lynch, S. E., Bitsko, R. H., & Blumberg, S. J. (2019). Prevalence and Treatment of Depression, Anxiety, and Conduct Problems in US Children. *J Pediatr, 206*, 256-267.e253. doi:https://doi.org/10.1016/j.jpeds.2018.09.021

Glasson, E. J., Buckley, N., Chen, W., Leonard, H., Epstein, A., Skoss, R., . . . Downs, J. (2020). Systematic Review and Meta-analysis: Mental Health in Children With Neurogenetic Disorders Associated With Intellectual Disability. *J Am Acad Child Adolesc Psychiatry, 59*(9), 1036–1048. doi:https://doi.org/10.1016/j.jaac.2020.01.006

Hayashi, A. S., Selia, E., & McDonnell, K. (2009). Stress and provider retention in underserved communities. *J Health Care Poor Underserved, 20*(3), 597-604. doi:https://doi.org/10.1353/hpu.0.0163

Healthy Steps Evidence Summary. (2017). Retrieved from https://ztt-healthysteps.s3.amazonaws.com/documents/5/attachments/HealthySteps_OutcomesSummary.FINAL.10.09.18.pdf?1599572344

Huffine, C (2012).Child and adolescent psychiatry. In McQuistion HL, Sowers WE, Ranz JM, Feldman JM (Eds.), *Handbook of Community Psychiatry*. London: Springer Science & Business Media.

Hysing, M., Elgen, I., Gillberg, C., Lie, S. A., & Lundervold, A. J. (2007). Chronic physical illness and mental health in children. Results from a large-scale population study. *J Child Psychol Psychiatry, 48*(8), 785-792. doi:https://doi.org/10.1111/j.1469-7610.2007.01755.x

Knitzer, J. O., Lynn. (1982). *Unclaimed Children: The Failure of Public Responsibility to Children and Adolescents in Need of Mentalh Health Services*: CDF Publications.

Menschner, C. a. M., Alexandra. (2016, April 2016). Issue Brief: Key Ingredients for Successful Trauma-Informed Care Implementation. Retrieved from https://www.samhsa.gov/sites/default/files/programs_campaigns/childrens_mental_health/atc-whitepaper-040616.pdf

Myers, K., Vander Stoep, A., Zhou, C., McCarty, C. A., & Katon, W. (2015). Effectiveness of a telehealth service delivery model for treating attention-deficit/hyperactivity disorder: a community-based randomized controlled trial. *J Am Acad Child Adolesc Psychiatry, 54*(4), 263-274. doi:https://doi.org/10.1016/j.jaac.2015.01.009

ProjectTEACH: Training and Education for the Advancement of Children's Health. Retrieved from https://projectteachny.org/

Pumariega, A. J. and Winters, N. C. (Ed.) (2003). The Handbook of Child and Adolescent Systems of Care: The New Community Psychiatry: Jossey-Bass.

Ranz, J. M., Vergare, M. J., Wilk, J. E., Ackerman, S. H., Lippincott, R. C., Menninger, W. W., . . . Sullivan, A. (2006). The tipping point from private practice to publicly funded settings for early- and mid-career psychiatrists. *Psychiatr Serv, 57*(11), 1640–1643. doi:https://doi.org/10.1176/ps.2006.57.11.1640

Richardson, L. P., Ludman, E., McCauley, E., Lindenbaum, J., Larison, C., Zhou, C., . . . Katon, W. (2014). Collaborative care for adolescents with depression in primary care: a randomized clinical trial. *Jama, 312*(8), 809–816. doi:https://doi.org/10.1001/jama.2014.9259

Røst, T. B., Clausen, C., Nytrø, Ø., Koposov, R., Leventhal, B., Westbye, O. S., . . . Skokauskas, N. (2020). Local, Early, and Precise: Designing a Clinical Decision Support System for Child and Adolescent Mental Health Services. *Front Psychiatry, 11*, 564205. doi:https://doi.org/10.3389/fpsyt.2020.564205

Shonkoff, J. P., & Garner, A. S. (2012). The lifelong effects of early childhood adversity and toxic stress. *Pediatrics, 129*(1), e232-246. doi:https://doi.org/10.1542/peds.2011-2663

Shucksmith, J., Jones, S., & Summerbell, C. (2010). The Role of Parental Involvement in School-Based Mental Health Interventions at Primary (Elementary) School Level. *Advances in School Mental Health Promotion, 3*(1), 18-29. doi:https://doi.org/10.1080/1754730X.2010.9715671

Silverstein, M., Hironaka, L. K., Walter, H. J., Feinberg, E., Sandler, J., Pellicer, M., . . . Cabral, H. (2015). Collaborative care for children with ADHD symptoms: a randomized comparative effectiveness trial. *Pediatrics, 135*(4), e858–867. doi:https://doi.org/10.1542/peds.2014-3221

Stormshak, E. A., Dishion, T. J., Light, J., & Yasui, M. (2005). Implementing family-centered interventions within the public middle school: linking service delivery to change in student problem behavior. *J Abnorm Child Psychol, 33*(6), 723-733. doi:https://doi.org/10.1007/s10802-005-7650-6

Stroul, B., & Friedman, R. (1986). A system of care for severely emotionally disturbed children and youth. Washington, DC: CASSP Technical Assistance Center, Center for Child Health and Mental Health Policy; Georgetown University, Child Development Center.

Van Cleave, J., Holifield, C., & Perrin, J. M. (2018). Primary Care Providers' Use of a Child Psychiatry Telephone Support Program. *Acad Pediatr, 18*(3), 266-272. doi:https://doi.org/10.1016/j.acap.2017.11.007

Van den Bergh, B. R. H., van den Heuvel, M. I., Lahti, M., Braeken, M., de Rooij, S. R., Entringer, S., . . . Schwab, M. (2020). Prenatal developmental origins of behavior and mental health: The influence of maternal stress in pregnancy. *Neurosci Biobehav Rev, 117*, 26–64. doi:https://doi.org/10.1016/j.neubiorev.2017.07.003

Vélez-Agosto, N. M., Soto-Crespo, J. G., Vizcarrondo-Oppenheimer, M., Vega-Molina, S., & García Coll, C. (2017). Bronfenbrenner's Bioecological Theory Revision: Moving Culture From the Macro Into the Micro. *Perspect Psychol Sci, 12*(5), 900-910. doi:https://doi.org/10.1177/1745691617704397

Winters, N. C., & Terrell, E. (2003). Case management: The linchpin of community-based systems of care. In A. J. Pumariega & N. C. Winters (Eds.), The handbook of child and adolescent systems of care: The new community psychiatry (pp. 171–200). Jossey-Bass/Wiley.

Yonek, J., Lee, C. M., Harrison, A., Mangurian, C., & Tolou-Shams, M. (2020). Key Components of Effective Pediatric Integrated Mental Health Care Models: A Systematic Review. *JAMA Pediatr, 174*(5), 487-498. doi:https://doi.org/10.1001/jamapediatrics.2020.0023

Yu, H., Kolko, D. J., & Torres, E. (2017). Collaborative mental health care for pediatric behavior disorders in primary care: Does it reduce mental health care costs? *Fam Syst Health, 35*(1), 46-57. doi:https://doi.org/10.1037/fsh0000251

Serving Elders in the Public Sector

Carl I. Cohen, Lucy Bickerton, Joyce Huang, Zoya Huda, Paige Marze, and Michael M. Reinhardt

The gray tsunami is upon us. Providers working in the public sector are confronting the demands of a rapidly growing aging population. It behooves community practitioners and policymakers to familiarize themselves with the tenets of geriatric psychiatry and with the resources available to provide high-quality comprehensive care. This chapter provides a brief guide to caring for older adults by describing the basic principles of geropsychiatry, key community resources, primary prevention strategies, and illustrations of successful innovative model programs, especially those incorporating integrated systems and age-friendly care.

Basic Principles of Geriatric Psychiatry for Community Practitioners

1. *Older adults are the most heterogeneous group in the population*. There are dramatic within-group differences among older people in their physical and mental health, functioning, social networks, political and religious beliefs, and so forth. Although we often categorize aged persons based on chronological age—e.g., the US Bureau of the Census (US Bureau of the Census 1996) defines "elderly" as 65 and over—there are marked differences in biological aging. This is especially true among persons with persistent and severe mental illness such as schizophrenia, who have a 15- to 20-year shortened life expectancy and are thought to undergo "accelerated" aging (Copeli and Cohen 2019). Although older adults are heterogeneous, they do share some common life experiences that may have psychosocial ramifications (so-called cohort effect). However, with an increasing proportion of older persons reaching very old age, the number of cohorts within the aging population has grown. For example, persons born in the 1930s grew up during the Great Depression and World War II, whereas those born after the war came of age during more prosperous times that included the cultural and social turmoil of the 1960s. Similarly, the oldest African Americans grew up during a period of oppressive racial segregation and discrimination that engendered considerable pessimism regarding social change, whereas "young-old" African Americans came of age during a period of social activism that resulted in civil rights legislation and the elimination of Jim Crow laws in the south.

   Clinical Implications: Mental and physical health care to older adults should not be

C. I. Cohen (✉) · L. Bickerton · J. Huang · Z. Huda · P. Marze · M. M. Reinhardt
SUNY Downstate Health University, Brooklyn, NY, USA
e-mail: carl.cohen@downstate.edu

W. E. Sowers et al. (eds.), *Textbook of Community Psychiatry*,
https://doi.org/10.1007/978-3-031-10239-4_47

determined solely by chronological age because of the marked diversity within this age group. However, living through similar historical periods can provide a common context for older adults of the same age.

2. *The demographics of aging are shifting*. The baby boomers (people born between 1946 and 1964) have had a profound impact on the number of elderly people aged 65 and over, which will double over the first third of the twenty-first century from 35 million (12.4% of the population) in 2000 to 72 million (20%) in 2030 (Federal Interagency Forum on Aging-Related Statistics 2012), at which point the number of elderly will exceed the number of children in the population. Persons aged 85 and over are the most rapidly growing segment of our population, and their numbers will double over the first quarter of the century and more than quadruple by 2050 to over 19 million persons. The older population is also becoming more diverse. For example, in the 2000 census, 16% of the elderly population was non-white (Blacks, Hispanics, Asians, Native Americans) or 5.8 million persons. In 2050, 36% of the elderly population will be non-white or 29.5 million persons. Thus, there will be a fivefold increase in the number of minority elders over the first half of the twenty-first century (Federal Interagency Forum on Aging-Related Statistics 2012).

   Clinical Implications: Community mental health providers can expect to be working with increasingly older and more diverse populations and that they must possess appropriate clinical skills and cultural knowledge if they are to deliver competent care.

3. *Assessment is different in older age*: The assessment of older adults must consider physical handicaps, cognitive difficulties, and problems in communication secondary to deficits in vision and hearing. Another key difference from younger persons is the likelihood that caregivers, both formal and informal, will be more involved in providing information and treatment.

   Clinical Implications: On initial examination, mental health clinicians should systematically assess cognition, psychiatric symptoms, physical illness, and daily functioning and then continue to closely monitor for the impact of treatment on these domains. Although these domains often affect each other, dysfunctions within the domains may have diverse etiologies and require different treatment strategies.

4. *Disorders may present differently*: Like physical disorders, the clinical presentations of psychiatric disorders may differ in older persons. For example, compared to younger persons, depression in older adults may present with fewer signs of sadness and with more symptoms of social withdrawal, somatic concerns, motor disturbances, and apathy (Haigh et al. 2018). Similarly, late-onset schizophrenia tends to disproportionately affect women and to have fewer negative symptoms and formal thought disorders (Cohen et al. 2020).

   Clinical Implications: Clinicians must be vigilant for more atypical symptoms in older adults.

5. *Pharmacological treatment may be different*: With increased age, there are changes in the absorption rate of medications, distribution of drugs as a result of an increase in adipose tissue relative to lean body mass, diminished metabolism in the liver, and declines in renal clearance.

   Clinical Implications: Dosages of medications may need to be lower than in younger persons, and considerations of side effects and drug interactions become more relevant (Kratz and Diefenbacher 2019). Ideally, it is best to prescribe drugs that do not undergo Phase I hepatic metabolism, but only Phase II hepatic metabolism (conjugation), since this process is not affected by aging. Because of changes in the distribution of drugs in the body, the fat-soluble drugs, which include many of the drugs used in psychiatry, tend to remain in the body longer and may cause toxicity. Conversely, water-soluble drugs such as lithium should be prescribed cautiously because of the diminution of total body water with age. Finally, some psychotropic drugs remain active (e.g., lithium, gabapentin, rivastigmine, paliperidone) until they are cleared by the kidney, and doses may need to be adjusted in older adults.

6. *The course of disorders may be different.* Among persons with schizophrenia, there is often a diminution in positive symptoms with age, whereas levels of co-occurring depression may remain the same or increase, and mild cognitive problems that occur early in the disorder may cross the threshold into dementia due to the normal age-related declines (Cohen et al. 2020). Depression in later life may present with subtypes (e.g., depression associated with cerebrovascular disease called "vascular depression," depression with dementia, depression associated with medical conditions) that are often more resistant to treatment, and older persons with major depression may be more prone to relapse or relapse sooner than their younger counterparts (Haigh et al. 2018).

   Clinical Implications: When treating persons with schizophrenia, it is important to be aware of changes in the severity and types of symptoms that occur with aging and to adjust treatment accordingly. In treating older adults with depression, it is important to determine the subtype of depression, because prognosis and treatment vary considerably depending on the etiology of the depression.

7. *Aging is characterized by both long-standing conditions and late-onset conditions that may become chronic.* There is increasing evidence that depression in older adults has a more chronic course than in younger adults. For example, over three-fifths of older persons attending specialized psychiatric services experienced a chronic course, and chronicity ranged from 20% to 50% among elders with presumably milder disorders being treated by primary care providers (Haigh et al. 2018). Moreover, the line between reversible and irreversible illnesses may become less distinct. For example, late-onset depression may be a prodromal sign of dementia or dementia masquerading as depression. Rates of dementia found on follow-up among persons with depression and cognitive problems in old age have ranged from 0% to 89% (Brodaty and Connors 2020).

   Clinical Implications: Although treatment can help reduce recurrence and levels of symptoms, the complex interaction of psychiatric and physical conditions may make full recovery less likely. Consequently, while the ultimate goal for all patients may be the remission of symptoms, sometimes treatment goals will have to be adjusted, and like some chronic physical disorders, persons may have to live with a modest level of symptoms.

8. *Nearly all older adults with psychiatric disorders will have comorbid conditions, although not all comorbidity is alike.* Some comorbid conditions can contribute substantially to disability and functional decline (e.g., severe osteoarthritis, heart disease, neurocognitive disorders, frailty), whereas other conditions have minimal effects on daily functioning (e.g., well-controlled hypertension or hypercholesterolemia). There is strong evidence of a reciprocal interaction between depression and many physical disorders (Haigh et al. 2018). In other words, depression is associated with a greater occurrence of physical illnesses, and physical disorders may lead to a greater incidence of depression.

   Comorbidity of different categories of symptoms is more common in older adults. For example, depression and anxiety often co-occur, and having more anxiety symptoms is a poor prognostic indicator for depression (Haigh et al. 2018).

   Moreover, underlying neuropathology may increase the likelihood of comorbid symptoms. Thus, vascular changes in the brain may increase cognitive deficits as well as depression ("vascular depression").

Similarly, in persons with dementia, roughly one-fourth manifest clinical depression, one-half have psychotic symptoms, and two-fifths to one-half have agitation or activity disturbances (Phan et al. 2019). One of the more significant health challenges involves persons with some combination of chronic pain, dementia, depression, anxiety, bereavement, multiple losses, social isolation, and poor nutrition (Flint 2002).

Clinical Implications: Treating mental illness in later life is more challenging because of the co-occurrence of physical and neurological disorders that manifest in more complex clinical presentations. Consequently, clinical response to standard treatments may be less robust in later life.

9. *Psychiatric illness must be understood within a social and biological context.*

   It is said that aging is a bit like gambling: the longer you go on, the more likely you are to lose. Thus, older adults must confront and deal with various losses, perhaps best summarized by the 4Ds of aging: disability, dependency, desertion (e.g., loss of close relationships as people move away or die), and death (e.g., one's own mortality and the death of others). Adjusting to these losses and stressors is a key to greater well-being in later life.

   Clinical Implications: For some adults who are physically healthy and have strong social resources, a useful strategy might be to encourage activities and engagement following losses of kin or friends. On the other hand, for persons with more disabilities and fewer resources, encouraging too much engagement may be unrealistic and further exacerbate feelings of worthlessness (Gubrium 1973).

10. *There is continuity in personality.* Each older person is a product of the lifelong effects of physiological, environmental, and psychological factors. Concerning the latter, although some changes occur across a lifespan, various personality traits (e.g., coping, sense of control, self-esteem, interpersonal skills) tend to be fairly stable over time, and they will affect how one deals with late-life stressors (Sadavoy 2009). Moreover, scientists have identified a "paradox of aging" that helps explain why older people can adapt to adverse events (Thomas et al. 2016). That is, while physical and cognitive functioning may decline with age, subjective well-being increases. Thus, persons in their 70s and 80s have higher well-being scores than any other age group. Compared to younger persons, older adults commonly recall past events more favorably, give more positive ratings to negative events, focus more on things that will yield greater well-being, and view their social networks more favorably.

    Clinical Implications: On the positive side, continuity means that most older persons have been able to successfully employ various coping strategies to manage their stressors over their lifespan (Sadavoy 2009). This is further strengthened by the older person's affinity toward positive rather than negative information. Consequently, therapists should aim to help gird up previously successful coping mechanisms. However, with increasing age and disability, earlier strategies may be less effective, and therapy must assist patients to develop new strategies to deal more effectively with the physical, cognitive, and social losses that occur in later life.

11. *The prevalence of psychiatric disorders in older adults and mental disorders is best viewed on a continuum.* A major issue in geriatric psychiatry is whether the official classification of psychiatric disorders accurately reflects the degree of psychiatric distress in the aging community. This stems in part from the fact that many older adults may present atypically, that comorbid physical and cognitive disorders may make the fulfillment of the diagnostic criteria more difficult, and that elders with psychiatric disturbances may cluster in certain settings so that they may not be adequately sampled (e.g., naturally occurring retirement communities,

assisted living facilities, and nursing homes). Increasingly, gerontologists view psychiatric disorders on a continuum and appreciate the clinical importance of subsyndromal or subthreshold disorders. This perspective overcomes some of the difficulties using formal diagnostic categories and acknowledges that many of these subthreshold categories are associated with poor functioning and outcomes. Typically, prevalence rates of specific disorders—major depression, anxiety, and psychoses—are roughly half of the levels found in younger samples. However, when symptom prevalences of these conditions are assessed, they are usually similar to younger persons (Cohen and Doumlele 2023). While dementia increases dramatically with age (the prevalence rate doubles every 5 years until age 90 and then may level off), it is also found on a continuum. Persons with mild neurocognitive impairment (MCI) have modest cognitive deficits (one to two standard deviations below their age peers) with minimal or no problems in daily functioning. Rates of MCI are nearly double the rates of dementia in elderly people, i.e., 17% versus 10% (Petersen et al. 2018).

Clinical Implications: Although rates of depressive, anxiety, and psychotic disorders may be lower in older adults, the rates of symptoms for each of these groups may be equal to younger persons. Thus, psychiatric and cognitive symptoms are common among older people and may cause dysfunction or distress, even when they do not meet the DSM-5 criteria. Thus, more so than in any other age category, it is important to not overly rely on strict diagnostic criteria and to focus on the clinical symptoms that are raising concern.

12. *It is essential to view the treatment goals for older adults with more severe and persistent mental illness in the context of a life course trajectory*. For more severe mental illnesses such as schizophrenia, it is now recognized that the disorder does not typically attain a stable end stage in later life. Rather, many people transition into and out of various states of clinical recovery. Cohen and Reinhardt (2020) identified a five-tier taxonomy of clinical recovery in older adults with schizophrenia in which 12% remained persistently in clinical recovery (defined as being in clinical remission and attaining community integration) at both baseline and follow-up (Tier 1) and 18% never met the criteria of clinical recovery (Tier 5). The remaining 70% moved between various states of remission and community integration over time (Tiers 2–4). For persons with severe mental illness, the ideal life trajectory can be viewed as a process moving from diminishing psychopathology and impaired functioning to normalization or "clinical recovery" to positive health and well-being ("successful aging"). The latter is a state that older adults may aspire toward, but often do not achieve. Among the general aging population, only one-fifth attain "successful aging," whereas, among persons with schizophrenia, only about 1 in 50 persons attain this status.

    Clinical Implications: We now recognize that for many persons with schizophrenia, middle and older age is associated with more clinical movement than had been previously believed and treatment should be specifically targeted to where the person is located on the clinical trajectory.

13. *Mental illness in older age is complex*: Items 1 through 12 suggest a high degree of complexity concerning the interaction of age and mental illness. For example, Flint (2002) observed that in later life there is a complex interplay between depression, anxiety, physical illness, cognitive impairment, personality factors, and life stress. Despite the increase in vulnerabilities to various social and physical losses, as suggested above, many elders have physiological, psychological, and social resources that offset these processes and avert unfavorable outcomes.

    Clinical Implications: In caring for older adults, each biological, psychological, and social element is likely to be more complex than in younger adults because longevity has provided more life experiences along with more opportunities for interactions among these elements. It is important to remember that older adults are survivors, having outlived many of those in their age cohort, and they have strengths that must be appreciated along with any shortcomings. Care must be personalized to each person's symptom complex and biography.

Meeting the Service Needs of Older Adults

By 2030, one in five Americans will be age 65 or older, and roughly 15 to 20% will have a psychiatric disorder (Everett 2019). The cost of untreated mental illness in the United States is estimated to be as much as $300 billion annually, and approximately half of that cost may be attributed to people aged 60 and over (Sisko et al. 2009; National Alliance on Mental Illness 2017). Untreated mental illness often decreases a person's ability to address their medical comorbidities, which is particularly pertinent for elderly populations, where medical comorbidities are common, and frailty leads to significant mortality and exacerbates burdens placed on their caregivers. In 2015, among a cohort of Medicare beneficiaries, $2.7 billion (of $64 billion total costs) was spent on mental illness, with an additional $5.5 billion spent on medical spending associated with mental illness (Figueroa et al. 2020). The authors found that patients with a diagnosis of serious mental illness not only incurred costs from mental health services but also spent one-third more on medical services for physical conditions than their counterparts with no mental illness.

While older adults with mental illness have many unmet needs, they have a lower rate of service use than adults in middle age and are less likely to perceive the need for mental health services. A cross-national literature review by Wells et al. (2020) identified several factors that contribute to the unmet mental health needs of older adults: (1) a triad of elements based on the perception by older people and providers that mental illness is an inevitable consequence of aging, that the need for psychiatric care declines with age, and negative (ageist) attitudes about older people; (2) older adults' self-perceptions of stigma about having a mental illness; (3) lack of affordability of psychiatric care and/or the lack of availability of appropriate care; and (4) the high reliance on family caregivers to shoulder the burden of mental distress. Although these were prominent themes in the literature, there have been inconsistencies in the findings concerning the older persons' utilization of mental health services and their views about using mental health treatment. Contrary to expectation, an analysis of attitudes about mental health using the National Comorbidity Survey-Replication (NCS-R) data found that older Americans did not have negative help-seeking attitudes or beliefs about the efficacy of treatment for mental health problems (Mackenzie et al. 2008). More than 80% of adults 55 and older had positive attitudes, and more than 70% had positive treatment beliefs. This finding suggested that the availability of resources and perception of need rather than negative attitudes are more likely explanations for older adults' lower rates of mental health service use.

The existing formal and informal support systems do not work well. While formal and informal sources provide adequate services for certain client needs, over 70% of the clients do not receive the correct type of help for some of their needs (Cummings and Kropf 2009). Research studies underscore the complex multilevel needs experienced by older adults with mental health problems as well as the heterogeneity of the aging population. There is a consensus that mental health service needs can be addressed by: (1) ensuring that care is more accessible as well as age and culturally appropriate; (2) educating and creating greater linkages among health professionals, mental health clinicians, and social service providers; (3) enhancing communication and collaborating with informal caregivers; and (4) adapting to an individual's changing levels of functioning over time (Nair et al. 2019).

Community Resources and Care

In Table 1, we present an overview of the services for older adults based on a person's functional level. On the vertical axis of the table is a measure of independence and self-functioning (mental and physical) divided into three categories: well, moderately impaired, and/or severely impaired. On the horizontal axis are three broad categories of needs: physical and mental health needs; self-maintenance needs such as dressing, grooming, cooking, transportation, cleaning, and handling money; and a more complex level involving social needs such as work roles, friendship, intimacy, and education. Thus, for example,

Table 1 Types of services available to elderly individuals

Functional level	Physical and mental health needs	Self-maintenance needs	Social needs
Well elderly (60% of population)	Mutual help groups Consumer health education Health insurance Health screening Screening for psychiatric symptoms, substance abuse, and prescribed drug misuse	Shared housing Converted boarding homes ECHO[a] units and "granny flats" Section 8 and Section 202 housing Elderly apartment complexes Retirement community Congregate meal program Nutrition education "Brown bag" programs	Senior center Voluntary association Senior Community Service Employment Program Foster parents and grandparents Senior companions Service Corps of Retired Executives Adult education
Moderately impaired (30% of population)	Outreach services Visiting nurse Crisis intervention teams Collaborative care programs Problem-solving techniques	Case management Home care services Congregate housing Foster care Vocational rehabilitation Assisted living Board and care homes Congregate housing Meals on Wheels Transportation services Escort services Chore services	Friendly visiting Telephone reassurance Strengthen informal social network
Severely Impaired (10% of population)	Multiple help groups for family Outreach services Visiting nurses Crisis intervention teams Inpatient psychiatric and medical care Collaborative care programs	Daycare Respite care Home care services Hospice Nursing home Meals on Wheels Protective services Case management	Friendly visiting Telephone reassurance Strengthen informal social Support network Social skills training

Source: Modified from Cohen and Boran (2004) and Cohen and Ibrahim (2012)
[a]*ECHO* Elder Cottage Housing Opportunity

a comparatively well older man who has recently lost his spouse might be helped by referrals to mental health services in the top left box and social and vocational services listed in the upper right box of Table 1. Similarly, a moderately impaired person with depression might benefit from various services in the middle row of the table.

Description of Community Services

In working with older adults, community clinicians should familiarize themselves with the various types of community services available to older adults. In Table 2, we describe the programs that can be used to address the various needs listed in Table 1.

Model Innovative Programs

Over the past two decades, a variety of innovative community treatment strategies for older adults with mental illness have advanced the field toward an appreciation of the importance of addressing both co-existing psychiatric and medical disorders. These programs can be divided into (a) collaborative programs, (b) case management strategies, (c) self-management techniques, and (d) some combination of the three. New technology is also being used to help elders and to engage and train community practitioners. Some of these endeavors are described in the next section.

Collaborative initiatives that integrate mental health, primary care, and pertinent community supports have the potential to ease the accessibility issues faced by older adults and to foster cross-discipline knowledge transfer to address complex situations such as severe depression or suicidality (e.g., Unützer et al. 2002; Bruce et al. 2004; Horgan et al. 2009). Case manager strategies typically use persons with clinical backgrounds to provide guidance, counseling, and skills training to older clients concerning psychiatric and physical health, to promote appropriate care by primary care providers, and to enhance interdisciplinary communication. The principal goal is to improve the outcome of care (e.g., Bartels et al. 2014). Self-management strategies train older psychiatric patients to assume greater responsibility for their physical health as well as to improve coping abilities to deal with psychiatric stress (e.g., Bartels et al. 2015; Green et al. 2015; Druss et al. 2018).

Much of the focus of collaborative care programs and case management approaches for older people have been directed toward primary healthcare providers (Unützer et al. 2002; Bruce et al. 2004; Horgan, Le Clair, and Puxty 2009). For example, the World Health Organization (2004) asserts that the treatment of common mental disorders such as depression should be done in primary healthcare settings. Several writers (Lester et al. 2004) have contended that the integration of health and mental health care within primary healthcare settings is the best option for psychiatric care and that these settings may be the logical sites for "medical homes" for persons with mental illness. Some of the reasons for focusing on primary care settings is that they are the predominant site of care for most psychological problems (e.g., anxiety, depression), that consumers are more satisfied when their physical and mental health care are integrated into the primary healthcare setting, and primary health care is a better fit with the typical way a majority of consumers present their undifferentiated mental health problems. With this better fit, there may be greater treatment adherence and improved health outcomes. Although the range of mental health needs that appear in primary care settings often exceeds the capacity and skills of even well-trained primary care physicians, referral to an outside mental health professional is considered a poor alternative. Consequently, programs that create collaboration between primary care providers and mental health professionals may serve to improve the skills of primary care providers in dealing with the psychosocial aspects of care. Finally, there is compelling evidence indicating that collaborative care programs are cost-effective (Gilbody et al. 2006; Health Resources Services Administration 2019).

Table 2 Principal community services for older adults

Assistance and protection	
Information and referral (assistance) services	These activities are coordinated through the Administration on Aging (AOA) that requires each state to designate an agency for aging services. In some states, an independent office on aging has been established; in the remaining states, aging programs are part of a human services department. In most states, aging agencies designate smaller geographic service centers, termed area agencies on aging (AAA), to provide local communities with information and referral services. There are also a variety of voluntary and private resources that provide information and assistance, e.g., family services agencies, senior centers, and mental health associations
Case or care management	The primary aim of traditional case management is to help clients and families deal with a fragmented and complex system by locating and coordinating existing resources through a process that includes screening, assessment, case planning, linkage to services, advocacy, monitoring, and behavioral health. More recently, care managers are being used as part of a therapeutic team for psychiatric patients and may involve direct counseling, collaboration with primary care providers, and coordination of services (see section "Model Innovative Programs" below)
Adult Protective Services	These services serve persons who are incapable of performing functions necessary to meet the basic physical and health requirements, incapable of managing finances, dangerous to self or others, or exhibiting behavior that brings them into conflict with the community. Services may be provided with or without consent if guardianship is required. Such agencies may facilitate hospitalization or assist with various legal actions
Community care	
Respite care	Respite care is provided on a short-term basis (usually several hours to several weeks) to a dependent person in the community to relieve the caregiver. It includes five major categories: (1) in-home (e.g., home companions, homemakers, home healthcare workers), (2) in the community (e.g., adult daycare), (3) institutions caring for elderly individuals (e.g., adult homes, overnight stays) that provide 24-hour furnished accommodations, (4) hospitals, and (5) combination models. Religious organizations, nursing homes, home healthcare agencies, and voluntary agencies commonly organize these services
In-home healthcare services	This wide array of services can be grouped under three broad categories: (1) intensive or skilled services, e.g., wound care, catheters, tube feedings ordered by a physician and under the supervision of a nurse; (2) personal care or intermediate services for medically stable individuals who require assistance with activities of daily living; and (3) homemaker, chore, or basic services such as light housekeeping or meal preparation to persons with difficulties caring for their themselves but who can do more basic activities of daily living such as feeding or toileting. A new addition to the home healthcare model is Medicaid Consumer Directed Personal Assistance Program (CDPAP), available in many states, allows Medicaid to pay family or friends to provide the home care services and for the consumer to manage the selection, training, and scheduling of aides
Related in-home services	There are a variety of services for homebound elderly individuals that can complement or substitute for the in-home services described above. These may be offered by senior centers or other agencies and may include friendly visiting, telephone reassurance, emergency response systems, and chore services

(continued)

Table 2 (continued)

Adult daycare	Designed for at-risk persons who are mentally, physically, or socially impaired and who need day services to maintain or improve their level of functioning so that they can remain in or return to their own home. Such programs may also provide some respite for families. Programs are typically staffed by interdisciplinary professionals who provide participants with health monitoring, socialization and leisure activities, and assistance with ADLs. They are traditionally categorized into two broad types: health-oriented and social services-oriented. More recent classifications have focused more on the location of services: Auspice Model 1, includes outpatient day centers affiliated with nursing homes and rehabilitation centers that cater to physically dependent, older populations and are health-oriented (e.g., nursing, health assessments, social services, and physical, occupational, and speech therapies). Auspice Model 2, situated in an outpatient unit of a general hospital, social service, or housing agency. Most patients are younger than those in Model 1 and can perform activities of daily living; more than 40% have mental disorders. Services are more social and supportive (e.g., case management, professional counseling, transportation, nutrition, education, health assessment). Auspice Model 3, special-purpose centers that serve a single type of clientele such as blind or mentally ill persons, those with dementia, or veterans
Mutual aid (self-help) groups	Self-help or mutual help aid groups are very popular modalities comprising small groups formed voluntarily by people with one or more of these attributes: (1) they are composed of members who share a common condition, situation, heritage, symptoms, or experience; (2) they are largely self-giving and emphasize self-reliance; (3) they offer fact-to-face fellowship networking and are typically accessible without charge; and (4) they tend to be self-supporting rather than dependent on external funding. Examples include informational and emotional support groups, such as Alzheimer's caregiver groups, and political action groups, such as the Gray Panthers. Some self-help groups have been organized with the financial assistance of religious institutions, community organizations, and community mental health centers
Nutritional services	
Home delivery program ("Meals on Wheels")	Meals are delivered to the homes of individuals of any age who cannot prepare or obtain adequate nutrition. These are typically administered by nonprofit agencies or congregate meal programs that prepare, package, and deliver midday meals and occasionally cold suppers or snacks
Congregate meals program	Inexpensive meals served in a community setting such as a church, senior center, or school, for individuals who cannot prepare or obtain adequate nutrition. All persons aged 60 and older and their spouses of any age are eligible
"Brown bag" program	Various community groups provide volunteers who fill shopping bags for low-income elderly individuals
Transportation and escort	
Transportation services	Federally subsidized funding for transport (e.g., subsidized taxis, minibuses, and private cars) to assist with physician visits and errands
Escort services	Community agencies and police provide escorts to assist frail elderly individuals with errands and other activities
Shopping assistance	Senior centers and other senior organizations provide transport service to help elderly persons get to shopping centers
Volunteer and employment programs	
Retired Senior Volunteer Program	Volunteers aged 55 or older work in hospitals, nursing homes, senior centers, and other community programs
Foster Grandparents	Provides a small stipend to low-income individuals aged 55 or older to work with youths in need of supportive and affectionate adults; the program is conducted in schools, hospitals, drug treatment centers, correctional institutions, and/or childcare centers

(continued)

Table 2 (continued)

Senior Companions	This federally funded program provides a stipend and supplemental insurance for low-income persons aged 55 or over. Volunteers provide aid and friendship to elderly individuals who have difficulty with daily living tasks in nursing homes, hospitals, and private homes
Service Corps of Retired Executives	Allows retired professionals to assist small business owners who lack funds to pay for such services
Senior Community Service Employment Program	Authorized by the Older Americans Act, it requires participants to be aged 55 or older and have an income that is below 125% of the federal poverty line. The program employs participants in a variety of community service activities at nonprofit and public facilities, including schools, hospitals, daycare centers, and senior centers. The Senior Aides and the Green Thumb (in rural areas) programs are part of this funding
General community programs	
Adult education	Increasing numbers of elderly individuals are enrolling in tuition-waiver programs in colleges, adult education courses, and elder hostel programs
Senior centers	Participation in senior centers is appreciably greater than any other community-based service for elders. One model views the center as an informal social club or voluntary organization. The other model depicts the center as a multipurpose service provider or social services agency designed to meet a range of needs of frail elderly individuals, particularly poor and disengaged persons
Community housing	
Long-term care	
Nursing homes	These institutions can be divided into two broad categories: (1) skilled nursing facilities, which provide 24-hour nursing care and medical coverage for persons who require extensive care (reimbursement is provided by Medicaid and time-limited coverage by Medicare), and (2) intermediate care facilities that provide health-related care for persons who are more stabilized but require some medical and nursing supervision (not full time); costs are covered by Medicaid but at a reduced level for Medicare. New models of nursing have focused on enhancing the quality of life while providing clinical care. For example, the Green House Model offers small, residential-style homes for 10–12 residents who each have a private room and attached bath and share a central living space with an open kitchen, dining, and living area. A team of universal caregivers is responsible for the range of personal, clinical, and home care activities
Hospice	Provides a setting of comfort and relief from pain in a person's last weeks of a terminal illness. Hospices may be found as a hospital unit, a freestanding facility, an outpatient unit for counseling and medical visits, or a home care program
Board and care homes and residential care facilities (RCFs)	Both are generic terms that describe various types of housing with supportive long-term services exclusive of licensed nursing homes. They provide more support to residents than congregate housing or rooming houses. Homes typically provide three meals a day, laundry service, and 24-hour supervision; many also provide transportation services, cleaning of living areas, personal assistance, and arrangement of medical appointments. Traditionally, board and care homes and RCFs have fallen into one of three basic types: (1) homes serving residents with intellectual or developmental disabilities, (2) homes serving residents with mental illness, and (3) homes serving a mixed population of physically frail elderly, cognitive impaired elderly, and persons with mental illness. Most facilities are in the last category
Assisted living	Assisted living constitutes a new name for a rapidly expanding sector of the traditional board and care housing and residential care facility sector. These facilities are designed to accommodate frail elderly residents who can live independently but need assistance with activities of daily living
Congregate housing	Consists of apartment houses or group accommodations that provide limited health services and other support services (e.g., meals in a central dining room, heavy housekeeping, social services, recreational activities) to functionally impaired older persons who do not need routine nursing care. These facilities are somewhat less institutionalized than board and care residences

(continued)

Table 2 (continued)

Foster care	For older persons, particularly those with chronic mental illness, in need of care and protection in a substitute family; it provides socialization, stimulation, support, and protection. The number of paying residents is usually limited to four
Single room occupancy (SRO)-type housing for older people	SRO-type housing has been used to house specific target populations such as persons with mental illness or substance use disorders. Such units often provide on-site staffing and support
Elder Cottage Housing Opportunity (ECHO)	Also known as granny flats, accessory housing, and second-unit ordinances, these are ancillary structures for elderly persons that are permitted by special zoning variances to be placed on land belonging to the children of these individuals, thereby enabling the older person to receive informal care and support from his or her kin
Continuum of care and life-care facilities	These facilities offer multiple levels of care ranging in setting from one's own home to a nursing home. They provide private living units with ancillary services such as meals and health care. When there is a need for more intensive care, the resident may be transferred to a nursing home, often on the same site. As residents' health needs change over time, they can move through the levels of care in the community
Retirement communities	These are non-licensed, age-segregated communities of apartments or freestanding homes. Services are generally social (e.g., clubhouses, tennis courts) and do not routinely include health services
Elderly apartment complexes	These include public, nonprofit, and privately owned buildings for elderly individuals. Many have been built with Section 202 federal funds. They do not routinely provide health care, although they are required to provide a daily meal and to make available housekeeping, transportation, personal care, and chore services
Shared housing ("senior matching")	A social services agency matches occupant (owner/renter) with a renter, or the agency buys or rents units and then rents these units to others
Naturally occurring retirement communities (NORCs)	NORCs refer to buildings, apartment complexes, or neighborhoods that were not originally developed for older persons and where most residents have become elderly. The term has evolved to mean any building or neighborhood where more than half of the residents are over 60. Innovative programs for these older persons have been established that provide social work, case management, nursing, recreation, and educational enrichment
Geriatric mental health services	
Mental health crisis intervention services	These services provide rapid restabilization of a person's psychiatric symptoms and social adjustment. Crisis services are often hospital-based or tied to community mental health centers. Services may be delivered in the patient's home or at a designated place outside the home. Mobile units or home treatment teams may visit the home or maintain daily telephone contact
Community outreach	Such models of care involve a team of outreach workers that connect services to persons in non-institutional settings such as where they reside or spend significant amounts of time. These programs have been successful in meeting the mental health needs of traditionally underserved and disadvantaged elderly populations such as those with low-income, homeless persons, those residing in rural areas or public housing, or from racial and ethnic minority backgrounds
Psychiatric vocational rehabilitation	Although these programs underserve older patients, such programs should be considered as a treatment option for aging psychiatric patients. Two basic types of programs exist. Sheltered employment, also known as sheltered workshops or compensated work therapy programs, provides work opportunities for individuals who are not ready for competitive employment. Transitional employment provides real-work jobs with commercial establishments that are supervised by psychiatric or rehabilitation professionals
Geriatric psychiatry clinics and dementia centers	These programs typically offer multidisciplinary, comprehensive evaluations, and care for older adults. They are usually situated at large medical centers
Model innovative community care programs	As described below, these programs focus primarily on enhancing interdisciplinary collaboration and /or use case managers with clinical skills to provide guidance and counseling to older clients as well as to promote appropriate care by primary care providers and interdisciplinary communication

Source: Updated from Cohen and Boran (2004) and Cohen and Ibrahim (2012)

Technology and Community-Dwelling Older Adults

There are a variety of technologies now available that enable older adults to improve their health, age in place, and receive age-friendly care. These technologies span a wide range of forms and intended uses—humanoid care robots, personal devices, smart home systems and devices or software that enable telehealth connectivity. In-home sensing and monitoring devices cover everything from medical needs such as fall detection and medication adherence to personal or "quantified self" measurements focused on calorie and step counting, sleep quality, and air quality (Prendergast 2020). While personal devices that track activity and other biometrics appear to increase activity levels and mobility in older adults, the impact of activity tracking on mental health, quality of life, and cognitive health remains uncertain (Oliveira et al. 2020). These same personal devices may be used for audio and video connectivity to family and friends and be connected to smart home systems. Evidence suggests that smart home and home health monitoring systems may improve activities of daily living as well as cognitive, mental, and cardiovascular health (Liu et al. 2016). Unfortunately, economic and technological barriers have limited their implementation (Liu et al. 2016; Choi et al. 2019). Telehealth and telepsychiatric health have shown a great promise in improving access to care across multiple populations of older adults, but they face utilization hurdles including cost, legal, technological, remunerative, provider, and patient factors (Gentry et al. 2019). Technological advances have allowed the democratization of knowledge across community and provider settings alike by utilizing distance learning models that leverage technology to amplify clinical knowledge. For example, Project ECHO (Extension for Community Healthcare Outcomes) is a model of guided practice wherein community providers attend video conference-based sessions composed of brief didactics and case discussions focused on the evidence-based management of targeted health conditions. Project ECHO has shown promise in improving provider's geriatrics healthcare knowledge and patient outcomes (Bennett et al. 2018).

Primary Prevention

Although the principal focus of this chapter is on secondary prevention (i.e., early detection and intervention of disease) and tertiary prevention (i.e., minimizing effects of disease and disability), community mental health providers are often involved in developing primary prevention programs (i.e., prevention of disease occurrence). The Institute of Medicine (Gordon 1983) categorized primary prevention into three groups based on the level of clinical symptoms and the target population. As seen in Table 3, "universal prevention" focuses on asymptomatic people and uses broad-based initiatives such as health screenings, lifestyle recommendations, environmental protection, and improvements in local and national health systems. "Selective prevention" targets persons that still may be asymptomatic or pre-symptomatic with interventions that are more specific to their risk factors such as harm reduction, physician education, and medication reviews. Last, "indicated prevention" is directed at high-risk individuals with some symptoms (e.g., subsyndromal conditions) and uses more disease-specific interventions including psychotherapy, behavioral treatment, and pharmacotherapy within the context of an integrated care system.

Guiding Principles of Psychogeriatric Care for the "Ideal" Individual Program and Service System

In recent years, two overlapping themes have dominated the geriatric care literature as achievable visions for individual- and systems-level care: "integrated care" and "age-friendly" systems. The World Health Organization (2019) developed a framework entitled, "Integrated Care for Older People" (ICOPE), aimed at guiding health and social services for older people at the

Table 3 Primary prevention of mental illness in older adults

Intervention terminology	Approach	Target	Objectives	Examples
Universal prevention	Population	Entire population not identified based on individual risk	Implement broadly directed initiatives to prevent substance misuse, mental illness, and suicide-related morbidity and mortality through reducing risk and enhancing protective factors	Physical and mental health screening, health education, exercise, addressing vascular risk factors for dementia (obesity, diabetes, hyperlipidemia, hypertension smoking), optimize mobility and sensory capacity, diminishing social isolation, religiosity/spirituality, reducing firearms, enhancing health coverage, improving social safety net, improving environmental and climate issues, age-friendly communities, training of health and social system workers, coordinated multidisciplinary health systems
Selective prevention	Population; high-risk Individuals	Asymptomatic or pre-symptomatic individuals or subgroups with risk factors for substance misuse, mental illness, or suicide; individuals who have a higher-than-average risk of developing substance use or mental disorders; bereavement; post-stroke patients	Prevent morbidity and mortality by addressing specific characteristics that place older adults at risk	Physician advice and warnings, medication reviews, patient education, gatekeepers, caregiver support groups, addressing drug misuse, stress-reducing strategies, improve sleep hygiene, socialization activities
Indicated prevention	High-risk individuals	Individuals with detectable symptoms, subsyndromal disorders, and/or other primary risk factors for substance abuse, mental illness, or suicide	Treat/intervene with older individuals with precursor signs and symptoms to prevent the development of disorders or the expression of suicidal behavior	Psychosocial interventions such as problem-solving, reminiscence therapy, caregiver counseling, depression management, provider collaboration, CBT or IPT for depressive symptoms, interdisciplinary programs to address depressive symptoms and suicidality (see section "Model Innovative Programs")

References: Blow et al. (2005), Blazer et al. (2009), and Madhusoodanan et al. (2010)

clinical (micro-), service (meso-), and system (macro-) levels. At the micro-level, the focus is on ascertaining patient-centered goals and developing care plans that maximize their intrinsic capacity and functional ability. At the meso-level, the aim is to ensure that care is coordinated and delivered by a multidisciplinary team and to engage and empower people and communities toward community-based care. At the macro-level, the focus is on strengthening the governance and accountability of systems, developing policies for integrated care, protecting elders from abuse, ensuring that various stakeholders are involved in policy and service reviews, that care is delivered equitably, and creating workforces and financing to implement these policies.

Several of the recommendations for micro-level and meso-level services were inspired by the novel collaborative care approaches described in the earlier section on "Model Innovative Programs".

The Age-Friendly Health Systems framework advocates for modifications in geriatric care for primary treatment settings (e.g., routine use of geriatric screening tools, home visits, telehealth, use of physical therapy and exercise groups), hospitals (e.g., develop psychogeriatric services, acute care for elderly units, polypharmacy screening), community (e.g., age-friendly cafes and stores, walkways, reduced pollution, community screenings for geriatric disorders), public health systems (e.g., coordination of supports and services), as well as emergency departments, nursing homes, care transition teams, and palliative care (Health Resources Services Administration 2019). Preliminary research identified 17 evidenced-based models and programs serving older adults that were found to be guided by 13 core features, which were in turn distilled into the "vital few" elements (Institute for Healthcare Improvement 2019). The latter comprised the "four Ms" that is forming the essential core for guiding age-friendly practices in various community settings:

- "What matters" to the older adult, and using information elicited from each individual to guide care preferences and health outcome goals.
- "Medication" refers to the identification of the use of polypharmacy and inappropriate medication that can increase the likelihood of experiencing adverse effects for older adults with comorbid chronic diseases and is a significant predictor of hospitalization, nursing home placement, and impaired mobility.
- "Mentation" refers to the identification of psychiatric symptoms of depression, suicidality, anxiety, substance abuse, delirium, and cognitive impairment.
- "Mobility" refers to assessing limitations in mobility and predisposition to falls.

The IHI reviewed studies of age-friendly model programs and found that geriatric integrated systems significantly reduced inpatient utilization and ICU stays, and increased use of hospice care as well as patient satisfaction; also, there was a decrease in emergency department utilization and rehospitalization for persons with dementia (Institute for Healthcare Improvement 2019). The review found a 30% or more reduction in direct, indirect, and total hospital costs among patients who receive care to improve mobility. Simple improvements in communication between practitioners and patients were shown to successfully decrease the medication burden on older adults and improve health.

Conclusions

In the early years of this century, Leibowitz (2006) observed that a comprehensive and rationally designed geriatric mental healthcare system did not exist in the United States. Rather, a patchwork of fragmented and uncoordinated services had evolved in most communities. Although older adults are still often poorly served with respect to psychiatric care, health providers, policymakers, and funding agencies have gained an increased appreciation of the need for integrated, age-friendly care, largely driven by the demographic imperative of a rapidly expanding and diverse older populace. The dramatic growth in the number of older persons has created a crisis in geropsychiatric care. There are 54 million elderly people in the United States but fewer than 1300 practicing geriatric psychiatrists; two states have none (Health Resources Services Administration 2019). Consequently, community psychiatrists, primary care providers, and other healthcare professionals are being called upon to provide care and develop treatment programs for older adults. This chapter has provided a toolkit to assist community practitioners in their work with older adults.

Acknowledgment Partial support was provided by funding from HRSA GWEP U1QHP33077.

References

Bartels, S. J., Pratt, S. I., Aschbrenner, K. A., Barre, L. K., Naslund, J. A., Wolfe, R., Xie, H., McHugo, G. J., Jimenez, D. E., Jue, K., Feldman, J., & Bird, B. L. (2015). Pragmatic Replication Trial of Health Promotion Coaching for Obesity in Serious Mental Illness and Maintenance of Outcomes. *American Journal of Psychiatry*, *172*(4), 344–352. https://doi.org/10.1176/appi.ajp.2014.14030357

Bartels, S. J., Pratt, S. I., Mueser, K. T., Forester, B. P., Wolfe, R., Cather, C., Xie, H., McHugo, G. J., Bird, B., Aschbrenner, K. A., Naslund, J. A., & Feldman, J. (2014). Long-Term Outcomes of a Randomized Trial of Integrated Skills Training and Preventive Healthcare for Older Adults with Serious Mental Illness. *The American Journal of Geriatric Psychiatry*, *22*(11), 1251–1261. https://doi.org/10.1016/j.jagp.2013.04.013

Bennett, K. A., Ong, T., Verrall, A. M., Vitiello, M. V., Marcum, Z. A., & Phelan, E. A. (2018). Project ECHO-Geriatrics: Training Future Primary Care Providers to Meet the Needs of Older Adults. *Journal of Graduate Medical Education*, *10*(3), 311–315. https://doi.org/10.4300/JGME-D-17-01022.1

Blazer, D. G., Steffens, D. C., & Koenig, H. G. (2009). Mood disorders. In D. G. Blazer & D. C. Steffens (Eds.), In *The American psychiatric publishing textbook of geriatric psychiatry*. American Psychiatric Press.

Blow, F. C., Bartels, S. J., Brockmann, L. M., Van Citters, A. D. (2005). *Evidence-based practices for preventing substance abuse and mental health problems in older adults*. Older Americans Substance Abuse and Mental Health Technical Assistance Center.

Brodaty, H., & Connors, M. H. (2020). Pseudodementia, pseudo-pseudodementia, and pseudodepression. *Alzheimer's & Dementia: Diagnosis, Assessment & Disease Monitoring*, *12*(1). https://doi.org/10.1002/dad2.12027

Bruce, M. L., Ten Have, T. R., Reynolds, C. F., Katz, I. I., Schulberg, H. C., Mulsant, B. H., Brown, G. K., McAvay, G. J., Pearson, J. L., & Alexopoulos, G. S. (2004). Reducing suicidal ideation and depressive symptoms in depressed older primary care patients: a randomized controlled trial. *JAMA*, *291*(9), 1081–1091. https://doi.org/10.1001/jama.291.9.1081

Choi, Y. K., Lazar, A., Demiris, G., & Thompson, H. J. (2019). Emerging Smart Home Technologies to Facilitate Engaging With Aging. *Journal of Gerontological Nursing*, *45*(12), 41–48. https://doi.org/10.3928/00989134-20191105-06

Cohen, C. I., & Doumlele, K. (2023). Social Psychiatry: Aging. In R. R. Gogineni (Ed.), *World Association of Social Psychiatry Textbook of Social Psychiatry Historical, Cultural, Developmental, and Clinical Perspectives*. Oxford Press.

Cohen, C. I., & Ibrahim, F. (2012). Serving Elders in the Public Sector. In McQuisten H. L., Sowers W. E., Ranz J. M., Feldman J. M. (Ed.), *Handbook of Community Psychiatry*. Springer.

Cohen, C. I., & Boran, M. (2004). Integrated community services. In *Comprehensive review of geriatric psychiatry (3rd ed.)*. Norton.

Cohen, C. I., & Reinhardt, M. M. (2020). Recovery and Recovering in Older Adults with Schizophrenia: A 5-Tier Model. *The American Journal of Geriatric Psychiatry: Official Journal of the American Association for Geriatric Psychiatry*, *28*(8), 872–875. https://doi.org/10.1016/j.jagp.2020.03.008

Cohen, C. I, Freeman, K., Ghoneim, D., Vengassery, A., Ghezelaiagh, B., & Reinhardt, M. M. (2020). Advances in the Conceptualization and Study of Schizophrenia in Later Life: 2020 Update. *Clinics in Geriatric Medicine*, *36*(2), 221–236. https://doi.org/10.1016/j.cger.2019.11.004

Copeli, F., & Cohen, C. I. (2019). Medical issues in older persons with schizophrenia. In C. Cohen & P. Meesters (Eds.), *Schizophrenia and Psychoses in Later Life: New Perspectives on Treatment, Research, and Policy*. Cambridge.

Cummings, S. M., & Kropf, N. P. (2009). Formal and informal support for older adults with severe mental illness. *Aging & Mental Health*, *13*(4), 619–627. https://doi.org/10.1080/13607860902774451

Druss, B. G., Singh, M., von Esenwein, S. A., Glick, G. E., Tapscott, S., Tucker, S. J., Lally, C. A., & Sterling, E. W. (2018). Peer-Led Self-Management of General Medical Conditions for Patients With Serious Mental Illnesses: A Randomized Trial. *Psychiatric Services*, *69*(5), 529–535. https://doi.org/10.1176/appi.ps.201700352

Everett, A. (2019). *Bringing Awareness to the Mental Health of Older Adults*. https://blog.samhsa.gov/2019/05/20/bringing-awareness-to-the-mental-health-of-older-adults

Federal Interagency Forum on Aging-Related Statistics. (2012). *Older Americans Key Indicators*. US Gov Printing Agency.

Figueroa, J. F., Phelan, J., Orav, E. J., Patel, V., & Jha, A. K. (2020). Association of Mental Health Disorders With Health Care Spending in the Medicare Population. *JAMA Network Open*, *3*(3), e201210. https://doi.org/10.1001/jamanetworkopen.2020.1210

Flint, A. J. (2002). The Complexity and Challenge of Non-Major Depression in Late Life. *The American Journal of Geriatric Psychiatry*, *10*(3), 229–232. https://doi.org/10.1097/00019442-200205000-00001

Gentry, M. T., Lapid, M. I., & Rummans, T. A. (2019). Geriatric Telepsychiatry: Systematic Review and Policy Considerations. *The American Journal of Geriatric Psychiatry : Official Journal of the American Association for Geriatric Psychiatry*, *27*(2), 109–127. https://doi.org/10.1016/j.jagp.2018.10.009

Gilbody, S., Bower, P., Fletcher, J., Richards, D., & Sutton, A. J. (2006). Collaborative care for depression: a cumulative meta-analysis and review of longer-term outcomes. *Archives of Internal Medicine*,

166(21), 2314–2321. https://doi.org/10.1001/archinte.166.21.2314

Gordon, R. S. (1983). An operational classification of disease prevention. *Public Health Reports*, *98*(2), 107–109.

Green, C. A., Yarborough, B. J. H., Leo, M. C., Yarborough, M. T., Stumbo, S. P., Janoff, S. L., Perrin, N. A., Nichols, G. A., & Stevens, V. J. (2015). The STRIDE Weight Loss and Lifestyle Intervention for Individuals Taking Antipsychotic Medications: A Randomized Trial. *American Journal of Psychiatry*, *172*(1), 71–81. https://doi.org/10.1176/appi.ajp.2014.14020173

Gubrium, J. F. (1973). The Myth of the Golden Years. A Socio Environmental Theory of Aging. *THOMAS, SPRINGFIELD, ILL.* https://doi.org/10.2307/2063187

Haigh, E. A. P., Bogucki, O. E., Sigmon, S. T., & Blazer, D. G. (2018). Depression Among Older Adults: A 20-Year Update on Five Common Myths and Misconceptions. *The American Journal of Geriatric Psychiatry*, *26*(1), 107–122. https://doi.org/10.1016/j.jagp.2017.06.011

Health Resources Services Administration. (2019). *Preparing the Current and Future Health Care Workforce for Interprofessional Practice in Sustainable, Age-Friendly Health Systems*.

Horgan, S., Le Clair, K., & Puxty, J. (2009). Collaborative care: Addressing seniors' mental, physical and social health needs. *Synergy. Research and Education Mental Health.*, *13*(2), 1–3.

Institute for Healthcare Improvement. (2019). *Age-Friendly Health Systems: Guide to using the 4Ms in the care of older adults*. Institute for Healthcare Improvement.

Kratz, T., & Diefenbacher, A. (2019). Psychopharmakotherapie im Alter. *Deutsches Arzteblatt International*, *116*(29–30), 508–518. https://doi.org/10.3238/arztebl.2019.0508

Lebowitz, B. D. (2006). Mental health services. In S. R. Schulz, R, Noelker LS, Rockwood K (Ed.), *The Encyclopedia of Aging, 4th edition* (The Encycl). Springer.

Lester, H., Glasby, J., & Tylee, A. (2004). Integrated primary mental health care: Threat or opportunity in the new NHS? *British Journal of General Practice*, *54*(501), 285–291.

Liu, L., Stroulia, E., Nikolaidis, I., Miguel-Cruz, A., & Rios Rincon, A. (2016). Smart homes and home health monitoring technologies for older adults: A systematic review. *International Journal of Medical Informatics*, *91*, 44–59. https://doi.org/10.1016/j.ijmedinf.2016.04.007

Mackenzie, C. S., Scott, T., Mather, A., & Sareen, J. (2008). Older Adults' Help-Seeking Attitudes and Treatment Beliefs Concerning Mental Health Problems. *The American Journal of Geriatric Psychiatry*, *16*(12), 1010–1019. https://doi.org/10.1097/JGP.0b013e31818cd3be

Madhusoodanan, S., Ibrahim, F. A., & Malik, A. (2010). Primary prevention in geriatric psychiatry. *Annals of Clinical Psychiatry : Official Journal of the American Academy of Clinical Psychiatrists*, *22*(4), 249–261. http://www.ncbi.nlm.nih.gov/pubmed/21180656

Nair, P., Bhanu, C., Frost, R., Buszewicz, M., & Walters, K. R. (2019). A Systematic Review of Older Adults' Attitudes towards Depression and its Treatment. *The Gerontologist*, *60*(1), e93–e104. https://doi.org/10.1093/geront/gnz048

National Alliance on Mental Illness. (2017). *No Title*. https://www.nami.org/getattachment/Get-Involved/NAMI-National-Convention/Convention-Program-Schedule/Hill-Day-2017/FINAL-Hill-Day-17-Leave-Behind-all-(1).pdf

Petersen, R. C., Lopez, O., Armstrong, M. J., Getchius, T. S. D., Ganguli, M., Gloss, D., Gronseth, G. S., Marson, D., Pringsheim, T., Day, G. S., Sager, M., Stevens, J., & Rae-Grant, A. (2018). Practice guideline update summary: Mild cognitive impairment. *Neurology*, *90*(3), 126–135. https://doi.org/10.1212/WNL.0000000000004826

Phan, S. V., Osae, S., Morgan, J. C., Inyang, M., & Fagan, S. C. (2019). Neuropsychiatric Symptoms in Dementia: Considerations for Pharmacotherapy in the USA. *Drugs in R&D*, *19*(2), 93–115. https://doi.org/10.1007/s40268-019-0272-1

Prendergast, D. (2020). Ethnography, technology design, and the future of "aging in place". In J. Sokolovsky (Ed.), *The Cultural Context of Aging: Worldwide Perspectives. 4th Edition.* (pp. 130–150). Praeger.

Oliveira, JS., Sherrington, C., Zheng, E. R. Y., Franco, M. R., & Tiedemann, A. (2020). Effect of interventions using physical activity trackers on physical activity in people aged 60 years and over: a systematic review and meta-analysis. *British Journal of Sports Medicine*, *54*(20), 1188–1194. https://doi.org/10.1136/bjsports-2018-100324

Sadavoy, J. (2009). An integrated model for defining the scope of psychogeriatrics: the five Cs. *International Psychogeriatrics*, *21*(5), 805–812. https://doi.org/10.1017/S104161020999010X

Sisko, A., Truffer, C., Smith, S., Keehan, S., Cylus, J., Poisal, J. A., Clemens, M. K., & Lizonitz, J. (2009). Health Spending Projections Through 2018: Recession Effects Add Uncertainty To The Outlook. *Health Affairs*, *28*(Supplement 1), w346–w357. https://doi.org/10.1377/hlthaff.28.2.w346

Thomas, M. L., Kaufmann, C. N., Palmer, B. W., Depp, C. A., Martin, A. S., Glorioso, D. K., Thompson, W. K., & Jeste, D. V. (2016). Paradoxical Trend for Improvement in Mental Health With Aging. *The Journal of Clinical Psychiatry*, *77*(08), e1019–e1025. https://doi.org/10.4088/JCP.16m10671

U.S. Bureau of the Census. (1996). *Current Population Reports, Special Studies P23-190, 65+ in the United States*. U.S. Government Printing Office.

Unützer, J., Katon, W., Callahan, C. M., Williams, Jr, J. W., Hunkeler, E., Harpole, L., Hoffing, M., Della Penna, R. D., Noël, P. H., Lin, E. H. B., Areán, P. A., Hegel, M. T., Tang, L., Belin, T. R., Oishi, S., Langston, C., & for the IMPACT Investigators. (2002). Collaborative Care Management of Late-Life Depression in the

Primary Care Setting. *JAMA*, *288*(22), 2836. https://doi.org/10.1001/jama.288.22.2836

Wells, J., Kennedy, C., Bain, H., & Lee, S. H. (2020). The experiences of older adults with a diagnosed functional mental illness, their carers and healthcare professionals in relation to mental health service delivery: An integrative review. *Journal of Clinical Nursing*, *29*(1–2), 31–52. https://doi.org/10.1111/jocn.15067

World Health Organization. (2004). *Mental health policy, plans and programmes – Rev. ed.* World Health Organization.

World Health Organization. (2019). *Integrated care for older people (ICOPE) implementation framework: guidance for systems and services*. https://www.who.int/ageing/publications/icope-framework/en/

Rural Populations

Carolyn M. Rekerdres and Marisa A. Giggie

O beautiful for spacious skies,
For amber waves of grain,
For purple mountain majesties
Above the fruited plain!
America! America!
God shed His grace on thee
And crown thy good with brotherhood
From sea to shining sea!
Katherine Lee Bates, *America The Beautiful*

Introduction

The American cultural experience, since its inception, has been informed and enhanced by the vastness and magnificence of the American rural countryside. As the popular patriotic song recounts, Americans feel a collective sense of pride in the idea of an abundant and prosperous landmass spreading out "from sea to shining sea." In fact, 97% of American lands are still rural places in the United States (Census 2016). However, only about 14% of the American population lives in these places (Pender 2019). When discussing community psychiatry for these rural places, it is helpful to know what exactly is meant by the term "rural." Rural is defined as any geographic area that is not incorporated within a greater urban region. The US Census Bureau puts this quite plainly by saying, "rural … (is) what is not urban—that is, after defining individual urban areas, rural is what is left" (Ratcliffe et al. 2016). Psychiatrists should not be surprised therefore to discover that there is considerable modern confusion as to what rural America really *is* beyond the lack of urbanity.

In fact, any psychiatrist looking to develop a career in rural America must understand the changing reality that rural Americans have been facing moving from the twentieth century into the twenty-first century. Changes that have affected their economic, cultural, and physical health precipitate alarming increases in mortality and lower qualities of life (Cosby et al. 2019). Understanding these clearly is paramount for one to be able to provide proper, culturally competent care to persons living with serious mental illness in these regions. The social determinants of health seen in America more broadly are amplified in rural areas, and therefore the need for a highly trained psychiatric workforce with a strong knowledge base of the complex biopsychosocial realities of rural people has never been greater. This chapter will provide a road map for those bold souls who are eager for impact and autonomy in their work, those for whom the absence of cityscape signals the presence of possibility within the great American wilderness.

C. M. Rekerdres (✉)
East Texas Behavioral Health Network, Lufkin, TX, USA

M. A. Giggie
Psychiatry & Behavioral Medicine, The University of Alabama, Tuscaloosa, AL, USA

W. E. Sowers et al. (eds.), *Textbook of Community Psychiatry*,
https://doi.org/10.1007/978-3-031-10239-4_48

Demographics

Population is not evenly distributed within each county in the United States; therefore there is a controversy regarding how to measure rurality for research and policy purposes. There are three different governmental entities which each have different definitions of rural (the Office of Management and Budget (OMB), the US Census Bureau, and the US Department of Agriculture (USDA); this can be confusing for researchers and clinicians when it comes to grant writing and when trying to interpret location-specific data (Smith et al. 2013). The OMB definition is strictly done by counties, the US Census Bureau looks at smaller geospatial units identifying "census tracts" of population density, and the USDA has a complicated continuum with five categories of rurality (Smalley et al. 2014). According to the USDA definition, two thirds of rural people live in metro adjacent rural counties, and the other third reside in completely rural areas (Pender 2019). The figure below shows that the majority of US counties are, in fact, rural.

In the United States, people are moving in record numbers into suburbs and the unincorporated areas that surround them (Parker et al. 2018). This has confused the notion of rural even further. One might be aware of terms like "suburban sprawl" or "exurban" to describe these suburban-like developments characterized by new construction homes with fairly high residential density in previously rural areas distant from any other established urban cluster city. There are also the so-called "frontier" areas which number about 445 counties in the United States (Olson et al. 2018). Despite modern advances in technology, these areas may still have a lack of access to basic infrastructure such as running water, electricity, reliable cellular phone service, or broadband Internet.

In general, rural Americans are older, sicker, less educated, and poorer than their city-dwelling counterparts, and 48% of rural people live in the southern states (Ratcliffe et al. 2016). They have less access to healthcare in general, and there is an estimated unmet need of psychiatric prescribers in up to 96% of rural counties in the United States (Thomas et al. 2009). Demographically,

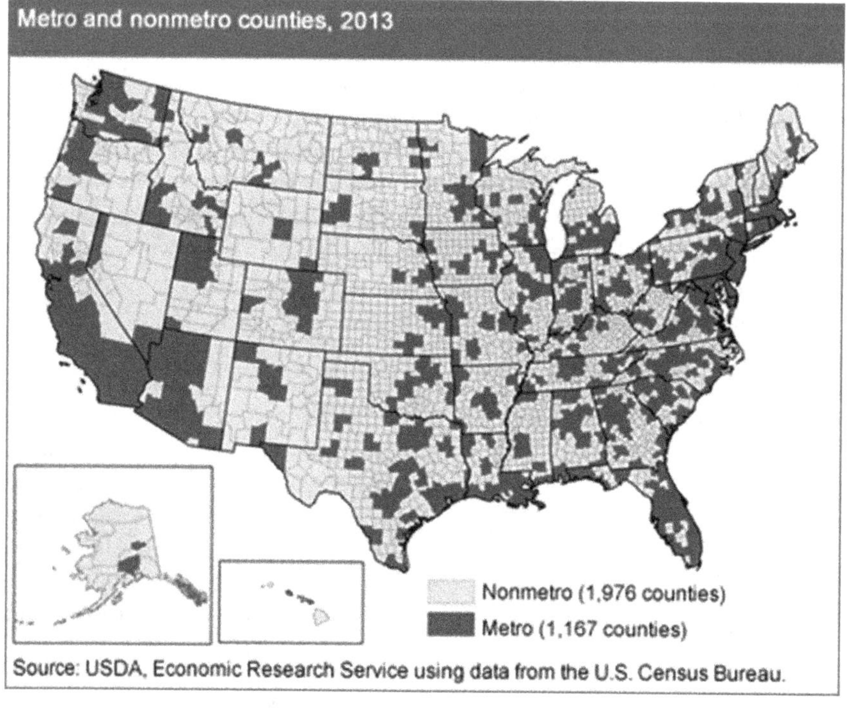

80% of rural Americans are still White, 9% Hispanics, 8% Black, and less than 2% are Native American or Asian (Cromartie 2018). Rural areas are more likely to have people unemployed at younger ages due to physical and mental health disability (Pender 2019). Native Americans are a small percentage of the overall rural population, but they are the only group in which the majority still choose to live in rural areas (Cromartie 2018). Notably, over 9 million Hispanics migrated to the United States between 2000 and 2010, and although the net rate of immigration declined over the next decade, the overall increase in Hispanic populations in rural areas has far outpaced any other racial group at a remarkable 19.2% (HAC 2020).

The rural experience is not an exclusively White, heteronormative experience. There are rural counties which have high percentages of Black residents in the so-called black belt of Mississippi, Alabama, Georgia, North and South Carolina, and Virginia. The sparsely populated border counties of the southwest have the highest rural clusters of Hispanics. And, in the four corners, the region of New Mexico, Arizona, Colorado, and Utah belong primarily to the sovereign Native American nations of the Navajo, Hopi, Ute, and Zuni tribes (HAC 2020). Also, data shows that LGBT prevalence in rural areas is equivalent to that within urban areas (somewhere between 4% and 5% of the adult population). Thus, 15–20% of LGBT people live in rural and work in rural areas across the country but like other racial minorities may face much higher rates of discrimination, justice inequities, and lack of culturally competent, high-quality healthcare (MAP 2019).

Culture

Statistically, rural people are more likely to be White, married, and religious and have lower levels of college educational attainment than people living in the cities (Parker et al. 2018). All of these areas have been shifting toward rates seen in cities, with the exception of college educational attainment in which the gap has been widening over the last two decades as urban rates of higher education have far surpassed the growth seen in rural areas (USDA, Rural Education at a Glance 2017). Social issues are certainly shifting too, with recent survey data showing that 40% of rural people report "never" or "rarely" going to church with an additional 15% saying they go only "occasionally" (Dillon and Henley 2008). Unexpectedly to many, rural regions now have the highest rate of children born to unwed mothers at 39% of all live births (Parker et al. 2018). Jobs in rural areas are changing too as agriculture, mining, fishing, forestry, hunting, and manufacturing now only make up only 21.7% of the labor force in rural areas. These industries now lag behind educational services, healthcare, and social assistance at 22.3% of the workforce (Census 2016).

When it comes to prevailing, cultural attitudes seen in rural areas, scholars have long argued that a self-selecting process occurred during early American settlement which rewarded traits of individualism and self-reliance, ultimately creating a persisting attitude of so-called rugged individualism that is common in rural areas (Bazzi et al. 2017). Rural culture is not homogenous though and cannot be generalized as monolithic.

However, as the 2016 and 2020 elections highlighted, a majority of rural people clearly identify more strongly ideologically with the leading economic and social philosophies of the early twentieth century than they do with those of the current twenty-first century. Donald Trump won the most rural counties in America by a full 35 points in 2020, which was an increase over the 32 percentage points that he won those areas in 2016 (Economist 2020). This has caused many in America to wonder why areas with poorer people, with lower rates of health insurance, higher rates of unemployment, a higher dependence on tax payer-supported incomes from healthcare, education, and social security/disability income would ever want to support a candidate whose main theme was one of less government interventions and fewer healthcare, food, and monetary benefits for the indigent. It's helpful therefore to remember what Alexis de Tocqueville wrote 200 years ago in his famous work, *Democracy in*

America. According to Tocqueville, "The Americans do not read the works of Descartes,... but they follow his maxims" (Tocqueville 1838).

The Enlightenment ideals of order, individual virtue and emphasis on man's innate, purely rational, and capability to master the external environment have been deeply entrenched in American culture since the founding of the United States. Almost a century later, Thomas Nixon Carver wrote a book in 1911 entitled *Principles of Rural Economics*. In it, he asserted the widely accepted laissez-faire economic ideas of the day saying: "In this kind of world it happens that success comes to those races which possess in the highest degree of economic virtues of industry, sobriety, thrift, forethought, reliability, knowledge of natural laws, and mutual helpfulness" (Carver 1911). In this view, freedom from aristocracy meant each man's success would be completely based on his level of virtue and effort. Survival at the meanest level was still a victory of liberty. This author, having lived in and among rural people most of her life, would like to assert that modern rural Americans have not read Thomas Nixon Carver – but they certainly do follow his maxims. That is to say, the majority of people living in rural areas do not know or care about the idea of upstream social determinants of health (racism, sexism, heterosexism, access to healthcare, socioeconomic status, intersectionality, education) and have been taught instead, whether directly or indirectly, brutal social Darwinism. From a healthcare standpoint, this mentality also creates a worrisome skepticism about the legitimacy of mental health treatment in general and leads to an additional barrier for engagement (Smalley et al. 2014). Despair and disappointment often arise when this cultural framework of meritocracy fails to explain their own personal struggles of trauma, health issues, addiction, and loss which coalesce into mental health issues. Honoring their values of order, rational thought, personality responsibility, duty, and stoicism can help reframe this difference of thinking into a strength for treatment and can enhance the treatment alliance.

Economics

Throughout the world, the twentieth century saw a decisive shift of population from rural areas into cities (Ritchie 2018). This change marked the first time in human history that more people lived in cities rather than rural areas. In general, people tended to move to cities as societies got richer from the urban wealth-producing activities that arose after the industrial revolution in the early twentieth century (Ritchie 2018).

In 1950, 40% of Americans in rural areas lived on a farm, and 30% of rural people worked in agriculture alone. The numbers today are very different. As agricultural work became more mechanized, fewer people were needed to do farm work, and people moved over time to metropolitan areas where more jobs were available. Manufacturing jobs, the other mainstay of rural employment fell from around 25% of all wage earners in America to only 12% following the Great Recession. 5.7 million jobs were lost between 2000 and 2010 alone (Bailey and Bosworth 2010). The average rate of poverty in rural areas is around 16%, with the southern region of the United States having rates at 20.5%. Black and Native peoples have a higher likelihood of being poor than White people in all areas of the United States, but in rural regions, this phenomenon is more pronounced, highlighting the increased effects of inequity found in rural regions where social services and access to healthcare are limited (Miller and Vasan 2020).

As shown in the figure below, many rural communities continue to be precariously dependent on industries like farming, oil and gas, mining, and manufacturing which are all prone to large-

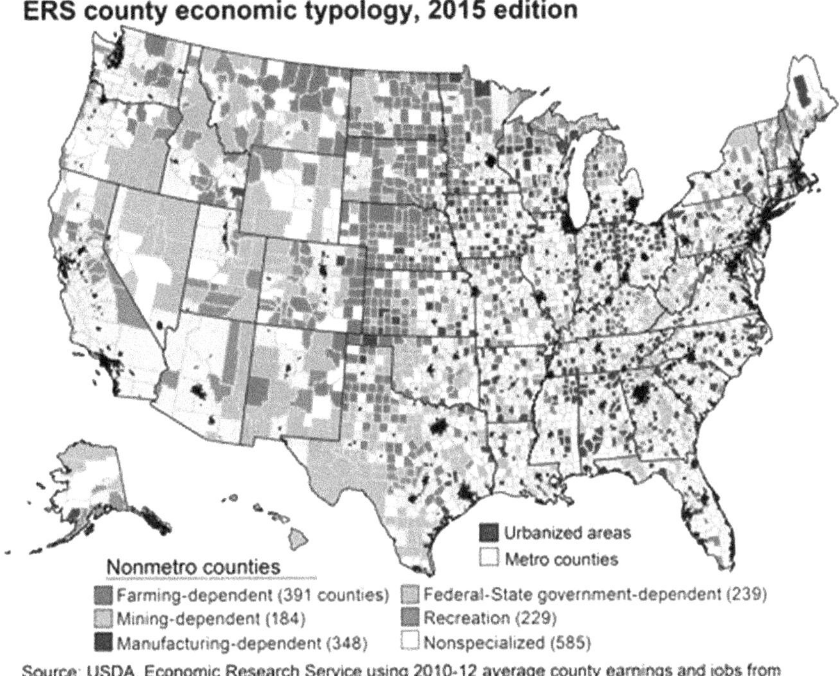

Rural Mortality and the Psychiatric Service Response

Until 1964, life expectancy and quality of life were higher in rural areas than in urban cities. Then, the rates of mortality equalized for about 20 years (Cosby 2008). But, after 1989 things started to change. Since that time, there has been a persistent and widening gap of mortality seen between rural and urban regions (Cosby 2008). In 2015, Angus Deaton and Anne Case published a ground-breaking paper pointing to a new pattern of increasing mortality and morbidity in non-Hispanic Whites (both urban and rural) aged 45–54. Disturbingly, this phenomenon which preceded the SARS COVID-19 pandemic as well has not been described in any other developed country in the world (Case and Deaton 2015). Three factors appear to account for the increased causes of death – end-stage alcohol-related deaths, accidental overdose (largely opiate and benzodiazepine), and suicide (Case and Deaton 2015). This phenomenon made news headlines and subsequently earned the moniker "deaths of despair." Rural America is Whiter and older and has less access to healthcare and higher rates of disability than urban areas, and so many of these deaths have been clustered in rural areas. In addressing this public health emergency, mental health workers in rural areas are frontline workers.

Despite an earlier cultural aversion seen in the early twentieth century against all substance use, rural Americans now have higher rates of alcohol misuse, tobacco use, and methamphetamine use than urban populations. Substance use is a well-known risk factor for suicide and is linked to mortality in that way as well. The rates of opiate and prescription drug abuse have risen dramatically in all areas of the United States but have been particularly devastating in rural regions (SAMSHA 2019). This has had dire consequences to overall health and quality of life for people living in rural America. Survey results show that over half of people living in rural areas believe that "drug use is a problem" in the area where they live (Parker et al. 2018).

Opiate SUD

The biggest rate increase in deaths from substance use disorders has been seen in the opiate crisis which accounts for two thirds of all accidental overdoses in the United States in the last decade (CDC 2020b). The CDC reports that over 450,000 people have died from opiate drug overdoses since the beginning of 1999 (with peak numbers being over 60,000 per year). The first wave of deaths was related to an increase in physician prescribing of narcotics; then, around 2010, a rise in heroin deaths began. This was finally followed by a startling spike in synthetic opiate overdoses in 2013 (CDC 2020b). This final rise was a consequence of both prescribed and illicit fentanyl flooding the market. Despite admirable decreases in prescribing patterns which was the result of efforts by the federal government at increasing physician awareness of inappropriate opiate prescribing, fentanyl is still widely available throughout the country (DEA 2019). In 2018, 70% of all overdose deaths involved an opiate drug. Rural areas with their inherent lack of substance use disorder treatment facilities have been hit hard with death rates from overdoses exceeding urban areas every year since 2006 (CDC 2020b).

Systems Case Study

Vermont is one of the most rural states in the nation with over 65% of the population living in rural areas that are harder to service with traditional, urban-based centers for substance use. In response to the growing number of deaths and persons affected by opioid substance use disorder, the state coordinated a complex hub and spoke program. They designated six different regional "hubs" with outlying rural clinics as the "spokes." Care coordinators were employed to facilitate patient navigation through the system. By providing compensated training for physicians to begin prescribing buprenorphine as a medication-assisted treatment and later supporting those physicians in the form of patient consultations from experts at the hubs, they have greatly increased the rural capacity to fight the opiate epidemic by increasing the number of data-waivered buprenorphine prescribers by 68% and offering behavioral supports in every region of the state where previously there were no coordinated resources available (Brooklyn et al. 2017).

Alcohol SUD

Despite the attention that suicide and opiate overdose deaths get, alcohol-related causes of death remain a higher absolute number of deaths in the United States each year. According to the CDC, there are approximately 95,000 alcohol-related deaths each year. Alcohol is a silent and persistent killer with steeply growing numbers of deaths within the last decade. Because it is toxic to almost all tissues in the human body, prolonged use leads to a significantly increased risk for acute and chronic toxicity in the form of neurologic destruction, heart failure, and most commonly liver failure (CDC 2020a). Additionally, the National Cancer Institute states that alcohol is known to increase the risk of oral cancers, cancer of the larynx, esophageal cancer, breast cancer, colorectal cancer, and liver cancer (CDC 2020a). An estimated 10,000-15,000 breast cancer deaths occur each year in the United States due to alcohol exposure (Nelso et al. 2013). Cancer outcomes have historically been poorer in rural regions due to lack of access, health insurance, and infrastructure so this risk is amplified in these regions (Smalley et al. 2014). The most alarming change in alcohol-related deaths has been the number of end-stage alcohol-related deaths reported following the Great Recession. The rates of increase have become astonishingly high in rural areas which saw a 51% increase in the rate of male deaths from 2005 to 2018. Women's rate of change was even higher (Spencer et al. 2020).

Methamphetamine SUD

Methamphetamine abuse has been rising across American and in rural areas over the last decade (SAMSHA 2019). In some rural areas, the prevalence of methamphetamine substance use disorders is well over double seen in urban, metro counties (SAMSHA 2019). Methamphetamine production has shifted away from domestic production due to effective law changes placing limits on purchased amounts of over-the-counter decongestants. This has unfortunately resulted in increased trafficking of extremely pure and potent methamphetamine from Mexico which appears to have an increased psychotomimetic effect (DEA 2019). Drug overdose-related deaths have increased 543% since 2005 as a result of increased use and potency (DEA 2019). Amphetamines are known to produce paranoia and can cause acute, substance-induced psychosis as well as a chronic psychotic disorder even after months to years of total abstinence. Psychosis, particularly seen as paranoid, persecutory delusions, and prominent ideas of reference, has been seen in 26–46% of individuals who meet criteria for methamphetamine dependence (Glasner-Edwards and Mooney 2016). These individuals are very likely to be involved in the legal system and are frequently seen by crisis teams in rural areas. Literature supports the use of antipsychotics in both acute and chronic treatment of amphetamine-related psychosis (Glasner-Edwards and Mooney 2016). Thus, psychiatric prescribers are needed desperately in rural areas to handle the increased demand in emergent presentations of psychosis that have been precipitated by this drug.

This case is an all-too-common presentation in rural areas where older patients are just as likely to be actively using drugs as younger patients. The risk for cerebrovascular events, seizures, work-related accidents, and domestic violence all increase significantly with methamphetamine use, and deaths and morbidity with this drug are likely not fully captured in current statistics. Methamphetamines are commonly mixed with opiates in industries that require a long period of time with extended concentration and physical labor – oil and gas, mining, farm work, heavy machinery operation, construction, and truck driving. These are all jobs that are prevalent in rural areas.

Suicide

Higher rates of rural suicide completion are a phenomenon that is seen consistently throughout the world with various contributing cultural, geospatial, and systemic forces at play (Hirsch et al. 2014). In the United States, the current rates of suicide in rural areas are 17.6 deaths per 100,000 population vs 12.5 per 100,000 in urban areas. An astonishing 60% of suicide completions in rural areas involve a firearm with hanging/suffocation being the second highest cause (Musgrove 2017). Non-Hispanic Native Americans have the highest risk for suicide with young people aged 15–34 – an alarming rate of 34.1 suicide deaths per 100,000 (Musgrove 2017). Well-established risk factors in urban areas, including a history of mental health issues, witnessing suicide, previous attempts, and a history of trauma, have been

Case Study

Mr. M is a 68-year-old Caucasian male who presents with his wife of 14 years for an initial evaluation via telemedicine at the community mental health clinic following a mobile crisis assessment 2 days prior for delusional thinking and threatening to shoot himself with a shotgun. He was able to make a safety plan, all acquired capability was removed from their home, and he was referred to an outpatient visit. His vital signs are within normal limits, and his BMI is 19.4. On social history, his highest level of educational attainment was 7th grade, and he has worked in the oil fields most of his life. He does have a remote history of 15 years of using "speed" in the 1980s–1990s but reports that he quit after that. His wife is present and appears supportive throughout the interview but becomes tearful and frustrated when the patient reports that he is convinced his wife is cheating on him and that this has made him feel depressed and pushed him to the point of wanting to kill himself. The patient was seen in the ER and had a negative head CT and unremarkable bloodwork so they discharged him. He has no focal neurological complaints and no pertinent past medical history or family history. On mental status examination, he is calm and cooperative and has a restricted demeanor. He has a logical TP in all things except the persistent, illogical belief that his wife is writing secret messages on their living room wall to an ex-boyfriend. He endorses feelings of hopelessness and extreme dysphoria and denies that he has ever had delusions, auditory hallucinations, or any thought disorder symptoms before. His wife corroborates this history. His attention and concentration are intact, and memory appears fair. Urine drug test reveals the presence of methamphetamines in the urine. After discussing the results of the study and educating the patient and his wife about the dangers of prolonged meth use, the patient rates his motivation level to quit as 9 out of 10, is willing to take antipsychotic medication to help with his "anxiety," and works with a peer support specialist. He will follow up in 2–4 weeks for follow up, and the need to continue antipsychotic treatment will be reassessed at each visit as well as the need to continue to safety plan for suicidal thoughts.

shown to impart higher risks of suicide in rural people too. The important risk factor of access to acquired capability appears to be especially important in areas with lower population density. At least one study in the state of Maryland showed that deaths by firearm accounted for the entire disparity of suicide rates in rural areas, where gun ownership is common, vs urban areas where gun ownership was less common. Veterans are another vulnerable group to suicide in the United States, and VA data shows a 20% higher rate of suicide in rural regions than urban areas (McCarthy et al. 2012).

Community psychiatrists should always assess for suicidal ideation at every mental health visit including a review of potential acquired capability for harm to self or others. When patients feel strongly about their right to own firearms, it is important to provide psychoeducation on safe firearm storage (gun safes are preferable; never store guns under a bed, in bedside table, or any place where a child could easily access them; never leave guns loaded) and work with families to store guns at a separate locked location if suicidal ideations are present. Anecdotally, it is noted that many rural, male patients fear mental health treatment due to misinformation they have been given which makes them think they will have their weapons automatically confiscated by the government if they engage in mental health treatment. Addressing these fears helps decrease stigma/misinformation about mental health treatment and increase participation in appropriate levels of evidence-based behavioral health interventions.

Serious Mental Illness Considerations

In the United States, it is estimated that over 40 million Americans suffer from a diagnosable mental illness other than substance use; the incidence is even higher in rural areas (FORHP 2017). Presentations may vary slightly than in urban areas, but the main differences in treating patients in rural areas come in the so-called 3 As: accessibility, affordability, and acceptability (Smalley et al. 2014). Accessing treatment, affording treatment, and getting beyond stigma are all unique challenges in rural areas. Rural Americans are more likely to use personal means of transportation (car, motorcycle, bike) than people in urban areas, so this can be additionally challenging for persons with intellectual and developmental disorders, patients with chronic psychosis, and those for whom medication side effects make it dangerous to drive (Mattson 2015). Only 0.5% of people living in rural areas use public transportation to get to work each day in America (Mattson 2015). Just getting patients and providers to and from clinic is one of the main challenges that community mental health centers face. In later parts of this chapter, we will look at some novel solutions utilizing technology that are helping to bridge the gap created by geospatial barriers. Affordability continues to be a challenge as rural Americans are less likely to be insured than those living in metropolitan areas (USDA 2018). Acceptability refers to the stigma against receiving mental health treatment that has been well documented for rural populations where self-reliance is seen in conflict with talking about one's problems or taking medication for mood or thought problems (Smalley et al. 2014).

It is also important to remember that mental health conditions affect people at all stages of life and therefore present in all age groups from preschoolers to nursing home residents. As people in rural areas tend to skew older, this means a larger unmet need of middle-aged and older persons with mental illness. An urban study in 2012 showed that 70% of older adults who experienced mood and anxiety disorders did not seek treatment from a qualified mental health provider (Byers et al. 2012). According to the University of Michigan's report on the current status of the American Psychiatric Workforce, there were about half as many geriatric psychiatrists in all of North Dakota, Mississippi, Wyoming, South Dakota, Oklahoma, Delaware, Alaska, Vermont, Utah, and Montana than the county of New Haven Connecticut alone (Beck et al. 2018). Community psychiatrists working in rural areas need to have a broad-based knowledge of psychiatry and be willing to practice with all age groups, dual diagnosis disorders, IDD populations, and ACT populations. This is both the challenge and the immense reward of working in rural areas as most physicians who love rural work state that they enjoy a role where they never get bored and have an opportunity to diagnose and treat a wide array of mental health conditions.

Child and Adolescent Population Considerations

Following the sentinel Kaiser Adverse Childhood Event (ACE) study published in 1998, the field of pediatric psychiatry has routinely recognized in the literature a predictable connection between early life trauma and later life mental health disorders and difficulty with functioning. According to government survey data, approximately 54.5% of rural adults report exposure to one ACE and almost 15% report exposure to four or more (Secretary 2018). There are similar later life disruptions seen in children with learning disorders who do not receive appropriate educational accommodations. One study revealed that despite dyslexia having a prevalence of about 10% of the US population, 48% of inmates in the Texas penitentiary system had dyslexia using validated assessment metrics (Moody 2000). This is in keeping with what has already been reviewed about families living in rural areas. Namely, they are poorer, substance abuse rates for adults and adolescents are high, children are more often born into single mother homes, and rural resources for education are lower than urban school districts due to economic factors. This, coupled with restricted access to child and adolescent psychiatric specialists in rural areas, creates a true emerging emergent situation for children and families living in these regions. In the state of Texas, for example, one sees that the state has the third highest number of child and adolescent trained psychiatrists (690) and yet over 180 counties in the state lack a single psychiatrist living there at all. By car, it could be 14–16 hours to drive the entire span of the state so commuting urban doctors to rural areas has not been a feasible solution to these inequities in the past.

Case Study

LL was an 11-year-old Black female living in a small town of about 1000 people. Her parents were respected members of the community, and she had no known health concerns. She had begun to feel extremely upset after she shared naked photos taken of and by herself with a boy in her class who subsequently shared them without her consent on social media. She felt unable to speak to anyone in her family or at her church due to fear of judgment, and the school's one counselor was a member of that church. The closest behavioral health provider was located 2 hours by car away. LL completed suicide via hanging, and her journal was later found that showed she had been experiencing intense feelings of depression and anxiety and felt she had no other options.

Sadly, the above case illustrates a new phenomenon – the rise of child suicide. Last year, three children under the age of 11 (two 9-year-olds and one 11-year-old) died by hanging in one author's service area, all three in rural areas and all three children of color. Suicide is now the leading cause of death in the United States for 10–14-year-olds (Underwood 2019). This rate tripled from 2007 to 2017 and is a national health crisis, affecting rural areas disproportionately (Mangrum 2019). Suicide is a mounting public health concern for all children and adolescents in the United States and remains the second leading causes of death for all children under 18, following accidental deaths (Cunningham 2018). Children in rural areas face higher levels of traumatic early life experiences and can be more isolated than children living in more dense regions. According to recent data, about one third of the nation's homeschooled children live in micropolitan or purely rural areas making their healthcare providers potentially the only place for abuse outcries and diagnosing developmental disorders, learning disorders, or other mental health disorders. Clearly, population-level planning is needed to help correct support rural children as they grow and develop into healthy adults.

Models of Financing Rural Mental Health

Rural communities rely upon traditional payer sources like Medicare, Medicaid, Children's Health Insurance Program, commercial insurance, and private pay, similar to other regions. However, rural areas differ by having more uninsured and publicly funded patients, due to higher rates of poverty and the working poor (USDA, United States Department of Agriculture Facts 2018). As previously mentioned, rural communities have suffered greatly during economic shifts of the past half century, with displacement of agricultural and manufacturing jobs by technology and cheaper overseas labor. This shift in the rural economic landscape has diminished tax bases, forcing austerity-level cuts of local public services. Typically, mental health services are some of the first services to be cut, a national trend that has affected rural areas disproportionately. A comprehensive federal approach to developing a robust mental health infrastructure in both cities and rural areas is lacking at this time.

Medicaid Expansion Through the Affordable Care Act (ACA)

The ACA of 2014 allowed states to expand minimum requirements for Medicaid eligibility to adults with incomes up to 133% of the federal poverty level, thus expanding the number of low-income people and working poor qualifying for this public insurance option (MAPAC 2020). Currently, 12 states, 8 of them in the south, chose not to expand Medicaid (Medicaid 2020). These states include Alabama, Georgia, Mississippi, Tennessee, South Carolina, North Carolina, Texas, Florida, Kansas, Wyoming, South Dakota, and Wisconsin. Since the Affordable Care Act was introduced in 2010, there have been 120 rural hospitals that have been forced to shut due to the economic non-viability of continuing operation in areas with high numbers of uninsured patients and low population density overall (Chartis 2020). The paradox of the non-Medicaid expansion state's insistence on not expanding government is that the health disparities that are further widening as a result no doubt increase overall healthcare costs for the states. It will never be fully known how many lives could have been saved during the SARS COVID-19 crisis if those 120 hospitals had remained open and been able to care for patients in their counties and regional areas during the pandemic.

States that expanded Medicaid coverage showed substantial drops in the uninsured rate, much more than those that did not, particularly for low- and moderate-income adults (Haley et al. 2018). In rural areas, being a Medicaid non-expansion state translates to gaps in affordable mental healthcare coverage and access, disproportionate to Medicaid expansion states. As of 2020, 12% of people in mostly rural areas lack health insurance compared to 9% nationwide (Bureau 2019). Furthermore, rural non-Medicaid expansion states have lower access to integrated substance use and mental health treatment and medication-assisted treatment (MAT) compared to expansion states, despite the disproportionate higher risk of opioid misuse and overdose in rural populations (Pro et al. 2020).

Medicaid expansion has the potential to improve access to care and quality for community mental health centers (CMHCs) in rural communities as evidenced by gains seen in Community Health Centers (CHCs). Between 2011 and 2015, CHCs in Medicaid expansion states showed an 11% decline in uninsured patients and 13% increase in Medicaid patients; rural CHCs in expansion states showed improvements in quality with more BMI and mammogram screenings and improved asthma and hypertension control (Cole et al. 2018). In the period after expansion (2014–2015), CHCs saw a 5% increase in total patient volume, more mental health visits, more Medicaid patients, and fewer uninsured patients compared to centers in non-expansion states (Han et al. 2017). Given the large distances that rural patients must traverse to obtain care, some predominately rural states have moved toward integrating CMHCs with CHCs as a way to reach rural patients in a more efficient, high-quality, low-cost manner.

Collaborative Care

Integrating professional mental health services with primary care in an integrated or collaborative model achieves the triple aim of public health – improved outcomes, patient satisfaction, and lower healthcare costs (Raney 2015). Given that the majority of people get their mental healthcare from their primary care physician, not a behavioral health professional, collaborative care (CC) makes sense from a population health perspective. The CC model approaches behavioral health delivery by integrating mental health with primary care either by integrating behavioral health into primary care settings or vice versa. Integration is *not* co-location, which alone has not improved patient outcomes at a population level (Uebelacker et al. 2009). Rather, integration involves a systematic population health approach utilizing behavioral health screenings at primary care visits, support for primary care physicians, integrated use of non-physician behavioral health professionals, and referral of more complex patients to a psychiatrist (without face-to-face visits with patients but case reviews with a care manager) for regularly scheduled meetings. Given the challenges rural communities face in recruiting and retaining qualified behavioral health professionals, telemedicine is an effective way of using off-site teams to staff the CC model, especially for harder-to-recruit specialty services like child and adolescent psychiatry and addiction services.

In 2017, Medicare began paying for collaborative care services, and in 2018, Medicare introduced the Psychiatric Collaborative Care Management CPT codes (99492–99494) and expanded coverage to include services provided in Rural Health Centers and Federally Qualified Health Centers, through the use of two G-codes (G0511, G0512). Since 2018, many state Medicaid programs and private payers are reimbursing psychiatric collaborative care management CPT codes (APA 2020). The APA has listed payers that have approved coverage for psychiatric collaborative care management on their website (APA 2020).

Grants

Multiple different federal and state agencies as well as non-profit organizations are involved in funding demonstration grants aimed at improving the delivery of mental health services in the rural United States. The most common federal agencies/organizations involved in these grants are the Health and Human Services Department (HHS), Substance Abuse and Mental Health Services Administration (SAMHSA), Health Resources and Services Administration (HRSA), Department of Education (DOE), Department of Justice (DOJ), and Indian Health Service (IHS). Also, hundreds of private non-profit organizations fund grants supporting rural mental health initiatives. Winning such grants, however, requires rural communities to collaborate with academic institutions and/or have leadership and resources to apply for grants. Given that most rural community mental health centers are working with limited state resources, few have the resources to support vibrant development programs.

Models of Care for Rural Mental Healthcare Delivery

Telemedicine

Telemedicine, the use of communication technology to provide clinical services to patients without an in-person visit, has been used in psychiatry since the late 1950s to address the lack of capacity and inequitable distribution of behavioral health services (Bhaskar et al. 2020). Psychiatry, due to its natural adaptability to audiovisual technology, has been a leader in the telemedicine field (Nesbitt 2012; Grady 2012). Studies have shown high levels of agreement between in-person and telepsychiatry diagnoses along with high satisfaction rates in psychiatric patients (Nesbitt 2012).

The coronavirus disease 2019 (COVID-19) pandemic has loosened prior telemedicine restrictions, accelerating its use worldwide, with the potential to expand behavioral health services to more rural and remote frontier communities. The rapid adoption of various technologies, due to COVID-19, driven by the need for social distancing, has catalyzed its potential to improve delivery, access, and efficiency to vulnerable and rural communities (Bhaskar 2020). Different models of telepsychiatry include (1) traditional referral and direct care, (2) collaborative care, (3) consultation, (4) consultation-liaison, and (5) curbside consultation (Bhaskar et al. 2020, Part 2).

Case Study: The Extension for Community Healthcare Outcomes (ECHO) Model to Address the Opioid Epidemic in Rural Communities

The tele-ECHO model is a type of telemedicine that uses a hub-and-spoke knowledge-sharing approach in which expert teams lead virtual clinics, improving the capacity to deliver evidence-based practices to underserved and remote communities (UNM 2020b; Arora et al. 2010). Developed at the University of New Mexico Health Sciences Center to train rural primary care physicians to treat hepatitis C patients, rural tele-ECHO clinics have expanded to provide technical assistance to increase CMHCs' and MHCs' capacity to treat other conditions as well as mental and substance use disorders. Most recently, the ECHO model has been used to address the opioid use disorder (OUD) epidemic, which has affected rural areas disproportionately (Holmes et al. 2020). Typically limited to 30 participants per session, several Opioid ECHO hubs have been launched to address barriers faced by primary care clinicians who care for patients with OUDs. Barriers included providing medication for addiction treatment (MAT), access to OUD treatment, stigmatizing language, access to psychiatric treatment, and the complex healthcare system.

The ECHO model effectively addresses these barriers, empowering participants to literally and figuratively meet OUD patients "where they are," coordinating with specialists to provide individualized and culturally sensitive, community-based access to a continuum of care (Bachhuber et al. 2017). Cross-discipline training and a better understanding of the respective roles and responsibilities across disciplines improve workflow, patient engagement and treatment, and operations of health centers (Joo et al. 2015; Gurewich et al. 2014). A study released in 2018 showed the application of the ECHO model targeting OUDs and showed a reduction in benzodiazepine and opioid usage, more so in individuals who participated in the ECHO program over the control group (Katzman et al. 2018). Quality Counts is a New England-based adaptation of the ECHO model that has partnered with more than 140 clinicians to offer programs related to opioids as well as working with community organizations to educate them on opioid-related deaths (Letourneau et al. 2019).

Certified Community Behavioral Health Center

On April 1, 2014, the Protecting Access to Medicare Act of 2014 (PAMA) passed into law, establishing criteria for demonstration grants for certified community behavioral health centers (CCBHCs) to improve community mental health services, funded as part of Medicaid (SAMHSA 2019, 2020). As of 2020, CCBHCs are in select states and offer an opportunity for communities to provide patient-centered community-based psychiatric services integrated with primary care. The initial eight states selected by HHS for demonstration programs are Minnesota, Missouri, New Jersey, New York, Nevada, Oklahoma, Oregon, and Pennsylvania (CCBHC 2020). CCBHCs must offer the following services: (1) crisis mental health services; (2) screening, assessment, and diagnosis; (3) patient-centered treatment planning; (4) outpatient mental health and substance use services; (5) outpatient clinic primary care screening and monitoring; (6) targeted case management; (7) psychiatric rehabilitation services; (8) peer support, counseling, and family support; and (9) intensive mental healthcare for those in the military and veterans.

Outreach and Assertive Community Treatment Teams

Assertive Community Treatment (ACT) services have a long track record of decreasing the need for hospital care, a scarce resource in rural areas. Therefore, rural ACT teams may be even more necessary there than in urban settings. However, the recommendation that an ACT team has a staff-to-patient ratio of 10–15:1, serving 50–100 people, poses challenges and opportunities in rural settings. Rural service areas may not have sufficient numbers of people with the most severe illnesses to develop full teams. Even if the numbers are present, they may live in dispersed areas, making core services such as outreach difficult. Rural ACT teams also are at risk for having a higher proportion of non-reimbursable activity owing to the extra travel involved. However, with telemedicine, a psychiatrist can still manage a standard caseload of ACT patients and be able to staff cases weekly with the team according to the fidelity model. This has allowed for the expansion of ACT services in areas where previously geospatial distances made it too difficult to coordinate ACT scheduling for doctor visits.

While the traditional ACT team includes a variety of specialized professionals, it lends itself well to rural settings as the model also emphasizes team members functioning as generalists within their scope of practice. An ACT team is typically available 24 hours a day, 7 days a week, but a 24-hour, 7-day per week coverage may be difficult to provide in a rural environment. For example, some team members may live at a great distant from the clinical site and patients' homes. Rural ACT recommendations have been modified to have a lower recommended staff to patient ratio of 8:1 and typically serve fewer people, as low as 42–50. In order to provide shift coverage and maintain the low ratio, a minimum of five mental health professionals are needed on each team (Allness 2010). The following case illustrates that intensive services, including ACT and specialized pharmacotherapy, can be provided in rural areas.

Mr. L, a 30-year-old single male with schizophrenia and cannabis dependence, lives in the eastern part of the county in his mother's home, about 30 miles from the county seat where the ACT office is located. The psychiatrist on the ACT team has been discussing a trial of clozapine, but the patient and his mother have raised concerns that Mr. L may be unable or unwilling to travel for weekly blood draws, as required with this medication. Arrangements are made by the ACT nurse for Mr. L to have his blood drawn at the family doctor's office, at a more manageable distance from his home. Contact with the ACT team also was increased during this time. A team member added a stop to Mr. L's house on his way home the day prior to blood draws. This served as a reminder but also allowed for encouragement and problem solving, such as when the family car was inoperable.

Case Study: Project Horseshoe Farm, Greensboro, Alabama

Project Horseshoe Farm started in 2007 in Greensboro, Alabama, a town of 2,200 in one of America's poorest regions, by a psychiatrist as a community outreach program (started as an after-school homework program) to build upon the strength of the local community, improve overall health of the most vulnerable, and prepare citizen service leaders for the future (Project Horseshoe Farm 2020). Recognizing that the current model of healthcare delivery falls short, this innovative program has designed a gap year for college graduates to work with community partners to provide mental healthcare, case management, education support, and leadership development in a grassroots community partnership. Since its inception, the program has expanded to Marion, Alabama, and Pomona, California. In 2009, Horseshoe Farm opened an Independent Living Program for women recovering from serious mental illness; in 2012, it opened a community center that provided nutritional, education, social, wellness, and medical support for people with mental illness in the community, providing a holistic approach to health in a rural community with limited resources. Funded by donations and community partners, and drawing upon the strengths of the local community, Horseshoe Farm has illustrated how to build a sustainable comprehensive mental health delivery program in a rural underserved area literally from the ground up with limited government support.

Mental Health Professional Workforce Development

Rural Psychiatry Programs and Tracks in Psychiatry Residency

The number of psychiatry residency programs offering rural tracks is increasing. The University of New Mexico started a rural track in 1991 and has retained 37% of its graduates in rural communities vs 10% from traditional tracks (Bohnam et al. 2014). The University of Texas Health Sciences Center at Tyler started an accredited rural psychiatry residency program in 2016 with several rural tracks being developed at psychiatry residency programs across the country like the State University of New York Upstate, University of Texas Southwestern, University of Utah (Rural

Idaho Track), Michigan State University (Rural Upper Peninsula Track), and West Virginia University. Furthermore, the number of residency slots in psychiatry has increased steadily between 2015 and 2020.

University-Based Programs

The University of Alabama School of Medicine, Tuscaloosa Campus, Behavioral Health Fellowship for Family Medicine

In 2009, the University of Alabama School of Medicine in Tuscaloosa started the first behavioral fellowship program for family medicine. Funded by the Alabama Family Practice Rural Health Board, graduates are required to practice in rural Alabama for 1 year after a year-long didactic and experiential training in the most common behavioral health concerns (CCHS 2020). Given that most people seek psychiatric treatment from their primary care physician, the goal of this program is to increase the capacity for psychiatric treatment in rural communities beyond traditional mental health professionals, which are lacking in most rural communities. The program has produced five graduates since its inception, with four of the five practicing in rural Alabama as of 2020.

University of California at Davis (UC-Davis) Integrated Program

UC-Davis has created an integrated telehealth program with rural primary care network. The UC health system collaborates with a community health network for rural Northeastern California, funded by grants from private and semi-public foundations (UC-Davis 2020). Since its inception, the program has incorporated screening instruments and outcome measures into the practice at multiple rural sites for depression, alcoholism, and anxiety disorders. UC-Davis' Center for Health and Technology also offers Rural-PRIME, a 5-year MD and master's degree to develop future physician leaders and target students from rural backgrounds (UC-Davis 2020).

The University of New Mexico (UNM)

The UNM Department of Psychiatry developed the Center for Rural and Community Behavioral Health in 1993 to provide "community-oriented services to underserved populations, engage in rural mental health training and workforce development, and to strengthen the behavioral health services research capacity in New Mexico" (UNM 2020a). The center trains psychiatry residents and fellows and serves as a recruitment and retention tool for rural New Mexico. Residents work 1–2 days per month up to 6 months per year in rural sites during the fourth year. The sites have included CMHCs, federally qualified health centers (FQHCs), HIS facilities, schools, and private practices. Rural psychiatry residents rotate with family medicine, pediatrics, and obstetrics-gynecology residents and dental interns in community training sites and provide "curbside consults" to their nonpsychiatric colleagues often seeing patients together as a team. Funding for the rural track comes through a contract with the state of New Mexico's Behavioral Health Services Division.

Conclusion

In summary, rural communities are broadly defined by their lack of a core urban center, but more importantly for community psychiatrists, they face significant challenges in providing accessible, high-quality, and affordable mental healthcare. These challenges present opportunities for those interested in both patient care and population health strategies to address the so-called mortality penalty now seen in the sparsely populated areas of the country. Rural Americans are less wealthy, less healthy, less educated, more disabled, and more likely to be uninsured than urban Americans. America's rural areas are faced with severe professional mental health and primary care manpower shortages. These communities have suffered disproportionately from the opioid and methamphetamine crisis with proportionately more deaths from overdoses than urban/suburban areas. Traditional farms and factories have been replaced with non-human worker technology or outsourced to cheaper foreign labor. Fewer federal and state resources are placed in these areas with fewer collaborations within academic medical centers.

Despite these significant problems, rural America offers satisfying careers for mental health workers and psychiatrists in general. Expansions in telehealth, integrated care models, and the tele-echo consultation models are ways for psychiatrists to be involved in rural communities even if they do not live there. Integration with primary care makes sense from a population health perspective and offers the additional benefit of working side by side with primary care colleagues who truly value the help. Medicaid expansion has improved services and lowered uninsured rates in expansion states. Rural communities are often close-knit and family focused and offer a well-compensated, validating, bucolic lifestyle for behavioral health practitioners. More psychiatry training programs are beginning to offer rural tracks to entice professionals to make rural psychiatry a lifetime career and collaborate with school systems to develop pipeline programs. This tribe of rural psychiatrists dedicated to elevating the forgotten people of our open spaces is ever growing and, thanks to technology, no longer geographically restricted. Finally, in these authors' own experiences, rural America today offers the same excitement, adventure, natural awe, and frontier spirit that has defined the bold American mindset for over 200,000 years and will certainly be an important field for this century.

References

Allness. "NAMI National Program Standards for ACT Teams." 31 October 2010. *A Manual for ACT Start-up*. www.nami.org/Template.cfm?Section=ACT-TA_Center.

APA. *Getting Paid in the Collaborative Care Model*. 20 November 2020. https://www.psychiatry.org/psychiatrists/practice/professional-interests/integrated-care/get-paid.

Arora, S, et al. "Expanding access to hepatitis C virus treatment-Extension for Community Healthcare Outcomes (ECHO) project: Disruptive innovation in specialty care." *Hepatology* (2010): 1124–1133.

Bachhuber, M et al. "Primary Care: On the Front Lies of the Opioid Crisis." 1 June 2017. *University of Pennsylvania Lennard Davis Institute of Health Economics*. http://Ldi.upenn.edu/brief/primary-care-front-lines-opioid-crisis.

Bailey, MN & Bosworth, BP. "Manufacturing Share of Real GDP Manufacturing Employment Share." *Journal of Economic Perspectives* (2010): 3–26.

Bazzi, S et al. "Frontier Culture: The Roots and Persistence of "Rugged Indificualism" in the United States." 2017.

Beck, A et al. "Estimating the Distribution of the U.S. Psychiatric Subspecialist Workforce Project Team." 2018.

Bhaskar. "Telemedicine Across the Globe-Position Paper form the COVID-19 Pandemic Health System Resilience PROGRAM (REPROGRAM) International Consortium (Part 1)." 2020.

Bhaskar, et al. "Telemedicine as the New Outpatient Clinic Gone Digital: Position Paper from the Pandemic Health System Resilience Program (REPROGRAM) International Consortium (Part 2)." 2020.

Bohnam, et al. "Training Psychiatrists for Rural Practice: a 20-year Follow-Up." *Academic Psychiatry* (2014): 623–626.

Brooklyn, JR et al. "Vermont Hub-and-Spoke Model of Care for Opioid Use Disorder: Development, Implementation, and Impact." *Journal of Addiction Medicine* (2017): 11(4).

Bureau, US Census. *America Counts: Stories Behind The Numbers*. 9 April 2019. https://www.census.gov/library/stories/2019/04/health-insurance-rural-america.html#:~:text=Residents%20of%20rural%20counties%20still,percent%20for%20mostly%20urban%20counties.

Byers, A et al. "Low Use of Mental Health Services among Older Americans with Mood and Anxiety Disorders." *Psychiatric Services* (2012): 66–72.

Carver, TN. *Principles of Rural Economics*. 1911.

Case A & Deaton, A. "Rising morbidity and mortality in midlife amonhg white non-Hispanic Americans in the 21st century." *Proceedings of the National Academy of Sciences of the United States of America*. National Academy of Sciences, 2015. 15078–15083.

CCBHC. 14 November 2020. https://www.center-4healthandsdc.org/the-ccbhc-program.html.

CCHS. *Behavioral Medicine Fellowship in Family Medicine*. 12 November 2020. https://fmr.ua.edu/fellowships/behavioral-health/.

CDC. "Alcohol and Public Health: Alcohol-Related Disease Impact (ARDI)." 2020a.

—. "Wide-ranging online data for epidemiological research (WONDER)." 2020b.

Census. *American Community Survey*. Washington DC: U. S. Department of Commerce, 2011–2015, 2016.

Chartis, The Chartis Center for Rural. 2020.

Cole, Megan, et al. "Medicaid Expansion and Community Health Centers: Care Quality and Service Use Increased for Rural Patients." *Health Affairs* (2018): 900–907.

Cosby, AG et al. "Growth and persistence of place-based mortality in the United States: The rural mortality penalty." *American Journal of Public Health* (2019): 155–162.

Cosby, AG. "Preliminary evidence for an emerging nonmetropolitan mortality penalty in the United States." *American Journal of Public Health* (2008): 1470–1472.

Cromartie, J. "Rural America at a Glance, 2018 Edition." November 2018. *USDA Economic Research Service.* https://www.ers.usda.gov/publications/pub-details/?pubid=90555.

Cunningham, RM. "The Major Causes of Death in Children and Adolescents in the United States." *New England Journal of Medicine* (2018): 2468–2475.

DEA. "National Drug Threat Assessment." 2019. www.dea.gov/documents/2020/01/30/2019-national-drug-threat-assessment.

Dillon, M and Henley, M. "Religion, Politics, and the Environment in Rural America." 2008.

Economist, The. "America's urban-rural partisan gap is widening." 2020. *The Economist Daily Chart.* https://www.economist.com/graphic-detail/2020/11/10/americas-urban-rural-partisan-gap-is-widening.

FORHP. "Rural Behavioral Health." 2017.

Glasner-Edwards, S & Mooney LJ. "Methamphetamine Psychosis: Epidemiology and Management." *CNS Drugs* (2016): 1115–1126.

Grady, Brian. "Promises and limitations in telepsychiatry in rural mental health care." *World Psychiatry* (2012): 199–201.

Gurewich, D, et al. "Managing care for patients with substance abuse disorders at community health centers." *Journal of Substance Abuse Treatment* (2014): 277–31.

HAC. *Rural Research Brief.* August 2020. http://www.ruralhome.org/sct-information/publications/68-rural-rn.

Haley, Jennifer, et al. *Adults' Uninsurance Rates Increased By 2018 Especially in States that did not Expand Medicaid – Leaving Gaps in Coverage, Access and Affordability.* 26 September 2018. https://www.healthaffairs.org/do/10.1377/hblog20180924.928969/full/

Han, Xinxin, et al. "Medicaid Expansion and Grant Funding Increases Helped Improve Community Health Center Capacity." *Health Affairs* (2017): 49–56.

Hirsch, JK et al. "Suicide in rural areas: An updated review of the literature." *Journal of Rural Health* (2014): 65–78.

Holmes, C, et al. "Project ECHO and Opioid Education: a Systematic Review." *Current Treatment Options in Psychiatry* (2020): 9–22.

Joo, JY, et al. "Community-based case management effectiveness in populkations that abuse substances." *International Nursing Review* (2015): 536–46.

Katzman, JG, et al. "Army and Navy ECHO PAin Telementoring Improves Clinician Opioid Prescribing for Military Patients: an Observational Cohort Study." *Journal of General Internal Medicine* (2018): 387–395.

Letourneau, LM, et al. "Supporting Physicians and Practice Teams in Efforts to Address the Opioid Epidemic." *The Annals of Family Medicine* (2019): Supplement 1.

Mangrum, M. *Suicide rate nearly tripled in children ages 10–14 from 2007–2017.* 27 October 2019.

MAP. *Movement Advancement Project.* April 2019. https://www.lgbtmap.org/rural-lgbt.

MAPAC. *Medicaid and CHIP Payment and Access Commission* . 12 November 2020. https://www.macpac.gov/subtopic/overview-of-the-affordable-care-act-and-medicaid/.

Mattson, J. "NDSU Upper Great Plains Transportation Institute." 2015. *Small Urban and Rural Center on Mobility.* https://www.ugpti.org/surcom/resources/transitfactbook/.

McCarthy, JF et al. "Suicide Among Patients in the Veteran Affairs Health System: Rurl-Urban Differences in Rates, Risks, and Methods." *American Journal of Public Health Supplement* (2012): 111–117.

Medicaid. *Status of State Medicaid Expansion Decisions: Interactive Map.* 2 November 2020. https://www.kff.org/medicaid/issue-brief/status-of-state-medicaid-expansion-decisions-interactive-map/.

Miller, CE & Vasan, RS. "The southern rural health and mortality penalty: A review of regional health inequities in the United States." *Social Science and Medicine* (2020): 113443.

Moody, KC. "Prevalence of Dyslexia among Texas prison inmates." *Texas Medicine* (2000): 69–75.

Musgrove, R. "National Advisory Committee on Rural Health and Human Services Understanding the Impact of Suicide in Rural America." 2017.

Nelso, DE et al. "Alcohol-attributable cancer deaths and years of potential life lost in the United States." *American Journal of Public Health* (2013): 641–648.

Nesbitt, Thomas. *The Role of Telehealth in an Evolving Health Care Environment: Workshop Summary.* Washington DC: National Academies Press, 2012.

Olson, Steve et al. "Achieving Rural Health Equity and Well-Being: Proceedings of a Workshop." *National Academies of Sciences, Engineering.* National Academies Press, 2018.

Parker, Kim et al. "What Unites and Divides Urban, Suburban, and Rural Communities: Amid widening gaps in politics and demographics, Americans in urban, suburban, and rural areas share many aspects of community life." 22 May 2018. *Pew Research Center Social & Demographic Trends.* https://www.pewsocialtrends.org/2018/05/22/what-unites-and-divides-urban-suburban-and-rural-communities/.

Pender, J. *Rural America AT A Glance.* 2019. https://www.ers.usda.gov/webdocs/publications/95341/eib-212.pdf?v=7864.9.

Project Horseshoe Farm. 27 November 2020. https://www.projecthsf.org/overview.

Pro, George et al. "The Role of State Medicaid Expansions in Integrating Comprehensive Mental Health Services into Opioid Treatment Programs: Differences Across

the Rural/Urban Continuum." *Community Mental Health Journal* (2020): Online accessed ahead of print.
Raney, Lori. *Integrated Care: Working at the Interface of Primary Care and Behavioral Health.* Washington DC: American Psychiatric Association Press, 2015.
Ratcliffe, M, et al. *Defining Rural at the US Census Bureau: American community survey and geography brief.* 1–8 December 2016. www.census.gov/geo/pdfs/reference/ua/Defining_Rural.pdf.
Ritchie, H. "Urbanization. Our World in Data." 2018.
SAMHSA. 14 November 2020. https://www.center-4healthandsdc.org/the-ccbhc-program.html.
SAMSHA. "National Survey on Drug Use and Health." 2019.
Secretary, E. "National Advisory Committee on Rural Health and Human Services Exploring the Rural Context for Adverse Childhood Experiences (ACEs)." 2018.
Smalley, K et al. *Rural Public Health: Best practices and Preventative Models.* Springer Publishing Company, 2014.
Smith, ML et al. "The Utility of Rural and Underserved Designations in Geospatial Assessments of Distance Traveled to Healthcare Services: Implications for Public Health Research and Practice." *Journal of Environmental and Public Health* (2013): 960157.
Spencer, M et al. "Rates of Alcohol-induced Deaths Among Adults Aged 25 and Over in Urban and Rural Areas: United States, 2000–2018: NCHS Data Brief." 2020.
Thomas, KC et al. "County-level estimates of mental health professional shortage in the United States." *Psychiatric Services* (2009): 1323–1328.
Tocqueville, A de. *Democracy in America. Book II.* G Dearborn and Co., 1838.
UC-Davis. *Psychiatry and Behavioral Sciences.* 20 November 2020. https://health.ucdavis.edu/cht/about-us/legacy.html.
Uebelacker, LA et al. "Treatment of Depression in a Low-Income Primary Care Setting with Collocated Mental Health Care." *Family Systems Health* (2009): 161–171.
Underwood, B. *Ohio Department of Health says suicide is the leading cause of death in kids aged 10–14.* 20 November 2019.
UNM. *Center for Rural and Community Behavioral Health.* 12 November 2020a. https://sociology.unm.edu/research/research-affiliates/profile/center-for-rural%2D%2Dcommunity-behavioral-health.html.
—. *Project ECHO The University of New Mexico.* 14 November 2020b. https://hsc.unm.edu/echo/.
USDA. "Rural Education at a Glance." 2017.
—. *United States Department of Agriculture Facts.* 2018. November 2020. Ers.usda.gov.

Clinical Issues and Programming for Sexual and Gender Minority Populations

Ronald Hellman

Introduction

As concepts of mental health and social change have evolved, social psychiatry has adapted and influenced the contemporary delivery of mental health care to the sexual and gender minority (SGM) community. With social transformation, integration, and advances in the knowledge base, a richer, holistic understanding of SGM individuals continues to emerge.

Psychiatrists who practiced prior to the extraordinary transition that took place when the American Psychiatric Association declassified homosexuality in 1973 witnessed how sexual orientation became a catalyst in redefining the nature of what constitutes a mental disorder (Bayer 1981). The histories of older SGM patients remind us of the different world in which they lived, perceived as ill, criminal, sinful, and unable to live an open and authentic life. Few classes of people within our society have undergone such dramatic change, even within the last decade.

Gender identity disorder remained in the DSMs after the declassification of homosexuality. It was a fixed concept implying an erroneous identification. It was finally declassified in 2013, replaced with gender dysphoric disorder, indicating a temporary dissatisfaction leading to emotional disruptions of clinical intensity. There are treatments that address these conditions, including hormones and surgery, which are increasingly recognized and covered by insurance. In addition, same-sex marriage, previously a fanciful notion, became a socially affirmed, legally recognized union in all states in 2015. LGBT employment discrimination became illegal nationwide in 2020. Our SGM colleagues felt pressured to remain in the closet through the 1970s to avoid jeopardizing their careers. Today, they are an open, active, and integrated group within the diverse community of psychiatry.

These gains are having complex effects on the well-being of SGM individuals. While the impact has been positive, for the most part, there have also been risks. Greater transgender visibility has resulted in social backlash and politicization reminiscent of the earlier gay rights struggle. Increasing acceptance of sexual and gender minorities has influenced the average age of disclosure to family and others, falling from the early 20s, in the 1970s, to the early teens today (Russell and Fish 2016). Lacking the relative autonomy of early adulthood, those who self-disclose during this earlier phase of development remain more dependent on families that may or may not be supportive. They can be more subject to peer pressure, bullying, and social isolation

R. Hellman (✉)
Icahn School of Medicine at Mount Sinai, New York, NY, USA

W. E. Sowers et al. (eds.), *Textbook of Community Psychiatry*,
https://doi.org/10.1007/978-3-031-10239-4_49

and more susceptible to religious and cultural messaging, with psychological effects that can extend into adulthood.

When assessing SGM stressors, community psychiatrists will find significant variation in the experience of SGM patients. Families and communities exhibit a spectrum of enlightenment and ignorance, wealth and poverty, tolerance and repudiation, and support and opposition. With this in mind, community mental health settings should be structured to engage the SGM patient with staff that are diverse and welcoming and with whom SGM clients can identify. Clinicians, who are able to demonstrate that the SGM patient is understood and who are aware of auxiliary resources that include SGM specialists, support groups, social networks, and culturally appropriate social services, will be the ones that have the most successful outcomes.

Standard therapeutic techniques can be adapted to SGM populations. For example, cognitive behavior therapy, previously modified to address other psychiatric presentations, is now available in a format that specifically targets sexual minority stress (Pachankis 2014). Absent therapeutic interventions that specifically address SGM issues, the treatment alliance may be tenuous, introducing an iatrogenic element to existing minority stress. This can only increase a client's reluctance to engage in mental health services and affects their adherence to treatment recommendations (Romanelli and Hudson 2017).

Sexual and Gender Minorities

There is no consensus on the number of terms that describe what is now recognized as a spectrum of gender identities and sexual orientations. These terms continue to evolve and expand. "LGBT" has been the most common moniker, but not infrequently includes those who are questioning, intersex, and asexual (LGBTQIA). As this becomes more unwieldy, "SGM" has become a preferred term (see Table 1 for a glossary of terms).

There is an increasing recognition that some individuals are identified as neither male nor female and a spectrum of nonbinary gender terms have taken hold. Some will be unfamiliar to the general clinician, but they are of significant psy-

Table 1 A glossary of terms

Ambiphilic: Attracted to males and females
Androphilic: Attracted to males
Arousal: Refers here to genital arousal as studied in clinical research
Asexual: Lack of attraction or sexual desire
Binegativity: Negative attitudes toward bisexuals
Bisexual: Attracted to males and females
Cisgender: Gender identity that is congruent with the sex assigned at birth
Gay: Attracted to people of the same gender
Gender identity: The mental conviction of being male, female, neither, or something in between
Gender non-conforming: Not fitting in with cultural expectations regarding gender
Gender role: Appearance and behavior based on cultural gender expectations
Gynephilic: Attracted to females
Heterosexism: The presumption that heterosexuality is superior to nonheterosexuality
Heterosexual: Attracted to the opposite sex
Homosexual: Attracted to the same sex
Homophobia: Anti-homosexual bias
Lesbian: A female attracted to females
LGBTQIA: Lesbian, gay, bisexual, transgender, questioning/exploring gender identity and/or sexual orientation, anatomically intersex, asexual
Nonbinary: Identifying as neither exclusively male nor female
Queer: Different from being exclusively heterosexual and cisgender
Romance/romantic: Referring to limerence or deep affection for another person
Sex assigned at birth: Based on external anatomy, may or may not be congruent with emerging gender identity
Sexual identity: A all-encompassing term that includes gender identity, sexual orientation, and gender role
Sexual orientation: Having to do with the gender(s) one is attracted to
SGM: Sexual and gender minorities, excludes the majority population that is cisgender and heterosexual
Trans: Short for transgender
Transfemale: A person born anatomically male whose gender identity is female
Transgender: Gender identity that differs from the gender assigned at birth
Transmale: A person born anatomically female whose gender identity is male
Transphobia: Negative bias toward transgender people

chological import to those who go by them, and they provide a window into the mind and physical presence of persons seen in clinical practice. In 2019, the National Institutes of Health officially expanded the definition of the term "SGM" to encompass the broadest umbrella possible of sexual and gender minority inclusivity (National Institutes of Health 2019).

Terms such as "nonheterosexual," "cisgender," "nonbinary," "trans," and "queer" have become more commonplace (Richards et al. 2016). With evidence that gender identity changes for some, and is inchoate for others, the binary "either or" conceptualization of gender is increasingly recognized as incomplete. The term "they," when used by a patient as a gender neutral pronoun, may induce both skepticism and a challenge in clinical communication due to its singular and plural denotations. Respectful acknowledgment of the individual's gender neutrality, continuing education to better understand the gender spectrum, and supervision will promote engagement.

Inquiry and discussion of these terms with the individual are critical to understanding who the patient is and how they see themselves (National LGBT Health Education Center 2020). When these preferences are noted in charts, they not only document a more knowing and inclusive assessment, they begin to address a form of medical discrimination experienced by SGM patients when they are addressed with inappropriate gender terms (Lykens et al. 2018).

LGBT subgroups refer to forms of naming that imply a cultural identification. A "transgender male" is likely to have a cultural identification with the transgender community. A similar person, who identifies simply as "male," may wish to be perceived only as a member of the general male population. A male identifying as "gay" tends to have a cultural identification with the gay community, while another male who engages in same-sexual behavior may be identified as "heterosexual" or "straight" if his primary cultural identification is with the heterosexual community.

SGM Prevalence

In men, sexual arousal is the most accurate depiction of sexual orientation, no matter the gender of attraction, whereas sexual orientation as assessed by the community psychiatrist is a label chosen by the patient that gives rise to variations in prevalence (Bailey et al. 2016). Almost all women show an equal arousal pattern to both sexes in research studies, but most women are identified as heterosexual or mostly heterosexual, while a minority is identified as bisexual. Males on the other hand are usually aroused by just one gender. Transfemales show the monogender male pattern of genital arousal to either males or females, in contrast to the cisfemale pattern of arousal to both males and females (Chivers 2004). The arousal pattern in transmales has not, as yet, been reported. A significant minority of transgender individuals report a change in the gender of attraction as they transition (Auer et al. 2014).

Most people are cisgender, meaning their gender assigned at birth and their gender identity are the same. The gender one is attracted to determines sexual orientation. Terms used for sexual orientation in transgender individuals can be confusing. A male who is attracted to females would be labeled as "heterosexual," but if that individual later acknowledges a female gender identity, they would be labeled "homosexual," since they now acknowledge having a female gender identity and they are attracted to females. The gender of attraction did not change, and this person could be said to have always been "gynephilic." People of any gender identification who are attracted to males are said to be "androphilic," and those attracted to both sexes, "ambiphilic."

Men who have sexual and romantic experience with both sexes exhibit a bisexual arousal pattern and are identified as bisexual. But some studies have found monosexual arousal patterns in these individuals despite their bisexual identity (Rosenthal et al. 2011). Bisexual arousal has also been found in some men who identify as gay. Arousal patterns detected in clinical laboratory research can differ from actual interpersonal situations, highlighting the complexities of physiological versus psychological arousal and identity. More women than men identify as bisexual, and they are more likely to retain that label. When same-sexual attraction is pursued, the bisexual label may be repressed (Bailey et al. 2016).

Just asking a patient if they are gay or straight elicits incomplete information because sexual identity is a multidimensional phenomenon that consists of how one identifies their own gender, how one prefers to be identified in the social realm regarding their sexual orientation, what one's inner sexual desire for any gender is, who one actually engages with sexually by gender, and gender role behavior. Inquiry about a homosexual *identity* evokes a positive response in about 2.8% of adult males and 1.4% of adult females. Preference for same-sexual *behavior* is elicited in about 4.9% of adult males and 7.5% of adult females, while 7.7% of adult males and 7.5% of adult females report same-sexual *desire* (Lauman et al. 1994). Coffman et al. (2017) addressed the common survey limitation regarding sensitive questions about sexuality, which are more likely to elicit socially desirable answers rather than honest answers. Using a novel method, they found that the prevalence of a non-heterosexual identity is 65% higher and the prevalence of same-sexual behavior is 59% higher than in previous surveys.

Bisexual identity in a 2017 population survey was 2.9% for adult males and 5.4% for adult females (National Center for Health Statistics 2017): bisexual behavior ranges from 5.8% to 8.6% in adult males and 3.8% in females (Laumann et al. 1994; Sandfort et al. 2001). Transgender identity, including those who do not seek hormones or surgery, may be as frequent as 1:200 (Olysager and Conway 2008). Estimates in young people who identify as transgender range from 0.17% to 1.3% (Connolly et al. 2016).

Prevalence of Mental Disorders in the SGM Population

Most SGM individuals do not have histories of clinically significant mental health issues. Even so, experiences of rejection, stigma, alienation, shame, harassment, and discrimination due to gender or sexual differences increase the risk for psychological distress and mental disorders. The anticipation of potential rejection and changes in relationships and cultural identifications that occur with disclosure of a minority sexual identity are significant stressors. Elevated rates of psychological distress, depression, anxiety, and suicidality (suicidality is discussed in more detail in the next section) are consistently reported in SGM research samples (Plöderl and Tremblay 2015). Gay and bisexual men are reported to have elevated rates of panic disorder, body image, and eating disorders (Cochran et al. 2003). Elevated suicide risk is a consistent finding (Cochran and Mays 2006; Skegg et al. 2003). The highest rates of psychiatric morbidity based on sexual orientation occur in those with a bisexual identity (Warner et al. 2004; Koh and Ross 2006). Higher rates of psychiatric comorbidities are associated with alcohol or tobacco use in gay, lesbian, and bisexual individuals compared to heterosexual individuals, with the highest rates in the bisexual group (Evans-Polce et al. 2020). Rates also tend to be higher in the young and elderly (Fredriksen-Goldsen et al. 2013; Semlyen et al. 2016).

Higher rates of depression, suicidality, trauma, drug misuse, and anxiety disorders are observed in transgender and gender nonconforming populations (Dhejne et al. 2016; Valentine and Shipherd 2018). Estimates are significantly related to the extent of social ostracism and the challenges of gender incongruence. Rates of psychiatric disorders have been reported to range as high as 20–50% for diagnoses of depression, anxiety, and suicidality, with a range of 26–62% for substance abuse. Elevated rates of eating disorders and body image disturbance have also been noted (Pfafflin 2007). Significant improvement to normative levels in many, with residual anxiety and mood disorders in some, is reported with gender-confirming interventions (Bränström and Pachankis 2020; Mueller 2020).

Risk factors in all SGM groups include gender nonconformity, family and social rejection, discrimination, verbal abuse, physical assault, and religious conflict (Diaz et al. 2001; Omoto and Kurtzman 2006; D'Augelli et al. 2002). Higher morbidity in the bisexual group has been linked to ostracization by heterosexual and homosexual groups (Volpp 2009) and concealment of bisexuality (Schrimshaw et al. 2013).

Suicidality

Suicidal ideation and attempts are of the highest concern for clinicians. Approximately four-fifths of individuals of minority sexual orientation have no history of suicidality, but rates are consistently higher than for the general population and significantly higher in those who identify as transgender.

There appears to be little difference in fatalities compared to the general population, but ideation and attempts are higher (Haas et al. 2011). Attempts are higher in adolescence when disclosure of sexual orientation results in abuse or homelessness, especially in Black and Latinx groups. In Whites, there is a closer association with psychiatric disorders.

The lifetime rate of suicide attempts in transmen and transwomen is over 40%, the highest rate of any known demographic group. Risk factors include younger age, racial and ethnic minority identity, gender nonconformity, disclosure to others, psychiatric disorders, HIV, experiences of rejection, violence, homelessness, and discrimination. Protective factors include social support, transition services, and safe environments (Sausa 2005; Connolly et al. 2016).

Intersectionality

The interplay between multiple, stigmatized social group identities and health disparities defines intersectionality. Non-response to survey questions on sexual orientation is greater among African American, Hispanic, and Asian Americans compared to non-Hispanic Whites (Kim and Fredriksen-Goldsen 2013). SGM individuals that are also members of other stigmatized groups have an increased risk for depression and other psychiatric and medical comorbidities (Cochran and Mays 1994; Trinh et al. 2017). Higher rates of alcohol consumption are reported in Black and Hispanic sexual minority women compared with White heterosexual women, with greater differences when race and sexual identity are considered together (Greene et al. 2020).

Higher rates of bisexual behavior and HIV risk are reported in Black and Latino men, because the stigma of homosexuality in these communities more often results in disavowal of a gay identity. Internalized homophobia results in lower rates of disclosure to female partners (Jeffries and Dodge 2007).

African American transgender individuals fare worse than those in other ethnic and racial groups (Grant et al. 2011). Older transgender individuals have greater fear of healthcare services and poorer mental health than non-transgender individuals (Fredriksen-Goldsen et al. 2014).

Intersectional awareness and inquiry by the clinician can deepen the minority patient's sense of feeling understood, heightening engagement with the treatment setting while sensitizing the clinician to the differential nature of stigma between social groups.

Education and Training

Surveys of psychiatric residents and residency directors indicate that residents would like more training in their work with SGM patients. More than half of residency programs surveyed provide 5 hours or less of total training on SGM topics, with an average of 1.21 hours per year, leaving residents feeling unprepared. Competency can be measured by using the LGBT-Development of Clinical Skills Scale (LGBT-DOCSS), which assesses clinical preparedness, attitudinal awareness, and basic knowledge. Nowaskie found that competency improves significantly with 5 hours of exposure per year and an average of 40 LGBT patients during the residency (Nowaskie 2020).

Numerous educational opportunities are just a computer click away. The Group for the Advancement of Psychiatry provides a complimentary curriculum (gap-lgbtq.org), as does the National LGBTQIA+ Health Education Center (https://www.lgbtqiahealtheducation.org/). There is now a wealth of personal stories on YouTube that can sensitize clinicians to SGM issues, including stories of coming out as gay or transgender and the experience of SGM seniors when homosexuality was illegal and a psychiatric disorder.

LGBT Cultural Identity and Mental Illness

Those who work in community psychiatry should be able to answer the following question: *Why should it matter to me if the patient is LGBT when I am treating an illness such as schizophrenia?*

The answer illustrates why it is essential to look beyond symptoms. LGBT patients with psychiatric disorders present to clinicians at different stages of LGBT psychological development and phases of the life cycle. If a person is just coming to terms with their sexual identity, mental illness can interfere with and constrain its maturation. If they are exploring, or have established themselves in the LGBT world, it can pull them away. If they have past experiences with psychiatric treatment, the extent to which their sexual identity had been affirmed, ignored, or devalued will influence their expectations in current and future psychiatric settings.

LGBT individuals with major mental illnesses are just as likely to be shunned in the LGBT community as in mainstream society. Many are not able to reintegrate within an LGBT community at large, placing greater responsibility on the mental health community to address their cultural needs through support groups, advocacy programs, and provision or referral to resources that provide socialization and peer support (Hellman and Klein 2004; Hellman et al. 2010).

Disclosure of sexual identity extends to interactions in the mental health setting. Social interactions on inpatient units, in day programs and outpatient settings, in group therapy, on residences, and with secretaries, nurses, personnel, and families constantly expose the SGM person to the possibility of homophobia (Herek 2000), transphobia (Shipherd et al. 2010), heterosexism (Simoni and Walters 2001), or accusations of not being open and truthful if they do not disclose (Ritter and Terndrup 2002). The ability of the SGM community to buffer such experience is curtailed when the SGM person experiences mental illness, because it is typically not equipped to engage those who are, for example, hallucinating, delusional, thought disordered, manic, or severely depressed. Fear of being stereotyped, misunderstood, or inadequately assessed and treated contributes to a reluctance to engage with healthcare services (Corrigan et al. 2003).

SGM patients tend to be identified less with mainstream treatment environments, because they are predominately heterosexual and cisgender (Lenning 2009). The dual alienation associated with major mental illness and sexual minority status contributes to a lack of well-being and reinforcement of the “patient” role. Unless there is evidence for inclusiveness through affirmation in the psychiatric setting, healing from mental illness can mean investing significant effort adapting to mainstream culture or remaining invisible regarding sexual and gender orientation. Strained therapeutic alliances subject SGM patients to greater risk for non-adherence and poorer psychiatric outcomes (Jamison 2006). However, SGM patients with years of prior treatment for major mental illness can show remarkable gains when relevant cultural programming is available (Hellman et al. 2010).

Clinical Cultural Communication with SGM People

The social exchange between the provider and the SGM patient is influenced by the beliefs and expectations of both. This complex, multicultural dyad influences the session bilaterally, facilitating or constraining the clinical process.

It is the responsibility of the physician to be alert to the multicultural nature of the encounter and to be able to sensitively understand and address barriers, such as differences in language, values, beliefs, and customs. Self-reflection, discussion, and supervision ensure a productive interaction, especially when these barriers operate unconsciously. For example, if a patient that does not conform to stereotypical expectations of gender appearance and behavior evokes counter-transference in the clinician, the physician may deny or minimize the issue in an attempt to maintain harmony in the session but unconsciously maintain distance by ignoring aspects of the patient, withholding compassion, shortening sessions, and providing substandard care. Self-reflection and discussion can provide insight into this marginalization, transforming barriers in the clinical relationship into opportunities for an empathic partnership.

SGM patient-clinician interaction can evoke personal issues that can affect the social exchange. What is the patient assuming about the clinician's sexual and gender orientation? Should this be disclosed, and if so, how and when? Does the relationship with colleagues and the culture of the psychiatric institution influence disclosure (Hellman et al. 2010)? What past experience and issues are evoked from the clinician's personal background during the encounter? Do personal traditions, assumptions, beliefs, and moral values conflict or agree? Are they creating barriers to a productive treatment alliance?

Cultural competence is an aspirational ideal throughout a professional career. A humane and compassionate approach with the SGM patient is as necessary as technical prowess in eliciting and treating symptoms. Connecting with SGM patients so they feel comfortable, safe, understood, and supported in an environment that allows them to flourish takes time, learning, supervision, experience, self-reflection, and an institutional effort to provide an inclusive and affirming environment.

The cultural match between the clinician and the SGM patient is based on the extent of shared cultural knowledge, experience, and identity. Shared cultural characteristics tend to elicit a sense of implicit trust and identification that can enhance a treatment alliance (Rogers and Bhowmik 1970). However, some patients with significant, internalized homophobia may be clinically more comfortable with a therapist who is not gay or not openly gay. But in this situation, there is a risk that cultural identity development will be inhibited if the clinician also shares significant, internalized homophobia.

SGM Identity Development

SGM individuals with mental illness present to community psychiatrists at different stages of sexual minority identity development. With few exceptions, SGM individuals are born and raised in heterosexual, cisgender environments. Although not invariable, an early sense of being different results in the development of self-protective defenses. This is less influential when the environment is supportive and inclusive. Efforts to conform to the dominant social expectations of families and communities result in intrapsychic conflict as same-sex attraction or transgender convictions emerge. Stigmatization, alienation, isolation, shame, and fear can hinder the maturation of sexual identity and social competence, nurturing protective efforts at deception and reactive perfectionism, where the individual strives to meet heterosexist and other cultural expectations.

In those developing a bisexual identity, there is the experience of a dichotomous gay-straight world that is perceived to be negatively biased toward them and monogamously inclined. The heterosexual world generally believes they are closeted gays and the gay world resents or ignores their heterosexual interest. Potential partners of either sex are suspicious of outside interests or mate sharing.

A 2002 survey found the public's attitude toward bisexuals to be more negative than toward other major demographic and political groups, including other sexual minorities. The negative attitudes toward those with a bisexual identity (binegativity) differed, depending on the current gender of the bisexual's partner and the sexual orientation of acquaintances (Herek 2002; Sarno et al. 2020). Transgender individuals must also contend with sexual orientation. The internal nature of sexual orientation contrasts with the deep link between subjective gender experience and its external physical manifestation. Sexual or romantic desire for another person can be hidden away, in contrast to signals of gender through physical appearance, clothing, and behavior.

The toll of hiding an emerging sexual identity can motivate exploration of a more genuine experience of intimacy and social presentation that serves to integrate behavior, appearance, and identity. A period of separation from the predominant culture, whose beliefs and values are now questioned, results in varying degrees of distancing from family and community of origin as a minority subculture is explored and internalized. Support and acceptance from the minority subculture instill pride, confidence, and enhanced self-esteem. Sexual identity progressively synthesizes with other aspects of identity as a process of coming out and reintegration into the larger world begins.

SGM identities usually differ from the sexual identities of family members and communities of origin, whereas the race and ethnicity one is born into are shared. This gives rise to the need to reconcile shared cultural givens with the emerging awareness of a minority sexual identity. One must reconcile, for example, being gay with negative religious teachings related to homosexuality and anti-gay beliefs in the family. When successful, the process promotes a balanced, multicultural identity. Ongoing cultural conflict can increase psychiatric vulnerability.

Assessing Sexual Identity, Sexual Practices, and Marital and Familial Status

Ascertaining *sexual identity* involves the collection of information on the patient's core; subjective conviction of being male, female, androgynous, or nonbinary; the gender(s) of sexual attraction; and the degree of comfort in the gender role. How one socially identifies their gender or sexual orientation may differ from their inner identification and sexual behavior (i.e., sexual desire, erotic fantasy, or romantic interest).

A single question on sexual identity is, therefore, likely to yield incomplete or misleading information. A repertoire of questions yields a more accurate characterization. A sampling of introductory questions below will help clinicians develop this repertoire.

Questions on sexual experience can be expanded to inquiry about age of occurrence, frequency, circumstance, and concerns about sexual practices and risk for sexually transmitted diseases. About half of SGM patients with severe mental illnesses have had no sexual partner in the past year (Hellman et al. 2002). For those who

Creating Dialogue

I am going to ask you some questions about your sexual health that I ask all my patients. They allow me to know more about how to keep you healthy, and your answers are strictly confidential (Potter 2010).

Do you have any concerns about your sexual or gender orientation or sexual practices?

To clarify gender orientation: Sometimes people have an issue with being male or female…

Have you ever desired to be a member of the opposite sex? *If yes,* what pronoun ["he" or "she"] do you prefer? Would you like me to use that?

Has your sexual experience been with men, women, both, or neither?

What is your sexual orientation?

Have you felt sexually attracted or fantasized about men, women, or both?

Have you been romantically involved with men, women, or both?

Have you been involved with anyone in the past year? *If yes*, what kind of sex did you engage in – oral, vaginal, anal, mutual masturbation? Anything else?

Are you using protection, like condoms?

When did you last have unprotected sex?

How many partners have you had in the past year?

(continued)

Do you have any children?

The people who come here sometimes have preferences regarding therapists, e.g. male or female, Hispanic, African-American, gay etc. Do you?

Tell me about your life from a gay [lesbian, bisexual, pansexual, non heterosexual, transgender, nonbinary] perspective.

Have you previously had psychiatric treatment?

If yes: What was that like from a sexual or gender minority (SGM) perspective? Did you feel comfortable and supported?

How has mental illness affected your life as an SGM person?

Are there any LGBT concerns that you would like to address here?

lack sexual experience or partners, questions that focus on sexual interest, desire, or appeal are more appropriate.

What we think we know about SGM sexuality often derives from cultural stereotypes (Hellman 2019). LGBT people may even question their own erotic interests because they have internalized these assumptions. A self-defined, authentic erotic identity experienced in sexually safe ways is a more appropriate framework for exploration of the contribution of sexuality to general mental well-being. This is also an opportunity to explore issues in common with other psychiatric patients, such as sexual side effects of medication and the lack of privacy and autonomy for some in residences and other living arrangements.

Assessment of romantic interest, emotional attachment, relationships, and commitments expands on the context of sexuality. LGBT patients may present with no marital history, a history of heterosexual or same-sex marriage, civil unions, domestic partnerships, and commitment ceremonies. All live in a world of opinions and emotions evoked by societal changes in beliefs and attitudes, legal options, and social status.

Child-rearing is a growing aspect of the SGM story. Approximately 15% of same-sex couples in the United States have children in their household (Flood et al. 2020). Marital alternatives, offspring, and child-rearing apply to the overall assessment.

General SGM Issues for the Community Psychiatrist

The diversity among SGM individuals warrants caution in formulating a clinical approach based on simple characterizations of these groups. SGM subgroups are subject to similar prejudices rooted in beliefs and traditions about sexuality and gender. Bias toward one subgroup tends to generalize to all four, and the subgroups often come together for social and political strength (Ferris 2006). But unique personal histories, including gender differences in rearing, socialization and physiology, stereotypes of gender and gender expectations, and gender-based differences that are reinforced in same-sexual erotic, romantic, social, and parental interactions, necessitate the development of SGM patient profiles that reflect these distinctions.

Initial assessment determines the extent to which these issues will be a focus of therapy or will just provide a context for it (Falco 1996).

Bisexual individuals are more likely to experience hostility from both the gay and straight worlds and face unique stereotypes regarding promiscuity, relational commitments, and community affiliations, with resulting internalization of binegativity (Weinberg et al. 1994). This generates complex decisions about when and where to disclose or conceal sexual orientation. These stressors result in higher rates of psychiatric problems in relation to other sexual orientation minorities (Feinstein and Dyar 2017). Lack of cultural affiliation with the gay community, and aloofness within the heterosexual community, enhances the risk of isolation and lack of support (Jeffries and Dodge 2007). Successful bisexual commitments are predicated upon open communication regarding sexual and emotional expectations and mutually agreed-upon rules regarding outside contacts (Deacon et al. 1996).

The desire to be a member of the opposite sex unites a diverse group under the umbrella of transgender phenomena. Transgender individuals may be heterosexual, bisexual, homosexual, or asexual. Transfemales and transmales are, respectively, biological males with a female identification and male-identified biological females. Some have a mixed gender identity and may refer to themselves as "genderqueer" or "two-spirited." The term "transgender" is broader than "transsexual" because it includes those who do not transition with hormones and surgery.

Physical alteration of the body can be an expensive process. Affordability, rather than subjective desire, can be the determining factor in transitioning. As a result, clinicians may see individuals born as males who state that they subjectively are identified and live as a woman despite retention of their male genitalia. Some, with transvestic fetishism, are heterosexual and are initially comfortable in their gender of birth. They cross-dress for erotic arousal but become progressively uncomfortable in their anatomical gender, as the erotic element fades and a cross-gender identity intensifies.

Gender dysphoria is distress related to gender incongruence between anatomy and gender identity. It can be intense and persistent in some but not others. When gender affirmation surgery is desired, it is typically the culmination of a process that includes living as a member of the opposite sex, with interventions that can include cross-gender hormone treatment, electrolysis, breast alteration, facial augmentation, and genital surgery. No psychiatric intervention can change gender identity.

Clinicians are not likely to see many of these individuals based on prevalence. However, gender atypical individuals face harassment, stigma and discrimination, gender dysphoria, and the significant challenges of gender transitioning, all of which can motivate a desire for help. Because cross-gender identity is rare, transgender individuals are frequently concerned they will not get appropriate mental health care in a mainstream community setting. Psychiatrists treating transgender individuals should be familiar with the *Standards of Care for the Health of Transsexual, Transgender, and Gender Nonconforming People* (Coleman et al. 2012), which provides guidelines regarding diagnosis, evaluation and documentation for transitioning, aspects of psychotherapy, education, and follow-up care.

In some transgender individuals, hormone therapy not only facilitates a gender transition but also diminishes anxiety and depression without the need for standard psychotropic medications. Cross-gender hormone therapy is associated with irreversible physical changes, medical side effects, and occasional affective lability or depression and should only be administered by physicians that are familiar with its risks, benefits, and management. Most psychiatrists will want to refer to an endocrinologist or gender specialist when hormones are a consideration (Coleman et al. 2012; Gooren and van de Waal 2007).

Careful facilitation must be balanced against unnecessary policing of gender transition. Psychiatrists not familiar with cross-gender issues should refer these patients to a gender specialist, but may, otherwise, address standard psychiatric issues.

Building Effective Programs for SGM Patients

From a specialization that once saw its mandate as changing sexual orientation, psychiatry continues to develop effective models of SGM healthcare delivery (Kidd et al. 2016; Pachankis 2014). Grassroots organizations provided some of the first interventions to address the mental health needs of the SGM community, taking a largely pragmatic approach before there was national leadership, medical education and training, and evidence-based guidelines (Byers et al. 2019). With the Covid-19 viral pandemic, telepsychiatry ascended to further meet the mental health needs of the SGM community (Whailbeh et al. 2020).

Effective programming does not have to involve additional funding. Start with the resources you have. Who is interested? Who already has experience and training? Which hours, on what days, and which space can be designated as a safe and confidential place for groups, socialization, and other activities?

Culturally competent care begins where a focus on the chief complaint leaves off. In its most elemental yet intersectional form, there resides a simple, clinical question: *Is there anything about your gender, sexual orientation, age, religion, race, or ethnicity that would be important for me to know in providing your care here? May I ask you some details?*

Patient presentations differ; demographics vary; staff exhibit all levels of training, interest, and comfort with SGM issues; programs differ in size, purpose, resources, and interventions; organizational cultures vary; and the list goes on. For these reasons, successful programming requires strategic planning. This can start with an overview of the health disparities that SGM individuals experience (Daniel et al. 2015).

It is recommended that staff and administrators meet to discuss the strengths and weaknesses of their organization as a resource to the SGM patient and community (Israel et al. 2011). Established criteria for SGM clinical competence can be reviewed, and time frames set to achieve specific goals. Feedback from SGM consumers, either informally or through an SGM consumer advisory committee and consultation with experts in the SGM community, can provide valuable feedback.

Articulation of an ideal vision of what the organization would hope to become, for example, a limited goal of developing an SGM staff resource, or a comprehensive one, such as a regional resource to SGM people with major mental illness, sets the organization on a path with a purpose. A statement of mission conveys how this would be done, say by the provision of culturally sensitive, core psychiatric, psychosocial, cultural, peer, and advocacy services to SGM patients or perhaps, simply, a monthly meeting on SGM issues.

Promotion of the vision by leaders in the organization, and the achievement of benchmarks as the mission is operationalized, helps the culture of the organization evolve as staff and administration witness the benefit to patients, experience enhanced professional pride with staff development, and realize greater institutional stature as the organization becomes a resource to the SGM community (Burkhart and Reuss 1993).

Because SGM patients are a minority in mainstream settings, comprehensive clinical programming may only be justified on a regional basis, in contrast with cultural competence, which should be a goal in all settings. When the number of SGM clients in the clinical setting is low, realistic service provision may only be possible on an individual basis. Programs of any size can designate interested staff as first-line referral resources. Over time, with ongoing in-service education and discussion of cases and issues, the competence of all staff will be enhanced, and staff resources will widen. SGM patients can be encouraged to connect with others through support and advocacy websites such as *rainbowheights.org*.

Practical Programming Suggestions

Objectives ensure that the mission to deliver effective SGM services will be achieved. Objectives provide an umbrella for specific actions that must be taken through a series of concrete tasks. The box below describes some useful objectives and tasks.

Conclusion

This chapter provides an overview of essential information for the community psychiatrist and mental health team treating SGM patients. The evidence-based literature in this area continues to expand, but it is not necessary to know everything about SGM people and culture in order to engage this population. It is necessary to know how to create an inclusive, friendly, respectful environment that can promote trust and identification, put the SGM patient at ease, and allow for the development of a dialogue that enhances the likelihood that relevant and sensitive information will be elicited and addressed. Standards of care

Creating Culturally Competent Programming

1. *Reduce sexual and gender minority (SGM) patient ambivalence, anxiety, and fear of mainstream settings (create an inclusive setting).*
   (a) Post a nondiscrimination of service notice in public spaces.
   (b) Include definition of families/significant others in policies – same-sex partners and parents, domestic partners, spouses.
   (c) Create a culturally inclusive brochure for the waiting room.
   (d) Put up an SGM poster in the waiting room.
   (e) Provide intake materials for patients that encourage sharing concerns with the assigned clinician about sexual orientation and gender (Cooper and Roter 2003).
   (f) Include gender identity/expression and sexual orientation in Patients' Bill of Rights.
   (g) Involve same-sex partners or a key, supportive SGM friend in care.
   (h) Broaden concept of "family" to include anyone that plays a significant supportive role.
2. *Create an inclusive staff environment*
   (a) Post nondiscrimination statement regarding staff hiring inclusive of sexual and gender orientation/expression.
   (b) Review methods of inquiry about traditional and nontraditional family arrangements.
   (c) Canvass clinical staff regarding SGM knowledge, clinical experience, cultural affiliation, and interest as first-line referral sources, and enhance diversity of the workforce, and provide supervision on SGM cases, quarterly in-service staff educational presentations, SGM journal discussion groups, SGM case conferences, discussion and supervision regarding clinician bias.
   (d) Enhance the cultural competence of ancillary staff with regular meetings; review the use of gender neutral terms; review strategies for fielding telephone inquiries; maintain confidentiality in public areas; create a policy for the use of bathrooms for transgender clients; integrate inclusive language in intake forms.
   (e) Include same-sex partners at social functions.
   (f) Meet and review diversity issues once a year.
3. *Empower SGM consumers*
   (a) Create an SGM consumer advisory committee.
   (b) Recruit and train SGM peer specialists for support, connection, and advocacy (Lecomte et al. 1999).
4. *Establish affiliation with the LGBT community*
   (a) Invite an SGM representative onto the community advisory board to guide inclusiveness and nondiscrimination, enhance cultural competence, and facilitate community referrals.
   (b) Clarify racial/ethnic profile of local SGM community and develop staffing reflective of the profile.
5. *Facilitate SGM sociocultural activities*
   (a) Organize a "Gender Day" event with transgender speaker presentation and discussion group on gender expression, and have a Gender Party.
   (b) Organize a "Lobby Day" event, arranging for LGBT consumer group to meet with government representatives who will impress legislators with importance of funding LGBT inclusive care.

(continued)

for SGM patients are now widely available and should ease the clinician's task of acquiring the requisite background.

Community psychiatry has progressively shifted in its views and obligations toward sexual minorities. This evolution continues as knowledge of SGM persons, and the most effective ways to help them, deepens. Collaborating with SGM patients is far from a narrow specialization, because it helps define who we are, both professionally and personally, challenging foundational assumptions about human identity and behavior while testing our ability to connect. It is work that expands our understanding of human experience, as we organize ourselves in the best way possible to enhance the well-being of those we serve.

References

Auer MK, Fuss J, Höhne N, Stalla GK, Sievers C (2014) Transgender transitioning and change of self-reported sexual orientation. PLoS One. 9(10): e110016. Published online 2014 Oct 9. https://doi.org/10.1371/journal.pone.0110016 PMCID: PMC4192544

Bailey JM et al (2016) Sexual orientation, controversy, and science, *Psychological Science in the Public Interest*, 17(2) 45–101

Bayer R (1981) Homosexuality and American Psychiatry, Basic Books, New York

Bränström R, Pachankis JE (2020) Reduction in mental health treatment utilization among transgender individuals after gender-affirming surgeries: A total population study. *Am J Psych* 177 (8): 727–734.

Burkhart PL, Reuss S (1993). *Successful Strategic Planning: A Guide for Nonprofit Agencies and Organizations*. Newbury Park: Sage Publications

Byers, D. S., Vider, S., & Smith, A. (2019). Clinical activism in community-based practice: The case of LGBT affirmative care at the Eromin Center, Philadelphia, 1973–1984. *American Psychologist, 74*(8), 868–881

Chivers ML (2004) A sex difference in the specificity of sexual arousal. *Psychological Science* 15(11):736–44

Cochran SD, Mays VM (1994). Depressive distress among homosexually active African American men and women. *Am J Psych*. 151:524–529

Cochran SD, Mays VM, Sullivan JG (2003). Prevalence of mental disorders, psychological distress, and mental health services use among lesbian, gay, and bisexual adults in the United States. *J Consult Clin Psychol*. 71(1):53–61.

Cochran SD, Mays VM (2006). Estimating prevalence of mental and substance-using disorders among lesbians and gay men from existing national health data. In, Omoto AM & Kurtzman HS (Eds.), Contemporary perspectives on lesbian, gay, and bisexual psychology. Sexual orientation and mental health: Examining identity and development in lesbian, gay, and bisexual people (p. 143–165). American Psychological Association

Coffman KB, Coffman LC, Keith M. Marzilli-Ericson (2017) The size of the lgbt population and the magnitude of anti-gay sentiment are substantially underestimated. *Management Science* 63 (10): 3168–3186

Coleman E, Bockting W, Botzer M, Cohen-Kettenis P, et al (2012). Standards of care for the health of transsexual, transgender, and gender-nonconforming people, version 7. *Int J of Transgenderism*, 13(4): 165–232. https://doi.org/10.1080/15532739.2011.700873

Connolly MD, Zervos MJ, Barone CJ, Johnson CC, et al (2016) The mental health of transgender youth: Advances in understanding. *J Adolesc Health*, 59(5):489–495

Cooper LA, Roter DL, (2003). Patient-provider communication: The effect of race and ethnicity on process and outcomes of healthcare. In Smedley BD, Stith AY, Nelson AR (Eds.) *Unequal Treatment: Confronting Racial and Ethnic Disparities In Health Care*. The National Academies Press: Washington, DC, 552–593.

Corrigan P, Thompson V, Lambert D, Sangster Y, Noel JG, Campbell J (2003). Perceptions of discrimination among persons with serious mental illness. *Psychiatric Services*, 54, 1105–1110

D'Augelli AR, Pilkington NW, Hershberger SL (2002). Incidence and mental health impact of sexual orientation victimization of lesbian, gay, and bisexual youths in high school. *School Psychology Quarterly*, 17(2):148–67

Daniel H, Butkus R et al (2015) Lesbian, gay, bisexual, and transgender health disparities: executive summary of a policy position paper from the American College of Physicians *Ann Intern Med*. 163(2):135–7

Deacon SA, Reinke L, Viers D (1996). Cognitive-behavioral therapy for bisexual couples: Expanding the realms of therapy. *The American J of Family Therapy*. 24(3):242–258

Dhejne C, Vlerken RV, Heylens G, Arcelus J (2016) Mental health and gender dysphoria: A review of the literature. *Int Rev Psychiatry*, 28(1):44–57

Diaz RM, Ayala G, Bein E, Henne J, Marin BV (2001). The impact of homophobia, poverty, and racism on the mental health of gay and bisexual Latino men: Findings from 3 US cities. *Am J Pub Health* 91:927–932

Evans-Polce RJ, Kcomt L, Veliz PT, Boyd CJ, McCabe SE (2020) Alcohol, tobacco, and comorbid psychiatric disorders and associations with sexual identity and stress-related correlates. *Am J Psych* 177 (11): 1073–1081

Falco KL (1996). Psychotherapy with women who love women. In, Cabaj RP, Stein TS (Eds.) *Textbook of Homosexuality and Mental Health*. Washington, DC: American Psychiatric Association Press

Feinstein BA, Dyar C (2017). Bisexuality, minority stress, and health. *Current sexual health reports*, *9*(1): 42–49.

Ferris JL (2006). The nomenclature of the community: An activist's perspective. In Shankle MD (Ed.), *The Handbook of Lesbian, Gay, Bisexual and Transgender*

Public Health: A Practitioner's Guide to Service. The Haworth Press, Binghamton, NY, 3–10.

Flood S, King M, Rodgers R, Ruggles S, Warren JR (2020) Integrated public use microdata series, current population survey: Version 8.0 [dataset]. Minneapolis, MN: IPUMS. https://doi.org/10.18128/D030.V8.0

Fredriksen-Goldsen KI, Kim HJ, Barkan SE, Muraco A, Hoy-Ellis CP (2013) Health disparities among lesbian, gay, and bisexual older adults: results from a population-based study. *Am J Public Health*.103(10):1802–1809.

Fredriksen-Goldsen K I, Cook-Daniels L, Kim H J, et al. (2014). Physical and mental health of transgender older adults: An at-risk and underserved population. *The Gerontologist*, 54(3), 488–50

Gooren LJ, Delemarre-van de Waal HA (2007). Hormone treatment of adult and juvenile transsexual patients. In, R Ettner, S Monstrey, Eyler AE (Eds.) *Principles of Transgender Medicine and Surgery*. Routledge: NY, 73–88

Grant JM, Mottet LA, Tanis J, Harrison J, Herman JL, Keisling M (2011) Injustice at every turn: a report of the national transgender discrimination survey. *National Center for Transgender Equality and National Gay and Lesbian Task Force*. Washington, DC.

Greene N, Jackson JW, Dean LT (2020) Examining disparities in excessive alcohol use among black and hispanic lesbian and bisexual women in the united states: an intersectional analysis. *J Stud Alcohol Drugs*. 81(4):462–470

Haas AP, Eliason M, Mays VM, et al (2011) Suicide and suicide risk in lesbian, gay, bisexual, and transgender populations: review and recommendations. *J Homosex*, 58:10–51.

Hellman, R.E., Sudderth, L., & Avery, A.M. (2002). Major mental illness in a sexual minority psychiatric sample. *Journal of the Gay and Lesbian Medical Association*, 6, 97–106.

Hellman RE, Klein E (2004) A program for lesbian, gay, bisexual, and transgender individuals with major mental illness, *J of Gay & Lesbian Psychotherapy*, 8(3–4): 67–82

Hellman RE, Klein E, Huygen C, Chew M, Uttaro T (2010). A study of members of a support and advocacy program for LGBT persons with major mental illness. *Best Practices in Mental Health: An International Journal*. 6(2): 13–26.

Hellman, RE (2019) The way of the world: how heterosexism shapes and distorts male same-sexuality, a thesis, *J of Gay & Lesbian Mental Health*. 23(3):349–359.

Herek GM (2000). The psychology of sexual prejudice. *Current Directions in Psychological Science*, 9, 19–22

Herek GM (2002) Heterosexuals attitudes toward bisexual men and women in the United States. *J Sex Res*. 39(4):264–74

Israel T, Walther WA, Gortcheva R, Perry JS (2011): Policies and practices for lgbt clients: Perspectives of mental health services administrators, *J of Gay & Lesbian Mental Health*, 15(2): 152–168

Jamison KR (2006). The many stigmas of mental illness. Lancet, 367: 533–534.

Jeffries IV, WL, Dodge B (2007). Male bisexuality and condom use at last sexual encounter: results from a national survey. *Journal of Sex Research*. 44(3): 278–289

Kidd SA, Howison M, Pilling M, Ross LE, McKenzie K (2016). Severe mental illness in LGBT populations: A scoping review. *Psychiatric Services* 67(7): 779–783.

Kim H J, & Fredriksen-Goldsen, KI (2013). Nonresponse to a question on self-identified sexual orientation in a public health survey and its relationship to race and ethnicity. *Am J of Public Health*, 103(1), 67–69

Koh AS, Ross LK. (2006). Mental health issues: a comparison of lesbian, bisexual and heterosexual women. *J Homosexuality* 51:33–57

Lauman, EO, Gagnon, JH, Michael, RT, Michaels, S (1994). *The social organization of sexuality: Sexual practices in the United States*. Chicago: University of Chicago Press.

Lecomte T, Wilde JB, Wallace CJ (1999) Mental health consumers as peer interviewers. *Psychiatric Services*. 50:693–695

Lenning E (2009). Moving beyond the binary: Exploring the dimensions of gender presentation and orientation. *International Journal of Social Inquiry*. 2 (2): 39–54

Lykens JE, LeBlanc AJ, & Bockting WO (2018). Healthcare experiences among young adults who identify as genderqueer or nonbinary. *LGBT health*, *5*(3): 191–196.

Mueller SC (2020) Mental health treatment utilization in transgender persons: what we know and what we don't know. *Am J Psych* 177 (8): 657–659.

National Center for Health Statistics (2017) Sexual orientation and attraction. Centers for Disease Control and Prevention. https://www.cdc.gov/nchs/nsfg/key_statistics/s_2015-2017.htm#sexualorientationandattractionNational

LGBT Health Education Center (2020) Neurodiversity & gender-diverse youth: An affirming approach to care. https://www.lgbtqiahealtheducation.org/wp-content/uploads/2020/08/Neurodiversity-and-Gender-Diverse-Youth_An-Affirming-Approach-to-Care_2020.pdf

National Institutes of Health (2019) Sexual and Gender Minority Populations in NIH-Supported Research, August 28, 2019, https://grants.nih.gov/grants/guide/notice-files/NOT-OD-19-139.html

Nowaskie D (2020) A national survey of U.S. psychiatry residents' LGBT cultural competency: The importance of LGBT patient exposure and formal education, *J of Gay & Lesbian Mental Health*, 24:4, 375–391.

Olysager F, Conway L (2008). Transseksualiteit komit vaker voor dan u denkt. Een nieuwe kijk op de prevalentie van trasnsseksualiteit in Nederland en Belgie (Transsexualism is more common than you think. A new look at the prevalence of transsexualism in the Netherlands and Belgium). *Tijdschrift voor Genderstudies (Dutch Journal for Gender Studies)*. 11(2):39–51

Omoto AM, Kurtzman HS (Eds.) (2006). *Sexual Orientation and Mental Health: Examining Identity and Development in Lesbian, Gay, and Bisexual People*. Washington, DC: American Psychological Association.

Pachankis, J E (2014). Uncovering clinical principles and techniques to address minority stress, mental health, and related health risks among gay and bisexual men. *Clinical Psychology: Science and Practice*, 21(4), 313–330.

Pfafflin F (2007). Mental health issues. In Ettner R, Monstrey S, Eyler AE (Eds) *Principles of Transgender Medicine and Surgery*. New York: Routledge

Plöderl M, Tremblay P (2015) Mental health of sexual minorities. A systematic review, *International Review of Psychiatry*, 27 (5): 367–385

Potter J (2010). Meeting the healthcare needs of LGBT populations: An end to invisibility. *Grand Rounds*. University of Louisville, Department of Medicine, April 8, 2010

Richards C, Bouman WP, Seal L, Barker MJ, Nieder TO, T'Sjoen G (2016) Non-binary or genderqueer genders, *Int Rev of Psych*, 28:1, 95–102

Ritter, K.Y., Terndrup, A.I. (2002). *Handbook of Affirmative Psychotherapy with Lesbians and Gay Men*. New York: The Guilford Press

Rogers EM, Bhowmik DK (1970). Homophily-heterophily: relational concepts for communication research. *Public Opinion Quarterly*, 34(4):523–538

Romanelli, M, Hudson K D (2017). Individual and systemic barriers to health care: Perspectives of lesbian, gay, bisexual, and transgender adults. *American Journal of Orthopsychiatry, 87*(6), 714–728.

Rosenthal A M, Sylva D, Safron A, Bailey J M (2011) Sexual arousal patterns of bisexual men revisited. *Biological Psychology*, 88, 112–115.

Russell ST, Fish JN (2016) Mental health in lesbian, gay, bisexual, and transgender (LGBT) youth. *Ann Rev Clin Psychol* 12 (1):465–487

Sandfort TGM, de Graaf R, Bijl RV, Schnabel P (2001). Same-sex sexual behavior and psychiatric disorders: Findings from the Netherlands mental health survey and incidence study (NEMESIS). *Archives of General Psychiatry, 58*(1): 85–91.

Sarno EL, Newcomb ME, Feinstein BA, Mustanski B (2020) Bisexual men's experiences with discrimination, internalized binegativity, and identity affirmation: Differences by partner gender. *Arch Sex Behav*. 49(5):1783–1798.

Sausa, LA (2005). Translating research into practice: Trans youth recommendations for improving school systems. *The Journal of Gay and Lesbian Issues in Education, 3*(1): 15–28.

Schrimshaw EW, Siegel K, Downing M, Jr., Parsons, JT (2013). Disclosure and concealment of sexual orientation and the mental health of non-gay-identified, behaviorally bisexual men. *Journal of Consulting and Clinical Psychology, 81*(1): 141–153

Semlyen J, King M, Varney J *et al* (2016) Sexual orientation and symptoms of common mental disorder or low wellbeing: combined meta-analysis of 12 UK population health surveys. *BMC Psychiatry* 16 (67). https://doi.org/10.1186/s12888-016-0767-z

Shipherd JC, Green KE, Abramovitz S (2010). Transgender clients: Identifying and minimizing barriers to mental health treatment. *Journal of Gay & Lesbian Mental Health*, 14, (2): 94–108

Simoni JM Walters KL (2001). Heterosexual Identity and Heterosexism: Recognizing Privilege to Reduce Prejudice. *Journal of Homosexuality*, 1(1): 157–173.

Skegg K, Nada-Raja S, Dickson N, Paul C, Williams S (2003). Sexual orientation and self-harm in men and women. *American Journal of Psychiatry*, 160:541–546

Trinh MH, Agénor M, Austin SB, Jackson CL (2017) Health and healthcare disparities among U.S. women and men at the intersection of sexual orientation and race/ethnicity: a nationally representative cross-sectional study. *BMC Public Health*.17(964) https://doi.org/10.1186/s12889-017-4937-9

Valentine SE, Shipherd JC (2018) A systematic review of social stress and mental health among transgender and gender non-conforming people in the United States. *Clin Psychol Rev*. 66:24–38.

Volpp SY (2009). Bisexuals. In, Ruiz P, Primm A (Eds.) *Disparities in Psychiatric Care: Clinical and Cross-Cultural Perspectives*. Philadelphia: Lippincott Williams and Wilkins

Warner J, McKeown E, Griffin M, Johnson K, Ramsay A, Cort C, King M (2004). Rates and predictors of mental illness in gay men, lesbians, and bisexual men and women: Results from a survey based in England and Wales. *Br J Psych* 185:479–485

Weinberg MS, Williams CJ, Pryor DW (1994). *Dual Attraction*. New York, NY: Oxford University Press.

Whaibeh E, Mahmoud H, Vogt EL (2020) Reducing the treatment gap for lgbt mental health needs: the potential of telepsychiatry. *J Behav Health Serv Res* 47: 424–431.

Migrant and Refugee Mental Health

Barbara Robles-Ramamurthy, Carissa Cabán-Alemán, Maria Rodriguez, Xinlin Chen, Eugenio M. Rothe, and Lisa R. Fortuna

Migration is a natural phenomenon that has occurred since the beginning of time. Migration—to flee harm, drought, or war or to pursue sustenance, fertile land, or trade routes—is a natural aspect of human life. What is not natural is *forced* displacement of people. By the mid-2020, forcibly displaced people worldwide surpassed an all-time high of 80 million. These numbers include 46 million internally displaced people, 26 million international refugees, and 4 million asylees (United Nations High Commission on Refugees 2020).

The United States celebrates its identity as a nation of immigrants with its welcoming poem by Emma Lazarus, *The New Colossus*, on the iconic Statue of Liberty. The nation's story is of pilgrims crossing the ocean to seek religious freedom. These cultural narratives often obscure the story of a different type of migration: forced displacement of native and African people. Slavery has been a foundational economic institution, backed by the state, robbing people of everything, including their wealth-producing labor and land. This institution remains in distinct though familiar modern-day iterations. While its players and context are different, the power dynamics and interdependent push and pull factors of migration today are not dissimilar to those throughout history.

Forced or involuntary migration may be attributed to human causes such as conflict or to so-called natural causes such as disasters. In practice, these are inter-connected, as conflict often arises over natural resources and human activity itself may trigger natural disasters such as long-term climate warming. The response (or lack of response) to a natural disaster can range from neglect to state violence, hence creating a political or humanitarian disaster. The drastic increase of forced displacement that has occurred in the decade of 2010–2020 is mainly due to conflicts in the Syrian region, sub-Saharan Africa, the inflow

B. Robles-Ramamurthy (✉)
Long School of Medicine at the University of Texas Health San Antonio, San Antonio, TX, USA
e-mail: roblesramamu@uthscsa.edu

C. Cabán-Alemán · E. M. Rothe
Herbert Wertheim College of Medicine at Florida International University, Miami, FL, USA
e-mail: ccabanal@fiu.edu; erothe@fiu.edu

M. Rodriguez
Florida Immigrant Coalition, Miami, FL, USA
e-mail: Maria@flic.org

X. Chen
NYU Grossman School of Medicine, New York, NY, USA

Public Psychiatry Fellow at Columbia University, New York, NY, USA
e-mail: chenx5@nychhc.org

L. R. Fortuna
Department of Psychiatry, University of California San Francisco, Zuckerberg San Francisco General Hospital and Trauma Center, San Francisco, CA, USA
e-mail: lisa.fortuna@ucsf.edu

W. E. Sowers et al. (eds.), *Textbook of Community Psychiatry*,
https://doi.org/10.1007/978-3-031-10239-4_50

of Rohingya refugees to Bangladesh, and the displacement of Venezuelans (International Migration Law 2019).

This chapter begins with defining the various legal and social designations used for groups of migrant and refugee populations, as these legal and social definitions affect quality of life and mental health. Important sociocultural factors that influence mental health needs in immigrant and refugee populations are described along with a brief overview and examples of culturally tailored evidence-based treatments that have been found to be beneficial. The chapter concludes with an emphasis on the need for including affirmative and culturally responsive practices in clinical training and the importance of understanding and preventing vicarious trauma. Through the use of best practices, clinicians are able to optimize their clinical care of migrants and refugees while also maintaining their own wellness.

Defining the Populations: Migrant, Asylum Seeker, Refugee, and Other Important Populations

Not all displaced people can achieve the legal status of refugees. A refugee, as defined by the United Nations High Commissioner for Refugees, is a person who has a:

> ...well-founded fear of being persecuted for reasons of race, religion, nationality, membership of a particular social group or political opinion, is outside the country of his nationality and is unable or, owing to such fear, is unwilling to avail themselves of the protection of that country; or who, not having a nationality and being outside the country of his former habitual residence as a result of such events, is unable or, owing to such fear is unwilling to return to it. (United Nations High Commissioner for Refugees 1951)

This status is granted internationally before entry to the United States or other receiving countries. When refugees remain in their host country, they often move steadily toward full citizenship in their established new home.

Seeking asylum is a human right. Individuals may seek asylum due to fear of persecution or other reasons, as described in the definition of refugee status. While refugees request protection while still overseas, before entry into the United States, a person who requests protection within the first year of arrival is called an asylum seeker. In the United States, asylees achieve legal permanent residency and, in theory, are able to naturalize, i.e., become citizens, within 3 years.

Other persons may be granted temporary protected status (TPS), a designation by the US Citizenship and Immigration Services to eligible nationals of certain countries (or parts of countries), who are already in the United States due to ongoing armed conflict, environmental disaster, epidemic or other extraordinary, and temporary conditions. During a designated period, TPS beneficiaries are not deportable, can obtain a work permit, and may be granted travel authorization (US Citizenship and Immigration Services 2021). While nationals of some countries receive TPS for 2 or 3 years before their designation ends, others, such as Sudanese, Nicaraguans, Hondurans, and Salvadorans, have held TPS for almost two decades. Salvadorans make up 60% of the 437,000 TPS recipients (Congressional Research Service 2020). This is a precarious and temporary status which creates uncertainty, physically and emotionally, for TPS beneficiaries and their 250,000 US citizen children.

Children who entered the United States without authorization, i.e., undocumented, are known as "Dreamers" and if they meet the criteria of the 2012 Deferred Action for Childhood Arrivals (DACA) program are also conferred a temporary protection from deportation. It should be noted that DACA only applies to those who arrived in the United States after June 15, 2007. Similarly, these young people face the stress of uncertainty, as the designation has been challenged by litigation and political rhetoric. Additionally, they often carry the emotional and financial burden of supporting their undocumented parents and mixed-status families.

Deferred Enforced Departure is a status similar to DACA, recently granted to Venezuelans, the largest displaced population in this hemisphere as of this writing. It confers protection from deportation but no opportunity for permanency (unless an individual is otherwise qualified to adjust his or her status).

Documented migrants are foreign-born individuals who are legally admitted to the United States, as they were able to avail themselves of existing laws and to provide proper documentation. Unauthorized immigrants either entered without inspection or overstayed a visa such as a tourist, work, business, or student visa and were unable to extend or adjust their status.

Mixed-status families include family members with various immigration status. Typically, these families are made of parents who do not have legal status, while their children do, generally because they were born on US territory. A 2015 report found that approximately half a million US citizen children experienced apprehension, detention, and deportation of at least one parent in the course of about 2 years (Capps et al. 2015).

Hemispheric and Regional Migration: Central America's Northern Triangle

About 3.5 million immigrants in the United States come from Central America. In 2017, Central Americans were about 8% of the overall immigrant population in the United States, and people from the Central American Northern Triangle (Guatemala, Honduras, and El Salvador) represented 86% of Central Americans. They primarily cite insecurity and environmental challenges as the cause of their migration. For instance, civil wars in the Northern Triangle have led to a rise in the number of migrants since the 1980s. Hurricanes, such as Mitch in Honduras and Nicaragua in 1998, or earthquakes like the one that hit El Salvador in 2001 have been the sources of migration along with drought (Migration Policy Institute 2019). Overall, Hondurans and Guatemalans were estimated to be crossing in greater number as of 2018, even surpassing Mexicans that year (Restrepo et al. 2019).

While adult men are traditionally the majority of migrants, unaccompanied minors and families have been on the rise. In 2018, the Customs and Border Protection apprehended 38,000 minors and 104,000 traveling as families. People have been traveling in larger groups, including caravans of several hundreds or even several thousands of people. An estimated 30–34 million (38–43%) of the 80 million forcibly displaced persons globally are children below 18 years of age (United Nations High Commissioner for Refugees 2020). Conditions in the home country as well as the reception in the receiving country have lifelong and intergenerational impact on the psycho-social development of these children and their families.

Certain populations, in addition to unaccompanied children, face distinct circumstances in the migratory process. For indigenous populations, language and cultural adaptation may take longer as they adjust to new urban settings. Some LGBTQI migrants are able to successfully claim refugee or asylee status as members of a persecuted group. However, they may face specific challenges when engaging with the immigration administration, for example, regarding their gender marker on official documents. Structural stigma toward sexual minorities in receiving countries was associated with increased health risks, mitigated by time and language ability (Pachankis et al. 2017).

Sociocultural Factors Impacting the Mental Health of Immigrant Communities

Immigration and Sociopolitical Factors

Immigration in and of itself can be considered a social determinant of health. The intersection between immigration status and other factors, such as living and working conditions, detention, and deportation, and the association of different immigration classifications with eligibility for different types of benefits can affect the mental health of immigrants and their access to healthcare services. Structural factors such as racism and discrimination, financial difficulties, family and community separation, previous experiences of civil conflict, war, and other types of violence and trauma have also been implicated in the increasing risk of mental illness among immigrants. The interplay of these factors can impact an individual's risk of mental illness (Rodriguez et al. 2020).

Sociocultural Factors

Identity and culture are key factors to consider when addressing the mental health needs of immigrant communities. The history of immigrant communities is as complex and rich as the story and trajectory of their members and their descendants. Appreciating these differences and eliciting and respecting the way individuals define their cultural identity is critical for inclusion, engagement, and equitable access to care. It is also important to recognize and address specific stressors during pre-migration (e.g., history of abuse or violence; loss of social, familial, and material resources), migration (e.g., forced vs. voluntary, documented vs. undocumented immigrant status, length of distance traveled, trauma during migration), and post-migration (e.g., language proficiency, lack of employment or housing, discrimination, separation from family or friends, work exploitation) stages (Walker and Barnett 2007; Watters 2001).

One must also consider the level of acculturation with the dominant or host culture (How et al. 2017). Acculturation is a process resulting in shifts in an individual's identity, behaviors, values, and opinions that occurs through the contact that an immigrant person has with the new culture(s) in the host country. This process is influenced by the degree to which an individual is affiliated with their own culture versus the degree of their affiliation with the host culture (Berry 1997).

Cultural assimilation happens when an individual rejects or exchanges certain aspects of their original culture for that of the majority culture. Assimilation is the process of adapting effectively to the host culture which historically has been found to be a protective factor for positive mental health outcomes. *Integration*, sometimes called biculturalism, occurs when immigrants maintain important parts of their original cultural values while also adapting positively to the host culture. If the host society supports cultural diversity, acculturation and/or the development of bicultural identity can happen more smoothly. On the other hand, psychological acculturative stress is more likely if the host culture has an attitude of rejection toward other cultures or tries to eliminate diversity through policies that marginalize cultural minorities or force assimilation (Berry 1997). Simultaneously, some immigrants experience marginalization when they either reject their own culture or do not adopt the host culture.

Research has also identified some sociocultural factors that can protect the mental health of immigrant communities. The collectivistic approach to life in which group cohesiveness and well-being are valued over individual well-being can be protective for many immigrant communities. Family relationships and peer networks with other immigrants can also provide a buffering effect (Kim et al. 2012). Other studies have identified protective factors for refugees such as English proficiency, social support, community inclusion, connection to the culture of the host country, valuing of and connection to one's native culture, valued social roles, and access to resources to be predictors of refugee mental health (Goodkind et al. 2020). Other potential strengthening qualities include centrality of family ties and extended kindship (Valdivieso-Mora et al. 2016), as well as faith, spirituality, and religious attendance (Moreno and Cardemil 2016; Shaw et al. 2019).

Mental Health Needs, Community Psychiatry, and Treatments That Work

The Mental Health Needs of Migrants and Refugees

Research shows that immigrants to the United States are often initially healthier upon the first arrival compared with other immigrants who have remained in the host country for longer periods. In the literature, this has been referred to as the "healthy immigrant effect" or "the immigrant paradox." This phenomenon has been described in multiple immigrant groups, including Asian American, Africans, Afro-Caribbeans, and Latinx, and for a variety of mental health outcomes including psychosis, substance use, and depression (Alegria et al. 2008; Williams et al. 2007; Venters and Gany 2011; Takeuchi et al. 2007).

It is important to note that contradictory evidence exists to prevent the generalization of the immigrant paradox to all immigrants, particularly when discussing immigrant populations. For example, Alegria et al. (2008) found that this phenomenon cannot be generalized to all Latinx subgroups and all psychiatric disorders. Some evidence suggests that context and issues within the host society (racism, anti-immigrant sentiments, etc.) and their intersection account for this effect, rather than any intrinsic features regarding immigrants as individuals (Perez et al. 2008). As an example, migrating from an under-developed to a developed country has been found to be associated with higher rates of schizophrenia. This effect was more pronounced when the immigrants lived in an area where they were outnumbered by the majority group, likely resulting in worsening cultural isolation and marginalization (Zolokowska et al. 2001). Additionally, a systematic literature review of studies that assessed the prevalence and factors associated with depression and anxiety in adult war-refugees found that resettlement to the United States predicted higher rates of depression and anxiety (Bogic et al. 2015). Sociopolitical climate, especially anti-immigrant/refugee policies and xenophobia, can have a strong and negative impact on the mental health of resettled individuals.

Access to Care in Community Psychiatry

Immigrant populations utilize mental health services at lower rates than non-immigrants (Bauldry and Szaflarski 2017). The reasons for this can be understood at the levels of individual (health literacy, insight, socioeconomic reasons), interpersonal (stigma), institutional (racism, lack of cultural and linguistic competence in providers), and structural barriers (lack of insurance, transportation issues, clinic locations) explored below. These barriers reflect the existing inequality and oppression within a society, such as racism, sexism, and homophobia. This leads to worse health care for immigrants.

Mental health services are least utilized among people who are uninsured and undocumented. This highlights the intersection of structural and interpersonal barriers, spanning multiple levels of issues including economic, political, and cultural disenfranchisement that impact immigrants. Undocumented immigrants might not only have to address their own culture's stigma against mental illness and mental health treatment but also navigate a complex healthcare system without insurance and overcome the fear of being reported to immigration authorities and therefore face the possibility of deportation. For example, Derr (2016) reviewed studies describing the utilization of mental healthcare services by immigrant populations in the United States and found that limitations in healthcare system capabilities such as lack of linguistic and cultural competency by clinicians are important structural barriers to care. It also identified other significant barriers such as cultural stigma of mental health within immigrant communities, fear of deportation, unaffordable cost of services, lack of insurance, lack of knowledge about services, and communication challenges. Additional barriers to accessing care for immigrants included undocumented status, male gender, youth, and lack of insurance.

Clinical practice locations may negatively affect patient access. Clinical care provided through healthcare workers affiliated with places of worship, schools, and other public agencies can help mitigate the challenges posed by the inadequate placement of clinical practices. Enhancing telepsychiatry and teleservices capacity within community organizations and practices may provide a new model of care that may help address disparities in mental healthcare access due to practice location and transportation challenges.

People who end up seeking mental health treatment will often find themselves seeking care from mental health professionals who are most likely white and American-born. According to a study that assessed the ethnicity of US psychiatrists, practicing psychiatrists from historically under-represented backgrounds (URMs) are 10.4% of all psychiatrists, compared to 32% of the US population (Wyse et al. 2020). Although the proportion of URM resident physicians training in psychiatry increases every year, the number of URM faculty increases at a rate disproportionately four times slower.

According to the American Psychiatric Association, 27% of all practicing psychiatrists in the United States are international medical graduates, suggesting that a significant proportion of psychiatrists are themselves immigrants. However, disproportionately fewer are in faculty positions, leadership, or management roles. Specialized training in mental health for immigrant populations is not standard among psychiatry residency programs, nor are all community clinics and hospitals integrating awareness of racial oppression, history of imperialism and colonialism, and cross-generational trauma in their operational policies and practices. People who seek mental health treatment might find themselves getting care from providers who belong to the majority group, who do not share the same background, and who may apply a western biomedical model to explain experiences and symptoms which may not fit neatly under a DSM-5 diagnosis. A grave concern is not simply misdiagnosing or misunderstanding patients but the fact that a western biomedical gaze can risk reinforcing the same institutional and systemic oppression that exists outside the mental health system during an individual's time of emotional need or vulnerability.

A concept described in the literature is that of mistrust of the medical system, especially when discussing marginalized populations. Although this attitude has been previously described as a barrier to care, focusing on individual characteristics may result in missed opportunities to better explain this phenomenon and reach the populations in need. Language matters when discussing these concerns. Instead of discussing distrust, which places the burden of remediation on the individual, healthcare workers striving to regain the community's trust must assess and openly discuss the trustworthiness of institutions and its practices. From coercive sterilizations to withholding of treatment, as in the infamous Tuskegee Study, medicine has a past of exploiting and experimenting on minority groups, which cannot be ignored (Nuriddin et al. 2020). To improve access to and quality of care for historically under-served groups and immigrants, mental health providers must demonstrate awareness of this history to patients who may bring it up while actively challenging its long-ranging impacts on an administrative level.

High Rates of Trauma and Variable Clinical Presentations: The Need for Cultural Humility

The mental health needs of immigrant patients depend on a variety of factors, including the context resulting in their migration, their migratory journey, legal status in the United States, level of acculturation, family, and other social support. Due to sociopolitical factors, nearly all immigrants in the United States will experience a certain level of discrimination and will be more likely to belong to a low socioeconomic household and to experience unemployment. Additionally, almost all immigrants will have experienced a certain level of family separation, as most have left extended family in their home countries. The concepts of acculturation, acculturative stress, and assimilation will also be felt to some extent by all immigrants, potentially affecting their mental health. Depending on the severity of factors such as financial stress, racism, and discrimination, the negative impact may be higher in some individuals than others.

Although all immigrants experience the above stressors in some form, there is a differentiation between immigrants whose journeys were not forced and those who migrated to the United

States fleeing violence or persecution. Asylum seekers, refugees, exiles, and unaccompanied immigrant children have high rates of traumatic experiences that span their pre-migratory, peri-migratory, and post-migratory process. Rates of PTSD, depression, and anxiety disorders are higher in recently resettled refugees compared to their non-war-affected counterparts. Estimates show that one in five refugees of war may experience psychiatric illness such as depression, anxiety, or posttraumatic stress disorder (PTSD), even 5 years or longer after displacement (Fazel et al. 2005). Exiles, or individuals barred from their country often due to political reasons, are a special population that has been under-studied. Matos et al. (2008) found that a quarter of adult Cuban exiles self-reported symptoms of trauma and depression, more than 60% reported frequent thoughts related to the family separation and emotional distress experienced during the process of becoming exile.

Unaccompanied children are an especially vulnerable group in the immigrant population. Minors tend to migrate unaccompanied by a caregiver due to home or community violence, threat of war, threat of recruitment as child soldiers or enslavement, or after the death of their guardian (Ehntholt and Yule 2006). These children have high rates of peri-migratory trauma, with studies documenting that up to one-third had a history of sexual trauma prior to their migration to the United States (Betancourt et al. 2012). They are also at higher risk of experiencing traumatic experiences during their migratory journey (Women's Refugee Commission 2012), during their stays in refugee camps (Rothe et al. 2002), and during the initial period of resettlement (National Immigrant Justice Center et al. 2014). This is a highly vulnerable immigrant population that has been found to present with higher levels of psychological distress when compared to accompanied immigrant children, with up to 30% of them experiencing PTSD (Betancourt et al. 2012).

Children who have been separated from their families, as was increasingly seen after the zero-tolerance policy went into place under the Trump administration, have been found to have high levels of anxiety and depression compared to immigrant children who did not experience family separation (Suarez-Orozco et al. 2011). Additionally, even if the child is reunified with their natural family, they may experience further traumatic experiences through reunification-related stress. Changes in family composition and dynamics, as well as the possibility that the caregivers may feel guilty or ashamed of allowing the child to migrate independently, could impact the caregivers' ability to validate the child's emotional distress upon reunification.

Factors such as age, gender, legal status, socioeconomic level, English proficiency, and migration history may impact the clinical presentation of immigrants. These factors not only affect the way patients express symptoms and their needs but also clinicians' ability to engage the patient, take a thorough history, display empathy, and address mental health needs as one would with non-immigrant patients.

Culturally Tailored Treatments

A concept in health care that can help clinicians to provide high-quality mental health care for immigrants and refugees is cultural humility, which guides clinical practice by encouraging learning about a person's identity in their own words (Tervalon and Murray-García 1998). The principle behind this concept is to understand that "culture" does not imply a fixed identity or body of discrete traits. Instead, cultural factors are perceived as an ever-changing system of notions and actions that persons can choose from, shaped by the specific social context in which it is generated. However, it is not possible to predict the beliefs and behaviors of individuals solely based on their cultural background (Hunt 2001). Knowing as much as possible about a person's background is highly valuable, but it is not necessarily useful without a simultaneous process of self-reflection and commitment to lifelong learning in which clinicians become comfortable letting go of the false sense of security that stereotyping brings. This process mediates enough flexibility and humbleness for clinicians to recognize when they do not know or understand their patient's belief system. Understanding the cultural background of others using humility as an approach instead of as a mastered subject and searching for resources that might facilitate this understanding can make a significant difference in the rapport of clinicians with their immigrant patients and enhance the quality of the treatment they obtain (Cabán-Alemán 2017). For detailed discussion in this regard, please also see chapter "Cultural and Linguistic Competence".

Cultural adaptations of evidence-based psychotherapeutic treatments have been created and found to be helpful in addressing mental health needs of refugees and immigrants. Cognitive behavioral therapy interventions have been adapted to meet the cultural needs of immigrant populations with positive results in symptom reduction of certain conditions. The Integrated Intervention for Dual Problems and Early Action (IIDEA) is a ten-session intervention that incorporates cognitive therapy and mindfulness to address symptoms of depression, anxiety, posttraumatic stress, and co-occurring substance use problems. This intervention has been studied in Latinx immigrants with positive outcomes in mental health symptoms and significant improvements in mindful awareness, therapeutic alliance, and illness self-management (Fortuna et al. 2020; Alegria et al. 2019).

Multiphase model of psychotherapy (MMP) and counseling, social justice, and human rights are culturally responsive interventions that aim to address the unique challenges of refugees. It incorporates psychotherapeutic concepts to address trauma and the psychological responses seen with pre-migratory stress, displacement, acculturation, and the patient's cultural conceptualization of mental illness and recovery. Additionally, MMP engages the clinician in assessing their own personal biases and political countertransference, which makes this a unique intervention (Bemak and Chung 2015; Chung et al. 2011).

For children and their families, therapeutic modalities must be adept to assess family structure and functioning. Cognitive behavioral therapy (CBT) for traumatic stress has been studied as a school-based, multi-level CBT intervention that includes individual and group psychoeducational components addressing acculturation stress and cultural trauma. It is delivered by educators and mental health providers and has been found to reduce symptoms of PTSD and depression in immigrant youth (Kataoka et al. 2003). Narrative exposure therapy, studied in the Netherlands, is another intervention that has demonstrated positive effects in addressing symptoms of trauma in child immigrants (Schauer et al. 2011). It incorporates storytelling of the child's life, opening up the opportunity to narrate multiple traumas as these children oftentimes do not have one index trauma. This process promotes habituation of emotional responses when discussing trauma and improves insight into the relationship between past traumatic experiences and current psychological functioning. Child-parent psychotherapy has been found to be effective in addressing mother-child attachment (Lieberman and Van Horn 2008).

A psychotherapeutic model to address refugee child mental health needs in the context of humanitarian crises has been previously described by Rothe (2008). It includes three main aims: (1) to decrease hyperarousal symptoms and protect the patient's neuroendocrine system, (2) to help the patient construct a cohesive narrative of events during the peri-traumatic period, and (3) to enable the clinician to be an advocate for the refugee children and their families. Personal empowerment, connecting patients to community agencies, and psychoeducation are key components of this approach that aims to create a strong foundation as the patient and their families continue to navigate challenging situations requiring psychological agility and adaptation.

Predictors of treatment outcomes for refugees with PTSD have been identified, although data is limited. Factors associated with improvement in symptoms included higher baseline symptoms, high level of functioning, young age at arrival to host country, full-time employment, and reunified family status (Sonne et al. 2021). Prevention and treatment models that incorporate community members, a multidisciplinary team, and systems of care approach have been shown to be effective in addressing the mental health needs of immigrants and refugee youth (Abdi 2011). Approaches that include validation, mutual support, and the processing of common migration and adaptation experiences have been found to be protective (Abdi et al. 2012).

Practical Applications in Community Mental Health Care

Addressing the Social Determinants of Health for Immigrants and Refugees

When developing and implementing community-focused interventions to address the mental health of persons that are or were refugees or immigrants, it is very helpful to have an ecological perspective that focuses on multiple levels of context. This includes the microsystem or immediate environment of the patient (e.g., living situation, family, school, work), the ecosystem around the microsystem (other formal and informal social structures), and the macrosystem (economic, political, legal, and other social systems) that together affect a patient's health and development, emphasizing improvement of fit between patients and their environments.

Poverty, racism, and migration-related stress are social determinants of the mental health of immigrants and refugees. Attention to these social determinants arguably eclipses even necessary primary and behavioral health care, as it critically affects basic survival and well-being. Interprofessional collaborations are crucial to provide effective mental health treatment and address the needs of immigrant communities (How et al. 2017). These collaborative services must include a very wide range of human services, usually led by community-based organizations, including those that are faith-based. Such services must include legal support, vocational development, nutritional or dietary services, housing assistance, English as second language resources, tutoring, and access to any public entitlements that could be available.

Clinical Applications and Advocacy

Cultural and structural humility assist mental health practitioners to become culturally and structurally competent, as they help recognize how social, cultural, and structural determinants result in inequities and shape health and illness before, during, and after the clinical encounter (Metzl and Hansen 2014). The clinical model of "affirmative practice" is a key approach for serving immigrant and refugee populations. Originating from work with LGBTQI communities, affirmative practice refers to a range of models that serve to create supportive healthcare environments in which individuals can safely express their identity, with the services they receive acknowledging and countering the oppressive contexts people often experience in more conventional care (Mendoza et al. 2020). Therefore, affirmative care with immigrant and refugee individuals includes practicing with cultural humility to understand beliefs, values, and strengths while also validating that social disparities, discrimination, and racism have an impact on well-being. Some examples of how to cultivate affirmative care practices include working collaboratively with communities in services planning; paying attention to the relevant and central aspects of cultural, social, and political narratives; honoring and facilitating an understanding of patients' expressed needs, priorities, and preferences; identifying sociocultural factors that influence care; and engaging supportive cultural networks (Mendoza et al. 2020). No matter how well-educated psychiatrists and other behavioral health clinicians are, one cannot expect clinicians to fully understand a patient's culture and experience of oppression or to have the ability to predict their social needs. Therefore, structural and cultural humility are imperative, further reducing clinician unconscious bias and facilitating affirmative practice.

Optimizing Clinical Skills: Sociopolitical Countertransference and Vicarious Trauma

Experiences of systemic oppression may result in distrust of the healthcare system. Patients who are mistrustful of a medical provider, system, or treatment options may present as disengaged or guarded and have challenges adhering to clinical recommendations. Structurally and culturally competent clinicians ought not to interpret these presentations as signs of patient disinterest or inability to engage with treatment. Instead, one must engage in trauma-informed care that incorporates a sociopolitical lens, enabling the patient to express their needs in their own way and to take their time in trusting and engaging with a recommended treatment plan. Struggling with this often arouses negative countertransference.

Simultaneously, mental health clinicians may find themselves having to comply with unrealistic clinical service expectations, particularly in settings where vulnerable populations such as asylum seekers, refugees, and immigrants are encountered. Overly full clinic days, limited resources to address the social determinants of health, and limited availability of support and supervision by peers can result in the moral injury associated with burnout. Specifically, in the clinical care of migrants and refugees, clinicians can be vulnerable to displacing frustrations with the system in which they work onto patients, creating emotional or cognitive barriers to fully engage in the care of patients with such complex presentations and circumstantially high need. Clearly, countertransference is a tool that cannot be ignored, and it offers potential opportunity to advocate for systemic change.

Another dimension of countertransference is the role of vicarious trauma: the experience of exposure to trauma through the narratives of the patients we treat. This must be taken into consideration when treating vulnerable populations such as migrants, asylum seekers, and refugees. Vicarious trauma has been associated with negative outcomes such as compassion fatigue and lack of intimacy, as well as positive outcomes such as vicarious posttraumatic growth (Rizkalla and Segal 2020). Adequate training and supervision can support a clinician's ability to maintain mental well-being while working with traumatized patient populations (Finklestein et al. 2015). Clinicians inspired to work with migrants, refugees, and asylum seekers can find unique opportunities to engage in meaningful work as they learn clinical skills and systems-based practices necessary to serve this population. Some opportunities include participation in national organizations within psychiatry, such as the American Psychiatric Association and its Council on Minority Mental Health and Health Disparities, and the minority caucuses. As medical trainees, one can also become involved with the national organization Physicians for Human Rights, which trains physicians to assess and document trauma and torture to support asylum seeker's claims in immigration court. A team approach can be helpful to prevent the negative outcomes from vicarious trauma, foster the use of sociocultural and political conceptualization, and make the best use of trauma-informed care practices. Supervision and debriefing opportunities can decrease the mental load carried by mental health providers. Group and individual supervision can improve accountability, which is a necessary tool for mental health providers to maintain the use of trauma-informed care practices and reduce the negative effects of countertransference reactions.

Conclusion

Provision of mental health treatment to migrants and refugees can be challenging within the current medical system. Clinicians looking for opportunities to gain clinical, research, advocacy, and administrative skills needed to establish unique mechanisms and provide quality mental health care often find creative ways to find and engage in health equity work by seeking collaborators and/or clinical models to learn from. Participation with community agencies serving this population and networking with mentors even outside our own institution are some ways one can acquire the knowledge and experience to serve this vulnerable population. However, all mental health clinicians have an opportunity to optimize their clinical skills when working with migrant and refugee populations by practicing the skills and clinical approaches presented in this chapter. It is also important to understand how the sociocultural-political climate and resulting policies can negatively impact immigrant and refugee patients' mental health. It is within the purview of the mental health field to engage in a higher level of community and political engagement to advocate for policy changes and cultivate models of care that aim to reduce or extinguish the barriers to care that patients often face.

References

Abdi, S., Barrett, C., Blood, E.A., Betancourt, T.S., Ellis, B.H. Miller, A.B. (2012). Multi-tier mental health program for refugee youth. Journal of Consulting and Clinical Psychology, 81, 1, 129–140.

Abdi, S. (2011). New directions in refugee youth mental health services: overcoming barriers to engagement. J Child Adolesc Trauma, 4, 1, 69–85.

Alegría, M., Canino, G., Shrout, P.E., et al. (2008). Prevalence of mental illness in immigrant and non-immigrant U.S. Latino groups. *Am J Psychiatry*, 165, 359–369.

Alegría, M., Falgas-Bague, I., Collazos, F., et al. (2019). Evaluation of the integrated intervention for dual problems and early action among Latino immigrants with co-occurring mental health and substance misuse symptoms: a randomized clinical trial. JAMA Netw Open, 2, 1.

Bauldry, S. and Szaflarski, M. (2017). Immigrant-based disparities in mental health care utilization. *Socius: Sociological Research for a Dynamic World*, 3, 1–14.

Bemak, F. and Chung, R.C.-Y. (2015). Counseling refugees and migrants. In P.B. Pedersen, W.J. Lonner, J.G. Draguns, J.E. Trimble, and M.R. Scharron-del Rio (Eds.), *Counseling across cultures* (7th ed., pp 323–346). Thousand Oaks, CA: Sage.

Berry, J.W. (1997). Immigration, acculturation, and adaptation. *Applied Psychology,* 46(1), 5–34.

Betancourt, T.S., Newnham, E.A., Layne, C.M., Kim, S., Steinberg, A.M., Ellis, H., Birman, D. (2012). Trauma history and psychopathology in war-affected refugee children referred for trauma-related mental health services in the United States. *J Trauma Stress*, 25(6), 682–90.

Bogic, M., Njoku, A., Priebe, S. (2015). Long-term mental health of war-refugees: a systematic literature review. *BMC International Health and Human Rights*, 15, 1–41.

Cabán-Alemán, C. (2017). Cultural Humility. In J. Tse & S.Y. Volpp (Eds.), *A Case-based Approach to Public Psychiatry* (pp 29–36). Oxford University Press.

Capps, R., Koball, H., Campetella, A., Perreira, K., Hooker, S., Pedroza, J.M. (2015). Implications of immigration enforcement activities for the wellbeing of children in immigrant families. Urban Institute and Migration Policy Institute. Retrieved January 25, 2021, from https://www.urban.org/sites/default/files/alfresco/publication-exhibits/2000405/2000405-Implications-of-Immigration-Enforcement-Activities-for-the-Well-Being-of-Children-in-Immigrant-Families.pdf

Chung, R.C.-Y., Bemak, F., Kudo Grabosky, T. (2011). Multicultural-social justice leadership strategies: Counseling and advocacy with immigrants. *Journal of Social Action in Counseling and Psychology*, 3, 86–102.

Congressional Research Service. (2020). Temporary Protected Status: Overview and Current Issues. Retrieved January 26, 2021, from https://crsreports.congress.gov/product/pdf/RS/RS20844

Derr A.S. (2016). Mental health service use among immigrants in the United States: A systematic review. *Psychiatric Services*, 67(3), 265–274.

Ehntholt, K.A. and Yule, W. (2006). Practitioner review: assessment and treatment of refugee children and adolescents who have experienced war related trauma. *J Child Psychol Psychiatry* 47, 1197–1210.

Fazel, M., Wheeler, J., Danesh, J. (2005). Prevalence of serious mental disorder in 7000 refugees resettled in Western countries: A systematic review. *Lancet*, 365, 1309–14.

Finklestein, M., Stein, E., Greene, T., Bronstein, I., Solomon, Z. (2015). Posttraumatic Stress Disorder and Vicarious Trauma in Mental Health Professionals. *Health & Social Work*, 40(2), 25–31.

Fortuna, L.R., Falgas-Bague, I., Ramos, Z., Porche, M.V., Alegría, M. (2020). Development of a cognitive behavioral therapy with integrated mindfulness for Latinx immigrants with co-occurring disorders: Analysis of intermediary outcomes. *Psychol Trauma*, 12(8), 825–835.

Goodkind, J.R., Bybee, D., Hess, J.M., et al. (2020). Randomized Controlled Trial of a Multilevel Intervention to Address Social Determinants of Refugee Mental Health. *American Journal of Community Psychology,* 65 (3–4), 272–289.

How, P.C., Lo, P., Westervelt, M., et al. (2017). Refugees and Immigrants. In J. Tse & S.Y. Volpp (Eds.), *A Case-based Approach to Public Psychiatry* (pp 179–186). Oxford University Press.

Hunt, L. (2001). *Beyond cultural competence: applying humility to clinical settings*. Park Ridge Center Bulletin, 24, 3e4.

International Migration Law. (2019). Glossary on Migration, No 34. Geneva, Switzerland. Retrieved January, 25, 2021 from https://publications.iom.int/system/files/pdf/iml_34_glossary.pdf

Kataoka, S.H., Stein, B.D., Haycox, L.H., Wong, M., Escudero, P., Tu, W., Zaragoza, C., Fink, A. (2003). A school-based mental health program for traumatized Latino immigrant children. *Journal of the American Academy of Child and Adolescent Psychiatry*, 43, 3, 311–318.

Kim, J., Suh, W., Kim, S., Gopalan, H. (2012). Coping strategies to manage acculturative stress: Meaningful activity participation, social support, and positive emotion among Korean immigrant adolescents in the USA. *International Journal of Qualitative Studies on Health and Well-Being*, 7, 1–10.

Lieberman, A. F. and Van Horn, P. (2008). *Psychotherapy with infants and young children: Repairing the effects of stress and trauma on early attachment*. New York, NY: Guilford Press.

Matos, H.C., Rothe, E.M., Pumariega, A.J., Lewis, J.E. (2008). Trauma historico, perdidas y separaciones: un estudio piloto para evaluar los problemas especificos de la salud mental de los exiliados. Revista Latinoamericana de Psiquiatria, 9, 10–18.

Mendoza, N. S., Moreno, F. A., Hishaw, G. A., Gaw, A. C., Fortuna, L. R., Skubel, A., Porche, M. V., Roessel, M. H., Shore, J., Gallegos, A. (2020). Affirmative Care Across Cultures: Broadening Application. *Focus (American Psychiatric Publishing)*, *18*(1), 31–39.

Metzl, J. M. and Hansen, H. (2014). Structural competency: Theorizing a new medical engagement with stigma and inequality. *Social Science & Medicine*, 103, 126–133.

Migration Policy Institute. (2019). Central American Immigrants in the United States. Retrieved January 20, 2021, from https://www.migrationpolicy.org/article/central-american-immigrants-united-states-2017

Moreno, O. and Cardemil, E. (2016). The role of religious attendance on mental health among Mexican populations: A contribution toward the discussion of the immigrant health paradox. Am J Orthopsychiatry, 88, 1, 10–15.

National Immigrant Justice Center, Esperanza Immigrant Rights Project, Americans for Immigrant Justice, Florence Immigrant and Refugee Rights Project, ACLU Border Litigation Project. (2014). Systemic abuse of unaccompanied immigrant children by U.S. Customs and Border Protection. Retrieved January 26, 2021, from, http://www.immigrantjustice.org/sites/immigrantjustice.

Nuriddin, A., Mooney, G., White, A.R. (2020). Reckoning with histories of medical racism and violence in the USA. *The Lancet*, 296: 949–951.

Pachankis, J., Hatzenbuehler, M., Berg, R., Fernandez-Davila, P., Mirandola, M., Marchus, U. et al. (2017). Anti-LGBT and anti-immigrant structural stigma: an intersectional analysis of sexual minority men's HIV risk when migrating to or within Europe. *Journal of Acquired Immuno Deficiency Syndromes*, 76, 4, 356–366.

Pérez, D. J., Fortuna, L., Alegria, M. (2008). Prevalence and correlates of everyday discrimination among US Latinos. *Journal of Community Psychology*, 36(4), 421–433.

Restrepo, D., Sutton, T., Martinez, J. (2019). Getting Migration in the Americas Rights: A National Interest-driven approach. Center for American Progress. Retrieved January 12, 2021, from https://www.americanprogress.org/issues/security/reports/2019/06/24/471322/getting-migration-americas-right/

Rizkalla, N. and Segal, S. (2020). Refugee trauma work: Effects on intimate relationships and vicarious posttraumatic growth. *Journal of Affective Disorders*, 276, 839–847.

Rodriguez, D.X., Hill, J., McDaniel, P. (2020). A scoping review of literature about mental health and well-being among immigrant communities in the United States. *Health Promotion Practice*. Advance online publication.

Rothe, E.M., Castillo-Matos, H., Busquets, R. (2002). Posttraumatic stress symptoms in Cuban adolescents refugees during camp confinement. *Adolesc Psychiatry*, 26, 97–124.

Rothe, E.M. (2008). Psychotherapy model for treating refugee children caught in the midst of catastrophic situations. *Journal of the American Academy of Psychoanalysis and Dynamic Psychiatry*, 36, 4, 625–642.

Schauer, M., Neuner, F., Elbert, T. (2011). Narrative exposure therapy: A short team treatment for traumatic stress disorders (2nd ed). Cambridge, MA: Hogrefe Publishing.

Shaw, S.A., Peacock, L., Ali, L.M., Pillai, V., Husain, A. (2019). Religious coping and challenges among displaced Muslim female refugees. Affilia, 34, 4, 518–534.

Sonne, C., Lykke, E., Silove, D., Palic, S., Carlsson, J. (2021). Predictors of treatment outcomes for trauma affected refugees: Results from two randomized trials. *Journal of Affective Disorders*, 282, 194–202.

Suarez-Orozco, C., Bang, H.J., Kim, H.Y. (2011). I felt like my heart was staying behind: Psychological implications of family separations & reunifications for immigrant youth. *Journal of Adolescent Research*, 26(2), 222–257.

Takeuchi DT, Zane N, Hong S, et al. (2007). Immigration-related factors and mental disorders among Asian Americans. *Am J Public Health*, 97:84–90.

Tervalon, M. and Murray-Garcia, J. (1998). Cultural humility versus cultural competence: A critical distinction in defining physician training outcomes in multicultural education. Journal of Health Care for the Poor and Underserved, 9, 2, 117–125.

United Nations High Commissioner for Refugees. (1951). Convention and Protocol Relating to the Status of Refugees, Article 1, A(2).

United Nations High Commissioner for Refugees. (2020). Refugee Statistics. Retrieved January 25, 2021, from https://www.unhcr.org/refugee-statistics/

U.S. Citizenship and Immigration Services. (2021). Temporary Protected Status. Retrieved January 25, 2021, from https://www.uscis.gov/humanitarian/temporary-protected-status

Valdivieso-Mora, E., Peet, C.L., Garnier-Villarreal, M., Salazar-Villanea, M., Johnson, D.K. (2016). A systematic review of the relationship between familism and mental health outcomes in Latino population. Front Psychol, 7, 1632.

Walker, P.F. and Barnett, E.D. (2007). *Immigrant medicine*. St. Louis, MO. Saunders/Elsevier.

Watters, C. (2001). Emerging paradigms in the mental health care of refugees. *Social science & medicine*, 52(11), 1709–18.

Williams, D.R., Gonzalez, H.M., Neighbors, H., Nesse, R., Abelson, J.M., Sweetman, J., Jackson, J.S. (2007). Prevalence and distribution of major depressive disorder in African Americans, Caribbean blacks, and non-Hispanic whites: results from the National Survey of American Life. *Archives of General Psychiatry*, 64(3), 305–315.

Women's Refugee Commission. 2012. Forced from home: The lost boys and girls of Central America. Retrieved January 20, 2021, from www.womensrefugeecommission.org/component/zdocs/document?id=844-forced-from-home-the-lost-boys-and-girlsof-central-america.

Wyse, R., Hwang, W.-T., Ahmed, A.A., Richards, E., Deville C, (2020). Diversity by Race, Ethnicity, and Sex within the US Psychiatry Physician Workforce. *Acad Psychiatry*, 44(5), 523–530.

Venters, H. and Gany, F. (2011). African immigrant health. *J Immigr Minor Health*, 13(2), 333–344.

Zolokowska, K., Cantor-Graae, E., McNeil, T. (2001). Increased rates of psychosis among immigrants to Sweden: Is immigration a risk factor for psychosis? Psychological Medicine, 31, 669–678.

Part VIII

Development and Administration of Services

Transforming Mental Health Systems and Programs

Michael F. Hogan and Wesley E. Sowers

> There is nothing more difficult to take in hand, more perilous to conduct, or more uncertain in its success, than to take the lead in the introduction of a new order of things. Because the innovator has for enemies all those who have done well under the old conditions, and lukewarm defenders in those who may do well under the new. This coolness arises partly from fear of the opponents, who have the laws on their side, and partly from the incredulity of men, who do not readily believe in new things until they have had a long experience of them. (Niccolo Machiavelli 1513)

Introduction

Some things don't change. Machiavelli's observation is as true today as it was in 1513. As we contemplate an update of this chapter for this second edition of the *Handbook/Textbook of Community Psychiatry*, the final report of the President's New Freedom Commission on Mental Health (NFC; New Freedom Commission 2003) can again be used to model the processes of "transformational" change. As we look for ways to improve our systems of care, *how* to achieve that kind of significant change remains a vexing problem for advocates and for anyone who accepts responsibility in a mental health program or system.

The work of a presidential commission is scarcely a typical example of a mental health leadership challenge or management problem, but the processes employed were not markedly distinct from efforts that take place on a more modest scale. Short-term task forces, special committees, and work groups happen all the time at every level of the mental health system—both within organizations and across them. Any professional or advocate interested in change is likely to participate in such an effort, and many of us will lead one. Examining the processes, successes, and limitations of the NFC's work offers a framework for other efforts to implement new systems to improve the outcomes of services. It may also illuminate the challenges of ongoing leadership in mental health organizations and systems. The chapter will also use some findings from the Innovation Diffusion and Adoption Research Project (IDARP) (Panzano and Roth 2006; Panzano et al. 2005). This was a multi-year study of change in mental health organizations—specifically the factors associated with success in launching and successfully completing a change (the adoption of one or more evidence-based practices) in community mental health agencies. And finally, some lessons from general management and group dynamics are included to help provide guidance for change efforts. In the interest of addressing contemporary challenges, we

M. F. Hogan (✉)
Case Western Reserve University, School of Medicine, Delmar, NY, USA

W. E. Sowers
University of Pittsburgh Medical Center, Western Psychiatric Hospital, Pittsburgh, PA, USA
e-mail: sowerswe@upmc.edu

W. E. Sowers et al. (eds.), *Textbook of Community Psychiatry*,
https://doi.org/10.1007/978-3-031-10239-4_51

will end the chapter considering some of the major issues facing mental health services today and some of the measures that have been taken to advance the implementation of related changes.

A Framework for Leading Change: First, Identify Changes That *Should* Be Made That *Can* Be Made

Anyone leading a change effort must wrestle with the tension between what should be done and what can be done. Our positive instincts and much of the management literature challenge us to aim high; in discussing successful companies, Collins and Porras (1994) cite the importance of Big, Hairy, Audacious Goals (BHAGs). But aiming high in improving mental health care does not guarantee success. Indeed, the history of mental health reform in the United States is that lofty aims are often defeated. Political scientists Marmor and Gill (1989) pointed out that the demands of good care for people with mental illness and the realities of the American political system clash in a way that suggests that truly successful reforms are unlikely in this country. Good mental health care requires coordination and integration of services, demanding a shared approach across levels of government (federal, state, local) and across areas of governmental responsibility (e.g., mental health and health care, housing, income support policies). Yet the nature of American democracy, with its focus on balanced powers and divided responsibilities, mitigates against strong action—especially on behalf of a politically weak minority like people with mental illness.

Some of the more notable efforts to reform/transform mental health care in America illustrate this problem. Dorothea Dix championed construction of asylums for people with mental illness in the nineteenth century, winning the passage of legislation establishing a national construction program for state asylums in 1854. However, President Franklin Pierce vetoed the bill as an unwarranted exercise of federal powers, setting a lukewarm tone for federal leadership on mental health that has persisted until the present. Reforms that followed were often limited or compromised. For example, the community mental health center (CMHC) program proposed by President Kennedy sought to establish local community centers across the country. But the CMHC program was only partially and weakly implemented and bypassed the state agencies responsible for mental health care. Centers that received funding were given 7-year start-up grants rather than ongoing support, and by the time the program was converted to a block grant to the states in 1981, only a fraction of the needed centers had been established. Another example is seen in the 1980 Mental Health Systems Act. This legislation seemed an exception; it provided national leadership to improve mental health care based on strong recommendations of President Carter's mental health commission. However, the legislation lasted only about a year; it was eviscerated in President Reagan's first budget. The balance of powers inherent in American democracy makes changing mental health care—at the federal, state, or local level—a challenging proposition. In this context, finding a balance between what *should be done* and what *can be done* is a particularly important consideration in changing mental health services. President Bush made this balance explicit for the NFC, saying in his speech announcing the effort "the commission will make recommendations *that can be implemented, and they will be implemented*" (Bush 2002a).

Selecting a target for change that is significant yet feasible is essential. The first part of this "change equation" goes to the heart of leadership: *what is it that should be done*. In many cases of organizational change, the broad direction of change is prescribed. A higher authority may mandate that something is addressed. An incident may reveal a quality-of-care problem that must be corrected. But even in these situations, the target of change must be selected—and choosing this goal or guiding its choice is delicate and important.

In clinical care, an assessment suggests what the treatment should be. As the Institute of Medicine noted in defining evidence-based practice (2001), treatments should be consistent with the best current research on care for a condition, acceptable to the patient/consumer, and shaped by the practitioner's skills and training. This framework has relevance for choosing the direction of change for organizations. Choosing a direction for change in organizations is as critical a decision as choosing the right treatment in clinical care. Change for a mental health organization must move the organization in a valued direction, consistent with the evidence about the prevalence and distribution of need, and those interventions that are effective. Certainly, there are alternative directions that might be suggested: the way we're used to doing things, the approach that is easiest, or the path of least resistance. But the task of leadership is to frame a direction that is *right* in terms of current knowledge and our best values. One aspect of leadership responsibility is to consider emerging scientific knowledge. For example, there is a substantial new knowledge of the effectiveness of targeted preventive interventions, especially for children (O'Connell et al. 2009). Leaders should use this knowledge to shape approaches to care.

The other considerations in the IOM's definition of evidence-based practice are also relevant to organizational change. Just as a treatment must be acceptable to an individual—considering personal preferences and cultural norms—the direction of change in an organization must be acceptable to the organization itself (e.g., the staff and board) and also to key players in the environment (funders, partners, advocates). Launching a program that is desirable but which no one will pay for is scarcely a wise decision. And, just as treatments must be delivered in a fashion consistent with a clinician's skill set and training, the changes taken on by an organization must be feasible for that organization in terms of current capabilities. Of course, the ultimate goal of the chosen strategies may be to *improve* or *expand* the capabilities of the organization, but leaders must recognize that this objective can only be realized in a step-wise manner.

Similar factors are crucial in the decision-making process to determine whether or not to adopt an evidence-based practice. The Innovation Diffusion and Adoption Research Project (IDARP) suggested that significant decisions in an organization often involve accepting substantial risk. Leaders must weigh the value of change to their organization and assess whether it can be successfully implemented. An organization's capacity for change can be bolstered by experience; earlier successes in making changes increase an organization's willingness to try and ability to make changes (Panzano and Roth 2006). The study also indicates that an organization's capacity and willingness to make change can be increased via actions that leaders can take: creating an environment conducive to learning, promoting a positive management attitude toward change, and dedicating resources to the change process. These findings illustrate a central facet of change—leadership is central, and what leaders do or don't do makes a difference.

The challenge of proactive leadership is not simply to dictate a direction for change that "works" in the mind of the person in charge. Defining a direction—like launching a course of treatment—involves a dialogue and collaborative process with the participants. The leader must have a good idea about the general direction but must also orchestrate the change process to bring people along, expand their vision of what is acceptable, and build capabilities and confidence to make the change. Some of the tactics used during the NFC process should be relevant to shaping and sizing the direction of change in local or statewide efforts.

Engage Shareholders in Return for Their Support

In the case of the NFC (and other similar processes), this meant meeting individually as well as collectively with all the major mental health advocacy organizations. Eager for input, they agreed to work together to submit ideas for consideration and generally pledged their support. The support of these organizations and the general lack of contentiousness that resulted created a "safe space" for the NFC to do its work while informing the commission about considerations that would make recommendations more acceptable. Dialogue with shareholders is an essential step while launching a change effort. Often, mental health constituents are as concerned about whether they are consulted as they are about many details of change.

Engage Key Administrators and Decision-Makers in Advance of the Recommendations

The key officials to engage depend on the context of the change effort you are involved in (e.g., local or statewide, internal to an agency or public). With the NFC, engagement meant a round of meetings with senior federal officials in the participating agencies and with members and senior staffers of Congress. In this process, the limits of influence were painfully clear. While involved White House staff and leadership in the Substance Abuse and Mental Health Services Administration (SAMHSA) were very supportive, there was no mandate to other federal agencies to commit to policy change, and support from the different agencies varied. And the general reaction from Congress—aside from some activist leaders—was "This is an initiative of the Administration. We'll wait and see if it amounts to anything. If it does, they'll make recommendations, and we'll decide. Meanwhile we're working on *our* agenda." It is important to recognize and inform those who have power even when proposed changes seem peripheral to their main concerns. These efforts may have limited value in the short term, but gaining buy-in is essential in any change effort where preparation must lead to action.

Managing the Change Process: Timing, Process, and Organization

Timing is everything in change. Just as in a game of chess, every change scenario has a beginning, middle, and end. Different tactics must be employed in the different stages of change, and different success factors are involved in each. In the beginning, the leader must set the direction, develop expectations and boundaries, and create a management process to get the work done. In the middle of a change process, the work must be carried out while unanticipated issues are dealt with—without losing focus or momentum. In the end game, the transition to the implementation phase must be planned and executed, and an orderly ending to the change process itself achieved and celebrated.

The Beginning or Opening Phase of a Change Process

In the beginning stage, as in the opening of a chess game, the possibilities are wide open. Based on a strategy and direction, the leader makes the initial moves that establish a strong position while expending the minimum necessary resources. An example from the NFC process was using time in the very first commission meeting to focus on the recently completed Surgeon General's report (1999). A presentation by senior scientific editor of the report (Howard Goldman MD), at a time in the process when members were eager to become a working group and get started on their task, led to a quick agreement to use the Surgeon General's report as a foundation. This was an efficient way to establish a good direction and conserved energy that might have been wasted in reviewing countless other issues and reports. It allowed the NFC to move forward quickly. Participants in a change process are often quite willing to reasonably defer to the leader on many issues at the beginning and taking advantage of this while launching change is essential.

A key activity in the early stage of any change effort is to develop a clear plan and approach to get the work done. For example, establishing subcommittees to work on specific aspects of the desired change provides an efficient structure for completing a plan. The subcommittees provide a framework that can be used to set deadlines and accountability for key tasks. Members of the committee can chair or co-chair a subcommittee, giving them ownership of the subcommittee work. Securing resources to do the work of change—which may involve tasks outside of an organization's normal day-to-day activities—is also essential. For example, appointed members of the NFC were generally local mental health practitioners, advocates, and administrators rather than national "policy wonks." Therefore, consultants with a national perspective on each subcommittee's topic were provided to advise members and provide an initial policy analysis for consideration. Because "fresh eyes" are frequently valued, in many cases, the advice of experts from outside the organization is more highly valued than that of experts from within, even when an internal expert may be the more respected outside their own home base.

A final essential element of any change process is to establish boundaries or norms for participation. This may be accomplished via informal group meals to develop camaraderie or occasional supportive visits from higher leadership emphasizing the need to work together and focus on the mission. Meeting individually with each of the committee members before getting started helps form an alliance and creates "buy-in."

The Middle Game

In chess, the major considerations for the middle game are to enhance your position while preserving resources. Similarly, in a change process effort, you must get the work done, manage resources, and deal with issues that emerge. Key issues in the middle of the NFC process were to maintain a very active liaison with constituencies, keep work going on 15 subcommittees, and deliver an *Interim Report* (New Freedom Commission 2002) on time. The Interim Report, with its stark and candid assessment that "the system is a shambles," communicated to stakeholders that the NFC's view of the system would be unsparing. It raised expectations for the final report and thus strengthened receptivity to the commission's message. Transparency in disclosure of a committee's or work group activities will provide a foundation for an implementation process. This also allows the group to prepare for negative reactions and to plan more effectively for the roll-out of the plan.

Unexpected issues will arise in any change process. Adjustments must be made as events demand them. The middle part of a change process within an agency or system—as opposed to a task force or commission—may be even more complex: timelines or commitment to the change effort may be threatened by the need to meet ongoing challenges. Assuring that there are adequate resources to manage the change process is essential. These structures will encounter difficulties if they depend entirely on voluntary contributions of time by participants. Even adequate and comfortable space and refreshments are often meaningful to those who do donate their time. The provision of support staff to aid the work of the committee is an important element as well. In the case of the NFC, SAMHSA Administrator Charles Curie created an additional position of Deputy Executive Director and recruited a long-time colleague who was a strong manager of details. Additionally, he provided a budget for consultative and logistical support. Inevitably, a change process will include twists, turns, and demands that raise resource questions. Managing these is essential for the process to succeed.

The End Game

Obviously one core challenge for the end stage of a change process—as in the game of chess—is achieving closure, whether this means agreement on a plan or recommendations or completing a report. This task may be made more difficult when participants have bonded and want to continue their work—even if the time has come to end the process. This dilemma is an aspect of normal group dynamics, which we will discuss later in the chapter—and can lead to conflict over recommendations that is due to less substantive disagreement and more to the fact that agreement means the end of the process. Another challenge in any change process is to manage the transition from planning change to implementing it. This was a group process challenge for the NFC because the commission was explicitly time limited and had no role in implementation. But it also meant the end of the work was the end of the effort.

Learning from other change efforts can help in planning the end game. A lesson for the NFC leadership was that work products from Carter's mental health commission subsequently catalyzed change, sometimes in a fashion that went beyond formal recommendations. Koyanagi and Goldman (1991) described how issues discussed during the Carter commission were carried on by federal staff and advocates, finding their way into the government's National Plan for the Chronically Mentally Ill. Implementation of these actions led to many incremental but significant changes in policy, even during the Reagan administration. The NFC tactic of multiple subcommittees, each staffed by a consultant, was also an attempt to emulate this success. We hoped that candid subcommittee reports not subject to the federal "clearance" process could become part of a national advocacy strategy. This was only a partial success. For reasons that are still not clear, only 5 of the 15 subcommittee reports were published by SAMHSA. On the other hand, the consultants who had advised the subcommittees retained intellectual property rights to their initial reports. Many were edited and submitted to the journal *Psychiatric Services* and published independently as policy papers—e.g., Cook (2006), O'Hara (2007). This kept the recommendations alive in the mental health community.

Another tactic in wrapping up the planning phase of change is to ensure that recommendations have a "home" in an entity that can carry out implementation. In the case of the NFC, the Center for Mental Health Services (CMHS) in SAMHSA was charged with coordinating implementation activities and development of an "Action Agenda" for change. In their study of implementation success, Panzano et al. (2005) found a range of factors that contributed to success across the whole implementation period. These included consistent top management support (balanced by freedom in the organization to express doubts), availability of technical assistance when needed, and dedicated resources—to assist with implementation and to monitor its effectiveness. In the end stages of planning a change, these issues must be considered in the transition to implementation.

Group Process as a Vehicle and Metaphor of Change

Mental health services and the mental health system—like human groups and organizations generally—are complex, "open systems." The behavior of complex systems is unpredictable and counterintuitive. Actions that appear strong may fail because they lead to strong resistance (e.g., passage of the Mental Health Systems Act), while apparently "weak" actions can lead to substantial change…*if* they are the right actions at the right time in the right place (Senge 2006).

While the complexity of human systems and attempting to change them is daunting, mental health leaders interested in change are perhaps better prepared than many realize. This is because group work is a common element in mental health treatment, and the fundamentals of group dynamics are perhaps the core competencies of change. Interactions in groups (work groups, committees, task forces) are a dominant part of organizational life and the heart of any change process. We must bring the skills of group leadership to the challenges of leading change. While a broad review of group dynamics is beyond the scope of this chapter, illustrating several fundamental elements of task group behavior will demonstrate the centrality of group leadership skills in the change process.

Students of group behavior know that some of the most important initial work on the behavior of groups working on a task was conducted by Wilfred Bion. Psychoanalyst Bion's observations of group dynamics were based on observation and experience with psychotherapy groups. Nonetheless, his observations are deeply relevant to all human groups including leadership teams and corporate boards. Bion (1948) concluded that human groups can only be understood if one appreciates that there are really two "groups" functioning at the same time. The portion of the group's energy devoted to the work he described as the task group, while other group energies form the "basic assumption group," referring to the emotional—and perhaps unconscious—aspect of the process. This portion of any group's activities may be devoted, for example, to *dependency* ("who's in charge here, why are we meeting?") or *fight-flight* (e.g., the group delays beginning its work or refuses to come to closure because doing so might end the work and thus the group's existence).

Bion's observations are fully in play in any change process that involves groups, committees, or meetings—in short in any change process. The most obvious—yet often ignored—implication is that leaders must pay attention to the unconscious and emotional side of groups if they are to function effectively. Efforts to build friendship, trust, and working relationships pay off in productivity and the quality of the work. While the NFC's leadership used a number of conscious efforts to build group identity, an unscripted example from the process of the NFC illustrates the byplay between the emotional side of a group's work and the task side. The example has to do with how the term "transformation" became the consensual rallying cry of the commission.

Surrounded by flip charts in a long and exhausting meeting near the end of the NFC's work, the discussion turned to how to frame or label the changes that the group was calling for. It was an exhausting discussion. The term "reform" seemed old and tired. State-level change efforts have used terms like California's "realignment," but these didn't resonate deeply. Many ideas were raised and abandoned. The group was tired. After a long discussion, in a moment of pregnant silence, SAMHSA Administrator Charley Curie—interestingly, the only social worker member of the commission, asked "what about *transforming* the system?" The Commission quickly and by acclimation decided on "transformation" as a descriptor of change.

How does this story serve as an example understanding group dynamics as a framework for change? The choice of "transformation" as a theme by the Commission members was a classic example of group decision-making and of leadership. For various reasons, partly political und unknown to most members, Charley Curie wanted to use the term "transformation" in the report. We are often in this position, wanting to get our key idea included in a decision. How does one know how to achieve this? The story offers a good example. Solutions offered early in a decision process will often be passed over, often for reasons that illustrate Bion's distinction between "task" and "basic assumption" dynamics. A group that has not "formed" (either early in a process or early in a specific meeting) is unlikely to evaluate a suggestion based on its merits. Even if the conversation seems like a rational evaluation of the proposal, what may be going on is likely more reflective of an unconscious exercise in group formation. The effective leader will help the group form a healthy identity, providing an opportunity for everyone to be heard/feel a part of the process. (I am constantly surprised how much the simple step at the beginning of a group process asking people to share who they are, and what they bring to/expect from the work, helps normalize group behavior.) Also, because of the basic assumption dynamics present in every group, suggestions made by the leader are especially significant. Substantive suggestions made by formal leaders early in the process will often be adopted—or rejected—based on a seemingly superficial discussion. The underlying issue is not the content of the proposal but a group formation problem. So leaders must be careful about their role in introducing content. In the case of the NFC, Curie played a very low-key role as an equal member of the group rather than as the administrator of the lead federal agency (SAMHSA). This, ironically, made his role as a commission member more effective.

The other lesson in this little episode has to do with timing. In a group process, since emotional/basic assumption forces are often dominant, when ideas or solutions are introduced has a lot to do with how the group receives them. It is said that Henry Kissinger was a master negotiator and that one of his tactics was to hold very long negotiating sessions with plenty of water on the table—which he would not drink. Somehow, ideas offered near the end of a meeting are more likely to be accepted simply because the group is ready to end/move on. Kissinger's ploy simply strengthened the impulse. Curie's timing illustrated how an idea offered at the right time is likely to be accepted. So the NFC chose the term "transformation" in part because it was right but in part because it was offered at the right time in the right way by a leader—who happens to have had plenty of experience running treatment groups! Leaders must be aware of both the basic assumption and task aspects of group process and address both to achieve good decisions that are well accepted.

Implementation

We have focused on the process of identifying the subject for change and developing proposed solutions. In many ways the next step of implementation is an even greater challenge. Implementation requires a much broader buy-in and consensus building among often disparate stakeholders. The interests of these stakeholders are not always aligned in a way that facilitates an alliance. In the case of the NFC, its mandate did not include implementation. That task was assigned to various administrative entities at the federal, state, and local levels. After nearly two decades, the record is mixed. Leadership responsibility for coordinating federal follow-through fell to the Center for Mental Health Services (CMHS), which convened federal agency staff to develop an "Action Agenda" focused on implementation activities. A series of major grants to selected states provided several million dollars annually over a 5-year period and focused on an array of activities motivated by the commission's report. Seven state grants were awarded in the initial cycle, and two more grants followed in a second cycle, but outcomes in these states were uneven, and it is unclear whether these grants made a significant difference for implementation. In any case, support for implementation dwindled with changes in the federal administration after 2004.

The major impact of the commission's activities in the years since appears to have been in local communities and programs where the themes of recovery have resonated with most stakeholders. One example of this is the Allegheny County Coalition for Recovery (ACCR), an advocacy organization in Pittsburgh, Pennsylvania, that has evolved around this theme since its inception in 2001 (ACCR 2022). The mission of the ACCR is to "increase awareness of behavioral health recovery and to promote the use of recovery principles and practices in behavioral health services in Allegheny County." The ACCR brought together the full array of behavioral health stakeholders to participate in the evolution of the service system to the recovery-oriented care paradigm. It consists of five working committees: (1) public awareness, (2) education, (3) quality improvement, (4) collaborative for recovery dialogues, and (5) child and family. Each of these committees is co-chaired by a provider and a person in recovery or family member, and a Steering Committee provides oversight and governance. Through the work of these committees, the ACCR has developed a variety of materials and events that promote recovery and reduce the stigma associated with EH issues. Some of those accomplishments include (1) Guidelines for Developing Recovery Oriented Behavioral Health Systems, (2) Principles for Recovery Oriented Service Planning, (3) Consumer-Provider Dialogues: Guidelines for Preparation, (4) Recovery Education Tool-Kit, (5) Position Statement on the Universality of Recovery Principles, (6) Words Matter: A Guide for Using Person-First Language, (7) Recovery Walks, (8) Recovery Festivals, and (9) Cultural Sensitivity Training.

The ACCR is supported by county funds along with the Peer Support and Advocacy Network (PSAN) and Consumer Action Response Team (CART). PSAN provides a resource center for persons in recovery, a peer-to-peer warmline, and a peer professional training program (PSAN 2022). CART is a peer-administered evaluation program that surveys those who use services and provides feedback to the county's providers (CART 2017). These organizations have provided direction to providers of clinical services and has held them accountable for adherence to the model. They have markedly increased the voice of people in recovery in the administration of services (Sowers). Many other states and counties across the country have orchestrated similar transformations, largely inspired by the work of the NFC.

A key factor in sustaining the progress of such initiatives is commitment from leadership and stable financing. There are numerous examples of programs that are developed with the assistance of a demonstration grant from federal or state behavioral health administrations that are very successful over the period of the funding but are not sustainable due to their inability to generate revenue under current reimbursement mechanisms (see chapter "Financing of Community Behavioral Health Services"). Implementation of these programs should include plans for sustainability.

Contemporary Opportunities for Transformation

Despite the progress we have witnessed over the past 20 years, many challenges and opportunities remain in our systems of care. Several of the goals developed by the NFC have not yet been adequately addressed and will require ongoing efforts for implementation. The six goals set out in the recommendations were:

1. Recognition that mental health is a critical determinant of overall health.
2. Mental health care is driven by service users and families.
3. Disparities in mental health are eliminated.
4. Early screening and assessment of mental health is in place.
5. Excellent care is delivered, and research is accelerated.
6. Technology is in place to allow access to mental health care and information.

A thorough examination of progress on each of these goals is beyond the scope of this chapter, but it is worth looking at few areas in which progress has been made. An underlying issue that is determinant of the fragmentation and disparities identified by the NFC is the profit-driven system that is a uniquely American paradigm for financing services. In many cases, this has a direct impact on clinical decision-making and the intensity of services provided (see chapter "Financing of Community Behavioral Health Services"). One result of this structure has been extremely expensive care that fails to provide good outcomes. It is estimated that the United States spends at least twice as much of its GDP for health care as other developed countries, but most indicators of population health are much lower (Sowers 2022). Another way of expressing this is that our systems deliver a very low value product (i.e., Value = Quality/Cost).

Clearly, some transformation processes will take much longer than others, and while solutions may be ready for implementation, resistance to change holds them in abeyance until a critical event occurs. Since the 1990s there has been recognition that the costs of health care were becoming prohibitive. The profit-driven solution to this situation was to control costs of care by controlling access to it, resulting in the rise of managed care organizations and the development of medical necessity criteria (MNC) while also often stressing high-volume demands on behavioral health practitioners. However, this created an adversarial relationship between payers and providers, with the former managing resources and the latter managing treatment and services. Over time this dynamic has done little to reduce the cost of care, with quality of care diminishing in the eyes of many stakeholders. Historically, MNC have been most often proprietary tools that were perceived to serve the interests of the commercial insurers who drafted them (Shoyinka 2020).

In reaction to these circumstances, more equitable and clinically informed methods for finding the right balance between the quality of care and prudent use of resources have been viewed as needed. The development of the American Society of Addiction Medicine's Patient Placement Criteria (ASAM-PPC) in 1991 attempted to create a standard and a process to guide decisions regarding the level of care needed for people with addictive disorders (ASAM 2022). Now in its third edition, it's been used broadly and mandated in several states. This advancement has been accomplished through steady promotion by that organization and fierce advocacy from substance use treatment providers.

Similarly, in 1996, the American Association for Community Psychiatry (AACP) released a tool to manage value in mental healthcare systems. The Level of Care Utilization System for Psychiatric and Addiction Services (LOCUS) is a clinical assessment instrument that quantifies intensity of needs via numeric ratings. These ratings are then used to match needs to one of six levels of service intensity. LOCUS integrated a consideration of co-occurring substance use and/or physical health problems into its dimensional ratings along with social determinants of health (see chapter "Creating Value: Resource and Quality Management"). While both LOCUS and ASAM-PPC made steady progress through the first two decades of the twenty-first century, it was not until the 2018 decision by the ninth circuit court of CA in the suit of Wit v. United Behavioral Health that demand for these professionally developed criteria rose sharply. In that decision, both of these systems were recognized as professional standards. In response to this demand, organizations have attempted to meet them through the development of training and supportive materials, promotion of derivative tools, the formation of partnerships with professional organizations, and development of software to integrate with EMRs and facilitate clinical workflows. This transformation in the paradigm for making decisions about who gets what care helped advance all six of the NFC's goals, fertilized by a court decision and subsequent state legislative action mandating their use.

Another example of transformation that was set in motion by a critical incident is the multivariant assault on structural racism and other forms of discrimination within behavioral health systems. Although it has long been recognized that significant disparities exist between the health of minority populations (Blacks in particular) and that of Caucasians, cultural and structural competencies were given little attention in training programs, and the effects of both explicit and implicit biases remained problematic. The police killing of George Floyd in 2021, and the subsequent attention paid to other unjustified killings of Black people at the hands of both police and civilian vigilantes, gave additional impetus to the Black Lives Matter movement and significant reexamination of discrimination and structurally supported racism within behavioral health systems. Residency training programs have increasingly sought to incorporate more aspects of social justice and social determinants of health, which has been so central to the identity of community psychiatry. In 2021 the AACP developed the Self-Assessment for Modification of Anti-Racism Tool (SMART), which facilitates the process of scrutinizing practices within organizations that sustain disparities and the devaluation of minority stakeholders (Talley et al. 2021).

Several other areas ripe for transformative agendas are identified in other sections of this book. Chapter "Population Health, Prevention, and Community Psychiatry" lays out the need to extend this mainstay of community psychiatry into the curricula and consciousness of all of psychiatry. Other products of the profit-driven system are the accessibility constraints and often traumatic encounters the people seeking services often experience. Chapter "Inspiring a Welcoming, Hopeful Culture" describes how providers can offer services that are inviting and respectful. The integration of primary and behavioral health care has been initiated but still needs to become the mainstay of primary health care (see chapter "Integrated Care and Community Psychiatry"). Climate change and disaster response will become increasingly important in the years ahead, and it is not unlikely that our survival will depend on it. These issues are considered in detail in chapters "Climate Change: Impact on Community Mental Health" and "Disaster Victims and the Response to Trauma" of this book. Both ends of the political spectrum have recognized that our carceral systems generate and exacerbate mental illness and societal health (see chapter "Collaborative Reduction of Criminal Justice Involvement for Persons with Mental Illness").

Conclusion

Leading change in mental health services and systems is a paradox. On the one hand, every change process is unique to a particular time, place, and culture. On the other, there are patterns which can be learned and approaches that can be mastered to greatly increase the chances of success. This chapter has reviewed some principles of change. A crucial initial factor is choosing change targets and goals that are both relevant and achievable.

Timing is a crucial variable in any change process. Actions to be taken at the beginning, in the middle, and near the end of a change process must fit the stage of change; each phase presents distinct challenges and opportunities. Finally, group processes are at the heart of every organization and change effort. This is a comforting realization for mental health professionals who usually have training in group work. With attention and practice, the techniques in group leadership can be applied to work groups and change processes. Research on change in mental health agencies—specifically on the adoption of evidence-based practices by community programs—is also comforting. Many factors determined to influence the success of change are common sense.

"Transformation" has become more popular as a term for change since the NFC used the term in its 2003 report. It is probably appropriate as a label for change since it implies both substantial reform—surely still needed in mental health—and an approach that is not necessarily top-down or structural. Transformative change affects not just process or structure but alters how things are done. Like the process of recovery from mental illness, transformative change is a journey and a process that alters the nature of things. By approaching the task of change armed with knowledge and tools, we can accelerate it and achieve more lasting results.

References

AACP (2016) The Level of Care Utilization System (LOCUS) Available at: http://communitypsychiatry.org/resources/locus, Accessed April 5, 2022

ACCR (2022) Allegheny County Coalition for Recovery, Available at: http://coalitionforrecovery.org/committees/ Accessed April 4, 2022

ASAM PPC (2022) A brief history of ASAM Criteria PPC 2R, Available at: https://paulearley.net/articles/asam-criteria/ppc-history, Accessed April 5, 2022

Bion, W. R. (1948). Experiences in groups, Human Relations (I–IV). 1948–1951, Reprinted in Experiences in Groups (1961).

Bush, G.W. (2002a), Speech announcing President's New Freedom Commission on Mental Health. Albuquerque, NM, April 29, 2002

Bush, G. W. (2002b), Executive order 13263 of April 29, 2002. Federal Register, 67, (86) Friday, May 3, 2002.

CART (2017) The Consumer Action Response Team 2017 Annual Report, Available at: https://www.alleghenycountyanalytics.us/wp-content/uploads/2018/06/CART-2017-Annual-Report-Final-Draft.pdf Accessed April 4, 2022

Collins, J., and Porras, J. (1994) Built to last: Successful habits of visionary companies. New York: Harper Collins.

Cook, J.A. (2006) Employment barriers for persons with psychiatric disabilities: Update of a report for the President's Commission. Psychiatr Serv, 57: 1391 – 1405.

Department of Health and Human Services. Mental health: A report of the surgeon general. Rockville, MD: author, 1999.

Institute of Medicine. (2001) Crossing the quality chasm: A new health system for the 21st century. Washington, DC: National Academy Press.

Koyanagi, C., and Goldman, H. H. (1991) The quiet success of the national plan for the chronically mentally ill. Hosp Community Psychiatry 42:899–905.

Machiavelli, N. (1513) The Prince, translated by N.H. Thomson. Vol. XXXVI, Part 1. The Harvard Classics. New York: P.F. Collier & Son, 1909–14.

Marmor, T. R. and Gill, K.C. (1989) The political and economic context of mental health care in the United States. Journal of Health Politics, Policy and Law. 14(3):459–475

New Freedom Commission on Mental Health, (2003) Achieving the Promise: Transforming Mental Health Care in America. Final Report. DHHS Pub. No. SMA-03-3832. Rockville, MD: 2003.

New Freedom Commission on Mental Health, (2002) Interim Report to the President. Department of Health and Human Services, Rockville, MD

O'Connell, M. E., Boat, T., and Warner, K. E. (2009) Preventing Mental, Emotional, and Behavioral Disorders Among Young People Progress and Possibilities. Washington, D.C.: The National Academies Press

O'Hara, A. (2007) Housing for people with mental illness: Update of a report to the President's New Freedom Commission. Psychiatr Serv, 58: 907–913.

Panzano, P. and Roth, D. (2006). The decision to adopt evidence-based and other innovative mental health practices: Risky business? Psychiatric Services, Vol. 57, pp. 1153–1161.

Panzano, P., Seffrin, B., Chaney-Jones, S., Roth, D., Crane-Ross, D., Massatti, R, and Carstens, C. (2005) The innovation diffusion and adoption research project (IDARP): Moving from the diffusion of research results to promoting the adoption of evidence-based innovation in the Ohio mental health system. New Research in Mental Health (16). Columbus, OH: Ohio Department of Mental Health

PSAN (2022) Peer Support and Advocay Network, Available at: http://www.peer-support.org/ Accessed April 4, 2022

Senge, Peter M. (2006) The fifth discipline: the art and practice of the learning organization.: Random House, London

Shoyinka S, (2020) Innovative financing, Chapter 6 in Seeking value: balancing cost and quality in psychiatric care, Sowers and Ranz Editors. APPI Washington, DC

Sowers W, Trenney K, Knickerbocker S, and Schwartz M (2022 in press) The Voice of Recovery, Chapter 5 in the Textbook of Administrative Psychiatry, Saeed S Editor. American Psychiatric Association Press, Washington DC

Talley RM, Shoyinka S, Minkoff K; (2021) The Self-assessment for Modification of Anti-Racism Tool (SMART): Addressing structural racism in community behavioral health; Community Ment Health J 57(6):1208–1213. https://doi.org/10.1007/s10597-021-00839-0. Epub 2021 May 23.

Program Evaluation

Alison R. Thomas, Erinn E. Savage, Kathleen Hodgin, and Robert Savage

Introduction

In the nine years since the first edition of this book was published, the field of program evaluation has expanded substantially, as has the culture of accountability and data-driven decision-making. Such growth is evident in federal and state legislation, the emphasis on evidence-based practice in all professions, the requirement for evaluation officers for federally funded projects, and reporting to oversight and accrediting bodies (such as the Centers for Medicare and Medicaid Services, CMS). Accordingly, the need for demonstrating quality outcomes for community psychiatry and public mental health programs is more important than ever.

Yet adoption of robust program evaluation efforts varies widely across community mental health providers. While most laborers in the mental health field are conscientious and diligent in providing high-quality services, proving this and linking service delivery to desirable outcomes can be challenging. Not only must community mental health providers have a working knowledge of the core tasks of program evaluation, but they must also adhere to the spirit of accountability and continuous quality improvement inherent in modern program evaluation.

Broadly, four main trends characterize the modern conceptualization of evaluation. First, outcome-based evaluations increasingly focus on the best practice indicators that can be measured objectively. Although values and culture are important and necessary ingredients for organizational success, the worth of a program is now typically measured via operationalized (i.e., specifically defined) variables. Second, evaluations should include a diversity of outcomes, selected from a range of perspectives. This includes, but is not limited to, the groups that receive services, organizational leadership, and financial concerns. Third, organizations should take a diverse, inclusive, and collaborative approach to evaluation. This trend is reflected in program evaluation standards that recommend engaging a full range of program stakeholders in all steps of the evaluation process and may include administrators, support personnel, service recipients, and funders. Fourth, and perhaps the most difficult to put into practice, is the movement toward continuous quality improvement. Program evaluation, in this sense, should be incorporated as part of an iterative cycle that occurs on a regular basis. This trend emphasizes that evaluation practices are intended to improve process and outcomes, not just serve as data collection. Such integration

A. R. Thomas (✉) · K. Hodgin · R. Savage
University of Alabama at Birmingham, Birmingham, AL, USA
e-mail: alisonthomas@uabmc.edu; kathleenhodgin@uabmc.edu; rsavage@uabmc.edu

E. E. Savage
Washington State University, Pullman, WA, USA
e-mail: erinn.savage@wsu.edu

W. E. Sowers et al. (eds.), *Textbook of Community Psychiatry*,
https://doi.org/10.1007/978-3-031-10239-4_52

can be challenging because it typically involves cultural transformation, championed by organizational leadership, that becomes incorporated into the already crowded daily practice of frontline clinicians and staff (Schalock et al. 2014).

The mechanics of program evaluation can be daunting and will become moreso as the field of program evaluation expands with more nuanced methodologies and recommendations. In fact, the growth is so significant that, to fully review the wealth of available literature, theory, and texts would be impossible. This chapter aims to provide a summative review with the intention that all professionals who are involved in community mental health will be able to engage with the material and benefit from the discussion. To start, a recommended framework will be reviewed, followed by considerations particularly relevant to community mental health in the current climate, a review of the basic theory and key components of program evaluation, a description of the most common types of program evaluation, and, finally, a discussion of possible sources of data and data analysis.

The CDC Framework for Program Evaluation

In response to the growing need for regular, valid, and integrated program evaluation in public health organizations and the lack of a standardized practice, the CDC developed a framework for program evaluation in public health settings (US Dept. of Health and Human Services Centers for Disease Control and Prevention [CDC] 1999). Since its inception, the framework has become one of the most common models for program evaluation in many settings because it is manualized and openly available. The CDC Framework "is a practical, non-prescriptive tool, designed to summarize and organize the essential elements of program evaluation" (CDC 1999, p. 4). It provides a six-step structure that revolves around the four quality standards of designing and using evaluation (see Fig. 1):

1. Engage stakeholders
2. Describe the program
3. Focus the evaluation design
4. Gather credible evidence
5. Justify conclusions
6. Ensure use and share lessons learned

In this framework, the standard of *utility* refers to the usefulness of the information to the intended users of the evaluation. *Feasibility* holds evaluators accountable for being realistic, efficient, and diplomatic in their evaluation design. Ethical and legal behavior is encompassed in the standard of *propriety*, along with holding the welfare of the program stakeholders in mind. Evaluators are expected to be *accurate* in their findings as well as in their dissemination of the findings, including particular attention to the manner in which meaning can vary depending on which stakeholder group is receiving the information (see Gill et al. 2016 for an interesting summary and discussion of the cultural context of program evaluation).

While the guidelines suggest that the actual process may not be linear, a step cannot be considered complete until the prior steps are complete. For example, in practice, an organization may simultaneously engage stakeholders and describe the program. However, a program description would not be considered complete without input from all the stakeholders who will be participating in the evaluation. The self-study manual and additional resources are available at the CDC website: www.cdc.gov/eval/index.htm.

The CDC Framework utilizes logic models for describing a program (step 2). Logic models, to be explained in more detail further below, are visual depictions of how intended outcomes are related to the program activities (CDC 1999). Logic models are not meant for program design, but to capture the important program activities and link their relationship to intended outcomes. The program description, or logic model, is intended to help organizations focus the evaluation on the outcome(s) of most importance.

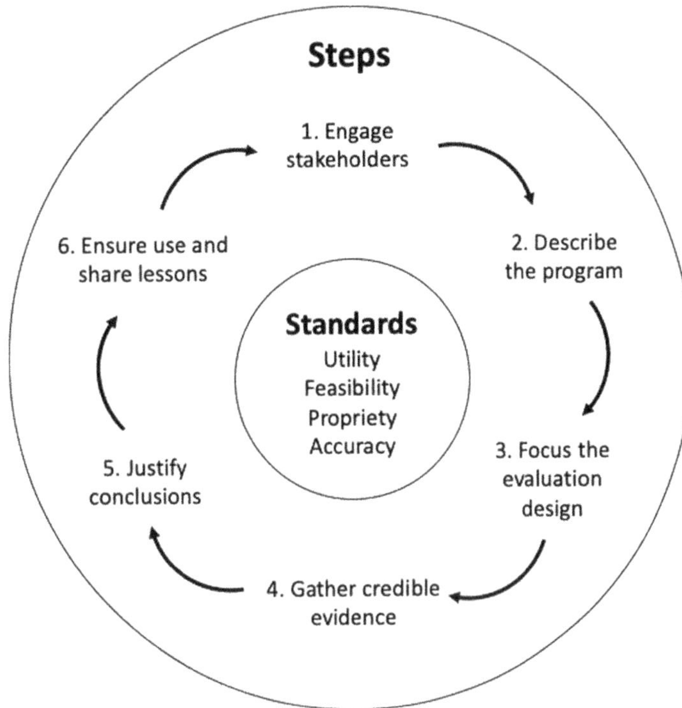

Fig. 1 CDC Framework steps and standards (CDC 1999, p. 4)

Considerations

Community Mental Health

Evaluation in the community mental health setting is often complicated by issues related to consumer participation, limitations in measurement and funding, and the fragmentation of healthcare systems. Community care often involves a wide range of stakeholders (e.g., providers, administrators, peer specialists, advocacy groups) who may value aspects of a program differently, and evaluations may be difficult to conduct when these stakeholders have conflicting goals. Gathering such information from relevant stakeholder groups prior to implementation can help address uncertainties early, increase buy-in, and inform selection of optimal implementation strategies (Cabassa et al. 2015). Further, though involvement of stakeholders in evaluations is often viewed positively, lack of clarity surrounding stakeholder role and level of expertise may diminish the credibility of findings. Studies have shown that findings are considered more credible when an evaluation is controlled by dedicated, trained evaluators vs. stakeholders, though this effect is reduced when stakeholder credibility is perceived as higher. Thus, stakeholder involvement should be considered carefully in evaluations and, when included, must be characterized clearly, as this information will better inform readers and may enhance credibility of findings (Jacobson and Azzam 2018).

In addition to the coordination of multiple organizations and stakeholders, any single organization is often composed of multiple smaller-scale programs. By paying attention to five areas, such organizations can overcome the challenges associated with choosing a specific focus and structuring results such that they are useful for all elements of a complex system. First, organizations must create a shared operational definition among all programs for outcomes of importance to ensure data is comparable across sites. Second, measures of change should be considered carefully as programs may be implemented and measured differently across sites; building common measures, such as magnitude of change, can usefully reduce or eliminate this challenge. Third, programs should provide sites with a specific reporting form to facilitate aggregating results across sites. Fourth, threading evaluation-oriented activities throughout daily practice can increase engagement in the evaluation process more organically. Finally, making research centers readily available to practice organizations can reduce the difficulty translating research into practice (e.g., state health departments; Nesbit et al. 2018).

Additional challenges in community mental health derive from consumer engagement. Community mental health clinics typically serve vulnerable populations with a diverse range of mental and physical health needs in addition to socioeconomic disadvantages. High rates of appointment no-shows, low consumer access to resources (phone/Internet, transportation, etc.), and other difficulties such as limited literacy and language barriers may make surveys and other forms of measurement efforts especially challenging to implement. Cognitive deficits and other impairments may also interfere with some individuals' ability to engage appropriately. Thus, tailoring evaluation methods to the target population that both anticipates and adapts to potential barriers to consumer engagement is key.

Despite increasing pressure for its greater incorporation, the use of quality improvement measures across mental health care remains limited. Although many measures are available, few are endorsed nationally due to similarity among measures, poor translation from research to practice, and limited supporting evidence for their role in improving the quality of care (Pincus et al. 2016). Scarcity of measures addressing some components of patient-centered care (such as mental health recovery) creates further problems. Further, information on the complex needs routinely encountered in community practice (e.g., housing, employment, education, etc.) is often not well integrated into mental health data systems, a task likely requiring intensive coordination across service providers (Kilbourne et al. 2018). In addition to development of a stronger evidence base, more coordinated investment and leadership are needed to guide quality measurement efforts, integration of data systems to provide more information on quality of care, and increased collaboration with consumers and staff in promoting quality improvement (Pincus et al. 2016). Limitations in quantitative measurement create inherent difficulty in choosing and assessing what is valued in mental health care; integrating both qualitative and quantitative methods may help overcome some of these limitations when evaluating community mental health programs (Luchins 2012).

Considerable constraints in resources and funding, including for evaluation, present further obstacles to mental health programs. A case study by Aby (2020) showcases the difficulty of implementing and sustaining primary care integration within a community mental health center after the end of federal grant support. Aby (2020) identified several barriers the center confronted, including inconsistencies in defining integrated care across the organization, lack of ongoing training and support in application of evidence-based practices (EBPs), discrepant regulations and policies associated with separate Medicaid funding streams for mental health and substance use treatment, and difficulties in changing organizational culture surrounding staff roles and communication. Case study findings suggested the need for increased staff flexibility, stronger interdisciplinary teamwork, and ongoing training, alongside systemic changes to promote congruence across agency and government regulations for patient care (Aby 2020). Further, the siloed nature of many mental health clinics and service providers can impede evaluation efforts. Depending on the target outcome, evaluations may require extensive collaboration with other organizations that are involved in meeting the complex needs of community mental health consumers (e.g., charitable agencies, primary and specialty healthcare clinics, local resource providers, etc.).

Cultural Competency

Just as cultural competency is emphasized in the delivery of services, cultural competency is equally important in program evaluation and development. Such efforts must consider the role of culture in order to be useful. In 2014, the Centers for Disease Control and Prevention (CDC) developed a guide for conducting program implementation and evaluation through a culturally competent lens (Gill et al. 2016). The guide recommends that evaluators prioritize including typically underrepresented groups in studies, communicate using terms with which communities involved in the program are familiar, explicitly define cultural competence as a component of the evaluation, and attempt to involve a diverse group of evaluators (Gill et al. 2016).

More broadly, cultural competency is essential (but not sufficient) for addressing the many health disparities faced by minorities. In the United States, health disparities for ethnic and racial minorities are well documented (Fiscella and Sanders 2016), and made more obvious by the disproportionate impact of the COVID-19 pandemic on Black, Latino, and Native American communities (Fortuna et al. 2020). Regarding mental health treatment specifically, individuals from racial and ethnic minority groups utilize services less often than whites, which has been attributed to several barriers such as cost, stigma, and language barriers. The 2014 National Healthcare Quality and Disparities Report, considered the most comprehensive measure of health disparities in the United States, found one of the largest disparities for Blacks, Hispanics, and Asians to be in the "treatment for depression among individuals with major depressive disorder" (Fiscella and Sanders 2016). Disparities in mental health treatment by individuals from historically oppressed groups may be underreported due to their pre-existing expectation of poorer care (Luchins 2012). In other words, when completing satisfaction surveys, individuals from racial and ethnic minority groups may report a higher quality of care, not because the care was necessarily satisfactory, but because their expectations for care were lower, compared to that of white consumers. This completion bias should be considered by program evaluators both when developing measures and analyzing outcome data.

Review of Purpose and Theory of Program Evaluation

Program evaluations seek to answer a range of questions, which are the principal guide for choosing the type of evaluation and analytic approach. Needs assessments compare and identify the gaps between an existing situation and the desired condition (Altschuld and Watkins 2014). Such assessments typically examine a targeted population to determine the presence, extent, characteristics, and effects of a problem for which a program is intended to address. For example, an evaluator for a program seeking to increase local access to mental health care may conduct a needs assessment to determine how many people within a certain community are unable to access care, identify characteristics of those individuals, and articulate the most common barriers. Once needs are identified, causal analysis and prioritization of needs alongside consideration of available assets and capacities then provide crucial information for potential solutions. Needs assessments are essential in defining a problem and laying groundwork for program development and implementation. Therefore, needs assessments usually occur in early stages of program development but may be embedded within evaluation of ongoing programs (Altschuld and Watkins 2014).

Interest in and evaluation of programs' theoretical underpinnings have grown from simply seeking to understand whether or not programs work, to also understand how they work. A program's theory is the conceptual foundation of how a program will reach its intended outcome (i.e., change mechanisms) and is assessed via program theory evaluation. Such evaluations focus on the adequacy or validity of a program's theory, (i.e., whether a program as designed has the potential to reach its intended outcome) and may identify program improvements, inform future evaluations, or point to alternative interventions. Evidence remains mixed about the practical value of program theory evaluation (Coryn et al. 2011). Nonetheless, program theory evaluation continues to grow. Often depicted graphically in diagrams or displayed in tables, program theories illustrate relationships between program processes (inputs, actions, and outputs) and outcomes (expected changes).

Logic analysis, a popular methodology, utilizes existing scientific knowledge to test the soundness of a program's theory through the following steps: (1) create a logic model to depict the particular program theory in question, (2) form a conceptual framework based on the existing evidence or expert guidance, and (3) evaluate the program theory by comparing the program as designed to the framework derived from scientific knowledge (Brousselle and Champagne 2011). Logic models are particularly useful for programs that utilize multiple activities to target an outcome or set of outcomes, such as public health or mental health problems which rarely have a single etiology. These models range widely from relatively simple and linear formats to more complex, contextualized models informed by systems thinking, with the latter having received increasing emphasis more recently. Notably, different groups of stakeholders will require different levels of detail. The CDC manual for a self-evaluation gives the example of a big picture (i.e., simplified) logic model (Fig. 2) for funding stakeholders who do not require implementation details.

Common Types of Program Evaluation

Implementation Evaluation and Program Fidelity

Implementation evaluation is a complex form of program evaluation designed to determine whether a program is being implemented as intended (Schalock et al. 2011). Two types of implementation evaluation include formative (used to guide the developmental stages of a program) and summative (used to evaluate the program once it has been implemented and typically addresses several outcomes) (Smith and Hasan 2020). The widespread call for utilizing EBPs has necessitated an increase in implementation evaluation. Several oversight groups and mental healthcare systems have engaged in efforts to systematically implement EBPs, often in partnership with researchers and other program stakeholders (Hermann et al. 2006b). Several issues impact the implementation of EBPs at the individual, organizational, and societal level, most notably the challenge of translating science into practice (Schalock et al. 2011; Schoenwald et al. 2011).

In community mental health, implementing evidence-based practice most commonly refers to treating patients with empirically supported treatments (ESTs). A well-researched EST demonstrating positive results in the research setting cannot be expected to produce the same results in clinical practice if the treatment is not implemented in the intended manner (e.g., if the clinician does not follow the treatment manual properly). Thus, implementation evaluation requires that evaluators measure program fidelity, which is "the degree to which a particular program follows…a well-defined set of interventions and procedures to help individuals achieve some desired goal" (Bond et al. 2000). In other words, fidelity refers to how well an intervention implemented in the clinical setting matches the intervention as it was intended (Hill et al. 2007). Several studies examining fidelity to Assertive Community Treatment (ACT), a commonly used treatment in community mental health, have indicated that higher fidelity is associated with more

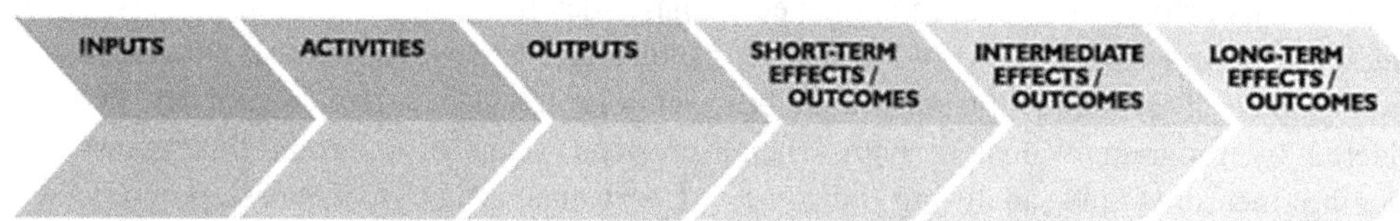

Fig. 2 CDC basic program logic model (CDC 2011, p. 27)

positive outcomes, including decreased hospitalizations, less time in the hospital, and greater treatment retention (McGrew et al. 1994; McHugo et al. 1999). Research has indicated that, even when provided with a manualized format, administrators often make changes to treatment, even though they report knowing they should not (Hill et al. 2007). Thus, reliable measures that assess fidelity are important and can be impactful. The National Institute of Mental Health (NIMH) has acknowledged the importance of fidelity assessment and has increased funding aimed to develop fidelity measures that will examine treatment integrity and monitor outcomes (NIMH 2011). Effective program fidelity monitoring can be incorporated into feedback systems for continuous improvement and evaluation at multiple organizational levels (Schoenwald et al. 2011).

Modified observational coding systems, practitioner reports, and client reports are all important for efficiently and effectively measuring fidelity in the delivery of evidence-based psychotherapy. Fidelity measures should be both effective (i.e., accurately measure what they intend to measure) and efficient (i.e., simple to administer). Effectiveness is accomplished by using well-validated measures, but because the development and administration of such measures are both labor and cost-intensive, fidelity assessment can be inefficient (Schoenwald et al. 2011). This inefficiency makes fidelity assessment in the "real world" an ongoing challenge, which isn't surprising given that fidelity measures were originally designed and used entirely for research.

As their purpose has expanded for use in implementation evaluation in non-research settings, fidelity measures have become more "high stakes," impacting decisions about program funding and even the hiring and firing of personnel (Schoenwald et al. 2011). Regarding cost efficiency, remote fidelity assessments (i.e., conducted via phone) can be as effective as on-site assessments, which significantly lowers cost and increases accessibility to fidelity assessment for settings with limited resources (Rollins et al. 2017). Effective, efficient, and accessible fidelity measures are essential to the advancement of both EST research and to ensuring a high level of care in community mental health settings (Teague et al. 2012; Schoenwald et al. 2011). However, strict treatment fidelity may not be the best practice when working with culturally diverse patients; rather, providers can use their observations in clinical work to inform research questions, with the goal of ultimately improving care (Weisner and Hay 2015).

Outcome-Based Evaluation

In addition to exploring needs and theory, evaluations can be used to assess intervention implementation to determine whether it is delivered as intended. This can help organizations avoid unnecessary use of resources, address unanticipated barriers in program application, and understand why a program succeeded or may have fallen short. Community-based mental health programs are typically evaluated using such methods, namely, outcome-based evaluations (OBEs). The purpose of OBE is to evaluate whether these programs are providing adequate education, health care, and human services to the intended population and to report effectiveness and efficiency to program stakeholders (Roberts and Steele 2005; Schalock 2001). OBE helps programs and policymakers understand social problems affecting communities, the types of services needed, service utilization, and effectiveness of those services (Gowin and Millman 1981). OBE can also provide information on service outcomes (e.g., health and psychological outcomes) and patient satisfaction (Roberts and Steele 2005). Schalock et al. (2014) recommend that OBE be both collaborative (i.e., utilizing input from all program stakeholders) and integrative (i.e., ongoing self-assessment that leads to continuous improvement).

Effectiveness analysis – one of the most commonly used OBE techniques – aims to evaluate whether the program has met the intended goals. Results are specifically intended to inform programmatic changes. This type of evaluation strives to be pragmatic, cost-effective, and practical. It reduces the ethical problems associated with techniques that use experimental and control conditions (e.g., subjects in control conditions may not receive active treatment). Typically, comparison designs are used, including comparing people to themselves before and after treatment, pre-post treatment exposure comparisons, or longitudinal status comparisons.

Of course, as the number of assumptions made by researchers increases, so too do limitations on the precision, certainty, and generalizability of the analysis. Despite these limitations, these analyses provide essential information that can be used for data-based management, reporting, and program change purposes (Schalock 1995, 2001).

Impact evaluation is another OBE used to determine whether a given program made a difference as compared to either no program or an alternative program (Schalock 1995, 2001). Specifically, it aims to determine whether outcomes can be directly attributed to the program (Gertler et al. 2016). Ideally, an impact evaluation will answer both whether the difference a program made is significant and whether that difference would have occurred in the absence of the program, both of which impact the decision to continue funding and operating the program in question (Schalock 1995, 2001).

Cost-effectiveness evaluation, the most complex type of OBE, seeks to uncover whether a program's impact is large enough to justify the cost of implementing the program. This form of OBE utilizes comparative analyses of varied treatment programs/models and related operational expenses in order to determine the most effective treatment relative to the cost of the program (Wolff et al. 1997). For mental health care in particular, cost and resources required can vary drastically across programs, depending on factors such as treatment type, program setting, and type of provider. Several categories are considered when evaluating a program's cost-effectiveness, including potential costs to the society when mental health difficulties go untreated (Shearer et al. 2016). Evidence of cost-effectiveness is increasingly necessary to secure funding (please see Rabarison et al. 2018, for a specific tool to support cost analysis).

Benchmarking is a form of OBE in which an organization utilizes existing data sets to compare its operations to those of similar organizations. Fortunately, data sets that lend themselves to benchmarking are readily available in the United States. Most government-run and publicly funded agencies are required to provide open access to certain general information such as consumer demographics, services provided, accessibility, and spending. Programs collect this information and provide access to it through their websites, publications, and direct requests. National performance measurement guidelines (Ganju 2006) and international benchmarks of mental health care (Hermann et al. 2006c) provide additional guidance. Financial and operational benchmarks can be used by organizations internally to set goals and target areas of quality improvement, as well as by external researchers seeking to identify the best practices in mental health (Rushing and Lefkovitz 2008). Historically, mental healthcare programs have suffered from a significant deficit in data. A 2006 project attempted to address this by developing several consensus-based, process-oriented measures from which benchmarks were developed (Hermann et al. 2006a). They looked at measures such as usage of several antidepressant treatments, antipsychotic treatments, and mood stabilizers. Six other measures involved follow-up visit parameters. They concluded that statistical benchmarks can be developed for quality-related data points and that incorporating such benchmarks into quality improvement activities leads to better mental health care and improved consumer outcomes (Hermann et al. 2006a).

Measurement-based quality improvement (MBQI) represents another type of OBE. Quality improvement and quality management efforts range from small projects of limited scope and a few key goals to more complex efforts in evaluating the structural, process, and outcome components of quality of care (Donabedian 2005). National initiatives, funders, and oversight bodies have largely promoted the growth of MBQI implementation, and hospitals, clinics, insurance plans, and other mental health organizations have increasingly incorporated routine MBQI to systematically identify areas of concern and strengthen quality of care (Hermann et al. 2006b). Used to evaluate a wide variety of aspects of clinical mental health care, MBQI measures can assess program structure (e.g., staff and facility characteristics), processes (e.g., degree of evidence-based practice), and outcomes (e.g., improvement in symptoms, quality of life; Kilbourne et al. 2018). MBQI is also closely related to evidence-based practice implementation (EBPI; Hermann et al. 2006b).

Despite widespread calls for adoption of MBQI in mental health, it remains underutilized for several reasons, including the absence of an agreed-upon systematic method to measure quality of care and issues with validity of process measures. Weaknesses in policy and technological infrastructure, gaps in evidence supporting mental health quality measures, and inconsistent training and support across professions present additional barriers to MBQI in mental health (Kilbourne et al. 2018). More recently, efforts within the United States to bolster mental health MBQI (and EBPI) include the Veterans Health Administration's informatics approach to improve mental healthcare quality and performance (Schmidt et al. 2017), the increasing use of value-based payment models, utilization of mobile technologies, and initiatives from CMS to integrate mental health and primary care (Kilbourne et al. 2018).

Goal-Free Evaluation

In contrast to the popular outcome-based evaluations, there is a growing, but not new, interest in goal-free evaluation (GFE). First articulated by Michael Scriven in the 1970s, GFEs are carried out without any information regarding programmatic goals with the purpose of supporting a broad range of potential outcomes. Scriven was concerned that with knowledge of intended outcomes, relevant unintended outcomes may be overlooked. In the earliest iterations of GFE, evaluators purposely avoided any knowledge that could indicate the program's goals, and evaluation procedures often included a middle man between the evaluator and the program stakeholders (Youker et al. 2017). The four general principles of GFE are:

1. Identify relevant effects to examine without referencing goals and objectives.
2. Identify what occurred without the prompting of goals and objectives.
3. Determine if what occurred can logically be attributed to the program or intervention.
4. Determine the degree to which the effects are positive, negative, or neutral.

In a discussion of modern GFEs, Youker et al. (2017) noted that, despite a lull in publications utilizing GFE, several methodologies that appear to be goal-free in spirit and "goal-dismissive" in practice have emerged more recently. They identified four goal-dismissive evaluation strategies (defined as strategies in which evaluators treat the intended outcomes with indifference when constructing evaluation goals): most significant change, outcome harvesting, participatory assessment of development, and qualitative impact protocol (Youker et al. 2017).

The advantage of GFEs compared with outcome-based evaluations is that they exhibit less bias because the evaluator has less alliance with program stakeholders. The very purpose of GFEs is to avoid or consciously counter any information about intended outcomes that could emphasize some outcomes more than others. The strength of such a stance is a more accurate and broader evaluation. However, when determining evaluation aims, limited resources need to be directed toward questions that justify resources already spent toward specific outcomes, argue for further resources for intended outcomes, and perhaps fulfill specific reporting requirements. Thus, GFE is much less utilized than OBE. When GFEs are used, they are typically performed in conjunction with OBEs (Youker et al. 2017).

Data Sources

We have discussed a range of methodologies for program evaluation. Some methodologies automatically utilize certain sets or types of data. For example, program fidelity and implementation evaluations have standardized variables and measures to assess the target outcomes (both targets of the intervention and alignment of activities with the manual). When using a methodology without prescribed data sources or procedures, such as impact evaluation, programs and evaluators have a range of options. Two common sources of data are surveys and databases (e.g., administrative data, federal or state databases). As programs become increasingly data-driven, large databases are growing in all dimensions. Similarly, the emphasis on consumer experience has led to a plethora of survey measures, as well as tools for collecting that data.

Surveys are a direct method for gathering feedback from program stakeholders, are typically less time-intensive than interviews, and tend to be simple to administer and relatively cheap. However, using survey data comes with two potential sources of bias: nonresponse bias and response bias. Nonresponse bias is introduced when survey nonresponders share some kind of common trait that relates to their choice not to participate. For example, when giving a satisfaction survey at a community mental health center, patients who are not satisfied with their treatment may be more likely to decline to participate than those who are satisfied. Thus, survey results will be skewed toward higher levels of satisfaction. Response bias refers to errors in data that result from the manner in which participants respond to the questions, which arises when the meaning of questions is ambiguous and changes over time or when participants are motivated to respond a certain way to influence how the interviewer/raters feel about the participant (i.e., social desirability bias) or themselves (e.g., rating providers highly to spare their feelings). Even anonymous surveys do not necessarily eliminate biases based on how the participant feels (Barnow and Greenberg 2019).

Administrative databases are often used to access data related to financial matters, demographics, and a wide range of other information (e.g., insurance, work status). Moreover, administrative databases exist at nearly all levels of organizations, whether you need data about a specific hospital or clinical program, a state-wide system, or a federal program. The primary challenge of administrative databases is noncoverage. Evaluators have no control over what data was collected or how the variables are defined, such that a specific outcome of interest may not be gathered in the database or that the outcome is assessed differently in the database than suits the purpose of the evaluation. For example, one study accessed unemployment insurance (UI) data at the federal level to assess the impact of a training voucher program on earnings. They compared survey data to administrative data and found that survey data indicated a statistically significant impact and administrative data did not. They explored possible explanations and noted that the UI database does not include data for some job statuses, such as self-employment, multiple jobs, work that is out of state, and working while receiving lower UI (Moore et al. 2019). Evaluators should use multiple sources of data and remember that outcome and impact are not always the same (e.g., examining the outcome of employment status does not speak to the impact on earnings).

Data Analysis

Evaluators use data analysis to make sense of and communicate data with program stakeholders. Though analytical methods in evaluation have largely been informed by social science's use of randomized controlled trials, the complexity of evaluating multidimensional programs over time often renders such methods inappropriate in real-world settings (Gao et al. 2019). Keeping in mind this possible challenge, many methods of analysis are available for evaluators to examine and interpret program data, and the evaluation questions are central in guiding the choice of analytic method (Treasury Board of Canada, Secretariat 1998). Descriptive statistics are commonly used to summarize and compare quantitative (i.e., numeric) program data in tables, graphs, and charts. For example, the means, frequency distribution, and correlations of quantitative variables (e.g., survey data, performance metrics, etc.) are often used to describe program and population characteristics. Such descriptive statistics allow evaluators to concisely present often large and overwhelming amounts of data. From descriptive statistics, meaningful patterns may emerge to aid administrators in making decisions and identifying potential areas of concern or achievement. Inferential statistics can also be used to infer conclusions from a particular sample or set of data to a larger population. T-tests, for example, are commonly used to compare means at two time points (e.g., before and after program participation) or between two different groups. More advanced approaches employ predictive analytics to anticipate program outcomes via statistical modeling. For example, evaluators may use predictive modeling to identify which clients may be least or most likely to benefit from a program. These models may also be embedded within care systems to assist staff in ongoing decision-making and evaluation (Filhn et al. 2014).

Though quantitative methods can assist evaluators in assessing observable findings, they come with limitations related to bias, reliability, and validity. An overreliance on quantitative measurement of care may obscure how well a program is truly performing; a mixed-methods approach that integrates qualitative data can help address limitations of either approach while increasing the validity of overall findings (Luchins 2012). Qualitative data refers to non-numeric written information typically gleaned from interviews, focus groups, document review, or direct observation. Qualitative approaches can be more time-intensive and costly than quantitative methods but can also enrich evaluations with valuable contextual detail. They may be especially useful when either established measures are inappropriate or do not exist for a given construct. In program evaluation, qualitative methods are likely to play a greater role in developing program theory, gathering details for implementation, understanding program impact, and presenting more accessible reports of findings (US Department of Health and Human Services 2016).

Conclusion

Although this chapter focuses on summarizing the mechanics of program development, our purpose is serving individuals with significant mental health challenges by supporting the professionals and organizations who have chosen to serve them. The organized delivery of mental health services is becoming an increasingly complex task. This is particularly true of community settings which face a rising demand for services in the setting of financial cutbacks. While challenging, this level of complexity and oversight is necessary to ensure that we are using limited resources responsibly and intentionally. In that process, we risk losing sight of our primary purpose for the sake of meeting requirements, standards, and specific agendas. We must also be thoughtful about the challenge of balancing what we measure and what we value. Quantitative measures may not reflect the qualitative aspects of valued outcomes. Thus, using a "mixed-methods" approach, which is less likely to only represent a better a score on a measure, brings us closer to impacting what we value.

Additional Resources

The CDC has a well-developed program development system and a wide range of associated resources: www.cdc.gov/eval/index.htm.

The National Association of State Mental Health Program Directors (NASMHPD) offers various supports for all levels of program stakeholders: www.NASMHPD.org.

The NASMHPD Research Institute, Inc. (NRI) is associated but independent and focuses on research. This includes collection and dissemination of data and support for mental health groups: http://www.nri-inc.org/.

The National Quality Forum (NQF; www.qualityforum.org) evaluates measurement instruments for use in healthcare. Summary reports for specific areas, e.g., behavioral health, can be found here: http://www.qualityforum.org/News_And_Resources/Endorsement_Summaries/Endorsement_Summaries.aspx.

The Centers for Medicare and Medicaid Services (CMS) provides a compendium of quality measures for both general and mental health care: https://www.cms.gov/Medicare/Quality-Initiatives-Patient-Assessment-Instruments/QualityMeasures.

References

Aby, M. A. (2020). Case study of implementing grant-funded integrated care in a community mental health center. *Journal of Behavioral Health Services & Research, 47*, 293–308. https://doi.org/10.1007/s11414-019-09671-7

Altschuld, J. W., & Watkins, R. (2014). A primer on needs assessment: More than 40 years of research and practice. *New Directions for Evaluation, 2014*(144), 5–18. https://doi.org/10.1002/ev.20099

Barnow, B. S. & Greenberg, D. H. (2019). Special issue editors' essay. *Evaluation Review, 43*(5), 231–265. https://doi.org/10.1177/0193841X19865076

Brousselle, A., & Champagne, F. (2011). Program theory evaluation: Logic analysis. *Evaluation and Program Planning, 34*(1), 69–78. https://doi.org/10.1016/j.evalprogplan.2010.04.001

Bond, G. R., Evans, L., Salyers, M. P., Williams, J., & Kim, H. W. (2000). Measurement of fidelity in psychiatric rehabilitation. *Mental Health Services Research, 2*, 75–87.

Cabassa, L. J., Gomes, A. P., & Lewis-Fernández, R. (2015). What would it take? Stakeholders' views and preferences for implementing a health care manager program in community mental health clinics under health care reform. *Medical Care Research and Review: MCRR, 72*(1) 71–95. https://doi.org/10.1177/1077558714563171

Coryn, C. L. S., Noakes, L. A., Westine, C. D., & Schröter, D. C. (2011). A systematic review of theory-driven evaluation practice from 1990 to 2009. *American Journal of Evaluation, 32*(2), 199–226. https://doi.org/10.1177/1098214010389321

Donabedian, A. (2005). Evaluating the quality of medical care. 1966. *The Milbank Quarterly, 83*(4), 691–729. (Original work published 1966). https://doi.org/10.1111/j.1468-0009.2005.00397.x

Fihn, S. D., Francis, J., Clancy, C., Nielson, C., Nelson, K., Rumsfeld, J., Cullen, T., Bates, J., & Graham, G. L. (2014). Insights from advanced analytics at the Veterans Health Administration. *Health Affairs, 33*(7), 1203–1211. doi: https://doi.org/10.1377/hlthaff.2014.0054

Fiscella, K., & Sanders, M.R. (2016). Racial and Ethnic Disparities in the Quality of Health Care. *Annual Review of Public Health, 37*(1), 375–394. https://doi.org/10.1146/annurev-publhealth-032315-021439

Fortuna, L. R., Tolou-Shams, M., Robles-Ramamurthy, B., & Porche, M. V. (2020). Inequity and the disproportionate impact of COVID-19 on communities of color in the United States: The need for a trauma-informed social justice response. *Psychological Trauma: Theory, Research, Practice, and Policy*. https://doi.org/10.1016/S2468-2667(20)30164-X

Ganju, V. (2006). Mental health quality and accountability: the role of evidence-based practices and performance measurement. *Administration and Policy in Mental Health, 33*(6), 659–665.

Gao, X., Shen, J., Wu, H., & Kreen, H. Y. (2019). Evaluating program effects: Conceptualizing and demonstrating a typology. *Evaluation and Program Planning, 72*, 88–96. https://doi.org/10.1016/j.evalprogplan.2018.10.008

Gertler, P. J., Martinez, S., Premand, P., Rawlings, L. B., & Vermeersch, C. M. (2016). *Impact evaluation in practice*. The World Bank.

Gill, S., Kuwahara, R., & Wilce, M. (2016). Through a culturally competent lens: Why the program evaluation standards matter,. *Health Promot Pract., 17*(1), 5–8. https://doi.org/10.1177/1524839915616364

Gowin, D., & Millman, J. (1981). Toward reform of program evaluation. *Educational Evaluation and Policy Analysis, 3(6),85–87.*

Hermann, R. C., Chan, J. A., Provost, S. E., & Chiu, W. T. (2006a). Statistical benchmarks for process measures of quality of care for mental and substance use disorders. *Psychiatric Services, 57*(10), 1461–1467.

Hermann, R. C., Chan, J. A., Zazzali, J. L., & Lerner, D. (2006b). Aligning measurement-based quality improvement with implementation of evidence-based practices. *Administration and Policy in Mental Health, 33*(6), 636–645.

Hermann, R. C., Mattke, S., Somekh, D., Silfverhielm, H., Goldner, E., Glover, G., et al. (2006c). Quality indicators for international benchmarking of mental health care. *International Journal of Quality in Health Care, 18 Suppl 1*, 31–38.

Hill, L. G., Maucione, K., & Hood, B. K. (2007). A focused approach to assessing program fidelity. *Prevention Science, 8*, 25–34.

Jacobson, M. R., & Azzam, T. (2018). The effects of stakeholder involvement on perceptions of an evaluation's credibility. *Evaluation and Program Planning, 68*, 64–73. doi: https://doi.org/10.1016/j.evalprogplan.2018.02.006

Kilbourne, A. M., Beck, K., Spaeth-Rublee, B., Ramanuj, P., O'Brien, R. W., Tomoyasu, N., & Pincus, H. A. (2018). Measuring and improving the quality of mental health care: A global perspective. *World Psychiatry, 17*(1), 30–38. doi: https://doi.org/10.1002/wps.20482

Luchins, D. (2012). Two Approaches to Improving Mental Health Care: Positivist/quantitative versus skill-based/qualitative. *Perspectives in Biology and Medicine, 55*, 409–34.

McGrew, J. H., Bond, G. R., Dietzen, L., & Salyers, M. (1994). Measuring the fidelity of implementation of a mental health program model. *Journal of Consulting and Clinical Psychology, 62*, 670–678.

McHugo, G. J., Drake, R. E., Teague, G. B., & Xie, H. (1999). Fidelity to assertive community treatment and client outcomes in the New Hampshire dual disorders study. *Psychiatric Services, 50*, 818–824.

Moore, Q., Perez-Johnson, I., & Santillano, R. (2019). Decomposing differences in impacts on survey- and administrative-measured earnings from a job training voucher experiment. *Evaluation Review, 42*(5–6), 515–549. https://doi.org/10.1177/0193841X18799434

National Institute of Mental Health. (2011). 2012 *Budget report.* Retrieved from http://www.nimh.nih.gov/about/budget/cj2012.pdf.

Nesbit, B., Hertz, M., Thigpen, S., Castellanos, T., Brown, M., Porter, J., & Williams, A. (2018). Innovative methods for designing actionable program evaluation. *J Public Health Manag Practi., 24*(Suppl 1), S12–S22. https://doi.org/10.1097/PHH.0000000000000706

Pincus, H. A., Scholle, S. H., Spaeth-Rublee, B., Hepner, K. A., & Brown, J. (2016). Quality measures for mental health and substance use: Gaps, opportunities, and challenges. *Health Affairs, 35*(6), 1000–1008. https://doi.org/10.1377/hlthaff.2016.0027

Rabarison, K. M., Marcelin, R. A., Bish, C. L., Chandra, G., Massoudi, M. S., & Greenlund, K. J. (2018). Cost analysis of Prevention Research Centers: Instrument development. *J Public Health Manag Pract., 24*(5), 440–443. doi: https://doi.org/10.1097/PPH.0000000000000706

Roberts, M. & Steele, R. (2005). Program evaluation approaches to service delivery in child and family mental health. In Handbook of Mental Health Services for Children, Adolescents, and Families. EBSCO Publishing NetLibrary; printed on 2/14/2011 3:32 pm via University of Alabama-Birmingham eISBN:9780306485602.

Rollins, A. L., Kukla, M., Salyers, M. P., McGrew, J. H., Flanagan, M. E., Leslie, D. L., Hunt, M. G., & McGuire, A. B. (2017). Comparing the costs and acceptability of three fidelity assessment methods for Assertive Community Treatment. *Adm Policy Ment Health, 44,* 810–816. https://doi.org/10.1007/s10488-016-0785-7

Rushing, S. & Lefkovitz, P. (2008). Learning from top performers. *Behav Healthc, 28(2)*, 28, 30–31.

Schalock, R. L. (1995). Outcome-based evaluation. New York: Plenum Press.

Schalock, R. L. (2001). Outcome-based evaluation, second edition. EBSCO Publishing-NetLibrary; printed on 2/28/2011 3:12pm via University of Alabama-Birmingham eISBN:9780306464584.

Schalock, R. L., Lee, T., Verdugo, M., Swart, K., Claes, C., van Loon, J., & Lee, C. S. (2014). An evidence-based approach to organization evaluation and change in human service organizations evaluation and program planning. *Evaluation and program planning, 45*, 110–118.

Schalock, R. L., Verdugo, M. A., and Gomez, L. E. (2011). Evidence-based practices in the field of intellectual and developmental disabilities: An international consensus approach. *Evaluation and Program Planning*, 34(3), 273–82. https://doi.org/10.1016/j.evalprogplan.2010.10.004

Schmidt, E. M., Krahn, D. D., McGuire, M. H., Tavakoli, S., Wright, D. M., Solares, H. E., Lemke, S., & Trafton, J. (2017). Using organizational and clinical performance data to increase the value of mental health care. *Psychological Services, 14*(1), 13–22. doi: https://doi.org/10.1037/ser0000098

Schoenwald, S. K., Garland, A. F., Chapman, J. E., Frazier, S. L., Sheidow, A. J., & Southam-Gerow, M. A. (2011). Toward the effective and efficient measurement of implementation fidelity. *Administration and Policy in Mental Health, 38*(1), 32–43. doi: https://doi.org/10.1007/s10488-010-0321-0

Shearer, J., McCrone, P., & Romeo, R. (2016). Economic evaluation of mental health interventions: A guide to costing approaches. *PharmacoEconomics, 34,* 651–664. https://doi.org/10.1007/s40273-016-0390-3

Smith, J. D. & Hasan, M. (2020). Quantitative approaches for the evaluation of implementation research studies. *Psychiatry Res., 283*, 112521. https://doi.org/10.1016/j.psychres.2019.112521

Teague, G. B., Mueser, K. T., & Rapp, C.A. (2012). Advances in fidelity measurement for mental health services research: four measures. *Psychiatr Serv., 63*(8), 765–771.

Treasury Board of Canada, Secretariat. (1998). *Program Evaluation Methods.* Public Affairs Branch.

U.S. Department of Health and Human Services, Administration on Children, Youth, and Families. (2016). *Qualitative research methods in program evaluation: Considerations for federal staff.* https://www.acf.hhs.gov/sites/default/files/acyf/qualitative_research_methods_in_program_evaluation.pdf

U.S. Department of Health and Human Services Centers for Disease Control and Prevention. (1999). *Morbidity and Mortality Weekly Report: Framework for program evaluation in public health.* https://www.cdc.gov/eval/framework/index.htm

U.S. Department of Health and Human Services Centers for Disease Control and Prevention. Office of the Director, Office of Strategy and Innovation. (2011). *Introduction to program evaluation for public health programs: A self-study guide.* https://www.cdc.gov/eval/guide/index.htm

Weisner, T. S. & Hay, M. C. (2015). Practice to research: Integrating evidence-based practices with culture and context. *Transcultural Psychiatry, 52*(2), 222–243. doi: https://doi.org/10.1177/1363461514557066

Wolff, N., Helminiak, T., Morse, G., Calsyn, R., Klinkenberg, D., & Trusty, M. (1997). Cost-effectiveness evaluation of three approaches to case management for homeless mentally ill clients. *American Journal of Psychiatry, 154(3)*, 341–348.

Youker, B. W., Ford, K., & Bayer, N. (2017). Dismissing the goals: A comparison of four goal-dismissive goal-free evaluations. *Evaluations and Program Planning, 64*, 1–6. https://doi.org/10.1016/j.evalprogplan.2017.05.007

Creating Value: Resource and Quality Management

Wesley E. Sowers and Joe Parks

Introduction

In previous chapters of this book, we have considered the evolution of behavioral health services over time, influenced by both ethical/philosophical and economic factors. On the one hand, we agree that service development should be driven by quality concerns and outcomes. More recently, the choices of the people using services has also become an important source of influence. On the other hand, we have had to recognize that there is expense associated with the provision of quality services and that our resources are not unlimited. Over the last three or four decades, the conflict between these opposing concerns has been intensifying, and it would appear that this tug of war could continue indefinitely. As the costs of providing care rise and economic conditions deteriorate, these issues become even more prominent. Psychiatrists and other behavioral health practitioners, working primarily in publicly funded programs, find themselves in the middle of these struggles and thus are obliged to think about how they can use available resources wisely and fairly while maintaining an acceptable standard of care. It is only through these endeavors that we can efficiently use resources to provide the needed care to the greatest number of people (Frank and McGuire 2005; Pincus et al. 2007).

In this chapter, we will consider the tension between service provision and resource use and then examine various approaches to guide service intensity decision-making or put more simply how we decide who gets what. We will then consider the elements of rational service-resource management, the goal of which is to maintain a reasonable balance between the two. We will refer to this balance as "value." After considering the nature of value and how it has evolved, the chapter will discuss medical necessity criteria and, specifically, the Level of Care Utilization System (LOCUS) and its Child and Adolescent counterpart (CALOCUS). These instruments were developed by the AACP to guide and create consistency in service intensity decision-making and to help establish a rational balance between quality care and the efficient use of resources, thereby helping clinicians and payers to effectively maximize value (AACP 1996).

The Scope and Evolution of Resource Management

Active decision-making about resource management occurs at all levels of health care including patients, individual providers, healthcare organi-

W. E. Sowers (✉)
Western Psychiatric Hospital, University of Pittsburgh Medical Center, Pittsburgh, PA, USA

J. Parks
Missouri Institute for Mental Health, University of Missouri St Louis, St. Louis, MO, USA
e-mail: JoeP@thenationalcouncil.org

W. E. Sowers et al. (eds.), *Textbook of Community Psychiatry*,
https://doi.org/10.1007/978-3-031-10239-4_53

zations, and payers both contracted and governmental. It is fairly common for each of the different levels to disagree with the resource management choices of the others. Resource management can be conceptualized as occurring in two broad categories, resource allocation and resource optimization. Resource allocation activities are commonly referred to as coverage determination, utilization management, and medical necessity by payers and referred to as treatment planning and scheduling by healthcare providers. Resource optimization activities which seek to reduce the cost and improve the quality of the outcomes of the allocated resources are commonly referred to as care coordination and care management by both payers and providers. The individual resource allocation decisions at every level are biased by the particular incentives and constraints of the decision-maker at that level. The larger scope of resource allocation decisions across all stakeholders will be considered first.

Patients make resource allocation decisions when they decide what level of health insurance coverage they will purchase or what level of healthcare services they will buy directly out of their own budget. For public sector patients, they make a resource allocation decision when they decide how much time and administrative burden they will undergo to establish and maintain coverage. They allocate their time and limited income for transportation costs when they decide which providers to make and keep appointments with. It is common for patients to decide that they are not willing to allocate the amount of time and effort required to adhere to treatment recommendations made by their psychiatrists.

Individual psychiatrists make resource allocation decisions when they decide how many hours of work they will do and what types of patients they will see. They make resource allocation decisions when they decide how frequently they will see individual patients and how much time they will schedule for each appointment. Since there are a fixed number of psychiatrists, if they were to see patients more frequently and for longer appointments, it would mean that some other needy people would not be seen by a psychiatrist at all.

Community mental health centers and other healthcare organizations routinely develop an individualized treatment plan for all patients, which could also be referred to as a "individualized utilization management plan." Individualized treatment plans stipulate specific types and amounts of services and have a formal approval process. Community mental health centers make large-scale resource allocation decisions when they decide how much and what kind of staff they hire. This has ramifications for their budget as much as decisions regarding what programs to include or not include in their service array. These large-scale decisions have indirect, but important, influence on the service types and intensities included on each individualized treatment plan, which are commonly determined to a large extent by the services that are feasible, convenient, and profitable for that healthcare organization to provide. In other words, what services are paid for and the way they are paid for determine what is provided at least as much as the specific needs of a particular patient in most cases.

Managed care companies and other insurers make large-scale utilization management decisions by how much of their capitation payment budget to allocate to behavioral health as opposed to other healthcare services such as pharmacy or general medical care. That budgeting decision also puts indirect, but significant, influence on the type of medical necessity criteria used for prior authorizations and subsequently on the type and quantity of services approved for an individual patient.

Prior to the implementation of Medicaid and Medicare in the late 1960s, most of the payments for services to providers of behavioral health treatments were mostly accomplished through global funding. State hospitals or community mental health centers received a global annual allocation and budgeted accordingly. Their executive team had a very wide discretion on allocation decisions. The implementation of fee-for-service payment methodology under Medicare and Medicaid, followed by rapidly spreading commercial coverage for behavioral health conditions, leads to the development of a broader service array, but the costs associated with providing these services expanded along with them (Sharfstein et al. 1993; Boyle and Callahan 1993). These conditions lead to a rapid rise in the cost of providing care that eventually sent funding entities (local and regional governments and employers) scrambling for ways to contain costs. The development of managed care organizations was a solution that did cause a needed realignment of what constituted necessary care and eliminated some of the excesses of past practices, but in many cases, cost reduction took precedence over quality of care. Since that time, the healthcare industry has been struggling to find a path to the right balance of cost and quality or "value."

Defining Value

Value is most simply the product of quality divided by cost. How and what we measure for cost and quality is less straightforward and introduces levels of complexity into discussions of what outcomes are desired. Imagine that someone is admitted to the hospital due to suicidal ideation. Most would agree that a quality outcome would be transitioning that individual back to the community without further thoughts of self-harm. Hospital care is expensive, so if this could be accomplished within 3 days, it would be less expensive than it would be if it took 7 days. If outcomes were the same, then we would consider the former a better value. Likewise, we might be able to accomplish this outcome in a residential treatment facility rather than a hospital, which would be less costly and also a better value. Determinations of value become more complex when there is disagreement about what the best outcomes are. Various stakeholders in the behavioral health system (service users, providers, payers, purchasers, suppliers) will often have different ideas about what outcomes are most important and what resources should be expended to achieve them. These differences are due in large part to differences in "personal values," those ideas, beliefs, customs, affiliations, desires, or materials that define individuals or communities. Further complexities are encountered when indirect social costs and outcomes are considered (Fage et al. 2020). These differences and complexities must be addressed to achieve a common vision for value enhancement in large systems of care. For clinical interactions in community psychiatry, decisions regarding the use of resources and desired outcomes can be more concrete. These will be the primary focus of this chapter.

Several issues will be relevant to the consideration of value enhancement in community psychiatry. The efficient operation of systems of care and positive outcomes are undermined by fragmentation of services and the lack of continuity of care that results (Sowers 2020a). Administrative expense has a significant impact on the value derived from provided services as well. It is estimated that 25–30% of healthcare expenditures are spent on administrative activities (Michael 2020). A significant portion of these expenditures are related to the profit-driven nature of the US health system. The extraction of profit by healthcare companies is only a small part of the cost that this arrangement generates. Other expenses are generated by overtreatment (i.e., maximizing billable actions) and undertreatment (i.e., denial of payment for needed care), but administrative costs, in the form of excessive regulations, complex billing requirements, micromanagement by payers, and other insurance-related activities, account for about half of these expenses (Jiwani et al. 2014; Berwick and Hackbarth 2012).

The Evolution of Value Management

In the past, decisions regarding the location and intensity of treatment were left almost exclusively to the physician. People with severe mental illnesses were treated in state hospitals when they were considered to be very ill or in the community with limited professional support when they were considered to be fairly stable. The criteria used to make these decisions were not well defined or consistent, but the doctors' orders were rarely questioned. With a growing sensitivity to civil rights and social justice following World War II, the restrictiveness and frequently poor conditions of state institutions, along with the high cost of maintaining them, resulted in the release of many more people with severe mental illness to the community. The advent of psychotropic medications is also seen as a factor facilitating this shift. Both the community and the patients were ill prepared for this change, however, and as a result, needs of many people were left unmet. Public systems began to develop a broader service array, but little thought was given to the costs associated with providing these services by the practitioners who prescribed them (Sharfstein et al. 1993; Boyle and Callahan 1993).

There were several factors that contributed to this lack of awareness. Psychiatric residency training programs rarely made reference to cost issues, and most were situated in resource-rich (university) environments. Physicians became accustomed to thinking about benefits relative to risks, but not costs. A good bit of expense can be generated in attempting to maximize benefits when there is limited risk, with very little added benefit. With no limits on what insurers would pay for, "doing more" was hard to resist and value declined as a result. Systems (hospitals) did not discourage this perspective, because they too would be paid more if more were done! Professional liability was another part of the equation, fanning the flame of "over" treatment or what has been called defensive medicine (Mello et al. 2010). Even in systems that were publicly funded, providers were generally paid for the services that *they* decided were necessary with very little scrutiny of whether they actually were needed or effective. More intensive care was often equated with "better" care, although there was no substantial evidence to support this belief, and it often conflicted with the desires of its recipients (Frank et al. 1996; Brosowski 1991; Lesage and Tansella 1993). These factors contributed to the soaring costs of medical care in the latter part of the twentieth century and, to a large extent, still do today.

During this same period, technological advances and the growth of expensive pharmacological interventions brought health care to a point where it was becoming prohibitively expensive. Entities paying for health care began to scrutinize the care being prescribed and to consider ways increase accountability and to control costs. Companies specializing in managing resources quickly sprung up and emerged as the predominant solution to the cost problem. These companies would contract with paying entities to regulate the resources being used for health services. Although they are commonly referred to as managed *care* companies, their real function is to manage *resources* (Roman and Morrison 1997). Their profit and performance, in contrast to providers, are derived from limiting *payment* for services as much as possible. Although they did not make clinical decisions directly, their decisions regarding payment had a direct impact on clinical care. Providers could not afford to provide services that were not paid for (Backlar 1996).

Among the methods commonly used by managed healthcare plans to control costs and thus remain financially profitable are the following:

- Contracting exclusively with providers willing to offer their services at discounted rates.
- Monitoring the use of basic and ancillary services furnished by network providers and using incentives to reward below-average use and disincentives to discourage excess (above-average) use.
- Discouraging the excessive use of tests and prescription medications.
- Requiring plan participants to obtain a referral (prior authorization) from their primary care physician to gain access to specialty services reimbursable under the plan.
- Requiring providers to assume part of the financial risk of cost overruns for services they control, directly or indirectly.
- The development of medical necessity criteria and the micromanagement of health conditions. These techniques are generally referred to as utilization review.

Medical Necessity Criteria

To be successful in containing costs, it was important for resource management companies to determine when and what services were absolutely necessary to adequately treat a defined condition and which were not. Criteria sets were created, primarily through "expert" consensus, to indicate the conditions for which payment would be provided and under what circumstances. The development of these medical necessity criteria in behavioral health, as in physical health, arose from the desire to control costs, and to do so, at least on the surface, in a way that was uniform, responsible, and driven by outcomes.

The term "medical necessity" originated in the physical health treatment environment and the appropriateness of its application to behavioral health has often been questioned. For physical health problems, a specific illness or injury may require a specific type of treatment regimen to reduce or eliminate their impact, and these interventions can be fairly easily quantified and tested for efficacy. This evidence-based approach to designating the need for specific interventions is fairly distinct from what is available in behavioral health. In behavioral health, rather than defining specific interventions or procedures for a condition, medical necessity criteria try to address how to use a spectrum of interventions for a given syndrome and with what intensity they should be applied. The array of services that may be designated for a particular diagnosis is still largely intuitive and based upon an individual's constellation of needs. Even though attempts are made to develop a broader database of outcomes associated with particular types of treatment approaches for given conditions, the complexity of developing a strong evidentiary base is orders of magnitude greater for behavioral health services because of the multiple factors that influence these outcomes (Gregoire 2000).

Despite these limitations, in behavioral health, attempts have been made to codify which clients fit best into existing treatment programs or program "types" as a way to insure that costly services are not used when they are not necessary. The concept of "level of care" envisioned a gradient of service intensities from community-based outpatient services at the low end to highly structured hospital-based care at the high end. Traditional formulations of medical necessity criteria generally follow a format in which a particular type of treatment program is described, often along with some minimum requirements for staffing and operations. This is usually followed by a diagnostically driven criteria set which defines particular characteristics of persons who are appropriate for admission to the described program, another set describing how one remains eligible for continuing treatment in the program, and a third set describing how a client qualifies for "discharge" from the program.

These attempts at injecting some objectivity into the level of care or service intensity decision-making processes are simplistic, but they are not simple. Providers and service users find them difficult to access and understand. In many cases they are seen as rigid, unclear, and not connected to clinical activities such as assessment and treatment planning. In addition, they are inconsistent with person-centered (individualized) services. As a result, this approach is increasingly seen as obsolete in the context of our evolving service environment (Goldman et al. 1997; Shoyinka 2020; Witt v United Behavioral Health 2019; Sowers 2020b).

Utilization Management

Utilization management is "a set of techniques used by or on behalf of purchasers of healthcare benefits to manage healthcare costs by influencing patient care decision-making through case-by-case assessments of the appropriateness of care prior to its provision" (Institute of Medicine 1989). In other words, it is the evaluation of the "appropriateness" or medical necessity of healthcare services, procedures, and facilities, according to criteria adopted or developed by the paying entity. The use of proprietary medical necessity criteria instead of medical guidelines developed by professional societies that are publicly available is most common. Two commonly used UM criteria frameworks are the McKesson InterQual criteria (Mitus 2008) and MCG (previously known as the Milliman Care Guidelines) (Sebastian 2014). Utilization management processes scrutinize decisions regarding program admissions, treatment planning, discharge planning, and continuing stay eligibility with concurrent clinical reviews and peer reviews. UM may be done prospectively, retrospectively, or concurrently. For cases in which the patient or provider disagrees with the payer's denial of services, an appeals process must be in place and can be initiated by either. Utilization review separates cost decisions from direct care decisions setting up an adversarial relationship between payer and provider. It also creates enormous expense on both the payer and provider sides related to its staffing and administration, thus reducing the value of services by diverting these funds from quality-enhancing activities.

Instruments for Management of Services and Resources

The emergence of "managed care" companies and of medical necessity criteria in behavioral health had some impact on costs, and particularly on the practice of physicians, who were now compelled to justify their decisions regarding the care they prescribed (Frank and Garfield 2007; Rabinowitz et al. 1995). This arrangement of having an outside entity making decisions about payment was not popular however, and clinicians frequently perceived their decisions as mercenary and clinically insensitive (Jellineck and Nurcombe 1993). One of the difficulties of this system was that there were a multitude of managed care companies, each developing its own distinct set of medical necessity criteria, which were often cumbersome or difficult to access. This made it very difficult to become familiar with any one of them. The use of multiple criteria sets creates inconsistency in clinical thinking and suggests a lack of integrity and justice in clinical care. Case-by-case scrutiny of clinical decisions by a third party was also a costly process, using resources that would otherwise be available for services (Cutler 2018; Jellineck and Nurcombe 1993; Sabin 1994).

The challenge then became one of developing systems of management that would enhance the wise use of resources and eliminate the use of unnecessary services while limiting aspects of third-party resource management that were costly and disruptive to quality care. To meet this challenge, standardized methods for assessing service needs and an array of services for meeting them, which were broadly agreed upon by all stakeholders, were needed (Glazer and Gray 1996; Uehara et al. 1996). There are several advantages that come from creating a common language and a common methodology for thinking about clinical needs and resource utilization (AACP 1996; Nudelman and Andrews 1962). It allows for the development of consistent and rational clinical thinking and provides integrity to service provision (Uehara et al. 2003). Communication is facilitated, and elements of treatment planning are more easily identified and implemented. Finally, when the interests of both cost-efficiency and quality care are considered in the development of standards, the need for oppressive scrutiny of all clinical decisions is eliminated along with the associated expenses (Gibbons et al. 2008). Occasional audits are then sufficient to assure that standards are being applied appropriately (Sowers 2020b).

Clinical rating scales had been in use for some time, developed by clinical researchers to quantify the severity of symptoms or disability in their subjects (Overall and Gorham 1962; McLellan et al. 1980). While these instruments could be used to provide some measure of a person's needs, they were often narrowly focused on particular diagnostic categories or populations. For example, the Multnomah Community Ability Scale (Barker et al. 1994) provided ratings of function in several categories for persons with severe mental illness and was useful in developing treatment plans, but like other similar instruments, it provided no guidance for prescribing services to adequately meet these identified needs (Overall and Gorham 1962; McLellan et al. 1980; Derogatics 1994).

Responding to the need for an instrument linking needs to services, professional organizations, service researchers, and resource management companies began to make attempts to do so. The Level of Need-Care Assessment Method (LONCA) used needs profiles along with demographic and epidemiologic information to calculate costs and resource use within systems of care, but its complexity limited its usefulness for clinical decision-making (Srebnik et al. 1998; Uehara et al. 1996). The American Society of Addiction Medicine developed the ASAM Patient Placement Criteria for persons with substance use disorders in the 1990s, and its use is widely established today. It uses six dimensions to assess clinical status and to create profiles that are employed to determine service needs. In its most recent iteration, nine levels of service intensity are defined to meet identified needs. It also attempts incorporate mental and physical health issues into the assessment process, broadening the scope of its utility (ASAM 2013).

Several other instruments were developed following this basic design; dimensional assessment leading to a needs profile used to determine eligibility for admission, continuing care, and discharge for defined levels of care (Glazer and Gray 1996). Some of these developed rating scales for the assessment dimensions that provided a quantitative method for determining eligibility for defined levels of service intensity, making the matching process somewhat simpler (Kazarian and Joseph 1994; Roy-Byrne et al. 1998). The assessment dimensions used by these instruments varied in number and content, but elements such as safety, social and role function, symptom severity, and environment were common to most. A continuum of care with levels of service intensity was generally described, rather than the more specific program-related descriptions used in previous iterations of medical necessity criteria. Despite these advances, no single approach emerged that was comprehensive, practical, accessible, integrative, reliable, and broadly accepted (Goldman et al. 1997; Sowers et al. 2003).

The foregoing account of evolving practices to manage resources and services is brief and simplified but provides a context for the remainder of this chapter which will consider the development of the Level of Care Utilization System (LOCUS) and the Child and Adolescent Level of Care Utilization System (CALOCUS) by the AACP in the middle and late 1990s. The development of these instruments was intended to meet demands for a single standard that would provide practical and rational service-level recommendations (Sowers 1998). After more than two decades of use, they have emerged as the leading candidates to meet these demands (Witt v. UBH 2019). The management of value, both for the treatment of individuals and for assuring that resources are used in a manner that maximizes the health status of the population, is offered by these tools (Sowers 1998).

The Design of LOCUS and CALOCUS

The design of LOCUS began with a conception of rational care and service management. Many of the elements of this concept have been alluded to earlier:

- Maintains a balance between quality and cost concerns
- Informed by evidence or outcomes
- Operates with a full array or continuum of services
- Facilitates individualized, person-centered service planning
- Sets standards that are broadly acceptable and uniformly applied
- Used does not require significantly more time or expense
- Allows integrated value management by service providers

A few of these elements require some further elaboration. (1) Most systems will have some gaps in the continuum of services that they can offer, but to manage resources wisely, services that can meet identified needs efficiently are necessary. (2) Individualization means that rather than trying to fit a person's needs into predetermined service constructs, a unique plan is tailored to meet that individual's needs. (3) Value will be enhanced if administration of management systems does not add greatly to expenses (e.g., micromanagement) and drain valuable resources from service provision. Systems that allow providers to make decisions about both care and resource use, perhaps with some guidance and assumption of risk (i.e., value-based contracting), are most efficient because they eliminate redundancies and micromanagement, which are costly (Shoyinka 2020).

With this concept in mind, the AACP designers attempted to identify principles to guide the development of an instrument that would complement and facilitate this model of rational management. Ten principles were derived through a review of existing instruments and an amalgam of personal experiences. These principles are summarized below:

1. *Simple*: Instruments should be easily understood and used, requiring little additional time to apply or extensive training to use.
2. *Dimensional*: Instruments should provide an approach and structure for assessment that facilitates consistent clinical thinking and objective decision-making.
3. *Concise*: Dimensions should be clearly and succinctly defined, minimizing the number, complexity, and redundancy of factors considered.
4. *Integrative*: Dimensions should be relevant to both substance use disorders and other psychiatric disturbances and reflect their interaction with each other and physical health issues.
5. *Relevant*: Observable behavior related to symptom severity or functional impairment should be used in dimensional assessments rather than diagnostically based formulations.
6. *Quantifiable*: Numeric dimensional ratings enhance communicability and interactivity between variables and reflect the dynamic nature of clinical circumstances over time.
7. *Flexible*: Service continuum definitions should be flexible and adaptable to a variety of systems for broad application.
8. *Person centered*: Criteria selection defines individual needs that translate easily into service plans.
9. *Collaborative and empowering*: Allows consumers and their significant others to participate with providers in assessment and the development of service recommendations.
10. *Reliable and valid*: Level of care recommendations should be made reliably and should provide valid responses to the clinical and social circumstances.

Assessment Dimensions

Building on these principles, the AACP workgroup completed the design of the LOCUS. LOCUS uses six assessment dimensions. One of these dimensions is composed of two subscales, giving a total of seven scales which must be completed. Each of these scales is rated from 1 to 5 with specific criteria for each increment in rating. A composite score is obtained which ranges from 7 to 35 and weighs prominently in the determination of the level of care recommendations. The six evaluation dimensions are described briefly below:

I. *Risk of harm* – This rating reflects the degree to which a person is at risk for harming themselves or others. This risk may be due to suicidal or homicidal ideations or due to impaired judgment or impulse control resulting from intoxication or otherwise altered mental states. Criteria for this rating include factors such as suicidal or homicidal thoughts, intentions, ambivalence, history of attempts, impulsivity, and availability of means. Criteria are also included that indicate the degree to which one's ability to keep themselves safe is impaired.

II. *Functional status* – This rating measures a person's level of function relative to their baseline functional status. The criteria consider the ability to interact with others, to maintain hygiene and activities of daily living, and to fulfill role responsibilities and physical functions, such as sleep and weight fluctuations.

III. *Medical, addictive, and psychiatric co-morbidity* – This rating measures potential complications to the course of the presenting or most prominent condition due the co-existence of additional disorders. The criteria specify the degree to which the presence of additional disorders prolongs the course, increases the severity of, or impedes the ability to recover from the presenting condition. Withdrawal syndromes are considered as medical co-morbidity in this context.

IV. *Recovery environment* – This dimension contains two subscales: level of stress and level of support. Criteria for ratings on the stress scale include interpersonal conflicts or harassment, life transitions, interpersonal or material losses, environmental threats, and perceived pressures to perform. On the support scale, criteria delineate the degree to which support is available from family, friends, and professional sources and the likelihood that these supports will be able to participate in care.

V. *Treatment and recovery history* – This scale considers past experience and response to treatment and the durability of any recovery achieved. Criteria for this rating include the intensity of treatment experienced, the degree of success, and the extent and durations of recovery periods. Recent experiences and responses are weighed more heavily than more remote episodes.

VI. *Engagement and recovery status* – This rating measures a person's capacity for change, and criteria on this scale include the ability to recognize one's difficulties, current stage in the process of change, one's ability to engage with potential sources of aid, and the ability to accept responsibility for maintaining health.

The same assessment process may be used for initial placement recommendations, for determination of continuing care needs at a particular level, and to guide transitions between levels of care. The system is based on a dynamic understanding of the course of an illness, and so the assessment should be repeated as frequently as indicated clinically. There will be some cases where behaviors will change very rapidly (i.e., a person who presents with intoxication and who sobers up over the course of several hours) and other cases where circumstances are unchanged for extended periods of time (i.e., a person with schizophrenia who is stabilized with treatment and support). In general, ratings will need to be repeated most frequently during periods of greatest acuity and instability.

Levels of Care

Six "levels of care" are defined by these instruments. Each level of the service continuum is described in terms of four variables: (1) care environment, (2) clinical services, (3) support services, and (4) crisis resolution and prevention services. The LOCUS levels of care are better conceived of as levels of resource intensity. Each describes a flexible array of services which, taken individually, may span more than one level of care. For example, case management may be used in levels II, III, and IV, and supported housing is available in levels I through IV. Although there will be some overlap between adjacent levels of care with respect to the "menus" of services offered, and significant variability in the constellation of services required by a person at the particular level of care (reflecting the individualization of the service plan), *on average* service utilization becomes progressively more intensive (and expensive) as one moves from the lower to the higher levels of care. A description of each level of care follows:

1. *Recovery maintenance and health management* – This is the least intensive level of care and is designed for persons who have completed treatment at a more intensive level of care and who require minimal professional support to maintain their recovery. Clients at this level of care might vary in their needs from monthly to biannual visits to support their recovery. Services may be provided in a clinic or in the community, and facilitation of access to social support services may be provided if necessary.
2. *Low-intensity community-based services* – These are provided to persons who have active, but not significantly disabling disor-

ders. Clinical contacts will usually occur once every 1–4 weeks and may include a variety of treatment modalities. They will often be provided in a clinic-type setting but may be provided in various community settings as well. Extensive case management will generally not be required, but supported housing may be needed in some cases. Access to other types of supportive services can be facilitated.

3. *High-intensity community-based services* – These are intended for persons who require more intensive support but are able to live in the community. Services may be provided in a clinic or may be community based. Professional contacts will usually occur several times per week, often in extended sessions. Multi-modal treatments and easy access to clinical services at all hours should be available. Case management and supported housing will frequently be employed. Access to other supportive services will be facilitated as needed.
4. *Medically monitored non-residential services* – These are the most intensive of the outpatient options and are appropriate for persons who are capable of living in community settings but only with significant support and intensive treatment and case management. A structured treatment setting with clinical contacts for extended periods on most days is available with 24-h availability of clinical staff by phone. A variety of treatment modalities can be employed, and necessary supportive services can be arranged, including services such as day care for dependent children. Partial hospital and ACT programs could be part of a plan for care at this level.
5. *Medically monitored residential services* – Treatment and other supportive services are provided in the context of a residential setting, but the facility is not locked. Treatment is provided on site, and most contact with the community takes place in the context of some type of supervision. The setting provides adequate living space and ensures that all material needs are met. The facility is staffed 24 h daily, medications are monitored, and psychiatric contacts should occur about once per week. Structured social, educational, and rehabilitative activities may be employed as needed.
6. *Medically managed residential* – This is the most intensive level of care available and will be provided in the context of a secure setting capable of providing close monitoring and in extreme cases seclusion and/or restraint. Psychiatric, nursing, and medical services will be available on site or in close proximity 24 h daily with a capacity to respond quickly when needed. Physician contact will generally occur on a daily basis, and medication will be administered by the staff. Multi-modal treatment will be available. All material needs will be provided, as well as support of activities of daily living. Liaison with community-based resources and supports will be an essential element of provided services.

Although not a level of care per se, *basic services for prevention and health management* are also defined. These basic services are available to persons at all levels of care in the continuum as well as community members who have not required any ongoing forms of care recently. They include a variety of activities related to the prevention of illness or the minimization of distress during periods of crisis such as screening programs, outreach to high-risk populations, supporting victims of trauma, education, consultation with primary care providers, and environmental assessments. Although some of these services may be provided in a centralized location, most of them will occur in community locations.

Placement Decisions

Criteria are provided for each level of care indicating the most appropriate dimensional ratings for the particular level of care and the composite scores required for eligibility. In some cases, independent criteria (such as suicidal intentions) are indicated which supercede other require-

AACP LEVEL OF CARE DETERMINATION GRID

Dimensions \ Level of Care	Recovery Maintenance Health Management Level 1	Low Intensity Community Based Services Level 2	High Intensity Community Based Services Level 3	Medically Monitored Non-Residential Services Level 4	Medically Monitored Residential Services Level 5	Medically Managed Residential Services Level 6
I. Risk of Harm	2 or less	2 or less	3 or less	3 or less	④ 3	⑤ 4
II. Functional Status	2 or less	2 or less	3 or less	3 or less	④* 3	⑤ 4
III. Co-Morbidity	2 or less	2 or less	3 or less	3 or less	④* 3	⑤ 4
IV A. Recovery Environment "Level of Stress"	Sum of IV A + IV B is 4 or less	Sum of IV A + IV B is 5 or less	Sum of IV A + IV B is 5 or less	3 or 4	4 or more	4 or more
IV B. Recovery Environment "Level of Support"				3 or less	4 or more	4 or more
V. Treatment & Recovery History	2 or less	2 or less	3 or less	3 or 4	3 or more	4 or more
VI. Engagement & Recovery Status	2 or less	2 or less	3 or less	3 or 4	3 or more	4 or more
Composite Rating	10 to 13	14 to 16	17 to 19	20 to 22	23 to 27	28 or more

❍ indicates independent criteria - requires admission to this level regardless of composite score

* Unless sum of IV A and IV B equals 2

Fig. 1 AACP Level Of Care Determination Grid

ments and automatically recommend the described LOC. A simplified methodology for arriving at placement recommendation is provided in two forms. A placement grid summarizes placement criteria for each level of care and provides a very accurate estimate of the LOC recommendation (Fig. 1). A level of care decision tree is also provided and comprises the algorithm which determines the definitive LOCUS recommendation. A computer-assisted version has also been developed incorporating the decision tree algorithm to provide the placement recommendation instantly following completion of ratings in all six dimensions (Sowers et al. 1999). The selected criteria in each dimension can be collected at the end of the assessment to create a client profile of needs, which will guide the treatment planning process.

Child and Adolescent Level of Care Utilization System (CALOCUS)

The CALOCUS was developed in 1998 and follows the general format of the LOCUS for adults. It is modified to incorporate principles of child and adolescent development, a family and youth empowerment focus, and an emphasis on community-based systems of care (Sabin and Daniels 1999). Developmental disabilities are added to the co-morbidity scale, and the concept of resiliency is added to the treatment/recovery history scale. Two alternate subscales were developed for the engagement dimension, one for youth and the other for primary caretaker. Only one of these scales is selected, depending on the clinical circumstance (Sowers et al. 2003). Likewise, the levels of care in CALOCUS are modified reflecting wrap-around approaches and the broader community service collaboration required to meet children's needs. The similarities between the two instruments make transitions between child and adult service systems go more smoothly and help bridge the gap between the two treatment communities. They both encourage a consistent and intuitive clinical thinking process, which is useful regardless of what service system is involved. Both instruments use the same scoring system and the same algorithm to guide placement recommendations. Both have established their reliability when scored by a variety of clinicians and the validity of their recommendations.

Extended Applications

Although these instruments were developed primarily to guide service intensity placement decisions, the potential for their broader application is easily apparent. The dynamic nature of the composite and dimensional scores when plotted against time allows tracking of the course of illness and disability as well as service utilization. This information is valuable not only for the clinical care of individuals but, when taken in aggregate, is quite useful for system-wide service planning. It is possible to see what the demand for services at each level of care will be over time and where deficits in the system's capacity lie. This information can also be used to provide guidance in setting rates for value-driven reimbursement rates. Average costs for care at a particular level of care can be calculated for the reference population overall and for particular demographics within it. These can be translated into per diem or episode of care rates within each level (Sowers 2020b).

Another aspect of the design and use of these instruments that has become increasingly valuable is their ability to facilitate collaborative interactions between the service user and the service provider. Using language that is easily accessible even to those with limited reading skills, they allow the service user to meaningfully participate in the assessment process. The profile that results from the assessment provides a coherent, intuitive, and fully transparent rationale for the level of care recommendations (Sabin and Daniels 1999), which is very useful in facilitating interactions between payers and providers. These recommendations are based on a consistent application of an objective process that reduces the influence of clinician or system bias. This process is designed to reduce discriminatory assignment of services that may result from idiosyncratic or prejudicial decision-making. In addition, the dimensional and quantitative measures of need translate very easily into a prioritized listing of the issues that need to be addressed in the recovery plan to allow a service user to progress to lower levels of service need.

In providing a framework upon which a person-centered treatment plan may be built, a truly client-driven planning process can be realized without the need for prohibitive expenditure of clinicians' time and productivity. A fully integrated clinical record is obtained with the addition of progress documentation keyed to the issues in the treatment plan, creating a continuum from assessment to treatment plan to progress notation to transition planning. This will also result in continuity of documentation from one level of care to the next when used across the system of care (Sowers et al. 2003). More information on the integrated person-centered treatment plan in relation to LOCUS is presented in chapter "Person-Centered Recovery Planning as a Roadmap to Recovery".

The LOCUS/CALOCUS design is easily adaptable to computer applications and integration into electronic medical records. LOCUS/CALOCUS software provides placement recommendations immediately after scores are entered and additional software uses the scores to suggest issues that should be addressed in the treatment plan. It is then able to provide a series of menus with suggestions for strengths, objectives, actions, measures, and interventions that can be selected or customized by the service user and provider to construct a person-centered recovery plan in which everyone has an investment. The interactive and collaborative process encouraged by LOCUS/CALOCUS is further facilitated by their inclusion in the EMR. It provides a solid foundation for implementation of recovery-oriented systems of care.

Although these instruments have never been validated as outcome instruments, many users have suggested their usefulness for this purpose. Whether or not they are used formally or informally in this way, we have seen that LOCUS and CALOCUS are useful not only for their intended purpose of guiding service intensity assignments but also a variety of other clinical functions, most importantly in providing a framework for recovery-oriented services, rapidly becoming a priority for most systems of care.

Conclusion

Value has been elusive in health care, and the unique characteristics of emotional health care make its measurement more complex and fraught by the competing interests of various stakeholders. A large part of the expense associated with EHC in the United States is related to profit-driven systems, charged with controlling the costs of care, being separated from those who provide care. This generates a great amount of administrative expense and in many cases under-treatment of the complex disorders that are present in individuals seeking treatment. Creating a balance between the competing interests of cost and quality is responsible for creating value. The use of clinical tools such as LOCUS and CALOCUS will enable clinicians and the systems in which they work to maximize the value of the services they deliver.

References

American Association of Community Psychiatrists (1996), Level of Care Utilization System for psychiatric and addiction services. Pittsburgh. www.communitypsychiatrist.org

ASAM (2013) American Society of Addiction Medicine Criteria, Mee-Lee D, Shulman G, Fishman M, and Gastfriend D Editors, Change Companies publishers, Carson City, NV

Backlar P (1996) Managed mental health care: conflicts of interest in the provider/client relationship. Community Mental Health Journal 32(101-106).

Barker, S., Barron, N., McFarland, B.H. & Bigelow, D.A. (1994). A community ability scale for chronically mentally ill consumers, part I: reliability and validity. Community Ment Health J, 30, 363-8

Berwick DM, Hackbarth AD (2012): Eliminating waste in US health care. JAMA. 307(14), 1513-1516.

Boyle PJ, Callahan D, (1993) Minds and hearts: priorities in mental health services. Hasing Cent Rep 23 (supp): S3-23

Brosowski A (1991) Current mental health care environments: why managed care is necessary. Prof Psychol Res Pract 22:6-14

Cutler DM, Ana A, Colin B, Ernest B (2018). Introduction to Measuring and Modeling Health Care Costs. Measuring and Modeling Health Care Costs. White paper Available at: https://scholar.harvard.edu/files/cutler/files/c13093.pdf. Accessed July 2022. Chicago: The University of Chicago

Derogatics, LR (1994) Symptom Checklist-90-R: administration, scoring and procedural manual 3rd Ed. Minneapolis: National Computer Systems

Fage B, Sapra M, and Balfour M (2020): Defining and Measuring Value, Chapter 1 in Seeking Value: Balancing Cost and Quality in Psychiatric Care, Sowers and Ranz Editors, APPI publishers, Washington, DC, pp 3-22

Frank RG, Huskamp HA, McGuire TG, Newhouse JP (1996) Some economics of mental health "carve outs" Arch Gen Psychiatry 53: 933-7

Frank RG, McGuire TG (2005) Economics and Mental Health, Handbook of Health Economics, Culyer AJ and Newhouse JP Editors, Chpt 16 pp 893-954 Elsevier Press, Amsterdam

Frank RG, Garfield RL (2007) Managed behavioral health care carve outs: past performance and future prospects. Annual Rev. of Public Health 28: 303-320

Gibbons C, Dubois S, Ross S, Parker B, Morris K, et al (2008) Using the resident assessment instrument-mental health (RAI-MH) to determine levels of care for individuals with serious mental illness. J. of Beh. Health Services and Research 35:60-70

Glazer, W.M. & Gray, G.V. (1996). Psychometric properties of a decision-support tool for the era of managed care. J Ment Health Admin, 23:226-33.

Goldman RL, Wier CR, Turner CW, & Smith CB (1997) Validity of utilization management criteria for psychiatry. American Journal of Psychiatry 154, 349-355

Gregoire TK, (2000) Factors associated with level of care assignment in substance abuse treatment, Journal of Subst. Abuse Treatement 18:241-248

Institute of Medicine (1989), Controlling Costs and Changing Patient Care?: The Role of Utilization Management, Washington, DC, USA: National Academies Press, doi:https://doi.org/10.17226/1359, ISBN 978-0-309-04045-7 PMID 25144100.

Jellineck MS, Nurcombe B (1993) Two wrongs don't make a right: managed care, mental health and the marketplace. JAMA 270:1737-9

Jiwani A, Himmelstein D, Woolhandler S, and Kahn JG;. (2014) Billing and insurance-related administrative costs in United States' health care: synthesis of micro-costing evidence. BMC Health Serv Res. 13;14:556

Kazarian, S.S., & Joseph, L.W. (1994). A brief scale to help identify outpatients' level of need for community support services. Hosp Community Psychiatry, 45. 935-7.

Lesage AD, Tansella M (1993) Comprehensive community care without long stay beds in mental hospitals: trends from an Italian good practice area. Can J Psychiatry 38: 187-94

Mello M, Chandra A, Gawande AA, and Studdert DM (2010): National costs of the medical liability system. Health Aff (Millwood) 29(9): 1569–1577

Michael E: A third of US health care spending stems from administrative costs, Healio, January 6, 2020. Available at www.healio.com/news/primarycare/2020016/a--third-of-us-health-care-spending-stems-from-adminstrative-costs/, Accessed June 20, 2020

Mitus, A. J. (2008). The birth of InterQual: evidence-based decision support criteria that helped change healthcare. Prof Case Manag, 13(4), 228-233

McLellan AT, Luborsky L, Woody GA, O'Brien CP (1980) An improved diagnostic evaluation instrument for substance abuse patients: the Addiction Severity Index. Journal Nerv Ment Dis 168:26-33

Nudelman PM, Andrews LM (1962) The "value added" of not-for-profit health plans. N Eng J Med 334:1057-9

Overall KE. Gorham DR (1962) The Brief Psychiatric Rating Scale, Psychol Rep 10-799-812

Pincus HA, Page AE, Druss B et al, (2007) Can psychiatry cross the quality chasm? Improving the quality of health care for mental and substance use condition, Am J Psychiartyr 164:712-719

Rabinowitz, J., Slyuzberg, M., Salamon, I., Dupler, S., Kennedy, R.S. & Steinmuller, R. (1995). A method for understanding admission decision making in a psychiatric emergency room. Psychiatr Serv, 46. 1055-60

Roman, B. & Morrison, A. (1997) Utilization Management. Managed Mental Health Care in the Public Sector. A Survival Manual (K. Minkoff, D. Pollack, eds.), Chapter 13, 151-168, Harwood Academic Publishers, The Netherlands.

Roy-Byrne, P., Russo, J., Rabin, L., Fuller, K., Jaffe, C., Ries, R., Dagadakis, C. & Avery, D. (1998). A brief medical necessity scale for mental disorders: reliability, validity, and clinical utility. The Journal of Behavioral Health Services & Research, 25:4 November, pp 412-424

Sabin JE. (1994) A credo for ethical managed care in mental health practice. Hosp. Community Psychiatry 45: 859-69

Sabin JE, Daniels N. (1999); Public sector managed behavioral health care: meaningful consumer and family participation. Psychiatric Services 50: 883-885

Sebastian, Michael (2014). "Hearst's New Health Division is a Departure from Magazines and TV". AdAge. Retrieved April 14, 2018.

Sharfstein SS, Stoline AM, Goldman HH, (1993) Psychiatric care and health insurance reform. Am J Psychiatry 150:7-18

Shoyinka, S (2020) Innovative Financing: Incentivizing Value, Chapter 6 in Seeking Value: Balancing Cost and Quality in Psychiatric Care, Sowers and Ranz Editors, APPI publishers, Washington, DC pp 137-159

Sowers, W. (1998). Level-of-Care Determinations in Psychiatry. Harvard Rev Psychiatry, 5:286-90.

Sowers W, George C, Thompson K: (1999) Level of Care Utilization System for Psychiatric and Addiction

Services (LOCUS): a preliminary assessment of reliability and validity. Community Mental Health Journal 35:545–563

Sowers WE, Pumariega A, Huffine C, Fallon T, (2003) Best practices: level of care decisions making in behavioral health services, the LOCUS and the CALOCUS Psychiatr Serv 54:1461-1463, November

Sowers, W (2020a): The Current System: The Mess We're In, Chapter 3 in Seeking Value: Balancing Cost and Quality in Psychiatric Care, Sowers and Ranz Editors, APPI publishers, Washington, DC pp 55-77

Sowers, W (2020b): A Value Vision for Health Care Reform, Chapter 22 in Seeking Value: Balancing Cost and Quality in Psychiatric Care, Sowers and Ranz Editors, APPI publishers, Washington, DC, pp 563-590

Srebnik, D., Uehara, E. & Smukler, M. (1998). Field test of a tool for level-of-care decisions in community mental health systems. Psychiatric Services, 49:91-97

Uehara E.S., Smukler, M., & Newman, F.L. (1996). Linking resource use to consumer level of need: field test of teh level of need-care assessment (LONCA) method. J Consult Clin Psychol, 62. 695-709

Uehara ES, Srebnik D, Smukler M (2003): Statistical and consensus-based strategies for grouping consumers in mental health level-of-care schemes. Administration and Policy in Mental Health 30:287-306

Wit v. United Behavioral Health (2019), Available at: https://www.govinfo.gov/content/pkg/USCOURTS-cand-3_14-cv-02346/pdf/USCOURTS-cand-3_14-cv-02346-10.pdf, Accessed April 13, 2021

Telehealth and Technology

Flávio Casoy, Robert Cuyler, and Avrim B. Fishkind

While in the first two decades of the twenty-first century, the widespread use of telehealth in community psychiatry was considered a far-fetched goal, the COVID-19 global pandemic made telehealth the norm across most community mental health systems. Public and nonprofit agencies leapt over previously insurmountable barriers to rapidly implement telehealth services in an effort to decrease the spread of COVID-19 while continuing care for millions of individuals who depend on mental health services. Previous concerns that the clinical workforce in community mental health agencies would not be able to adapt to new technologies, that community mental health patients would receive worse care in the transition from in-person to virtual care, or perhaps most critically that funders would not reimburse telehealth on par with in-person visits were proven unfounded. However, the rapid transformation due to the COVID-19 crisis exposed significant equity issues in access to broadband data and video-equipped smartphones. Remarkable shifts in delivery of mental health services were documented in response to the COVID-19 pandemic. By the fall of 2020, 41% of all behavioral health visits were provided via telehealth, substantially greater than any other specialty. This same survey showed a 14% reduction in behavioral health visits (both in-person and telehealth) compared to a pre-pandemic period (Mehrotra et al. 2020). The decrease in the overall number of visits, coupled with widespread anecdotal reports of the decrease of no-show rates in agencies that adopted telehealth, suggests that while many mental health agencies excelled at adopting telehealth options for clients, others struggled with the transition, resulting in a likely initial decrease in overall access to services in the early part of the COVID-19 pandemic.

Telehealth has long been used in psychiatry. In 1956, Cecil Wittson of the Nebraska Psychiatric Institute described using one-way, closed-circuit television transmission to provide psychiatric training to students at the Medical College of Nebraska (Wittson et al. 1961). In 1957, the instructional network was expanded to Iowa and North and South Dakota with the ability to transmit audio in both directions. Simultaneous audio and video transmission debuted in 1959 with subsequent improvement in consultation, diagnostic assessment, and even group psychotherapy.

In 1968, the National Institute of Mental Health funded the first microwave relay resulting in direct consultation from Dartmouth's Department of Psychiatry to a patient in a rural affiliate hospital. Dwyer described a project in

F. Casoy (✉)
Brooklyn, NY, USA

R. Cuyler
Freespira, Inc., Houston, TX, USA
e-mail: cuyler@freespira.com

A. B. Fishkind
Empathic Soul Health, Houston, TX, USA

W. E. Sowers et al. (eds.), *Textbook of Community Psychiatry*,
https://doi.org/10.1007/978-3-031-10239-4_54

1973 in which psychiatrists from the Massachusetts General Hospital used closed-circuit television to see patients at the nearby airport (Dwyer 1973). This project was noteworthy for the first use of the term "telepsychiatry" and the use of remote-controlled cameras to pan, tilt, and zoom.

Since the mid-1970s, telehealth has gradually expanded in acceptance and become more embedded in community psychiatry networks as obstacles have slowly been overcome. These obstacles include licensure-based restrictions on practice across state lines, limited reimbursement by insurers, uneven availability of sufficient bandwidth in mental health settings, ease of the use of equipment and lack of available technical support, cost of videoconferencing equipment, and robust privacy protection. While historically telehealth was delivered between two different institutional settings, the great advances in personal video telecommunication equipment through personal laptops, tablets, and smartphones have greatly increased the feasibility of delivering services to patients across a broader spectrum of locations, including the home. These advances have also helped overcome clinicians' fears on whether it is possible to form close therapeutic relationships over a video screen (Bunnell et al. 2020). This chapter will describe considerations in the implementation of telehealth throughout community mental health systems.

Advantages of Telehealth

First, telehealth can make mental health provider agencies more adaptive and more flexible to the service needs of the community. For too many people in the United States, psychiatric care is accessed, if at all, through emergency services where the experience is often involuntary, overwhelming, lacking in community-based follow-up, and too often dehumanizing. Telehealth creates significant opportunities to allow for patients to access care in more comfortable settings with well-trained and high-quality professionals. With the current technology, telepsychiatry can be used to extend the reach of the community mental health system to a variety of settings. This is done by providing services to persons who have poor access to mental health services (e.g., patients living in frontier, rural, or medically underserved urban areas, as well as patients with physical disabilities impairing movement, patients below the poverty line, patients who are incarcerated, patients with inadequate or non-existent access to public transportation, and those who reside overseas). There is also widespread evidence that telehealth can be used to treat a wide range of psychiatric diagnoses in different patient populations (Banshur et al. 2016).

Second, modes of communication are forever evolving in new directions. Readily available videoconferencing systems can provide high-definition communication between patient and clinician and, at its best, can provide a face-to-face encounter that is as satisfying as an in-person visit. Additionally, patients and clinicians are increasingly using email, text messaging, as well as Internet chat rooms, forums, phone counseling, e-therapy, online workbooks, shared electronic health records, mobile-based applications, and others. Clinicians are also using social media platforms such as Facebook and Twitter, along with private websites, to disseminate information and educational materials about mental health. Their patients may interact with these materials in addition to therapeutic interactions. Adolescents and young adults increasingly expect to interact with their clinicians virtually, just as they interact with their friends, schools, universities, and workplaces.

Togetherall, also known as the Big White Wall, is an example of an extremely innovative approach to telehealth that was started in 2007 through the UK National Health Service and has expanded around the world and is beginning to make incursions into several parts of the United States. It is a web-based platform that allows users to interact with each other anonymously in multiple components, including an online peer-support network that is moderated 24/7 by licensed professionals; a mechanism for users to journal thoughts and feelings or take validated screening instruments; self-help guided courses with psychoeducation resources; a platform for users to engage with licensed clinicians by text, voice, or video for direct psychotherapy; and a mechanism for licensed professionals to identify users in any of the components who are at risk and engage them directly. Such innovative uses of telehealth allow individuals to more easily access care and avoid spiraling into a crisis (Hensel et al. 2019; Hyatt 2015).

Third, telehealth makes it possible for community psychiatrists to work in multiple settings in the same day, thereby allowing agencies to optimize their staff psychiatrists' time. For example, a psychiatrist may do a morning clinic at a jail-based program, 2 h of supervision and rounding with an ACT team, and 2 h of seeing emergency consults with a mobile crisis team. Agencies can organize services to be delivered by a pre-arranged schedule or requested on-demand.

Fourth, community mental health also involves treatment planning, education, and training components. Telehealth systems, with capacity for simultaneous multiple users, can bring together usually distant parts of a treatment team for planning or case conferences, for instance, to a counselor at school, a clinic psychiatrist, or family members at home. In this way, treatment can progress more quickly and efficiently, and problem issues such as splitting can be better avoided. Outreach can be done to sister agencies to provide psychoeducation and prevention-oriented interventions. Training and clinical supervision can be provided for psychiatric residents and other trainees.

Finally, telemedicine is capable of meeting the goals of the Institute of Healthcare Improvement's Triple Aim of advancing population health, improving experience of care, and reducing per capita cost (Whittington et al. 2015). Patients can now be seen via computer tablets pre-crisis, in crisis in emergency departments, and post-crisis to assist with linkage to outpatient care. This is a radical change in outpatient psychiatric care, enabling the psychiatrist to not only be in many actual places at one time but also to provide care to patients across the spectrum of clinical acuity.

Achieving the Triple Aim: Three Telehealth Examples

Between 2010 and 2020, an explosion in the use of telepsychiatry in areas other than one-to-one outpatient contact has occurred. The first example comes from using telepsychiatry in medical emergency departments, intensive care units, and medical/surgical hospital floors. Skilled mental health assessments are done in real time (improved access), with vastly lower costs to hospitals due to decreased lengths of stay, decreased personnel (sitters), legal, pharmacy, and transportation costs, and with higher customer satisfaction for both patients and practitioners (Torrey et al. 2012; Bullard et al. 2009).

One study showed that the average cost of assessing and boarding a psychiatric patient in the emergency department incurred total costs of $2264 dollars (Nicks and Manthey 2012). A study shortly thereafter showed availability of emergency telepsychiatry consults reduced length of stay from 26.3 h to 8.2 h, time from order of consult to seeing a psychiatrist was reduced from 14 to 2.6 h, and door to consult time reduced from 19.6 h to 5.9 h (Southard et al. 2014). The statewide South Carolina Telepsychiatry Program has shown that implementing telepsychiatry in emergency departments saved $3006.00 per admission while achieving a 200% increase in aftercare participation (Narasimhan et al. 2015).

Another example is Project ECHO (Extension for Community Health Outcomes), a teleconsultation, tele-education, and tele-mentoring model for enhancing primary care treatment of underserved patients (Zigmond 2013; Feiden 2014). ECHO is a guided practice model that reduces health disparities in underserved and remote areas of the state and nation and in multiple countries around the world. The ECHO model uses a hub-and-spoke knowledge-sharing approach where expert teams lead virtual clinics, amplifying the capacity for providers to deliver evidenced-based care to their rural and underserved communities (Zhou et al. 2016). The goal is to help develop the expertise of primary care practitioners to treat the mental health and substance use issues of their patients via mentoring. A good example is New Mexico's Integrated Addictions and Psychiatry (IAP) teleECHO program where primary care teams (the "spoke") joined a weekly, 2-h videoconference with a team including a psychiatrist, addiction specialist, licensed clinical social worker, and case manager (the "hub") (Komaromy et al. 2016). An introductory lecture on a pertinent topic was followed by a review of case presentations and recommendations. In 2016, IAP collected 299 surveys from their spoke participants. Amongst the outcomes, 93% reported "information would be useful in caring for their own patients," and 77% reported changes in patient's treatment planning. Project ECHO arrangements have been applied in a variety of clinical situations and locations, including in nursing home use of restraints and antipsychotics, treatment of opioid use disorder in mental health clinics, psychiatric treatment in rural communities, chronic pain programs, and others.

The third example is field-based, first-responder programs. At the time of the writing of this chapter, there are seven telehealth first-responder programs in the United States, with many others in the planning stage. The programs differ in a variety of ways, including in type of clinicians providing the service (master's-level clinicians, psychiatrists, psychologists), technology used (iPads, telemedicine software), and end user (police and/or EMS). Programs also vary by administrative structure (collaboration with mental health agency or first-responder run) and funding sources (government contracts, foundation grants, or Medicaid-reimbursed). The services are relatively new, and some are still in the pilot program stage. The most developed is Project CORE, a collaboration between the Sheriff's Department and the local mental health authority in Harris County, Texas – a region of 4.5 million residents (Harris County Sheriff's Office 2020). In a 1-year study in 2019, 20 sheriff's deputies completed 361 telehealth evaluations with a master's-level clinician backed by a psychiatrist if needed. Forty-two percent of patient interventions resulted in resolution on the scene, with 57% being transported to a medical or psychiatric emergency center. Only 1% of patients were transported to a criminal justice facility. In terms of access, 46% of consumers were first encounters with mental healthcare services. Cost savings from jail diversion were $780,000; in 89% of calls, telehealth providers were able to educate the consumer about available community resources previously unknown to them. Deputies reported an average 88% decrease in time spent on mental health encounters, leaving them more time to police their community (Blackburn et al. 2020).

Telemedicine Technology and Environment

In earlier days of telehealth, adapting to the technology was a daunting task that required personnel with technical expertise and expensive audiovisual conferencing equipment. Today, video communication between friends, families, at school, and at work is widespread for much of the population. Clinicians based in institutional settings or their homes often already have strong wireless networks and computers or tablets equipped with high-quality cameras and microphones. The Best Practices in Videoconferencing-Based Telemental Health issued by the American Psychiatric Association (APA) and American Telemedicine Association (ATA) states that clinicians and agencies should select videoconferencing applications that have appropriate verification, confidentiality, and security parameters necessary to ensure privacy and sufficient data bandwidth to ensure adequate video resolution and audio quality. Agencies should also have contingency plans in the event of a technology breakdown that disrupts a session or prevents an encounter (e.g., telephone access) (Shore et al. 2018).

A major problem remains for a significant portion of our patients who do not have adequate access to technologies or data plans that provide sufficient bandwidth. The essential challenge of access to broadband data has become less of an issue for patients who access telehealth services in clinics and other institutional settings; but many of the most vulnerable patients have limited or no access to phone minutes, data plans, or video technology, making universal implementation of home-based telehealth services impossible. This lack of access to technology at home emerged in the COVID-19 crisis as a critical social determinant of poorer health outcomes (Ramsetty and Adams 2020). A review of approximately 150,000 unique patients in a large urban academic medical setting documented inequities in telemedicine access to older, Asian, non-English-speaking, female, Black, Latinx, and low-income individuals during the early stages of the COVID-19 pandemic (Eberly et al. 2020).

This multidimensional problem includes inequities in the built environment in the form of (1) inadequate broadband infrastructure, (2) differences in social or cultural expectations on the use of technologies in different interactions, (3) inequities in digital literacy and education about changing technologies, (4) economic inequality leading to difficulties with keeping up with hardware upgrades and compatibility of software, and (5) implementation of different technologies in school, work, healthcare, and other settings that make it difficult for an individual to keep up with all the different requirements (Hensel et al. 2019). For this reason, increasing the proportion of adults with broadband Internet was included as a baseline objective in the Healthy People 2030 initiative (US Department of Health and Human Services Office of Disease Prevention and Health Promotion, 2020). There is no easy way for community mental health agencies to overcome this digital divide, particularly for the most vulnerable and difficult-to-engage patients. During the COVID-19 crisis, the Centers for Medicare and Medicaid Services (CMS), and many state governments relaxed regulations governing telehealth and allowed telephone visits in lieu of requiring video or in-person encounters (Centers for Medicare and Medicaid Services, 2020). While this regulatory relaxation significantly increased access and maintained continuity of services during the crisis, its efficacy and long-term impacts on patients remain unknown.

Consulting Room Environment

There has been much discussion about the environment of the telemedicine consulting room. In general, the room should be treated as any mental health consultation room. There should be no unauthorized access, and the room should be soundproof with no outside line of sight. APA and ATA Best Practices recommend that patient and provider cameras should be placed at eye level with the face clearly visible to the other person. The physical space should be adjusted to maximize lighting, comfort, and ambiance (Shore et al. 2018). Clinicians who work from home offices must ensure a professional-looking background and privacy throughout all clinical encounters. When patients are seen in non-institutional settings, the clinician must ask the patient about privacy and coach the patient to optimize the environment so the best possible mental status exam can be obtained.

Agencies must develop workflows that ensure that patients and clinicians are appropriately identified at every encounter (Shore et al. 2018). Any other participants in the session must also be identified and introduced. At every session, clinicians should verify the address of the patient's current location and confirm alternate means of contact, such as telephone, text message, or email. Clinicians should also verify contact information for other clinicians, family members, or friends who could be contacted in case of emergency. As during in-person sessions, clinicians must always clarify the frame and ensure that patients understand and agree with the purpose of the session and what will be discussed.

Legal and Ethical Considerations

Telepsychiatry raises multiple legal and ethical questions by nature of the different locations of the patient and community psychiatrist. Some issues are more concrete, such as licensure requirements for the physician. Other issues are more abstract, such as the nature of the doctor-patient relationship in a virtual encounter. Still others raise physician responsibility questions, such as the physician's actions in the case of interrupted patient care sessions.

Licensure and Credentialing

Licensure, DEA registration, and credentialing remain legal obstacles in telehealth. In general, physicians must be licensed and possess a DEA registration in the state where the patient resides. Hospitals and agencies credential clinicians to practice as members of a defined medical staff. This makes it very difficult for a single psychiatrist using a telehealth platform to treat patients across state lines or in multiple, unrelated hospitals. Federal systems such as the Veterans Administration, Department of Defense, Indian Health Services, and others may allow a physician who is licensed in one state to practice across state lines when carrying out their federal duties (Kels and Kels 2013). Growing interstate licensure compacts may ease this barrier in the coming years. Agencies should also work with their malpractice insurance carriers to ensure their clinicians are adequately covered if they are seeing patients spread over multiple sites and geographic regions.

E-security, Privacy, and Confidentiality

With regard to data security and privacy, the delivery of mental healthcare via telehealth is subject to the Health Insurance Portability and Accountability Act (HIPAA) and state laws. Specialized substance use programs may also be subjected to the increased privacy protections of 42 CFR Part 2. Agencies will commonly contract with a third-party vendor to provide a telehealth platform. This may be integrated with or separate from other electronic systems, such as an electronic health record. Agencies must enter into HIPAA business associate agreements (BAAs) to ensure compliance with applicable laws. Platforms that cannot enter into BAAs may not have the capacity to fully meet legal requirements. Table 1 lists some platforms that offer BAAs and healthcare-grade encryption (US Department of Health and Human Services 2021).

Table 1 Telehealth platforms that offer HIPAA business associate agreements

Skype for business/Microsoft Teams
Updox
VSee
Zoom for healthcare
Doxy.me
Google G Suite Hangouts Meet
Cisco Webex Meetings/Webex Teams
Amazon Chime
GoToMeeting
Spruce Healthcare Messenger

Confidentiality and privacy are important for both clinicians and patients. No recordings should be made either telephonically or via teleconferencing without written or otherwise documented consent. Safeguards must be taken to protect any communications including email, instant messaging, and texting.

Informed Consent

It is important to address security, privacy, and confidentiality through informed consent. Different states may have different laws or regulations on consent for telehealth services, and agency policy and practice must adhere to these. Consent may be obtained by the clinician conducting the telehealth session or by other clinicians onsite with the patient. Such forms generally resemble a typical psychiatric informed consent template, with additional items that relate to telehealth (see Table 2). Consent may be obtained at intake and does not necessarily need to be repeated prior to each telehealth visit.

Prescribing Medications

When prescribing medications, clinicians must be aware of and abide by all applicable federal and state laws governing prescriptions, including

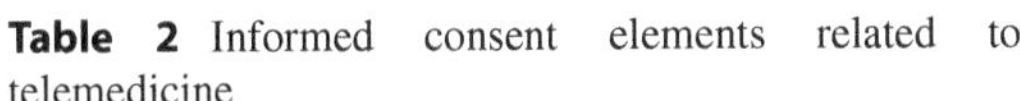

Table 2 Informed consent elements related to telemedicine

☐ My healthcare provider has explained to me how the videoconferencing technology may be used to conduct my visit. I understand that this consultation will not be the same as an in-person patient/healthcare provider visit due to the fact that I will not be in the same room as my healthcare provider
☐ I understand there are potential risks to this technology, including interruptions, unauthorized access, and technical difficulties. I understand that this video consultation is done over a secure communication system that is almost impossible for anyone else to access, but that since it is still a possibility, I accept the very rare risk that this could affect confidentiality. I understand that my healthcare provider(s) or myself can discontinue the telemedicine consult/visit if it is felt that the videoconferencing connections are not adequate for the situation.
☐ I understand that the specialist may need a healthcare person sitting in the room with me during the consultation to assist in the consultation and to help provide for continuity of care.
☐ I understand that my healthcare information may be shared with other individuals at my institution for scheduling and billing purposes. Others may also be present during the consultation other than my healthcare provider and the consulting healthcare provider in order to operate the video equipment. The abovementioned people will all maintain confidentiality of the information obtained. I further understand that I will be informed of their presence in the consultation and thus will have the right to request the following: (1) omit specific details of my medical history/physical examination that are personally sensitive to me, (2) ask non-medical personnel to leave the telemedicine examination room, and/or (3) terminate the consultation at any time.
☐ I have had the alternatives to a telemedicine consultation explained to me, and in choosing to participate in a telemedicine consultation, I understand that some parts of the exam involving physical tests may be conducted by individuals at my location at the direction of the consulting healthcare provider.
☐ I understand that none of the consultation will be recorded or photographed.

the Ryan Haight Online Pharmacy Consumer Protection Act of 2008. This Act, enacted prior to the widespread use of telehealth technologies, requires physicians working via telehealth platforms to see their patients in person at least once every 2 years in order to prescribe controlled substances (Drug Enforcement Administration 2020). One of the provisions of the 2018 SUPPORT for Patients and Communities Act requires the Drug Enforcement Administration (DEA) to activate a special registration for physicians and nurse practitioners to prescribe controlled substances via telemedicine without an initial in-person exam. As of this writing, the DEA has yet to put the special registration into effect (115th Congress 2018). In response to the opioid overdose epidemic, DHHS allows a DATA 2000 waivered clinician to prescribe buprenorphine via telehealth without an initial in-person encounter, provided the patient has a concurrent in-person evaluation by a non-waivered but DEA-registered physician, nurse practitioner, or physician assistant, and that the two clinicians maintain a collaborative relationship throughout the course of care of the patient receiving buprenorphine (Department of Health and Human Services 2018).

Emergencies

Care delivery via telemedicine introduces additional hurdles for management of emergencies. Clinicians must always have a plan of how to deal with clinical emergencies that occur during or in between encounters (Shore et al. 2018). Individual clinicians are responsible to know and be able to access crisis services in the patient's location, as well as understand local mental hygiene laws, including requirements for involuntary commitment and duty to warn laws. When emergencies occur when patients are in institutional settings, such as a clinic or hospital, the remote clinician must have a clear way to contact local staff. When patients are served in their own home or settings without other clinical staff, appropriate planning must be put in place to ensure timely intervention, such as utilizing emergency contacts or ensuring patients understand there is a lower threshold for calling 911.

In the case of technology failure (e.g., hardware malfunction, loss of Internet, loss of power), agencies should establish and communicate protocols for alternate communication, such as a telephone call or contacting a family member or peer.

Supervision and Quality Assurance

Agencies who implement telehealth services either develop their own programs by directly hiring staff who provide virtual services (either entirely or hybrid with in-person encounters) or contract with a third-party vendor to provide virtual services. Payment arrangements with contractors include on-demand pay-per-encounter, hourly rates for when a clinician is on shift, a flat monthly or weekly fee to cover services, or a combination of these (e.g., a flat fee for a certain number of encounters and a pay-per-encounter if there are extra encounters in a given period). Agencies must plan and implement methods for integrating remote clinicians into the "culture" of the organization and allow for remote clinicians to collaborate with each other and with onsite staff through formal staff meetings, patient rounds, live trainings, or some other mechanism. Agencies who contract with third-party vendors should include in business contracts the requirement that remote clinicians participate in collaborative meetings with patients' other clinicians.

Quality or professionalism problems in remote clinicians may not become immediately apparent to the agency due to reduced opportunities for informal contacts with other agency staff. Accordingly, agencies must also develop mechanisms to provide oversight or clinical supervision to their remote clinicians. This may include chart reviews, shared patients, virtually "sitting in" during new patient evaluations, obtaining patient and family feedback, or obtaining feedback from other staff who interact with the clinician.

Community mental health agencies should carefully weigh the pros and cons of contracting a third-party agency to provide telehealth services instead of directly hiring remote staff. Working through a contracted third party may significantly increase the difficulty of ensuring continuity of care, integration of the remote clinician into the rest of the clinical team, and clinical supervision. On the other hand, working with an established telehealth agency may allow faster onboarding of clinicians, access to clinicians already experienced in virtual care, broader range of specialty focus, and coverage for evenings, weekends, and absences. Agencies who chose to contract with third-party telehealth vendors should carefully assess prospective vendors to ensure compatibility of operational and clinical philosophies and practices.

Clinical Considerations

While most patients can benefit from care that is exclusively virtual, many will need to always be seen in person or have a mix of in-person and virtual visits. Clinicians must conduct a careful and deliberative assessment of each patient to determine what is the correct approach. Some treatments, such as administration of long-acting injectables, collection of specimens for laboratory testing, or physical exams, need to occur in person. Community mental health agencies also often treat a large segment of the population that historically have not been able to engage with traditional ambulatory care. These individuals, particularly those enrolled in assertive community treatment or forensic linkage programs, may need more in-person encounters to successfully engage them. As mentioned, individuals who do not have adequate access to technologies that allow telehealth encounters will need in-person services or the possibility of engaging in clinic-based telehealth services. Table 3 lists factors to consider when determining appropriateness of telehealth encounters (New York State Office of Mental Health 2020). Telehealth use in psychosocial or vocational rehabilitation programs is new, and further research is needed to understand how to best deliver it.

Other Modalities of E-Mental Health

With the explosive growth of bandwidth and smart devices, development and availability of behavioral health mobile applications have commensurately increased. One recent review estimated that more than 10,000 mental or behavioral health apps are available for download by consumers. The study authors find that this rapidly growing sector generally lacks a robust evidence

Table 3 Factors to consider when determining appropriateness of telehealth encounters

Clinical factors and personal preference
Cognitive capacity, especially as it relates to the ability to engage in remote care and to navigate remote platforms
Requirement for treatments or interventions that can only be performed in person (such as administration of long-acting injectable antipsychotic, blood draw for clozapine, dispensation of methadone, etc.)
Strength of relationship, engagement, and continuity of care. Is the patient new to the program? Was there a recent change in clinician assignment?
Ability to take a more active role during virtual sessions than may be needed during an in-person session
Static and dynamic risk factors, such as risk for suicide or self-injurious behavior, risk for violence, new housing instability, impact of substance use, re-entry from incarceration, increased frequency of emergency department or hospital admissions, etc.
Frame setting and discussion of circumstances if an individual can no longer be safely managed through telehealth, individual is aware in-person services may be required
Ability to identify and implement effective safety plans
Comorbidities or medical risk factors that may impair transportation to in-person services or connection to virtual encounters
Risks associated with in-person encounters (infections, falls, etc.)
System factors
Access to crisis services
Access to technology (phone ownership, data plan, minutes, broadband access, etc.); ability to establish a private space without interruptions
Access to reliable transportation
Complexity around transitions in care; avoiding interruptions in care as patients switch providers or programs
For individuals returning to the community from prison or other forensic settings, it is recommended that in-person warm handoffs occur on the day of release to ensure safe transition to housing and access to psychiatric medication, food/clothing, and telephone for telehealth contacts. Many patients will require in-person assistance to reconnect to services as they readjust to the community environment

base as well as guidance for consumers and professionals to optimally guide adoption at the individual level. Many of these apps imply that the evidence-based benefits of well-established interventions, such as cognitive-behavioral therapy or mindfulness, transfer to these electronic systems without substantiating these claims with published evidence (Carlo et al. 2019). Many apps take a psychoeducation approach to stress management, meditative or breathing exercises, and cognitive restructuring practices. Emphasis in the platforms may be general or condition specific (e.g., depression, anxiety, eating disorder, insomnia, etc.).

Adoption of digital behavioral platforms by patients can take many routes: (1) an individualized recommendation by the clinician, (2) adoption into the treatment workflow by the provider agency, (3) adoption by the patient and subsequently disclosed to the clinician, or (4) adoption by the patient without disclosure to the clinician. The impact of these digital platforms on mental health outcomes remains largely unknown, except as anecdotal reports. The nature of app-based interventions suggests that the risk of adverse effects is likely limited. However, potential risks of adoption by consumers may include the use of a behavioral health app instead of more effective "traditional" care, resulting in delay of care during periods of escalating acuity or decompensation or confusion stemming from contradictions in the clinician-driven versus app-driven approaches or recommendations. When recommending a particular app, clinicians and agencies must consider how the developers will use data gathered through the use of the app and ensure that patients understand the implication of the terms in user agreements as part of the informed consent conversation.

When we look more broadly at available digital therapeutics beyond the "app store" download, a variety of delivery methods are emerging. Certain platforms offer "virtual" encounters supplemented with individualized between-visit homework that is reviewed by the clinician on a regular basis. Some hybrids mix real-time videoconference visits with between-session text exchanges, while others pair consumers with "health coaches" who guide and support consumer use. Other platforms offer text-only interaction between consumer and clinician, with an expectation of text frequency and response time designated in terms of service, and often available on a tiered pricing model. Text-only counseling exists in a regulatory "grey zone." Some platforms offer text counseling by licensed clinicians, but the platform terms of service may define the encounter as advice and does not establish a "doctor-patient" relationship. Other platforms may offer anonymous participation by consumers which makes intervention in case of emergency impossible.

An additional emerging model consists of prescription software or digital platforms for specific diagnoses. These have effectiveness and safety data that are sufficient to obtain FDA clearance. While the field is accustomed to physicians prescribing medications or specific devices (such as glucometers), the notion of prescription software is completely new. Such platforms are treated similarly to medical devices and are available only by authorization by a physician. One example is Pear Therapeutics' reSet and reSet-O. This is a digital platform that provides adjunctive CBT in a contingency management approach for substance use and opioid use disorder, respectively (Pear Therapeutics, n.d.). Another example, also by Pear, is Somryst for chronic insomnia; this application interfaces with both patients and clinicians and delivers CBT for insomnia (Pear Therapeutics, n.d.). Freespira Inc. has an FDA-cleared device and online platform that trains patients on how to manage panic and posttraumatic stress disorders (Freespira, n.d.). Akili Interactive's EndeavorRx is a digital platform-based "videogame" that is FDA-cleared for the treatment of childhood ADHD (Akilli, n.d.). It is likely more similar platforms will emerge. While the prescription digital platforms lack the almost infinitely scalable nature (and low cost) of app-store interventions, they are nevertheless more scalable than our limited professional workforce, lend themselves to virtual deployment to improve access to care, can be relied on to deliver interventions as designed, and offer automated adherence and outcomes tracking. It is important for mental health clinicians to understand the evidence behind these interventions prior to widespread implementation.

The process to obtain FDA clearance for prescription software is similar to the process the FDA uses to clear medical devices – and is quite different from the FDA's process to approve medications. Clearing a medical device or piece of software, particularly if it is categorized as Class I or II, does not involve a rigorous review of the data. Class I devices generally pose the lowest risk to patients; examples include bandages, oxygen masks, tongue depressors, etc. Prescription software or other online applications are generally considered Class II, as are blood pressure cuffs or EKG machines. All FDA-cleared digital platforms have publicly available information on a database that clinicians can use to review the evidence behind a given digital platform or software. Brand-new applications (e.g., Pear's reSet) can be found on the "de novo" database (US Food and Drug Administration, 2021a), and applications for products claiming to be substantially equivalent to existing products (e.g., Pear's reSet-O) can be found on the "510(k) Premarket Notification" database (US Food and Drug Administration, 2021b). These types of interventions and platforms will likely become part of how our patients will access mental health services. Future research is critical to determine how they can be optimally used and to prevent potential negative outcomes.

Conclusion

The dynamics of the COVID-19 pandemic provoked rapid and massive changes in knowledge of, availability of, and acceptance of telehealth, with behavioral health services at the leading edge. Telehealth encounters went from rare to ubiquitous in a matter of months, with rapid regulatory and benefit changes to facilitate adoption. At this writing, it is uncertain whether some, most, or all the substantive changes will be permanently adopted at the federal and state levels, as well as by commercial insurers determining post-pandemic policy.

Projecting ahead, we can reasonably assume that telehealth services will be much more widely available, with services extending to remote and urban institutional locations as well as to patients' homes. As payment mechanisms continue to evolve from the historic in-person office-visit model, development of hybrid care models is likely, with fluid and individualized blends of in-person, virtual, synchronous/asynchronous, video, text, and app elements available. As younger populations of consumers and practitioners demand that behavioral health incorporates ever-evolving smart devices and on-demand availability (as with all other aspects of life), community psychiatry must both adapt to these changes, safeguard quality of care, and preserve access to communities caught on the wrong side of the digital divide.

Disclosures Dr. Fishkind is a consultant for Orbis Health, Inc. Dr. Cuyler is the Chief Clinical Officer of and owns shares in Freespira Inc. Dr. Cuyler was a consultant for BrainCheck Inc. Dr. Casoy does not have any disclosures to report.

References

Akili. (n.d.) *EndeavorRx*. Retrieved January 27, 2021, from https://www.endeavorrx.com/

Banshur, R. L., Shannon, G. W., Banshur, N., & Yellowlees, P. M. (2016). The Empirical Evidence for Telemedicine Interventions in Mental Disorders. *Telemed J E Health*, *22*(2), 87-113. https://doi.org/10.1089/tmj.2015.0206

Blackburn, A. G., Brusman-Lovins, L. L., Goltz, H. H., & Smith, D. S. (2020). *Process Evaluation of the Harris County Sheriff's Office Tele-Health/CORE Pilot Program: Final Report Submitted to Arnold Ventures*. Harris County Sheriff's Office. Retrieved January 20, 2021, from http://www.harriscountycit.org/wp-content/uploads/Arnold-Final-Report-11.04.20.pdf

Bullard, M., Villa-Roel, C., Bond, K., Vester, M., Holroyd, B., & Rowe, B. (2009). Tracking emergency department overcrowding in a tertiary care academic institution. *Healthc Q*, *12*(3), 99-106. 10.12927/hcq.2013.20884

Bunnell, B. E., Barrera, J. F., Paige, S. R., Turner, D., & Welch, B. M. (2020, 11 17). Acceptability of Telemedicine Features to Promote Its Uptake in Practice: A Survey of Community Telemental Health Providers. *Int J Environ Res Public Health*, *17*(22), 8525. doi: https://doi.org/10.3390/ijerph17228525

Carlo, A. D., Ghomi, R. H., Renn, B. N., & Arean, P. A. (2019, June 17). By the numbers: ratings and utilization of behavioral health mobile applications. *npj Digit. Med*, *2*(54). https://doi.org/10.1038/s41746-019-0129-6

Centers for Medicare and Medicaid Services. (2020). *COVID-19 Emergency Declaration Blanket Waivers for Health Care Providers*. enters for Medicare and Medicaid Services. Retrieved January 27, 2021, from https://www.cms.gov/files/document/summary-covid-19-emergency-declaration-waivers.pdf

Department of Health and Human Services. (2018). *Telemedicine and Prescribing Buprenorphine for the Treatment of Opioid Use Disorder*. Department of Health and Human Services. Retrieved November 28, 2020, from https://www.hhs.gov/opioids/sites/default/files/2018-09/hhs-telemedicine-hhs-statement-final-508compliant.pdf

Drug Enforcement Administration. (2020). Implementation of the Ryan Haight Online Pharmacy Consumer Protection Act of 2008. *Federal Register*, *85*(190), 61594-61601. https://www.govinfo.gov/content/pkg/FR-2020-09-30/pdf/2020-21310.pdf

Dwyer, T. (1973). Telepsychiatry: Psychiatric consultation by interactive television. *Am J Psychiatry*, *130*(8), 865-9. https://doi.org/10.1176/ajp.130.8.865

Eberly, L. A., Kallan, M. J., & Julien, H. M. (2020). Patient Characteristics Associated With Telemedicine Access for Primary and Specialty Ambulatory Care During the COVID-19 Pandemic. *JAMA Network Open*, *3*(12). https://doi.org/10.1001/jamanetworkopen.2020.31640

Feiden, K. (2014). *Project ECHO: Bridging the gap in health care for rural and underserved communities*. Robert Wood Johnson Foundation. Retrieved 27 January, 2021, from https://www.rwjf.org/en/library/research/2014/04/project-echo%2D%2Dbridging-the-gap-in-health-care-for-rural-and-unde.html

Freespira, Inc. (n.d.) *Freespira*. Retrieved January 27, 2021, from https://freespira.com/

Harris County Sheriff's Office. (2020). *Project CORE: About our Program*. Retrieved January 20, 2021, from https://www.harriscountycit.org/3846-2/

Hensel, J. M., Shaw, J., Ivers, N. M., Desveaux, L., Vigod, S. N., Cohen, A., Onabajo, N., Agarwal, P., Mukerji, G., Yang, R., Nguyen, M., Bouck, Z., Wong, I., Jeffs, L., Jamieson, T., & Bhatia, R. S. (2019). A Web-Based Mental Health Platform for Individuals Seeking Specialized Mental Health Care Services: Multicenter Pragmatic Randomized Controlled Trial. *J Med Internet Res*, *21*(6). https://doi.org/10.2196/10838

Hyatt, J. (2015). *Big White Wall: Expanding Mental Health Access Through The Digital Sphere*. HealthAffairs Blog. Retrieved November 27, 2020, from https://www.healthaffairs.org/do/10.1377/hblog20150601.048059/full

Kels, C. G., & Kels, L. H. (2013). Portability of Licensure and the Nation's Health. *Military Medicine*, *178*(3), 279-84. https://doi.org/10.7205/MILMED-D-12-00390

Komaromy, M., Duhigg, D., Metcalf, A., Carlson, C., Kalishman, S., Hayes, L., Burke, T., Thornton, K., & Arora, S. (2016). Project ECHO (Extension for Community Healthcare Outcomes): A new model for educating primary care providers about treatment of substance use disorders. *Substance Abuse*, *37*(1), 20-4. https://doi.org/10.1080/08897077.2015.1129388.

Mehrotra, A., Chernew, M., Linetsky, D., Hatch, H., Cutler, D., & Schneider, E. C. (2020). *The Impact of the COVID-19 Pandemic on Outpatient Care: Visits Return to Prepandemic Levels, but Not for All Providers and Patients*. The Commonwealth Fund. Retrieved January 27, 2021, from https://www.commonwealthfund.org/publications/2020/oct/impact-covid-19-pandemic-outpatient-care-visits-return-prepandemic-levels

Narasimhan, M., Druss, B. G., Hockenberry, J. M., Royer, J., Weiss, P., Glick, G., Marcus, S. C., & Magill, J. (2015). mpact of a Telepsychiatry Program at Emergency Departments Statewide on the Quality, Utilization, and Costs of Mental Health Services. *Psychiatric Services*, *66*(11), 1167-72. https://doi.org/10.1176/appi.ps.201400122

New York State Office of Mental Health. (2020). *New York State Office of Mental Health Infection Control Manual for Public Mental Health System Programs*. Guidance on COVID-19. Retrieved January 27, 2021, from https://omh.ny.gov/omhweb/guidance/covid-19-guidance-infection-control-public-mh-system-sites.pdf

Nicks, B. A., & Manthey, D. M. (2012). The impact of psychiatric patient boarding in emergency departments. *Emergency Medicine International, 2012*. https://doi.org/10.1155/2012/360308

115th Congress. (2018). *H.R.6 - SUPPORT for Patients and Communities Act*. Congress.Gov. Retrieved January 20, 2020, from https://www.congress.gov/bill/115th-congress/house-bill/6

Pear Therapeutics. (n.d.) *reSET & reSET-O*. Retrieved January 27, 2021, from https://peartherapeutics.com/products/reset-reset-o/

Pear Therapeutics. (n.d.) *Somryst*. Retrieved January 27, 2021, from https://peartherapeutics.com/products/somryst/

Ramsetty, A., & Adams, C. (2020). Impact of the digital divide in the age of COVID-19. *J Am Med Inform Assoc.*, *27*(7), 1147-48. https://doi.org/10.1093/jamia/ocaa078

Shore, J. H., Yellowlees, P., Caudill, R., Johnston, B., Turvey, C., Mishkind, M., Krupinski, E., Myers, K., Shore, P., Kaftarian, E., & Hilty, D. (2018). *Best Practices in Videoconferencing-Based Telemental Health*. American Psychiatric Association. Retrieved November 27, 2020, from https://www.psychiatry.org/psychiatrists/practice/telepsychiatry/blog/apa-and-ata-release-new-telemental-health-guide

Southard, E. P., Neufeld, J. D., & Laws, S. (2014). Telemental health evaluations enhance access and efficiency in a critical access hospital emergency department. *Telemed J E Health*, *20*(7), 664-8. https://doi.org/10.1089/tmj.2013.0257

Torrey, E. F., Fuller, D. A., Geller, J., Jacobs, C., & Ragosta, K. (2012). *No Room at the Inn: Trends and Consequences of Closing Public Psychiatric Hospitals*. The Treatment Advocacy Center. Retrieved January 27, 2021, from https://www.treatmentadvocacycenter.org/storage/documents/no_room_at_the_inn-2012.pdf

US Department of Health and Human Services. (2021). *Policy changes during the COVID-19 Public Health Emergency*. Retrieved January 27, 2021, from https://www.telehealth.hhs.gov/providers/policy-changes-during-the-covid-19-public-health-emergency/?section=1,2#providing-telehealth-services-for-medicare-patients

US Department of Health and Human Services Office of Disease Prevention and Health Promotion. (2020). *Increase the proportion of adults with broadband internet — HC/HIT-05*. Healthy People 2030. Retrieved November 28, 2020, from https://health.gov/healthypeople/objectives-and-data/browse-objectives/neighborhood-and-built-environment/increase-proportion-adults-broadband-internet-hchit-05

US Food and Drug Administration. (2021a). *Device Classification Under Section 513(f)(2)(De Novo)*. Retrieved January 28, 2021, from https://www.accessdata.fda.gov/scripts/cdrh/cfdocs/cfPMN/denovo.cfm

US Food and Drug Administration. (2021b). *510k Premarket Notification*. Retrieved January 28, 2021, from https://www.accessdata.fda.gov/scripts/cdrh/cfdocs/cfpmn/pmn.cfm#:~:text=A%20510(K)%20is%20a,not%20subject%20to%20premarket%20approval

Whittington, J. W., Nolan, K., Lewis, N., & Torres, T et al. (2015). Pursuing the Triple Aim: The First 7 Years. *Milbank Q*, *93*(2), 263-300. https://doi.org/10.1111/1468-0009.12122

Wittson, C., Affleck, D., & Johnson, V. (1961). Two-way television in group therapy. *Mental Hospitals*, *12*(10), 22-23.

Zhou, C., Crawford, A., Serhal, E., Kurdyak, P., & Sockalingam, S. (2016). The impact of project ECHO on participant and patient outcomes: a systematic review. *Academic Medicine*, *91*(10), 1439-1461. https://doi.org/10.1097/ACM.0000000000001328

Zigmond, J. (2013). Teaching by telementoring: Project ECHO advancing physicians' skill sets. *Modern Healthcare*, *43*(37), 28-9.

The Medical Director in Community-Based Mental Healthcare

Patrick S. Runnels, Joe Parks, Ken Hopper, and Jules M. Ranz

Introduction

De-institutionalization and the development of community-based care for the severely mentally ill began in the United States in the late 1950s and accelerated in the second half of the 1960s (Mechanic and Rochefort 1990). In the late 1970s, literature specifically concerned with the role of the psychiatrist in the community mental health system began to appear (Winslow 1979; Ribner 1980; Langsley and Barter 1983; Donovan 1980). The picture this literature presented was distinctly negative. Focused in particular on the federal community mental health center (CMHC) program – which had a high profile and on which data was collected – the literature documented both that the average number of full-time equivalent psychiatrists per center dropped from 3.1 to 2.4 between 1970 and 1975 (Winslow 1979) and that the proportion of CMHCs run by psychiatrists dropped rapidly from over 50% in 1971 (Pollack 1992) to 26% in 1977 (Ribner 1980) and to 8% in 1985 (Knox 1985).

A number of compounding factors contributed to this situation. Given that psychiatrists were by far the most expensive members of the staff, CMHCs were incentivized to maximize their role as prescribers, a task they alone could perform. At the same time, social engineering and prevention were increasingly supplanting the medical model for addressing the problems associated with mental illness, buoying the rise of social workers (who were also significantly less expensive) into leadership dominance. Because psychiatrists were not traditionally trained in administration and often lacked the knowledge and skills required to navigate a fiscal, political, and regulatory environment that was becoming ever more complex, their central role as administrators in community mental health settings

P. S. Runnels (✉)
Case Western Reserve University School of Medicine, Shaker Heights, OH, USA

Population Health, University Hospitals, Shaker Heights, OH, USA
e-mail: patrick.runnels1@uhhospitals.org

J. Parks
National Council on Mental Wellbeing, Washington, DC, USA

Missouri Institute of Mental Health, University of Missouri, St. Louis, St. Louis, MO, USA
e-mail: joep@thenationalcouncil.org

K. Hopper
Texas Christian University/University of North Texas Health Science Center, Fort Worth, TX, USA

The Hopper Group, Fort Worth, TX, USA
e-mail: k.c.hopper@tcu.edu

J. M. Ranz
NYS Psychiatric Institute/Columbia, University Medical Center, New York, NY, USA

Department of Psychiatry, Columbia University College of Physicians and Surgeons, New York, NY, USA
e-mail: jmr1@columbia.edu

W. E. Sowers et al. (eds.), *Textbook of Community Psychiatry*,
https://doi.org/10.1007/978-3-031-10239-4_55

faded. And since psychiatrists could earn far higher incomes in private practice, they also had a strong financial incentive to leave the CMHC setting entirely (Sharfstein 2000).

Yet, in the 1980s and 1990s, a new wave of biologic research and the arrival of a much wider range of medical treatment options increased the demand for psychiatrists in CMHCs (Beigel 1984; Okin 1984). Meanwhile, as funding for CMHCs shifted from grants to third-party payors (principally Medicaid), parties responsible for those dollars had an interest in strong medical oversight of the specific services being reimbursed. This led to regulations that tied reimbursement to a requirement for medical supervision (Diamond et al. 1995). As a result, a new leadership role for psychiatrists – titled "medical director" – emerged (Pollack and Cutler 1992; Ranz et al. 1997; Stein 1998; Diamond et al. 1991).

A survey of psychiatrist job descriptions in CMHCs (Diamond et al. 1995) revealed that an official medical director position existed in 142 of 214 (69%) respondents. Meanwhile, a survey of the American Association of Community Psychiatrists (AACP) a few years later mirrored that finding among psychiatrists, with 58% of 286 respondents identifying as medical directors (Ranz and Stueve 1998). That same year, the AACP published Guidelines for Psychiatric Leadership in Organized Delivery Systems for Treatment of Psychiatric and Substance Disorders (AACP 1995) with the dual goals of codifying existing practice and promoting the continued growth and evolution of psychiatric leadership.

Now, more than two decades later, the medical director role in CMHCs is ubiquitous around the country. This is thanks in no small part to advocacy by the AACP paired with the emergence and growth of Public and Community Psychiatry Fellowships, and its apotheosis is best exemplified by the creation of the Medical Director Institute embedded within the National Council for Wellbeing, the predominant advocacy organization for CMHCs. In this new environment, concerns about the quality and supply of medical director candidates stand alongside concerns about whether or not CMHC leaders around the country truly embrace an expanded and substantive role for medical directors.

The History of the Medical Director Role

More than a century ago, hospital medical staffs started electing their own "chiefs of staff" to represent the needs of physicians to hospital administrators. As hospital administration became more complex, hospital leadership saw the need to appoint physician administrators to both liaise with and communicate leadership decisions to the medical staff, shifting the role from elected representation of the staff to include appointed representation of the leadership. By 1966, this appointed role was formally called the hospital medical director, and physicians filling that role spent the bulk of their time – if not all of it – performing administrative duties, including the central role of line authority over medical staff (Ranz et al. 2000a, b).

A parallel process played out in community mental health centers. While CMHCs were initially run by psychiatrists, as the director role shifted to non-physicians, the term medical director was used as a title for a senior psychiatrist appointed by the administration. Yet, the term medical director remained informal, near absent in the literature as late as the 1980s, a likely reflection of the relative sparsity of such a formal role across CMHCs. Psychiatrists working in community mental health settings often felt they were pigeonholed into the very narrow role of medication management, one of the few roles that only they could perform (Ranz et al. 2000a, b).

The American Association of Community Psychiatrists was formed in the mid-1980s by psychiatrists who felt marginalized, looking to impact the work of CMHCs in a more robust way. In 1995, they published the guidelines for the role of the medical director in CMHCs, which has since been updated and is outlined later in this chapter. By outlining a formal job description, the AACP accomplished two things. First, they created a standard and taxonomy for which to study psychiatric leadership in community mental health settings, which subsequently led to more formal scholarly attention. But perhaps more importantly, they created a role conceptualization that inspired psychiatrists to envision and negotiate their' roles anew in CMHCs across the country and around the world (Ranz et al. 2000a, b).

Current Requirements for a Medical Director as the Standard of Care

While The Joint Commission accreditation requirements do not explicitly require a named medical director, the presence of such a role is implied. Specifically, The Joint Commission Guide to Leadership Standards (JCHO 2009) states:

> …to fail to adequately incorporate into the organization's leadership the licensed independent practitioner leaders who can evaluate and establish direction for the clinical care and decision making of licensed independent practitioners throughout the organization, is to create a fundamental gap in the leadership's capability to achieve the organization's goals with respect to the safety and quality of care, financial sustainability, community service, and ethical behavior.

and

> A chief medical officer may be a member of both the senior managers and the medical staff.

Moreover, NCQA accreditation standards for managed care organizations require a medical director. Certified Community Behavioral Health Clinics are also required to have a medical director, and organizations with full-time medical directors have a higher performance, specifically characterized by leadership that is working together and communicating the institution's goals effectively to all levels of the organization (Weber 2001). The 100 top hospitals are selected annually based on seven critical parameters for each of the 6200-plus US hospitals with 25 or more beds. They include the previous year's risk-adjusted patient mortality and complication rates, severity-adjusted average patient lengths of stay, expenses, profitability, proportional outpatient revenue, and asset turnover ratio (a measure of facility and technological peace-keeping ability). The winners are selected from five comparable size groupings – small, medium, and large community, teaching, and large academic hospitals. Conspicuous among the winners at every level are physician-led organizations. Even in the majority of hospitals headed by non-physician administrators, however, the managerial capabilities of medical directors are the key to success. The most common characteristic of these award-winning hospitals is that the leadership is working together and communicating the institution's goals effectively to all levels of the organization.

The Medical Director Responsibilities and Subtypes

The responsibilities of the medical director in community mental health are catalogued in the AACP model job description, as follows (American Association of Community Psychiatrists 1995):

Model Job Description for the Medical Director

Unless the chief executive officer (CEO) is properly trained and qualified to serve this purpose, the medical director has ultimate authority and responsibility for the medical/psychiatric services of the system. Specifically, this includes responsibility for:

1. Assuring that all system patients receive appropriate evaluation, diagnosis, treatment, medical screening, and medical/psychiatric evaluation whenever indicated and that all medical/psychiatric care is appropriately documented in the medical record.
2. Assuring psychiatric involvement in the development, approval, and review of all policies, procedures, and protocols that govern clinical care.
3. Ensuring the availability of adequate psychiatric staffing to provide clinical, medical, and administrative leadership and clinical care throughout the system.

4. Developing job descriptions for staff psychiatrists that are comprehensive and permit involvement in therapeutic and program development activities, as well as application of specific medical expertise.
5. Recruiting, evaluating, and supervising physicians (including residents and medical students) and overseeing the peer review process.
6. Assuring that all clinical staff receives appropriate clinical supervision, staff development, and in-service training.
7. Assuring, through an interdisciplinary process, the appropriate credentialing, privileging, and performance review of all clinical staff.
8. Providing direct psychiatric services.
9. Advising the CEO regarding the development and review of the system's programs, positions, and budgets that impact clinical services.
10. Assisting the CEO by participating in a clearly defined and regular relationship with the board of directors.
11. Participate with the CEO in making liaisons with private and public payors, in particular with medical directors or equivalent clinical leadership in payor organizations.
12. Assuring the quality of treatment and related services provided by the system's professional staff, through participation (directly or by designee) in the system's ongoing quality assurance and audit processes.
13. Providing oversight to ensure appropriate continuum of programs, level of care criteria, standards of practice, and psychiatric supervision for each program. Internal review of the level of care determinations and appeal of adverse UR decisions is an additional component of this process.
14. Participating in the development of a clinically relevant, outcome evaluation process.
15. Providing liaison for the system with community physicians, hospital staff, and other professional and agencies with regard to psychiatric services.
16. Developing and maintaining, whenever possible, training programs in concert with various medical schools and graduate educational programs.

The medical director, by licensure, training, and prior clinical/administrative experience, shall be qualified to carry out these functions and shall have an approximate minimum of 50% of his/her time allocated to administration. In all but the smallest settings, this position should be no less than 32 hours per week.

Surveys about the medical director position that classified the activity of psychiatrists into three categories – (1) direct clinical service, (2) clinical collaboration (meaning clinical consultation or supervision), and (3) administration – found that, in practice, the medical director position falls into two distinct subtypes (Ranz et al. 1997; Ranz et al. 2000a, b). The medical director exists not only at the *agency level*, as the AACP model job description tends to imply, but at the *program level* as well. As one would expect, agency medical directors engage in administrative tasks more than program medical directors. Though not addressed in the survey, the clinical/administrative split for agency medical directors varies widely, with some agency medical directors spending the majority of their time providing direct clinical service, while others provide very little direct clinical service. While reasons for this variation have not been formally studied, a diminished administrative footprint stems from two main issues, as cited by CMHC CEOs during a focus group conducted by the Medical Director Institute of the National Council for Mental Wellbeing in 2018: a perceived lack of physician leadership competence (which is often accurate) and psychiatric staffing shortages.

Meanwhile, the survey found that program medical directors do the same amount of direct clinical service as staff psychiatrists (suggesting that the bulk of their time remains clinical) but that they do significantly more clinical collaboration and administration and have greater job satisfaction. As to whether the program director title was merely ceremonial, the survey authors observed:

> Because clinical caseloads are not lower for program medical directors, one might wonder whether creating such a position amounts to little more than having the title of medical director on paper, but not in reality. In fact, the position of medical director legitimizes and facilitates the performance of collaborative activities that are associated with higher job satisfaction. Nonetheless, it is worth considering that some of the increased satisfactions may indeed come from the title alone. The perceptions created among staff by a job title such as "medical director" include an expectation of leadership, and if the person filling the position has true leadership and administrative skills, he or she will almost certainly be looked to for guidance. (Ranz 1997, p. 919)

Even though the respondents indicated that this greater job satisfaction is due to the performance of clinical collaboration, job satisfaction was actually correlated tightly with the performance of administrative tasks across both medical director classifications (Ranz and Stueve 1998).

Informal Authority in the Role of Medical Director

The surveys also found that the medical director's span of authority at both the agency and program levels divides into three categories – (1) authority over medical staff alone, (2) authority over medical staff and other clinical staff, and (3) authority over all staff, clinical and administrative (Ranz et al. 2000a, b). While the policy manual or table of organization may grant some formal authority over non-psychiatric clinical staff and other associated non-clinical staff, in practice this designation means formal line authority typically applies only to a limited number of high-risk, agency-wide clinical decisions.

The majority of a medical director's authority over the non-psychiatric clinical staff must be exercised informally instead. This informal authority derives from three primary sources: (1) the presence of a formal title, (2) the status of the medical degree, and (3) the proximate relationship of the medical director to the agency CEO. The relationship between the medical director and the CEO can be used externally to navigate problems in a community mental health center's environment and internally to guide clinical treatment across multiple domains, generate quality improvement initiatives, and guide program development. Since projects require general clinical staff to engage in new tasks, the medical director cannot bring ideas to fruition alone. Practically, this means that promoting change and advancing clinical care are reliant as much on managing relationships as they are on executing tasks (Bass 2008). Change happens at the speed of trust (Covey 2006); whatever vision a medical director has for improving or transforming care will only get as far as the trust they engender in others through appropriate relationship management. The medical director must convince the CEO, other clinical and administrative leaders, and key clinical stakeholder groups that a given idea is worthwhile, then develop a collaborative strategy to accomplish implementation (Eilenberg et al. 2000).

Medical Director for Governmental Authorities

Even though the state agency responsible for mental health services, referred to as a State Mental Health Authority (SMHA), is among the largest healthcare organizations in the country, some either do not have a medical director or, if they do, do not utilize them to lead statewide clinical innovation, resolve clinical issues, and influence non-clinician executives to establish organizational policies that support good clinical outcomes for patients and service consumers. The SMHA medical director's primary role is as the department's senior clinical leader, in which they are responsible for establishing and maintaining the department's standards of care on both clinical and programmatic levels, providing leadership and mentorship to clinical staff, and oversee the department's quality management program. As such, the medical director must be an inclusive clinical leader, not a "medical" leader in the narrower sense, i.e., just a leader of physicians (NASMHPD 2009).

In addition to direct clinical leadership, the SMHA medical director must provide advice and counsel to the commissioner and executive team regarding a broad range of clinical, policy, and programmatic issues, including direct involvement in the development of the department's strategic direction. In this role, they are also one of the department's essential troubleshooters, being available to be dispatched by the commissioner to manage difficult and complex situations that arise in the course of administering an SMHA. Through their professional expertise and knowledge, they provide clinical credibility for the department related to a wide range of internal and external audiences, constituencies, customers, regulatory bodies, other state agencies, etc. When highly visible "critical incidents" occur, they stand side by side with the commissioner, lending professional expertise, credibility, and authority to unfortunate and very public situations which can be difficult to manage from a public relations and political point of view. As part of their other functions (in areas related to clinical risk management activities), the medical director should significantly contribute to the prevention of such incidents.

Beyond the overarching role described above, the broad range of additional functions to which the SMHA medical director may be assigned, depending upon the needs of the agency and the preferences of the commissioner, includes:

- Identifying, selecting, and implementing clinical evidence-based practices, "best practices," and "best programs," etc.
- Developing (and implementing) statewide clinical policies, procedures, protocols, practice standards, etc.
- Consultation regarding difficult/controversial individual cases or situations
- Providing input and direction for special populations and specialty programs, e.g., individuals with co-occurring mental health and substance abuse disorders, forensics, and programs for individuals with brain injury or developmental disabilities, young adult programs, sex offender treatment programs, etc.
- Utilization management, levels of care determinations, arbitration of clinical appeals, etc.
- Overseeing recruitment and retention of psychiatrists and other medical and clinical professionals
- Overseeing the pharmacy benefit:
  - Formulary management
  - Implementation of medication algorithms
  - Monitoring of physician prescribing practices
- Developing, implementing, and evaluating new programs, delivery systems, etc.
- Overseeing and maintaining the linkage between the general health system – including primary care – and the behavioral healthcare system
- Providing linkage to professional and academic communities
- Providing linkage to accrediting and monitoring bodies and agencies

The Medical Director Role in Managed Behavioral Healthcare

As noted earlier, NCQA accreditation standards for managed care organizations require a medical director. Many clinical, quality, and oversight structures exist "in mirror" to care delivery systems. Escalated utilization management (UM) and/or quality trends identified by the health plan have been traditionally addressed in joint meetings (often referred to as joint operating committees or JOCs) between hospitals and health plans. Representation for both sides typically includes both medical directors and the CEO/regional managers (administrators) of both entities. Traditionally, the medical directors represent UM, clinical, and quality perspectives, while administrators represent contract and financial perspectives.

Few articles have been published specifically on the topic of the managed behavioral healthcare medical director, but one testimonial by Juliana Ekong provides an honest picture of the work involved (Ekong 2008). Notably, she highlighted the specific work of utilization management, which occupied 60% of her time. While she rendered denials quite rarely (consistent with the literature on managed care), when she did deny authorization, she was confident that she was preventing tight resources from being misallocated. At the same time, she highlights a problem known to all managed care medical directors: a situation where medical necessity is not met, but realistic and suitable alternative levels of care are not present. In this very specific service availability gap, the medical director must balance patient need, reality, legalities, and the culture of the managed care organization. Recent court rulings have also provided some footing and guidance for managed care organizations. Unfortunately, coverage and availability of services across the full continuum of care are incomplete in many areas, even when such levels of care are reimbursed. The treatment setting, intensity, and push toward resilience are a tricky balance that can be thwarted when patients "overstay" certain levels of care. The medical director can be instrumental in finding, promoting, and facilitating treatment methods and venues to close the gaps in care structurally and functionally.

As has occurred on the care delivery side over the last 20 years, managed care medical directors have increasingly found opportunity to be included in primary program design, operational planning, and the oversight of outcomes and staff performance. Naturally, a diverse array of leadership and management skills, such as human-to-human connectivity, communication, influence, budget/finance, and team leadership, have become increasingly important to executing the role well. Medical leaders often exert influence through matrixed organizational structures, e.g., the COO and the medical director, might both have accountability for physician staff positions. Despite the presence of matrix organizational structures, hierarchical, authoritarian, and/or overly competitive cultures can negate the formal and informal authority of the medical director. As a result, physicians are increasingly being given authority over both clinical operations and clinical quality/strategy, leading to more substantial roles with aligned accountability and authority.

The title chief medical officer (CMO) has become increasingly popular over the past 20 years. In managed care settings, the CMO would attend and participate in senior leadership strategic planning meetings while leading and setting standards for one or several medical directors (who report to the CMO). The movement in managed care organizations toward a "seat at the table" for physicians to provide strategic vision, operational planning, and management is indeed welcome. In these roles, they contribute to clinical design which serves patient health and well-being and also have opportunities to acquire the qualities and competencies that make their voice a trusted and impactful one.

As the role of medical directors and CMOs has expanded, authority and accountability have not always been aligned, such that physician leaders are often made accountable for results without having formal authority over the individuals or domains most responsible for achieving those results. The role of medical director is one of the *influencers* in the longitudinal relationship with providers. Denials can be issued, but common ground and understanding can and should be found for the effective management of care. In one real-world example, a managed care medical director was able to gradually find common ground with the medical director of a substance abuse residential program regarding the appropriate use of intensive outpatient care (IOP) services. The tone of review calls turned from hostile to collaborative with time, and the agenda became an honest discussion about clinical need and medical necessity match. Trust was built through demonstration that tactics were not deployed simply "in search of a denial." The only route to shared quality goals is through a trusting relationship and the influence such relationships create with providers.

Value-Based Care and the Future of the Medical Director Role

For decades, our healthcare system has been on an unsustainable track, with healthcare inflation far outpacing overall inflation, roughly doubling the percentage of GDP spent on healthcare from 9.2% in 1980 to 17.7% in 2018 (CMS 2021). Despite this massive increase in healthcare spending, outcomes in the United States rank well below many nations that spend significantly less (Commonwealth Fund 2021). Much of the discrepancy between spending and outcomes has been attributed to a lack of accountability in reimbursement.

When the Affordable Care Act became law in 2009, it targeted the foundational fee-for-service model that had both fueled increased spending and incentivized the marginalization of high-risk patients into public systems of care, where their long-term need for high-cost, low reimbursement services could be offloaded onto stand-alone community mental health centers and state hospitals. Whereas individuals with severe mental illness had been effectively excluded from the rest of the healthcare system prior to passage of the law (with dire consequences; individuals with severe mental illnesses die as much as 25 years younger than age-matched peers without them), new payment models that incentivize effective management of all chronic disease have stimulated providers to focus on comorbid physical illness alongside mental illness and substance use disorders.

Value-based payment mechanisms connect reimbursement for services rendered to both cost and quality standards across an attributed population. The primary lever for accomplishing this goal is financial: incentives for achieving set targets and disincentives for failure to do so (see chapter "Financing of Community Behavioral Health Services"). To be sure, at this early stage, successful models that provide high-quality care at lower cost have yet to emerge. Nonetheless, the trend toward value-based care portends a future in which previously marginalized populations with severe mental illness and substance use disorders experience access care in integrated settings.

In this environment, physician leadership will take on a new urgency with new dimensions and contours. Demand for effective psychiatrist leaders will grow as CMHCs (and hospital partners) are incentivized to shift toward minimizing unplanned care in emergency rooms and inpatient psychiatric and medical units. Mature integration with primary care will require clinical supervision of social workers around physical disease and physical health clinicians around behavioral disease. This will undoubtedly call for psychiatrists to bridge knowledge and culture gaps in a larger diversity of settings. Demand by large healthcare systems to develop effective communication and trust in managing difficult cases will increase the need for effective liaising and partnership building by individuals who fully grasp the intricacies of how such systems operate. Strategic planning in this emerging healthcare environment will require psychiatrists to learn new skills related to budgeting and finance, as well as innovation in developing new clinical pathways and managing new partnerships that would previously have been unthinkable, like large health systems starting their own community mental health centers or serving as a convener for multi-provider collaborators to establish unified crisis intervention or diversion centers for individuals with mental illness and substance use disorders.

In this future world, the value of a great medical director will grow significantly, but responsibility for pursuing new knowledge and managing personal growth in leadership skills will be prerequisites for success. We are likely entering a period where previously distinct worlds – state hospital systems, CMCHs, large health systems, mental health crisis services – are ready to collide; the reverberations will last for decades. Future medical directors can be excited about the opportunities to help lead this transformation yet must be prepared to meet the challenges that lie ahead.

References

American Association of Community Psychiatrists: "Guidelines for Psychiatric Leadership in Organized Delivery Systems for Treatment of Psychiatric and Substance Disorders. *Community Psychiatrist*, Autumn 1995, pp 6–7. Posted at http://www.communitypsychiatry.org/publications/clinical_and_administrative_tools_guidelines/leadership.aspx

Bass BM (2008). The Bass Handbook of Leadership: Theory, Research, and Managerial Applications, 4th Edition. New York: Free Press.

Beigel A (1984). The Remedicalization of community mental health. *Hospital and Community Psychiatry*, 35, 1114–1117.

Center for Medicare and Medicaid Services (2021). Accessed on January 2nd, 2022 at https://www.cms.gov/Research-Statistics-Data-and-Systems/Statistics-Trends-and-Reports/NationalHealthExpendData/NationalHealthAccountsHistorical

Commonwealth Fund 2021. Mirror, Mirror 2021: Reflecting Poorly – Health Care in the U.S. Compared to Other High-Income Countries. Last accessed on January 2nd 2022 at https://www.commonwealthfund.org/publications/fund-reports/2021/aug/mirror-mirror-2021-reflecting-poorly?utm_source=alert&utm_medium=email&utm_campaign=Improving+Health+Care+Quality

Covey SMR (2006). The Speed of Trust: The One Things That Changes Everything. Simon and Schuster Free Press, New York.

Diamond R, Stein LI, Susser E (1991). Essential and non-essential roles for psychiatrists in community mental health centers. *Hospital and Community Psychiatry* 42: 187–89.

Diamond R, Goldfinger S, Pollack D, Silver M (1995). The role of psychiatrists in community mental health centers: a survey of job descriptions. *Community Mental Health J* 31: 571–77.

Donovan C (1980). Problems of psychiatric practice in community mental health centers. *Am J Psychiatry* 139: 456–60.

Eilenberg J, Townshend EJ, Oudens E. (2000). Who's in charge here anyway? Managing the management split in mental health organizations. *Administration and Policy in Mental Health* 27: 287–97.

Ekong JI (2008). The Role of a Behavioral Health Medical Director in Medicaid Managed Care. *Psychiatric Quarterly* 79: 33–42.

Knox, MD (1985). National Register Reveals Profile of Service Providers. National Council News (National Council of Community Mental Health Centers), September, p. 1.

Langsley D, Barter J (1983). Psychiatric roles in the community mental health center. *Hospital and Community Psychiatry* 34: 729–33.

Mechanic D. Rochefort D. (1990). De-institutionalization: appraisal of a reform. *Ann Rev Sociology* 16:301–27.

National Association of State Mental Health Program Directors. The Role of the Medical Director in a State Mental Health Authority: A Guide for Policymakers December 2009. Accessed on January 2nd, 2022 at http://nasmhpd.org/sites/default/files/The%20Role%20of%20the%20Medical%20Director%20-%2012-09.pdf

Okin, R (1984). How community mental health centers are coping. *Hospital and Community Psychiatry* 35, 1118–1125.

Pollack D, Cutler D (1992). Psychiatry in community mental health centers: everyone can win. *Community Mental Health J* 28: 259–67.

Ranz J, Eilenberg J, Rosenheck S (1997). The psychistrist's role as medical director: task distributions and job satisfaction. *Psychiatric Services* 48: 915–20.

Ranz JM, Stueve A (1998): The role of the psychiatrist as program medical director. *Psychiatric Services* 49:1203–7.

Ranz JM, Stueve A, Rosenheck S (2000a): The role of the psychiatrist as medical director: A survey of psychiatric administrators. *Administration and Policy in Mental Health* 27 (5): 299–312.

Ranz J, McQuistion HL, Steuve A (2000b). The role of the community psychiatrist as medical director: a delineation of job types. *Psychiatric Services*: 930–32.

Ribner DS. Psychiatrists and community mental health: current issues and trends. Hosp Community Psychiatry 1980 May;31(5):338-41. doi: 10.1176/ps.31.5.338.

Sharfstein SS (2000). Whatever Happened to Community Mental Health? *Psychiatric Services* 51 (5): 616–20.

Stein LI (1998). The community psychiatrist: skills and personal characteristics. *Community Mental Health J* 34: 437–45.

Weber D (2001). Physicians Lead the Way at America's Top Hospitals. *Physician Executive*, 27(3): 24–9.

Winslow WW. The changing role of psychiatrists in community mental health centers. Am J Psychiatry 1979 Jan;136(1):24–7. doi: 10.1176/ajp.136.1.24..

Financing of Community Behavioral Health Services

Sosunmolu Shoyinka, Wesley E. Sowers, and Hunter L. McQuistion

Introduction

The US healthcare system is one of the most advanced in the world. It has led innovation in technology, pharmaceuticals, service design, and other areas. Yet it is also the most expensive in the world. Despite the high levels of expenditure, outcomes remain poorer than in other similarly developed economies.

The COVID-19 pandemic of 2020–2022 was linked with a global increase in mental health distress (Kaiser Family Foundation 2021). This resulted in an increased demand for services (Center for Disease Control 2020; American Psychological Association 2021), with a renewed focus on the funding and provision of mental health services. Unfortunately, demand has continued to outstrip the supply of behavioral health services (National Council for Mental Wellbeing 2021b). Additionally, access problems continue to disproportionately impact marginalized populations and underserved regions of the USA (Cohen's Veteran Network and National Council for Behavioral Health 2018).

There has rarely been a greater need or opportunity for psychiatric thought leadership to navigate this critical era of change. However, to be effective as leaders and change agents, psychiatrists serving in both clinical and administrative leadership roles must have a working understanding of healthcare financing. This is because the structure and delivery of healthcare services are often derived directly from the way those services are funded. Thus, to improve the way services are delivered often requires changes in funding mechanisms. This chapter will introduce how mental health services are funded in community behavioral health organizations.

Behavioral Healthcare Financing in the USA: A Complex Conundrum

Healthcare financing in the USA is complex. This can be attributed to many factors, including tension over the role of government vs. the private business sector in health care, tension between service-user/participant choice, and the need for cost containment and larger systemic questions around whether health care should be an entitlement or a privilege. It also arises from the multiplicity of funding sources, payers, and payment

S. Shoyinka (✉)
Department of Behavioral Health and Intellectual Disability Services, Philadelphia, PA, USA
e-mail: sosunmolu.shoyinka@phila.gov

W. E. Sowers
University of Pittsburgh Medical Center, Pittsburgh, PA, USA
e-mail: sowerswe@upmc.edu

H. L. McQuistion
New York University Grossman School of Medicine | NYU Langone Health, New York, NY, USA
e-mail: hunter.mcquistion@nyulangone.org

W. E. Sowers et al. (eds.), *Textbook of Community Psychiatry*, https://doi.org/10.1007/978-3-031-10239-4_56

models. To emphasize the point, beyond pure clinical services, there are even a wide range of independent, and largely uncoordinated, governmental agencies that contribute to aspects of overall welfare for people with behavioral health challenges, from housing to nutrition (Frank and Glied 2006). Funding models range from the easily understood, but cumbersome, fee-for-service framework to complex payment structures and cost management mechanisms that are much more obscure regarding their derivation. Government sources such as Medicare, Medicaid, and local government grants/funds play a major, and increasing, role in the financing of behavioral health services (Medicaid.gov 2020). Although the principles of community psychiatry may be applied in the private sector, most of the funding for community mental health services comes from public payment sources such as these.

Additionally, healthcare costs in the USA significantly outstrip those in other similarly developed countries, accounting for nearly 18% of the GDP in 2017 (Centers for Medicare and Medicaid Services NHE Fact Sheet 2022). However, population health outcomes in the USA lag those of other developed countries (Commonwealth Fund 2019). Key strategies for increasing value (outcome relative to cost) have been to restructure funding in ways that incentivize providers to focus on access and population health outcomes rather than volume of care provided (as is the case under fee for service systems). Examples of these strategies include initiatives such as the Medicare Access and CHIP Reauthorization Act of 2015 (MACRA) and the Merit-Based Incentive Payment System (MIPS), Alternative Payment Models, and Accountable Care Organizations. These arrangements will be considered in more detail later in the chapter.

The Mental Health Parity and Addiction Equity and the Affordable Care Acts have expanded insurance coverage to millions of Americans (Winkelman and Chang 2018). The American Rescue Plan Act of 2021 (National Council for Mental Wellbeing 2021b) contained provisions that aimed to significantly strengthen funding for mental health and addiction treatment services as the demand for mental health and addiction treatment services continued to rise in the aftermath of COVID-19 (CDC 2020). Despite the possibility of increased funding to meet the rising demand for services, the continued shortage of trained behavioral health clinicians to deliver mental health and addiction services threatens the systems' ability to meet these needs (American Psychological Association 2021).

This chapter will discuss the essential structural components of financing of public behavioral health services through public funding mechanisms. It will then review newer funding strategies that hold promise for the future of behavioral health financing.

The Role of Psychiatrists in Community Settings

Community psychiatrists play different roles in treatment settings. These range from providing direct care, advocacy, policy creation, education, and training to serving in leadership roles as medical directors or chiefs of service. Psychiatrists that serve in leadership roles often find their jobs to be more stimulating (Ranz et al. 2001) and are less likely to succumb to burnout than those who do not. Additionally, organizations that have learned to integrate the expertise of clinically trained leaders within their executive decision-making teams outperform those that haven't (McKinsey 2021). However, to succeed in these roles, psychiatrists must understand the business goals, financing, and operations of the organization in addition to the clinical mission. An integral aspect is understanding the financing of healthcare services within the purview of the agency.

How Mental Health and Addiction Treatment Services Are Funded

Behavioral health funding, like all healthcare funding in the USA, is funded through a complex blend of governmental, private, and other sources. Since the passage of Medicare and Medicaid in

1965, government funding has grown to become the predominant source of funding for behavioral health treatment in the USA, with private insurance, self-pay, and philanthropy contributing but a small portion (Medicaid.gov 2020). People with behavioral health issues are less likely to be working and thereby obtaining employer-based health insurance. At the same time, members of impoverished communities are more likely to have mental health problems (see chapter "Social and Political Determinants of Health and Mental Health").

Government Funding of Mental Health Services

Government funding of public behavioral health services occurs at the federal, state, and local levels. Often behavioral health treatment providers receive a mixture of funding from various sources. Public contributions are derived through taxation at the federal and/or state levels, supporting programs such as Medicare, the Veterans Administration, Indian Health Service, Medicaid, Federal Insurance Exchanges, and Children's Health Insurance Program (CHIP).

Federal Funding

Medicare

Medicare is a federal health insurance program for persons aged 65 or older, those of any age living with end-stage renal disease or aged less than 65 but with certain disabilities. Medicare's straightforward design and administration provides a foundation to understand government health financing mechanisms.

Medicare is funded through social security taxes paid to the government by employers and employees. Part A covers hospital-based care for the elderly and disabled. Medicare Part B pays for physician services, while Part D covers prescription drugs. Part B and D are paid for by federal taxes and small monthly premiums from beneficiaries (CMS 2019).

Medicare Advantage (also known as Part C) is a comprehensive ("bundled") alternative to Medicare. These "bundled" plans include Part A, Part B, and usually Part D. Medicare Advantage plans often offer extra benefits over regular Medicare such as vision, hearing, and dental services. Premiums are higher, while out-of-pocket expenses are usually lower.

Veterans Administration (VA)

VA benefits provide access to comprehensive healthcare services for individuals who have served in the US military, national guard, or reserves and were released/discharged under conditions other than dishonorable. Out-of-pocket costs are significantly limited to small copayments for health care or prescription drugs. All services are prepaid (US Dept of Veterans Affairs, 2021). The VA is funded through the Military Construction, Veterans Affairs, and Related Agencies (MILCON-VA) appropriations bill for the federal budget annually.

Indian Health Service

Like the VA, the Indian Health Service (Indian Health Service 2019) is a single, comprehensive federal health service delivery system for American Indians and Alaska Natives that provides direct medical and public health services to members of federally recognized Native American tribes and Alaska indigenous people. The Indian Health Service is funded yearly with US Congressional appropriation, with IHS administering these funds by both direct operating allocation and grant opportunities for special projects. In FY 2020, the IHS behavioral healthcare budget was almost 336.5 million dollars, with over 2/3 of that funding dedicated to substance and alcohol services. This remained flat for FY2021 (Indian Health Service 2022). Global IHS funding levels have been criticized as chronically insufficient to meet quality demands, though its FY2019 designation offered partial relief through the mechanism of designation as "payer of last resort," permitting IHS facilities to divert cost to a patient's public or private insurance carrier, if extant (Khetpal et al. 2022).

Federal Block Grants

The Federal Mental Health Block Grant (MHBG) program provides funds to state mental health authorities and requires states to create a comprehensive state mental health plan developed by a statewide planning council. This funding stream arguably has both advantages and disadvantages. It is flexible in that it is not subject to federal Medicaid regulations. Thus, it can support planning and program administration in ways that fee for service designs, like Medicaid, cannot provide (SAMHSA 2021). However, it is also vulnerable to states' prioritization for this grant allocation, with some states potentially yielding greater efficiency and vision than others. The MHBG program is relatively small. For fiscal year 2018, the total MHBG allotment for the states and territories was $722 million (RAND Corporation 2018). This rose to three billion allocated to SAMHSA for FY 2022 as part of the American Rescue Plan during the COVID-19 pandemic. Total spending for mental health care by the US government was about $225 billion in 2019 (US Dept. of Health and Human Services 2021).

Insurance Exchanges

The insurance exchanges were created under the Affordable Care Act and combine federal, state, and private/commercial insurance functions. Individuals who are self-employed or who do not receive insurance through their employment and do not qualify for Medicare or Medicaid may purchase insurance via these exchanges. People can choose from a range of government-standardized healthcare benefit plans offered by private insurers participating in the exchange. The exchanges offer purchasers an opportunity to compare and purchase plans through a single platform. Insurers in the exchanges offer several types of plans with variable degrees of coverage and cost sharing. Exchanges lower cost by pooling the risk of participating individuals. Lower-income earners are eligible for subsidies from the Federal government. Subsidies, in the form of premium tax credits and cost-sharing reductions for purchasers, are available to individual purchasers on a sliding scale according to income. Small businesses may be eligible for small business health insurance tax credits when they purchase coverage for their employees through the exchange (HealthCare.gov 2020).

Federal Safety Net Programs

Finally, federal and state safety net programs such as Social Security, housing subsidies (e.g., section "Behavioral Health Financing Today"), food stamps, prescription medication coverage, and unemployment are disproportionally accessed by and support individuals with mental health, addiction, and intellectual disability needs. In this sense, they can be considered indirect funding of mental health support services.

State Funding

Medicaid

Medicaid insures low-income Americans and is jointly funded and administered by the federal and state governments (Medicaid.gov 2020) and provides health insurance for low-income Americans. It is the primary source of state funding for mental health and addiction treatment services. Medicaid was significantly expanded in most states under the Affordable Care Act and is available to all citizens and legal residents with family income below 133% of the federal poverty line in expansion states.

Over the past several years, Medicaid has been increasingly characterized by its use of managed care formats, and it is estimated that as of mid-2019, 69% of Medicaid beneficiaries were covered by managed care plans for their general health care. Keen interest by commercial health insurance companies to contract with state Medicaid authorities has accompanied this trend. As part of this, there is an increasing penetration into behavioral health services by Medicaid managed care plans, including carve-outs tailored to those with serious mental illnesses (Kaiser Family Foundation 2022).

Eligibility for Medicaid is based on a means test, which includes annual household income and a consideration of assets. Income eligibility requirement for Medicaid is determined by each state. A state's Medicaid plan defines which services are covered by Medicaid. There is significant variability in the scope of covered services from state to state. Poorer states generally provide a lower per capita allocation of funding for Medicaid than wealthier states. The portion of Medicaid funds paid by the federal government is referred to as the Federal Medical Assistance Percentage or FMAP (Medicaid.gov 2020). States are funded at different levels, and FMAP rates have a statutory minimum of 50% and maximum of 83%. The FMAP is based on a formula that provides higher reimbursement to states with lower per capita incomes relative to the national average. Thus, for every dollar the state spends on Medicaid, the federal government matches at a rate that varies year to year.

It is well understood that over the past generation, state funding for behavioral health services, and especially for mental health, has migrated from state general funds to Medicaid. From a fiscal perspective, this maneuver permits states to reduce costs of delivering care from 100% budget outlay to their respective FMAP quotients. While theoretically there is greater regulatory restriction through "Medicaidization," the range of qualified services is potentially high, especially if states elect to pursue so-called federal Medicaid waivers to broaden the palette of offered services, often enhancing reimbursement rate structures, too. An example of such a waiver is for intensive outpatient treatment programming in New York State that permits these programs to receive higher reimbursement and multiple daily clinic contacts, avoiding the customary single visit per day limitation and creating greater flexibility of care.

The Children's Health Insurance Program (CHIP)

CHIP is another federal-state health insurance program, specifically for uninsured children in low-income families whose income is still too high to qualify the entire family for Medicaid and who do not have other forms of insurance that would otherwise cover these dependents (State Children's Health Insurance Program 2019). Pregnant women with low incomes and children of state employees may also qualify. The eligibility limits and benefits for CHIP vary by state, and state entities may administer the program either as part of Medicaid or as an independent entitlement. The federal funding methodology also follows an FMAP formula, though the federal share is much greater than that for Medicaid itself.

State General Funds

Prior to the introduction of large-scale Medicaid behavioral healthcare funding, states funded many local community provider programs through contracting mechanisms, often termed Community Support Programs. These were sometimes vetted and administered through local governing units.

At this point, full state funding continues to be required for intermediate and long-term hospitalization, typically for state hospital systems. In no small part, this may be traced to the 1854 presidential veto of a bill that that would have otherwise created national social welfare policy and funded real estate acquisition for construction of asylums. It has perpetuation in the so-called IMD (Institutions of Mental Disease) Exclusion, which blocks federal funding for free-standing psychiatric institutions over 16 beds. It is noteworthy that in 2018, the federal Centers for Medicare and Medicaid Services created a Medicaid waiver, too, for states to submit IMD demonstration projects (Modern Healthcare 2018).

Local Government Funding

City and county governments typically contribute a share of the state's FMAP quotient. Also, through local tax levy, they may also fund mental health services through grants and subsidies as program funds. They are often a payer of last resort for uninsured individuals. Localities may also fund mental health services indirectly through financing of supports and services in settings such as schools, housing programs, criminal justice/corrections, child, family services, etc.

Private Health Insurance

Privately funded coverage is provided primarily through employer-sponsored plans in the USA. Employers and employees share the costs, with employers typically paying most of the premium that purchases health insurance for their employees. Plans with greater choice, lower out-of-pocket contributions (deductibles and copays), and more covered services tend to be more expensive than those with restricted networks, higher out-of-pocket charges and fewer covered services. Because private insurance plans are nearly always for-profit entities, they are motivated to maintain financial health. This may conflict with quality imperatives and emphasize cost control through strategies like medication formulary restrictions, restrictive medical necessity criteria, and pre-authorization processes. Private insurers provide relatively little coverage for community mental health. However, it should be noted that in recent years, many states have contracted with private, for-profit Managed Care Organizations (MCOs) to manage their Medicaid benefits. As a result, many public sector programs experience cost-cutting pressures like those seen in the private sector.

Insurance of Last Resort

Individuals and families who cannot afford health insurance do not meet criteria for Medicaid, or other government funding make up the majority of the uninsured in the USA. This category also includes undocumented immigrants and individuals who have a criminal record. When these individuals become ill, they are generally cared for in publicly funded programs, which can vary greatly in range of benefits from state to state, and even locality to locality. Many of these uninsured or underinsured individuals are served through Federally Qualified Health Centers (FQHC), which are funded through the Health Resources and Services Administration. These organizations receive federal prospective payments based on the yearly anticipated costs of serving their complex patient population; their mission is to meet the health needs of underserved and vulnerable patients such as those who are homeless, are migratory and seasonal agricultural workers, and are residents of public housing. Individuals seeking services in FQHCs may be required to pay sliding scale fees. Services offered include primary and preventative care, embedded behavioral health resources, subsidized pharmacy services, and dental care (Health Resources and Services Administration 2021).

Certified Community Behavioral Health Clinics (CCBHCs) are a new class of federally subsidized providers and are funded by the federal Substance Abuse and Mental Health Services Administration. They are analogous to FQHCs and are charged with providing comprehensive behavioral health services, including 24-h crisis care, rehabilitation, case management, peer support, and primary care screening and monitoring to the local community. They may provide these services directly or contract with partner organizations to complete the required service array (Substance Abuse and Mental Health Services Administration 2021).

Behavioral Health Financing Today

Fee for service (FFS) payment remains the dominant method for covering the costs of community-based behavioral health care in the USA today even for patients enrolled in managed care programs. Payers establish a set of covered (reimbursable) services and set compensation (rates) for those services. Rates often vary by provider type. Third-party payers (entities that serve as intermediaries between service users and providers to manage and pay for healthcare expenses) collect premiums (or taxes, in the case of government plans) and provide payments on behalf of the insured. Providers bill the third-party payer for services delivered, and the insured often pay a predetermined portion of the cost of services received. Payments to managed care plans are prospective, as distinct from reimbursement for FFS payments.

FFS ensures accountability that services are delivered. However, it limits services to what is "covered" under that person's insurance plan. This has often historically excluded certain services that are extremely important to ensuring best outcomes, such as care coordination. This creates a disincentive to providers from delivering those services. Additionally, FFS decouples payment from outcomes and so may incentivize providers to prioritize providing a high volume of billable services regardless of the quality of care. It also discourages providers from creating individualized responses to their clients' needs since some of the required services may not be reimbursed. Most providers cannot afford to provide uncompensated care.

Foundational Concepts in Behavioral Health Financing

Due to the limitations of the fee-for-service model, other methods of compensation have been developed over time. This includes bundled payments, prospective payments, and pay-for-performance (P4P) arrangements. These models share a common goal of incentivizing cost-effective, quality care by aligning incentives to reward high-quality wise use of resources. They enjoy varied penetration within behavioral health marketplace. To fully understand these models, familiarity with some basic concepts is useful (Shoyinka 2021).

Risk Assuming risk means accepting financial responsibility to operate within available resources and liability for any expenses that exceed them. A major threat to those bearing risk is unanticipated costs from catastrophic events or unexpectedly high utilization. Private insurers, government entities, and providers may each take on risk. Managed Care Organizations may assume (1) no risk, in which the managed care company provides administrative services only; (2) limited risk, wherein potential loss and profit are restricted for the behavioral health managed care company; and (3) full risk, wherein the company assumes full financial risk for a population and stands to profit if costs are kept low. Whatever entity bears risks will have an incentive to operate efficiently to either maximize profit or to stay within budget for nonprofit organizations.

Incentives This refers to the use of strategies and techniques that reward desired practices and outcomes while discouraging (or not rewarding) undesired practices and outcomes, often through fiscal and other penalties.

Value-Based Reimbursement (VBR) In value-based reimbursement arrangements, payment is structured to reward healthcare *outcomes* rather than simply reimbursing services provided. These arrangements provide an incentive for a focus on quality rather than revenue. They generally use bundled payments that are tied to quality measures and require the provider to bear some degree of risk for outcomes of care.

Bundled Payments Bundling involves establishing a predetermined payment rate for all service inputs (including ancillary costs such as food and support services) for the medically necessary treatment of a condition. These services are then billed at the single pre-negotiated rate after they are provided. This billing structure simplifies payment and reduces the administrative burden of billing for each service provided by clarifying what providers can expect to be paid. It also encourages efficiency and creativity in service planning. "Per diem" payments for intensive treatment settings such as hospitalizations and residential treatments are one example of bundled payments. Case rates for Assertive Community Treatment (ACT) teams are another example of bundled payments.

Episode of Care Payments (also known as episode-based payment, case rate or DRG) is a type of bundled payments used to reimburse healthcare providers "on the basis of expected costs for clinically-defined episodes of care" (Yuan et al. 2017). In this arrangement, the provider is aware in advance the amount of payment they will receive for the episode of care. Reimbursement is based on average costs of an episode of care at a specific level of service intensity (such as an inpatient admission) for each DRG. Although often paid retrospectively, they can also be a prospective payment.

Prospective payments are a fixed amount made in advance of service delivery. Payment amounts are calculated from the resources historically needed to treat a particular condition. These may be based on regional average costs of care and classification systems such as diagnosis-related groups (DRGs) which are frequently used for this purpose (Krinsky et al. 2017). They may also be used for payment of capitated payment arrangements.

Capitation Within this arrangement, risk-bearing entities (such as providers or MCOs) contract with a payer (government or insurer) to provide all required care for a defined population. In exchange for assuming this responsibility, they receive fixed, predetermined payments for each member of that population (a per member, per month rate), regardless of actual need. The capitation is based on actuarial data predicting the number of members who are likely to need care of various kinds, and how intense that care is likely to be (Yuan et al. 2017). Payments may be risk-adjusted to reflect the intensity of need of the group on whose behalf the payments are made. For example, agencies serving people who are identified with severe illnesses and who require a large amount of treatment or services to meet their needs would fall into a high-risk group that would be reimbursed at a higher rate.

Program Funding or Global Payments Under this prospective payment arrangement, specific programs operated by a healthcare system or provider are funded through a fixed prepayment to provide care for all persons served over a specified time. This single payment is based on a prospective budget that covers all treatment and services and may include diagnostic tests, prescription drugs, and supports. These programs may be held accountable to obtain targeted outcomes to maintain funding. This type of arrangement is often used as "start-up/investment" funds for innovative programs (e.g., uses of these funds include supporting staff hiring, acquisition of office space, equipment, etc.) while developing other funding systems (e.g., billing insurance) for sustainability.

Alternative Payment Models (APMs)

Innovations that tie payment to quality/outcomes have been a major focus of value enhancement strategies with managed care formats exemplary in this manner. These alternative payment models (APMs) include prospective payment arrangements with case-mix adjustments, pay-for-performance (P4P), shared savings, capitated payment models, and full-risk advanced payment models (Self and Coffin 2016). They leverage measurement-based care and technology and foster flexibility in care delivery with an eye toward cost containment. Several APMs focus specifically on behavioral health services (Mauri et al. 2017). Various types of APMs will now be considered (Shoyinka 2021).

Pay for Performance (P4P) Under P4P, providers can earn a "reward" payment over and above routine reimbursement (e.g., through FFS) by demonstrating a measurable improvement in clinical outcomes. These arrangements carry little risk to the provider. They can be used to incentivize very specific services or outcomes, such as preventive screening, enhancing patient satisfaction, or achieving certain quality outcomes. P4P has been tied to HEDIS (Healthcare Effectiveness Data and Information Set) measures, such as 7- or 30-day follow-up after hospitalization or screening for diabetes and antidepressant medication adherence (Unutzer et al. 2012).

Shared Savings Shared savings programs incentivize providers under FFS to lower cost of care by improving coordination of care to meet quality metrics. Actual spending is calculated against projected spending for a wide range of health services and settings. When specific cost and quality benchmarks are realized, the provider can "share" in the savings with its payer (Ouayogodé et al. 2017). This is generally a designated percentage of the difference between the projected and actual cost of the services provided.

MACRA and MIPS The Medicare Access and CHIP Reauthorization Act of 2015 (MACRA) potentially transforms healthcare practices by establishing new payment methodologies for Medicare beneficiaries. MACRA and the Merit-Based Incentive Payment System (MIPS) create an incentive for physicians to utilize measurement in routine care delivery. MIPS is the measurement component of MACRA. It specifies measurement requirements for providers. Currently, providers must submit data on six quality measures (including one outcome measure) that are approved by the Center for Medicare and Medicaid Services (CMS). The Hospital-Wide, 30-Day, All-Cause Unplanned Readmission (HWR) Rate for the Merit-Based Incentive Payment Program (MIPS) is one example. Clinicians have over 206 measures to choose from and must collect a full calendar year of data. Additionally, although providers are not restricted to measures listed in the specialty sets that apply to them, it may be helpful to consider those sets consider when selecting measures.

This system creates a monetary incentive for providers to track and demonstrate improved quality of care (CMS.gov 2019). Physicians must participate in MIPS if they meet certain requirements, such as billing more than a specified amount for Part B covered professional services. They, however, may be excluded from these programs or may request exemptions under certain circumstances (e.g., natural disasters, pandemics).

Accountable Care Organizations (ACOs) ACOs are typically formed by large medical centers or a consortium of healthcare provider organizations that contract with a payer to serve a defined patient populations with services and programs while meeting specific quality and cost benchmarks over a set period. They are an example of Global Funding on a large scale. Essentially, an ACO assumes both clinical responsibility and financial risk for an assigned beneficiary population that would otherwise be reimbursed through a fee-for-service (FFS) arrangement. Accountability for quality of care is required and monitored through the establishment of outcome benchmarks. A shared risk and/or savings arrangement is often part of the funding scheme. If the ACO can provide care at a lower cost than predicted based on historical data, all, or part, of the savings are retained by the organization. With full risk arrangements, when costs exceed the threshold, the ACO bears the loss.

APMs for Behavioral Health

Given the high service utilization and need for multiple supports and/or care coordination associated with severe mental illness, a variety of payment mechanisms have been proposed for this population. These arrangements typically include the costs of behavioral and physical health services (both inpatient and outpatient), care coordination, medication, and all ancillary services (Mauri et al. 2017). The New York State Health and Recovery Plan (NYS HARP) is an example of this all-inclusive bundled rate financing. Under NYS HARP, Medicaid Managed Care organizations are paid an enhanced rate to cover these services (New York State Office of Mental Health Health Action and Recovery Plans 2019).

Another type of APM bundles costs of care according to the level of service intensity and the average cost of care at that level per day or episode of care. Service planning and prescribed services are left to the discretion of the provider within predetermined parameters for each level of care. Service intensity "necessity" tools are used to identify the level of services required. Tools developed by professional organizations such as the Level of Care Utilization System (LOCUS) developed by the American Association for Community Psychiatry (AACP) and their derivatives are the most widely used tools of this type (see chapter "Creating Value: Resource and Quality Management"). This approach saves money in the long term by facilitating care coordination, improving engagement, and promoting flexibility in treatment. It reduces the administrative burden of billing and by delegating risk to providers it eliminates the need for concurrent reviews. It also helps to ensure that people can access the services that they need in a timely manner, thus reducing long-term costs related to recidivism or from the complications of delayed treatment.

Patient-Centered Opioid Addiction Treatment Payment (P-COAT): P-COAT is designed to incentivize the utilization of medication-assisted treatment (MAT) by eliminating barriers such as prior authorization and FFS billing. Bundled payments under this model cover three phases of care: patient assessment and treatment planning, initiation of MAT, and maintenance of MAT. These bundles cover medication, psychological treatment, and coordination of social services necessary to remain in treatment following initiation. For individuals who drop out or terminate treatment early, monthly maintenance of MAT payments are made to the team to facilitate reengagement (American Society for Addiction Medicine 2018).

Next-Generation Healthcare Financing Models

Additional innovations in paying for healthcare services being considered and piloted for the enhancement of value in health care include the following:

Value-Based Insurance Design (V-BID) (Choudhary et al. 2010; Shoyinka 2021) V-BID incentivizes service users to adhere to their service plan and recommended care guidelines by developing variable consumer out-of-pocket costs. By making curative services more expensive relative to preventative ones, members are motivated to use less expensive primary care and preventative services. For example, reduced co-pays, or even discounts or rebates, are leveraged to incentivize the use of preventative services such as smoking cessation, cancer screening, or medication for chronic conditions (such as HTN) over curative services such as elective surgery. Participation in health promotion and secondary prevention programs may also qualify members for premium discounts.

HMOs Incorporating Socioeconomic Determinants of Health HMOs like Kaiser, Geisinger, and Community Behavioral Health are beginning to incorporate community health programs that target social determinants of health. By addressing social determinants which are linked to negative health outcomes (e.g., unsafe housing linked to respiratory disease), these plans realize savings in the form of avoided costs of downstream care of complex/advanced conditions. Examples of services paid for include housing, healthy nutrition, employment, and programs that prevent mental illness and addiction.

A Look at the Future of Behavioral Health Financing

These well-intended APMs have not yet had a significant impact on the overall value (quality/cost ratio) achieved in our health systems. This is at least due in part to the continued dominance of FFS reimbursement as a method of paying for community-based services. A sustainable financing model that ensures equitable, adequate funding of quality-focused behavioral health services is essential for driving change. This funding must also allow flexibility in planning services for improved outcomes. The ability to measure the outcomes of care is central to both quality and cost containment. In other words, funding must be tied to quality metrics to calculate value (Shoyinka 2021). Suggested strategies include:

Delegated Risk and Bundling Mechanism Shifting some or all risk to providers may offer the greatest opportunity for flexibility with accountability in health care. Various types of bundled payments accomplish this when tied to measurable outcomes. Bundling has the potential to enhance quality by allowing providers the leeway to customize services as needed.

Efficiency Integration of services reduces redundancies and simplifies administration. Integrated financing streams and licensing will also increase efficiency. There must be incentives to reduce barriers to consolidations of fragmented services.

Analytics and Informatics Data collection and analysis for actionable insights (analytics) are the backbone of health financing and population health management. Analytics can be used to isolate segments of the population, identify cost trends, and predict future utilization. This facilitates targeted interventions and further analysis, potentially reducing waste and improving efficiency. Furthermore, technologies can revolutionize data management by facilitating information sharing in health care. The capacity to store information about transactions in a secure and indelible way must be supported by financing plans. These technologies can reduce fragmentation, improving integration and reducing cost. Meaningful outcome metrics that address the values of all stakeholders can be tracked and monitored.

Social Determinants Reducing their negative impact will require addressing health at a true population level through integration of financing for social welfare and health care. Inclusion of measures to ensure that basic needs are met in addition to those that focus on medical necessity criteria, such as LOCUS, is one step in that direction, but financing plans will need to develop clear incentives that enhance primary prevention, as well (Geisinger Medical Center Geisinger–Shamokin Area Community Hospital Community Health Needs Assessment 2022).

Conclusion

The funding of contemporary community mental health services is complex. The establishment of a simple and universal coverage scheme for all health services remains elusive, and it appears that it will remain so in the foreseeable future. Equity of benefits and improvement in population health are unlikely to be fully achieved until this is in place. As a result, coverage for community mental health services is composed of multiple sources with different rules that render funding difficult to understand, particularly for busy clinicians providing direct service. For instance, while moving through daily patient care, it can be challenging to be nuanced in assigning correct billing codes using apparently byzantine criteria. This can unintentionally affect a program's fiscal viability. Obtaining adequate funding for behavioral health services historically has been challenging. The COVID-19 pandemic provided opportunity to advocate for sustained, equitable funding to improve access to quality behavioral health treatment, and some increase in funding was realized as a result. An example of this is the emergence of greater billing flexibility for telepsychiatry, increasing some aspects of efficiency and patient access (Avalone et al. 2021). Advances in funding methods, such as the APMs that offer opportunity to better balance cost and quality, and significant restructuring of the payment system in ways that balance risk, incentives, and quality are needed to assure overall value in the services we provide.

References

American Psychological Association (2021): Worsening Mental health crisis pressures psychological workforce. 2021 COVID 19 practitioner survey. Available at https://www.apa.org/pubs/reports/practitioner/covid-19-2021. Accessed December 22nd, 2021

American Society of Addiction Medicine (2018). Patient Centered Opioid Addiction Treatment. Alternative Payment Model. Available at https://www.asam.org/docs/default-source/advocacy/asam-ama-p-coat-final.pdf?sfvrsn=447041c2_2. Accessed March 21, 2022.

Avalone L, Barron C, King C, Linn-Walton R, Lau J, McQuistion, HL et al (2021) Rapid telepsychiatry implementation during COVID-19: increased attendance at the largest health system in the United States. Psychiatric Services 72, 708-711.

Centers for Disease Control and Prevention: Mental Health, Substance Use, and Suicidal Ideation During the COVID-19 Pandemic — United States, June 24–30, 2020. Available at https://www.cdc.gov/mmwr/volumes/69/wr/mm6932a1.htm?s_cid=mm6932a1_x#T1_down. Accessed December 22nd, 2021.

Centers for Medicare and Medicaid Services December 1, 2019. Medicare general Information. Available at https://www.cms.gov/Medicare/Medicare-General-Information/MedicareGenInfo/index.html. Accessed March 21, 2022.

Centers for Medicare and Medicaid Services 2017 National Health Expenditure Fact Sheet. April 26th, 2019. Available at https://www.cms.gov/research-statistics-data-and-systems/statistics-trends-and-reports/nationalhealthexpenddata/nhe-fact-sheet.html. 04/26/2019. Accessed December 22nd, 2021.

Centers for Medicaid and CHIP services July 12th, 2022. Available at https://www.medicaid.gov/. Accessed December 12th, 2022.

Centers for Medicare and Medicaid Services. The Medicare Access and CHIP reauthorization Act. December 1, 2021. Available at https://www.cms.gov/medicare/quality-initiatives-patient-assessment-instruments/value-based-programs/macra-mips-and-apms/macra-mips-and-apms.html. Accessed March 21, 2022.

Choudhry NK, Rosenthal MB, Milstein A (2010). Assessing the evidence for value-based insurance design. Health Affairs (Millwood). Health Affairs 29, No. 11: 1988–1994.

Cohen Veterans Network, National Council for Behavioral Health. America's Mental Health. October 10, 2018. Available at https://www.cohenveteransnetwork.org/wp-content/uploads/2018/10/Research-Summary-10-10-2018.pdf. Accessed 6/11/19. Accessed December 21st, 2021.

Commonwealth Fund. U.S. Health Care from a Global Perspective (2019). Higher Spending, Worse Outcomes? https://www.commonwealthfund.org/publications/issue-briefs/2020/jan/us-health-care-global-perspective-2019. Accessed December 22nd, 2021.

Frank RG, Glied SA (2006). *Better But Not Well: Mental Health Policy in the United States Since 1950*. Johns Hopkins University Press, Baltimore, USA.

Healthcare.gov. (2020). Small Business Health Care Tax Credit and the SHOP Marketplace. Available at: https://www.healthcare.gov/small-businesses/choose-and-enroll/shop-marketplace-overview/. Accessed March 21st 2022.

Health Resources and Services Administration August 2021. Available at https://bphc.hrsa.gov/about/what-is-a-health-center/index.html. Accessed March 21, 2022.

Geisinger Medical Center Geisinger–Shamokin Area Community Hospital Community Health Needs Assessment. Available at https://www.geisinger.org/-/media/OneGeisinger/pdfs/ghs/about-geisinger/chna/2021/Geisinger-Community-Medical-Center-Community-Health-Needs-Assessment-2021.pdf. Accessed March 21, 2022.

Indian Health Service. Available online at IHS.gov https://www.ihs.gov/. Accessed December 22, 2019.

Indian Health Service. Available online at http://www.ihs.gov/budgetformulation/congressional justifications/. Accessed January 6, 2022.

Kaiser Family Foundation (2021). The Implications of COVID-19 for Mental Health and Substance Use. Available at https://www.kff.org/coronavirus-covid-19/issue-brief/the-implications-of-covid-19-for-mental-health-and-substance-use/. Accessed December 21st, 2021

Kaiser Family Foundation (KFF) (2022). 10 Things to Know About Medicaid Managed Care. Available at https://www.kff.org/report-section/10-things-to-know-about-medicaid-managed-care-issue-brief/, Accessed March 20, 2022.

Khetpal V, Roosevelt J, Adashi EY. A federal Indian health insurance plan: fulfilling a solemn obligation to American Indians and Alaska Natives in the United States. Preventive Medicine Reports 25, 2022. Available online Dec. 16, 2021

Krinsky S, Ryan AM, Mijanovich T, Bluestein (2017). Variation in Payment Rates under Medicare's Inpatient Prospective Payment System. Health Serv Res. 52: 676–696.

Medicaid.Gov; Behavioral Health Services. Available at https://www.medicaid.gov/medicaid/benefits/behavioral-health-services/index.html. Accessed December 21st, 2020.

Mauri A, Harbin H, Unutzer J, Carlo A, Ferguson R, Schoenbaum M. Payment Reform and Opportunities for Behavioral Health: Alternative Payment Model examples. Thomas Scattergood Behavioral and Peg's Foundation September 2017. Available at https://www.scattergoodfoundation.org/wp-content/uploads/yumpu_files/Scattergood_APM_Final_digital.pdf. Accessed December 22nd 2021.

McKinsey and Company. The rapid evolution of the payer Chief Medical Officer. Available at https://www.mckinsey.com/industries/healthcare-systems-and-services/our-insights/the-rapid-evolution-of-the-payer-chief-medical-officer. Accessed December 21st, 2021.

Modern Healthcare, CMS plans to overturn Medicaid ban on mental health facility pay, November 13, 2018. Available at https://www.modernhealthcare.com/article/20181113/NEWS/181119988/cms-plans-to-overturn-medicaid-ban-on-mental-health-facility-pay. Accessed January 7th, 2022.

National Council for Mental Wellbeing. Demand for Mental Health and Addiction Services Increasing as COVID-19 Pandemic Continues to Threaten Availability of Treatment Options. Available Online at https://www.thenationalcouncil.org/press-releases/demand-for-mental-health-and-addiction-services-increasing-as-covid-19-pandemic-continues-to-threaten-availability-of-treatment-options/. Accessed 12/22/21.

National Council for Mental Wellbeing. Medicaid. Available online at https://www.thenationalcouncil.org/topics/medicaid/. Accessed December 22, 2021a.

National Council for Mental Wellbeing. American Rescue Plan Funding for Community Based Mental Health Services. Available online at https://engage.thenationalcouncil.org/communities/community-home/digestviewer/viewthread?GroupId=67&MessageKey=02406421-7cc6-4f6f-8ea2-f276662e3372&CommunityKey=83fe128a-4d3e-4805-88dc-5acfaef5d555&tab=digestviewer&ReturnUrl=%2Fcommunities%2Fcommunity-home%2Fdigestviewer%3FCommunityKey%3D83fe128a-4d3e-4805-88dc-5acfaef5d555&gclid=CjwKCAiAtouOBhA6EiwA2nLKH4xG_eEmDrrY2JR0oUCL4lDjNmK11A3X-qefyJGei8APaAMBLNboYaRoCgI4QAvD_BwE. Accessed December 22nd 2021b.

New York State Office of Mental Health Health Action and Recovery Plans (2019). Available at https://www.omh.ny.gov/omhweb/bho/harp.html. Accessed March 21, 2022.

Ouayogodé MH, Colla CH, Lewis VA (2017). Determinants of Success in Shared Savings Programs: An Analysis of ACO and Market Characteristics. Healthc (Amst). 5:53–61.

RAND corporation (2018). Federal Block Grants to States for Mental Health, Substance Abuse, and Homelessness Potential Improvements to Funding Formulas. Available Online at https://www.rand.org/content/dam/rand/pubs/research_briefs/RB10000/RB10049/RAND_RB10049.pdf, Accessed December 25th 2021.

Ranz, J, Stueve, A, McQuistion, H (2001). The Role of the Psychiatrist: Job Satisfaction of Medical Directors and Staff Psychiatrists. *Community Ment Health J* **37,** 525–539.

Self R, Coffin, JA (2016). Creating Loose Alternative Payment Model Guiding Principles: A Brief Overview. *The Journal of Medical Practice Management: MPM, 32*(1), 6–8.

Shoyinka, S.O (2021). Innovative Financing, Incentivizing Value, in W.E Sowers, J.M Ranz. Seeking Value Balancing Cost and Quality in Psychiatric Care (pp 137-164) Washington D.C. American Psychiatric Publishing.

State Children's Health Insurance Program 2019. Available Online at https://www.benefits.gov/benefit/6173. Accessed December 21st, 2021.

Substance Abuse and Mental Health Services Administration. Certified Community Behavioral Health Organization. Available online at https://www.samhsa.gov/grants/grant-announcements/sm-21-013. Accessed December 22nd. 2021.

Substance Abuse and Mental Health Services Administration. Community Mental Health Services Block Grant. Available online at https://www.samhsa.gov/grants/block-grants/mhbg. Accessed December 22nd, 2021.

Unützer J, Chan Y, Hafer E, Knaster J, Shields S, Powers D, et al (2012) Quality Improvement with Pay-for-Performance Incentives in Integrated Behavioral Health Care. Am J Public Health. 102 : 41–45.

US. Dept of Health and Human Services May 2021. Available online at https://www.hhs.gov/about/news/2021/05/18/hhs-announces-3-billion-in-american-rescue-plan-funding-for-samhsa-block-grants.html. Accessed December 25th, 2021.

US Dept of Veterans Affairs (2021). Available online at https://www.va.gov/health/. Accessed December 22nd, 2021.

Winkelman TNA, Chang V (2018). Medicaid Expansion, Mental Health, and Access to Care among Childless Adults with and without Chronic Conditions. J Gen Intern Med. 33 (3): 376–383.

Yuan B, He L, Meng Q, Living J. Payment methods for outpatient care facilities Cochrane Database Syst Rev. 3; 2017.

Workforce Development in Community Psychiatry

Jeffrey C. Eisen

Building and retaining a high-performing team of psychiatrists dedicated to the biopsychosocial needs of highly complex and complicated patient population challenges even the most seasoned organizational leaders. Given the many barriers that limit the growth and development of a psychiatric team, it is imperative that organizations create and formalize ongoing, intentional strategies to recruit and retain a strong set of clinicians to meet the significant demand for community-based behavioral health services.

The objective of this chapter is threefold: (1) to review systemic challenges that affect workforce development in community psychiatry; (2) to consider practical, tangible approaches to recruitment and retention of a psychiatry workforce in community-based behavioral health; and (3) to describe broad actions that the field can collectively take to ensure that the workforce can adequately deliver quality care to those in need.

Case Study, Part 1: Mountain Behavioral Health

Mountain Behavioral Health is a major provider of mental health and substance use disorder treatment in the Pacific Northwest, serving approximately 18,000 individuals annually across a wide array of programs and services, including health centers, residential, street, crisis-based, and criminal justice interfacing programs and services.

Newly arrived Chief Medical Officer, Dr. Jason Ellis, MD, found seven full-time equivalent (FTE) open positions, reflecting a daunting task at hand. In getting to know the team, he recognized that all members of the psychiatry group were part-time employees, with some working as few as 4 h per week for the organization. Each psychiatric provider worked independently, with limited supervision or opportunities for collaboration among one another, or with the broader team of therapists and case managers. Salaries had not been reconsidered in several years, and the benefits package did not include allocations for continuing medical education (CME) days or dollars. The team appeared fragmented and disconnected from the broader integrated behavioral health approach toward which the organization was working. They expressed frustration and exhaustion. The team did acknowledge adequate time for assessments (60 min) and follow-up appointments (30 min), and while they felt comfortable with their caseloads, they recognized

J. C. Eisen (✉)
Department of Psychiatry, Oregon Health & Science University, Portland, OR, USA

Behavioral Health Network, MultiCare Health System, Tacoma, WA, USA
e-mail: jeffreyeisen@alumni.stanfordgsb.org

W. E. Sowers et al. (eds.), *Textbook of Community Psychiatry*,
https://doi.org/10.1007/978-3-031-10239-4_57

that there was little space in the schedule for new patients who needed care and treatment.

- What factors beyond the limited numbers of psychiatrists affect the ability to develop the community psychiatry workforce?
- How do broader, systemic challenges that exist in the field of psychiatry affect the circumstances described at Mountain Behavioral Health?

Systemic Barriers to Workforce Development in Community Psychiatry

Challenges facing the field of psychiatry, and more broadly, the practice of medicine, directly affect the ability to recruit and retain psychiatrists for work in community settings. Furthermore, community psychiatry is disproportionately affected by these factors based upon characteristics unique to this psychiatric specialization.

Supply and Demand Gap in Psychiatry

A 2018 study conducted by the American Association of Medical Colleges (AAMC) reported that there are 28,000 practicing psychiatrists in the United States (Japsen 2018). At face value, this may seem like a significant number. However, three in five psychiatrists are 55 years of age or greater, and it is expected that by 2025, demand may outstrip supply by 6090–15,600 psychiatrists nationwide (Weiner 2018). The supply of psychiatrists working with public sector insured populations already has seen a decline of 10% from 2003 to 2013 (Weiner 2018).

As described in a 2017 study by the National Council for Behavioral Healthcare, the psychiatric workforce is unevenly distributed across the country, noting that 77% of counties are underserved and 55% of states have an extreme shortage of child and adolescent psychiatrists (National Council Medical Director Institute 2017). The study further notes that 40% of the psychiatry workforce practices in cash-only private practices, which further limits the workforce for community-based behavioral health organizations (National Council Medical Director Institute 2017).

From 2001 to 2015, psychiatry residents increased by approximately 5%, suggesting an increase in the pipeline of medical students into the profession (Japsen 2018). This rate, however, does not match the expected decline of practicing psychiatrists over the next decade.

Effects of Reimbursement Limitations

The effects of low reimbursement and lack of payment parity are widespread and pervasive, affecting organizations and psychiatrists alike. It is an unfortunate irony that for psychiatry, low reimbursement rates for the provision of psychiatric care, particularly public sector-based care, are not sufficient to cover the cost of care provided (National Council Medical Director Institute 2017). This illogical reality does not hold for the vast majority of other medical specialties, or for other industries beyond medicine. Rarely, if ever, would an auto manufacturer sell a vehicle for a price less than that which it costs to produce it.

As a result of low rates, or without alternative payment models (see chapter "Creating Value: Resource and Quality Management") that provide more comprehensive approaches to revenue generation, a community mental health organization will frequently lose money on each psychiatrist hired. This in turn limits the number of psychiatrists that an organization may hire despite the demand, which limits needed access. Psychiatrists may also feel pressure to see more patients per hour and/or to carry higher overall caseloads, as organizations attempt to recoup the cost of the providers.

Physician Burnout and the Quadruple Aim

The rising prevalence of physician burnout represents a public health crisis, with providers reducing hours or leaving direct care due to the effects of ongoing work-related stress. Physician burnout, a work-related syndrome involving emotional exhaustion, depersonalization, and a sense of reduced personal accomplishment, is prevalent internationally (West et al. 2018). Rates of burnout symptoms associated with adverse effects on patients, the healthcare workforce, costs, and physician health exceed 50% in studies of both physicians-in-training and practicing physicians (West et al. 2018). Two in five psychiatrists are experiencing professional burnout (American Psychiatric Association 2020), a concerning rate that accelerates plans to retire early. The pursuit of non-direct care healthcare positions with consulting firms, payers, or other private sector organizations, or leaving the field altogether, further depletes the availability of psychiatrists. This short supply of psychiatric providers creates challenges in recruitment and retention. Active approaches to address the risks associated with burnout provide a foundation for workforce development efforts at individual, organizational, and systemic levels.

Taking on a leadership role that includes administrative activities can be new for many physicians, given that the skills associated with such work are not emphasized in medical school or residency programs and are often viewed from afar while providing clinical care. When physicians find themselves working in roles for which they were not sufficiently trained, they face a greater risk of burnout (Kumar 2016). Hence, specific training and education on leadership and administration, particularly workforce development, for physicians has become increasingly important.

The Institute for Healthcare Improvement (IHI) developed the Triple Aim framework to help healthcare organizations address health system performance in three dimensions – improving the patient experience of care (including quality and satisfaction), improving the health of populations, and reducing the per capita cost of care (Institute for Healthcare Improvement 2020a, b). Because of heightened concerns regarding physician burnout and the imperative to address systemic healthcare inequities and disparities, IHI has suggested that organizations evolve from the Triple Aim to the Quadruple Aim, adding an additional objective to elevate joy in work (Institute for Healthcare Improvement 2020a, b).

Health Inequity, Representation, and Implications for Workforce Development

The psychiatric work force suffers from a lack of disparity within its workforce as well as its inability to reflect the communities in which it serves. Only 10.4% of practicing psychiatrists are Black, LatinX, or Native American, as compared to 32.6% of the US population (Nitkin 2020). In addition, 38.5% of practicing psychiatrists are women versus 50.8% of the US population (Nitkin 2020). Trends indicate a reduction in underrepresentation, and the field is more diverse than other medical specialties. However, poor representation of minority populations among practicing psychiatrists, including psychiatry faculty and fellows, continues and is an ongoing concern (Wyse et al. 2020). The trend of increased minority representation among residents is not replicated among fellows and faculty (Wyse et al. 2020).

Without intentional equity, diversity, and inclusion (EDI), efforts that work toward correcting these disparities, organizations, and institutions continue to have difficulty in all segments of the workforce pipeline, including attracting individuals to the field, recruiting and retaining minority providers, and, importantly, developing culturally relevant and specific programs and services that ultimately reduce health inequities and improve outcomes.

However, mission statements and mandates supporting EDI efforts cannot achieve such goals without reform and redesign of structures that contain practices and policies which, unintentionally or otherwise, perpetuate racism and lead to a lack of progress in diversity and inclusion (Sudak and Stewart 2020). Particularly in community psychiatry, where individuals pursue work as part of a mission-driven objective of working to correct inequities and improve the lives of individuals often marginalized from traditional avenues of care, providers are less likely to sign on to, or stay in, a role where these efforts are not prioritized by an organization or where change is perceived as futile (Sudak and Stewart 2020).

Case Study: Part 2

Dr. Ellis recognized that filling open roles was only one part of the challenge. He thought about the importance of hiring the *right* providers – those with passion for community psychiatry and, in particular, those who are invested in and reflective of the communities served by Mountain Behavioral Health – rather than any available provider. He wondered whether this would be possible in an environment where the demand for psychiatric providers far exceeds the supply of available providers.

He also wanted to ensure that current providers would remain on board and not jump at the opportunity to join another organization. Dr. Ellis aspired to keep new hires for the long term, rather than as temporary participants in care, which could have detrimental effects on team morale and quality of care provided to patients. He hoped to build a diverse, talented team that is engaged in the mission of Mountain and where individuals view themselves as having a future at the organization. This required a defined, focused strategy in collaboration with human resource partners and the entire psychiatry team.

The vignette suggests the following questions:

- What areas of concern did Dr. Ellis identify that can affect the ability to hire and maintain a robust team of psychiatrists?
- What framework might Dr. Ellis use to organize his thoughts around this effort?
- How are recruitment and retention defined? In what ways are they unique, and in what ways might the recruitment and retention activities serve one another?
- What specific, practical tactics might Dr. Ellis pursue to successfully recruit psychiatrists for his community-based organization?
- What are the primary factors that affect employee retention?

Definitions and a Simple Strategic Framework

Recruitment refers to the overall process of identifying, attracting, screening, interviewing, and presenting offers to suitable candidates for jobs within an organization (Smart Recruiters 2020). *Retention* is defined as the ability to maintain or keep employees in an organization and is often referred to by the percentage of employees kept in positions over a certain period of time (Mitchel 2020). For example, if 80% of employees are retained in their roles over a 1-year period of time, then 20% of employees turned over or left the organization in a given year. Both definitions suggest the importance of the development of a long-term strategy and a defined process to address these needs rather than solely considering the hiring tactics necessary to achieve workforce development goals.

Recruitment is generally viewed as an external activity, searching for outside candidates for roles, while retention is primarily internally focused with current employees. While there are unique approaches to recruitment and retention, many specifics of each overlap and serve one another. For instance, recruiting for leadership roles in an organization often occurs internally. Similarly, the development of a strong retention program can enable the ability to recruit candidates who view these internal efforts favorably for their career growth, development, and satisfaction as they consider career choices and opportunities.

The Join-Stay-Leave model is a simple framework for organizing employee recruitment and retention efforts (VSkills Tutorial 2020). It enables an evaluation of the internal and external environments that can shape hiring efforts and serve as a source of reflection for how to better the needs of one's workforce. It essentially serves as a "three-legged stool" of workforce development efforts. The three questions posed by the model include:

- Why does someone *join* my organization?
- Why does someone *stay* in the organization?
- Why does someone *leave* the organization?

Leaders can learn a great deal about the strengths and weakness of their teams and organizations by conducting this three-part assessment. Conversely, not gathering data about one leg of the "three-legged stool" may result in not effectively developing strategies to recruit and retain a quality workforce.

Recruitment Approaches

The medical literature, a primary resource for psychiatrists and psychiatry leaders, contains little about practical, concrete aspects of recruiting qualified professionals. However, human resources-based publications, and physician recruiting specialists in particular, provide a wealth of information with regard to how to develop one's recruitment strategy and course of action.

A Consistent Plan

One mistake that is commonly seen in physician recruiting efforts is viewing each hire independently, pursuing an ad hoc hiring approach to fill the open role, and then ending recruiting efforts altogether when positions are successfully filled. This leaves an organization vulnerable to ebbs and flows in staffing, as well as changes in demand that might be experienced within a community or population. A consistent, longer-term approach can consider internal staffing and external community needs, the refining of roles over time, benefits and compensation review, and, importantly, the development of internal and external collaborative partnerships that are vital given the ongoing limited supply of candidates across communities (Medicus Firm 2018).

Position Review

A core component of a recruitment plan includes review of salary and benefits. These factors can rapidly change in hiring environments where there is a distortion in provider supply and demand, particularly applicable to community psychiatry. Development of policies and procedures to ensure benefits beyond salary itself can be compelling as well. This may include such tactics as considering bonuses for additional skills gained, such as a second language or the ability to prescribe buprenorphine. CME dollars or days may be standard in academic environments but can be limited or absent in community settings, as well as reimbursement of licenses and provision of malpractice insurance. If possible, time can also be allocated for research or leadership and administrative activities.

Internal and External Partnerships

The pressure to successfully hire to meet a great community demand can often fall to one person in a community organization, such as a Medical Director or a Human Resources Manager. This process is more likely to result in the achievement of its hiring goals with a team effort that is invested in its success. It begins with inviting multiple medical and nonmedical, clinical team members into the process. This can be accomplished with such methods as inquiring as to what characteristics team members would like to see in their peers, developing specific sets of interview questions, brainstorming how and where to find potential candidates, and holding brief, *regular* meetings to discuss current openings and potential candidates, or to consistently include this in a standing team meeting.

Partnering with a Human Resources (HR) professional enables both the HR and the medical teams to share their unique areas of expertise with one another. Medical providers are able to utilize their own personal and professional networks that can lead to highly qualified candidates whose clinical experiences and interpersonal skills are well known. Similarly, HR professionals build the external brand of the organization by developing relationships with candidates and physician organizations and provide great support in many forms, including locating and screening candidates, coordinating interviewing efforts, and selling the opportunities to candidates. This offsets the clinical demands of the medical team that reduce their abilities to consistently attend to the recruiting effort.

It is important to note that not all community-based behavioral health organizations have a medical director to be the point person from which these efforts can be directed. Limited funding and reimbursement under a Medicaid fee-for-service model has led to the reduction in administrative, non-direct revenue-generating time for individuals who provide medical services. This affects both the ability to recruit and to retain psychiatrists, as described later. Recent Alternative Payment Methodologies, including the Certified Community Behavioral Health (CCBHC) Prospective Payment System, has emphasized the allocation of medical director hours to more fully address the needs of patients, and the broader needs of the organization in its provision of psychiatric services (National Council for Behavioral Health 2015).

Utilizing an Equity Lens

The importance of a psychiatry workforce that reflects the communities it serves cannot be understated. Building a team with an emphasis on equity, diversity, and inclusion requires an intentional, consistent effort that begins with listening and learning from both psychiatric staff and clients regarding historical and current structural racism and marginalization that exists broadly across the healthcare system, and more specifically within psychiatry and the organization itself (Sudak and Stewart 2020). With this foundation, the development of an action plan with specific workforce development goals can lay the groundwork for a recruiting effort.

Ideally, this plan derives from a broader organizational racial equity plan that is embedded in the mission, vision, and values of an organization. Executive support of such efforts is critical to and predictive of the success of such a plan, as an executive team's support sends an important message about the importance and priorities around EDI efforts. Nonetheless, the dedication of a medical team and HR partnership in the implementation of such a plan can still deliver results of great benefit to patients and the broader community.

A number of specific tactics can enable the infusing of an equity lens into recruiting efforts. Developing an EDI Recruitment Committee that, among many activities, places a representative on an interview team to specifically ensure consideration of EDI goals helps to ensure intentionality and consistency in hiring. Interview questions that specifically speak to understanding a candidate's own self-perceptions related to race and ethnicity, comfort level in working with a diverse set of patients, and understanding of culturally relevant and specific approaches can provide valuable information in hiring decisions. Given the dearth of psychiatrists in many communities, it can be difficult to resist the temptation to hire the first available and qualified candidate. However, holding positions open long enough to allow a diverse set of candidates to apply can lead to long-term success in one's hiring goals. Networking widely to seek out a range of candidates is key to this approach.

The Right Candidate Versus Any Candidate

As noted, the hiring of any available candidate – based on the pressure to find providers to meet considerable demand – may provide some initial relief but ultimately hinders a long-term, team building strategy. From the patient-centered perspective, the arrival and departure of a psychiatrist affect the therapeutic alliance and treatment efforts. The expense of hiring, as well as the expense associated with onboarding new psychiatrists to a team, can be formidable. Therefore, assessing the qualifications and fit with the culture of an organization should remain a priority even in times of shortage (Rappleye 2015). Utilizing short-term strategies such as temporary providers may be necessary in combination with an ongoing recruiting plan.

Role of Technology

Changes in technology have had enormous effects on the delivery of psychiatric care, particularly amidst the COVID-19 pandemic, which led to further proliferation of telepsychiatry and the relaxation of regulations to enable ongoing reimbursement of such services (see chapter "Telehealth and Community Psychiatry"). Technology offers great benefits to recruiting efforts as well. The creation of an organizational telehealth program enables the hiring of staff from anywhere in the country, without individuals having to relocate if they do not desire to do so. This opens up a much greater pool of candidates than in the past by enabling a recruitment process that spans well beyond the region in which an organization is located. Telehealth also promotes improved work-life balance for psychiatrists by allowing providers to work from home or in a clinic-home hybrid model, which can be a strong selling opportunity for recruiters.

Scope of Practice and the Development of a Psychiatry Team: Partnership with Advanced Practice Professionals (APPs) in Workforce Development

For many organizations, and more broadly for the overall delivery of psychiatry across communities, building a team with a hybrid of psychiatric providers has been an essential workforce development strategy to meet the demand for services. Given the national and worldwide shortage in psychiatrists, as previously described, utilization of APPs as partners with psychiatrists can provide not only additional direct care support but also expertise in patient care approaches given the nursing experience that many APPs carry as part of their past work experience.

The inclusion of other professionals who provide psychiatric medication-based services to patients has evolved over time. While not unique to psychiatry, the roles of advanced practice registered nurses (APRNs), physician assistants (PAs), and pharmacists have filled voids particularly noticeable in community settings that can be isolated and underserved (Runnels 2021). Many factors are attributed to this trend, including a persistent lack of access to psychiatric services, the psychiatric workforce shortage, and, unfortunately, limited reimbursement leading to motivation to find more cost-effective means of care.

Today, APPs have emerged as instrumental in the delivery of psychiatric care across community settings (Runnels 2021). Along with this has emerged opportunities for the growth and development of APPs, including APPs serving as Medical Directors that provide administrative leadership and clinical supervisory support to their colleagues.

Controversy and tension do exist with the expansion of providers addressing the psychiatric needs of patients. As the field of psychiatry considers the value proposition of the psychiatrist within the behavioral health field, opportunity exists to recruit a larger base of providers, fostering increased professional collaboration and consideration of how these disciplines together can deliver accessible, high quality care (Runnels 2021).

Recruitment-Retention Interrelationships

As stated, factors that attract candidates to positions also can help retain them. It is well described that salary is only one factor in recruiting and retaining professionals – in many cases, it is not the most important factor, and is a factor that wanes in importance over time (Chamberlain

2017). Few psychiatry salaries can keep someone in a role that experiences ongoing dissatisfaction (Chamberlain 2017).

Working on continuous internal improvements, and advocating with organization leadership as to the integral role of psychiatry in community-based settings, is critical to ensure that providers join the community psychiatry workforce and stay in the workforce versus pursuing other avenues of income, including in private practice and non-direct care industries. Expanding EDI efforts beyond recruiting by developing and maintaining efforts to include, advance, and address the well-being of diverse colleagues after joining an organization is of particular importance (Sudak and Stewart 2020).

Retention Factors

Community psychiatrists face numerous vulnerabilities that affect one's work satisfaction, and the most dedicated providers face the greatest risk of burnout (Seppälä and Moeller 2018). Large caseloads, pressure to reduce time with patients, and extensive documentation requirements add burdens that directly affect quality of care. Without adequate supervision or collaborative opportunities with fellow providers, the work can become increasingly isolating. This isolation is exacerbated by the complex and challenging nature of community psychiatry, where there are limited opportunities for interactions with other psychiatrists, the high level of complex needs of the patient population, as well as substantial socioeconomic disparities that affect quality of life and health outcomes. These aspects of the work can challenge even the most committed community psychiatrist.

Das and Baruah (2013) conducted an extensive review of the published literature on workforce retention. They describe multiple factors associated with the successful retention of employees within organizations, all of which relevant to community psychiatry. These include the areas that follow.

Compensation

While compensation has been found to have a negative effect on turnover, it is also notable that compensation is *not* consistently one of the primary factors influencing the decision to leave one's role (Noah 2008; Ramlall 2003). This has multiple implications, first and foremost that leaders need to consider multiple approaches to retention of staff and, furthermore, that intangible benefits can be as important to cultivate over time as the presented benefits and compensation package. Therefore, the remainder of this section is dedicated to describing numerous intangible benefits that have been found to enhance the overall experience of work (Hewitt 2002).

Leadership

The common saying that people do not leave a job, they leave a boss, continues to hold true. In a national study, 57% of respondents left a job because of their supervisor, and an additional 32% seriously considered leaving because of their direct manager (DDI 2019). When employees left because of a lack of quality work or the opportunity to grow in an organization, they cited their manager as the person who could have helped ameliorate these concerns (Goler et al. 2018). Therefore, strong leadership is essential to employee retention efforts.

The lack of a strong medical director role in many community-based behavioral health organizations exacerbates such concerns, as it leaves psychiatric providers without a resource for support when needed. A medical leader can also assure consistent individual and/or peer-based supervision that can uphold quality care and assist in navigating administrative or other cross-disciplinary matters. Conversely, leaders can also ensure that providers have the autonomy they desire to direct care in a manner of greatest benefit to patients, and in line with their training and licensure.

Public psychiatry fellowships serve an important role in providing the framework and experiences that enable psychiatrists to successfully take on leadership roles in community settings. Following the launch of the first program at Columbia University, the presence of public psychiatry fellowships has grown over time, numbering over 20 nationwide (see chapter "Public and Community Psychiatry Fellowships").

The fostering of medical director roles in community settings can have significant positive effects on the satisfaction of both psychiatric providers and those that hold medical director roles (Ranz and Stueve 1998). In a study of public psychiatry fellowship alumni, both program medical directors and staff psychiatrists asserted that participation in clinical collaboration tasks led to increased satisfaction. Psychiatrists found benefit in having a greater sense of involvement with their community mental health colleagues. However, a reexamination of that data concluded that, notwithstanding those assertions, it was the performance of administrative (and not clinical collaboration) tasks that correlated with higher job satisfaction (Ranz and Stueve 1998).

Work-Life Balance

Acknowledgment of priorities outside of work, and providing some flexibility to address such needs and interests, can improve balance, increase workforce participation and engagement, and increase productivity and reduce costs (Ashford et al. 1989). The development of policies and procedures to support such efforts enables the actualization of these benefits. For example, development of telehealth approaches during the COVID-19 pandemic has enabled flexibility for both patients and providers. Patients who have access to technology can attend appointments from a variety of locations, which has multiple effects, from saving time and money on transportation to solving childcare needs. Providers also can benefit from work-from-home arrangements, which support balance and flexibility.

Recognition and Appreciation

Fostering a culture of recognition and appreciation can go a long way toward maintaining a dedicated team of providers. Recognition refers to giving positive feedback for performance. It is conditional, based upon specific achievement, and the feedback can be tangible, such as a bonus or promotion, or intangible, such as praise for a job well done. Appreciation, while similar, is based upon the inherent value or personal worth of an individual or team. The results of recognition and appreciation are significant – individuals feel validated and understood, leading to greater trust and connection (Robbins 2019).

Participation in Decision-Making

Participation in decision-making consists of two key components – having a voice *and* being heard. Creating a culture where individuals feel that they can speak up with regard to that which works well and that which needs improvement, and where they are rewarded for such behavior, takes time and energy to foster yet is the key to continuous quality improvement within an organization. This endeavor only succeeds if ideas are considered and/or acted upon. Helping teams and individuals understand which ideas may be immediately actionable, which are indeed possible and take time, and where there may be limits or boundaries to that which can be modified (and how those ideas may be refined to become actionable) can lead to conversations that spark collective investment in a team's efforts, and also transparently conveys the opportunities and challenges associated with change.

Opportunity for Growth

Each psychiatrist on a team may have different thoughts and plans with regard to their career goals. Some direct care providers may seek promotion to a leadership position. Others may view growth as developing their skills and acumen in the direct care of patients, such as enhancing knowledge in treatment of substance use disorders, understanding new approaches to psychopharmacology, or building skills in new modalities of care including transcranial magnetic stimulation (TMS) or electroconvulsive therapy (ECT). Policy and advocacy work are additional areas of interest for many providers. Understanding and being able to deliver on the short- and long-term goals of team members provide a signal to providers that the organization is invested in them and provide motivation for providers to maintain their commitment to the work.

Training and Development

As described above, training and development is an important component of growth opportunities for providers, allowing the maintenance of current skills and the development of new skills and knowledge of care and treatment. The CME requirement for ongoing licensure and board certification further supports the need for ongoing training but is not universally provided as a benefit to psychiatrists in community organizations. Organizations can find it difficult to provide CMEs for internal trainings due to the complex requirements associated with offering CME-certified programming. This is a barrier that is less prevalent for other behavioral health professional certifications, enabling organizations to offer CEs but not CMEs, even if the training is relevant to medical professionals. Partnering with a university or other organization that is accredited to offer CMEs provides one avenue to make CMEs more accessible; providing CME dollars or days as part of a compensation package enables providers the autonomy to direct their learning as they see fit.

Provision of regular individual or group supervision also enables providers the opportunity to gain insights and learn new skills, which is particularly useful in a community psychiatry setting where cases can be particularly complex. Supervision further allows the ability for providers to process transferential and countertransferential feelings about the patients they serve, enabling self-reflection and greater self-understanding. Importantly, supervision provides support and connection with others that can ameliorate risks of burnout and maintain engagement.

Case Study: Part 3

Dr. Ellis rolled up his sleeves and got to work on developing the medical team at Mountain Behavioral Health. He took the time to listen and learn from the medical team, respecting the culture as it currently existed before embarking on quick changes that could lead to resistance. He actively participated in organization-wide racial equity efforts to seek intentional improvements that would best serve patients and the medical team.

He developed a biannual all-medical team meeting to enable didactic training as well as administrative matters, build connections between providers, and offer breakout groups to identify areas for improvement and share ideas. He identified providers with interest in developing leadership skills and allocated a few hours per week for these individuals to serve as point persons for their areas of responsibility, such as for the organization's health centers and residential programs; these positions evolved to program Medical Director roles, in which they continued to provide a significant percentage of patient care while maintaining the point person representation. This team met one to two times monthly to consider clinical and administrative matters, with specific emphasis on reviewing and implementing a consistent recruiting and retention strategy that emphasized equity, diversity, and inclusion principles. This team also partnered with the People & Culture (Human Resources) department to review regional standards in benefits and compensation.

Group and individual supervision was instituted, as well as expanding annual performance evaluations to the medical team. He was not able to overcome the requirements of CME accreditation but, after much advocacy, was able to offer CME dollars and days as part of the overall benefits and compensation strategy. He also was able to purchase a best clinical practices database from which providers could receive CMEs for searching for and reviewing articles. A telepsychiatry program was developed amidst the COVID-19 pandemic that provided increased flexibility for providers and patients, with plans to continue the hybrid approach, with advocacy with payers for continued parity in reimbursement with in-person care.

Clinically specific improvements were initiated based on needs identified by the medical team and asked for by patients. A new, in-house pharmacy vendor was identified after numerous concerns arose regarding medication dosage and distribution accuracy. Collaboration with other behavioral health team members was encouraged and enhanced, with a specific emphasis on care coordination for complex, co-occurring physical and mental health concerns.

The filling of the empty seven positions started slowly, but over time, the efforts gained momentum. The recruitment and retention work gained recognition across the region, and word spread among providers, leading to increased applications for open roles. After two-and-a-half years of effort, all seven full-time roles were filled, and, in a first for the organization, multiple candidates needed to be considered for roles that opened due to retirement or performance management.

Calls to Action

The 2001 convening of concerned patients, family members, providers, and policymakers led to the formation of the Annapolis Coalition on the Behavioral Health Workforce, which led to the development of a national action plan for workforce development across all sectors of the behavioral health field (Hoge et al. 2009).

With the support of the Substance Abuse and Mental Health Services Administration (SAMHSA), the coalition proposed goals to develop the behavioral health workforce. By broadening the concept of workforce, communities and individuals with lived experience have increased ability to describe their needs, thereby informing psychiatry and nonpsychiatric behavioral health professionals as to optimal care and treatment practices. Strengthening the behavioral health workforce emphasizes improving recruitment and retention strategies, including provider development via leadership and training. Building infrastructure, including a national research and evaluation effort, enables technical assistance, data collection, and analysis necessary to implement and monitor progress related to workforce development efforts (Hoge et al. 2009; Schoenwald et al. 2010).

Similar themes, with an increased emphasis on leveraging policy-based initiatives to strengthen the psychiatry workforce, emerged from a 2017 report on the psychiatric shortage published by the National Council for Behavioral Healthcare Medical Director Institute (MDI). The MDI convened a broad group of "practitioners, administrators, policymakers, researchers, innovators, educators, advocates, and payers" charged with identifying the root causes of the concern, finding solutions, and listing actionable approaches that can be taken at the national, regional, and local levels (National Council Medical Director Institute 2017).

An important conclusion drawn from the effort was that "increasing the number of psychiatrists – *by itself* – would not be sufficient to improve access and the quality of care." The solutions, they asserted, derive from a range of efforts designed that affect every aspect of care delivery – not only growing the workforce but also increasing the efficiency of delivery of psychiatric services, including care coordination and information exchange; implementing models of integrated care; training medical students, residents, and the current workforce in new models of care; adopting effective payment structures that adequately reimburse psychiatrists for the cost of care; and actively working to reduce the percentage of psychiatric providers who engage in cash-only, private practices (National Council Medical Director Institute 2017).

With this in mind, strategies to expand the capacity of a limited psychiatry workforce have emerged, most notably the development of team-based care approaches. Originally developed within primary care practices, the adaptation of a team-based care framework for behavioral health considers the many potential roles that exist in the successful delivery of psychiatric care within behavioral health settings. Utilization of medical assistant, nursing, and care coordinator roles in tandem with psychiatric providers can enable each of these professionals to work at the top of their skill sets, thereby enabling psychiatrists to focus their attention on areas for which they offer their greatest skills. This can allow for increased satisfaction in work, reduced time required in administrative, non-patient care activity, and create a more efficient patient flow to the satisfaction of both patients and providers (National Council Medical Director Institute 2020).

The psychiatry workforce crisis, and more broadly, the significant lack of community behavioral health providers nationwide, has been widely described and discussed. The prediction of a shortage of psychiatrists has come to fruition, with greater shortages expected over time. Macro, policy-based initiatives, in combination with practical, local recruiting and retention efforts tailored to specific patient populations and geographies, are necessary components of an overall strategy to consider and successfully address community psychiatry workforce growth and development.

References

American Psychiatric Association (2020). *Well-being and Burnout.* Retrieved from https://www.psychiatry.org/psychiatrists/practice/well-being-and-burnout

Ashford, S., Lee, C., & Bobko, P. (1989). Content, Causes, and Consequences of Job Insecurity: A Theory-based Measure and Substantive Test. Academy of Management. Journal, 32(4), 803-829. https://doi.org/10.2307/256569

Chamberlain, A. (2017, January 17). *What Matters More to Your Workforce Than Money.* Retrieved from https://hbr.org/2017/01/what-matters-more-to-your-workforce-than-money

Das, B.L., & Baruah, M. (2013). Employee Retention: A Review of Literature. International Organization of Science and Research (IOSR) Journal of Business and Management, (14)2, 8-16. https://doi.org/10.9790/487X-1420816

DDI (2019, December 9). *New DDI Research: 57 Percent of Employees Quit Because of Their Boss.* Retrieved from https://www.prnewswire.com/news-releases/new-ddi-research-57-percent-of-employees-quit-because-of-their-boss-300971506.html

Goler, L., Gale, J., Harrington, B., & Grant, A. (2018, January 11). *Why People Really Quit Their Jobs.* Retrieved from https://hbr.org/2018/01/why-people-really-quit-their-jobs

Hewitt, P. (2002). High Performance Workplaces: The Role of Employee Involvement in a Modern Economy. Retrieved from http://www.berr.gov.uk/files/file26555.pdf

Hoge, M.A., Morris, J.A., Stuart, G.W., Huey, L.Y., Bergeson, S., Flaherty, M.T., Morgan, O., Peterson, J., Daniels, A.S., Paris, M., & Madenwald, K. (2009). A National Action Plan for Workforce Development in Behavioral Health. Psychiatric Services, 60(7), 883-7. https://doi.org/10.1176/ps.2009.60.7.883

Institute for Healthcare Improvement (2020a). *IHI Triple aim Initiative.* Retrieved from http://www.ihi.org/Engage/Initiatives/TripleAim/Pages/default.aspx

Institute for Healthcare Improvement (2020b). *The Triple Aim or the Quadruple Aim? Four Points to Help Set Your Strategy.* Retrieved from http://www.ihi.org/communities/blogs/the-triple-aim-or-the-quadruple-aim-four-points-to-help-set-your-strategy

Japsen, B. (2018, February 25). *Psychiatrist Shortage Escalates As U.S. Mental Health Needs Grow.* Retrieved from https://www.forbes.com/sites/brucejapsen/2018/02/25/psychiatrist-shortage-escalates-as-u-s-mental-health-needs-grow/?sh=6e1f5fdb1255

Kumar, S. (2016). Burnout and Doctors: Prevalence, Prevention and Intervention. Healthcare, 4(3), 37. https://doi.org/10.3390/healthcare4030037

Mitchel, M. (2020, August 4). The Building Blocks of a Successful Employee Retention Strategy. Retrieved from https://www.smartrecruiters.com/blog/the-building-blocks-of-a-successful-employee-retention-strategy/

Medicus Firm (2018, December 31). *7 Ways to Set Up 2019 for Physician Recruiting Success.* Retrieved from https://www.themedicusfirm.com/news/7-ways-to-set-up-2019-for-physician-recruiting-success

National Council for Behavioral Health (2015, June). Appendix III - Section 223, Demonstration Programs to Improve Community Mental Health Services Prospective Payment System (PPS) Guidance. Retrieved from https://www.thenationalcouncil.org/wp-content/uploads/2015/06/Appendix-III-CMS-PPS-Guidance.pdf?daf=375ateTbd56

National Council Medical Director Institute (2017, March 28). Retrieved from https://www.thenationalcouncil.org/wp-content/uploads/2017/03/Psychiatric-Shortage_National-Council-.pdf?daf=375ateTbd56

National Council Medical Director Institute (2020, January). Retrieved from https://www.thenationalcouncil.org/wp-content/uploads/2021/01/010521_

Psychiatric_Workflow_Team-based_Care_Toolkit.pdf?daf=375ateTbd56

Nitkin, K. (2020, August 31). *Johns Hopkins Study Shows Need for More Diversity in Psychiatry.* Retrieved from https://www.hopkinsmedicine.org/news/articles/johns-hopkins-study-shows-need-for-more-diversity-in-psychiatry

Noah, Y. (2008). A Study of Worker Participation in Management Decision Making Within Selected Establishments in Lagos, Nigeria. Journal of Social Science, 17(1): 31-39. https://doi.org/10.1080/09718923.2008.11892631

Ramlall, S. (2003). Managing Employee Retention as a Strategy for Increasing Organizational Competitiveness, Applied H.R.M. Research, 8(2), 63-72.

Ranz, J., & Stueve, A. (1998). The Role of the Psychiatrist as Program Medical Director. Psychiatric Services, 49(9), 1203-1207. https://doi.org/ https://doi.org/10.1176/ps.49.9.1203

Rappleye, E. (2015, July 30). *8 strategies to recruit and retain top physicians.* Retrieved from https://www.beckershospitalreview.com/hospital-physician-relationships/8-strategies-to-recruit-and-retain-top-physicians.html

Robbins, M. (2019, November 12). *Why Employees Need Both Recognition and Appreciation.* Retrieved from https://hbr.org/2019/11/why-employees-need-both-recognition-and-appreciation

Runnels, P. (2021). Psychiatric Workforce Development. *Seeking Value: Balancing Cost and Quality in Psychiatric Care,* 359-394

Schoenwald, S.K., Hoagwood, K.E., Atkins, M.S., Evans, M.E., & Ringeisen, H. (2010). Workforce Development and the Organization of Work: The Science We Need. Administration and Policy in Mental Health and Mental Health Services, 37(1-2), 71-80. https://doi.org/10.1007/s10488-010-0278-z

Seppälä, E., & Moeller, J. (2018, May 16). *1 in 5 Highly Engaged Employees is at Risk of Burnout.* https://hbr.org/2018/02/1-in-5-highly-engaged-employees-is-at-risk-of-burnout

Sudak, D.M., & Stewart, A. J. (2020). Can We Talk? The Role of Organized Psychiatry in Addressing Structural Racism to Achieve Diversity and Inclusion in Psychiatric Workforce Development. Academic Psychiatry, published online in advance of print, 12 January 2021. https://doi.org/10.1007/s40596-020-01393-9

Smart Recruiters (2020). *Recruitment.* Retrieved from https://www.smartrecruiters.com/resources/glossary/recruitment/

VSkills Tutorial (2020). *Join-Stay-Leave Model.* Retrieved from https://www.vskills.in/certification/tutorial/join-stay-leave-model/

Weiner, S. (2018, February 12). *Addressing the escalating psychiatrist shortage.* Retrieved from https://www.aamc.org/news-insights/addressing-escalating-psychiatrist-shortage

West, C.P., Dyrbye, L.N., & Shanafelt, T.D. (2018). Physician Burnout: Contributors, Consequences and Solutions. Journal of Internal Medicine, 283(6), 516-529. https://doi.org/10.1111/joim.12752.

Wyse, R., Hwang, W.T., Ahmed, A.A., Richards, E., & Deville, C Jr. (2020). Diversity by Race, Ethnicity, and Sex within the US Psychiatry Physician Workforce. Academic Psychiatry, 44(5), 523-530. https://doi.org/10.1007/s40596-020-01276-z

Practical Ethics for Practicing Clinicians

John S. Rozel and Darcy M. Moschenross

Introduction

The work of community psychiatry places professionals in a complex and overlapping territory where clinical interests, patient rights, state laws, professional rules, and cultural frames all meet and blend. While much of the work of a community psychiatrist lies unambiguously in the domain of ethical practice, there are borders where ethical principles are more difficult to apply. While efforts should always be made to stay within the precepts of ethical practice, few practitioners would doubt that there are times where such boundaries become ambiguous and complex.

And yet, for all the intellectual richness of the interplay between community psychiatry and medical ethics, most community psychiatrists find their time best spent engaging and working with their patients through the course and management of their illnesses and stressors. For most, community psychiatry is an immensely practical science: work done in the streets, clinics, and emergency departments of our neighborhoods, usually far removed from access to traditional medical ethics consultation services. Ethics committees can be quite useful when available, but they may take more time than is practical for the practitioner. Attention is inevitably and necessarily given to practical matters of clinical management and safety than to matters of philosophy and ethics.

Arguably, one of the necessary skills of community psychiatrists is their ability to interact with patients nimbly, compassionately, and effectively, in a time and manner most conducive to their full participation in care. This engagement benefits from creativity and flexibility. While caring for our patients ethically is critical, the reality is that we often face complex ethical questions with less-than-ideal resources and support. This chapter is intended to support frontline community psychiatrists in making ethical decisions quickly in the real world.

J. S. Rozel (✉)
University of Pittsburgh, Pittsburgh, PA, USA

Resolve Crisis Services of UPMC Western Psychiatric Hospital,
Pittsburgh, PA, USA
e-mail: rozeljs@upmc.edu

D. M. Moschenross
University of Pittsburgh, Pittsburgh, PA, USA

Psychiatric Consult Liaison Service, UPMC Western Psychiatric Hospital, Pittsburgh, PA, USA
e-mail: moschenrossdm@upmc.edu

Not All Ethical Problems Are Difficult

When many people think about medical ethics, their minds leap to complex cases – the outliers and extreme cases they have struggled with

W. E. Sowers et al. (eds.), *Textbook of Community Psychiatry*,
https://doi.org/10.1007/978-3-031-10239-4_58

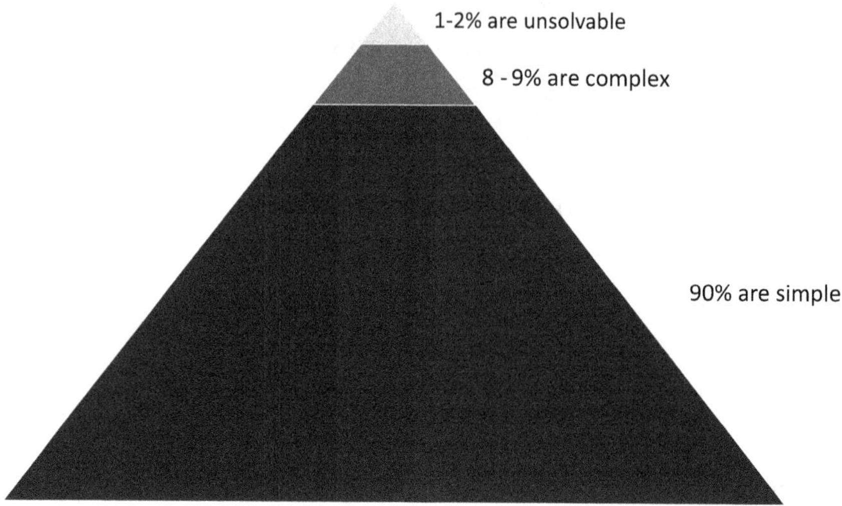

Fig. 1 The hierarchy of difficulty in ethical problems

before. The reality is that the most difficult cases are the most exceptional: they are uncommon and are not routine. Clinicians encounter a myriad of ethical decisions every day and navigate the overwhelming majority of them without difficulty and, often, without a second thought. A small subset is difficult, but resolvable and an even smaller subset may be unsolvable. Consider, as an arbitrary breakdown and as a modified Pareto principle (i.e., the 80:20 principle, where a small number of cases require a disproportionate amount of attention) as outlined in Fig. 1.

90% of Ethical Issues Are Simple

They are easily and appropriately resolved with little effort or thought. For example, obtaining informed consent, supporting client autonomy, or not breaching our various duties and responsibilities are actions done routinely and with little conscious ethical consideration. (For example: patient – "If I give you cash, then will you prescribe me 180 Xanax for my depression?" Psychiatrist: "Nope.")

8–9% of Ethical Issues Are Complex

These require consideration of the issues, the stakeholders, and a thoughtful application of various rules and laws to lead to an appropriate outcome. These issues are solvable but require effort – and, perhaps, more time than is typically readily available in routine clinical practice.

1–2% of Ethical Issues Are Unsolvable

These tend to defy even the most astute analysis. No matter how cleverly current laws and rules are applied, the answer remains substantively unsatisfactory. New rules or laws created for the specific problem are likely to be similarly flawed. Clinicians must recognize these problems for what they are, and not be overly concerned about leaving them unsolved. Clinical work is demanding – and the substance of such work may be undermined by inappropriate expenditures to solve extraordinarily complex conundrums.

Thus, the best application of ethical thinking in community psychiatry may best be spent on the second cluster: complex but solvable situations. The first group requires little conscious attention. The third, once recognized, can be carefully and deliberately set aside, recognizing that even great effort will result in solutions which are imperfect or untimely. As difficult as it can be to accept, not every clinical dilemma has a solution that is both clearly ethical and clinically satisfying.

Preliminary Considerations

Before engaging in ethical analysis, two considerations should be addressed by the clinician. First, is there a cultural or cognitive bias which is skewing the perception of the ethical problem, or even a cultural misunderstanding which is creating a conflict and an ethical problem? Second, is there an easy solution that is otherwise being missed because of the (mis)classification of the conflict as an ethical issue?

Bias Check

An array of biases can interfere with ethical decision-making. These potential biases include errors of judgment related to decision-making (often referred to as cognitive biases) and biases relating to perspectives influenced by culture, race, gender, and similar factors (often referred to as implicit biases). Both cognitive and implicit bias can impact ethical analysis, and implicit biases, in and of themselves, can create highly volatile clinical situations through misunderstanding and antagonizing patients. Clinicians may benefit from exploring how their own biases manifest and influence their clinical approach and ethical analysis.

The tools and precepts of modern American and Western medical ethics need to be recognized as just that: the product of our contemporary culture, more specifically, the product of a modern society where autonomy and liberty are central moral values and social goals (Charlesworth 1993). Many of the critical questions in psychiatric ethics hinge on the challenges of supporting autonomy in the face of illnesses which can powerfully subvert autonomy and self-awareness (Prigatano 2009). As such, psychiatric ethics often becomes a subset – a specialized territory within the broader territory of medical ethics – due to the conflicts arising between autonomy and autonomy-subverting illnesses.

Psychiatric illnesses have intrinsically psychosocial and cultural attributes as well as being a matter of clinical concern. As we approach more relational issues of psychiatric ethics –individual rights vs. community interests, privacy, and coercion – the focus on autonomy may yield less satisfactory answers. While the Western canon of bioethics can be tremendously useful in addressing these issues, it must also be recognized that using this Western cultural perspective exclusively may be an incomplete approach. Bioethics has never been homogenous or static: as a field, it grows and evolves both because of increased understanding of the subject and because the issues which are addressed change. The lessons of feminist and African American bioethics – including the importance understanding power, oppression, and the impact of systemic bias – blend naturally with many of the core values we recognize in our work in community psychiatry (Griffith 2007; Martin 2001). Indeed, in an era where we are better recognizing culture as an intersectional concept, we are also recognizing that living with mental illness creates an added layer of identity and meaning for all of our patients which community psychiatrists need to understand to ethically and effectively care for our patients (Crenshaw 1989; Oexle and Corrigan 2018).

Further, our own subjective biases anchored in stereotypes of ability and disability, race, religion, gender, culture, and other characteristics that differentiate "us" from "them" can impact our ethical decision-making (Jecker 2001; Louw 2016). The impact of these biases, when applied to complex cases, can make it difficult to effectively analyze an ethical problem. In formal bioethics, systematic analysis of cases can help mitigate these risks (Agich 2001). At a practical level, a basic reflective question may help reduce the impact of these biases: is there something about the cultural, gender, or other distinctions in this case leading me to make assumptions based on my own background or values? In a systematic analysis, expressing recognition of the adverse impact of implicit bias in health care can be a critical first step to improving decisions (Sukhera et al. 2020).

Work Smarter, Not Harder

While careful ethical analysis can be a useful tool, it consumes the clinician's time and attention. And even with tremendous use of these finite resources, ethical analysis is not guaranteed to yield ethically and clinically satisfactory outcomes. Discretion can be the better part of valor: sometimes risks are created by entering into unnecessary ethical analyses when it could be simpler to avoid those quandaries. Common foibles including overthought ethical analysis and misunderstanding decision-making responsibility are briefly explained below.

The appeal of constructing a complex ethical rationalization for a clinically desired course of action can take on a momentum of its own. Convoluted ethical reasoning and overly intricate plans can be made instead of simpler, less ambiguous ones. To wit, Ockham's razor can be applied to ethical decision-making as well as scientific explanations: all things being equal, given a choice between a complex ethical solution and a simpler one, the simpler choice may be preferred. For example, a clinician concerned about the well-being of a patient may go through convoluted reasoning to reframe the facts of a case to fit the regional rules about involuntary commitment for inability to care for self. In doing so, the clinician runs the risk of angering a patient who sees their autonomy being stripped from them and believing that even though the patient's living situation may not be improved, the responsibility of addressing that risk would then fall to the inpatient team to resolve. Or the clinician can simply explore easier, clinically pragmatic solutions which require substantially less ethical acrobatics to justify. The clinician can express their concerns to the patient and find a collaborative solution, persuade the patient to voluntarily admit themselves, or engage family to provide added supports. Put simply: basic clinical engagement can often be preferred over complex and ethically challenging – or dubious – reasoning.

At times, psychiatrists have paternalistically assumed responsibility for a decision when it is more appropriately made by the patient or their proxy. Not every clinical dilemma is ours to solve. Many physicians are prone to the bias and the assumption that, through their authority and paternalistic traditions, they can and should be making decisions that will lead to the best outcomes for their patients. In truth, in the absence of a small number of exceptions, our patients retain autonomy and the right to make their own decisions. For example, a psychiatrist is extremely concerned about a patient's decision to move in with a relative who may be exploiting them for their benefits. In the absence of criteria for involuntary interventions or reassignment of benefits to a payee, the psychiatrist may have no legal standing to enforce a change in this living arrangement.

Some ethical questions can be avoided with early planning and explanation of clinic practices to patients. Clearly drafted policies provide at least an initial position in the face of a number of common ethical questions. Clearly explained clinic rules, shared in advanced with patients and their immediate supports, can become a useful anchor point for future decisions. When can or should a provider call an emergency contact? How are cancellations and refill requests handled? Are emotional support animal letters written, and if so, with what standards? When and how is information shared with or received from family members? This process is in many ways simply an extension of informed consent. Used consistently, it can be an easy route through potentially murky ethical waters.

Case Study: When to Write a Letter

A patient is referred to a psychiatrist for one-time consultation. She is a 24 year old female with history of depression, currently not in treatment, but asks them to sign Family and Medical Leave Act paperwork so she can have unlimited, flexible days off during the month. She has some vague symptoms (poor sleep, low mood). The psychiatrist makes multiple recommendations for treatment to improve her mood, but she does not seem particularly interested (discussion of behavioral activation, improving sleep habits, etc.*) and does not want to engage in therapy. She refuses to* *answer the psychiatrist's inquiry about the reasons these work stipulations are needed. She starts to demand that the psychiatrist write the letter. The psychiatrist explains that they have insufficient evidence or information to complete the form or that doing so is not in the patient's best clinical interest in terms of recovery from depression.*

The session ultimately deteriorates and the patient leaves, as angry and frustrated with the psychiatrist as the psychiatrist is with the patient. Reviewing the situation with a colleague, the psychiatrist notes that as a private practitioner they have no standard rubric to approach completion of such forms. They prepare language for their website and new patient materials that explains that disability related paperwork is only completed for patients who have been engaged in treatment with the psychiatrist and a therapist for at least 6 weeks. The psychiatrist understands that this is an arbitrary limitation but that it may help prevent such conflicts in the future.

Who Has Decision-Making Authority?

It can be difficult to resist the urge to resist poor decisions made by our patients when we have better solutions. The urge to "fix" can be hard to disconnect from; indeed, it is at the very core of our identity as physicians and healers. But we must respect that people are their own beings and their decisions can deviate from our own. This deviation does not necessarily make those decisions wrong and that can be a helpful lesson for the practitioner. Clinicians sometimes confuse their disagreement with a patient's decision as a reason to find a way to subvert the patient's autonomy. But this is not an ethically supportable position relative to current clinical values and standards. As recovery-oriented care has become broadly recognized, appropriate alternatives that support autonomy are more commonly employed, such as a plan to work with the patient to improve their understanding of the ramifications of their choices – or simply being ready to support the patient should their chosen course of action fail.

Autonomy is a central value and a central goal in modern psychiatry. Ultimately, patients who have capacity to make decisions are legally and ethically permitted to do so. Shared decision-making can be a helpful tool to find and focus on common ground between patient and provider. Coercion should be avoided as it sets up many barriers for therapeutic relationships. It can create a false narrative of patient decision-making: "if you do not agree to this, then I will 'be forced to' intervene on your behalf, so you *should* agree." Respect for autonomy can be a great boon to the therapeutic relationship and promote discussions about values, historical choices, and allow for greater understanding of the decision-making structure of the patient.

Letting go of the false belief that psychiatrists have control over the behaviors and choices of patients is one layer. A second is recognizing that, at times, when a patient's judgment is profoundly impaired, decision-making authority does not automatically revert to the psychiatrist or the psychiatrist's preferences. The structure of surrogate decision-making and substitute judgment may exist as a result of laws or policies in place based on jurisdictional rules or the use of advanced directive tools. These fall under the rubric of rules and tools.

An Ersatz Approach to Ethical Decision-Making

Clinical ethical dilemmas can be challenging and intellectually engaging – even to the point of distraction or distress. Following a consistent problem-solving approach in resolving ethical challenges can improve the quality and consistency of the decisions and reduce the time and stress needed to address them. A simple approach for ethical decision-making, tailored for use in settings where decisions need to be made quickly, compassionately, and in the absence of extensive consultative resources, is offered below. As an iterative process, a formal consultative program would reinforce and support this model with more extensive subject matter expertise from

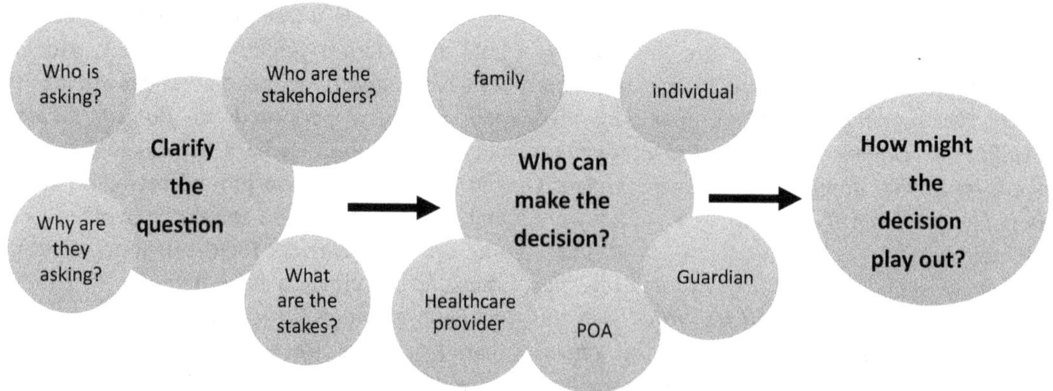

Fig. 2 Decision-making process

professionals with formal medical ethics and consultation training.

There are three essential steps to use when working through ethical quandaries. First, clarify the question to be sure one understands what actually needs to be resolved. Second, use the rules and tools of your environment. Third, use the "core four" principles of medical ethics (beneficence, autonomy, justice, nonmaleficence) to help guide you when the rules and tools do not apply (Fig. 2). These will be laid out in more detail later in this chapter.

First, Clarify the Question

People often approach ethicists with what appear to be ethical questions but in fact are just a jumbled, messy clinical dilemma that has raised everybody's anxiety. First and foremost, who is asking and what are they asking? Who are the stakeholders? Once the question has been clarified, who has the actual authority to make a decision? Not every difficult decision is the clinicians to make: often the most difficult decisions in health care need to be made by our patients or their families.

To give an example, on consult-liaison services, psychiatrists clarify the question to increase the likelihood of actually tackling the dilemma of concern. For example, consultation-liaison psychiatrists are asked to weigh in on decision-making capacity, often mistaken for global competence by other practitioners. Once we are able to clarify and narrow down the focus, the question of specific decision-making capacity is much easier to answer and respects patient autonomy by minimizing any possible restrictions on their choices.

Second, Use Rules and Tools

Much of psychiatric and medical ethics is not abstract decision-making: often, there are clear and concrete rules and laws that must be followed. One hopes the allure of clinical ethics is not diminished by this revelation. The patient's mom is begging the clinician not to call Child Protective Services (CPS) about the child abuse because she is finally clean and might relapse without her kids to motivate her – all the details in the world become moot because there is a law that tells clinicians what to do (report). Psychiatrists work within communities and work within the hierarchy of rules and laws that govern the treatment of our patients and our profession. Sometimes established laws and rules may supersede how one might proceed if one were to strictly follow loose rules of medical ethics (however, most codes of medical ethics stipulate that general adherence to applicable laws and regulations are presumed to be ethical.).

Generally, there is a hierarchy of such rules. Federal statutes enacted by the legislature, regulations articulated by agencies, and common law

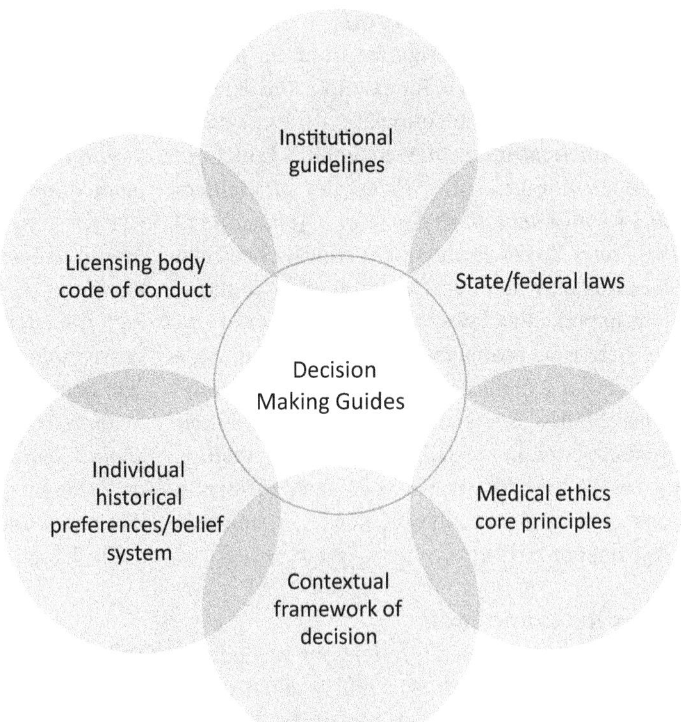

Fig. 3 Rules and tools of decision-making

prescribed by court decisions will generally supersede state level equivalents, which will, in turn, supersede professional rules or standards. The various laws, regulations, and common-law court rules have developed over time and are incapable of having prepared rules or guidance for every situation. However, when they do apply, they should be used in the absence of a clear reason not to (Fig. 3).

Legal Rules and Tools

Laws are enacted by state or federal legislatures and may cover topics such as when to report child abuse and how old a person needs to be to consent to treatment. Court rulings are decisions of appellate and supreme courts that define certain legal standards in a given jurisdiction, such as Jaffee v Redmond where the Supreme Court recognized therapist-client privilege. Regulations are rules promulgated by a state or federal agency but are not approved by the legislature or executive; the Health Insurance Portability and Accountability Act (HIPAA) privacy rules are regulations.

In general, adherence to prevailing and applicable statutes, regulations, and court rulings is considered ethical. Deviation from these rules without clear justification is fraught with ethical and legal risk. That said, laws, regulations, and court opinions may not apply to all situations encountered by clinicians. Sometimes the guidance from legal, regulatory, or court sources will conflict with professional ethical standards. It will then fall upon our own ethical analysis to resolve the situation. For example, a patient witnessed an assault and is called as a witness. One of the attorneys subpoenas the psychiatrists to testify about the patient, and the patient does not wish the psychiatrist to testify. Even in the face of a subpoena, the psychiatrist may wish to consult with their own legal counsel and risk management team prior to responding to the subpoena. It would generally be wise to have a long discussion with legal counsel before defying a court order, but there are situations where it may be reasonable to refuse and the psychiatrist may prevail (*In re B* 1978).

Professional Rules and Tools

Codified ethical rules originate from our professional associations; see, for example, the detailed American Psychiatric Association's annotations of the American Medical Association's Principles of Medical Ethics (*The Principles of Medical Ethics with Annotations Especially Applicable to Psychiatry* 2013). Professional ethical codes and standards may help resolve ambiguities or omissions in prevailing laws or regulations. For example, there is no formal law or regulation guiding a psychiatrist's public speech about non-patients. A psychiatrist is asked by a journalist for their opinion about an elected official. While there is no law to prohibit such a statement, there is a clear rule prohibiting such statements (Appelbaum 2017).

Policy Rules and Tools

There are often hospital policies or procedures that can guide us, such as a policy about documenting informed consent for medications in minors. These policies can serve as a useful structure for interpreting and applying complex or ambiguous laws or regulations in a consistent manner across an organization.

Case Study: Pharm for Thought

The Wellness Clinic is a new community behavioral health practice that is opening within an underserved community. It plans to operate on a sliding scale and will predominantly serve a struggling community. The group is an offshoot of a larger health system but operates independently. The office consists of two psychiatrists, four therapists, and two case managers all with equal partnership in the practice. The larger health system has decided to go "pharm free" (no involvement with pharmaceutical industry representatives) but has left the decision up to the Wellness Clinic to decide for themselves.

After a rousing debate, the clinic providers are at a standstill, they recognize that going pharm free may help to remove bias in prescribing practices, but they worry that forgoing free samples would be detrimental to the community, in which some members struggle to pay for medications or are uninsured. Ultimately, the team decides on a policy of limited engagement with pharmaceutical representatives, standard language for discussing the implications of using sample medication with patients, with an explicit directive for prescribing generic medication as first line treatment when appropriate. The policy also mandates that linkages to improved medical benefits for clients be facilitated. This represents a reasonable balance of ethical principles including beneficence *(clients will benefit from the availability of medication),* justice *(everyone should have access to available treatments according to need) and* nonmaleficence *(serving one's own interests rather than the patient's). See* Table 1.

When in Doubt, Use the Core Four

Any student of contemporary American medical ethics is likely familiar with Beauchamp and Childress's four principles: autonomy, beneficence, nonmaleficence, and justice (Beauchamp and Childress 2019). These four concepts reflect Beauchamp and Childress's synthesis and interpretation of contemporary medical ethics and are broadly recognized as seminal precepts in the

Table 1 Core principles of medical ethics

Autonomy	Respect for individual's capacity to act on their own behalf without outside control, and supporting those decisions
Beneficence	The concept of our overarching duty to be of benefit to our patients, with intention of trying to remove harm from patient's path
Nonmaleficence	The principle that we not intentionally cause harm or pain to an individual through our actions. This is what standard of care is based upon, as we set out a level of care that minimizes/avoids risk of harm to individuals
Justice	The principle of equal treatment for all similarly situated individuals requires distributing care and resources equally

field (Shea 2020). Any ethical decision should generally adhere to these principles just as it should adhere to established law, regulation, or procedure. However, Beauchamp and Childress's principles are arguably broad precepts. In practical clinical scenarios, more specific "rules and tools" can be more practical: it is easier to adhere to the simple rule that it is wrong to trade a prescription for controlled substance for sexual favors than to work through an analysis of beneficence and nonmaleficence.

Any experienced practitioner has had experiences where they have encountered complex situations where there is no clearly applicable rule or there is conflict or ambiguity in the available rules and tools. The ambiguities may arise because the issue at hand is not covered in existing rules and tools or the ambiguities arise because the application of those rules and tools yields and unsatisfactory solution. In such situations, it may be quite reasonable to seek a solution that may be a novel product of the application of the core four principles.

It should be stressed that adherence to established laws and regulations is generally, at first approximation, ethical (*The Principles of Medical Ethics with Annotations Especially Applicable to Psychiatry* 2013). When those rules and tools apply without conflict or concern, adherence to those rules is ethically preferred over de novo analysis with these core principles. Determining whether or not there are applicable rules and tools should precede an application of the core four principles.

Case Study: Peeking Behind the Curtains

One afternoon, during a break between patients, a therapist is perusing social media. A post by a person lamenting about how weird it is that they are never comfortable talking about a number of sensitive topics with their therapist but are comfortable talking about them online has gone viral. The therapist is taken aback – the patient in the post is immediately recognized as her long term client and she had felt that they had a good rapport. The therapist correctly recognizes that looking further at the postings of the patient could be intrusive and feels awkward about disclosing the information she unintentionally already learned. A quick perusal of available ethical rules offers no further guidance.

Ultimately the therapist feels that not to disclose what was learned would be contrary to the precepts of autonomy and beneficence. At the next appointment the therapist discloses what she inadvertently found. They spend the session processing the inadvertent exposure to this information and the therapist emphasizes her respect for the client's right not to share some information, she has concerns that the client must feel there were important things in her life that she did not want to disclose in therapy. The client reassures the therapist that there is nothing to worry about, and that it was just a joke to her friends. The therapist continues to be unsure in future sessions if the client is fully disclosing her concerns but does not want to push past the comfort of the client to disclose sensitive information.

Advanced Planning and Mental Health Advanced Directives

As noted above, decision-making under stress may not yield the most rational or ethical outcomes. Most experienced clinicians can identify any number of clinical and ethical challenges that they struggled with early in their career but which they now handle routinely and with little effort. Often this is because the challenging decision-making processes with the early cases helped them develop rules and pathways for managing similar patterns. Often, this is a learning process with varying degrees of awareness (Kahneman 2013). There is great value to making these "lessons learned" explicit, memorializing them in policy for future use for the individual clinician or the clinic itself in the form of policies or guidelines. Even in work as highly cognitive and variable as clinical psychiatry, there are tremendous benefits to developing standards when possible (Staats and Upton 2011). At times, there may not be a perfect answer, and accepting an available choice at least allows a reference point for future decisions (or intentional, mindful deviance from that original plan). Additionally, the process of writing out one's thoughts (in a clinical note or a clinic's policies) may provide a useful reflective practice as one considers options and alternatives (Simon and Shuman 2009). Put colloquially, while excessive (obsessive) planning can be problematic and lead to analysis paralysis, the adage that a failure to plan is planning to fail has merit as well.

At an individual level, the use of mental health advance directives can be clinically and ethically invaluable. In many ways, they embody a number of the core precepts of modern psychiatric ethics: centering patient autonomy and preserving it against the usurpation of illness, expanding dialogue and shared understanding between patient and provider, and codifying and memorializing informed consent. Any planning tool that helps the patient and the treatment team explicitly discuss and understand the patient's preferences and needs in the care of their illness offers value for empowering patients, clinical planning, support of informed consent, facilitation of understanding between parties, promotion of autonomy, preservation of decisional rights, and rehearsal of crisis and contingency planning (Srebnik and Fond 1999). These are clinically useful, ethically sound, and recovery-centered benefits. There is evidence that the use of these tools can improve clinical outcomes and reduce coercive and involuntary interventions (Thornicroft et al. 2010). Advance planning can range from simple safety plans to formal and (in some jurisdictions) legally binding advance directive documents. Local legal standards and customs can have a substantial impact on development, implementation, and adherence to mental health advance directives (Henderson et al. 2008). There is an opportunity for improved standardization across regions through the use of model statutes (Clausen 2014).

Memorializing in writing any complex ethical decision-making process – whether through the development of a complex care plan for an individual patient or establishing a clinic policy – can help as a reminder of past efforts to resolve the problem and simplify efforts to solve similar problems in the future. As an added benefit, a well-crafted medical record (or clinic policy) can help mitigate liability in the event of malpractice litigation or other adverse external review. Bad outcomes may be inevitable, but demonstration of appropriate efforts at ethical decision-making can help in the defense of practitioners. Medical malpractice has been likened to high school math: even if the final answer is wrong, one still gets credit for showing the work (Rozel and Zacharia 2021).

Case Study: Mental Health Advance Directives

Ms. Smith is a 42 year old with schizoaffective disorder bipolar type. Several years ago, during an admission to Memorial Hospital, she was assaulted by another patient and, since then, has had varying degrees of post-traumatic stress disorder symptoms. She had been stable and in treatment with an outpatient clinic affiliated with Memorial Hospital since then. Several weeks ago, she ran out of her medications and, having lost phone service due to financial stressors, was unable to reach her treatment team for support. She decompensated severely and her landlord contacted a mobile crisis team who, in turn, had her involuntarily committed to Memorial Hospital for inability to care for self and aggression. Ms. Smith was immediately upset about being at Memorial and was fixated on this for much of the admission. The admission ended up being prolonged and marked by repeated aggression by her on the unit, but ultimately helped restore her to her normal level of functioning.

On her first follow up, she tells her therapist how frightened she was going back to Memorial Hospital and that she would have signed in voluntarily, but "all those mobile clinicians wanted to do was take me to Memorial." She compellingly described substantial activation of her PTSD and, in hindsight, it is apparent that those trauma symptoms substantially disrupted and undermined her treatment. Her therapist reflects to Ms. Smith, "I'm really sorry you had that experience. You are identifying some pretty good reasons why an admission to Memorial would be really unhelpful if you need that level of care in the future." The therapist arranges for Ms. Smith to work with a peer specialist to craft a Mental health Advanced Directive. One of the critical elements is that if Ms. Smith requires admission, that she should go to Charity or City Hospital instead of Memorial Hospital. Ms. Smith reviews the Mental Health Advance Directive with her therapist and psychiatrist who, in turn, make sure that it is available in the electronic health record and that the Mobile Crisis Team and local Emergency Departments have copies as well.

Ethical Outcomes Are Not Necessarily Clinically Optimal Outcomes

Clinicians often encounter situations where the ethically optimal outcome does not clearly overlap with clinically ideal goals – a patient who wishes to stop an effective medication, for example. Part of the physician's role has always been to advocate and encourage optimal decision-making while promoting patient autonomy. A coerced decision (or assent to the directive of a provider) often does not lead to sustained adherence or improved clinical rapport. When the patient does not feel invested in a decision, they are not invested in persisting with the offered plan.

Involuntary hospitalization or outpatient commitment may be a necessary and important intervention in some circumstances, but it runs the risk that patients will object and resist further. It creates perilous heuristic challenges: do we involuntarily commit a patient today, knowing they may be alienated from the treatment team and perhaps treatment itself? Can there be an allowance for short-term risk – forgoing an involuntary commitment, accepting a risk of short-term harm – in hopes that such an act of trust promotes future engagement and collaboration? In short, can short-term risk be used in some way to barter for long-term recovery (Rozel 2020)? Arguably, to respect recovery means to allow patients the right to take risk in their own life and experience the dignity of failure (Mitchell 1994).

But how far can a clinician go to engage, persuade, or even induce certain types of behavior? At the most extreme, involuntary commitment and court-ordered treatment are possible. Involuntary commitment can be invaluable in some extreme cases, but it is not a useful general tool for routine management of people with psychiatric illness (Mulvey et al. 1987; Segal 2017). Most psychiatric treatment can and should be delivered in voluntary settings – and yet, most effective psychiatric treatment still involves some degree of direction by the provider to the patient. Given the intrinsic power differential between patient and provider, being directive without being coercive can be challenging.

Many of the most effective therapeutic approaches balance this conflict, blending the influence of the provider with the autonomy of the patient, quite effectively. Motivational Interviewing, Dialectical Behavior Therapy, and Collaborative Problem Solving, for example, are all modalities with well-developed ground rules for when and how to direct patient behavior or enforce consequences for nonadherence (i.e., limit setting). Yet, these therapeutic modalities are all expressly grounded in the paradigm of supporting and developing healthy self-determination and autonomy in the patient. The use of deception, intimidating and clinically unnecessary contingencies, withholding of information, and withholding of needed or desired objects as tools of motivation are all clearly more coercive and less ethically appropriate. Effective strategies in clinical engagement are reflected in the canons of de-escalation and negotiation which may also serve as useful resources for clinicians hoping to improve their ability to ethically influence patient behavior (Cialdini 2009; Fisher et al. 2011; Richmond et al. 2012).

Conclusion

Striving to provide ethical care is an essential and rewarding part of practice. That community psychiatry may offer more ethical challenges is arguably a strength and not a limitation of such work: it implies that practitioners are intentionally seeking to work with the most challenging cases, to wit, those of people most in need of care and most likely to have been left behind by other parts of the social services safety net. By careful navigation of ethical issues when possible – and embracing ambiguity and uncertainty when necessary – recovery-oriented and person-centered care can be consistently achieved. While some clinicians may balk and even become anxious at the mere contemplation of tackling ethical problems, solving ethical problems in clinical psychiatry can be far less complex than may be feared. It is hoped that this chapter has provided practical and clear guidance for solving ethical problems in community psychiatric practice.

References

Agich, G. J. (2001). The Question of Method in Ethics Consultation. *The American Journal of Bioethics*, *1*(4), 31–41. https://doi.org/10.1162/152651601317139360

Appelbaum, P. S. (2017). Reflections on the Goldwater Rule. *The Journal of the American Academy of Psychiatry and the Law*, *45*(2), 228–232.

Beauchamp, T. L., & Childress, J. F. (2019). *Principles of Biomedical Ethics* (8 edition). Oxford University Press.

Charlesworth, M. J. (1993). *Bioethics in a liberal society*. Cambridge University Press.

Cialdini, R. B. (2009). *Influence: Science and practice* (5th ed). Pearson Education.

Clausen, J. A. (2014). Making the Case for a Model Mental Health Advance Directive Statute. *Yale J. Health Pol'y L. & Ethics*, *14*, 1.

Crenshaw, K. (1989). Demarginalizing the Intersection of Race and Sex: A Black Feminist Critique of Antidiscrimination Doctrine, Feminist Theory and Antiracist Politics. *University of Chicago Legal Forum*, *1989*(1), Article 8.

Fisher, R., Ury, W., & Patton, B. (2011). *Getting to yes: Negotiating agreement without giving in* (3rd ed., rev. ed). Penguin.

Griffith, E. E. H. (2007). Personal Narrative and an African American Perspective on Medical Ethics. In L. Prograis & E. D. Pellegrino (Eds.), *African American bioethics: Culture, race, and identity* (pp. 105–125). Georgetown University Press.

Henderson, C., Swanson, J. W., Szmukler, G., Thornicroft, G., & Zinkler, M. (2008). A Typology of Advance Statements in Mental Health Care. *Psychiatric Services*, *59*(1), 63–71. https://doi.org/10.1176/ps.2008.59.1.63

In re B, 394 A. 2d 419 (Supreme Court 1978).

Jecker, N. S. (2001). Uncovering Cultural Bias in Ethics Consultation. *American Journal of Bioethics*, *1*(4), 49–50.

Kahneman, D. (2013). *Thinking, fast and slow*. Farrar, Straus and Giroux.

Louw, B. (2016). Cultural competence and ethical decision making for health care professionals. *Humanities and Social Sciences*, *4*(2–1), 41–52.

Martin, N. (2001). Feminist Bioethics and Psychiatry. *Journal of Medicine and Philosophy*, *26*(4), 431–441. https://doi.org/10.1076/jmep.26.4.431.3008

Mitchell, G. (1994). The dignity of risk and the right to failure: One profile of patient-focused care. *Perspectives (Gerontological Nursing Association Canada)*, *18*(3), 10.

Mulvey, E. P., Geller, J. L., & Roth, L. H. (1987). The promise and peril of involuntary outpatient commitment. *American Psychologist*, *42*(6), 571–584. https://doi.org/10.1037/0003-066X.42.6.571

Oexle, N., & Corrigan, P. W. (2018). Understanding Mental Illness Stigma Toward Persons With Multiple Stigmatized Conditions: Implications of Intersectionality Theory. *Psychiatric Services*, *69*(5), 587–589. https://doi.org/10.1176/appi.ps.201700312

Prigatano, G. P. (2009). Anosognosia: Clinical and ethical considerations. *Current Opinion in Neurology*, *22*(6), 606–611. https://doi.org/10.1097/WCO.0b013e328332a1e7

Richmond, J. S., Berlin, J. S., Fishkind, A. B., Holloman, G. H., Zeller, S. L., Wilson, M. P., Rifai, M. A., & Ng, A. T. (2012). Verbal De-escalation of the Agitated Patient: Consensus Statement of the American Association for Emergency Psychiatry Project BETA De-escalation Workgroup. *Western Journal of Emergency Medicine*, *13*(1), 17–25. https://doi.org/10.5811/westjem.2011.9.6864

Rozel, J. S. (2020). Identifying and Understanding Legal Aspects of Emergency Psychiatry Unique to Different Jurisdictions. In M. J. Fitz-Gerald & J. Takeshita (Eds.), *Models of Emergency Psychiatric Services That Work* (pp. 165–175). Springer International Publishing. https://doi.org/10.1007/978-3-030-50808-1_16

Rozel, J. S., & Zacharia, M. (2021). Risk Management in Behavioral Emergencies: Liabilities, Duties and EMTALA [Chapter]. In L. S. Zun, M. P. Wilson, & K. Nordstrom (Eds.), *Behavioral Emergencies for Healthcare Providers*. Springer.

Segal, S. P. (2017). Assessment of outpatient commitment in randomised trials. *The Lancet Psychiatry*, *4*(12), e26–e28. https://doi.org/10.1016/S2215-0366(17)30286-9

Shea, M. (2020). Forty Years of the Four Principles: Enduring Themes from Beauchamp and Childress. *The Journal of Medicine and Philosophy: A Forum for Bioethics and Philosophy of Medicine*, *45*(4–5), 387–395. https://doi.org/10.1093/jmp/jhaa020

Simon, R. I., & Shuman, D. W. (2009). Therapeutic Risk Management of Clinical-Legal Dilemmas: Should

It Be a Core Competency? *Journal of the American Academy of Psychiatry and the Law Online*, *37*(2), 155–161.

Srebnik, D. S., & Fond, J. Q. L. (1999). Advance Directives for Mental Health Treatment. *Psychiatric Services*, *50*(7), 919–925. https://doi.org/10.1176/ps.50.7.919

Staats, B. R., & Upton, D. M. (2011). Lean Knowledge Work. *Harvard Business Review*, *89*(10), 100–110.

Sukhera, J., Watling, C. J., & Gonzalez, C. M. (2020). Implicit Bias in Health Professions: From Recognition to Transformation. *Academic Medicine*, *95*(5), 717–723. https://doi.org/10.1097/ACM.0000000000003173

The Principles of Medical Ethics with Annotations Especially Applicable to Psychiatry. (2013). American Psychiatric Association.

Thornicroft, G., Farrelly, S., Birchwood, M., Marshall, M., Szmukler, G., Waheed, W., Byford, S., Dunn, G., Henderson, C., Lester, H., Leese, M., Rose, D., & Sutherby, K. (2010). CRIMSON [CRisis plan IMpact: Subjective and Objective coercion and eNgagement] protocol: a randomised controlled trial of joint crisis plans to reduce compulsory treatment of people with psychosis. *Trials*, *11*, 102. https://doi.org/10.1186/1745-6215-11-102

Part IX

Shaping the Future

Medical Student and Resident Education in Community Psychiatry

Kathleen A. Clegg

The Need for More Clinicians and Enhanced Education in Community Psychiatry

There is broad agreement that there is a shortage of well-trained, committed psychiatrists working in the public sector. Many would agree that the quality of education and training for professionals in this sector significantly influences the quality and quantity of psychiatrists choosing to practice in publicly funded settings. Therefore, this chapter focuses on medical student and resident education in community psychiatry and what can be done to improve the effectiveness and attractiveness of professional preparation for careers in this field, so as to attract more medical students and residents into community psychiatry.

Two aspects of medical school curricula and placements offer significant opportunities for enhancement. While more has been added to medical school and psychiatry residency curricula about issues related to community psychiatry such as social determinants of health, and the importance of interdisciplinary practice, there is still much more focus on advances in the neurosciences and biologic treatment. Introducing community psychiatrists as faculty early in the education of medical students could spur interest in the field. Second, most medical student clerkship placements and most psychiatry residency placements continue to take place in hospital settings, despite the fact that the vast majority of persons living with mental illness are living and receiving mental health services in the communities in which they live.

K. A. Clegg (✉)
Case Western Reserve University School of Medicine, Cleveland, OH, USA

University Hospitals Cleveland Medical Center, Cleveland, OH, USA
e-mail: Kathleen.clegg@uhhospitals.org

Community Psychiatry in Medical Schools

Medical schools vary greatly in the amount of the curricula dedicated to psychiatry in general and to community psychiatry, in particular.

In the first year of medical school, most schools offer a course that teaches the basics of "behavioral science" and has included topics such as the doctor-patient relationship, the clinical interview, ethical issues facing physicians, and many of the cultural and societal issues that patients face. Newer additions to these behavioral science curricula include the population health approach to health and the importance of social determinants of health. In the Case Western

W. E. Sowers et al. (eds.), *Textbook of Community Psychiatry*,
https://doi.org/10.1007/978-3-031-10239-4_59

Reserve University Medical School curriculum, the first block of the Foundations of Medicine and Health curriculum includes content on topics such as Population Health, Epidemiology, Biostatistics, Bioethics, and Heath Disparities. Per the Liaison Committee on Medical Education (LCME) Guidelines, 124 US Medical Schools include content on Social Determinants of Health in first- and second-year Medical School curricula (AAMC 2018–19).

Moreover, while some schools involve psychiatrists in these first-year courses, many schools rely almost entirely on primary care faculty practicing in areas such as family medicine and internal medicine to perform this function. From the perspective of psychiatry, it would be better to include more psychiatry faculty, including community psychiatry faculty, in the teaching teams for these first-year courses. It would strengthen these courses for all medical students to include more psychiatrists because psychiatrists in general, and community psychiatrists in particular, tend to be expert in the behavioral science dimensions of medical care.

Further, medical students could be exposed to general psychiatrists and community psychiatrists earlier in their education, and this would likely have a positive impact on career choice. In fact, a Canadian study found that the duration of pre-clerkship exposure to psychiatry predicted the number of students selecting psychiatry as their first choice as a discipline (Lau et al. 2015).

Other topics that are particularly important in community psychiatry, such as adherence, adaptive and maladaptive behavioral responses to stress and illness, patient-centered communication, cultural competence, system-based practice, healthcare policy/economics, healthcare disparities, access to care, and issues of social justice can be found in the content description of the Social Sciences component of the United States Medical Licensing Examination (USMLE 2020).

In support of these recent changes to the behavioral science curricula in the first 2 years of medical school, it has been stated that "the professional identity of the physician who was successful in the acute disease era of the twentieth century will not be effective in the complex chronic disease era of the twenty-first century. Medical schools and residency programs must restructure their views of basic and clinical science and workplace learning to give equal emphasis to the science and skills needed to practice in and lead in complex systems" (Lucey 2013).

In the second year of medical school, most schools have a course covering psychopathology, as well as basic psychopharmacology. In many medical schools, this course may be the first time a medical student has been exposed to a psychiatrist. Historically, there has been greater consensus about what topics should be covered in these basic science courses. However, moving in the opposite direction, despite increased interest in the topics listed above as included in the USMLE content outline, the amount of time dedicated to teaching behavioral science may actually be reduced. Sometimes this happens when the second-year psychopathology course is combined with a neuroscience course. And once again, since community psychiatrists are underrepresented in most academic medical centers (McQuistion et al. 2004), a community psychiatrist seldom teaches such courses.

However, on the positive side, some medical schools offer electives on Introduction to Mental Health to first- and second-year medical students. At Case Western Reserve School of Medicine in Cleveland, Ohio, this course includes topics such as Mental Disorders as a Public Health issue, Addiction and Motivational Interviewing, and Trauma. Discussions include the challenges of stigma, social determinants of health, and an appreciation of patient's lived experience vs. focusing on diagnostic and treatment algorithms.

In the third year of medical school, students are required to complete a series of core clerkships in a number of areas of medicine, specifically Internal Medicine, Surgery, Pediatrics, Obstetrics/Gynecology, and Psychiatry (AAMC 2019–20).

The importance of the clerkship experience cannot be overemphasized, as some studies have shown the clerkship experience has been shown to be a critical factor in medical students' career choices (Clardy et al. 2000) and consideration of psychiatry as a career (Lyons and Janca 2015). Most medical students do not go on to pursue careers in psychiatry, though the psychiatry clerkship is the point in their clinical education where all medical students learn about the clinical care of persons with psychiatric diagnoses that clinicians in every field of medicine encounter. There are issues with the duration and nature of this clerkship in American medical schools that clearly require updating.

No governing or regulatory body mandates the amount of time spent on each clerkship experience, but psychiatry clerkships tend to be shorter than clerkships in other fields (Rosenthal et al. 2005). The average length of US medical school psychiatry clerkships had been gradually declining, from 6.4 weeks in 1982 to 6 weeks in 1999 and to 5.5 weeks in 2010 (Lau et al. 2015). Per the Liaison Committee on Medical Education (LCME) Annual Medical Questionnaire Part II, the average length of the psychiatry clerkship in 2018–2019 was down to 5.1 weeks, but the average number of weeks spent on a psychiatry clerkship in 2019–2020 was up slightly at 5.6 weeks (AAMC 2019–20). The short duration of the psychiatry clerkship is particularly unfortunate in that every practicing physician encounters an increasing number of patients with psychiatric disorders, as the prevalence of such disorders is steadily increasing, most recently in response to the COVID-19 pandemic (WHO 2022).

Per the LCME, in 2018–2019, 97% of US Medical Schools have separate required psychiatry clerkships (AAMC 2019–20). However, some schools have experimented with combining clerkships such as the psychiatry and neurology clerkships. This has been done in many schools in order to respond to shortened clerkship lengths, as opposed to necessarily addressing overlap between the clinical practices of psychiatry and of neurology. Many schools that have attempted such integration have ended up with courses and/or clerkships that are juxtaposed in the curriculum, but not truly integrated. For instance, in an 8-week neuropsychiatry clerkship, frequently the clerkship experience is divided as 4 weeks of neurology and 4 weeks of psychiatry rather than 8 weeks of a truly integrated experience.

Other schools tried "merging" the psychiatry clerkship with other medical specialties such as family medicine or primary care. While there is merit to collaborative teaching and learning, and in training future physicians in integrated care (Cowley et al. 2014), merging psychiatry clerkships with other clerkships risks psychiatry being marginalized with the psychiatry portion being further shortened.

Increasing numbers of persons with psychiatric disorders are treated in community and other outpatient settings, and, in fact, the bulk of general psychiatric practice occurs in outpatient environments. Nevertheless, many schools offer insufficient basic clerkship time in outpatient environments, still fewer offering exposure to community mental health or other public sector psychiatry settings. Most psychiatry clerkships are conducted in inpatient settings, despite increasingly shorter lengths of stay that focus on acute stabilization rather than full symptom remission and recovery. This leads to medical students not learning sufficiently about the "real-world" practice of psychiatry. One way to alter this situation is for psychiatry departments to appoint community psychiatrists as clerkship directors, with explicit encouragement to establish community mental health placements that better represent modal psychiatric practice. Another response that many medical schools have taken has been to develop and implement Longitudinal Clinical Programs, with a subset of these being Longitudinal Integrated Clerkships. These Longitudinal Integrated Clerkships address the suggestions in the Lancet Commission Report in 2010 that medical education "develop curricula that will serve patient and population needs, foster better understanding of the clinical context, emphasize continuous care over episodic encounters and broaden training venues beyond inpatient care" (Gheihman et al. 2018).

Finally, in the fourth year of medical school, students have the opportunity to take electives in order to explore areas in which they might like to further their learning and education. For some students, the fourth year and these electives may be the first opportunity to investigate community psychiatry as a career option.

On the other hand, it can be argued that, in many ways, this point in the curriculum may be "too late" to substantially influence a student's career choice, as students are already beginning to interview for residency positions in the first few months of their fourth year of medical school. Another trend further reduces the career exploration value of fourth-year electives, in which medical students use several of their fourth-year electives solely as "audition" months to enhance their chances of matching in a residency program at one of these sites. More proactive advising regarding a well-rounded fourth year may address the issue of the "audition" electives.

Still, many medical schools do continue to offer electives in a number of subspecialty fields of psychiatry, such as child psychiatry, forensic psychiatry, psychosomatic medicine or consult-liaison psychiatry, gero-psychiatry, and community psychiatry. In those programs where an elective in community psychiatry is offered, it may include exposure to a unique population such as people with mental illness and homelessness, or those living with HIV/AIDS. And students may be exposed to various treatment settings and modalities such as those offered by mobile crisis teams, crisis shelters, clubhouse models, and drop in centers.

The preceding discussion of community psychiatry topics and the role of community psychiatry faculty in undergraduate medical education might justifiably be viewed as the enumeration of a distressing set of negative trends. However, each area of concern can also be viewed as identifying a strategic pressure point, that is, an opportunity that can be utilized by resourceful psychiatry, and especially community psychiatry, faculty to improve medical education and encourage more students to enter psychiatry.

Folding Community Psychiatry Into the Psychiatry Residency Curriculum

Psychiatry residencies are governed by the rules of the American Council on Graduate Medical Education (ACGME) and the Residency Review Committee, which define competencies that must be achieved by psychiatry residents in the course of the 4 years of their training, having moved away from dictating the amount of time a resident must spend in various treatment settings and toward a more competency-based approach to residency education. The ACGME Psychiatry Milestones, which are "intended to provide a framework for the assessment of the development of the resident in key dimensions of the elements of physician competence in a specialty or subspecialty," were updated and went into effect in 2021 (ACGME 2020). This approach focuses on a resident's performance and the demonstration of learning outcomes. The goal of this shift is to help residents develop greater competence as a physician and to improving the quality of the patient care they are actually able to deliver. The six competencies identified by the ACGME continue to include the following broad themes: Medical Knowledge, Patient Care, Interpersonal and Communication Skills, Professionalism, Systems-Based Practice, and Practice-Based Learning and Improvement.

It turns out that this competency-based approach actually makes it easier to think about creative ways to fold community psychiatry into curricula offered to all residents by a department of psychiatry. Admittedly, folding extended, comprehensive community psychiatry training into the training of all psychiatry residents may sound like a radical proposal. But, working with clients in a community psychiatry setting requires an especially broad set of interpersonal and clinical skills. It is thus an ideal setting to learn and acquire these competencies. And community psychiatry settings tend to provide especially accessible and welcoming training site opportunities for both medical students and residents because the assistance medical students and residents provide tends to be more highly valued in these settings than in other outpatient settings.

Further, one of the six prescribed competency areas, systems-based practice, can be one of the more difficult areas to address. Community psychiatry is quintessentially systems based. Community psychiatry practice settings are typically multidisciplinary and team-based in approach to service delivery and therefore are especially appropriate for the development of competence in the systems-based approach to practice.

An illustration of the advantages of folding community psychiatry into the training of all psychiatry residents follows, but first, a brief history of training in community psychiatry.

In the early 1960s, most community psychiatrists were trained in state hospitals, and university-based training programs were just developing. After the Community Mental Health Centers Construction Act in October, 1963, mental health care began the transition from state hospitals to the community, and many community psychiatrists made this transition along with their patients. By the late 1960s and early 1970s, the transformation of the base of training from the state hospital to the university hospital was well under way, with patchy efforts across the country, such as a pioneering community psychiatry program at Albert Einstein College of Medicine in the Bronx (McQuistion and Rosenheck 2006).

Due to the "Mental Health Systems Act" in 1980, which was a result of the second presidential commission to study the mental health system in the USA, the National Institute of Mental Health began to fund statewide community support grants to recognize state mental health programs and to train core mental health disciplines to improve the community support service systems in the states. Very quickly, training grants followed for psychiatry residency programs. In 1979, Shore, Kinzie, and Bloom published an article describing required educational objectives in community psychiatry (Shore et al. 1979). In 1981, Cutler et al. described an Oregon Health Sciences University program where residents received training in working with community support systems for chronically mentally ill persons (Cutler et al. 1981). In 1988, a model community psychiatry curriculum for psychiatry residents in Wisconsin was also described (Factor et al. 1988).

In 1991, states and universities began to collaborate in the training of psychiatrists to work in their public sector, both hospital and community (Talbott et al. 1991). Some public-academic partnerships have played a role in addressing the severe shortage and maldistribution of child and adolescent psychiatrists in the USA, emphasizing collaboration via consultation, education, and support to primary care providers and to general psychiatrists and psychiatric nurse practitioners (Gabel and Sarvet 2011). Public-academic collaboration continues to the present time. A successful model of this type of public academic collaboration has been underway at Case Western Reserve University, in Cleveland, Ohio, since 1990, as now described.

Community Psychiatry at Case Western Reserve University

Case Western Reserve University (CWRU) has a comprehensive model of training in community psychiatry that may be useful for readers to draw upon. The residency training program in psychiatry at University Hospitals Cleveland Medical Center (UHCMC) incorporates community psychiatry as a major component during the second half of the residency program for all residents. The first 2 years of residency include the required in-patient psychiatry experiences as well as a rotation in psychosomatic medicine/consult-liaison psychiatry. Second-year residents begin to experience outpatient psychiatric practice through participation in a "Psychiatry Access Clinic." This clinic was established with the goal of improving fast access to outpatient psychiatric appointments through time-limited consultations of one to four visits, after which time patients usually return to their primary care provider for ongoing care. First- and second-year residents can also participate in the Public and Community Psychiatry Special Interest Group, organized by psychiatry residents. Activities include presentations by Community Psychiatry faculty and providers about topics relevant to community psychiatry.

The community psychiatry experience, during the third and fourth years, takes advantage of the existence of a community-based educational program in community psychiatry that has been in operation for over 30 years, the Public Academic Liaison Program (PAL). PAL is a collaboration between University Hospitals Cleveland Medical Center, the UHCMC Department of Psychiatry, and the Alcohol, Drug and Mental Health Services (ADAMHS) Board of Cuyahoga County, Ohio, in metropolitan Cleveland. It provides clinical and training opportunities for psychiatry residents and medical students, supervised by full- and part-time faculty – most of whom also provide clinical services, throughout Cuyahoga County. The University and ADAMHS both consider this program to be an excellent and valued example of responsible community service on the part of the CWRU School of Medicine and University Hospitals Cleveland Medical Center.

Initially, the PAL Program involved a limited number of general psychiatry residents and faculty, but it quickly grew to include all general and child psychiatry residents. The ADAMHS Board administers numerous community agencies ranging from small specialty programs in housing, vocational rehabilitation, and homeless and crisis services to large "case management" or "community support service" agencies. Over the past 30 years, PAL has provided hundreds of thousands of hours of clinical service in-service training and educational services while developing comprehensive and model curricula for undergraduate, graduate, and postgraduate medical education in community mental health services. The objectives of the PAL program have been to educate psychiatry residents in community psychiatry with the goal of graduates of the program staying and working in Cuyahoga County, the Ohio county in which the city of Cleveland is located (Public Academic Liaison (PAL) Program 2020). This goal has been realized several fold, as PAL graduates now comprise a majority of psychiatric providers within this system, and many agencies have PAL graduates serving as the medical directors of the agencies.

PAL residents, clinical faculty, and full-time faculty provide psychiatric services at several of the larger ADAMHS-associated agencies and collaborate in the provision of regular in-service trainings for agency staff.

For over two decades on a biannual basis, the Case Western Reserve University-University Hospitals Cleveland Medical Center Department of Psychiatry hosted the "All- Ohio Institute on Community Psychiatry," a statewide celebration of community mental health services. It has typically drawn more than 450 multidisciplinary participants from around the state. This large meeting has offered large group plenary and lecture sessions, and a number of small group workshops, showcases, and poster presentations focused on current clinical, political, and financial issues challenging community mental health service providers throughout the state. The All-Ohio Institute provided a major opportunity for community-based practitioners from around the Ohio to share their innovations, in a continuing education activity that also showcased the latest thinking and innovations of experts at the state's medical schools, teaching hospitals, and local and state government agencies. A number of national community psychiatry experts regularly participated as plenary speakers and workshop facilitators. And the Institute provided trainees a local, regional forum in which to present workshops and showcase presentations or posters. Trainees had the opportunity to network with academic community psychiatry faculty as well as psychiatrists practicing in public settings in the community throughout Ohio.

Structure and Operation of the CWRU Community Psychiatry Curriculum

Utilizing ACGME's competency themes of Patient Care, Medical Knowledge, Practice-Based Learning and Improvement, Interpersonal and Communication Skills, Professionalism, and Systems-Based Practice, the following sections describe the goals and objectives of the community psychiatry curriculum embedded in this 2-year experience and how they are integrated with residents' clinical responsibilities. Text Boxes 1 and 2 outline these goals and objectives.

Learning objectives are divided by core competency and further subdivided by postgraduate year, beginning in the PGY 3 year, when residents first enter the community mental health center setting. PGY 3 goals and objectives continue into the fourth year of training with a "layering on" of additional skills, responsibilities, and independence of clinical practice. Additionally, PGY 4 residents are expected to function as "senior residents," participating in the training and education of the junior residents and medical students. Here, only the "layered on" goals and objectives are included:

Text Box 1: PGY4 Goals in Community Psychiatry

Patient Care

- Meet the objectives of the PGY 3 in the community setting independently, seeking supervision as appropriate.

Medical Knowledge

- Plan and implement in-service sessions for community mental health center staff, psychiatry residents, and medical students.

Practice-Based Learning and Improvement

- Identify an area for improvement in the clinical setting, and plan and implement a performance improvement project.

Interpersoal and Communication Skills

- Continue to engage in therapeutic and ethically sound relationships with patients and function effectively as part of the interdisciplinary team.

Professionalism

- Continue to demonstrate professional behaviors with patients, families, staff, peers, and supervisors, and serve as a role model for PGY 3 residents starting in the community mental health center setting.

Systems-Based Practice

- Identify, plan, and implement an advocacy effort.

Patient Care

In the Case Western Reserve University (CWRU)-University Hospitals Cleveland Medical Center (UHCMC) Psychiatric Residency Program, residents typically follow a caseload of 20–40 clients, in community mental health center settings. Their caseload is monitored and controlled for volume and variety of experience. Residents perform psychiatric diagnostic evaluations and provide ongoing care for their caseload of patients. Supervision is provided on-site by experienced, board-certified faculty, who see the patient following the resident evaluation. Residents have the opportunity to work with a multidisciplinary team including Advanced Practice Registered Nurses (APRNs), psychologists, psychiatric nurses, social workers, counselors, vocational counselors, and community support service providers (case managers) and are considered a part of the team. The central role of the interdisciplinary team in community mental health settings is emphasized.

Most people seen by psychiatry residents are receiving case management services for serious and persistent mental disorders, and many receive other services as well, such as counseling, housing support, vocational, and crisis services. Residents primarily participate in diagnostic assessment and medication management and develop comprehensive biopsychosocial treatment plans in collaboration with the other members of the community treatment team (psychiatrist, psychotherapist, psychiatric nurse, and social worker). They may perform disability evaluations and other specialized assessments under supervision and also have experiences in crisis intervention, partial hospitalization programming, group therapy, and supportive psychotherapy. Leadership and educational experiences accrue from their involvement in the multidisciplinary team. Optional experiences include emergency psychiatry, outreach crisis

Text Box 2: PGY3 Goals in Community Psychiatry

Patient Care

- Exhibit appropriate knowledge of the patient.
- Gather not only a past psychiatric history and but also past experience with the mental health system.
- Gather information from a variety of sources: e.g., records, family members, case managers, outside agency records.
- Generate an appropriate differential diagnosis.
- Develop and present biopsychosocially informed formulations.
- Develop sound therapeutic decision-making skills, and implement appropriate treatment plans.
- Work with a team of professionals as well as patients' families and support systems to implement treatment plans.
- Monitor for treatment response, and adjust the treatment plan according to the needs of each individual patient.
- Perform indicated basic health maintenance screening.
- Identify when the need exists to refer patients for medical or surgical care.
- Counsel and educate patients with regard to diagnosis and recommended treatment.

Medical Knowledge

- Demonstrate knowledge of the major mental health disorders, as well as common comorbid medical diagnoses.
- Demonstrate a working knowledge of psychopharmacology, including measures to address adherence issues.
- Understand the complexities of working with patients with substance use disorders/dually diagnosed patients.
- Demonstrate knowledge of indicated laboratory monitoring because of the use of psychiatric medications.
- Demonstrate knowledge of the variety of treatments available in the community setting.
- Actively pursue independent learning and apply current medical-based knowledge and best evidence-based community practices to foster recovery.

Practice-Based Learning and Improvement

- Integrate feedback in order to improve patient care.
- Identify areas for performance improvement.
- Outline a plan for implementation of a performance improvement project.
- Attend presentations and meetings with a focus on practice-based learning and improvement.

Interpersonal and Communication Skills

- Create and sustain therapeutic and ethically sound relationships with patients.
- Maintain appropriate boundaries.
- Gather collateral information.
- Elicit and communicate information using a range of communication skills.
- Demonstrate cultural competence.
- Work effectively within a systems-based, recovery-oriented, and patient-centered practice managed through a diverse treatment team.

Professionalism

- Meet universal standards of professionalism work effectively with all members of the treatment team.
- Show respect for patients at all times.
- Ensure that patient autonomy is respected through the process of informed consent.

(continued)

treatment of tobacco use disorder, co-occurring substance use disorders and psychiatric disorders, relapse prevention training, motivational interviewing, and interface between pain and addiction.

Forensic Psychiatry This series covers suicide and violence risk assessment in outpatient psychiatry, police and psychiatry, correctional psychiatry, and utilization of diversion centers; female offenders, malingering, and psychiatric malpractice; and stalking, expert witness, competency to stand trial, and the insanity defense.

Integrated Care Presentations of integrated care practice from multiple perspectives such as women's mental health, pediatrics and child psychiatry, primary care and psychiatry, neurology and psychiatry, and psych oncology.

Trauma and Trauma-Informed Care Trauma-related disorder phenomenology, trauma-related disorder diagnoses, neuroscience of PTSD, evidence-based treatment of PTSD, trauma-related disorder formulation, trauma-related disorder and childhood abuse, trauma-related disorders in children, and complex trauma.

Social Determinants of Health and Healthcare Disparities In addition to incorporating information about social determinants of health and health disparities in each topic area, there is also a residency wide presentation on burnout and minoritized caregivers.

PGY 4 Year

In the fourth year of residency, there is a layering on of more advanced and complex issues in the above areas. Also included is a special presentation for the PGY 4 residents on the psychological impact of racism.

Practice-Based Learning and Improvement

In the community mental health center setting, residents systematically analyze practice performance to identify opportunities for improvement, develop an improvement plan, implement and monitor the plan, and incorporate changes that result in improvement into practice in sustained ways. The resident develops the ability to learn from and continuously apply what is learned from these activities. Many resident groups have chosen to complete their required PGY3 Quality Improvement project in the community mental health settings in which they work. Examples include studying utilization of newer and more costly antipsychotics upon discharge from the hospital into community mental health settings, the rate at which the recommended metabolic monitoring is being done in individuals treated with second-generation antipsychotics in community settings, and identifying barriers when not done, and screening for trauma in the hospital setting and in follow-up services in the community.

Interpersonal and Communication Skills

The multiculturally diverse populations served in the community mental health centers give residents recurring opportunities to employ interpersonal and communication skills, the fourth core competency. They create and maintain therapeutic and ethically sound relationships with patients in settings that include multimodal diagnosis, multicultural diversity, and lower social-economic privileges. They learn to maintain appropriate boundaries in the therapeutic relationship while appreciating therapeutic flexibility within the limited resources that are prevalent in lower-income community settings. They learn the awareness, ability, and benefit of gathering collateral information to refine diagnosis and treatment planning. They gain ability to thoroughly elicit and clearly communicate information using a range of communication skills, including nonverbal effective listening, as well as explanatory, questioning, and writing skills, all within the context of a diverse cultural, social, and educational milieu. They learn to understand the wealth of benefits of having the ability to communicate with patients in a culturally sensitive manner. They learn to work effectively within the context of a system-based, recovery-oriented, and patient-centered practice managed through a diverse treatment team of supervisors, physicians, case managers, nurses, and office staff.

Professionalism

The sensitivity and integrity necessary to meet the many demands of working in a community mental health center setting allow residents ample opportunity to continue to refine their skills in the area of professionalism. They continue to be required to meet universal standards of professionalism including promptness, appropriate appearance and demeanor, and responsibility in supervision (planning, arriving on time, reading recommended materials, being open to feedback, and utilizing feedback in future patient care).

They learn to work effectively with all members of the treatment team, respecting office staff, nurses, therapists, and case managers as all having a critical role in patient care. They practice demonstrating the value of respect for clients at all times and help maintain the dignity of patients who are often demoralized by poverty and stigmatizing past histories such as substance abuse histories and/or legal system involvement. They continue to balance respect for patient confidentiality with responsibilities to report on progress to third parties such as probation officers or child welfare officials.

Systems-Based Practice

Residents develop a working understanding of how the practice of psychiatry and its delivery are influenced by healthcare organizations as well as community bias with regard to mental health care. They learn to serve as the coordinator of care, since many times a community mental health center is the only place patients have to receive any kind of healthcare services. The patients served in the community mental health centers may lack health insurance; many are covered by Medicaid or Medicare, so implementing a risk/benefit analysis with regard to cost is essential. Residents participate in team meetings where they advocate for quality patient care in systems that will best insure the patient's safety, meet the mental and physical healthcare needs of the patient, and for social services provided by an array of organizations that will enhance optimal quality of life for their patients.

They become knowledgeable about resources available in the community such as food pantries, shelters, primary care clinics, and clothing donations sites and help clients access those resources. Additionally, residents must regularly consider how to best distribute resources within the community mental health system, particularly when considering the limited availability and funding for high-cost services and medications weighed against the clinical severity of symptoms their patients experience. Such risk-benefit analyses are often at the center of the care they deliver. Residents have the benefit of onsite supervision by full-time or clinical faculty as they implement these elements of systems-based practice. Some residents have chosen an "Advocacy Elective" that focuses on approaching advocating for mental health care at the broader level, by involvement with professional organizations, legislative activities, courts, etc. to raise awareness and educate others about inequities and stigma regarding mental health treatments and patients receiving psychiatric treatment.

Future Directions in Medical Student/Resident Education in Community Psychiatry

Ideally, medical students ought to be introduced early in training to the field of community psychiatry and the social issues affecting the provision of health care, including mental health care. One of the best ways to do this, given the powerful impact on recruitment, is to include psychiatrists, and in particular community psychiatrists, in the teaching faculty. They could be included as faculty teaching coursework in the "Foundations of Medicine," sometimes referred to as the Doctoring course, or Doctor-Patient Relationship course, that typically occurs in the first year.

Community psychiatrists should also be part of faculty teaching the second-year medical school course on Human Behavior and Psychopathology or its equivalent. Community psychiatrists and exposure to community psychiatry should be integral to the third-year clerkship experience. Community psychiatrists have expertise in a number of areas important for the education of medical students, such as working as a member of an interdisciplinary team and addressing the needs of individuals with serious and persistent mental illnesses with limited resources in the context of the family and community. It will be particularly important that community psychiatrists teaching in psychiatry clerkships be highly competent and passionately committed to the field of community psychiatry which, as noted, has evidence of being the biggest predictor of which field a medical student decides to pursue for residency.

As for psychiatry residency training, residents should graduate from residency prepared to provide clinical care in community psychiatry settings, having been educated about challenges facing people with serious and persistent mental illnesses and the evidence-based/promising practices used in treatment. Residents should be well versed in the recovery-oriented services and be able to work closely and supportively with people to attain their goals beyond merely helping them manage the symptoms of psychiatric illness. Residents should have access to quality on-site supervision during their community psychiatry rotations by a faculty member who is a dedicated community psychiatrist, with expertise working in public and community settings. Residents should also have exposure to different settings in the community and have the opportunity to work with a diversity of faculty in order to get a broad view of community psychiatry as a career choice. Faculty should seek to retain residents to take positions in local community mental health centers after graduation to provide much needed clinical care and to supervise residents themselves in order to develop a steady supply of quality supervisors for the perpetuation of these programs. Some of these graduates may choose to continue training in community psychiatry fellowships that educate graduates to assume leadership positions in community psychiatry as well as participate in research that furthers the knowledge base in community psychiatry.

There are a number of pressing issues regarding the future of education and training in community psychiatry. They deserve considerable discussion, systematic research, and innovative experimentation.

1. Integrated Care

Given the recognition that the psychiatric workforce is insufficient to meet the mental health needs of the US population, integrated care programs are increasingly important as a way to utilize the expertise of psychiatrists and allow them to participate in meeting the mental health needs of a larger percentage of the population by partnering with primary care providers. Given their expertise in providing care collaboratively, community psychiatrists will be increasingly called upon to function in a consultative and/or educational role with primary care providers. Medical school and psychiatry residency curricula will need to include education in integrated care, teaching the core principles of collaborative care, namely, patient-centered care, evidence-based care, measurement-based treatment to target, population-based care, and accountable care (Raney 2015).

In 2015, a review of General and Child and Adolescent Psychiatry Resident Training in Integrated Care reported that 26% of general psychiatry residency programs offered integrated care rotations (Reardon et al. 2015), a number that clearly needs to increase.

2. Trauma-Informed Care

Trauma-informed care, as defined by the Substance Abuse and Mental Health Services Administration (SAMHSA), refers to care that involves "these key elements: (1) realizing the prevalence of trauma; (2) recognizing how trauma affects all individuals involved with the program, organization or system, including its own workforce; and (3) responding by putting this knowledge into practice." Community psychiatrists have long recognized the impact of trauma in the populations they serve and have had an awareness of how symptoms and behavior may have developed as a result of trauma. This awareness is a foundation for providing trauma-informed care that emphasizes safety, choice, and empowerment and is strengths based, as well as providing leadership in the creation of trauma-informed systems of care (SAMHSA 2014).

3. Social Determinants of Health and Healthcare Disparities

Community psychiatrists have been aware of the negative impact of social determinants of health such as poverty, homelessness, food insecurity, unemployment, and discrimination on mental health. The World Health Organization (WHO) report Closing the Gap in a Generation makes the point that social determinants of health lead to health inequities (WHO 2008). Community psychiatrists can use their unique skill set to impact clinical care, including preventative programs, as well as to effect public policy. The skills necessary to engage at this level should be incorporated into medical school and psychiatry residency curricula (Shim and Compton 2018).

4. Impact of Long-Term Disasters Such as the COVID-19 Pandemic and Climate Change

Public and community psychiatrists will be called upon to be in the forefront of disaster mental health services, given the significant prevalence of immediate and long-term mental health sequelae resulting from such events. Now that we are coming to appreciate that one of the primary long-term public health impacts of natural and man-made disasters concerns mental health, community psychiatrists likely will be called upon to assume significant leadership roles on disaster response teams as an expression both of their expertise and of their commitment to public health and preventative mental health. Community psychiatrists may be asked to devote a greater proportion of their time in the immediate aftermath of disasters, using their crisis intervention skills to help large numbers of individuals and families to effectively utilize a diverse array of existing supports in the community in order to better cope with the residue of traumatic experiences. When the symptomatology of psychiatric disorders is identified during the acute phase of disasters, community psychiatrists will be asked to play a lead role in mental health triage and treatment, taking good advantage of their experience with the availability of limited resources. Community psychiatrists will be called upon to educate first responders and healthcare providers about the concepts of compassion fatigue and vicarious trauma, which are significant mental health concerns following disasters. Therefore, training in disaster mental health services must be incorporated into psychiatry residency training curricula.

While much of the research on disaster mental health has focused on the impact of one-time disasters, further study is necessary to better understand the impact on the mental health of individuals and communities due to long-term or "chronic" disasters such as the COVID-19 pandemic and the effects of climate change, which has been shown to be causing more erratic and frequent weather-related phenomena (Taquet et al. 2020).

The mental health effects of climate change may be directly related to the weather events resulting in loss of loved ones and bereavement, increased substance use, and an exacerbation of preexisting mental health issues. The trauma associated with physical damage, need for migration, and disruption of communities can contribute to increased anxiety, fear, and distress. Vulnerable populations, such as those cared for by community psychiatrists, are at increased risk of impact from climate change. Climate change and long-term disasters generally can serve to increase health disparities and inequities. Community psychiatrists can and should play a major role in combatting climate change, and education about climate change and the psychological and psychiatric sequelae should be included in the education of medical students and residents, including psychiatry residents (Coverdale et al. 2018).

Conclusion

- Community psychiatrists have long embraced many values and principles that are just now being recognized by mainstream US medicine as crucial factors affecting health.
- Community psychiatrists have always practiced population health, in that effort is made to engage clients that did not show up at the community mental health center for care and treatment, in addition to providing treatment to the clients who did show up for care.
- Community psychiatrists have recognized the value of the interdisciplinary team, working alongside Advanced Practice Registered Nurses, psychiatric nurses, counselors, social workers, case managers, and peer support specialists to provide comprehensive, holistic care to clients.
- Community psychiatrists have recognized the importance of providing integrated care, so that clients reluctant to go elsewhere for primary care could have access to primary care at the setting in which they were most familiar and comfortable, usually the community mental health center.
- Community psychiatrists have paid attention to the social determinants of health, such as poverty, community violence, food insecurity, homelessness, unemployment, healthcare disparities, and systemic racism, as major factors contributing to health, and worked to minimize these in the communities they served.
- Community psychiatrists have long recognized that trauma is pervasive in populations affected by mental health challenges and understand the far-reaching effects of trauma, thereby working toward providing trauma-informed care that works to minimize the possibility of re-traumatization and empowers clients as active collaborators in their health care.

In summary, having embraced these principles for decades, community psychiatrists are well poised to serve as medical leaders in health-care systems in the twenty-first century. And education to prepare practitioners in this field will be challenged to rise to new heights of integration, cutting-edge practice, and ongoing innovation.

Acknowledgments The author wishes to acknowledge the contribution of David L. Cutler, MD concerning the history of training of medical students and psychiatry residents in community psychiatry.

References

AAMC Average Required Weeks for Psychiatry, LCME Annual Questionnaire Part II 2009–10, 2014–15, 2019–20. [aamc.org/data-reports/curriculum-reports/interactive-data/clerkship-week-requirements-curriculum-year] accessed 3/6/2022.

AAMC Percentage of Medical Schools with Separate Required Clerkships by Discipline: Psychiatry, LCME Annual Questionnaire Part II 2011–12 through 2019–20. [aamc.org/data-reports/curriculum-reports/interactive-data/clerkship-requirements-discipline] accessed 3/6/2022.

AAMC Number of US Medical Schools Reporting Social Determinants by Academic Level, AAMC Curriculum Inventory 2018–19 [aamc.org/data-reports/curriculum-reports/interactive-data/social-determinants-health-academic-level] accessed 3/6/2022.

Accreditation Council for Graduate Medical Education (ACGME). (2020). *Psychiatry Milestones.*

Clardy, J., Thrush, C., Guttenberger, V., Goodrich M, Burton R.(2000). The junior year psychiatric clerkship and medical students' interest in psychiatry. *Academic Psychiatry 24*, 35-40.

Commission on Social Determinants of Health: Closing the Gap in a Generation: Health Equity through Action on the Social Determinants of Health. Final Report. Geneva, World Health Organization (2008). https://www.who.int/social_determinants/final_report/csdh_finalreport_2008.pdf

Coverdale, J.,Balon, R., Beresin, E. et al. (2018). Climate change: a call to action for the psychiatric profession. *Academic Psychiatry 42,* 317-323. https://doi.org/10.1007/s40596-018-0885-7

Cowley, D., Dunaway, K., Forstein, M., et al. (2014). Teaching psychiatry residents to work at the interface of mental health and primary care. *Academic Psychiatry 38* (4), 398-404.

Cutler, D.L., Bloom J.D., Shore, J.H. (1981). Training psychiatrists to work with community support systems for chronically mentally ill persons. *American Journal of Psychiatry, 138* (1), 98-101.

Factor R., Stein, L. Diamond R. (1988). A model community psychiatry curriculum for psychiatry residents. *Community Mental Health Journal, 24*, (4), 310-27.

Gabel S, Sarvet B. (2011) Public-academic partnerships: Public-academic partnerships to address the need for child and adolescent psychiatric services. *Psychiatric Services, 62*(8):827-829. doi: https://doi.org/10.1176/ps.62.8.pss6208_0827. PMID: 21807821

Gheihman, G., Jun, T., Young, G.J., et al. (2018). A review of longitudinal clinical programs in US medical schools. *Med Educ Online*, *23*,(1), 1444900. https://doi.org/10.1080/10872981.2018.1444900.

Lau, T, Zamani, D, Lee, E, et al. (2015). Factors affecting recruitment into psychiatry: a Canadian experience. *Academic Psychiatry,* 39(3), 246-52. DOI https://doi.org/10.1007/s40596-014-0269-6.

Lucey, C.R. (2013). Medical education: Part of the problem and part of the solution. *JAMA Intern Med,* 173,1639–1643.

Lyons, Z. and Janca, A. (2015). Impact of a psychiatry clerkship on stigma, attitudes toward psychiatry and psychiatry as a career choice. *BMC Medical Education 15*(34) DOI https://doi.org/10.1186/s12909-015-0307-4.

McQuistion, H.L., Ranz, J.M., Gillig, P.M. (2004). A survey of American psychiatry residency programs concerning education in homelessness. *Academic Psychiatry*, 28, 116-121.

McQuistion H.L & Rosenheck, S.D. (2006). Heroes in community psychiatry: C. Christian Beels and the evolution of community psychiatry in New York City. *Community Mental Health J, 42*(6), 513-520.

Public Academic Liaison (PAL) Program Provider Service Plan. (2020). Report to the Alcohol Drug and Mental Health Services (ADAMHS) Board of Cuyahoga County by University Hospitals Cleveland Medical Center.

Raney, L. ed. (2015). *Integrated care: working at the interface of primary care and behavioral health.* American Psychiatry Publishing.

Reardon, C.L., Bentman, A., Cowley, D.S. et al. (2015). General and child and adolescent psychiatry resident training in integrated care: a survey of program directors. *Academic Psychiatry 39***,** 442–447. https://doi.org/10.1007/s40596-015-0315-z

Rosenthal, R., Levine, R., Carlson, D., Clegg, K., and Crosby, R. (2005). The “shrinking” clerkship: characteristics and length of clerkships in psychiatry undergraduate education. *Academic Psychiatry*, 29,47-51.

Shim, R and Compton, M. (2018). Addressing the social determinants of mental health: If not now, when? If not us, who? *Psychiatric Services*, *69*, 844-846. doi:https://doi.org/10.1176/appi.ps201800060.

Shore, J.H., Kinzie, J.D., Bloom J.D.(1979). Required educational objectives in community psychiatry. *American Journal of Psychiatry, 13* (2), 193-195.

Talbott, J.A, Bray, J.D., Flaherty, L., Robinowitz, C.B., Taintor, Z.(1991). State university collaboration in psychiatry: The Pew Memorial Trust Program. *Community Mental Health Journal 27* (6) 425-440.

Taquet, M., Luciano, S., Geddes, J.R., et al. (2020). Bidirectional associations between Covid-19 and psychiatric disorder: retrospective cohort studies of 62,354 Covid -19 cases in the USA. *Lancet Psychiatry 1-11* https://doi.org/10.1016/S2215-0366(20)30462-4

United States Department of Health and Human Services, Substance Abuse and Mental Health Services Administration, Center for substance Abuse Treatment. (2014). *Trauma-Informed Care in Behavioral Health Services*, Treatment Improvement Protocol (TIP) Series 57.

United States Medical Licensing Examination (USMLE). (2020). *United States Medical Licensing Examination Content Outline*. Usmle.org/pdfs/usmlecontentoutline.pdf

World Health Organization press release (2022) https://www.who.int/news/item/02-03-2022-Covid-19-pandemic-triggers-25-increase-in-prevalence-of-anxiety-and-depression-worldwide

Public/Community Psychiatry Fellowships

Stephanie M. Le Melle and Jules M. Ranz

Introduction

Psychiatrists are popularly viewed as seeing patients in a private office practice setting. However, a 2006 survey of APA members demonstrated that early and mid-career psychiatrists now spend more time in publicly funded organizational settings than in private practice. Nonetheless, psychiatric training is still oriented toward careers in private practice, with little dedicated training for psychiatrists to work in organizational settings (Ranz et al. 2006).

Public funds (e.g., Medicare, Medicaid, VA, and State Mental Health Authorities) in 2019 comprised 62.7% of all mental health services in the USA (Open Minds 2020). This is up from 58% in 2006 (SAMHSA 2010). These government funds support myriad services in countless nonprofit and even private for-profit organizations. These organizations have mandates to use their public funding to serve the poor and people with serious mental illness and complex needs. Public money, appropriately, is distributed via a political process and comes with strings attached, such as contracts for specific services to mandated target populations, certification and accreditation standards, and mechanisms of fiscal accountability. As these public funding streams changed over time, so did the need to train clinicians to run and work in these organizations. The political and social changes from 1960s to 2020s swing from social consciousness and civil rights, to medicalized care, to criminalization of people with behavioral health needs, and to the recovery movement. Fiscal changes, prompted by these political changes, greatly influence clinical services. Clinical leaders need to know what kinds of services will best fulfill the mandates of the time and justify public expenditures. Clinical leaders and managers need to know how to create and maintain behavioral organizations as the political/fiscal needs change. It is this need that spurred the development of postdoctoral fellowships in public/community psychiatry.

There have been several phases to fellowship training for public/community psychiatrists:

Phase 1: 1960s to 1970s – fellowship training focused on mental health consultation, created in the wake of downsizing of mental health

S. M. Le Melle (✉)
Public Psychiatry Fellowship of NYS Psychiatric Institute/Columbia University Medical Center, New York, NY, USA

Department of Psychiatry, Columbia University College of Physicians and Surgeons, New York, NY, USA
e-mail: stephanie.lemelle@nyspi.columbia.edu

J. M. Ranz
Public Psychiatry Fellowship of NYS Psychiatric Institute/Columbia University Medical Center, New York, NY, USA

Department of Psychiatry, Columbia University College of Physicians and Surgeons, New York, NY, USA

NYS Psychiatric Institute, New York, NY, USA

W. E. Sowers et al. (eds.), *Textbook of Community Psychiatry*,
https://doi.org/10.1007/978-3-031-10239-4_60

institutions and movement of treatment to the community.

Phase 2: 1980s to 2000s – the initial growth and development of fellowship training focused on people with serious mental illness.

Phase 3: 2000 to 2010 – the fiscal and structural adaptations of fellowships to meet local needs.

Phase 4: 2010 to 2020 – the increased interest and demand for community psychiatrists in diverse systems of care.

Phase 1: Early History of Public and Community Psychiatry Fellowships 1960s–1970s

The landmark 1963 Federal Community Mental Health Centers Act (CMHC) listed "mental health consultation" as one of five basic services to be provided by all community mental health centers. As a result, there was a marked development of training programs in this method in the mid-1960s (Caplan 1970). With the downsizing of asylums and mental health institutions, people with "chronic mental illness" now referred to as people with "significant mental health needs" were left to seek care in communities. The CMHC Act provided federal funds to support the development of mental health outpatient clinics. This shift necessitated a different approach to care. Psychiatrists, who had been the clinical leader in hospital settings, had to learn how to provide treatment in the community with a multidisciplinary team. These new community teams were primarily run by nonpsychiatrists. The deinstitutionalized people needing care, outside of a custodial system, had to also find ways to live in the community. This required programs to address coordination of care, rehabilitation, socialization, housing, and other social determinants of health.

The early programs were also heavily influenced by clinicians who were psychodynamically trained. As a result of this orientation, treatment practice in community clinics tended to focus on psychotherapy, and the treatment of people with "minor mental disorders and problems coping with life crisis" like depression, anxiety, personality disorders, and PTSD who were the majority of patients appears in these clinics. There was also an academic divide between the libertarian view and the medical/biological view. At one end was the libertarian belief that psychiatry was influencing social control over people "who didn't fit social norms" and that psychiatry should focus more on social reform to address poverty, housing, and other social determinants of health. At the other end was the medical/biological view that mental illness was inherited and therefore not easily changed, a chronic condition requiring lifelong, intensive treatment (Bonita Weddle, New York State Archives, 1998, #70).

Most of the early fellowships tended toward the libertarian view and called themselves community psychiatry training programs, and some used the term social and community psychiatry, emphasizing the blending of the concepts of social psychiatry with the practices of community psychiatry. Thus, a program at the Albert Einstein College of Medicine in the Bronx, NY, used the term social and community psychiatry, "to train psychiatrists in the techniques of practice involved in community psychiatry and to teach the core content pertaining to social and cultural factors that promote mental health or contribute to mental illness, which comprises social psychiatry" (Pattison 1972). Two of these early programs used the term public health to describe their programs.

In the 1960s, the term "community" generally referred to community outreach. Currently, it refers to psychiatrists working in the community. The term "community" also conveys a commitment to the community of people being served, and by extension, the community of people and their providers.

In distinction, the term public which as we will see came into use in the early 1980s conveys the practice of working in municipal, state, and federal organizational settings. The term has also been extended to include publicly funded nonprofit organizational settings, which encompasses the majority of psychiatric care delivered in organization settings. Finally, the term public conveys a responsibility to provide care to public sector patients: people living in poverty (especially single-parent families, the elderly, and children), and adults with serious mental illness, substance abuse, and other complex needs. There are other specialty populations served in the public sector: homeless adults and families, people with behavioral health needs and criminal justice involvement, immigrants, people with behavioral health needs and other chronic medical illnesses, and people suffering from complex trauma and adverse childhood experiences. The terms "public" and "community" are now used interchangeably by fellowship training programs.

A report titled Education for Community Psychiatry (1967) issued by the Group for the Advancement of Psychiatry (GAP) documented the training programs in existence in the mid-1960s. These programs were 1–2 years in length and combined didactic training with field experiences. Areas of focus reflected the diversity of services that were being developed at that time: consultation, prevention, program planning, and research activities in community settings. A minority of the program emphasized administration. These fellowship programs are listed in Table 1.

The Social and Community Psychiatry Training program at the University of California, Los Angeles (UCLA), was particularly well documented (Karno et al. 1974). It was a 2-year post-residency program originally leading to an MPH degree. The program attempted to integrate social science and public health disciplines within the same program. The program, which received support from the National Institute of Mental Health, began on July 1, 1962. As of 1972, the level of funding had risen as a reflection of the growing demand and provided stipends and teaching support for 12 fellows-in-training, 6 at each level of the 2-year program. By 1972, the program had graduated 44 psychiatrists. Support from the National Institute of Mental Health (NIMH) ended in 1974, and at that time, the program was disbanded, but its "core community practicum experience and coursework" were transferred into the general residency training program. Two other programs at Columbia and Harvard were also described in separately published manuscripts (Bernard 1964; Caplan 1970).

These fellowships provided a framework for teaching clinicians the skills needed to transition people from institutional care to publicly funded care in community settings.

None of the early programs survived more than a decade, probably because of the drying up of federal support for these programs.

Phase 2: Columbia Public Psychiatry Fellowship 1980s–2000

There is no evidence of any dedicated postdoctoral public or community psychiatry training program functioning during the mid- to late 1970s. During the Reagan administration's first budget in 1980, there were significant cuts. One of funding streams cut was CMHC funding. The funding was shifted to the states in the form of block grants through NIMH. Several states, including New York and California, took advantage of this shift in public funds to block grants with mandates to use public funds to focus more on people with serious mental illness. The Young Adult Chronic Patient: overview of a population (Pepper et al. 1981) describes the new population of young people, with serious mental illness, who had never been "institutionalized" and were now living in the community. As a result of funding shifts and the required focus on people with serious mental illness, fellowship programs created after 1980 began to shift their focus and structure to address the needs of this new population of patients.

The NYS Office of Mental Health, wishing to promote dedicated training for psychiatrists interested in careers serving people with serious mental illness, provided funding to start the Columbia University Public Psychiatry Fellowship (PPF) in 1981 (Ranz et al. 1996). This new PPF was distinct from the earlier program at Columbia and still exists today. The Columbia PPF trains ten fellows per year and serves as the model for virtually all other public and community psychiatry training programs currently in existence. A small number of other programs

Table 1 Phase 1 - Early fellowship programs

	#Fellows/#Years	Postgraduate social and community psychiatry training programs	Education for community psychiatry (1967)[a]
		Courses	**Field placement structure**
Albert Einstein College of Medicine – The Social and Community Psychiatry Fellowship	3–5 fellows in 1- to 2-year program	Social psychiatry, communications theory, epidemiology, and research design	Individually tailored, but each fellow spent time in a day hospital, a family therapy seminar, a community consultation service, and conducting a small research project
Boston State Hospital	2 PGY 4/5 psychiatrists for 1-year program	Training focused on psychiatric leadership in community services. "Intensive social psychiatry seminar work"	Training a variety of hospital and community settings, with options for training in brief treatment, home treatment, family therapy, consultation, mental health planning (with the Department of Mental Health of the State of Massachusetts)
Columbia University – The Traineeship in Community and Social Psychiatry	4–5 fellows in 2-year program with an MS or MPH available	Legal aspects of psychiatry, hospital administration, consulting, communication, ward management, social psychiatry, government processes, and epidemiology	Supervised field placements chosen from settings that emphasize prevention, rehabilitation, and community planning
Massachusetts General Hospital (MGH) – Training in Community Mental Health for Psychiatrists	2 "clinician-practitioner-administrators" in 1- to 2-year program	Community processes, epidemiology, crisis intervention, consultation, group dynamics, research and communication, plus "some emphasis on administration"	The ratio of time devoted to didactic to practical experiences was 40/60. Field experiences took place at various units of MGH, especially the Human Relations Service of Wellesley, Inc.
Menninger Foundation – The Post-residency Fellowship in Community Psychiatry	4 fellows in 2-year program	"Consultants, administrators and investigators of psychosocial phenomena". Consultation, group and family dynamics, collaboration and communication, research and epidemiology	Fellows placed in at least two of five divisions: Law and Psychiatry, Religion and Psychiatry, School Mental Health, Industrial Mental Health, Psychosocial Research. Each division offered field experiences. Each fellow carried out a research project
The Institute of the Pennsylvania Hospital Community Psychiatry	2 fellows in 1- to 2-year program	"Continuing seminar on all aspects of social psychiatry, including prejudice and discrimination, community crises and disorganization, urban renewal, hospitalization and administrative practices"	Court agencies, adoption agencies, hospitals, halfway houses, schools, and Department of Welfare

(continued)

Table 1 (continued)

The University of California in Los Angeles (UCLA) – The Social and Community Psychiatry Training Program	7 fellows in a 2-year program leading to MPH	Consultation, preventive psychiatry, research, epidemiology and "recommended therapeutic practices for the treatment of existing and future community mental health problems"	Courses covered social sciences, social psychiatry, community structure, consultation, epidemiology, administration, social class and culture (No mention of field placements)
There were an additional five programs training psychiatrists alongside other MH professionals:			
Name of program	**#Fellows/#Years**	**Courses**	**Field placement structure**
Center for Training in Community Psychiatry and Mental Health Administration (Berkeley CA)	3 psychiatrists at PGY4 or PGY5 level alongside 205 trainees, 88 of which were psychiatric residents	Didactic training An MPH was available	"Affiliations with field work placements"
Harvard Medical School Educational Program in Community Mental Health of the Laboratory of Community Psychiatry[b]	10–18 psychiatrists, psychologists, social workers, and nurses in a 1-year program	Halftime in seminars covering research methodology, administration, consultation, group process, legal aspects, and preventive psychiatry	Half time was spent in "supervised field experiences and participation in community mental health research and practice"
Johns Hopkins Public Health-Mental Health	7–10 "mental hygiene specialists" (psychiatrists, psychologists, nurses and social workers) among 70 students	1 year of training in biostatistics, epidemiology, prevention, and administration	(No mention of field placements)
Langley Porter Community Mental Health Training Program	Psychiatrists and psychologists in a 1–2 year program. Psychiatrists were supported by NIMH stipends	"Methods and Practices" and "Principles and Theory" in Community Mental Health Field	"Intensive study of a particular problem relevant to community mental health" and an "opportunity for observation and participation in …community mental health service"
Yale – Public Health Psychiatry	"Not more than 6–8 students" including psychiatrists, psychologists, social workers, and RNs in a 2-year program leading to an MPH	Epidemiology, community psychiatry, social psychiatry, biostatistics, and methodology of social research	The program focused on program development and evaluation, and research. Field work experience was provided

[a]Education for Community Psychiatry (1967), Formulated by the Committee on Medical Education, Group for the Advancement of Psychiatry, Volume VI, Report #67

[b]This program was originally created by Gerald Caplan in the mid-1950s at the Harvard School of Public Health and transferred to the Laboratory of Community Psychiatry in 1964 (Caplan)

training one to two fellows each were started in the 1980s and 1990s, but none of these small programs survive today.

In contrast to the first phase of fellowships, the Columbia fellowship purposely chose to use "Public" in their title. In a personal communication from C. Christian Beels, MD, the founder of the PPF program, to Jules M. Ranz MD, the former fellowship director, Dr. Beels writes:

> The reason for choosing Public rather than Community or Social psychiatry was the connotation that the other names had acquired in the 60's. Grob (1994) wrote that social and community psychiatry had become associated both with the "community mental health center" movement, a federal effort to get states to take up the cause of the severely mentally ill, and with an effort to improve mental health outcomes indirectly by community organizing and improvement of the social environment. We used the word "Public": to convey our commitment to working for existing public (usually state or city) institutions already charged with the care of the long-term mentally ill, the addicted, and the poor or homeless. The problem with the social and community psychiatry movement was that it never really figured out how to be a psychiatrist to a community. There was much discussion about how to deal with homelessness, for example, but few plans to actually provide and supervise homes until nonprofit community-based agencies began to provide government funded services for the homeless in the 1970s. I would add that an important reason for using the word "public" was that it was clearly the opposite of "private," as in private practice and corporate profit. The image of the psychiatrist as civil servant seemed important (Beels, personal communication).

According to the PPF website (ppf.hs.columbia.edu): Public and Community Psychiatry encompasses the care of people with serious and complex behavioral health needs in multiple community service systems typically publicly funded through Medicaid, Medicare, and local grants and contracts. The PPF mission statement reflects the changing focus on the training of psychiatrists, the population served, and the funding streams:

> The mission of the Columbia Public Psychiatry Fellowship is to train post residency psychiatrists to become clinical, administrative and academic leaders in the field of Public/Community Psychiatry who will serve people with behavioral health needs that require more complex levels of care and to impact the practice of publicly-funded behavioral health nationally, through fostering the career development of fellows and alumni as well as promoting the development of a network of public/community psychiatry fellowships around the country.

Early published surveys showed that 97% of PPF alumni continued to work in the public sector, 67% in leadership roles, mostly as program medical directors (i.e., of clinics, recovery and rehab programs, and ACT teams) (Ranz and Stueve 1998). These values have remained relatively constant over the years and in 2020 were 98% and 60%, respectively. Throughout the 1-year program, each of ten fellows spend 3 days a week working in one public mental health hospital or agency. At their job sites, fellows assume some of the responsibilities of a leadership role by running team meetings, participating in program planning, analyzing budgets, and initiating internal program evaluations. The Columbia model encourages fellows, at the end of the fellowship year, to continue in their jobs and move from part-time employees to full-time employees. This expectation benefits both the fellows and the organizations. Fellows are encouraged to apply for positions as program medical directors at their job sites after completion of the fellowship year, as the next logical step toward public sector leadership careers.

Phase 3: 2000–2010 Growth and Collaboration Between Fellowships

The needs of the people served in the public mental system became more complex in the 1990s. HIV, substance abuse, homelessness, the overincarceration of people with mental illness, immigration, and the consumer movement all impacted the political/social atmosphere of the 1990s. In 2000, The Young Adult Chronic Patient: A Look Back (Cournos and Le Melle 1990) reflects on the changes in community/public mental health since Pepper's paper 10 years earlier. People with serious mental illness now had to navigate multiple system of care outside of the mental health system to get their needs met. This required that community/public psychiatrists have a more extensive understanding of systems and act as "boundary spanners." This was particularly true at the interface between mental health, substance abuse, and the criminal justice system (Steadman

1992). In 2010, the Treatment Advocacy Center reported that there were three times more mentally ill people in jails and prison then in hospitals (Torrey et al. 2010, TAC report). It was not enough to focus on mental health needs alone. It also became apparent that people with serious mental illness were dying from medical illness at higher rates and 14 to 32 years sooner than the general public (Colton and Manderscheid 2006). Knowledge of the criminal justice system and medical treatment became essential in the treatment of people with serious illness in the community. These were not topics typically covered in psychiatric training. Therefore, fellowships began to focus more on the concepts of boundary spanning and collaborative care.

As of 2011, there were 14 fellowship programs in existence and 2 in the serious planning stages. A program was created at Case Western in 2000 and became somewhat dormant until restarted in 2009. Another program was created at Emory in 2001. All the others were created between 2005 and 2011, partly sparked by recent interest on the part of several states in developing fellowships in public psychiatry to meet the growing need for psychiatrists. In 2007, Pennsylvania awarded "Center of Excellence" status (a model developed in Ohio) to three academic centers at the University of Pittsburgh, Lake Erie, and the University of Pennsylvania with mandates and funding to create public sector fellowships with PPF as model. In 2004, California created dedicated mental health funds created by the Mental Health Services Act (Proposition 63, levying a 1% state tax on incomes of $one million or more). Some of these funds were earmarked for training of mental health professionals. In 2012, a program was created in San Diego in the spirit of Proposition 63, though with other funds.

Programs were started at Yale and the Durham VA in 2007 and at NYU in 2008. In 2010, programs were started at the University of Texas South Western in Dallas, Texas (USTW), the University of NC-Chapel, Florida, and Alabama, and in 2011, a program was started at the University of California in San Francisco (UCSF). Six of the existing programs have been run by Columbia PPF alumni (Columbia, NYU, Case Western, UTSW, UCSF and Penn).

The Core Elements of a Public Psychiatry Fellowship

Public/community psychiatry fellowships are recognized as subspecialty training in psychiatry but not accredited by the Accreditation Council for Graduate Medical Education (ACGME). This actually allows the fellowships to adapt and change as the needs of the people served and the community needs change. In addition, this allows fellowships to choose a variety of fiscal models, including flexibility with regard to fellows' salaries (see below). As new fellowships were developed, to provide some standardization, the Columbia fellowship became the model for program development. The Columbia PPF began consulting with developing programs and shared their curriculum with the new programs. In 2008, in response to these requests, the Columbia PPF faculty developed 7 core elements considered as essential for fellowship training program (Ranz et al. 2008).

1. *Academic curriculum covering the essential topics in public psychiatry*, including the Structure of Public Psychiatry, The Role of the Psychiatrist, Recovery-Oriented Care; Systems-Based Practices; Internal Program Evaluation; Healthcare Disparities, Special Populations of people affected by substance use, trauma, homelessness; Fiscal Management; and Public Mental Health Advocacy including presentations by people with lived experience.
2. *Application of concepts taught in the academic curriculum by fellows to job placements*, through formal written presentations to other fellows and faculty: Congruence Model analysis of job placement organization; Systems-Oriented Clinical Case; Budget; Advocacy and Internal Program Evaluation. Fellows take feedback from these presentations to job site supervisors as suggestions to inform system change.

3. *Presentations by guest speakers illustrating topics covered in the academic curriculum.*
4. *Practicum in mental health administration.* Sessions teaching basic concepts in mental health administration and leadership interspersed with case presentations by alumni who are medical directors in public sector organizations addressing management problems to which fellows and faculty suggest strategic solutions.
5. *Placement in one public mental health organization throughout the year* to achieve a comprehensive clinical and management experience. Fellows select the agency for which they work 3 days a week throughout the fellowship year. Agencies are chosen with regard to their willingness to allow fellows to assume leadership roles and their track record of providing positive experiences to previous fellows.
6. *Weekly meetings with a faculty preceptor for individual support in academic and field placement experiences.*
7. *Mentorship and other ongoing support from faculty beyond the fellowship year* through *above presentations, consultations, reunions, fellowship website, and list serve.*

In addition, the authors indicated that, in recognition of the importance of group process, new programs are encouraged to start with at least two fellows. If funds were only available for one fellow, a 2-year program was recommended ensuring a minimal group process between first and second year fellows. To guarantee a reasonably complete curriculum, the authors also recommended classes be scheduled a minimum of 1 day per week. If class time has to be limited to one-half day per week, a 2-year program is again recommended. The faculty from the Columbia Public Psychiatry Fellowship continue to consult in the development of other fellowships nationally and make available their didactic curriculum for other fellowships.

The core elements and the soon-to-follow American Association of Community Psychiatry (AACP) Guidelines for Community Psychiatry Fellowships became the standards for fellowship development.

AACP Guidelines for Community Psychiatry Fellowships

The publication of the Columbia Core Elements and the renewed interest in developing fellowship programs nationally inspired the American Association of Community Psychiatrists to develop "*Guidelines for Developing and Evaluating Public and Community Psychiatry Training Fellowships*" (AACP 2008).

> The purpose of the AACP guidelines is to create a vision for training of psychiatrists that incorporates the capacity to promote health and wellness through a comprehensive conceptualization of human experiences and an integrated, holistic approach to treatment and services. This vision includes elements needed to re-establish psychiatry's strong position in leadership and consultation.

These five elements are derived from the PPF Core Elements, though described in more detail in the AACP guidelines:

Academic curriculum covering the essential topics in public psychiatry,
Application of concepts taught in the academic curriculum by Fellows to job placements
Presentations by guest speakers illustrating topics covered in the academic curriculum.
Practicum in mental health administration
Placement in one public mental health organization throughout the year

Other Elements of Fellowship Program Design

1. *Systems management skills.* Some fellows or programs emphasize participation in larger systems administering behavioral health care.
2. *Community, consumer, or family advocacy.* Programs or individual fellows may wish to develop a public health focus by enhancing organizational skills useful in advocating for change or empowerment of various stakeholder groups.
3. *Recovery/resiliency-oriented services.* In response to the consumers/people with lived experience empowerment movement, and the

growth and acceptance of recovery-oriented treatment and care, people with lived experience are more invested in directing their own care and making choices about the services they receive. As recovery-oriented transformation efforts gain momentum at the federal, state, and local levels, it is essential that fellows have a thorough understanding of recovery and resiliency principles and knowledge of how services can be delivered in a manner that supports them.

4. *Healthcare equity, cultural humility.* It is crucial that programs and fellows obtain competence in the treatment of diverse cultural groups, develop humility and sensitivity to the relevant needs of different groups, and address these needs in clinical practice or in transforming systems of care in a manner that reduces the obstacles to receiving evidence-based, competent care for all.

Phase 4: 2011 to 2020 Continued Increase in Number and Diversification of Fellowships

From 2011 to 2020, the number of public/community fellowships (PPFs) has increased from 15 programs, in 2012, to approximately 25 nationally in 2020. New programs have been started in Florida, Illinois, Massachusetts, Michigan, New York, Pennsylvania, Ohio, Virginia, and Washington State. This was partly due to the general shortage of psychiatrist nationally. More specifically, there is a general need for more well-trained psychiatrists to provide treatment and care for underserved populations and for people with serious mental illness and complex needs in community settings (Thompson et al. 2017). This shortage is exacerbated further by the fact that psychiatrists working in private practice often do not accept insurance. This further limits options for people who cannot afford to pay out of pocket or who need a team approach to their care. This is particularly apparent in low-income communities and rural settings.

There are several other factors that may have contributed to this increase and diversification of fellowships. These factors can be viewed through three lenses: (1) recovery model of care lens – desire to step out of the medical model and into a person-centered recovery model; (2) systems-based practice lens – a growing frustration with the siloed systems of health care, disconnected social service systems, growth of the criminal justice system, and the general desire for coordinated systems of care; and (3) social justice lens – belief that behavioral and general health care is an essential component of social justice.

Recovery lens: Many applicants to PPFs describe feeling limited by the "medical model" of care which focuses on the treatment of illness rather than on health. Applicants also desire to understand the whole person and to join with people in their recovery. PPF fellows are looking for careers in psychiatry that allow them to practice beyond simply being "prescribers." Approaching care and treatment through a "recovery lens" allows fellows to use all of their skills as psychiatrists to help people live their best lives. The concept of a "recovery model of care" is still not an ACGME-required milestone (ACGME Milestones 2020). There is only a single reference to SAMHSA's recovery model of care, in the community-based program milestone and a comment about "shared decision-making" in the information sharing milestone. Principles of recovery-oriented care are a primary feature of PPF training, and this recovery-oriented training has attracted more applicants.

Systems-Based Practice Lens: Medical education in the USA is focused on specialty training. This has led to the development of systems of health care that are based on specialization. This has resulted in fragmentation of our healthcare delivery system including behavioral health care (Emery 2012). People with chronic illness and complex needs have to navigate multiple systems of care to get their needs met. In medical school and residency, trainees have to navigate these systems with clients but are not routinely taught the tools that they need to do so nor are they taught the skills needed to lead change in these systems of care. PPFs training focuses on systems-based practice and teaches fellows how to understand, improve, and become leaders in health organizations. Fellowships, therefore, attract applicants who are drawn to leadership and management and who are willing to "think outside of the box" to improve our siloed systems of care. Principles for understanding and teaching SBP have been developed and are being incorporated into both fellowship and residency training (Le Melle et al. 2013).

Social Justice Lens: There has been increased concern and activism among applicants regarding social justice. The Affordable Care Act, Parity Legislation, Black Lives Matter, immigration issues, and, most recently, COVID-19, all have highlighted healthcare disparities and social injustice in our healthcare systems. All of the fellowships focus on the impact of social determinants of health and health inequities and encourage fellows to be involved in advocacy to address disparities. The concepts of health equity are taught in fellowship didactics and reinforced in fellows' clinical work, research, and systems change projects. Many early career psychiatrists are drawn toward opportunities to participate in clinical settings where there is encouragement to discuss and address health equity and social justice. This training prepares the fellows to become change leaders throughout their careers and to advocate for change at local, state, and national levels.

Models of Funding and Diversification of Fellowships

Regarding funding, fiscal challenges contributed to the closing of many fellowships and the diversification of others. A spectrum of fiscal models is currently being used to fund PPFs (Le Melle et al. 2012). At one end of the spectrum, the fellowship training institution pays the full salary of fellows, and at the other end, the job site agency pays the full salary (junior faculty model or part-time attending model). Intermediary strategies involve sharing of the salary between fellowship training institutions and job site agencies. In all programs, the structural arrangements involve fellows providing clinical work in various community settings and having protected time for didactic learning, fellowship presentations, and supervision. The time allotted for clinical and didactic work varies depending on the fiscal structure. There are tradeoffs to be considered with each model including the PPFs ability to balance clinical work requirements with protected time for training, competitive salaries, and the potential to stay on in the rotation or job after completing the fellowship.

Many academic programs have struggled to maintain grant funding for fellowships, and sustainability of academic institutional funding can vary from year to year. So, in recent years, the "junior attending" model has become more popular. In this model, fellows are hired within their academic institutions or hospital affiliates and work as junior attendings. This model, however, can pose a problem with the recognition of "a fellow" in the academic institution where they are employed. Graduate Medical Education (GME) offices, which monitor and regulate training programs, often do not know what to do with a "Fellow" who is also an "Attending." Some programs have been able to negotiate recognition of fellows hired as attendings as "postgraduate fellows." In some fellowships, jobs as attendings are based on availability of position in the system. Examples of fellowships using this model are UCSF, UCSD, Yale, NYU, and UTSW.

The model of using contracts for clinical services in community programs is also popular. In this model, the academic institution is contracted to provide clinical services, performed by fellows, to specific community programs. This contractual arrangement can cover a partial or full salary for a fellow. Fellows may work in one or multiple community programs depending on the contract. This model also allows fellows to work outside of their academic institutions and enables community programs greater access to fellowship trained psychiatrists. An example of a fellowship using this model is U Penn.

The model of fellows hired as "part-time psychiatrist" allows fellows to choose competitive jobs, working part time, in community programs or academic centers. Fellows devote the remainder of their time to academic pursuit in the fellowship. This is the new model used by Columbia

Public Psychiatry Fellowship. Fellows are hired, by community programs or academic institutions, with negotiated competitive salaries, for 0.6 full-time equivalents (3 days a week). Fellows work as fully licensed attending psychiatrists with all of the autonomy, responsibility, and privilege of an attending psychiatrist in the community program. They then spend the remaining 2 days a week in didactics, supervision, and in carrying out their fellowship projects.

This model allows fellows to choose their "jobs," and their job site agencies make an initial investment in a part-time psychiatrist who will likely become full time after completing fellowship training. Columbia is fortunate to also have a New York State Office of Mental Health contract to support the academic programming and a small stipend to supplement fellows' income during the fellowship. This model, in general, poses a minimal financial burden for the academic program and also allows for greater collaboration with a larger number and more diverse community programs. The Columbia program chose a .6FTE model because they offer 2 full days of didactics and programing, thus accounting for a 40-h work week. In other programs with less didactic and program time, a .7FTE or .8FTE might be a better model and allow fellows to earn a higher salary.

Steiner (2014) designates the Columbia model "Multiple Funding Sources and Sites," commenting that in addition to the advantages listed above, "A potential disadvantage is the lack of direct oversight or control by the fellowship director over the quality of the experience at those sites." She includes Yale and UCSF as examples of "single-source funding," in which one host agency provides all the funding and work sites. She comments that the advantage of this model is better oversight over the clinical experiences, with the disadvantage being reliance on a single source of funding. Finally, she lists Alabama and UCSD as grant-funded programs. The obvious appeal of grant funding incorporates its own disadvantage that it is inevitably time limited. She concludes that "the PPFs… identities and future success are dependent on the financial and workforce development relationships they have established within their own local, state, and academic homes."

Another recent fiscal model is the inclusion of PGY3 and four residents as PPF fellows. In this case, the residents continue to be paid and receive benefits through their residency training program and are given protected time to participate in the PPF didactics and projects. Other programs are beginning to develop public/community psychiatry residency tracks instead of, or in addition to, fellowship programs. In this model, the fiscal cost is entirely absorbed as part of the residency training program.

There are some tradeoffs with this model. Resident fellows must use their elective time to attend fellowship activities which take away their opportunity to explore other areas of training typical done as electives. Clinical systems tend to treat residents as trainees and limit administrative responsibilities and opportunities to "be at the table" where policy and other decisions are made. This limits the residents' opportunity to truly take on leadership roles which are a key focus of PPF fellowship training. Residents are also required to fulfill all of their other residency-required activities which can dilute the fellowship experience.

Collaboration of Public/Community Psychiatry Fellowships

Since 2008, directors of public/community psychiatry fellowships have been meeting at the Institute for Psychiatric Services (IPS) conference annually. In 2009, potential applicants were invited to attend the meeting. A yearly survey has served to create a common database for all programs. *Starting* in 2020, partly due to the COVID-19 pandemic, two meetings per year have been planned. One meeting, during the IPS annual meeting, will continue to include applicants, current fellows, and directors. This meeting serves as an opportunity for fellowships to present their programs, recruit applicants, and encourage network building among fellows. In addition, a second meeting, held remotely online, allows directors to focus on strategy and program development. Through this network, alumni of the programs have the opportunity to consult with each other, share clinical and administrative pearls, find jobs, and produce academic work. Many of the alumni have become medical directors and chief medical officers of programs and organizations. They have taken leadership roles at state and national levels in managed care organizations. Some have become leaders in state-level behavioral health agencies, and others provide excellent clinical care for people with complex needs in underserved areas. All alumni are also strongly encouraged to join the larger network of community providers through the AACP. An updated list of fellowships is maintained on the AACP website. (https://sites.google.com/view/aacp123/training-consultation/fellowship-training-opportunities)

As noted above, public/community psychiatry fellowships are not eligible for ACGME accreditation. In lieu of such accreditation, the AACP Board sought for a way to provide highly qualified public and community psychiatrists recognition. Accordingly, in 2014, the AACP launched the AACP Board Certification in Community and Public Psychiatry Exam, hosted on the APA website. Graduates of Public/Community Psychiatry Fellowships are eligible to take the exam upon completion of their fellowships. Other psychiatrists need to work for 2–5 years in public or community psychiatry settings before becoming eligible to take the exam.

Conclusion: A Growing Network of Public/Community Psychiatry Fellowships

Through the adoption of the Core Elements and AACP Guidelines and the biyearly network meetings, it is hoped that the newly developed public/community psychiatry fellowships and future fellowships will be sustained through their inception and continued implementation. The new training programs have increased the number of psychiatrists trained and prepared to meet the recruitment needs of the community and public sector behavioral health programs, organizations, and agencies. As fellowships expand their programs and begin to include advanced practice nurses and family practice physicians into this growing collaborative, we hope to integrate behavioral health in all aspects of health care.

It is anticipated that interaction within the network of public/community psychiatry fellowships will improve the overall quality of training among all programs, ultimately producing a new generation of psychiatrists in public sector and community leadership positions, who will deliver recovery-oriented, justice- and equity-informed, high-quality care in community settings.

Finally, we wish to acknowledge the programs that have published articles about their fellowships (Ranz et al. 1996; Kotwicki and Compton 2010; Sowers and Marin 2014; Runnels and Ronis 2014; Runnels and Ruggiero 2015; Mangurian et al. 2014; Shtasel et al. 2015) and hope to encourage other fellowship directors to publish articles describing the uniqueness of their programs.

References

AACP Guidelines for Community Psychiatry Fellowships (2008). https://drive.google.com/file/d/0B89glzXJnn4cVjZ3bXdPS21VUlE/view Accessed December 23, 2020.

ACGME Milestones Guidelines for Residents and Fellows (2020) https://www.acgme.org/Portals/0/PDFs/Milestones/MilestonesGuidebookforResidentsFellows.pdf Accessed December 23, 2020

Bernard V.W. (1964) Education for Community Psychiatry in a University Medical Center (with Emphasis on the Rationale and Objectives of Training, pp 82-122, in Handbook of Community Psychiatry and Community Mental Health, edited by Leopold Bellak, Grune and Stratton NY

Caplan G. (1970) The Theory and Practice of Mental Health Consultation. Basic Books, Inc. NY Chapter 13: Training in Mental Health Consultation

Colton C.W. and Manderscheid R.M. (2006). Congruencies in Increased Mortality Rates, Years of Potential Life Lost, and Causes of Death Among Public Mental Health Clients in Eight States. Prev Chronic Dis. 3(2): A42. Published online 2006 Mar 15. PMCID: PMC1563985, PMID: 16539783

Cournos F, Le Melle S.M., (1990): The Young Adult Chronic Patient: A Look Back, Psychiatric Services 51:8 pp996-1000, 2000

Education for Community Psychiatry (1967), Formulated by the Committee on Medical Education, Group for the Advancement of Psychiatry, Volume VI, Report #67

Emery N (2012), https://www.theatlantic.com/health/archive/2012/07/our-unsustainable-culture-of-medical-specialization/260504/

Grob G. (1994) The Mad Among Us. The Free Press: New York

Karno M, Kennedy J.G.,Lipschultz S (1974): Community Psychiatry at UCLA: A Decade of Training. American Journal of Psychiatry 131:601-4

Kotwicki R.J., Compton M.T. (2010). Key features of a unique community psychiatry fellowship: the emory university fellowship in community psychiatry/public health. Community Mental Health J. Aug;46(4):403-8

Le Melle S, Mangurian C, Ali O.M., Giggie M.A., Hadley T, Lewis M.E., Runnels P, Sowers W, Steiner J.L., Trujillo M, Ranz J.M. (2012). Public psychiatry fellowships: a developing network of public-academic collaborations. Psychiatric Services;63(9):851-4.

Le Melle S, Arbuckle M, Ranz J, Integrating Systems-Based Practice, Community Psychiatry, and Recovery Into Residency Training, Academic Psychiatry 37(1):35-7 2013

Mangurian C, Shumway M, Dilly J. (2014). Mental Health Services Research Training for the Next Generation of Leaders in the Public Health Sector: A Case Study of the UCSF/SFGH Public Psychiatry Fellowship. Academic Psychiatry.

Open Minds (2020, May 13). 2019 U.S. Mental Health Spending Topped $225 Billion, With Per Capita Spending Ranging From $37 In Florida To $375 In Maine - OPEN MINDS Releases New Analysis. https://www.prnewswire.com/news-releases/2019-us-mental-health-spending-topped-225-billion-with-per-capita-spending-ranging-from-37-in-florida-to-375-in-maine%2D%2Dopen-minds-releases-new-analysis-301058381.html

Pattison E.L. (1972) Residency Training Issues in Community Psychiatry. American Journal of Psychiatry 128:1097-1102,

Pepper B, Kirshner MC, Ryglewicz H (1981): The young adult chronic patient: overview of a population. Hospital and Community Psychiatry 32:463-469, Abstract, Google Scholar

Ranz JM, Rosenheck S, Deakins S: Columbia University's Fellowship in Public Psychiatry. *Psychiatric Services* 47:512-516, 1996

Ranz J.M., Stueve A (1998): The role of the psychiatrist as program medical director. *Psychiatric Services* 49:1203-7

Ranz JM, Vergare MJ, Wilk JE, et al (2006). The Tipping Point From Private Practice to Publicly Funded Settings for Early- and Mid-Career Psychiatrists, *Psychiatric Services* 57:1640-1643

Ranz J.M, Deakins S.M., Le Melle S.M., Rosenheck S.D., Kellermann S.L. (2008). Core Elements of a Public Psychiatry Fellowship, Psychiatric Services 59(7):718-20.

Runnels P, Ronis R. (2014). Expanding the playing field: public and community psychiatry fellowship and beyond. Community Mental Health Journal

Runnels P, Ruggiero R. (2015) Collaborative Training in Fellowship: Implications for Psychiatric Workforce Development. Academic Psychiatry, Published Online March

SAMHSA (2010). Mental Health, United States, 2008. HHS Publication No. (SMA) 10-4590

Shtasel D, Hobbs-Knutson K, Tolpin H, Weinstein D, Gottlieb GL (2015). Developing a Pipeline for the Community-Based Primary Care Workforce and Its Leadership: The Kraft Center for Community Health Leadership's Fellowship and Practitioner Programs. Academic Medicine Sep;90(9):1272-7.

Sowers W, Marin R. (2014) A community engaged curriculum for public service psychiatry fellowship training. Community Mental Health J. Jan;50(1):17

Steiner J.L., Giggie M.A., Koh S, Mangurian C, Ranz J.M. (2014). The Evolution of Public Psychiatry Fellowships. Academic Psychiatry, 38(6):685-9.

Steadman, H.J. (1992) Boundary spanners: A key component for the effective interactions of the justice and mental health systems. *Law Hum Behav* **16,** 75–87 https://doi.org/10.1007/BF02351050

Torrey F, Kennard A, Eslinger D, Lamb R, Pavle J, More Mentally Ill Persons Are in Jails and Prisons Than Hospitals: A Survey of the States, Treatment Advocacy Center (2010) https://www.treatmentadvocacycenter.org/storage/documents/final_jails_v_hospitals_study.pdf

Thompson K, Flaum M, Pollack D (2017) https://www.psychiatrictimes.com/view/crisis-public-service-psychiatric-workforce

Weddle, Bonita (1998) Mental Health in New York State, 1945 – 1998. Albany: New York State Archives, pp. 16, 26-31

Mentoring and Supervision in Community Psychiatry

Hunter L. McQuistion, Paul Rosenfield, and Patrick S. Runnels

Introduction

Learning while being taught by example and encouragement is central to becoming a physician. In Western medicine, this tradition in craft development dates at least to Hippocrates and has evolved as medical education began its journey of scholastic formalization in C.E. ninth century, at Schola Medica Salernitana, near the Italian city of Salerno. Even as subsequent history has reflected formal curricular standardization, with medicine acquiring the benefit of a scientific core to help people strive for and maintain well-being, learning how to implement this formal knowledge in the real world has developed through relationships with teachers. These relationships are powerful in guiding students as they master clinical skills. Such relationships extend to mentorship, which lies at the heart of medical education. While learning through these relationships, apprentices – protégés, or mentees – find their career paths and are also modeled for their own turn as future supervisors and mentors.

As we describe through this chapter, mentorship in psychiatry has range and depth, and so we choose the term "mentee" rather than the more classic, "protégé," which has apprentice-like connotation more typically existing in some research environments. This chapter focuses on how psychiatrists develop skills through different levels of involvement with mentors and form professional identity and embrace their trajectory with the help of those senior colleagues committed to their growth and success. Moreover, because of the clinical and systems nature of most community psychiatric practice, our emphasis here is on how community psychiatrists experience being mentees and mentors and how this process can unfold. Classically, in psychiatric education, mentorship can begin in medical school or earlier. It has an evolutionary quality, arguably most commonly beginning with finding a resonant relationship with a supervisor during residency. Developing through training and early career, the relationship can evolve into friendship as the mentee moves forward. The process also models a future mentorship role. After discussing basic tenets of mentorship, we will embark on our detailed discussion at the beginning of many mentorship experiences: clinical supervision in residency. We will then turn to focusing on the process and challenges of mentorship.

We dedicate this chapter to Joel Feiner, MD.

H. L. McQuistion (✉)
New York University Grossman School of Medicine | NYU Langone Health,
New York, NY, USA

P. Rosenfield
Psychiatry Education and Training, Mount Sinai Morningside/West,
New York, NY, USA

Icahn School of Medicine at Mount Sinai, New York, NY, USA

P. S. Runnels
Population Health – Behavioral Health, University Hospitals, Cleveland, OH, USA

Department of Psychiatry, Case Western Reserve School of Medicine,
Cleveland, OH, USA

W. E. Sowers et al. (eds.), *Textbook of Community Psychiatry*,
https://doi.org/10.1007/978-3-031-10239-4_61

Mentoring

Meditations on mentoring often begin with considering Book I of *The Odyssey*, in which Athena, Greek goddess of wisdom and intelligence, appears in the form of Mentes to Telemachus, Odysseus' son. Telemachus is ill-prepared to face his mother's parasitic suitors, who assume that Odysseus will never return to Ithaca. Mentes is an old friend of Odysseus', and Athena assumes his form to advise Telemachus and instill *menos*, or moral strength. This occurs without his father's direct influence. Mentes is therefore an interlocutor, a divine conduit of ancestral skill and wisdom. Mentes brings additional qualities to his counsel, too: knowledge and experience not specifically derived from Telemachus' family background and the basic education from which it flows. These newly offered gifts develop the mentee's incomplete state, giving additional strength so they may blaze their own path.

As such, "mentorship is profession-agnostic" (Chopra and Saint 2017) and in Western culture, arguably it has navigated through the medieval guild system's development of craft, with the passing on of trade secrets. In recent history, mentorship has been actively developed in the business community and described in its literature at least since the 1970s. Within medicine, the tradition is old, but the professional literature, especially in psychiatry, is not robust. For example, a Google Scholar search for "psychiatry mentorship" or "psychiatry mentoring" yielded under 25 publications since 2000, covering disparate aspects of peer-level and individual mentorship, accenting residency and research. Though we cite some through this chapter, none were specific to community or public psychiatry.

A definitive literature review of mentorship in medicine, and particularly psychiatry, is not within this chapter's scope, but it is noteworthy that Sambunjak and colleagues' (2006) systematic review identified 3640 potentially related articles published between 1991 and 2006. Only 42 studies quantitatively measured the impact of mentoring on trainees and faculty. They concluded that mentorship can have "an important influence on personal development, career guidance, career choice, and research productivity" though there is as yet little data to support it, so further study is indicated.

While mentorship's history is for a great part oral, one small study of interdisciplinary academic faculty members found that 98% of respondents ($n = 16$) endorsed lack of mentoring as either the first or second most important factor hindering professional progress (Jackson et al. 2003) and study survey of 596 full-time US medical school faculty reported that those who had mentors had greater job satisfaction (Palepu et al. 1996).

A Base for Mentorship: Clinical Supervision of Residents

Graduate medical education is the crucial step of professional development between medical school and autonomous clinical practice. It is in this vital phase of the continuum of medical education that residents learn to provide optimal patient care under the supervision of faculty who not only instruct but serve as role models of excellence, compassion, professionalism, and scholarship (ACGME 2020a, b).

Psychiatry residency training includes a wide range of experiences that provide the scaffolding for medical school graduates to build their competence as psychiatrists over 4 years. While residents attend lectures and grand rounds, they learn most from the direct clinical work on their various rotations. Supervisors on these rotations advise, teach, guide, and support the residents throughout their training. In this textbook's 2012 edition, the late Joel Feiner wrote wisely about supervision:

> Particularly in outpatient work, a pairing is likely to be made through assignment by the training program director who matches the interests of the trainees and faculty. The mandate is not necessarily defined clearly, but in many cases this lack of definition allows for a creative interaction and evolution. The faculty member may serve as a person to assist the resident in adapting to the program or to psychiatry in general. Meetings may be regular but are often arranged on an as needed basis and usually they are entirely optional. Assignments and selection may be made based upon areas of interest or experience.

Effective supervisors typically spend significant time with each resident, helping to translate and make sense of clinical encounters, offering advice on good care, explaining the importance of the therapeutic alliance, ensuring clear and timely documentation, modeling professionalism, and facilitating residents' development of their own clinical intuition, skill, and ability to learn independently. From among these supervisors, residents find role models and may discover them as lifelong mentors and colleagues. In this way, the residency supervision experience models important dimensions of mentorship.

Supervisors who teach and demonstrate the foundational community psychiatry principles of person-centered, evidence-based, trauma-informed, recovery-oriented care can have an impact on residents' ability to help patients reach their goals rather than just treat symptoms. Residents who learn from their supervisors to formulate their patients in a biopsychosocial framework are better prepared to provide holistic care that can integrate neurobiological findings, psychological theories, and the impact of social determinants of health. We discuss here some basic elements and types of supervision and various strategies to infuse the values of community psychiatry into training.

Residents are expected to receive supervision appropriate to their level of training. Through the course of residency, oversight tapers and autonomy and responsibility increase as a function of the resident's demonstration of competence. This competence includes professional behaviors, teamwork, communication skills, and understanding of systems.

The settings in which residents rotate, from inpatient and emergency departments to outpatient clinics and specialized settings, may determine the nature of the supervision. Junior residents usually start their training in emergency and inpatient settings where patients are experiencing an acute illness episode or psychological crisis. They develop the capacity to assess a patient's situation and imminent risk effectively, decide whether to admit or discharge the patient, quickly establish a therapeutic relationship, initiate treatment, and figure out a disposition plan for ongoing care. Supervisors in these settings play a major role, as they model the type of care residents will emulate. Ideally, residents learn from supervisors how to do careful evaluations, contact collateral sources of information (especially family and other providers), formulate the issues in a holistic manner, engage their patients effectively, educate them about their illness and treatment, and provide hope and access to ongoing care and resources. Supervisors may demonstrate interview skills or provide feedback to residents about their interviews, ask questions to help residents conceptualize the issues, and guide them in their clinical decision-making.

On inpatient units, consult-liaison services and emergency rooms, residents present patients in rounds, interview patients with attendings, and meet together to discuss assessments and plans. Residents tend to see most outpatients on their own and have more autonomy with decision-making in the moment. Supervisors typically meet with residents weekly, participate directly in some patient encounters, provide feedback about case formulations and treatment decisions, discuss the therapeutic relationship, and help anticipate next steps. As alluded to above, there is a distinction between general supervisors who oversee the overall caseload, psychotherapy supervisors who focus on a small number of therapy cases, and other supervisors who work in research or specialized clinics.

The Dreyfus model of professional development guides thinking about the general developmental process of training from beginner (with a more rigid, rule-based approach) to competent clinician to expert (with more capacity to handle complexity and primary responsibility). Newman et al. (2016) describe how to apply this to psychiatric training and supervision. For beginners, the task of the supervisor is to provide more concrete and immediate feedback and help residents develop basic interviewing, diagnostic, and therapeutic skills. When residents have achieved a higher competency level, supervisors can address more subtle skills and situations such as treating a patient with co-occurring diagnoses or complex trauma. As residents become more expert, supervision continues to help them develop a more nuanced understanding of their own work, as well as more advanced teaching skills for medical students and junior residents. These authors conducted focus groups of both supervisors and residents on their perceptions of supervision. They found residents prefer more structure, instruction, and feedback, while attendings prefer to encourage residents to set the agenda and to talk about the MMR.

The ACGME Milestones Project (ACGME 2013) built on this developmental approach to chart the expected growth of residents through training. Five levels of competence are described with anchor points across 22 domains within the larger categories of patient care, medical knowledge, systems-based practice, practice-based learning and improvement, professionalism, and interpersonal and communication skills. Figure 1 demonstrates the progression in competence with performing a psychiatric evaluation, from collecting basic information to efficiently acquiring a history to eliciting subtle findings and serving as a role model. Residents progress through these levels as they gain clinical experience and greater expertise, with the help of their supervisors. Another tool utilized to measure competence is the clinical skills verification exam, an observed interview by a board-certified psychiatrist. On three separate occasions, residents must perform an effective interview, establish a therapeutic doctor-patient relationship, and provide a clear case presentation, at the standard level of quality of a practicing psychiatrist in the community.

In order for residents to learn and progress, they must have feedback. Two key forms of feedback are described. *Formative* feedback is usually provided in the midst of a rotation; the supervisor provides helpful advice about how the resident might develop during the rest of the rotation. For example, the supervisor may inform the resident that a risk assessment should be more comprehensive and then discuss with the resident a way to modify the interview next time. *Summative* feedback summarizes the quality of work on a rotation, often for an evaluative purpose. Each of these forms of feedback may be related to clinical skills, professional behavior, documentation style, or procedural technique, to name a few examples. A well-known "sandwich" model of feedback surrounding the "meat" of constructive criticism with the "bread" of praise or positive feedback (Dohrenwend 2002) has been updated in recent years by the "ask-tell-ask" model, in which the supervisor asks the learner for their self-assessment, then provides ("tells") feedback that is responsive to the learner. This would be characterized by acknowledging their concerns and sharing both something they did well and one or two areas for improvement, along with focused teaching about the interaction. Next, the supervisor asks how the learner heard this feedback and together works on a plan for improvement (French et al. 2015).

Systems-based practice (SBP) is a core competence within the milestones that community psychiatrists are especially adept at teaching. This competence includes understanding patient safety and quality improvement, system navigation for patient-centered care (such as providing safe transitions across levels of care and demonstrating awareness of population-based health), and the physician's role within the healthcare system, such as healthcare financing, shared decision-making and advocacy. Ranz et al. (2012) describe four SBP roles that allow residents to implement SBP into their work: team member, information integrator, resource manager, and patient care advocate. Clinical supervisors can guide residents in how to communicate and collaborate with a range of providers, family members, and patients to create an effective team. This includes how to integrate the information across different disciplines and parts of the healthcare system to create a coherent and safe plan of care. In pursuit of health and recovery, residents also need to learn how to implement cost-effective care and access available community resources, advocating for their patients in dealing with systems and healthcare disparities. LeMelle et al. (2013) describe how supervision is an essential aspect of teaching residents to integrate SBP and principles of recovery into their work. Moving beyond the focus on psychotherapy and medication management, their team has trained supervisors in the four SBP roles to help

Patient Care 1: Psychiatric Evaluation **A:** Gathers and organizes findings from the patient interview and mental status examination **B:** Gathers and organizes data from collateral sources **C:** Screens for risk and integrates risk assessment into the patient evaluation				
Level 1	Level 2	Level 3	Level 4	Level 5
Collects general medical and psychiatric history and completes a mental status examination	Efficiently acquires an accurate and relevant history and performs a targeted examination customized to the patient's presentation	Uses hypothesis-driven information gathering to obtain complete, accurate, and relevant history	Elicits and observes subtle and unusual findings	Serves as a role model for gathering subtle and accurate findings from the patient and collateral sources
Collects relevant information from collateral sources	Selects appropriate laboratory and diagnostic tests	Interprets collateral information and test results to determine necessary additional steps	Interprets collateral information and test results to determine necessary additional steps in the evaluation of complex conditions	
Screens for risk of harm to self, to others, or by others	Engages in a basic risk assessment and basic safety planning	Incorporates risk and protective factors into the assessment of imminent, short, and long-term patient safety and the safety of others	Incorporates risk and protective factors into the assessment of complex patient presentations, including eliciting information not readily offered by the patient	Serves as a role model for risk assessment
Comments:				Not Yet Completed Level 1 ☐ Not Yet Assessable ☐

Fig. 1 ACGME Milestones Project 2.0. https://mentee.acgme.org/Portals/0/PDFs/Milestones/PsychiatryMilestones2.0.pdf?ver=2020-03-10-152105-537 (accessed 12/8/20; used by permission)

emphasize a holistic approach to patients and the systems they navigate.

Supervisors informed by community psychiatry's focus on systems of care help residents develop an awareness of the history and structures of mental health care, considerations about access to care, and social determinants of health. There are a range of strategies to do so. Supervisors can help residents think holistically about their patients with a recovery-oriented biopsychosocial model. They can assign residents to complete a comprehensive formulation to understand their patients as people with unique personal goals, rather than just listing the DSM-5 diagnosis and its criteria or utilizing a purely psychodynamic formulation. The importance of social determinants of health (see the chapter "Social and Political Determinants of Health and Mental Health") such as childhood adversity in the form of abuse or neglect in the home, or poor education and systemic racism is addressed along with genetic and neurobiological factors and psychological defenses. As such, a useful exercise to help residents understand the lived experiences of their patients is a "person-centered systems evaluation," which entails obtaining a robust social history and an opportunity for residents to ask patients in depth about their personal experiences with the educational system, housing or homelessness, the legal system, social relationships, and their own understanding of their illness experience and their given diagnoses (LeMelle et al. 2013). Finely tuned skills can be instilled with supervisors using the DSM 5 Cultural Formulation (see the chapter "Cultural and Linguistic Competence") helping residents as they acquire basic cultural competence.

Castillo et al. (2020) have proposed an additional milestones competency in structural competency, health equity, and social responsibility to deepen residents' appreciation of health disparities and how they impact their patients. Supervisors trained in these areas can help residents identify the economic, policy, and institutional structures that influence health. Through this deeper understanding, residents may more easily pursue advocacy roles. Some residency programs have created community psychiatry tracks to enhance the clinical experience and training for those interested in future careers in the public sector. These often entail community-based rotations, faculty mentorship, opportunities for scholarly work, participation in professional organizations, and formal didactics (Reardon et al. 2014).

Residents become supervisors themselves as they take on senior roles with medical students or junior residents in the hospital or engage in systems outside the hospital. In addition to modeling themselves after their own supervisors, they should be taught supervision skills such as how to provide feedback effectively. After conducting a systematic review of curricula on residents as teachers, Post et al. (2009) recommended an evidence-based strategy for supervision called the One-Minute Preceptor, also called the Five Microskills for Clinical Teaching, originally presented by Neher et al. (1992):

1. Get a commitment (ask the learner for their impression).
2. Probe for supporting evidence (ask the learner to explain their impression).
3. Teach general rules (preceptor provides teaching on the subject).
4. Reinforce what was done right (preceptor provides positive feedback).
5. Correct mistakes (preceptor identifies areas for improvement).

The Active Ingredients of Successful Mentoring

We now discuss important formative elements of the mentor-mentee relationships (MMR) and their attendant issues in mentor-mentee collaboration. In addition to literature sources, we draw on our own – and gratefully – junior and senior colleagues' experiences. They have most generously shared their thoughts with us so we may tease out the nature of successful MMRs.

A useful working definition of mentoring is "a dynamic, reciprocal relationship in a work environment between an advanced career incumbent (mentor) and a beginner…aimed at promoting the development of both" (Healy and Weichert 1990). We have described that this relationship frequently develops in residency, but it can initiate across different settings and even professional lines. For example, one of this chapter's author's mentors, also his boss, was a civil rights attorney leading a community-based organization who exemplified values of social justice, intellectual precision, imagination, and moral strength.

Many psychiatric colleagues will say that they have had a series of mentors, too. They are senior to the colleague and are identified as philosophically and intellectually compatible, also sharing personal and professional values. Mentorship skill and professional position also signal to the mentee that the relationship might also be helpful to advance his or her career in some way. Some MMRs may begin before medical school and emerge informally. At one extreme, colleagues have noted that having a parent within the profession provides not only a model but also a mentor. Alternatively, one psychiatrist described being in college and developed a key MMR with a person running a lab. Since that person had no role model within their family, this mentor offered counsel and encouragement for a career in medicine and helped them to build confidence. These early mentorships, especially with a physician, can be highly formative, heavily influencing the future psychiatrist's practice, habits, and manner.

Examples of the range of MMRs over the course of training and early career include a senior psychiatric colleague who advises on the business aspect of practice or clinical approach. There are different levels of mentorship, beginning with sort of an admiration from afar (no formal relationship but with intermittent personal contact) to having a key person for career advice, to obtaining a close technical and professional advisor. Because of this range, some even advocate for a semantic differentiation between "mentor" and "sponsor" (Ayyala et al. 2019). The latter would embrace the more committed professional relationship, with the "sponsor" actively promoting the mentee's future. Features would include offering first authorship on a manuscript, working closely on the mentee's funding application, actively helping in networking efforts, and helping with meritorious employment.

Regardless of level, mentorship is defined by certain key attributes. These include trustworthiness, enthusiasm, moral and ethical stature, compassion, empathy, knowledge, wisdom, and intellect. Communicating a sense of selflessness and offering opportunities and guidance without transactional pretext are essential. Cho and colleagues (2011) reviewed 29 medical, nursing, dentistry, and pharmacy school nominations for a lifetime mentorship award and noted these attributes. These authors also highlighted other essential operational themes, or traits, of availability, career guidance, work-life balance support, and commitment to leave a legacy for the formation of future mentors.

Availability

Because we are referring to a human relationship, successful mentors must be available to mentees in a meaningful and longitudinal manner. This goes well beyond any regularly scheduled meetings, which must be prioritized by the mentor, extending to ad hoc counsel. Here is a representative quotation (Cho et al. 2011):

> [He] is always accessible to anyone who sought him out for help. He had an open-door policy. Even though he was extremely busy, he always found time to talk with me.

In the face of a mentor's demanding schedule, this attribute can require discipline and also frank self-appraisal about whether taking on this role is feasible in terms of time, because without availability, there can be an unintentional message of devaluation. Availability serves as affirmation to the mentee that the mentor is, in the words of another mentee, "very interested and really connected," as well as immediately helpful with a sudden issue. Clearly, this is especially important if the issue is personal.

The longitudinal aspect of availability has been cited in research (Cho et al. 2011). One psychiatrist, who has been instrumental in developing the longstanding fellowship in Public Psychiatry at Columbia, considers mentoring a central dimension of the program, and mentorship extends as far into a mentee's career as needed (Ranz et al. 2008).

For public and community psychiatry in particular, mentorship has special importance. In addition to interest in science and healing, physicians typically enter with a public service mission that involves social justice and destigmatization, with interests in professional collaboration, public policy, administrative roles, and, for some, academics. Employment opportunities can therefore be understood as remarkably wide in community psychiatry. However, because many community psychiatrists work in clinical settings, such as community-based organizations, often isolated from other physicians and subject to service demands that may be more volatile than in other clinical roles, they can also experience greater professional isolation. Quality of employment life is dependent on a range of factors in this regard, such as public funding and institutional financial pressures affecting occupational roles, professional relationships, and quality care. These vicissitudes often beg for a port in an occupational storm, sometimes just as a sounding board, other times to garner detailed advice from the senior colleague who really knows the mentee.

Career Guidance

Solid advice develops along with the relationship and the basis for this is *quality meeting time* that results in tangible effects on the mentee's career. For example, these meetings can cover problem-solving around navigating professional politics or reviewing challenging clinical situations, or they might involve designing publication projects, the nitty-gritty support of editing drafts, advising in their own supervision of trainees, or shaping actual or potential job descriptions.

An area where physicians struggle is long-term planning in the early-career phase that starts right after training. After completing the 8- to 9-year gauntlet of post undergraduate education, psychiatrists often look forward to being a "finished product." Yet, without clear consideration of career trajectory, they risk feeling either stuck or unfulfilled as career progresses, with little understanding of how to evolve.

Boyatzis (2008) described a mechanism for effectively avoiding this pitfall through Intentional Change Theory, which involves a series of steps that a mentor can aid in developing, with the mentee moving through phases of defining an "ideal self" and arriving at a "real self" that eschews a mentee's perceived externally derived but nonvital expectations through encouraging the development of a 10-year personal and professional vision statement, combined with successive 3- to 5-year learning agendas. This process requires reflection on strengths and weakness, values, personal history related to both how they developed and what resonated with them in the past, and passions.

In the context of community psychiatry, personal vision, learning agendas with experimentation, and practice might include domains of scholarship, teaching, administrative responsibilities, program planning, evaluation, or epidemiological research. The most successful mentors operate within the framework of a *resonant relationship* with mentees (Boyatzis et al. 2019). Resonant relationships are based on authentic connection and positive emotional tone. Resonant work then is marked by the mentor's ability to identify and focus on the mentee's strengths and goals, working in partnership to achieve objectives. Honest feedback about missteps as well as pushing people out of their comfort zones are important but must always be delivered through the frame of compassion. Accentuating strengths builds necessary trust and confidence in the relationship, enabling the mentor to encourage course corrections that the mentee can take the lead in devising and navigating. As in any relationship, the ability to be a good listener is so paramount that it enables a mentee to have confidence to seek guidance from a trusted colleague about a personal situation or issue that has some, even if only tangential relevance to career, particularly when the issue invokes anxiety or highlights personal failures. This arrangement quintessentially embodies the mentor as a deep interlocutor: father's old friend, Mentes, carrying Athena's wisdom and, by association, parental trust.

A final consideration is the development of social capital, often referred to as networking. Mentees benefit from having a core mentorship circle but must be encouraged to expand it beyond one or two core mentors. Furthermore, each mentor should provide something unique to the mentee. While it is valuable to engage with supportive like-minded people, developing psychiatrists should also be encouraged to seek a diverse set of peers who can offer opportunities to be challenged and gain access to new resources (Claridge 2018).

One manner in which a mentor can help ensure mentees are developing a good network structure with high-quality, foundational network relationships is to invite a mentee to join professional meetings and encourage them to be involved in relevant professional organizations. This broadens perspective and helps in making important collegial friendships that can last through a career. For community psychiatry, this is illustrated within the American Association for Community Psychiatry (AACP) where, for example, there is an informal tradition wherein Board of Directors members have often introduced mentees to the AACP in order to be able to closely identify with the field and then sometimes become organizational leaders themselves. In larger organizations, such as the American Psychiatric Association or the Group for Advancement of Psychiatry, residents have entered competitive honorary fellowship programs that help in networking and in turn introduce them to mentors. Moreover, because community psychiatry has so many interdisciplinary threads, mentors should access mentees to organizations and public agencies whose membership is focused beyond psychiatry itself, such as consumer and family organizations and public policy gatherings, or even beyond behavioral health, as is exemplified by the emergence of climate change activism.

Work and Life Balance

A 2017 survey noted that 92% of millennial physicians ranked work-life balance as a top priority (Rogawski and Rogawski 2018). Mentors can be crucial in guiding mentees in this regard. From a purely relational viewpoint, mentees must perceive respect for their time, lest they begin to feel exploited by demands from the mentor. Beyond this, for mentors to effectively address these concerns, they must have a firm grasp of the systemic factors that interfere with well-being.

The first are related to how physician hours affect quality care. In 1989, after a highly publicized emergency department patient death, the State of New York enacted a law limiting resident work hours (NYS Dept of Health, 11/14/2018). This helped generate related research (Lockley et al. 2004), and in 2003, the ACGME issued national duty hour limits (Accreditation Council for Graduate Medical Education 2004). Nonetheless, the demands of both patient care broadly and administrative systems more specifically have continued to lead to upsurges in compassion fatigue and professional burnout (Summers et al. 2020).

Specifically, the impact of the information revolution has gradually shifted our sense of how to accomplish work productivity (Newport 2021). As modes of communication have made everyone more accessible, communication – for example, through email or tasks in electronic medical records – has become a dominant form of getting work done. Rather than devoting concentrated time to thoroughly completing specific tasks and projects, we respond to dozens or even hundreds of inputs every day. This leaves us constantly shifting attention between multiple tasks, a process both cognitively exhausting and remarkably less efficient (Leroy 2009).

It leads to a feeling of working much harder and a reality of working more hours while paradoxically getting less meaningful work done. And because these media are so ubiquitous in our lives, with the effect of making us feel connected all the time, our online and offline lives merge (Floridi 2014).

This particularly affects those who work in the already time-intensive profession of medicine, causing greater blur between work and home. It can result in a sense of less time for oneself and loved ones, with hours spent online communicating and charting in transit, at home, and even on holidays. The COVID-19 pandemic likely accentuated this, too, by presenting increased service demands, with telepsychiatry mushrooming (see the chapter "Telehealth and Community Psychiatry") and online contact with colleagues occurring in almost any physical location. Some argue that video visits present special challenges of increased effort for psychiatrists because their clinical contacts require high degrees of emotional as well as intellectual presence. These challenges are accentuated in public sector psychiatry, where caseloads often have the highest demands in terms of patient need and volume, themselves presenting risks for emotional detachment.

Therefore, mentors must help strategize with mentees how to prevent technological "job-creep" into their personal world, while at the same time not themselves contributing to the anxiety produced by excessive virtual communication. In this manner, less frequent but concentrated periods of engagement can be far more effective for processing career and personal growth than frequent short contacts that leave little time for focused consideration.

The third factor is generational nuance. At this time, the majority of early career psychiatrists are Millennials (i.e., Generation Y), born roughly between the early 1980s and 2000s. This generation, and its older Generation X cohort, while more comfortable with technology than its predecessors, did experience life prior to the current ultra-digitalized reality, with 64% in one large survey, for example, stating that if they spent less time on social media, they would be healthier (Deloitte & Touche 2019). Controlling work and work-life balance has often been ascribed to Millennials (Deloitte & Touche 2016), perhaps reflecting sensitivity to the stresses of technology noted above. Encouragingly, this generation has also been described as altruistically focused (https://en.wikipedia.org/wiki/Millennials), with up to 60% considering a public service career, also ascribing itself to the importance of relationships, including with supervisors (Myers and Sadaghiani 2010). While this presents opportunities for mentors, it also requires a sensitivity to what extent a mentee embraces these generational needs, particularly for Baby Boom and Generation X mentors, who were often raised and trained with a strong ethic of "work first," but often also experienced a world with fewer distractions, less indebtedness, and ladders of advancement more directly linked to extra work.

Finally, in 2019, 40.2% of the 38,770 psychiatrists in the USA were women, compared with 51% of all psychiatric residents and fellows (American Association of Medical Colleges 2020). This demographic shift is affecting how psychiatry conceptualizes its occupational profile, one that expands beyond traditional gender roles and affects double-income, married, and partnered professionals who share family responsibilities. While each person dictates their own sense of how career fits into lifestyle, family life and child-rearing add compelling rationale to respect and encourage balance between work and nonwork. Sambunjak et al. (2006) found that women perceived greater difficulty finding mentors than male colleagues. For women, evidence suggests that having a same-sex mentor leads to greater career satisfaction, though this need not render a policy of keeping MMRs sexually homogeneous, as indicated by this observation (Levenson et al. 1991):

> My mentor during nephrology fellowship was male and completely understanding [vis-a-vis] stresses of both job and home. His household was a two career household with children and he definitely carried equal responsibility.

Research Mentorship

A discussion of mentorship in psychiatry cannot be complete without noting its role in building research careers, relevant to community psychiatrists who also strongly identify with the academy. Because the knowledge base in research scholarship builds on itself, developing a network of colleagues with similar interests is critical, not only for cross-fertilization of ideas but more elementally for a career to advance. Research mentorship is key to this process, having two important functions: collegial and technical. The function of collegiality, in particular, along with the active ingredients described above, such as networking, is universal to all MMRs. In academia, finding a tenure-track faculty position happens frequently through a professional network of people with similar intellectual pursuit, fueled by collegial acknowledgment of ability.

In academic psychiatry, two sets of research mentees have been described. The first arrives with a developed sense of technical competency (e.g., those with PhDs as well as MDs). Mentorship under these circumstances is less directive and narrowly instructive, with dialogue and support that begins at a high level of conceptual discussion and, in turn, may be more laissez-faire. In such cases, even critiquing drafted grant applications may not be overly time-consuming for the mentor. More commonly, however, academically oriented community psychiatrists may assume less intensive roles in research or join efforts peripherally as part of a larger research group. The process may begin as a resident, fellow, or in early career when a motivated individual has keen interest in a subject, but relatively less experience in actually formulating a functional research question, constructing coherent methodology, expertly designing an analytic plan, and then executing it. For example, the mentee may depend on a mentor for close guidance on writing a grant application, including reviewing grant submission drafts to achieve competitiveness.

Because of concern about an overall dwindling supply of researchers, some academic departments have developed articulated research mentorship programs (Kupfer et al. 2009), including training in services research (Yager et al. 2007). Regardless, a senior person not only educates their junior colleague in elements of technique but importantly helps the mentee to rigorously develop ideas for their own research, critically but supportively offering counsel as the person develops the craft of investigation and deepens intellectual curiosity and rigor. Importantly, efforts within this relationship must be focused on the mentee's growth, not on the mentor's need for someone to merely do a service of labor for the mentor's projects, although aspects of service within the mentor's projects can serve as a learning tool.

Benefits for Mentors

The benefits and satisfactions of being a mentor are manifold. If managed in a way that helps a person's development, as an apprentice, a mentee can indeed be directly involved in the mentor's work. If working as an assistant to a mentor's grant or research project, the relationship not only helps the mentee's career development but provides valuable service to the mentor. This is particularly important in busy service program environments, when a clinical leader needs an able and motivated junior colleague to take leadership, and be tutored, on a project. This can work particularly well in the context of program evaluation, in which the mentee manages aspects of program process and outcome, while also collecting and analyzing data. The mentor is guide and consultant while helping to shape the expertise and skill set of the mentee. However, this only works well when there is active mentorship support and availability, fostering a sense of project "ownership" in the mentee, and allowing for the mentor's feedback.

Beyond this, as one senior mentor has expressed, the most valuable benefit may be a reciprocal learning process. A mentor conveys knowledge and wisdom to their mentee but acquires certain wisdom themselves. For example, through what can be a mutual Socratic process, a mentor can not only learn about their own management style but also enhance their understanding of advances in clinical and digital technologies and emerging social movements as they affect psychiatry. New approaches to behavioral health policy and issues concerning race and gender may also be absorbed by the mentor. Included in this is the possibility of understanding the views and values of another generation at close range. Examples of these subtleties include evolving interprofessional roles within behavioral health care and workloads. Crucially, it feeds an adaptive need for generativity (Erikson 1950), which includes the professional maturation of a next generation and also helps form the next cohort of mentors who have derived an identity from their experiences as mentees.

Challenges to the Mentor-Mentee Relationship

Among challenges to the relationship, the most striking is also the most basic: getting the right fit. This is particularly true if the relationship is meant to be primary and supremely consequential, in which the mentor is expected to be a primary guide for the mentee, such as in research environments. Yet, the challenge extends beyond this. As noted above, in psychiatry, mentees acquire mentors more naturalistically and also for different aspects of their professional lives. Mentors must gauge the nature and level of what potential mentees wish to receive from the relationship and whether the mentor's time will serve the purpose. Active mentorship interest in the mentee is important, but the mentee must be equally active and responsible. Diffidence, frequent lateness to meetings, a certain willfulness, and failure to follow through on assignments bode poorly.

Associated with this is managing conflict. Both literature (Rodenhauser et al. 2000) and experience indicate, as in all human relationships, that conflicts between mentor and mentee need attention without delay, as avoiding it undermines necessary trust, potentially destroying the nature of the relationship. A key relational aspect in all MMRs is maintaining alignment of goals (O'Donnell, 2017). An example is when the mentor as manager must carry out a policy, procedure, or other administrative necessity, sometimes reflecting service demands or fiscal realities about which the mentee may disagree. This especially occurs when a mentor is also an administrative supervisor within an explicit power relationship. In such cases, in addition to the mentor's being able to listen to the substance of a disagreement (and possibly altering course), there is opportunity to examine a conflict's administrative or systemic causes, with Socratic discussion, yielding an advance in the mentee's understanding of the issue. In the discussion, the mentor may also gain insight into how to optimally manage future controversy with the mentee or other staff.

An extremely important aspect of fit involves racial, ethnic, sexual orientation, and gender concerns. As noted above, a female psychiatrist's career satisfaction may well be enhanced by having a same-sex mentor, offering role modeling and counsel in career goals, as well as being able to understand potential gender-based discrimination. Most dramatically, and as described in the chapter "Cultural and Linguistic Competence", the reality of systemic racism permeates our culture, including medicine and psychiatry, and is frequently displayed in subtle forms (Wilkerson 2020). While through honesty, humility, and change there is hope that our future society will render it unnecessary, Black and other racially and ethnically underrepresented junior colleagues must be permitted, or better, encouraged, to seek out similarly racially or ethnically identified mentors as they may be available, either locally, through professional organizations, or elsewhere. This arrangement permits sharing mutual experiences that other race/ethnicity mentors have not had. Such mentorship offers the mentee powerful reification of what is professionally possible and how to attain it. As one example of among many, these MMRs combat an experiential struggle with an "imposter syndrome," described as a person of color sensing they must appear to always be perfect or possess supercompetence, with accompanying painful self-doubt, feeling the need to overcome subtle but pervasive judgment (Ellis et al. 2020). This crucible requires support from a knowing senior person who shows what doors can be opened. It also helps a mentee form personal and professional pride while defining and meeting a self-defined goal of success and satisfaction.

People who identify as LGBTQ+ can have analogous experiences and benefit from those who have genuine respect for them or who themselves have successfully managed professional bias regarding sexual orientation or identity. Just as their Black, Latinx, Asian, or Indigenous colleagues do within their own MMRs to enlighten dominant cultural caste members about attitude and discrimination, these MMRs have vehicular capacity in educating binary heterosexuals. This helps advance social progress, with the ultimate beneficiaries being patients who then receive culturally competent care.

Another, more circumstantial, challenge involves an emerging trend among Millennial physicians to not stay in a single organization or job through their careers to the degree that prior generations had. Frequent transitioning can have the effect of impeding naturalistic long-term MMRs. In turn, residency supervisors and directors should purposefully explore how to encourage long-term mentor relationship efforts to thrive across multiple mentee job transitions. How to do this without lapsing into assigning mentors to residents and fellows takes thoughtful programming, especially given that at least one study found that residents who themselves initiated the mentor relationship (versus being assigned) were more likely to agree that their mentors had a positive impact on their research, publications, and scholarly projects (Amonoo et al. 2019). These generational circumstances also open a door for professional organizations to develop mentorship activities, even though they can sometimes be challenging because of often brief interactions at professional meetings. Such challenges require systematic problem-solving.

Finally, a common MMR challenge concerns personal boundaries. On the part of the mentor, the risk of boundary violations may hover over misplaced parental protectiveness, infantilizing the mentee, but can concern sexual or romantic issues too. Many MMRs become close and may appropriately involve the mentee sharing personal issues, such as deaths in close family, child-rearing challenges, or marital or other relationship challenges. Romantic attraction on the part of either half of the relationship may occur. Professional ethics regarding romantic and sexual transgression are clear, with even apparently minor boundary crossings leading to risk of exploitation in a power relationship. Averting boundary violations requires more than ethical mandates. It requires knowledge of one's own psyche and taking heed of contemporaneous personal challenges that may affect the MMR. This permits the MMR to continue its alignment with professional goals while offering flexibility to supportively discuss how mentee personal realities and challenges affect career.

Conclusion

Mentorship can begin anywhere in the process of a person's development, even from first glimmers of interest about career, and then extending across its life span. We have focused on mentorship attributes and mentee needs that occur in the early formation of their identity as a psychiatrist, especially in public and community psychiatry. Mentorship itself is an ancient institution. Though times change, even currently as digital technology decreases a sense of personal space to engage in thought, mentorship will continue to be integral to learning about our work and ourselves. The mentor-mentee relationship offers a rare opportunity for two committed people to sit, discuss, and plan mutually satisfying intellectual and career development, gaining and offering support and, in turn, helping a profession to flourish. This is particularly important in psychiatry, the practice of which depends on contemplating complexity as it relates not only to the underpinnings of psychiatric disorders and patient well-being but also in mapping the many paths psychiatrists can take in their careers.

References

Amonoo HL, Barreto EA, Stern TA, Donelan K (2019). Residents' experiences with mentorship in academic medicine. Acad Psychiatry, 43(1):71-75.

American Association of Medical Colleges. Physician Specialty Data Report (2020) Available at: https://www.aamc.org/data-reports/workforce/interactive-data/active-physicians-sex-and-specialty-2019, https://www.aamc.org/data-reports/interactive-data/acgme-residents-and-fellows-sex-and-specialty-2019

Accreditation Council for Graduate Medical Education (ACGME). The ACGME's Approach to Limit Resident Duty Hours 12 Months After Implementation: A Summary of Achievements, 2004. Available at: https://www.acgme.org/Portals/0/PFAssets/PublicationsPapers/dh_dutyhoursummary2003-04.pdf

Accreditation Council for Graduate Medical Education (ACGME) (2013). Implementing Milestones and Clinical Competency Committees. Available at https://www.acgme.org/globalassets/PDFs/ACGMEMilestones-CCC-AssesmentWebinar.pdf

ACGME Common Program Requirements for Residency (2020a). Available at: https://www.acgme.org/Portals/0/PFAssets/ProgramRequirements/CPRResidency2020.pdf

ACGME Psychiatry Milestones 2.0 (2020b). Available at: https://www.acgme.org/Portals/0/PDFs/Milestones/PsychiatryMilestones2.0.pdf?ver=2020-03-10-152105-537

Ayyala MS, Skarupski K, Bodurtha JN, González-Fernández M, Ishii LE, Fivush B, Levine RB (2019). Mentorship is not enough: exploring sponsorship and its role in career advancement in academic medicine. Acad Med, 94(1):94-100.

Boyatzis RE. Leadership development from a complexity perspective (2008). Consulting Psychology Journal: Practice and Research, 60(4), 298-313

Boyatzis RE, Smith M, Van Oosten E (2019). *Helping People Change: Coaching with Compassion for Lifelong Learning and Growth*. Harvard Business Review Press, Boston, USA.

Castillo EG, Isom J, DeBonis KL, Jordan A, Braslow JT, Rohrbaugh R (2020). Reconsidering Systems-Based Practice: Advancing Structural Competency, Health Equity, and Social Responsibility in Graduate Medical Education. Acad Med, 95(12):1817-1822.

Cho CS, Ramanan RA, Feldman MD (2011). Defining the ideal qualities of mentorship: a qualitative analysis of the characteristics of outstanding mentors. Am J Med, 2011; 124:53-458.

Chopra V, Saint S. 6 things every mentor should do (2017). Harvard Business Rev. https://hbr.org/2017/03/6-things-every-mentor-should-do

Claridge T. Functions of social capital – bonding, bridging, linking (2018). Social Capital Research, p1–7. https://d1fs2th61pidml.cloudfront.net/wp-content/uploads/2018/11/Functions-of-Social-Capital.pdf?x66629

Deloitte & Touche. The Deloitte Global Millenial Survey 2016. https://www2.deloitte.com/al/en/pages/about-deloitte/articles/2016-millennialsurvey.html

Deloitte & Touche. The Deloitte Global Millennial Survey 2019. https://www2.deloitte.com/cn/en/pages/about-deloitte/articles/2019-millennial-survey.html

Dohrenwend, A. (2002). Serving up the feedback sandwich. Family Practice Management, 9(10), 43.

Ellis J, Otugo O, Landry A, Landry A. Interviewed while Black (2020). New Engl Jnl Med. 383(25):2401-2404.

Erikson EH (1950). *Childhood and Society*, WW Norton& Co., New York

Floridi L (2014). *The 4th Revolution: How the Infosphere is Reshaping Human Reality*. Oxford University Press, Oxford, UK.

French JC, Colbert CY, Pien LC, Dannefer EF, Taylor CA (2015). Targeted feedback in the milestones era: utilization of the ask-tell-ask feedback model to promote reflection and self-assessment. J Surg Educ, 72(6):e274-9.

Healy CC, Welchert A (1990). Mentoring relations: a definition to advance research and education. Educ Res, 19:17-21.

Jackson VA, Palepu A, Szalacha L, Caswell C, Carr PL, Inui T (2003). "Having the right chemistry": a qualitative study of mentoring in academic medicine. Acad. Med. 78:328–334.

Kupfer DJ, Schatzberg AF, Grochocinski VJ, Leslie O. Dunn LO, Kelley KA, et al (2009). The Career Development Institute for Psychiatry: an innovative, longitudinal program for physician-scientists. Acad Psychiatry, 33:313–318.

LeMelle S, Arbuckle MR, Ranz JM (2013). Integrating systems-based practice, community psychiatry, and recovery into residency training. Acad Psychiatry, 37(1):35-7.

Leroy S (2009). Why is it so hard to do my work? The challenge of attention residue when switching between work tasks. Organizational Behavior and Human Decision Processes, 109:168-81.

Levinson W, Kaufman K, Clark B, Tolle SW (1991): Mentors and role models for women in academic medicine. West J Med, 154:423-426.

Lockley SW, Cronin JW, Evans EE, Cade BE, Lee CJ, et al (2004). Effect of reducing interns' weekly work hours on sleep and attentional failures. N Engl J Med, 351:1829-1837.

Myers KK, Sadaghiani, K (2010). Millennials in the workplace: a communication perspective on millennials' organizational relationships and performance. J Bus Psychol, 25:225–238.

Neher JO, Gordon KC, Meyer B, Stevens N (1992). A five-step "microskills" model of clinical teaching. J Am Board Fam Pract, 5(4):419-24.

Newman M, Ravindranath D, Figueroa S, Jibson MD (2016). Perceptions of Supervision in an Outpatient Psychiatry Clinic. Acad Psychiatry, 40(1):153-6.

Newport C (2021). *A World Without E-Mail: Reimagining Work in an Age of Communication Overload*. Portfolio/ Peguinrandomhouse, New York City, USA.

New York State Department of Health, 11/14/2018, Title: Section 405.4 – Medical Staff. https://regs.health.ny.gov/content/section-4054-medical-staff

Palepu A, Friedman RH, Bame RC, Carr PL, Ash AS, et al (1996). Medical faculty with mentors are more satisfied (Abstract). J Gen Int Med, 11, April (supplement):107.

O'Donnell BRJ (2017). When Mentorship Goes Off Track. *The Atlantic,* July 28, 2017. https://www.theatlantic.com/business/archive/2017/07/mentorship-fails-psychology/535125/

Post RE, Quattlebaum RG, Benich JJ III (2009). Residents-as-teachers curricula: a critical review. Acad Med, 84(3):374–380.

Ranz JM, Deakins SM, LeMelle SM, Rosenheck SD, Kellermann SL (2008). Public-academic partnerships: core elements of a public psychiatry fellowship. Psychiatr Services, 59(7):718-20.

Ranz JM, Weinberg M, Arbuckle MR, Fried J, Carino A, McQuistion HL et al (2012). A four factor model of systems-based practices in psychiatry. Acad Psychiatry, 36(6):473-8.

Reardon CL, Factor RM, Brenner C, Singh P, Spurgeon J (2014). Community psychiatry tracks for residents: A review of four programs. Community Mental Health J, 50(1):10-16.

Rodenhauser P, Rudisill JR, Dvorak R (2000). Skills for mentors and proteges applicable to psychiatry. Acad Psychiatry, 24:14–27.

Rogawski DS, Rogawski MM (2018). Generational differences in mentoring relationships. JAMA, 320(10):1037.

Sambunjak D, Straus SE, Marušic A. (2006) Mentoring in academic medicine: a systematic review. JAMA, 296:1103-1115.

Summers RF, Gorrindo T, Hwang S, Aggarwal R, Guille C (2020). Well-being, burnout, and depression among North American psychiatrists: the state of our profession. Am J Psychiatry, 177:955–964.

Wilkerson I (2020). *Caste: The Origins of Our Discontents*, Random House, New York City, USA.

Yager J, Waitzkin H, Parker T, Duran B (2007). Educating, training, and mentoring minority faculty and other trainees in mental health services research. Acad Psychiatry, 31:146–151.

International Trends in Community Mental Health Services

Alan Rosen, Roberto Mezzina,
and Jacqueline Maus Feldman

Introduction

This chapter will provide summaries of the state of community mental health in some countries around the world, allowing readers to compare and contrast the nature of services and to further understand the successes and challenges of innovative programing. We cannot hope to provide an exhaustive international survey of the rest of the world in such a short space, but the table (see Table 1 at the end of the chapter) and the section on global psychiatry redress this to some extent. We will describe examples from countries of which we have the most firsthand knowledge and focus on some leading-edge innovations and systems reforms. Although the countries discussed are different on many levels, it is intriguing to note that there are consistent themes across these nations: (1) movement away from institutional hospital-centricity; (2) greater provision of mental health services in the community; (3) providing supported housing and purposeful and productive activity (e.g., work); (4) emphasis on human rights and facilitating individual choice and control, voluntary or least restrictive care; (5) family education and consultations wherever possible; (6) committed leadership enabling lived experience empowerment, stigma reduction and

A. Rosen (✉)
Australian Health Services Research Institute,
University of Wollongong,
Wollongong, NSW, Australia

Brain & Mind Centre, University of Sydney,
Sydney, NSW, Australia

Far West NSW LHD Mental Health Services,
Broken Hill, NSW, Australia

The Mental Health Services [Themhs] Conference/
Themhs Learning Network of Australia & New
Zealand, Balmain, NSW, Australia

Transforming Australia's Mental Health Service
System [TAMHSS] Inc., Balmain, NSW, Australia

Former Inaugural Deputy Commissioner, Mental
Health Commission of New South Wales, 2013–15,
Sydney, NSW, Australia
e-mail: alan.rosen@sydney.edu.au

R. Mezzina
International Mental Health Collaborating Network,
Exeter, UK

World Federation of Mental Health,
Woodbridge, VA, USA

Former Director, Diparimento di Salute Mentale,
WHO Collaborating Centre for Research and
Training in Mental Health, Trieste, Italy

J. M. Feldman
Department of Psychiatry and Behavioral
Neurobiology, University of Alabama at Birmingham,
Birmingham, AL, USA
e-mail: jfeldman@uabmc.edu

W. E. Sowers et al. (eds.), *Textbook of Community Psychiatry*,
https://doi.org/10.1007/978-3-031-10239-4_62

Table 1 Brief survey of notable examples of community mental health services

Nigeria, Ghana, and Zimbabwe	The origin of contemporary community mental health services owes a huge debt to Dr. Tom Lambo in Nigeria. Lambo initiated a system of village care of individuals identified as acutely or severely mentally ill. It relied on occupants of several villages taking these individuals into their homes as lodgers for a very small fee, while a combination of nurses, doctors, and local traditional healers jointly provided care in the villages with a 24-h on-call service providing emergency cover from the main village. Unfortunately, this system was dismantled after rebuilding of the Aro psychiatric hospital was completed (Asuni 1967; Adewunmi 2002). In recent years, WHO has initiated very promising human rights-based interventions in countries like Ghana, while NGOs with international support are trying to support recovery and work opportunities in Togo, Sierra Leone and other countries to abolish the archaic use of chaining people to trees. The "Friendship Bench" is a CBT-related problem-solving and communal support group program for depression, training grandmothers as local lay health workers (LHW's) originating in Zimbabwe, with growing RCT evidence of effectiveness (Chibanda et al. 2016; Riley 2018; WHO 2021) and dissemination to other countries, especially in Africa.
Palestinian territories	Since 2004, the WHO and various European Union donors have supported an ambitious program of development of mental health services in the West Bank and Gaza (Bassam 2005). The main thrust of the plan entailed developing local community mental health centers located close to primary care centers, in each of the regions of the West Bank and Gaza, and extensive retraining of the practitioner workforce. It established family and service-user associations including public awareness campaigns to help overcome stigma, discrimination and misunderstanding. It also developed a new mental health legislation to protect human rights (WHO 2006; Palestinian National Authority 2004). Sustaining these improvements and reform of the old psychiatric hospitals in Bethlehem in the West Bank and in Gaza City, which continue consuming most of the relatively small mental health budget, remain as continuing challenges (WHO-AIMS 2006).
Israel	Comprehensive community mental health service reform had been delayed except for some crisis intervention and trauma-related developments and community rehabilitation initiated by family organizations. A mental health insurance reform was launched in July 2015, transferring responsibility for treating patients with mental illness from the government to four nationally mandated health maintenance organizations. Prior to this reform, separation between physical and mental health care exacerbated disparities in psychiatric service funding and availability. The mental health reform was intended to closely link physical health and mental health and by doing so to reduce (hopefully) the visibility and subsequent impact of stigma (Cohen et al. 2020).
Sri Lanka and Indonesia	Both have undertaken a widespread process of deinstitutionalization following the disaster caused by Tsunami in 2006 and have developed community services based on primary care which include mental health (and also mobile) components (WHO 2016).
Malaysia	In Malaysia, the Permai Hospital in Johor Bahru has developed a grassroots program to stop the use of restraints, alongside work-integration schemes and good quality pilot community-based services.

India	Parts of rural India have excelled at low-cost community village-based rehabilitation (Thara et al. 2008). "The Banyan" recovers homeless women with severe mental illness from the streets and supports them in a process of housing, social integration, and community engagement. Another program implemented the WHO "Quality Rights" Initiative on a large scale with the creation of peer support groups.
China & Hong Kong	China has begun to devolve from institutionally based mental health services to community health centers. In some places, outpost centers have been established in large residential blocks or complexes. Community-based individual and group family sessions focus on psychoeducational, traditional herbal remedies, and improving marriage prospects (Xiong et al. 1996) as well as more orthodox psychopharmacology (Rathbone et al. 2007). Some Chinese Psychiatrists have been dually trained in Western and traditional Chinese medicine. In Hong Kong, despite the persistence of western-style psychiatric hospitals, and recent political upheaval, community-based programs are being developed including Work Employment Social Enterprises (WISEs) (Po-Ying and Chan 2010) and Early Intervention in Psychosis for young people (Chen et al. 2019) as well as often NGO-based individual, family, and group rehabilitation and support programs.
Japan	Japan is still stuck in one of the most immobile hospital-based systems worldwide, despite regional efforts to embed reforms. The number of beds is huge (about 340.000), and the ownership of private hospitals is usually in the hands of psychiatrist directors. Only initial steps have been taken toward reducing the average length of stay and creating community care facilities (Hiroto et al. 2013; Cohen et al. 2020), although international dialogue to assist change is ongoing.
Brazil and Argentina	In the 1970's–1980's Brazil and Argentina, the influence of Italian reforms was greater than elsewhere in the world (Delgado 1991). Basaglia's impact in Brazil was enormous (Basaglia 2000; Venturini et al. 2020) in tune with the political movements of that time. The first federal reform law was applied in the 1980s with the creation of Community Mental Health Services, with all states phasing out of mental hospitals (Nicacio 1990). In the 1990s, a very innovative program of community services formed using resources of a former private hospital. Their National Health Law (Larrobla and Botega 2001) guaranteed full citizenship to people with mental health problems and fostered the growth of community-based services (CAPS), a clear shift from psychiatric hospitals to community-based services (Tykanori 2011). While about 19,000 beds were closed in hospitals, 3000 long-stay beds were created in group-homes and in short-stay beds in CMHCs with linkage of public mental health to housing, work, and income generation in a national program of poverty eradication (Tykanori 2011). The government of Lula Da Silva (2003–2010) was committed to the creation of a national health service with equal access for all citizens (Caldas de Almeida and Cohen 2008). Unfortunately, more recent ultraconservative policies have undermined this fundamental transformation and curtailed community mental health development. Training in Integrative Community Therapy, a large group dialogic intervention offered within communities, has been widely networked in Brazil (purportedly with 40,000 facilitators) and now elsewhere to facilitate communal discussions of mental health and drug and alcohol problems, as well as common concerns, fears and anxieties to build interpersonal recovery, emotional resilience and solidarity, as a loose informal social movement co-led by Brazilian psychiatrist Adalberto Barreto (https://www.visiblehandscollaborative.org/). Argentina developed some pilot models of public community service in Cordoba in the late 1980s and the 1990s. In Rio Negro, a regional law developed a network of effective community services and work cooperatives (Cohen and Natella 1995). This was one of the first reforms to successfully implement an integrated mental health system with no psychiatric hospital with extensive psychosocial rehabilitation and patient participation. In 2008, more than 25,000 inpatients were still in Argentinian mental hospitals (CELS 2009). In 2010, with a new mental health law, the closure of mental hospitals became a goal, and a network of community-based services was envisioned (Mauri and Barcala 2020). Unfortunately, the implementation of this vision has been very slow.

(continued)

Table 1 (continued)

Chile and Peru	Chile (Minoletti et al. 2012; Minoletti 2016) with its system of primary care centers and teams and Peru (Peru Ministerio de la Salud 2021) are undertaking a rapid transition from outmoded psychiatric institutions to modern Community Mental Health Centers, inspired by the Italian model. In general, WHO/PAHO data show that the reduction in psychiatric hospitals has recently occurred in this part of the world faster than elsewhere.
Czech Republic and Belgium	Both these countries have chosen to develop community teams to provide some alternatives to hospitalization. The Czech reforms, supported by structural European funds, combines a welfare component in these teams that promotes social integration. The Belgian reform (Jacob et al. 2016; Borgermans et al. 2018) promotes wide ranging mobile teams which are only loosely linked with private hospitals with no clearly defined catchment areas.
Germany	Despite having well-resourced welfare and health organizations, most mental health services are still heavily hospital based, usually poorly integrated with separate community mental health services. Hospital-centric systems, occasionally with community outreach components, often take a lead role in coordinating different care providers for individuals with long-lasting conditions, often with high levels of inpatient occupancy (Brunn et al. 2021; Cruz-Arez 2021).
France	Lille has developed mental health service reforms with a particular emphasis on supporting social inclusion through foster families for persons in crisis, a wide variety of residential solutions and promoting products of artists with lived experience of mental illness (Roelandt 2010, 2016) France has otherwise failed to substantially reduce the role of psychiatric hospitals (Brunn et al. 2021). However, it has issued a new law for reinforcing the decentralization of welfare and health services, and the government began evaluating the WHO good practice examples of Trieste and Lille in 2019
Spain	Spain began to close their asylums and developing community services (Aparicio Basauri 2010; Salvador-Carulla et al. 2010) around the same time as Italy. There were 120 psychiatric hospitals in 1975, with 91 still functioning in 2003, coexisting with a mix of community services. There was a national heath law in 1986, but regional models varied as they were autonomous (Aparicio Basauri and Sanchez Gutierrez 2002). Job orientation and supported employment in the open market have commonly been provided, as are day hospitals, rehabilitation communities, and community mental health teams, with small general hospital psychiatric units (Lopez 2004). The successful implementation process of ACT (TAC) teams throughout Spain has resulted in a national network of teams with an annual TAC conference (Martinez-Jambrina J, 2009, & personal communications, 21 June, 2021)
The Netherlands	Ari Querido pioneered a citywide mobile crisis team with follow-up management in the 1930s, with a focus on social factors precipitating mental disorders (Querido 1935). Nonetheless, the Netherlands' mental health care remains dependent on hospital-based care, although there are policies aimed at its reduction, being hindered by (mostly insurance-based) financial systems that favor remuneration of hospitalization over outpatient care. The Netherlands have implemented hybrid FACT teams (flexible assertive community treatment and general community teams) (Keet et al. 2019). However rigorous controlled evidence of effectiveness has not yet been established, and FACT fidelity to model appears to depend on a detailed external inspection system, wherever it exists. Yet, FACT could provide practical solutions for rural teamwork and smoother transitions to less intensive care (Rosen et al. 2015; Killaspy and Rosen 2022; Bond and Drake 2015). Netherlands clinicians initiated the European Community Mental Health Services Provider EUCOMS Network (Keet et al. 2019) to combine evidence-based service delivery systems with recovery orientation, peer workers, and other community mental health reforms.

Sweden and Denmark	Sweden closed most of its asylums and pioneered a 24-h "social psychiatry" service in Stockholm. The general trend is toward evidence-based and clinically orientated community mental health services. A strong service user movement with involvement in care actively advocates for human rights. A 1994 law separating health care from social welfare programs still lets vulnerable individuals "slip between the cracks" (Topor 2020) Similar reforms in Denmark have been at an impasse, split between an institutional highly biological-orientated hospital psychiatry and fairly advanced services run by local municipalities.
Finland	The world-renowned program of Open Dialogue originated here, centered in rural Western Lapland, but a hospital-based psychiatric system remains dominant in Finland (Wahlbeck K & Salvador-Carulla, personal communications, 3–4 July 2015). Research of Open Dialogue has been hampered possibly by problematic methodology, theoretical ambiguity of its "fidelity criteria," and tacit encouragement of outpatient or private practice more than its outreach components (Mueser 2019; Bergstrom et al. 2018; Rosen et al. 2020a; Waters et al. 2021). Whether it is an effective alternative to good practice guidelines, acute care of psychosis has not yet been established. Many of the principles on which it is based have parallels in crisis intervention (e.g., rapid response, home visiting, family and resource network involvement, nonjudgmental dialogue, and negotiation) with more emphasis in Open Dialogue on tolerating uncertainty, ensuring all voices are heard ("polyphony"), sharing of responsibility, and avoiding clinical dominance.

advocacy; (7) expansion of the mental health professional and peer workforce, supporting interdisciplinary integrated teamwork; (8) holistic and comprehensive assessment addressing social determinants; (9) providing trauma-informed, recovery-oriented treatment across the life span; (10) optimal balance between in-person or home delivery care and telehealth or digitally augmented care; (11) culturally respectful global mental health approaches integrated in general health services. Structural reform of mental health services is easier to achieve than improvements in service quality. Success comes when leadership is shared and inspired, trustworthy, and transparent, and when political exigencies and funding are stable and predictable. Accomplishing all or most of these objectives is rarely seen in countries around the world. In these national profiles, we will be describing the attempts of several countries to achieve them.

Oceania

The histories of Australian and New Zealand psychiatry are entwined with the impact of European (British) invasion and settlement, initially in Australia, in 1788, to form penal colonies to alleviate the overcrowding of English jails; this generated a masculine-dominated, individualistic culture. As European settlement in Australia and New Zealand expanded, the colonists began to struggle over land and resources with the original inhabitants, some of whom had been there over 60,000 years. Culturally congenial methods of working with indigenous peoples are being integrated into mental health services of both countries, i.e., increasingly training and employing indigenous clinical professionals, support workers, and traditional healers. With accelerating immigration from many parts of the developed and developing world since the 1950s, both countries have become increasingly multicultural in their approaches.

Australia

Australia serves as an example of a country whose mental health provision structure has been evolving from institutional to community-based care. We will trace its trajectory over the last 50 years.

Reform Implementation By the mid-1950s, occupation of psychiatric institutions reached its peak in Australia, much like the USA. A random controlled trial (Hoult et al. 1984) replicating the research of Stein and Test (1980) and Polak and Kirby (1976) demonstrated that acute mental health care for people with severe and complex disorders could be shifted safely and effectively from institutions to mobile community teams that are available around the clock. This became the core of the community mental health reforms proposed in the Richmond Report (1983) in the most populous state, New South Wales (NSW). Crisis and assertive community treatment teams, residential programs, and community support services were developed to meet complex needs.

The First Australian National Mental Health Policy was endorsed in 1992. It provided initial transitional (bridging) funding as part of the National Mental Health Strategy. Communities of practice networks (teams of similar functions from different regions swapping experiences and solutions) emerged in NSW, and then nationally, ultimately through the support of The Mental Health Services (TheMHS) Conference of Australia and New Zealand. There have been five distinct phases of the National Mental Health Strategy over 27 years (1993–2020) (Department of Health and Family Services 2002; Australian Health Ministers' Advisory Committee 2003;

Department of Health and Aging 2005; Rosen 2006a, b; Rosen et al. 2012a). The first phase effectively accelerated deinstitutionalization in the first 5 years, but these strategies have since lost much of their momentum (O'Halloran and O'Connor 2015). National Mental Health Service Standards based on the world's first fully integrated community and hospital (Rosen et al. 1995) became the national basis for integration and accreditation of all mental health facilities. However, subsequent regressive revisions of the national mental health service standards (Miller et al. 2009; Rosenberg 2010) diminished full consultation with stakeholders and diluted the national strategy (Miller et al. 2009; Rosen and Sweet 2016).

Recovery Support Services Following intensive advocacy, individuals with severe and complex mental health disorders were included in the National Disability Insurance Scheme (NDIS), with personal budget packages allowing individuals and their families to exercise choice of rehabilitation supports from the NGO or private sector. Pilot sites were developed starting in 2013, but only with substantial national implementation since 2020. Too many people with moderate rehabilitation needs (80% of Australians with psychiatric disability) are still excluded, but hopefully, this may now be addressed by a new federal government from mid-2022 which demonstrates a greater commitment to the NDIS.

Workforce Australian governments are beginning to focus belatedly on a nationally consistent workforce training system, which should include interdisciplinary team-based upskilling, supervision, pastoral support, and mentoring system for professionals and support workers, including peer workers operating in interdisciplinary teams. For example, a proposed national mental health workforce institute has been endorsed by a prominent government committee with a high priority for implementation (Teesson et al. 2021). As a result, people with lived experience and family peer workers with "Recovery College" or technical college certificate qualifications are being employed increasingly (Byrne et al. 2021). Aboriginal Mental Health Workers (Brideson and Rosen 2013) are being trained and integrated as well, especially by Aboriginal community-controlled primary health services, NGOs, and the public sector. Active Australian participation is growing in internationally connected networks of people with lived experience and family educators, researchers, peer practitioners, and thought leaders (Byrne et al. 2021; Rosen et al. 2020c).

Advocacy Mental Health Australia coproduced reports that reinforced the need for reform (Groom et al. 2003; Human Rights and Equal Opportunity Commission 2005). The Mental Health Services (TheMHS) Conference (www.themhs.org) (Andrews 2005) has provided a melting pot for deliberation between all stakeholder interests. It provides binational (Australia and New Zealand) forums involving members of all mental health professions, peer workers, service users, family, indigenous, and transcultural stakeholders. It promotes an inclusive, human rights approach (Rosen et al. 2012a). It also convenes the annual Australasian mental health service achievement awards for interdisciplinary team innovations and implementation research.

Global pioneers and champions of early intervention (EI) programs for young people with mental illnesses in Australia include Professors Patrick McGorry, Eoin Killacky (jobs and careers), Andrew Chanen (personality disorders), Ian Hickie (online applications and modeling), and Dr. Jackie Curtis (physical health algorithms for EI) (McGorry and Jackson 1999; Byrne and Rosen 2014; Rosen et al. 2016). Australia has increased public awareness of mental health and illness through media campaigns, schools, and workplaces, expanding mental health literacy and ability to access resources (e.g., Rosen et al. 2000). Mental Health First Aid, a mental health equivalent of a physical first aid course originated by Betty Kitchener in Australia (Jorm et al.

2019), has been widely disseminated to develop mental health lay resource people in many walks of life, in the UK, Canada, the USA, Ireland, and many other countries and translations.

Politics Following the examples of New Zealand, and then Canada, several independent statutory reform-oriented standing mental health commissions have formed, state and federal, to revive movement toward evidence-based, consumer and family congenial, recovery-oriented mental health care, and suicide prevention (Rosen et al. 2004, 2010b; Rosen 2012; Rosenberg and Rosen 2012a, b). Despite some advances, they have not yet overcome fragmentary, poorly integrated, and underfunded mental health services. They lack affordable services for the "missing middle" (not severe enough for public psychiatric services, but too complex for primary care) (National Mental Health Commission 2014; National Productivity Commission 2020; Royal Commission into Victoria's Mental Health System 2021). Of these, the reforms in the State of Victoria have the most momentum with committed state funding. In other areas, federal funding streams and management structures have become even more separated into silos with poor coordination between them: public sector specialist clinical services funded by the states, primary mental health care, private professional, and nongovernment support services partly funded directly by federal government, some via the NDIS.

Implications These trends reflect the uneven but incremental evidence-based shift of the center of gravity of mental health services and resources from hospital-centric with occasional outreach when convenient for staff, to community-based services where people in need live, with in-reach to hospital only as necessary (Rosen et al. 2020a, b).

Mental health services are being eroded or have never developed sufficient breadth (Rosen et al. 2010a). Even after sporadic spending spurts, Australia has still lagged far behind similar Western countries (e.g., the UK and USA) in terms of the proportion of national health budget (e.g., 7.6% from 2016 to 2020, slightly more than Canada) spent on mental health services (Rosen et al. 2010a, b; AIHW 2022). Support of consumers, carers, and workforce is a critical factor in the success of mental health reforms (Whiteford & Buckingham 2005). Mental health commissions should be effective conduits to governments of all stakeholder voices and needs. As the only nation where both federal and most state and territory governments have implemented reform-oriented commissions, Australia is in a unique position to determine what coordinated efforts between them could achieve – almost like an opportunistic natural experiment. Eventually if stronger, more independent, focused, and combined voices of Australian mental health commissions are heard and heeded, governments could still restore momentum and coherence to Australian mental health reforms (Rosen et al. 2010b; Rosen 2012; Rosenberg and Rosen 2012a, b; Van Spijker et al. 2019).

New Zealand

New Zealand has had the benefit of being a close observer of the high-level decision-making of Australian reforms, and learning from their mistakes, they were able to improve that process. In the absence of private sector services, New Zealand created health services using public sources and nongovernmental organizations (NGOs).

Innovations New Zealand's Mental Health Commission, operating since 1996, was the *first* worldwide to adopt a system-wide reform agenda as its priority (New Zealand Mental Health Commission 1998, 2001). It closely monitored the quality of all mental health services. Recovery-oriented competencies, workforce development (O'Hagan 2001), and grassroots strategies for challenging stigma ("Like Minds, Like Mine" (2022) http://www.likeminds.org.nz/page/5-Home) were evaluated.

One of the most important initial achievements of the New Zealand Commission was to produce the Blueprint (New Zealand Mental Health Commission 1998), a detailed plan to offer mental health services with a recovery agenda to be developed in regular consultations with all stakeholders, including indigenous peoples. Financial commitment to the Blueprint from an incoming government enhanced the caliber and consistency of mental health services remarkably (New Zealand Mental Health Commission, 2010). As a result, by 2012, more than 80% of mental health services were provided in the community with 30% of mental health budgets spent on strict contracts with the NGO sector to enhance community services (Rosen et al. 2010b). New Zealand's per capita expenditure on mental health far exceeded Australia's, by more than 100% of public and NGO funding. However, the impact of the 2008 global financial crisis was much more severe in New Zealand than in Australia, and the budgets of both public and NGO services were cut back. Consequently, the pioneering, reform-focused, world-renowned New Zealand Mental Health Commission was "disestablished" in 2012 except for its Chair Commissioner, left in a Health and Disability Complaints Commission.

In 2014, the Ministry contracted with three organizations: (1) Te Rau Matatini, (2) the National Centre for Māori Health and Māori Workforce Development and Excellence, and (3) Le Va a Pasifika (Pacific Islander) Mental Health Support Organization, to establish a national Māori and Pasifika Community Suicide Prevention Program. Addressing unacceptable rates of compulsory orders for Māori became a priority (Director-General's report 2016), as noted in the following examples:

Te Pou o te Whakaaro Nui The long-standing New Zealand national government-funded center of evidence-based workforce development for the mental health, addiction, and disability sectors (https://www.tepou.co.nz/training-development).

Equally Well A Te Pou initiative that is a collaborative group of organizations and individuals with a common goal of reducing physical health disparities of those living with mental disorders and/or addictions.

He Ara Oranga (Pathways to Wellness) The Mental Health & Addictions Inquiry (New Zealand Government 2018, (https://mentalhealth.inquiry.govt.nz/inquiry-report/he-ara-oranga/) was commissioned by a new Labor Government to recommendations that were reported in 2018. Its mission is (1) to take a whole-of-government approach to well-being, tackling social determinants, and supporting prevention activities that impact on multiple outcomes; (2) to markedly improve access, wait times, and quality of care to a broader proportion of the population; (3) to provide more systematic attention to Māori and Pacific Islander mental and physical health and well-being, strengthening ties to family, tribal identity, language, spirituality, and addressing social determinants; (4) to undertake a mental health human rights focused reframing of mental health laws to honor their international treaty obligations; (5) to reduce involuntary care and eliminating restraints; and (6) to establish a new reform-oriented standing Commission to act as a watchdog at an arm's length from government, providing leadership and oversight of mental health and well being (Howie A, pers.comm. 13 May 2021).

New Zealand's current government has been highly responsive to mental health needs, promptly implementing the recommendations of the Mental Health Inquiry, particularly by enhancing well-being programs across all departments, based on both Māori and health economic approaches (e.g., Dalziel et al. 2018), and reestablishing a Mental Health and Well-Being Commission (https://www.mhwc.govt.nz).

Efforts to achieve the goals of expanding access and choice have included being able to access specialist services, and the provision of a broader menu and flexible choice of and self-referral to therapeutic roles by primary health organizations and general practices. This entails training counselor/behavioral health consultants, peer/cultural health coaches, and peer and community support workers to address practical needs. The public embrace of these approaches has been most encouraging, far exceeding IAPT (Improving Access to Psychological Therapies) (D. Codyre, personal communication, 20 April 2020; Appleton-Dyer and Andrews 2018).

Britain and Ireland

The UK

In 1998, the UK Secretary of State for Health Frank Dobson noted that, "Care in the community has failed" (Burns and Priebe 1999), referring to the process in the UK of deinstitutionalization, the closure of the old mental asylum system, and transfer of patients to the community. While movement into the community for some patients had been beneficial (Leff et al. 2000), for others it had led to homelessness and dislocation from care and their familiar community (Craig 1998). Dobson recognized that simply discharging many long-stay hospital residents (155,000 in 1954 to less than 20,000 in 1998) into the "nonsystem" of community living without consistent care had been a mistake (Keown et al. 2008).

In 1999, the National Service Framework (NSF) for Mental Health was published, (Department of Health 1999) outlining a quality framework for services. This was accompanied by NSF's detailed strategic approach to implementation of community care, known as the NHS (National Health Service) Plan (Department of Health 2000). The NSF clearly spelled out for the first time a blueprint for community-based mental health services. The NSF's NHS Plan for Mental Health set out, again for the first time in the UK, a clear and progressive national mental health policy. Importantly, it included a prescriptive, centrally driven, performance-managed, and relatively well-funded 10-year plan of implementation.

The performance management dimension involved clear targets, centralized monitoring, and primary care-based entities called Primary Care Trusts (PCTs). The latter involved payment by results and development of more competitive quasi-market forces. NHS Trusts (the main entity of public mental health) were redeveloped as more locally responsive "business" entities, which shifted planning away from a top-down direction and toward integration of health and social care functions.

In addition, priority was given to expanding and reforming the existing workforce through the introduction of new roles and tackling traditional problems. Collaboration with professional and accrediting bodies and higher education institutions along with the introduction of progressive workforce training and educational methodologies were part of the plan. These efforts were enhanced by funding of over $ two billion (US) annually under the leadership of the National Institute for Mental Health in England (National Institute for Mental Health in England 2004). This was a partial redirection of savings from the closure of over 130 psychiatric institutions in England. Workforce reform led to an expansion of new roles in the practitioner workforce, including 1000 new primary care mental health workers, 500 additional "gateway" workers to work with primary care providers, 3000 support workers, many with lived experience, and 14,000 additional clinical roles, including consultant psychiatrists, clinical psychologists, and 10,000 mental health nurses. These reforms pushed for 24-h per day/7 days per week community treatment with on-demand accessibility, early detection and prevention, consumer-centered care, evidenced-based practices, and care coordination (Department of Health 2007).

A multidisciplinary approach with greater promotion of self-management and peer support was planned. In 2008, the IAPT (Improving Access to Psychological Therapies) program was launched with teams of graduate psychologists offering team-supervised cognitive behavioral therapy (CBT) based on primary healthcare practices (https://www.england.nhs.uk/mental-health/adults/iapt/). Colocated in general practices, these teams mainly of graduate psychologists maintain strict fidelity criteria. However, waiting times for admission to these services can vary between 6 and 124 days, its reach to most needy populations is limited, and the uptake penetration for them is still too low (D. Codyre, personal communication, 20 April, 2021).

New Horizons, the UK's 2010 national mental health policy, was built on these NSF achievements with a greater focus on self-management, emphasizing social outcomes of work, housing, and inclusion (Department of Health 2009). It aimed at driving up quality and increasing choice, through encouraging a "plurality of providers." The use of direct payments and individual service-user budgets were to open the market to alternative providers, increasing choice, with a greater emphasis on outcomes. General practitioners' willingness and capacity to be gatekeepers and determine need was a limitation. With many providers involved, coherent pathways to care, integration, and whole system functioning would be challenging. Other challenges that lie ahead included how a national health service with a tradition of providing clinical treatment could deliver much more on outcomes, such as employment and housing, requiring greater integration and closer work with public welfare. Collaboration with the voluntary sector and other stakeholders would be required. However, by 2015, only 14 percent of adults surveyed felt they were provided with the right response when in crisis, and only around half of community teams were able to offer an adequate 24/7 crisis service (Care Quality Commission, 2019, 2021). By 2019, low fidelity to evidence guidelines was found in over a third of crisis teams (Lamb et al. 2019).

The Health and Social Care Act 2012 created a new legal responsibility for the NHS to deliver "parity of esteem" between mental and physical health by 2020. Parity of esteem was meant to ensure as much focus on mental as physical health and that people with mental health problems receive equal standard of care. However, this benchmark was not met in the designated time frame (Care Quality Commission, 2021).

Assertive Community Treatment

The more recent demise of "Assertive Outreach" (Assertive Community Treatment) teams in England, based on a dubious reading of the evidence, proved costly, and was arguably politically motivated and discriminatory. The influential UK Schizophrenia Commission Report (2012) called for investment in high-quality services to deliver evidence-based treatments for people with long-term psychosis. Ironically, this report did not include anything about the need to invest in Assertive Community Treatment (ACT) teams. It specifically recommended extension of principles of early intervention to support people experiencing ongoing psychosis but ignored fidelity guidelines specifying an ACT pathway for these individuals (Rosen et al. 2013). Financial constraints and some flawed evaluations in the UK led to the remodeling of English ACT teams and their integration into standard care) (Killaspy and Rosen 2013, 2022; Rosen et al. 2013). However most UK purported studies of or proxies for ACT did not meet the ACT fidelity standards established in the USA, Australia, and Canada. Subsequently, many affected individuals were sent from major city hospitals to distant inpatient facilities, dislocated from their families and familiar environments. This was using up the resources that could have been used for community-based rehabilitation services. This disinvestment in ACT in England has deprived many individuals and their families of the intensive support they needed and discouraged research to inform the intelligent evolution of the ACT model within different contexts (Rosen et al. 2013).

A review of UK mental psychiatric rehabilitation services (Rethink Mental Illness & Royal College of Psychiatrists 2020) demonstrated that fewer than one in four mental health trusts employed a dedicated community mental health rehabilitation team to help these patients in their local area. Some UK community rehabilitation teams have endeavored to retain many features of mobile ACT teams, but overall disinvestment in services for this complex needs group has been detrimental, prompting some moves toward rebuilding of community rehabilitation services for them (H. Killaspy, personal communication, 18 February 2021).

Rehabilitation Research

Research and practice promoting the recovery movements led by professors Mike Slade (Nottingham University) and Geoff Shepherd (Sainsbury Trust) now routinely include experts with lived experience, often trained in peer-run Recovery Colleges (Whitley et al. 2019). Of individuals living with severe mental illnesses, 90% were supported by the community mental health services. However, within these services, there is lack of access to, or very long waits for, most of the key interventions recommended by NICE (the National Institute of Clinical Excellence), such as psychological therapies. A review of UK mental psychiatric rehabilitation services in 2020 (Rethink Mental Illness & Royal College of Psychiatrists 2020) demonstrated that nearly half of regional services which had decommissioned beds revealed that they also had placed patients out of area, 75% had no plans to reduce the number of patients with enduring mental health problems being sent often hundreds of miles from home, as such placements were "now routine, despite their negative impacts," and fewer than 25% of mental health trusts employ a dedicated community mental health rehabilitation team to help these patients in their local area. Disappointingly, 25% of people using secondary mental health services do not know who is responsible for coordinating their care or participated in treatment planning. Almost 20% had not had a formal meeting to review their care plan in the previous 12 months.

The Early Intervention in Psychosis (EIP) Program

This program in England was co-led by Drs. David Shiers and Jo Smith, developing EIP NICE guidelines. Meaningful Lives (supporting young people with psychosis in education training employment and career development) and Healthy Active Lives (HeAL) led to physical health monitoring protocols for GPs, EIPs, and community mental health teams. They convened initially in the UK, together with Australians Jackie Curtis and Eoin Killackey, utilizing widespread international translations, declarations, and adoption of the "Bondi Algorithm" and the "Lester Resource," which are concise graphic physical monitoring protocols for GPs and EIP mental health team (Shiers and Smith 2014; Byrne and Rosen 2014; Curtis et al. 2012).

Multiple leaders facilitated deployment of social movements as powerful dissemination tools in evidence-based knowledge translation (e.g., via the related IRIS initiative), which also disseminated understanding of the uses of "woodshedding" in recovery (Shiers et al. 2009; Iris Initiative 2018).

Crisis Intervention

The evidence-based practice guidance for Crisis Intervention teams in the UK is well developed via the Cochrane Collaboration and NICE guidelines. The Crisis Care Concordat, launched by the Department of Health in February, 2014, has triggered joint agreements at the local level between the police, social care, mental health, and ambulance services to improve how professionals work together. Achievements so far include a significant drop in the number of people being detained in police cells during mental health crises. In October, 2014, the government announced access and waiting time standards for some mental health services, the first time such targets had been set for mental health, psychological therapies, and early intervention (EIP). The majority of people with first episode psychosis were to access EIPs within 2 weeks of first presentation for comprehensive EIP care.

A report of an independent taskforce to NHS England (2016) and the NHS Long Term Plan (2019) developed a 10-year strategy to improve and widen access to care for children and adults. It promised to transform mental health care so more people could access treatment by increasing funding for a range of mental health services matched to their age- and gender-related needs. It would also make it easier and quicker for people of all ages to receive mental health crisis care around the clock (Sashidharan S.P., pers. comm. 6 March 21).

Ireland

The Republic of Ireland is a high-income European country. The population has been growing in recent years and has passed 4.83 million. In the middle of the twentieth century, the country had an extremely high rate of institutionalization. In 1961, there were 7.3 psychiatric beds per 1000 population. This was possibly the highest provision in the world (Kelly 2016). A national mental health policy called *A Vision for Change* (AVFC) was launched in 2006. This was a progressive document that envisioned a wide range of community-based inputs and a shift to a recovery philosophy within services. While a good deal of progress has been made and many of the initiatives proposed in AVFC have been implemented, it is widely accepted that there is much left to do (Cullen and McDaid 2017). In 1963, there were 19,801 people in psychiatric hospitals in the country. By 2017, this figure had dropped to 2324, a fall of 88% (Daly and Craig 2018). Ireland now has one of the lowest beds to population ratios in Europe. However, the economic crash of 2007/2008 hit Ireland hard, and community mental health service development suffered. With poor community services in place, some people are now calling for more beds.

An updated national policy called *Sharing the Vision* was launched (Department of Health, Ireland 2020) providing an overview of recent developments in the country. National Clinical Programmes (NCPs) for mental health in various stages of implementation include (i) assessment and management of service users presenting to emergency departments following self-harm; (ii) the national clinical program for eating disorders; and (iii) an early intervention in psychosis model of care. As in other countries, the voluntary sector now plays an important role in service provision in Ireland. Nongovernmental organizations (NGOs) and recovery colleges provide workshops and training on healthy living, mental health awareness, resilience, Mental Health First Aid and trauma-informed care, peer support, and service user involvement at national and regional level are being incorporated (Bracken P. pers. comm. 20 February 2021).

Italy

A Short History of Law 180

Learning from the experience of the historical and decisive anti-institutional movement in Italy is fundamental. This movement began with the pioneering experiences of Franco Basaglia and others in the 1960s and 1970s. Initially improving care conditions of inpatients of asylums, then promoting their freedom, and finally closing these institutions, Basaglia's influence led to Italy's renowned psychiatric reform Law 180 in 1978 and ultimately had a considerable impact on community mental health system reforms in other countries (Sashidharan et al. 2019a, b).

Italy was the first in the world to mandate halting all admissions to mental hospitals (where more than 100,000 inpatients were confined in 1970) and to severely limit involuntary care. Inpatient units were limited to 15 beds and attached to general hospitals, while most clientele were cared for by community mental health centers and/or relocated to community dwellings, serviced initially by institutional staff and later by social cooperatives providing human services to "hosted" residents. It led to the healthcare goal plans of the 1990s and generated the political clout necessary to finally close all psychiatric hospitals and bring the Asylum Era to an end in the country by 2000. A well-staffed local CMHC, open up to 24/7, can be the core of an effective one-stop shop for all psychiatric requirements of its catchment areas (Mezzina 2018).

The existence of six forensic ("judiciary") psychiatric hospitals in Italy was extended until they could be replaced by small units (no more than 20 beds each (Barbui and Saraceno 2015)). Forensic inpatient beds fell from 1400 in 2008 to 652 in the range of residential facilities (Corleone

2018). The closure of all forensic hospitals occurred a year later. Social acceptance of the reform law and a general decrease of stigma attached to psychiatry mark a series of fundamental changes in public attitudes. After some initial strong resistance, families began to advocate strongly for improved community services as it was demonstrated that family burden was much lower relative to European countries (Basaglia 2000; Magliano et al. 2002).

Compulsory treatments dropped dramatically after 1978 as an immediate effect of Law 180, and Italy attained the lowest annual rate of these events in Europe (15 per 100,000) (Ministero della Salute 2018). Many general hospital units are still inadequate and continue the use of mechanical restraints, even though there is a wide campaign to abolish them. Some regions also use short- and medium-term admissions to private hospitals (De Girolamo et al. 2007). Sheltered community-based residences expanded to more than 17,000 places by the end of the 1990s (De Girolamo et al. 2002) and to about 30,000 by 2018 (Starace and Baccari 2018). In Italy, rehabilitation and reintegration of former long-term patients in transitional community residential settings is more extensive than in any other Western country, although the quality of care varies by region regarding the range of staff coverage (up to 24 h) and community inclusion. The development of personal recovery-oriented planning with associated healthcare individual budgets has been shown to speed up the move toward independent living, with provision of daily life supports in some regions (Ridente and Mezzina 2016).

For people with mental health problems, recovery includes citizenship and social reintegration. Social cooperatives have been developed that provide work activities, such as gardening, building, cleaning, hotel, restaurant, radio station and tailoring businesses, as a vehicle to enhance such reintegration. These are social enterprises which try to be competitive in the market. All workers are voting members of these cooperative businesses. More than 8500 such cooperatives are now operating in Italy. These enterprises must include at least 30% disabled service users to qualify for tax benefits that sustain a viable business (Leff and Warner 2006).

Trieste: An Exemplary Model Fully Implemented

Trieste is one practical example of how the Italian movement achieved deinstitutionalization. In other countries, the situation is conceptualized as a bed-reduction process, limiting institutional resources (as a mere de-hospitalization; De Leonardis et al. 1986). In Trieste, there was a gradual relocation of the economic and human resources to create 24-h CMHCs and community living for former inpatients. The institutional hierarchy was dismantled and replaced by a more flexible organization, with a critical paradigm shift, from a narrow focus on mental illness to the whole person's needs (Rotelli 1988; Bennett 1985; Mezzina 2014, 2016).

According to the WHO (World Health Organization) (WHO 2001), Trieste's 50 years of experience in the field of mental health is a proven success. After a 9-year process, there was the creation of a system of open door, open access community services which completely replaced the old asylum (Dell'Acqua and Cogliati Dezza 1986; Dell'Acqua 2010; Mezzina 2014; Muusse and Van Rojien 2015). CMHCs were made fully responsible for small catchment areas of 60,000 on average, working 24 h/7 days per week with a small number (6–8) of "hospitality" (crisis respite) beds for an effective crisis care (Mezzina and Johnson 2008; Mezzina 2014, 2016). The organization and philosophy of these CMHCs were based on the principles of (1) non-selection of demand (i.e., not based on particular diagnoses, severity thresholds, or other exclusion criteria); (2) non-hospitalization; (3) service flexibility and mobility; and (4) the involvement of multiple comprehensive resources, such as a wide range of welfare provisions, in the therapeutic and support programs (Mezzina and Vidoni 1995).

The budget of the Trieste Mental Health Department was 37% of the former psychiatric hospital. In Trieste, 94% of the mental health budget is spent in the community with only 6% of the budget going to a six-bed general hospital-based service which acts as an emergency first aid station at night (Mezzina 2020). The wide range of responses include (1) supported community accommodation for individual and small groups; (2) job training and placement for about 300 service users annually; and (3) a range of day center activities, including sport and cultural events. About 150 people are supported by personal budgets in the areas of housing, work, and social inclusion each year (Mezzina et al. 2019).

This experimental WHO pilot area of deinstitutionalization in 1974 (Bennett 1985) demonstrated that a city like Trieste can manage and provide a safe environment and provide maximum safeguards for individual freedom. The system became a regional model in Friuli Venezia Giulia and was implemented in other parts of Italy. Over the past 50 years, all forms of intrusive practices have been abolished, including physical restraint and ECT, using compulsory treatments only when absolutely unavoidable (from 7 to 9 per 100,000 inhabitants annually). There are continuous efforts to avoid incarceration of people with mental illness. The rate of suicide rate halved, from 25 per 100,000 in the mid-1990s, to 12 per 100,000 in 2003 (Dell'Acqua et al. 2003). With a dedicated prevention program, Trieste's suicide rate is on a par with other Mediterranean countries, with much less compulsion and hospital admissions (Mezzina 2010, 2014).

The comparative impact of the Trieste model of care has been limited by uncoordinated regional policies and by the fact that Italian mental health care is still severely underfunded with only 3.6% of the overall health budget allocated for mental health (Starace and Baccari 2018). It has inspired and sometimes shaped service reforms in other countries. It is an exemplary model for the recovery and human rights movements (WHO 2021).

Current regional government policies are posing a major threat to Trieste and the Friuli-Venezia Giulia Region. Cuts in 24 hrs community mental health services and staff, with the possible retreat to more inpatient care, may open the potential for privatization. This happens at a time when the COVID-19 has demonstrated the dire need for more community health systems (Mezzina et al. 2020; Sashidharan 2022; Frances 2021). This could hamper any possibility of developing a comprehensive mental health service network across the whole country, and internationally, that has been long awaited by stakeholder organizations (Mezzina 2018; United Nations 2020; International Mental Health Collaborating Network 2021).

North America and the Caribbean

Cuba

It is difficult to penetrate the mental health service provision in Cuba because of a paucity of written descriptions or published research. It has been reported (Gorry 2013) that 25% of the Cuban population is depressed, that suicide is in the top ten causes of death, and that the rate of alcoholism is increasing. In 1995, in recognition of the importance of mental health, and in the face of limited access and few coordinated services, the Havana Charter was developed: psychiatric care was integrated with primary care and focused on the development of neighborhood clinics that offered prevention, treatment, and rehabilitation.

People would seek health care at neighborhood clinics and be referred to specialty mental health clinics if need be. While the move to integrated care has improved access, particularly in urban areas (101 community mental health offices exist), Cuba continues to struggle with access in rural clinics. There are 17 specialized psychiatric hospitals, but access to outpatient care is always a concern. However, the creation of local day hospitals has helped those transitioning back to the community and allows for more intense community-based care. There is growing understanding of the importance of including family members in community care and stabilization of patients. As with other medical specialties in Cuba, access to and quality of care is much more assured at the primary healthcare level than at the specialty psychiatry level.

Access to a variety of pharmaceutical products has been limited by the level of poverty and the US embargo. Workforce issues are reflected in less than adequate numbers of mental health professionals (in 2012, there were 1051 psychiatrists = <10/100,000 psychiatrists for 11.26 million population). While access to medication is free in the hospital, outpatient medications must be paid for, and there is limited access to medications for those living with psychoactive substances use disorders. Concern has also been expressed about declining services for the expanding elderly population. There are some positive results regarding a significant subset of the population utilizing and responding to natural/traditional approaches to treatment (ACN 2022). More contentious as potential contributors to well-being are widespread locally inclusive communal projects, like urban communal vegetable gardens and cooperative house-building initiatives by "micro-brigades," possibly motivated more by political ideology, the prospect of food insecurity, shortages of affordable housing, and tradespeople (Marsh 2020; Minoff 2015).

Caribbean

Multiple island nations as well as land-locked countries are included in this survey (e.g., Bahamas, Turks & Caicos, Belize, Guyana, Surinam, Trinidad, Tobago). Schizophrenia and depression top the list in terms of clinical presentations. It is noted that the prevalence of mental illness seems high and that services are absent or inaccessible in most places. Sixty percent of those with symptoms of mental illness are unable to access services. An average of only 3% of their health budget is expended on mental health across the region. Care is typically centralized; some nations offer mainly hospital care for mental illness (where rates of seclusion and restraint appear high), while others offer only outpatient care.

Poverty and economic instability combined with overwhelming stigma and discrimination contribute to development of depression and disincentives to seek care. The increasing population, anxiety, and stress related to the consequences of climate change, trauma, disasters, social decline, and the lack of political leadership all negatively impact attempts at improvement in the development of plans and policies. Some innovations are moving systems of care forward: consideration of day hospitals, increased nonprofessional workforce development, and integrative care (primary care and psychiatry) have been instituted in some locations (enhancing access). The mental health workforce is limited, though numbers of psychiatric nurses are climbing significantly. Surprisingly, access to psychotropic medication is relatively good, and medication seems affordable for most (WHO 2011b).

Exceptionally, the Dominican Republic is now a WHO model for LMIC's mental health services. Its asylum was closed in the 1990s with ongoing support from Trieste. It was repurposed as an open rehabilitation center, with other functions completely replaced by a comprehensive range of services, from primary care to community care, encompassing general hospitals acute units, crisis services with respite beds, day centers, supported living, and outpatient psychiatric and psychological care (Plan Nacional de Salud Mental: República Dominicana 2019).

Mexico

It is reported that at least 17% of the Mexican population is living with at least one psychiatric diagnosis. Workforce development and access to mental health services are challenges faced across the nation, particularly in rural areas. One study reflects in the Jalisco region found that there are limited numbers of outpatient clinics, and those that do exist are often long distances from those patients who need them, creating barriers to access.

MD staffing (psychiatrists) is inadequate (3.71/100,000). In the face of limited outpatient mental health services, it is difficult to address the challenge of mental illness. The need for an expanded array of services has been identified (Carmona-Huerta et al. 2021). A nonprofit group of organizations has formed the Red Voz Pro Salud/Borgan Project to increase access to mental health services by combatting stigma with psychoeducation. They report that Mexico ranks second in the world in level of stigma associated with mental health services, 40% of the population lacks insurance, and that Mexican youth have twice the numbers of mental disorders when compared to the USA and Canada. Red Voz Pro Salud is working to provide education (via NAMI family-to-family lessons, social media, advocacy with political leadership) to tackle stigma (Daniels 2022).

Canada

Canada has an impressive record of community mental health innovation and of being early replicators and adopters of evidence-based initiatives (Fenton et al. 1979; Wasylenki et al. 1985, 1993). Earlier programmatic examples include collaboration of greater Vancouver's "Car 87" joint mental health and police crisis intervention team with Venture House, a community sited 24-h low-key respite facility (Torrey et al. 1993). Other key initiatives include crisis intervention and integrated care delivered in naturalistic settings (Mercier 1990; Fenton et al. 1979), system-wide implementation of ACT in Ontario (George et al. 2009), and Quebec (Latimer and Nadeau 1998), as well as early psychosis intervention teams (Malla et al. 2005). A national Mental Health Commission (MHCC) was launched in 2007, developing a national mental health strategy to support movement toward community-based care, recovery orientation, a knowledge exchange center, community awareness, and anti-stigma campaign (Mental Health Commission of Canada 2015; Goldbloom and Bradley 2012). Programs focusing on developing and adapting evidence-based practice of providing homes and support services for those living with mental illness who were homeless ("Chez Soi" housing) were launched by MHCC in 2009 with considerable success, supported by a sizeable federal research and implementation grant to MHCC enabling large-scale research supporting its effectiveness (Latimer et al. 2020). "Housing First"-type programs are being widely disseminated, partly based on these studies.

In 2015, 15.8 billion dollars were spent on mental health (private and public funding) which is only 7% of the total healthcare budget (much less that England or France). Barriers to care included stigma, membership in some demographic groups (child/adolescent, rural, Indigenous), and lack of public funding (especially psychotherapy services). In 2017, $950 million dollars were paid for private practice therapists, while 30% of those needing these services had to pay out of pocket. At the same time, it was reported that the unmet needs of those with mental health problems were responsible for $51 billion dollars in additional healthcare spending, lost productivity, and decreased quality of life. It was reported that there was a 75% increase in emergency room mental health services since 2007. Extended wait times for mental health services peaked, especially for children; the average wait time for intensive services was 92 days.

In 2017, the government (federal and provincial) responded by drafting and accepting the Common Statement of Principles in Shared Health Priorities, which seeks to increase mental health priorities by (1) increasing mental health spending to 9% of health costs; (2) maximizing the use of technology (e.g., the use of telehealth mental health, which has proven especially helpful during the COVID pandemic); (3) increasing the mental health workforce; (4) improving stable housing opportunities; (5) developing and using "stepped care" (utilization of primary care resources first and establishing policies and procedures for integrated care); (6) promulgating early intervention; and (7) increasing access to therapy (Moroz et al. 2020).

Global Community Mental Health Practices of the Future

The Global Mental Health movement (Patel and Prince 2010; WHO (mh-GAP) 2019a) is still largely dominated by Western models of care. Low- and medium-income countries often have national mental health systems severely limited by a paucity of resources. Many of these countries have systems that still retain asylums and other forms of long-term institutionalization (WHO 2011a). Task-shifting approach from psychiatric clinicians to primary care disciplines (Patel and Prince 2010) appears to be an effective strategy when combined with a development approach addressing the social determinants of poor health and the environmental contexts (Sashidharan et al. 2016). Global mental health is still in a process of growth and development. This has much to do with operationalizing the premises of deinstitutionalization overcoming colonial legacy in many LMIC (low- and middle-income countries). This transition must be combined with retention of human and economic resources to be converted into community supports and services. Cultural sensitivity must be respected through a "two-ways" or "two worlds" approach to implementation, combining least restrictive Western evidence-based interventions with expert traditional healing, extended kinship support and guided progression through rites of passage (Rosen 2006b, Gayaa Dhuwi (Proud Spirit) Declaration (https//:www.gayaadhuwi.org.au/resources/the-gayaa-dhuwi-proud-spirit--declaration/, Durie M, Foreword, in NiaNia W, Bush A, Epston D, Collaborative and Indigenous Mental Health Therapy: Tataihono, Routledge, New York, 2017, (https://www.routledge.com/Collaborative-and-Indigenous-Mental-Health-Therapy-Tataihono-Stories/NiaNia-Bush-Epston/p/book/9781138230309).

Any effective community mental health care can only be realized with a sincere process for phasing out psychiatric hospitals. The WHO reports that 80% of resources are still spent in psychiatric hospitals worldwide (WHO Atlas 2021; Saxena et al. 2011), while a clear gap still exists between the need for care and the available services. Even in Europe, only few countries are considered by WHO to have a full range of services for people with mental illness living in the community. Up to 50.3% of those with severe illness did not receive any treatment within the prior year in developed countries, while in developing countries, these data were much higher – 76–85% (WHO 2004a, b; Economist Intelligence Unit (2014).

The "balanced care model" (Thornicroft and Tansella 2013) was proposed, and although unintended by these authors, it can be misconstrued to suggest that the evidence base for psychiatric hospitalization is as strong as intensive community care and to support the persistence of standalone hospital-based services (Rosen et al. 2018, 2020b). The Lancet Psychiatry-WPA Future of Psychiatry Commission's uncritical endorsement of the balanced care model (Lancet Mental Health Group 2007; Bhugra et al. 2017) implies such scientific justification for hospital care, which is unwarranted. Virtually all rigorous studies have demonstrated the superiority of high-fidelity mobile outreach community mental health systems over hospital-based care (Rosen et al. 2018, 2020a). The evidence supports an integrated mental healthcare ecosystem model, shifting of the center of gravity of services toward a greater proportion of community care (Rosen et al. 2020a).

One important aspect of newly implemented mental health policies in several countries was the integration of mental health into primary care. Cuba was the first to include mental health in primary care as the basis of the new mental health system and to implement this strategy at the national level. The existence of a network of primary care covering the entire population was certainly a factor that greatly facilitated this strategy, but arguably (Caldas de Almeida and Cohen 2008), it would never have been implemented without a detailed mental health plan, making it possible to train professionals, create specific programs, and develop new facilities in the community.

Beyond the relevant issue of expanding coverage, the concept of comprehensive services organized in several steps, from self-care to specialist services (WHO 2003, 2011a), doesn't seem to "get" or convey the real issue of the need to transform cultures and practices. The Global Mental Health Action Plan (WHO 2020) points out four objectives, two of which deserve extra emphasis:

1. To strengthen effective leadership and governance for mental health with a highly consultative interdisciplinary leadership team.
2. To provide comprehensive, integrated, and responsive mental health and social care services in community-based settings and the empowerment of persons with mental disorders and psychosocial disabilities.

Regarding these objectives, the World Health Organization states:

> Community-based service delivery for mental health needs to encompass a recovery-based approach that puts the emphasis on supporting individuals with mental disorders and psychosocial disabilities to achieve their own aspirations and goals," while "more active involvement and support of service users in the reorganization, delivery and evaluation and monitoring of services is required so that care and treatment become more responsive to their needs. Greater collaboration with 'informal' mental health care providers, including families, as well as religious leaders, faith healers, traditional healers, school teachers, police officers, and local nongovernmental organizations, is also needed (WHO 2020).

and sometimes also welfare workers, pharmacists, hairdressers, real estate agents, and helpline workers.

Conclusion

Are we destined to fight the same battles to save community mental health over and over again? For example, although a celebrated global and WHO beacon of mental health reform, the fate of Trieste mental health services and many years of humane Italian reforms again hang in the balance (Frances 2021; Sashidharan 2022), and too many Australian community mental health services have suffered funding diversion and retraction to hospital sites (Rosen et al. 2012b). A shift of the center of gravity of mental health services to community-based care is squarely supported by worldwide evidence and is long overdue in many countries. However, community teams and facilities do not have a high public profile, so they are vulnerable to variable and chronic underfunding and recurrent attempts to dismantle them on the basis of faux economy of scale (Rosen et al. 2010a). Some dismiss community mental health reforms as having a marked ideological component and being extremely dependent on and vulnerable to political shifts (Caldas de Almeida and Cohen 2008). However, inpatient bed-preoccupied institutionally centered services have been defended on the basis of habit, ideology, and political expediency for several centuries (Rosen et al. 2020b).

The WHO has embraced for many years now a clear direction toward a comprehensive mental health service system, where hospital beds should be better located in general hospitals or community residential respite facilities. Long-term institutions were even officially (WHO 2009) considered as the relics of the past. The Global MH Action Plan encompasses some of the principles of the community mental health movement: facilitating an integrated multisectoral and interdisciplinary approach, where those with lived experience and family members become empowered and engaged in co-leadership. Services should actively facilitate both recovery and human rights agendas (Rosen et al. 2012a; Rosen and O'Halloran 2014; Mezzina et al. 2019; Rosen et al. 2020a; WHO Quality Rights 2019b).

Community mental health services have been strengthened and enriched by empowering of individuals with lived experience and their families as advocates and mutual support networks, and the accelerating valuing and inclusion of peer workers in interdisciplinary teams. These networks have now engaged the mental health services sector in the quest to include lived experience leadership and research at every level of the system: teams, services, organizations, and governments (Byrne and Wykes 2020; Jones et al. 2021).

Too many lower- and middle-income countries' mental health systems are still concentrated in postcolonial asylums and other forms of total institutions (Raja et al. 2021). The data in the WHO Mental Health Atlas (WHO 2021) and DESDE Atlas (Salvador-Carulla et al. 2013; Romero-López-Alberca et al. 2019; Rosen et al. 2020a, b) demonstrate that the availability of much evidence-based community components of service for moderate to severe and complex mental illness is still limited to higher-income countries. To complete deinstitutionalization of mental health care (WHO 2021a), we must converge human rights, person-centered, and recovery approaches with comprehensive, strong, accountable, and responsive community-centric services. The centrality of innovative and cost-effective service arrays based in local communities, with in-reach to acute care transitional admissions only as needed, should replace the hospital-centric approaches of the past.

There is a true paradigm shift from a reductionist biological-medical approach to treating mental illness to a model that helps people with mental health problems in their journey of recovery and social inclusion (Mezzina 2005). This entails a mental health care ecosystems approach at both micro and macro levels (Rosen et al. 2020a) facilitating human rights, ensuring freedom, choices, opportunities (Mezzina et al. 2019, Rosen et al. 2012); transcultural awareness, respect, safety and responsiveness; and community alternatives, from entering to leaving the service network (Rosen 2006a, b); while addressing the mental health impacts of warfare, climate change, environmental and economic disasters in small communities to large populations.

Acknowledgments Many thanks to Mr. Paul O'Halloran (Australia), coauthor of the original chapter, who was not able to join us for this revision; Drs. Sashi Sashidharan, David Shiers, Jo Smith Norton, Peter Byrne and Professor Helen Killaspy (UK) for new inputs or ongoing discussions; Dr. Pat Bracken (Ireland); Professor Sir Mason Durie, Drs Andrew Howie, Alister Bush and David Codyre, Ms. Janet Peters, Mr. David Epston and Mr. Hayden Wano (New Zealand); Professors Pat Dudgeon, Luis Salvador-Carulla, Patrick McGorry and Helen Herrman, Drs Louise Byrne, Michael Dudley and Paul Fanning, Mr. Doug Holmes, Mr. Tom Brideson, Ms. Viv Miller (Australia); Drs Nev Jones, David Pollack and Ken Thompson (USA); and Dr. Wes Sowers, USA, for patient editing and encouragement. Also partly updated from Rosen A et al. (2015). International Trends in Community-Oriented MHS, Ch 15, in Mpofu E, ed., Community-Oriented Health Services, New York: Springer, 2015.

References

ACN Cuban News Agency. (2022). Santiago de Cuba reports on 2021 mental health program (8 February 2022). Available www.cubanews.acn.cu/sciences/16360-santiago-de-cuba/ Accessed 09 March 2022.

Adewunmi A (2002). Community psychiatry in Nigeria. *Psychiatric Bulletin*, *26*, 394-395.

AIHW (Australian Institute of Health & Welfare) (2022). Mental Health Services in Australia: Expenditure on mental health-related services, https://www.aihw.gov.au/reports/mental-health-services/mental-health-services-in-australia/report-contents/expenditure-on-mental-health-related-services

Andrews G (2005). Editorial. The crisis in mental health: The chariot needs one horseman. *Medical Journal of Australia*, 182, 372–373.

Aparicio Basauri, V, Sanchez Gutierrez, E. (2002). Psychiatric reform in Spain. *The International Journal of Mental Health*, 31, 14-29.

Aparicio Basauri, V. (2010). Deinstitutionalisation in mental health and primary care in Spain. In Toresini L & Mezzina R (Eds.) *Beyond the Walls. Deinstitutionalisation in the European Best Practices in Mental Health.* Meran: Alpha & Beta: Meran.

Appleton-Dyer, S., Andrews, S. (2018). Fit for the Future: An Evaluation for the Enhanced Integrated Practice Teams, New Zealand: Synergia, Report for Ministry of Health, New Zealand.

Asuni, T. (1967). Aro Hospital in perspective. *American Journal of Psychiatry*, 124, 71-78.

Australian Health Ministers' Advisory Committee (2003). *National Mental Health Plan 2003–2008*. Canberra: Commonwealth of Australia.

Barbui, C., & Saraceno, B. (2015) Closing forensic psychiatric hospitals in Italy: a new revolution begins. *BJPsych*, 206, 445–446. doi: https://doi.org/10.1192/bjp.bp.114.153817

Basaglia, F.O. (2000). *Conferenze Brasiliane* Basaglia, FO, Giannichedda MG (Eds). Milano: Raffaello Cortina Editore.

Bassam, A. A. (2005). An update on mental health services in the West Bank: Community mental health services in the West Bank, Jerusalem. *Isr. J.Psychiatry*, 42, 81–83.

Bennett, D. H. (1985). The changing pattern of mental health care in Trieste. *International, Journal of Mental Health,* 14, 7-92.

Bergstrom, T., Seikkula, J., Alakare, B., et al. (2018). The family-oriented open dialogue approach in the treatment of first-episode psychosis: Nineteen-year outcomes. *Psychiatry Research*, 270, 168 – 175.

Bhugra, D., Tasman, A., Pathare, S., et al. (2017) The WPA-Lancet Psychiatry Commission on the Future of Psychiatry. *Lancet Psychiatry,* 4, 775–818.

Bond, G.R. and Drake, R.E. (2015). The critical ingredients of assertive community treatment. *World Psychiatry*, 14(2), 240-242.

Borgermans, L., Jacob, B., Coture, M., De Bock, P. (2018). Multisectoral Mental Health Networks in Belgium: An example of successful mental health reform through service delivery redesign. WHO, Regional Office for Europe.

Brideson T, Rosen A, (2013). Programme for Aboriginal mental health professionals: An evaluation. Symposium. *The Mental Health Services (TheMHS) Conference of Australia & New Zealand*, August, 2013.

Brunn, M., Kratz, T., Padge, M., Clement, M. C., Smyrl, M. (2021). Why are there so many hospital beds in Germany? *Health Management Services Research*, https://journals.sagepub.com/doi/10.1177/

Burns, T., Priebe, S. (1999). Mental health care failure in England: Myth and reality. *British Journal of Psychiatry*, 174, 191-2.

Byrne, L., Roennfeldt, H., Davidson, L., et. al. (2021). To disclose or not to disclose? Peer workers impact on a culture of self-disclosure for mental health professionals with lived experiences. *Psychological Services*, 19(1), 9-18.

Byrne, L., & Wykes, T. (2020): A role for lived experience mental health leadership in the age of COVID-19. *Journal of Mental Health*, 29(3), 243-246. DOI: https://doi.org/10.1080/09638237.2020.1766002

Byrne, P., & Rosen, A. (eds.) (2014) Early Intervention in Psychiatry*:* EI of nearly everything for better mental health. Oxford: Wiley-Blackwell.

Caldas de Almeida, J. M., Cohen, A., eds (2008), Innovative mental health programs in Latin America & the Caribbean. Washington, DC: Pan American Health Organization.

Care Quality Commission (CQC). (2021). *A new strategy for the changing world of health and social care – CQC's strategy from 2021*. Available https://www.cqc.org.uk/sites/default/files/Our_strategy_from_2021.pdf Accessed 10 April 2022.

Care Quality Commission, (CQC) UK, (2019). *Thematic Reports on Acute & Crisis Services, and Access to Mental Health Care 2019*. Available https://www.cqc.org.uk/publications/themes-care/thematic-review-mental-health-crisis-care https://www.cqc.org.uk/news/stories/cqc-reports-need-better-access-mental-health- care-support

Carmona-Huerta, J et al. (2021). Community mental health care in Mexica: A regional perspective from a mid-income country. *International Journal of Mental Health Services*. 65, 7-11.

Centro de Estudios Legales y Sociales (CELS). (2009). *Derechos Humanos in Argentina: Informe*. Buenos Aires: SigloVeintuino Editores.

Chen, E. Y. H., Chan, S. K.-w., Chang, W.-c., Hui, C. L.-m., Lee, E. H.-m., Lo, T.-l., Chong, C. S.-y., Yeung, W.-s., Ng, R. M.-k., Cheung, E. F.-c., Chung, D. W.-s., & Poon, L. T. (2019). Early intervention for psychosis: Perspective after 15 years of development. In E. Y. H. Chen, A. Ventriglio, & D. Bhugra (Eds.), *Early intervention in psychiatric disorders across cultures* Oxford: Oxford University Press. Pg 87-100. https://doi.org/10.1093/med/9780198820833.003.0008

Chibanda, D., Weiss, H. A., Verhey, R., Simms, V., Munjoma, R., Rusakaniko, S., Chingono, A., Munetsi, E., Bere, T., Manda, E., Abas, M., & Araya, R. (2016). Effect of a primary care-based psychological intervention on symptoms of common mental disorders in Zimbabwe: a randomized clinical trial. *JAMA*, 316, 2618–2626.

Cohen, A. A., Magnezi, R., Weinstein, O. (2020). Review and analysis of mental health reforms in several countries: Implementation, comparison and future challenges. *Ann Psychiatry Treatm*, 4(1), 013-024. DOI: https://doi.org/10.17352/apt.000015

Cohen, H., Natella, G. (1995). *Trabajar en salud mental, la desmanicomilizacion en Rio Negro* [Working on mental health, the deinstitutionalization in Rio Negro]. Buenos Aires: Lugar Editorial. In Spanish.

Corleone F. (2018) *Manicomi Criminali. La rivoluzione aspetta la riforma*, Quaderni del Circolo Rosselli, Pacini Editore, Pisa, n. 1, 141-157.

Craig, T. (1998) Homelessness and mental health. *Psychiatric Bulletin*, 22, 195-197.

Cruz-Arez, G. (2021) From Fragmentation to Integration of MHS: Comparing working in Germany and Mexico, Public Policy in Psychiatry Section Symposium, World Psychiatric Association Congress, Colombia.

Cullen, K., McDaid, D. (2017). Evidence review to inform the parameters for a refresh of A Vision for Change (AVFC). A wide-angle international review of evidence and developments in mental health policy and practice. https://www.gov.ie/en/publication/4664bf-evidence-review-to-inform-the-parameters-for-a-refresh-of-a-vision-f/?referrer=/blog/publications/evidence-review-to-inform-the-parameters-for-a-refresh-of-a-vision-for-change/

Curtis, J., Newall, H. D., Samaras, K, (2012). The heart of the matter: cardiometabolic care in youth with psychosis. Early Intervention in Psychosis Journal. 6(3), 347-353. https://doi.org/10.1111/j.1751-7893.2011.00315.

Dalziel, P., Saunders, C., Saunders, J. (2018). Wellbeing economics: The Capabilities Approach to Prosperity. Palgrave: MacMillan. https://doi.org/10.1007/978-3-319-93194-4

Daly, A., & Craig, S. (2018). HRB Statistics Series 38. Activities of Irish Psychiatric Units and Hospitals 2017 Main Findings. Dublin: Irish Health Research Board.

Daniels, S. "The Borgan Project" Red Voz Pro Salud and mental health in Mexico. Available: https://borgan-project.org/tag/mental-health-in-Mexico. Accessed 17 February, 2022.

De Girolamo, G., Barbato, A., Bracco, R., et al. (2007). Characteristics and activities of acute psychiatric in-patient facilities: National survey in Italy. *British Journal of Psychiatry,* 191, 170–77.

De Girolamo G, Picardi A, Micciol R., et al (2002). Residential care in Italy: national survey of non-hospital facilities. *British Journal of Psychiatry 181*:220–225.

De Leonardis, O., Mauri, D., Rotelli, F. (1986). Deinstitutionalization: a different path. The Italian Mental Health Reform. *Health Promotion*. WHO: Cambridge University Press, 151-165.
Delgado, J. (Ed.) (1991). *A Loucura Na Sala de Jantar*. Sao Paulo.
Dell'Acqua, G., Cogliati Dezza, M. G. (1986). The end of the mental hospital: A review of The psychiatric experience in Trieste. *Acta Psychiatrica Scandinavica*, 316, 45-69.
Dell'Acqua, G., Belviso, D., Crusiz, C., Costantinides, F. (2003). Trieste e il suicidio: un progetto di prevenzione. *Quaderni Italiani di Psichiatria, 22*, 11-23.
Dell'Acqua G (2010). Trieste: History of a transformation. In Toresini L., Mezzina R. (eds) *Beyond The Walls. Deinstitutionalisation in the European Best Practices in Mental Health.* Meran: Alpha & Beta.
Department of Health. (2007). *Mental Health: New Ways of Working for Everyone: Developing and Sustaining a Capable and Flexible Workforce*. London: Department of Health.
Department of Health. (1999). *National Service Framework for Mental Health: Modern Standards and Service Models*. London: Department of Health.
Department of Health. (2009). *New Horizons: A Shared Vision for Mental Health*. London, UK: Department of Health.
Department of Health. (2000). *The NHS Plan-Mental Health*. London: Department of Health.
Department of Health and Aging (2005). *National Mental Health Report 2005. Summary of Ten Years of Reform Under the National Mental Health Strategy 1993–2003*. Canberra: Commonwealth of Australia.
Department of Health and Family Services (2002). *National Practice Standards for the Mental Health Workforce. National Mental Health Strategy.* Canberra: Commonwealth of Australia.
Department of Health, Ireland. (2020). Sharing the Vision: A Mental Health Policy for Everyone, 2020. https://www.gov.ie/en/publication/2e46f-sharing-the-vision-a-mental-health-policy-for-everyone/
Director-General Mental Health. (2016), Annual Report 2016: Māori and the Mental Health Act, New Zealand Government. https://www.health.govt.nz/publication/office-director-mental-health-annual-report-2016
(The) Economist Intelligence Unit, Mental Health and Integration. (2014). A provision for supporting people with mental illness: A comparison of 30 European countries. *The Economist*, suppl. 2014.
Fenton, F. R., Tessier, L., Struening, E. L. (1979). A Comparative Trial of Home and Hospital Psychiatric Care: One-Year Follow-up. *Arch Gen Psychiatry/ JAMA Psychiatr,* 36(10), 1073-1079. doi:https://doi.org/10.1001/archpsyc.1979.01780100043003
Frances, A. (2021). Save Trieste's mental health system. *The Lancet*. Published Online July 14, 2021 https://doi.org/10.1016/S2215-0366(21)00252-2.
George, L, Durbin, J, Koegl, C. (2009). System-wide implementation of ACT in Ontario; An Ongoing improvement effort. *The Journal of Behavioral Health Services and Research*. 36:309-319.
Goldbloom, D., Bradley, L. M. (2012). The Mental Health Commission of Canada: The first five years. *Mental Health Review Journal*, 17(4), 221-228.
Gorry, C. (2013) Community mental health services in Cuba. *MEDICC Review*. 15, 11-14.
Groom, G., Hickie, I., Davenport, T. (2003). *'Out of Hospital, Out of Mind!' A Report Detailing the Mental Health Services in Australia in 2002 and Community Priorities for National Mental Health Policy for 2003–2008.* Canberra: Mental Health Council of Australia.
Hiroto, I., Frank, R. G., Nakatani, Y., Fukuda, Y. (2013). Mental Health Care Reforms in Asia: The Regional Health Care Strategic Plan: The Growing Impact of Mental Disorders in Japan. Psychiatric Services, 4(7), 617-619. Link: https://bit.ly/39rtgYl
Hoult, J., Rosen, J., Reynolds, I. (1984). Community-oriented treatment compared to psychiatric hospital-oriented treatment. *Social Science and Medicine*, 18, 1005-1010.
Human Rights and Equal Opportunity Commission. (2005). *Not for Service: Experiences of Injustice and Despair in Mental Health Care in Australia.* Canberra: Mental Health Council of Australia.
International Mental Health Collaborating Network. (2021). *Big issues identified by Covid 19 requiring a Fundamental Change in Mental Health - A Local and Global Action Following Covid-19.* https://imhcn.org/wp-content/uploads/ActionPlanCoalitionApril2021.pdf
Iris Initiative, UK. (2018). Relapsing and Persistent Psychosis. Available Woodshedding-poster1.pdf (iris-initiative.org.uk). Access 20 April 2022.
Jacob, B., Macquet, D., & Natalis, S. (2016). Mental health care reform in Belgium: Presentation of a model. *L'information psychiatrique*, 92, 731-745.
Jones, N., Atterbury, K., Byrnez, L., Carras, M., Brown, M., Phalen, P. (2021) Lived Experience, Research Leadership, and the Transformation of Mental Health Services: Building a Researcher Pipeline Psychiatric Services in Advance. doi: https://doi.org/10.1176/appi.ps.202000468)
Jorm, A. F., Kitchener, B. A., Reavley, N. J. (2019). Mental Health First Aid training lessons learned from the global spread of a community education program, World Psychiatry, 18, 2, 142-143.
Keet, R., de Vetten-Mc Mahon, M., Shields-Zeeman, L., et al. (2019) Recovery for all in the community: Position paper on principles and key elements of community- based mental healthcare. BMC Psychiatry, 19, 174. https://doi.org/10.1186/s12888-019-2162-z
Kelly, B. (2016). Hearing Voices. *The History of Psychiatry in Ireland.* 2016. Dublin: Irish Academic Press.
Keown, P., Mercer, G., Scott, J. (2008). Retrospective analysis of hospital episode statistics, involuntary admissions under the Mental Health Act 1983, and number of psychiatric beds in England 1996-2006. *BMJ,* 337, 1837.

Killaspy, K., Rosen, A. (2013, 2022). Case management and assertive community treatment. Chapter 15 in Thornicroft, G., Drake, R. E., Gureje, O., Mueser, K. T., Szmukler, G., eds, Oxford: Oxford Textbook of Community Mental Health, 2nd edition: 2013, 3rd edition: in press, 2022.

Lamb, D., Lloyd-Evans, B., Fullarton, K., et al. (2019) Crisis resolution and home treatment in the UK: A survey of model fidelity using a novel review methodology. *International Journal of Mental Health Nursing*. https://doi.org/10.1111/inm.12658

Lancet Global Mental Health Group (2007). Scale up services for mental disorders: a call for action. Global Mental Health Series 6. *Lancet*, 370, 1241–52.

Larrobla, C., & Botega, N. (2001). Restructuring mental health: A South American survey. *Social Psychiatry and Psychiatric Epidemiology*, 36(5), 256-59.

Latimer. E. A., Rabouin, D., et al. (2020). Cost-effectiveness of housing first with assertive community treatment: Results from the Canadian At Home/Chez Soi trial. Psychiatric Services (online), 71(10).

Latimer, E, Nadeu, L. (1998). Cost-effectiveness of assertive community treatment for the seriously Mentally ill in Quebec, Canada. International Society of Technology Assessment in Health Care. In *Annual meeting of the international society of technology assessment in health care*. Montreal, Canada: Quebec Health technology Assessment Council. (Vol 14, pg 97).

Leff, J., Trieman, N., Knapp, M., Hallam, A. (2000). The TAPS Project: A report on 13 years of research, 1985-1998. *Psychiatric Bulletin*, 24, 165-168.

Leff, J., Warner, R. (2006). *Social Inclusion of People with Mental Illness*. Cambridge: University Press.

"Like Minds, Like Mine. (2022) Available http://www.likeminds.org.nz/page/5-Home Accessed 10 April 2022.

López, M. (2004). Alternativas comunitarias ante el estigma y la discriminación. La experiencia de Andalucía (España). *Acta psiquiát psicol Am lat.* 50, 99-109.

Magliano, L., Marasco, C., Fiorillo, A., et al. (2002). The impact of professional and social network support on the burden of families of patients with schizophrenia in Italy. *Acta Psychiatrica Scandinavica*, 106, 291–298.

Malla, M. K., Norman, R. M. G., Joober, R. (2005). First-episode psychosis, early intervention, and outcome: What have we learned? *Canadian Journal of Psychiatry*. 50:881-891.

Marsh, S. (2020). Facing crisis, Cuba calls on citizens to grow more of their own food. Reuters, JUNE 30, 2020, 4:47 AM. https://www.reuters.com/article/us-health-coronavirus-cuba-urban-gardens-idUSKBN2402P1

Martinez-Jambrina, J. J. (2009). The implementation of assertive community treatment in Spain. *European Psychiatry*, 24, (Supplement 1), S1149. Issue S1: 17th EPA Congress - Lisbon, Portugal, Abstract book DOI: https://doi.org/10.1016/S0924-9338(09)71382-3

Mauri, D., and Barcala, A. (2020). From the asylum to community mental health services: The path to human rights. In *From Asylum to Community. Basaglia's International Legacy*, Burns, T., & Foot, J., eds., Oxford: Oxford University Press, 129-145.

McGorry, P. D., Jackson, H. J. (Eds.) (1999). *The Recognition and Management of Early Intervention: A Preventive Approach*. Cambridge: Cambridge UP.

Mental Health Commission of Canada. (2015). *Guidelines for recovery-oriented practice*. Available: https://www.mentalhealthcommission.ca/wp-content/uploads/drupal/MHCC_RecoveryGuidelines_ENG_0.pdf. Accessed 10 April 2022.

Mercier, C. (1990). The evaluation of intervention programs in their natural milieu. *Canadian Journal of Program Evaluation*. 5, 1-16.

Mezzina, R. (2005). Paradigm shift in psychiatry: processes and outcomes. In Ramon, S., Williams, J. E. (Eds.). *Mental Health at the Crossroads. The Promise of Psychosocial Approach*. Aldershot: Ashgate.

Mezzina, R. (2010). Outcomes of deinstitutionalisation in Trieste. In Toresini, L., Mezzina, R. (Eds), *Beyond the walls. Deinstitutionalisation in the European Best Practices in Mental Health*. Meran: Alpha & Beta.

Mezzina, R. (2014). Community mental healthcare in Trieste and beyond. An "open door-no restraint" system of care for recovery and citizenship. *The Journal of Nervous and Mental Disease* 202:440-5.

Mezzina, R. (2016). Creating mental health services without exclusion or restraint but with open doors - Trieste, Italy. La santé mentale en France et dans le monde. *L'Information Psychiatrique*, 92 (9), 747-54.

Mezzina, R. (2018). Forty years of the Law 180: the aspirations of a great reform, its success and continuing need. *Epidemiology and Psychiatric Sciences*, 27, 336–345.

Mezzina, R. (2020). Basaglia after Basaglia: recovery, human rights, and Trieste today. In *From Asylum to Community. Basaglia's International Legacy*, Burns, T., & Foot, J., eds., Oxford: Oxford University Press, 43-67.

Mezzina, R., Johnson, S. (2008). Home Treatment and "Hospitality" within a Comprehensive Community Mental Health Centre. In Johnson, S., Needle, J., Bindman, J. P., Thornicroft, G. (Eds). *Crisis Resolution and Home Treatment in Mental Health*. Cambridge: Cambridge University Press. Ch 20: 251-266.

Mezzina, R., Rosen, A., Amering, M., Javed, A. (2019). The practice of freedom: Human rights and the global mental health agenda. In Javed, A., Fountoulakis, K. N., eds, *Advances in Psychiatry*. New York: Springer International Publishing AG, part of Springer Nature, 483-515. https://doi.org/10.1007/978-3-319-70554-5_30

Mezzina, R., Sashidharan, S. P., Rosen, A., Killaspy, H., Saraceno, B. (2020). Mental health at the age of coronavirus: Time for change. *Social Psychiatry and Psychiatric Epidemiology*, 55, 965-968.

Mezzina, R., Vidoni, D. (1995). Beyond the mental hospital: crisis and continuity of care in Trieste. a four-year follow-up study in a community mental health centre.

The International Journal of Social Psychiatry, 41, 1-20.

Miller, V., Rosen, A., Gianfrancesco, P., Hanlon, P. (2009). Australian national standards for mental health services: A blueprint for improvement. *International Journal of Leadership in Public Services.* 5, 25-42.

Ministero della Salute. (2018) *Rapporto salute mentale. Analisi dei dati del Sistema InformativoperlaSaluteMentale*, https://www.salute.gov.it/imgs/C_17_pubblicazioni_2932_allegato.pdf

Minoff, N, (2015) A socialist vision fades in Cuba's biggest housing project. Washington Post, Dec 29. 2015. https://www.washingtonpost.com/sf/world/2015/12/29/a-socialist-vision-fadesin-cubas-biggest-housing-project/

Minoletti, A. (2016). The reform of mental health services in Chile: 1991- 2015. *L'information psychiatrique*, 92, 761-766. https://doi.org/10.1684/ipe.2016.1549

Minoletti, A, Sepúlveda, R., and Horvitz-Lennon, M. (2012). Twenty Years of Mental Health Policies in Chile. Lessons and Challenges. *The International Journal of Mental Health,* 41, 21–37. DOI: https://doi.org/10.2753/IMH0020-7411410102

Moroz, N., Moroz, I., D'Angelo, M. S. (2020). Mental health services in Canada: Barriers and cost-effective solutions to increase access. *Healthcare Management Forum.* 33, 282-287.

Mueser K T. (2019). Taking Issue: Is more rigorous research on "Open Dialogue" a priority? Psychiatric Services, 70(1), 1-1. https://doi.org/10.1176/appi.ps.70101

Muusse, C., & Van Rojien, S. (2015). *Freedom First. A study of the experience with community-based mental health care in Trieste, Italy, and its significance for the Netherlands.* Trimbos Instituut, Utrecht.

National Institute for Mental Health in England (2004). *Mental Health Workforce Strategy.* London: Department of Health.

National Mental Health Commission. (2014) Contributing lives, thriving communities. National Review of Mental Health Programmes and Services. Canberra: Australian Government.

National Productivity Commission. (2020). Mental Health Inquiry Final Report, Australian Government, Commonwealth of Australia.

New Zealand Government. (2018). He Ara Oranga: Report of the Government Inquiry into Mental Health and Addiction. Wellington, NZ: New Zealand Government.

New Zealand Mental Health Commission (1998). *Blueprint for Mental Health Services in New Zealand: How things need to be.* Wellington: Mental Health Commission, New Zealand Government.

New Zealand Mental Health Commission. (2010). *Statement of Intent 2010–2013.* Wellington: Mental Health Commission: New Zealand Government.

New Zealand Mental Health Commission (2001). *Strategic Plan 2001–2003: Building on the Blueprint.* Wellington: Mental Health Commission, New Zealand Government.

NHS England. (2016). The Five Year Forward View for Mental Health: A report of the independent taskforce to NHS in England. England: The Mental Health Task Force. www.england.nhs.uk/mentalhealth/taskforce.

NHS Long Term Plan. (2019). Mental Health Implementation Plan 2019/20 – 2023/24. https://www.longtermplan.nhs.uk/wp-content/uploads/2019/07/nhs-mental-health-implementation-plan-2019-20-2023-24.pdf.

Nicacio F (Ed.) (1990). *Desinstitucionalizaçao.* Sao Paulo: Hucitec.

O'Hagan, M. (2001). *Recovery competencies for New Zealand mental health workers.* Wellington: Mental Health Commission.

O'Halloran, P., & O'Connor, N. (2015). Time to invest in developing community mental health services. *Australasian Psychiatry: Bulletin of Royal Australian and New Zealand College of Psychiatrists*, 24(3), 268-271.

Palestinian National Authority, Steering Committee on Mental Health. (2004). Plan *on the Organization Of Mental Health Services in the Occupied Palestinian Territory*

Patel, V., & Prince, M. (2010). Global mental health: A new global health field come of age. *Journal of the American Medical Association*, 303(19), 1976-1977.

Peru Ministerio de Salud (2021). *Centros de Salud Mental Comunitaria (CSMC).* Lima: Peru Ministry of Health. www.minsa.gob.pe/salud-mental/. Accessed 11 November 2021.

Plan Nacional de Salud Mental: República Dominicana 2019-2022. (2019). Santo Domingo: Ministerio de Salud Pública; https://repositorio.msp.gob.do/handle/123456789/1660).

Polak, P. R., Kirby, M. W. (1976) A model to replace psychiatric hospitals. Journal of Nervous and Mental Disease. 162. 13-22.

Po-Ying, A, & Chan, K. T. (2010). The social impact of work integration social enterprise in Hong Kong. *International Social Work*, 50, 33. DOI: https://doi.org/10.1177/0020872809348950

Querido, A. (1935). Community mental hygiene in the city of Amsterdam. *Mental Hygiene*, 19, 177-193.

Raja, T., Tuomainen, H., Madan, J., Mistry, D., Jain, S., Easwaran, K., Singh, S. P. (2021). Psychiatric hospital reform in low- and middle-income countries: a systematic review of literature. *Soc Psychiatry Psychiatr Epidemiol.* 56(8), 1341-1357. doi: https://doi.org/10.1007/s00127-021-02075-z. Epub 2021 Apr 21. PMID: 33884439; PMCID: PMC8316186.

Rathbone, J., Zhang, L., Zhang, M. M., et. al. (2007). Chinese herbal medicine for schizophrenia: Cochrane systematic review of randomized trials. *British Journal of Psychiatry,* 190, 379-384.

Rethink Mental Illness & Royal College of Psychiatrists, (2020). In sight and in mind: Making good on the promise of mental health rehabilitation. https://www.rethink.org/media/3571/insightandinmind_rehabreport_rethinkmentalillness_rcpsych_february-2020.pdf

Richmond, D. T. (1983). Richmond report: Inquiry into health services for the psychiatrically ill and developmentally disabled. NSW: Department of Health NSW, Division of Planning Research.

Ridente, G., Mezzina, R. (2016). From residential facilities to supported housing: The personal health budget model as a form of coproduction. *The International Journal of Mental Health,* 45, 1-12.

Riley, A, **A.** (2018). Friendship Bench in Zimbabwe is Starting a Revolution in Mental Health. Available: https://mosaicscience.com/story/friendship-bench-zimbabwe-mental-health-dixon-chibanda-depression. Accessed on 06 April, 2022.

Roelandt, J. (2016). How an innovative citizen psychiatry experiment became a WHO reference center for mental health in the community. *L'information psychiatrique*, 92, 711-717.

Roelandt, J. L. (2010). The East Lille mental health service experience: Citizen psychiatry integrated in the city. In Toresini, L., Mezzina, R. (Eds): *Beyond the Walls Deinstitutionalisation in the European Best Practices in Mental Health.* Meran: Alpha & Beta.

Romero-López-Alberca, C., Gutiérrez-Colosía, M. R., Salinas-Pérez, J. A., et al. (2019). Standardised description of health and social care: A systematic review of use of the ESMS/DESDE (European Service Mapping Schedule/ Description and Evaluation of Services and Directories). Review/Meta-analyses: European Psychiatry. *European Psychiatry,* 61, 97–110.

Rosen, A. (2006a). Australia's national mental health strategy in historical perspective: Beyond the frontier. *International Psychiatry*, 3, 19-21.

Rosen, A, (2012). Mental Health Commissions of Different Sub-species. Can they effectively propagate mental health service reform? Provisional taxonomy and trajectories. Editorial Review. *Mental Health Review Journal,* 17(4), 167-179. https://doi.org/10.1108/13619321211289344

Rosen, A. (2006b). The Australian experience of deinstitutionalization: The effect of Australian culture on the development and reform of its mental health services. *Acta Psychiatrica Scandinavica,* 113, 1–9.

Rosen, A., Beels, C., Beels Newmark, M. (2020c). Is interdisciplinary role models and pastoral mentors helping us find viable pathways to our collective. *International Journal of Narrative Therapy and Community Work.* Dulwich Centre Publications, Issue No.4. www.dulwichcentre.com.au.

Rosen, A., Byrne, P., Goldstone, S., McGorry, P. (2016) Early Intervention for Better Mental Health Services. Chapter 99 in *Psychiatry*, Fourth Edition. Edited by Tasman, A., Kay J., Lieberman, J. A., First, M. B., & Riba, M. B. New York: John Wiley & Sons, Ltd.

Rosen, A., Gill, N. S., Salvador-Carulla L, (2020a). The future of community psychiatry and community mental health services, *Current Opinion in Psychiatry*, 33(4), 375-390, doi: https://doi.org/10.1097/YCO.0000000000000620 https://protect-au.mimecast.com/s/dt8tCL7EwMfRmg5O8IBzGyu?domain=journals.lww.com

Rosen, A., Goldbloom, D., McGeorge, P. (2010b). Mental health commissions: Making the critical difference to the development and reform of mental health services, clinical therapeutics. In Naber, D., Pincus, H. (Eds.). *Current Opinion in Psychiatry*, 6, 593-603.

Rosen, A., Gurr, R., Fanning, P. (2010a). The future of community-centred health services in Australia: Lessons from the mental health sector. *Australian Health Review*, 34, 106–115.

Rosen, A., Gurr, R., Fanning, P., Owen, A. (2012b) The future of community-centred health services in Australia: 'When too many beds are not enough.' *Australian Health Review*, 36, 239–243.

Rosen, A., Killaspy, H., Harvey, C. (2013). Specialisation and marginalisation: how the Assertive Community Treatment debate impacts on individuals with complex mental health needs. *The Psychiatrist*, 37, 345-348.

Rosen, A., McGorry, P., Hickie, I., Groom, G., et al. (2004). Australia needs a mental health commission. *Australasian Psychiatry*, 12, 213–219.

Rosen, A., Mezzina, R., Shiers, D, (2018). Why so few specific recommendations for psychiatry's future? Response to D Bhugra et al, Lancet Psychiatry Commission on the Future of Psychiatry, *Lancet Psychiatr*. 5, 16-17.

Rosen, A., Parker, G., Miller, V. (1995). Area Integrated Mental Health Services (N.S.W.), & AIMHS Quality Assurance and Standards Project. (1995). *AIMHS standards: Area integrated mental health service standards*. Chatswood, N.S.W: Area Integrated Mental Health Services Standards Project.

Rosen, A., O'Halloran, P. (2014) Recovery entails bridging the multiple realms of best practice: Towards a more integrated approach to evidence-based clinical treatment and psychosocial disability for mental health recovery, (Theme paper), *East Asian Archives of Psychiatry*, 24, 104-109.

Rosen, A., O'Halloran, P., Mezzina, R., Thompson, K. (2015). International trends in community oriented mental health services, Ch 15 in Mpofu E, ed, *Community Oriented Health Services: Practices across Disciplines*. New York: Springer.

Rosen, A., Rock, D., Salvador-Carulla, L. (2020b). The Interpretation of Beds: More bedtime stories or maybe they're dreaming? *Australian & New Zealand Journal of Psychiatry,* 54(12), 1154-1156.

Rosen, A., Rosen, T., McGorry, P. (2012a). The Human Rights of People with Severe and Persistent Mental Illness: Can Conflicts between Dominant and Non-Dominant Paradigms be reconciled? in Dudley, M., Silove, D., Gale, F., eds. *Mental Health and Human Rights*, Oxford: Oxford University Press.

Rosen, A., & Sweet, M. (2016). Turnbull government warned that cuts to youth mental health services are "a national tragedy in the making." *Croakley Health Media*. https://www.croakey.org/turnbull-government-warned-that-cuts-to-youth-mental-health-services-are-a-national-tragedy-in-the-making/ Accessed 09 April 2022.

Rosen, A., Walter, G., Hocking, B., Casey, D., et al. (2000). Combating psychiatric stigma: An overview of contemporary initiatives. *Australasian Psychiatry*, 8, 19–26.

Rosenberg, S. (2010). Why the new national mental health service standards are an opportunity lost. https://blogs.crikey.com.au/croakey/2010/11/01/why-%20the-new-national-mental-health-service-standards-are-an-opportunity-lost/

Rosenberg, S., Rosen, A, (2012a). It's raining mental health commissions – prospects and pitfalls in driving mental health reform. *Australasian Psychiatry*, 20(1), 85-90.

Rosenberg, S., Rosen, A, (2012b). Can mental health commissions really drive reform? Towards better resourcing, services, accountability and stakeholder engagement, *Australasian Psychiatry*, 20(3), 193-8.

Rotelli, F. (1988). Changing Psychiatric Services in Italy. In Ramon S., Giannichedda, M.G. (Eds.) *Psychiatry in Transition. The British and Italian Experiences.* London: Pluto Press, 182-190.

Royal Commission into Victoria's Mental Health System (2021). Melbourne: State of Victoria. www.rcvmhs.vic.giv.au/ Accessed 04 April 2022.

Salvador-Carulla, L., Alvarez-Gálvez, J., Romero, C., Gutiérrez-Colosía, M. R., Weber, G., et al. (2013). Evaluation of an integrated system for classification, assessment and comparison of services for long-term care in Europe: the eDESDE-LTC study.

Salvador-Carulla, L., Costa-Font, J., Cabases, J., McDaid, D., Alonso, J. (2010). Evaluating Mental Health Care and Policy in Spain. *J Ment Health Policy Econ,* 13, 73-86.

Sashidharan, S. P. (2022). Why Trieste Matters. Editorial. *BJ*, 220, 52-53. doi: https://doi.org/10.1192/bjp.2021.149

Sashidharan, S., Mezzina, R., & Puras, D. (2019a). Reducing coercion in mental healthcare. *Epidemiology and Psychiatric Sciences*, 28(6), 605-612. doi:https://doi.org/10.1017/S2045796019000350

Sashidharan, S. P., Mezzina, R., Saraceno, B., Rosen, A., Davidson, L., Frances, A, Kendall, T. (2019b). Franco Basaglia's impact on Anglophone psychiatry: A response to Burns T, Essay: Franco Basaglia: a revolutionary reformer ignored in Anglophone psychiatry, *Lancet Psychiatry*, 62, 95-96.

Sashidharan, SP, White R, Mezzina R, Jansen S, Gishoma D. (2016). Global mental health in high-income countries. *Br J Psychiatry,* 209(1), 3-5. doi: https://doi.org/10.1192/bjp.bp.115.179556. PMID: 27369474.

Saxena, S., Lora, A., Morris, J., et al. (2011). Mental health services in 42 low- and middle-income countries: a WHO-AIMS cross-national analysis. *Psychiatric Services*, 62(2), 123-125.

Schizophrenia Commission Report. (2012). *The Abandoned Illness: A Report from the Schizophrenia Commission.* London: Rethink Mental Illness.

Shiers, D., Rosen, A., Shiers, A. (2009). Beyond early intervention: can we adopt alternative narratives like 'Woodshedding' as pathways to recovery in schizophrenia? *Early Intervention in Psychiatry*, 3, 163-171.

Shiers, D., Smith, J., (2014) Early intervention and the power of social movements: UK development of early intervention in psychosis as a social movement and its implications for leadership, in Byrne, P., & Rosen, A, *Early Intervention in Psychiatry: EI of Nearly Everything*, Oxford: Wiley Blackwell.

Starace & Baccari, F. (eds). (2018). Quaderno 4 SIEP – La salute mentale in Italia. Analisi dei trend 2015-2017. https://siep.it/wp-content/uploads/2019/10/QEP_volume-4_def.pdf

Stein, L. I., & Test, M. A. (1980). Alternatives to mental hospital treatment. I. Conceptual Model, treatment programs, and clinical evaluation. *Archives of General Psychiatry*, 37, 392-397.

Teesson, M., Rosen, A., Miller, V. (2021). Australian National Workforce Institute for Mental Health [ANWIMH] Initiative, Commonwealth of Australia Parliament, House of Representatives Select Committee on Mental Health & Suicide Prevention, Submission, Testimony, and Supplementary Report in Hansard, High Priority Recommendation No.10, Final Report, October 2021.

Thara, R., Padmavati, R., Aynkran, J. R., John, S. (2008). Community mental health in India: A rethink. *International Journal of Mental Health Systems*, **2,** 11. doi:https://doi.org/10.1186/1752-4458-2-11.

Thornicroft, G., Tansella, M. (2013). The balanced care model: the case for both hospital-and community-based mental healthcare. *Br J Psychiatry*. 202, 246 – 248.

Topor, A. (2020) Deinstitutionalization, the welfare state, and social engineering: Basaglia in the Swedish context. In *From Asylum to Community. Basaglia's International Legacy*, Burns, T., & Foot, J., eds., Oxford: Oxford University Press, 333-345

Torrey, E. F., Bigelow, D. A., Sladen-Drew, N. (1993). Quality and cost of services for seriously mentally ill in British Columbia and the United States. *Hospital and Community Psychiatry*, 44, 943-950.

Tykanori, R. (2011). Closing the mental health gap in Brazil-2011. Mental Health Coordination, Ministry of Health, Brazil. Geneva: WHO mhGAP Programme,

United Nations. (2020). *United Nations Policy Brief: Covid-19 and the Need for Action on Mental Health.* https://www.un.org/sites/un2.un.org/files/un_policy_brief_covid_and_mental_health_final.pdf.

Van Spijker, B. A., Salinas-Perez, J. A., Mendoza, J., Bell, T., Bagheri, N., Furst, M. A., Reynolds, J., Rock, D., Harvey, A., Rosen, A., Salvador-Carulla, L. (2019). Service availability and capacity in rural mental health in Australia: Analysing gaps using an Integrated Mental Health Atlas. *Aust New Zeal J Psychiatry*, 28, 1–13. https://doi.org/10.1177/000486741985780

Venturini, E., Brandao Goulart, M. S., Amarante, P. (2020) The optimism of practice. The impact of Basaglia's thoughts on Brazil. In *From Asylum to Community.*

Basaglia's International Legacy, Burns, T., & Foot, J., eds., Oxford: Oxford University Press, 113-128

Wasylenki, D. A., et al. (1985). Impact of a case manager program on psychiatric aftercare. *The Journal of Nervous and Mental Disease,* 173, 303-308.

Wasylenki, D. A, et al. (1993). The hostel outreach program: Assertive case management for homeless mentally ill persons. Clark Institute of Psychiatry, Toronto, Ontario, Canada. *Hospital and Community Psychiatry,* 44, 848-853.

Waters, E., Ong, B., Mikes-Liu, K., McCloughen, A., Rosen, A., Mayers, S., Sidis, A., Dawson, L., Buus, N. (2021). Open Dialogue, need-adapted mental health care, and implementation fidelity: A discussion paper, *International Journal of Mental Health Nursing,* 30, 805–813. doi: https://doi.org/10.1111/inm.12866

Whiteford, H., Buckingham, W. J. (2005). Ten years of mental health service reform in Australia: Are we getting it right? *Medical Journal of Australia, 182,* 396–400.

Whitley, R., Shepherd, G., Slade, M. (2019). Recovery colleges as a mental health innovation. *World Psychiatry,* 182),141-142. DOI:https://doi.org/10.1002/wps.20620.

World Health Organization-AIMS. (2006). *Report on Mental Health System in West Bank And Gaza.* West Bank and Gaza: WHO and Ministry of Health, Palestinian National Authority.

World Health Organization. (2009). Approaching *Mental Health Care Reform Regionally:The Mental Health Project for South-eastern Europe (SEE). Copenhagen, Denmark:* WHO Regional Office for Europe.

World Health Organization (2020). Comprehensive Mental Health Action Plan (2013-2030). https://www.who.int/initiatives/mental-health-action-plan-2013-2030.

World Health Organization, (2021a). *Guidance and technical packages on community mental health services: Promoting person-centred and rights-based approaches.* https://www.who.int/publications/i/item/guidance-and-technical packages-on-community-mental-health-services

World Health Organization. (2003). Investing in mental health. World Health Organization. https://apps.who.int/iris/handle/10665/42823

World Health Organization. Mental Health Atlas 2020 (2021) https://www.who.int/publications/i/item/9789240036703.

World Health Organization. (2016). mhGAP Intervention Guide for Mental, Neurological and Substance Use Disorders in Non-Specialized Health Settings: Mental Health Gap Action Programme (mhGAP): Version 2.0. Geneva: World Health Organization.

World Health Organization. (2019a). mhGAP Intervention Guide - Version 2.0 for mental, neurological and substance use disorders in non-specialized health settings, https://www.who.int/publications/i/item/9789241549790

World Health Organization (2019b) Quality Rights materials for training, guidance and Transformation. Geneva: WHO.

World Health Organization. (2004a). *Report on a Joint Council of Europe/WHO Meeting in The Framework of The Stability Pact Initiative for Social Cohesion.* Zagreb, Croatia: WHO.

World Health Organization. (2001). *Stop exclusion – Dare to care.* World Health Day 2001. Department of Mental Health and Substance Abuse, Geneva: WHO. WHO/NMH/MSD/WHD/00.2.

World Health Organization. (2011a). The Optimal Mix of Services for Mental Health. WHO Pyramid Framework. Geneva: World Health Organization.

World Health Organization. (2011b). *WHO Report on mental health systems in the Caribbean region.* Geneva: WHO.

World Health Organization. (2004b). World Mental Health Survey. Prevalence, severity, and unmet need for treatment of mental disorders in the World Health Organization World Mental Health Surveys. *JAMA,* 291, 2581–2590. doi: https://doi.org/10.1001/jama.291.21.2581

Xiong, W., Phillips, M. R., Wang, R., Dai, Q., et al (1996). Family-based intervention for schizophrenic patients in China: A randomised controlled trial. *British Journal of Psychiatry,* 165, 239-247.

Community Psychiatry: Past, Present, and Future

Wesley E. Sowers, Hunter L. McQuistion, Jules M. Ranz, Jacqueline Maus Feldman, and Patrick S. Runnels

Introduction

With the final chapter of this book, we hope to use many of the concepts developed in its chapters to construct a concise and coherent vision of what community psychiatry is and what it can be. In this construction, the pillars of community psychiatry will be revisited along with the historical roots of the systems that have been in place in recent times. Against this backdrop, the elements of our major systems of care can be evaluated regarding their effectiveness in meeting the needs of individuals and communities. An environmental analysis, assessing both the strengths and weaknesses of community psychiatry as a discipline, as well as the threats and opportunities that it must prepare for, will be provided. In conclusion, we will consider the strategies that may be useful in meeting the challenges that lie ahead and that must be confronted if our vision for community psychiatry is to become reality.

W. E. Sowers (✉)
University of Pittsburgh Medical Center, Pittsburgh, PA, USA
e-mail: sowerswe@upmc.edu

H. L. McQuistion
New York University Grossman School of Medicine | NYU Langone Health, New York, NY, USA
e-mail: hmcquist@chpnet.org

J. M. Ranz
Columbia University, Vagelos College of Physicians and Surgeons, New York, NY, USA
e-mail: Jmr1@cumc.columbia.edu

J. M. Feldman
University of Alabama at Birmingham, Gravois Mills, MO, USA
e-mail: jfeldman@uabmc.edu

P. S. Runnels
Department of Psychiatry, Case Western Reserve School of Medicine, Shaker Heights, OH, USA
e-mail: patrick.runnels1@UHospitals.org

Historical Factors: Past to Present

Culture

While American society is extremely diverse and it would be simplistic to suggest a monolithic view of mental health that penetrates the many subcultures that make it up, there are many beliefs and attitudes that have been pervasive at any point in time. These pervasive attitudes and beliefs have been quite variable over time and have had significant influence on the treatment and policies related to those with mental illnesses and/or substance use disorders. They are evident in the representation of people with MI in theater, cinema, and literature, as well as in the structures created in reaction to their presence. Mental illnesses have for the most part been considered quite differently from other health problems as there has usually been a degree of shame associated with all types of emotional disturbances.

W. E. Sowers et al. (eds.), *Textbook of Community Psychiatry*,
https://doi.org/10.1007/978-3-031-10239-4_63

The prevailing reaction of the states toward people with MI in the nineteenth century was to remove these individuals from mainstream society. The era of the asylums, which began with an emphasis on "moral treatment" (with some similarities to what we now term recovery-oriented care), devolved by the early twentieth century into an isolative, custodial model as institutions became overcrowded and unable to treat large numbers of the old and infirm for which they were not designed (Thompson 1994). As financial pressures grew and new treatment modalities became available that allowed the release of many patients from state hospitals by the mid-century, communities were not well prepared to receive them and were slow to develop adequate services to meet their needs. As a result, many of these patients ran into legal trouble, became homeless, or involved with substance use, causing further stigmatization and discrimination from an unwelcoming public. The shame associated with substance use spawned the Alcoholics Anonymous movement, which discouraged public disclosure from, and identification of, individuals with addictions (White 1998). Confidentiality laws were developed in response to the discrimination suffered by people with all kinds of emotional disturbances.

Attitudes toward people with MI have shifted gradually in the latter part of the twentieth century and into the early part of the twenty-first century. The recovery movement has asserted the rights of people with mental illnesses and their ability to regain capacity to make positive contributions to society and the economy. More people, including those who work in the mental health and substance use fields, have been comfortable coming "out" with their identity as people who have suffered with MI or SU. Nonetheless, there remains significant stigma associated with these conditions and overt and subtle forms of discrimination still persist (Feldman 2012).

Costs of Care

The costs of providing care for people with emotional disturbances have traditionally resided with families first, and when they have been unable or unwilling to provide the needed care, local and state governments have had to bear the cost. People with these disorders were often met with cruel or punitive measures to control them and found few opportunities to improve their condition. The establishment of state mental hospitals in the latter part of the nineteenth century following the crusade of Dorthea Dix shifted the burden of paying for care directly to the states. Conditions were quite variable from hospital to hospital and state to state, but the costs of maintaining these institutions grew as greater numbers of people were admitted, many of whom were demented or had other forms of cognitive decay. States became anxious to find other sources to pay for the care of this population (Thompson 1994).

This relief finally came from the federal government, which had for a long time refused to accept responsibility for paying for the care of people with MI. The Community Mental Health Centers Act of 1963 made federal money available to catchment areas established across the country to build mental health centers, which would provide services in the community rather than in hospitals. The establishment of Medicare and Medicaid in 1965 provided a further source of revenue to these catchment areas via the Federal Medical Assistance Percentage. It incentivized states to decrease the census of their state hospitals since this funding was not applicable to services provided there. This "deinstitutionalization" gradually compelled states to develop more comprehensive community services to extend the tenure of people with mental illness in homes in the community, rather than having them become homeless or ending up in the penal system where the states would again bear the full burden of expense for their care (Sastry 2021; Everett et al. 2012).

In the latter part of the twentieth century, there was growing dissatisfaction at the federal and state levels with the global funding arrangements within the catchment areas. The perception was that there was a lack of accountability for how this money was used, and that people with severe mental illnesses were not getting their needs met.

This dissatisfaction led to a transition of community mental health (CMHC) funding from federal grants to fee for service (FFS) payments from Medicaid in which narrowly defined service elements were reimbursed for each instance they were provided. In addition, recipients were longer restricted to the CMHCs of their catchment area, ostensibly creating competition between providers. These changes provided greater accountability, but it severely limited flexibility and creativity from the CMHCs (Shoyinka 2021). These FFS arrangements have been predominant through the early part of the twenty-first century and have forced CMHCs to focus on billable services and to require high volumes of patient contact from those professionals (particularly psychiatrists) that generate revenue. Since demands have been greater than the supply of services, competition has done little to improve the satisfaction of service users (Sowers 2020; Everett et al. 2012).

The rising costs of care also became a particular concern during this period. By the 1980s, cost management started to become a priority for many states, as it was with private sector insurers. They began to transfer their risk (and costs) to private resource management companies who stood to profit by limiting care and services. These arrangements often had disastrous results with regard to the quality of care and the treatment opportunities available for people with severe mental illnesses and/or substance use disorders. Flexibility and creativity for the CMHCs were further limited by these upheavals, and this often made it difficult to sustain the evidence-based practices (EBPs) established through grant funding when those funds expired during the latter part of the twentieth century. Administrative silos have created distinct funding streams for particular types of services, making the integration of care for people with co-occurring illnesses (mental health, substance use, physical health) more difficult (Everett et al. 2012). Since the 2010s, there have been attempts to reign in some of the excesses of cost containment. There has been increased experimentation with alternative funding mechanisms that encourage innovation and flexibility while maintaining accountability to established outcome measures. Placing greater risk in the hands of providers creates incentives for them to contain costs while pursuing these outcomes. The survival of these arrangements will depend to some degree on the evolution to the healthcare system in the years ahead (Shoyinka 2021; Mauri et al. 2017).

Demographics

Although the USA is one of the wealthiest countries in the world, that wealth has always been unevenly distributed between the rich and poor. While its constitution promises liberty and equality, exploitation and oppression have plagued this nation, as it has many others, throughout its history. It is a nation of immigrants, often described as a great melting pot, but new arrivals have been variably welcomed and have often suffered derision and abuse for many years before assimilation and acceptance into a mainstream society. Many ethnic or racial groups (primarily people of color) have long been, and remain, part of an underclass that is structurally maintained and deprived of equal opportunity and protection by the plutocracy. Economic and political forces have long played a significant role in determining the complexion of this diverse and segregated society.

The past half century has brought measurable contraction in the middle class, especially in its purchasing power, with a now well-known widening gap between the rich and the mass of families struggling to support themselves (Pew Research Center 2018). The pandemic of 2020 made the consequences of these disparities painfully obvious. Unmet basic needs (food, shelter, income) have a significant impact on emotional health and increase the incidence of Adverse Childhood Experiences (ACEs) and victimization. The sequelae of trauma, discrimination, and persecution have led to significant disparities in health, wealth, and quality of life between the privileged members of society and a growing underclass (Rodenbach 2021; Picket and Wilkinson 2007). This underclass has found it increasingly difficult to succeed in an economically divided society and often suffer from illnesses that are sometimes referred to as "diseases of despair" (i.e., violence, suicide, substance use, crime, apathy, chronic anger).

Social structures have further entrenched these disparities by limiting opportunities and creating barriers to the successful engagement in the legitimate economy. Rates of incarceration in the USA are among the highest in the world and disproportionately impact people of color and impoverished communities (Mauer 2011). The ramifications of this circumstance extend far beyond the damage to an individual's life, however devastating that might be. It affects their families, communities, public safety, emotional health, and financial security. The resources available for education, and by extension its quality, are determined locally and based on tax revenues. Those revenues are decidedly lower in impoverished communities, limiting opportunities for higher education and access to well-paying jobs. Underemployment and hopelessness are common in these circumstances, and participation in alternative illegal economies appears to be the only means of escape to many. Once again, people of color and impoverished families are most severely affected. Access to health care, healthy foods, transportation, legal resources, and healthy recreational activities are all adversely affected in distressed communities (Picket and Wilkinson 2009).

These demographic shifts have created increased demand for services in publicly financed mental health facilities. One of the tenets of community psychiatry has always been the recognition that social justice equates with social health. It follows that treatment and empowerment of underserved populations and communities are part of what is needed to achieve greater balance. Public psychiatry began in state institutions, but as people were moved out of these hospitals and into the community, new venues and modalities of care were needed. The subspecialty of community psychiatry emerged from this. Through the work of psychiatrists in mental health centers, jails, and prisons, substance use treatment programs, homeless shelters, and in the streets, an identity was created. Community psychiatry may be considered a primary care specialty, but its emphasis on community health, prevention, empowerment, and advocacy creates a more complex profile and sets it apart from that simple formulation. These elements are essential aspects of establishing a social order that respects the rights and meets the needs of all members of the larger community.

Politics

The demographic shifts discussed above are obviously related to political determinants that have overridden the constitutional intentions of the US republic. Even as the words of the Constitution and the Bill or Rights were being written, large portions of the population were excluded from its protections and from participation in political processes. Putting aside these deliberate transgressions, the two-party system and the assertion of states rights in the federation have been the source of conflicting interests and great antagonisms. The stalemates resulting from partisan squabbles have made it difficult to pass needed legislation and take advantage of opportunities to find non-partisan solutions to urgent problems. While this has been markedly limiting in the early part of this century, it has plagued American politics of most eras.

The veto by President Pierce of legislation that would have established a role for federal governments financing of mental health care in 1854 and the Mental Health Centers Act of 1963, which did the opposite over 100 years later, is one example of the shifting winds of politics and how they affect mental health care (Feldman 2012). The availability of resources to treat mental illness and substance use disorders has been a very small part of the healthcare budget, despite evidence that it is one the major sources of disability. The Federal Medical Assistance Percentage (FMAP) is the degree to which the federal government contributes to a state's Medicaid expenses. These matches have been available for 75 years with the intention of equalizing the quality of care across state borders. Despite the greater contributions in federal matching funds to poorer states, large disparities remain in per capita spending for Medicaid and behavioral health services from state to state. Fragmentation in the administration and financing of various service sectors has resulted in competition for resources and the formation of discreet funding streams that interfere with attempts to integrate care for the large number of people with coexisting and chronic health problems (Everett et al. 2012).

Although it appears that we have come a long way from the days when people with mental illness were imprisoned and shackled, US prisons and jails have become the most common receptacle for people with mental illness and substance use (Pinals 2017). Many of those inmates are victims of severe mental illness, substance use, and the "diseases of despair." The incarceration of these individuals only exacerbated these conditions and placed many in a seemingly endless cycle of homelessness, hospitalization, and incarceration (Dvoskin et al. 2017). As noted earlier, this has had a significant impact on the communities from which they come. The "War on Drugs," waged throughout most of the latter twentieth century, has actually been a war on the people that use them and has been a major contributor to the swollen prison population. At the same time, it did little to ebb the flow of illegal substances into US communities. Little was done to reduce the harm caused by substances until they touched more affluent members of society. It has only been since the 2010s that the fallacy of punitive solutions to social problems has become more widely recognized and politicians on both ends of the political spectrum have sought penal reform and harm reduction strategies. Although adequate resources are not yet available to meet the demand for treatment, there is now greater recognition in political circles of its advantages over punishment.

Unlike most developed countries, the USA has allowed market forces and for-profit business interests to be the major drivers of the structure and priorities of the healthcare system. This has been increasingly responsible for the poor outcomes and high costs of services in the USA. Corporate interests have always had significant influence in American politics, but their influence has grown steadily over the years since the rapid industrialization of the Gilded Age in the late nineteenth century. Politicians have been beholden to corporate donations for their election and reelection, and this has made it very difficult to reform health care so it is less costly and more responsive to the needs of the population. Both public and private payers have often limited coverage of mental health and substance use disorders with the dubious belief that this will minimize their expenses. The Mental Health Parity ACT of 2007 attempted to equalize coverage for behavioral health (BH) care with respect to physical health coverage, but change has come about slowly as health plans have resisted full parity and enforcement has been difficult. Restrictive medical necessity criteria used by managed care organizations have maintained these disparities, but recent lawsuits and additional legislation in many jurisdictions have begun to unravel the web of obstacles to the access to comprehensive BH services (Wit v. UBH 2019).

Science

Unlike most other diseases, the pathophysiology of emotional health problems has remained obscure throughout medical history. Through most of its existence as an identified medical specialty in the nineteenth century until the middle of the twentieth century, there were very few proven treatments that fit into a biologic model of mental illness. Despite this, many crude physical treatments were devised and carried out, mostly serving to subdue and control people with emotional disturbances. Prefrontal lobotomies, ice baths, and insulin shock are a few examples of this.

During this same period, the development of humanistic and intellectual therapies was developed based on theories of the "mind" rather than the "brain." Although these approaches struggled to produce evidence for their effectiveness and had limited application for people with more severe mental illnesses, they had great appeal to well-educated and affluent elements of society. These two paradigms divided the psychiatric community, and their relative dominance varied much like how a pendulum swings over this period.

While this dialectic continues into the present era, significant changes occurred beginning in the second half of the twentieth century that changed the content of the discussion. One was the advance of psychotherapy research, which was shown to be effective for certain clinical syndromes. At the same time, ongoing elucidation of the neurophysiology of the brain, the biologic aspects of human behavior became more compelling. The resulting development of pharmacologic agents, which to varying degrees mitigated the symptoms of emotional disturbances, further contributed to the legitimization of biologic treatments and a decided swing of the pendulum back in the direction of a "medical model" for mental illness. Combined with the high cost of psychiatric services compared to those of other mental professionals, this shift has resulted in psychiatry taking a more limited role, focusing mostly on medication management, with less training in and fewer opportunities to engage in various psychotherapies and especially psychosocial treatments.

Despite this shift, it was during this same period that community psychiatry solidified its identity with the establishment of CMHCs, community funding by localities, and especially Medicaid to support community-based treatment. This development brought with it greater recognition of environmental influences on emotional health, the interaction of co-occurring illnesses, the development of psychosocial rehabilitation, and an increased emphasis on the emotional health of communities and prevention. Community psychiatrists did not eschew treatment with medication but rather saw it as one element of more comprehensive service planning. Engel (1980) articulated this holistic approach as the biopsychosocial model of the determinants of mental illnesses. In partnership with those in recovery from mental illnesses and substance use, a recovery-oriented paradigm for clinical care evolved that emphasized hope, collaboration, and affiliation. This approach was codified in the President's New Freedom Commission Report in 2003 (Hogan 2003) and in the SAMHSA Recovery to Practice initiative that was funded from 2008 to 2016 (AACP/APA 2012).

During this same period, EBPs in community psychiatry have expanded greatly. Services research has been the basic science of community psychiatry, and many non-pharmacologic EBPs have been identified. The limitations of biologic treatment in alleviating the symptoms related to emotional disturbances arising from social determinants of mental health such as poverty, discrimination, and social disruption have become evident, and the simplification of unnecessary polypharmacy and assistance with medication discontinuation has become an integral part of community psychiatric practice.

Professional Identity

Psychiatry had its origins as a specialty with the formation in 1844 of The Association of Medical Superintendents of American Institutions for the Insane in Philadelphia. Many of these facilities provided "Moral Treatment," in which clients were treated with kindness and encouraged to engage in productive and social activities. Despite this promising start, the profession and the treatment it provided diverged considerably from this beginning for more than 100 years. Many psychiatrists continued to work in state hospital settings during this period, but treatment moved steadily toward control and custodial care. It was not until the latter part of the twentieth century that humanistic, recovery-oriented services (ROS) once again became a prominent aspect of community psychiatry (Sastry 2021; Amadeo 2018).

The establishment of CMHCs in the late 1960s created a new venue for psychiatric treatment and the opportunity to develop creative approaches to meeting the needs of people with severe mental illness. Group therapies, family therapy, and the development of supportive services grew out of this new environment. It also brought psychiatrists working in these settings into closer contact with the communities in which they served, and with that, a greater awareness of the environmental factors, such as poverty, violence, and racism, that had an impact on emotional health. These developments took place in the context of social disruption related to the civil rights movement, the unrest related to the Viet Nam War, and the expansion of a drug culture in neglected communities. This experience was the backdrop for the incorporation of social justice and a public health emphasis into the mindset of the psychiatrists working in these settings.

Psychiatrists played a prominent role in the leadership and administration of community mental health centers at their inception. By the 1980s however, reduced funding, lack of adequate training for those roles, and the need to maximize billing in FFS systems forced many psychiatrists out of those roles. These changes were the impetus for the formation of the American Association of Community Mental Health Center Psychiatrists in 1985, later becoming the American Association of Community Psychiatrists in 1987, and more recently the American Association for Community Psychiatry (AACP) in 2019. These name changes reflect the evolving focus of the organization. While the initial formation revolved around defining the leadership role of community psychiatrists, the organization quickly moved toward an emphasis on serving underserved populations and disrupted communities and currently on its collaboration with other stakeholders in delivering psychiatric care. The AACP developed a series of clinical tools, service guidelines, and position statements regarding systems of care that brought this subspecialty recognition, even though only a small percentage of community psychiatrists actually became members.

The systems in which community psychiatrists worked were far from ideal. In most cases, resources were scarce, and it was no easy task to obtain all of the services that were required to get people on the road to good health. Clearly, beyond the clinical interventions that were deployed to address emotional health issues, it was also necessary to advocate for both individual clients and system changes in the face of political, social, and cultural barriers. Although advocacy activities were not necessarily part of mainstream psychiatric identity, it has been a hallmark of community practitioners as they work with the members of society who have the greatest need. The AACP and several other national and local organizations have often joined together to promote needed changes in systems of care.

These influences coalesced to create an identity unique to community psychiatrists, consisting of:

- A relationship-centered, recovery-oriented approach to clinical care
- An emphasis on prevention, health promotion, and community health
- Advocacy for social justice and equal opportunity
- A focus on comprehensive integrated systems of care
- Provision of leadership and interdisciplinary, interagency, and community collaboration

In the early part of the twenty-first century, interest in community psychiatry has grown rapidly. In 2007, there were two advanced training programs in public and community psychiatry, but by 2022, there were 26, training over 60 psychiatrists annually to work in community service settings. In 2010, the AACP began offering a certification examination to eligible community psychiatrists. The need for psychiatrists in community settings far exceeds the supply, and greater numbers of psychiatrists are spending at least part of their time in these community settings, even if they do not actively identify as community psychiatrists or embrace all of its principles. Community psychiatry may be variably defined, but its principles would serve all of psychiatry well. It is a primary care psychiatry, which calls its members to be proficient in a variety of ways, to meet the needs of the communities they serve.

A Vision for the Future of Community Mental Health and Psychiatry

Throughout this book, the basic building blocks of community psychiatry have been laid out and applied to the construction of a comprehensive vision of community mental health. This section will attempt to offer a coherent and concise overview of that vision and its relationship to psychiatry in general and health care overall.

Clinical Care

Providing clinical care to underserved populations has been the hallmark of community psychiatry throughout its evolution. With the development of psychiatric rehabilitation and recovery-oriented services, collaborative and empowering relationships became a dominant part of the clinical approach, with motivational interviewing incorporated as a framework for achieving them. Continuing to move clients out of custodial and restrictive circumstances and putting them on track to achieve their full potential will continue to be a priority. Facilitation of autonomy, hope, and affiliation will provide a pathway to meaningful and fulfilling lives. A holistic view of individual health must include the capacity to address physical health issues as well as those of emotional health and to draw the lines that will allow clients to connect them.

Systems of Care

Clinical care can only be as good as the systems in which it is delivered. The service system must evolve in a manner that assures that a comprehensive service plan can be delivered. A comprehensive array of services must be available that allow these service plans to be customized to individual needs. This will include the ability to provide adequate shelter, nourishment, and resources that allow all individuals to access needed services and live safely. The efficient use of resources, eliminating administrative waste, judicious use of expensive interventions, and value conscious prescribing will help offset some of the expense of expanded services.

The financing of services must be realigned to provide incentives for provider organizations to offer high-quality care as their prime goal, while exploiting available funding to achieve it as best as fiscal realities can absolutely tolerate, and doing so without excessive administrative oversight. This realignment will encourage innovation and allow providers to design the services that best meet the client's and community's needs. Integration of financing for mental health, physical health, and substance use services will help assure that every entryway is the right one and that all people in need will be welcomed. Such value-based reimbursement arrangements that eliminate the cumbersome and inefficient fee for service funding should prevail.

Training of professionals entering the field, as well as those who have worked in the trenches for many years, must incorporate the principles and skills that help define community psychiatry. Early career psychiatrists and trainees must have access to supervision and mentors that can prepare them to practice effectively in the community and allow them to work collaboratively with other members of the healthcare team. Opportunities for transdisciplinary training will be an essential aspect of new training initiatives.

Prevention and Community Health

A complete vision for community mental health cannot be realized without an emphasis on prevention and its relationship to overall community health. Primordial prevention will include the local economy and jobs, the status of human rights, housing stock, broad social welfare policy, and universal environmental engineering to assure that communities are safe (i.e., free of toxins and violence) and allow residents to access the resources (i.e., nutritious food and housing) and services that they need. They are augmented by primary prevention efforts such as aspects of basic primary care, nutrition, and broad psychoeducational interventions. These efforts will reduce exposure to adverse childhood experiences (ACEs) and diseases of despair. Associated stress reduction will mitigate the manifestations of illness experienced by those with severe mental illnesses. The reduction in the incidence of illness will also allow systems to meet the needs of individuals who do become ill more effectively.

Healthy communities provide significant supports to their residents in the form of social and recreational activities, youth programs, religious affiliations, advocacy activities, and assistance to those in need. Bringing resources and professionals experienced in community organization to distressed communities will reduce the detrimental health effects their residents experience. Enhancing education and employment opportunities will also strengthen the community's capacity to thrive.

Community psychiatrists and other behavioral health clinicians may not have a direct role in primordial or primary prevention activities or in strengthening communities, but their understanding of the impact of the factors that contribute to illness will allow them to be more empathic and fashion their clinical activities more realistically. They can participate in selective and indicated prevention efforts that will provide critical attention to those at greatest risk. Routine secondary prevention activities (i.e., screening, early detection, and treatment) will be especially helpful in primary care settings. Incorporation of these interventions will allow them to contribute to the reduction in the prevalence of illnesses in the communities they serve. Training must provide this perspective and focus a greater percentage of its instruction on prevention and health promotion rather than illness.

Public Policy and Social Justice

Envisioning an ideal social order for community mental health and well-being cannot be constructed without consideration of the inequities sustained by current social policy and the discriminatory practices that adversely affect all members of society, either directly or indirectly. Among the most egregious factors associated with community distress are the discriminatory and punitive criminal justice system, and the disparate quality of education, employment, and health care for the privileged relative to the underclass. Gun violence, the war on drug users, and the suppression of participation of the underclass in a distorted democratic process are also significant factors associated with social decay.

Reduction and elimination of these factors are critical aspects of the prevention agenda described above. Community mental health professionals must play an active role in changing the political agenda in partnership with the individuals and communities that they serve. Concerted advocacy and community awareness will emanate from a shared vision for a more harmonious future and leadership from the mental health professional community in bringing it to fruition. Compiling convincing evidence of the negative impact of the existing disparities on people of privilege will be required to enact needed changes for a safer, less wasteful, and less threatening social order. The unfortunate impact of climate change, institutional violence toward underclasses, and the pandemic of 2020 will create opportunities to make this case more convincingly.

This vision for community psychiatry and mental health ought to be the vision for psychiatry in general. Although there will no doubt be an ongoing need for psychiatric specialists in areas such as research, forensics, pharmacology, or refractory conditions, transforming general psychiatry to embody the knowledge and skills enumerated here would produce a workforce that is better suited to function in a system oriented toward primary care, which will be required to meet the needs of the population. These ideals should not be confined to a small group of psychiatrists bold enough to expand their scope of practice.

A Contemporary Perspective on the Environment of Community Psychiatry

Twenty years into the twenty-first century, the complexion of community mental health has undergone significant changes. The provision of adequate psychiatric care requires creative thinking for many of the challenges that lie ahead. It has become clear that the scope of psychiatric practice must extend beyond *psychiatrists*, and new models for the profession must emerge. This section will use a modified format of a SWOT (strengths, weaknesses, opportunities, and threats) analysis to consider the environment from which this new paradigm will be formed. As is often the case, the line between strengths and weaknesses or opportunities and threats can be a thin one in a dynamic environment. In the best scenario, planners will attempt to use their strengths to overcome some of their weaknesses and turn threats into opportunities. For that reason, this section will first look at weaknesses and threats, followed by strengths and opportunities.

Weaknesses

Psychiatrists who identify as community psychiatrists can see themselves as mavericks, outside the established order of the profession. With this perception comes a reluctance to join guild organizations such as the American Psychiatric Association. This mindset has hampered the ability of the AACP, which has fashioned its mission differently from guild groups, to achieve penetration with its vision and to recruit and effectively grow the organization. This has arguably limited its capacity to fully promote the agenda of community psychiatry.

In addition, the value of community psychiatry has not been widely recognized by administrative and management professionals working in the field, and many of the positions available in the public sector have been poorly compensated and supported. FFS funding created direct service volume, or "productivity" pressures that were unrewarding to many practitioners and exposed them to potential burnout. Although these conditions have become somewhat less common, and well-trained psychiatrists have become more adept at negotiating more favorable working conditions, some of these negative perceptions associated with community practice persist.

Another factor that has limited attraction to community psychiatry is a lack of prestige or respect that community psychiatrists receive within the psychiatric community at large. This has been most significant in the academic settings where most psychiatrists are trained. Grants for services research are more limited than for those related to biologic research and so they are less valued by psychiatric departments. Well-trained community psychiatrists with faculty positions often have limited time allocated for teaching, leaving trainees with little exposure to role models and mentors. Space in the curricula of training programs often devote minimal time to topics related to community psychiatry, indicative of how these topics are valued. This is not lost on trainees.

These factors have limited the strength of the workforce and the discipline. Without significant numbers of well-trained community practitioners joining together to promote the agenda of community psychiatry, the political influence of the field and the organization that represents it is diminished.

Threats

There are several issues and conditions that may stand in the way of progress toward solidifying a prominent place for community psychiatry in the healthcare spectrum. While some of these items may have immediate and predictable aspects, many of them loom in the future, and it is difficult to determine their evolution and impact. This discussion will begin with those which are most apparent.

Political polarization and power struggles have made it difficult to move legislation of any kind forward. Conservative political forces have stood in opposition to measures that would establish universal health insurance. Progressive interests are more likely to support these measures, but a politicized judicial system could further complicate the establishment of any successful legislative intervention.

If this scenario, with its related issues of social welfare, is not disrupted, societal unrest could grow, correctional reform could flounder, and homelessness may continue to plague individuals and communities. In our view, corporate interests will continue to set the health care and social agenda. While these conditions create the diseases of despair that community psychiatrists are best equipped to manage, need will outstrip the supply of these professionals, and resources will likewise be inadequate.

Complicating the need for a larger, more diverse, and well-trained workforce is the relative academic conservatism of many departments of psychiatry and their associated training programs. It may prove difficult to penetrate the content of these programs and reopen the narrowed scope of practice that has been promulgated by professional training curricula. While the American Psychiatric Association has elected officers who have been leaders in community psychiatry in recent years, their influence is transient with a 1-year term, and the permanent administrative leadership has not robustly embraced the principles of community psychiatry as well. For example, The Institute for Psychiatric Services, a major community-oriented conference held annually by the APA, had been under attack from within the organization for many years, and its survival was chronically uncertain. The meeting was reorganized and renamed the Mental Health Services Conference in 2021, but whether it will continue to support the aims of community psychiatry has not been determined at the time of this writing. This is one example of the lack of support for the community psychiatry agenda from the profession's strongest organization.

The pandemic of 2020 created some dramatic changes in lifestyles that were very stressful for individuals, particularly for those living in crowded urban environments. It is not yet clear the extent to which the effects of isolation, economic disruption, unemployment, and fear will have a lasting impact in the years to come. It has become clear however that exposure to infection and other environmental toxins falls disproportionately on minorities and people of lower economic status. Leaving a portion of the population without health insurance, and otherwise vulnerable to environmental threats, adversely affects the entire population. Similarly, the impact of climate change has been of growing concern as it creates increasing social and economic changes that threaten to overwhelm the systems that serve impoverished populations, community psychiatry among those that will be taxed.

Strengths

Community psychiatry has made great progress in establishing a sturdy identity. It has largely overcome a past in which it was not uncommon to find that many in the mental health community had difficulty defining the field. Its elements were splintered, often identified with other designations, such as *public* psychiatry or *social* psychiatry. Part of this newly established identity has been rooted in public service and relationship building, characteristics that are attractive to many medical students entering the profession. Recovery-oriented care is now well established as its philosophy of care, providing a coherent paradigm that extends beyond clinical care and will guide adherents in a variety of activities that define community psychiatry (e.g., leadership, advocacy, program development, and quality improvement).

The development of a well-trained workforce through dedicated training programs is a growing asset. Collaboration with allied professionals has strengthened the capacity of the system to accommodate expanding needs. There are now well-established resources for community psychiatric practice. Evidence-based practices, clinical guidelines, and decision supports tools are part of that expanded catalogue. Services research provides a mechanism to grow the scope of resources further. The knowledge base for the application of the principles of community psychiatry has been well defined through training curricula and a certification examination. While the number of psychiatrists remains far from adequate, the percentage working in community settings is growing, along with interest in advanced training.

The AACP provides a home base for clinicians who identify with community psychiatry and has ably represented the interests of the field. It has taken an active role in promoting social justice, cultural sensitivity, and trans-professional reforms, which enhances community psychiatry's appeal to minority clinicians. This diversification will better serve multicultural communities as they grow.

Opportunities

The growing interest and practice of community psychiatry creates some opportunities to change some of the vulnerabilities described above. As a larger percentage of psychiatric care is delivered in publicly financed service centers, the need for an expanded and well-trained workforce will continue to increase. Graduates of fellowships in community psychiatry are more likely to take faculty positions in academic centers, increasing the exposure trainees will have to the discipline and the availability of mentors to nurture their interests. The presence of more community psychiatrists in academic settings will also open up possibilities for curriculum reform with greater inclusion of skills (group facilitation, leadership, program planning, consultation, advocacy, etc.) and topics to prepare graduates of general adult and child psychiatry programs to work more effectively in the community and be better prepared to practice in a new treatment environment.

This latter point relates to another opportunity that healthcare reform could provide. As the strength of the psychiatric workforce increases, pressure to make necessary changes in the system can be expanded. The growing need for psychiatric care will require a refashioning of the scope of practice for the profession even if the numbers of medical students choosing psychiatry grows significantly. With a large portion of the current workforce approaching retirement, reliance on allied professional prescribers must grow, and psychiatrists will be called upon to spend a greater portion of their time in consultation and supervision and for curricula to provide a wider range of expertise. Advancing technology will change the way that many services are delivered to expand access to psychiatric care. The pandemic of 2020 demonstrated what can be accomplished via remote platforms. New arrangements for reimbursement will be required to support this changing work environment.

The social unrest and protest, fomented by the pandemic, violence directed toward people of color, and signs of relentless climate change, may be a force that will open doors for social change that will better meet the needs of the disenfranchised and oppressed members of the population. Advocacy from community psychiatrists for change within the profession and in the structure of its institutions will be more compelling in this environment. Issues such as penal reform, gun control, and eradication of homelessness can be more clearly connected to their impact on public health and the well-being of all members of society.

Realizing the Vision: Strategies for Progress

It is not as difficult to imagine an ideal environment for community mental health as it is to figure out how to achieve it. There are clearly some opportunities that would move the field closer to that ideal, but also some factors that threaten to block any progress toward it. As noted earlier, the challenge will be to use the strengths of CP in a thoughtful planning process to overcome some of those barriers. Multiple strategies and an incremental, step-by-step process may be needed to develop communities ready for the challenges the future holds.

First-Person Strategies

Some of the issues identified in the vision can be addressed simply, by individual community psychiatric clinicians. Relationship building, recovery-informed care, evidence-based and cost-conscious prescribing, holistic service planning, and the use of motivational techniques are a few of the basic interventions that individual psychiatrists can engage in without a significant increase in resources or "permission" from the system. Self-education or CME activities will enable the acquisition of necessary knowledge and skills to deliver this care. Those who are committed to meaningful change will find a variety of voluntary activities that can further these goals. Advocacy may take several forms, ranging from helping individual patients to access the services and resources they need for recovery, to the active education and persuasion of the public and elected officials regarding the social and policy issues that must be in place. These activities will be considered further in the following sections.

Local Systems Strategies

On a local level, psychiatric care providers work in systems that are imperfect. In some cases, these local systems are constrained from making changes by the larger systems in which they reside, but in many cases, opportunities for improvement exist. Even in the context of high-volume demands, psychiatrists can often find time and encouragement to participate in program development and quality improvement activities, particularly when they are knowledgeable about the systems in which they work and understand the financial realities that must be addressed. Clearly, psychiatrists will be most effective in these activities in collaboration with others who have similar values and concerns. Transdisciplinary consensus and action in collaboration with local advocacy organizations composed of people in recovery and/or their family members will have greater impact than a narrowly defined interest group.

While there may be limits to the expansion of public funding for clinical and supportive services, engagement with private foundations and grant applications may offer some opportunities to meet growing needs for services and for the development of innovative programming. Developing an evidence base for this programming will increase the chances for their survival beyond the life of grant funding. However, data gathering must extend beyond academic settings and the limited availability of grant funding. Data-driven care can permeate all services and demonstrate their value to the system, or the lack thereof. Development of clinical systems that reduce fragmentation (e.g., common electronic health record, unified treatment plans, unified service intensity criteria, and especially integrated, value-based funding) can be implemented on local levels with concerted efforts by stakeholders.

Perhaps the most effective strategy for system transformation is also the most difficult to achieve. Engagement with the community, particularly those which community mental health clinicians typically serve, is often fraught by perceptions formed from years of neglect, discrimination, and exclusion. Building trust and developing partnerships can be a slow and painful process, but one that is necessary and worthwhile. Perceptions and mistrust that exist locally are often determined by structures and policies kept in place by larger systems, which will now be considered.

Larger System Strategies

Many of the changes that arc critical to the pathway toward healthy communities are obstructed by public policy and laws that emanate from local, state, and federal governments. While divided and contentious government often creates stalemates when progressive policies are considered, compelling arguments for just social policy, based on sound data may be a basis for consensus and bipartisan support. Moral indignation and self-righteous scolding will find little purchase, but respectful engagement with those with apparently incongruous political views may result in the discovery of common ground and create opportunities for incremental changes. Epidemiologic information related to demographic variables will be an important element for success. Because American politicians always have a view toward the next election, public opinion in their districts can have a significant impact. In that regard, public education around the implications of inequalities and injustice may shift voter's perspectives.

Efforts to engage politicians and change public opinion will be most successful when broad collaboration with multiple stakeholders is in place. Community psychiatrists must overcome their reluctance to "join" in order to have a stronger voice and increase their influence. Organizations like the American Association for Community Psychiatry and the Global Alliance for Social Justice in Mental Health (formerly Orthopsychiatry) attempt to develop a coalition of professionals to advocate for the elements of the community mental health agenda, but they need to grow their membership to be successful. Penetration of other organizations such as the American Psychiatric Association or the American Medical Association will be crucial to the effort to shift their agendas to be more in tune with community mental health rather than professional interests.

Voters' decisions are often based on personal interests and emotional responses to the events and circumstances of their environment. These responses and perceptions have become increasingly influenced by confusion regarding the accuracy of the information to which they are exposed. Misinformation and propaganda have become part of their daily lives and have fostered a mistrust of science. Changing those responses is difficult. The pandemic of 2020 and the economic disruption associated with it, growing protest over discriminatory laws and their enforcement, and calamities associated with climate change will help illustrate how each voter is negatively affected, and using that illustration to change voting behavior may give greater success to public education efforts. It can only succeed through the discovery of consensus and broad promotion of the prevailing wisdom.

Closing the Book

Sixty-two chapters later we have come to the end of this textbook. The length of the book has grown along with the breadth of the topics considered in this second edition. Our hope is that this project will provide an ongoing resource for professionals working to promote community mental health and especially for community psychiatry. The continued recognition of its professional identity and the values it represents will eventually determine the success of the vision laid out in this final chapter. The definition of that identity has grown and embodies the ideals of many who have chosen to go into medicine. An increased understanding of the significance of emotional health issues in the overall health of individuals and communities will hopefully attract these individuals to join us in our pursuit of healthy communities that are inclusive, supportive, and fair for everyone.

References

Amadeo, K. (2018). Deinstitutionalization, Its Causes, Effects, Pros, and Cons. Available at https://www.thebalance.com/deinstitutionalization-3306067. Accessed July 27, 2019.

AACP/ APA (2012) Recovery to Practice: Recovery oriented care in psychiatry curriculum, available at https://www.communitypsychiatry.org/resources/recovery-to-practice Accessed October 16, 2021

Everett A, Sowers W, and McQuistion H (2012) Financing of community behavioral health services in Handbook of Community Psychiatry, McQuistion H, Sowers W et al. Editors, Springer Science, New York, pp 45-60

Feldman JM (2012) History of community psychiatry in Handbook of Community Psychiatry, McQuistion H, Sowers W et. al. Editors, Springer Science, New York, pp 11-18

Dvoskin, JA, Brown, MC, Metzner, JL, et al. (2017) The structure of correctional mental health services, in Principles and Practice of Forensic Psychiatry, 3rd edition. Edited by Rosner R, Scott CL. New York, CRC Press, pp 529-549

Engel G (1980) The clinical application of the biopsychosocial model. *Am J Psychiatry.* 1980;137:535–544.

Hogan FH (2003) The President's New Freedom Commission Report: Recommendation to transform mental health care in America. Psychiatric Services 54: 1467-1474

Mauer M (2011) Addressing racial disparities in incarceration. The Prison Journal 91 (3 suppl): 87S-101S

Mauri A, Harbin S, Unitzer J et al. (2017) Payment reform and opportunities for behavioral health: altnerative payment model examples. Scattergood Foundation Available at https://www.thekennedyforum.org/app/uploads/2017/09/Payment-Reform-and-Opportunities-for-Behavioral-Health-Alternative-Payment-Model-Examples-Final.pdf Accessed October 15, 2021

Pew Research Center, September 6, 2018. Middle class is stable in size, but losing ground financially to upper-income families. Available at https://www.pewresearch.org/fact-tank/2018/09/06/the-american-middle-class-is-stable-in-size-but-losing-ground-financially-to-upper-income-families/ Accessed March 28, 2022.

Pickett KE, Wilkinson RG (2009) The spirit level: why greater equality makes societies stronger. New York, NY: Bloomsbury Press

Pickett KE, Wilkinson RG (2007) Child wellbeing and income inequality in rich societies: ecological cross sectional study. BMJ 335(7629):1080-1086, 2007

Pinals, DA (2017) Jail diversion, specialty court, and reentry services: Partnerships between behavioral health and justice systems, in Principles and Practice of Forensic Psychiatry, 3rd edition. Edited by Rosner R, Scott CL. New York, CRC Press, pp 237-246

Rodenbach KE (2021) Social determinants of health in Seeking Value: Balancing Cost and Quality in Psychiatric Care Sowers W and Ranz J Editors, American Psychiatric Association Publishing, Washington DC pp 81-108

Sastry D (2021) Evolution of funding and quality control in health care in Seeking Value: Balancing Cost and Quality in Psychiatric Care Sowers W and Ranz J Editors, American Psychiatric Association Publishing, Washington DC pp 27-54

Shoyinka S (2021) Innovative financing: incentivizing value in Seeking Value: Balancing Cost and Quality in Psychiatric Care Sowers W and Ranz J Editors, American Psychiatric Association Publishing, Washington DC pp 137-164

Sowers W (2020), The current system: the mess we are in, in Seeking Value: Balancing Cost and Quality in Psychiatric Care Sowers W and Ranz J Editors, American Psychiatric Association Publishing, Washington DC pp 55-80

Thompson JW (1994) Trends in the development of psychiatric services, 1844-1994, Hosptal and Community Psychiatry Vol 45 No 10 pp 987-992

White, W. L. (1998). Slaying the dragon: The history of addiction treatment and recovery in America. Chestnut Health Systems/Lighthouse Institute, pp 393-395

Wit vs. United Behavioral Health Feb 28th 2019. Available at https://www.courtlistener.com/recap/gov.uscourts.cand.277588/gov.uscourts.cand.277588.418.0.pdf. Accessed Oct. 10, 2021

Index

W. E. Sowers et al. (eds.), *Textbook of Community Psychiatry*, https://doi.org/10.1007/978-3-031-10239-4

Q

R

S

T

CPSIA information can be obtained
at www.ICGtesting.com
Printed in the USA
LVHW061258020723
751366LV00002B/9